SCOTT FORESMAN

SOCIAL STUDIES

REGIONS

Teacher's Edition

Editorial Offices: Glenview, Illinois • Parsippany, New Jersey • New York, New York
Sales Offices: Parsippany, New Jersey • Duluth, Georgia • Glenview, Illinois • Coppell, Texas • Ontario, California • Mesa, Arizona

ISBN: 0-328-08164-7

4 5 6 7 8 9 10 V064 12 11 10 09 08 07 06 05

Authors, Consultants, and Reviewers

Scott Foresman Social Studies was developed by a team with extensive experience as educators, authors, and researchers. Their goal was to provide social studies materials that help your students become active, informed, and responsible citizens.

PROGRAM AUTHORS

Dr. Candy Dawson Boyd
Professor, School of Education
Director of Reading Programs
St. Mary's College
Moraga, California

Dr. C. Frederick Risinger
Director, Professional Development and Social Studies Education
Indiana University
Bloomington, Indiana

Dr. Allen D. Glenn
Professor and Dean Emeritus
College of Education
Curriculum and Instruction
University of Washington
Seattle, Washington

Dr. Geneva Gay
Professor of Education
University of Washington
Seattle, Washington

Sara Miranda Sanchez
Elementary and Early Childhood Curriculum Coordinator
Albuquerque Public Schools
Albuquerque, New Mexico

Dr. Carole L. Hahn
Professor, Educational Studies
Emory University
Atlanta, Georgia

CONTRIBUTING AUTHORS

Rita Geiger
Director of Social Studies and Foreign Languages
Norman Public Schools
Norman, Oklahoma

Dr. Carol Berkin
Professor of History
Baruch College and the Graduate Center,
The City University of New York
New York, New York

Dr. M. Gail Hickey
Professor of Education
Indiana University–Purdue University
Fort Wayne, Indiana

Dr. James B. Kracht
Associate Dean for Undergraduate Programs and Teacher Education
College of Education
Texas A & M University
College Station, Texas

Lee A. Chase
Staff Development Specialist
Chesterfield County Public Schools
Chesterfield County, Virginia

Dr. Bonnie Meszaros
Associate Director
Center for Economic Education and Entrepreneurship
University of Delaware
Newark, Delaware

Dr. Valerie Ooka Pang
Professor of Teacher Education
San Diego State University
San Diego, California

Dr. Jim Cummins
Professor of Curriculum
Ontario Institute for Studies in Education
University of Toronto
Toronto, Canada

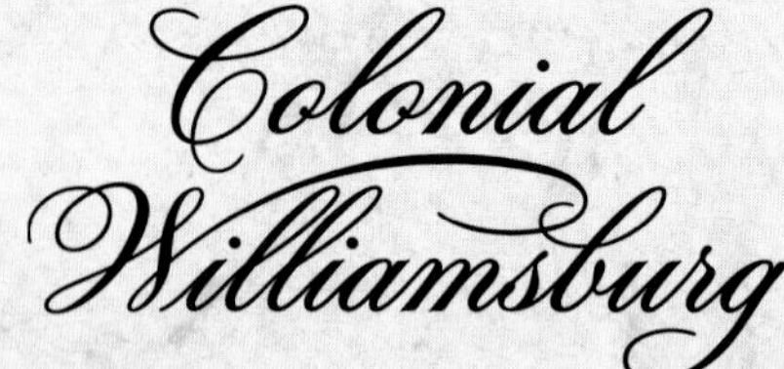

The world's largest living history museum is now a contributing author to Scott Foresman Social Studies!

CONTENT CONSULTANTS

Catherine Deans-Barrett
World History Specialist
Northbrook, Illinois

Dr. Michael Frassetto
Studies in Religions
Independent Scholar
Chicago, Illinois

Dr. Gerald Greenfield
Hispanic-Latino Studies
History Department
University of Wisconsin, Parkside
Kenosha, Wisconsin

Dr. Frederick Hoxie
Native American Studies
University of Illinois
Champaign, Illinois

Dr. Cheryl Johnson-Odim
Dean of Liberal Arts and Sciences
and Professor of History
African American History Specialist
Columbia College
Chicago, Illinois

Dr. Michael Khodarkovsky
Eastern European Studies
University of Chicago
Chicago, Illinois

Robert Moffet
U.S. History Specialist
Northbrook, Illinois

Dr. Ralph Nichols
East Asian History
University of Chicago
Chicago, Illinois

CLASSROOM REVIEWERS

Diana Vicknair Ard
Woodlake Elementary School
St. Tammany Parish
Mandeville, Louisiana

Sharon Berenson
Freehold Learning Center
Freehold, New Jersey

Betsy Blandford
Pocahontas Elementary School
Powhatan, Virginia

Nancy Neff Burgess
Upshur County Schools
Buckhannon-Upshur Middle School
Upshur County, West Virginia

Gloria Cantatore
Public School #5
West New York, New Jersey

Stephen Corsini
Content Specialist in
Elementary Social Studies
School District 5 of Lexington
and Richland Counties
Ballentine, South Carolina

Sally L. Costa
Hellen Caro Elementary School
Pensacola, Florida

Deanna Crews
Millbrook Middle School
Elmore County
Millbrook, Alabama

LuAnn Curran
Westgate Elementary School
St. Petersburg, Florida

Kevin L. Curry
Social Studies Curriculum Chair
Hickory Flat Elementary School
Henry County, McDonough, Georgia

Sheila A. Czech
Sky Oaks Elementary School
Burnsville, Minnesota

Louis De Angelo
Office of Catholic Education
Archdiocese of Philadelphia
Philadelphia, Pennsylvania

Dr. Trish Dolansinski
Paradise Valley School District
Arrowhead Elementary School
Glendale, Arizona

Dr. John R. Doyle
Director of Social Studies Curriculum
Miami-Dade County Schools
Miami, Florida

Dr. Roceal Duke
District of Columbia Public Schools
Washington, D.C.

Sherill M. Farrell
Hillsborough County Schools
Valrico, Florida

Peggy Flanagan
Roosevelt Elementary School
Community Consolidated School
District #64
Park Ridge, Illinois

Mary Flynn
Arrowhead Elementary School
Glendale, Arizona

Su Hickenbottom
Totem Falls Elementary School
Snohomish School District
Snohomish, Washington

Allan Jones
North Branch Public Schools
North Branch, Minnesota

Brandy Bowers Kerbow
Bettye Haun Elementary School
Plano ISD
Plano, Texas

Martha Sutton Maple
Shreve Island School
Shreveport, Louisiana

Lyn Metzger
Carpenter Elementary School
Community Consolidated School
District #64
Park Ridge, Illinois

Marsha Munsey
Riverbend Elementary School
West Monroe, Louisiana

Christine Nixon
Warrington Elementary School
Escambia County School District
Pensacola, Florida

Cynthia K. Reneau
Muscogee County School District
Columbus, Georgia

Brandon Dale Rice
Secondary Education
Social Science
Mobile County Public
School System
Mobile, Alabama

Liz Salinas
Supervisor
Edgewood ISD
San Antonio, Texas

Beverly Scaling
Desert Hills Elementary
Las Cruces, New Mexico

Madeleine Schmitt
St. Louis Public Schools
St. Louis, Missouri

Barbara Schwartz
Central Square
Intermediate School
Central Square, New York

Melody Stalker
Escambia County School District
Pensacola, Florida

Rich Content

Every chapter in Scott Foresman Social Studies provides rich, comprehensive content that captures your students' imagination and makes them eager to learn more.

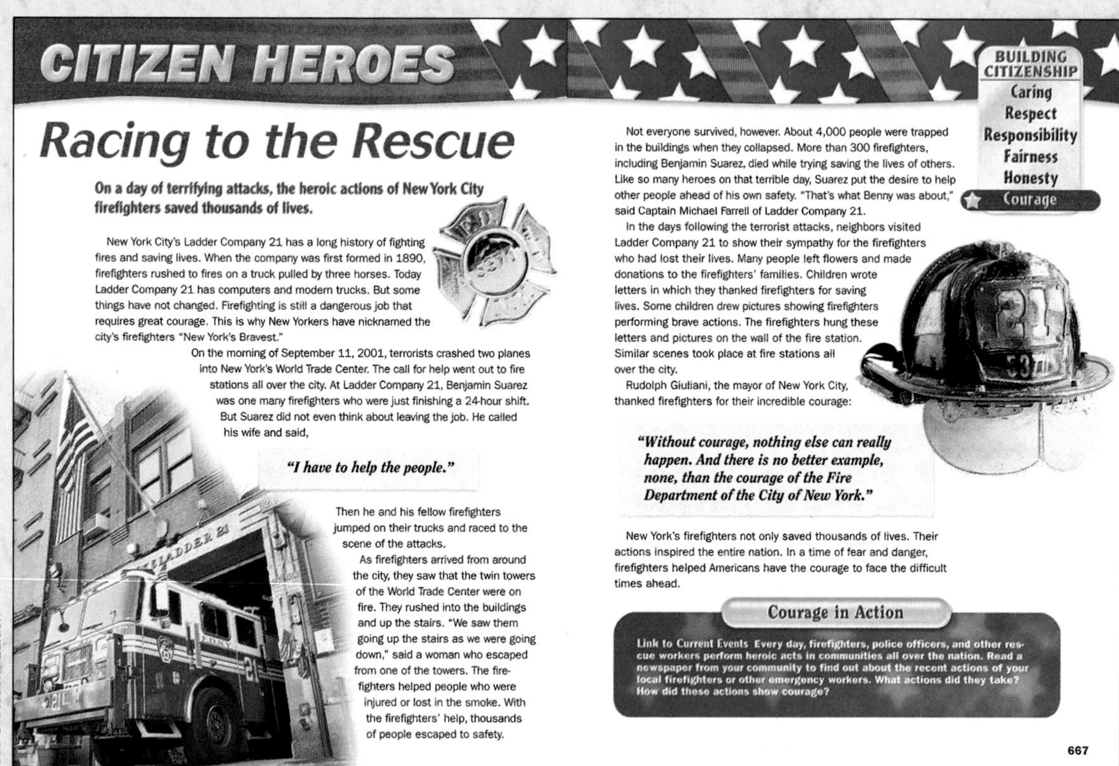

Grade 5 Student Edition

CITIZEN HEROES

BUILDING CITIZENSHIP
Caring
Respect
Responsibility
Fairness
Honesty
Courage

Racing to the Rescue

On a day of terrifying attacks, the heroic actions of New York City firefighters saved thousands of lives.

New York City's Ladder Company 21 has a long history of fighting fires and saving lives. When the company was first formed in 1890, firefighters rushed to fires on a truck pulled by three horses. Today Ladder Company 21 has computers and modern trucks. But some things have not changed. Firefighting is still a dangerous job that requires great courage. This is why New Yorkers have nicknamed the city's firefighters "New York's Bravest."

On the morning of September 11, 2001, terrorists crashed two planes into New York's World Trade Center. The call for help went out to fire stations all over the city. At Ladder Company 21, Benjamin Suarez was one many firefighters who were just finishing a 24-hour shift. But Suarez did not even think about leaving the job. He called his wife and said,

"I have to help the people."

Then he and his fellow firefighters jumped on their trucks and raced to the scene of the attacks.

As firefighters arrived from around the city, they saw that the twin towers of the World Trade Center were on fire. They rushed into the buildings and up the stairs. "We saw them going up the stairs as we were going down," said a woman who escaped from one of the towers. The firefighters helped people who were injured or lost in the smoke. With the firefighters' help, thousands of people escaped to safety.

Not everyone survived, however. About 4,000 people were trapped in the buildings when they collapsed. More than 300 firefighters, including Benjamin Suarez, died while trying saving the lives of others. Like so many heroes on that terrible day, Suarez put the desire to help other people ahead of his own safety. "That's what Benny was about," said Captain Michael Farrell of Ladder Company 21.

In the days following the terrorist attacks, neighbors visited Ladder Company 21 to show their sympathy for the firefighters who had lost their lives. Many people left flowers and made donations to the firefighters' families. Children wrote letters in which they thanked firefighters for saving lives. Some children drew pictures showing firefighters performing brave actions. The firefighters hung these letters and pictures on the wall of the fire station. Similar scenes took place at fire stations all over the city.

Rudolph Giuliani, the mayor of New York City, thanked firefighters for their incredible courage:

"Without courage, nothing else can really happen. And there is no better example, none, than the courage of the Fire Department of the City of New York."

New York's firefighters not only saved thousands of lives. Their actions inspired the entire nation. In a time of fear and danger, firefighters helped Americans have the courage to face the difficult times ahead.

Courage in Action

Link to Current Events Every day, firefighters, police officers, and other rescue workers perform heroic acts in communities all over the nation. Read a newspaper from your community to find out about the recent actions of your local firefighters or other emergency workers. What actions did they take? How did these actions show courage?

667

Citizen Heroes

Famous people and everyday citizens show your students how they can make a difference by putting good citizenship skills into action.

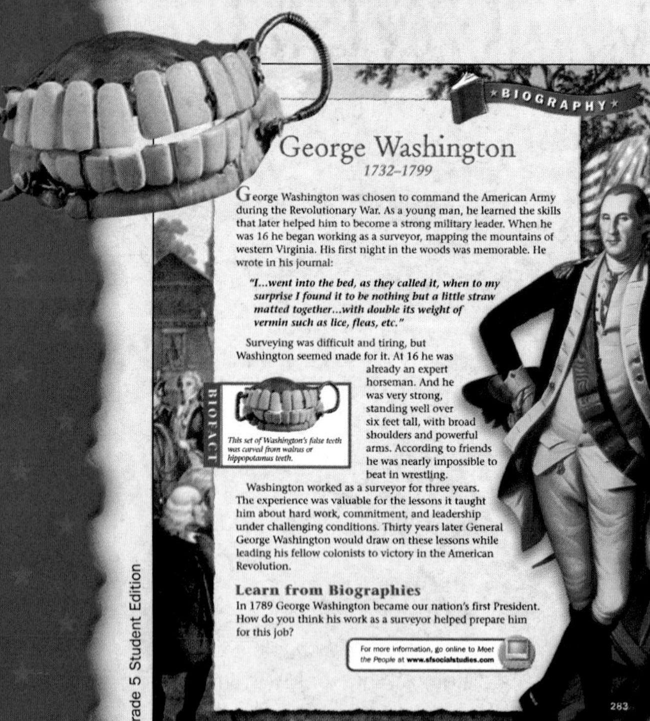

Grade 5 Student Edition

BIOGRAPHY

George Washington
1732–1799

George Washington was chosen to command the American Army during the Revolutionary War. As a young man, he learned the skills that later helped him to become a strong military leader. When he was 16 he began working as a surveyor, mapping the mountains of western Virginia. His first night in the woods was memorable. He wrote in his journal:

"I...went into the bed, as they called it, when to my surprise I found it to be nothing but a little straw matted together...with double its weight of vermin such as lice, fleas, etc."

Surveying was difficult and tiring, but Washington seemed made for it. At 16 he was already an expert horseman. And he was very strong, standing well over six feet tall, with broad shoulders and powerful arms. According to friends he was nearly impossible to beat in wrestling.

BIOFACT

This set of Washington's false teeth was carved from walrus or hippopotamus teeth.

Washington worked as a surveyor for three years. The experience was valuable for the lessons it taught him about hard work, commitment, and leadership under challenging conditions. Thirty years later General George Washington would draw on these lessons while leading his fellow colonists to victory in the American Revolution.

Learn from Biographies

In 1789 George Washington became our nation's first President. How do you think his work as a surveyor helped prepare him for this job?

For more information, go online to *Meet the People* at **www.sfsocialstudies.com**

283

Colorful Biographies

Fascinating stories enhance your students' understanding by personalizing history and bringing key figures to life.

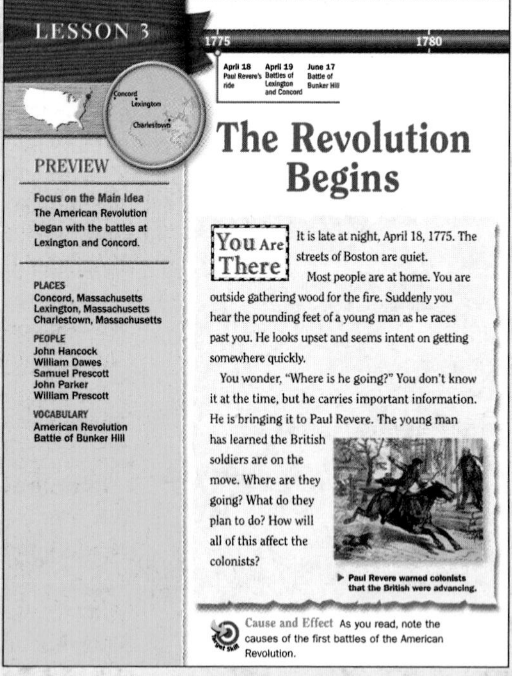

Grade 5 Student Edition

LESSON 3

PREVIEW

Focus on the Main Idea
The American Revolution began with the battles at Lexington and Concord.

PLACES
Concord, Massachusetts
Lexington, Massachusetts
Charlestown, Massachusetts

PEOPLE
John Hancock
William Dawes
Samuel Prescott
John Parker
William Prescott

VOCABULARY
American Revolution
Battle of Bunker Hill

The Revolution Begins

You Are There It is late at night, April 18, 1775. The streets of Boston are quiet.

Most people are at home. You are outside gathering wood for the fire. Suddenly you hear the pounding feet of a young man as he races past you. He looks upset and seems intent on getting somewhere quickly.

You wonder, "Where is he going?" You don't know it at the time, but he carries important information. He is bringing it to Paul Revere. The young man has learned the British soldiers are on the move. Where are they going? What do they plan to do? How will all of this affect the colonists?

▶ Paul Revere warned colonists that the British were advancing.

Target Skill **Cause and Effect** As you read, note the causes of the first battles of the American Revolution.

You Are There

Riveting selections build excitement and bring your students right into the lesson. Each piece puts children in the middle of the action, keeping them motivated and engaged.

Economics

Economics is the study of how people produce, distribute, and use goods and services.

Economics in Washington

Seattle

Pike Place Market
Seattle, Washington

You Are There You've never seen so much food or smelled so many different scents in your life. It's noisy and busy. People rush past you in a hurry, carrying bags of bread and flowers. You stop to look around. Restaurant chefs, local people, and tourists like you fill the streets of the enormous farmer's market in Seattle. "Heads up!" you hear, just in time. A giant fish whooshes by your head. Thirty feet away, a man behind a counter catches it and wraps it for a customer. The people selling fish shout and joke with one another. It's only Tuesday morning. The market is just getting started!

Economics at Work at the

Pike Place Market

Since it was built in 1907, many consumers have come to Pike Place Market. **Consumers** are people who buy and use products. **Products** are things that are made and sold. People like the products at Pike Place because they are usually fresher and more affordable. Producers, such as farmers or fishermen, can sell their goods directly to consumers at Pike Place. Supermarkets spend money to ship, display, and sell their products. This means they may have to charge more for the products in the stores. Foods at Pike Place are not shipped from far away or displayed in stores.

The best stalls are given to shopkeepers who have been selling at the market for the longest time.

Seattle is located between the fertile farmland of California and the fishing waters of Alaska. It has some of the world's best fresh food.

Fast Facts:

- During the 1960s, consumers began shopping more in supermarkets. The Pike Place Market was almost closed and demolished.
- More than 20,000 people visit the market on weekdays. More than 37,000 people visit on Saturdays.

Link to You

What products do you buy directly from a producer?

E4 E5

Grade 5 Student Edition

Explore the United States

Gripping narrative and museum-quality art draw your students into the text and show the major social studies strands at work across our nation.

Research Skills

Colonial Williamsburg

Living History from Colonial Williamsburg
www.history.org

Think Like a Historian

Written records are a way for us to learn about the past. Historians search libraries for letters, diaries, and other records. Documents written by the people who saw the events, places, and people of the past are called primary sources. Primary sources help us understand what life was like long ago.

Nicholas Cresswell traveled in Virginia in 1777. This is how he described the city of Williamsburg.

"This is the finest town I have seen in Virginia . . . It consists of one principal street about a mile long, very wide and level with a number of good buildings, the Capitol at the end of the street and the College at the other . . ."

"The Capitol is the place where all public business is done, the Colonial Assembly meets, &c . . . In the Capitol is a fine marble statue of the late Governor . . ."

"The Governor's Palace is a good brick building, but it does not make a grand appearance."

"Here is only one Church, none the grandest, and I suppose there may be about 250 houses in town."

Capitol

Governor Botetourt

Governor's Palace

Bruton Parish Church

College of William and Mary

Write a description of your neighborhood. Use details that will help people in the future understand what life was like there. What does it look like? Who lives there? What events take place there?

H4 H5

Grade 5 Student Edition

Colonial Williamsburg

Exciting full-color spreads from the world's largest living history museum provide unique opportunities for your students to connect with the past.

Direct Reading and Writing Instruction

Scott Foresman Social Studies provides explicit reading and writing instruction that builds understanding and prepares your students for high-stakes testing.

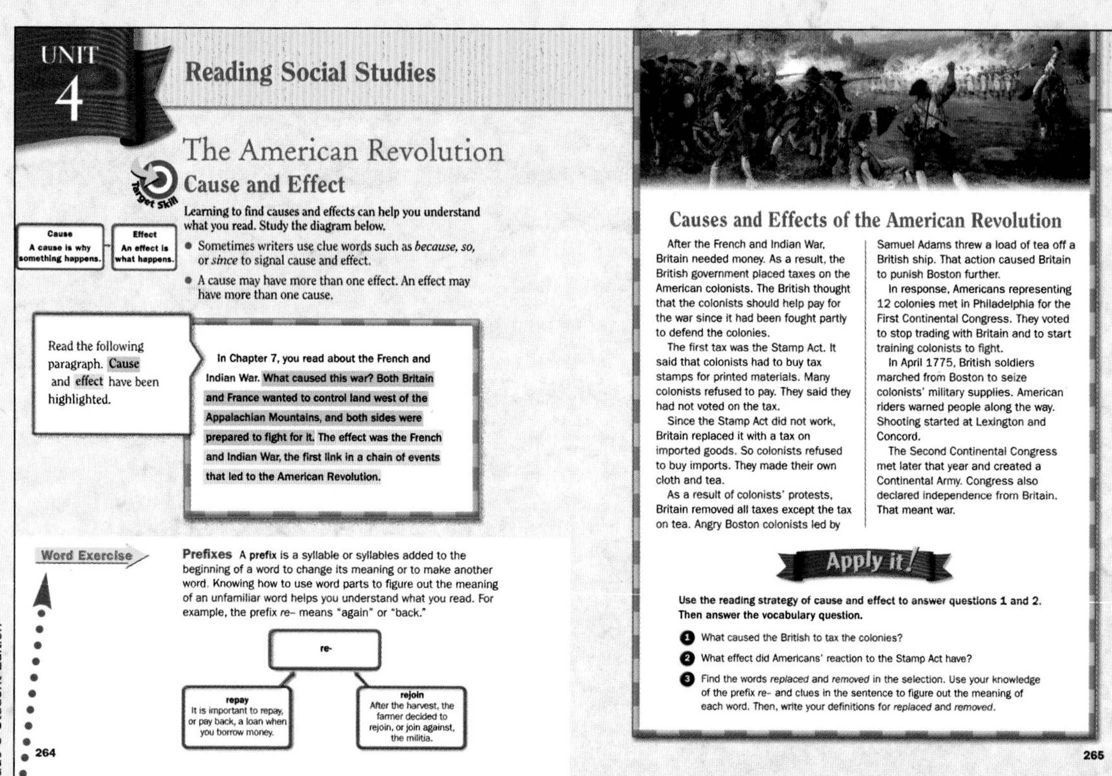

UNIT 4

Reading Social Studies

The American Revolution

Cause and Effect

Cause	Effect
A cause is why something happens.	An effect is what happens.

Learning to find causes and effects can help you understand what you read. Study the diagram below.

- Sometimes writers use clue words such as *because, so,* or *since* to signal cause and effect.
- A cause may have more than one effect. An effect may have more than one cause.

Read the following paragraph. Cause and effect have been highlighted.

In Chapter 7, you read about the French and Indian War. What caused this war? Both Britain and France wanted to control land west of the Appalachian Mountains, and both sides were prepared to fight for it. The effect was the French and Indian War, the first link in a chain of events that led to the American Revolution.

Word Exercise

Prefixes A prefix is a syllable or syllables added to the beginning of a word to change its meaning or to make another word. Knowing how to use word parts to figure out the meaning of an unfamiliar word helps you understand what you read. For example, the prefix *re-* means "again" or "back."

re-

repay It is important to repay, or pay back, a loan when you borrow money.

rejoin After the harvest, the farmer decided to rejoin, or join against, the militia.

264

Causes and Effects of the American Revolution

After the French and Indian War, Britain needed money. As a result, the British government placed taxes on the American colonists. The British thought that the colonists should help pay for the war since it had been fought partly to defend the colonies.

The first tax was the Stamp Act. It said that colonists had to buy tax stamps for printed materials. Many colonists refused to pay. They said they had not voted on the tax.

Since the Stamp Act did not work, Britain replaced it with a tax on imported goods. So colonists refused to buy imports. They made their own cloth and tea.

As a result of colonists' protests, Britain removed all taxes except the tax on tea. Angry Boston colonists led by Samuel Adams threw a load of tea off a British ship. That action caused Britain to punish Boston further.

In response, Americans representing 12 colonies met in Philadelphia for the First Continental Congress. They voted to stop trading with Britain and to start training colonists to fight.

In April 1775, British soldiers marched from Boston to seize colonists' military supplies. American riders warned people along the way. Shooting started at Lexington and Concord.

The Second Continental Congress met later that year and created a Continental Army. Congress also declared independence from Britain. That meant war.

Apply it!

Use the reading strategy of cause and effect to answer questions 1 and 2. Then answer the vocabulary question.

1. What caused the British to tax the colonies?
2. What effect did Americans' reaction to the Stamp Act have?
3. Find the words *replaced* and *removed* in the selection. Use your knowledge of the prefix *re-* and clues in the sentence to figure out the meaning of each word. Then, write your definitions for *replaced* and *removed*.

265

Grade 5 Student Edition

Look for the Target Skill!

Every unit teaches a key Target Skill that helps students read for understanding. The Target Skill icon appears throughout the text and identifies opportunities for reading instruction, practice, and application.

Teach the Target Skill

Direct reading instruction at the beginning of each unit helps your students develop reading and comprehension skills throughout the social studies content.

Word Exercise

Built-in vocabulary instruction ensures student comprehension of key social studies terms.

READING SKILL

Cause and Effect

In the Lesson Review, students complete a graphic organizer like the one below. You may want to provide students with a copy of Transparency 20 to complete as they read the lesson.

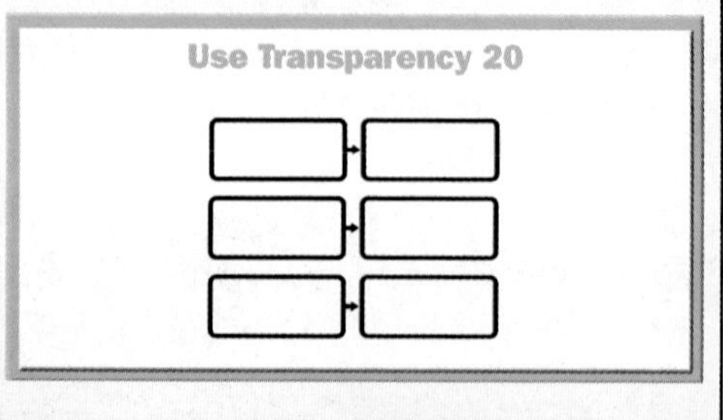

Grade 5 Teacher's Edition

Practice the Target Skill

Research-based strategies, such as using graphic organizers, assist your students in practicing the target skill.

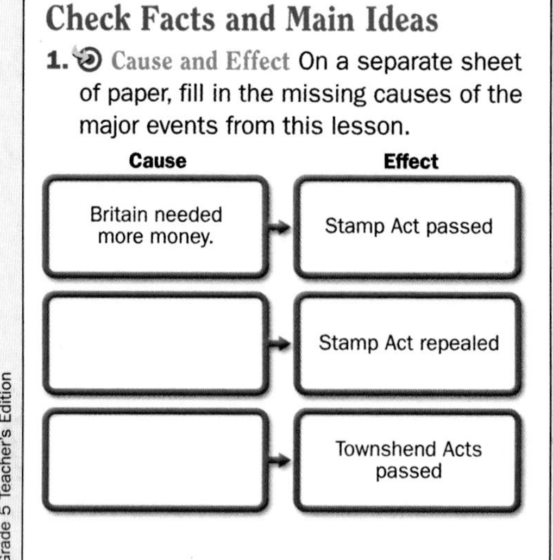

LESSON 1 REVIEW

Check Facts and Main Ideas

1. Cause and Effect On a separate sheet of paper, fill in the missing causes of the major events from this lesson.

Cause	Effect
Britain needed more money.	Stamp Act passed
	Stamp Act repealed
	Townshend Acts passed

Grade 5 Teacher's Edition

Apply the Target Skill

Lesson, Chapter, and Unit Reviews ensure that your students can apply the target skill independently.

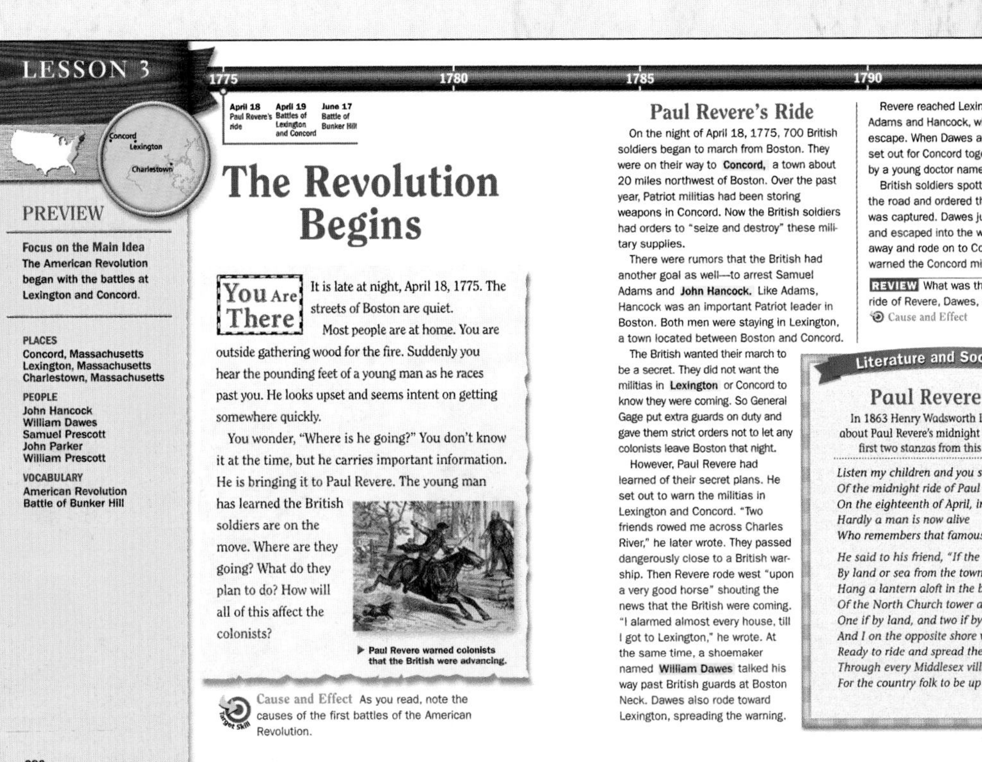

LESSON 3

PREVIEW

Focus on the Main Idea
The American Revolution began with the battles at Lexington and Concord.

PLACES
Concord, Massachusetts
Lexington, Massachusetts
Charlestown, Massachusetts

PEOPLE
John Hancock
William Dawes
Samuel Prescott
John Parker
William Prescott

VOCABULARY
American Revolution
Battle of Bunker Hill

The Revolution Begins

You Are There It is late at night, April 18, 1775. The streets of Boston are quiet.

Most people are at home. You are outside gathering wood for the fire. Suddenly you hear the pounding feet of a young man as he races past you. He looks upset and seems intent on getting somewhere quickly.

You wonder, "Where is he going?" You don't know it at the time, but he carries important information. He is bringing it to Paul Revere. The young man has learned the British soldiers are on the move. Where are they going? What do they plan to do? How will all of this affect the colonists?

▶ Paul Revere warned colonists that the British were advancing.

Cause and Effect As you read, note the causes of the first battles of the American Revolution.

286

Paul Revere's Ride

On the night of April 18, 1775, 700 British soldiers began to march from Boston. They were on their way to **Concord,** a town about 20 miles northwest of Boston. Over the past year, Patriot militias had been storing weapons in Concord. Now the British soldiers had orders to "seize and destroy" these military supplies.

There were rumors that the British had another goal as well—to arrest Samuel Adams and **John Hancock.** Like Adams, Hancock was an important Patriot leader in Boston. Both men were staying in Lexington, a town located between Boston and Concord.

The British wanted their march to be a secret. They did not want the militias in **Lexington** or Concord to know they were coming. So General Gage put extra guards on duty and gave them strict orders not to let any colonists leave Boston that night.

However, Paul Revere had learned of their secret plans. He set out to warn the militias in Lexington and Concord. "Two friends rowed me across Charles River," he later wrote. They passed dangerously close to a British warship. Then Revere rode west "upon a very good horse" shouting the news that the British were coming. "I alarmed almost every house, till I got to Lexington," he wrote. At the same time, a shoemaker named **William Dawes** talked his way past British guards at Boston Neck. Dawes also rode toward Lexington, spreading the warning.

Revere reached Lexington first. He warned Adams and Hancock, who prepared their escape. When Dawes arrived, he and Revere set out for Concord together. They were joined by a young doctor named **Samuel Prescott.**

British soldiers spotted the three riders on the road and ordered them to stop. Revere was captured. Dawes jumped from his horse and escaped into the woods. Prescott got away and rode on to Concord, where he warned the Concord militia to get ready.

REVIEW What was the effect of the ride of Revere, Dawes, and Prescott? Cause and Effect

Literature and Social Studies

Paul Revere's Ride

In 1863 Henry Wadsworth Longfellow wrote about Paul Revere's midnight ride. Below are the first two stanzas from this famous poem.

Listen my children and you shall hear
Of the midnight ride of Paul Revere,
On the eighteenth of April, in Seventy-five;
Hardly a man is now alive
Who remembers that famous day and year.

He said to his friend, "If the British march
By land or sea from the town to-night,
Hang a lantern aloft in the belfry arch
Of the North Church tower as a signal light,—
One if by land, and two if by sea;
And I on the opposite shore will be,
Ready to ride and spread the alarm
Through every Middlesex village and farm,
For the country folk to be up and to arm."

287

Grade 5 Student Edition

repeal

to cancel

Vocabulary Cards

Flashcards with key terms and definitions make it easy to extend vocabulary practice and help all students access the content.

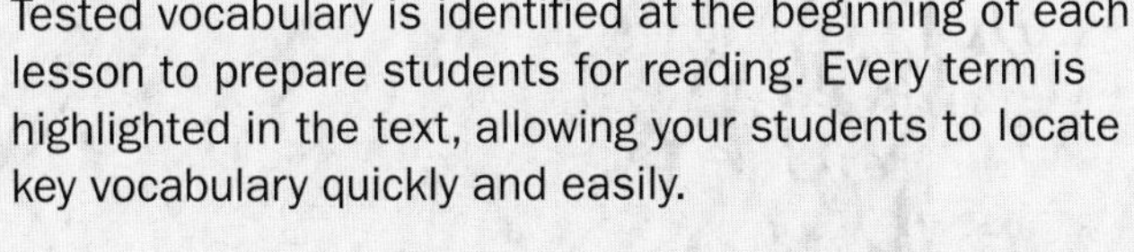

Vocabulary Preview

Tested vocabulary is identified at the beginning of each lesson to prepare students for reading. Every term is highlighted in the text, allowing your students to locate key vocabulary quickly and easily.

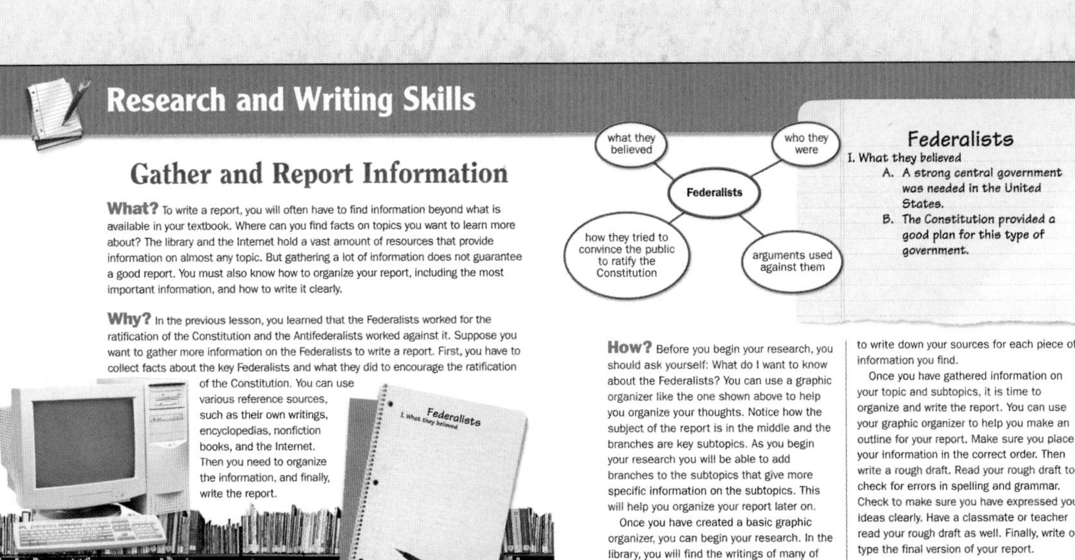

Research and Writing Skills

Gather and Report Information

What? To write a report, you will often have to find information beyond what is available in your textbook. Where can you find facts on topics you want to learn more about? The library and the Internet hold a vast amount of resources that provide information on almost any topic. But gathering a lot of information does not guarantee a good report. You must also know how to organize your report, including the most important information, and how to write it clearly.

Why? In the previous lesson, you learned that the Federalists worked for the ratification of the Constitution and the Antifederalists worked against it. Suppose you want to gather more information on the Federalists to write a report. First, you have to collect facts about the key Federalists and what they did to encourage the ratification of the Constitution. You can use various reference sources, such as their own writings, encyclopedias, nonfiction books, and the Internet. Then you need to organize the information, and finally, write the report.

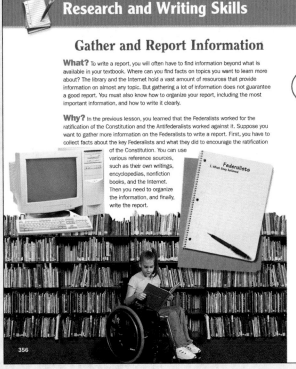

B. The Constitution provided a good plan for this type of government.

How? Before you begin your research, you should ask yourself: What do I want to know about the Federalists? You can use a graphic organizer like the one shown above to help you organize your thoughts. Notice how the subject of the report is in the middle and the branches are key subtopics. As you begin your research you will be able to add branches to the subtopics that give more specific information on the subtopics. This will help you organize your report later on.

Once you have created a basic graphic organizer, you can begin your research. In the library, you will find the writings of many of the Federalists as well as encyclopedias that have information on almost any subject. They are organized alphabetically by topic. To find information on the Federalists, you might look up Federalists, the Constitution, or United States history. You can use the library's catalogue to find nonfiction books on the Federalists. A historical atlas, which contains maps and information about the past, might be a helpful resource as well. The Internet contains online encyclopedias and many Web sites with historical information. Remember to write down your sources for each piece of information you find.

Once you have gathered information on your topic and subtopics, it is time to organize and write the report. You can use your graphic organizer to help you make an outline for your report. Make sure you place your information in the correct order. Then write a rough draft. Read your rough draft to check for errors in spelling and grammar. Check to make sure you have expressed your ideas clearly. Have a classmate or teacher read your rough draft as well. Finally, write or type the final version of your report.

Think and Apply

1. Write the steps for gathering and reporting information in order.
2. What subjects might you look up in an encyclopedia if you needed to write a report on the Bill of Rights?
3. Why is it important to write a rough draft?

356

357

Grade 5 Student Edition

Research and Writing Skills

Complete lessons guide your students through the process of researching a topic and presenting their findings.

WRITING

Write a Letter About the Stamp Act, TE p. 269
Write a Letter to King George, TE p. 273
Link to Writing, PE/TE pp. 273, 300
Write a Newspaper Article, TE p. 280
Write a Dialogue, TE p. 297
Analyze Hancock's Statement, TE p. 300
Create a Poem, TE p. 309
Create Persuasive Slogans, TE p. 311
Write an Appreciation Letter, TE p. 315
Different Points of View, TE p. 319

Grade 5 Teacher's Edition

Daily Writing Opportunities

who they were

how they tried to convince the public to ratify the Constitution

Writing activities throughout the text improve your students' writing skills and encourage them to think critically and apply what they learned. A special Rubric section in the Teacher's Edition aids you in evaluating student work.

Purposeful Skills Instruction

Scott Foresman Social Studies provides built-in skills lessons that enhance social studies content and teach essential learning and testing skills.

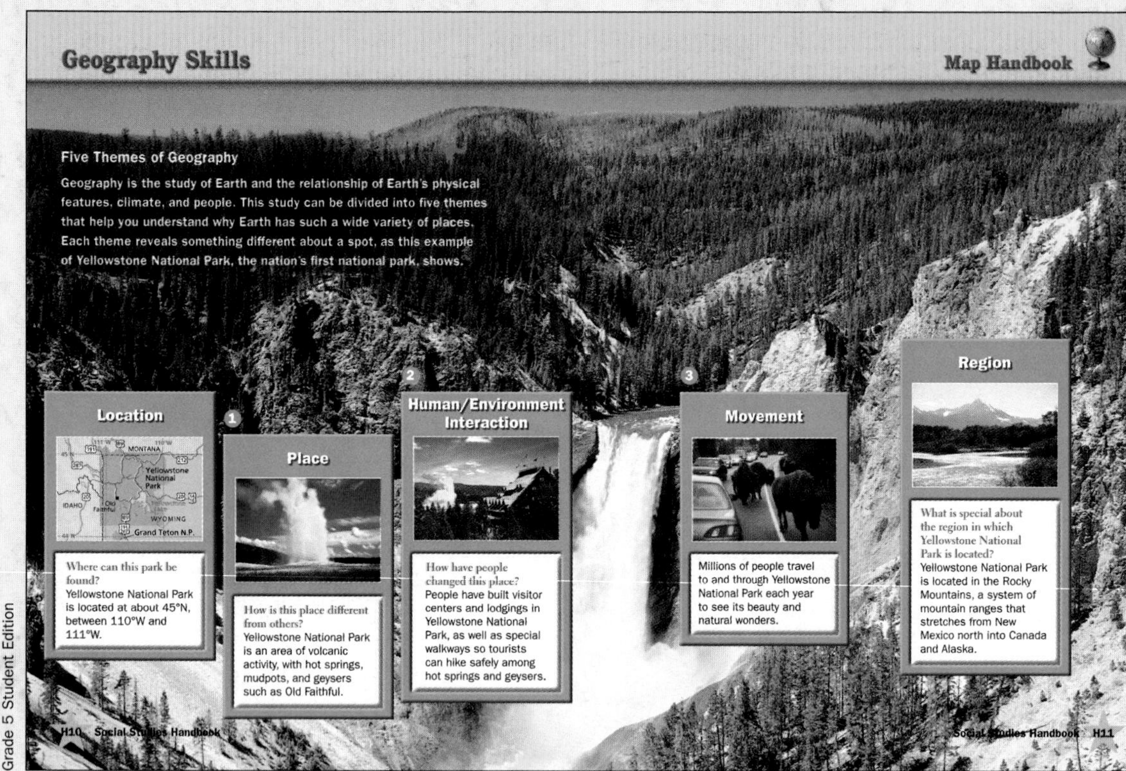

Geography Skills

Map Handbook

Five Themes of Geography

Geography is the study of Earth and the relationship of Earth's physical features, climate, and people. This study can be divided into five themes that help you understand why Earth has such a wide variety of places. Each theme reveals something different about a spot, as this example of Yellowstone National Park, the nation's first national park, shows.

Location

Where can this park be found?
Yellowstone National Park is located at about 45°N, between 110°W and 111°W.

1 **Place**

How is this place different from others?
Yellowstone National Park is an area of volcanic activity, with hot springs, mudpots, and geysers such as Old Faithful.

2 **Human/Environment Interaction**

How have people changed this place?
People have built visitor centers and lodgings in Yellowstone National Park, as well as special walkways so tourists can hike safely among hot springs and geysers.

3 **Movement**

Millions of people travel to and through Yellowstone National Park each year to see its beauty and natural wonders.

Region

What is special about the region in which Yellowstone National Park is located?
Yellowstone National Park is located in the Rocky Mountains, a system of mountain ranges that stretches from New Mexico north into Canada and Alaska.

H10 Social Studies Handbook — Social Studies Handbook H11

Grade 5 Student Edition

Map Handbook

This special section at the beginning of the book reviews geography skills from the previous year and provides direct map and globe skill instruction essential for learning social studies.

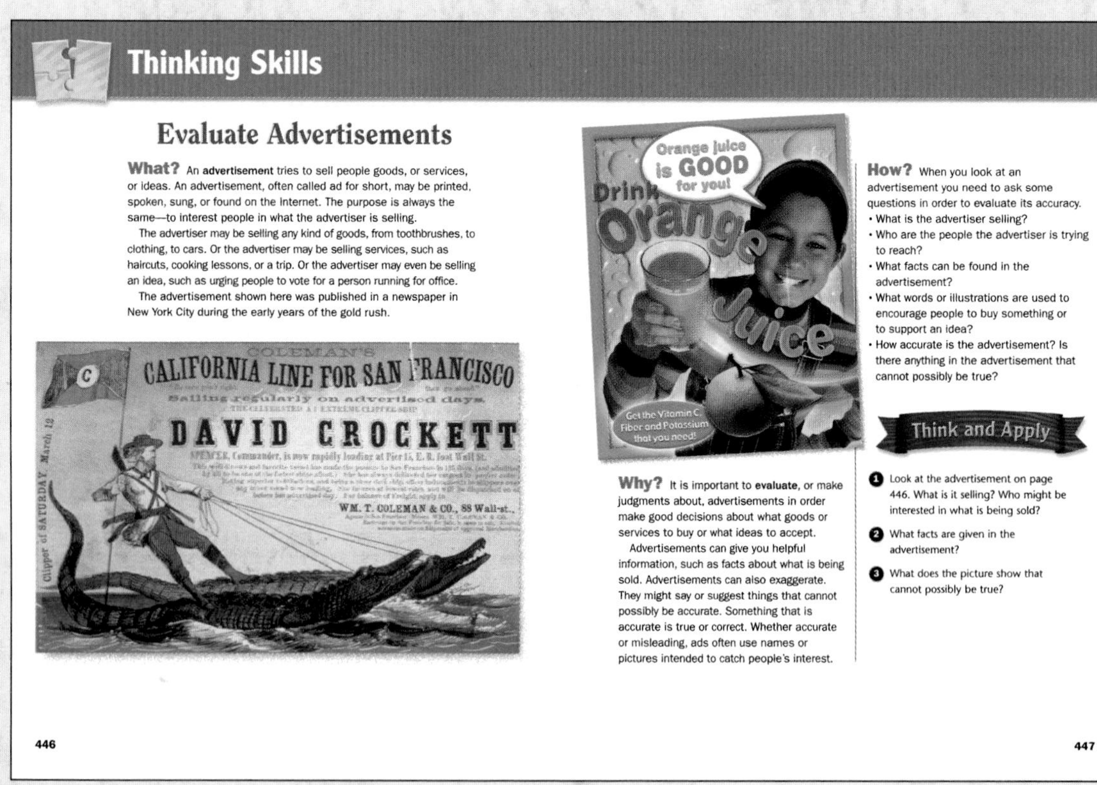

Thinking Skills

Evaluate Advertisements

What? An **advertisement** tries to sell people goods, or services, or ideas. An advertisement, often called ad for short, may be printed, spoken, sung, or found on the Internet. The purpose is always the same—to interest people in what the advertiser is selling.

The advertiser may be selling any kind of goods, from toothbrushes, to clothing, to cars. Or the advertiser may be selling services, such as haircuts, cooking lessons, or a trip. Or the advertiser may even be selling an idea, such as urging people to vote for a person running for office.

The advertisement shown here was published in a newspaper in New York City during the early years of the gold rush.

Why? It is important to **evaluate**, or make judgments about, advertisements in order make good decisions about what goods or services to buy or what ideas to accept.

Advertisements can give you helpful information, such as facts about what is being sold. Advertisements can also exaggerate. They might say or suggest things that cannot possibly be accurate. Something that is accurate is true or correct. Whether accurate or misleading, ads often use names or pictures intended to catch people's interest.

How? When you look at an advertisement you need to ask some questions in order to evaluate its accuracy.

- What is the advertiser selling?
- Who are the people the advertiser is trying to reach?
- What facts can be found in the advertisement?
- What words or illustrations are used to encourage people to buy something or to support an idea?
- How accurate is the advertisement? Is there anything in the advertisement that cannot possibly be true?

Think and Apply

1. Look at the advertisement on page 446. What is it selling? Who might be interested in what is being sold?
2. What facts are given in the advertisement?
3. What does the picture show that cannot possibly be true?

446 — 447

Grade 5 Student Edition

Thinking Skills

Thinking skills are taught, practiced, and applied throughout each lesson to help students become critical thinkers and problem solvers.

- Solve a Problem
- Make a Decision
- Classify
- Identify Point of View
- Make Generalizations
- Evaluate Advertisements
- Recognize Fact and Opinion
- Make Inferences
- Detect Bias
- Determine Accuracy of Information

Chart and Graph Skills

Read a Cross-Section Diagram

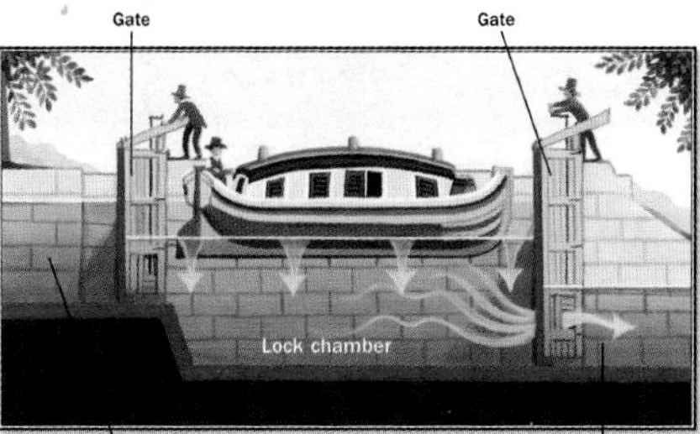

What? A **cross-section diagram** is a drawing that shows a view of something as if you could slice through it. Cross-section diagrams can be used to show you how something works.

Why? It is difficult to understand how a device works if you cannot see inside it. In a cross-section diagram, the artist "removes" part of the outside so that you can see how the inside works. A cross-section diagram helps you see how canals like the Erie Canal work.

How? To use a cross-section diagram, you have to study the drawing carefully. Read the labels to identify each part of the diagram.

The diagram on this page shows how a boat moves from higher to lower water in the lock of a canal. A lock is a section of a canal that is closed off so that water can be removed or added. The water coming in or going out changes the level of the water in the lock so that a boat can be moved higher or lower.

Look at the cross-section diagram. Notice that the boat has to be moved to a lower water level. Locate the gates that will keep the boat in the lock while the water level is being changed. Notice where the boat will go after the water level has been changed.

Think and Apply

1. What is the purpose of a canal lock?
2. What do the lock gates do?
3. This cross-section shows how a boat is moved from a higher water level to a lower water level. How do you think a lock could be used to move a boat from a lower water level to a higher water level?

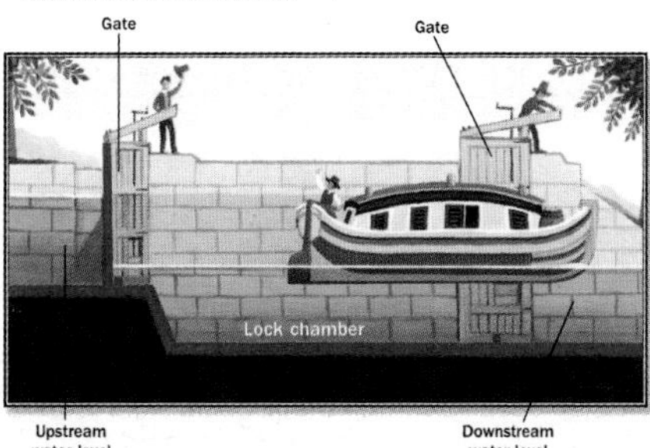

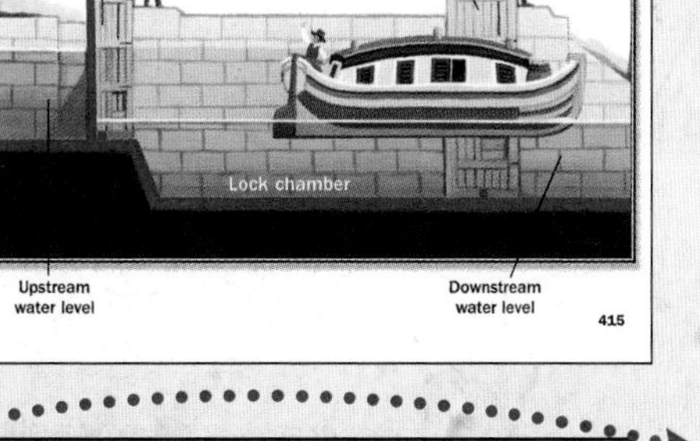

414 415

Grade 5 Student Edition

Chart and Graph Skills

Informative lessons teach your students how to read and interpret the types of data and graphic information that appear on high-stakes testing.

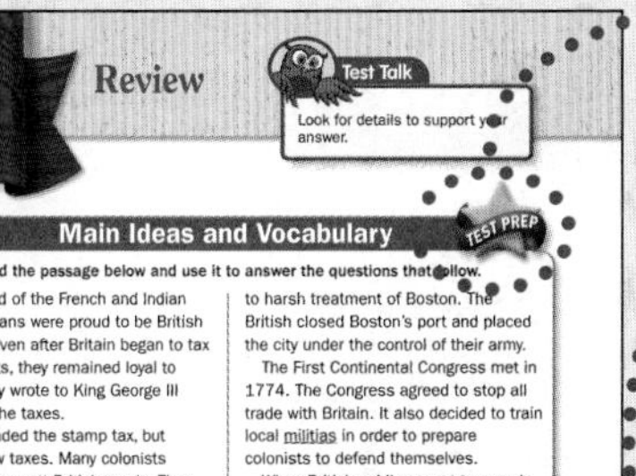

UNIT 4 Review

Test Talk

Look for details to support your answer.

Main Ideas and Vocabulary

326

Grade 5 Student Edition

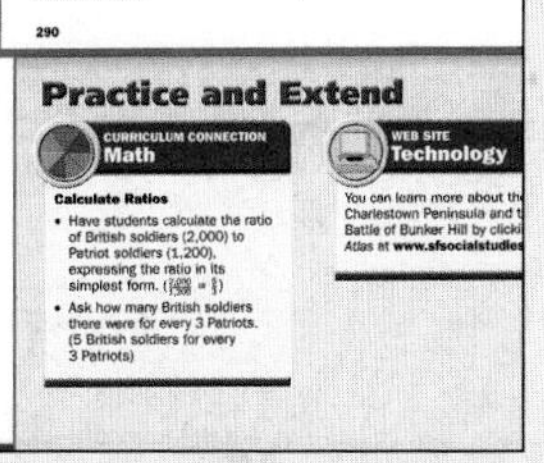

Test Talk

Locate Key Words in the Question

13 Why might the Patriots have waited to fire until the British got close? Have students identify the key words in the question. If necessary point out that *waited* and *close* are both key words. The Patriots could do more damage this way. **Make Inferences**

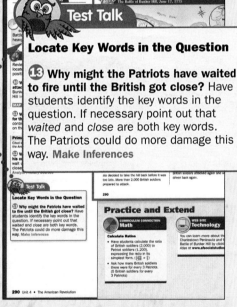

Practice and Extend

290 Unit 4 • The American Revolution

The gold star identifies test-prep opportunities.

Test Prep

Look for the Test Prep and Test Talk logos throughout Scott Foresman Social Studies to identify where key test-taking strategies are taught and practiced.

SCOTT FORESMAN DIFFERENCE

Map and Globe Skills

Using Latitude and Longitude

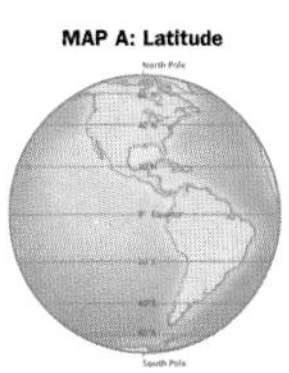

MAP A: Latitude

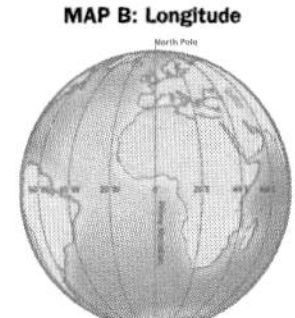

MAP B: Longitude

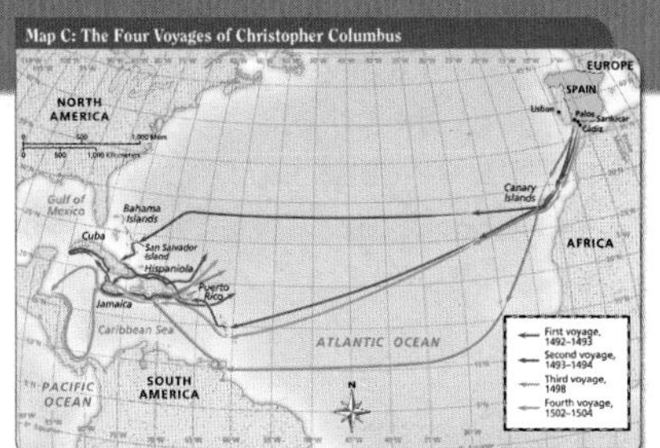

Map C: The Four Voyages of Christopher Columbus

Think and Apply

Internet Activity

140 141

Grade 5 Student Edition

Map and Globe Skills

Throughout the text, map and globe skills are taught, reviewed, and practiced to help build geographic literacy.

Easy to Plan, Easy to Teach

Scott Foresman Social Studies provides lessons in a clean, organized format that maximizes your teaching effectiveness and ensures that no child is left behind.

iTE
Online Teacher's Edition with connections to print ancillaries

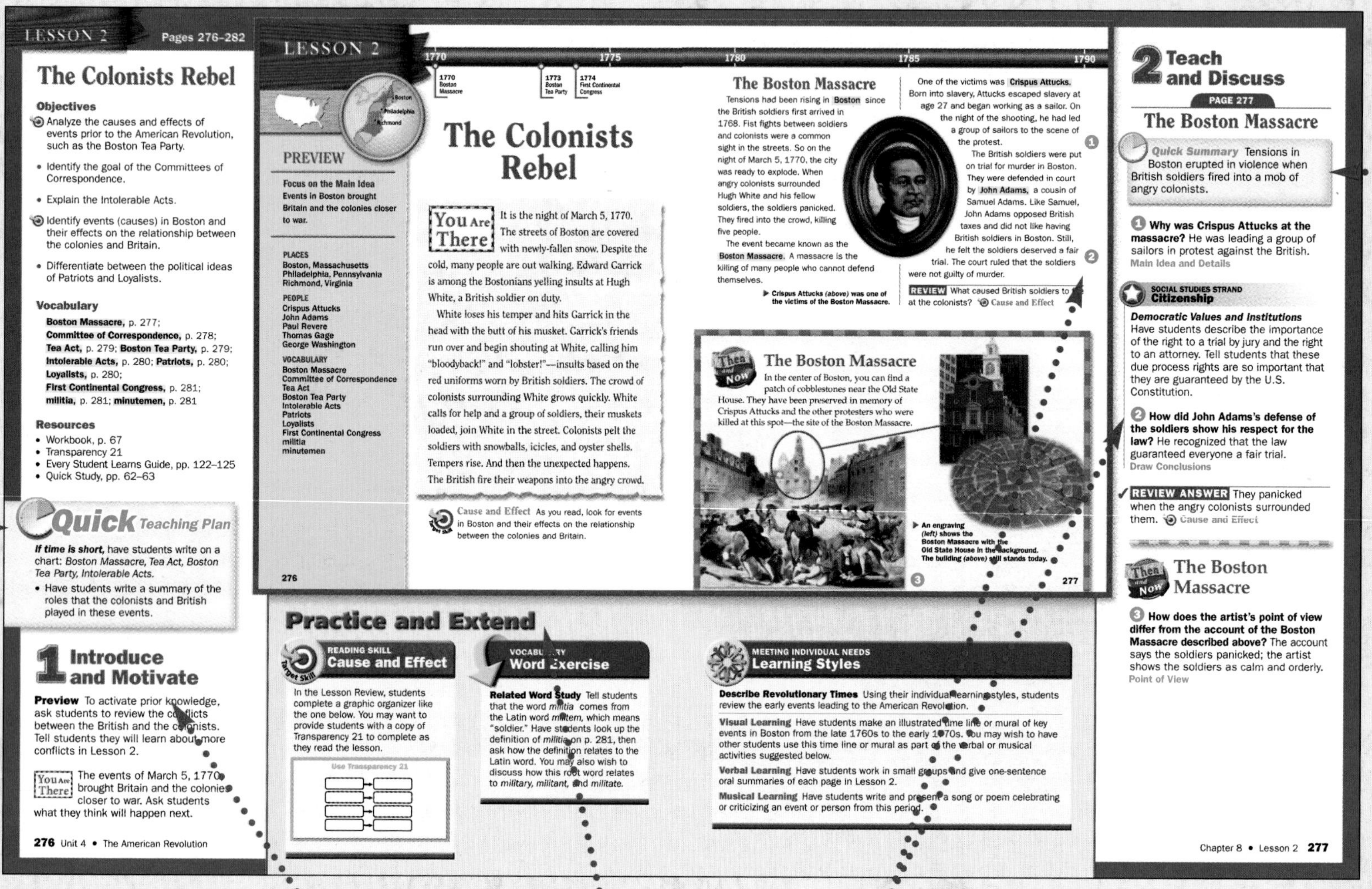

LESSON 2 Pages 276–282

The Colonists Rebel

Objectives

- Analyze the causes and effects of events prior to the American Revolution, such as the Boston Tea Party.
- Identify the goal of the Committees of Correspondence.
- Explain the Intolerable Acts.
- Identify events (causes) in Boston and their effects on the relationship between the colonies and Britain.
- Differentiate between the political ideas of Patriots and Loyalists.

Vocabulary

Boston Massacre, p. 277; **Committee of Correspondence**, p. 278; **Tea Act**, p. 279; **Boston Tea Party**, p. 279; **Intolerable Acts**, p. 280; **Patriots**, p. 280; **Loyalists**, p. 280; **First Continental Congress**, p. 281; **militia**, p. 281; **minutemen**, p. 281

Resources

- Workbook, p. 67
- Transparency 21
- Every Student Learns Guide, pp. 122–125
- Quick Study, pp. 62–63

Quick Teaching Plan

If time is short, have students write on a chart: *Boston Massacre, Tea Act, Boston Tea Party, Intolerable Acts.*

- Have students write a summary of the roles that the colonists and British played in these events.

1 Introduce and Motivate

Preview To activate prior knowledge, ask students to review the conflicts between the British and the colonists. Tell students they will learn about more conflicts in Lesson 2.

You Are There The events of March 5, 1770, brought Britain and the colonies closer to war. Ask students what they think will happen next.

LESSON 2

1770 Boston Massacre | 1773 Boston Tea Party | 1774 First Continental Congress

1770 | 1775 | 1780 | 1785 | 1790

PREVIEW

Focus on the Main Idea
Events in Boston brought Britain and the colonies closer to war.

PLACES
Boston, Massachusetts
Philadelphia, Pennsylvania
Richmond, Virginia

PEOPLE
Crispus Attucks
John Adams
Paul Revere
Thomas Gage
George Washington

VOCABULARY
Boston Massacre
Committee of Correspondence
Tea Act
Boston Tea Party
Intolerable Acts
Patriots
Loyalists
First Continental Congress
militia
minutemen

The Colonists Rebel

You Are There It is the night of March 5, 1770. The streets of Boston are covered with newly-fallen snow. Despite the cold, many people are out walking. Edward Garrick is among the Bostonians yelling insults at Hugh White, a British soldier on duty.

White loses his temper and hits Garrick in the head with the butt of his musket. Garrick's friends run over and begin shouting at White, calling him "bloodyback!" and "lobster!"—insults based on the red uniforms worn by British soldiers. The crowd of colonists surrounding White grows quickly. White calls for help and a group of soldiers, their muskets loaded, join White in the street. Colonists pelt the soldiers with snowballs, icicles, and oyster shells. Tempers rise. And then the unexpected happens. The British fire their weapons into the angry crowd.

Cause and Effect As you read, look for events in Boston and their effects on the relationship between the colonies and Britain.

276

The Boston Massacre

Tensions had been rising in Boston since the British soldiers first arrived in 1768. Fist fights between soldiers and colonists were a common sight in the streets. So on the night of March 5, 1770, the city was ready to explode. When angry colonists surrounded Hugh White and his fellow soldiers, the soldiers panicked. They fired into the crowd, killing five people.

The event became known as the Boston Massacre. A massacre is the killing of many people who cannot defend themselves.

► Crispus Attucks (above) was one of the victims of the Boston Massacre.

One of the victims was Crispus Attucks. Born into slavery, Attucks escaped slavery at age 27 and began working as a sailor. On the night of the shooting, he had led a group of sailors to the scene of the protest. 1

The British soldiers were put on trial for murder in Boston. They were defended in court by John Adams, a cousin of Samuel Adams. Like Samuel, John Adams opposed British taxes and did not like having British soldiers in Boston. Still, he felt the soldiers deserved a fair trial. The court ruled that the soldiers were not guilty of murder. 2

REVIEW What caused British soldiers to fire at the colonists? Cause and Effect

Then and Now: The Boston Massacre

In the center of Boston, you can find a patch of cobblestones near the Old State House. They have been preserved in memory of Crispus Attucks and the other protesters who were killed at this spot—the site of the Boston Massacre.

► An engraving (left) shows the Boston Massacre with the Old State House in the background. The building (above) still stands today. 3

277

2 Teach and Discuss

PAGE 277

The Boston Massacre

Quick Summary Tensions in Boston erupted in violence when British soldiers fired into a mob of angry colonists.

1 **Why was Crispus Attucks at the massacre?** He was leading a group of sailors in protest against the British. Main Idea and Details

SOCIAL STUDIES STRAND **Citizenship**

Democratic Values and Institutions Have students describe the importance of the right to a trial by jury and the right to an attorney. Tell students that these due process rights are so important that they are guaranteed by the U.S. Constitution.

2 **How did John Adams's defense of the soldiers show his respect for the law?** He recognized that the law guaranteed everyone a fair trial. Draw Conclusions

REVIEW ANSWER They panicked when the angry colonists surrounded them. Cause and Effect

Then and Now: The Boston Massacre

3 **How does the artist's point of view differ from the account of the Boston Massacre described above?** The account says the soldiers panicked; the artist shows the soldiers as calm and orderly. Point of View

Practice and Extend

READING SKILL **Cause and Effect**

In the Lesson Review, students complete a graphic organizer like the one below. You may want to provide students with a copy of Transparency 21 to complete as they read the lesson.

Use Transparency 21

VOCABULARY **Word Exercise**

Related Word Study Tell students that the word *militia* comes from the Latin word *militem*, which means "soldier." Have students look up the definition of *militia* on p. 281, then ask how the definition relates to the Latin word. You may also wish to discuss how this root word relates to *military, militant,* and *militate.*

MEETING INDIVIDUAL NEEDS **Learning Styles**

Describe Revolutionary Times Using their individual learning styles, students review the early events leading to the American Revolution.

Visual Learning Have students make an illustrated time line or mural of key events in Boston from the late 1760s to the early 1770s. You may wish to have other students use this time line or mural as part of the verbal or musical activities suggested below.

Verbal Learning Have students work in small groups and give one-sentence oral summaries of each page in Lesson 2.

Musical Learning Have students write and present a song or poem celebrating or criticizing an event or person from this period.

Quick Teaching Plan

If time is short, use the Quick Teaching Plan to teach lesson objectives quickly and cover the core content and skills.

Complete Lesson Plan

A familiar three-step lesson plan helps you deliver effective lessons that reach all your students.

Practice and Extend

Additional teaching strategies help you meet the needs of every student in your classroom.

Numbered Answers

Questions are keyed to the Student Edition to help you quickly guide students to the correct answer.

Quick Summary

Clear, concise lesson summaries save you valuable classroom instruction time.

✓ Ongoing Assessment

If... students do not understand the British and colonists' views of the Intolerable Acts,	**then...** have students make a list of the punishments Britain placed on Boston and another list of the actions colonists planned as a result of these punishments.

ExamView®
Test Bank CD-ROM
All Questions and Answers in English and Spanish

Assessment Opportunities

Ongoing Assessment
"If/then" models help you diagnose needs and prescribe practice at point of use.

Formal Assessment
Lesson, Chapter, and Unit Reviews give you multiple chances to assess your students' learning and provide test-taking practice.

ExamView Test Bank CD-ROM
Create customized tests and study guides in English and Spanish. Format tests to resemble state and national tests, administer them online, and receive immediate feedback.

Portfolio Assessment
Leveled Practice Activities, Workbook pages, and Curriculum Connections give you multiple ways to assess your students' understanding.

Performance Assessment
Hands-on Unit Projects, Internet Activities, Performance Assessment Notes, Write and Share Opportunities, and Scoring Guides allow you to assess your students' performance in a variety of ways.

Quick Study
- Complete Lesson Summaries for Easy Access
- Key Vocabulary Defined
- Review Sheets with Graphic Organizers

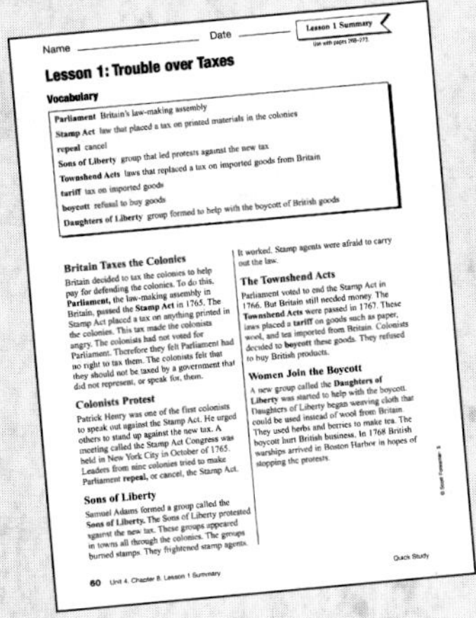

Lesson 1: Trouble over Taxes

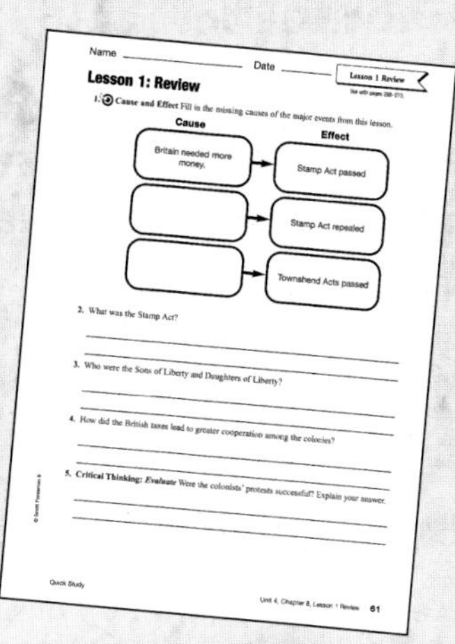

Lesson 1: Review

Quick Study

Easy-to-read summaries of every lesson ensure access to content, vocabulary, and skills. Review sheets with graphic organizers test every lesson objective and assess your students' understanding.

MEETING INDIVIDUAL NEEDS
Leveled Practice

Write a Letter About the Stamp Act Ask each student to write a letter about the effects of the Stamp Act.

Easy As a colonist, write a letter to a friend listing four things you want or need that the Stamp Act will affect. **Reteach**

On-Level As a colonist, write a short letter to Prime Minister Grenville. Explain how the Stamp Act affects you and why you oppose it. **Extend**

Challenge As Prime Minister Grenville, explain in a letter to a colonist how the Stamp Act will affect government income, why the government needs additional income, and why the act is fair. **Enrich**

For a Lesson Summary, use Quick Study, p. 60.

BUILD BACKGROUND
ESL Support

Make Comparisons Write on the board the average high and low temperatures for your area. Then provide current weather charts and maps from the newspaper or Internet for students to use in comparing temperatures in different areas.

Beginning Have students point out three places that have higher temperatures than your area and three areas that have lower temperatures. Help them record the information on a two-column chart with the headings *Cooler Than Our Community* and *Hotter Than Our Community*.

Intermediate Model comparison statements such as *The weather today is hotter in* _____ *than in our community.* Have students choose various places and make statements comparing the weather there to the weather in your community.

Advanced Have students study the weather maps and look for patterns that relate temperatures to location. Ask them to describe patterns that they notice.

For additional ESL support, use Every Student Learns Guide, pp. 10–13.

Meeting Individual Needs

Leveled practice helps you match your instruction with students' needs. Each lesson promotes active participation from all your students by providing the same type of activity at three instructional levels.

ESL Support

Research-based ESL strategies at point of use provide effective teaching suggestions for your Beginning, Intermediate, and Advanced language learners. Explore word meanings, usage, and form as well as cognates, etymologies, and more!

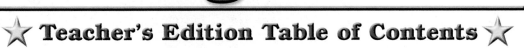

Teacher's Edition Table of Contents

Explore the United States E1

Table of Contents iii

Social Studies Handbook H2

Unit 1 *Living in the United States* 1a

Unit 2 *The Northeast* 95a

Unit 3 *The Southeast* 157a

Unit 4 *The Midwest* 223a

Unit 5 *The Southwest* 291a

Unit 6 *The West* 359a

Reference Guide R1–R78

Teacher Resources

Facing Fear: Helping Students Cope with Tragic Events TR1–TR2

School-to-Home Letters TR3–TR14

Calendar Activities TR15–TR28

Writing Rubrics TR29–TR38

Unit Bibliographies TR39–TR44

Graphic Organizers TR45–TR70

Index TR71–TR76

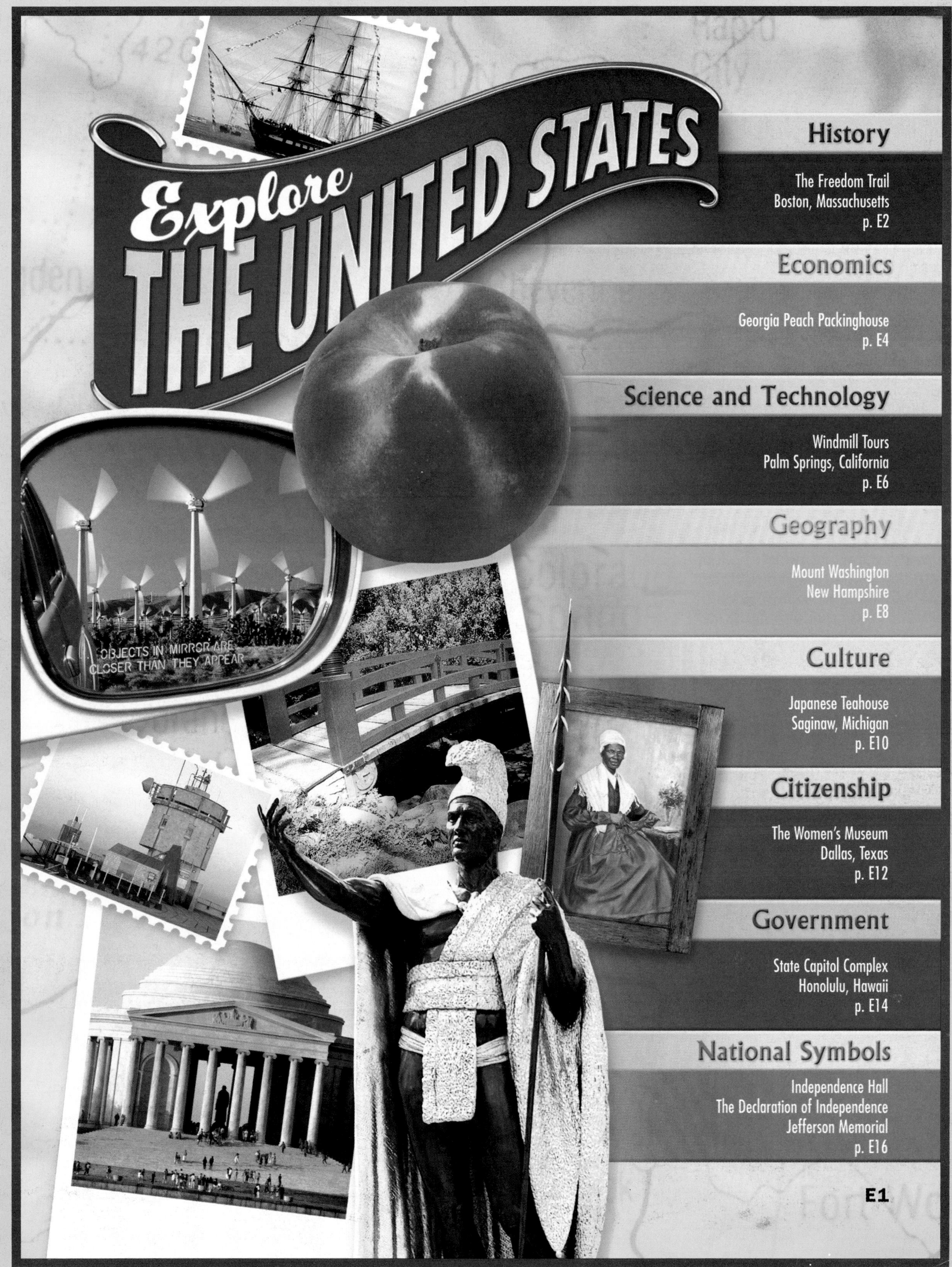
Explore
THE UNITED STATES
OBJECTS IN MIRROR ARE
CLOSER THAN THEY APPEAR

History

The Freedom Trail
Boston, Massachusetts
p. E2

Economics

Georgia Peach Packinghouse
p. E4

Science and Technology

Windmill Tours
Palm Springs, California
p. E6

Geography

Mount Washington
New Hampshire
p. E8

Culture

Japanese Teahouse
Saginaw, Michigan
p. E10

Citizenship

The Women's Museum
Dallas, Texas
p. E12

Government

State Capitol Complex
Honolulu, Hawaii
p. E14

National Symbols

Independence Hall
The Declaration of Independence
Jefferson Memorial
p. E16

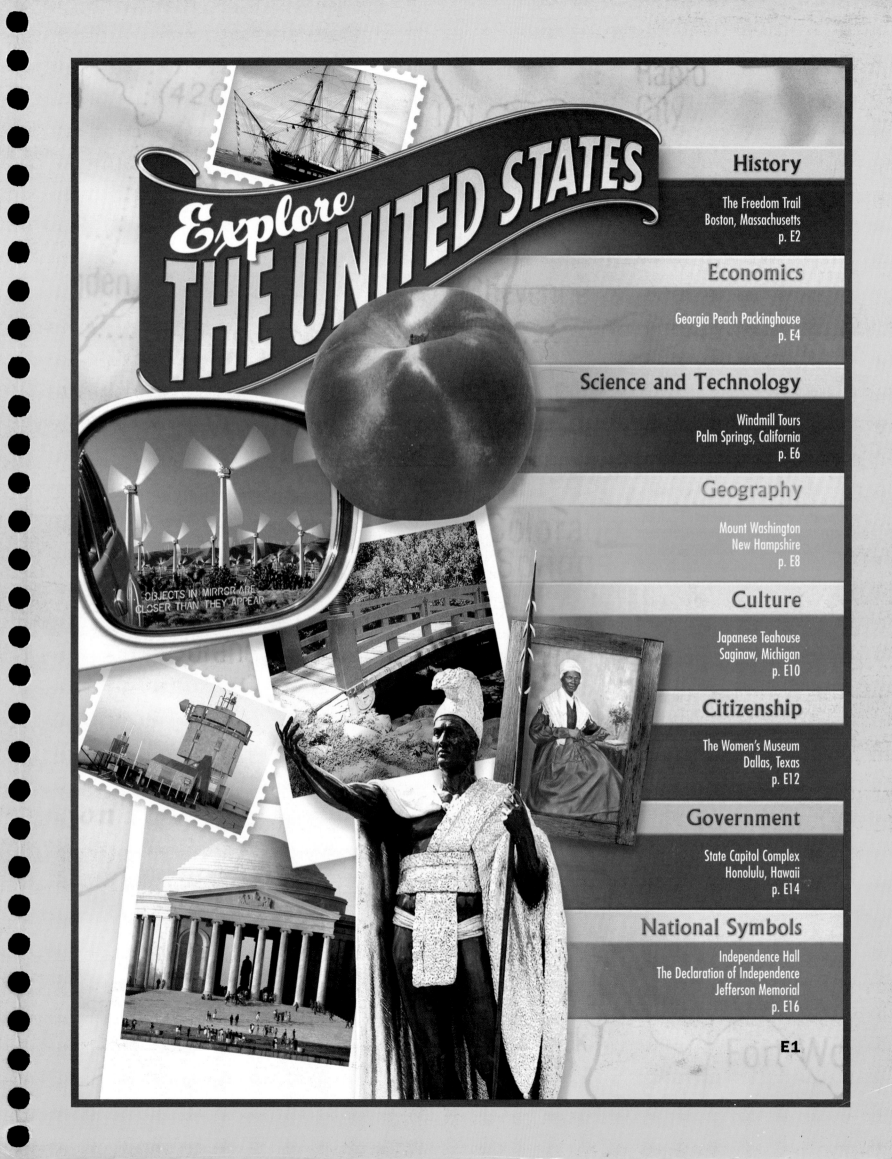

History

Objectives

- Identify important sites and events in American history.
- Explain the importance of preserving historic sites.

Vocabulary

freedom the power to do, say, and think as you want

preserve keep something from being harmed or changed

1 Introduce and Motivate

Preview To activate prior knowledge, ask students what they know about people, places, and events, such as John Adams, Samuel Adams, Bunker Hill, the Boston Tea Party, and Paul Revere's midnight ride. Explain that many important events in American history took place in Boston.

You Are There Have students look at the pictures of some of the historic places on the Freedom Trail as shown on the travel brochure on pages E2–E3. Discuss which sites they would most like to visit, and why.

History

History is the study of events that happened in the past.

The Freedom Trail
Boston, Massachusetts

You Are There You're following the Freedom Trail through the narrow streets of Boston. You have to really watch your step since the sidewalks are made of brick. Wow! Most of these buildings are really old! Many were built before the United States became a country. You can picture what life was like here more than 200 years ago. You pass by the Old South Meeting House, where colonists held protests. You find Paul Revere's home, where he began his famous journey. You stand where a battle began at Bunker Hill. You can almost hear the firing of the cannons.

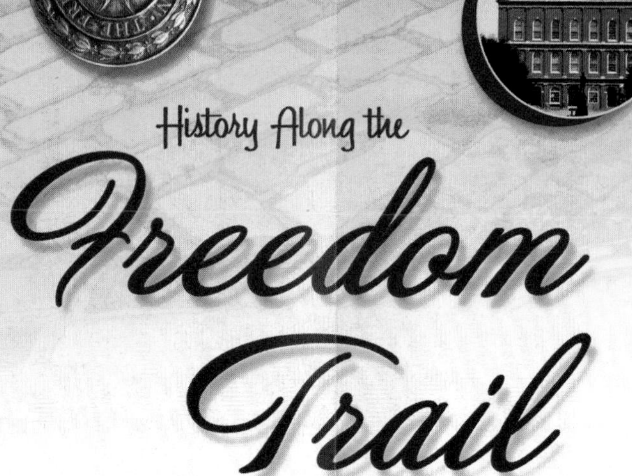

THE FREEDOM TRAIL BOSTON
Faneuil Hall
History Along the
Freedom
Trail

The Freedom Trail is a walking tour of sixteen historic places. Boston is one of the oldest cities in the United States. It was once part of a colony ruled by Great Britain. Many people in Boston fought for freedom from British rule. **Freedom** is the power to do, say, and think as you want. Each site on the Freedom Trail was important to the fight for freedom and the birth of our country.

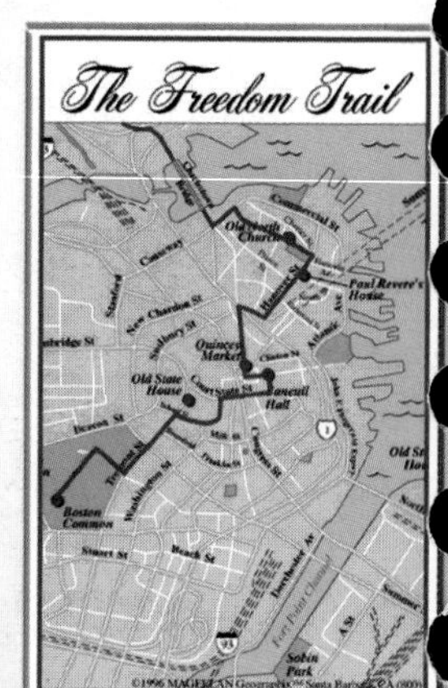

Practice and Extend

FYI SOCIAL STUDIES
Background

About the Freedom Trail

- Boston was colonized by the British in 1630.
- A Boston newspaper columnist, as a way to showcase and preserve the city's historic sites, conceptualized the Freedom Trail in 1951.
- Four million people visit the Freedom Trail every year.
- Following the Freedom Trail, visitors can see the graves of John Hancock, Samuel Adams, Paul Revere, Crispus Attucks, and others.

History in Massachusetts

Boston

Bunker Hill Monument

A painted line connects the sixteen sites on the Freedom Trail.

USS *Constitution*

Paul Revere warned other colonists of a British attack the night before the American Revolution began. His house, the oldest wooden building in Boston, is a stop on the Freedom Trail.

Fast Facts:

- The Freedom Trail was created in 1958. It has helped preserve historic sites in Boston. **Preserve** means to keep something from being harmed or changed.
- The Freedom Trail starts at our country's oldest public park, called the Boston Common. Long ago the people of Boston used to graze sheep and cattle there.

Link to You

What historic buildings in your community have been preserved?

E3

2 Teach and Discuss

Map Study Have the students use the maps on p. E3. to locate Boston and Massachusetts. Ask them to turn to the Atlas map on pp. R12–R13. Have them identify the states that surround Massachusetts.

Read the text on pp. E2–E3 with students. Then discuss the following questions:

What are some sites on the Freedom Trail? Possible answers: The Old South Meeting House; Paul Revere House; Boston Common; Bunker Hill; Faneuil Hall

Why do you think it was called the Freedom Trail? Possible answer: Because each site was important to the fight for freedom from British control

Why do you think the Freedom Trail was created? Possible answers: To preserve historic sites in Boston; to educate people about the history of Boston

3 Close and Assess

Have students discuss the impact of the Freedom Trail on people's understanding of history. Do they think the preservation of sites on the Freedom Trail was important?

Link to You

Have students use the History graphic organizer to develop a list of historic buildings in their community. Answers will vary.

CURRICULUM CONNECTION
Writing

Use Graphic Organizers

- Use the History graphic organizer to help students answer the Link to You question.
- Direct students to use pictures and words in their answers.
- Have students share their answers with a partner or in a small group.

Organizer, p. E17

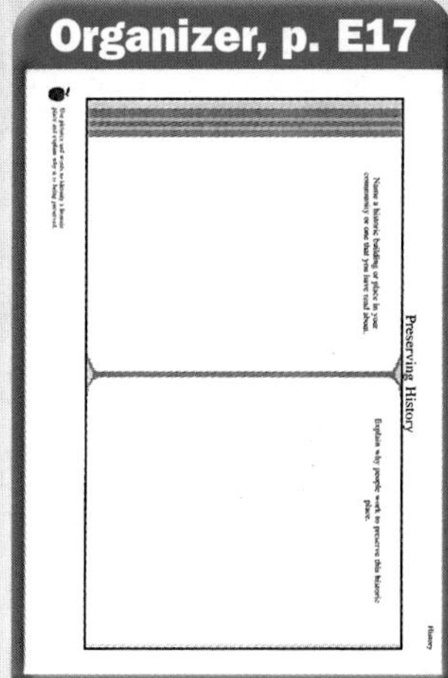

Economics

Objectives
- Explain the impact of technological progress on the growth of industry.
- Describe the production and delivery process of a product.
- Define profit and how it might change if there are more opportunities to sell a product.

Vocabulary

produce grow or make

profit money made from a business

transport deliver

1 Introduce and Motivate

Preview To activate prior knowledge, ask students to think about where the fruit they eat comes from and how it reaches their stores. Explain that the travel brochure on pp. E4–5 explains how Georgia peaches get from orchards to stores.

You Are There Ask students to think about some of the products they buy or use on a daily basis. Discuss the processes these products might have gone through before being purchased.

Economics

Economics is the study of how people produce, distribute, and use goods and services.

Georgia Peach Packinghouse

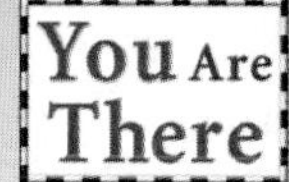

You Are There It's a hot summer day in Georgia. You're at a peach packinghouse. Hundreds of peaches roll past you. They were picked this morning and brought here by tractor. Each one is inspected. You watch as the peaches are washed, rinsed, and dried. They are inspected again. Peaches that are too small or bruised are removed. Then the good peaches are packed up in boxes. You know that once they are loaded into cold trucks, they will be on their way to stores.

E4

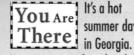

Get a taste of economics at work in the **Peach Packinghouse!**

Years ago, the peaches **produced**, or grown, in Georgia could only be sold at nearby stores or stands. If peaches were shipped too far away or got too hot, they would spoil. Only people near the orchards could buy them fresh. The **profits**, or money made by the business, were small. Now peaches can be packed in refrigerated trucks. They are **transported**, or delivered, to places all over the country. Today, the state of Georgia earns about $35 million a year from the sale of peaches.

Practice and Extend

FYI SOCIAL STUDIES **Background**

Georgia's Peach Industry
- Georgia has long been known as the Peach State. Another name it has is "Empire State of the South," to indicate its importance in industrial and economic development in the southern states.
- Peachtree Street is an important street in Atlanta, Georgia.
- While machines are used during some stages of processing peaches, most are still hand-picked and hand-packed.
- Peaches are processed and shipped quickly. Many arrive in stores within a day of being picked.

Economics in Georgia

Peach Region

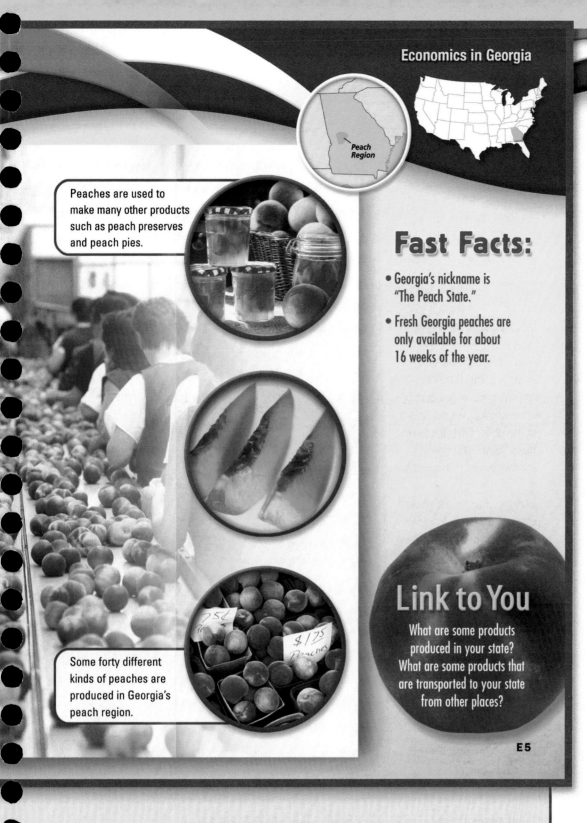

Peaches are used to make many other products such as peach preserves and peach pies.

Some forty different kinds of peaches are produced in Georgia's peach region.

Fast Facts:

- Georgia's nickname is "The Peach State."
- Fresh Georgia peaches are only available for about 16 weeks of the year.

Link to You

What are some products produced in your state? What are some products that are transported to your state from other places?

E5

2 Teach and Discuss

Map Study Have the students use the maps on p. E5 to locate Georgia and its peach growing region.

Read the text on pp. E4–E5 with students. Then discuss the following questions:

What happens to a peach before you buy it in the store? It is picked, transported by tractor, inspected, washed, rinsed, dried, inspected again, sorted, packed, refrigerated, and shipped.

How did refrigerated trucks change the peach business in Georgia? They allowed peaches to be shipped outside of Georgia, which caused profits to grow.

How does the peach business affect the economy of Georgia? Possible answers: Georgia earns $35 million a year from peaches; the Georgia peach business provides many jobs.

3 Close and Assess

Explain to students that profits are the money made on a business *after all expenses have been paid.* Discuss various expenses a peach business might have.

Link to You

Have students use the Economics graphic organizer to show what products come from your state, and what products are transported to your state. Answers will vary.

CURRICULUM CONNECTION
Writing

Use Graphic Organizers

- Use the Economics graphic organizer to help students answer the Link to You question.
- Direct students to use pictures and words in their answers.
- Have students share their answers with a partner or in a small group.

Organizer, p. E18

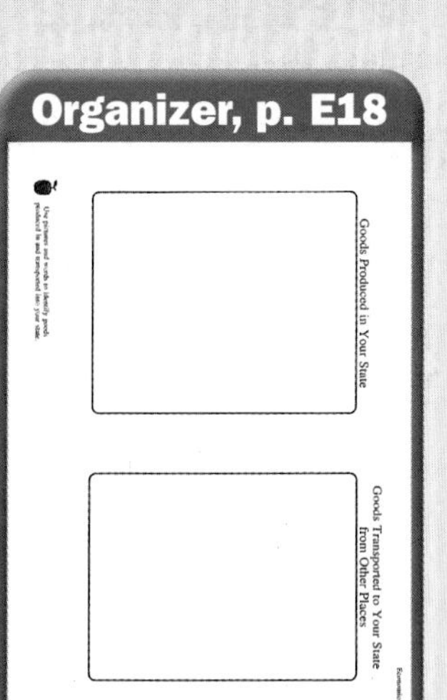

Science and Technology

Objectives
- Explain how natural forces can be used to create energy.
- Give examples of ways changes in technology has improved peoples' lives.

Vocabulary

modern newer

electricity the kind of energy that can power a light bulb or TV

1 Introduce and Motivate

Preview To activate prior knowledge, ask students if they know how electricity is created. Explain that they will be learning about one way electricity is made.

You Are There After reviewing the pictures on the travel brochure shown on pp. E6–E8, ask students what kinds of places they think usually have windmill farms. Have them explain their ideas.

Science and Technology

Science and technology change people's lives. These changes bring opportunities and challenges.

Windmill Tours
Palm Springs, California

You Are There The wind whips through your hair as you stand in the desert. A "sea of giants" surrounds you. Each one stands more than 100 feet tall with long powerful arms. As you gaze up at one of them, the sun reflects off the white metal. You squint. These "giants" are windmills, and they are using the wind to make electricity. As wind turns the blades, or arms, of the windmill, energy is produced. As you get ready to leave, you look behind you. The windmills are spinning almost silently. The wind rustles your hair again as you wave good-bye to the giants.

E6

Nature Meets Technology at

WINDMILL TOURS

Windmills are a good example of nature and technology working together. The windmill farm near Palm Springs, California, is in one of the windiest places in the state. More than 3,000 windmills line the valley. Wind power spins their blades. Engines inside these **modern**, or newer, windmills turn the wind's energy into electricity. An engine is a machine that uses movement to make power. **Electricity** is the kind of energy that can power a light bulb or TV.

Windmills have been used for hundreds of years. Modern windmills make more energy than older ones do.

Practice and Extend

FYI SOCIAL STUDIES **Background**

About Windmill Farms
- The windmill farm is in the San Jacinto Mountains, where the entrance to the Coachella Valley creates a natural wind tunnel.
- Coachella Valley winds switch direction midday. Half of the farm's windmills face east, to catch the morning winds, and the other half face west, for the afternoon winds.
- The largest windmills at the farm are 20 stories high. Each one can produce enough power for 2000 homes.
- Windmill "farmers" make a living by selling electricity to utility companies.
- California, Texas, and Iowa are some of the states in the U.S. with the greatest wind power capacity.

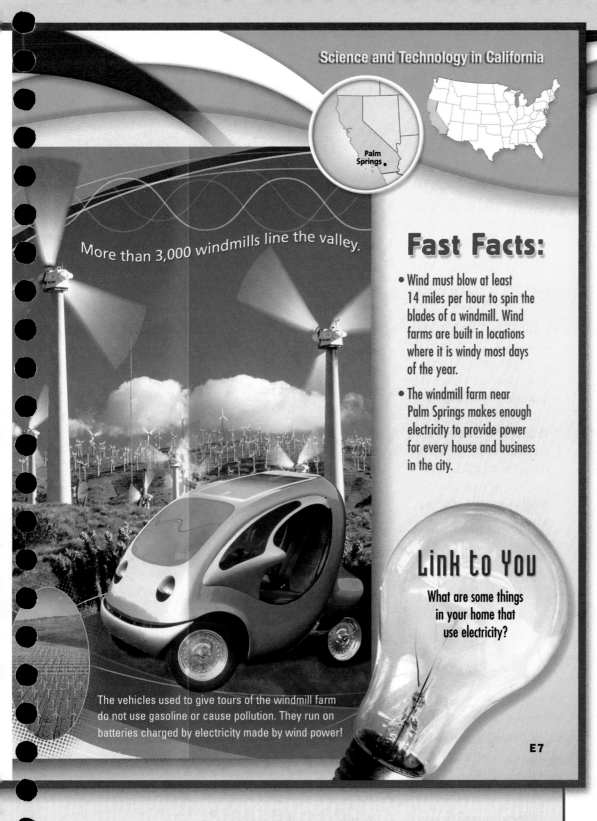

Palm Springs

More than 3,000 windmills line the valley.

Fast Facts:

- Wind must blow at least 14 miles per hour to spin the blades of a windmill. Wind farms are built in locations where it is windy most days of the year.
- The windmill farm near Palm Springs makes enough electricity to provide power for every house and business in the city.

Link to You

What are some things in your home that use electricity?

The vehicles used to give tours of the windmill farm do not use gasoline or cause pollution. They run on batteries charged by electricity made by wind power!

2 Teach and Discuss

Map Study Have the students use the maps on p. E7 to locate Palm Springs and California.

Read the text on pp. E6–E7 with students. Then discuss the following questions:

What does the engine inside the windmill do? Turns the wind's energy into power

Why is this valley in California a good place to produce energy using windmills? Because it is one of the windiest places in state

How are modern windmills different from older ones? Possible answers: Modern windmills make more energy; they look very different.

What are some other things that use the power of the wind to move? Possible answers: Sailboats; kites; hang gliders

3 Close and Assess

The city of Palm Springs, California, gets all of its electricity from wind. Ask students to consider whether or not their own community could use windmills to create electricity.

Link to You

Have students use the Science and Technology graphic organizer to list items that use electricity. Possible answers: Lights; refrigerator; television; stereo; computer.

CURRICULUM CONNECTION

Writing

Use Graphic Organizers

- Use the Science and Technology graphic organizer to help students answer the Link to You question.
- Direct students to use pictures and words in their answers.
- Have students share their answers with a partner or in a small group.

Organizer, p. E19

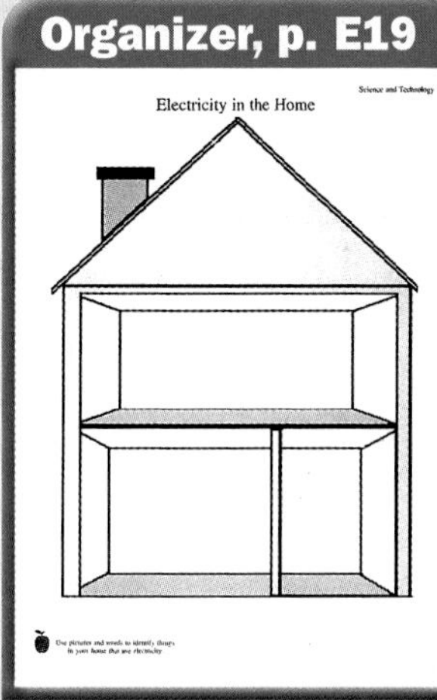

Geography

Objectives

- Explain differences between temperature and weather.
- Explain how a place's geography affects its weather.
- Identify and explain unique weather patterns.

Vocabulary

weather the temperature and other conditions at a certain time and place

range a group of mountains

temperature how hot or cold a place gets

1 Introduce and Motivate

Preview To activate prior knowledge, ask students to explain what they think the relationship is between the words *weather* and *temperature.* Using the pictures as clues, have students predict what they will learn about this location.

You Are There Ask students to describe the coldest or windiest places they have ever visited. Have them compare their experiences with the photographs and descriptions of Mount Washington on the travel brochure shown on pp. E8–E9.

Geography

Geography is the study of the relationship between Earth's physical features, climate, and people.

Mount Washington
New Hampshire

You Are There You're standing at the top of a snow-covered mountain. It's one of the windiest spots in the world! The wind howls against the windows of the observatory. You are safe and warm behind the thick glass of the building. Outside, you can see icicles that stick out sideways, straight off the building. You see people struggling to stand up straight against the wind. You take one last look out the window. Then you bundle up in your winter coat. You step outside, point the top of your head into the wind, and put one foot forward.

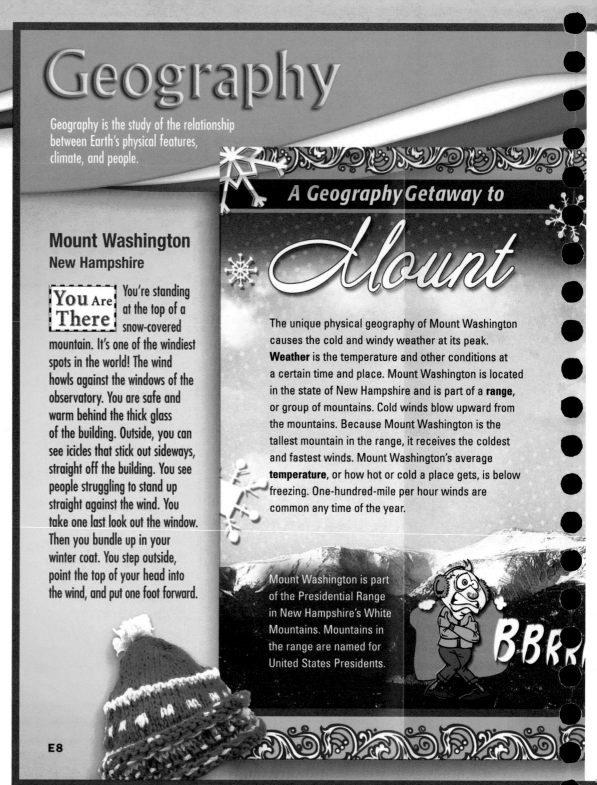

A Geography Getaway to Mount

The unique physical geography of Mount Washington causes the cold and windy weather at its peak. **Weather** is the temperature and other conditions at a certain time and place. Mount Washington is located in the state of New Hampshire and is part of a **range**, or group of mountains. Cold winds blow upward from the mountains. Because Mount Washington is the tallest mountain in the range, it receives the coldest and fastest winds. Mount Washington's average **temperature**, or how hot or cold a place gets, is below freezing. One-hundred-mile per hour winds are common any time of the year.

Mount Washington is part of the Presidential Range in New Hampshire's White Mountains. Mountains in the range are named for United States Presidents.

BBRR

E8

Practice and Extend

SOCIAL STUDIES
Background

About Mount Washington

- The Presidential Range includes mountains named for other U.S. Presidents, such as Adams, Jefferson, Madison, and Monroe.
- The Mount Washington Observatory was founded in 1932, when scientists began recording the peak's unusual weather.
- You can reach the top of Mount Washington on a special railway that carries passengers up and down the steep mountain. For the 3 mile trip up the mountain, the steam engine uses up 2,000 pounds of coal and more than 1,000 gallons of water. Part of the ride is so steep that people seated in the front of the passenger car are 14 feet higher than passengers at the rear of the car.

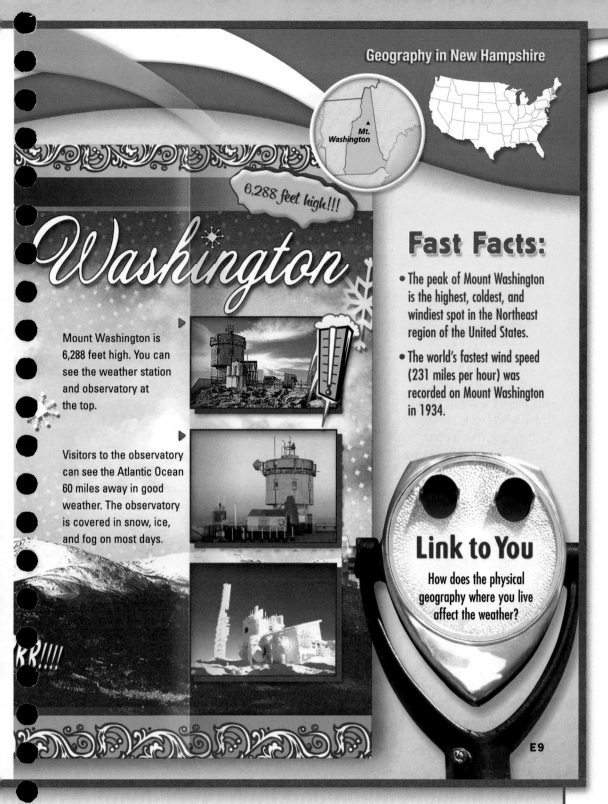

Mt. Washington

6,288 feet high!!!

Washington

Mount Washington is 6,288 feet high. You can see the weather station and observatory at the top.

Visitors to the observatory can see the Atlantic Ocean 60 miles away in good weather. The observatory is covered in snow, ice, and fog on most days.

Fast Facts:

- The peak of Mount Washington is the highest, coldest, and windiest spot in the Northeast region of the United States.
- The world's fastest wind speed (231 miles per hour) was recorded on Mount Washington in 1934.

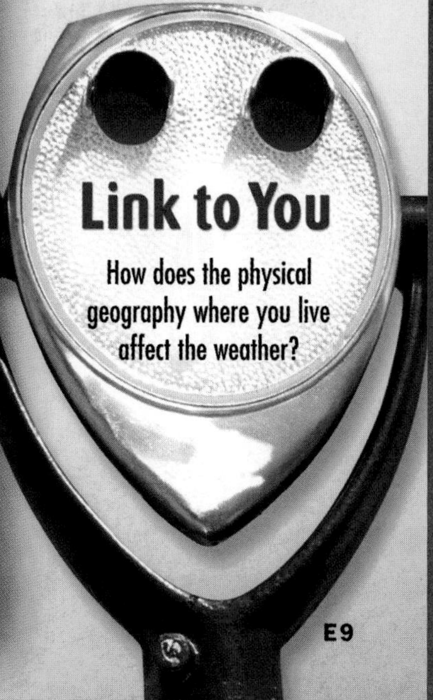

Link to You

How does the physical geography where you live affect the weather?

E9

2 Teach and Discuss

Map Study Have the students use the maps on p. E9 to locate New Hampshire and Mount Washington. Tell the students that visitors can see the Atlantic Ocean from the top of the mountain on a clear day. Have students turn to the Atlas map on pp. R14–R15 and find Mount Washington. Ask them to name the state they would look across to see the Atlantic Ocean. They would look across Maine.

Read the text on pp. E8–E9 with students. Then discuss the following questions:

Why is it so windy at the top of Mount Washington? Because cold winds blow upward from the other mountains in the range

What is at the top of Mount Washington? An observatory and a weather station

Why do you think people built a weather station on Mount Washington? Possible answer: Because the weather on Mount Washington is so unusual

3 Close and Assess

Have students identify other locations in the United States that have unique or extreme weather. Discuss how the geography of these regions impacts their weather.

CURRICULUM CONNECTION
Writing

Use Graphic Organizers

- Use the Geography graphic organizer to help students answer the Link to You question.
- Direct students to use pictures and words in their answers.
- Have students share their answers with a partner or in a small group.

Organizer, p. E20

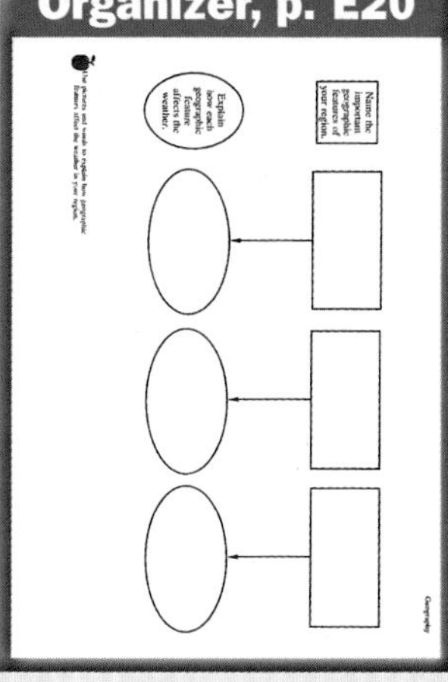

Link to You

Have students use the Geography graphic organizer to help them answer the question. Possible answers: It is hot because we live in the South, which is closer to the equator; it is windy because we live near a lake; there is a lot of snow because we live in the mountains.

Culture

Objectives

- Identify and describe traditions from cultures around the world.
- Recognize the diversity of cultures and traditions within the United States.

Vocabulary

symbol object that represents an idea

authentic done in a traditional way

1 Introduce and Motivate

Preview To activate prior knowledge, ask students if they know someone who drinks tea. Ask students if that person drinks tea hot or cold. Have them look at the pictures on the travel brochure shown on pp. E10–E11. Tell the students that they are going to learn about a Japanese tea house and how tea is served there.

You Are There Ask the students to describe ceremonies in which they might have taken part that remind them of the Japanese Tea Ceremony.

Culture

Culture includes the customs, traditions, behavior, and values of a group of people.

Japanese Tea House and Friendship Garden
Saginaw, Michigan

You Are There The gong sounds and the tea ceremony, or "Way of Tea" begins. Taking off your shoes, you enter the tatami (tah TAH mee), or woven straw mat, tearoom. Then you walk toward the scroll and flowers and sit to admire them. You move next to your hostess, and wait as she prepares the tea in the traditional way, as it has long been done in Japan. While you watch, she adds boiling water to the tea and whisks it. When the tea is ready, you receive the tea bowl, then turn it twice and sip the tea. It is delicious!

Let your friendships blossom...

Japanese Tea House and Friendship Garden

The Friendship Garden is a traditional Japanese garden. The Garden and Tea House were built as symbols of friendship between the cities of Saginaw (SA-gi-naw), Michigan, and Tokushima (TOH-koo-shee-mah), Japan. A **symbol** is an object that represents an idea. People come here to learn about Japanese culture. Visitors can participate in an authentic Japanese tea ceremony in the Tea House. **Authentic** means done in a traditional way.

E10

Practice and Extend

FYI SOCIAL STUDIES Background

The Japanese Tea Ceremony

- Only a dozen authentic Japanese tea houses exist in the United States. The tea house in Saginaw is considered to be one of the finest outside of Japan.
- The Japanese tea ceremony is frequently called the *chado* (CHAH-doh).
- The basic principles of an authentic Japanese tea ceremony are Wa-Kei-Sei-Jaku, or harmony, respect, purity, and tranquility.
- The tea house in Saginaw holds ceremonies for beginners, to teach visitors the basic traditions of a tea ceremony.

Culture in Michigan

Saginaw

Fast Facts:

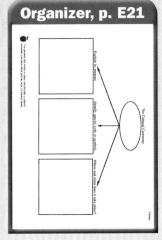

- No nails or paint are used in the construction of an authentic Japanese tea house.
- Japanese tea houses have very low doors. Guests must bend down to enter them.

Craftsmen from Japan helped build the Tea House in Saginaw. It looks like an authentic tea house from Japan.

Link to You

Have you ever seen or taken part in a cultural ceremony? What made it memorable?

E11

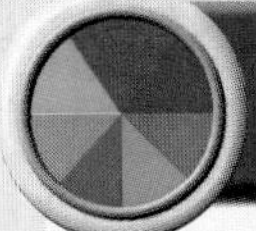

CURRICULUM CONNECTION Writing

Use Graphic Organizers

- Use the Culture graphic organizer to help students answer the Link to You question.
- Direct students to use pictures and words in their answers.
- Have students share their answers with a partner or in a small group.

Organizer, p. E21

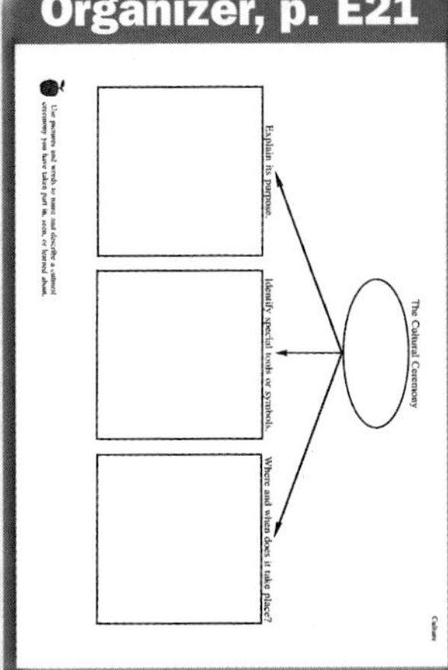

2 Teach and Discuss

Map Study Have students use the maps on p. E11 to locate Saginaw and Michigan. Ask them to turn to the world map in the Atlas on p. R5 and locate Japan.

Read the text on pp. E10–E11 with students. Then discuss the following questions:

What is a *tatami*? A woven straw mat

What do the Japanese Tea House and Friendship Garden symbolize? Friendship between the cities of Saginaw and Tokushima

What are some things that make the tea house authentic? Possible answers: No nails or paint were used in construction; the doors are very low; the tea ceremony is done in the traditional way.

3 Close and Assess

Ask students to identify cultures they are interested in. Have them suggest ways that they could learn about the customs of these cultures.

Link to You

Have students use the Culture graphic organizer to describe a cultural ceremony that they have seen or taken part in. Answers will vary.

Citizenship

Objectives

- Identify rights and responsibilities of U.S. citizenship.
- Explain how people sometimes have to work to gain their rights.

Vocabulary

rights things you are allowed to do

equality having the same rights as others

1 Introduce and Motivate

Preview To activate prior knowledge, ask students why it is important to be treated equally. Have students give examples of times they felt they did or did not have equality. Tell them that the travel brochure shown on pp. E12–E13 describes a museum where people can learn about some women who have helped gain equality for women in the United States.

You Are There Sojourner Truth risked her life to speak out for women's right to vote. Ask students why the right to vote is important.

Citizenship

Citizenship is the rights, privileges, and duties that a member of a nation has.

The Women's Museum

Dallas, Texas

You Are There You look into the eyes of Sojourner Truth's photograph. You remember learning that this brave woman fought hard for equal rights of citizenship. It was illegal for women to vote at the time this photograph was taken. Women were turned away from elections. Others were put in jail or even beaten for trying to vote. Sojourner Truth gave speeches about equality all over the country. You pause and look at her photograph again. You wonder if you could have been that brave.

Honor Citizenship and Equality at The Women's Museum

WOMEN HONOR EQUALITY CITIZEN

E12

Practice and Extend

SOCIAL STUDIES Background

Women's Rights and the Women's Museum

- The exhibits of the Women's Museum highlight women's achievements in fields such as science, sports, invention, health, literature, comedy, and politics.
- Sojourner Truth was born into slavery in upstate New York around 1797. She became legally free in 1827. She gave her famous "Ain't I a Woman?" speech at the 1851 Women's Rights Convention in Akron, Ohio. The nineteenth amendment, granting women the right to vote, was passed on August 18, 1920.
- The Women's Museum offers classes in math, science, and computer technology.
- The museum has a 70-foot-long Harmony Wisdom Wall with postings of quotes and sayings. Before being permanently installed, the wall toured eleven U.S. cities.

The Women's Museum in Dallas, Texas, has exhibits that honor women who fought for equal rights of citizenship. **Rights** are things you are allowed to do. Although women have gained many rights over the years, some still fight for equality. **Equality** means having the same rights as others. The museum inspires visitors today to become responsible citizens and leaders by teaching about strong women.

Companies and individual citizens donated money to open the museum.

The colorful "Electronic Quilt" greets visitors at the entrance. Thirty-five television screens show images from the museum's exhibits.

Fast Facts:

- The Women's Museum in Dallas tells the stories of more than 3,000 American women.
- More than 100,000 people have visited the Women's Museum since it opened in 2000.

What rights do you have as a citizen? What responsibilities come along with those rights?

E13

2 Teach and Discuss

Map Study Have the students use the maps on p. E13 to locate Texas and Dallas.

Read the text on pp. E12–E13 with students. Then discuss the following questions:

Why was voting such an important right to Sojourner Truth and other women in the 1800s? Possible answer: Women wanted to have the same rights as others; women wanted to have a vote in their government.

How does the Women's Museum honor women? Possible answer: By providing exhibits about women who worked to achieve equal rights

How does the Women's Museum help people to be better citizens? Possible answer: The museum teaches people to become leaders by following the example of women from history.

3 Close and Assess

Tell the students that along with the rights of citizenship, comes responsibilities. Ask the students to identify some of their responsibilities as citizens of their class and school.

Link to You

Have students use the Citizenship graphic organizer to describe the rights and responsibilities of a citizen. Answers will vary.

CURRICULUM CONNECTION
Writing

Use Graphic Organizers

- Use the Citizenship graphic organizer to help students answer the Link to You question.
- Direct students to use pictures and words in their answers.
- Have students share their answers with a partner or in a small group.

Organizer, p. E22

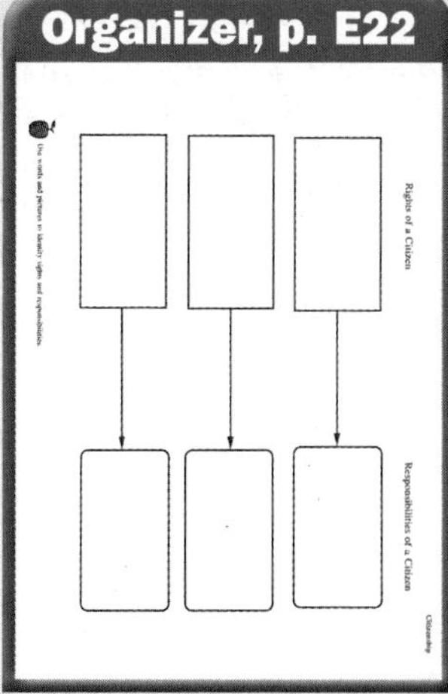

Government

Objectives

- Identify and define the differences between a monarchy and a constitutional government.
- Identify ways in which the government in Hawaii has changed since the 1800s.

Vocabulary

monarch king or queen

constitution written plan of government

1 Introduce and Motivate

Preview To activate prior knowledge, ask students what they think it would be like to live in a kingdom. How would their lives be different? Tell students that the travel brochure on pp. E14–E15 will help them learn about Hawaii's government, which was once a kingdom ruled by kings and queens.

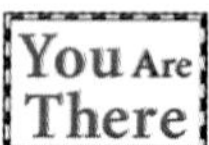

Remind students that each state has its own capitol building. Ask students how Hawaii's State Capitol might be similar to or different from their own state's capitol.

2 Teach and Discuss

Map Study Have students look at the maps on p. E15 to locate Hawaii and Honolulu. Point out that the map showing the location of Hawaii relative to the mainland states is not drawn to scale. Have students turn to the Atlas map on pp. R10–R11 to see a map that is drawn to scale and shows how far Hawaii is from the mainland.

Government

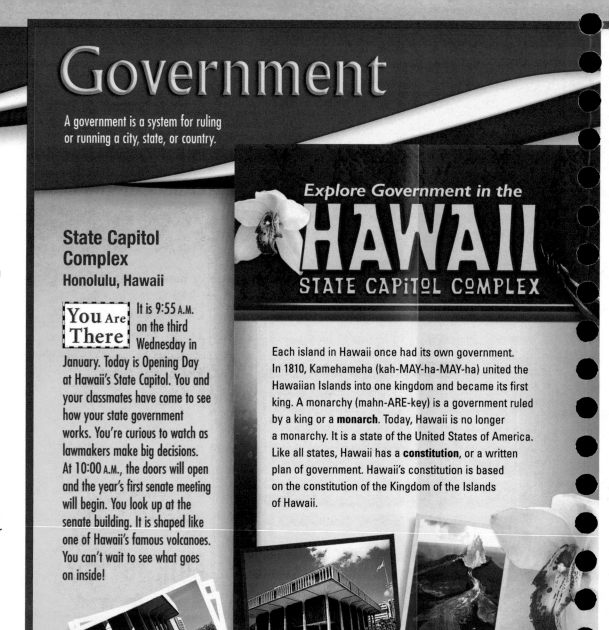

A government is a system for ruling or running a city, state, or country.

Explore Government in the

HAWAII STATE CAPITOL COMPLEX

State Capitol Complex
Honolulu, Hawaii

You Are There It is 9:55 A.M. on the third Wednesday in January. Today is Opening Day at Hawaii's State Capitol. You and your classmates have come to see how your state government works. You're curious to watch as lawmakers make big decisions. At 10:00 A.M., the doors will open and the year's first senate meeting will begin. You look up at the senate building. It is shaped like one of Hawaii's famous volcanoes. You can't wait to see what goes on inside!

Each island in Hawaii once had its own government. In 1810, Kamehameha (kah-MAY-ha-MAY-ha) united the Hawaiian Islands into one kingdom and became its first king. A monarchy (mahn-ARE-key) is a government ruled by a king or a **monarch**. Today, Hawaii is no longer a monarchy. It is a state of the United States of America. Like all states, Hawaii has a **constitution**, or a written plan of government. Hawaii's constitution is based on the constitution of the Kingdom of the Islands of Hawaii.

Hawaii's Capitol is in Honolulu, on one of the state's eight islands, Oahu (oh-AH-hoo). Hawaii is the only island state in our country.

E14

Practice and Extend

SOCIAL STUDIES
Background

Government in Hawaii

- The Kingdom of Hawaii lasted from 1810 to 1893, and was ruled by King Kamehameha I, II, III, IV, and V, followed by King Lunalilo, King Kalakaua, and Queen Lili'uokalani.
- Queen Lili'uokalani was overthrown in 1893. Hawaii was annexed to the United States in 1898, but did not become a state until 1959.
- The architecture of the Hawaii State Capitol Complex is symbolic, representing the state's islands, palm trees, and volcanoes.

Government in Hawaii

Honolulu

Visit the ONLY island state in our country!!!

Fast Facts:

- Hawaii became our fiftieth state in 1959.
- Hawaii is the only U.S. state that was once a monarchy.

Link to You

How does your state's government work for you?

KAMEHAMEHA I

King Kamehameha ruled the Kingdom of the Islands of Hawaii for many years. His palace was located in Honolulu.

E15

Read the text on pp. E14–E15 with students. Then discuss the following questions:

What are some unique things about Hawaii and its government? Possible answers: Hawaii is the only island state; it is the only state that was once a monarchy; Hawaii's constitution was based on the constitution of the Kingdom of the Islands of Hawaii.

What are some differences between a monarchy and a government with a constitution? Possible answer: In a monarchy, one person makes decisions for everyone. In a government with a constitution, the people participate in their government.

When did Hawaii become a state? How many states were there at that time? 1959; 49

3 Close and Assess

About 200 years ago, the Hawaiian Islands were not united under a single government. Ask students what they think life in Hawaii might have been like during that time. How might life have changed when Hawaii became united under one kingdom and, later, a state?

Link to You

Have students use the Government graphic organizer to help them explain how the state government works for them. Possible answer: The state government makes decisions that affect our schools, taxes, and laws.

CURRICULUM CONNECTION
Writing

Use Graphic Organizers

- Use the Explore Government graphic organizer to help students answer the Link to You question.
- Direct students to use pictures and words in their answers.
- Have students share their answers with a partner or in a small group.

Organizer, p. E23

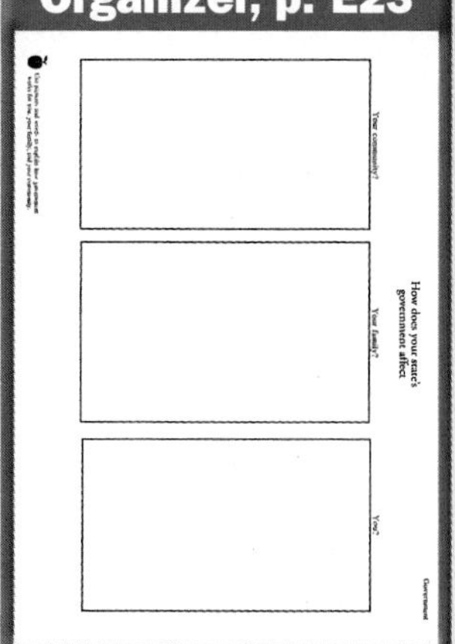

National Symbols

Objectives
- Explain the history and meaning of some national symbols.
- Identify important documents, places and people in American history.

1 Introduce and Motivate

Preview To activate prior knowledge, ask students what they know about the birth of the United States. Explain that they will be learning about some people and places that were important in America's struggle for independence.

2 Teach and Discuss

What is important about the Declaration of Independence? Possible answer: It declared the colonies free from British control.

Why do you think Independence Hall is sometimes called "the birthplace of the nation"? Possible answer: Colonial leaders met there to plan the future of the new nation; The Declaration of Independence and the United States Constitution were both signed there.

What were some of the important contributions that Thomas Jefferson made to our country? Possible answers: Authoring the Declaration of Independence; being a President of the United States

3 Close and Assess

Ask students to write about why they think national symbols are important. Have them explain why they think so many people visit national landmarks, such as the Jefferson Memorial and Independence Hall.

National Symbols

Independence Hall
Philadelphia, Pennsylvania

◀ Many important events in United States history took place in Independence Hall. This stately, red brick building is a symbol of our nation's birth. Colonial leaders met here to plan the future of the new nation. The Declaration of Independence and the United States Constitution were both signed here.

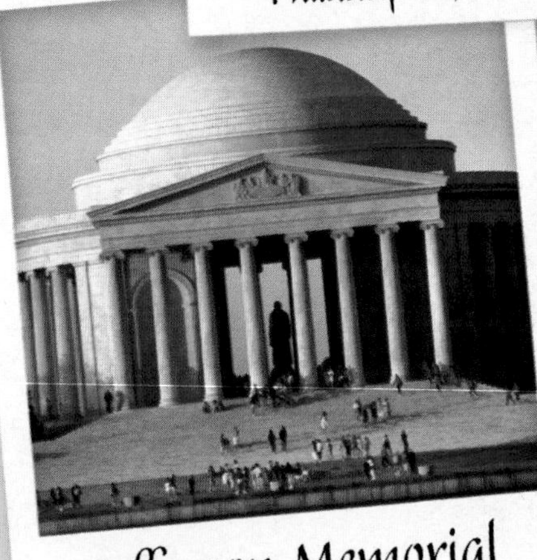

Jefferson Memorial
Washington, D.C.

▲ The Jefferson Memorial honors Thomas Jefferson, an author of the Declaration of Independence and the third President of the United States. The memorial is a symbol of gratitude for Jefferson's contributions to our country.

The Declaration of Independence

▲ The Declaration of Independence is a document that declared the colonies free from British control. The document was signed in Independence Hall in 1776. It is a symbol of our nation's freedom.

E16

Practice and Extend

CURRICULUM CONNECTION
Writing

Use Graphic Organizers
- Use the National Symbols graphic organizer to help students learn about important symbols.
- Help students choose U.S., state, and community symbols to describe on their graphic organizers.
- Have students share their work with a partner or in a small group.

Organizer, p. E24

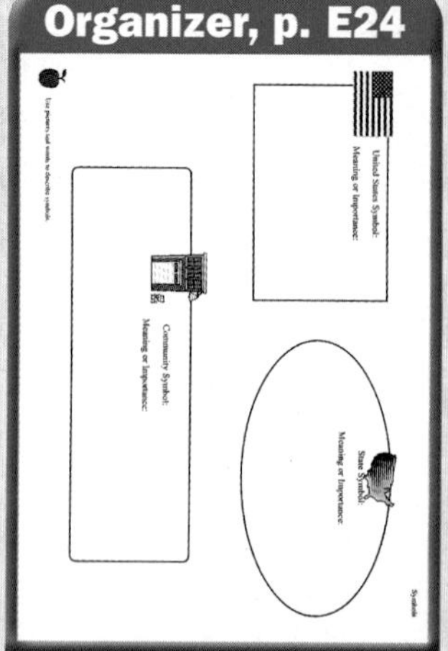

Preserving History

Name a historic building or place in your community or one that you have read about.	Explain why people work to preserve this historic place.

Use pictures and words to identify a historic place and explain why it is being preserved.

Goods Produced in Your State

Goods Transported to Your State from Other Places

Use pictures and words to identify goods produced in and transported into your state.

Electricity in the Home

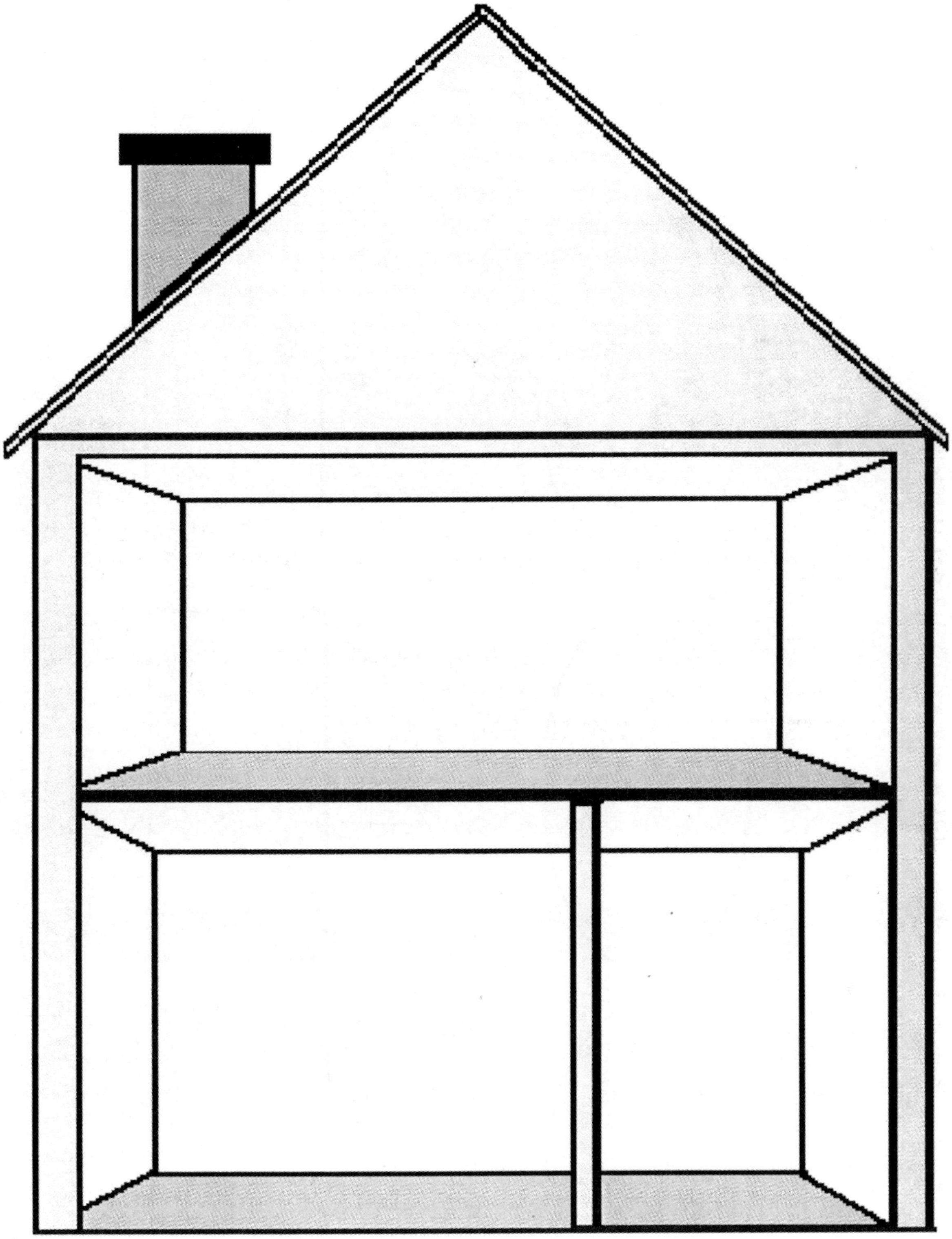

Use pictures and words to identify things in your home that use electricity.

Geography

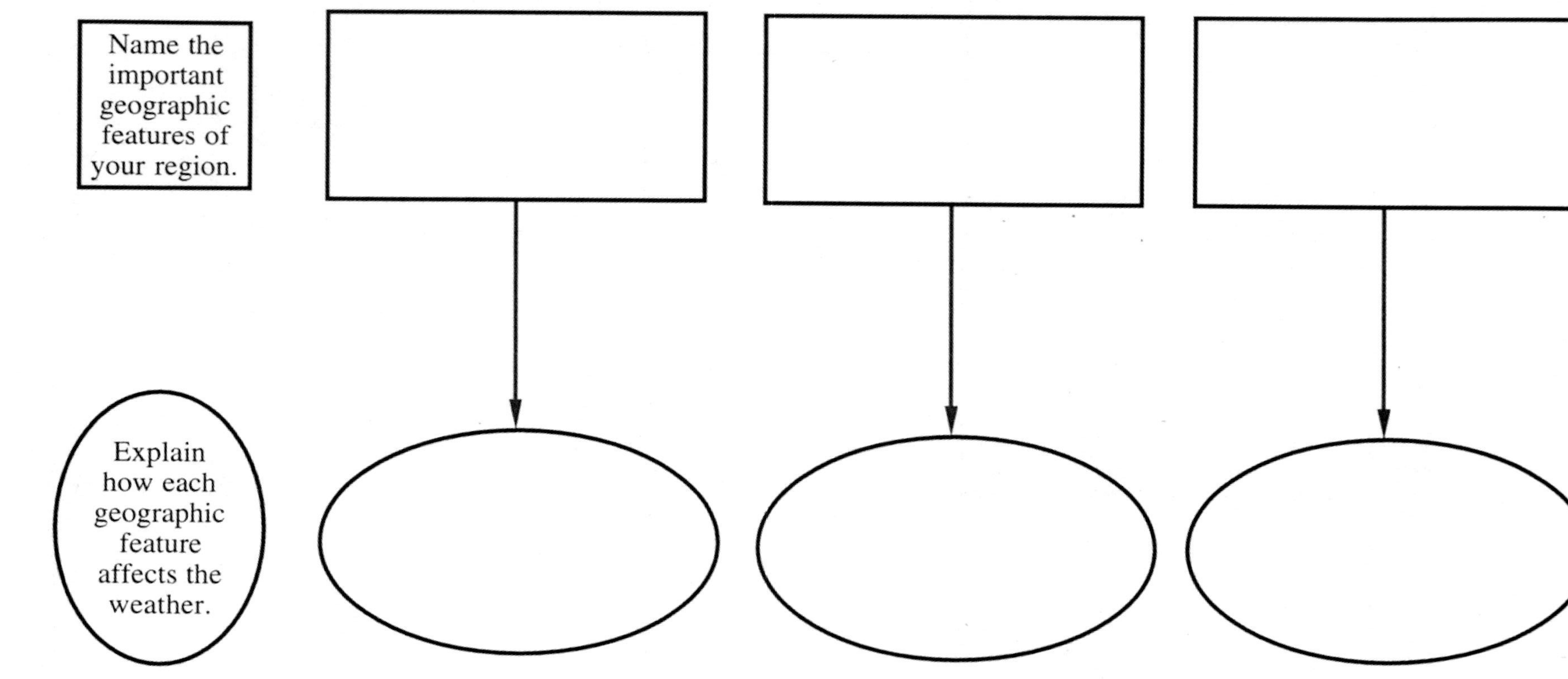
Name the important geographic features of your region.
Explain how each geographic feature affects the weather.

Use pictures and words to explain how geographic features affect the weather in your region.

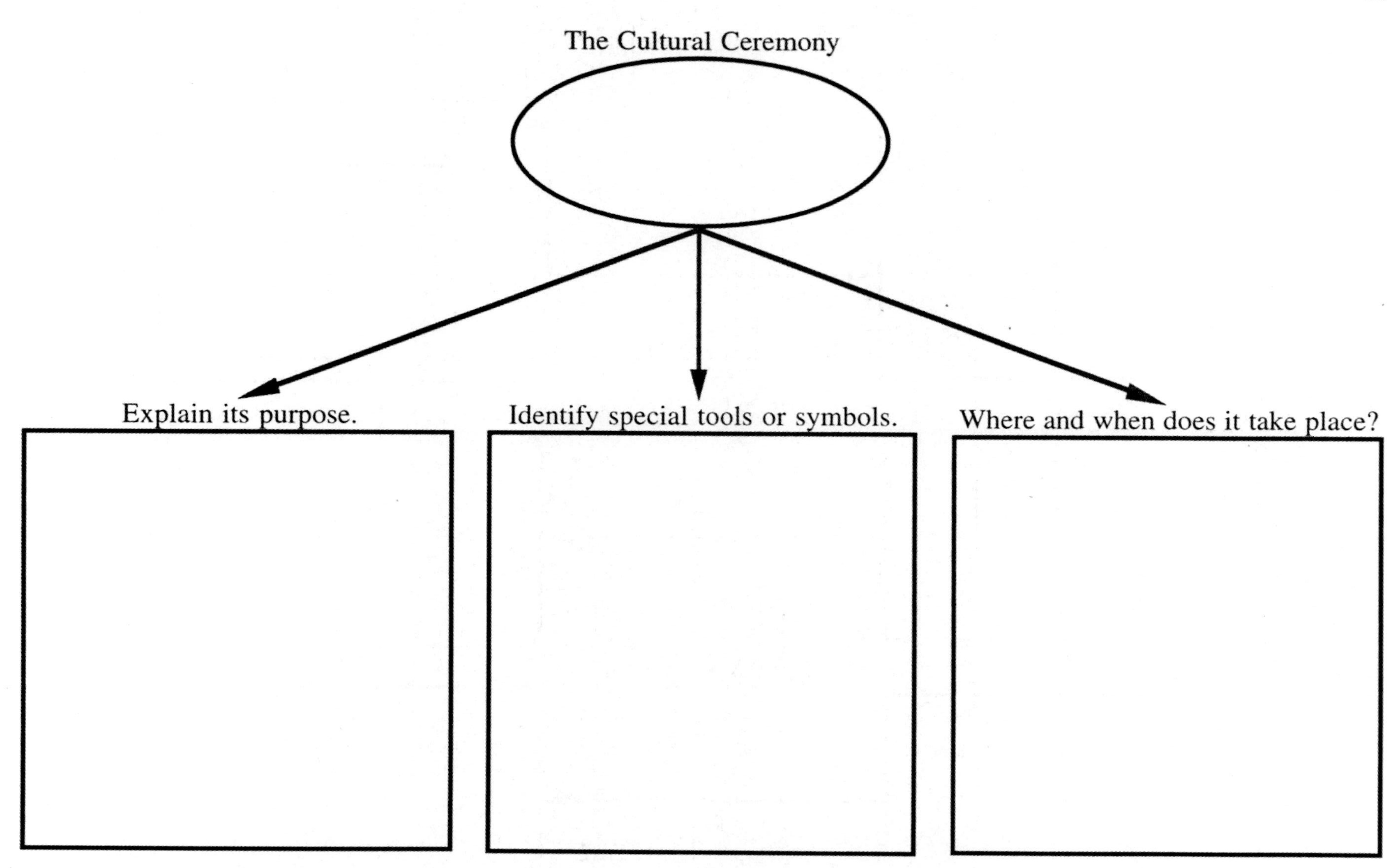
The Cultural Ceremony
Explain its purpose.
Identify special tools or symbols.
Where and when does it take place?

Use pictures and words to name and describe a cultural ceremony you have taken part in, seen, or learned about.

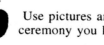

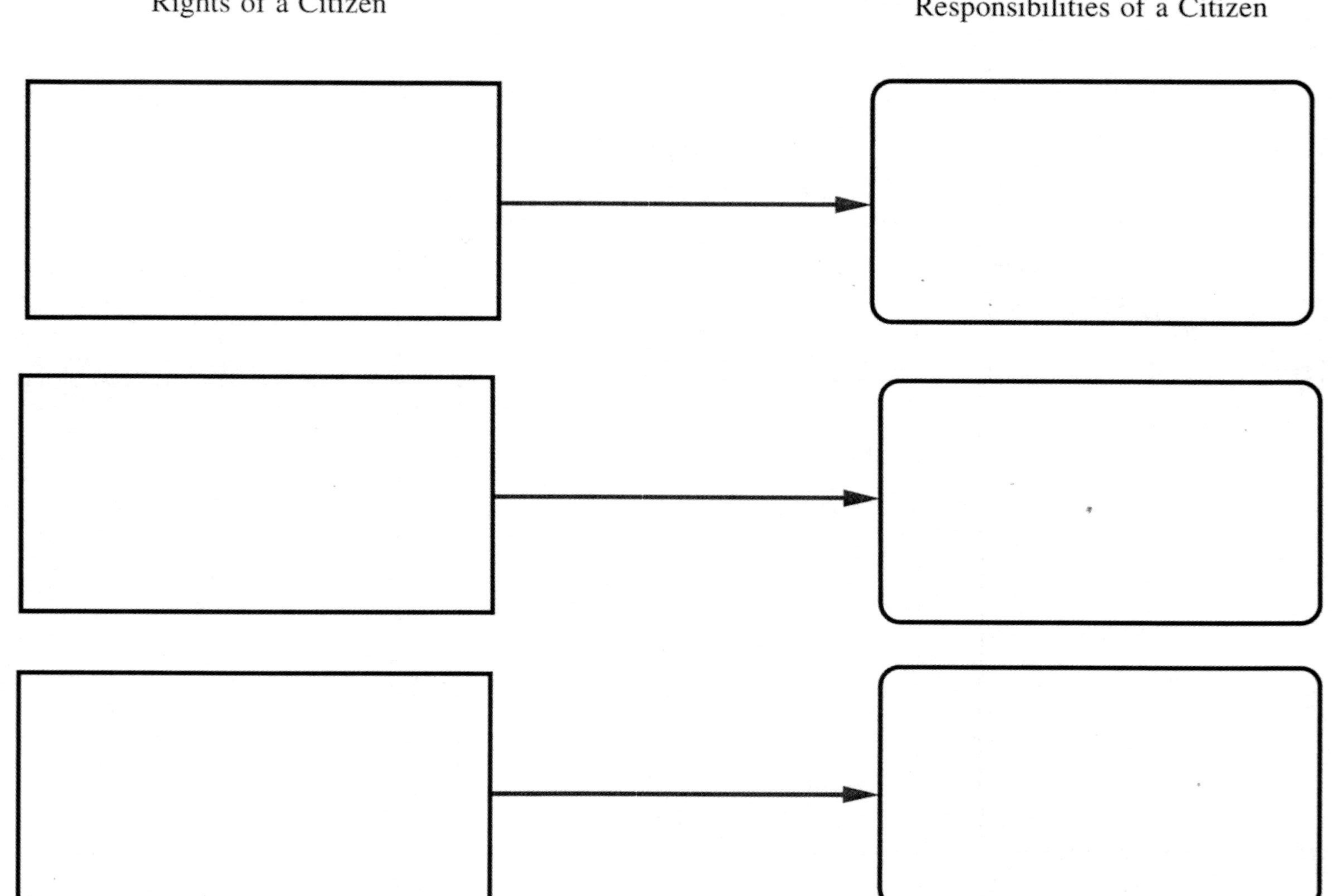

Use words and pictures to identify rights and responsibilities.

How does your state's government affect

Your community?	Your family?	You?

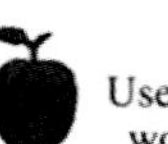
Use pictures and words to explain how government works for you, your family, and your community.

Symbols

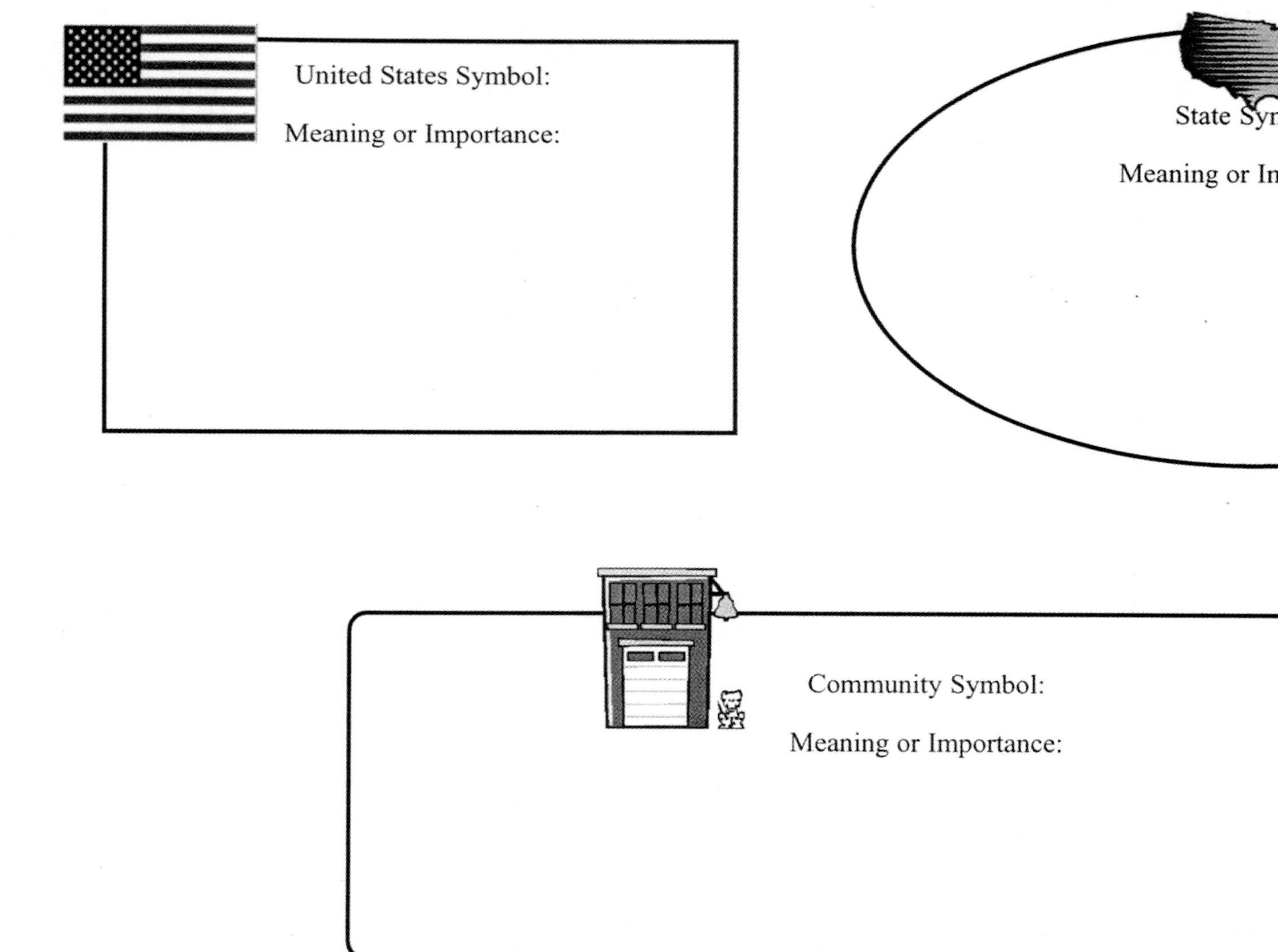

Use pictures and words to describe symbols.

kidspiration This graphic organizer is also available for use on your school computers. Find this activity and a 30-day Kidspiration trial at www.inspiration.com/sf.

SCOTT FORESMAN

PROGRAM AUTHORS

Dr. Candy Dawson Boyd
Professor, School of Education
Director of Reading Programs
St. Mary's College
Moraga, California

Dr. Geneva Gay
Professor of Education
University of Washington
Seattle, Washington

Rita Geiger
Director of Social Studies and Foreign Languages
Norman Public Schools
Norman, Oklahoma

Dr. James B. Kracht
Associate Dean for Undergraduate Programs and Teacher Education
College of Education
Texas A&M University
College Station, Texas

Dr. Valerie Ooka Pang
Professor of Teacher Education
San Diego State University
San Diego, California

Dr. C. Frederick Risinger
Director, Professional Development and Social Studies Education
Indiana University
Bloomington, Indiana

Sara Miranda Sanchez
Elementary and Early Childhood Curriculum Coordinator
Albuquerque Public Schools
Albuquerque, New Mexico

CONTRIBUTING AUTHORS

Dr. Carol Berkin
Professor of History
Baruch College and the Graduate Center
The City University of New York
New York, New York

Lee A. Chase
Staff Development Specialist
Chesterfield County Public Schools
Chesterfield County, Virginia

Dr. Jim Cummins
Professor of Curriculum
Ontario Institute for Studies in Education
University of Toronto
Toronto, Canada

Dr. Allen D. Glenn
Professor and Dean Emeritus
Curriculum and Instruction
College of Education
University of Washington
Seattle, Washington

Dr. Carole L. Hahn
Professor, Educational Studies
Emory University
Atlanta, Georgia

Dr. M. Gail Hickey
Professor of Education
Indiana University-Purdue University
Fort Wayne, Indiana

Dr. Bonnie Meszaros
Associate Director
Center for Economic Education and Entrepreneurship
University of Delaware
Newark, Delaware

CONTENT CONSULTANTS

Catherine Deans-Barrett
World History Specialist
Northbrook, Illinois

Dr. Michael Frassetto
Studies in Religions
Independent Scholar
Chicago, Illinois

Dr. Gerald Greenfield
Hispanic-Latino Studies
History Department
University of Wisconsin, Parkside
Kenosha, Wisconsin

Dr. Frederick Hoxie
Native American Studies
University of Illinois
Champaign, Illinois

Dr. Cheryl Johnson-Odim
Dean of Liberal Arts and Sciences and Professor of History
African American History Specialist
Columbia College
Chicago, Illinois

Dr. Michael Khodarkovsky
Eastern European Studies
University of Chicago
Chicago, Illinois

Robert Moffet
U.S. History Specialist
Northbrook, Illinois

Dr. Ralph Nichols
East Asian History
University of Chicago
Chicago, Illinois

CLASSROOM REVIEWERS

Diana Vicknair Ard
Woodlake Elementary School
St. Tammany Parish
Mandeville, Louisiana

Sharon Berenson
Freehold Learning Center
Freehold, New Jersey

Betsy Blandford
Pocahontas Elementary School
Powhatan, Virginia

Nancy Neff Burgess
Upshur County Schools
Buckhannon-Upshur Middle School
Upshur County, West Virginia

Gloria Cantatore
Public School #5
West New York, New Jersey

Stephen Corsini
Content Specialist in Elementary Social Studies
School District 5 of Lexington and Richland Counties
Ballentine, South Carolina

Deanna Crews
Millbrook Middle School
Elmore County
Millbrook, Alabama

LuAnn Curran
Westgate Elementary School
St. Petersburg, Florida

Kevin L. Curry
Social Studies Curriculum Chair
Hickory Flat Elementary School
Henry County, McDonough, Georgia

Sheila A. Czech
Sky Oaks Elementary School
Burnsville, Minnesota

Louis De Angelo
Office of Catholic Education
Archdiocese of Philadelphia
Philadelphia, Pennsylvania

Dr. Trish Dolasinski
Paradise Valley School District
Arrowhead Elementary School
Glendale, Arizona

Dr. John R. Doyle
Director of Social Studies Curriculum
Miami-Dade County Schools
Miami, Florida

Dr. Roceal Duke
District of Columbia Public Schools
Washington, D.C.

Peggy Flanagan
Roosevelt Elementary School
Community Consolidated School District #64
Park Ridge, Illinois

Mary Flynn
Arrowhead Elementary School
Glendale, Arizona

Sue Gendron
Spring Branch ISD
Houston, Texas

Su Hickenbottom
Totem Falls Elementary School
Snohomish School District
Snohomish, Washington

Allan Jones
North Branch Public Schools
North Branch, Minnesota

Brandy Bowers Kerbow
Bettye Haun Elementary School
Plano ISD
Plano, Texas

Martha Sutton Maple
Shreve Island School
Shreveport, Louisiana

Lyn Metzger
Carpenter Elementary School
Community Consolidated School District #64
Park Ridge, Illinois

Marsha Munsey
Riverbend Elementary School
West Monroe, Louisiana

Christine Nixon
Warrington Elementary School
Escambia County School District
Pensacola, Florida

Cynthia K. Reneau
Muscogee County School District
Columbus, Georgia

Brandon Dale Rice
Secondary Education Social Science
Mobile County Public School System
Mobile, Alabama

Liz Salinas
Supervisor
Edgewood ISD
San Antonio, Texas

Beverly Scaling
Desert Hills Elementary
Las Cruces, New Mexico

Madeleine Schmitt
St. Louis Public Schools
St. Louis, Missouri

Barbara Schwartz
Central Square Intermediate School
Central Square, New York

Editorial Offices:
- Glenview, Illinois
- Parsippany, New Jersey
- New York, New York

Sales Offices:
- Parsippany, New Jersey
- Duluth, Georgia
- Glenview, Illinois
- Coppell, Texas
- Ontario, California
- Mesa, Arizona

www.sfsocialstudies.com

1 2 3 4 5 6 7 8 9 10 V057 13 12 11 10 09 08 07 06 05 04

Contents

Social Studies Handbook

H2 **Citizenship Skills**
H4 **Colonial Williamsburg**
H6 **Research Skills**
H10 **Geography Skills**

Unit 1 — Living in the United States

2 **Begin with a Primary Source**
4 **Welcome to the United States**
6 Reading Social Studies: Summarize

Chapter 1 — 8 The Regions of the United States

10 **Lesson 1 Regions and Landforms**
16 **Here and There** Highest and Lowest Landforms
18 **Lesson 2 Climate**
24 Map and Globe Skills: Read Inset Maps
26 **Lesson 3 Regional Resources**
32 **DK The United States and North America**
34 **Chapter 1 Review**

Chapter 2 — 36 We All Live Together

38 **Lesson 1 Americans All**
45 **Biography** *Fiorello La Guardia*
46 **Lesson 2 We the People**
53 **Biography** *Daniel Inouye*

54 Map and Globe Skills: Read a Time-Zone Map
56 **Lesson 3 The Strengths of Our Freedoms**
60 **Citizen Heroes:** Doing the Right Thing
62 **Chapter 2 Review**

Continued

Chapter 3 — 64 Earning and Learning

66 **Lesson 1 The Land of Plenty**

72 **Lesson 2 Trade Then and Now**

74 **Literature and Social Studies** *Josefina Saves the Day*

80 **Lesson 3 Transportation and Communication**

83 **Map Adventure** Assembling a Computer

86 **Map and Globe Skills:** Use a Road Map and Scale

88 **Chapter 3 Review**

90 **End with a Song:** "America"

92 **Unit 1 Review**

94 **Discovery Channel School:** Unit 1 Project

Nov–Dec

UNIT 2 The Northeast

96 **Begin with a Primary Source**

98 **Welcome to the Northeast**

Target Skill 100 **Reading Social Studies:** Sequence

Chapter 4 102 Land and Water in the Northeast

104 **Lesson 1 The Beautiful Northeast**

107 **Literature and Social Studies** "Stopping by Woods on a Snowy Evening"

110 **Chart and Graph Skills:** Read a Cross-Section Diagram

112 **Lesson 2 Resources of the Northeast**

116 **Lesson 3 The Plentiful Sea**

118 **Then and Now** Nantucket

120 **Here and There** Bay Life

122 **Chapter 4 Review**

Chapter 5 124 People of the Northeast

126 **Lesson 1 The Narragansett People**

130 **Lesson 2 The Land of New Beginnings**

134 **Chart and Graph Skills:** Use a Vertical Time Line

136 **Lesson 3 Taking a Stand**

139 **Biography** ***Elizabeth Cady Stanton***

140 DK **Winning the Right to Vote**

142 **Lesson 4 Cities Grow and Change**

144 **Map Adventure** Northeastern Landmarks

147 **Biography** ***Andrew Carnegie***

148 **Citizen Heroes:** Capturing History

150 **Chapter 5 Review**

152 **End with a Poem:** "Niagara"

154 **Unit 2 Review**

156 Discovery School **Discovery Channel School:** Unit 2 Project

Jan

Feb

UNIT 3

The Southeast

158 **Begin with a Primary Source**

160 **Welcome to the Southeast**

162 **Reading Social Studies:** Main Idea and Details

Chapter 6 164 The Land of the Southeast

166 **Lesson 1 Coastal Plains to the Mountains**

170 **Map and Globe Skills:** Read Elevation Maps

172 **Lesson 2 Sunlight and Storms**

174 **Map Adventure** Visiting Lighthouses

176 DK **Hurricanes**

178 **Lesson 3 Wildlife and Resources**

179 **Literature and Social Studies** *The Yearling*

184 **Chapter 6 Review**

Chapter 7 186 People and Events that Shaped the Southeast

188 **Lesson 1 The Cherokee**

193 **Biography** *Sequoyah*

194 **Lesson 2 Early History of the Southeast**

197 **Then and Now** Monticello

200 **Citizen Heroes:** Speaking Out

202 **Lesson 3 The Nation Divided**

207 **Biography** *Rosa Parks*

208 **Thinking Skills:** Identify Fact and Opinion

210 **Lesson 4 The Glittering Cities**

214 **Here and There** Spoleto Festival of Two Worlds

216 **Chapter 7 Review**

218 **End with a Song:** "Shenandoah"

220 **Unit 3 Review**

222 **Discovery Channel School:** Unit 3 Project

Feb

Mar

UNIT 4

The Midwest

224 **Begin with a Primary Source**

226 **Welcome to the Midwest**

Target Skill 228 **Reading Social Studies:** Cause and Effect

Chapter 8 230 Water and Land of the Midwest

232 **Lesson 1 A Route to the Sea**

238 **Issues and Viewpoints** Zebra Mussel Invasion

240 **Chart and Graph Skills:** Compare Line and Bar Graphs

242 **Lesson 2 The Badlands of South Dakota**

246 **Lesson 3 Bountiful Midwestern Farms**

250 **Here and There** Big Farms and Little Farms

252 **Chapter 8 Review**

Chapter 9 254 People of the Midwest

256 **Lesson 1 The Ojibwa**

260 **Citizen Heroes:** Keeping a Culture Strong

262 **Research and Writing Skills:** Use a Search Engine on the Internet

264 **Lesson 2 The Fur Trade**

267 **Biography** *Jean Baptiste Point Du Sable*

268 Colonial Williamsburg Trading for Goods

270 **Lesson 3 Building Farms**

273 **Literature and Social Studies** *On the Banks of Plum Creek*

275 **Biography** *John Deere*

276 **Lesson 4 Hub of the Nation**

277 **Then and Now** Cahokia

279 **Map Adventure** Lewis and Clark Expedition

283 **Biography** *Mark Twain*

284 **Chapter 9 Review**

286 **End With a Song:** "I've Been Working on the Railroad"

288 **Unit 4 Review**

290 **Discovery Channel School:** Unit 4 Project

UNIT 5

The Southwest

292 **Begin with a Primary Source**
294 **Welcome to the Southwest**
296 **Reading Social Studies:** Draw Conclusions

Chapter 10
298 **Land and Resources of the Southwest**

300 **Lesson 1 A Land of Canyons**
305 **Biography** ***John Wesley Powell***
306 **Thinking Skills:** Make Generalizations
308 **Lesson 2 Climates in the Southwest**
310 **Literature and Social Studies** "The Desert Is Theirs"
312 **Here and There** Giant Plants
314 **Lesson 3 Oil and Technology**
318 **Citizen Heroes:** Flying to Help
320 **Chapter 10 Review**

Chapter 11
322 **The People of the Southwest**

324 **Lesson 1 The Navajo**
329 **Biography** ***Henry Chee Dodge***
330 **Research and Writing Skills:** Identify Primary and Secondary Sources
332 **Lesson 2 Spanish Influence**
335 **Then and Now** "Remember the Alamo!"
338 **Lesson 3 Ranches and Drivers**
341 **Map Adventure** The Chisholm Trail
344 **DK Cowboys and Cowgirls**
346 **Lesson 4 • Living in the Desert**
349 **Biography** ***Willis Haviland Carrier***
350 **Issues and Viewpoints** Save "America's Main Street"?
352 **Chapter 11 Review**

354 **End with Literature:** *Cowboy Country*
356 **Unit 5 Review**
358 **Discovery Channel School:** Unit 5 Project

Apr

May

UNIT 6

The West

360 **Begin with a Primary Source**

362 **Welcome to the West**

364 **Reading Social Studies:** Compare and Contrast

Chapter 12 366 The Land of the West

368 **Lesson 1 A Land of Mountains**

374 **DK When a Mountain Explodes**

376 **Research and Writing Skills:** Take Notes and Write Outlines

378 **Lesson 2 Climates in the West**

384 **Lesson 3 Resources of the West**

385 **Literature and Social Studies** "Ripening Cherries"

389 **Biography** ***Seth Lewelling***

390 **Chapter 12 Review**

Chapter 13 392 Living in the West

394 **Lesson 1 The Tinglit**

398 **Here and There** Masks Tell a Story

400 **Lesson 2 Exploration and Growth**

402 **Map Adventure** In Search of Gold

404 **Then and Now** Bodie, California

407 **Biography** ***Levi Strauss***

408 **Map and Globe Skills:** Understand Latitude and Longitude

410 **Lesson 3 Business and Pleasure**

416 **Citizen Heroes:** Building a City

418 **Chapter 13 Review**

420 **End with a Song:** "Sweet Betsy from Pike"

422 **Unit 6 Review**

424 **Discovery Channel School:** Unit 6 Project

May

June

Reference Guide

Atlas	R2
Geography Terms	R16
Facts About Our Fifty States	R18
Symbols of the United States	R24
Our National Anthem	R26
United States Documents: The Declaration of Independence	R28
Facts About Our Presidents	R32
Learn About Your State	R36
Gazetteer	R45
Biographical Dictionary	R52
Glossary	R56
Index	R63

★BIOGRAPHY★

Fiorello La Guardia	**45**
Daniel Inouye	**53**
Elizabeth Cady Stanton	**139**
Andrew Carnegie	**147**
Sequoyah	**193**
Rosa Parks	**207**
Jean Baptiste Point Du Sable	**267**
John Deere	**275**
Mark Twain	**283**
John Wesley Powell	**305**
Henry Chee Dodge	**329**
Willis Haviland Carrier	**349**
Seth Lewelling	**389**
Levi Strauss	**407**

Maps

Regions of the United States 11
Average Temperatures in January in the United States 19
Average Precipitation in a Year Throughout the United States 20
Climate Areas of the United States 22
The United States 24
The United States 25
Routes of European Explorers 40
Expansion of the United States 41
Time Zones of the United States 54
Road Map of Ohio and Pennsylvania 86
Power Plants on the Niagara River 105
Resources of the Northeast 114
European Immigration 133
States and Landforms of the Southeast 167
Elevations of the Southeast 170
Average January Temperatures in the Southeast 173
Agriculture in the Southeast 181
The Trail of Tears 191
Where Explorers Traveled 195
Waterways Connect Regions 234
Average Yearly Rainfall in the United States 247
The Voyage of Marquette and Jolliet 265
Railroad Lines Around 1870 281
Average Temperatures in the Southwest During May 309
The Long Walk 326
Coronado's Expedition 333
Dams in the Phoenix Area 347
Elevations in the West 372
Average January Temperatures in the West 381
Agricultural Products of the West Region 387
Claims to the Pacific Coast in the Early 1800s 401
Gold Rush Claims 403
Latitude and Longitude in the West 409
Trade and the Pacific Rim 414

Skills

Reading Social Studies

Summarize 6
Sequence 100
Main Idea and Details 162
Cause and Effect 228
Draw Conclusions 296
Compare and Contrast 364

Map and Globe Skills

Read Inset Maps 24
Read a Time-Zone Map 54
Use a Road Map and Scale 86
Read Elevation Maps 170
Understand Latitude and Longitude 408

Thinking Skills

Identify Fact and Opinion 208
Make Generalizations 306

Research and Writing Skills

Use a Search Engine on the Internet 262
Identify Primary and Secondary Sources 330
Take Notes and Write Outlines 376

Chart and Graph Skills

Read a Cross-Section Diagram 110
Use a Vertical Time Line 134
Compare Line and Bar Graphs 240

Fact File

My Region 30
Immigration Information 42
Three Levels of Government 49
Money in the United States 75
The Appalachian Trail 106
Main Crops of the Midwest 248
Grand Canyon Facts 303
Oil and Its Products 315
Populations of Major Cities in the West 413

Citizen Heroes

Doing the Right Thing 60
Capturing History 148
Speaking Out 200
Keeping a Culture Strong 260
Flying to Help 318
Building a City 416

Issues and Viewpoints

Zebra Mussel Invasion 238
Save "America's Main Street"? 350

Then and Now

Nantucket 118
Monticello 197
Cahokia 277
"Remember the Alamo!" 335
Bodie, California 404

Here and There

Highest and Lowest Landforms 16
Bay Life 120
Spoleto Festival of Two Worlds 214
Big Farms and Little Farms 250
Giant Plants 312
Masks Tell a Story 398

Literature and Social Studies

Josefina Saves the Day 74
"Stopping by Woods on a Snowy Evening" 107
The Yearling 179
On the Banks of Plum Creek 273
"The Desert Is Theirs" 310
"Ripening Cherries" 385

Map Adventure

Assembling a Computer 83
Northeastern Landmarks 144
Visiting Lighthouses 174
Lewis and Clark Expedition 279
The Chisholm Trail 341
In Search of Gold 402

Graphic Organizers

Summarize	6
Summarize	15
Summarize	23
Main Idea and Details	31
Chapter 1 Summary	34
Main Idea and Details	44
Summarize	52
Summarize	59
Chapter 2 Summary	62
Summarize	71
Summarize	79
Summarize	85
Chapter 3 Summary	88
Sequence	100
Sequence	109
Sequence	115
Sequence	119
Chapter 4 Summary	122
Sequence	129
Sequence	133
Compare and Contrast	138
Cause and Effect	146
Chapter 5 Summary	150
Main Idea and Details	162
Main Idea and Details	169
Main Idea and Details	175
Main Idea and Details	183
Chapter 6 Summary	184
Main Idea and Details	192
Main Idea and Details	199
Main Idea and Details	206
Main Idea and Details	213
Chapter 7 Summary	216
Cause and Effect	228
Cause and Effect	237
Cause and Effect	245
Cause and Effect	249
Chapter 8 Summary	252
Cause and Effect	259
Cause and Effect	266
Cause and Effect	274
Cause and Effect	282
Chapter 9 Summary	284
Draw Conclusions	296
Draw Conclusions	304
Draw Conclusions	311
Draw Conclusions	317
Chapter 10 Summary	320
Cause and Effect	328
Draw Conclusions	337
Draw Conclusions	343
Cause and Effect	348
Chapter 11 Summary	352
Compare and Contrast	364
Compare and Contrast	373
Compare and Contrast	383
Summarize	388
Chapter 12 Summary	390
Summarize	397
Draw Conclusions	406
Compare and Contrast	415
Chapter 13 Summary	418

Charts, Graphs, Tables & Diagrams

Diagram: The Rain Cycle 21
Diagram: The Three Levels of Government 48
Diagram: The Three Branches of Government 50
Diagram: Free Trade and Profit 76
Diagram: Communication and Transportation 84
Read a Cross-Section Diagram 110
Diagram: How a Lock Works 235
Line Graph: Population of Illinois, 1850–2000 240
Bar Graph: Population of Illinois, 1850–2000 240
Bar Graph: Populations of Michigan and Missouri, 1850–1900 241
Diagram: Oil and Its Products 315
Diagram: A Spanish Mission 334
Diagram: The Cascade Rain Shadow 382
Bar Graph: Metro Area Population Growth, 1990–2000 413
Circle Graph: Metro Area Populations, 2000 413

Time Lines

How the United States Grew 38
Early History of the Northeast 130
Famous Inventions Time Line 135
The Abolition and Women's Rights Movements 136
Chapter 5 Review 150
European Contact with the Cherokee 188
Growth of Settlements in the Southeast 194
The Civil War 202
Chapter 7 Review 216
The Fur Trade 264
Transportation in the Midwest 276
Chapter 9 Review 284
The Navajo 324
Spanish Influence on the Southwest 332
The Cattle Industry in the Southwest 338
Living in the Desert 346
Chapter 11 Review 352
Growth of the West 400
Chapter 13 Review 418

Citizenship Skills

The following aspects of citizenship should be discussed with students. Help students determine ways in which the personal attributes described apply to their lives.

Respect

1 **How can you show respect?** Possible answers: I can listen without interrupting; I can be understanding of people's feelings; I can congratulate people for trying and for succeeding. **Apply Information**

Fairness

2 **What does it mean to "play fair"?** Take turns, follow the rules, and respect other players **Main Idea and Details**

Caring

3 **How is the student in the picture showing that she cares?** She is thinking about what someone else needs. She is pushing the woman in the wheelchair. **Analyze Pictures**

Responsibility

4 **What are some ways you act responsibly?** Possible answers: I do my work at school; I do my chores at home; I play safely and follow the rules; I keep my promises to others. **Apply Information**

Courage

5 **What are some courageous things you have seen students do?** Possible answers: Give a speech; perform onstage; try something new; help others in danger; work hard to recover from an injury or illness **Apply Information**

Honesty

6 **Describe some benefits of being honest.** Possible answers: People will trust you; you might be considered for important responsibilities. **Apply Information**

Citizenship Skills

There are six ways to show good citizenship: through respect, fairness, caring, responsibility, courage, and honesty. In your textbook, you will learn about people who used these ways to help their community, state, and country.

1 **Respect**
Treat others as you would want to be treated. Welcome differences among people.

2 **Fairness**
Take turns and follow the rules. Listen to what other people have to say.

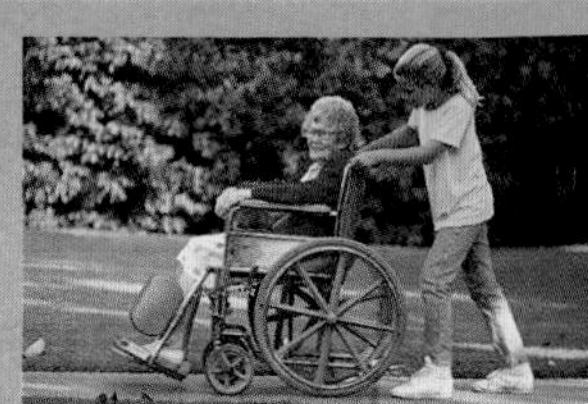

3 **Caring**
Think about what someone else needs.

4 **Responsibility**
Do what you are supposed to do and think before you act.

5 **Courage**
Do what is right even when the task is hard.

6 **Honesty**
Tell the truth and do what you say you will do.

Practice and Extend

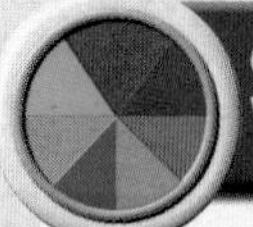

CURRICULUM CONNECTION
Writing

Write About Good Citizenship

- Have students keep a *Good Citizens in Action* log. They can list actions they see at school and in the community.
- Each week have students discuss their observations.
- Create a display summarizing commendable actions. Have students make awards honoring good citizens.
- Have students write articles about good citizens.

SOCIAL STUDIES STRAND
Citizenship

Citizen Heroes

In Grade 4, students will read about the following Citizen Heroes.

- Seth and Sam: *Honesty*
- Ethan: *Responsibility*
- Sarah and Angelina Grimké: *Courage*
- Joseph Podlasek: *Respect*
- Jerrie Cobb: *Caring*
- Thomas Bradley: *Fairness*

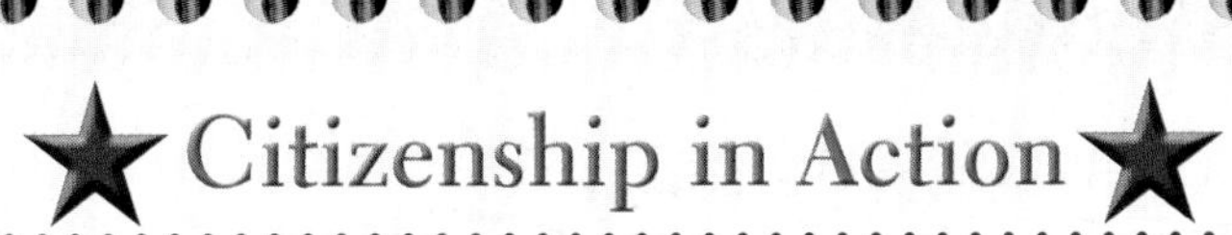

★Citizenship in Action★

Good citizens make careful decisions. They solve problems in a logical way. How will these students handle each situation as good citizens?

Decision Making

The students are choosing a pet for their classroom. The following steps will help them make a decision.

1. **Tell what decision you need to make.**
2. **Gather information.**
3. **List your choices.**
4. **Tell what might happen with each choice.**
5. **Act according to your decision.**

Problem Solving

Sometimes students argue at recess over whose turn it is to have a ball. The fourth-graders can use the following steps to help them solve the problem.

1. **Name the problem.**
2. **Find out more about the problem.**
3. **List ways to solve the problem.**
4. **Talk about the best way to solve the problem.**
5. **Solve the problem.**
6. **Then figure out how well the problem was solved.**

Social Studies Handbook H3

CURRICULUM CONNECTION
Literature

Analyze Decisions

- Have students analyze the decision-making and problem-solving scenarios presented in fables and fairy tales, such as "Stone Soup" and "The Little Red Hen."
- Help students identify the steps taken in the tales to reach each decision or solution.
- Have students consider other solutions. Have them tell what they would do if faced with the same decision or problem.

CURRICULUM CONNECTION
Music

Write a Song

- Have groups of students write a song about citizenship.
- Encourage them to review pp. H4 and H5 to get ideas for lyrics.
- Students can use the melody of a familiar song, or they can use their own melody.
- Remind students to write a song with a positive message.
- Invite students to share their songs.

★Citizenship in Action★

As students read about the situations on p. H5, have them incorporate their ideas into the models of decision making and problem solving.

Decision Making

Discuss the decision-making scenario. Help students make a careful decision.

1. A decision must be made to determine what kind of pet to choose.
2. Students can read books or call pet shops to learn about possible pets.
3. Choices might include a rabbit, fish, turtle, snake, or bird.
4. Students should consider the cost, care, and other factors for each pet.
5. Have the class vote for their choice.

Problem Solving

Discuss the problem-solving scenario. Help students solve the problem in a logical way.

1. The problem is that students are arguing over whose turn it is to have the ball.
2. Have the players explain their reasons for wanting the ball.
3. Possible solutions: Set a time limit for each person to play with the ball; have students use the ball together.
4. Have students share their opinions about each possible solution.
5. Students should choose the solution they feel is best.
6. Have students evaluate the solution that they choose.

Citizenship Throughout History

As students learn more about U.S. history and geography in this book, have them identify decisions and problems that people have had to make and solve.

Think Like a Historian

Objectives

- Use primary sources, including written documents, to learn about the past.
- Explain how written records help us learn about a place or understand what life was like long ago.

1 Introduce and Motivate

- Explain to students that diaries and other personal accounts are primary sources that help us learn about life in the past.
- Explain to students that many different kinds of information are written in letters, diaries, and journals. That information can tell us what people of the past were thinking and feeling, where they traveled, the people they met, and even what they saw.
- Ask students what kinds of information they would write in a letter, diary, or journal to describe a place they might visit.

2 Teach and Discuss

- **Street Scene** In the 1700s, Williamsburg was the capital of the colony of Virginia. This photograph shows a group of people gathered in front of a store on the Duke of Gloucester Street, the busy main street of Williamsburg. Have students describe the main street in their city.
- **Capitol** This is a photograph of the reconstructed Capitol building in Williamsburg, Virginia. In the 1700s, Virginia's colonial government—the House of Burgesses and Governor's Council—met here. Even today, each state has a capitol building where the state government conducts its business. Ask students to identify their state's capitol city.

Research Skills

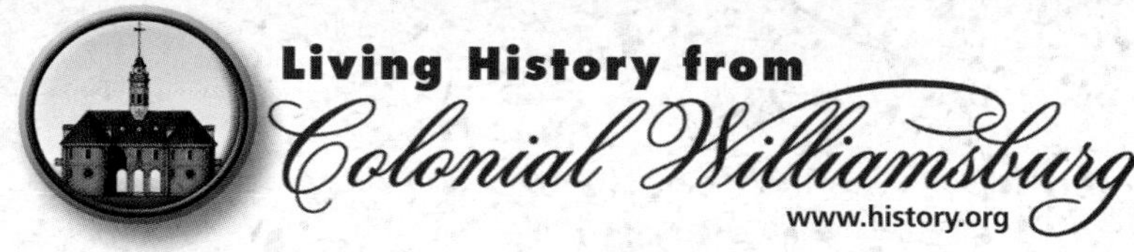

Think Like a Historian

Written records are a way for us to learn about the past. Historians search libraries for letters, diaries, and other records. Documents written by the people who saw the events, places, and people of the past are called primary sources. Primary sources help us understand what life was like long ago.

Nicholas Cresswell traveled in Virginia in 1777. This is how he described the city of Williamsburg.

"The Capitol is the place where all public business is done, the Colonial Assembly meets, &c . . . In the Capitol is a fine marble statue of the late Governor . . ."

"This is the finest town I have seen in Virginia . . . It consists of one principal street about a mile long, very wide and level with a number of good buildings, the Capitol at the end of the street and the College at the other . . ."

H4

Practice and Extend

FYI SOCIAL STUDIES Background

Primary Sources *by Dr. William E. White, Colonial Williamsburg Historian*

- Written records are a historian's most important tools. Letters, journals, diaries, account books, government records, newspapers, and other documents help us understand the people, places, and events of the past.
- No single document provides a complete account of the past. Like detectives, historians piece together small clues from many different sources to discover the whole story. Not everyone agrees about what they've seen or experienced. Nicholas Cresswell was impressed by Williamsburg. Thomas Jefferson, who also wrote a description of Williamsburg, thought its buildings were old-fashioned and ugly.
- A document that has been hidden in a library or someone's personal papers can change our ideas about what actually happened in the past. History is a story that is still unfolding.

"The Governor's Palace is a good brick building, but it does not make a grand appearance."

"Here is only one Church, none the grandest, and I suppose there may be about 250 houses in town."

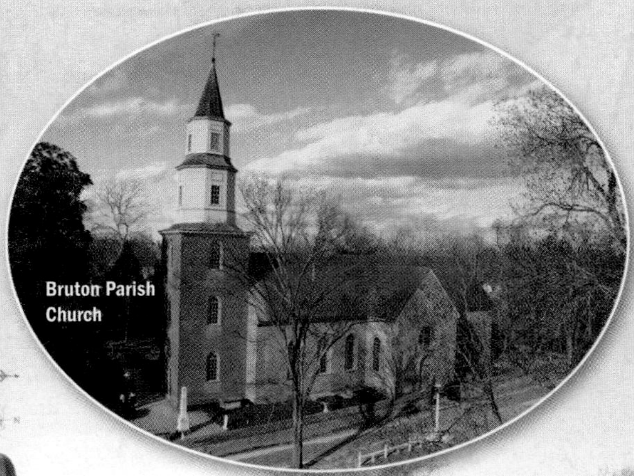

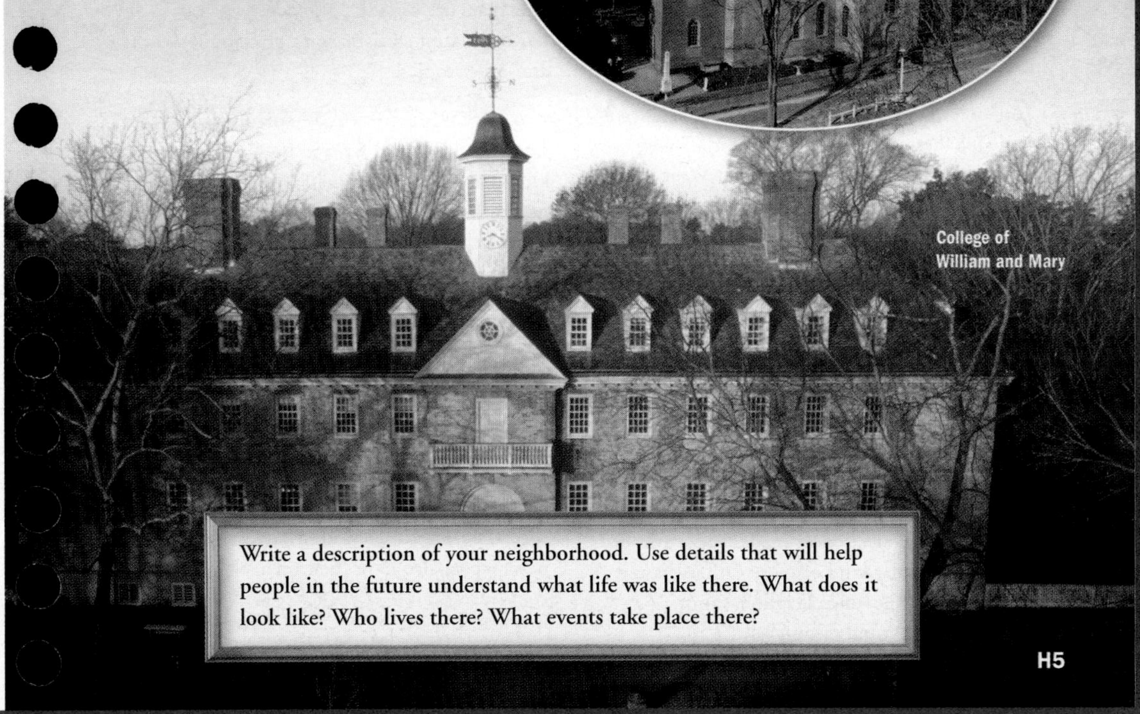

Write a description of your neighborhood. Use details that will help people in the future understand what life was like there. What does it look like? Who lives there? What events take place there?

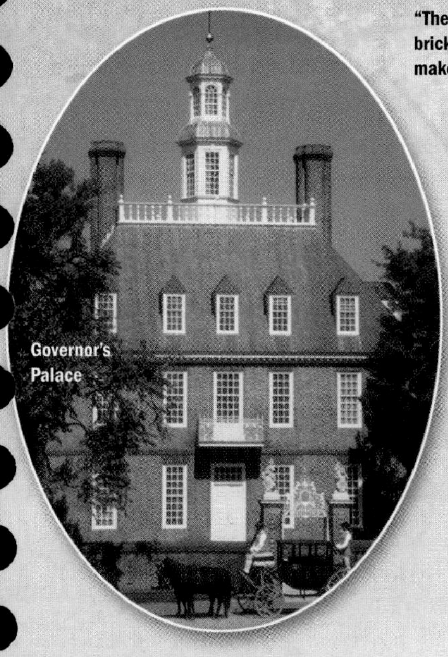

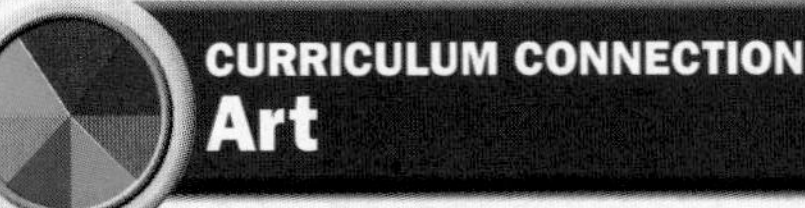

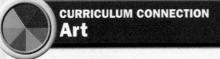

CURRICULUM CONNECTION
Art

Travel Sketches

- Explain to students that even today travelers sometimes make sketches of places they visit.
- Have students choose a familiar public building from their community. Have students create a sketch of that building that includes a short description.

- **Governor's Palace.** This is a photograph of the reconstructed Governor's Palace in Williamsburg, Virginia. The royal governor, or the King of England's representative in the colony, lived here.
- **Bruton Parish Church.** In the 1700s, the Anglican Church, or Church of England, was the official government church in Williamsburg. Church and government were not separate in the 1700s. Today our government guarantees the freedom of religion, and most cities and towns have many different places of worship. Ask students to identify places of worship in their community.
- **College of William and Mary.** This is a photograph of the Wren building at the College of William and Mary. William and Mary, established in 1693, is the second oldest college in the United States. In the 1700s, young gentlemen from wealthy families attended the college. Ask students if they can name any colleges or universities in their area or state.

3 Close and Assess

- Explain to the students how Nicholas Cresswell's descriptions tell us about the way Williamsburg, Virginia, looked in 1777. Written documents, such as letters, diaries, and journals help historians understand how people of the past lived and what places of the past looked like.
- As a class, discuss the types of buildings that have been constructed in students' community.
- Using the Nicholas Cresswell descriptions of Williamsburg as a model, have students choose several buildings in their neighborhood or community and write two or three sentences describing each building and its uses.

Identify Primary and Secondary Sources

- Ask students to categorize the following items as either a *Primary Source* or a *Secondary Source.*
  - ▶ a diary entry from an astronaut on the first trip to the moon *(Primary Source)*
  - ▶ a science book about space travel *(Secondary Source)*
  - ▶ an interview with a professional football player *(Primary Source)*
- Have students list other primary and secondary sources in their school and community.

Print Resources

Use Encyclopedias and Dictionaries

- Show students a set of encyclopedias. Based on the guide letters and volume numbers, ask students to find the volume they would use to research such topics as the Rocky Mountains or Cape Hatteras.
- Ask students to look in a dictionary to find a word they do not know. They should pronounce the word, spell it, and describe its meaning.

Use Atlases and Almanacs

- **What information can you find in an atlas?** Maps that show elevation, crops, and natural resources. Main Idea and Details
- **How is an almanac different from an encyclopedia?** An almanac is published yearly and provides facts and figures; an encyclopedia is a collection of articles on various topics. Compare and Contrast

Use Nonfiction Books and Periodicals

- **Why is it important to check the copyright date of nonfiction books and periodicals when conducting research?** To make sure that the book or periodical is not outdated. Make Inferences

*When you need to find information for a report or a project, you can use three main resources: **Print Resources, Technology Resources,** and **Community Resources.***

The information you find can be from either primary or secondary sources. Primary sources are documents that were written by people who lived at that time or who were at an event and saw it. Journals, diaries, letters, and photographs are all primary sources.

Secondary sources are descriptions of an event written by people who have researched the event. These people tell what they learned from reading about the event and looking at primary sources, but they were not there. Look for both kinds of sources when you do research.

Print Resources

A reference tool is any source of information. Books are reference tools. Libraries often have reference books such as atlases, almanacs, dictionaries, and encyclopedias. Usually, reference materials cannot be checked out of the library, but you can use them to look up information while you are at the library.

An encyclopedia is a collection of articles, listed alphabetically, on various topics. When you need information quickly, an encyclopedia is a good choice. Electronic encyclopedias, available on the Internet or CD-ROM, have sound and video clips in addition to text.

A dictionary is an alphabetical collection of words, their spellings, their meanings, and their pronunciations. If you find a word you don't understand, you can look it up in a dictionary. Many dictionaries also include abbreviations, names, and explanations of well-known people and places.

An atlas is a collection of maps. Some atlases have one particular kind of map. Others have a variety of maps showing elevation, crops, population, or natural resources.

An almanac is a book or computer resource that lists facts about a variety of topics. Almanacs are usually organized in sections by topic. Much information is given in charts, tables, and lists. Almanacs are usually updated every year, so they have the latest statistics on population, weather, and other topics.

A nonfiction book is a book on a topic that was researched and written by someone who knows about that topic. In a library, all nonfiction books are numbered and placed in order on the shelves. Books on the same subject are grouped together. You can search for a book in the library's catalog by title, subject, or author. The call number of the book will guide you to the area of the library where you will find the book. A librarian can help you.

A periodical, such as a newspaper or a magazine, is published on a regular basis, usually daily, weekly or monthly. Most libraries have a special periodical section. Many magazines and newspapers also have their own Web sites.

Practice and Extend

BUILD BACKGROUND
ESL Support

Explore Print Resources Collect a variety of print resources for students to compare. If possible, include resources written in students' home languages.

Beginning Make a picture chart showing differences among print resources. Include short, simple descriptions. For example, *almanac: shows lots of charts, tables, and lists.* Refer to the chart to help students use the resources.

Intermediate Have students make a label for each kind of resource. Then have them sort a collection of resources by type, placing each resource under the correct label. Check for understanding by asking simple questions about specific resources.

Advanced Have students look up the name of their state in a dictionary, atlas, almanac, and encyclopedia to compare the kinds of information in each. Then have students complete sentences such as *An encyclopedia provides information about* ________.

Technology Resources

You can use technology such as the Internet, CD-ROMs, databases, television programs, and radio programs as sources of information.

The Internet is a system of linked computers that can store information for others to find and use. The World Wide Web, which is part of the Internet, has a great deal of information.

Before you search for information on the Web, plan your research. If you want to research your community or neighborhood, write down some words or names of places you can use to search the Web. If you have not used the Internet before, you might want to ask a librarian, teacher, or parent for help.

To find a search engine to begin your research, click on SEARCH or NET SEARCH at the top of your screen. Type one of your subject words or terms into the search engine field. Then click SEARCH or GO. The computer will list Web sites about your topic. You can try different search engines for more complete results.

Web sites have Uniform Resource Locators, or URLs. A URL is like an address. If you already know the address of a site that might have information you need, type it in the LOCATION/GO TO box in the upper left corner of the screen. Here is an example of a URL: www.sfsocialstudies.com.

It is important to check all information you find on the Web to make sure it is accurate. Try to find at least three reliable sources that give similar information. Once you find a reliable Web site, you can mark it so that you can find it again. Click BOOKMARKS at the top of your screen and choose ADD BOOKMARK.

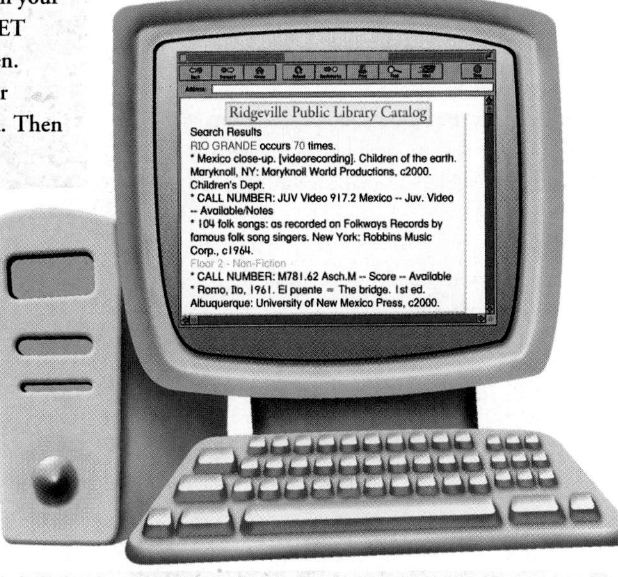

WEB SITE
Technology

Safety on the Internet

- Teach students never to give out personal information—including their name, address, phone number, age, race, family income, school name or location, or friends' names—without permission.
- Teach students never to share their password, even with friends.
- Warn students never to arrange a face-to-face meeting with someone they meet online without first talking with a parent or teacher.
- Students should never respond to messages that make them feel uncomfortable. They should ignore the sender, end the communication, and tell a teacher, parent, or other trusted adult right away.
- Tell students never to use bad language or send mean messages online.
- Make sure students know that people they meet online are not always who they say they are, and online information is not private.

Technology Resources

Discuss the Internet

- To establish guidelines for your students' safe and responsible use of the Internet, use the *Scott Foresman Internet Guide.*
- **How is the Internet useful?** The World Wide Web, which is part of the Internet, provides a great deal of information. **Main Idea and Details**
- **Why is it important to check the information given at a Web site? How can you check the information?** Anyone can make a Web site, so the information may not be accurate; try to find out if a reliable person or organization provided the information, and find other reliable sources that give the same facts. **Main Idea and Details**

Use a Search Engine

- Have students list the steps to follow when using a search engine as you write the steps on the board. Review the steps to be sure they are in the right order.
- Have students use a search engine to find three reliable Web sites that give the same facts about a tourist attraction in Washington, D.C., such as the Washington Monument. Have students list or print out the facts and the Web site addresses.
- **What should you do if a search engine gives you a long list of possible Web sites? How can you find what you need without spending hours checking every site on the list?** Possible answers: Do another search using a more specific search term; read the descriptions of the listed Web sites to find the ones that are more likely to give you the information that you need. **Evaluate**

Community Resources

Interviews

- You may wish to ask a local historian to come and speak to the class about your community's history or another topic.
- Have students complete the steps under **Plan ahead.** Find background information for students to use to prepare questions.
- As students conduct the interview, remind them to follow the steps under **Ask/Listen/Record.** When students have completed their initial line of questioning, have them review the information they have gathered.
- Remind students to follow the steps under **Wrap-up.** Ask students to prepare a thank-you note to present to their guests.

Surveys

- Have students conduct a survey of their classmates about a topic that they choose.
- Students should use either yes/no questions or short-answer questions as they gather information.
- Have students tally people's answers.
- Students should analyze their data and interpret what they have discovered.
- Have students write about what they found out or make graphs to display their data.

Write for Information

- Have groups of students work together to compose e-mail letters requesting information from a community resource.
- Have students proofread their letters and correct any errors in spelling, punctuation, grammar, and sentence structure.

Community Resources

The people in your community are good sources of information.

Interviews

An interview is a good way to find out what people in your community know. This means asking them questions about the topic you are researching. Follow these steps:

Plan ahead

- List the people you want to interview.
- Call or write to ask if you can interview them. Let the person know who you are and why you need information.
- Agree on a time and place to meet.
- Find out about the topic.
- Write a list of questions to ask.

Ask/Listen/Record

- Ask questions clearly.
- Listen carefully. Be polite. Do not interrupt.
- Write notes so that you will remember what was said. If possible, use a tape recorder.

Wrap-up

- Thank the person when you are finished.
- Send a thank-you note.

Surveys

A survey is a list of questions that you ask people, recording everyone's answers. This gives you an idea about what people in your community know, think, or feel about a subject. You can use yes or no questions or short-answer questions. Make a tally sheet with a column for answers to each question. Follow these steps:

- Write down a list of questions.
- Decide where you want to conduct the survey and how many people you want to ask.
- Use a tally sheet to record answers.
- After the survey, look through the responses and write what you found out.

How long have you lived in the neighborhood?	What has changed the most?	What has changed the least?	What do you like most about living here?
30 years	There used to be cornfields at the end of the street.	People still feed ducks at the pond in the park.	People are still friendly.
12 years	There are several tall buildings now.	Our track team is still first in the district.	I have lots of friends here.

Write for Information

Another way to get information from people or organizations in your community is to e-mail or write a letter asking for information. Follow these steps:

- Plan what you want to say.
- Tell who you are and why you are writing.
- Thank the person.
- Be neat and careful about spelling and punctuation.

Practice and Extend

SOCIAL STUDIES STRAND
History

Gather Personal Accounts of Local History

- Arrange for students to interview senior citizens at a retirement home or community center. Students can conduct interviews in person, by phone, or via e-mail. Remind them to follow the steps listed on p. H8.
- Have them introduce themselves and the purpose of the interview in a letter.
- Students might review time lines and other references to find important state and national events in the mid- to late twentieth century. Have students ask questions about people's memories of these events.
- During the interview, students should be respectful, listen carefully, and take notes. They should note dates of events discussed. Have students also list any primary sources such as diary entries shared during the interview.
- Ask students to share the information they gather. Give them the option of creating a time line, writing a summary, or giving an oral report.

Writing a Research Report

Prewrite

- Decide on a topic for your report. Your teacher may tell you what kind of report to research and write, and how long it should be.
- Write down questions about the topic for which you want to find answers.
- Use different sources to find information and answers for your questions. Be sure to write down all your sources. This list of sources is called a bibliography.
- Take notes about what you learn from your sources.
- Review the notes you have taken from all your sources.
- Write down the main ideas you want to write about. Two or three main ideas are enough for most reports.
- Make an outline, listing each main idea and some details about each main idea.

Write a First Draft

- Using your outline, write what you have learned, using sentences and paragraphs. Each paragraph should be about a new idea.
- When you use exact words from your sources, give credit to that source. Write down the sources from which you got the information. This list of sources will become part of your bibliography.

Revise

- Read over your first draft. Does it make sense? Do you need more information about any main idea?
- Change any sentences or paragraphs that do not make sense. Add anything that will make your ideas clear.
- Check your quotations to make sure they are accurate.

Edit

- Proofread your report. Correct any errors in spelling, grammar, capitalization, sentence structure, and punctuation.

Publish

- Add pictures, maps, or other graphics that will help make your report interesting.
- Write or keyboard a final copy as neatly as possible.

Writing a Research Report

Follow the Writing Process

- Have students write a research report about the history of their school or neighborhood.
- Students should first complete the steps listed under **Prewrite** on p. H9. Remind them to use the resources they learned about on pp. H6–H8.
- Show students how to take notes and complete an outline. Point out that notes may be phrases and need not be complete sentences.
- Remind students to keep a record of the specific sources they use. Have students use their list to create a bibliography for their report.
- After students complete the prewriting, they should complete the steps listed under **Write a First Draft,** then the steps listed under **Revise.** You may ask students to review their peers' papers as they revise their drafts.
- Finally, ask students to complete the steps listed under **Edit** and **Publish.** Remind students to use standard grammar, spelling, sentence structure, and punctuation in their final draft.

CURRICULUM CONNECTION
Art

Present Information Visually

- Explain to students that pictures can sometimes help readers understand research reports. For example, a flowchart can show the steps in the life cycle of a frog. A drawing of a red-winged blackbird can show exactly where the red is on the bird's wings.
- Have pairs or small groups of students read each other's research reports.
- Students can then work together to identify which parts of the reports—if any—would be good places to add a diagram or a picture.
- Allow students to share with the class summaries of their research reports and explain where and why a diagram or a picture could be used.
- Students may wish to make diagrams, drawings, or photographs and add them to their reports.

Five Themes of Geography

From *"Guidelines for Geographic Education: Elementary and Secondary Skills,"* prepared by the Joint Committee on Geographic Education of the National Council for Geographic Education and the Association of American Geographers

Location

Describing a *location* involves finding the relative or exact position of a place.

- Show students a map of the United States. Have them locate Wyoming and name the states that border it. Then have students name the state that is north of Wyoming. (Montana)
- Point out the lines of latitude and longitude on the map. Have students find Grand Teton National Park, using a classroom map.

Place

Describing a *place* involves identifying distinguishing features and comparing them with features of other areas (natural or human-made).

1 How is Grand Teton National Park different from a park in your community? Possible answer: Grand Teton National Park has steep mountains, a large lake, and forests; unlike our local park, it does not have grassy fields and playground equipment. Compare and Contrast

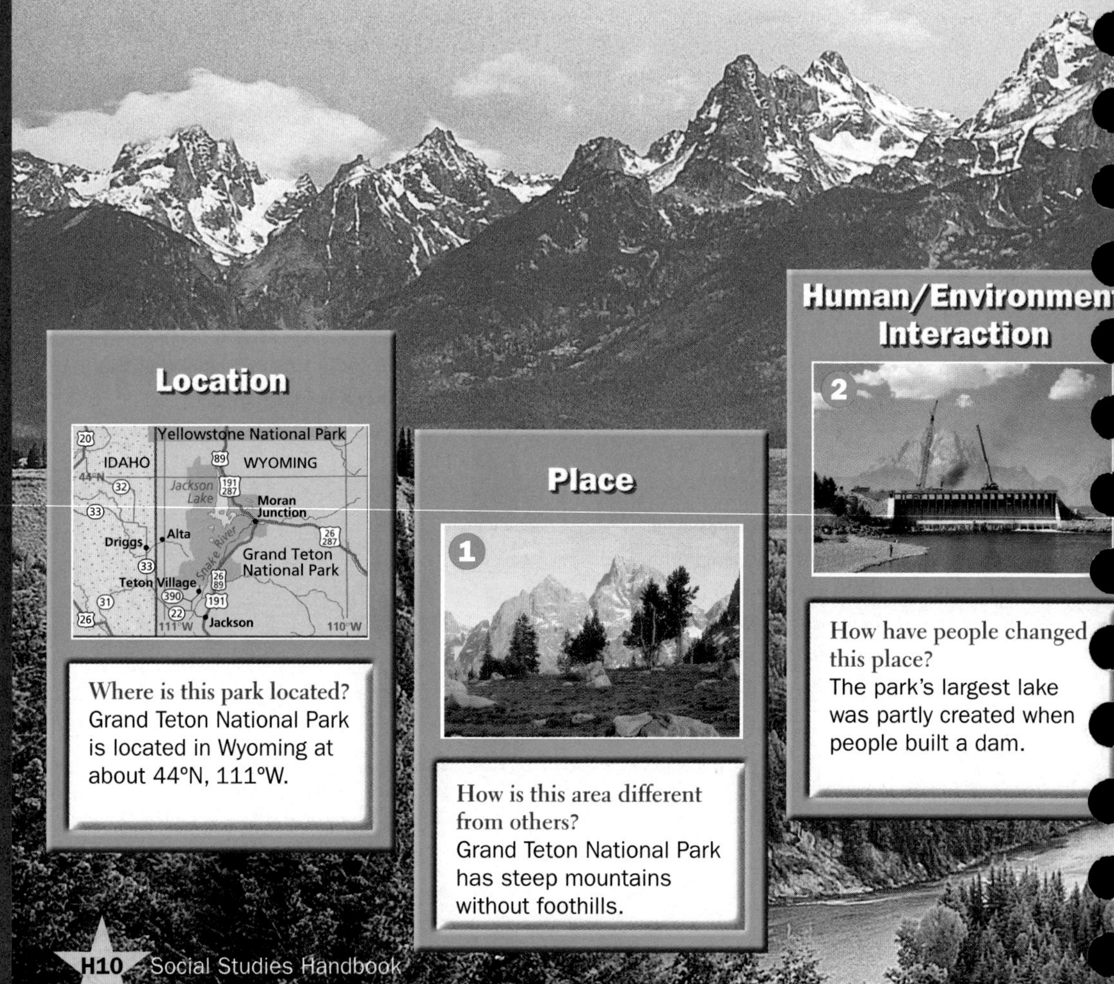

Geography Skills

Five Themes of Geography

Geography is the study of Earth. This study can be divided into five themes that help you understand why Earth has such a wide variety of places. Each theme reveals something different about a spot, as the following example of Grand Teton National Park shows.

Location

Where is this park located?
Grand Teton National Park is located in Wyoming at about 44°N, 111°W.

Place

1

How is this area different from others?
Grand Teton National Park has steep mountains without foothills.

Human/Environment Interaction

2

How have people changed this place?
The park's largest lake was partly created when people built a dam.

H10 Social Studies Handbook

Practice and Extend

SOCIAL STUDIES Background

The Essential Elements of Geography

From the National Council for Geographic Education

- **The World in Spatial Terms** Geography studies the relationships between people, places, and environments by showing information about them in a spatial context.
- **Places and Regions** The identities of individuals and cultures can be found in particular places and regions.
- **Physical Systems** Physical processes shape Earth's surface and interact with flora and fauna to create, sustain, and change ecosystems.
- **Human Systems** Human activities help shape Earth's surface. Human structures and settlements are part of Earth's surface, and humans control portions of Earth's surface.
- **Environment and Society** The physical environment is modified by human activities, many having to do with the pursuit of Earth's natural resources. Human activities are also influenced by Earth's physical features and processes.
- **The Uses of Geography** Knowledge of geography enables people to develop an understanding of the relationships between people, places, and environments over time.

Movement

3

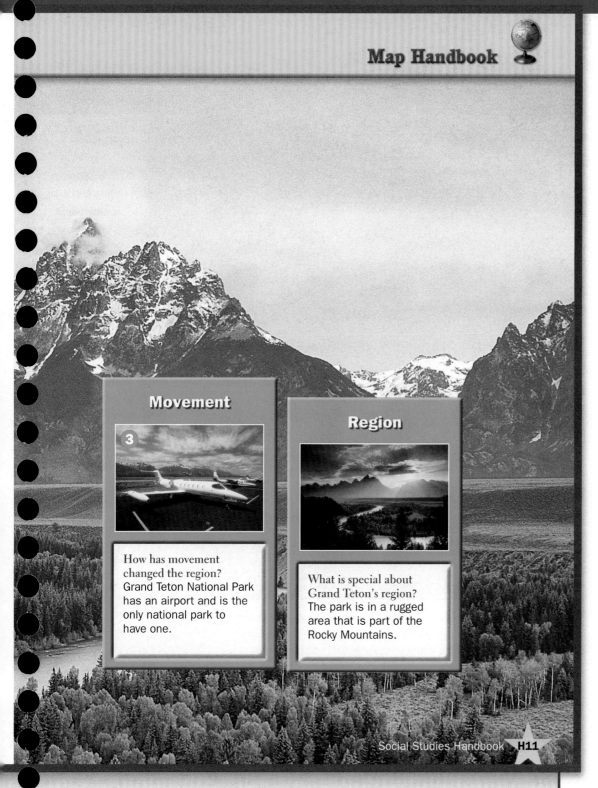

How has movement changed the region?
Grand Teton National Park has an airport and is the only national park to have one.

Region

What is special about Grand Teton's region?
The park is in a rugged area that is part of the Rocky Mountains.

SOCIAL STUDIES STRAND
Geography

Analyze the Continental Divide

- Have students use print or online resources to learn more about the Continental Divide.
- Have them identify the location of the Continental Divide in Grand Teton National Park and discuss what it represents.
- On an outline map of the United States, have students draw the path of the Continental Divide. Have them use arrows to show the direction rivers flow on each side of this imaginary line.
- On their outline maps, ask students to label the states through which the Continental Divide passes.

Human/Environment Interaction

Interaction between humans and the environment involves people influencing (changing) and being influenced by their surroundings.

2 How have people changed the environment in your community? Possible answer: People have built bridges and roads, and they have built communities with homes, schools, and businesses. Draw Conclusions

Movement

Discuss the theme of *movement*—ways in which people, goods, and information move from one place to another.

3 How has the movement of people and goods changed since the first European settlers came to your state? The first European settlers did not use cars, trucks, planes, or trains. They used ships and horse-drawn wagons. Compare and Contrast

Region

The common features that make an area special help to comprise a *region.*

- Display pictures of different regions in the United States, including mountains, plains, woodlands, and so on. Have students compare and contrast the regions. You may wish to find pictures of different regions from the units in this book. Point out different landforms and vegetation.
- Use the map on pp. R14–R15 at the back of the Pupil Edition to highlight some of the physical features that comprise regions in the United States.

Additional Resources

The following resources can be used throughout Grade 4 to teach and reinforce geography skills.

- Intermediate Big Book Atlas
- Student Atlas
- Outline Maps
- Desk Maps
- Map Resources CD-ROM

What Does a Globe Show?

Use a Globe

- Point out that only half a globe is shown on p. H12.
- Have students use a globe to find and list Earth's seven continents (Asia, Africa, North America, South America, Antarctica, Europe, and Australia) and four oceans (Pacific Ocean, Atlantic Ocean, Indian Ocean, and Arctic Ocean) on the board.
- Note: Some people now consider the Southern Ocean to be the world's fifth ocean.
- Have students use the list to determine which continents and oceans are shown on p. H12 and which are not.

4 **How does a globe differ from a photograph or map of Earth?** A globe is a small, round (spherical) copy of Earth; you must turn it to see all the different continents and oceans.
Compare and Contrast

5 **What imaginary line runs halfway around Earth from the North Pole to the South Pole? What imaginary line runs east and west around the middle of Earth?** The prime meridian; the equator
Interpret Maps

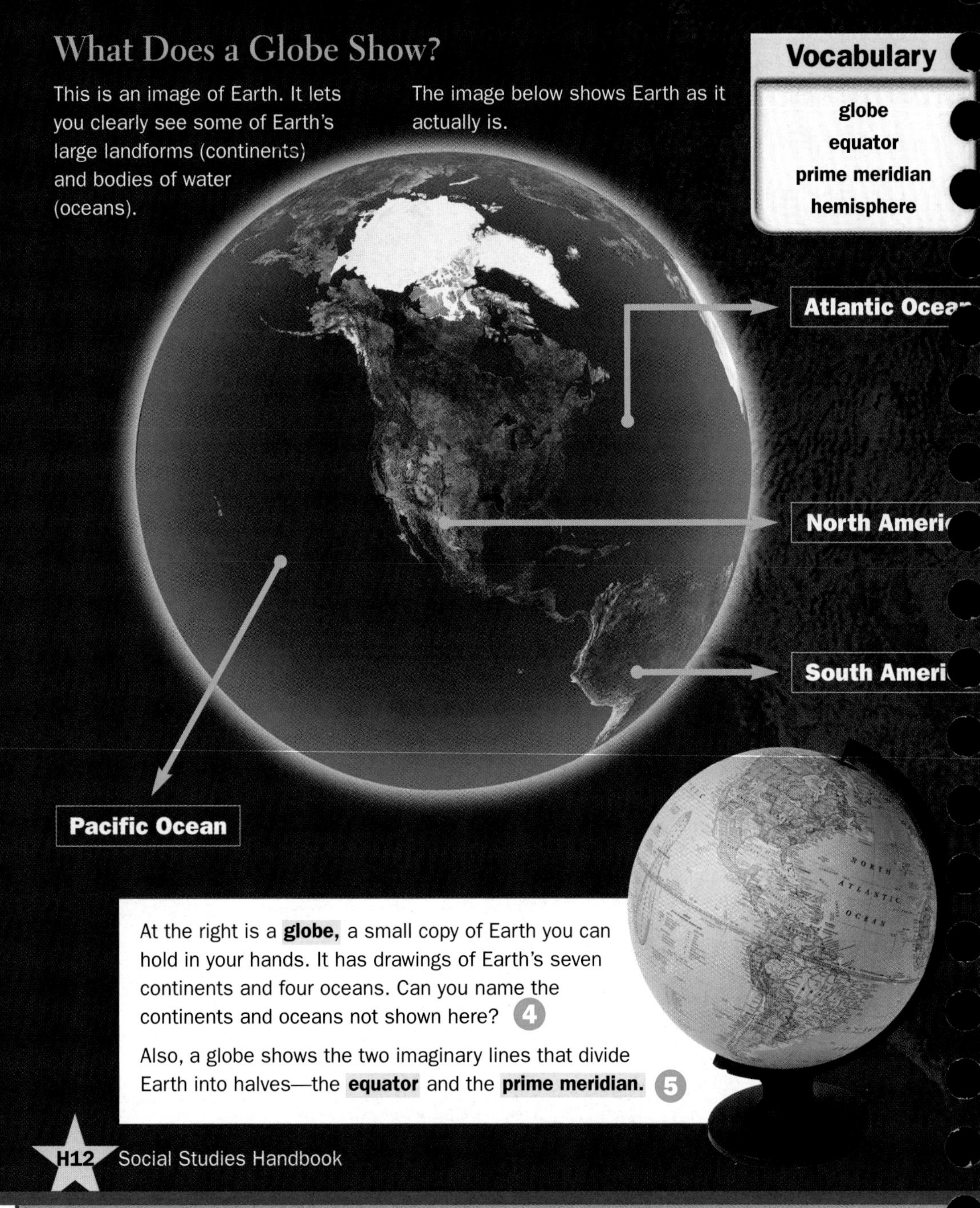
Geography Skills
What Does a Globe Show?
This is an image of Earth. It lets you clearly see some of Earth's large landforms (continents) and bodies of water (oceans).
The image below shows Earth as it actually is.
Vocabulary
globe
equator
prime meridian
hemisphere
Atlantic Ocea
North Ameri
South Ameri
Pacific Ocean
At the right is a globe, a small copy of Earth you can hold in your hands. It has drawings of Earth's seven continents and four oceans. Can you name the continents and oceans not shown here? 4
Also, a globe shows the two imaginary lines that divide Earth into halves—the equator and the prime meridian. 5
H12 Social Studies Handbook

Practice and Extend

SOCIAL STUDIES
Background

The Continental Drift Theory

- The continental drift theory was first presented in 1912 by Alfred Wegener.
- According to the theory, Earth's surface was once made up of a single continent, called Pangaea, that eventually fragmented and drifted apart to form seven continents.
- The theory explains why the eastern coast of South America and the western coast of Africa seem to fit together like pieces of a jigsaw puzzle.
- Many scientists today support the continental drift theory. They theorize that the planet's solid outer shell consists of huge rigid plates (tectonic plates) that move continuously. As the plates move, they carry the continents and the ocean floor with them.
- Some scientists estimate that the relative positions of the continents move at a rate of about 0.5 to 4 inches a year.

Hemispheres: Northern and Southern

You can see only half of Earth or of a globe at a time. Half views of Earth have names—**hemispheres**—and the illustration at left below shows Earth separated into these views at the equator. The **Northern Hemisphere** is the half north of the equator, which circles Earth halfway between the poles. However, there is only one way to see the Northern Hemisphere all at once. You have to turn a globe until you are looking down directly at the North Pole. The picture at the top right shows that view.

What are the only continents not found, at least in part, in the Northern Hemisphere?*

The **Southern Hemisphere** is the half of Earth south of the equator. The picture below turns the globe until you are looking down directly at the South Pole. You see all of the Southern Hemisphere. Which hemisphere—northern or southern—contains more land?

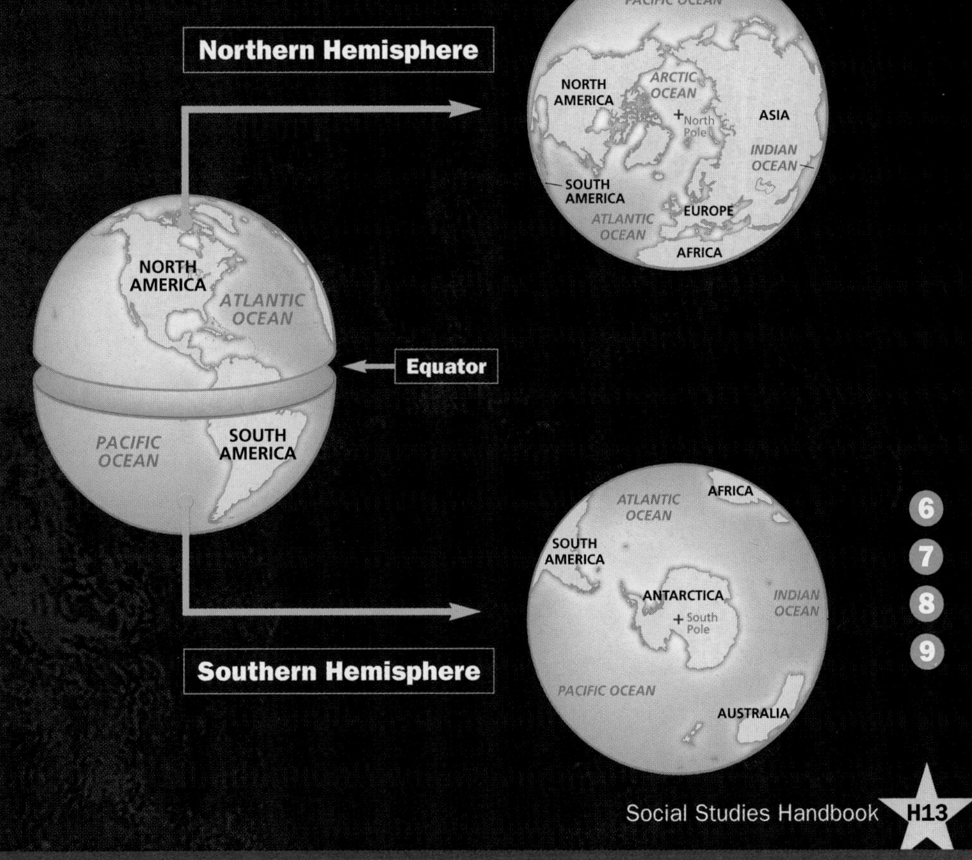

Hemispheres: Northern and Southern

Identify Hemispheres

- Have students use a globe and the pictures on p. H13 to determine the continents and oceans located in the Northern Hemisphere.
- Then have students identify continents and oceans located in the Southern Hemisphere.
- Point out that, although the equator divides Earth into equal halves, the Northern Hemisphere has more land.

6 **Which continents are located in both the Northern and Southern Hemispheres?** South America, Africa, Asia Interpret Maps

7 **Which continents are located entirely in the Southern Hemisphere?** Australia, Antarctica Interpret Maps

8 **Which ocean is located entirely in the Northern Hemisphere?** The Arctic Ocean Interpret Maps

9 **Why do you think the country of Ecuador in South America was given that name?** Make sure that students locate Ecuador on a map or globe. Because it lies on the equator (the name comes from the Spanish word meaning "equator") Draw Conclusions

Vocabulary

globe: a small copy of Earth with continents and oceans labeled

equator: an imaginary line halfway between the North and South Poles that divides Earth into two equal parts

prime meridian: an imaginary line that goes from the North Pole to the South Pole through Greenwich, England

hemisphere: one of two equal parts of Earth; the Northern and Southern Hemispheres are separated by the equator, and the Eastern and Western Hemispheres are separated by the prime meridian

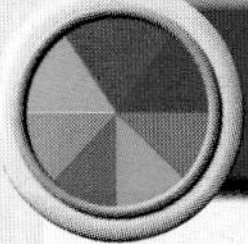

CURRICULUM CONNECTION
Art

Make a Globe

- Have students use papier-mâché, a round balloon, a black felt-tip marker (fine point), and tempera paint to make a replica of a globe.
- Students should cover the inflated balloon with at least four layers of papier-mâché (newspaper strips dipped in a mixture of flour and water). *Caution:* Students should wear cover goggles when handling inflated balloons.
- After the globes have dried overnight, have students paint on green-colored continents and blue-colored oceans. Suggest that they draw outlines of the continents before painting them.
- Display commercial globes for students to refer to as needed. You also may wish to provide copies of world maps.
- After the painted globes have dried overnight, have students label the continents and oceans and draw the equator and the prime meridian.

Hemispheres: Western and Eastern

- Tell students that the prime meridian, unlike the equator, extends only halfway around Earth.
- Have students look at the pictures on p. H14 and identify the continents and oceans located in the Western and Eastern Hemispheres.

10 **Which continents are located almost entirely in the Western Hemisphere?** North America, South America Interpret Maps

11 **Which continents are located entirely or almost entirely in the Eastern Hemisphere?** Europe, Africa, Asia, Australia Interpret Maps

12 **Which ocean is *not* located in both the Eastern and Western Hemispheres?** The Indian Ocean Interpret Maps

- Have students use what they know about the Northern, Southern, Eastern, and Western Hemispheres to answer the following questions.

13 **What is the only continent that is located almost entirely in the Southern and Western Hemispheres?** South America Interpret Maps

14 **In which hemispheres is Africa located?** Northern, Southern, Eastern, and Western Interpret Maps

Geography Skills

Hemispheres: Western and Eastern

Earth has two other hemispheres. They are formed by dividing Earth into halves a different way, along the prime meridian. The prime meridian is an imaginary line that runs from the North Pole to the South Pole. It passes through Greenwich, England, an area of London. The **Eastern Hemisphere** is the half east of the prime meridian. The prime meridian passes through which continents?

The **Western Hemisphere** is the half of Earth west of the prime meridian. Which two continents are found entirely within this hemisphere? Which of the four oceans is not found in this hemisphere? In which two hemispheres is the United States found?

Vocabulary

degree
latitude
longitude

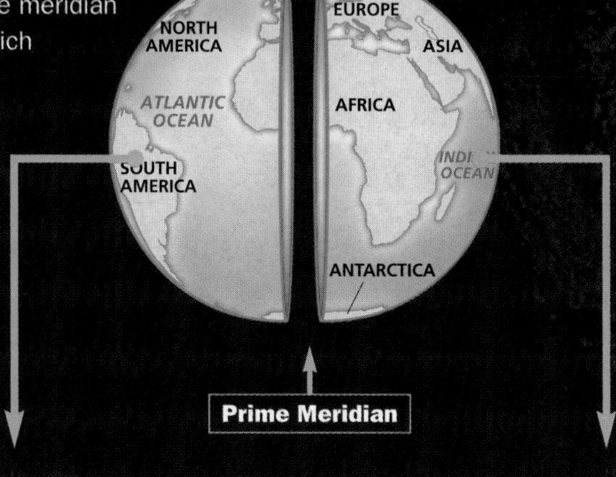

Prime Meridian

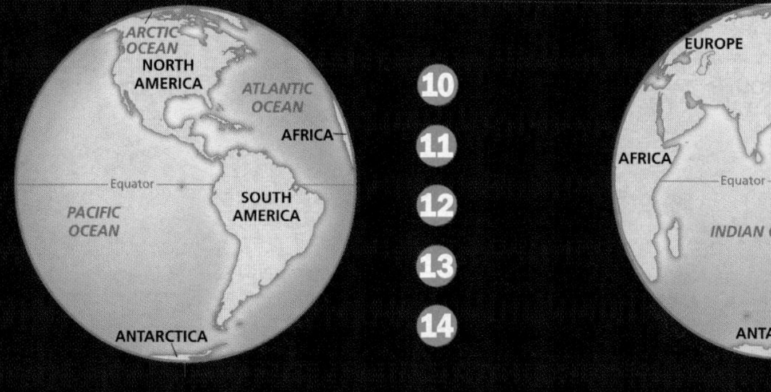

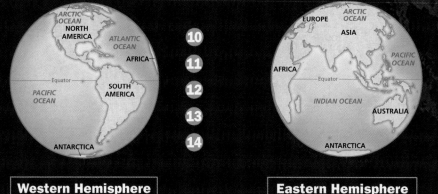

Western Hemisphere

Eastern Hemisphere

Practice and Extend

ACCESS CONTENT
ESL Support

Explore Hemispheres Students use geography terms and a globe.

Beginning Give each student a plastic-foam ball to serve as a globe. Have students draw the equator. Have students write geography terms they have learned on self-stick notes. Then have students place the self-stick notes on their globes in the appropriate places.

Intermediate Have students make the globe from the "Beginning" activity but also draw the prime meridian. Have students label their globes with self-stick notes on which they have written the names of hemispheres, continents, oceans, and other geography terms.

Advanced Use a commercial globe to review the four hemispheres with students. Then have volunteers give clues to lead students to a specific continent or ocean on the globe, for example: *This place is in the _____ Hemisphere; it is (close to, far from) the equator; it is an (ocean, continent); its name begins with the letter _____.*

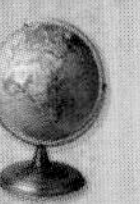

Understand Latitude and Longitude on a Globe

Mapmakers created a system for noting the exact location of places on Earth. The system uses two sets of imaginary circles crossing Earth. They are numbered in units called **degrees.**

Lines of **latitude** are the set of circles that go east and west. The equator is 0 degrees (0°) latitude. From there, the parallel circles go north and south. They get smaller and smaller until they end in dots at the North Pole (90°N) and the South Pole (90°S). The globe below at the left is tilted to show latitude lines 15° apart up to the North Pole. Most of the United States falls between which degrees of latitude?

Lines of **longitude** are the set of half-circles that go north and south. They are all the same size. The prime meridian is 0° longitude. However, from there, the degrees fan out between the North and South poles. They are not parallel and go east and west for 180°, not just 90°. The globe below at the right shows longitude lines 15° apart. They meet at 180° on the other side of Earth directly behind the prime meridian. Most of Africa falls between which degrees of longitude?

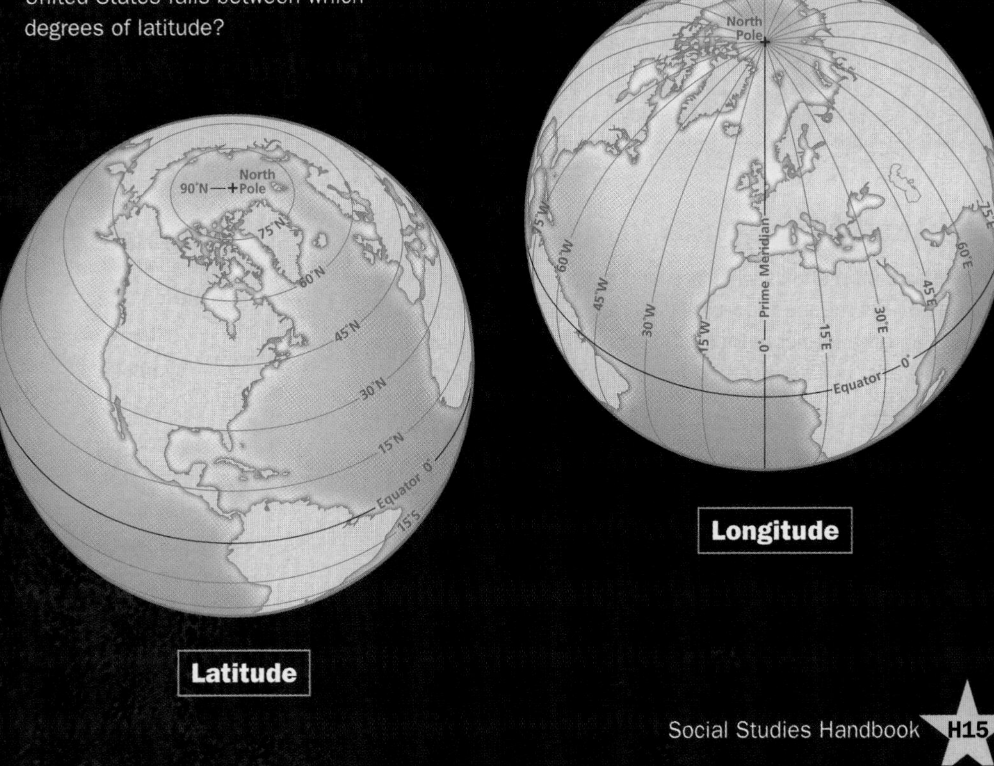

Longitude

Latitude

Understand Latitude and Longitude

Use Latitude and Longitude

- Have students find the equator and the prime meridian on the pictures of the globe.
- Name a specific line of latitude or longitude. Have students use the pictures on p. H15 to determine what continents or oceans are located on that line.
- Name two lines of latitude or longitude. Have students use a map or a globe that shows political boundaries to determine what countries are located between those two lines.
- Point out that some maps may show lines of latitude and longitude at increments of 2°, 5°, 10°, or 20°, rather than 15°.
- Tell students that lines of latitude are parallel and that lines of longitude meet, or converge, at the North Pole and the South Pole. If necessary, have students trace with their finger lines of latitude and then lines of longitude on a globe or on one of the pictures on this page.
- Students will learn more about lines of latitude and longitude on p. H21.

Vocabulary

degree: the unit of measure in the system used to describe exact locations on Earth

latitude: imaginary circles that go east and west around Earth

longitude: imaginary circles that go north and south around Earth and all meet at the North and South Poles

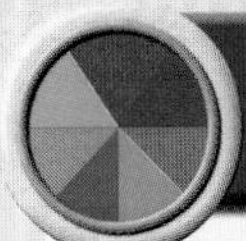

CURRICULUM CONNECTION
Science

Identify Positions of Celestial Objects

- The astronomer's system of locating objects in the sky is similar to the geographer's system of locating places on Earth.
- Astronomers use the celestial sphere—an imaginary sphere that represents the entire sky—to identify the positions of stars and other celestial bodies. The observer on Earth is at the center of that sphere.
- The celestial equator, which is an extension of Earth's equator into space, is halfway between the celestial poles, which are directly above Earth's poles.
- The celestial sphere is also divided by imaginary lines similar to the lines of latitude and longitude on a globe. Just as latitude and longitude help describe locations on Earth, these lines on the celestial sphere help identify positions of celestial bodies.

Use a Political Map

Have students identify the various features of the map on this page. Then have them compare the map with other maps in this book and point out similarities and differences.

15 **According to the map on this page, what Texas city is located very near Mexico's northern border? What city is the capital of New Mexico?** El Paso; Santa Fe
Interpret Maps

16 **What kind of map would you use to see state borders clearly? How does that kind of map make it easy to do that?** Political map; Different states have different colors.
Main Idea and Details

15

Political Map

A **political map** shows what humans have created on Earth's surface. This means that a political map can show borders that divide an area into countries, states, and counties. It can also show cities, roads, buildings, and other human-made elements. 16

A map's **title** tells what a map is about. What is the title of this map?

A map's **symbols** are lines, small drawings, or fields of color that stand for something else. The map's **key,** or legend, is a small box that tells what each symbol stands for. What do the stars stand for on the map?

Sometimes a map has a **locator,** a small map in a box or circle. It locates the main map in a larger area such as a state, country, continent, or hemisphere. In what larger area is the Southwest region shown?

Vocabulary
- political map
- title
- symbol
- key
- locator
- physical map
- compass rose
- cardinal direction

Practice and Extend

CURRICULUM CONNECTION
Math

Using Math with Social Studies

- Tell students that they can use math to interpret social studies information.
- They might use multiplication to interpret a map scale. If they are reading a map scale where the ratio of inches on the page to miles in the real world is 1:50, multiplying the number of inches between points by 50 will tell them how many miles apart the places are in the real world.
- Have students calculate the distances between different places on the map on this page.

Southwest Region of the United States: Physical

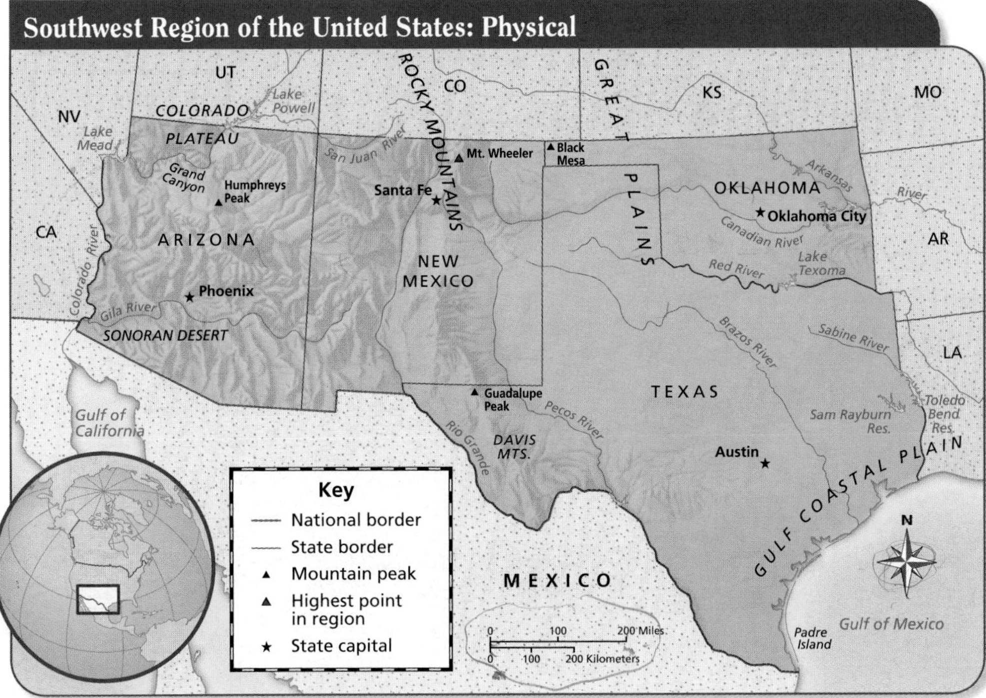

Physical Map

A **physical map** shows the major landforms and water on an area of Earth's surface. 17 What are some examples of mountains, a desert, rivers, and gulfs on the physical map of the Southwest region on this page? Notice that a physical map can have a few elements of a political map.

A **compass rose** is a fancy design with four large pointers that show the **cardinal directions.** The north pointer, which points toward the North Pole, is marked with an **N**. East is to the right, south is opposite north, and west is to the left. What direction is the Gulf of Mexico from the Gulf of California?

Four other features common on maps are intermediate directions, scale, grid, and latitude and longitude. They are covered in detail on the following pages.

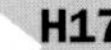

Use a Physical Map

- Point out to students that the southwestern United States has a great contrast of physical regions—high mountains, large deserts, and plains.
- Ask students to name some of the main landforms in the physical map on this page.
- Have students identify map features that appear on both the physical map on this page and the political map on page H16. (title, key, symbols, locator, compass rose, scale)

17 **What kind of map would you look at to see where deserts are located? Why?** A physical map, because it shows landforms **Main Idea and Details**

Vocabulary

political map: a map that shows the locations of cities, states, and countries

title: a line that tells what a map is about

symbol: a small drawing, line, or color that stands for something else

key: a map feature that tells what all of the symbols mean

locator: a small map that shows where the main map is located within a larger area

physical map: a map that shows landforms and bodies of water

compass rose: a pointer on a map that shows the four major directions

cardinal direction: one of the four major directions

SOCIAL STUDIES Background

History of Mapmaking

- Except for maps made by Ptolemy in ancient Greece, few accurate maps were produced before the Middle Ages. Mainly they were sketches based on guesses.
- In the 1300s, voyages of discovery, the development of compasses, the rediscovery of Ptolemy's maps, and advances in surveying contributed to the making of better maps.
- France and England conducted national surveys in the 1700s that made still better maps possible.
- Modern mapmakers use the products of a variety of new technologies, including satellite images and remote sensing data.

Intermediate Directions

Ask students the following questions:

18 **What map feature helps you find directions that are northwest, northeast, southeast, and southwest?** A compass rose Main Idea and Details

19 **Why does a compass rose show intermediate directions? Why aren't the cardinal directions enough?** Possible answer: Including intermediate directions makes it possible to describe directions more exactly. Main Idea and Details

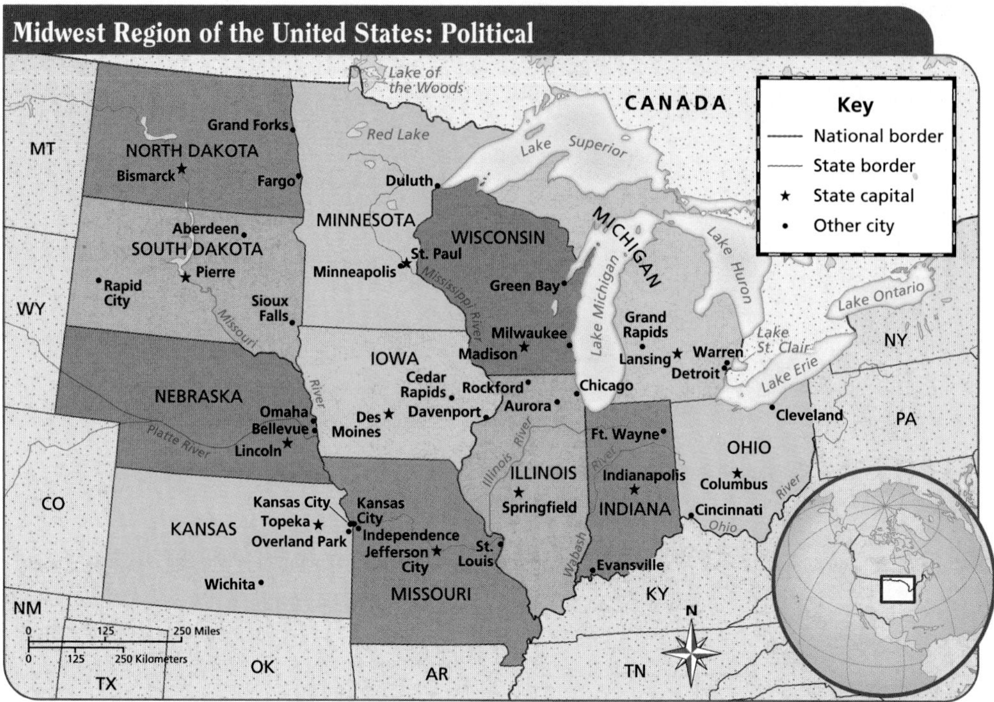

Intermediate Directions

As you just reviewed, a compass rose is a pointer that shows the four cardinal directions. Look at the compass rose on the map on this page. In addition to showing the large cardinal directions, it shows smaller points that are midway between them. 18
These are the **intermediate directions.** 19

Each intermediate direction shares the names of the cardinal directions on either side of it. For example, the intermediate direction between north and east is called northeast. The intermediate directions are **northeast, southeast, southwest,** and **northwest.** Which state is southeast of Nebraska? Which is northeast of Iowa? What direction is Madison, Wisconsin, from Columbus, Ohio?

Vocabulary

- intermediate direction
- northeast
- southeast
- southwest
- northwest
- scale

Practice and Extend

CURRICULUM CONNECTION
Writing

Write Directions

- Have pairs of students create directions for hikers to find a small waterfall in a state park of their own invention.
- Have partners first draw an illustrated map of the park and then write the directions.
- The directions should have hikers start at a specific landmark in the park, such as an unusual landform or building, and then use numbered steps and both cardinal and intermediate directions. For example: "Step 1—Start at the old railroad bridge and walk ten steps north. Step 2—Cross the creek and then walk fifteen steps northeast."
- Have students share their maps and directions with the class.

Major Mountain Ranges and Peaks of the Northeast Region

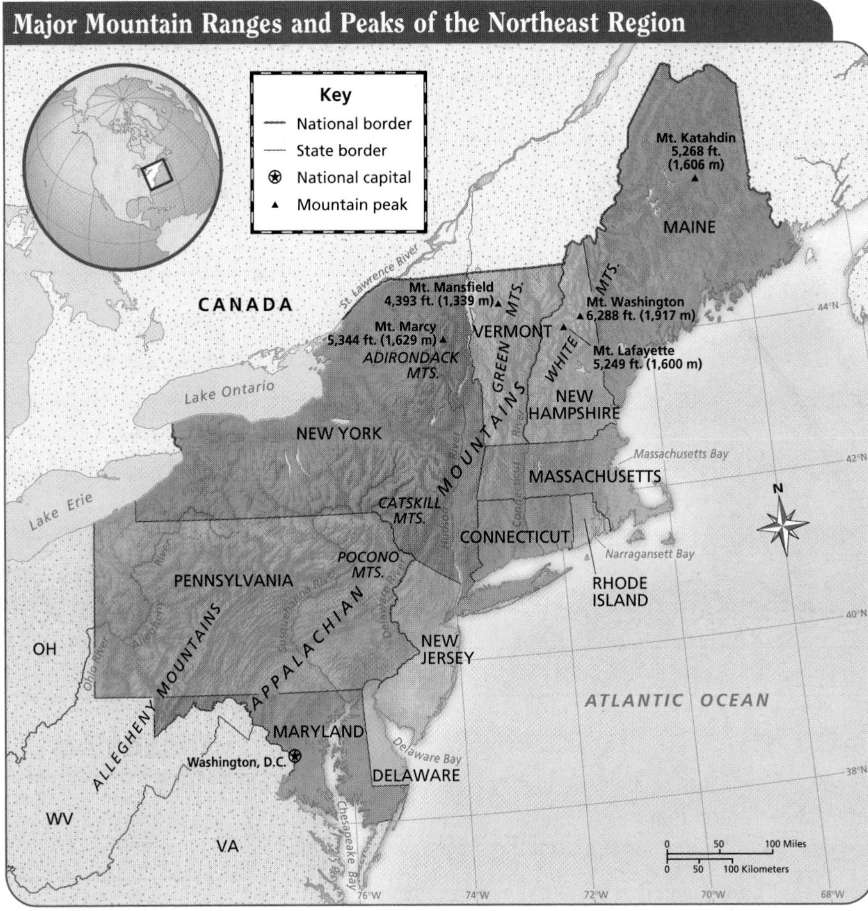

Use Scale

A **scale** will help you figure out how far it is in real miles or kilometers from one point on a map to another. Starting at 0, a scale marks off tens, hundreds, or even thousands of miles. The measurement chosen depends on the size of the area shown. One way to use the scale is to hold the edge of a scrap of paper under the scale and copy the scale onto it. Then you can place your copy directly on the map and measure the distance between two points. Use the scale on the map above to help you find out about how far it is in miles from Mt. Katahdin to Mt. Washington. Is this a political or a physical map? 20

Use Scale

Calculate Distances Between Cities

- Have students use a sheet of paper to copy the scale on p. H19 in the manner described in the text.
- List on the board pairs of mountain peaks shown on the map on this page. Have students use the scale to measure and calculate the distance between each pair of mountain peaks. Demonstrate the process before having students work independently.
- Encourage students to check their calculations with a partner before you list the correct answers on the board.
- Make sure students understand that different maps may use different scales. The scale used depends on the size of the area a map represents.

20 **Why might maps use different scales?** Because the scale chosen depends on the size of the area shown; when a map shows a large area that has been greatly reduced, a small unit of measurement may represent a long distance. **Analyze Information**

Vocabulary

intermediate direction: one of the four directions that are halfway between the cardinal directions

northeast: the intermediate direction on a compass that is midway between north and east

southeast: the intermediate direction on a compass that is midway between south and east

southwest: the intermediate direction on a compass that is midway between south and west

northwest: the intermediate direction on a compass that is midway between north and west

scale: a ratio relating the distance between two points on a map to the actual distance between the two places represented by those points

CURRICULUM CONNECTION
Math

Compare and Use Scales

- Have students compare the scales used on a map of their state, a map of the United States, and a world map. Ask students why one inch or one centimeter does not represent the same distance for all three maps. (An inch or a centimeter may represent a greater distance when a larger area is shown on a map.)
- Have students use the scale on a map of their state to find the distance (miles or kilometers) between the state capital and another city. Then have students use a U.S. map and a world map to find this distance.
- Ask students what was the same about finding the distance on the three maps. (Possible answers: The number of miles between the cities, using a ruler to measure the distance; using the scale to find out how many miles the distance represented)
- Ask students what was different about finding the distance on the three maps. (The measurement in inches)

Use a Grid

Play a Grid Guessing Game

- Model how to use the grid system on p. H20 to find the Civic Opera House on the map. Have students follow along in their books.
- Have students use the grid system to locate other places on the map.
- Make sure students understand that each letter-number combination identifies a square region, not just the point where the lines cross.
- Have students play a guessing game. Tell them a letter-number combination for the location of a place on the map. Have them use the grid to identify the place. If there is more than one place within that square region, include a clue along with the letter-number combination. For example: *I am in a city-government building located in C3. Where am I?* (Possible answer: City Hall)

Make a Grid Map

- Have students use inch-square or large-grid graph paper to make a map of a fictitious zoo or amusement park.
- Have them use letters and numbers to label the rows and columns of grid squares.
- Students should draw symbols on the map to show the locations of major sites, such as animal exhibits or park rides. Remind them to include a map legend or an index.
- Students can exchange maps and quiz each other about what is located at different letter-number combinations on their maps.

Vocabulary

grid: a system of rows of imaginary squares on a map

index: an alphabetical listing of places shown in a map

Geography Skills

Downtown Chicago, Illinois

Kinzie St. · Wrigley Building · Merchandise Mart · N · Chicago River · Wacker Dr. · Michigan St. · Franklin St. · LaSalle St. · Dearborn St. · Randolph St. · City Hall · Daley Plaza · Wabash Ave. · Lakefront Millennium Park · Civic Opera House · Wacker Dr. · Madison St. · Monroe St. · Adams St. · Art Institute of Chicago · Sears Tower · Orchestra Hall · 0 · 1/8 · 1/4 Mile · 0 · 1/8 · 1/4 Kilometer

Rows: A, B, C, D · Columns: 1, 2, 3, 4, 5

Index

- Art Institute of Chicago **D5**
- City Hall **C3**
- Civic Opera House **C1**
- Daley Plaza...... **C3**
- Merchandise Mart.......... **A2**
- Orchestra Hall.... **D4**
- Sears Tower **D1**
- Wrigley Building... **A4**

Use a Grid

A city map shows the streets of a city. It might also show some points of interest or natural features. What natural feature do you see on this map? Point to and name a street in downtown Chicago.

This map also has a **grid.** A grid is a system of rows of imaginary squares on the map. The rows of squares are numbered and lettered along the edges of the map. You can use an index to find places where rows of numbers and letters cross. An **index** is an alphabetical listing of places. The number-letter combination attached to each place tells you where the two rows cross. Here you can find the place you are looking for.

Look down the index until you find "Sears Tower." It is located in grid square D1. Find the "D" row on the map and move your finger over to where the "1" row crosses it. Now find the City Hall in the same way.

Vocabulary

grid

index

Practice and Extend

Decision Making

Use a Decision-Making Process

- Write the addresses of three fictitious garage sales and a different starting time for each sale. Have students use that information and a map of their community—with a grid and index of street names. **Suppose you want to go to these sales on the same day. Each sale starts at a different time. The sooner you get to each one, the better the bargains you will find. What route will you follow?**
- Students should use the decision-making process to decide what route to take from their home or from school to each garage sale. They must begin by using the grid and the index to find each location. For each step in the process, have students discuss and write about what must be considered. Write the steps above on the board or read them aloud.

1. Identify a situation that requires a decision.
2. Gather information.
3. Identify options.
4. Predict consequences.
5. Take action to implement a decision.

Some National Park Service Sites of the Southeast Region

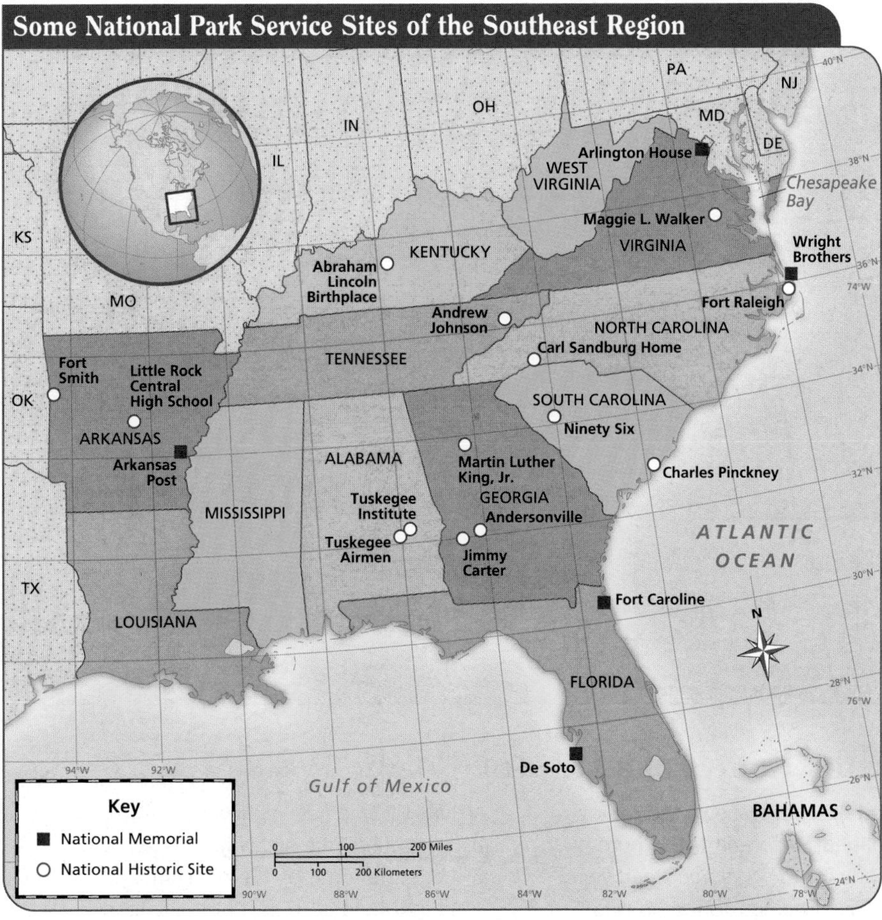

Use Latitude and Longitude for Exact Location

Lines of latitude and longitude are like city-map grid rows. When they are used on a map, the lines are numbered in degrees along the edges. Each point where east-west latitude and north-south longitude cross is an exact location. If a place is found at or nearly at where latitude and longitude lines cross, the place takes those two numbers as its exact location.

In the map above the exact location of Tuskegee Airmen National Historic Site is almost 32°N, 86°W. The Andersonville site is nearly 32°N, 84°W. What two sites are found at nearly 36°N, 76°W?

MEETING INDIVIDUAL NEEDS

Leveled Practice

Use Latitude and Longitude Have students complete the following activities using a map or globe that indicates both latitude and longitude.

Easy Have students choose one line of latitude or longitude and trace its path around the globe. Students should write the names of any continents, countries, or major cities on or near the line. **Reteach**

On-Level Tell students that you are planning a trip around the world. List the latitude and longitude of different places, but not the names. Have students use a map or globe to figure out the places you might visit. **Extend**

Challenge Have students choose destinations for their own trip around the world. They can write an itinerary of places using only latitudes and longitudes, not names. Have partners exchange itineraries and name the places on each other's routes. **Enrich**

Use Latitude and Longitude for Exact Location

Find the Latitude and Longitude of Places in the Southeast

- Review with students what they learned about latitude and longitude on p. H15.
- Model how to use the map on p. H21 to identify the locations of the Andersonville National Historic Site (about 32°N, 84°W) and the Tuskegee Airmen National Historic Site (about 32°N, 86°W).
- Help students identify the place found almost exactly at 34°N, 82°W (Ninety Six National Historic Site). Clarify to students that some places lie near, but not exactly on, the point where lines of latitude and longitude cross.
- Make sure students understand that the lines of latitude and longitude, rather than the regions between the lines, are labeled.
- After students understand how to use the map, have them identify the approximate latitude and longitude of various places in the Southeast, such as the Wright Brothers National Memorial (about 36°N, 76°W) and the Martin Luther King, Jr., National Historic Site (about 34°N, 84°W).

Geography Skills

Follow the Route of a Historic Road

- Explain to students that the National Road was the nation's first highway that was paid for entirely by the federal government.
- Discuss with students what the impact of the National Road was for settlement of the West, trade, and the growth of cities along its route.

21 **Through which states did U.S. Route 40 pass?** New Jersey, Delaware, Maryland, Pennsylvania, West Virginia, Ohio, Indiana, Illinois, Missouri, Kansas, Colorado, Utah, Nevada, California
Interpret Maps

Geography Skills

21

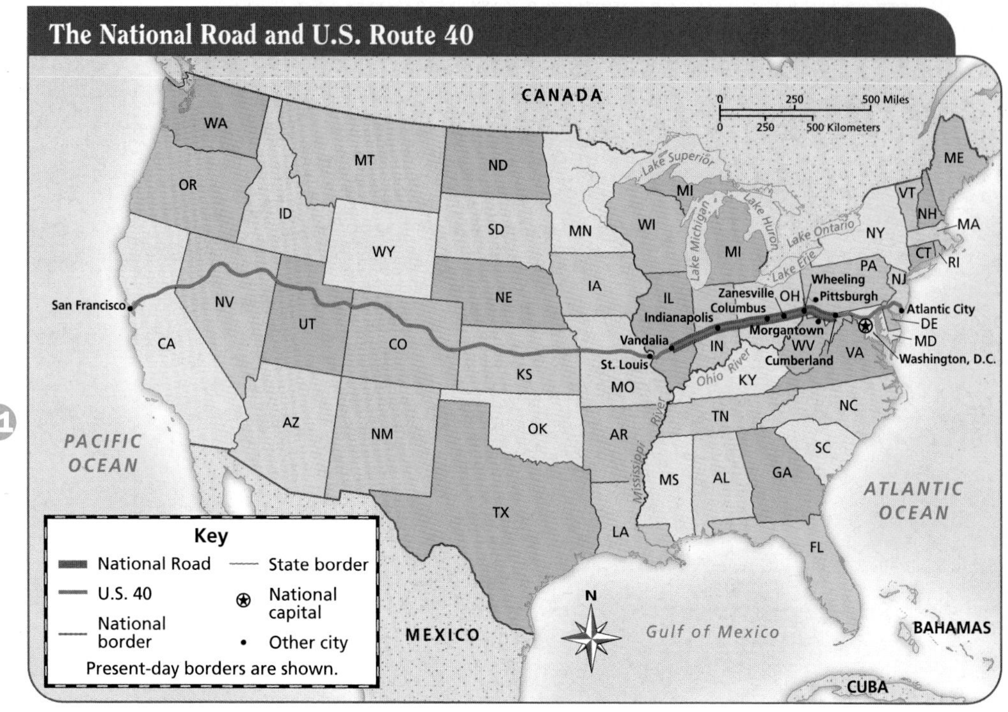

Follow the Routes of a Historic Road

The map on this page shows the routes of the old National Road and U.S. Route 40. Federal funds for the National Road were approved when Thomas Jefferson was president. Construction began in Cumberland, Maryland, in 1811. By the 1830s, stagecoaches and wagons followed the National Road through several states. What city lay at the western end of the old National Road in the 1800s? Which states did the National Road pass through?

In the 1920s a new highway, U.S. Route 40, was built. This highway covered much of the same route as the old National Road in the eastern part of the United States. By the 1950s, U.S. Route 40 stretched 3,220 miles from coast to coast. Later, the Interstate highway system was created. About 800 miles of U.S. 40 were discontinued. Today U.S. 40 ends in the west in Utah.

Practice and Extend

CURRICULUM CONNECTION
Math

- When the National Road was in operation in the mid-1800s, stagecoaches traveling on it could cover 60 to 70 miles per day.
- Ask students to consult the map scale and calculate how many days it would have taken a stagecoach to complete the trip from Wheeling, West Virginia, to Terre Haute, Indiana. (about six days)

SOCIAL STUDIES
Background

U.S. Route 40

- By 1880 railroads carried many people and goods. The National Road was seldom used and was in disrepair.
- Forty years later, few U.S. highways had all-weather surfaces that could handle automobile traffic.
- In 1921 Congress called for the construction of a better highway system. Roads running mainly east and west, such as Route 40, had even numbers, while those running mainly north and south had odd numbers.
- By the 1950s, U.S. Route 40 ran about 3,220 miles from Atlantic City, New Jersey, to San Francisco, California.
- Route 40 was largely replaced by a new national Interstate highway system after 1956. Today its westernmost point is in Silver Creek Junction, Utah.

★ Unit 1 ★

Vocabulary Routines

The following examples of reading and vocabulary development strategies can be used to instruct students about unit vocabulary.

BEFORE READING

Related Word Study

Words With Suffixes The structural analysis of words that contain a suffix can be accomplished by calling attention to the base word and the suffix that has been added. This will help students determine the meanings of words with suffixes.

We know that the word **communicate** *means "to give or exchange information." The suffix* **-ion** *can mean "act of" or "result of." When we add* **-ion** *to* **communicate**, *we create a new word:* **communication**. *Based on the meanings of* **communicate** *and* **-ion**, *what would you guess is the meaning of* **communication?** (the act of giving or exchanging information) This routine can also be used with the Unit 1 vocabulary words precipitation, elevation, and transportation. (explain that the *-ation* in transportation means the same thing as *-ion*)

Now think about the word **produce**. *When we add the suffix* **-er** *to produce, we create the word* **producer**. *The suffix* **-er** *means "person or thing that." So producer means "person who produces." What would you guess is the meaning of the vocabulary word* **consumer?** (person who consumes)

communicate	+	-ion	=	communication
produce	+	-er	=	producer

DURING READING

Context Clues

Use Context Clues As students read, encourage them to look at the words and sentences around any unfamiliar words. Explain that these words and sentences are called the word's context. Sometimes context clues offer enough information for students to determine the meaning of an unfamiliar word, but sometimes students will also need to use what they already know.

Point out that vocabulary words are defined in the text, but not everything students read will have definitions. Demonstrate how context clues can be used, and have students practice in a situation where they can check the definition to confirm their guesses. For example, after reading page 43 you could say, *Look at the word* **immigrant**. *Do the words around the word* **immigrant** *help you understand what it means? What clues can you find?* (Immigrants have come to the United States throughout the country's history. Many people in the United States are immigrants or the descendants of immigrants. Some came by choice and some did not.) Using these clues, how might you define immigrant?

AFTER READING

Individual Words

Possible Sentences Use this routine with students after you have read the lesson. Point out a vocabulary word and then use it in a sentence. Ask students if the sentence is possible or not. Have students explain their reasoning. This example is from chapter 2, lesson 3.

In the lesson we have just read, we read about a **passport**. *I want you to think about what* **passport** *means. Now I'm going to use* **passport** *in a sentence. Tell me if my sentence makes sense or not. We traveled in a ship to a* **passport**. (That doesn't make sense. A passport is not a place. It is a government document that people use to travel to foreign countries.) *Does this sentence using* **taxes** *make sense? Every April I pay my taxes.* (That makes sense. Taxes are something people pay to the government.)

Living in the United States

UNIT 1

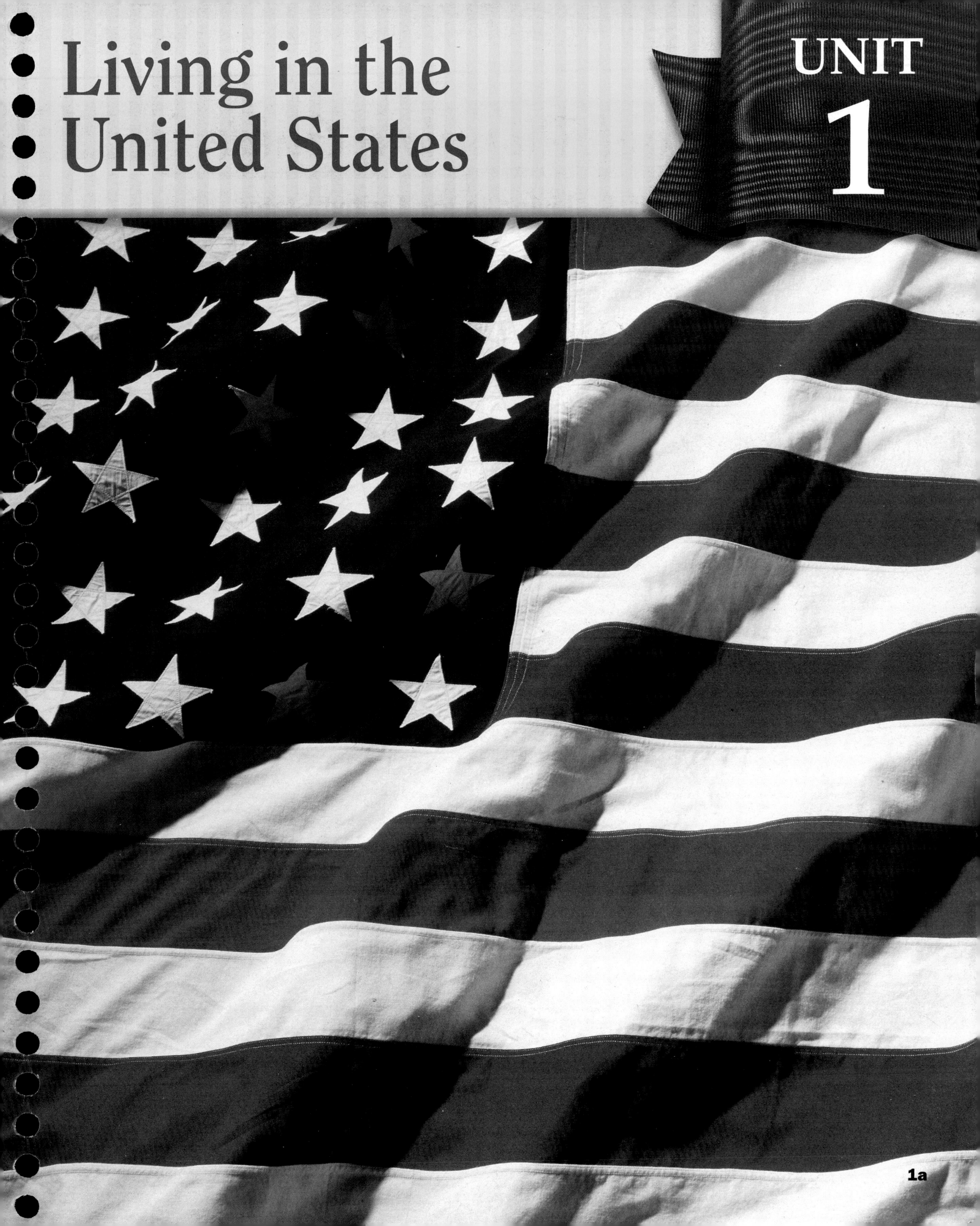

UNIT 1

Unit Planning Guide

Unit 1 • Living in the United States

Begin with a Primary Source pp. 2–3

Welcome to the United States pp. 4–5

Target Skill **Reading Social Studies, Summarize** pp. 6–7

Chapter Titles	Pacing	Main Ideas
Chapter 1 **The Regions of the United States** pp. 8–33 ✓ **Chapter 1 Review** pp. 34–35	9 days	• The United States is divided into five regions. • Many factors influence climate, which varies from region to region. • Each region has special resources.
Chapter 2 **We All Live Together** pp. 36–61 ✓ **Chapter 2 Review** pp. 62–63	9 days	• The United States is a diverse nation made up of people from many different backgrounds and cultures. • The government of the United States gives citizens the power to elect representatives who make and enforce laws. • Citizens have rights as well as responsibilities.
Chapter 3 **Earning and Learning** pp. 64–87 ✓ **Chapter 3 Review** pp. 88–89	7 days	• America's rich resources have drawn many people to the continent and to specific regions throughout our history. • People trade for the goods and services that they need and want. • The regions of the United States and the nations of the world depend on one another.

End with a Song pp. 90–91

✓ **Unit 1 Review** pp. 92–93

✓ **Unit 1 Project** p. 94

✓ = **Assessment Options**

The Constitution unites citizens under a common plan of government.

Resources	Meeting Individual Needs
• Workbook, pp. 2–6 • Every Student Learns Guide, pp. 2–13 • Quick Study, pp. 2–7 • Transparencies 1, 6, 8, 24–28 • Workbook, p. 7 ✓Chapter 1 Content Test, Assessment Book, pp. 1–2 ✓Chapter 1 Skills Test, Assessment Book, pp. 3–4	• ESL Support, TE pp. 11, 21, 29 • Leveled Practice, TE pp. 12, 19, 31 • Learning Styles, TE p. 30 ✓Chapter 1 Performance Assessment, TE p. 34
• Workbook, pp. 8–12 • Every Student Learns Guide, pp. 14–25 • Quick Study, pp. 8–13 • Transparencies 1, 5, 6, 29–30 • Workbook, p. 13 ✓Chapter 2 Content Test, Assessment Book, pp. 5–6 ✓Chapter 2 Skills Test, Assessment Book, pp. 7–8	• Leveled Practice, TE pp. 40, 48, 58 • ESL Support, TE pp. 42, 50, 57 • Learning Styles, TE p. 43 ✓Chapter 2 Performance Assessment, TE p. 62
• Workbook, pp. 14–18 • Every Student Learns Guide, pp. 26–37 • Quick Study, pp. 14–19 • Transparencies 5, 6, 31–34 • Workbook, p. 19 ✓Chapter 3 Content Test, Assessment Book, pp. 9–10 ✓Chapter 3 Skills Test, Assessment Book, pp. 11–12	• Leveled Practice, TE pp. 67, 73, 82, 86 • Learning Styles, TE pp. 68, 78 • ESL Support, TE pp. 70, 75, 81 ✓Chapter 3 Performance Assessment, TE p. 88

Providing More Depth

Additional Resources

- Trade Books
- Family Activities
- Vocabulary Workbook and Cards
- Social Studies Plus! pp. 4–29
- Daily Activity Bank
- Read Alouds and Primary Sources pp. 1–17
- Big Book Atlas
- Student Atlas
- Outline Maps
- Desk Maps

Technology

- AudioText
- Video Field Trips: Taking Care of the Earth
- Songs and Music
- Digital Learning CD-ROM Powered by KnowledgeBox (Video clips and activities)
- MindPoint® Quiz Show CD-ROM
- ExamView® Test Bank CD-ROM
- Teacher Resources CD-ROM
- Map Resources CD-ROM
- SF SuccessNet: iText (Pupil Edition online), iTE (Teacher's Edition online), Online Planner
- **www.sfsocialstudies.com** (Biographies, news, references, maps, and activities)

To establish guidelines for your students' safe and responsible use of the Internet, use the Scott Foresman Internet Guide.

Additional Internet Links

To find out more about:

- Mt. Everest, visit **www.pbs.org**
- House of Representatives, visit **www.house.gov**
- Computers, visit **www.pbs.org**

Unit 1 Objectives

Beginning of Unit 1

- Use primary sources to acquire information. (p. 2)
- Identify the different geographic regions of the United States. (p. 4)
- Describe specific details about the different regions of the United States. (p. 4)
- Analyze information by summarizing. (p. 6)

Chapter 1

Lesson 1 Regions and Landforms pp. 10–15

- Identify the five major regions of the United States.
- Describe the major landforms of each region in the United States.
- Explain the difference between regional and state boundaries.
- Analyze differences in landforms around the world. (p. 16)

Lesson 2 Climate pp. 18–23

- Explain the difference between weather and climate.
- Describe the climate of each region in the United States.
- Describe the three main factors that affect the climate of an area.
- Describe the major types of climates around the world.
- Identify the purpose of inset maps. (p. 24)
- Interpret information in inset maps. (p. 24)

Lesson 3 Regional Resources pp. 26–31

- Explain how each region's resources shaped the industries that grew there.
- Explain the difference between renewable and nonrenewable resources.
- Describe resources of the student's own region.
- Explain how people can be considered resources.
- Identify landforms, climates, and resources in the United States and North America. (p. 32)

Chapter 2

Lesson 1 Americans All pp. 38–44

- Describe what is known about the people who were living in America when Columbus arrived.
- Explain why explorers and settlers came to North America.
- Explain how the land belonging to the United States grew from the Atlantic Ocean to the Pacific Ocean.
- Analyze the contributions of citizens such as Fiorello La Guardia. (p. 45)

Lesson 2 We the People pp. 46–52

- Explain what the Constitution is and why it is important.
- Identify the three levels of government.
- Describe the responsibilities of each of the three branches of government.
- Explain how the Constitution can be changed.
- Identify individuals who have displayed the characteristics of good citizenship. (p. 53)
- Use a time-zone map to calculate times at specific locations. (p. 54)

Lesson 3 The Strengths of Our Freedoms pp. 56–59

- Identify two ways that a person can become a citizen of the United States.
- Identify three types of services that are paid for by taxes.
- Identify at least three responsibilities of U.S. citizens.
- Explain why voting is an important responsibility in the United States.
- Identify individuals who have demonstrated honesty. (p. 60)

Chapter 3

Lesson 1 The Land of Plenty pp. 66–71

- Explain what might have drawn the first Americans to North America.
- Explain why Americans decided to move westward in the 1800s.
- Describe what happened in the late 1800s to change the way people lived and worked.

Lesson 2 Trade Then and Now pp. 72–79

- Describe how goods and services were traded by barter.
- Explain how a business makes a profit.
- Explain the difference between supply and demand.

Lesson 3 Transportation and Communication pp. 80–85

- Explain what it means for regions to be economically interdependent.
- Describe what globalization is and why countries of the world depend on each other.
- Describe how fast transportation and communication have made national and world trade possible.
- Explain how to use a road map. (p. 86)
- Use a map scale to determine distances between places on a road map. (p. 86)

End of Unit 1

- Identify significant examples of music about the United States. (p. 90)
- Describe different features of a region. (p. 94)

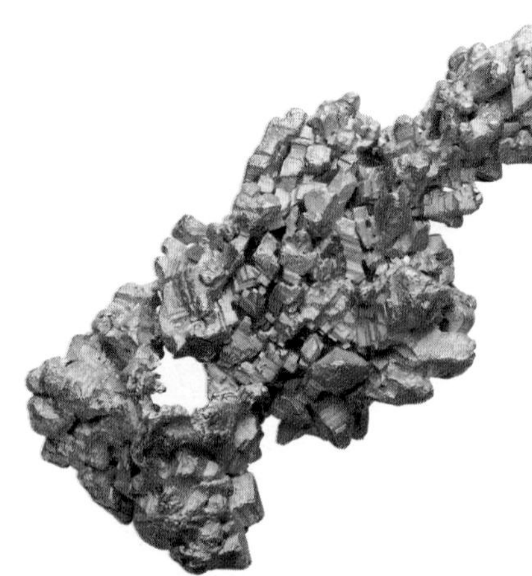

European explorers first came to North America in search of gold and other riches.

Assessment Options

✓ Formal Assessment

- **Lesson Reviews,** PE/TE pp. 15, 23, 31, 44, 52, 59, 71, 79, 85
- **Chapter Reviews,** PE/TE pp. 34–35, 62–63, 88–89
- **Chapter Tests,** Assessment Book, pp. 1–12
- **Unit Review,** PE/TE pp. 92–93
- **Unit Tests,** Assessment Book, pp. 13–16
- **ExamView® Test Bank CD-ROM**

✓ Informal Assessment

- **Teacher's Edition Questions,** throughout Lessons and Features
- **Section Reviews,** PE/TE pp. 11, 13, 15, 19–21, 23, 27–31, 39–44, 47–48, 51–52, 57, 59, 67, 69, 71, 73–74, 76–79, 81–82, 85
- **Close and Assess,** TE pp. 7, 15, 17, 23, 25, 31, 33, 44–45, 52–53, 55, 59, 61, 71, 79, 85, 87, 91

Ongoing Assessment

Ongoing Assessment is found throughout the Teacher's Edition lessons using an **If...then** model.

If = students' observable behavior,	**then** = reteaching and enrichment suggestions

✓ Portfolio Assessment

- **Portfolio Assessment,** TE pp. 1, 2, 93
- **Leveled Practice,** TE pp. 12, 19, 31, 40, 48, 58, 67, 73, 82, 86
- **Workbook Pages,** pp. 1–20
- **Chapter Review: Write About It,** PE/TE pp. 35, 63, 89
- **Unit Review: Apply Skills,** PE/TE p. 93
- **Curriculum Connection: Writing,** PE/TE pp. 31, 44, 71; TE pp. 20, 45, 47, 60, 74, 79, 85, 91

✓ Performance Assessment

- **Hands-on Unit Project** (Unit 1 Performance Assessment), TE pp. 1, 35, 63, 89, 94
- **Internet Activity,** PE p. 94
- **Chapter 1 Performance Assessment,** TE p. 34
- **Chapter 2 Performance Assessment,** TE p. 62
- **Chapter 3 Performance Assessment,** TE p. 88
- **Unit Review: Write and Share,** PE/TE p. 93
- **Scoring Guides,** TE pp. 93–94

Test Talk

Test-Taking Strategies

Understand the Question

- **Locate Key Words in the Question,** PE/TE p. 92, TE p. 49
- **Locate Key Words in the Text,** TE pp. 12, 74

Understand the Answer

- **Choose the Right Answer,** Test Talk Practice Book
- **Use Information from the Text,** TE p. 50
- **Use Information from Graphics,** TE p. 68
- **Write Your Answer to Score High,** TE p. 23

For additional practice, use the Test Talk Practice Book.

Featured Strategy

Locate Key Words in the Question

Students will:

- Find the key words in the question.
- Turn the key words into a statement that begins "I need to find out. . ."

PE/TE p. 92, **TE** p. 49

Curriculum Connections

Integrating Your Day

The lessons, skills, and features of Unit 1 provide many opportunities to make connections between social studies and other areas of the elementary curriculum.

Social Studies

READING

Reading Skill—Summarize, PE/TE pp. 6–7, 10, 18, 46, 56, 66, 72, 80

Lesson Review—Summarize, PE/TE pp. 15, 23, 52, 59, 71, 79, 85

Link to Reading, PE/TE pp. 59, 79

WRITING

Celebrate Climate, TE p. 20

Link to Writing, PE/TE pp. 31, 44, 71

Create a Campaign Speech, TE p. 45

Write to a Government Official, TE p. 47

Analyze the Effects of Your Decisions, TE p. 60

Write a Report, TE pp. 74, 85

Create a Pamphlet, TE p. 79

Compare Songs, TE p. 91

MATH

Use Scale, TE p. 25

Calculate Exchange Rates, TE p. 74

Calculate Time, TE p. 83

LITERATURE

Read About the Regions, TE p. 4

Read About the Highest and Lowest Landforms, TE p. 17

Read About the Growth of the United States, TE p. 41

SCIENCE

Explore Meteorology, TE p. 20

Link to Science, PE/TE pp. 23, 85

Research the Role of Government in Science, TE p. 49

Examine Time Zones, TE p. 55

Make an Industry Time Line, TE p. 71

Examine How Computer Chips Are Made, TE p. 83

Make a Communication Time Line, TE p. 84

MUSIC / DRAMA

Discover the United States in Song, TE p. 13

Personify a Region, TE p. 28

Sing About Traditions, TE p. 44

Deliver the Gettysburg Address, TE p. 47

Use Skits to Present an Idea, TE p. 61

Create a Sales Presentation, TE p. 84

Write a Song, TE p. 91

ART

Interpret the Picture, TE p. 3

Discover the United States in Pictures, TE p. 13

Link to Art, PE/TE pp. 15, 52

Make a Bill of Rights Poster, TE p. 52

Create Graphics for Supply and Demand, TE p. 77

 Look for this symbol throughout the Teacher's Edition to find **Curriculum Connections.**

Professional Development

Effective Strategies for Teaching Social Studies

by Fred Risinger, Ph.D.
Indiana University

In the past two decades, educational research has begun to focus on the relationship between teacher behaviors and instructional methods on student achievement. By following a series of steps, teachers can help students acquire the knowledge and skills essential for understanding.

The following examples can be found in the Teacher's Edition.

1. **Introduce lessons with clear goals.** Research strongly suggests that success for children in learning tasks is directly related to: (1) previous success on similar tasks; and (2) an awareness of what is expected of him or her.

   The Introduce and Motivate activity on the first page of each lesson relates new content to students' existing knowledge. The Objectives list (also on the first page) clearly defines what students are expected to master.

2. **Make ideas clear and useful.** Teachers should try to use terms that are as precise as possible. Illustrating generalizations with examples helps students understand concepts.

   Whenever possible, teachers are provided with examples or possible answers to help guide student understanding.

3. **Ensure elaboration.** For many students, providing more examples or additional information can make all the difference in understanding a topic better. Using the literature resources recommended in this program is an excellent way to elaborate and explain the topic.

   The Bibliography on p. 1h and the Literature Curriculum Connection features throughout the text provide teachers with a wealth of additional resources.

4. **Guide learning with questions.** Questions provide a teacher with the information to both elicit and guide how young children think and practice.

   The Teach and Discuss section of each three-part lesson plan provides teachers with questions covering a wide variety of skills which are appropriate for all levels of learners.

ESL Support

by Jim Cummins, Ph.D.
University of Toronto

In Unit 1, you can use the following fundamental strategies to help ESL students expand their language abilities.

Activate Prior Knowledge

There is general agreement among psychologists that prior experiences provide the foundation for interpreting new information. Thus, in social studies, the more students know about a topic, the more they are likely to understand related text. This expands their knowledge base and, in turn, enables them to understand even more concepts and vocabulary.

It is important to activate students' prior knowledge because students may not realize what they know about a particular topic or issue.

Visuals in texts, such as pictures of artifacts, posters, and photographs, can be used to stimulate discussion about aspects of their meaning and to encourage students to predict what the text is likely to be about.

Opportunities to write about what we know, such as "quick write" activities and dialogue journals, allow students to relate meaning to print and validate their own experiences.

Graphic organizers enable students to record and organize prior knowledge or to capture the results of class brainstorming and discussion.

The following examples in the Teacher's Edition will help you activate the prior knowledge of ESL students:

- ***Apply Climate Words** on p. 21 has students apply climate concepts and terms to places where they have lived.*
- ***Celebrate Immigration** on p. 42 has students examine the concept of immigration by reporting on their own family's immigration to the United States.*

Read Aloud

"Across America"
by Stephanie Nelson

I set out across the nation
To see what I could see
I passed by hills and mountains
And mighty redwood trees
From plains so flat and winds so cold
To beaches in the sun
I'll not forget the things I've seen
Or the things I've done

Read Alouds and Primary Sources

- *Read Alouds and Primary Sources* contains additional selections to be used with Unit 1.

Bibliography

Recycle! A Handbook for Kids, by Gail Gibbons (Little Brown & Co., ISBN 0-316-30943-5, 1996) **Easy**

The Story of Money, by Betsy Maestro (William Morrow, ISBN 0-688-13304-5, 1995) **Easy**

The Story of the White House, by Kate Waters (Scholastic Trade, ISBN 0-590-43334-2, 1992) **Easy**

America's Top 10 Natural Wonders, by Edward Ricciuti (Blackbirch Marketing, ISBN 1-56711-192-0, 1997) **On-Level**

Bold Journey: West with Lewis and Clark, by Charles Bohner (Houghton Mifflin Co., ISBN 0-395-54978-7, 1985) **On-Level**

Shh! We're Writing the Constitution, by Jean Fritz (PaperStar, ISBN 0-698-11624-0, 1997) **On-Level** ***ALA Notable Book***

How the Weather Works, by Michael Allaby (Reader's Digest Assn., ISBN 0-7621-0234-9, 1999) **Challenge**

Legends of Landforms: Native American Lore and the Geology of the Land, by Carole Garbuny Vogel (Millbrook Press, ISBN 0-7613-0272-7, 1999) **Challenge**

Where Do You Think You're Going, Christopher Columbus?, by Jean Fritz (PaperStar, ISBN 0-698-11580-5, 1997) **Challenge** ***ALA Notable Book***

Globalization and the Challenges of the New Century: A Reader, Patrick O'Meara, Howard D. Mehlinger, and Matthew Krain, eds. (Indiana University Press, ISBN 0-253-21355-X, 2000) **Teacher reference**

It Happened in the White House: Extraordinary Tales from America's Most Famous Home, by Kathleen Karr (Hyperion Press, ISBN 0-7868-1560-4, 2000) **Teacher reference**

Undaunted Courage: Meriwether Lewis, Thomas Jefferson, and the Opening of the American West, by Stephen E. Ambrose (Touchstone Books, ISBN 0-684-82697-6, 1997) **Teacher reference**

***Discovery Channel School* Video**

The Frontier Discover how two cultures clashed to create a new balance. (Item # 716704E, 26 minutes)

- To order *Discovery Channel School* videos, please call the following toll-free number: 1-888-892-3484.
- Free online lesson plans are available at **DiscoverySchool.com.**

Look for this symbol throughout the Teacher's Edition to find **Award-Winning Selections.** Additional book references are suggested throughout this unit.

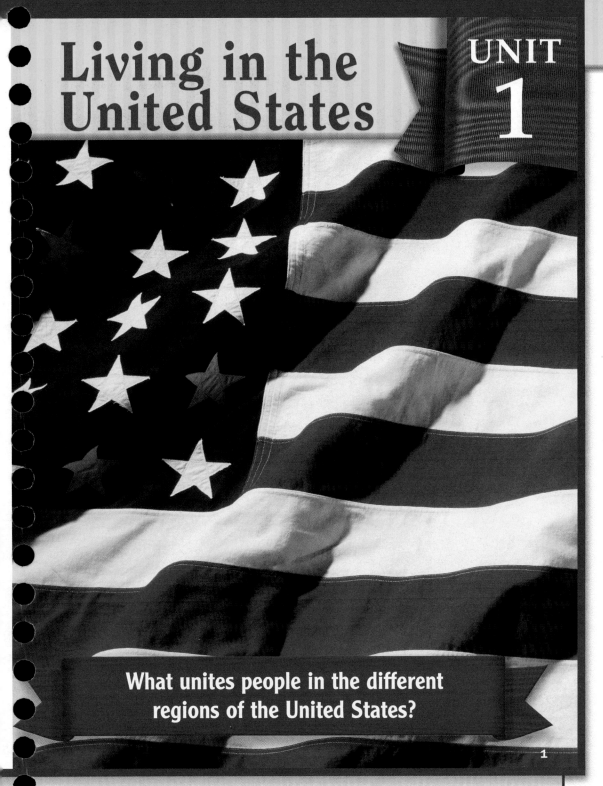

Living in the United States

UNIT 1

What unites people in the different regions of the United States?

1

Practice and Extend

Hands-on Unit Project

✓Unit 1 Performance Assessment

- The Unit Project, *Eye on Our Region,* found on p. 94 is an ongoing performance assessment project to enrich students' learning throughout the unit.
- This project, which has students creating a video tour of their region, may be started now or at any time during this unit of study.
- A performance assessment scoring guide is located on p. 94.

Living in the United States

Unit Overview

This land of varied regions, climates, landforms, and resources was settled by people from all over the world, eventually united by the ideas of democracy and tolerance. The Constitution of the United States and other laws protect our rights, and the economy provides us with an opportunity to earn a living.

Unit Outline

Chapter 1 ***The Regions of the United States*** pp. 8–35

Chapter 2 ***We All Live Together*** pp. 36–63

Chapter 3 ***Earning and Learning*** pp. 64–89

Unit Question

- Have students read the question under the picture.
- To activate prior knowledge, ask students what types of things bring people together in a family, school, or community.
- On paper, have students brainstorm a list of preliminary answers to the unit question.
- Create a class list of students' responses.

✓Portfolio Assessment Keep this list to review with students at the end of the unit on p. 93.

Begin with a Primary Source

Objective

- Use primary sources to acquire information.

Resource

- Poster 1

Interpret the Primary Source

- Tell students that the primary source is a verse from the well-known American folk song "This Land Is Your Land." Ask students if they know the song. If so, have a volunteer lead the class in singing it.
- Point out that Woody Guthrie chose to include U.S. symbols that would be familiar to most people living in the United States. Ask students to name other well-known American symbols that Guthrie might have used in his song.

✓**Portfolio Assessment** Remind students of the list of ideas they began on p. 1. As students read Unit 1, have them revise the class list. Review the list at the end of the unit on p. 93.

UNIT 1

Begin with a Primary Source

2

Practice and Extend

SOCIAL STUDIES
Background

About the Primary Source

- Born in Oklahoma in 1912, Woody Guthrie grew up in the shadow of the Great Depression. Over time, the search for work took him to places such as Texas, California, Oregon, and New York. "This Land Is Your Land" describes many of the things he saw during his travels.
- When Guthrie was a boy, his mother was sent to an asylum and his father left home to find work. When Woody was about 16 years old, he joined his father in West Texas.
- In his lifetime, Woody Guthrie wrote more than 1,000 songs, many poems, two books, and hundreds of articles and essays. "This Land Is Your Land" is one of his most famous works.

"This land is your land, this land is my land,
From California, to the New York island, 1
From the redwood forest to the Gulf Stream waters; 2
This land was made for you and me."—Woody Guthrie, from "This Land Is Your Land"©

3

Interpret the Picture

- Point out to students that no one knows who made the first U.S. flag, but historians believe it may have been designed by Congressman Francis Hopkinson and sewn by Betsy Ross.
- On June 14, 1777, the Continental Congress passed the first Flag Act, proclaiming that "the flag of the United States be made of thirteen stripes, alternate red and white" and that "the union be thirteen stars, white in a blue field."
- Tell students that the current 50-star flag was designed by an Ohio high school student. In 1958, as the U.S. government considered adding Alaska and Hawaii to the union, student Robert G. Heft designed a 50-star flag for a school project. His flag had five rows of six stars and four rows of five stars. The boy sent his flag to his congressman, who got the design accepted. The United States officially adopted Heft's 50-star flag design on August 21, 1959.

1 **What do you think the 13 stars on the first official U.S. flag represented?** The 13 original colonies **Hypothesize**

2 **What do you think might happen to the flag design if the United States adds more states in the future?** Possible answer: It may be redesigned to include more stars to represent the new states. **Predict**

SOCIAL STUDIES
Background

About Flag Etiquette

- The flag should be raised briskly and lowered slowly.
- Citizens should salute the flag by placing their right hand over their heart.
- Ordinarily the flag should be displayed only between sunrise and sunset. It should be illuminated if displayed at night.
- When displayed with flags of states, communities, or organizations, no flag should be larger than the U.S. flag, no flag should be placed above it, and the U.S. flag should be the first raised and the last lowered.
- When the flag is lowered, no part should touch the ground or any other object other than receiving hands and arms.

Welcome to the United States

Objectives

- Identify the different geographic regions of the United States.
- Describe specific details about the different regions of the United States.

Resource

- Poster 2

Research the Regions

Each of the regions featured on these pages is an important part of the United States. Have students do research using online or library resources to find out the answers to the following questions.

- **What is one important geographic feature shared by the Northeast, Southeast, Southwest, and West regions?** Possible answer: A seacoast
- **Name at least two major Midwestern cities located on the shores of a Great Lake and name the Great Lake each is near.** Possible answers: Duluth, Minnesota, Lake Superior; Chicago, Illinois, Lake Michigan; Milwaukee, Wisconsin, Lake Michigan; Detroit, Michigan, Lake Erie; Toledo, Ohio, Lake Erie; Cleveland, Ohio, Lake Erie
- **What major mountain range extends through much of the West? The Northeast?** Possible answers: Rocky Mountains; Appalachian Mountains

Students may wish to write their own questions about these regions for the rest of the class to answer.

UNIT 1

Welcome to the United States

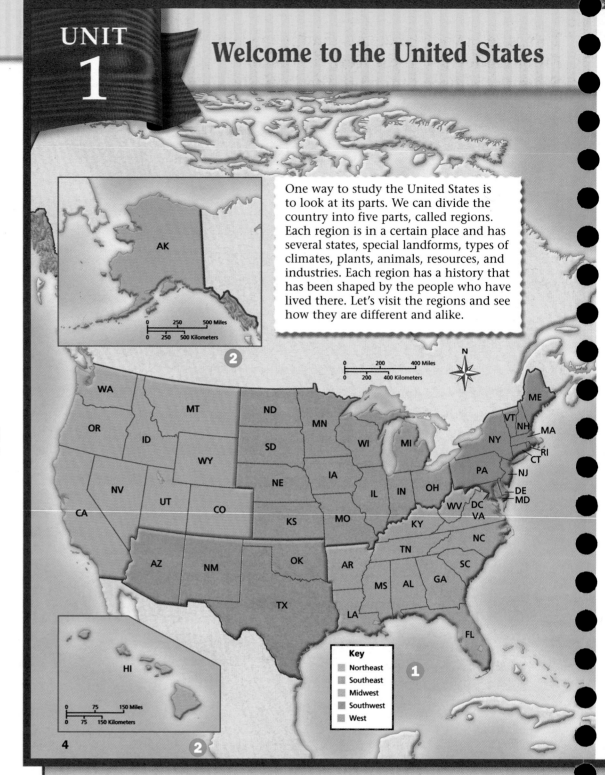

One way to study the United States is to look at its parts. We can divide the country into five parts, called regions. Each region is in a certain place and has several states, special landforms, types of climates, plants, animals, resources, and industries. Each region has a history that has been shaped by the people who have lived there. Let's visit the regions and see how they are different and alike.

Key: Northeast, Southeast, Midwest, Southwest, West

4

Practice and Extend

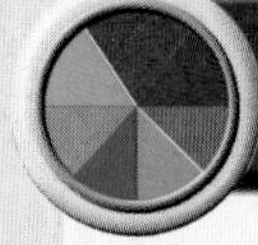

CURRICULUM CONNECTION
Literature

Read About the Regions

Use the following informational texts to extend the content.

Indians of the Northeast, by Colin G. Callaway (Facts on File, ISBN 0-8160-2389-1, 1991) **Easy**

Dog Days of the West, by Vivian Sathre (Lyrick Publishing, ISBN 1-57064-336-9, 1998) **On-Level**

Meet the Wild Southwest: Land of Hoodoos and Gila Monsters, by Susan J. Tweit (Graphic Arts Center Publishing Co., ISBN 0-88240-468-7, 1995) **Challenge**

Midwest

Northeast

West

3

Southeast

Southwest

4

5

For more information, go online to the *Atlas* at **www.sfsocialstudies.com.**

5

WEB SITE
Technology

Students can learn more about places in this unit by clicking on *Atlas* at **www.sfsocialstudies.com.**

Discuss the Regions

Have students use the pictures and captions to answer the following questions.

1 **How does the map on p. 4 show that certain states are included within a region?** All the states in a region are the same color. Interpret Maps

2 **Which region includes two states not connected to the rest of the United States? Name these two states.** West; Alaska and Hawaii Interpret Maps

3 **What can you conclude about the West by looking at the picture on p. 5?** Possible answer: It contains mountain ranges. Draw Conclusions

4 **What type of weather would you expect to experience in the part of the Southwest shown in the picture?** Possible answer: Hot and dry Analyze Pictures

5 **Look at the pictures on this page. Would you conclude that the regions of the United States are more alike or different? Explain.** Possible answers: Alike, because they all are located within the United States and the people who live there are similar; Different, because they all have different climates and landforms Generalize

Read About the Regions

The regions shown here are discussed in the text on the following pages in Unit 1.

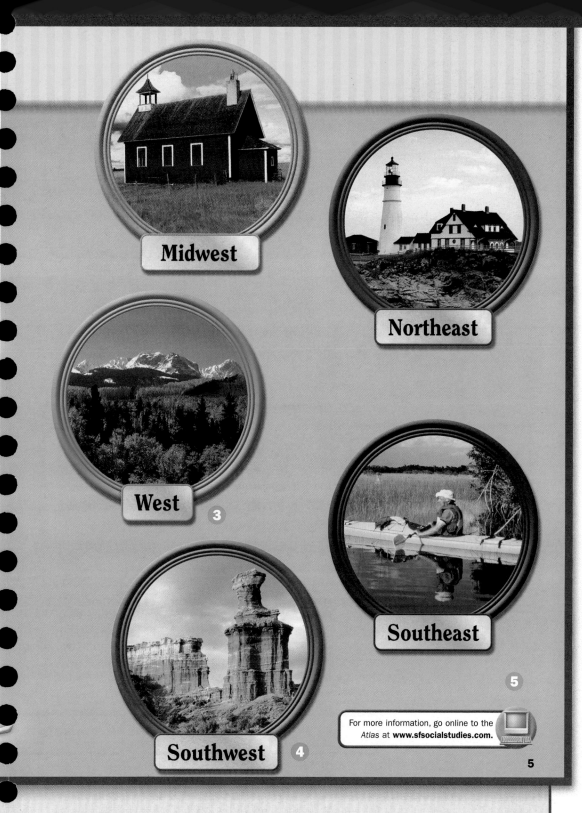

- The Northeast, pp. 12, 14, 28, 68
- The Southeast, pp. 12, 14, 28
- The Midwest, pp. 11–14, 27–28, 68, 81
- The Southwest, pp. 11, 13–14, 27–28, 68
- The West, pp. 11, 13, 15, 28, 68

Reading Social Studies

Summarize

Objective

Analyze information by summarizing.

Resource

- Workbook, p. 1

About the Unit Target Skill

- The target reading skill for this unit is Summarize.
- Students are introduced to the unit target skill here and are given an opportunity to practice it.
- Further opportunities to summarize are found throughout Unit 1.

1 Introduce and Motivate

Preview To activate prior knowledge, ask students how they might tell a friend about a book, television show, or soccer game. Tell students that, rather than describing every detail about the topic, they should concentrate on communicating the most important information.

UNIT 1

Reading Social Studies

Living in the United States

Summarize

- Summarizing will help you recall and organize information.
- Choose important details or events as you read.
- Leave out unimportant details or events.
- Use only a sentence or two in a summary.

Detail | Detail | Detail

Summary
A summary is a short statement that tells the main ideas of an article or story.

Read the following paragraph. The most important ideas have been highlighted.

The United States is divided into five regions. The regions are the Northeast, the Southeast, the Midwest, the Southwest, and the West. These regions have many different landforms. They also have different climates. The five regions are surrounded by both land and water.

Summary: The five regions of the United States have different landforms and climates.

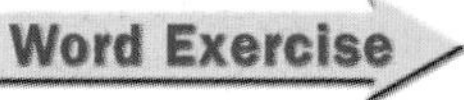

Superlatives A **superlative** is a form of a word or a combination of words that shows the greatest something can be. *Best* is a superlative of *good*. *Fastest* is a superlative of *fast*. Sometimes a superlative is made by adding the *-est* ending to an adjective. The passage says that the hottest climates are found in the West. The word *hottest* is made by adding *-est* to the word *hot*.

hot + -est = hottest

6

Practice and Extend

ACCESS CONTENT

ESL Support

Demonstrate Summarizing Have students practice summarizing the purpose of specific information sources, such as books, newspapers, magazines, Web sites, computer programs, or television shows.

Beginning Write the word "Information" in the inner circle of a web on the board and have students brainstorm its meaning. Then have them work in pairs to generate sources of information and write these on the spokes of the web.

Intermediate Have students work in pairs using a two-column chart to list advantages and disadvantages for two of the sources of information they have identified. Students should then use their charts to give a verbal summary of different information sources.

Advanced Have students write a paragraph summarizing the sources from which they get information and what they like and dislike about each source.

The United States: Vast and Varied

The United States covers most of the southern part of the continent of North America. It is surrounded by both water and land. The Pacific Ocean is to the west and the Atlantic Ocean is to the east. Mexico and the Gulf of Mexico are to the south, and Canada and the Great Lakes are to the north. The United States is more than 3.5 million square miles in land area. It would take more than two days and nights of non-stop driving to cross this country from coast to coast. The main part of the country is so large that it crosses four different time zones. Alaska and Hawaii are in two additional time zones.

Across the five regions of the United States, landforms and climates can be very different. Farmlands stretch through the Midwest. Warm, sandy beaches line the Southeast, and tall, jagged mountains rise in the West. Climates range from freezing cold to dangerously hot. In one day it could be snowing in the Northeast, raining in the Southwest, and as hot as 100° F in the West. Even within each region, landscape and climate can be different. For example, the West region has the highest and lowest landforms in the United States as well as the hottest and coldest areas.

Apply it!

Use the reading strategy of summarizing to answer questions 1 and 2. Then answer the vocabulary question.

1. What is the most important idea in paragraph one?
2. Which sentence is the better summary of the passage?
   a. The United States is a big country, and the five regions have different landscapes and climates.
   b. The United States is so large that it has five regions.
3. The superlative form of the word *hot* is *hottest*. What other superlative words can you find in the passage? From what words are they formed?

7

Standardized Test Prep

TEST PREP

- Use Workbook p. 1 to give students practice with standardized test format.
- Chapter and Unit Tests in the Assessment Book use standardized test format.
- Test-taking tips are contained in the front portion of the Assessment Book Teacher's Edition.

Also on Teacher Resources CD-ROM.

Workbook, p. 1

Summarize Use with Pages 6–7.

Directions: Read the passage. Fill in the circle next to the correct answer.

The United States is made up of many unique landforms. These landforms are as varied as the different regions that make up the United States.

Caves are one type of landform. Mammoth Cave in Kentucky is the longest recorded cave system in the world. It has more than 300 miles of passages. Carlsbad Caverns in New Mexico is another cave system. It began forming 60 million years ago and is known for its large chambers and geological structures.

Mountains are another type of landform. The two largest mountain ranges in the United States are the Rocky Mountains in the West and the Appalachian Mountains in the East. Some of the smaller mountain ranges include the Great Smoky Mountains in Tennessee and North Carolina and the Sierra Nevada in California and Nevada.

Much of the United States coastline is made up of beaches. Some of the most popular beaches are Laguna Beach in California, Palm Beach in Florida, and South Padre Beach in Texas.

1. Which sentence best summarizes the passage?
   Ⓐ Most landforms in the United States are located in the West.
   Ⓑ The United States has several mountain ranges.
   Ⓒ There are many different types of landforms in the United States.
   Ⓓ Most landforms were formed millions of years ago.
2. Which detail does NOT contribute to a summary of the passage?
   Ⓐ One type of landform is a cave.
   Ⓑ Much of the United States is made up of beaches.
   Ⓒ The United States has a number of mountain ranges.
   Ⓓ Carlsbad Caverns began forming 60 million years ago.
3. What is the main idea of the third paragraph?
   Ⓐ The two largest mountain ranges in the United States are the Rocky Mountains and the Appalachian Mountains.
   Ⓑ The United States has a number of mountain ranges.
   Ⓒ Much of the United States coastline is made up of beaches.
   Ⓓ The United States is made up of many unique landforms.

Notes for Home: Your child learned how to summarize a passage.
Home Activity: With your child, read a short newspaper article. Have your child orally summarize the article.

2 Teach and Discuss

- Explain that a paragraph, passage, poem, or song often includes a summary sentence. Point out that the author may include a summary statement to help readers remember and organize important information.
- Have students read the sample paragraph on p. 6. Confirm that they can identify the summary sentence and details.
- Then have students read the longer practice sample on p. 7 and answer the questions that follow. Have students support their interpretations or conclusions with examples from the text.
- Ask students why, when studying geography, it is important to be able to summarize. (To develop a mental picture of an area, or to classify different aspects of an area, we need to be able to summarize information about it.)

Superlatives

Word Exercise

Students should be able to find the superlative words *highest, lowest,* and *coldest* in the passage. Help them understand that these words are formed from *high, low,* and *cold*. Tell students that recognizing the purpose of superlatives can help a reader better understand the meaning of what they read. Write the following words on the board and ask students to change them into superlatives: *fast, sweet, rich, poor, cool.*

3 Close and Assess

Apply it!

1. The United States is a huge country.

2. A

3. Highest, lowest, coldest

CHAPTER 1

Chapter Planning Guide

Chapter 1 • The Regions of the United States

Locating Places pp. 8–9

Lesson Titles	Pacing	Main Ideas
Lesson 1 **Regions and Landforms** pp. 10–15	3 days	• The United States is divided into five regions.
Here and There: Highest and Lowest Landforms pp. 16–17		• The world is made up of landforms in high and low places.
Lesson 2 **Climate** pp. 18–23	3 days	• Many factors influence climate, which varies from region to region.
Map and Globe Skills: Read Inset Maps pp. 24–25		• An inset map is a smaller map related to the main map used to show a different scale from the main map.
Lesson 3 **Regional Resources** pp. 26–31	3 days	• Each region has special resources.
DK **The United States and North America** pp. 32–33		• The United States and North America have many different landforms, climates, and resources.
✓ **Chapter 1 Review** pp. 34-35		

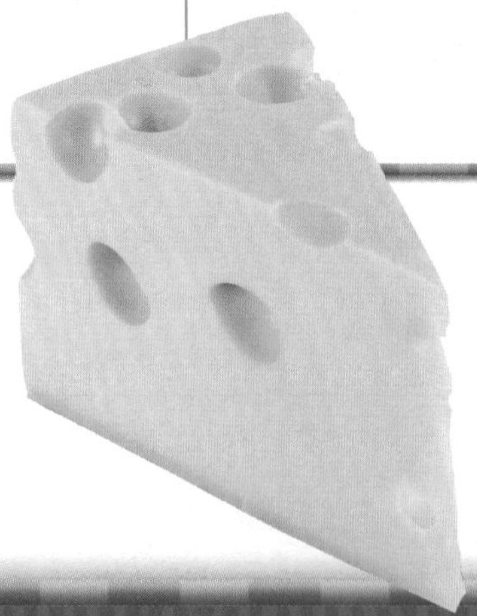

◀ **The regions of the United States produce a wide variety of goods. The Midwest is a producer of cheese and other dairy products.**

✓ = **Assessment Options**

People in different parts of the United States can experience a wide variety of weather conditions. ▶

Vocabulary	Resources	Meeting Individual Needs
region, landform, mountain, plain, desert, canyon, plateau, boundary, sea level	• Workbook, p. 3 • Transparencies 6, 24 • Every Student Learns Guide, pp. 2–5 • Quick Study, pp. 2–3	• ESL Support, TE p. 11 • Leveled Practice, TE p. 12
weather, climate, precipitation, temperature, humidity, equator, elevation, tropical climate, polar climate, subarctic climate, temperate climate, inset map	• Workbook, p. 4 • Transparencies 8, 25–28 • Every Student Learns Guide, pp. 6–9 • Quick Study, pp. 4–5 • Workbook, p. 5	• Leveled Practice, TE p. 19 • ESL Support, TE p. 21
natural resource, raw material, process, harvest, industry, manufacturing, product, capital resource, agriculture, conserve, renewable resource, recycle, nonrenewable resource, human resources, service	• Workbook, p. 6 • Transparency 1 • Every Student Learns Guide, pp. 10–13 • Quick Study, pp. 6–7	• ESL Support, TE p. 29 • Learning Styles, TE p. 30 • Leveled Practice, TE p. 31
	✔Chapter 1 Content Test, Assessment Book, pp. 1–2 ✔Chapter 1 Skills Test, Assessment Book, pp. 3–4	✔Chapter 1 Performance Assessment, TE p. 34

Providing More Depth

Additional Resources

- Vocabulary Workbook and Cards
- Social Studies Plus! pp. 12–17
- Daily Activity Bank
- Big Book Atlas
- Student Atlas
- Outline Maps
- Desk Maps

Technology

- AudioText
- MindPoint® Quiz Show CD-ROM
- ExamView® Test Bank CD-ROM
- Teacher Resources CD-ROM
- Map Resources CD-ROM
- SFSuccessNet: iText (Pupil Edition online), iTE (Teacher's Edition online), Online Planner
- **www.sfsocialstudies.com** (Biographies, news, references, maps, and activities)

To establish guidelines for your students' safe and responsible use of the Internet, use the Scott Foresman Internet Guide.

Additional Internet Links

To find out more about:

- The Great Lakes, visit **www.great-lakes.net**
- Hawaii, visit **www.state.hi.us**
- Environmental Protection Agency, visit **www.epa.gov**

Key Internet Search Terms

- Mt. McKinley
- weather
- recycling

Workbook Support

Use the following Workbook pages to support content and skills development as you teach Chapter 1. You can also view and print Workbook pages from the Teacher Resources CD-ROM.

Workbook, p. 1

Use with Pages 6–7.

Summarize

Directions: Read the passage. Fill in the circle next to the correct answer.

The United States is made up of many unique landforms. These landforms are as varied as the different regions that make up the United States.

Caves are one type of landform. Mammoth Cave in Kentucky is the longest recorded cave system in the world. It has more than 300 miles of passages. Carlsbad Caverns in New Mexico is another cave system. It began forming 60 million years ago and is known for its large chambers and geological structures.

Mountains are another type of landform. The two largest mountain ranges in the United States are the Rocky Mountains in the West and the Appalachian Mountains in the East. Some of the smaller mountain ranges include the Great Smoky Mountains in Tennessee and North Carolina and the Sierra Nevada in California and Nevada.

Much of the United States coastline is made up of beaches. Some of the most popular beaches are Laguna Beach in California, Palm Beach in Florida, and South Padre Beach in Texas.

1. Which sentence best summarizes the passage?
   - Ⓐ Most landforms in the United States are located in the West.
   - Ⓑ The United States has several mountain ranges.
   - ● There are many different types of landforms in the United States.
   - Ⓓ Most landforms were formed millions of years ago.
2. Which detail does NOT contribute to a summary of the passage?
   - Ⓐ One type of landform is a cave.
   - Ⓑ Much of the United States is made up of beaches.
   - Ⓒ The United States has a number of mountain ranges.
   - ● Carlsbad Caverns began forming 60 million years ago.
3. What is the main idea of the third paragraph?
   - Ⓐ The two largest mountain ranges in the United States are the Rocky Mountains and the Appalachian Mountains.
   - ● The United States has a number of mountain ranges.
   - Ⓒ Much of the United States coastline is made up of beaches.
   - Ⓓ The United States is made up of many unique landforms.

Notes for Home: Your child learned how to summarize a passage.
Home Activity: With your child, read a short newspaper article. Have your child orally summarize the article.

Use with Pupil Edition, p. 6

Workbook, p. 2

Use with Chapter 1.

Vocabulary Preview

Directions: Match each vocabulary term to its meaning. Write the number of the term on the line before the definition. Not all words will be used. You may use your glossary.

1. region
2. landform
3. mountain
4. plain
5. desert
6. canyon
7. plateau
8. boundary
9. weather
10. climate
11. precipitation
12. temperature
13. humidity
14. equator
15. elevation
16. tropical climate
17. polar climate
18. subarctic climate
19. temperate climate
20. natural resource
21. raw material
22. process
23. harvest
24. industry
25. manufacturing
26. product
27. capital resource
28. agriculture
29. conserve
30. renewable resource
31. recycle
32. nonrenewable resource
33. human resource
34. service

28 using the soil to raise crops or animals
6 deep valley with steep rocky walls
32 natural resource that cannot be replaced
21 thing we change or process so people can use it
2 natural feature on Earth's surface
34 job that a person does for others
13 amount of moisture in the air
24 form of business
31 use something again
10 weather of a place averaged over a long period of time
1 area in which places share similar characteristics
20 something in the environment that people can use
15 how high a place is above sea level
33 person who makes products or provides services
7 large, flat, raised area of land
26 something that people make or grow
11 amount of rain or snow that falls
29 use resources carefully
14 imaginary line that circles the center of Earth from east to west
17 coldest type of climate on Earth

Notes for Home: Your child learned the vocabulary terms for Chapter 1.
Home Activity: Fourteen of the vocabulary terms were not used in this activity. With your child, find the terms in this chapter and define them.

Use with Pupil Edition, p. 8

Workbook, p. 3

Use with Pages 10–15.

Lesson 1: Regions and Landforms

Directions: Complete the chart using the landforms and descriptions in the box. You may use your textbook.

- contains only four states
- rich farmland in Arkansas and Louisiana created by Mississippi and Red Rivers
- highest and lowest landforms and temperatures in United States
- Mississippi, Ohio, and Missouri Rivers flow through
- Appalachian Mountains run through Maine
- home to deserts and canyons
- mostly hilly and rocky along the Atlantic coast; good farmland to the west
- Mammoth Cave system in Kentucky
- some rolling hills, such as Smoky Hills in Kansas
- Rocky Mountains in New Mexico and part of Texas
- includes Alaska and Hawaii
- bordered by four of five Great Lakes
- fertile, green valleys and heavy forests
- Atlantic Coastal Plain
- Death Valley

Region	Landforms and descriptions
Northeast Region	**Appalachian Mountains run through Maine; mostly hilly and rocky along the Atlantic coast; good farmland to the west**
Southeast Region	**Atlantic Coastal Plain; rich farmland in Arkansas and Louisiana created by Mississippi and Red Rivers; Mammoth Cave system in Kentucky**
Midwest Region	**Mississippi, Ohio, and Missouri Rivers flow through; some rolling hills, such as Smoky Hills in Kansas; bordered by four of five Great Lakes**
Southwest Region	**contains only four states; home to deserts and canyons; Rocky Mountains in New Mexico and part of Texas**
West Region	**highest and lowest landforms and temperatures in United States; fertile, green valleys and heavy forests; includes Alaska and Hawaii; Death Valley**

Notes for Home: Your child learned about the five regions of the United States and the landforms that are unique to each one.
Home Activity: With your child, use information from this lesson to compare and contrast the region in which you live with the other regions in the United States.

Workbook — Lesson Review 3

Use with Pupil Edition, p. 15

Workbook Support

Workbook, p. 4

Use with Pages 18–23.

Lesson 2: Climate

Directions: Answer the following questions on the lines provided. You may use your textbook.

1. How are weather and climate alike? How are they different?

   Alike: both are determined by temperature and precipitation; Different: weather is the condition of the air at a certain time and place, and climate is the weather of a place averaged over a long period of time.

2. Summarize the cycle of water from oceans, rivers, streams, and lakes into the air and back to the sea.

   Energy from the sun changes some water into water vapor. When air cools, the vapor forms small drops. Together these drops form clouds. Tiny drops join together and grow. The bigger drops become precipitation and fall to the ground or into oceans and lakes. Then the cycle starts over.

3. What three major factors affect the climate of a place?

   the distance a place is from the equator, how far a place is from a large body of water, and elevation

4. Identify and describe four basic types of climates and give an example of each.

   tropical—usually very warm all year, near the equator, southern tip of Florida and Hawaii; polar—coldest climate, North and South Poles; subarctic—short, warm periods in summer, parts of ground covered in snow most of the year, parts of Alaska; temperate—between tropical and subarctic climates, moderate temperature, Arizona

Notes for Home: Your child learned about the climate of the United States.
Home Activity: With your child, create a chart to record the weather in your community for a week. Discuss any climate patterns you see.

Use with Pupil Edition, p. 23

Workbook, p. 5

Use with Pages 24–25.

Read Inset Maps

Directions: In the spaces provided, draw a map of your classroom. Draw an inset map that shows the location of your classroom in your school. Then answer the questions that follow.

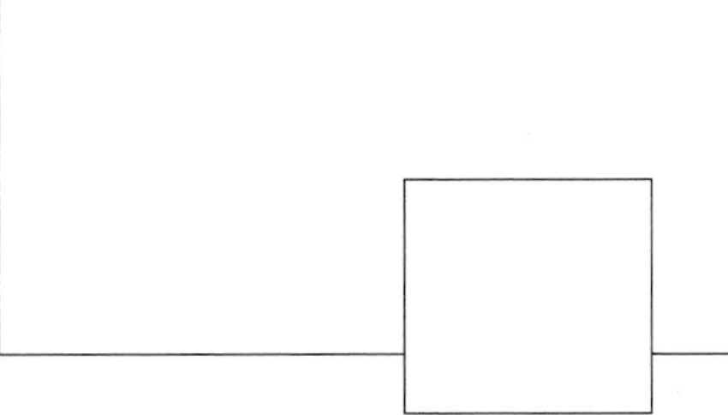

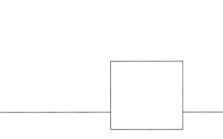

1. How does the inset map relate to the main map you drew?

   Possible answer: The inset map shows where my classroom is located within the school building.

2. What can you learn from the inset map that you could not find out from the main map?

   Possible answers: Location of classroom in the school building, nearest exits, main school entrance

3. What can you learn from the main map that you could not find out from the inset map?

   Possible answers: Location of items in the classroom, such as my seat and my teacher's desk

Notes for Home: Your child learned to read inset maps.
Home Activity: With your child, use an atlas to locate a map of your state or another state that includes an inset map. Notice which cities have been shown in inset maps. Discuss why it is important for an atlas to include inset maps.

Use with Pupil Edition, p. 25

Workbook, p. 6

Use with Pages 26–31.

Lesson 3: Regional Resources

Each of the five regions of the United States has special resources.

Directions: Classify each resource as Renewable or Nonrenewable. Then write at least one region in which each resource can be found. You may use your textbook.

1. livestock **Renewable; Possible answers: Midwest, West, Southwest, Northeast, Southeast**
2. cotton **Renewable; Possible answers: Southeast, Southwest**
3. corn **Renewable; Possible answers: Midwest, Northeast, Southeast, Southwest**
4. fish **Renewable; Possible answers: Northeast, West, Southeast**
5. timber **Renewable; West**
6. silver **Nonrenewable; West**
7. natural gas **Nonrenewable; Possible answers: Southwest, West**
8. coal **Nonrenewable; Possible answers: Northeast, Southeast**
9. gold **Nonrenewable; West**
10. oil **Nonrenewable; Southwest**
11. sugarcane **Renewable; Southeast**
12. rice **Renewable; Southeast**
13. wheat **Renewable; Possible answers: Midwest, Southwest, West**

Notes for Home: Your child learned about the special resources of each region of the United States and the effect of these resources on industry.
Home Activity: With your child, make a list of all the human resources with whom you or your child has had contact today.

6 Lesson Review Workbook

Use with Pupil Edition, p. 31

Workbook, p. 7

Use with Chapter 1.

Vocabulary Review

Directions: Circle the vocabulary term that best completes each sentence. You may use your textbook.

1. A line or natural feature that divides one area from another or one state from another is a (**boundary**, plain, desert).
2. Manufacturing is an important (process, elevation, **industry**), or form of business, in the Northeast region.
3. A (region, natural resource, **landform**) is a natural feature on Earth's surface, such as a mountain or a river.
4. A (mountain, plateau, **canyon**) is a deep valley with steep rocky walls.
5. A tree is a (**renewable resource**, nonrenewable resource, product) because it can be replaced.
6. A pilot checks the (recycle, humidity, **weather**), or the condition of the air at a certain time and place, to avoid flying into a dangerous storm.
7. An area with a (**tropical climate**, temperate climate, subarctic climate) is usually very warm all year.
8. The warmest climates are in places nearest to the (polar climate, **equator**, precipitation), an imaginary line that circles the center of the Earth from east to west.
9. A (**natural resource**, region, capital resource) is something in the environment that people can use.
10. To (service, **conserve**, harvest) means to use resources carefully.
11. A (human resource, **raw material**, region) is something we change or process so that people can use it.
12. (**Climate**, Manufacturing, Temperature) is the weather of a place averaged over a long period of time.

Notes for Home: Your child learned the vocabulary terms for Chapter 1.
Home Activity: With your child, make flashcards for the vocabulary terms in this chapter. Write each term on one side of an index card or small piece of paper and the definition on the other side.

Use with Pupil Edition, p. 34

Assessment Support

Use the following Assessment Book pages and TestWorks to assess content and skills in Chapter 1. You can also view and print Assessment Book pages from the Teacher Resources CD-ROM.

Assessment Book, p. 1

Chapter 1 Test

Part 1: Content Test

Directions: Fill in the circle next to the correct answer.

Lesson Objective (1:1)

1. Which of the following is NOT one of the five major regions in the United States?
● East
Ⓑ West
Ⓒ Southeast
Ⓓ Northeast

Lesson Objective (1:2)

2. Which landform is found in the Midwest region?
Ⓐ canyons
● plains
Ⓒ mountains
Ⓓ deserts

Lesson Objective (1:2)

3. Which of the following landforms is found in the Southwest region?
Ⓐ Death Valley
Ⓑ Appalachian Mountains
Ⓒ Great Lakes
● Grand Canyon

Lesson Objective (1:3)

4. How are regional boundaries different from state boundaries?
Ⓐ They do not divide areas of land.
Ⓑ They can only be seen on a map.
Ⓒ They are often marked by signs.
● They are not set by rules or laws.

Lesson Objective (1:3)

5. How are regional boundaries often determined?
Ⓐ number of states
Ⓑ historical events
● major landforms
Ⓓ state laws

Lesson Objective (2:1)

6. How is climate different from weather?
Ⓐ It includes only temperature.
Ⓑ It varies in different parts of the United States.
Ⓒ It can change every day.
● It is based on weather averaged over a long period of time.

Lesson Objective (2:1)

7. What are the two major factors of weather and climate?
● temperature and precipitation
Ⓑ temperature and elevation
Ⓒ humidity and precipitation
Ⓓ temperature and elevation

Lesson Objective (2:3)

8. Which of the following is NOT a factor that affects climate?
Ⓐ distance from the equator
● population
Ⓒ elevation
Ⓓ distance from a large body of water

Lesson Objective (2:4)

9. What type of climate describes an area that is usually very warm all year?
Ⓐ polar
Ⓑ subarctic
Ⓒ temperate
● tropical

Use with Pupil Edition, p. 34

Assessment Book, p. 2

Lesson Objective (2:2)

10. Which of the following describes the climate in much of the Southwest region?
● hot and dry
Ⓑ cold and snowy
Ⓒ cold and rainy
Ⓓ mild and wet all year

Lesson Objective (3:1)

11. Which is one of the most valuable resources of the Northeast region?
Ⓐ trees
● coal
Ⓒ corn
Ⓓ cotton

Lesson Objective (3:1)

12. Which of the following is NOT a major resource of the Southwest region?
Ⓐ oil
● gold
Ⓒ cotton
Ⓓ natural gas

Lesson Objective (3:2)

13. How is a renewable resource different from a nonrenewable resource?
Ⓐ It can be recycled.
Ⓑ It may run out one day.
● It can be replaced.
Ⓓ It is found in the earth.

Lesson Objective (3:2)

14. Which of the following is an example of a nonrenewable resource?
Ⓐ soil
Ⓑ trees
● oil
Ⓓ water

Lesson Objective (3:4)

15. What are human resources?
● people who make products or provide services
Ⓑ types of fuel that are created by people
Ⓒ minerals that people take out of the ground to make energy
Ⓓ resources that are used by people every day

Use with Pupil Edition, p. 34

Assessment Support

Assessment Book, p. 3

Part 2: Skills Test

Directions: Use complete sentences to answer questions 1–5. Use a separate sheet of paper if you need more space.

1. Name and describe the region of the United States in which you live. Which landforms are found in this region? **Summarize**

   Possible answer: I live in the Southwest region. This region contains beautiful deserts and canyons carved by the Colorado River. Part of the Rocky Mountains, the Grand Canyon, and the Colorado Plateau are in this region.

2. Is it important for individual states to have specific boundaries? Explain. **Point of View**

   Possible answer: Yes, states need specific boundaries. People need to know in which state they live because state laws apply only to the areas within those boundaries.

3. How do climate and resources affect businesses in an area? Give an example. **Cause and Effect**

   Possible answer: Many businesses develop to take advantage of the climate and resources in an area. Agriculture is important in the Southeast region because the fertile soil and warm climate make it good for farming.

Use with Pupil Edition, p. 34

Assessment Book, p. 4

4. In which area of the United States do you live? What is the climate like there? What are some of the resources found there? **Analyze Information**

   Possible answer: I live in Barrow, Alaska, in a subarctic climate. We have snow on the ground most of the year and few warm days in summer. Some of the resources here are fish, timber from forests, and water.

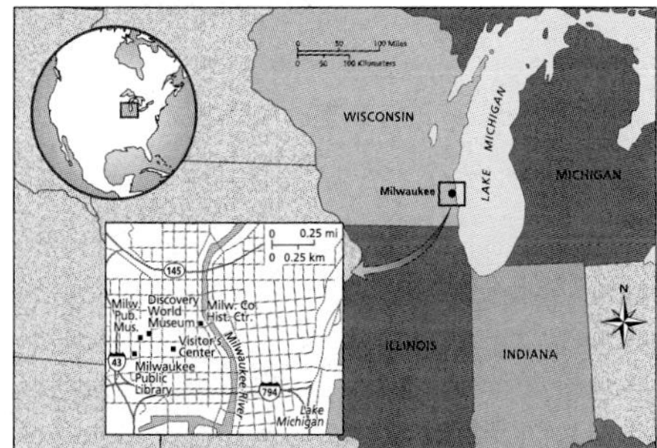

Milwaukee and Surrounding Areas

5. You and your family are planning a trip to Milwaukee. How can each of the three types of maps help you plan your trip? **Read Inset Maps**

   Possible answer: The large map shows me that Milwaukee is in the state of Wisconsin. The round inset map helps me see where in the United States Wisconsin is. The square insert map shows where some interesting places are in Milwaukee to visit.

Use with Pupil Edition, p. 34

CHAPTER 1

The Regions of the United States

Chapter 1 Outline

- **Lesson 1, *Regions and Landforms,*** pp. 10–15
- **Here and There: *Highest and Lowest Landforms,*** pp. 16–17
- **Lesson 2, *Climate,*** pp. 18–23
- **Map and Globe Skills: *Read Inset Maps,*** pp. 24–25
- **Lesson 3, *Regional Resources,*** pp. 26–31
- DK ***The United States and North America,*** pp. 32–33

Resources

- Workbook, p. 2: Vocabulary Preview
- Vocabulary Cards
- Social Studies Plus!

Regions and Landforms: Lesson 1

Ask students if they know in which region their town is located. Ask them to describe how their home region compares to the one in the picture.

Climate: Lesson 2

Have students examine the region shown in the picture. Ask them what they think the climate is like in that region. Have students explain the reasoning behind their conclusions.

Regional Resources: Lesson 3

Point out that this is a picture of one of Vermont's many forests. Ask students how the presence of forests might impact the environment, people, and economy of a region.

CHAPTER 1

The Regions of the United States

Lesson 1

Regions and Landforms
Each region of the United States has a variety of landforms and boundaries.

1

Lesson 2

Climate
Many factors influence climate, which varies from region to region.

2

Lesson 3

Regional Resources
Each region has special resources.

3

8

Practice and Extend

Vocabulary Preview

- Use Workbook p. 2 to help students preview the vocabulary words in this chapter.
- Use Vocabulary Cards to preview key concept words in this chapter.

Also on Teacher Resources CD-ROM.

Workbook, p. 2

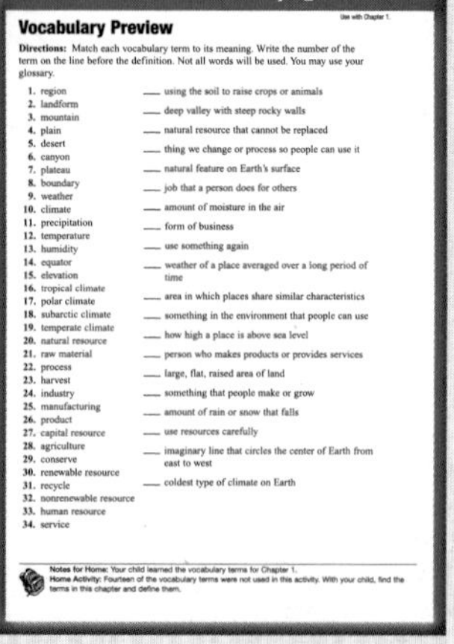

Vocabulary Preview — Use with Chapter 1.

Directions: Match each vocabulary term to its meaning. Write the number of the term on the line before the definition. Not all words will be used. You may use your glossary.

1. region
2. landform
3. mountain
4. plain
5. desert
6. canyon
7. plateau
8. boundary
9. weather
10. climate
11. precipitation
12. temperature
13. humidity
14. equator
15. elevation
16. tropical climate
17. polar climate
18. subarctic climate
19. temperate climate
20. natural resource
21. raw material
22. process
23. harvest
24. industry
25. manufacturing
26. product
27. capital resource
28. agriculture
29. conserve
30. renewable resource
31. recycle
32. nonrenewable resource
33. human resource
34. service

___ using the soil to raise crops or animals
___ deep valley with steep rocky walls
___ natural resource that cannot be replaced
___ thing we change or process so people can use it
___ natural feature on Earth's surface
___ job that a person does for others
___ amount of moisture in the air
___ form of business
___ use something again
___ weather of a place averaged over a long period of time
___ area in which places share similar characteristics
___ something in the environment that people can use
___ how high a place is above sea level
___ person who makes products or provides services
___ large, flat, raised area of land
___ something that people make or grow
___ amount of rain or snow that falls
___ use resources carefully
___ imaginary line that circles the center of Earth from east to west
___ coldest type of climate on Earth

Notes for Home: Your child learned the vocabulary terms for Chapter 1.
Home Activity: Fourteen of the vocabulary terms were not used in this activity. With your child, find the terms in this chapter and define them.

Locating Places

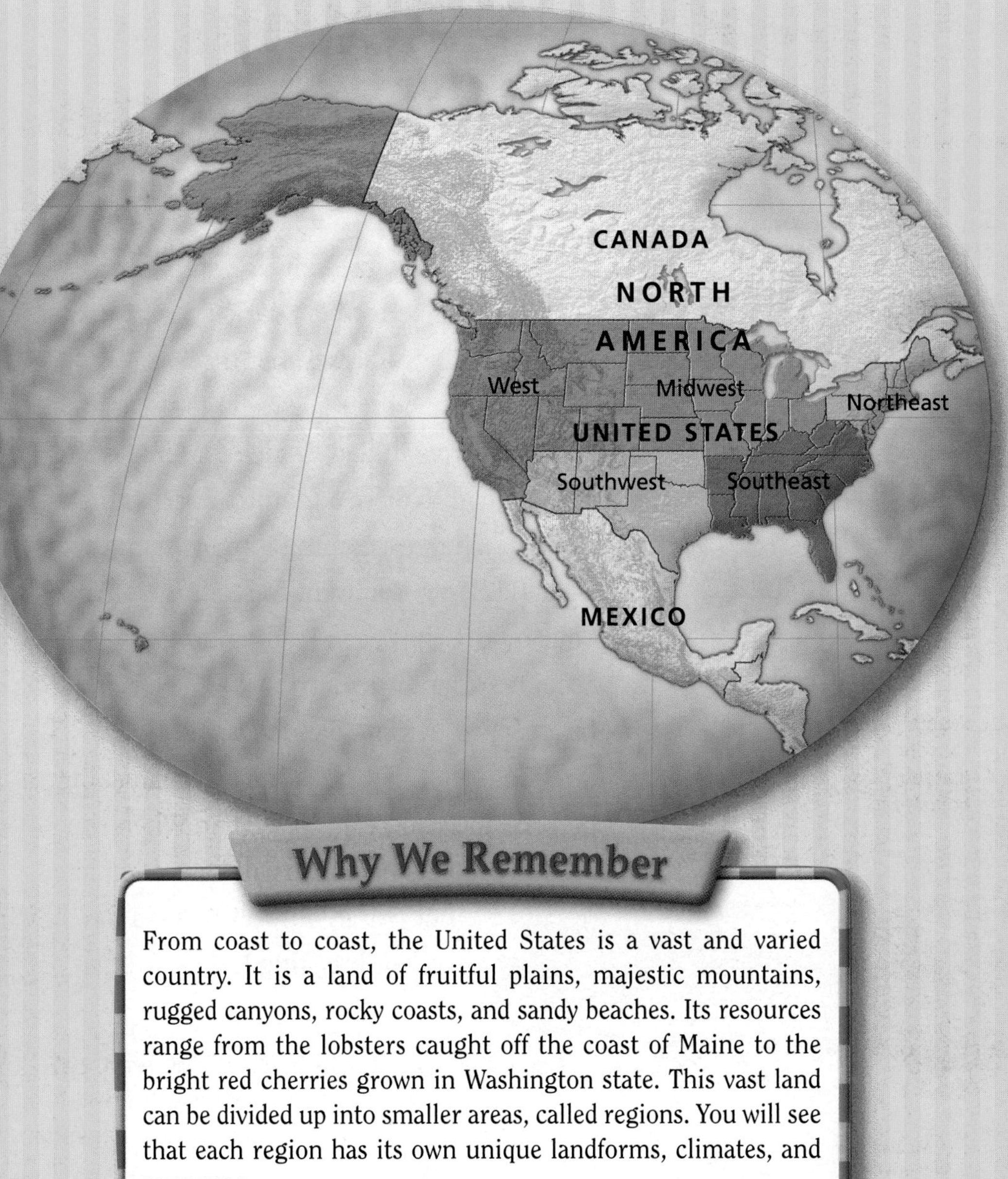

Why We Remember

From coast to coast, the United States is a vast and varied country. It is a land of fruitful plains, majestic mountains, rugged canyons, rocky coasts, and sandy beaches. Its resources range from the lobsters caught off the coast of Maine to the bright red cherries grown in Washington state. This vast land can be divided up into smaller areas, called regions. You will see that each region has its own unique landforms, climates, and resources.

9

WEB SITE
Technology

can learn more about the regions, landforms, and climates of the United States by clicking on as at **www.sfsocialstudies.com.**

SOCIAL STUDIES STRAND
Geography

Mental Mapping On a simple outline map of the United States,have students use crayons or different colored pencils to rough in the areas they think are the following regions: West, Southwest, Midwest, Southeast, and Northeast. Discuss with students how they chose these areas as the regions named.

Locating Places

- Have students examine the pictures shown on p. 8 for Lessons 1, 2, and 3.

Why We Remember

- Have students read the "Why We Remember" paragraph on p. 9 and ask them why they think the United States is fortunate to have such diversity in its resources throughout the country.
- Tell students that the varied landforms, climates, and resources of the United States have inspired people to write many poems, songs, and stories about the land.
- Encourage students to suggest other images of the United States that they find especially beautiful.

Regions and Landforms

Objectives

- Identify the five major regions of the United States.
- Describe the major landforms of each region in the United States.
- Explain the difference between regional and state boundaries.

Vocabulary

region, p. 11; **landform,** p. 11; **mountain,** p. 12; **plain,** p. 12; **desert,** p. 13; **canyon,** p. 13; **plateau,** p. 13; **boundary,** p. 14

Resources

- Workbook, p. 3
- Transparency 6
- Every Student Learns Guide, pp. 2–5
- Quick Study, pp. 2–3

Quick Teaching Plan

If time is short, have students create a chart of information from this lesson.

- Have students create a two-column chart with the headings *Regions* and *Landforms.*
- Tell students to complete the chart by recording details as they read the lesson independently.

1 Introduce and Motivate

Preview To activate prior knowledge, point to various geographic regions on a map of the United States and ask for volunteers who have lived in or visited each to briefly describe what they saw there. Tell students they will learn more about each region as they read Lesson 1.

Ask students what types of crops, landforms, people, and other resources Alice Ramsey might have seen if she had traveled through their home region.

LESSON 1

PREVIEW

Focus on the Main Idea
The United States is divided into five regions.

PLACES
Northeast region
Southeast region
Midwest region
Southwest region
West region
Washington, D.C.

VOCABULARY
region
landform
mountain
plain
desert
canyon
plateau
boundary

Regions and Landforms

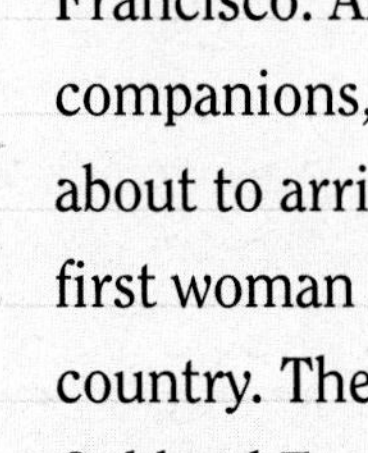

It is August 6, 1909. You and your family are standing in a crowd on Market Street in San Francisco. Alice Ramsey, her three traveling companions, and her Maxwell motorcar are about to arrive in San Francisco. Alice is the first woman to drive a motorcar across the country. They are coming into town on the Oakland Ferry. You want to see this woman. Your mother has been reading newspaper accounts about Alice's trip to you. Nothing has stopped her, not bad roads, not bad directions, not flat tires. She is one amazing person! You can't wait to see her. When she gets here, she will have completed her trip in only 59 days—a record-breaking time!

▶ A Maxwell motorcar like the one driven by Alice Ramsey

Summarize As you read, pay attention to details that will help you summarize the lesson.

10

Practice and Extend

READING SKILL
Summarize

In the Lesson Review, students complete a graphic organizer like the one below. You may want to provide students with a copy of Transparency 6 to complete as they read the lesson.

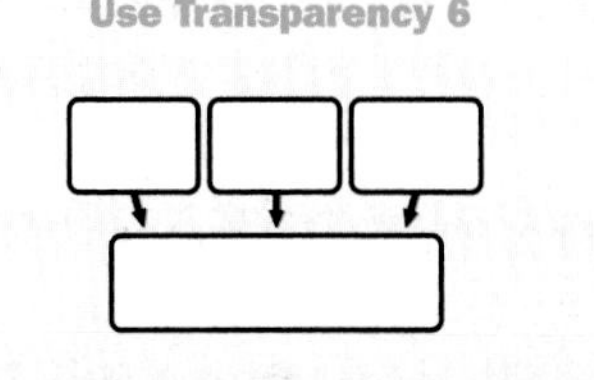

VOCABULARY
Related Word Study

Have students use the text, library, or Internet to locate pictures of mountains, plains, deserts, canyons, and plateaus to use as a reference to draw their own illustrations of these landforms. Then have students make "Landforms" charts consisting of the name of each landform, a picture of it, and a description of it in the students' own words.

Regions of the United States

Alice Ramsey would be surprised to see the road system that now covers the United States and allows travelers to visit almost every part of this vast and varied country. To help us understand the United States, we can divide the country into five different regions. A **region** is an area in which places share similar characteristics. Places within a region may share certain landforms. A **landform** is a natural feature on Earth's surface, such as a mountain or a river. 1

Areas within a region also may be completely different from each other. For example, the West has snow-covered mountains, fertile valleys, shining lakes, and an island state. The Midwest has fertile plains and the Great Lakes. In the Southwest you will find deserts and the largest canyon in the United States. 2

Use the map below to find the states and landforms for each region. Find your state on the map.

REVIEW Summarize the differences in landforms among the West, the Midwest, and the Southwest regions. Summarize

MAP SKILL

Regions of the United States

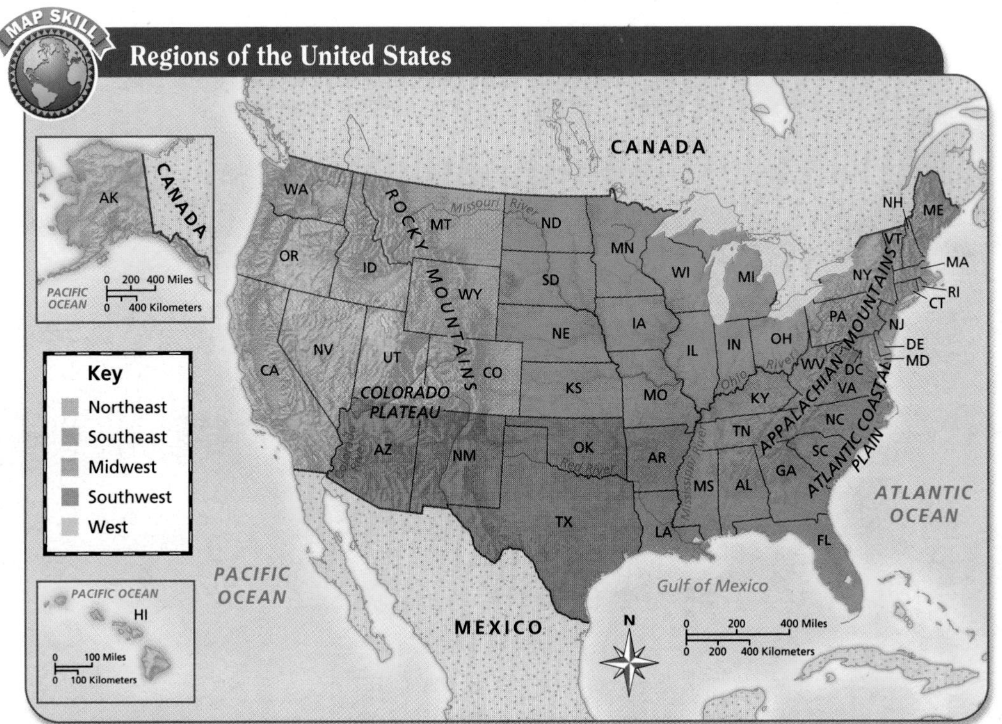

▶ This map of the United States is divided into five regions. 3

MAP SKILL Understand Cardinal Directions ***What direction would you travel from the West to the Midwest?***

2 Teach and Discuss

PAGE 11

Regions of the United States

Quick Summary Places within a region share certain characteristics, but they also may have different landforms and their own qualities.

1 **Name two examples of landforms in our state.** Answers should accurately reflect landforms in your state. Possible answers: Mountains, valleys, islands, plains, deserts, canyons Categorize

2 **Are all parts of a region exactly alike? Explain.** No; some areas of a region may have similar characteristics or landforms, but other areas may have different characteristics.
Main Idea and Details

✓ **REVIEW ANSWER** The West has mountains, lakes, and valleys; the Midwest has fertile plains and the Great Lakes; and the Southwest has deserts and a large canyon. Summarize

MAP SKILL

Regions of the United States

3 **Which regions of the United States border Mexico?** The West and Southwest
Interpret Maps

MAP SKILL Answer Possible answer: East

ACCESS CONTENT

ESL Support

Examine Direction Words Help students better understand the region names by exploring the words *north, south, east, west, northeast, southeast, northwest,* and *southwest.*

Beginning On a classroom map, place a pin showing the location of your community. Have students come to the map and respond as you call out instructions such as "Point to a location north of our community."

Intermediate Have students create their own sentences identifying a place in relation to your community, such as "___ is north of our community." Have students share their sentences with a partner.

Advanced On a map of the world, have students identify the locations of places where they have lived or visited in relation to your community.

For additional ESL support, use Every Student Learns Guide, pp. 2–5.

PAGES 12–13

Landforms of the Regions

Quick Summary Each region of the United States has distinctive landforms, ranging from mountains to deserts to wetlands.

Test Talk

Locate Key Words in the Text

4 **Through what two regions do the Appalachian Mountains run?** Have students locate key words in the text that match key words in the question. The Northeast and the Southeast
Main Idea and Details

5 **What creates rich farmland in the Southeast?** The Mississippi and Red Rivers Main Idea and Details

6 **Which region has the world's largest known cave system?** The Southeast Main Idea and Details

7 **In which region are mountains *not* an important landform?** The Midwest
Analyze Information

Landforms of the Regions

The **Northeast region** contains part of the oldest mountain range in the country—the Appalachian Mountains. A **mountain** is a very high landform, often with steep sides. The Appalachian Mountains run all the way from Georgia
4 in the Southeast through Maine in the Northeast and into Canada. The Northeast region is mostly hilly and rocky along the Atlantic coast but has good farmland to the west.

In the **Southeast region** the Appalachian Mountains gradually flatten eastward into the Atlantic Coastal Plain. A **plain** is a large area of mostly flat land that is often covered with grass. West of the mountains, Louisiana and Mississippi have plains leading into the Gulf of Mexico. The Mississippi and Red Rivers flow through the region, creating rich farmland in states like Arkansas and
Louisiana. The world's largest known 5
cave system is the Mammoth Cave
system in Kentucky. It's almost 350 6
miles long!

The **Midwest region** has flat, grassy plains and large areas of forest. There
are some rolling hills, such as the 7
Smoky Hills in Kansas. Big rivers, such as the Mississippi, Ohio, and Missouri, flow through this region.

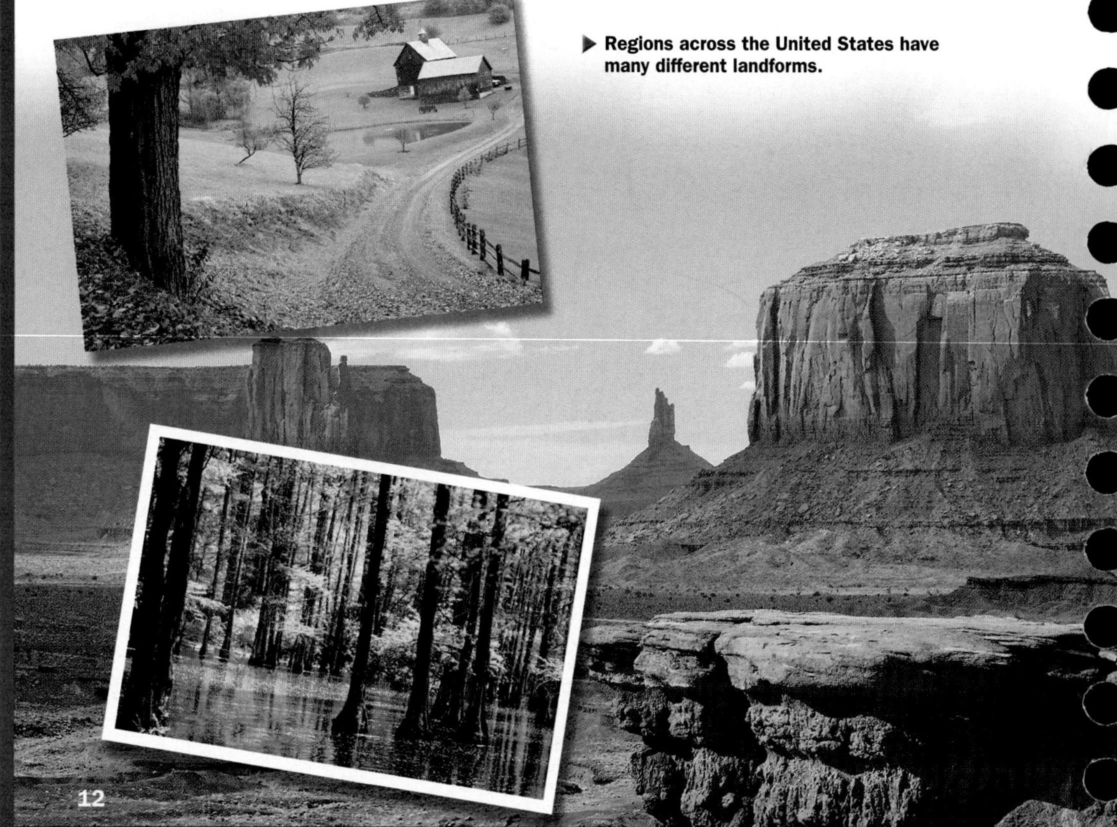

▶ Regions across the United States have many different landforms.

Practice and Extend

MEETING INDIVIDUAL NEEDS
Leveled Practice

Identify Landforms Help students create a bulletin board display of different landforms in the United States.

Easy Have students find pictures of at least five types of landforms and create a bulletin-board display. **Reteach**

On-Level Have students write one sentence that describes each of the landforms their classmates included in the display. Have them post their sentences beside the pictures. **Extend**

Challenge Have students choose a landform identified by their classmates, find out more about it, and write a descriptive paragraph about it. Have them post their paragraphs beside the related pictures. **Enrich**

For a Lesson Summary, use Quick Study, p. 2.

Four of the five Great Lakes—Lake Erie, Lake Huron, Lake Michigan, and Lake Superior—border parts of the Midwest. They are large bodies of
8 fresh (not salty) water.

The **Southwest region** has only four states in it. It is home to beautiful deserts and canyons. A **desert** is an area that gets very little rain. A **canyon** is a deep valley with steep rocky walls. Over time, the Colorado River has slowly carved the red land into canyons. Only about the thickness of a credit card is shaved from the walls of the Grand Canyon every five years. The depth of the Grand Canyon is equal to 80 four-story houses!

The canyons of the Southwest are found in an area called the Colorado Plateau. A **plateau** is a large, flat, raised area of land. The Rocky
9 Mountains run from the West region into the Southwest, through New Mexico. To the east of these mountains are flat plains.

The **West region** is a region of extremes. The highest and lowest temperatures in the United States have been recorded in the West. The highest temperatures were recorded in
Death Valley, California, and the lowest 10
in Alaska.

The highest and lowest landforms in the United States are in the West. The highest landform is Mt. McKinley in Alaska, and the lowest is Death Valley
in California. The coastal mountains 11
border the Pacific coast, and white sandy beaches run along part of the Pacific Ocean. There are fertile, green valleys in Oregon and California. Other areas are heavily forested, such as western Oregon and Washington. The West region also includes Alaska and Hawaii.

REVIEW List five types of landforms found in the United States.
Summarize

13

8 How are the Great Lakes like the oceans? How are they different? Alike: Both are large bodies of water, though the oceans are much larger than the Great Lakes; Different: The oceans lie along the coasts, while the Great Lakes are inland. The ocean is salty, but the freshwater Great Lakes are not.
Compare and Contrast

9 How are canyons different from plateaus? A plateau is a large, flat, raised area of land, and a canyon is a deep valley with steep, rocky walls.
Compare and Contrast

10 Summarize the characteristics of the West region. Possible answer: The West is a region of extremes.
Summarize

11 What are the highest and lowest landforms in the United States? In what region can they be found? Highest: Mt. McKinley in Alaska; Lowest: Death Valley in California; Both are found in the West.
Main Idea and Details

✓ **REVIEW ANSWER** Possible answers: Mountains, plains, caves, deserts, canyons, plateaus, beaches, valleys
Summarize

CURRICULUM CONNECTION
Art

Discover the United States in Pictures

- Help students find books with images that celebrate the American landscape.
- Have students choose one picture for each region to illustrate a landform from that region.
- Then, for each region, have students share their chosen pictures, identify the subject and artist, and explain why they think the picture represents the region.

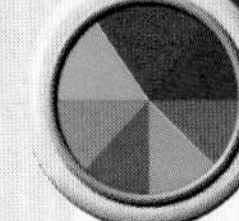

CURRICULUM CONNECTION
Music

Discover the United States in Song

- Have small groups research songs that celebrate the United States or its regions and landforms.
- Encourage students to begin with "America the Beautiful."
- Have each group create an audio montage of excerpts—sung by themselves or taken from other recordings—that conveys its impression of the United States.

PAGES 14–15

Boundaries

Quick Summary State boundaries are legal borders with exact measurements. However, regional boundaries are less exact and may vary from one source to another.

12 **Name the two natural features and the two state boundaries that form the borders of Florida.** Natural: Atlantic Ocean and Gulf of Mexico; State: the southern boundary lines of Georgia and Alabama **Categorize**

13 **How were state boundaries determined in the United States?** They were set by the government. **Main Idea and Details**

14 **Why might you find different regional borders in another book?** Because regional boundaries are not set by any rule or law or marked by signs **Apply Information**

15 **How might a person be in more than one state at the same time?** The person could stand on the spot where the boundaries of states meet. **Analyze Pictures**

Ongoing Assessment

If... students have difficulty imagining how a person could be in multiple places at once,	**then...** direct their attention to the picture at the top of p. 15.

Boundaries

A **boundary** is a line or natural feature that divides one area from another or one state from another. For example, the boundaries of the state of Florida include two natural features—the Atlantic Ocean and the Gulf of Mexico. Florida's northern boundary line also includes the southern boundaries of
12 Georgia and Alabama.

The lines that make boundaries around the states in the United States are found only on maps. If you rode to the border of your state, you would not actually see a line drawn in the ground. But you might see a sign welcoming people to your state.

State boundaries are legal borders with exact measurements around each state. These boundaries were set by
13 the government. The United States is divided into fifty states plus the District of Columbia, which is land set aside for the nation's capital, **Washington, D.C.** Each state has a

▶ Marina on Kentucky side of the Ohio River near Louisville. The other side of the river is Indiana.

government that allows the state officials to make choices about state issues, such as education and laws.

Regional boundaries are not set by any rule or law. In fact, you may see regions named or marked in different
ways than they are in this book. 14
Regional boundaries are sometimes based on the major landforms of the area. For example, the Northeast is mostly hilly and rocky with farmland in the western part of the region. The Southeast is mostly rolling hills, mountains, and plains bordered by beaches. The Midwest is mostly plains and lakes while the Southwest is mostly plateaus and canyons.

▶ State-line sign welcoming visitors to Utah

Practice and Extend

Decision Making

Use a Decision-Making Process

- Have students consider the following decision-making scenario: **Ellis Island is famous for being the place where millions of immigrants first entered the United States. An 1834 border agreement gave the three-acre island to New York, but the submerged areas to New Jersey. Over time, part of the harbor was filled in, and the island grew to 27 acres. Which state should own Ellis Island?**
- Students should use the decision-making process above to decide who should own the island. For each step in the process, have students work in small groups to discuss and write about what must be considered as they make their decision. Write the steps on the board or read them aloud.

1. **Identify a situation that requires a decision.**
2. **Gather information.**
3. **Identify options.**
4. **Predict consequences.**
5. **Take action to implement a decision.**

FYI SOCIAL STUDIES Background

About the Ownership of Ellis Island

- After students reach a decision in the Decision-Making activity at left, tell them that in 1998 the Supreme Court ruled that New York owned the original three acres of Ellis Island. It also ruled that New Jersey owned the filled-in portions of the island.

▶ At the Four Corners Monument, you can put your feet in Utah and Colorado, and your hands in New Mexico and Arizona!

The West includes perhaps the greatest variety, from the desert of Death Valley in California to the snow-covered peaks of Mt. McKinley in Alaska.

Regardless of the way in which the regions may be divided, regional boundaries are different from state boundaries—they are not marked with signs.

REVIEW Describe the two different types of boundaries. Summarize

Summarize the Lesson

- **There are five regions in the United States.**
- **Each region is made up of various landforms.**
- **Regional boundaries can be based on similar landforms. State boundaries are set by the government.**

LESSON 1 REVIEW

Check Facts and Main Ideas

1. Summarize On a separate sheet of paper, summarize each of the other four regions into graphic organizers like the one below.

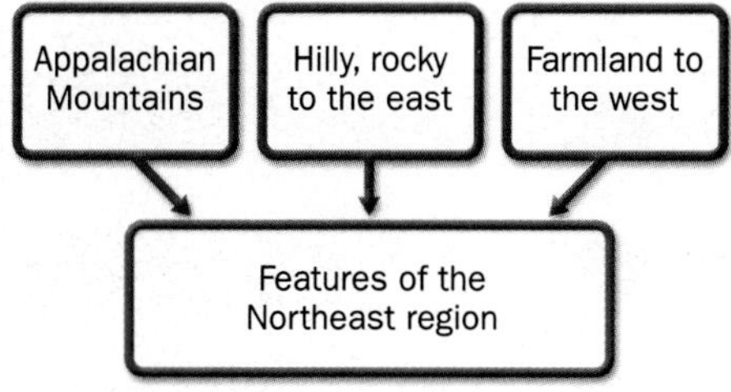

2. Name some of the landforms found in each region.
3. How do regional and state **boundaries** differ?
4. In which **region** or regions do you find each of the following: the Appalachian Mountains, the Mammoth Cave System, the Great Lakes, and the Rocky Mountains?
5. **Critical Thinking:** ***Make Inferences*** Choose one region and explain how the **landforms** of that region might affect how people work and play there.

Link to Art

Draw a Landform Choose one landform discussed in this lesson and make a drawing of it. Tell why people might want to visit it.

✓ **REVIEW ANSWER** Natural boundaries such as oceans occur in nature and can provide borders to a state. State boundaries are legal borders with exact measurements. Summarize

Summarize the Lesson

Have student volunteers take turns reading the three main points. As each point is read, have students provide specific examples.

✓ **LESSON 1 REVIEW**

1. Summarize For possible answers, see the reduced pupil page.
2. Possible answers: Northeast: mountains; Southeast: coastal plains; Midwest: grassy plains; Southwest: deserts and canyons; West: coastal mountains
3. Regional boundaries are determined by grouping states with similar characteristics. State boundaries have fixed borders with exact measurements. State borders were set by the government.
4. Appalachian Mountains: Northeast and Southeast; Mammoth Cave System: Southeast; Great Lakes: Midwest and Northeast; Rocky Mountains: West
5. **Critical Thinking: *Make Inferences*** Possible answers: The cold weather and mountain range in the Northeast might encourage people to ski, hike, and mine ore in the mountains; because there is a lot of water surrounding the Southeast, people might swim and fish along the coast.

Link to Art

Encourage students to reexamine the illustrations in this lesson and to include other details from their own experience or imagination.

SOCIAL STUDIES STRAND
Geography

Natural Features as Boundaries

- Point out that rivers are natural features that can form boundaries.
- Have students use the classroom map to determine what river marks the boundary between New Hampshire and Vermont (Connecticut River), between Mississippi and Arkansas (Mississippi River), between Arizona and California (Colorado River), and between Kentucky and Indiana (Ohio River).

Workbook, p. 3

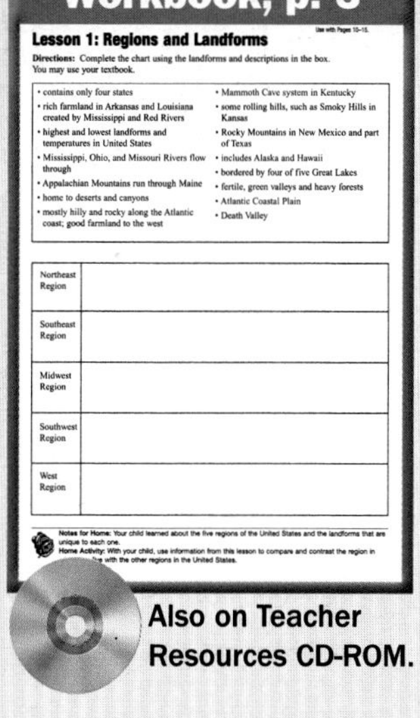

Lesson 1: Regions and Landforms

Use with Pages 10–15.

Directions: Complete the chart using the landforms and descriptions in the box. You may use your textbook.

- contains only four states
- rich farmland in Arkansas and Louisiana created by Mississippi and Red Rivers
- highest and lowest landforms and temperatures in United States
- Mississippi, Ohio, and Missouri Rivers flow through
- Appalachian Mountains run through Maine
- home to deserts and canyons
- mostly hilly and rocky along the Atlantic coast; good farmland to the west
- Mammoth Cave system in Kentucky
- some rolling hills, such as Smoky Hills in Kansas
- Rocky Mountains in New Mexico and part of Texas
- includes Alaska and Hawaii
- bordered by four of five Great Lakes
- fertile, green valleys and heavy forests
- Atlantic Coastal Plain
- Death Valley

Northeast Region	
Southeast Region	
Midwest Region	
Southwest Region	
West Region	

Notes for Home: Your child learned about the five regions of the United States and the landforms that are unique to each one.
Home Activity: With your child, use information from this lesson to compare and contrast the region in [illegible] with the other regions in the United States.

Also on Teacher Resources CD-ROM.

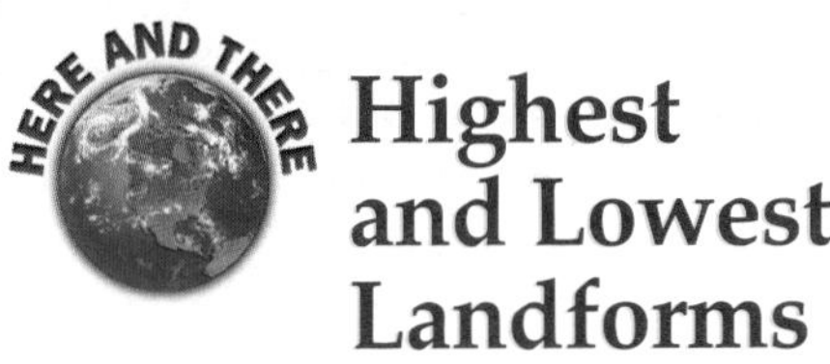

Highest and Lowest Landforms

Objective

- Analyze differences in landforms around the world.

1 Introduce and Motivate

Preview To activate prior knowledge, ask students to name the highest (or tallest) place they have ever visited. Ask them how they think that place compares to Mt. McKinley, the highest mountain in the United States.

Ask why it might be interesting to know how other places in the world compare to the highest and lowest places they have visited.

2 Teach and Discuss

1 How were the Himalayas formed? Two pieces of land collided and pushed the sea floor up higher and higher over millions of years. Summarize

SOCIAL STUDIES STRAND
Science • Technology

Tell students that fossils are the hardened remains or impressions of a plant or animal that lived in an earlier time.

2 How might fossils of sea creatures end up on Mt. Everest or other mountains? They might have been on the portion of sea floor that got pushed upward to form a mountain. Hypothesize

3 What type of landform found on both coasts of the United States lies at sea level? A beach Draw Conclusions

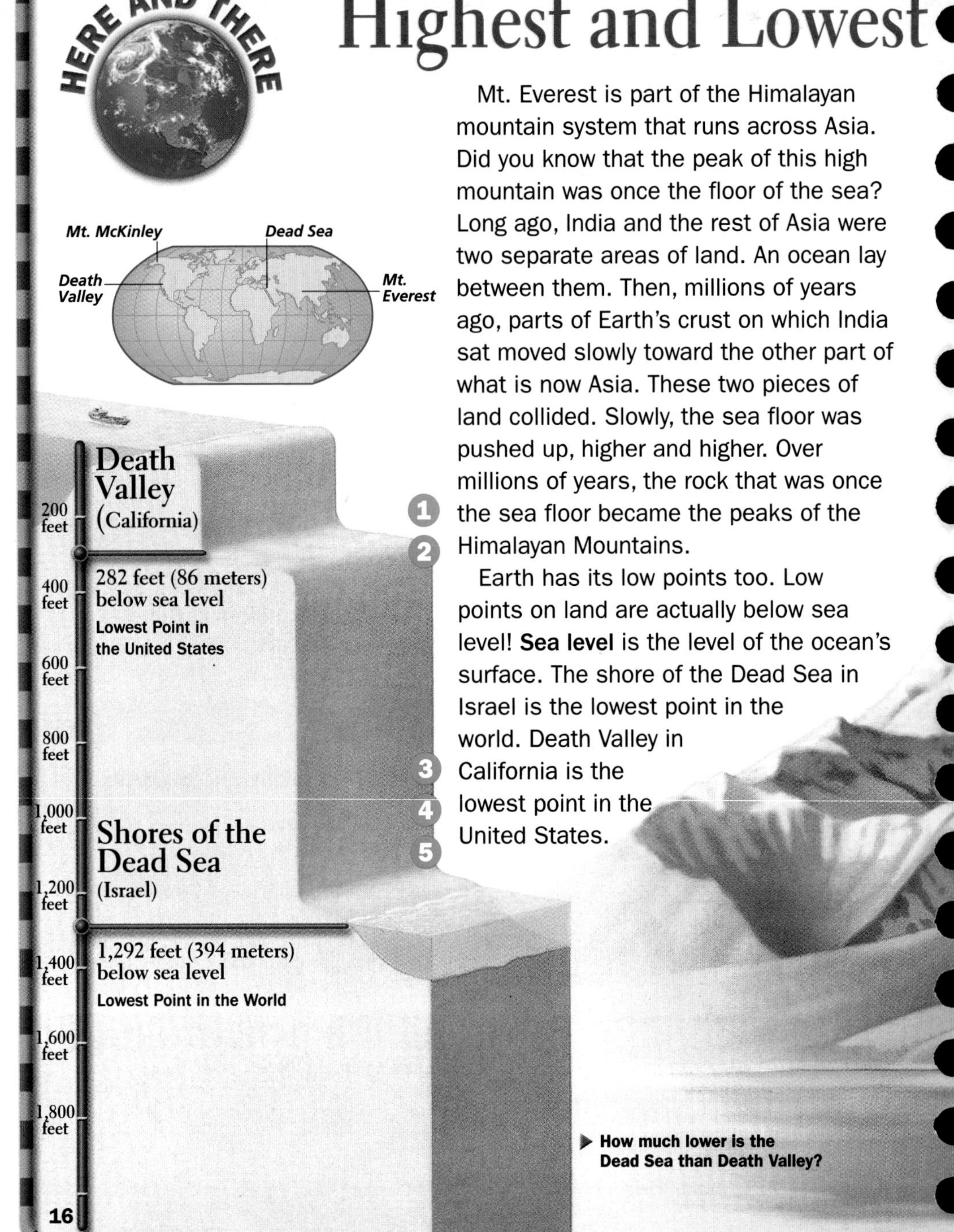

Highest and Lowest

Mt. Everest is part of the Himalayan mountain system that runs across Asia. Did you know that the peak of this high mountain was once the floor of the sea? Long ago, India and the rest of Asia were two separate areas of land. An ocean lay between them. Then, millions of years ago, parts of Earth's crust on which India sat moved slowly toward the other part of what is now Asia. These two pieces of land collided. Slowly, the sea floor was pushed up, higher and higher. Over millions of years, the rock that was once
1 the sea floor became the peaks of the
2 Himalayan Mountains.

Earth has its low points too. Low points on land are actually below sea level! **Sea level** is the level of the ocean's surface. The shore of the Dead Sea in Israel is the lowest point in the world. Death Valley in
3 California is the
4 lowest point in the
5 United States.

▶ How much lower is the Dead Sea than Death Valley?

16

Practice and Extend

SOCIAL STUDIES
Background

About the Highest and Lowest Points

- The Tibetan name for Mt. Everest is Chomolungma, or "Goddess Mother of the World"; the Native American name for Mt. McKinley is Denali, or "The High One."
- The first people to reach the summit of Mt. Everest were Edmund Hillary of New Zealand and Tenzing Norgay, a Nepalese Sherpa. The two reached the summit in 1953. Because the Sherpas have adapted to conditions at high altitudes, they have guided explorers since the 1920s.
- Both the Dead Sea and Death Valley lie in deserts. The name "Dead Sea" dates back more than 2,000 years; Death Valley was named in 1849 by a group of pioneers who crossed it. It became a national park in 1994.

Landforms

Mt. Everest
(Nepal)

29,035 feet
(8,850 meters)
Highest Mountain in the World

▶ How much higher is Mt. Everest than Mt. McKinley?

25,000 feet

Mt. McKinley
(Alaska)

20,320 feet
(6,194 meters)
Highest Mountain in the United States

15,000 feet

10,000 feet

5,000 feet

17

4 What are the highest and lowest points in the United States? in the world? United States: highest—Mt. McKinley, lowest—Death Valley; World: highest—Mt. Everest, lowest—Dead Sea **Interpret Maps**

5 Why do you think the lowest points in the United States and the world have the words *Death* and *Dead* in their names? Possible answer: Because both are in very hot desert areas where relatively few forms of life can survive **Make Inferences**

Answers to Captions

The Dead Sea is 1,010 feet (308 m) lower than Death Valley. Mt. Everest is 8,715 feet (2,656 m) higher than Mt. McKinley.

3 Close and Assess

Have students create a scale drawing of Mt. Everest and Mt. McKinley as shown here. Then have them research and add the highest point in their state, using the same scale.

WEB SITE
Technology

Students can find out more about places on these pages by clicking on *Atlas* at **www.sfsocialstudies.com.**

CURRICULUM CONNECTION
Literature

Read About the Highest and Lowest Landforms

Use the following texts to extend the content.

Death Valley National Park, by David Petersen (Children's Press, ISBN 0-516-26095-2, 1997) **Easy**

The Dead Sea: The Saltiest Sea, by Aileen Weintraub (PowerKids Press, ISBN 0-8239-5637-7, 2001) **On-Level**

To the Top of Everest, by Laurie Skreslet and Elizabeth MacLeod (contributor) (Kids Can Press, ISBN 1-55074-721-5, 2001) **Challenge**

Climate

Objectives

- Explain the difference between weather and climate.
- Describe the climate of each region in the United States.
- Describe the three main factors that affect the climate of an area.
- Describe the major types of climates around the world.

Vocabulary

weather, p. 19; **climate,** p. 19; **precipitation,** p. 19; **temperature,** p. 19; **humidity,** p. 20; **equator,** p. 21; **elevation,** p. 21; **tropical climate,** p. 22; **polar climate,** p. 22; **subarctic climate,** p. 22; **temperate climate,** p. 23

Resources

- Workbook, p. 4
- Transparency 8
- Every Student Learns Guide, pp. 6–9
- Quick Study, pp. 4–5

Quick *Teaching Plan*

If time is short, have students read the lesson independently and then work in pairs to summarize the lesson's information.

- Have students write a one- or two-sentence summary of each section.
- Encourage students to compare their summaries with those on p. 23.

1 Introduce and Motivate

Preview To activate prior knowledge, ask students how they might know what to pack for a trip to another part of the United States. (Check the climate of the area.) Tell students they will learn more about climate as they read Lesson 2.

Ask students to brainstorm the types of difficulties a businessperson might face if he or she had to travel all around the United States during the winter months.

LESSON 2

PREVIEW

Focus on the Main Idea
Many factors influence climate, which varies from region to region.

VOCABULARY
weather
climate
precipitation
temperature
humidity
equator
elevation
tropical climate
polar climate
subarctic climate
temperate climate

▶ Weather radar shows a cold front along the East Coast of the United States.

Climate

You Are There It is the end of December. You and your family are relaxing in the main lounge of your motel in Honolulu, Hawaii. You have just come back from a hiking trip through the Manoa Valley on the island of Oahu. There you saw streams, flowering trees, and a 200-foot waterfall.

Your brother is watching a weather program on television. You see images of a snowstorm in Kansas. Minutes later, the image of an ice storm in New York State fills the screen. Trees are bent over under the weight of ice. But outside your motel in Honolulu, the weather is 75 degrees and sunny. You are amazed at the variety of climates across the United States!

Summarize As you read, look for things that affect climate in the United States.

Practice and Extend

READING SKILL
Summarize

In the Lesson Review, students complete a graphic organizer like the one below. You may want to provide students with a copy of Transparency 8 to complete as they read the lesson.

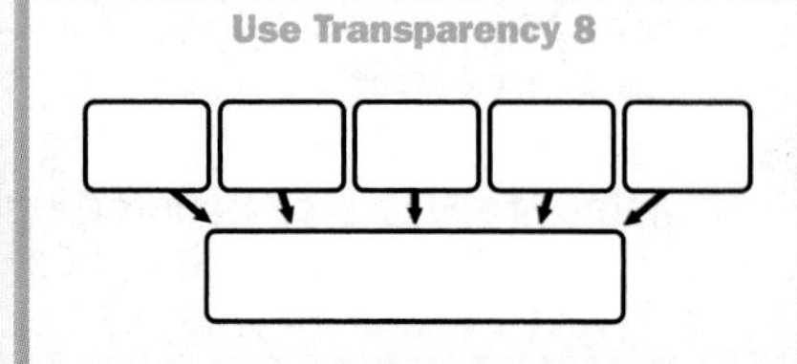

VOCABULARY
Context Clues

Discuss the meaning of the word *climate* with students. Write *tropical climate, polar climate, subarctic climate,* and *temperate climate* on the board. Point out that each term includes the word *climate*. Discuss what the words added to *climate* tell us. Help students develop definitions of each term in their own words and record these definitions in their writing journals.

Weather and Climate

In one way or another, we all pay attention to weather. You may just glance outside to see whether you will need an umbrella. Other people must pay more attention to weather when it directly affects their jobs or safety. For example, a pilot checks the weather to avoid flying into a dangerous storm.

Weather is the condition of the air at a certain time and place. Today's weather might be sunny and warm. Yesterday's weather might have been rainy and windy.

Climate is the weather of a place
1 averaged over a long period of time. Climate includes the changes in weather that happen during seasons of the year. A farmer needs to know about the climate of an area in order to know what crops to plant and when to plant them.

Two major factors of weather and climate are precipitation and temperature. **Precipitation** is the amount of rain or snow that falls. **Temperature** is how warm or cold a place is. 2 3

Climate varies around the United States. In Florida, for example, temperatures are warm, and it rarely snows. And while Illinois can get very hot in summer, it can be very cold in winter and snow a great deal.

The map below shows how different the weather can be around the country. It shows average temperatures throughout the country in the month of January.

REVIEW Why is it important to know what the weather is going to be? **Draw Conclusions**

MAP SKILL

Average Temperatures in January in the United States

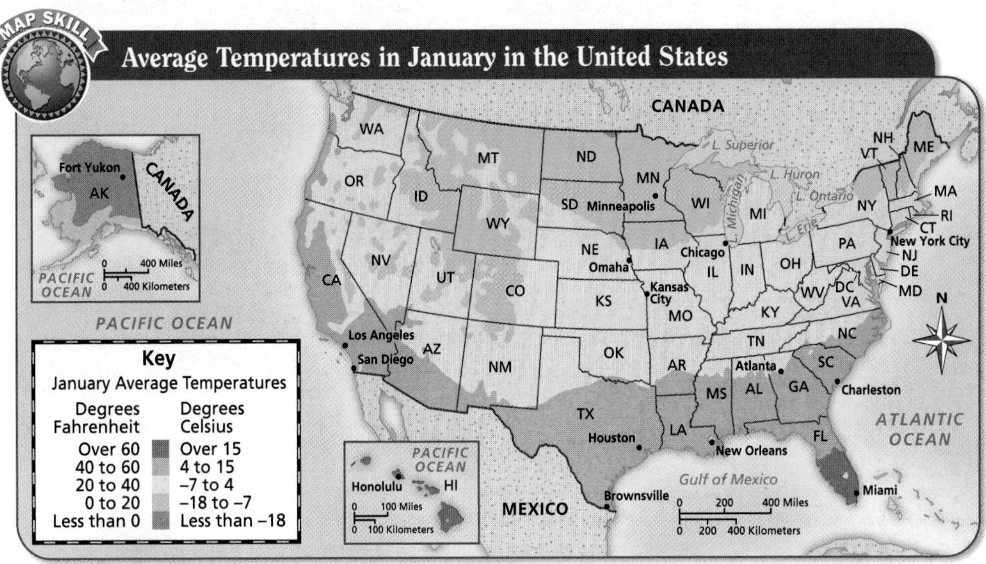

▶ Temperatures vary greatly across the United States.

MAP SKILL Use a Map Key *What is the average range of temperatures in degrees Fahrenheit for Houston in January?* 4

2 Teach and Discuss

PAGE 19

Weather and Climate

Quick Summary Weather is the condition of the air at a certain time and place, while climate is the weather of a place averaged over a long period of time. Both are affected by temperature and precipitation.

1 Summarize the main difference between weather and climate. Weather refers to the conditions at a certain time and place. Climate is the average weather of a place over a longer period of time. **Summarize**

2 Why would a farmer need to know about the climate of an area? To know what crops to plant and when to plant them. **Main Idea and Details**

3 Besides *cold* and *warm,* what other words do people often use to describe the weather? Possible answers: Freezing, chilly, brisk, pleasant, hot, steamy, broiling (Note: You may wish to have students organize their list on a continuum, ranging from words that describe the coldest days to those that describe the hottest days.) **Express Ideas**

✓ **REVIEW ANSWER** Possible answers: To decide what to wear, what activities to do; for safety reasons **Draw Conclusions**

MAP SKILL

Average Temperatures in January in the United States

4 According to the map, which state has the coldest January average temperature? Which states have the warmest January average temperature? Coldest: Alaska; warmest: Hawaii **Interpret Maps**

MAP SKILL Answer 40 to 60 degrees Fahrenheit

MEETING INDIVIDUAL NEEDS

Leveled Practice

Compare Weather Reports Have students compare different types of weather reports.

Easy Have students watch a local TV weather report and list the types of information it conveys. **Reteach**

On-Level Have students read a weather forecast in an almanac and compare it to a typical televised or newspaper weather report. Ask students in what instances might each forecast or report be more useful. **Extend**

Challenge Have students examine a weather map in a newspaper, analyze its symbols and key, and explain to the class how to read it. **Enrich**

For a Lesson Summary, use Quick Study, p. 4.

PAGE 20

Water in the Air

Quick Summary The sun converts water from oceans, lakes, rivers, and streams into water vapor, which can form into drops that fall back to the earth as rain or snow.

5 **What makes water vapor in the air form into small drops?** Cooling of the air **Apply Information**

6 **What happens in clouds before rain or snow can fall?** Tiny drops of water join together and form big drops. **Sequence**

✓ **REVIEW ANSWER** Energy from the sun changes some water from oceans, lakes, rivers, and streams into water vapor. **Summarize**

Average Precipitation in a Year Throughout the United States

7 **What is the range of average annual precipitation in the Northeast region?** Between 20–60 inches **Interpret Maps**

MAP SKILL Answer 40–60 inches (100–150 centimeters)

Water in the Air

Water in the air is another major part of climate. About three-quarters of Earth is covered by water. Even though you cannot see it, the air around us contains water too. **Humidity** is the amount of moisture in the air.

How does water get from the ground into the air? Energy from the sun changes some water from oceans, lakes, rivers, and streams into a gas that rises into the air. This invisible gas is called water vapor. When air cools, the water vapor can form small
5 drops. The drops gather together to
form clouds. Within the clouds, the tiny
drops join together and grow. The big
6 drops fall to the ground as
precipitation—rain or snow. The water in the air that can become rain in warm temperatures can become snow and ice in cold temperatures.

Rain falls into oceans, lakes, and onto the ground. Rain falling on land flows into rivers and streams and back to the seas and lakes. Then the cycle starts over again.

Different parts of the United States receive different amounts of precipitation. The map below shows the average amount of precipitation in the different parts of the United States.

REVIEW Describe how water gets into the air. **Summarize**

MAP SKILL

Average Precipitation in a Year Throughout the United States

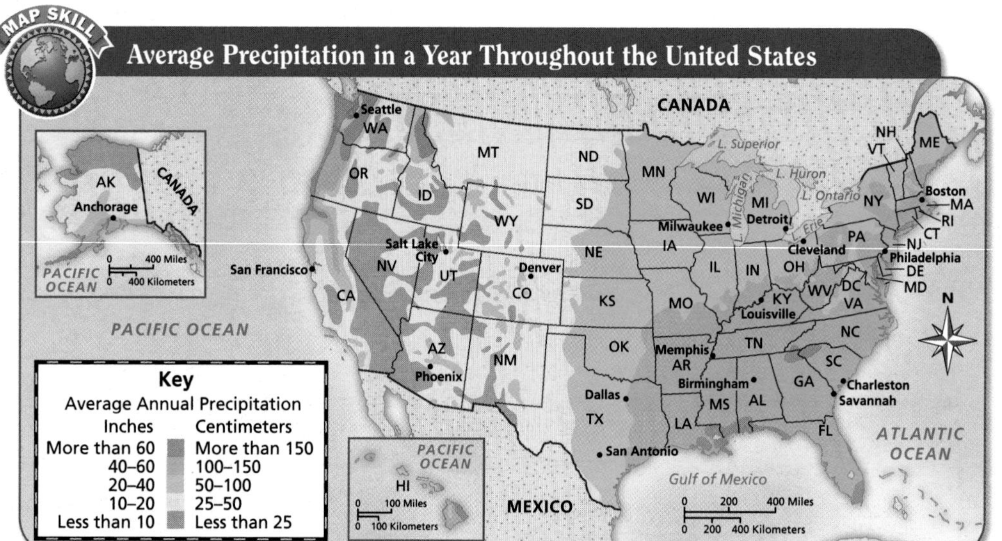

7 ▶ **Annual precipitation amounts vary from less than 10 inches to more than 60 inches.**

MAP SKILL Use a Map Key ***What is the average precipitation in centimeters in a year for Memphis?***

20

Practice and Extend

CURRICULUM CONNECTION
Science

Explore Meteorology

- Tell students that many professional weather forecasters are trained meteorologists.
- Have students research the definitions of *meteorology* (the study of weather) and *climatology* (the study of climates).
- Ask students to write a paragraph comparing and contrasting these two fields of science.

CURRICULUM CONNECTION
Writing

Celebrate Climate

- Have students write a poem about the climate of your region or some other region they have lived in or visited.
- Direct students to devote a stanza to each weather pattern they want to describe.
- Encourage students to include facts in each stanza of their poem.

What Causes Climate?

The climate of a place depends on its location. One factor is the distance a place is from the equator. The **equator** is an imaginary line that circles Earth halfway between the North and South Poles. The warmest
8 climates are in places nearest to the equator. These areas are usually warm all year.

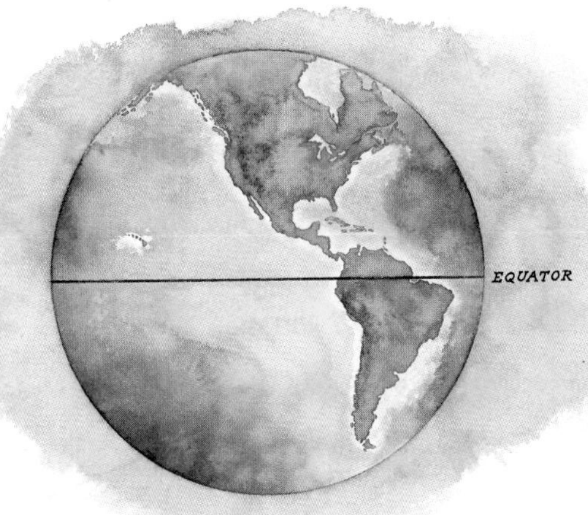
EQUATOR

A second factor that affects climate is how far a place is from a large body of water, such as an ocean. Places near an ocean usually have a milder climate than places far away from it. 9
Land heats and cools faster than water. So in summer, water is cooler than land, and cool air from above the water cools the land nearby. In winter, the land is colder and the water is warmer, so the air from above the water warms the land. A place such as the state of Kansas, which is far from an ocean, is not affected by large bodies of water as much as a state on the Pacific coast.

The third factor that affects climate is elevation. **Elevation** tells how high a place is above sea level. Mountain climates are generally colder because the temperature is lower the higher you go. Very high mountains can have snow and ice throughout the year. 10

REVIEW How does a place's location affect its climate?
Main Idea and Details

The Rain Cycle

In cool air, water vapor changes into small drops of water in clouds.
Sun
Cloud
Energy from the sun changes water into water vapor, an invisible gas in the air.
Water drops fall to Earth as rain or snow.
Lake

ACTIVATE PRIOR KNOWLEDGE
ESL Support

Apply Climate Words Help students relate climate concepts to places with which they are familiar.

Beginning Create flashcards with key terms from this lesson such as *humid, wet, dry, warm, cold, high, low, near water,* and *far from water.* Have students choose flashcards that describe their current community.

Intermediate Have students use key terms from this lesson to state one or two facts about the climate of a different country.

Advanced Have students create a two-column chart labeled *Community* and *Climate*. Then have them fill in the chart with details about the climate in their current community and two other communities.

For additional ESL support, use Every Student Learns Guide, pp. 6–9.

PAGE 21

What Causes Climate?

Quick Summary The climate of a place depends on its location—its distance from the equator, its distance from a large body of water, and its elevation.

8 **What parts of the earth have the coldest climates?** The places that are farthest from the equator, such as the North Pole and the South Pole
Make Inferences

✓ **Ongoing Assessment**

If... students have difficulty associating cold climates with distance from the equator,

then... point to a classroom globe or the picture on this page and ask, "If the warmest places are near the equator, where would the coldest places be?"

SOCIAL STUDIES STRAND
Science • Technology

Distance from a large body of water can affect weather as well as climate. That is one reason people often head to the ocean or a lake in the summertime.

9 **Boston and Worcester, Massachusetts, are about the same distance from the equator, but Boston is on the Atlantic Ocean, while Worcester is about 40 miles inland. Which city do you think will be warmer in summer? colder in winter?** Worcester; Worcester Apply Information

10 **Is it possible to find snow on a very tall mountain near the equator? Why or why not?** Yes; Because the temperature is lower the higher you go above sea level Draw Conclusions

✓ **REVIEW ANSWER** Climate is affected by distance from the equator, distance from a large body of water, and elevation. Main Idea and Details

PAGES 22–23

Types of Climates

Quick Summary The United States has many different climates: a few areas are tropical or subtropical; most are temperate; and parts of Alaska are subarctic or polar.

11 **If subtropical climates are near tropical climates, and subarctic climates are near polar climates, what might be another name for a polar climate?** An arctic climate
Make Inferences

12 **How might you describe a polar climate?** It is cold most of the year. The ground is covered with snow most of the year. Make Inferences

13 **What five types of climates can be found in the United States?** Tropical, subtropical, temperate, subarctic, and polar Summarize

MAP SKILL

Climate Areas of the United States

14 **What type of climate covers most of the United States?** Temperate
Analyze Maps

MAP SKILL Answer California

Types of Climates

The United States has many different climates. An area with a **tropical climate** is usually very warm all year. Places with tropical climates are near the equator. The rays of the sun strike Earth most directly in this area. In the United States only the southern tip of Florida and Hawaii have a tropical climate. Some areas have a subtropical climate, which is not as warm as a
11 tropical climate.

Areas around the North and South Poles have a **polar climate.** It is the coldest climate. A very small part of the United States, in Alaska, has a polar climate. Most parts of Alaska have a **subarctic climate** because they are closer to the North Pole. Warm periods in summer are short, and parts of the state are covered in snow for most of 12
the year.

▶ Palm trees grow in Hawaii's tropical climate.

MAP SKILL

Climate Areas of the United States

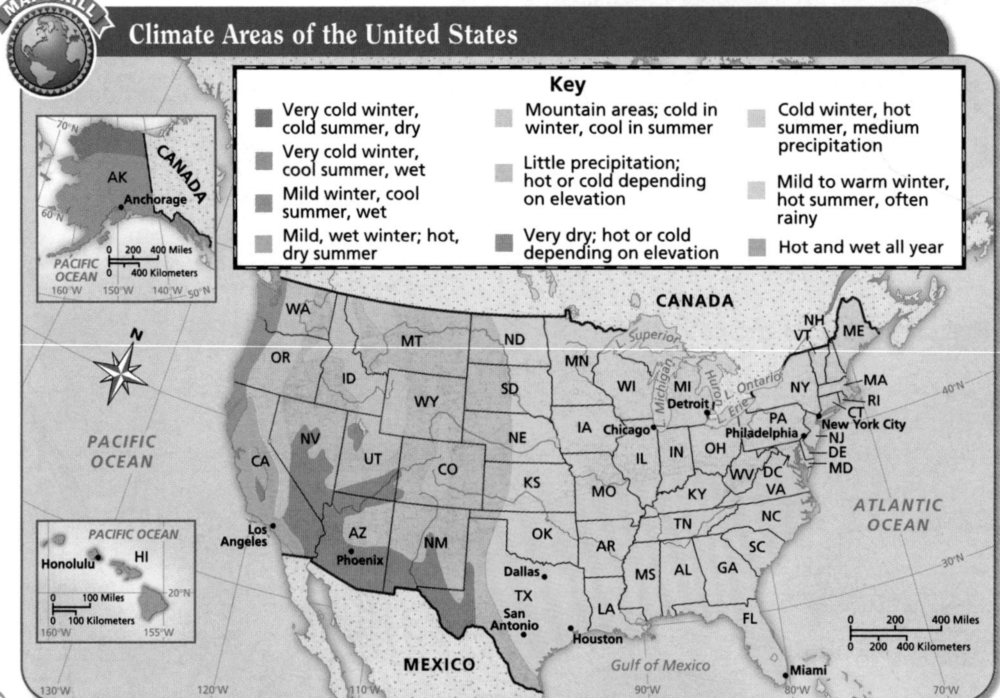

13
14 ▶ The climates in the United States range from very cold winters with cool and dry summers to areas that are hot and wet all year.

MAP SKILL Use a Climate Map ***What state has the greatest variety of climates?***

Practice and Extend

SOCIAL STUDIES
Background

About Climate Data

- The National Climatic Data Center, located in Asheville, North Carolina, is the world's largest active archive of weather data.
- Each year, the NCDC responds to over 170,000 requests for climate information from around the world. It is the world's main source of information on climate history.
- The NCDC has gathered climate information from individual observers and ships at sea for more than 100 years. It maintains more than 320 million paper records, 2.5 million microfiche records, 500,000 tapes, and satellite images dating back to 1960.
- In the United States, the NCDC is supported by six Regional Climate Centers as well as State Climate Offices in all 50 states and Puerto Rico.

Temperate climates are between the tropical and subarctic climates. Temperate climates are moderate in temperature, neither very hot nor very cold. The map shows some climate areas of the United States.

REVIEW Find your state's type of climate on the map. Now, find another state, far from yours. Make a list of the differences and similarities between the two climates. Compare and Contrast

Summarize the Lesson

- **Weather is the condition of the air at a certain time and place, and climate is the pattern of weather over a long period of time.**
- **Precipitation and temperature are factors of climate.**
- **Distance from the equator, distance from a large body of water, and elevation affect climate.**
- **The United States has many different climates.**

▶ **Snow covers the ground for most of the year in Alaska.**

LESSON 2 REVIEW

Check Facts and Main Ideas

1. Summarize On a separate sheet of paper, make a diagram like the one shown. Fill in some details of each type of climate.

A temperate climate is moderate. | A tropical climate is warm all year. | A polar climate is the coldest. | A subarctic climate has some warm periods.

→ The world has four major climates.

2. Write a sentence describing the difference between **weather** and climate.
3. Describe the variations in **climate** in each region of the United States.
4. What are the three main factors that affect climate?
5. **Critical Thinking: *Looking for Pictures*** Choose two photos from this lesson and write a description about the weather of each place.

Link to Science

Learn About Plants Some plants grow well in some climates but cannot grow in others. Choose a climate shown on the map. Use reference materials to find out about the plants that grow well in the climate you chose.

23

✓ **REVIEW ANSWER** Students should accurately compare and contrast their state's climate to the climate of another state. Compare and Contrast

3 Close and Assess

Summarize the Lesson

Have students take turns reading the four main points. Then ask students to turn each statement into a question and answer each question with their book closed.

✓ **LESSON 2 REVIEW**

1. Summarize For possible answers, see the reduced pupil page.
2. Weather is the condition of air at a certain time and place, and climate is the average weather in a place over a long period of time.
3. Possible answers: Northeast—cold winter, hot summer, medium precipitation; Southeast—mild to warm winter, hot summer, often rainy; Midwest——cold winter, hot summer, medium precipitation; Southwest—very dry, hot or cold depending on elevation; West—mountain areas; cold in winter, cool in summer
4. Distance from the equator, distance from a large body of water, and elevation

Test Talk

Write Your Answer to Score High

5. **Critical Thinking: *Looking for Pictures*** Students should make sure that their written answer is focused and detailed. Answers will vary but should include descriptive words about the weather.

Link to Science

Encourage students to use at least two reference sources, perhaps an encyclopedia and a field guide, to do their research.

ISSUES AND VIEWPOINTS
Critical Thinking

Analyze a Viewpoint

- Some scientists believe that the average temperature of Earth is rising—a process called *global warming*. Believed by some scientists to be caused mostly by the burning of fuels, global warming may lead to changes in climate.
- Have students research and explain some of the differing viewpoints regarding the theory of global warming.

Workbook, p. 4

Lesson 2: Climate

1. How are weather and climate alike? How are they different?
2. Summarize the cycle of water from oceans, rivers, streams, and lakes into the air and back to the sea.
3. What three major factors affect the climate of a place?
4. Identify and describe four basic types of climates and give an example of each.

Also on Teacher Resources CD-ROM.

Read Inset Maps

Objectives

- Identify the purpose of inset maps.
- Interpret information in inset maps.

Vocabulary

inset map, p. 24

Resource

- Workbook, p. 5

1 Introduce and Motivate

What is an inset map? Ask students why geographers might want to focus on a specific part of a map. (To show more detail about that part) Then have students read the **What?** section of text on p. 24 to help set the purpose of the lesson.

Why read inset maps? Have students read the **Why?** section of text on pp. 24–25. Then ask students what inset map they might include if they prepared a map of the school campus. Ask them why they might include the inset map. (Possible answers: Their classroom; To show greater detail)

2 Teach and Discuss

How is the skill used? Examine with students the main map and the inset maps on p. 24.

- Have students read the **How?** section of text on p. 25.
- Make sure students understand that the maps of Alaska and Hawaii use a scale different from the main map, and the distance between these states and the other states is not shown.
- Ask students where Alaska and Hawaii would appear on a map of the entire United States if there were no inset maps. (They would appear in their true locations, which would show the distance between Hawaii and Alaska and the other states.)

Map and Globe Skills

Read Inset Maps

What? Maps show a large area on a small piece of paper. For example, you might find a map of the entire world printed on a sheet of paper no bigger than a page in this book. A map usually has a scale that shows how real distance compares with the distance shown on the map.

Sometimes a map needs to show places in different scales. For instance, to show all 50 states of the United States can be tricky. That is because two states, Alaska and Hawaii, will not fit easily
1 on a map with the other 48 states. These two states can be shown in separate small maps. Each small map may have a separate scale. Such smaller maps that are related to the main map are called **inset maps.**

Why? Inset maps give information about places that are too large, too small, or too far away to be shown on the main map.

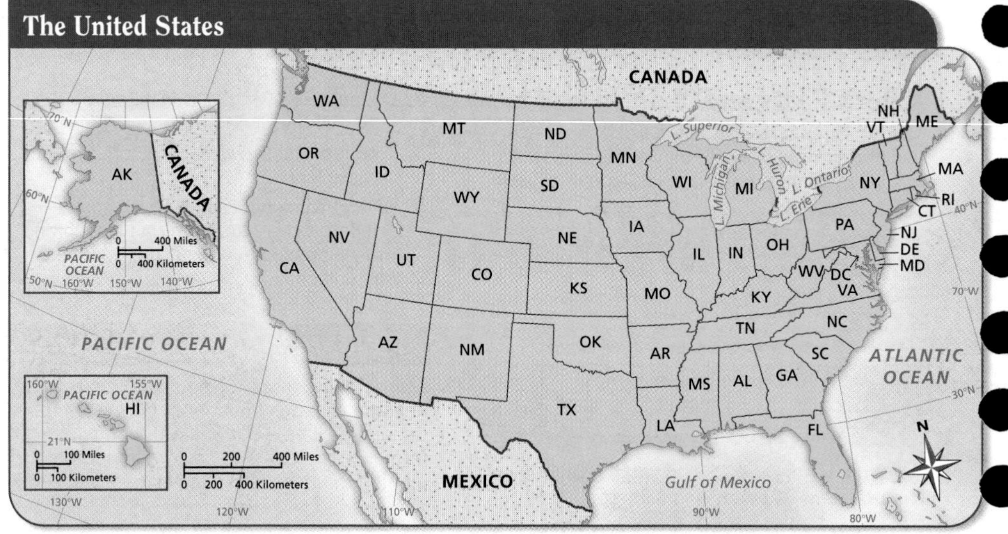

Practice and Extend

SOCIAL STUDIES STRAND
Geography

The following map resources are available:

- Big Book Atlas
- Student Atlas
- Outline Maps
- Desk Maps
- Map Resources CD-ROM

SOCIAL STUDIES STRAND
Geography

Examine Inset Maps Have students create a bulletin-board display of inset maps.

- If possible, include a community map that has an inset of a central business district, their school, or another special area.
- Include a state road map with insets of the major cities.
- As a class, examine the maps, discussing scale, the purpose of inset maps, and the relationship between inset maps and main maps.

For more information, go online to the *Atlas* at **www.sfsocialstudies.com.**

Some inset maps show how places relate to one another. This type of map might locate a country in a continent or a state within a region. Other inset maps give extra details. For example, a close-up map of a downtown section of a city can give details about the
2 city that cannot be shown on the
3 main map.

How? To read an inset map, first examine the main map. Notice its topic and its scale. Then study the inset map. Figure out how the inset map is related to the main map. Does it show a larger area? a smaller area? a distant area? What can you learn from the inset map that you could not find out from the main map?

Think and Apply

1. What does the main map on page 24 show? What do the **inset maps** show?
2. Why do you think the mapmaker decided to show the inset maps?
3. What other inset maps might be useful for a person looking at the main map?

The United States

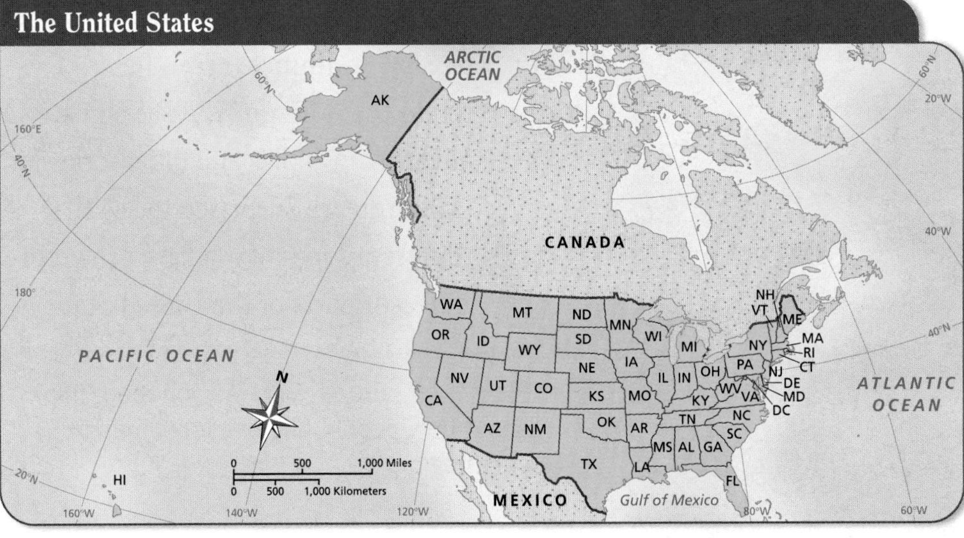

1 **Why would a map of the United States need to be much bigger if Alaska and Hawaii were shown on the main map rather than on an inset map?** Because Alaska and Hawaii are far away from the other 48 states **Analyze Information**

2 **How might you show detail about a state park while still showing where the park is located in the state?** Show a main map of the state and an inset map of the park. **Apply Information**

3 **What is the purpose of an inset map?** The purpose of the inset map is to give information about places that are too large, too small, or too far away to be shown on the main map. **Summarize**

3 Close and Assess

Think and Apply

1. The continental United States; Alaska and Hawaii
2. So the main map would not have to be large enough to include Alaska and Hawaii in their actual locations
3. Possible answers: A map of a specific state; a map of Washington, D.C., or another major city; a map of a major landform such as one of the Great Lakes or the Appalachian Mountains

CURRICULUM CONNECTION
Math

Use Scale

- Have students estimate the approximate size of the school grounds and main building(s).
- Have students create a map of the school grounds and building(s). Remind them to include a map scale.
- Ask students to add an inset map of a specific area of the school using a different scale.
- Have students explain to their classmates the scale they used in the main map and the scale they used in the inset.

Workbook, p. 5

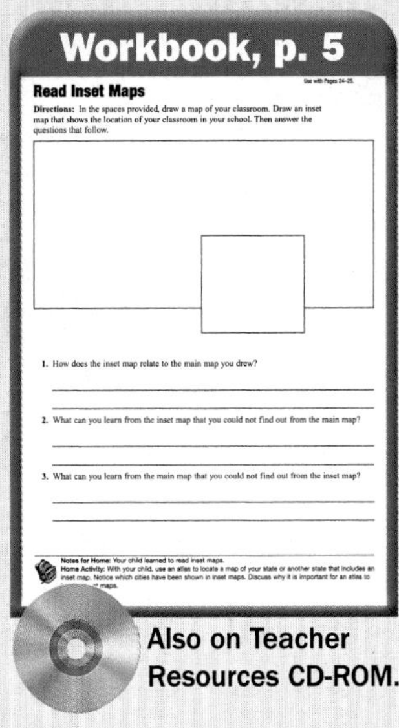
Read Inset Maps

1. How does the inset map relate to the main map you drew?
2. What can you learn from the inset map that you could not find out from the main map?
3. What can you learn from the main map that you could not find out from the inset map?

Also on Teacher Resources CD-ROM.

Regional Resources

Objectives

- Explain how each region's resources shaped the industries that grew there.
- Explain the difference between renewable and nonrenewable resources.
- Describe resources of the student's own region.
- Explain how people can be considered resources.

Vocabulary

natural resource, p. 27; **raw material,** p. 27; **process,** p. 27; **harvest,** p. 27; **industry,** p. 28; **manufacturing,** p. 28; **product,** p. 28; **capital resource,** p. 28; **agriculture,** p. 28; **conserve,** p. 29; **renewable resource,** p. 29; **recycle,** p. 29; **nonrenewable resource,** p. 29; **human resources,** p. 31; **service,** p. 31

Resources

- Workbook, p. 6
- Transparency 1
- Every Student Learns Guide, pp. 10–13
- Quick Study, pp. 6–7

Quick Teaching Plan

If time is short, have students use the vocabulary list on p. 26 as a study outline.

- Tell students to watch for the vocabulary words as they read the lesson independently and to record a definition for each as they read.

1 Introduce and Motivate

Preview Ask students to name important businesses in their state. Explain that these businesses depend on resources in the region. Tell students they will learn more about resources as they read Lesson 3.

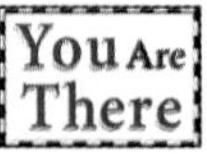

Ask students if they have ever taken a cross-country trip. What sights did they see while traveling through different regions?

LESSON 3

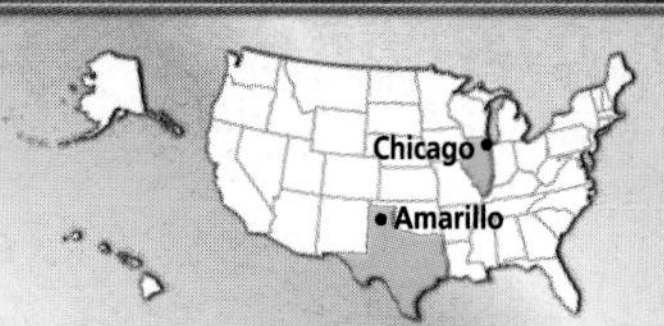

PREVIEW

Focus on the Main Idea
Each region has special resources.

VOCABULARY
natural resource
raw material
process
harvest
industry
manufacturing
product
capital resource
agriculture
conserve
renewable resource
recycle
nonrenewable resource
human resources
service

Regional Resources

A huge herd of brown cattle thunders by you for what seems like a full five minutes. You and your family are driving by a cattle ranch just outside of Amarillo, Texas. You are on the first leg of a long car trip to Chicago, Illinois. This is the first long trip you have ever taken, and boy, are you excited! In central Oklahoma, you see huge fields of golden wheat that ripple in the wind. You pass a farm in Missouri where pigs run to the fence to watch your car pass by. In Illinois, green fields of corn stretch to the horizon. You see signs advertising apples and blueberries for sale. You are surprised to see that different types of food are grown in different parts of the United States.

Main Idea and Details As you read, think about how people use the resources in each region.

Practice and Extend

READING SKILL
Main Idea and Details

In the Lesson Review, students complete a graphic organizer like the one below. You may want to provide students with a copy of Transparency 1 to complete as they read the lesson.

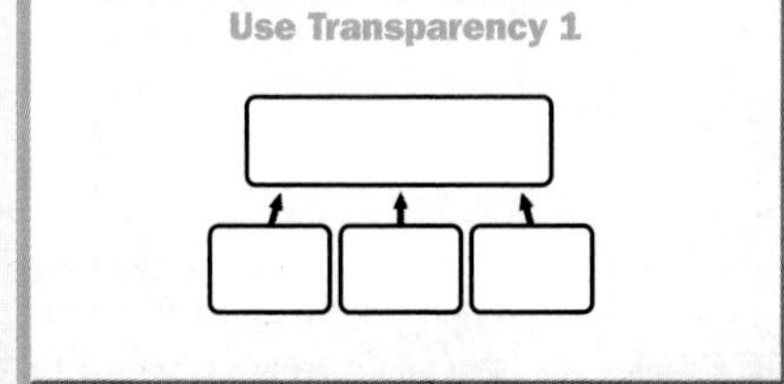

VOCABULARY
Related Word Study

One can often determine a word's meaning by examining prefixes and suffixes. Explain that the prefix *re-* means "once more, again," then ask what students think *renew* means (new again). (You may also wish to point out the use of *re-* in *recycle*.) Point out that the suffix *-able* means "can be done," then ask what *renewable* means (can be made new again). Finally, relate that *non-* means "not." Then ask what *nonrenewable* means (cannot be made new again).

Natural Resources

You have read about the landforms and climates that make each of the five United States regions special. Each region also has materials known as natural resources. A **natural resource** is something in the environment that people can use. Forests, soil, water, and plants are
1 examples of natural resources.

We can turn natural resources into raw materials. **Raw materials** are natural resources that have been
2 changed or **processed** so that people can use them to make other products. For example, we can change an oak tree, which is a natural resource, into lumber, which is a raw material. Then the lumber can be used to build homes or furniture. 3

Some farmers in the Midwest and Southwest grow wheat. When the wheat is **harvested,** or cut for use, it is not ready to be eaten or sold to grocery stores. The wheat is a raw material that is processed into flour. The flour is then used to make such food items as bread, cake, and pancakes.

In the picture below look at all the various raw materials used to make a breakfast.

REVIEW Why are natural resources turned into raw materials?
Main Idea and Details

4

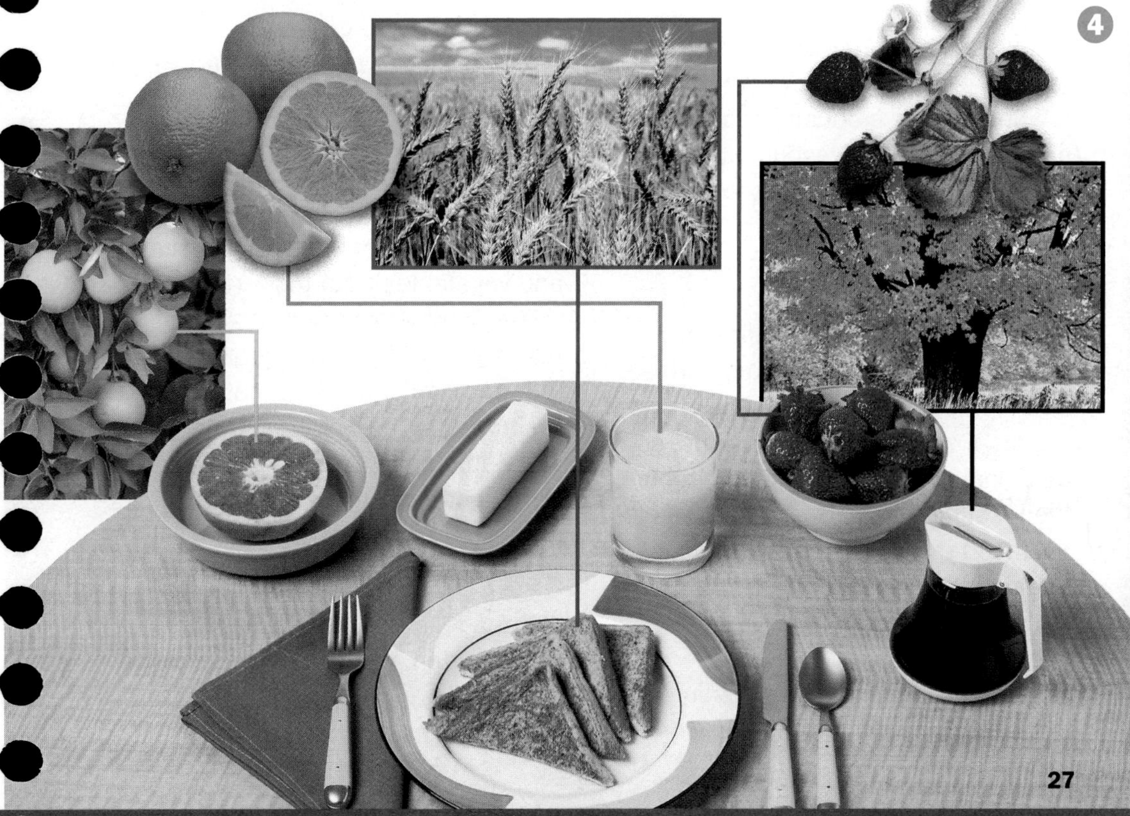

27

2 Teach and Discuss

PAGE 27

Natural Resources

Quick Summary Each region of the United States has natural resources. These resources can be turned into raw materials that can, in turn, be used to make other products.

SOCIAL STUDIES STRAND
Economics

Natural resources come from the environment—the land, water, or even the sky.

1 **What are two examples of natural resources that come from the land?** Possible answers: Trees and soil Main Idea and Details

2 **How do raw materials become the products we use?** They are processed. Main Idea and Details

3 **What must happen to oak trees before they can be used to build furniture or homes?** They must be processed into lumber. Sequence

✓ **REVIEW ANSWER** Possible answer: To make them easier to use in the creation of different products Main Idea and Details

4 **Does your home state produce any of the products shown in the picture of breakfast foods?** Possible answers: Local farms produce wheat, which is processed into flour, which is then used to make bread. Analyze Pictures

FYI SOCIAL STUDIES
Background

About Natural Resources

- Laws define who owns natural resources in the United States.
- In the East, those who own lands on a stream can take water from it. In the West, "prior appropriation"—those who used it first—is a factor in determining water rights.
- In the United States, minerals generally belong to the landowner. The General Mining Law of 1872 gives some mineral rights on federal lands to those willing to extract the minerals.

PAGE 28

Using Resources

Quick Summary The resources in each region help shape the businesses and industries that grow there.

Decision Making

5 **If you wanted to start a business in an area that has dense forests, what type of business might you start? Why?** Possible answers: Lumber business; paper mill; any type of business that uses wood; Because wood is readily available in the area Make Decisions

6 **Name two industries that are found in the Northeast.** Fishing and manufacturing Analyze Information

7 **What crops are grown in the Southeast? Why might these crops grow well there?** Cotton, sugarcane, and rice; The crops need warm weather to grow, and the Southeast has a warm climate. Main Idea and Details

8 **How did the natural resources of the Southwest affect the industries that developed there?** The cattle industry and oil manufacturing industry grew in the Southwest because of the plentiful grazing areas and the presence of oil in the region. Cause and Effect

✓ **REVIEW ANSWER** Possible answers: Trees: lumber; Cotton: cloth; Livestock: meat products; Fertile fields: crops Draw Conclusions

Using Resources

5 The resources in each region helped shape the businesses that grew there. The Northeast region was the nation's first center of industry. An **industry** is a form of business. For example, manufacturing is an industry. **Manufacturing** means making products to sell. **Products** are things that people make or grow.

When making products, people also need to use capital resources. **Capital resources** are things that people make in order to produce products. Tools, machines, and factory buildings are capital resources.

Manufacturing is important in the Northeast, but other industries are as well. Some parts of the Northeast are too rocky and hilly for large farms, so other industries have been built around the resources of the region. Fishing is an important industry along the coast. Coal is a natural resource also found in the Northeast, so industries that
6 use coal developed there.

Soil is a valuable natural resource. In the Southeast, many people work in agriculture. **Agriculture** is using the soil to raise crops or animals. In the Southeast, farmers grow crops such as sugar cane, cotton and rice. These crops grow well in the warm climate. 7 Cotton grown in the region is processed into cloth and then manufactured into clothing.

The fertile soil of the Midwest plains makes this region a great place to grow large crops of corn, soybeans, and wheat. Many people in the region raise cows and hogs. From the cows' milk, people make dairy products, such as cheese and butter. The Midwest also has large cities with manufacturing and other industries.

People moved to the West in search of silver, gold, and other valuable metals. Today, resources in the West include cattle that graze on the grassy plains; timber from the thick forests; fish from the ocean; and fruits, nuts, and vegetables from the fertile valleys.

The Southwest region has wide-open plains where cattle also graze. Cotton grows in its fields. Major natural resources of the Southwest are oil and natural gas. Many factories were built there to manufacture products from these resources. 8

REVIEW How might people use the following resources: trees, cotton, cattle, and fertile fields? Draw Conclusions

28

Practice and Extend

ISSUES AND VIEWPOINTS
Critical Thinking

Reduce, Reuse, Recycle

Explain to students that there are different ways to conserve resources. They might *reduce,* or cut down on, the number of resources they use; *reuse,* or use again, a resource that someone has already used; or *recycle,* or reprocess a resource into the same or a different product. Have students use this information to answer the following questions.

- Which type of conservation saves the most resources?
- Which type of conservation creates new kinds of industries?
- Which type of conservation do thrift shops and antique stores practice most?
- How do you think people might use each type of conservation in their everyday lives?

CURRICULUM CONNECTION
Drama

Personify a Region

- Divide the class into five groups and assign each group a region of the United States.
- Tell group members to work together to prepare a short speech entitled "I Am the (Region)." In the speech, have them identify the landforms, climates, and resources of their region.
- Have students take turns reading lines from their speech.
- Encourage them to use visuals as they present their speech.

Renewable and Nonrenewable Resources

▶ Oil is pumped from the ground.

"Close the refrigerator door!" "Turn off the lights when you leave!" Did you ever hear people say these things? They want to conserve resources. **Conserve** means to use resources carefully.

Some of the natural resources you've just read about are renewable and some are not. A **renewable resource** can be replaced. When we cut down trees to build houses or make furniture, we can plant more trees. Trees are renewable resources. But trees take a long time to grow, so
9 we have to conserve them.

Soil and water are also renewable resources. We can use the same soil over and over to plant crops if we keep the soil nourished. Water is reused too. As you learned in the previous lesson, water rises into the air and then falls back down as rain. Just as we must conserve trees, we must be careful with soil and water. All of our renewable resources can be damaged by pollution. Pollution can make water dirty, harm trees and other plants, and damage soil. 10

We can recycle resources as well as conserve them. **Recycle** means to use something again. People recycle 11 materials such as paper, metal and plastic.

Nonrenewable resources cannot be replaced. There is a limited amount of each nonrenewable resource. When this type of resource runs out, there is no more.

Fuels such as coal, natural gas, and oil are nonrenewable resources. These fuels can be burned to make the energy we use to heat and light our homes, move our cars, and cook our food. Since these fuels are nonrenewable resources, it is important to conserve them by walking sometimes instead of driving, turning off lights we're not using, and closing the refrigerator door. 12

REVIEW Why should you try to conserve resources? Draw Conclusions

29

PAGE 29

Renewable and Nonrenewable Resources

Quick Summary Renewable resources can be replaced; nonrenewable resources cannot. Both can be protected, conserved, and recycled.

9 **If trees are a renewable resource, why might people choose to conserve them?** Because they take a long time to grow **Main Idea and Details**

10 **Why should people be careful to prevent pollution?** Because pollution can make water dirty, harm trees and other plants, and damage soil **Main Idea and Details**

11 **Why might people choose to recycle as well as conserve?** Because new items can be made from used materials **Make Inferences**

Problem Solving

12 **How do both renewable and nonrenewable resources become more scarce? How can people prevent this problem?** People use too much of the resources; By conserving and recycling the resources **Solve Problems**

✓ **REVIEW ANSWER** Possible answer: Because, if a resource runs out, we might not be able to make certain types of products that we need or want **Draw Conclusions**

ACCESS CONTENT

ESL Support

Examine Abstract Concepts Help students understand the concepts of renewable and nonrenewable resources.

Beginning Help students work in pairs to create a two-column resources chart labeled *Renewable* and *Nonrenewable.* Then have them draw pictures or write words to complete the chart with resources described in this section.

Intermediate Have pairs of students do research in the library to make a list of renewable and nonrenewable resources.

Advanced Have students complete the intermediate activity and then share their findings with the class.

For additional ESL support, use Every Student Learns Guide, pp. 10–13.

PAGE 30

What About Your Region?

Quick Summary Maps, books, encyclopedias, the Internet, and people are all sources that contain information about regions.

13 **What sources might you use to find out information about your region?** Maps, encyclopedias, the Internet, people in the community, books
Main Idea and Details

✓ **REVIEW ANSWER** Possible answer: It can help me organize important information about my region.
Summarize

FACT FILE
My Region

14 **Name one other state that is located in the same region as your state.** Students should accurately identify another state in their region.
Analyze Information

✓ **Ongoing Assessment**

If... students are not able to name another state within their region,	**then...** have them use the map of the United States and its regions on p. 11 to locate a state in their region.

15 **Do you think all of your classmates will name the same three landforms for your region? Why or why not?** Possible answer: No; Because there are many different landforms in my region
Draw Conclusions

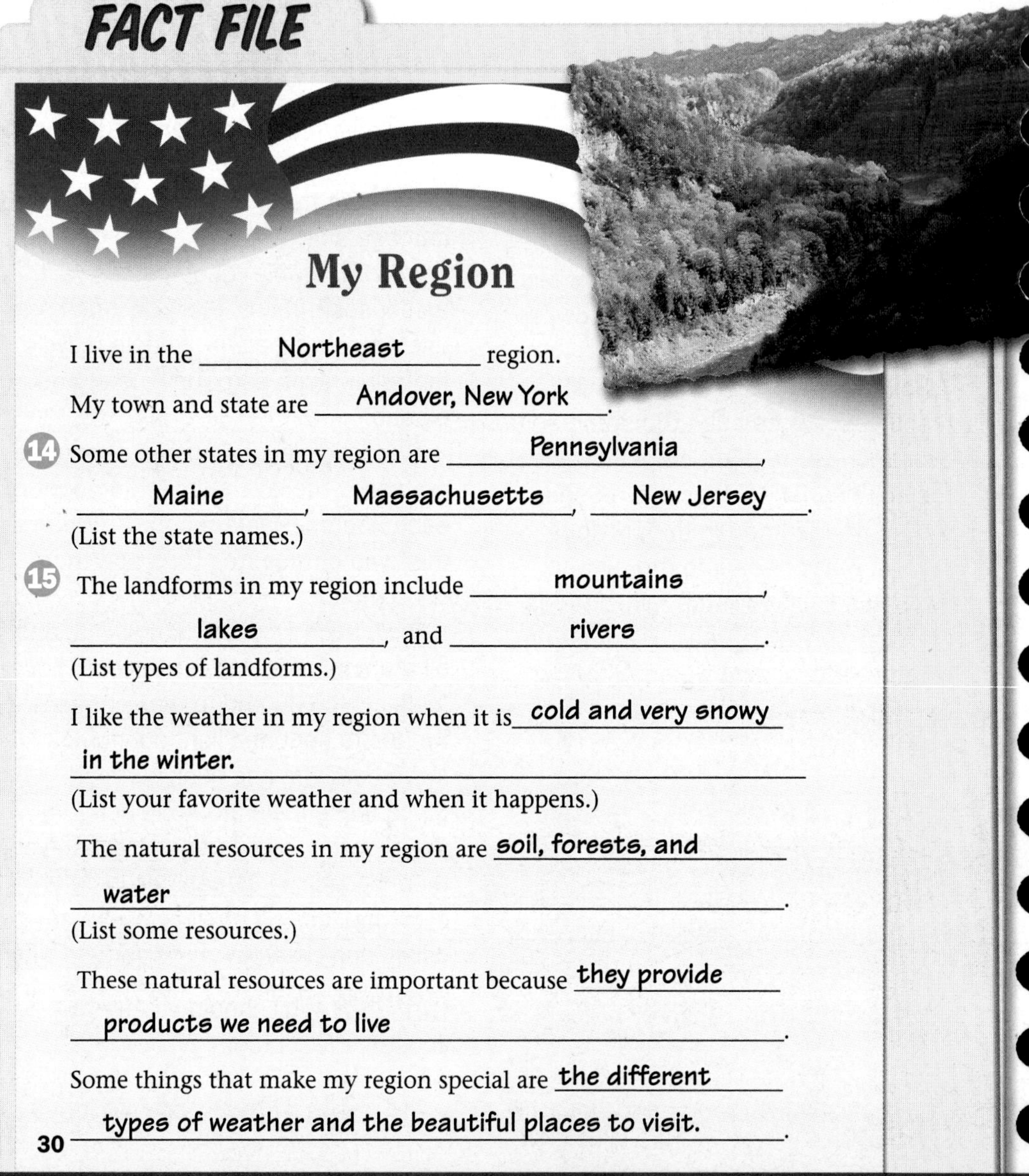

What About Your Region?

Use the information from this chapter and other sources, such as maps, encyclopedias, the Internet, people in your community, and books to fill out a form like the one below. 13

Then choose another region you would like to visit and explain why you would like to visit it and what you would do there.

REVIEW How can a form like the one below help you summarize facts about your region? Summarize

FACT FILE

My Region

I live in the Northeast region.

My town and state are Andover, New York.

14 Some other states in my region are Pennsylvania, Maine, Massachusetts, New Jersey.
(List the state names.)

15 The landforms in my region include mountains, lakes, and rivers.
(List types of landforms.)

I like the weather in my region when it is cold and very snowy in the winter.
(List your favorite weather and when it happens.)

The natural resources in my region are soil, forests, and water.
(List some resources.)

These natural resources are important because they provide products we need to live.

Some things that make my region special are the different types of weather and the beautiful places to visit.

30

Practice and Extend

MEETING INDIVIDUAL NEEDS
Learning Styles

Explore Your Region Allow students to use their individual learning styles to learn more about their region.

Logical Learning Have students collect statistical information about their state or region and present their data in circle graphs or bar graphs. For example, students might research how many people work in various industries or how weather and climate vary throughout the year.

Artistic Learning Have students create a collage that visually expresses the unique qualities of their region.

Auditory Learning Have students collect quotations from family and friends telling what is interesting about their region.

A Most Valuable Resource

You have read about natural and capital resources. Another very important resource is all around you, and is found in every region. **Human resources** are the people who make products or provide services. **Services**
16 are jobs that people do for others.

People do service work everywhere. Teaching, repairing things, taking care of people, delivering products, and building houses are some kinds of service work.

REVIEW List some examples of service work. Main Idea and Details

Summarize the Lesson

- **A natural resource is something from the environment that people can use.**
- **Each region has special resources.**
- **Renewable resources can be replaced and nonrenewable resources cannot.**
- **People use capital resources to make products and provide services.**
- **Human resources are people who make products or provide services.**

LESSON 3 REVIEW

Check Facts and Main Ideas

1. Main Idea and Details On a separate sheet of paper, make a diagram like the one below. Fill in the main idea.

Agriculture is important across the United States.

- Southeastern and Southwestern farmers grow cotton.
- Midwestern farmers grow corn and wheat.
- Western farmers grow fruits, nuts, and vegetables.

2. Why are people considered resources?
3. What is the difference between a **renewable** and a **nonrenewable resource?**
4. What resources are found in your region?
5. **Critical Thinking:** ***Make Inferences*** How do all the resources in a region help **industries** develop and grow?

Link to Writing

Write a Business Plan Suppose that you are going to start a small company that manufactures a simple product. What resources will you need? Write a plan that describes all the resources you will use and how you plan to make the product. Use the words **manufacture** and **product** in your business plan.

MEETING INDIVIDUAL NEEDS
Leveled Practice

Celebrate Human Resources Have students compile a display of human resources at school.

Easy Have students either find photos and magazine pictures or draw pictures of people who provide services in your school. **Reteach**

On-Level Have students write captions for each of the pictures, identifying the name and title of each person and the service he or she provides. **Extend**

Challenge Have students interview the people and add excerpts to the display. **Enrich**

For a Lesson Summary, use Quick Study, p. 6.

Workbook, p. 6

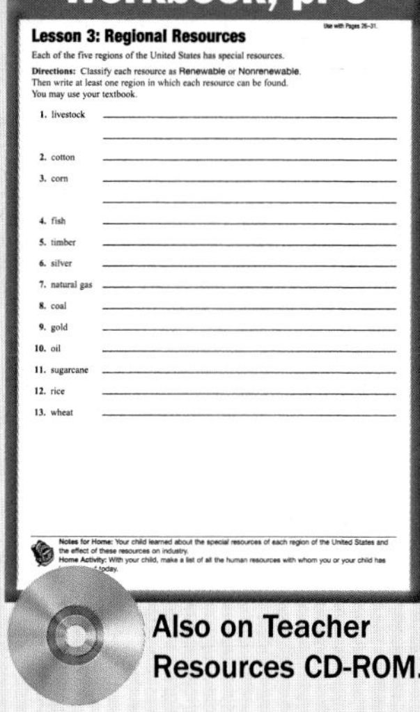

Lesson 3: Regional Resources

Each of the five regions of the United States has special resources.

Directions: Classify each resource as Renewable or Nonrenewable. Then write at least one region in which each resource can be found. You may use your textbook.

1. livestock
2. cotton
3. corn
4. fish
5. timber
6. silver
7. natural gas
8. coal
9. gold
10. oil
11. sugarcane
12. rice
13. wheat

Also on Teacher Resources CD-ROM.

A Most Valuable Resource

Quick Summary Human resources are the people who make products or provide services.

16 **How are people like other types of resources? How are they different?** Possible answers: Alike: both natural resources and human resources are used to make things; Different: natural resources are used for raw materials; people have skills. Compare and Contrast

✓ **REVIEW ANSWER** Possible answers: Teaching, performing health-care work, repairing things Main Idea and Details

3 Close and Assess

Summarize the Lesson

Have students read the main points of the lesson. Then ask students to list specific examples of resources for each point.

✓ **LESSON 3 REVIEW**

1. **Main Idea and Details** For possible answers, see the reduced pupil page.
2. Possible answer: People are valuable resources because they can make products and provide services.
3. A renewable resource can be replaced, but a nonrenewable resource cannot be replaced.
4. Answers should reflect natural, capital, and human resources available in your students' home region.
5. **Critical Thinking: *Make Inferences*** Industries are often set up in a region where the natural resources and workers are available. The growth of these industries often encourages the development of other industries.

Link to Writing

You may wish to have students choose a product made from natural resources available in their home region. Business plans should use the words *product* and *manufacture* correctly.

Dorling Kindersley

The United States and North America

Objective

- Identify landforms, climates, and resources in the United States and North America.

1 Introduce and Motivate

- Remind students that landforms and climates are not bound by the national, state, or regional borders that humans have determined.
- As a class examine the map on this page. Ask volunteers to name landforms that stretch across at least one such border.
- Point out that when places have similar landforms, they often have similar climates and resources. For example, many places near the Rocky Mountains have cool climates and large forests.
- Have students choose two similar landforms on the map and list what these two areas might have in common.

2 Teach and Discuss

1 Look at the map on this page. How can you tell where the Rocky Mountains and Appalachian Mountains are located? Possible answers: They look like bumpy areas on the map; they are labeled **Interpret Maps**

DORLING KINDERSLEY CHILDREN'S ATLAS

The United States and North America

The major landforms of the United States extend to its neighbors in North America. Mountains and plains reach north into Canada and south into Mexico. Huge chains of mountains run down the eastern and western sides of North America. The Appalachian Mountains are on the east, and the Rocky Mountains are on the west. Between the mountains, the land is mostly flat. The northern areas have large forests, while the central parts of the Great Plains are covered with flat, grassy lands.

Each region within the United States has its own types of landforms and range of climates. Climate and resources affect all the living things within a region. People use the resources in many ways.

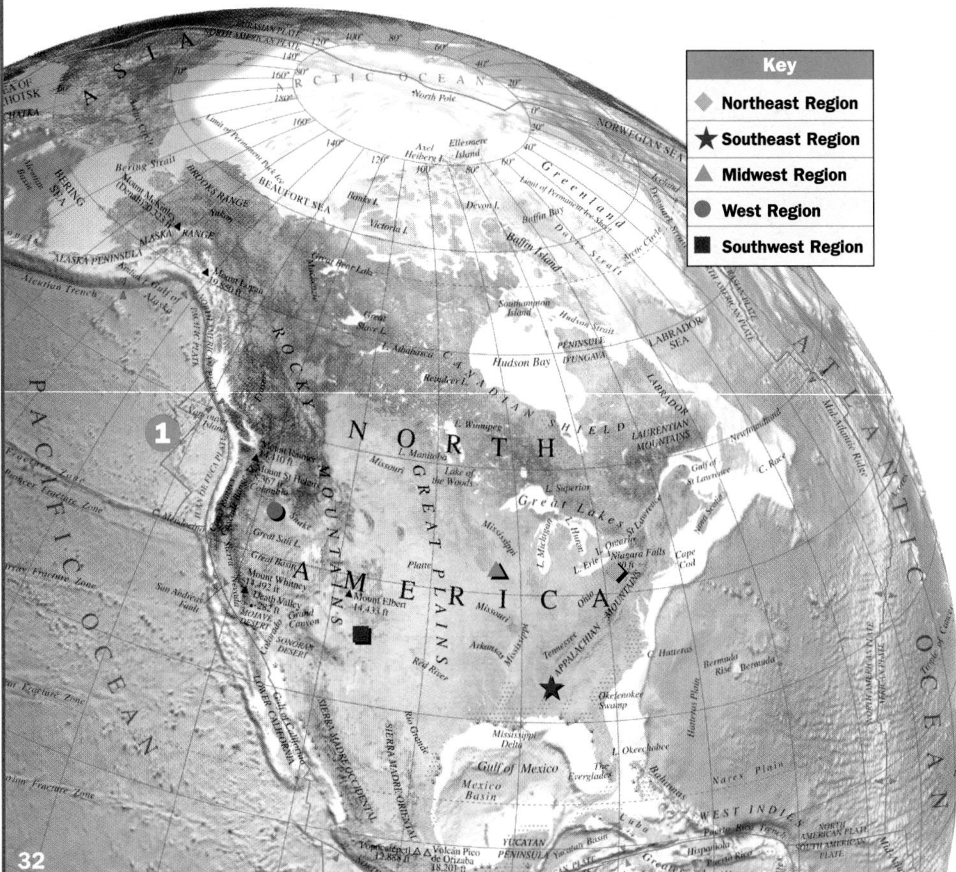

32

Practice and Extend

SOCIAL STUDIES
Background

About Atlases

- Tell students that this map of North America was taken from an atlas. Explain that an atlas is a book of maps that may include illustrations, tables, or other related information.
- Point out that *atlas* also has another meaning. According to Greek mythology, Atlas was a giant who supported the heavens on his shoulders. You may wish to show students a picture of Atlas.
- Tell students that early mapmakers often put a picture of this Greek god on the front pages of their books. That is how books of maps came to be known as atlases.
- You may wish to have students examine the Building Geography Skills section at the front of their book and the Atlas at the end of their book.

West

● **The Pacific Coast**
Waves crash along the rocky coast of Oregon. 4

West

● **Big Cities**
Its climate and resources have brought many people to Los Angeles. The parts of the city and surrounding areas are linked together by a system of roads.

Southwest

■ **Homes Made of Clay**
Many homes in Taos, New Mexico are built of sun-dried clay brick, called adobe. The Pueblo people lived in this region a thousand years ago. They used the resources of the area to build homes. 5

Southwest

■ **Carved by the Wind**
These strangely shaped rocks are in Monument Valley, Arizona. They have been carved by the wind.

Midwest

▲ **Faces on the Hills**
The heads of four great American presidents—George Washington, Thomas Jefferson, Theodore Roosevelt, and Abraham Lincoln—have been carved onto Mount Rushmore in South Dakota.

Midwest

▲ **Water Birds**
Many types of water birds, like this loon, spend the summer on the quiet lakes of Minnesota. 3

Midwest

▲ **Prairie Lands**
Flat land, fertile soil, and hot summers make the Midwest prairies ideal for farming. 2

Southeast

★ **Wetlands**
The beautiful Okefenokee Swamp is a large wetland in Georgia. Its warm climate makes it a comfortable home for many animals, including alligators and snakes.

Southeast

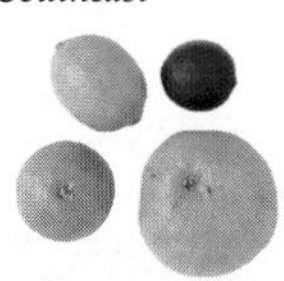

★ **Growing Fruit**
Florida and other parts of the Southeast have the right climate for growing citrus fruits. Farmers send their oranges, grapefruits, limes, and lemons all over the country.

Northeast

◆ **The Atlantic Coast**
Towns like this grew near the coast of the Atlantic Ocean. People who live here often use the resources of the sea. 4

Northeast

◆ **Traditional Farming**
Amish people live on this farm in Pennsylvania. They do not use any modern technology.

Southeast

★ **King Cotton**
The climate and soil of the Southeast are good for growing cotton. Large cotton farms can be seen in parts of the Southeast.

33

WEB SITE
Technology

Students can learn more about the states, communities, and landforms discussed on these pages by clicking on *Atlas* at **www.sfsocialstudies.com.**

2 What are three things that can make an area ideal for farming? Possible answers: Flat land, fertile soil, warm climate **Main Idea and Details**

3 What parts of the United States and North America might have wildlife similar to that found on the lakes of Minnesota? Possible answers: Other lakes, the Great Lakes, some Canadian lakes, parts of the wetlands of Georgia and Florida **Draw Conclusions**

4 What landforms and resources might parts of the Pacific coast and Atlantic coast have in common? Possible answer: Certain types of sea life **Compare and Contrast**

5 What types of resources did the people of Taos, New Mexico, use to build homes? Why did they not use trees? Sun-dried clay brick, called adobe; Possible answer: There are few trees in that area. **Make Inferences**

3 Close and Assess

- Have students refer to the lists they created earlier. Ask them if they might be able to add items to their lists after reading pp. 32–33.
- Have students use the Internet or print resources to research the characteristics of their chosen type of landform.
- Have students add information to their lists based on their research and what they read on these pages.

CHAPTER 1 REVIEW

Resources

- Assessment Book, pp. 1–4
- Workbook, p. 7: Vocabulary Review

Chapter Summary

For possible answers, see the reduced pupil page.

Vocabulary

1. e, **2.** c, **3.** l, **4.** g, **5.** i, **6.** a, **7.** b, **8.** j, **9.** k, **10.** h, **11.** f, **12.** d

CHAPTER 1 Review

Chapter Summary

Summarize

Target Skill

On a separate sheet of paper, make a diagram like the one shown. Fill in details about landforms in two more regions in the United States.

The West has the highest mountain and the lowest place.

The Northeast has part of the oldest mountain range.

The Southwest has deserts and canyons.

Each region has certain landforms.

Vocabulary

Match each word with the correct definition or description.

1. **boundary** (p. 14)
2. **region** (p. 11)
3. **plateau** (p. 13)
4. **desert** (p. 13)
5. **canyon** (p. 13)
6. **plain** (p. 12)
7. **climate** (p. 19)
8. **precipitation** (p. 19)
9. **humidity** (p. 20)
10. **elevation** (p. 21)
11. **capital resources** (p. 28)
12. **renewable resource** (p. 29)

a. a large area of flat land, often with grass

b. the pattern of a place's weather over time

c. an area with similar characteristics

d. a resource that can be replaced

e. a line or natural feature that divides one area from another

f. the things people make in order to produce products

g. an area that gets very little rain

h. how high a place is above sea level

i. a deep valley with steep rocky hills

j. the amount of rain or snow that falls

k. the amount of moisture in the air

l. a large, flat, raised area of land

34

Practice and Extend

Assessment Options

✓ Chapter 1 Assessment

- Chapter 1 Content Test: Use Assessment Book, pp. 1–2.
- Chapter 1 Skills Test: Use Assessment Book, pp. 3–4.

TEST PREP Standardized Test Prep

- Chapter 1 Tests contain standardized test format.

✓ Chapter 1 Performance Assessment

- Have students work in small groups to review information in this chapter.
- On an outline map of the United States, have students label each region and color each in a different color.
- Have students take turns adding details about landforms, climate, resources, or other information to each region of the map.

Facts and Main Ideas

1. What are the five regions of the United States?
2. What are three climate types?
3. Why do people try to conserve resources?
4. **Main Idea** What are some differences between the types of land in each region?
5. **Main Idea** How is climate affected by location?
6. **Main Idea** What are three main kinds of resources?
7. **Critical Thinking: *Ask Questions*** Write two questions about regions in the United States. Then write a short list of sources you might use to find answers.

Write About Geography

1. **Write a Region Riddle** Suppose that you are one of the United States regions. Without giving the name of the region, write a few hints. For example, if you were the West you could write, "I am the region with the tallest mountain." Exchange riddles with a classmate.
2. **Write an advertisement** for a particular place in the United States. Use illustrations and pictures from magazines to make your advertisement appealing.
3. **Write a travel article** explaining why someone should visit a region of your choice. Include locations you think are the most interesting.

Apply Skills

Use an Inset Map

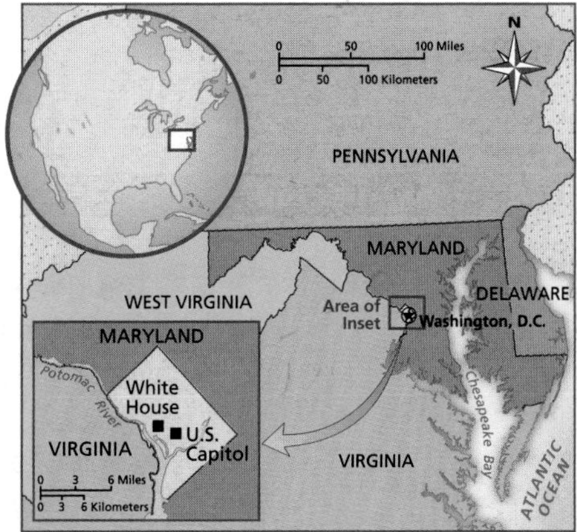

1. What is shown on the large map?
2. What is shown on the square inset map?
3. What is shown on the circular locator map?

Internet Activity

To get help with vocabulary and terms, select the dictionary or encyclopedia from *Social Studies Library* at **www.sfsocialstudies.com.**

Hands-on Unit Project

Unit 1 Performance Assessment

- See p. 94 for information about using the Unit Project as a means of performance assessment.
- A scoring guide is provided on p. 94.

WEB SITE Technology

For more information, students can select the dictionary or encyclopedia from *Social Studies Library* at **www.sfsocialstudies.com.**

Workbook, p. 7

Vocabulary Review Use with Chapter 1.

Directions: Circle the vocabulary term that best completes each sentence. You may use your textbook.

1. A line or natural feature that divides one area from another or one state from another is a (boundary, plain, desert).
2. Manufacturing is an important (process, elevation, industry), or form of business, in the Northeast region.
3. A (region, natural resource, landform) is a natural feature on Earth's surface, such as a mountain or a river.
4. A (mountain, plateau, canyon) is a deep valley with steep rocky walls.
5. A tree is a (renewable resource, nonrenewable resource, product) because it can be replaced.
6. A pilot checks the (recycle, humidity, weather), or the condition of the air at a certain time and place, to avoid flying into a dangerous storm.
7. An area with a (tropical climate, temperate climate, subarctic climate) is usually very warm all year.
8. The warmest climates are in places nearest to the (polar climate, equator, precipitation), an imaginary line that circles the center of the Earth from east to west.
9. A (natural resource, region, capital resource) is something in the environment that people can use.
10. To (service, conserve, harvest) means to use resources carefully.
11. A (human resource, raw material, region) is something we change or process so that people can use it.
12. (Climate, Manufacturing, Temperature) is the weather of a place averaged over a long period of time.

Notes for Home: Your child learned the vocabulary terms for Chapter 1.
Home Activity: With your child, make flashcards for the vocabulary terms in this chapter. Write each term on one side of an index card or small piece of paper and the definition on the other side.

Also on Teacher Resources CD-ROM.

Facts and Main Ideas

1. Northeast, Southeast, Midwest, Southwest, West
2. Possible answers: Polar, temperate, tropical, subtropical, subarctic
3. So they will last for a long time
4. Possible answers: The Midwest has plains; the West has mountains; the Southwest has canyons; the Northeast has rocky shorelines; the Southeast has coastal plains.
5. Possible answers: Being closer to the equator means higher temperatures; high elevations mean lower temperatures; being close to the ocean helps climate remain moderate.
6. Natural resources, capital resources, and human resources
7. Possible questions: What are the highest and lowest points of this region? What are the key industries in this region? Possible answers: Atlas, almanac, encyclopedia, the Internet, community resources

Write About Geography

1. After students exchange and discuss their riddles, you may wish to compile riddles in a "Name the Region" study game.
2. Tell students to decide to whom they want to appeal in their ads: business people? tourists? possible residents? This choice will help them focus the message of their ads.
3. Encourage students to use their textbook, an atlas, and other resources to identify interesting locations.

Apply Skills

1. Part or all of Pennsylvania, Maryland, Delaware, Virginia, West Virginia, and Washington, D.C.
2. Washington, D.C.
3. North America

CHAPTER 2

Chapter Planning Guide

Chapter 2 • We All Live Together

Locating Places pp. 36–37

Lesson Titles	Pacing	Main Ideas
Lesson 1 **Americans All** pp. 38–44	3 days	• The United States is a diverse nation made up of people from many different backgrounds and cultures.
Biography: Fiorello La Guardia p. 45		• Fiorello La Guardia, the son of immigrant parents, worked for fairness in government. He became a congressman and later mayor of New York City.
Lesson 2 **We the People** pp. 46–52	4 days	• Citizens of the United States elect representatives who make and enforce laws.
Biography: Daniel Inouye p. 53		• As a congressman and later a senator, Daniel Inouye worked for tolerance and respect among Americans.
Map and Globe Skills: Read a Time-Zone Map pp. 54–55		• Time-zone maps show time-zone boundaries.
Lesson 3 **The Strengths of Our Freedoms** pp. 56–59	2 days	• Citizens have rights as well as responsibilities.
Citizen Heroes: Honesty Doing the Right Thing pp. 60–61		• Children and adults should demonstrate honesty in their daily actions.
✓ **Chapter 2 Review** pp. 62–63		

As a congressman and mayor of New York City, Fiorello La Guardia worked for the fair treatment of immigrants.

✓ = Assessment Options

A compass like this one may have helped guide the first Europeans to North America.

Vocabulary	Resources	Meeting Individual Needs
immigrant culture	• Workbook, p. 9 • Transparencies 1, 29 • Every Student Learns Guide, pp. 14–17 • Quick Study, pp. 8–9	• Leveled Practice, TE p. 40 • ESL Support, TE p. 42 • Learning Styles, TE p. 43
government republic represent democracy citizen Constitution federal legislative branch Capitol executive branch White House judicial branch Supreme Court amendment Bill of Rights	• Workbook, p. 10 • Transparencies 5, 30 • Every Student Learns Guide, pp. 18–21 • Quick Study, pp. 10–11 • Workbook, p. 11	• Leveled Practice, TE p. 48 • ESL Support, TE p. 50
passport taxes jury	• Workbook, p. 12 • Transparency 6 • Every Student Learns Guide, pp. 22–25 • Quick Study, pp. 12–13	• ESL Support, TE p. 57 • Leveled Practice, TE p. 58
	✔Chapter 2 Content Test, Assessment Book, pp. 5–6 ✔Chapter 2 Skills Test, Assessment Book, pp. 7–8	✔Chapter 2 Performance Assessment, TE p. 62

Providing More Depth

Additional Resources

- Vocabulary Workbook and Cards
- Social Studies Plus! pp. 18–23
- Daily Activity Bank
- Big Book Atlas
- Student Atlas
- Outline Maps
- Desk Maps

Technology

- AudioText
- MindPoint® Quiz Show CD-ROM
- ExamView® Test Bank CD-ROM
- Teacher Resources CD-ROM
- Map Resources CD-ROM
- SFSuccessNet: iText (Pupil Edition online), iTE (Teacher's Edition online), Online Planner
- **www.sfsocialstudies.com** (Biographies, news, references, maps, and activities)

To establish guidelines for your students' safe and responsible use of the Internet, use the Scott Foresman Internet Guide.

Additional Internet Links

To find out more about:

- Lewis and Clark, visit **www.lewis-clark.org**
- The White House, visit **www.whitehouse.gov**

Key Internet Search Terms

- Juan Ponce de León
- United States Supreme Court
- Bill of Rights

Workbook Support

Use the following Workbook pages to support content and skills development as you teach Chapter 2. You can also view and print Workbook pages from the Teacher Resources CD-ROM.

Workbook, p. 8

Use with Chapter 2.

Vocabulary Preview

Directions: Match each vocabulary term to its meaning or description. Write the term on the line. Not all terms will be used. You may use your glossary.

immigrant	democracy	Capitol	amendment
culture	citizen	executive branch	Bill of Rights
government	Constitution	White House	passport
republic	federal	judicial branch	tax
represent	legislative branch	Supreme Court	jury

1. **legislative branch** part of the government that makes laws
2. **Supreme Court** highest court of the United States
3. **Constitution** written plan of government
4. **culture** way of life followed by a group of people
5. **Capitol** building at which the United States Congress meets
6. **amendment** change to the Constitution
7. **judicial branch** part of the government that interprets laws
8. **democracy** form of government in which citizens have a right to take part
9. **jury** panel of citizens who make decisions in a court of law
10. **republic** form of government in which leaders are elected to represent the voters
11. **represent** to make decisions for
12. **executive branch** part of the government that enforces laws
13. **federal** system of government in which national and state governments share power
14. **government** rules that people follow and the people who run the country
15. **Bill of Rights** first ten amendments to the U.S. Constitution

Notes for Home: Your child learned the vocabulary terms for Chapter 2.
Home Activity: With your child, select a brief newspaper or magazine article about the United States government. Have your child highlight or circle all the vocabulary terms that appear in the article and then define them in context as you read the article together.

8 Vocabulary Preview Workbook

Use with Pupil Edition, p. 36

Workbook, p. 9

Use with Pages 38–44.

Lesson 1: Americans All

Directions: Read the following descriptions and decide which culture group each one describes. Write NA (Native American), S (Spanish), or F (French). Some descriptions may apply to more than one group. You may use your textbook.

1. **S, F** looked for riches and new land
2. **NA** may have migrated from northern Asia, the South Pacific islands, or Australia
3. **S** explored parts of present-day Florida and New Mexico
4. **NA** occupied North America by the 1400s
5. **NA** lived in North America long before the Europeans came
6. **S** looked for a short route by sea to Asia

Directions: Answer the following questions on the lines provided.

7. How did the United States expand its borders to include 48 of today's 50 states?
Settlers traveled westward looking for good land. The United States purchased the Louisiana Territory from the French and Florida from Spain. England ceded the Oregon Territory. After the Mexican War, the U.S. purchased land from Mexico. Through these and other purchases, treaties, and wars, more territory was added.

8. What makes up the culture of a group of people?
Culture includes the food, clothing, music, art, religion, holidays, customs, stories, games, and languages of a group of people.

9. How does the motto *E pluribus unum* describe the people of the United States?
The people of the United States have come from different backgrounds and parts of the world but are united as a nation.

Notes for Home: Your child learned about the backgrounds of some of the cultural groups that make up the United States.
Home Activity: With your child, discuss the cultural heritage of your family.

Workbook Lesson Review 9

Use with Pupil Edition, p. 44

Workbook, p. 10

Use with Pages 46–52.

Lesson 2: We the People

Directions: Complete the following fact sheet about government in the United States. You may use your textbook.

U.S. Government Fact Sheet

Name of country: **United States (of America)**
Type of government: **Republic, representative democracy**
How government is run:
Citizens: **Elect leaders, follow laws**
Leaders: **Possible answers: Run the government, vote on laws**
Written plan of government: **Constitution of the United States of America**
How laws can be changed: **By amendment**
Number of levels of government: **3**
Level One **Local (village, town, city, county)**
Top Official: **Mayor or village manager**
Responsibilities: **Manage services, provide police and fire protection, run schools, and keep water supply clean and safe**
Level Two: **State**
Top Official: **Governor**
Responsibilities: **Runs state government**
Level Three: **National**
Top Official: **President**
Responsibilities: **Suggest laws, make budgets, select people to manage services**
Three branches of national government: **Legislative, executive, judicial**

Notes for Home: Your child learned about levels of government in the United States and the role elected officials play at each level.
Home Activity: With your child, research and identify the names of the local, state, and national officials elected to represent you. Write them on a sheet of paper.

Use with Pupil Edition, p. 52

Workbook Support

Workbook, p. 11

Use with Pages 54–55.

Read a Time-Zone Map

Directions: Answer the following questions on the lines provided.

1. What is one advantage of having time zones?

   Possible answers: To make clock time the same for large parts of Earth; to identify what time it is in another time zone

2. What does a time-zone map show?

   the boundaries of the time zones across a continent or for all of Earth

3. What is the relationship between a time zone and its neighboring time zones?

   Each time zone is an hour behind its neighbor to the east and an hour ahead of its neighbor to the west.

4. Why would an airline use a time-zone map? A federal government? A person calling from New York to Hawaii?

   Possible answers: To schedule flight departures and arrivals at the correct times; to know what time it is across the country and in other countries; to identify the best time to place a call

5. How are time zones marked on a time-zone map?

   Possible answers: By lines, shading, colors, clocks, or the names of the time zones

6. Look at the time-zone map on p. 54. How many time zones does the United States have? What are their names?

   six; Eastern, Central, Mountain, Pacific, Hawaii-Aleutian, Alaska

Notes for Home: Your child learned how to read a time-zone map.
Home Activity: With your child, look at the time-zone map on page 54. Help your child locate your state. Ask your child in which time zone your state is located. Do you have friends or relatives living in other states? If so, help your child locate those states and time zones.

Use with Pupil Edition, p. 55

Workbook, p. 12

Use with Pages 56–59.

Lesson 3: The Strengths of Our Freedoms

Directions: Complete the chart by using the terms in the box to classify the rights and responsibilities of United States citizens. Some terms will be used more than once. You may use your textbook.

Pay taxes	Make the communities and country a good place to live	Obtain a U.S. passport
Have freedom of press	Have a jury trial	Respect the Bill of Rights
Vote	Attend school	Speak freely
Serve on a jury		Obey U.S. laws
Worship freely		

United States Citizens

Rights	Responsibilities
Have freedom of press	**Pay taxes**
Vote	**Vote**
Worship freely	**Serve on a jury**
Speak freely	**Make the communities and country a good place to live**
Obtain a U.S. passport	**Attend school**
Have a jury trial	**Respect the Bill of Rights**
	Obey U.S. laws

Directions: Answer the following question on the lines provided. Which right identified above is also a responsibility? What conclusion can you draw?

Vote; Possible answer: Voting is very important. The government relies on its citizens to vote in order to represent the will of the people fairly.

Notes for Home: Your child learned about the rights and responsibilities of United States citizens.
Home Activity: With your child, discuss the most recent presidential election. In what ways can citizens exercise their rights and their responsibilities at election time?

Use with Pupil Edition, p. 59

Workbook, p. 13

Use with Chapter 2.

Vocabulary Review

Directions: Choose the vocabulary term from the box that best completes each sentence. Write the term on the line provided. Not all terms will be used. You may use your glossary.

immigrant	democracy	Capitol	amendment
culture	citizen	executive branch	Bill of Rights
government	Constitution	White House	passport
republic	federal	judicial branch	tax
represent	legislative branch	Supreme Court	jury

1. An official member of a country is a **citizen**.
2. A paper or booklet that gives a person permission to travel to foreign countries is a **passport**.
3. A person who comes to live in a new land is an **immigrant**.
4. A responsibility adult citizens have is to serve on a **jury**, or a panel of citizens who make decisions in a court of law.
5. The three levels of **government** in the United States are local, state, and national.
6. The founders of our country set up a plan for governing the nation in a document called the **Constitution** of the United States.
7. In a **republic** the leaders are elected to make decisions for those who elected them.
8. A **tax** is money the government collects to pay for its services, such as building roads, parks, and schools.
9. In a **federal** system of government, national and state governments share power.
10. An **amendment** is a change to the Constitution that is passed by Congress.
11. Food, clothing, music, art, religion, customs, and language are all examples of a group's **culture**.
12. The president lives and works in the **White House**.

Notes for Home: Your child learned the vocabulary terms for Chapter 2.
Home Activity: Have your child use each of the vocabulary terms in context to tell you about the system of government in the United States.

Use with Pupil Edition, p. 63

Assessment Support

Use the following Assessment Book pages and The test maker to assess content and skills in Chapter 2. You can also view and print Assessment Book pages from the Teacher Resources CD-ROM.

Assessment Book, p. 5

Chapter 2 Test

Part 1: Content Test

Directions: Fill in the circle next to the correct answer.

Lesson Objective (1:1)

1. According to some scientists, how did the first Americans arrive in North America?
- Ⓐ They sailed from Europe with Christopher Columbus.
- Ⓑ They slowly migrated from South America.
- ● They walked from Siberia to Alaska across the Bering Strait.
- Ⓓ They sailed from Africa in search of riches.

Lesson Objective (1:2)

2. Which of the following is NOT a reason why explorers and settlers came to North America?
- Ⓐ spread Christianity
- ● develop varied cultures
- Ⓒ find gold and riches
- Ⓓ claim land for their rulers

Lesson Objective (1:2)

3. What was the purpose of Christopher Columbus's first voyage to North America?
- ● find a short route by sea to Asia
- Ⓑ spread Christianity
- Ⓒ trade goods with Native Americans
- Ⓓ claim land for the United States

Lesson Objective (1:3)

4. Which is NOT a way that new territory was added to the United States?
- ● The U.S. took lands from Mexico and Canada after the Mexican War.
- Ⓑ Florida was purchased from Spain.
- Ⓒ The U.S. purchased the Louisiana Territory from the French.
- Ⓓ Britain gave up the Oregon Territory.

Lesson Objective (1:3)

5. How did the United States expand its territory from the Atlantic to the Pacific Oceans?
- Ⓐ conquering Mexican forces that controlled all the land
- Ⓑ making maps of the lands explorers discovered
- ● signing treaties, buying lands, and fighting wars
- Ⓓ trading lands with other countries

Lesson Objective (2:1)

6. What is the Constitution?
- Ⓐ nation's highest court
- Ⓑ building where the President lives
- Ⓒ United States Capitol
- ● written plan for the nation's government

Lesson Objective (2:2)

7. At which level of government do voters elect a mayor?
- ● local
- Ⓑ state
- Ⓒ national
- Ⓓ federal

Lesson Objective (2:3)

8. Which branch of government makes the nation's laws?
- Ⓐ executive
- ● legislative
- Ⓒ judicial
- Ⓓ state

Assessment Book — Unit 1, Chapter 2 Test **5**

Use with Pupil Edition, p. 62

Assessment Book, p. 6

Lesson Objective (2:3)

9. Which of the following is the head of the executive branch of government?
- Ⓐ Congress
- ● the President
- Ⓒ Supreme Court
- Ⓓ House of Representatives

Lesson Objective (2:4)

10. How can the United States Constitution be changed?
- Ⓐ in local elections
- Ⓑ by Supreme Court justices
- Ⓒ by an amendment passed by the President
- ● by an amendment approved by the states

Lesson Objective (3:1)

11. What is one way a person can become a citizen of the United States?
- ● being born in the United States
- Ⓑ getting a passport and traveling
- Ⓒ paying taxes and voting
- Ⓓ promising to live in this country

Lesson Objective (3:2)

12. Which is NOT a service that is paid for by taxes?
- Ⓐ maintaining roads
- Ⓑ making new parks
- Ⓒ building schools
- ● buying school supplies

Lesson Objective (3:3)

13. Which of the following is NOT a responsibility of all U.S. citizens?
- Ⓐ paying taxes
- Ⓑ obeying laws
- ● working for the federal government
- Ⓓ serving on a jury

Lesson Objective (3:3)

14. Which of the following is NOT a responsibility of U.S. children?
- Ⓐ learn how the U.S. government works
- ● vote
- Ⓒ learn about the history of the United States
- Ⓓ be educated

Lesson Objective (3:4)

15. Why is it important for Americans to vote?
- Ⓐ It helps them stay informed about current events.
- Ⓑ It is the only way that citizens can participate in government.
- ● It makes sure that the government represents the will of the people.
- Ⓓ It is a requirement to live in this country.

6 Unit 1, Chapter 2 Test — Assessment Book

Use with Pupil Edition, p. 62

Assessment Support

Assessment Book, p. 7

Part 2: Skills Test

Directions: Use complete sentences to answer questions 1–5. Use a separate sheet of paper if you need more space.

1. Who were the first Americans? **Summarize**

   Possible answer: They were ancestors of Native Americans who came to North America thousands of years before Europeans and other explorers settled in the area.

2. What effects of immigration can be seen in the United States? **Cause and Effect**

   Possible answers: Immigration has influenced the names of places across the country, helped our country's culture grow, and led to an appreciation for and tolerance of our differences.

3. In what ways do United States citizens make sure the government represents the will of the people? **Make Inferences**

   Possible answer: They can elect leaders to represent them, voice their opinions freely, and vote to make or change laws at all levels of government.

Use with Pupil Edition, p. 62

Assessment Book, p. 8

4. What might happen if all Americans ignored their responsibilities as citizens? **Hypothesize**

   Possible answers: People might not obey laws, pay taxes, or vote. The government might not function properly, laws might not be enforced, and there might not be enough money to pay for services people need and want.

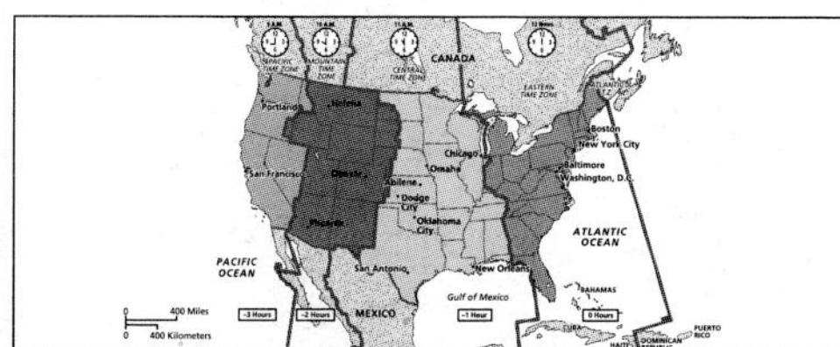

Time Zones of the United States

5. You just found out that your favorite singer is going to be on a live TV program this evening at 7:00 P.M. You live in Omaha. You want several of your friends to watch the same TV program. Your friends live in different cities, which are shown in the table. What time will the singer be on TV in each city? Use the information from the map to fill in the table. **Read a Time-Zone Map**

City	Time of TV Program
Omaha	7:00 P.M.
Phoenix	**6:00 P.M.**
San Antonio	**7:00 P.M.**
Portland	**5:00 P.M.**
Boston	**8:00 P.M.**

Use with Pupil Edition, p. 62

We All Live Together

Chapter 2 Outline

- **Lesson 1, *Americans All,*** pp. 38–44
- **Biography: *Fiorello La Guardia,*** p. 45
- **Lesson 2, *We the People,*** pp. 46–52
- **Biography: *Daniel Inouye,*** p. 53
- **Map and Globe Skills: *Read a Time-Zone Map,*** pp. 54–55
- **Lesson 3, *The Strengths of Our Freedoms,*** pp. 56–59
- **Citizen Heroes: *Doing the Right Thing,*** pp. 60–61

Resources

- Workbook, p. 8: Vocabulary Preview
- Vocabulary Cards
- Social Studies Plus!

Americans All: Lesson 1

Have students describe the groups of people represented in the picture (European explorers and Native Americans). Then ask students what the people in the picture might be thinking.

We the People: Lesson 2

Ask students to identify the building in the picture and its location (U.S. Capitol in Washington, D.C.) Then ask students to describe the activities that take place there.

The Strengths of Our Freedoms: Lesson 3

Ask students to describe the right shown in the picture (the right to vote). Ask students why they think this right is important.

CHAPTER 2

We All Live Together

Lesson 1

Americans All
Hundreds of years before the founding of our country, people from other lands made their way to North America.

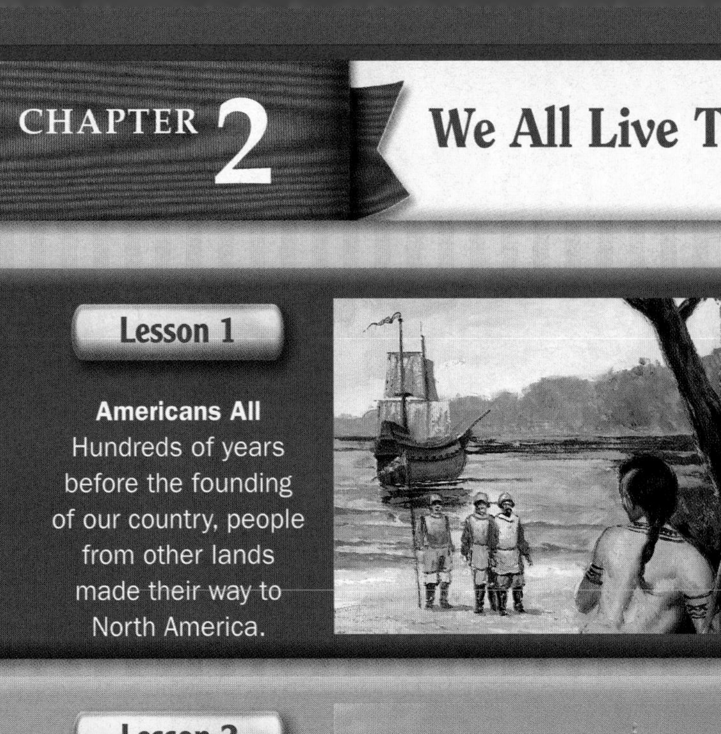

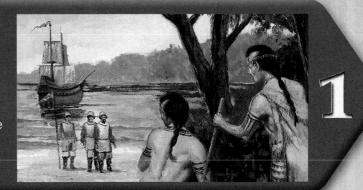

1

Lesson 2

We the People
Americans have a strong voice in how the government of the nation is elected, organized, and run.

2

Lesson 3

The Strengths of Our Freedoms
Everyone who lives in the United States has certain basic rights that are protected by our Constitution.

3

36

Practice and Extend

Vocabulary Preview

- Use Workbook p. 8 to help students preview the vocabulary words in this chapter.
- Use Vocabulary Cards to preview key concept words in this chapter.

Also on Teacher Resources CD-ROM.

Workbook, p. 8

Use with Chapter 2.

Vocabulary Preview

Directions: Match each vocabulary term to its meaning or description. Write the term on the line. Not all terms will be used. You may use your glossary.

immigrant	democracy	Capitol	amendment
culture	citizen	executive branch	Bill of Rights
government	Constitution	White House	passport
republic	federal	judicial branch	tax
represent	legislative branch	Supreme Court	jury

1. ______________ part of the government that makes laws
2. ______________ highest court of the United States
3. ______________ written plan of government
4. ______________ way of life followed by a group of people
5. ______________ building at which the United States Congress meets
6. ______________ change to the Constitution
7. ______________ part of the government that interprets laws
8. ______________ form of government in which citizens have a right to take part
9. ______________ panel of citizens who make decisions in a court of law
10. ______________ form of government in which leaders are elected to represent the voters
11. ______________ to make decisions for
12. ______________ part of the government that enforces laws
13. ______________ system of government in which national and state governments share power
14. ______________ rules that people follow and the people who run the country
15. ______________ first ten amendments to the U.S. Constitution

Notes for Home: Your child learned the vocabulary terms for Chapter 2.
Home Activity: With your child, select a brief newspaper or magazine article about the United States government. Have your child highlight or circle all the vocabulary terms that appear in the article and then define them in context as you read the article together.

Locating Places

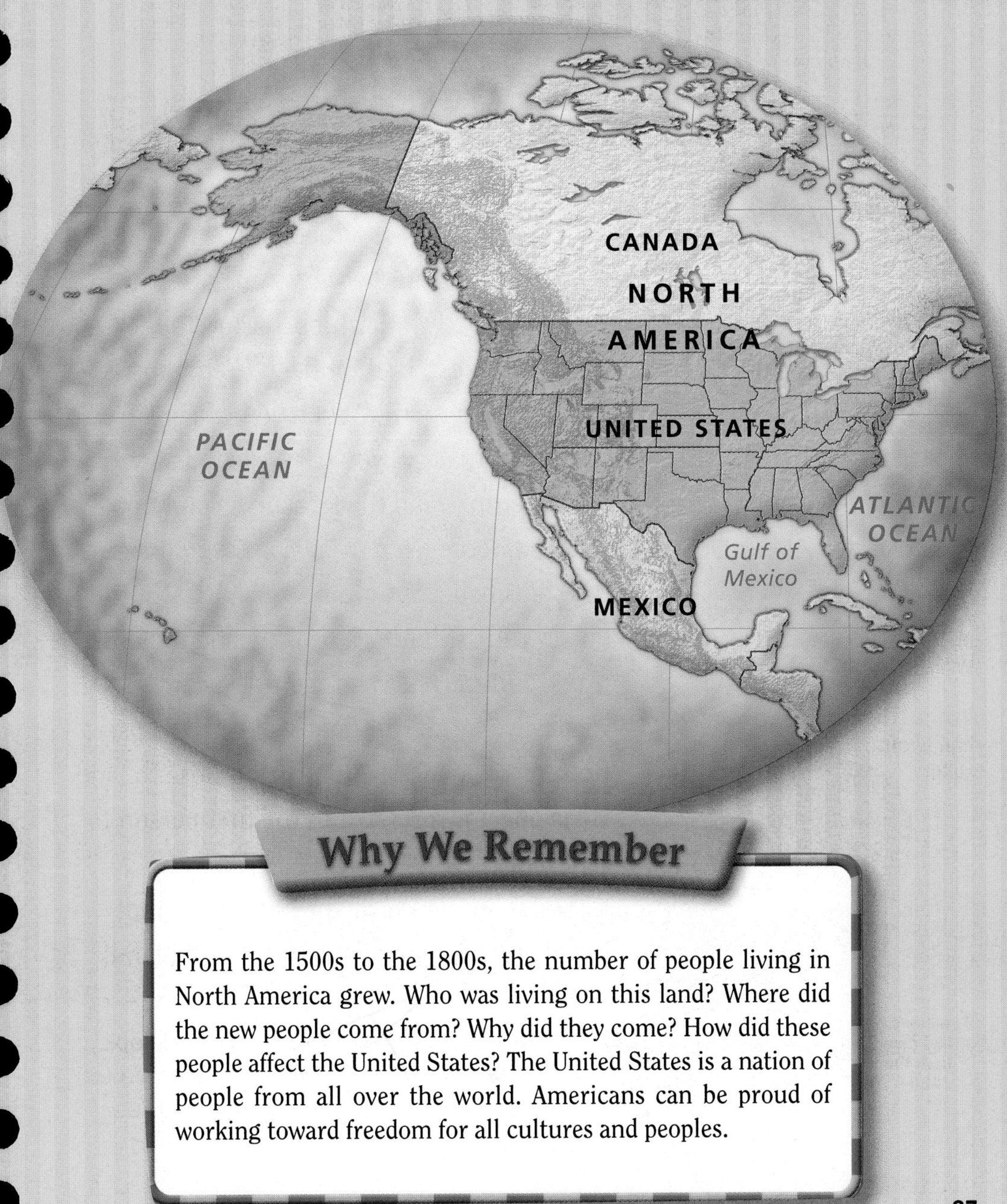

Why We Remember

From the 1500s to the 1800s, the number of people living in North America grew. Who was living on this land? Where did the new people come from? Why did they come? How did these people affect the United States? The United States is a nation of people from all over the world. Americans can be proud of working toward freedom for all cultures and peoples.

37

Locating Places

- Have students examine the pictures shown on p. 36 for Lessons 1, 2, and 3.

Why We Remember

Have students read the "Why We Remember" paragraph on p. 37 and ask why information in this chapter might be important to them. Have students work together to speculate about answers to the questions posed in the paragraph. Then ask them how they think life in the United States might be different if everyone who has immigrated had come from a single country.

WEB SITE
Technology

You can learn more about the capital of the United States by clicking on *Atlas* at **www.sfsocialstudies.com.**

SOCIAL STUDIES STRAND
Geography

Mental Mapping Have students draw an outline of their state from memory. Then, have them locate and label their community on the map. Discuss with students what makes their community different from others in their state, and in what ways it is similar to other communities.

Americans All

Objectives

- Describe what is known about the people who were living in America when Columbus arrived.
- Explain why explorers and settlers came to North America.
- Explain how the land belonging to the United States grew from the Atlantic Ocean to the Pacific Ocean.

Vocabulary

immigrant, p. 43; **culture,** p. 43

Resources

- Workbook, p. 9
- Transparency 1
- Every Student Learns Guide, pp. 14–17
- Quick Study, pp. 8–9

If time is short, have students create visual notes to summarize the lesson.

- Give students an outline map of North America.
- Tell them to read the lesson independently and record notes on their map.
- When students have completed their maps, have them compare their map with a partner's map.

1 Introduce and Motivate

Preview To activate prior knowledge, ask students what they know about Christopher Columbus. Tell students they will learn more about Columbus and others who helped shape our country as they read Lesson 1.

You Are There Remind students that the sailors had spent three months at sea with no guarantee of success. Discuss what the sailors might have been feeling before and after they finally spotted land.

LESSON 1

1500 — 1800 — 1850

- **1492** Columbus arrives in North America.
- **1803** The United States purchases the Louisiana Territory from France.
- **1819** The United States purchases Florida from Spain.
- **1845** Texas becomes a state.
- **185** The area that to become 48 of the 50 states is complete

PREVIEW

Focus on the Main Idea
The United States is a diverse nation made up of people from many different backgrounds and cultures.

PLACES
Bering Strait
Mississippi River
Louisiana Territory

PEOPLE
Christopher Columbus
Thomas Jefferson
Meriwether Lewis
William Clark

VOCABULARY
immigrant
culture

Americans All

You Are There It is October 1492. You are on the *Pinta,* one of the three ships in Christopher Columbus's exploration fleet. Columbus is on the *Santa María*. When you left Spain three months ago, you were excited about the adventure and the treasures you hoped to bring home from Asia. Now, everyone on the ships believes Columbus is lost. But then one of your shipmates runs up and tells you that Columbus has spotted tree branches with leaves and fruit floating by the ships. Columbus believes you must be close to land. He is offering a reward to the first person to spot land.

Suddenly, you hear the scream, "Land! Land!" Rodrigo de Triana has spotted land!

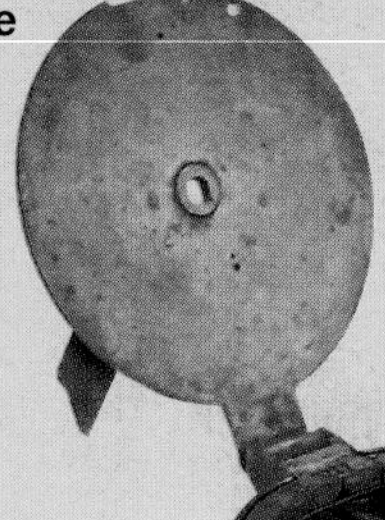

▶ A brass box and compass from the 1400s

Museum of the History of Science, Oxford

Main Idea and Details As you read, look for reasons why the United States came to include people of many different cultures.

38

Practice and Extend

READING SKILL
Main Idea and Details

In the Lesson Review, students complete a graphic organizer like the one below. You may want to provide students with a copy of Transparency 1 to complete as they read the lesson.

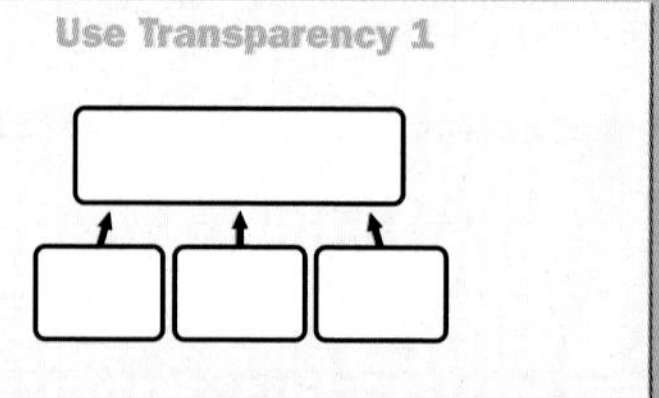

VOCABULARY
Related Word Study

Have students read the three sentences on page 43 that explain culture (through "Language is…"). On the board, create a word web with *culture* in the middle. Ask students which words in the text should be included in the web (*food, clothing, music, art, holidays, stories, games, language*). Then create one or more word webs to reflect either popular culture or the culture of your area or of students in the class.

The Earliest Americans

Although North America was a new world to Europeans, it was home to many people before **Christopher Columbus** arrived. When Columbus landed in America, he thought he had reached a group of islands between Asia and Australia. Those islands were known as the East Indies. Columbus therefore called the first North Americans he
1 saw "Indians." Today, we refer to these people and their descendants as Native Americans or American Indians. How did Native Americans' ancestors come to this land?

Early Americans came to this part of the world from other places. Scientists differ about when they came and where they came from. Some scientists think that the first Americans came from Asia. They might have come when much of the Northern Hemisphere was covered with ice. Some scientists think they might have walked across the **Bering Strait** on land that then connected what we now know as Siberia and Alaska.

Other scientists think that the first Americans sailed from northern Asia. Others think that the first Americans sailed from South Pacific islands or 2
Australia.

However they got here and whenever they came, people were living in North America over 11,000 years ago. Over time, they developed rich and varied cultures. Their cultures were shaped in part by the geography of the areas they settled. These early peoples became 3
the hundreds of different Native American groups that occupied North America by the 1400s.

REVIEW What are some different ideas scientists have about where the first Americans came from?
Main Idea and Details

▶ Workers at a site in Colorado search for objects that are thousands of years old.

4

39

SOCIAL STUDIES
Background

About Native Americans Today

- Almost 2.5 million people identified themselves as "American Indian" or "Alaska Native" in the 2000 census.
- There are about 275 Native American reservations in the United States. In these places, the tribal government acts as the local government authority.
- A 1924 act of Congress granted citizenship to all Native Americans who had not received citizenship by various means before then. Native Americans have the same right to vote and hold office as other U.S. citizens. They also have the same responsibility to pay taxes and to obey federal, state, and local laws.

2 Teach and Discuss

PAGE 39

The Earliest Americans

Quick Summary The first Americans may have traveled to North America over a land bridge from Asia, or they may have sailed here from Asia, the South Pacific, or Australia.

1 **Why did Columbus call the people he met "Indians"?** He thought he had reached the East Indies. (The people there were called "Indians.")
Cause and Effect

✓ **Ongoing Assessment**

If... students have difficulty understanding why people from other places are called Indians,	**then...** point to India on a classroom map or globe and ask what residents of that country are called.

2 **What two forms of transportation might have been used by the ancestors of the Native Americans to reach the Americas?** Walking, sailing
Main Idea and Details

3 **What was one factor that led to the development of varied cultures among Native Americans?** Possible answer: The varied geography of the areas they settled Cause and Effect

✓ **REVIEW ANSWER** Some scientists think the first Americans walked from Asia across the Bering Strait. Others think they sailed from Asia, the South Pacific islands, or Australia.
Main Idea and Details

4 **What are the workers in the picture searching for? Why do you think they are using screens to sift the sand?** They are searching for objects thousands of years old. Some of the objects might be very small. Analyze Pictures

PAGES 40–41

Explorers from Europe

Quick Summary Europeans traveled through many parts of North America during the 1500s and 1600s.

5 Why did European countries want a route by sea to Asia? They traded in Asia but the land routes were long and dangerous. They thought a sea route would be shorter. **Cause and Effect**

SOCIAL STUDIES STRAND
Geography

Europeans did sail to Asia, around the Cape of Good Hope on the southern tip of Africa. However, this route was long, and the many storms and rough seas made it very dangerous.

6 Why were some European countries looking for a western sea route to Asia? Because the sea route to the east around Africa was long and dangerous **Draw Conclusions**

MAP SKILL **Routes of European Explorers**

7 Which route did *not* pass through any part of what is now the United States? The route of Columbus **Interpret Maps**

MAP SKILL Answer By measuring along the Marquette and Jolliet line and doubling their answer to account for the return trip, students should obtain an answer between 2,000 and 2,400 miles.

8 Identify four European explorers to the Americas after Columbus, the country each represented, and the area each visited. Possible answers: Juan Ponce de León, Spain, Florida; Hernando de Soto, Spain, Florida; Francisco Vásquez de Coronado, Spain, Mexico and New Mexico; Jacques Marquette and Louis Jolliet, France, Mississippi River; Robert La Salle, France, Gulf of Mexico **Summarize**

✓ **REVIEW ANSWER** At first to find a short, safe route to Asia; later for gold and other riches, to claim land for their ruler, and to bring Christianity to the Americas **Main Idea and Details**

Explorers from Europe

Christopher Columbus and his fleet of ships arrived in 1492. His goal was to find a short route by sea to Asia. European countries, especially Spain, Portugal, France, and England, had been trading goods with China and India.
5 Traders traveled there over land, but
6 the routes were long and dangerous.

Columbus's voyages opened up a great age of exploration. European explorers came to the Americas in search of gold and other riches. These explorers also wanted to claim land for their rulers. The places they explored are shown on the map below.

In 1513 Spanish explorer Juan Ponce de León (Hwahn PAWN say de Lay AWN) landed in what is now Florida. He was hoping to find wealth and new lands. Ponce de León did not find the gold he was seeking. Another Spanish explorer, Hernando de Soto, also explored parts of what is now Florida. In 1539 his ships landed near what is now Tampa Bay. Francisco Vásquez de Coronado, a Spanish explorer who was seeking gold, traveled north from Mexico. In 1540 he explored parts of the area that is now New Mexico.

Explorers from France also came to North America for different reasons.

MAP SKILL **Routes of European Explorers**

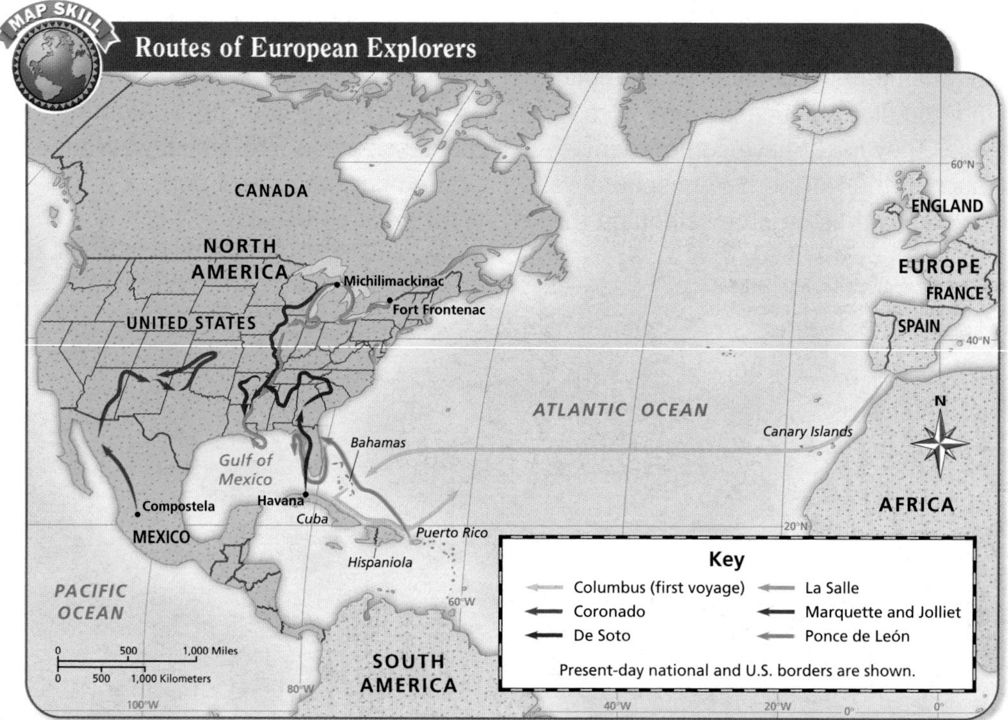

7 ▶ **European explorers traveled thousands of miles exploring North America.**

MAP SKILL **Use Map Scale** ***About how many miles did Marquette and Jolliet travel?***

Practice and Extend

MEETING INDIVIDUAL NEEDS
Leveled Practice

Create a Classroom Map Help students make an annotated map that reflects European exploration of North America.

Easy Have students work together to create a larger version of the map on p. 40 for display in the classroom. **Reteach**

On-Level Have students write one sentence summarizing the accomplishments of each of the explorers featured on their classmates' map, record their summaries on strips of paper, and add them to the map. **Extend**

Challenge Have each student choose one of the explorers and write a brief report on his expeditions. Post students' reports near the exploration map. **Enrich**

For a Lesson Summary, use Quick Study, p. 8.

In 1534 Jacques Cartier (Zhahk Kar TEE ay) came in search of riches. Others, like Jacques Marquette (Zhahk Mar KET), wanted to bring Christianity to the Americas. In 1673 he and Louis Jolliet (JOH lee et) explored the Mississippi River. As they traveled, Marquette drew maps of the region. Another French explorer, Robert La Salle, traveled the **Mississippi River** to the Gulf of Mexico. He
8 claimed land for France.

REVIEW Why did explorers come to the Americas? **Main Idea and Details**

▶ **Jacques Marquette**

The United States Grows

By the early 1700s, the Atlantic coast had many settlers. People traveled westward looking for good land. By 1783 the United States claimed land from the Atlantic coast to the Mississippi River.

Then, in 1803, the French sold land that was then called the **Louisiana Territory** to the United States. This included much of the land west of the Mississippi River to the Rocky Mountains.

9

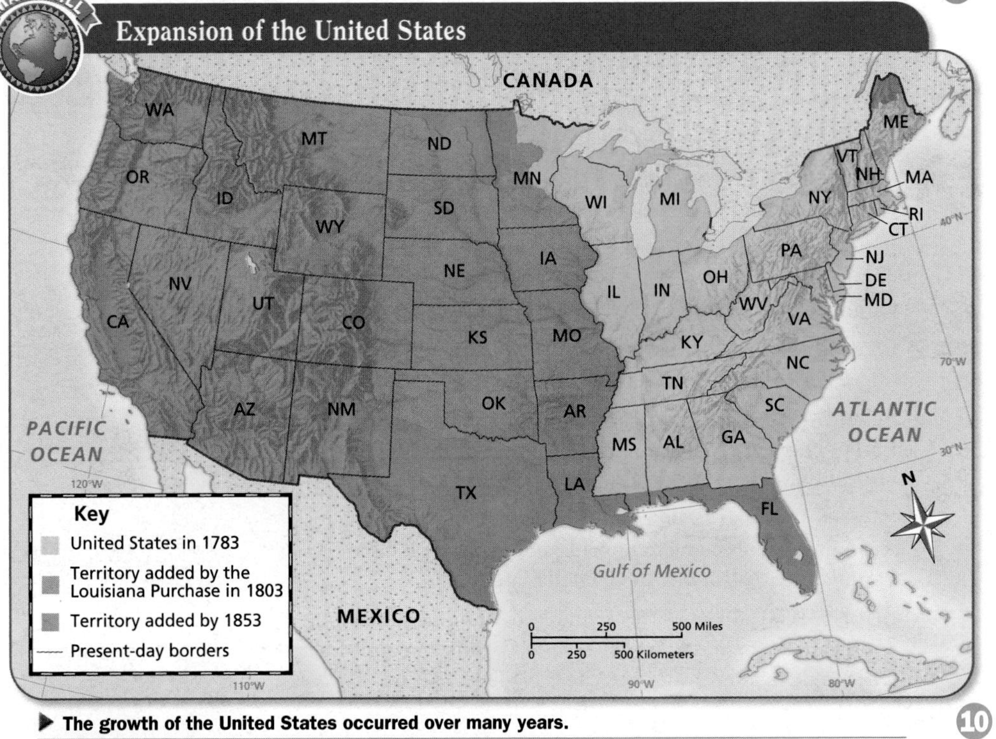

▶ **The growth of the United States occurred over many years.** 10

MAP SKILL Observe Change Through a Map ***How many years are represented by the changes shown on the map?***

PAGES 41–42

The United States Grows

Quick Summary In the 1700s and 1800s the United States acquired vast new territory. Lewis and Clark explored and described part of western North America.

9 **How did the United States acquire the Louisiana Territory? What lands were included in this territory?** The U.S. purchased the Louisiana Territory from France. It included much of the land west of the Mississippi River to the Rocky Mountains. **Main Idea and Details**

MAP SKILL

Expansion of the United States

10 **Territory that is part or all of which present-day states was added by the Louisiana Purchase?** Louisiana, Texas, Arkansas, Oklahoma, New Mexico, Missouri, Kansas, Colorado, Iowa, Nebraska, Wyoming, Minnesota, South Dakota, North Dakota, Montana **Interpret Maps**

MAP SKILL Answer Students should subtract 1783 from the current year to obtain the answer.

CURRICULUM CONNECTION

Literature

Read About the Growth of the United States

How We Crossed the West: The Adventures of Lewis & Clark, by Rosalyn Schanzer (National Geographic Society, ISBN 0-7922-6726-5, 2002) **Easy**

Girl of the Shining Mountains: Sacagawea's Story, by Connie Roop and Peter Roop (Hyperion Press, ISBN 0-7868-1323-7, 2003) **On-Level**

Westward Expansion: Primary Sources, by Tom Pendergast and Sara Pendergast (Gale Group, ISBN 0-7876-4864-7, 2001) **Challenge**

ISSUES AND VIEWPOINTS

Critical Thinking

Analyze Different Viewpoints

In the 1800s, many Americans believed it was their "Manifest Destiny"—"the way things obviously should become"—to expand the nation from sea to sea. Divide the class into two teams and have them debate the following viewpoints:

- **The United States should not have expanded beyond the original colonies.**
- **The United States should have expanded to the size it is today.**

Have students use both broad principles and specific examples to support their assigned viewpoint.

11 **Describe the growth of the United States from 1783 to 1853.** In 1803 the United States bought much of the land west of the Mississippi to the Rocky Mountains. In 1848 it purchased land from Mexico. By 1853 it had acquired all the land that would become 48 of the 50 states. **Sequence**

✓ **REVIEW ANSWER** By treaty, purchase, and war **Summarize**

FACT FILE

Immigration Information

12 **Based on the data in the Fact File, what generalization can you make about immigrants to the United States?** Possible answer: Immigrants have come to the United States from all over the world. **Generalize**

President Thomas Jefferson sent **Meriwether Lewis** and **William Clark** on an expedition to discover what was on the land that had been purchased. In 1804 Lewis and Clark began their trip on the Missouri River at St. Louis. Eighteen months later, they reached the Pacific Ocean. They made maps and kept journals about what they saw.

Between 1803 and 1853, the United States continued to expand. Through treaties, purchases, and wars, new territory was added. In 1819 the United States purchased Florida from Spain. Texas was added to the United States in 1845. The next year, England ceded, or gave up, the Oregon Territory. As a result of the Mexican War in 1848, the United States purchased a huge area of land from Mexico. Then, in 1853, with the purchase of more land, the area that would become forty-eight of the fifty states in the United States was complete. 11

REVIEW List some of the ways the United States grew from the Atlantic Ocean to the Pacific Ocean. **Summarize**

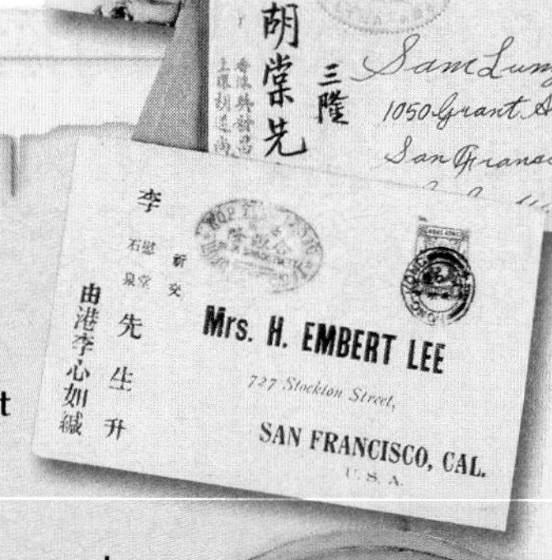

FACT FILE

Immigration Information

- ☑ Mid 1600s: Many people come to North America from England. About 50,000 people come during this time.
- ☑ Between 1730 and 1807: Over 40,000 Africans are brought to America against their will. In 1808 this practice is forbidden by law in the United States.
- ☑ Between 1860 and 1880: Nearly 200,000 Chinese workers come to the western United States. Many of them help to build railroads.
- ☑ Between 1880 and 1920: About 22 million immigrants from Europe come to the United States. Many pass through inspection stations at Ellis Island in New York City.
- ☑ Between 1910 and 1940: About 175,000 Chinese and other Asian immigrants come to Angel Island in San Francisco Bay and eventually enter the United States.
- 12 ☑ Between 1960 and the 1990s: Thousands of immigrants from Southeast Asian, South American, and Caribbean countries settle in the United States.

42

Practice and Extend

ACTIVATE PRIOR KNOWLEDGE

ESL Support

Celebrate Immigration Have students report on their own family's immigration to the United States. Be sensitive to the possibility that some students requiring ESL assistance may have been born in the United States.

Beginning Ask students to point out the countries that their families came from on a map, and tell something about the countries.

Intermediate Have students create a four-column chart, listing their name, native country, year their family immigrated, and where they first lived in the United States. They may also want to interview their classmates and add them to the chart.

Advanced Have students complete the intermediate activity and synthesize the interviews into an oral report, with visuals.

For additional ESL support, use Every Student Learns Guide, pp. 14–17.

Immigration

The English settlers who lived along the Atlantic coast in the 1600s were immigrants. An **immigrant** is a person
13 who comes to live in a new land. Not all the people, however, who came to North America had a choice. Many Africans were forced to come.

Immigrants have continued to come to the United States throughout its history. Most people living in the United States are immigrants or descendants of immigrants. Each immigrant group has helped our country's culture grow.

14 **REVIEW** Why have immigrants continued to come to the United States? Make Inferences

Cultural Riches

Culture is the way of life followed by a group of people. Food, clothing, music, art, religion, holidays, customs, stories, and games are all parts of a group's culture. 15

Language is another part of culture. Many words we use everyday show a variety of cultural influences. For example, the name *Kentucky* comes from the Iroquois Indian word *ken-tah-ten,* which means "land of tomorrow." The word *Michigan* received its name from the Chippewa Indian words for "great water." Lake Michigan is one of the largest fresh water lakes in the world. Florida received its name from the Spanish word *florida,* which means "flower."

Settlers named New York, New Jersey, and New Hampshire after places in England. Vermont got its name from the French words *vert mont*, which mean "green mountain." 16

REVIEW Why do you think the French named Vermont as they did? Draw Conclusions

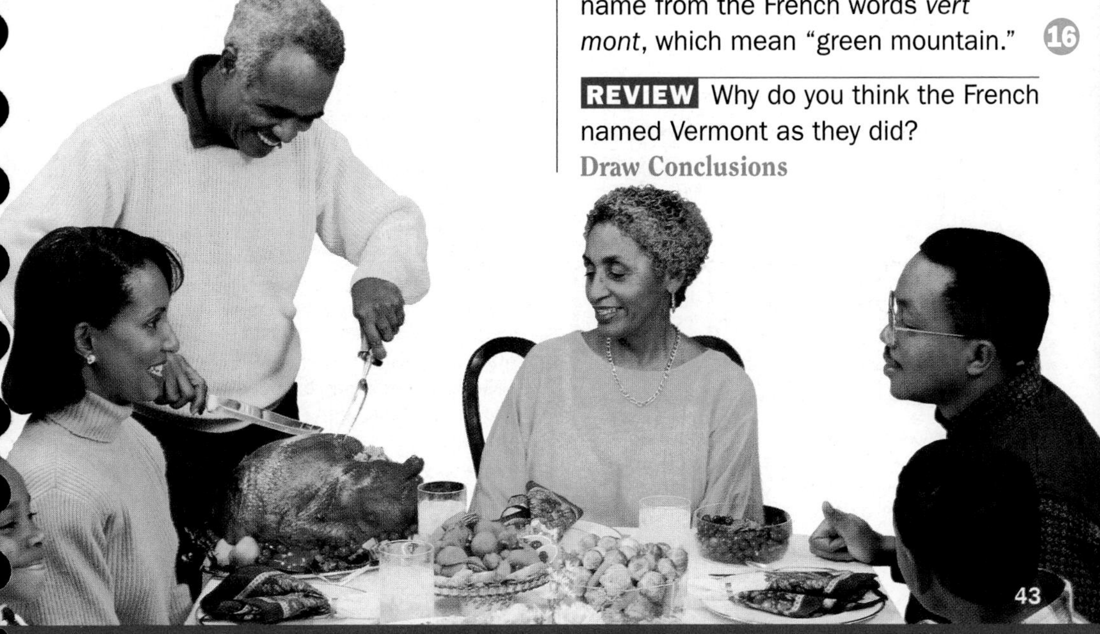

▶ Traditions and food are part of cultures across the United States.

43

PAGE 43

Immigration

Quick Summary Most people in the United States are descended from immigrants or are immigrants themselves.

13 **What is an immigrant?** A person who comes to live in a new land
Main Idea and Details

SOCIAL STUDIES STRAND
Government

In 1700 an estimated 250,000 people lived in what would later become the United States. In 1790 the new government conducted the first official census, or count, of the population. It counted 4 million people. According to the 2000 census, 281 million people now live in the United States.

14 **What do you think are two major causes of the increase in the U.S. population between 1790 and 2000?** Births and immigration Cause and Effect

✓ **REVIEW ANSWER** Possible answer: To work Make Inferences

Cultural Riches

Quick Summary Culture is the way of life followed by a group of people. U.S. place names come from a variety of languages.

15 **What are some parts of a group's culture?** Possible answers: Food, clothing, music, art, religion, holidays, customs, stories, games, and language
Main Idea and Details

SOCIAL STUDIES STRAND
Culture

16 **What are some place names that come from other languages? Name the language of origin for each word.** Possible answers: *Kentucky*—Iroquois, *Michigan*—Chippewa, *Florida*—Spanish, *New York*—English, *Vermont*—French
Main Idea and Details

✓ **REVIEW ANSWER** The mountains in the area are heavily forested.
Draw Conclusions

MEETING INDIVIDUAL NEEDS
Learning Styles

Celebrate Cultural Riches Using their individual learning styles, students explore the various cultures of the United States.

Visual Learning Have students create a display of flags of some of the countries of origin of U.S. immigrants.

Social Learning Have students prepare and demonstrate a group cultural activity, such as an Irish jig or an Asian dragon dance.

PAGE 44

Out of Many, One

Quick Summary A sense of respect has helped people from different cultures live together in the United States.

17 **What are some of the things that bind us together as Americans?** Our common traditions, our government and history, and respect for all people
Summarize

✓ **REVIEW ANSWER** *E pluribus unum*, which means "out of many, one"
Main Idea and Details

3 Close and Assess

Summarize the Lesson

Have students take turns reading the time line. After each item is read, have students provide details about that item.

✓ LESSON 1 **REVIEW**

1. **Main Idea and Details** For possible answers, see the reduced pupil page.
2. Native Americans; They had rich and varied cultures.
3. At first to find a short, safe route to Asia; later for gold and other riches, to claim land for their rulers, to bring Christianity to the Americas
4. Possible answers: By acquiring land by treaty, by purchase, and by war
5. **Critical Thinking: *Make Decisions*** Possible answers: To find freedom, new opportunities, rich resources, or a better way of life

Link to Writing

You might want students to work in small groups and to present their findings on a chart. Some groups might research other states in your region.

Out of Many, One

Even our country's motto, *E pluribus unum*, is a phrase from another language. It is Latin and means "out of many, one." You can see this motto on our coins. Out of many states comes one nation. Out of many different backgrounds comes one people, united as a nation.

What binds us together as Americans? Some Americans say that we are held together by our common traditions, such as celebrating American independence on the Fourth of July or sharing Thanksgiving dinner with our families. Other people say that our government and our history unite us. Many believe that the foundation of our unity is respect for all people. Our nation's laws seek to respect people, despite differences in culture or beliefs. This respect is America's key to bringing many people together to form one nation. 17

REVIEW What is our nation's motto and what does it mean?
Main Idea and Details

Summarize the Lesson

- **Pre-1492** Native American groups lived in North America for centuries.
- **1492** Columbus arrived in North America. Many more European explorers followed.
- **1803–1853** The United States grew with the addition of new lands.
- **Today** People continue to come to America from all over the world.

LESSON 1 **REVIEW**

Check Facts and Main Ideas

1. **Main Idea and Details** On a separate sheet of paper, write a sentence that states the main idea for the details given.

   People in North America have come from all over the world.

   - Europeans explored and settled North America.
   - Native Americans have been in North America for centuries.
   - **Immigrants** continue to come to the U.S.

2. Who was living in North America when Columbus arrived? What did you learn about these peoples? Use the word **culture** in your answer.
3. Why did European explorers and settlers come to North America?
4. How did the United States grow from the Atlantic Ocean to the Pacific Ocean?
5. **Critical Thinking: *Make Decisions*** Suppose you live in a different country. What might make you decide to move to the United States?

Link to Writing

Write About Your State Use encyclopedias and other books to find the answers to these questions. Write your answers and share them with the class.

Where did the name of your state come from?

Which Europeans first explored your state's region?

What words used today come from people who have lived in your region?

44

Practice and Extend

CURRICULUM CONNECTION
Music

Sing About Traditions

- Have students create a musical collage of songs that reflect our common traditions or history.
- Suggest examples such as "Take Me Out to the Ball Game" to celebrate traditions, or "The Star-Spangled Banner" to celebrate our history.
- Tell students that they can sing excerpts themselves, or prepare an audiotape based on recorded versions of the songs they choose.

Workbook, p. 9

Lesson 1: Americans All

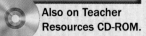

Also on Teacher Resources CD-ROM.

Fiorello La Guardia

1882–1947

Fiorello La Guardia (Fee uh REL oh Luh GWAHR dee uh) was the well-respected mayor of New York City from 1934 to 1945. His parents were Italian immigrants. Fiorello was born in New York City, but he spent much of his childhood in Arizona. His father was stationed with the army in Prescott, Arizona. There Fiorello met people from many different cultures. There were also children of all different backgrounds whose fathers were in the army. Sometimes children would make fun of Fiorello because his parents were immigrants.

BIOFACT

La Guardia read the Sunday comics over the radio to the people of New York City.

La Guardia became angry when he saw others being treated unfairly. For example, some companies sold the army rotten food to feed to soldiers. As a result of this,
1 his father died from eating spoiled meat. These things made La Guardia want to fight for fairness, especially in government.

After his father died, La Guardia and his mother moved back to Europe. While in Europe, he learned seven different languages. When he returned to New York City, one of his first jobs was helping immigrants. La Guardia continued helping people, first as a congressman
2 and later as mayor of the city.

Learn from Biographies

How do you think La Guardia's knowledge of languages helped him as mayor of New York City?

For more information, go online to *Meet the People* at **www.sfsocialstudies.com.**

45

Fiorello La Guardia

Objective

- Analyze the contributions of citizens such as Fiorello La Guardia.

1 Introduce and Motivate

Preview To activate prior knowledge, ask students to name their mayor (if there is a mayor in the student's community) and describe his or her duties.

Tell students that they will read about a mayor who worked to help immigrants move to the United States.

2 Teach and Discuss

1 How do you think La Guardia's years in Arizona affected his life? Possible answer: They gave him an understanding of people from many cultures, sympathy for the problems of immigrants, and a determination to fight for fairness, especially in government.
Draw Conclusions

SOCIAL STUDIES STRAND
Citizenship

2 What are two public offices to which La Guardia was elected? Congressman and mayor of New York City
Main Idea and Details

3 Close and Assess

Learn from Biographies Answer

Possible answer: Immigrants from many lands made their home in New York City. La Guardia's knowledge of several languages probably helped him communicate with these people.

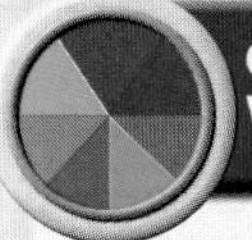

CURRICULUM CONNECTION
Writing

Create a Campaign Speech

- Have students work with a partner to write a speech for Fiorello La Guardia's first campaign for mayor.
- Have student pairs include a slogan based on this biography.
- Remind students that their speeches should be interesting, relevant, and persuasive.
- Have students perform their speeches aloud. Then have the class vote for the most persuasive speech.

WEB SITE
Technology

Students can find out more about Fiorello La Guardia by clicking on *Meet the People* at **www.sfsocialstudies.com.**

LESSON 2 Pages 46–52

We the People

Objectives
- Explain what the Constitution is and why it is important.
- Identify the three levels of government.
- Describe the responsibilities of each of the three branches of government.
- Explain how the Constitution can be changed.

Vocabulary

government, p. 47; **republic,** p. 47; **represent,** p. 47; **democracy,** p. 47; **citizen,** p. 47; **Constitution,** p. 48; **federal,** p. 48; **legislative branch,** p. 50; **Capitol,** p. 50; **executive branch,** p. 51; **White House,** p. 51; **judicial branch,** p. 51; **Supreme Court,** p. 51; **amendment,** p. 52; **Bill of Rights,** p. 52

Resources
- Workbook, p. 10
- Transparency 5
- Every Student Learns Guide, pp. 18–21
- Quick Study, pp. 10–11

Quick Teaching Plan

If time is short, have students create their own Fact Files for the lesson.
- Have students read the lesson independently and make a list of key facts for each section.
- Have students work in small groups to compare and discuss their fact lists. Allow students to revise their lists as necessary.

1 Introduce and Motivate

Preview To activate prior knowledge, ask students where they have heard the phrase "We the People." (The first words of the Constitution) Tell students they will learn more about the United States Constitution and our government as they read Lesson 2.

You Are There Ask students how the people in the story exercise their freedoms. (They meet openly, speak openly, and decide on their governmental leaders.)

LESSON 2

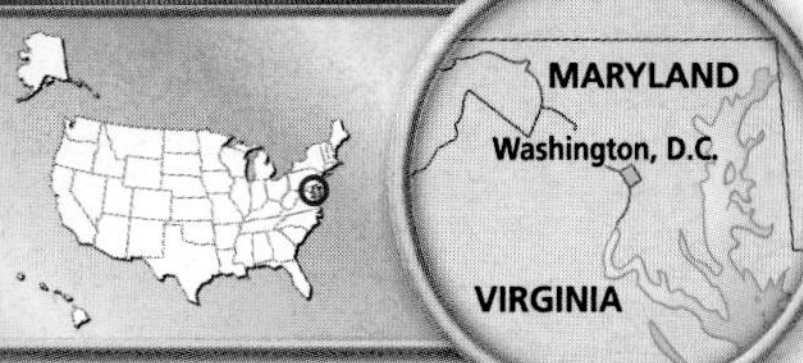

PREVIEW

Focus on the Main Idea
Citizens of the United States elect representatives who make and enforce laws.

PLACES
Washington, D.C.

VOCABULARY
government
republic
represent
democracy
citizen
Constitution
federal
legislative branch
Capitol
executive branch
White House
judicial branch
Supreme Court
amendment
Bill of Rights

We the People

You Are There People from all over town have gathered at your school tonight. They are here to talk about problems in the local park. They want to know why the mayor doesn't work harder to keep the local park clean and safe for everyone. You know that your mom has been thinking about this problem. You wait for her to speak up.

Once your mother starts talking, you notice that many people here seem to like her ideas. Later, a group of people stop to talk to your mom. She's as surprised as you are when you hear their request. They've just asked your mom to run for mayor.

Summarize As you read, look for details to summarize how the government of the United States is structured.

46

Practice and Extend

READING SKILL
Summarize

In the Lesson Review, students complete a graphic organizer like the one below. You may want to provide students with a copy of Transparency 5 to complete as they read the lesson.

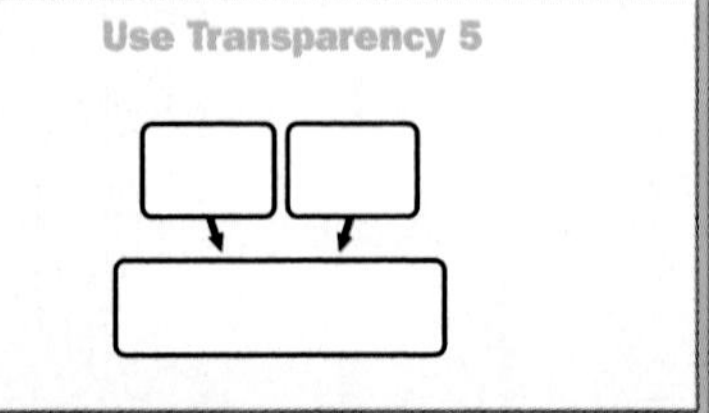

VOCABULARY
Related Word Study

Knowing the origins of words can help students better understand related words. *Citizen* comes from the Latin *civitatem*, meaning "citizenship, city, state." Related words are *civil*, which means "about citizens," and *city*. *Democracy* comes from the Greek *demos* (people) and *kratos* (rule). All words that end with *-ocracy* have to do with government. Students might guess (correctly) that *republic* is related to *public*. It comes from the Latin *res public*, which means "in the public interest."

A Government for the People

The **government** is made up of the rules, or laws, that we follow and the people who run our country. The government often does important jobs for us. For example, in many places the government makes sure that we have clean water to drink. The government builds and maintains our roads. It delivers our mail. It sets aside land for parks and playgrounds. The government tries to make sure that people
1 have safe, pleasant
2 places to live.

The United States is a republic. In a **republic,** the leaders are elected. The leaders **represent,** or make decisions for, the people who elected them. Our type of republic is also called a representative democracy. In a **democracy,** every citizen has a right to take part in government. A **citizen** is 3
an official member of a country. In the United States, the citizens elect the leaders who run the government. Our country follows a set of rules called laws. The elected leaders vote on the laws that all people must follow.

REVIEW Summarize the description of a republic. Summarize

▶ The United States Capitol in Washington, D.C. 4

2 Teach and Discuss

PAGE 47

A Government for the People

Quick Summary The United States is a republic—the people elect leaders to make laws, make decisions, and run the government.

1 **What are some of the jobs the government does?** Possible answers: Protects the water supply, builds and maintains roads, delivers mail, sets aside land for parks, and protects people **Main Idea and Details**

2 **Why is "government for the people" a good way to summarize these jobs?** Possible answer: Because all of these jobs benefit the people **Summarize**

3 **Explain how the term *representative democracy* describes the United States.** Possible answer: Citizens elect people to represent them in our government, a democracy. **Express Ideas**

4 **How do you think the picture on this page relates to the functions of our government?** Possible answer: The picture shows the inauguration of a leader—the President. **Analyze Pictures**

✓ **REVIEW ANSWER** A government in which people elect leaders to represent them **Summarize**

CURRICULUM CONNECTION
Drama

Deliver the Gettysburg Address

Explain to students that Abraham Lincoln described the United States as a "government of the people, by the people, for the people" in his 1863 Gettysburg Address. Point out that this brief speech has become one of the most famous in U.S. history.

- Have students research the text of the Gettysburg Address, practice it, and deliver it to the class.
- Remind speakers to speak loudly and clearly and to make eye contact with their listeners.

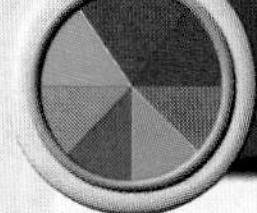

CURRICULUM CONNECTION
Writing

Write to a Government Official

- Have students list and discuss various things they believe government is doing right in their community and various things they would like to see improved.
- Have students write a letter to a local government official praising an accomplishment or suggesting a change.
- Tell students to state their point of view clearly and to support it with facts or reasons.

PAGE 48

Government by the People

Quick Summary The Constitution describes the structure of our government.

5 **In what way is the United States a government "by the people"?** Possible answer: Power in our government comes from the citizens who elect government leaders. Main Idea and Details

✓ **Ongoing Assessment**

If... students focus just on government leaders,	**then...** ask how government leaders get into office in the first place.

6 **What document explains how power is shared between the national and state government?** The Constitution Main Idea and Details

7 **What is a federal system of government?** A system in which the national and state governments share power Analyze Information

✓ **REVIEW ANSWER** Local, state and national Summarize

Government by the People

The founders of our country set up a very wise plan for governing our nation. This plan is a document called the **Constitution** of the United States of America.

The Constitution starts off with the words "We the People . . ." These three words show how important the idea of democracy is for the United States. The power of our government does not come from government leaders. It
5 comes from citizens who elect those leaders.

There are three levels of government in the United States. The first level is the local government. The local government includes village, town, city, and county governments. The second level is state government—the government set up by the people of each state.

The third level of government is the national government—the government of our entire country. The national government meets in the capital city of the United States, **Washington, D.C.**

The Constitution explains how the national and state governments share power. A system of government in which the national and state governments share power is called 6
a **federal** government. The Fact File 7
on the next page tells more about the three levels of government and the leaders at each level.

REVIEW What are the three levels of government in the United States? Summarize

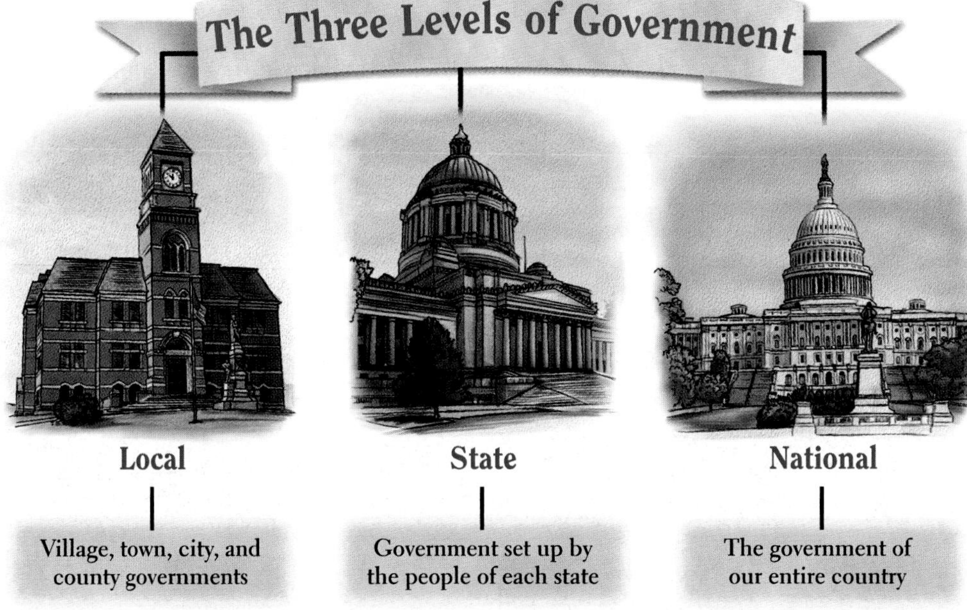

The Three Levels of Government
Local
Village, town, city, and county governments
State
Government set up by the people of each state
National
The government of our entire country

Practice and Extend

MEETING INDIVIDUAL NEEDS

Leveled Practice

Explore Local Government Have students analyze their local government.

Easy Have students research the names of the mayor and members of the town city council. If the students' community does not have a mayor or council, have students find the names of an elected county leader. Then have them write one duty of that local leader. **Reteach**

On-Level Have students create an organizational chart that identifies the roles of various local leaders. **Extend**

Challenge Have students interview a local leader. Help students prepare questions about how the leader was chosen, what the leader's duties are, and how the leader works with the other levels of government. **Enrich**

For a Lesson Summary, use Quick Study, p. 10.

FACT FILE

Three Levels of Government

National

★ The President of the United States is the head of the national government.

★ The President gets authority to run the country from the United States Constitution.

★ Presidential duties include suggesting laws, making budgets, and choosing people to manage the services that the country needs.

★ The President is also the commander-in-chief of the armed forces.

★ Most of a President's decisions must be approved by Congress.

State

★ State governments are run by governors.

★ Governors get authority to run their state governments from state laws and the state constitutions.

★ Most of the laws that affect our daily lives, like driving laws, come from state governments.

Local

★ A city, town, or village is run by a top official. This official is often called a mayor, but may have a different title, such as village manager. 8

★ Mayors get their authority from the people and the state constitutions.

★ Some mayors have the responsibility to appoint people to manage city services. 9

★ City services may include providing police and fire protection, running the schools, and making sure 10 that the water supply is clean and safe.

49

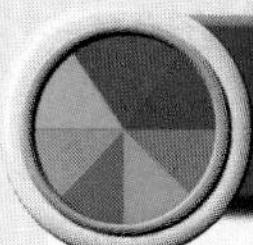

CURRICULUM CONNECTION
Science

Research the Role of Government in Science

- Have students explain the role of one of the state or federal government agencies involved in the sciences.
- If students need help finding a science-related agency, suggest the Environmental Protection Agency, the National Institutes of Health, or the U.S. Patent Office.
- Have students include in their explanation specific examples of their chosen agency's work.

FACT FILE
Three Levels of Government

Test Talk

Locate Key Words in the Question

8 **Who is the main leader in each of the three levels of government?** Ask students to look for key words in the question. Help students recognize that the key word *who* in the question refers to a person. Also point out that the word *each* tells them that their answer will have more than one part. National—president; State—governor; Local—mayor Summarize

Decision Making

9 **What are some decisions a president might have to make? a mayor?** Possible answers: What laws to suggest, how to allocate funds within a budget; which people to appoint to manage city services Make Decisions

10 **Which level of government is most concerned with the country's defense? with the daily services that people need? with laws that most affect people's daily lives?** National; Local; State Apply Information

The Three Branches of Government

Quick Summary The legislative branch makes laws. The executive branch enforces laws. The judicial branch interprets laws.

Test Talk

Use Information from the Text

11 **In which part of Congress are the states equal partners? What makes them equal?** Have students make notes about details from the text that answer the question. Have them reread the question and check their notes. Students should ask themselves, "Do I have enough information to answer the question?" If details are missing, have them go back to the text. In the Senate; Each state has the same number of senators: two. Apply Information

12 **In which branch of Congress do some states have more say than others? Explain your answer.** House of Representatives; States with more people have more members in the House. Apply Information

13 **What buildings serve as the centers for each of the three branches of the United States government?** Executive: the White House; Judicial: the Supreme Court; Legislative: the United States Capitol Analyze Information

The Three Branches of Government

The Constitution describes the organization of the national government. The United States government has three branches. These branches are the legislative branch, the executive branch, and the judicial branch.

The **legislative branch** is the part of the government that makes our nation's laws. Congress is the legislative branch of the United States government. Congress has two parts. One part of Congress is the House of Representatives, which is also called the House. The Senate is the other part of the United States Congress. The Congress meets in the building known as the United States **Capitol.**

The citizens of each state elect members to both the House of Representatives and the Senate. Each state has two senators. The senators are elected for six-year terms. The number of representatives for each state depends on the state's population. The larger the population, the more representatives a state has in the House of Representatives. For example, California has a large population, so it has fifty-two members in the House. Alaska has a small 11
population. It has only one member
in the House. Representatives are 12
elected for two-year terms.

13

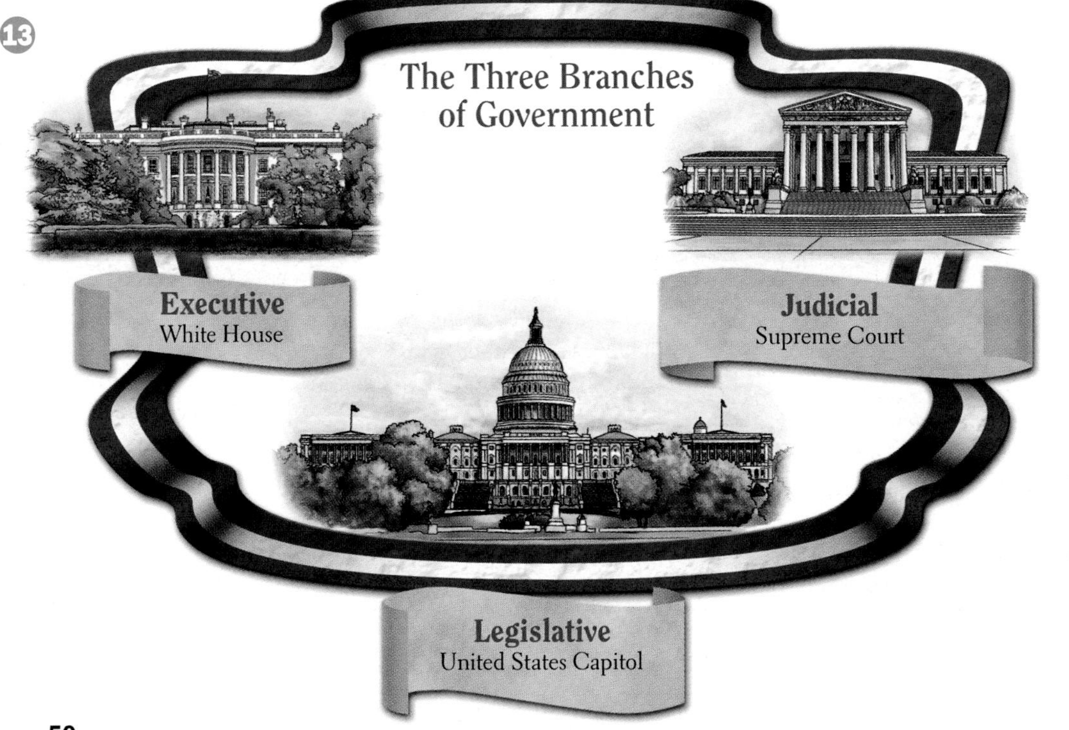

Practice and Extend

ACCESS CONTENT
ESL Support

Learn the Branches of Government Help students learn the names and functions of the branches of government.

Beginning Have students help you create a diagram of the three branches of government in a pocket chart, correctly organizing titles and details of each.

Intermediate Have students create a diagram illustrating the three branches of government, and explain their diagram to a classmate.

Advanced Have students work in pairs to write or present an oral presentation of each branch of government.

For additional ESL support, use Every Student Learns Guide, pp. 18–21.

Supreme Court Historical Society/Richard W. Strauss, Smithsonian Institute

▶ **The United States Supreme Court is made up of nine judges, appointed for life.**

The **executive branch** is in charge of enforcing our nation's laws. The President is the head of the executive branch. United States citizens vote to elect the President. The President serves a four-year term. A President can be reelected only once. The President lives and works in the **White House.** 14

The President has other duties besides enforcing the nation's laws. The President is in charge of our nation's armed forces. The President also suggests laws for Congress to pass.

The executive branch also includes the Vice-President. The Vice-President presides over, or heads, the Senate.

The **judicial branch** is in charge of interpreting our nation's laws. Judges in the federal courts decide whether the laws follow the Constitution. Our nation's highest court is called the **Supreme Court.** The nine judges who serve on the Supreme Court are called justices. Supreme Court justices and other federal court judges are appointed by the President and approved by the Senate. Once approved, all of these judges can keep their jobs for the rest of their lives. The United States Supreme Court meets in the Supreme Court building in Washington, D.C. 15 16

REVIEW Why do you think the President can be reelected only once? **Draw Conclusions**

SOCIAL STUDIES STRAND

History/Government

Only one U.S. President served more than two terms. That was Franklin Delano Roosevelt, who was elected four times: in 1932, 1936, 1940, and 1944. FDR did not serve the full 16 years because he died in 1945. Vice-President Harry S. Truman became President. To keep one person from serving so long, the Constitution was changed in 1951 to state that a President could only be elected two times.

14 **How might a President serve more than eight years?** If a President dies, resigns, or is removed from office, the Vice-President becomes President. Then that person could go on to win two elections. (Point out that the Constitution allows this possibility only if the Vice-President fills less than two years of the elected President's term.) **Predict**

15 **Compare and contrast how senators, representatives, the U.S. President, and the U.S. Supreme Court justices are chosen. Compare how long each serves.** Senators, representatives, and the President are elected, but Supreme Court justices are appointed. Senators serve 6-year terms, representatives 2-year terms, and Presidents 4-year terms; however, Supreme Court justices can serve for life. **Compare and Contrast**

16 **All three branches of government are concerned with what one key function of government?** Laws **Draw Conclusions**

✓ **REVIEW ANSWER** It prevents one person from becoming too powerful. **Draw Conclusions**

Decision Making

Use a Decision-Making Process

- Have students consider the following decision-making scenario: **A President can be elected only twice, but senators and representatives can be elected many times. Should there be a limit on how many terms these leaders can serve?**
- Students should use the decision-making process above to decide whether or not term limits are a good idea. For each step in the process, have students work in small groups to discuss and write about what must be considered as they make their decision. Write the steps above on the board or read them aloud.

1. **Identify a situation that requires a decision.**
2. **Gather information.**
3. **Identify options.**
4. **Predict consequences.**
5. **Take action to implement a decision.**

PAGE 52

The Flexibility of the Government

Quick Summary The U.S. government can be changed by laws and amendments.

17 Why is the amendment process important for the U.S. government? So that the Constitution can change as necessary Draw Conclusions

✓ **REVIEW ANSWER** So that people will not be afraid to express their ideas Draw Conclusions

3 Close and Assess

Summarize the Lesson

Have students take turns reading the three main points, distinguishing among the three terms and identifying the two major things the Constitution accomplished.

✓ **LESSON 2 REVIEW**

1. **Summarize** For possible answers, see the reduced pupil page.
2. Possible answers: The plan for governing our country; it describes the structure and functions of government.
3. Local government—provides community services; State government—involved with most laws that affect daily life; National government—the government of the entire country
4. Possible answer: Through amendments passed by Congress and approved by the states
5. **Critical Thinking: *Draw Conclusions*** Possible answer: The Constitution's plan of government is basic and flexible.

Link to Art

You may wish to have students work in groups, with each group making a poster of a different level of government.

The Flexibility of the Government

The United States government is flexible. That means that changes can occur. The government can be changed by laws and amendments. An **amendment** is a change to the Constitution. Amendments are passed by Congress and must then be approved by a majority of the states. 17

A number of amendments have been added to the Constitution since it was first written. The first ten amendments to the Constitution are known as the **Bill of Rights.** These amendments guarantee such freedoms as freedom of press, freedom of religion, and freedom of speech. Over time, our government has become a stronger, more representative democracy because of our amended Constitution.

▶ Congress in session

REVIEW Why was it necessary to have an amendment that guaranteed freedom of speech? Draw Conclusions

Summarize the Lesson

- **The United States government has three levels: local, state, and national.**
- **The United States government has three branches: legislative, executive, and judicial.**
- **The United States government is structured according to the Constitution. It lists duties of the branches and describes how power should be shared between the national and state governments.**

LESSON 2 REVIEW

Check Facts and Main Ideas

1. **Summarize** On a separate sheet of paper, make a chart like the one below. Use it to summarize the government's other two branches.

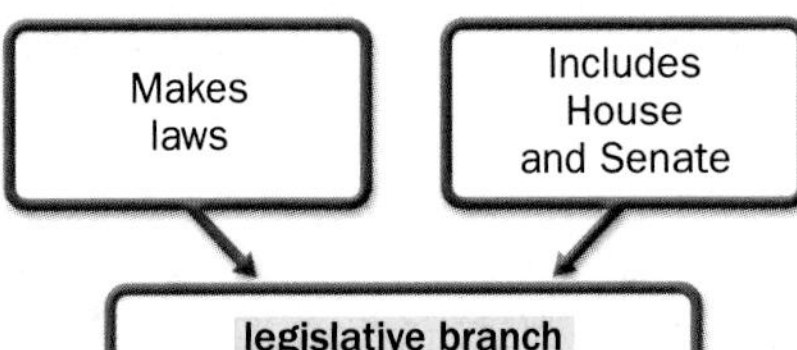

2. What is the United States Constitution, and why is it important?
3. Describe each of the three levels of **government.**
4. How can the **Constitution** be changed?
5. **Critical Thinking:** ***Draw Conclusions*** The United States Constitution was written in 1787. Since then, there have been fewer than thirty **amendments** to the Constitution. What does this say about the original Constitution as a plan for government?

Link to Art

Make a Poster Make a poster inviting people in your community to a meeting of your local government. Include details about the meeting, including where and when the meeting will be held.

52

Practice and Extend

CURRICULUM CONNECTION
Art

Make a Bill of Rights Poster

- Point out to students that many states would not agree to ratify, or approve, the Constitution until certain rights and freedoms were protected by a Bill of Rights.
- Divide the class into ten groups and have each group research one of the ten amendments in the Bill of Rights.
- Tell each group to create a poster explaining its assigned amendment in easy-to-understand language. Encourage groups to add descriptive pictures to their posters.
- Have each group present its poster to the class. Display posters in the classroom or library.

Workbook, p. 10

Lesson 2: We the People

Also on Teacher Resources CD-ROM.

Daniel Inouye 1924–

In 1959 Hawaii became a state. Daniel Inouye (ih NOH way) was Hawaii's first representative in Congress. He was also the first Japanese American to be elected to either the House or the Senate.

Inouye's father had moved from Japan to Hawaii. Inouye's mother grew up in Hawaii. As an adult, she encouraged her family to meet and vote on family matters. 1

Daniel valued this experience. He also valued the different races and cultures of Hawaii and often spoke out against disrespect of cultural differences.

BIOFACT

Because of his bravery in war, Inouye won the Congressional Medal of Honor, the highest award given by the United States government.

As a soldier in World War II, Inouye led troops in a battle to rescue his fellow American soldiers. During the battle, Inouye lost his right arm.

As both a representative and later as a senator from Hawaii, Inouye has continued to strengthen democracy by working for respect among all Americans.

> ***"You can make a difference in your lives and in the lives of others if you simply care enough to try...."*** 2

Learn from Biographies

An experienced politician once told Inouye that it was important to follow the Golden Rule: Treat others the way you want to be treated. Why is this good advice?

For more information, go online to *Meet the People* at **www.sfsocialstudies.com.**

WEB SITE
Technology

Students can find out more about Daniel Inouye by clicking on *Meet the People* at **www.sfsocialstudies.com.**

Daniel Inouye

Objective

- Identify individuals who have displayed the characteristics of good citizenship.

1 Introduce and Motivate

Preview To activate prior knowledge, ask volunteers to share what they know about Hawaii. Explain that people of many backgrounds live there.

2 Teach and Discuss

1 **How did the Inouye family practice democracy at home? Do you think all family decisions were decided democratically? Explain.** They held meetings in which they all voted on important family matters; Possible answers: Yes, because everyone's opinion matters; No, because there are some decisions that only the parents should make **Express Ideas**

Primary Sources

2 **How did Inouye act on his words?** Possible answers: By speaking out against the disrespect of cultural differences, by rescuing fellow soldiers, and by serving as a representative and a senator from Hawaii **Analyze Primary Sources**

3 Close and Assess

Learn from Biographies Answer

Possible answer: Yes, because the Golden Rule helps ensure fair and equal treatment for all people, regardless of race or culture

Read a Time-Zone Map

Objective

- Use a time-zone map to calculate times at specific locations.

Vocabulary

time zone, p. 54; **time zone map,** p. 55

Resource

- Workbook, p. 11

1 Introduce and Motivate

What is a time-zone map? Ask students what they think a time-zone map is. (A map that shows the boundaries of time zones.) Explain that it helps people know how much earlier or later the time is in other places. Then have students read the **What?** section of text on p. 54 to help set the purpose of the lesson.

Why understand time-zone maps? Have students read the **Why?** section of text on p. 55. Ask students for examples of situations when it might be important to understand time zones. (Possible answers: When making a phone call to a faraway relative, when planning a long trip)

2 Teach and Discuss

How is the skill used?

- Have students read the **How?** section of text on p. 55.
- Circulate among students and verify that they are identifying the colored bands as different time zones and that they associate each time zone with a clock at the top of the map.

Map and Globe Skills

Read a Time-Zone Map

What? Before railroads crossed the country, each town and city set its own time. People noted when the sun was at its highest point in the sky. At that time, people would set their clocks to noon. However, the sun appears to travel across the sky from east to west. So noon would be a different time in a neighboring area.

Having slightly different times in different towns caused trouble for people making train schedules. The railroads decided to establish time zones. A **time zone** is a region where one standard time is used. In each time zone, clocks are all set to the same time. The United States adopted this plan in the 1880s. It is the basic plan we use for setting our clocks today.

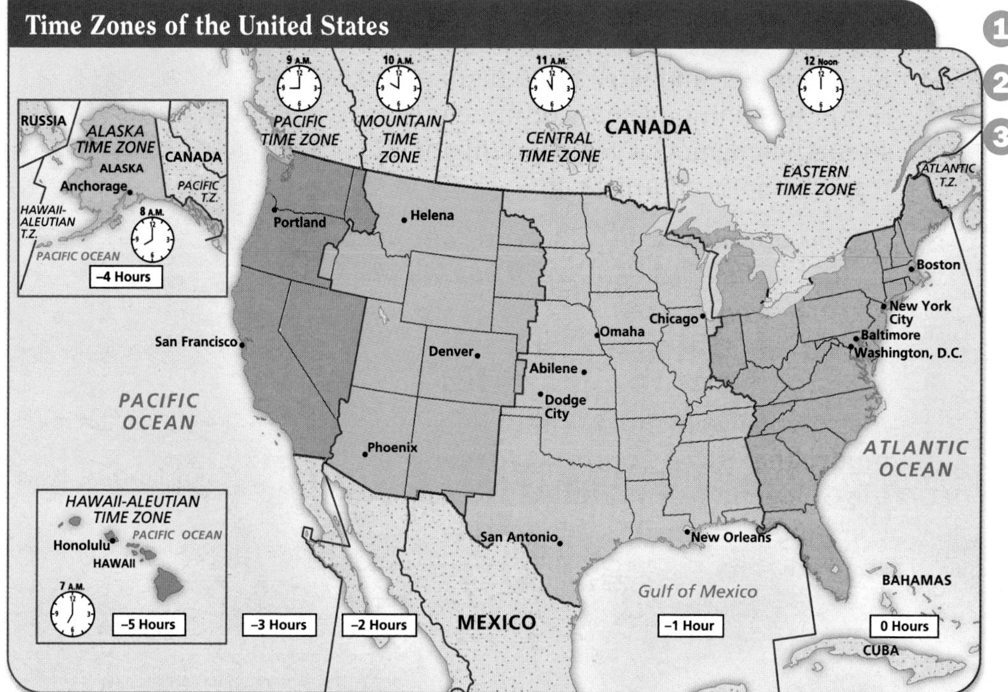

1
2
3

Practice and Extend

SOCIAL STUDIES **Background**

About Time Zones

- Each time zone is about 15° of longitude wide, but the boundaries angle in or out in places to keep certain areas together in one zone.
- The International Date Line runs approximately along the 180th meridian (the 180° longitude line). Each day first begins at the International Date Line.
- Travelers crossing the International Date Line heading west pass into the next calendar day; travelers heading east pass into the previous calendar day.

For more information, go online to the *Atlas* at **www.sfsocialstudies.com.**

Why? You can best understand time zones by looking at a time-zone map. A **time-zone map** shows the boundaries of the time zones across a continent or for the entire Earth. Earth is divided into 24 time zones. Each time zone is an hour behind its neighbor to the east and an hour ahead of its neighbor to the west.

How? Look at the time-zone map. Note that the boundaries of each time zone are drawn with purple lines. Each time zone is shaded with a different color. Find the clocks on the map. There is one clock for each time zone. Notice that the clocks show that the time in each zone is different by one hour from the time in the zone next to it. The names of the time zones are also given with each clock. What is the name of the time zone where you live?

Think and Apply

1. What time does this **time-zone map** show for the Pacific **time zone**? The Central time zone? The Eastern time zone?
2. When it is 10:00 A.M. in New York, what time is it in Portland?
3. If you lived in New York and you needed to call your friend in Portland at 8:00 P.M. Pacific time, what time would it be in New York when you called?

Hawaii

Texas

1 From east to west, name the time zones within the United States. Eastern, Central, Mountain, Pacific, Alaska, and Hawaii-Aleutian Interpret Maps

SOCIAL STUDIES STRAND
Science • Technology

Schedules often identify time zones with an abbreviation such as EST or CST.

2 What do you think the abbreviation EST stands for? CST? Eastern Standard Time; Central Standard Time Make Inferences

3 What time does your school begin in your time zone? As you are beginning school each day, what time is it in Hawaii? Answers should reflect an accurate calculation of time between students' home time zone and Hawaii. (If students' home time zone is in the Hawaii-Aleutian time-zone, both times would be the same.) Interpret Maps

3 Close and Assess

Think and Apply

1. 9 A.M.; 11 A.M.; 12 Noon
2. 7 A.M.
3. 11 P.M.

CURRICULUM CONNECTION
Science

Examine Time Zones

Have students examine a world time-zone map and answer the following questions:

- What is unusual about the marking of time zones in China? (Though China spans five time zones, the entire country is on the same time, eight hours later than Greenwich Time.)
- If it is 10 P.M. Tuesday in Toronto, what time and day is it in Los Angeles? (7 P.M. Tuesday)

Workbook, p. 11

Read a Time-Zone Map Use with Pages 54–55.

Directions: Answer the following questions on the lines provided.

1. What is one advantage of having time zones?
2. What does a time-zone map show?
3. What is the relationship between a time zone and its neighboring time zones?
4. Why would an airline use a time-zone map? A federal government? A person calling from New York to Hawaii?
5. How are time zones marked on a time-zone map?
6. Look at the time-zone map on p. 54. How many time zones does the United States have? What are their names?

Notes for Home: Your child learned how to read a time-zone map.
Home Activity: With your child, look at the time-zone map on page 54. Help your child locate your state. Ask your child in which time zone your state is located. Do you have friends or relatives living in other [illegible], help your child locate those states and time zones.

Also on Teacher Resources CD-ROM.

The Strengths of Our Freedoms

Objectives

- Identify two ways that a person can become a citizen of the United States.
- Identify three types of services that are paid for by taxes.
- Identify at least three responsibilities of U.S. citizens.
- Explain why voting is an important responsibility in the United States.

Vocabulary

passport, p. 57; **taxes,** p. 58; **jury,** p. 58

Resources

- Workbook, p. 12
- Transparency 6
- Every Student Learns Guide, pp. 22–25
- Quick Study, pp. 12–13

Quick Teaching Plan

If time is short, have students summarize the lesson in writing.

- Have students read the lesson independently and then write two short paragraphs beginning with "We, the people, have these rights," and "We, the people, have these responsibilities."
- Ask volunteers to read their paragraphs aloud, and then have the class discuss the relationship between citizens' rights and responsibilities.

1 Introduce and Motivate

Preview To activate prior knowledge, ask volunteers to name some rights people have. Tell students they will read more about the rights and responsibilities of citizens in Lesson 3.

You Are There Ask students what responsibility the students in the story fulfilled and what right they protected by fulfilling that responsibility.

LESSON 3

PREVIEW

Focus on the Main Idea
Citizens have rights as well as responsibilities.

VOCABULARY
passport
taxes
jury

The Strengths of Our Freedoms

You Are There Today we cleaned up the school yard so that our class can have our fall track and field competition outside. Abby, our class representative on the student council, told us that everyone needed to pitch in and make the school yard neat and clean.

Abby pointed out that with rights come responsibilities. With the right to decide on activities comes the responsibility to get the school ready for the special event. Together we filled thirty garbage bags with litter. When we finished, the school yard was spotless. Tomorrow we will have a special recess because we did our job as responsible citizens.

Summarize As you read, look for details to help you summarize the rights and responsibilities of all people living in the United States.

56

Practice and Extend

READING SKILL: Summarize

In the Lesson Review, students complete a graphic organizer like the one below. You may want to provide students with a copy of Transparency 6 to complete as they read the lesson.

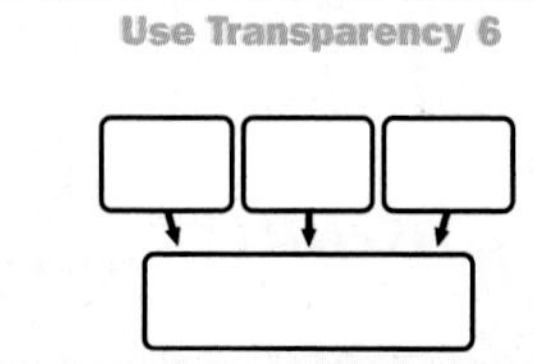

VOCABULARY: Context Clues

In the Student Edition, the context includes a definition for each vocabulary word. Have students read the definitions for the three vocabulary words, then have a discussion that uses these words in real-life contexts. You could ask if students have passports, if they have seen juries on TV or if family members have served on juries, or how much the sales tax is on the things they buy.

Our Constitutional Rights

As you have read, the Constitution guarantees United States citizens certain rights. A person who is born in the United States is a U.S. citizen. One can also become a citizen through a
1 process established by the government.

Four years after the Constitution was ratified, or approved, the Bill of Rights extended citizens' rights by guaranteeing freedoms such as freedom of speech, freedom of press, and freedom of religion. As time has passed, it has become necessary to make more changes. These changes have extended our rights even more.

For example, the Thirteenth Amendment ended slavery. Slavery
2 was legal when the Constitution was written. After the Civil War, it was not. On December 6, 1865, almost eight months after the war ended, the Thirteenth Amendment was ratified. It said, in part, "Neither slavery nor involuntary servitude...shall exist within the United States...." Servitude means that someone is forced to do work against his or her will.

On August 18, 1920, the Nineteenth Amendment was ratified. This amendment guaranteed women equal voting rights. For many years prior to this, many women and men had fought for this right. As with all of the amendments, once it was ratified, it became the law.

Another amendment that affected voting laws was the Twenty-Sixth Amendment. Ratified on July 1, 1971, this amendment gave citizens eighteen years of age and older the right to vote. Prior to this, a citizen had to be twenty-
one to vote. Again, many people had 3
fought for this amendment for a long time.

United States citizens have other rights as well. For example, a person can get a passport. A **passport** is a government document used in traveling to foreign countries. People who have United States passports can
visit countries throughout the world. A 4
United States passport shows people in other countries that the person is a United States citizen.

REVIEW List three special rights of United States citizens. Summarize

The Bill of Rights

PAGE 57

Our Constitutional Rights

Quick Summary Citizens of the United States have rights and responsibilities. Some of these are described in the Constitution and the Bill of Rights. All citizens have additional rights beyond those in the Bill of Rights.

1 **Name two methods by which a person can become a citizen of the United States.** By being born in this country or by going through a process established by the government
Main Idea and Details

2 **What part of the Constitution outlawed slavery?** Thirteenth Amendment Main Idea and Details

3 **What amendment to the U.S. Constitution changed the voting age?** Twenty-Sixth Amendment
Main Idea and Details

4 **Why do you think the right to obtain a passport is important to U.S. citizens?** Possible answer: Because, without that right, it would be harder to travel to foreign countries
Draw Conclusions

✓ **REVIEW ANSWER** Possible answers: Freedom of speech, freedom of the press, freedom of religion Summarize

EXTEND LANGUAGE
ESL Support

Explore the Meaning of *Amendment* Help students understand the meaning and applications of the word *Amendment*.

Beginning Lead students in pronouncing the word *Amendment*. Explain that it means "change." Then have students work in pairs to act out the process of *amending*, or changing, something.

Intermediate Have students choose one amendment discussed in the passage and explain it in their own words.

Advanced Have students do research to find out what rights were granted by the first ten amendments to the U.S. Constitution. Have them present their findings to the class.

For additional ESL support, use Every Student Learns Guide, pp. 22–25.

PAGES 58–59

Responsibilities as Americans

Quick Summary Citizens have certain responsibilities, including obeying laws, paying taxes when they are due, and serving on juries.

5 What are some of the ways you can show that you respect the rights of others? Possible answer: By letting people speak freely and freely practice their own religion Make Inferences

6 Why must people pay taxes? It is a responsibility that is required by law. Main Idea and Details

7 In the case of a jury trial, how does one person's responsibility protect another person's right? The responsibility to serve on a jury protects the right of people to a fair trial. Apply Information

8 Explain why voting is both a right and a responsibility. Possible answer: It is a right because it is something citizens age 18 and over are allowed to do. It is a responsibility because it is something citizens should do because it helps make sure the government represents the will of the people. Make Inferences

9 Why is getting an education an important responsibility? Possible answer: By learning about government and history, we learn how to make wise decisions. Main Idea and Details

Responsibilities as Americans

All people living in the United States should respect the rights of others. They must respect all of the rights guaranteed by the Bill of Rights. This means that you should respect the rights of people who have ideas that
5 are different from yours.

All people living in the United States are required to obey the laws of our country. Some laws require you to do particular things to fulfill your responsibilities as an American. For instance, people are required, by law, to pay the taxes they owe. **Taxes** are money the government collects to pay for its services, such as constructing
6 and maintaining our roads, parks, and
schools.

People pay taxes in several different ways. Taxes are taken out of paychecks. Taxes are added to the price of things you buy. Let's say you stop at a store to buy a soda that costs $1.00. You get to the cash register and find you have to actually pay $1.08. You may have just contributed toward new roads, fire and police protection, and maintaining your local park!

Another responsibility all adult citizens have is to serve on a jury when called upon. A **jury** is a panel of ordinary citizens who make decisions in a court of law. All Americans accused of a crime have a right to a jury trial. Serving on a jury is a way Americans
help protect their right to a fair trial. 7

All Americans should work to make their communities and their country a good place to live. This is a responsibility for everyone, regardless of age. Make a list of ways you can help out. Which are the best choices for you?

All adult citizens have the responsibility to vote. By voting, people show how they want our government to be run.

▶ The court recorder works as the lawyer addresses the jury.

58

Practice and Extend

MEETING INDIVIDUAL NEEDS
Leveled Practice

Create a Ring of Responsibility Have students record their ideas about children's responsibilities around the rim of a circle, cut it out, and display it on a bulletin board.

Easy Have students identify their responsibilities as members of a family. **Reteach**

On-Level Have students identify their responsibilities as members of a school community. **Extend**

Challenge Have students identify the responsibilities children can accept as citizens of their community. **Enrich**

For a Lesson Summary, use Quick Study, p. 12.

By voting, citizens make sure that the government represents the will of the
8 people.

To make good decisions when they vote, people need to be educated. Adults need to stay informed of issues by reading newspapers, watching TV news broadcasts, and going to public meetings.

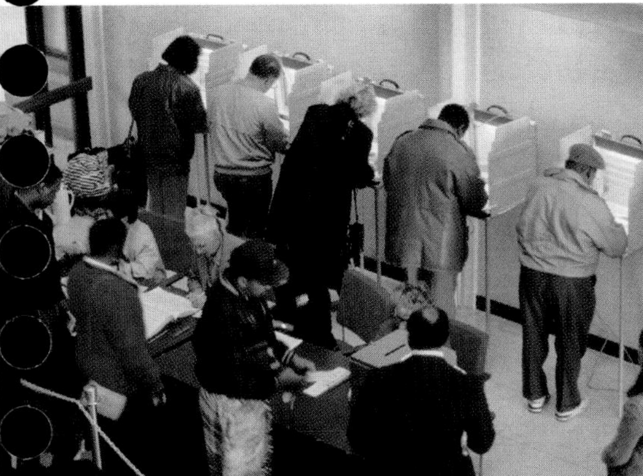

Children have responsibilities too. They are required by law to be educated. In school, they should learn about government and how it works. They should learn about our history. They should learn about decisions people have made that improve life for all Americans. 9

REVIEW How can you fulfill your responsibilities as a citizen?
Summarize

Summarize the Lesson

- **Everyone living in the United States has certain rights.**
- **People who are citizens of the United States have additional rights.**
- **Everyone who lives in the United States has certain responsibilities.**

▶ **Voting is an important responsibility.**

LESSON 3 REVIEW

Check Facts and Main Ideas

1. Summarize On a separate sheet of paper, copy and fill in a chart like the one below to summarize responsibilities of all United States citizens.

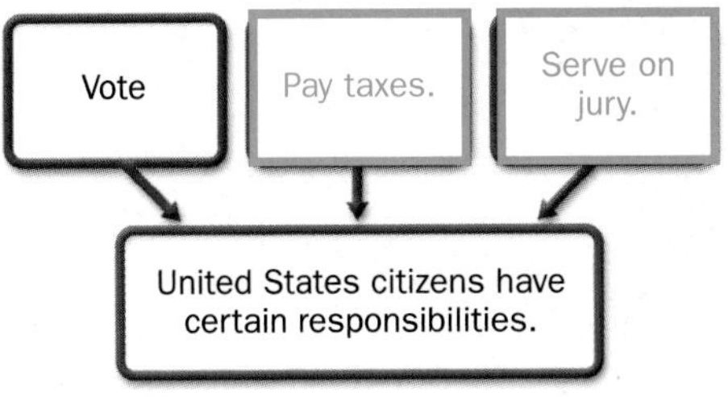

2. What are two ways that a person can become a citizen of the United States?
3. List three types of government services that are paid for by **taxes.**
4. Why is voting an important responsibility?
5. **Critical Thinking:** ***Evaluate Information*** If a person wants to run for President, he or she must be born a United States citizen. Give a possible reason for this requirement, and tell whether or not you think the requirement is a fair one.

Link to Reading

Read About the Bill of Rights Find a copy of the Bill of Rights. Choose one of the ten amendments in the Bill of Rights. Work with a partner to read the amendment. Use a dictionary to look up words you do not understand. Then summarize the rights granted in that amendment.

59

✓ **REVIEW ANSWER** Possible answer: By obeying laws and paying taxes when they are due; upon reaching age eighteen, by voting and serving on juries when you are asked Summarize

3 Close and Assess

Summarize the Lesson

Have students take turns reading the three main points. Then have students brainstorm examples of rights and responsibilities.

✓ **LESSON 3 REVIEW**

1. Summarize For possible answers, see the reduced pupil page.
2. By being born in the United States or by going through a process established by the government
3. Possible answers: Building and keeping up roads, parks, and schools
4. Voting ensures that the government represents the will of the people.
5. **Critical Thinking: *Evaluate Information*** Possible answer: A person born in another country might have a conflict of interest if the United States and the person's native country had a dispute; student's answer should be supported by reasons

Link to Reading

You may wish to divide the amendments among the students and have them present their summaries orally and in sequence.

FYI SOCIAL STUDIES Background

About the Rights of Citizens vs. Noncitizens

- Explain to students that many of the rights and freedoms outlined in the Constitution apply not only to citizens of the United States but also to noncitizens living in this country.
- Point out that the Declaration of Independence also names certain rights that all people possess. These include the rights to life, liberty, and the pursuit of happiness.
- In addition to these rights, U.S. citizens have additional rights and responsibilities, including the rights and responsibilities to vote, hold office, serve in the military, serve on a jury, and so on.
- As a class, discuss times when people may be denied certain rights, such as the right to bear arms or to freely assemble in prison or the right to yell "Fire!" in a crowded theater.

Workbook, p. 12

Lesson 3: The Strengths of Our Freedoms

United States Citizens

Rights	Responsibilities

Also on Teacher Resources CD-ROM.

Doing the Right Thing

Objective

- Identify individuals who have demonstrated honesty.

1 Introduce and Motivate

Preview To activate prior knowledge, have student volunteers describe a time when they did "the right thing." Ask students how they might know what is or is not the "right" thing to do in a given situation.

2 Teach and Discuss

1 **Why do you think the police came to Seth and Sam's home?** Possible answer: Because the boys' family called the police to report what they had found Draw Conclusions

2 **How do you think the check led the police to the owner of the money bag?** Possible answer: The check may have been made out to the person who owned the bag of money; the police may have called the person who wrote the check to find out more about the check's intended recipient. Make Inferences

3 **Do you think Seth and Sam returned the money only because of the reward? Explain your reasoning.** Possible answer: No; Seth and Sam did not know about the reward before they returned the money. They were trying to be honest citizens. Point of View

CITIZEN HEROES

Doing the Right Thing

Eight-year-old Seth and his brother Sam, five, were at the Sunland Park Mall in El Paso, Texas, on a Sunday in 1998. They entered a restroom where Sam found a bank deposit bag. When the brothers opened it, they saw the bag contained money. "It was exciting," Sam said. "There was a lot of money. We knew we couldn't keep it."

The boys decided to bring the bag to their father. Because the mall was about to close, the three took the money home with them. Police came to the family's El Paso home and counted out
the money on the kitchen table. 1
The total came to $23,399. The police also found a check among the money. The check gave the police a clue as to
who the owner was. 2
As it turned out, the money belonged to a builder in the area. He met with the family to thank the boys for
their honesty and to give 3
them a cash reward.

Practice and Extend

CURRICULUM CONNECTION
Writing

Analyze the Effects of Your Decisions

- Divide the class into pairs of students. Have each pair brainstorm a scenario in which they might have to make a decision like the one Seth and Sam made above.
- Have students write a paragraph describing the consequences of acting honestly (returning the item, reporting the incident, fixing the problem, and so on) in the scenario.
- Have students present their scenarios to the class. As a class, make generalizations about the consequences of acting honestly in everyday life.

Seth and Sam receive their awards for honesty.

"He was extremely grateful to my children for returning the money," the boy's mother, Lynette, said. "He told us that losing the money would have been damaging to his business." 4

Police called the boys' heroes for returning the money. 5 Seth responded, "We really didn't do anything special. My brother found the bag. When we opened it and saw all the money, we took it to my dad. We returned it to its rightful owner, which is what you're supposed to do."

"It felt good to return it because it wasn't our money."

Honesty in Action

Sometimes, doing the right thing can be hard. Write about someone who displayed honesty in a difficult situation. This person can be someone you know or a famous person from history.

CURRICULUM CONNECTION
Drama

Use Skits to Present an Idea

- Explain to students the phrase "Pay it forward." (When someone does something good for you, instead of paying that person back, you pay it *forward* by helping others.)
- Point out the national Pay It Forward Foundation (**www.payitforwardfoundation.org**) encourages students to involve their schools in doing good for others.
- As a class, develop three short, dramatic skits to illustrate the concept of paying it forward, how everyone can do it, and the potential effects on your school and community.
- Have students present their skits to the school. Encourage students to use the skits as a starting point for a local Pay It Forward chapter at their school.

4 **How do you think losing the money might have damaged the builder's business?** Possible answer: He probably needed the money to pay bills and employee wages and to buy supplies for his business. **Draw Conclusions**

SOCIAL STUDIES STRAND
Citizenship

5 **Why do you think the police called the boys heroes?** Possible answer: Seth and Sam helped save the builder's business. **Evaluate**

3 Close and Assess

Honesty in Action

- Encourage students to share their stories of people displaying honesty in difficult situations.
- As a class, discuss why most people would describe the people in their stories as honest. Discuss the value of having a reputation as an honest person.

CHAPTER 2 REVIEW

Resources

- Assessment Book, pp. 5–8
- Workbook, p. 13: Vocabulary Review

Chapter Summary

For possible answers, see the reduced pupil page.

Vocabulary

1. d, **2.** f, **3.** a, **4.** b, **5.** c, **6.** h, **7.** e, **8.** g

Vocabulary

1. executive branch

2. judicial branch

3. passport

4. jury

5. federal

CHAPTER 2 Review

Chapter Summary

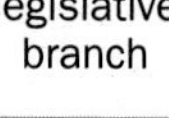

Summarize

Target Skill

On a separate sheet of paper, copy the chart. Use the details given to summarize information about the United States government.

legislative branch	judicial branch	executive branch

The government of the United States has three separate branches.

Vocabulary

Match each vocabulary word with its definition.

1. **culture** (p. 43)
2. **legislative branch** (p. 50)
3. **immigrants** (p. 43)
4. **government** (p. 47)
5. **Constitution** (p. 48)
6. **Bill of Rights** (p. 52)
7. **amendment** (p. 52)
8. **democracy** (p. 47)

a. people who come and live in a new land

b. the laws of a country and the people who run it

c. our nation's plan for governing

d. the way of life followed by a group of people

e. a change to something, such as the Constitution

f. the part of government that makes laws

g. a republic

h. the first ten amendments to the Constitution

Vocabulary

Fill in the blank in each sentence with the correct word from this list.

judicial branch (p. 51)
passport (p. 57)
federal (p. 48)
jury (p. 58)
executive branch (p. 51)

1. The president is the head of the __________ of government.
2. The main responsibility of the __________ of government is to interpret laws.
3. A __________ is an official document used in traveling to other countries.
4. A __________ is a panel of citizens that makes decisions in a court of law.
5. The sharing of power between the state and national governments is called a __________ system.

62

Practice and Extend

Assessment Options

✓ Chapter 2 Assessment

- Chapter 2 Content Test: Use Assessment Book, pp. 5–6.
- Chapter 2 Skills Test: Use Assessment Book, pp. 7–8.

TEST PREP Standardized Test Prep

- Chapter 2 Tests contain standardized test format.

✓ Chapter 2 Performance Assessment

- Have students work independently to record and summarize important information on a time line for Lesson 1, a chart for Lesson 2, and a list for Lesson 3.
- Then have pairs of students compare their work, discuss differences, and revise their summaries as necessary.
- Finally, put two pairs of students together and have them compare and discuss their work.

Facts and Main Ideas

1. What are three parts of a culture?
2. Why is our government called a representative democracy?
3. List two rights guaranteed to citizens in the United States.
4. **Main Idea** Why do people sometimes say that the United States is and has always been a land of immigrants?
5. **Main Idea** What are the three branches of the United States government, and what is the main job of each?
6. **Main Idea** How are the rights that United States citizens have connected to the responsibilities that they have?
7. **Critical Thinking:** ***Solve Problems*** Two friends of yours get into an argument over differences of opinion about an issue at school. What could you say that would help convince your two friends to show respect for each other's opinion?

Write About It

1. **Write a menu** for a holiday that you celebrate or would like to celebrate. Give a description of each food and tell how the food is related to the holiday.
2. **Write a job description** of a government official who serves in the national government. Use the Internet or other sources to gather information.
3. **Write an action plan** for a project that would improve your school or your community. Write down the steps for carrying out your project. For each step, tell who would be in charge and who would work on it. Finally, write up a time line or a schedule for the project.

Apply Skills

Read a Time-Zone Map

Answer the questions about this map.

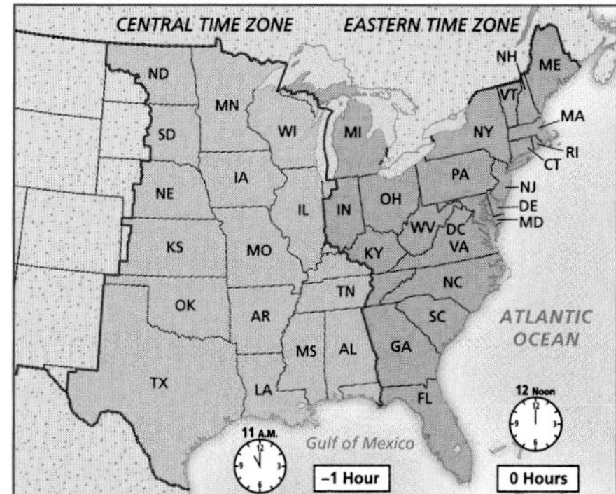

1. The President is giving a speech from the White House in Washington, D.C., at 7 P.M. You want to watch a live broadcast, and you live in Illinois. What time should you turn on your TV?
2. In what time zone will people be listening to the speech at 7 P.M.?
3. You want to talk about the broadcast with your uncle who lives in Wisconsin. What time would it be there if you called him at 8 P.M. in Illinois?

Internet Activity

To get help with vocabulary and terms, select the dictionary or encyclopedia from *Social Studies Library* at **www.sfsocialstudies.com.**

63

Hands-on Unit Project

✓ Unit 1 Performance Assessment

- See p. 94 for information about using the Unit Project as a means of performance assessment.
- A scoring guide is provided on p. 94.

WEB SITE
Technology

For more information, students can select the dictionary or encyclopedia from *Social Studies Library* at **www.sfsocialstudies.com.**

Workbook, p. 13

Use with Chapter 2.

Vocabulary Review

Directions: Choose the vocabulary term from the box that best completes each sentence. Write the term on the line provided. Not all terms will be used. You may use your glossary.

immigrant	democracy	Capitol	amendment
culture	citizen	executive branch	Bill of Rights
government	Constitution	White House	passport
republic	federal	judicial branch	tax
represent	legislative branch	Supreme Court	jury

1. An official member of a country is a ____________.
2. A paper or booklet that gives a person permission to travel to foreign countries is a ____________.
3. A person who comes to live in a new land is an ____________.
4. A responsibility adult citizens have is to serve on a ____________, or a panel of citizens who make decisions in a court of law.
5. The three levels of ____________ in the United States are local, state, and national.
6. The founders of our country set up a plan for governing the nation in a document called the ____________ of the United States.
7. In a ____________ the leaders are elected to make decisions for those who elected them.
8. A ____________ is money the government collects to pay for its services, such as building roads, parks, and schools.
9. In a ____________ system of government, national and state governments share power.
10. An ____________ is a change to the Constitution that is passed by Congress.
11. Food, clothing, music, art, religion, customs, and language are all examples of a group's ____________.
12. The president lives and works in the ____________.

Notes for Home: Your child learned the vocabulary terms for Chapter 2.
Home Activity: Have your child use each of the vocabulary terms in context to tell you about the system of government in the United States.

Also on Teacher Resources CD-ROM.

Facts and Main Ideas

1. Possible answers: Food, clothing, music, art, religion, holidays, games, language
2. Because our government is a democracy in which citizens elect people to represent their wishes
3. Freedom of speech and freedom of religion
4. Because many people who have settled here came from different countries. Even the American Indians came from somewhere else, according to scientists.
5. Legislative: makes laws; executive: enforces laws; judicial: interprets laws
6. A responsibility may protect a right: the responsibility to serve on a jury helps protect the right to a fair trial
7. Possible answer: Each of you has the right to voice your own opinion, but you also have the responsibility to respect one another's rights.

Write About It

1. You may wish to provide models of attractive, descriptive menus, and encourage students to present their information in a visually appealing way.
2. You may wish to narrow students' research by directing them to investigate either an elected official such as a representative or an appointed official such as a member of the President's Cabinet.
3. After students complete a draft of their plans, encourage them to walk through the steps in their imagination to see if they have included all the necessary information. If necessary, remind students to include funding sources or fund-raising methods.

Apply Skills

1. 6 P.M.
2. The Eastern time zone
3. 8 P.M.

CHAPTER 3

Chapter Planning Guide

Chapter 3 • Earning and Learning

Locating Places pp. 64–65

Lesson Titles	Pacing	Main Ideas
Lesson 1 **The Land of Plenty** pp. 66–71	2 days	• America's rich resources have drawn many people to the continent and to specific regions throughout our history.
Lesson 2 **Trade Then and Now** pp. 72–79	2 days	• People trade for the goods and services that they need and want.
Lesson 3 **Transportation and Communication** pp. 80–85	3 days	• The regions of the United States and the nations of the world depend on one another.
Map and Globe Skills: Use a Road Map and Scale pp. 86–87		• Road maps show the roadways of a particular area and can be used to plan the best route from one place to another.
✓ **Chapter 3 Review** pp. 88–89		

◀ **Computers and the Internet have made communication and trade easier in all regions of the United States.**

✓ = Assessment Options

◀ **Fertile soil and a mild climate allow many U.S. regions to grow corn and other crops in abundance.**

Vocabulary	Resources	Meeting Individual Needs
technology rural urban	• Workbook, p. 15 • Transparency 6 • Every Student Learns Guide, pp. 26–29 • Quick Study, pp. 14–15	• Leveled Practice, TE p. 67 • Learning Styles, TE p. 68 • ESL Support, TE p. 70
need want barter producer consumer economy free enterprise system profit supply demand opportunity cost	• Workbook, p. 16 • Transparencies 5, 31 • Every Student Learns Guide, pp. 30–33 • Quick Study, pp. 16–17	• Leveled Practice, TE p. 73 • ESL Support, TE p. 75 • Learning Styles, TE p. 78
transportation interdependent globalization communication	• Workbook, p. 17 • Transparencies 6, 32–34 • Every Student Learns Guide, pp. 34–37 • Quick Study, pp. 18–19	• ESL Support, TE p. 81 • Leveled Practice, TE p. 82
	• Workbook, p. 18	• Leveled Practice, TE p. 86
	✓ Chapter 3 Content Test, Assessment Book, pp. 9–10 ✓ Chapter 3 Skills Test, Assessment Book, pp. 11–12	✓ Chapter 3 Performance Assessment, TE p. 88

Providing More Depth

Additional Resources

- Vocabulary Workbook and Cards
- Social Studies Plus! pp. 24–29
- Daily Activity Bank
- Big Book Atlas
- Student Atlas
- Outline Maps
- Desk Maps

Technology

- AudioText
- MindPoint® Quiz Show CD-ROM
- ExamView® Test Bank CD-ROM
- Teacher Resources CD-ROM
- Map Resources CD-ROM
- SFSuccessNet: iText (Pupil Edition online), iTE (Teacher's Edition online), Online Planner
- **www.sfsocialstudies.com** (Biographies, news, references, maps, and activities)

To establish guidelines for your students' safe and responsible use of the Internet, use the Scott Foresman Internet Guide.

Additional Internet Links

To find out more about:

- California Gold Rush, visit **www.museumca.org**
- Great engineering achievements, visit **www.greatachievements.org**
- Money, visit **www.usmint.gov**

Key Internet Search Terms

- European explorers
- westward expansion
- globalization

Workbook Support

Use the following Workbook pages to support content and skills development as you teach Chapter 3. You can also view and print Workbook pages from the Teacher Resources CD-ROM.

Workbook, p. 14

Use with Chapter 3.

Vocabulary Preview

Directions: Circle the vocabulary term that best completes each sentence. You may use your glossary.

1. A (**producer**, consumer) is a person who makes goods or products to sell.
2. Trains provide (globalization, **transportation**) for the movement of goods, people, or animals from one place to another.
3. The money a business has left over after all the costs of the business are paid is the (**profit**, demand).
4. The development of the railroad in the 1800s was an example of (**technology**, economy), the development of scientific knowledge to solve problems.
5. Telephone and email are two forms of modern (transportation, **communication**).
6. If you choose to buy a baseball cap rather than a soccer ball, the soccer ball is your (**opportunity cost**, want).
7. If the (**demand**, supply) for a product suddenly increases, the price of the product may rise.
8. People who live in cities live in (rural, **urban**) areas.
9. Regions that depend on each other for goods, services, and resources are economically (**interdependent**, urban).
10. Something a person must have to live, such as food, is a (**need**, want).
11. A person who buys goods or services is a (producer, **consumer**).
12. The process in which a business makes something or provides services in different places around the world is (communication, **globalization**).
13. People who live in small towns or on farms live in (**rural**, urban) areas.
14. Something a person would like to have but can live without, such as a new CD, is a (need, **want**).
15. The United States (profit, **economy**) is based on a free enterprise system.
16. Some businesses (demand, **barter**) their goods and services in exchange for those they need or want.
17. Having a large (demand, **supply**) of a product can cause the price of the product to fall.
18. A (**free enterprise system**, globalization) is one in which businesses decide what goods to make or services to sell.

Notes for Home: Your child learned the vocabulary terms for Chapter 3.
Home Activity: With your child, analyze magazine ads or newspaper sales circulars. Have your child use as many vocabulary terms as possible to describe information in the ads.

Use with Pupil Edition, p. 64

Workbook, p. 15

Use with Pages 66–71.

Lesson 1: The Land of Plenty

Directions: Read each sentence below. One of the completions is NOT correct. Fill in the circle next to this answer. You may use your textbook.

1. When they migrated to the Americas, Native Americans found ________.
   - Ⓐ animals, fertile soil, and wild plants
   - ● Europeans had already settled the land
   - Ⓒ different resources in different regions
   - Ⓓ ways to use their local resources and trade for resources not available nearby
2. When Europeans came to the Americas, they ________.
   - Ⓐ settled along rivers near the coast
   - Ⓑ traded with Native Americans for resources found farther inland
   - ● gave Native Americans furs, seeds, and food
   - Ⓓ realized that the greatest resource in North America was the land
3. Producing crops and raising livestock became the nation's main economic activities because settlers ________.
   - ● could rely on resources from Europe
   - Ⓑ could clear trees and set up farms
   - Ⓒ could use the crops and the animals they raised to feed their families
   - Ⓓ could sell or trade extra farm products to others
4. Throughout the 1700s and early 1800s, people continued to move westward to ________.
   - Ⓐ find more land
   - ● live in cities
   - Ⓒ raise sheep and cattle
   - Ⓓ clear land for farms
5. The growth of industry in North America ________.
   - Ⓐ resulted from the continent's vast supply of raw materials
   - Ⓑ was influenced by advances in technology
   - Ⓒ caused many farmers to leave the land to seek better jobs in factories
   - ● caused people to move to rural areas

Notes for Home: Your child learned how natural resources affected the growth of agriculture and industry in the United States throughout the 1800s.
Home Activity: With your child, identify the natural resources located in the area in which you live. Brainstorm how life in your town might be different if the natural resources of your area were different.

Use with Pupil Edition, p. 71

Workbook, p. 16

Use with Pages 72–79.

Lesson 2: Trade Then and Now

Directions: On the lines provided, write words or phrases to complete the following paragraphs about Lesson 2.

1. In the early history of **the United States**, people **bartered (traded)** for the goods and services they **needed** and wanted. **Shells**, **stones**, and metal disks were early forms of money. In Egypt, people used **tiny bars of metal** as money. The Greeks produced the first **coins** as money. The Chinese used **paper** money instead of coins.
2. The economy of the United States is based on the **free enterprise system**. **Producers** make goods or products to sell, and they set the **prices** for those items. **Consumers** buy the goods or services they want. If a good or service sells for **more** than it cost to make or provide, the producer usually makes a **profit** on the sale.
3. In a free enterprise economy, a system of **supply and demand** balances the supply of a good or service against the **demand** for that item. Too great a supply may lead to **lower** prices. On the other hand, a shortage of an item may lead to **higher** prices for consumers.

Notes for Home: Your child learned how trade evolved and the basic principles of a free enterprise system.
Home Activity: With your child, look at different items that belong to him or her. Discuss reasons for your child's choices and the opportunity cost for each purchase. Discuss whether your child made good or poor choices.

Use with Pupil Edition, p. 79

Workbook Support

Workbook, p. 17

Use with Pages 80–85.

Lesson 3: Transportation and Communication

Directions: Complete the cause-and-effect chart with information from Lesson 3. You may use your textbook.

Cause		Effect
Trucks, trains, ships, and airplanes provide transportation from one place to another.	→	**Goods produced in one place can be sent to people in another.**
Different regions have different resources and climates.	→	Farmers in different regions grow different types of crops and produce different products.
No single region can produce everything that the people in that region need.	→	**Each region depends on other regions for goods, services, and resources.**
Many businesses have factories in places all around the world.	→	This allows people to use raw materials and resources to make and ship goods across the globe.
Communication and transportation have become faster.	→	**Companies can sell their goods and send information quickly to faraway places.**

Notes for Home: Your child learned how regions of the United States and other countries are interdependent.
Home Activity: Find a product manual, such as the owner's manual for an appliance. With your child, look through the manual to find the states or countries in which the components were made or assembled.

Use with Pupil Edition, p. 85

Workbook, p. 18

Use with Pages 86–87.

Use a Road Map and Scale

Directions: Answer the following questions on the lines provided.

1. What information does a road map show?
   roadways of a particular area, such as a city, state, or entire country
2. Which map would show greater detail: a road map of Canada or a road map of Washington, D.C.? Why?
   Washington, D.C.; There is more room for detail because Washington, D.C., is a smaller area than Canada.
3. Why do people use road maps?
   to plan routes from one place to another
4. What information does a map title or label give you? a map key? a map scale?
   the area shown on the map; symbols used to represent the different types of roads; how many miles (or km) each inch (or cm) on the map represents
5. Why is it important to understand the scale on a specific map?
   Without knowing the scale, you would find it difficult to use the map to figure out how far one place is from another.
6. Which of the following likely would not appear on a highway map of the United States: major interstates, major state highways, residential streets, or state boundaries? Why?
   residential streets; A road map of the United States is likely to show only major features, because the area is too large to show in great detail.

Notes for Home: Your child learned to use a road map and its scale.
Home Activity: With your child, look at another road map of the United States in an atlas or in this textbook. Compare it to the map on page 86. How are the two road maps alike? different?

18 Map and Globe Skills Workbook

Use with Pupil Edition, p. 87

Workbook, p. 19

Use with Chapter 3.

Vocabulary Review

Directions: Choose the vocabulary term from the box that best completes each sentence. Write the word on the lines provided. Then use the numbered letters to answer the clue that follows. Not all words will be used.

technology	barter	free enterprise system	opportunity cost
rural	producer	profit	transportation
urban	consumer	supply	interdependent
need	economy	demand	globalization
want			communication

1. Any money left over after all business costs are paid is a company's **p r o f i t**.
2. An **e c o n o m y** is how the resources of a country, state, region, or community are managed.
3. To trade one kind of goods or service for another is to **b a r t e r**.
4. A person who buys goods or services is a **c o n s u m e r**.
5. A person who makes goods or products to sell is a **p r o d u c e r**.
6. The amount of an item that sellers are willing to offer at different prices is its **s u p p l y**.
7. The movement of goods, people, or animals from one place to another is **t r a n s p o r t a t i o n**.
8. When two regions depend on one another for goods, services, and resources, they are said to be **i n t e r d e p e n d e n t**.

Clue: In what kind of economic system can businesses produce any goods or provide any service that they want?
f r e e e n t e r p r i s e s y s t e m
1 2 3 4 5 6 7 8 9 10 11 12 13 14 15 16 17 18 19 20

Notes for Home: Your child learned the vocabulary terms for Chapter 3.
Home Activity: Nine of the vocabulary terms for this chapter were not used in this exercise. Have your child identify and define the terms.

Use with Pupil Edition, p. 88

Workbook, p. 20

Discovery SCHOOL

Unit 1 Project Eye on Our Region

Directions: In a group, create a video tour of your region.

1. We focused on this topic: ____________________
2. We made a map of our region (on a separate sheet); we included these features:
   ___cities/towns ___resources ___landforms ___interesting sights
   ___weather ___other features: ____________________
3. These are some interesting facts about our topic:
   #1 ____________________
   #2 ____________________
   #3 ____________________
   #4 ____________________
   #5 ____________________
4. We drew pictures (on separate sheets); these are the descriptions of the pictures:
   ____

Gather atlases, maps, and other relevant resources from your school library to assist students in researching the region.

Checklist for Students
____ We chose a topic about our region.
____ We made a map of our region.
____ We wrote facts about the topic.
____ We drew pictures and described them.
____ We presented our video tour to the class.

Notes for Home: Your child learned about the region in which you live.
Home Activity: With your child, research your region by using the Internet or other resources at home or at a local library. Find interesting facts or pictures that might assist your child in his or her video tour.

Use with Pupil Edition, p. 94

Assessment Support

Use the following Assessment Book pages and The test maker to assess content and skills in Chapter 3 and Unit 1. You can also view and print Assessment Book pages from the Teacher Resources CD-ROM.

Assessment Book, p. 9

Chapter 3 Test

Part 1: Content Test

Directions: Fill in the circle next to the correct answer.

Lesson Objective (1:1)

1. What might have drawn the first Americans to North America?
   - Ⓐ Cheap land was for sale.
   - ● They followed a migrating herd of animals.
   - Ⓒ They wanted to live in a cooler climate.
   - Ⓓ They had heard of its abundance of water.

Lesson Objective (1:2)

2. Why did many settlers move westward during the early 1800s?
   - Ⓐ work in factories
   - Ⓑ follow migrating herds
   - ● find more land
   - Ⓓ build new buildings and cities

Lesson Objective (1:2)

3. Which 1848 discovery led many people to move to California?
   - Ⓐ farmland
   - Ⓑ steel
   - Ⓒ electricity
   - ● gold

Lesson Objective (1:3)

4. Which of the following is NOT a change that occurred in the late 1800s?
   - ● More people moved from cities to rural areas.
   - Ⓑ Industries grew near the sources of raw materials.
   - Ⓒ Many people left farming to work in the cities.
   - Ⓓ Railroads expanded across the country.

Lesson Objective (2:1)

5. How did people barter to get the things they needed?
   - ● They traded goods and services they had for those they needed.
   - Ⓑ They used money to buy goods and services.
   - Ⓒ They developed skills to make things for themselves.
   - Ⓓ They used valuable objects instead of money to buy things.

Lesson Objective (2:2)

6. What role do producers play in the economy?
   - Ⓐ They buy goods and services from other businesses.
   - ● They make goods or products to sell for a profit.
   - Ⓒ They control the shipment of goods from one place to another.
   - Ⓓ They decide what items of value can be used as money.

Lesson Objective (2:2)

7. How does a business make a profit?
   - Ⓐ It buys goods and services from other businesses at a high price.
   - Ⓑ It does not pay the workers who make the products.
   - ● It sets the price for its goods or services high enough to pay for its costs and to have money left over.
   - Ⓓ The government limits what goods a business can produce.

Assessment Book   Unit 1, Chapter 3 Test 9

Use with Pupil Edition, p. 88

Assessment Book, p. 10

Lesson Objective (2:3)

8. In a free enterprise economy, a business operates on what system?
   - Ⓐ barter for services
   - ● supply and demand
   - Ⓒ exchange of goods for shells
   - Ⓓ opportunity cost

Lesson Objective (2:3)

9. What might happen if a business makes more of a product than people want to buy?
   - Ⓐ The price of the product will likely increase.
   - ● The price of the product will likely decrease.
   - Ⓒ The producer will stop selling the product.
   - Ⓓ Consumers will ask the producer to make more of the product.

Lesson Objective (2:3)

10. If the supply of a popular product is much less than the demand for it, what likely will happen to the price?
    - ● It likely will go up.
    - Ⓑ It likely will go down.
    - Ⓒ People likely will pay any price.
    - Ⓓ People will buy more.

Lesson Objective (2:1, 2)

11. Which is NOT a way in which people contribute to the nation's economy?
    - Ⓐ learning the skills needed in the workplace
    - Ⓑ producing goods and services
    - Ⓒ buying and selling goods
    - ● trading by barter

Lesson Objective (3:1)

12. How are the regions of the United States interdependent?
    - Ⓐ They now barter for goods and services.
    - Ⓑ They do not depend on one another for goods.
    - Ⓒ They produce similar goods and services.
    - ● They rely on one another for goods, services, and resources.

Lesson Objective (3:1, 3)

13. How does transportation help economically interdependent regions?
    - Ⓐ It helps producers take orders from consumers.
    - ● It helps the interdependent regions get the resources they need.
    - Ⓒ Companies can no longer track what is sent from one place to another.
    - Ⓓ Computers and the Internet help companies conduct business daily.

Lesson Objective (3:2)

14. Which of the following is an example of globalization?
    - ● The parts of a computer are made all around the world.
    - Ⓑ Dairy farms in Wisconsin make ice cream from milk.
    - Ⓒ A local pizza restaurant holds a fund-raiser to support a worldwide cause.
    - Ⓓ Bob's Bike Shop is located on 321 Main Street in Yellow Springs.

Lesson Objective (3:3)

15. Which of the following factors has NOT increased world trade?
    - Ⓐ globalization
    - ● barter
    - Ⓒ communication
    - Ⓓ transportation

Use with Pupil Edition, p. 88

Assessment Book, p. 11

Part 2: Skills Test

Directions: Use complete sentences to answer questions 1–5. Use a separate sheet of paper if you need more space.

1. How did life in the United States change between the 1700s and the late 1800s? **Compare and Contrast**

   Possible answer: In the 1700s, most people in the United States lived in rural areas and farmed. In the late 1800s, industries grew rapidly. Many people began moving to cities, and people began to work in factories instead of on farms.

2. Which advancements in technology in the late 1800s are seen in the United States today? **Generalize**

   Possible answer: Linking the country by railroad, producing electricity, making steel, and using natural resources to run engines

3. In order, how did the United States economy evolve, or change, from a system of barter to a global economy? **Sequence**

   Possible answer: People bartered to trade goods and services. Then people began using shells, stones, and disks as money so they could buy and sell products without trading. As transportation and communication improved, businesses were able to make and sell their products in more places and in other countries.

Use with Pupil Edition, p. 88

Assessment Book, p. 12

4. How do both supply and demand affect the price of goods and services people buy? **Cause and Effect**

   As supply increases, more products exist that need to be sold, and the price may go down. As demand increases, people are willing to pay more for a product, so the price may go up.

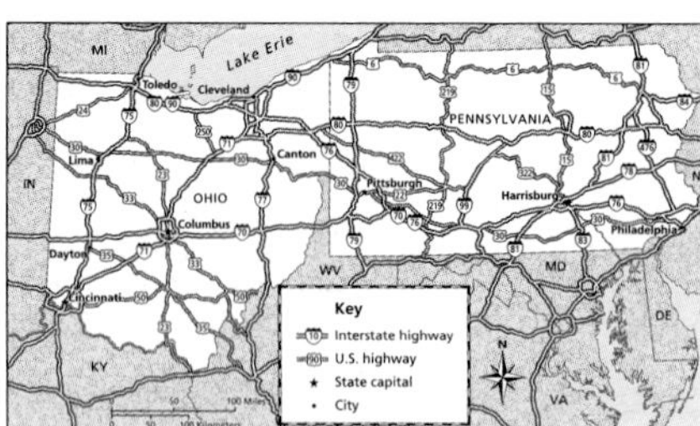

Road Map of Ohio and Pennsylvania

5. A friend is planning to travel from Philadelphia to Cleveland. He wants to know how far the trip is. You can help him find out by completing the table. **Use a Road Map and Scale**

Route	Estimated Distance	
	Miles	Kilometers
Philadelphia to Harrisburg	95	153
Harrisburg to Pittsburgh	180	290
Pittsburgh to Cleveland	120	193
TOTAL from Philadelphia to Cleveland	395	636

Use with Pupil Edition, p. 88

Assessment Support

Assessment Book, p. 13

Unit 1 Test

Part 1: Content Test

Directions: Fill in the circle next to the correct answer.

Lesson Objective (1–1:1)

1. Which of the following is NOT one of the five major regions in the United States?
- Ⓐ Northeast
- Ⓑ Midwest
- Ⓒ Southeast
- ● Northwest

Lesson Objective (1–1:3)

2. Which of the following sometimes determines regional boundaries?
- Ⓐ laws
- ● major landforms
- Ⓒ political decisions
- Ⓓ weather

Lesson Objective (1–2:1)

3. How is weather different from climate?
- Ⓐ Weather is based on a pattern over a long period of time.
- Ⓑ Weather includes temperature and precipitation.
- ● Weather can change every day.
- Ⓓ Weather does not vary in different parts of the United States.

Lesson Objective (1–2:3)

4. Which of the following is a factor that affects climate?
- Ⓐ natural resources
- Ⓑ humidity
- Ⓒ state boundaries
- ● elevation

Lesson Objective (1–3:2)

5. How do renewable resources differ from nonrenewable resources?
- ● They can be replaced.
- Ⓑ They are limited.
- Ⓒ They are found in the earth.
- Ⓓ They can be recycled.

Lesson Objective (2–1:1)

6. From where do some scientists believe the first Americans arrived?
- Ⓐ Africa
- ● Asia
- Ⓒ France
- Ⓓ England

Lesson Objective (2–1:2)

7. Why did some European explorers travel to North America?
- Ⓐ open a trade route to South America
- ● find wealth and land
- Ⓒ learn new languages
- Ⓓ learn more about Christianity

Lesson Objective (2–2:1)

8. What is the Constitution?
- Ⓐ building where the President lives
- Ⓑ nation's highest court
- ● written plan for the nation's government
- Ⓓ branch of government that enforces law

Assessment Book — Unit 1 Test **13**

Use with Pupil Edition, p. 92

Assessment Book, p. 14

Lesson Objective (2–2:3)

9. What is the main responsibility of the judicial branch of government?
- ● interpret laws
- Ⓑ make laws
- Ⓒ pass laws
- Ⓓ enforce laws

Lesson Objective (2–3:3)

10. Which of the following is NOT a responsibility of U.S. citizens?
- Ⓐ respect the nation's laws
- ● get a passport
- Ⓒ serve on a jury
- Ⓓ vote

Lesson Objective (3–1:2)

11. Why did many people in the United States move westward in the 1700s and early 1800s?
- ● find more land and set up farms
- Ⓑ follow migrating herds of animals
- Ⓒ find jobs in factories
- Ⓓ move to larger cities

Lesson Objective (3–1:3)

12. What happened in the late 1800s to change the way people lived and worked?
- Ⓐ The demand for farm products increased in U.S. cities and in Europe.
- Ⓑ Few people came to the United States.
- ● Advances in technology helped industries grow.
- Ⓓ Europeans began trading with Native Americans.

Lesson Objective (3–2:2)

13. What is a profit?
- ● the money left over after a business has paid all its costs
- Ⓑ the cost of the resources used to make a product
- Ⓒ limits placed on the number of goods and services provided
- Ⓓ system in which the government decides which goods a business provides

Lesson Objective (3–3:1)

14. Why are many regions of the United States economically interdependent?
- Ⓐ They use newer modes of transportation.
- Ⓑ They no longer communicate with one another.
- Ⓒ They all accept the same types of money.
- ● They rely on one another for goods and services.

Lesson Objective (3–3:2)

15. How does globalization affect the economy?
- Ⓐ allows businesses to communicate
- Ⓑ requires businesses to trade products
- ● ties countries together economically
- Ⓓ sets up a transportation system between countries

Use with Pupil Edition, p. 92

Assessment Book, p. 15

Part 2: Skills Test

Directions: Use complete sentences to answer questions 1–5. Use a separate sheet of paper if you need more space.

1. Why do some people believe that it is important to conserve resources? **Point of View**

Possible answer: Many resources may run out. Others cause pollution, so we should use them less. By conserving resources, we can make them last longer.

2. Who were the first Americans and from where might they have come? **Summarize**

Possible answer: The first Americans were Native Americans who came to North America long before European explorers arrived. They may have come from Asia, the South Pacific islands, or Australia.

3. Why is it important for citizens of the United States to understand their rights and responsibilities? **Draw Conclusions**

Possible answer: The U.S. government gets its power from its people. Citizens must understand their rights and responsibilities so they can make wise voting decisions and pay for services people need.

Use with Pupil Edition, p. 92

Assessment Book, p. 16

4. How have improved transportation and communication affected world trade? **Cause and Effect**

They have allowed companies to communicate with businesses in other countries, transport goods from one place to another more easily, and get almost anything they need or want.

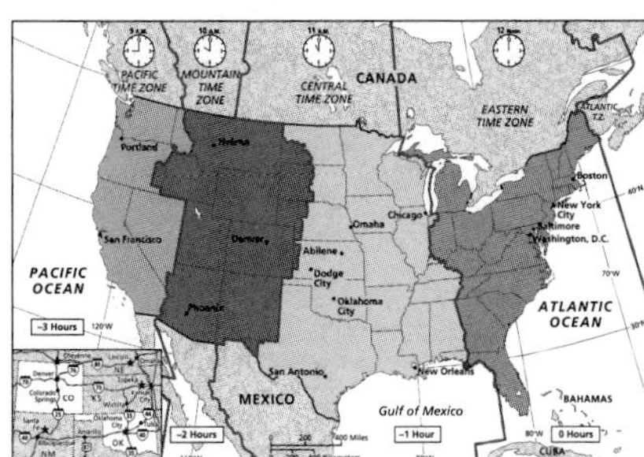

Road Map of Colorado and Oklahoma

5. A bus is traveling from Denver to Oklahoma City. It leaves Denver at 4:00 P.M.

a. What time is that in Oklahoma City? **Read a Time-Zone Map** 5:00 P.M.

b. What major highways will the bus take to get from Denver to Oklahoma City? **Read Road Map and Scale** Routes 70 and 135

c. How might having both the time-zone map and insert map help you if you were making this trip? **Read Inset Maps**

Possible answer: The inset map will help me figure out what routes to take and how long the trip will take. The time-zone map can help me figure out what the local time will be when I arrive in Oklahoma City.

Use with Pupil Edition, p. 92

Earning and Learning

Chapter 3 Outline

- **Lesson 1, *The Land of Plenty,*** pp. 66–71
- **Lesson 2, *Trade Then and Now,*** pp. 72–79
- **Lesson 3, *Transportation and Communication,*** pp. 80–85
- **Map and Globe Skills: *Use a Road Map and Scale,*** pp. 86–87

Resources

- Workbook, p. 14: Vocabulary Preview
- Vocabulary Cards
- Social Studies Plus!

The Land of Plenty: Lesson 1

This is a picture of a wheat field. Ask students what types of riches they can identify in the picture. Have them explain why these items are considered riches.

Trade Then and Now: Lesson 2

This is a historical photograph of a midwestern trading post near the Mississippi River. Ask students how they think a trading post might have been different from a modern store.

Transportation and Communication: Lesson 3

This is a picture of an airport. Ask students how air travel helps people and companies in the United States do business around the world.

CHAPTER 3 Earning and Learning

Lesson 1

The Land of Plenty
What makes up our riches? The answer to this question has changed over the years.

1

Lesson 2

Trade Then and Now
People have used different methods of trading in different places and at different times.

2

Lesson 3

Transportation and Communication
The United States does business with countries all over the world.

3

Practice and Extend

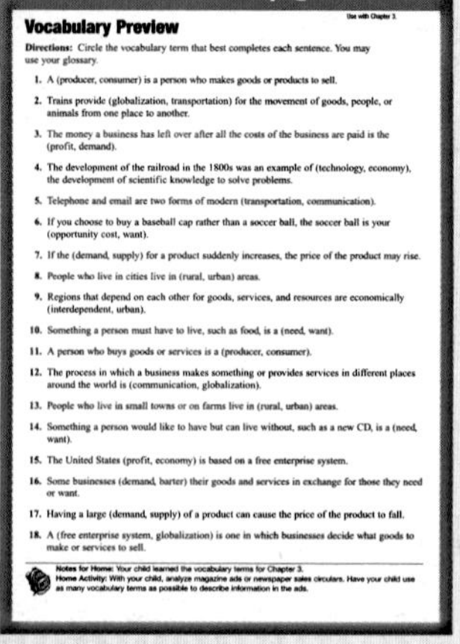

Vocabulary Preview

- Use Workbook p. 14 to help students preview the vocabulary words in this chapter.
- Use Vocabulary Cards to preview key concept words in this chapter.

Also on Teacher Resources CD-ROM.

Workbook, p. 14

Use with Chapter 3.

Vocabulary Preview

Directions: Circle the vocabulary term that best completes each sentence. You may use your glossary.

1. A (producer, consumer) is a person who makes goods or products to sell.
2. Trains provide (globalization, transportation) for the movement of goods, people, or animals from one place to another.
3. The money a business has left over after all the costs of the business are paid is the (profit, demand).
4. The development of the railroad in the 1800s was an example of (technology, economy), the development of scientific knowledge to solve problems.
5. Telephone and email are two forms of modern (transportation, communication).
6. If you choose to buy a baseball cap rather than a soccer ball, the soccer ball is your (opportunity cost, want).
7. If the (demand, supply) for a product suddenly increases, the price of the product may rise.
8. People who live in cities live in (rural, urban) areas.
9. Regions that depend on each other for goods, services, and resources are economically (interdependent, urban).
10. Something a person must have to live, such as food, is a (need, want).
11. A person who buys goods or services is a (producer, consumer).
12. The process in which a business makes something or provides services in different places around the world is (communication, globalization).
13. People who live in small towns or on farms live in (rural, urban) areas.
14. Something a person would like to have but can live without, such as a new CD, is a (need, want).
15. The United States (profit, economy) is based on a free enterprise system.
16. Some businesses (demand, barter) their goods and services in exchange for those they need or want.
17. Having a large (demand, supply) of a product can cause the price of the product to fall.
18. A (free enterprise system, globalization) is one in which businesses decide what goods to make or services to sell.

Notes for Home: Your child learned the vocabulary terms for Chapter 3.
Home Activity: With your child, analyze magazine ads or newspaper sales circulars. Have your child use as many vocabulary terms as possible to describe information in the ads.

Locating Places

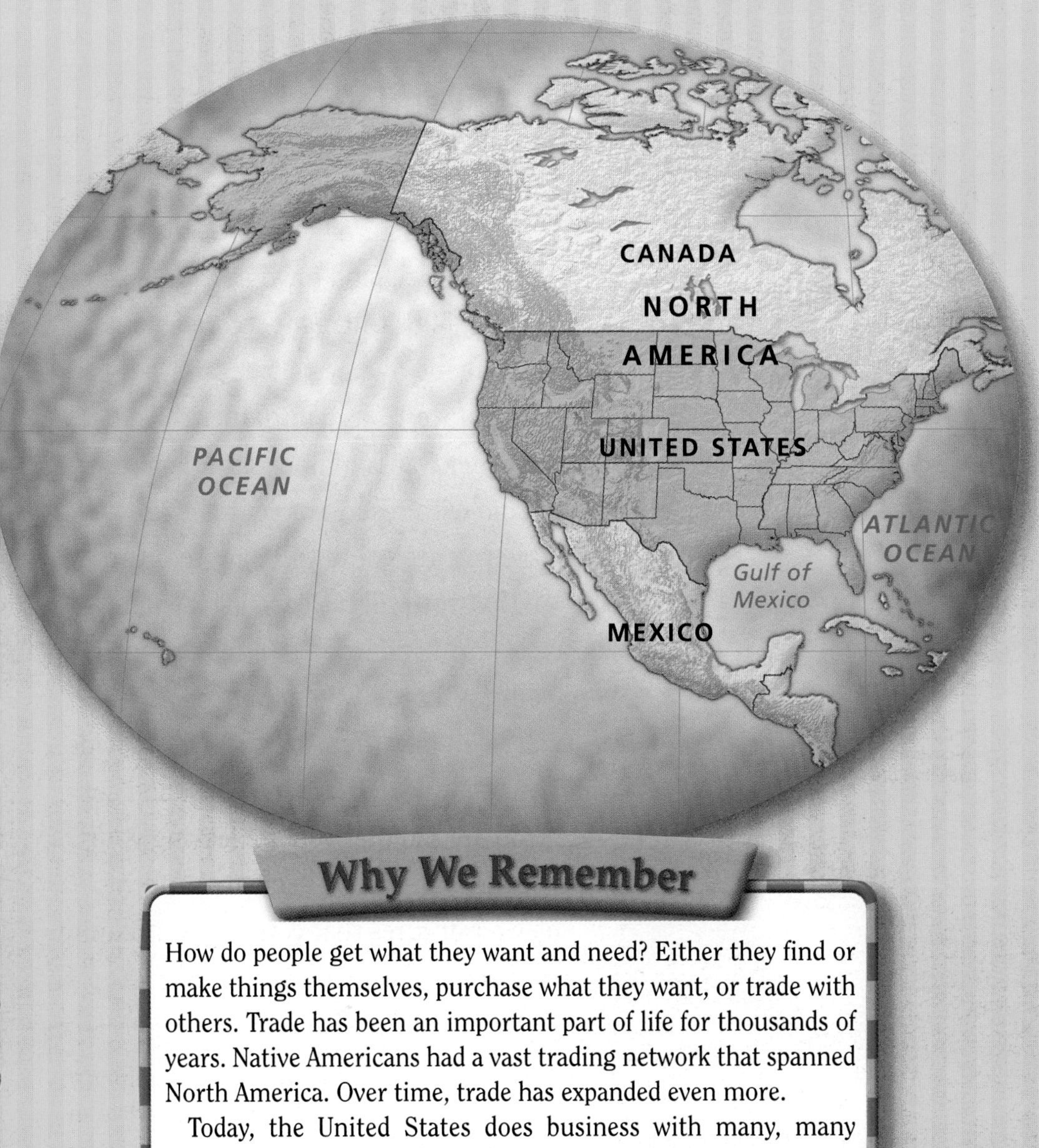

Why We Remember

How do people get what they want and need? Either they find or make things themselves, purchase what they want, or trade with others. Trade has been an important part of life for thousands of years. Native Americans had a vast trading network that spanned North America. Over time, trade has expanded even more.

Today, the United States does business with many, many different nations. Learning basic ideas about economics is important for understanding our nation and our world.

65

WEB SITE
Technology

You can learn more about places where resources are found and goods are made by clicking on *Atlas* at **www.sfsocialstudies.com.**

SOCIAL STUDIES STRAND
Geography

Mental Mapping Have students draw a map of a local shopping center or, if their community has one, a main commercial street. Have them label the stores and other places of business. Discuss with students what goods and services are traded at the businesses on their maps.

Locating Places

- Have students examine the pictures shown on p. 64 for Lessons 1, 2, and 3.

Why We Remember

Have students read the "Why We Remember" paragraph on p. 65 and ask why the concepts of trade and economics in this chapter might be important to them. Have them look at the labels on their clothing, their backpacks, and other items in the classroom to find out where each item was made. Then ask students to consider how life might be different for them if the United States did not do business with other countries.

The Land of Plenty

Objectives

- Explain what might have drawn the first Americans to North America.
- Explain why Americans decided to move westward in the 1800s.
- Describe what happened in the late 1800s to change the way people lived and worked.

Vocabulary

technology, p. 70; **rural,** p. 71; **urban,** p. 71

Resources

- Workbook, p. 15
- Transparency 6
- Every Student Learns Guide, pp. 26–29
- Quick Study, pp. 14–15

Quick Teaching Plan

If time is short, have students create a three-column chart with the headings: *Period, Main Occupations,* and *Important Resources.*

- In the *Period* column have students write: *First Americans, Early European Settlers, 1700–1870,* and *1870–1920.*
- Have students complete the chart as they read the lesson independently.

1 Introduce and Motivate

Preview To activate prior knowledge, ask students why the United States might be called the "Land of Plenty." Tell students they will learn more about the role natural resources have played in United States history as they read Lesson 1.

Ask students why this family is moving from New England to the West. Then ask students if they think people move for the same reasons today.

LESSON 1

The Land of Plenty

PREVIEW

Focus on the Main Idea
North America's rich resources have drawn many people to the continent and to specific regions of what today is our country.

VOCABULARY
technology
rural
urban

You Are There You are living in a small New England town in the 1850s. It's the night before your family is moving to a new place far away, "the land out west," as your father calls it.

Your father wants to find better land to farm—land with resources yet to be used. The place you are going will have many more trees so that you will have wood all winter to keep you warm and wood to build that new barn your father has wanted for so long. The new place will have rich soil that will provide wonderful, abundant fields of wheat and corn.

You are sad that you are leaving your friends, but you are excited about the new adventures that you and your family will have.

▶ A covered wagon that once traveled the Oregon Trail

Target Skill **Summarize** After you read, summarize the reasons that people want to live in certain places.

66

Practice and Extend

READING SKILL Summarize

In the Lesson Review, students complete a graphic organizer like the one below. You may want to provide students with a copy of Transparency 6 to complete as they read the lesson.

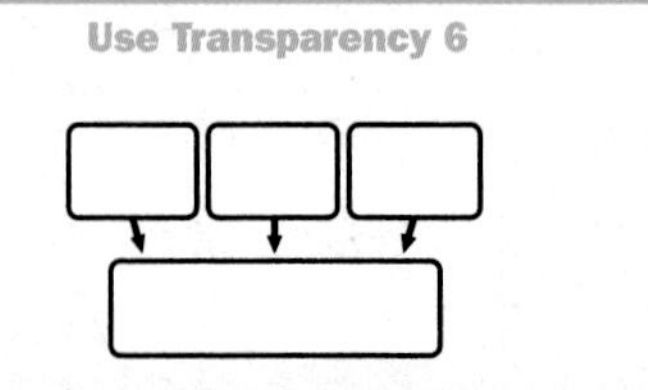

VOCABULARY Related Word Study

Have students read the definition of *technology* on page 70. Then tell them that technology is one member of a large word family. The Greek word *techne* means "art, skill, craft," and from this word we get *technology, technical, technician,* and *technique*. Encourage students to look up each of these words, or read them the definitions. Then discuss how the idea of art, skill, or craft relates to each word's definition.

A Land of Riches

When the first Americans came to North America, they arrived at a place full of natural resources. What they found convinced them to stay. They very likely came to this continent by accident, probably following a migrating herd of animals during a hunt. Once here, they found game
1 animals, fish, fertile soil, and wild plants in abundance.

While some first Americans settled in one area and farmed, many continued to move and spread across North America. Different resources were available in different regions. Each group found ways to use their local resources. Sometimes the first Americans traded over very long
2 distances for resources that were not available nearby.

In the early 1500s, Europeans also came to the Americas. Like the first Americans, they too were attracted to the continents by their rich resources.

In North America, the Europeans at first settled along the rivers near the
coast. They traded with the Native 3
Americans for resources found farther inland. But the Europeans began to move farther west and they, like the first Americans, settled in certain areas and farmed the rich land.

REVIEW What were some of the resources that convinced the first Americans to stay?
Main Idea and Details

Museum of Mankind, London

▶ These engraved knives were used for cutting blocks of snow by Native American groups living in cold regions.

▶ The first Americans hunted mammoths and other large mammals.

2 Teach and Discuss

PAGE 67

A Land of Riches

Quick Summary The first Americans found rich resources when they came to this continent. Later, European settlers were attracted by the same resources.

1 **What did the first Americans find when they came to this continent?** Possible answers: Fish and other animals, fertile soil, wild plants
Main Idea and Details

2 **Why did trade develop among different Native American groups?** Different resources were available in different regions. Groups traded for resources that were not available nearby.
Analyze Information

3 **How did Native Americans help the early European settlers?** They traded with them for resources found farther inland. **Main Idea and Details**

✓ **REVIEW ANSWER** Fish and other animals, fertile soil, and wild plants
Main Idea and Details

MEETING INDIVIDUAL NEEDS
Leveled Practice

Compare the First Americans and European Settlers Ask students to identify similarities and differences between the first Americans and the first European settlers.

Easy Have students write three sentences comparing or contrasting the two groups. **Reteach**

On-Level Have students complete a Venn diagram to compare the two groups. **Extend**

Challenge Have students make a list of possible difficulties the Native Americans and the first European settlers might have faced when they began to trade with one another. **Enrich**

For a Lesson Summary, use Quick Study, p. 14.

PAGES 68–69

Moving Westward

Quick Summary In the 1700s and 1800s, agriculture, including raising livestock, was the main economic activity. Overcrowding in cities along the Atlantic coast encouraged people to move westward in search of more land.

4 **How could farmers in the 1700s and 1800s earn money?** They could sell their extra farm products to others. Main Idea and Details

Test Talk

Use Information from Graphics

5 **What can you observe from the picture about the settlers who moved westward in the 1800s?** Tell students to use details from the picture to support their answer. They traveled by covered wagons drawn by horses. Analyze Pictures

6 **Why did settlers begin moving westward?** Cities along the Atlantic coast had become crowded. They moved to find more land. Main Idea and Details

▶ Wagon trains traveling west took many settlers to new homes.

Culver Pictures 5

Moving Westward

By the 1700s European settlers realized that the greatest resource available in North America was the land. The settlers themselves were another great resource. They cleared trees and set up farms. They could use the crops they grew and the animals they raised to feed their families. They could sell or trade their
4 extra farm products to others. There was an increase in demand for farm products due to the growing cities in North America and Europe. Producing crops and raising livestock soon came to be the nation's main economic activity.

Throughout the 1700s and the 1800s, people continued to come to North America to make a better life for themselves and their families. Cities along the Atlantic coast had become crowded. Settlers moved westward to find more land. They moved into places 6
in the Midwest where they carved out farms on the plains. They moved into the Southwest where they raised sheep and cattle. Everywhere they moved, they cleared land for farms.

68

Practice and Extend

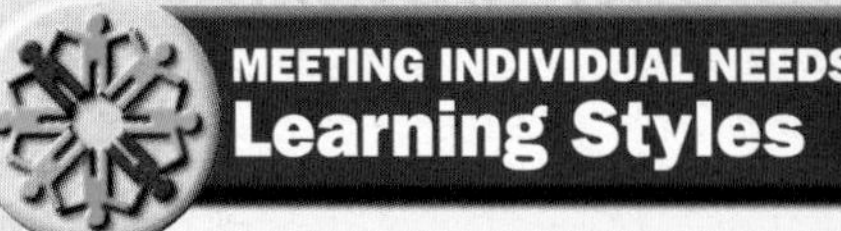

MEETING INDIVIDUAL NEEDS
Learning Styles

Describe the Settlement of the West Using their individual learning styles, students describe the settlement of the West.

Kinesthetic Learning Have students research, write, and present a skit about a family moving westward on a wagon train in the 1800s.

Visual Learning Have students use an almanac to label an outline map of the United States with the year each state was settled. Tell them to use different colors for the 1600s, 1700s, and 1800s.

Musical Learning Have students research or write a jingle or song that people on a wagon train might have sung during their journey.

Another resource drew people westward. In 1848 a man in California found gold in a stream running through the land of his employer. Within months, tens of thousands of excited people were heading to the area to "strike it rich." Few people became wealthy in the rush to California for gold, but many stayed in the region. This caused a population boom along the West Coast. 7

REVIEW Why did agriculture become the main economic activity in America? Summarize

Plentiful fields of wheat such as this are part of many Midwest farms.

The discovery of gold in California caused many people to move west.

Lithograph by Currier & Ives

8

SOCIAL STUDIES STRAND
Geography

Have students locate Sacramento, California, on a map. Then tell them that gold was first discovered at Sutter's Mill, which is about 35 miles northeast of Sacramento on the American River.

7 **How did the discovery of gold affect the settlement of the West Coast?** It caused the population to grow rapidly. Cause and Effect

✓ **REVIEW ANSWER** America had much fertile land and many people to work on it. Summarize

8 **Look at the photo. Do you think the people searching for gold had an easy or difficult life? Why?** Possible answer: It was difficult because they had to work outside in the dirt and water, and a lot of effort usually went into finding just a little gold. Analyze Pictures

SOCIAL STUDIES
Background

About the California Gold Rush

- James W. Marshall, a carpenter, was building a sawmill for John Sutter when he discovered gold. To make the river deep enough for the sawmill's waterwheel, he had to dig a hole in the riverbed. When he looked at the dirt from the river, he saw glittering gold.
- California gold seekers were called "forty-niners" because most of them came to the West in search of gold in 1849.
- Most miners lived in tents and lean-tos. Food and many other supplies were expensive and difficult to obtain.
- By 1849 about 80,000 people had come to California to search for gold. In 1850 California had the necessary population to request statehood.

PAGES 70–71

Growth of Industry

Quick Summary Use of natural resources and technological advances led to rapid industrial growth in the late 1800s and early 1900s. By 1920, the rural economy of the United States had been transformed into an urban, industrial economy.

H SOCIAL STUDIES STRAND
History

Point out that the railroad encouraged the rapid settlement of the West. The first transcontinental rail line was completed in 1869.

9 **How did the railroad contribute to the economic growth of the United States?** It linked the resources of the West to the markets in the East.
Apply Information

Ongoing Assessment

If... students have difficulty understanding how a railroad might affect the economy,	**then...** have them brainstorm how people's lives changed after the transcontinental railroad was completed.

10 **What natural resources were important in the industrial growth of the United States? Why?** Iron, coal, and oil; Iron and coal made it possible to create new technologies and build industry. Coal and oil were used to run engines and new machines.
Draw Conclusions

Growth of Industry

While settlers were moving steadily westward, industries were rapidly growing in other parts of the country. America was found to be rich in iron and coal, the raw materials necessary for industry.

By 1870 railroad workers had laid train tracks from coast to coast. Railroads linked resources of the West
9 to markets in the East. The railroad was one example of a new technology. **Technology** is the development and use of scientific knowledge to solve practical problems.

Advances in other technologies occurred in the latter half of the century. For example, people came up with a new process of making steel that made it cheaper to produce. By the 1900s steel plants began turning out the steel frameworks that made skyscrapers, cars, and other new products possible.

New ways to produce electricity were also developed. Electricity powered lights and machines, such as the elevator. People learned how to drill deep underground for oil. This provided another source of power to run machines.

Coal, electricity, and oil were used to run engines and the new machines that were being invented. All these technologies led to the growth of
other industries. 10

The rapid growth of industries changed the way people lived and worked in the United States.

70

Practice and Extend

ACCESS CONTENT
ESL Support

Conceptualize Word Meanings Explain the concepts of "rural" and "urban" through simple phrases and visuals.

Beginning Brainstorm a list of words and meanings on the board that could describe urban and rural areas. Have students create a two-column word bank with the English word on the left side and a picture on the right side.

Intermediate Show photos of urban and rural areas. Have students create a two-column chart to list features of the two different environments in both English and their first language.

Advanced Ask students if they would rather live in a rural or urban area and have them give reasons for their choice. You also may wish to have students classify different places where they may have lived as either rural or urban.

For additional ESL support, use Every Student Learns Guide, pp. 26–29.

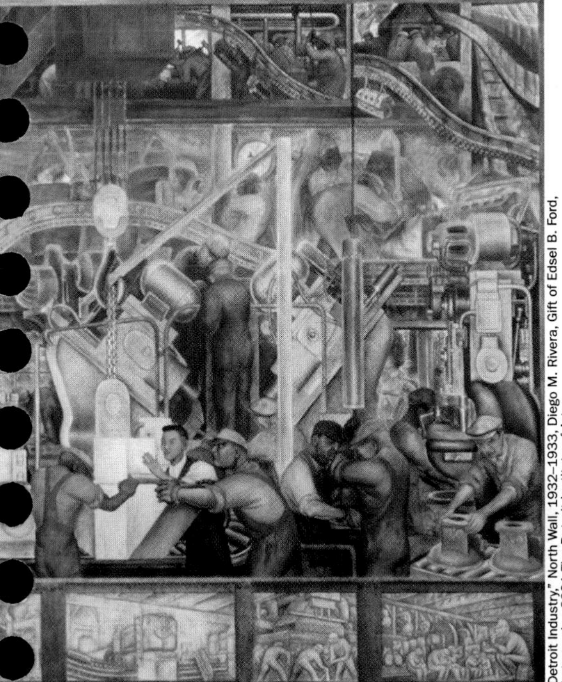

"Detroit Industry," North Wall, 1932–1933, Diego M. Rivera, Gift of Edsel B. Ford, photograph—2001 The Detroit Institute of Arts

▶ **This famous painting is titled "Detroit Industry."**

Cities were centers for most of the new industries that arose in the late 1800s.

People came to the cities to find work. Many farmers left the land. They looked for better jobs in factories. In 1870 the United States was a **rural** nation. Most Americans lived in small towns or on farms. By 1920 the United States had become an **urban** nation with most of the people living in cities. 11

REVIEW How and why did the economy of the United States change in the late 1800s? Summarize

Summarize the Lesson

- **America's resources have attracted people from different countries and enabled many to build better lives.**
- **The growth of agriculture contributed to the movement of people from one region to another.**
- **Our economy has changed from an agricultural economy to an urban industrial economy in the centuries since the founding of our nation.**

LESSON 1 REVIEW

Check Facts and Main Ideas

1. Summarize On a separate sheet of paper, write a sentence summary. Use the words **urban, rural,** and **technology** in your summary.

People lived by hunting and gathering. → Settlers moved to farms in the Midwest. → Industries grew rapidly. → As people moved from rural to urban areas, technology increased.

2. Why did the first Americans come to this continent?
3. What caused Americans to decide to move westward in the 1800s?
4. What happened in the late 1800s to change the way people lived in the United States?
5. **Critical Thinking:** ***Analyze Information*** Think of a product that is in your classroom. Make a list of the resources that were needed to make this product.

Link to Writing

Write a Diary Entry Suppose you are with some of the first Americans traveling in search of food. You stop every night to rest, but each new day the journey begins again. Write about some of the adventures, dangers, and challenges you might face.

71

11 What is the difference between a rural and an urban nation? In a rural nation, most people live in small towns or on farms. In an urban nation, most people live and work in cities. Compare and Contrast

✓ **REVIEW ANSWER** Possible answer: Industries grew and many farmers left the land and went to work in factories. These changes were caused by the discovery of raw materials, the growth of railroads that linked different regions, and advances in technology (new steel-making process, new ways to produce electricity, new ways of getting oil, new machines). Summarize

Summarize the Lesson

Have students take turns reading aloud the three main points. Then ask them what all of these points have in common. (The movement of people)

✓ **LESSON 1 REVIEW**

1. Summarize For possible answers, see the reduced pupil page.
2. Perhaps by accident, but they stayed because of the rich resources they found here
3. To find land; to own their own farms; the gold rush
4. Railroads expanded, new technologies were developed, industries grew, and people moved to the cities for better jobs in factories.
5. **Critical Thinking: *Analyze Information*** Answers might include wood and other products used in making chairs, desks, paper, and pencils.

Link to Writing

Diary entries should be as descriptive as possible while keeping in mind what North America might have been like long ago.

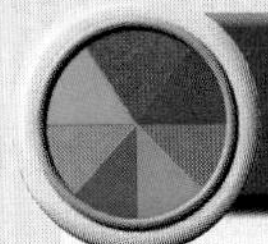

CURRICULUM CONNECTION
Science

Make an Industry Time Line

- Have students use the Internet, an almanac, or an encyclopedia to find five inventions created between 1870 and 1920 that contributed to industrial growth. For example, students might list the incandescent light bulb, the assembly line, the automobile, or the airplane.
- Have students use their research to make a *Growth of Industry* time line.

Workbook, p. 15

Lesson 1: The Land of Plenty

Also on Teacher Resources CD-ROM.

Trade Then and Now

Objectives

- Describe how goods and services were traded by barter.
- Explain how a business makes a profit.
- Explain the difference between supply and demand.

Vocabulary

need, p. 73; **want,** p. 73; **barter,** p. 73; **producer,** p. 74; **consumer,** p. 74; **economy,** p. 76; **free enterprise system,** p. 76; **profit,** p. 76; **supply,** p. 77; **demand,** p. 77; **opportunity cost,** p. 78

Resources

- Workbook, p. 16
- Transparency 5
- Every Student Learns Guide, pp. 30–33
- Quick Study, pp. 16–17

Quick Teaching Plan

If time is short, have students make a class picture book illustrating trade and basic economic principles.

- Have students draw a picture illustrating the main idea or vocabulary of each section and write a caption.
- Have students staple their papers together to create the book.

1 Introduce and Motivate

Preview To activate prior knowledge, ask students if they have ever made a trade. Then ask students why the Native Americans began trading and with whom they traded. Tell students that they will learn more about trade and how it affects the economy in Lesson 2.

Have students work in small groups to write a conclusion for this situation. Then ask groups to role-play their situation for the class and discuss why some trades might be successful while others are unsuccessful.

LESSON 2

Trade Then and Now

PREVIEW

Focus on the Main Idea
People trade for the goods and services that they need and want.

PLACE
St. Louis, Missouri

VOCABULARY
need
want
barter
producer
consumer
economy
free enterprise system
profit
supply
demand
opportunity cost

You Are There You are a fur trapper in the 1600s. It's early fall, time to stock up before winter comes. You have collected several fur pelts, and you need to trade them for sacks of corn and wheat. You've traveled a long distance to reach the nearest trading post.

A farmer with sacks of grain catches your eye. He says he needs pelts to make clothing to keep his family warm in the winter. You have extra pelts to trade. He has extra sacks of grain to trade. You wonder how many pelts the farmer wants for his extra sacks of corn and wheat.

Summarize As you read, look for details to help you summarize how trade has changed over time.

72

Practice and Extend

READING SKILL
Summarize

In the Lesson Review, students complete a graphic organizer like the one below. You may want to provide students with a copy of Transparency 5 to complete as they read the lesson.

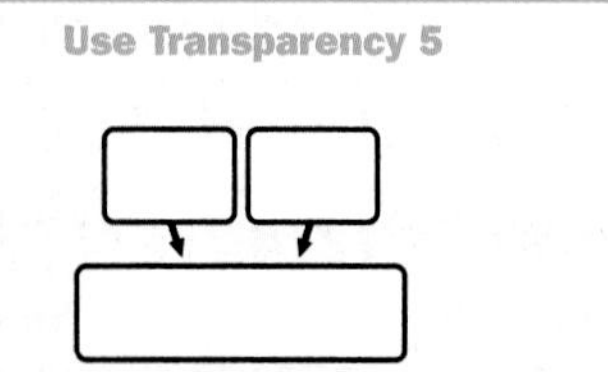

VOCABULARY
Context Clues

Write on the board the word pairs *need/want, producer/consumer,* and *supply/demand*. Have students find the definitions of each word in the text, then discuss how the words in each pair are related. Ask students to give examples from their own lives when possible to illustrate the concepts. (I *need* clothes, but I *want* the toy.)

Trading for Needs and Wants

Early in the history of the United States, people traded for the goods and services that they needed and wanted. A **need** is something that a person must have to live. People need
1 food, clothing, and shelter. A **want** is something that a person would like to
2 have, but can live without. People want things to make their lives easier and more comfortable.

People often bartered for what they needed and wanted. To **barter** is to trade one kind of goods or service for another. For example, people may have
3 bartered fur pelts for food they needed. In the early 1800s, **St. Louis, Missouri,** grew because people came there to trade for fur.

In other situations, people skilled at building things may have bartered their services for another kind of service. For example, a person might help someone build a house. In exchange for that service, the building owner might help the other person harvest a crop.

In ancient times, people used shells, stones, and round metal disks as money. A person who was willing to sell something exchanged that good or service for a certain number of the shells, stones, or metal disks. In time, however, people relied less on bartering as a way of trading.

REVIEW Describe a time when you have bartered with a friend.
Apply Information

Painting by Alfred Fredericks

▶ This famous painting shows a European explorer trading with Native Americans.

73

2 Teach and Discuss

PAGE 73

Trading for Needs and Wants

Quick Summary People began trading because there were goods and services they needed or wanted. In the past, people used bartering to trade one kind of good or service for another.

1 **What basic needs did people trade for in the past?** Food, clothing, and shelter Main Idea and Details

2 **Would you classify popcorn as a need or want? Why?** A want; Because it is something a person would like to have but can live without Categorize

SOCIAL STUDIES STRAND
Economics

Point out that goods are physical things you can touch and feel, like objects in a store. Services are not physical objects.

3 **How might you obtain a good or service if you did not have any money?** Possible answer: You could barter for it. Draw Conclusions

✓ **REVIEW ANSWER** Students may describe instances when they traded baseball cards, comic books, video games, or food. Apply Information

MEETING INDIVIDUAL NEEDS
Leveled Practice

Identify Needs and Wants Help students understand the difference between needs and wants.

Easy Show students pictures of different goods and services and have them classify each as a need or want. **Reteach**

On-Level Have students create a personal list of their needs and wants. Tell them to rate them from the most important to the least important. Ask volunteers to explain their ratings. **Extend**

Challenge Have students create a skit between a parent and a child based on this situation: You need a new pair of jeans. The ones you want cost $65.00. **Enrich**

For a Lesson Summary, use Quick Study, p. 16.

PAGE 74

Using Money

Quick Summary The Egyptians, Greeks, and Chinese began using money thousands of years ago. Today consumers use paper bills, metal coins, and checks to buy products and services.

4 **Who invented the type of money we use today?** The Greeks invented the first coins, and the Chinese invented paper money. **Analyze Information**

5 **Why do you think people need money?** Possible answer: To buy the things they need and want **Summarize**

6 **How do producers decide on a price at which to sell their products?** Possible answer: They decide on a price that covers their costs and gives them a profit and that they think the consumers are willing to pay. **Draw Conclusions**

Test Talk

Locate Key Words in the Text

7 **How do you think consumers might influence the pricing of goods and services?** Tell students that some questions combine what they know with what the text tells them. The answer comes from the *text* and *you.* Suggest students look for the words *consumer, price, goods,* and *services* to help them find the answer. Possible answer: Consumers might not want to buy goods and services that cost too much. Therefore, producers have to sell things at a price that consumers will want to pay. **Hypothesize**

✓ **REVIEW ANSWER** Producers make goods or supply services. Consumers buy a good or service. **Compare and Contrast**

Literature and Social Studies

8 **Did Josefina's papa feel as though he made a good trade or a bad trade for the mules? Explain.** A good trade; Because he could buy the sheep directly with silver instead of trading the mules for goods and the goods for sheep **Evaluate**

Using Money

The use of money goes back thousands of years. About 2500 B.C., the early Egyptians used tiny bars of metal as money. Around 700 B.C., Greek cities produced flat pieces of metal with a picture or design on them. These are considered the first coins used as money. The Chinese, who had a shortage of metal, came up with the idea of paper money about 1,400 years ago. 4

Today, in the United States and in most countries around the world, people use paper bills, metal coins, and checks as money. Our money is divided into dollars and cents. People use this money to buy things that they need and want. 5

People who make goods or products to sell are called **producers.** A person who buys goods or services is a **consumer.** Producers in the United States can set the prices for the goods that they have made or for a service that they want to sell. This price covers 6 their costs of production. Producers also think about what consumers are willing to pay in dollars and cents for the products or services. 7

REVIEW Tell the difference between a producer and a consumer. **Compare and Contrast**

Literature and Social Studies

Josefina Saves the Day

by Valerie Tripp

Josefina Saves the Day is a story about a girl who lived in New Mexico in the 1820s. In this part of the story, Josefina's papá decides to trade his mules. He is excited because Señor Patrick has found people to buy the mules. Read to find out what he will get in return.

"I have good news. Señor Patrick has found traders who want to buy all of our mules."

"My friends will be glad to get the mules," said Patrick quickly. "Mules are sturdy. They do better than oxen on the wagon trails. Oxen are fussy eaters. They have delicate feet, and they get sunburned." Patrick pointed to his own red nose and joked, "Just like me!"

Everyone laughed, and Patrick went on. "I can get you silver for the mules," he said.

Silver! This was lucky indeed. Normally, Papá would have traded the mules for the goods from the americanos. Then he would trade the goods for sheep. Josefina knew Papá must be pleased. It would be much easier to buy the sheep they needed with silver. 8

Practice and Extend

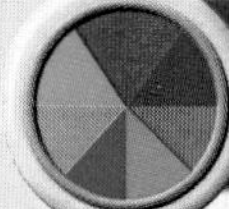

CURRICULUM CONNECTION Writing

Write a Report

- Have students research how cash, debit cards, and credit cards are used to buy goods and services.
- Students may wish to visit bank Web sites to explore different uses for debit and credit cards.
- Then have them prepare a report explaining which type of payment to use for different purchases.
- Encourage students to include charts and pictures in their reports.

CURRICULUM CONNECTION Math

Calculate Exchange Rates

- Have students look in a newspaper for the current exchange rates for the U.S. dollar, Japanese yen, Mexican peso, and the Euro.
- Then ask students to figure out how much a bicycle that costs $80.00 in the United States currency might cost if it were paid for in yen, pesos, or Euros.

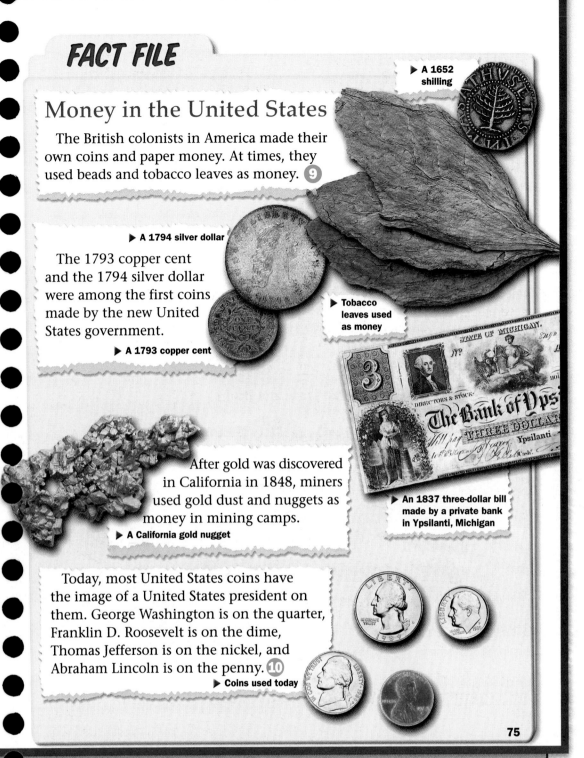

FACT FILE

Money in the United States

The British colonists in America made their own coins and paper money. At times, they used beads and tobacco leaves as money. (9)

▶ A 1652 shilling

▶ Tobacco leaves used as money

▶ A 1794 silver dollar

The 1793 copper cent and the 1794 silver dollar were among the first coins made by the new United States government.

▶ A 1793 copper cent

After gold was discovered in California in 1848, miners used gold dust and nuggets as money in mining camps.

▶ A California gold nugget

▶ An 1837 three-dollar bill made by a private bank in Ypsilanti, Michigan

Today, most United States coins have the image of a United States president on them. George Washington is on the quarter, Franklin D. Roosevelt is on the dime, Thomas Jefferson is on the nickel, and Abraham Lincoln is on the penny. (10)

▶ Coins used today

75

EXTEND LANGUAGE

ESL Support

Examine Word Meanings Have students explore the meanings of *consumer* and *producer.*

Beginning Use simple phrases, gestures, or pictures to portray various consumers and producers. Have students respond to each example with the appropriate label.

Intermediate Invite students to give examples of consumers and producers. Then brainstorm with students synonyms for these terms (e.g. *maker, manufacturer, buyer, customer*).

Advanced Ask students to use a dictionary to find two words that are related to *consume* and *produce* and to share their definitions with the class.

For additional ESL support, use Every Student Learns Guide, pp. 30–33.

FACT FILE

Money in the United States

(9) **Why do you think beads and tobacco leaves sometimes were used as money in the colonies?** Possible answer: Because these items were valued by many colonists and Native Americans **Draw Conclusions**

(10) **Why do you think the first U.S. coins did not have pictures of U.S. presidents on them?** Possible answer: Because at that time there had only been a few U.S. presidents **Hypothesize**

PAGE 76

Free Trade

Quick Summary The economy of the United States is based on the free enterprise system. To make a profit, businesses sell goods or services.

11 **What costs are included in the price of a product?** The costs of the natural resources, machinery, and workers used to make the product Main Idea and Details

12 **Why might a company sell a shirt for $20.00 when it only costs $15.00 to make it?** The company wants to make a profit. Draw Conclusions

13 **Why is it important for a business to make a profit?** Possible answer: So that the business owners can improve the business and buy the things they need and want Apply Information

✓ **REVIEW ANSWER** An economy based on a free enterprise system allows people and businesses to choose what they will produce and sell. In countries that do not have a free enterprise system, the government makes these decisions. Compare and Contrast

DIAGRAM SKILL Answer Natural resources, capital resources, and human resources

Free Trade

In the United States our economy is based on the free enterprise system. An **economy** is the resources of a country, state, region, or community and how the resources are managed. A **free enterprise system** is one in which businesses have the right to produce any goods or provide any service that they want. The government does not tell these businesses what they can produce or sell. People or businesses decide what they want to make and sell.

Not every country in the world has a free enterprise system. Some governments limit what goods businesses can produce and what services businesses can provide. Some governments even choose which businesses can provide certain goods or services. In the United States, business people usually produce and sell goods or services in hopes of making a profit. A **profit** is the money a business person has left over after all the costs of the business are paid.

For example, if a business makes and sells T-shirts, it has to pay for the costs of the natural resources. It also pays for the capital resources—the machinery used to make the product. It has to pay the workers—the human resources—who make the shirts. 11
When the business sells the shirts, it sets the price so that it can pay for all of its costs and still have money left over. The money left over is its profit.

Free Trade and Profit

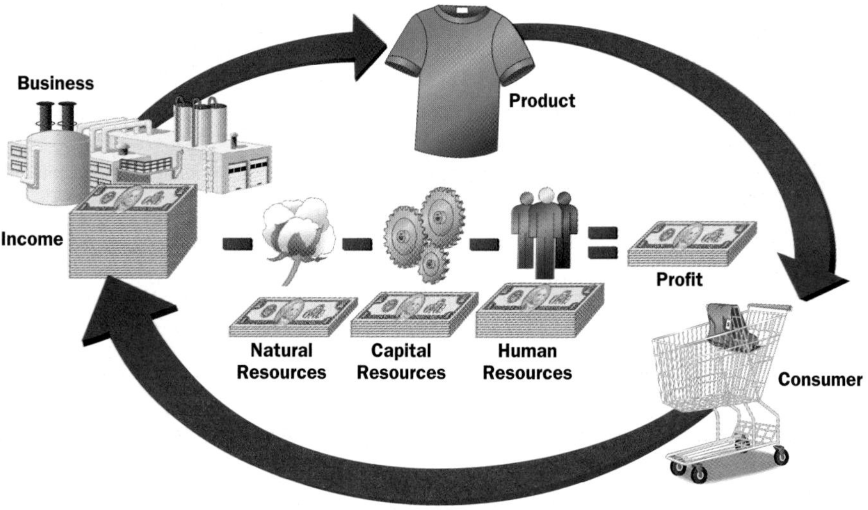

▶ **Many factors affect profit.**

DIAGRAM SKILL ***What factors that affect profit are shown in this diagram?***

76

Practice and Extend

Decision Making

1. **Identify a situation that requires a decision.**
2. **Gather information.**
3. **Identify options.**
4. **Predict consequences.**
5. **Take action to implement a decision.**

Use a Decision-Making Process

- Have students consider the following decision-making scenario: **Suppose you are the owner of a business that makes fruit juices and your profits are down. What can you do to encourage more people to buy your product?**
- Students should use the decision-making process above to decide how to increase their profits. For each step in the process, have students work in small groups to discuss and write about what must be considered as they make their decision. Write these steps on the board or read them aloud.

▶ Clearance signs are common sights when supply of a product is high.

12 Business owners use their profits to improve their businesses and to buy
13 the things that they need and want.

REVIEW How is an economy based on a free enterprise system different from one that is not? Compare and Contrast

The Amount of a Product

In a free enterprise economy, businesses operate based on a system of supply and demand. The quantity of an item that sellers are willing to offer at different prices is called the **supply.** Usually, if a business has made too much of one particular product, there is a large supply. The price of the product may go down. For example, if a business makes more robot dogs than people want to buy, the business may have to lower the price to try to get more people to buy 14 the robots.

The quantity of an item that consumers are willing to buy at different prices is the **demand.** Sometimes demand increases because consumers want more of a product for various reasons. Then, the demand is great, and since the supply is low, the price for the product goes up. If people really want this product, they may be willing to pay a higher price to get it. 15

REVIEW How might an increase in supply benefit a customer? Draw Conclusions

The Amount of a Product

Quick Summary In a free enterprise economy, the price of a product is based on the supply and demand for that product.

14 **Why might a toy store have a sale on robot dogs?** It might have a large supply of the robots and hope the sale would make more people want to buy them. Make Inferences

15 **What effect could an increase in demand for a product have on the price of that product?** The price could go up. Cause and Effect

✓ **Ongoing Assessment**

If...	**then...**
students have difficulty understanding the concept of supply and demand,	give them a specific example of what happens to the price of a popular toy when many people want it, but there are not enough for everyone.

✓ **REVIEW ANSWER** The price might decrease. Draw Conclusions

CURRICULUM CONNECTION
Art

Create Graphics for Supply and Demand Have students develop graphics to illustrate the economic principle of supply and demand.

- Have students work in groups of three or four to brainstorm a graphical way to show the relationship between supply, demand, and price. Suggest that students include symbols such as dollar signs and arrows to make their graphics easy to understand.
- Tell the groups to create a poster of their chosen design.
- Have each group present its completed poster to the class. Discuss whether each graphic is accurate and easy to understand. Allow groups to revise their posters as needed.

PAGE 78

Making Choices

Quick Summary People have to make choices about what to buy with their money. An opportunity cost is what people give up when they choose to buy one thing over another.

16 **Why is it important for people to make careful choices when spending their money?** Because they cannot have everything they want Make Inferences

✓ **REVIEW ANSWER** Possible answer: I had to choose between new tires for my bicycle or getting a new video game. I chose the tires. The opportunity cost was the video game. It was a good choice because I use my new tires to ride my bike with my friends and I enjoy biking more than playing video games. Make Decisions

Decision Making

17 **If you only had enough money to go to one of the places in the picture, which one would you choose? Why?** Answers should include reasons for choosing one place over another. Make Decisions

Making Choices

You probably can't buy everything
16 that you want. You have to make choices. Suppose you are at a fair. You have just enough money either to buy a ticket for a ride that you really want to take or to buy a stuffed toy at the dinosaur exhibit. You are just going to have to choose. If you choose to buy the toy, you can't take the ride. If you choose the ride, you can't buy the toy.

You decide that you are going to take the ride. You'll always be able to remember how much fun the ride was. The toy that you didn't buy is called your opportunity cost. An **opportunity cost** is what you give up when you choose one thing over another.

REVIEW Think of a choice that you had to make. What was your opportunity cost? Did you make a good choice or not? Make Decisions

17

Practice and Extend

MEETING INDIVIDUAL NEEDS
Learning Styles

Making Choices Using their individual learning styles, students apply a decision-making process to an economic scenario.

Kinesthetic Learning Have students write and present a short skit about someone making a decision to buy something.

Visual Learning Have students create a cartoon strip about someone making an economic choice.

Logical Learning Have students make a list of the pros and cons of buying a new DVD or a sweatshirt.

▶ Home computers are becoming more and more common.

Facing the Future

We can all contribute to our nation's economy. If you buy something, you are a consumer. Every time you buy something, you make a contribution to the economy of the United States.

When you get older and begin working, you will also help the economy by producing goods or services. Preparing yourself for work is very important. You need to study and go to school to learn the skills that you will
18 need as an adult in the workplace.

Our country is changing every day. New kinds of technology make the country a better place to live and work. Over the years, use of home computers has grown. Computers help us communicate quickly, do research, bank, and purchase products. The computer industry is creating new ways to work. What do you want to do when you grow up? What are some ways that you can prepare yourself for what you want to do?

REVIEW What are some ways that you can help the economy? Summarize

Summarize the Lesson

- **Goods and services have been traded by barter and money.**
- **Our free enterprise system is based on supply and demand.**
- **You help the economy when you are a careful producer and consumer.**

LESSON 2 REVIEW

Check Facts and Main Ideas

1. Summarize On a separate sheet of paper, fill in the summary statement for the details.

Businesses choose what to produce. | Businesses operate on supply and demand.

→ The United States economy is based on the free enterprise system.

2. How does a business make a **profit?**
3. What is the difference between **supply** and **demand?**
4. How were goods and services traded by **barter?**
5. **Critical Thinking:** ***Draw Conclusions*** How have computers affected the economy of the United States?

Link to Reading

Read a Fable Read the story of "Jack and the Beanstalk." Tell the class what Jack got in return for his mother's cow. Decide if Jack's trade was a good one or a bad one. Explain why you think so.

79

CURRICULUM CONNECTION
Writing

Create a Pamphlet

- Have students work in groups to create a pamphlet for other students on how to be a responsible consumer.
- Tell students to include a list of economic "Dos and Don'ts" in their pamphlets.
- When all groups have completed their pamphlets, allow them to compare and revise them.

Workbook, p. 16

Lesson 2: Trade Then and Now

Also on Teacher Resources CD-ROM.

PAGE 79

Facing the Future

Quick Summary Consumers contribute to the economy by buying goods. Workers contribute by producing goods or services.

18 **In what ways can you prepare yourself for work?** Study, go to school, learn certain skills Main Idea and Details

✓ **REVIEW ANSWER** By buying goods and by learning skills people need in the workplace Summarize

3 Close and Assess

Summarize the Lesson

Have students create a crossword puzzle using the vocabulary words and other important terms from this lesson. Then have them exchange and solve each other's puzzles.

✓ **LESSON 2 REVIEW**

1. Summarize For possible answers, see the reduced pupil page.
2. It sets the prices of its goods and services high enough or reduces its costs so that it has money left over after paying all its costs.
3. Supply is the amount of an item that sellers are willing to offer at various prices. Demand is the amount of an item that consumers are willing to buy at various prices.
4. A person makes a good or provides a service and barters it in exchange for another good or service.
5. **Critical Thinking: *Draw Conclusions*** Possible answers: They have changed the way we purchase products; they have created new jobs.

Link to Reading

Possible answer: At first Jack's trade seemed to be a bad one—a few beans for a cow. But it turned out that Jack had gotten magical beans, and he found a valuable goose as a result of his trade.

Transportation and Communication

Objectives

- Explain what it means for regions to be economically interdependent.
- Describe what globalization is and why countries of the world depend on one another.
- Describe how fast transportation and communication have made national and world trade possible.

Vocabulary

transportation, p. 81; **interdependent,** p. 81; **globalization,** p. 82; **communication,** p. 84

Resources

- Workbook, p. 17
- Transparency 6
- Every Student Learns Guide, pp. 34–37
- Quick Study, pp. 18–19

Quick Teaching Plan

If time is short, have students make a list of the effects of modern transportation and communication on trade and the economy. Tell students to write two items on their lists after reading each section.

1 Introduce and Motivate

Preview To activate prior knowledge, ask students to name some forms of transportation and communication people use today. Tell students that they will learn more about how transportation and communication affect business and the economy as they read Lesson 3.

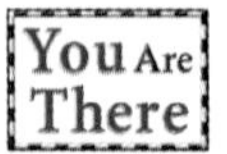

Ask students what forms of transportation were used to send the mail across the country in 1860. Then have students compare the meaning of "express mail" in 1860 and today.

LESSON 3

PREVIEW

Focus on the Main Idea
The regions of the United States and the nations of the world depend on each other.

VOCABULARY
transportation
interdependent
globalization
communication

▶ **Pony Express riders carried mail in sturdy leather pouches such as this one.**

St. Joseph Museum, Missouri

Transportation and Communication

You Are There It's 1860. William H. Russell's company has just hired you for the Pony Express. They need fast horse riders to get mail from Missouri to California. Mail takes from three weeks to six months to get across the country, either over land on trains and stagecoaches or by ship all the way around South America!

Your part of the route begins at Fort Kearny, Nebraska. You race toward the Rocky Mountains. When you arrive at the Platte station, your legs are wobbly and your horse is tired. First you hand the mail pouch to the next rider. Then you sit down to eat some beans and bacon before heading back. Even though the mail still has hundreds of miles to go, it will arrive in ten days. Now that's express!

Summarize As you read, look for details to help you summarize how transportation and communication help the economy.

Practice and Extend

READING SKILL Summarize

In the Lesson Review, students complete a graphic organizer like the one below. You may want to provide students with a copy of Transparency 6 to complete as they read the lesson.

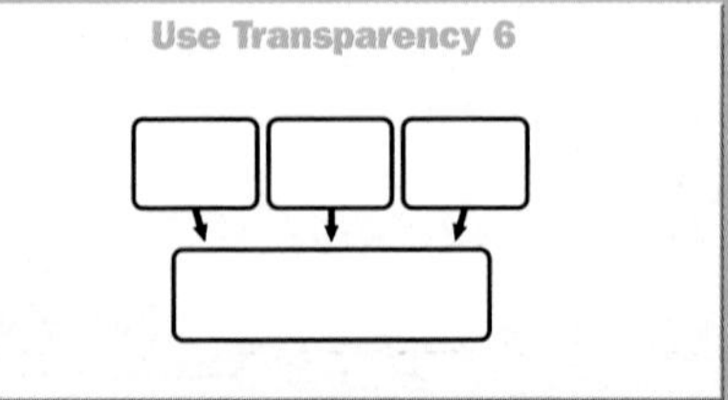

VOCABULARY Individual Word Study

Write *globalize* on the board. Ask students what a globe is. Then explain that the suffix *-ize* means "to make," so *globalize* means "to make global." Tell students that a word can have more than one suffix. Write *globalization* on the board, and explain that *-ation* means "act of or process of." Discuss the meaning of the word with the suffix (process of making global). You may also discuss *transport* and *-ation* and *communicate* and the *-ion* ending, which also means "act of."

From Across the USA

The days of mail delivery by horseback are long gone in the United States. Today a letter sent from the state of Washington can arrive in Washington, D.C., overnight! How? Trucks, trains, ships, and airplanes provide transportation across the states. **Transportation** is the moving of goods, people, or animals from one
1 place to another.

Why do we want to move goods across the states? Products grown in one state can be sent to people living in another state. For example, someone living in New York can buy Georgia peaches in their local grocery store. As you learned in Chapter 1, different regions have different climates. Because of differences in resources and climates, farmers grow different types of crops and produce different products in different regions.

No single region can produce everything that people in that region need and want. Each region depends on other regions for goods, services, and resources. When regions depend on one another in this way, they are economically **interdependent.** 2

Transportation helps the interdependent regions get almost anything they need and want. What would happen if we didn't have transportation? You could not get mail. If you lived in the Midwest, you would find mostly wheat and corn in the stores. You wouldn't find bananas or orange juice. If you lived in a community far from factories, you couldn't buy books, tennis shoes, or clothes.

REVIEW What does it mean for regions to be economically interdependent? Main Idea and Details

▶ A Pony Express rider (right) leaves St. Joseph, Montana on his way to California.

EXTEND LANGUAGE
ESL Support

Examine Word Meanings Have students explore the prefix *inter-*, which means "between or among."

Beginning Use a map to demonstrate the meaning of *international.* Then invite students to use the map to demonstrate the meanings of *interregional* and *interstate.*

Intermediate Ask students to use dictionaries to find three words that use the prefix *inter-* and to share their definitions with the class.

Advanced Have students give examples of how people in their communities also are interdependent.

For additional ESL support, use Every Student Learns Guide, pp. 34–37.

2 Teach and Discuss

PAGE 81

From Across the USA

Quick Summary The regions of the United States are economically interdependent because they have different climates and resources. Various forms of transportation are used to move goods between regions.

1 **What is *transportation*?** The moving of goods, people, or animals from one place to another. Main Idea and Details

2 **What causes different regions to be economically interdependent?** Possible answers: They have different climates and resources. No single region can produce everything that the people in that region need or want. Cause and Effect

✓ **REVIEW ANSWER** Regions depend on other regions for different products and resources. Main Idea and Details

PAGE 82

Around the World

Quick Summary Modern transportation has made possible the globalization of many businesses, making most countries of the world economically interdependent.

3 **How is the computer manufacturer in the text an example of the world's economic interdependence?** The manufacturer gets silicon from Germany, computer chips from Malaysia, and steel parts from Poland. **Analyze Information**

SOCIAL STUDIES STRAND
Culture

Point out that some people are against globalization because they fear American influence will change their national culture. American fast-food chains can be found in many of the world's capitals. People around the world also watch American movies and TV programs.

4 **Why do you think many U.S. businesses are in favor of globalization?** Possible answer: They might want to have greater access to resources and to consumers so they can make a larger profit. **Make Inferences**

✓ **REVIEW ANSWER** Computer parts are made in different countries and then sold to other countries around the world. **Main Idea and Details**

Around the World

The regions of the United States are economically interdependent. But trade and commerce stretch much farther than the borders of our country. Most of the countries of the world are tied together economically.

To understand how countries depend on each other, take a close look at a product you might find in your classroom or library: a computer. A computer works because it has a set of tiny electrical circuits called chips. The chips are made of silicon. The raw silicon might come from Germany. The design for the circuits might have been planned in Oregon, in the United States. The circuits might have been placed on the chips in Malaysia—a country in Asia.

The chips would have been sent to factories in different places where different computer parts are made. Some parts might have been made in Virginia. Other parts might have been made in England. The steel for the case around the computer might have been made in Poland. The computer might have been put together in Idaho. It might have been packaged in a big box made in Wisconsin and then sent to your school. 3

The making of your computer is an example of globalization. **Globalization** of businesses means that goods are produced using resources, raw materials, and services from several countries. Many businesses have factories in many places or use goods produced by other businesses. These companies also sell their products to businesses all around the world. With modern transportation, especially airplanes, companies can send goods halfway around the world in a day or two. 4

REVIEW Tell how the making of a computer is an example of globalization. **Main Idea and Details**

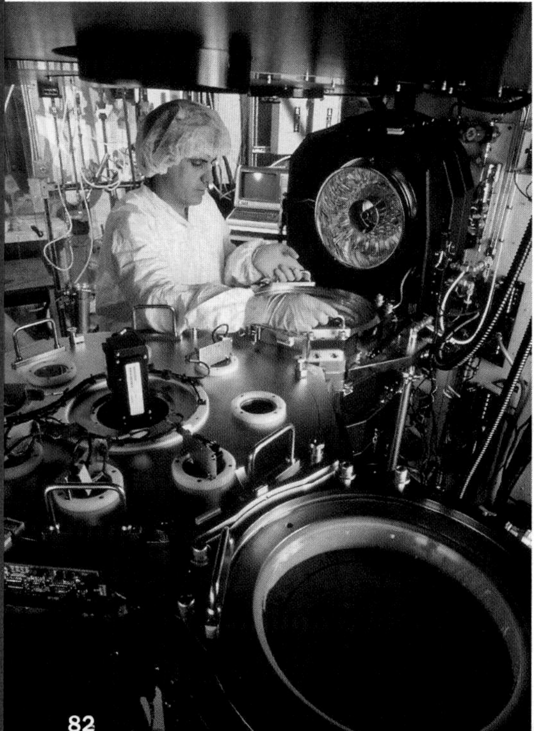

▶ The manufacturing of computer parts requires very clean conditions. Dust and other dirt particles cannot get into the final product.

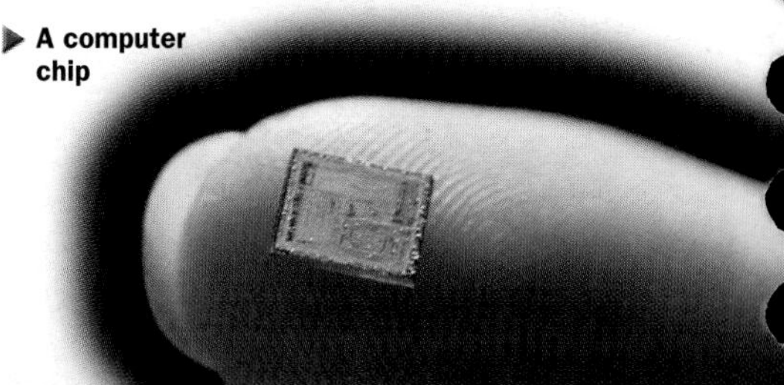

▶ A computer chip

82

Practice and Extend

MEETING INDIVIDUAL NEEDS
Leveled Practice

Evaluate the Effects of Modern Transportation Ask students to explain how modern transportation affects businesses and trade.

Easy Have students make a list of three effects of modern transportation on businesses and trade. **Reteach**

On-Level Have students write a paragraph on how modern transportation affects businesses and trade in the United States and around the world. **Extend**

Challenge Have students research and write a report on the effects of a transportation shutdown (airports, train stations, and bus stations). **Enrich**

For a Lesson Summary, use Quick Study, p. 18.

Map Adventure

Transportation has helped make globalization work. For example, a business can purchase raw materials or manufactured parts for a computer from several countries. The final product is then usually assembled in one place. Part of the trail of the making of a computer is shown below on the map. Study the trail and then answer the questions.

1. What parts came from Europe?
2. On the map below, what traveled the farthest to reach Idaho?
3. In which country will the computers be assembled?

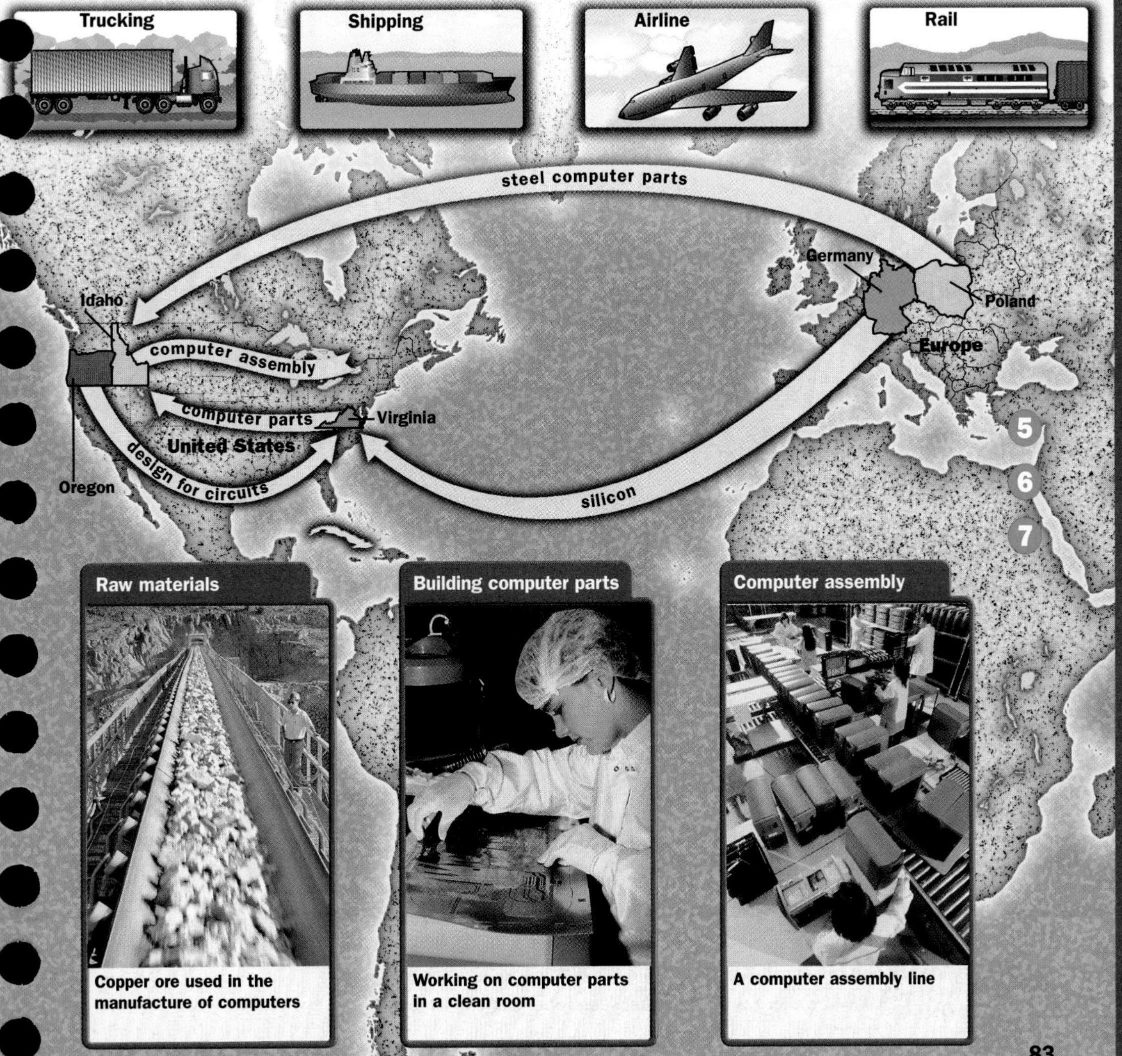

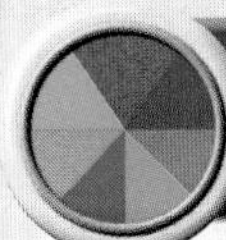
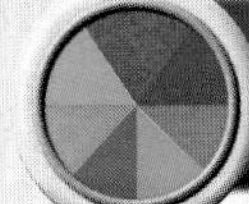

Copper ore used in the manufacture of computers

Working on computer parts in a clean room

A computer assembly line

83

Map Adventure

5 According to the map, how many countries are involved in producing these particular computers? Three Interpret Maps

6 Which country on this map produces silicon? To what country does it ship the silicon? Germany; United States Interpret Maps

7 According to this map, what computer-related product is made in Virginia? Computer parts Interpret Maps

Map Adventure Answers

1. Silicon, steel computer parts
2. Steel computer parts (Answer based only on Map Adventure)
3. United States

CURRICULUM CONNECTION Science

Examine How Computer Chips Are Made

- Have students work in small groups to research how computer chips are made. Suggest students use online resources.
- Have groups use their research to create a flowchart showing the steps involved in the process.
- Examine groups' flowcharts as a class, revising them as necessary.

CURRICULUM CONNECTION Math

Calculate Time

- Tell students to suppose that the computers described in the Map Adventure are packaged in boxes made in a box factory in Wisconsin, 1,700 miles from the assembly plant in Idaho. Ask students how long it would take a truckload of boxes to get to Idaho if the truck goes (a) 65 mph or (b) 55 mph. (a little over 26 hours; almost 31 hours)
- Tell students that the boxes can be flown the same distance in only a few hours but at a higher cost. Ask them which is the better economic choice and why.

PAGES 84–85

Communication

Quick Summary Fast communication is important to local, national, and world trade. It helps businesses and suppliers sell their goods, and it helps consumers communicate their wants and needs.

8 **Why is it possible to have bananas from Costa Rica and grapes from Chile for sale in supermarkets throughout the United States?** Possible answer: Fast transportation makes it possible to sell goods—even those that can spoil—far from where they are produced.
Apply Information

9 **Describe the process shown in the diagram beginning with the manufacturing of Brand X and ending with a consumer leaving the supermarket having purchased the product.** Brand X is manufactured at a factory, shipped to a retail store (supermarket), and advertised on TV. A consumer sees the advertisement, goes to the supermarket, buys the product, and then leaves the store.
Sequence

DIAGRAM SKILL **Answer** Two arrows are needed to show two steps. One arrow shows the consumer going to the supermarket to buy Brand X. The other arrow shows the consumer leaving the supermarket after buying Brand X.

Communication

Suppose that it's the late 1800s. You live on a dairy farm in Wisconsin. Your cows give you plenty of milk that you make into great ice cream. Everyone says you should sell your ice cream all over the country. Could you do that? Even though railroads are a part of everyday life, trains can't get goods to people's front doors. Even if they could, your ice cream would be melted and spoiled upon arrival.

Transportation in the 1800s was not fast. Airplanes had not been invented yet. Even if you decided to sell your ice cream to nearby places, the telephone and radio had only just been invented. To take orders, advertise, and get the
8 goods to your customers, you need fast transportation and communication.

Communication is the way that people send and receive information. Fast communication helps local, national, and world trade. Suppliers communicate with stores to tell them about available goods. Consumers communicate with businesses to tell them what they want.

Fast communication and transportation are especially important for companies that sell goods that can spoil, such as fruit and milk. With today's fast communication and transportation, these companies can sell their goods in faraway places. The illustration below shows a possible path that goods can take to get to the consumer.

Communication and Transportation

9

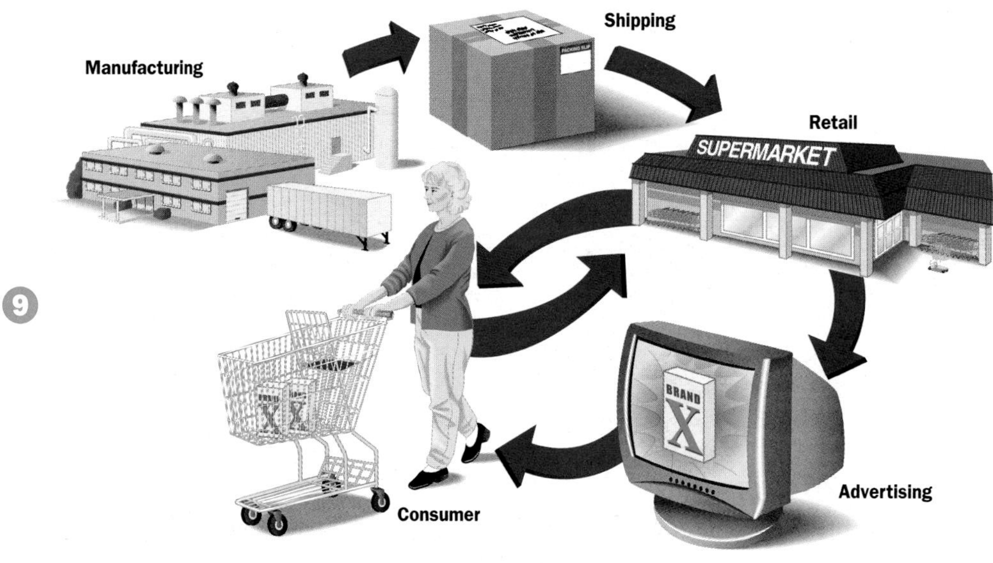

▶ Communication and transportation play a role in getting goods to the consumer.

DIAGRAM SKILL *Why are there two arrows between retail and consumer?*

84

Practice and Extend

CURRICULUM CONNECTION
Science

Make a Communication Time Line

- Have students research and create a time line of communication from 1800 to today.
- Tell students to include the following information on their time lines: telegraph (1837), Pony Express (1860), telephone (1876), Internet (ARPA) (1969), cell phone (1979), and handheld computer (1996).
- Encourage students to include additional information from their research.

CURRICULUM CONNECTION
Drama

Create a Sales Presentation

- Have students create a sales presentation for a cell phone or a handheld computer.
- First have them cut out or photocopy a picture of one of these devices from a magazine or newspaper. Tell them that their presentations should explain the features of the device, how it will help people do business, and what it will cost.

Today, people can communicate instantly by telephone. With wireless telephones, people can make long distance calls from almost anywhere. They can make business decisions on the spot. People also communicate using their computers. With the Internet, people can send and receive messages and documents very quickly. Computers allow companies to do business easily over long distances. 10

REVIEW Why are fast transportation and communication important for world trade? Summarize

Summarize the Lesson

- **Because no region can produce everything it needs, all the regions of the United States are economically interdependent.**
- **The globalization of businesses means that goods are produced using resources, raw materials, and services from several countries.**
- **Fast transportation and communication have made local and world trade easier.**

LESSON 3 REVIEW

Check Facts and Main Ideas

1. Summarize On a separate sheet of paper, copy the diagram. Fill in the details that lead to the summary.

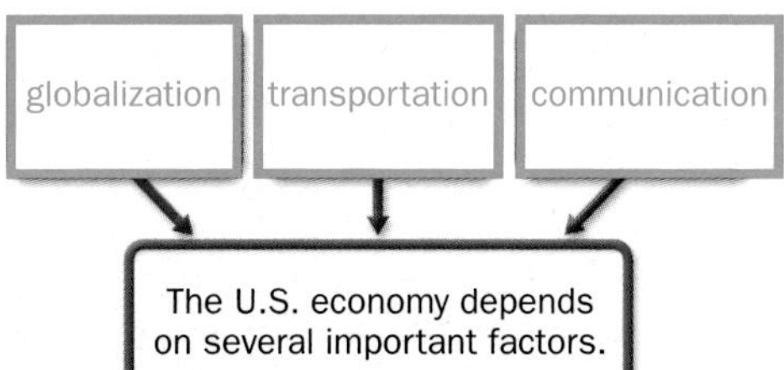

2. Give an example of a way that your region is economically **interdependent** with other regions in the United States.
3. What is an example of a way that your region helps the world economy?
4. How have **transportation** and **communication** been important in the growth of trade around the world?
5. **Critical Thinking:** ***Identify Opinions*** A newspaper ran a story about **globalization.** Part of the story said, "Globalization is not good for the economy of the United States. American companies have built factories in foreign countries." Which sentence is an opinion? Which is a fact?

Link to Science

Learn About Transportation Go to the library to find a book about the history of transportation. Make a time line to show how transportation has changed from the founding of our country in 1776 to the present.

CURRICULUM CONNECTION
Writing

Write a Report

- Have students research telecommuting, video phones, and videoconferencing. Tell them to write a report about how these technologies have changed the way people work and conduct business.
- Then have students speculate about how communication will change in the next 100 years.

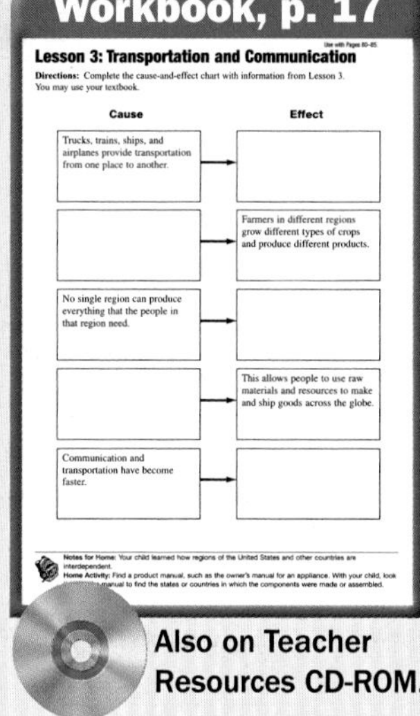

Workbook, p. 17

Use with Pages 80–85.

Lesson 3: Transportation and Communication

Directions: Complete the cause-and-effect chart with information from Lesson 3. You may use your textbook.

Cause	Effect
Trucks, trains, ships, and airplanes provide transportation from one place to another.	
	Farmers in different regions grow different types of crops and produce different products.
No single region can produce everything that the people in that region need.	
	This allows people to use raw materials and resources to make and ship goods across the globe.
Communication and transportation have become faster.	

Notes for Home: Your child learned how regions of the United States and other countries are interdependent.
Home Activity: Find a product manual, such as the owner's manual for an appliance. With your child, look through the manual to find the states or countries in which the components were made or assembled.

Also on Teacher Resources CD-ROM.

10 How does the Internet help people do business? It allows them to send and receive messages and documents quickly. Summarize

✓ **REVIEW ANSWER** Possible answer: They make it possible for companies to sell products all around the world in a timely fashion. Summarize

3 Close and Assess

Summarize the Lesson

Have students read the three main points and discuss how modern trade differs from trade in the early 1800s.

✓ **LESSON 3 REVIEW**

1. Summarize For possible answers, see the reduced pupil page.
2. Possible answer: Wheat grown in my region is processed into flour and sent to other regions to make different products. In one of those regions, some of the flour is used to make the cake mix that is sold in my local supermarket.
3. Possible answers: Producers from my region buy machines and materials from other regions and countries and produce goods consumers in other regions buy. Also, consumers from my region buy products from around the world.
4. Fast transportation makes it possible for goods to be sold around the world quickly. Fast communication makes it possible for producers and consumers around the world to send and receive important information related to buying and selling.
5. **Critical Thinking: *Identify Opinions*** Opinion: Globalization is not good for the U.S. economy. Fact: American companies have built factories in foreign countries.

Link to Science

Time lines might include the steamship (1783), the transcontinental railroad (1869), the car (1885), the plane (1903), and the space shuttle (1981).

Use a Road Map and Scale

Objectives

- Explain how to use a road map.
- Use a map scale to determine distances between places on a road map.

Vocabulary

road map, p. 86

Resource

- Workbook, p. 18
- Transparency 34

1 Introduce and Motivate

What is a road map? Ask students how people who drive cars might use a road map. (To find out which roads they can take from one place to another) Then have students read the **What?** section of text on p. 86 to help set the purpose of the lesson.

Why use a road map? Have students read the **Why?** section of text on pp. 86–87. Ask them what highways or major roads a road map of their community might include and have them tell what cities or other areas they connect.

2 Teach and Discuss

How is this skill used? Examine with students the map on p. 86 and have them identify the symbols in the map key. Then work through the example from the text, using the map scale.

- Review with students how to read half-inch and inch markers on a ruler.
- Point out that a map scale is usually given in miles and kilometers.

Map and Globe Skills

Use a Road Map and Scale

What? **Road maps** are maps that show roadways of a particular area, such as a city, a state, or an entire country. Maps that show a large area, like an entire country, include fewer types of roads because there is less room for detail. A road map of the United States, therefore, will show mostly major highways. On maps that show a small area, such as a city, more detail is included. City road maps include major highways, major paved streets, and certain side streets in local neighborhoods.

Why? People use road maps to plan routes from one place to another. Business travelers may want to figure out which route is fastest, while tourists might want to find a route that will take them through scenic areas.

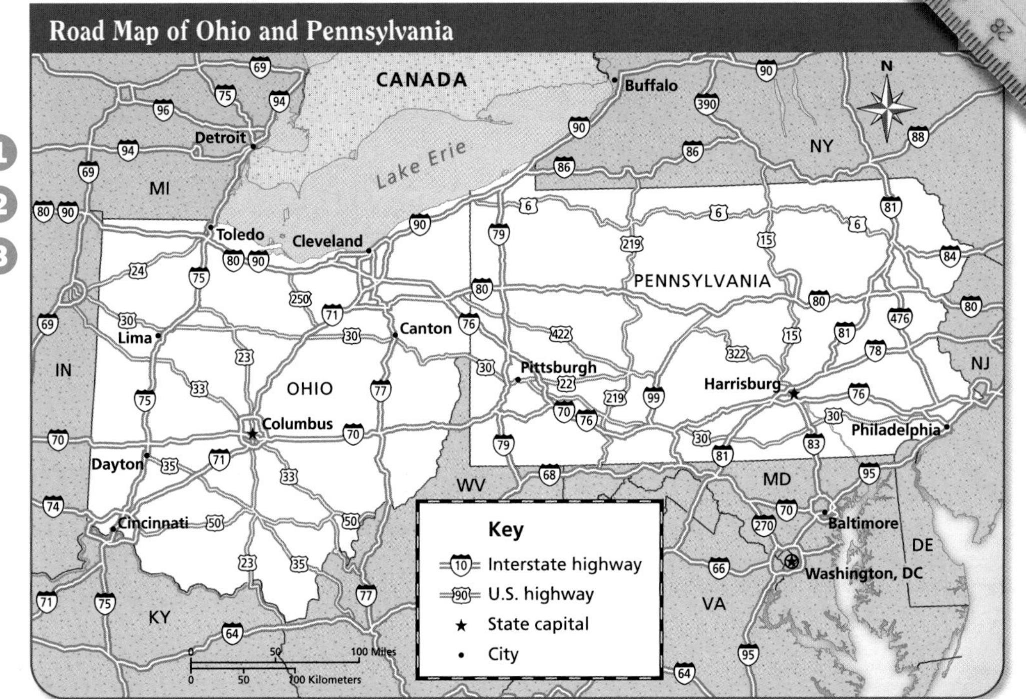

Practice and Extend

MEETING INDIVIDUAL NEEDS
Leveled Practice

Calculate Distance Have students practice using map scales to calculate distance.

Easy Have students calculate the distance between the capital of your state and the capital of a distant state, using a map of the United States in their textbook atlas. **Extend**

On-Level Have students look at a road map of their state and read the map scale. Have them calculate distances between various cities. **Reteach**

Challenge Have students plan a one-week road trip. Tell them to highlight their route on a map. Then have them list their destination and the distance they will travel each day. **Enrich**

For more information, go online to the *Atlas* at **www.sfsocialstudies.com.**

Others use road maps for local destinations, such as a trip to the museum or to a friend's house, or to find the best route to the airport.

How? First determine the area shown. Look for the map's title or label. This map's title indicates that this map shows Ohio and Pennsylvania. Then study the map key. Identify the symbols used to represent the different types of roads. According to the key for this map, double blue lines represent interstate highways. Find the road numbered "70" on the map. This road is shown as a double blue line, which means road "70" is an interstate highway.

After identifying the symbols in the key, you should identify the scale. The scale tells how many miles (or km) each inch (or cm) represents. For example, the scale for this map shows that one inch represents about 80 miles across land. If you measured with a ruler along Route 33 on the map, you'd find that Columbus is about an inch from the city of Lima. This means that if you were to drive on Route 33 from Columbus to Lima, you would travel almost 80 miles. Understanding scale is an important part of using a road map. Without knowing the scale, it would be nearly impossible to use the map to figure out just how far one place is from another.

Think and Apply

Suppose that you want to visit Greenfield Village near Detroit, Michigan. You are in Cleveland, Ohio. Use the **road map** on page 86 to find the answers.

1. What major highways would you take to get from Cleveland to Detroit?
2. About how many miles is it from Cleveland to Toledo? from Toledo to Detroit?
3. How many miles would your cousin from Cincinnati have to travel to meet you in Detroit?

87

- Explain that the different sizes of lettering on a road map usually indicate which places are large and which are small.
- Have students read the **How?** section of text on p. 87.

1 What major highway would you take from Toledo, Ohio, to Cincinnati, Ohio? Interstate highway 75 **Interpret Maps**

2 About how many miles is it from Dayton, Ohio, to Lima, Ohio? About 70 miles as measured on the map (Background: Actual driving distance is nearly 5 miles greater) **Interpret Maps**

3 About how many miles is it from Harrisburg, Pennsylvania, to Columbus, Ohio? About 320 miles as measured on map (Background: Actual driving distance is over 360 miles.) **Interpret Maps**

3 Close and Assess

Think and Apply

1. Interstate 80–90 west to Interstate 75 north
2. About 110 miles; about 50 miles
3. About 240 miles

WEB SITE
Technology

Students can find out more by clicking on *Atlas* at **www.sfsocialstudies.com.** Help students identify key search terms.

Workbook, p. 18

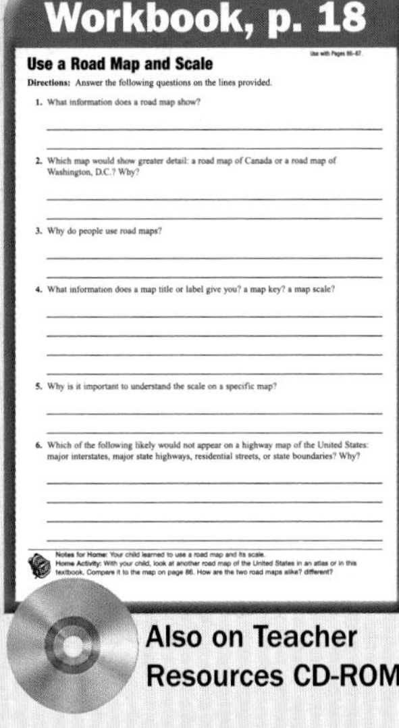

Use with Pages 86–87.

Use a Road Map and Scale

Directions: Answer the following questions on the lines provided.

1. What information does a road map show?
2. Which map would show greater detail: a road map of Canada or a road map of Washington, D.C.? Why?
3. Why do people use road maps?
4. What information does a map title or label give you? a map key? a map scale?
5. Why is it important to understand the scale on a specific map?
6. Which of the following likely would not appear on a highway map of the United States: major interstates, major state highways, residential streets, or state boundaries? Why?

Notes for Home: Your child learned to use a road map and its scale.
Home Activity: With your child, look at another road map of the United States in an atlas or in this textbook. Compare it to the map on page 86. How are the two road maps alike? different?

Also on Teacher Resources CD-ROM.

Resources

- Assessment Book, pp. 9–12
- Workbook, p. 19: Vocabulary Review

Chapter Summary

For possible answers, see the reduced pupil page.

Vocabulary

1. e, **2.** l, **3.** h, **4.** c, **5.** k, **6.** a, **7.** d, **8.** g, **9.** b, **10.** f, **11.** j, **12.** i

CHAPTER 3 Review

Chapter Summary

Summarize

Copy the diagram on a separate sheet of paper. Use the terms listed in the chart in a summary statement about the economy of the United States.

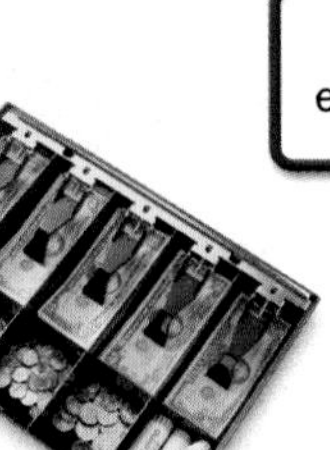

Free enterprise | Supply and demand | Prices

The U.S. economy is a free enterprise system. Prices are based on supply and demand.

Vocabulary

Fill in the blank in each sentence with the correct vocabulary word from the list below.

a. **producer** (p. 74)
b. **barter** (p. 73)
c. **opportunity cost** (p. 78)
d. **urban** (p. 71)
e. **rural** (p. 71)
f. **consumer** (p. 74)
g. **supply** (p. 77)
h. **free enterprise system** (p. 76)
i. **demand** (p. 77)
j. **interdependent** (p. 81)
k. **globalization** (p. 82)
l. **technology** (p. 70)

1. The countryside is considered a _______ area.
2. Putting scientific knowledge to practical use is called _______.
3. Businesses in a _______ have the right to produce any goods they want.
4. When you choose one thing over another, what you give up is the _______.
5. The process of making parts of a product in different places around the world is called _______.
6. A person who makes goods to sell is a _______.
7. Cities are _______ areas.
8. The amount of an item that sellers are willing to offer at different prices is the _______.
9. To trade one kind of goods or service for another is to _______.
10. A person who buys things is called a _______.
11. When regions depend on one another, they are economically _______.
12. The amount of an item that consumers are willing to buy at different prices is called the _______.

88

Practice and Extend

Assessment Options

✓ Chapter 3 Assessment

- Chapter 3 Content Test: Use Assessment Book, pp. 9–10.
- Chapter 3 Skills Test: Use Assessment Book, pp. 11–12.

Standardized Test Prep

- Chapter 3 Tests contain standardized test format.

✓ Chapter 3 Performance Assessment

- Have students work in small groups to create nine questions for a Question-and-Answer relay.
- Tell groups to write three original questions (with answers) for each lesson in Chapter 3.
- Have groups form two teams and compile their questions.
- Have teams take turns asking questions. If one team answers incorrectly, the other team keeps asking questions. The first team to ask all its questions wins.

Facts and Main Ideas

1. List some resources that Native Americans or European settlers found in North America.
2. What is the difference between bartering and using money?
3. Why are transportation and communication very important in our modern economy?
4. **Main Idea** How did America's rich resources affect early settlement?
5. **Main Idea** How might a change in supply or a change in demand affect the price of objects?
6. **Main Idea** How are economic interdependence and globalization related to one another?
7. **Critical Thinking:** ***Draw Conclusions*** Having a healthy economy is important for our country. Why is this true?

Write About Economics

1. **Write an Ad** Suppose you are selling a product or service. Describe your product or service. Tell why the product or service is useful or important. List the price and explain why the price is a good one.
2. **Write a Newspaper Article** Write about certain goods that are in short supply. Many consumers wish to purchase these goods. Tell why the goods are in limited supply and why consumers want to buy them. Be sure to tell what will happen to the price for the goods.
3. **Write a Brochure** Tell why a particular type of business should move to your region. Think about the resources your region has and decide which type of new businesses would do well in your region. Discuss the communication and transportation networks in your region.

Apply Skills

Use a Road Map

Look at the map below. Then answer the questions.

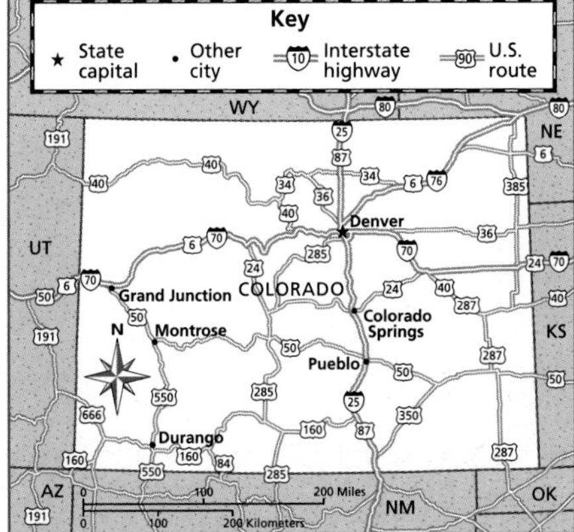

1. What information does this map give?
2. What is the scale of this map?
3. About how many miles is it from the New Mexico border to the Wyoming border traveling on Interstate 25?

Internet Activity

To get help with vocabulary and terms, select the dictionary or encyclopedia from *Social Studies Library* at **www.sfsocialstudies.com.**

89

Hands-on Unit Project

✓ Unit 1 Performance Assessment

- See p. 94 for information about using the Unit Project as a means of performance assessment.
- A scoring guide is provided on p. 94.

WEB SITE Technology

For more information, students can select the dictionary or encyclopedia from *Social Studies Library* at **www.sfsocialstudies.com.**

Workbook, p. 19

Vocabulary Review

Also on Teacher Resources CD-ROM.

Facts and Main Ideas

1. Possible answers: Southwest: grazing land; West: gold; Southeast: farmland; Northeast: fish
2. Barter: people trade one kind of good or service for another; Money: people exchange money for goods or services
3. Transportation and communication make national and world trade possible.
4. Many people came to the Americas in search of resources and settled here.
5. When supply increases, the price often decreases. When demand increases, the price often increases.
6. Possible answer: Globalization means that a company produces or sells its goods and services throughout the world. This causes countries to depend on one another for goods and services—to be interdependent.
7. Possible answer: When the economy is healthy, people have jobs and spend money, which creates a demand for goods or services. This demand, in turn, creates more jobs.

Write About Economics

1. Encourage students to use pictures and persuasive language in their ads.
2. Remind students to use descriptive language in their newspaper articles. They may want to include a picture.
3. Encourage students to look at their community's or state's Web site or to contact their local chamber of commerce for information about their region.

Apply Skills

1. It gives information about roads in Colorado.
2. About $1\frac{1}{4}$ inches represents 200 miles or 1 inch represent about 150 miles
3. About 290 to 300 miles

America

Objective

- Identify significant examples of music about the United States.

Resources

- Transparency 35

1 Introduce and Motivate

Preview To activate prior knowledge, ask students why they think the song "America" was written. Then ask students to name other songs that celebrate the United States.

2 Teach and Discuss

1 **Do you think "America" is a fitting tribute to George Washington? Why or why not?** Possible answer: Yes; It talks about the ideals that led to American Independence, and George Washington was an important figure in that struggle. Point of View

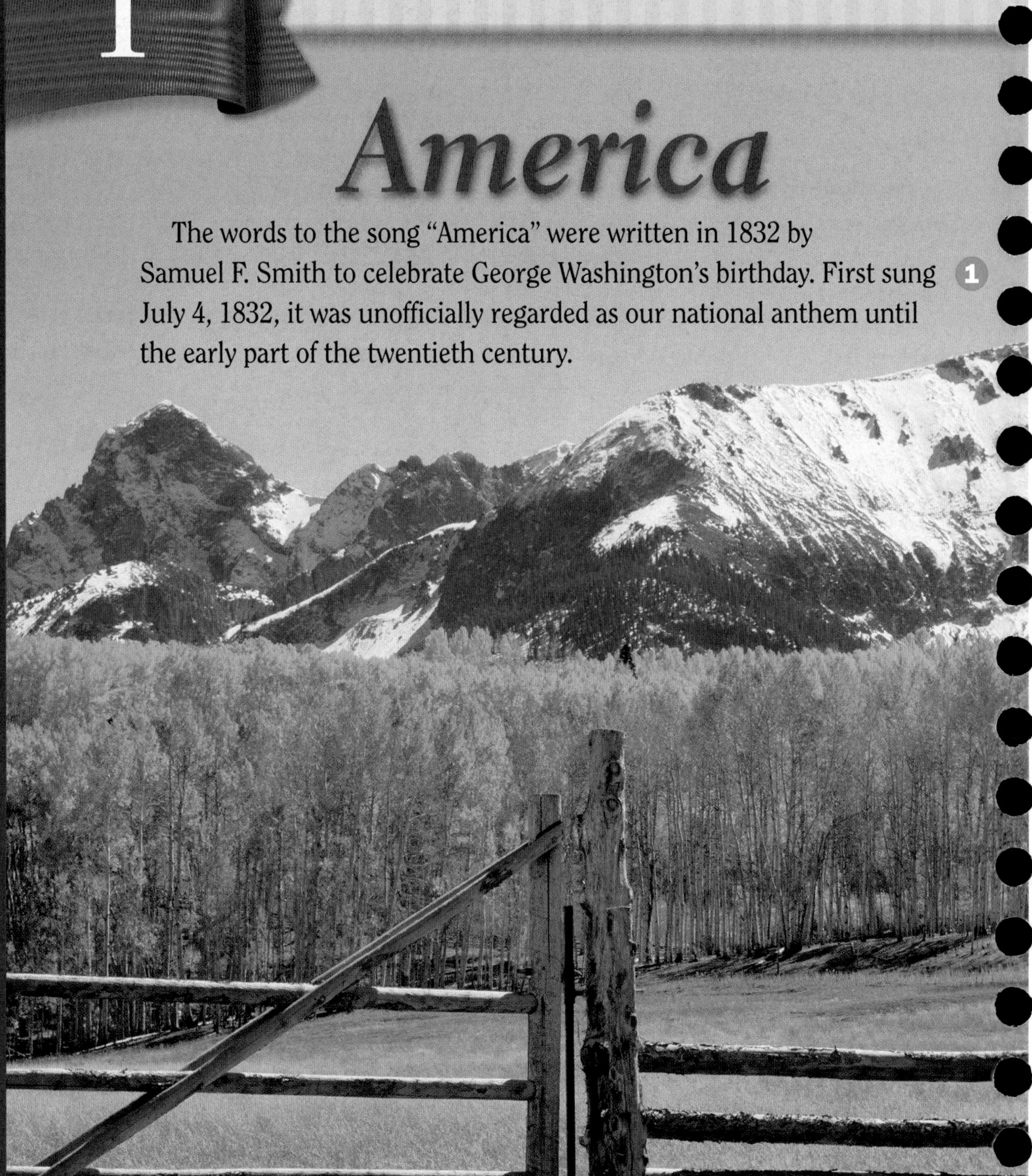

UNIT 1 End with a Song

America

The words to the song "America" were written in 1832 by Samuel F. Smith to celebrate George Washington's birthday. First sung 1 July 4, 1832, it was unofficially regarded as our national anthem until the early part of the twentieth century.

90

Practice and Extend

SOCIAL STUDIES
Background

About "America"

- "America" often is known by its first line, "My Country 'tis of Thee." The title "America" can only be traced back to 1890 when Samuel F. Smith, the author, added the title to a handwritten copy of the music.
- Smith borrowed the tune for "America" from a German song called "God Save the King." The same tune had already been used for England's "God Save the Queen" and several other American songs, including "God Save the President," "God Save George Washington," and "God Save the Thirteen States."
- Once Smith discovered the tune, he wrote the complete lyrics of "America" in less than 30 minutes' time.

AUDIO CD
Technology

Play the CD, *Songs and Music,* to listen to "America."

Words by Samuel Francis Smith

America

Traditional Melody

1. My coun - try! 'tis of thee, Sweet land of lib - er - ty, Of thee I sing; Land where my fa - thers died, Land of the Pil - grims' pride, From ev - 'ry moun - tain-side Let free - dom ring!

2. My na - tive coun - try, thee, Land of the no - ble free, Thy name I love; I love thy rocks and rills, Thy woods and tem - pled hills; My heart with rap - ture thrills Like that a - bove.

2 3

91

2 **What landforms are mentioned in the song?** Mountainsides, rills (small streams), hills **Analyze Primary Sources**

3 **How do you think this song might unite people in different regions of the United States?** Possible answer: The song refers to "America" as a whole, rather than divided into specific regions or states. Also, people may feel united by their patriotism when they sing this song. **Draw Conclusions**

3 Close and Assess

- Have students discuss ways to perform this song. Students who play musical instruments may be interested in playing the song for the class.
- Ask students what they can learn about the United States by studying the lyrics on p. 91. (Possible answers: It is a land of liberty and freedom. It has mountains, hills, rills (small streams), and woods.

CURRICULUM CONNECTION
Writing

Compare Songs

- Hand out a copy of the song "God Bless America" or "America the Beautiful." Ask students to write a paragraph comparing the lyrics of that song with "America."
- Have students imagine that "The Star-Spangled Banner" had never been written. Have them write a second paragraph explaining which song they might choose as a national anthem and why.

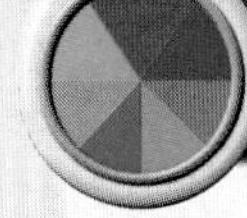

CURRICULUM CONNECTION
Music

Write a Song

- Have students work in groups to write a song or jingle about the United States of America.
- Ask groups to perform their songs for the class and have students identify the different features of the United States noted in each song.
- You may wish to have the class vote on one song and perform it as a group for the student body.

UNIT 1 Review

Resource

- Assessment Book, pp. 13–16

Main Ideas and Vocabulary

1. c, **2.** d, **3.** d, **4.** b

Test Talk

Locate Key Words in the Question

Use Main Ideas and Vocabulary, Question 2, to model the Test Talk strategy.

Find the key words in the question.

Have students ask themselves, "Who, or what is this question about?" The words that tell *who,* or *what* the question is about are key words. The words *regions* and *in the passage* are key words in this question.

Turn the question into a statement.

Students should use the key words in a sentence that begins "I need to find out …."

Terms

1. e, **2.** a, **3.** b, **4.** d, **5.** c

UNIT 1 Review

Test Talk

Narrow the answer choices. Rule out answers you know are wrong.

Main Ideas and Vocabulary

TEST PREP

Read the passage below and use it to answer the questions that follow.

The United States is divided into regions. A region is an area defined by similar characteristics. The five regions of the United States are the Northeast, the Southeast, the Midwest, the Southwest, and the West.

Landforms help make the five regions different from one another. The Northeast has seacoasts and the Appalachian Mountains. The Appalachian Mountains also run through the Southeast. The Southeast has coastal areas and plains. The Midwest is mostly grassy plains. Like the Northeast, the Midwest also has land shaped by glaciers. The Southwest has canyons, high plateaus, and some deserts. The Rocky Mountains just touch the Southwest. The West also includes the Rocky Mountains and some deserts. But unlike the Southwest, the West has a seacoast and a second range of mountains called the Cascade Mountains.

Climate differences also help make the regions distinct. The southern regions tend to be warmer than the northern regions. The regions that are lower in elevation tend to be warmer than the higher regions.

Each region has different resources. Resources are used to produce goods that people need or want. Some of the resources are related to the landforms and climates of a region.

The resources of each region contribute to the region's economy. Each region gets some things that it needs from other regions and sends things to other regions. For this reason, the regions are economically interdependent.

1. In the passage, the word region refers to
   - **A** an area with only one kind of landform
   - **B** an area with only one kind of culture
   - **C** an area of similar characteristics
   - **D** an area that is distinct from other areas on other continents

2. What are the regions listed in the passage?
   - **A** the plains and the plateaus
   - **B** the Appalachian Mountains, the Rocky Mountains, and the Cascade Mountains
   - **C** the Atlantic coast, the Pacific coast, and the coast of the Gulf of Mexico
   - **D** the Northeast, the Southeast, the Midwest, the Southwest, and the West

3. In the passage, the word resources means
   - **A** a mine
   - **B** a person
   - **C** the way a particular area, like a country, manages its goods and services
   - **D** something that can be used to produce goods that people want

4. What is the unstated main idea of the passage?
   - **A** People disagree on how the United States should be divided into regions.
   - **B** The five regions of the United States are distinct in their landforms, climate, resources, and economies.
   - **C** The equator determines climate.
   - **D** The five regions of the United States have similar characteristics.

92

Practice and Extend

Assessment Options

✓Unit 1 Assessment

- Unit 1 Content Test: Use Assessment Book, pp. 13–14.
- Unit 1 Skills Test: Use Assessment Book, pp. 15–16.

Standardized Test Prep

- Unit 1 Tests contain standardized test format.

✓Unit 1 Performance Assessment

- See p. 94 for information about using the Unit Project as a means of Performance Assessment.
- A scoring guide for the Unit 1 Project is provided in the teacher's notes on p. 94.

Test Talk

- Test Talk Practice Book

WEB SITE Technology

For more information, you can select the dictionary or encyclopedia from *Social Studies Library* at **www.sfsocialstudies.com.**

Terms

Match each word with the correct description or definition.

1. **elevation** (p. 21)
2. **plateau** (p. 13)
3. **economy** (p. 76)
4. **legislative branch** (p. 50)
5. **landform** (p. 11)

a. a raised, flat area of land

b. how the resources of a place are managed

c. feature on Earth's surface

d. the branch of government that makes our nation's laws

e. how high above sea level a place is

Apply Skills

Make a Map Game Ask an adult for old road maps or an old atlas. Pick one of the maps to use for a board game. Find or make playing pieces for your game. Decide where the starting and ending points will be. Make playing cards for the game. The cards could give directions for moving on the map. Decide on other rules for moving pieces along the map. Try out your game with a friend. After your trial game, revise the cards or the rules to improve the game.

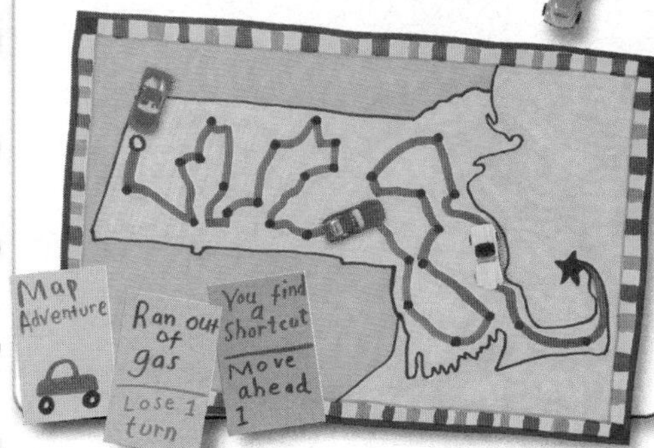

Write About It

Design a Museum Exhibit As a class, design a museum exhibit about economics. Decide on a topic for your exhibit. You might consider designing an exhibit about methods of trading, about money, or about our nation's economy at any point in history. Decide what will be in your exhibit. Then divide into three groups. One group will describe the objects or displays in the exhibit. One group will write the labels to go with the objects or displays. One group will read the descriptions and the labels together and edit them. As you write and edit, make sure that the main idea you want to teach about economics is clear.

Read on Your Own

Look for books like these in the library.

93

Revisit the Unit Question

✓Portfolio Assessment

- Have students look at their lists of ideas about what unites people in different regions of the United States.
- Give students the opportunity to work with a partner to revise and edit their lists.
- Have students independently write a summary expressing how their own ideas about what unites people in different regions of the United States may have changed over the course of this unit.
- Have students add these lists and summaries to their Social Studies Portfolio.

Apply Skills

- Have students make at least ten playing cards for the game.
- Tell students to highlight on their maps the routes that are mentioned on the playing cards.
- Use the following scoring guide.

✓Assessment Scoring Guide

Map Game	
6	Clearly defines rules. Prepares playing pieces and ten or more playing cards with clear, accurate directions. Identifies starting and ending point on map.
5	Clearly defines rules. Prepares playing pieces and up to ten playing cards with accurate directions. Identifies starting and ending points.
4	Clearly defines rules. Prepares playing pieces and up to ten playing cards with accurate directions.
3	Includes all the necessary game parts, but a few directions on the playing cards are unclear or inaccurate.
2	Fails to explain many directions. Parts of the game are missing.
1	Directions on cards are illegible or inaccurate. Creates only a few game parts.

If you require a 4-point rubric, adjust accordingly.

Write About It

- Have students use the Internet or library resources to research the topic of their exhibit.
- Encourage students to include pictures or make models of the objects chosen for their exhibit.

Read on Your Own

Have students prepare oral reports using the following books.

Ellis Island: New Hope in a New Land, by William J. Jacobs. (Simon & Schuster, ISBN 0-684-19171-7, 1990) **Easy**

Quilted Landscape: Conversations with Young Immigrants, by Yale Strom (Simon & Schuster, ISBN 0-689-80074-6, 1996) **On-Level**

Native American Rock Art: Messages from the Past, by Yvette La Pierre (Lickle Publishing, ISBN 1-56566-064-1, 1994) **Challenge**

Eye on Our Region

Objective

- Describe different features of a region.

Resource

- Workbook, p. 20

Materials

poster board or large sheets of paper; pencils, crayons or other coloring materials; travel guides and other books or magazines about your region

Follow This Procedure

- Tell students they will create storyboards to make a video tour about their region. Explain that people who make videos first draw storyboards, or pictures of what they will shoot for their video.
- List possible topics: geographic location; industries and agriculture; natural resources; weather and climate; plants or animals; populations of cities and towns; and historic milestones.
- Divide students into groups. Have each group choose a unique topic.
- Have students list facts and make a map of their region.
- Invite each group to take the class on their "video tour."
- Use the following scoring guide.

✓ Assessment Scoring Guide

Eye on Our Region	
6	Provides accurate, vivid descriptions and illustrations of regional features in logical sequence
5	Provides accurate descriptions and illustrations in logical sequence
4	Provides mostly accurate descriptions and illustrations in logical sequence
3	Provides mostly accurate descriptions and illustrations, but sequence may not be entirely logical
2	Provides few accurate descriptions and illustrations, and sequence may not be entirely logical
1	Provides no accurate descriptions and few clear illustrations in no particular sequence

If you require a 4-point rubric, adjust accordingly.

UNIT 1 Project

Eye on Our Region

Take visitors on a video tour of your region. Show what's great about it.

1 **Form** a group and choose an interesting topic about your region.

2 **Make** a map of your region.

3 **Make** a list of facts about your topic. Draw pictures that illustrate your facts. Write a sentence or two to describe each picture.

4 **Put** your group's pictures together. Put them in the order in which you will show them. Use your map as an introduction. This is your video tour to share with the class.

Internet Activity

Learn more about geography. Go to **www.sfsocialstudies.com/activities** and select your grade and unit.

Practice and Extend

Hands-on Unit Project

✓ Performance Assessment

- The Unit Project can also be used as a performance assessment activity.
- Use the scoring guide to assess each group's work.

WEB SITE Technology

Students can launch the Internet Activity by clicking on *Grade 4, Unit 1* at **www.sfsocialstudies.com/activities.**

Workbook, p. 20

Also on Teacher Resources CD-ROM.

★ Unit 2 ★

Vocabulary Routines

The following examples of reading and vocabulary development strategies can be used to instruct students about unit vocabulary.

BEFORE READING

Individual Word Study

Compound Words Instructing students on how to determine the meaning of a compound word by breaking it down can help them figure out the meaning of the compound word and assist in reading comprehension. Explain that compound words are made up of two smaller words. Some compound words are combined into one word, some are separate words, and some are connected by a hyphen. Remind students that, once they have guessed a meaning, they need to make sure it fits the context. Chapter 4 contains several compound words: *lighthouse, vineyard, watermen,* and *crab pot.*

Think about the word **lighthouse.** *How do you know that this word is a compound word? Right.* **Lighthouse** *is a compound word because it is made up of two smaller words. How do the two words in* **lighthouse** *help us figure out the meaning?* (*Light* means "a form of energy that the eye can see." House means "a building for any purpose.") *So if we bring these two words together, what definition can we come up with for lighthouse?* ("a building whose purpose is to give off light to help people see.")

lighthouse	=	light	+	house
watermen	=	water	+	men

DURING READING

Related Word Study

Related Words As students read the text, suggest pairs or groups of words and ask students how the words are related. For example, *bay* and *inlet* in Chapter 4, Lesson 3 or abolitionist and slave in Chapter 5, Lesson 3.

Look at the words **abolitionist** *and* **slave.** *Think about what an* **abolitionist** *and a* **slave** *are. How are these words related?* (A slave is a person who is owned as the property of another person. Abolitionist is related to slave because an abolitionist wants to get rid of slavery and free slaves.) *Make a page for these words in a vocabulary journal, and write a definition for each word. Then compare the meanings of the words and write two or three sentences summarizing how they are related.* After reading p. 117 say, *We have just finished reading about* **bays, inlets, watermen,** *and* **crab pots.** *How would you group these words?* (I would put *bay* and *inlet* together because they are both found on coastlines. I would put *watermen* and *crab pots* together because watermen use crab pots.)

AFTER READING

Context Clues

Sentence Completions To reinforce word meanings, have students fill in blanks in sentence stems. To help students determine the correct words to fill in, use sentences that relate strongly to the missing word. For example, write the words *vineyard, bog, sap, minerals,* and *quarry* on the board. Below that, write the following sentences and have students supply the missing words (in parentheses).

- *The grapes from the ___ will be used to make wine.* (vineyard)
- *When you walk through a ___, be careful because the ground is spongy and wet.* (bog)
- *Last year, we got enough ___ from our trees to make several gallons of maple syrup.* (sap)
- *Granite is composed of several different types of ___.* (minerals)
- *All the marble in this building came from the same ___.* (quarry)

Read the words on the board. Think about what each one means. Then pick a word to complete each sentence. Remember to look for context clues to confirm your choices. Explain your answers.

The Northeast
UNIT
2

UNIT 2

Unit Planning Guide

Unit 2 • The Northeast

Begin with a Primary Source pp. 96–97

Welcome to the Northeast pp. 98–99

Target Skill **Reading Social Studies, Sequence** pp. 100–101

Chapter Titles	Pacing	Main Ideas
Chapter 4 **Land and Water in the Northeast** pp. 102–121 ✓ **Chapter 4 Review** pp. 122–123	6 days	• The Northeast region is one of incredible scenery and magnificent natural formations. • The Northeast produces products for the world to enjoy. • Chesapeake Bay and other bays in the Northeast provide seafood for millions.
Chapter 5 **People of the Northeast** pp. 124–149 ✓ **Chapter 5 Review** pp. 150–151	10 days	• The Narragansett lived in the Northeast region before European settlers came to North America. • The Northeast saw the beginnings of the American Revolution, the writing of our nation's Constitution, and the start of many new lives as immigrants arrived in the United States. • The Northeast was the birthplace of the abolitionist movement and the women's rights movement. • Northeastern cities and their industries have grown and changed.

End with a Poem pp. 152–153

✓ **Unit 2 Review** pp. 154–155

✓ **Unit 2 Project** p. 156

Former slaves such as Frederick Douglass helped the abolitionist movement flourish in the Northeast and spread throughout the Union.

✓ = **Assessment Options**

The Northeast is known as a major supplier of lobster and other shellfish.

Resources	Meeting Individual Needs
• Workbook, pp. 22–26 • Every Student Learns Guide, pp. 38–49 • Transparencies 9, 10, 11, 36, 37 • Quick Study, pp. 20–25 • Workbook, p. 27 ✓ Chapter 4 Content Test, Assessment Book, pp. 17–18 ✓ Chapter 4 Skills Test, Assessment Book, pp. 19–20	• ESL Support, TE pp. 105, 114, 117 • Leveled Practice, TE pp. 108, 110, 113, 118 • Learning Styles, TE p. 119 ✓ Chapter 4 Performance Assessment, TE p. 122
• Workbook, pp. 28–34 • Every Student Learns Guide, pp. 50–65 • Transparencies 10, 11, 14, 15, 38, 39 • Quick Study, pp. 26–33 • Workbook, p. 35 ✓ Chapter 5 Content Test, Assessment Book, pp. 21–22 ✓ Chapter 5 Skills Test, Assessment Book, pp. 23–24	• ESL Support, TE pp. 128, 131, 137, 143 • Leveled Practice, TE pp. 129, 132, 134, 138, 145 • Learning Styles, TE p. 141 ✓ Chapter 5 Performance Assessment, TE p. 150

Benjamin Franklin and many other great leaders and inventors called the Northeast region home.

Providing More Depth

Additional Resources

- Trade Books
- Family Activities
- Vocabulary Workbook and Cards
- Social Studies Plus! pp. 32–51
- Daily Activity Bank
- Read Alouds and Primary Sources pp. 18–34
- Big Book Atlas
- Student Atlas
- Outline Maps
- Desk Maps

Technology

- AudioText
- Video Field Trips: Exploring the Northeast
- Songs and Music
- Digital Learning CD-ROM Powered by KnowledgeBox (Video clips and activities)
- MindPoint® Quiz Show CD-ROM
- ExamView® Test Bank CD-ROM
- Colonial Williamsburg Primary Sources CD-ROM
- Teacher Resources CD-ROM
- Map Resources CD-ROM
- SF SuccessNet: iText (Pupil Edition online), iTE (Teacher's Edition online), Online Planner
- **www.sfsocialstudies.com** (Biographies, news, references, maps, and activities)

To establish guidelines for your students' safe and responsible use of the Internet, use the Scott Foresman Internet Guide.

Additional Internet Links

To find out more about:

- Blue Crabs, visit **www.vims.edu**
- Andrew Carnegie, visit **www.pbs.org**
- Susan B. Anthony, visit **www.susanbanthonyhouse.org**

Unit 2 Objectives

Beginning of Unit 2

- Use primary sources to acquire information. (p. 96)
- Identify objects and places of interest in the Northeast. (p. 98)
- Analyze information by sequencing events. (p. 100)

Chapter 4

Lesson 1 The Beautiful Northeast
pp. 104–109

- Identify the two Great Lakes between which Niagara Falls is located.
- Identify the two main features for which Niagara Falls is known.
- Identify the three main mountain ranges in the northeastern part of the Appalachian Mountains.
- Identify the two states in the Northeast that do not border the Atlantic Ocean.
- Describe the operations of a hydroelectric power plant. (p. 110)

Lesson 2 Resources of the Northeast
pp. 112–115

- Identify key steps in the production of maple syrup.
- Explain why grapes grow well in certain areas of the Northeast.
- Identify the largest lake of the Finger Lakes.
- Explain why water is essential to the production and growth of cranberries.

Lesson 3 The Plentiful Sea
pp. 116–119

- Define the name of the people who fish Chesapeake Bay.
- Explain how pollution from a factory gets into Chesapeake Bay.
- Explain why Chesapeake Bay is important to the Northeast.
- Describe actions a resident of the Chesapeake Bay area could take to help preserve the bay.
- Identify marine creatures native to Shark Bay. (p. 120)

Chapter 5

Lesson 1 The Narragansett People
pp. 126–129

- Describe key events that affected the Narragansett way of life once European settlers arrived.
- Define *sachem*.
- Describe what goods the Europeans and Native Americans traded.
- Explain why the Iroquois Confederacy was established.

Lesson 2 The Land of New Beginnings pp. 130–133

- Identify events leading from colonization up to the founding of the United States.
- Identify cities in the Northeast that have been capitals of the United States.
- Identify the city in the Northeast where most European immigrants arrived in the 1800s.
- Explain why immigrants came to the United States.
- Analyze a vertical time line to acquire information. (p. 134)

Lesson 3 Taking a Stand
pp. 136–138

- Explain similarities and differences between the abolitionist movement and the women's rights movement.
- Explain the meaning of the word *abolitionist.*
- Identify important women's rights reformers.
- Explain why reformers fought to win voting rights for women.
- Explain how Elizabeth Cady Stanton came to be involved in women's rights. (p. 139)
- Use visual artifacts to acquire information. (p. 140)

Lesson 4 Cities Grow and Change
pp. 142–146

- Explain why northeastern cities developed where they did.
- Identify and explain the importance of places that make tourism a major industry in northeastern cities.
- Describe how Pittsburgh's industries, like those of other northeastern cities, have changed over the years.
- Describe the relationship between the people and the economies of northeastern cities.
- Explain key events that shaped Andrew Carnegie's life. (p. 147)
- Describe how citizens of New York City have shown responsibility on and after September 11, 2001. (p. 148)

End of Unit 2

- Analyze the poem "Niagara," by Carl Sandburg. (p. 152)
- Understand the experiences of Native Americans or early settlers in America. (p. 156)

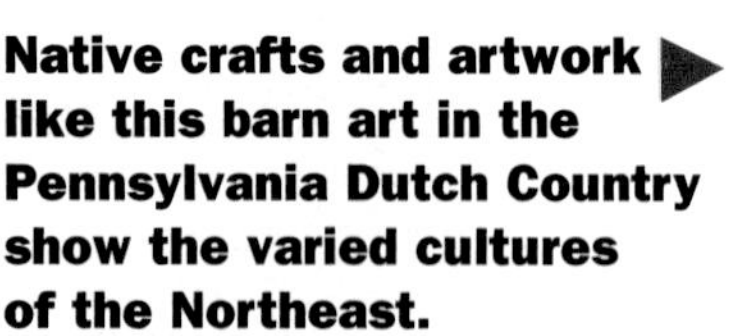

Native crafts and artwork like this barn art in the Pennsylvania Dutch Country show the varied cultures of the Northeast.

Assessment Options

✓ Formal Assessment

- **Lesson Reviews,** PE/TE pp. 109, 115, 119, 129, 133, 138, 146
- **Chapter Reviews,** PE/TE pp. 122–123, 150–151
- **Chapter Tests,** Assessment Book, pp. 17–24
- **Unit Review,** PE/TE pp. 154–155
- **Unit Tests,** Assessment Book, pp. 25–28
- **ExamView® Test Bank CD-ROM**

✓ Informal Assessment

- **Teacher's Edition Questions,** throughout Lessons and Features
- **Section Reviews,** PE/TE pp. 105, 107, 109, 113, 115, 117–119, 127–129, 131, 133, 137–138, 143–146
- **Close and Assess,** TE pp. 101, 109, 111, 115, 119, 121, 129, 133, 135, 138–139, 141, 146–147, 149, 153

Ongoing Assessment

Ongoing Assessment is found throughout the Teacher's Edition lessons using an **If...then** model.

If = students' observable behavior,

then = reteaching and enrichment suggestions

✓ Portfolio Assessment

- **Portfolio Assessment,** TE pp. 95, 96, 155
- **Leveled Practice,** TE pp. 108, 110, 113, 118, 129, 132, 134, 138, 145
- **Workbook Pages,** pp. 21–36
- **Chapter Review: Write About It,** PE/TE pp. 123, 151
- **Unit Review: Apply Skills,** PE p. 155, TE p. 154
- **Curriculum Connection: Writing,** PE/TE pp. 109, 133; TE pp. 106, 140, 144, 146

✓ Performance Assessment

- **Hands-on Unit Project** (Unit 2 Performance Assessment), TE pp. 95, 123, 151, 156
- **Internet Activity,** PE p. 156
- **Chapter 4 Performance Assessment,** TE p. 122
- **Chapter 5 Performance Assessment,** TE p. 150
- **Unit Review: Write and Share,** PE/TE p. 155
- **Scoring Guides,** TE pp. 155–156

Test Talk

Test-Taking Strategies

Understand the Question

- **Locate Key Words in the Question,** TE p. 107
- **Locate Key Words in the Text,** PE/TE p. 154, TE p. 117

Understand the Answer

- **Choose the Right Answer,** Test Talk Practice Book
- **Use Information from the Text,** TE p. 114
- **Use Information from Graphics,** TE p. 111
- **Write Your Answer to Score High,** TE p. 133

For additional practice, use the Test Talk Practice Book.

Featured Strategy

Locate Key Words in the Text

Students will:

- Make sure that they understand the key words in the question.
- Find key words in the text that match key words in the question.

PE/TE p. 154, **TE** p. 117

Curriculum Connections

Integrating Your Day

The lessons, skills, and features of Unit 2 provide many opportunities to make connections between social studies and other areas of the elementary curriculum.

Social Studies

READING

Reading Skill—Sequence, PE/TE pp. 100–101, 104, 112, 116, 126, 130

Lesson Review—Sequence, PE/TE pp. 109, 115, 119, 129, 133

Link to Reading, PE/TE pp. 119, 146

Read Carl Sandburg's Work, TE p. 153

WRITING

Create a Slide Show of the Appalachian Trail, TE p. 106

Link to Writing, PE/TE pp. 109, 133

Create a Suffrage Time Line, TE p. 140

Write a Travel Itinerary, TE p. 144

Write a Description, TE p. 146

MATH

Calculate Averages, TE p. 135

LITERATURE

Read About the Region, TE p. 98

Read About Northeastern Resources, TE p. 115

Read Biographies, TE p. 139

SCIENCE

Analyze Ecological Threats, TE p. 109

Link to Science, PE/TE p. 115

Explore Shark Bay, TE p. 121

Research Diseases, TE p. 128

MUSIC / DRAMA

Listen to Niagara Falls, TE p. 105

Present a Dramatic Reading, TE p. 107

Present a Dramatization, TE p. 133

Stage a Disaster Drill, TE p. 148

Perform a Folk Song, TE p. 153

ART

Interpret Fine Art, TE p. 96

Link to Art, PE/TE p. 129

Create a Protest Button, TE p. 140

Promote Libraries, TE p. 147

Create an Emergency-Action Poster, TE p. 148

Look for this symbol throughout the Teacher's Edition to find **Curriculum Connections.**

Professional Development

Preparing Twenty-First Century Citizens

by Carole Hahn, Ed.D.
Emory University

We want students to know concepts such as "democracy," "government," "rights," and "responsibilities of citizens." We want them to learn about the political history of their country. We want young people to become well informed about issues that citizens face today and that students are likely to encounter as adults. Because we want students to be knowledgeable citizens, we must spend time teaching them powerful ideas in social studies lessons.

Students need to develop a commitment to the ideals contained in the Declaration of Independence and the Constitution and Bill of Rights, ideals reiterated in the suffragists' Seneca Falls Declaration and Martin Luther King, Jr.'s "Letter from Birmingham Jail." At the same time, young people need to realize that the nation has not always lived up to its ideals and that it is the responsibility of each generation to work to improve society for the next generation.

As we give students practice in analyzing issues and ask them to take the perspectives of others across time and space, we will help them to appreciate their role as global citizens, as well as citizens in the national, local, and ethnic communities of which they are a part.

- *On p. 131 of the Teacher's Edition, students use a map to locate places associated with the birth of the United States, including the original 13 colonies, and cities such as Plymouth and Lexington, Massachusetts; Philadelphia, Pennsylvania; New York City, New York; and Washington, D.C.*
- *On p. 133 of the Teacher's Edition, students analyze the experiences of immigrants arriving at Ellis Island in 1900 and brainstorm ways to remove language barriers and other potential difficulties facing new immigrants today.*

ESL Support

by Jim Cummins, Ph.D.
University of Toronto

In Unit 2, you can use the following fundamental strategy to help ESL students expand their language abilities.

Extend Language

Academic English is fairly predictable because many words are derived from Latin and Greek. You can help students use these word origins to understand the language of social studies. Focus on meaning, form, and use. This can be illustrated with reference to the word *community*.

Focus on meaning. Have your students brainstorm words directly related to the word *community*. Then, explore the meaning of different word forms. Thus, a verb related to *community* is *communicate;* an adjective is *common*.

Focus on form. If students learn the typical patterns for forming nouns and adjectives from verbs, they can recognize them when they appear in text. Rather than learning just one word in isolation, students learn entire *word families*.

Focus on use. Have students explore the uses of particular words through brainstorming as a class or small group, exploring such categories as general uses, idioms, metaphorical use, proverbs, advertisements, puns, and jokes.

The following examples in the Teacher's Edition will help you extend the language abilities of ESL students:

- ***Examine Compound Nouns** on p. 105 helps students recognize the meanings of familiar words when they appear in compound nouns, such as* waterfall, hydropower, cross-section, *and* hydroelectricity.
- ***Examine Prefixes** on p. 143 has students identify the meanings of the prefixes* im- *and* ex- *and determine how they affect the root words to which they are attached.*

Read Aloud

Tourist
by Petey Bean

I travel the land with camera in hand
Looking for something to see.
I've found a place of beauty and grace
Surrounded by water and trees.
"Leaf Peeper" I'm called, after I visit the falls
And point my camera up to the sky.
The leaves of the trees are no longer in greens
As the fall season passes on by.
After two weeks, I leave the Northeast.
The colors and food fill my mind.
Though my time here is through, I say unto you,
I might travel back here sometime!

Read Alouds and Primary Sources

- *Read Alouds and Primary Sources* contains additional selections to be used with Unit 2.

Bibliography

Dancing on the Sand: A Story of an Atlantic Blue Crab, by Kathleen M. Hollenbeck (Soundprints Corp Audio, ISBN 1-568-99730-2, 1999) **Easy**

The Tower to the Sun, by Colin Thompson (Knopf, ISBN 0-679-98334-1, 1997) **Easy**

Way to Go, Alex! by Robin Pulver (Albert Whitman & Company, ISBN 0-807-51583-3, 1999) **Easy**

Awesome Chesapeake: A Kid's Guide to the Bay, by David Owen Bell (Tidewater Publishing, ISBN 0-870-33457-3, 1994) **On-Level**

Famine, by Christopher F. Lampton (Millbrook Press, ISBN 1-562-94317-0, 1994) **On-Level**

Sojourner Truth: Ain't I a Woman? by Patricia C. McKissack and Fredrick McKissack (Scholastic Trade, ISBN 0-590-44691-6, 1994) **On-Level** ***ALA Notable Book, Coretta Scott King Honor Book***

Roger Williams, by Mark Ammerman (Barbour Publishing, ISBN 1-557-48761-8, 1996) **Challenge**

Waterman's Boy, by Susan Sharpe (Simon & Schuster, ISBN 0-027-82351-2, 1990) **Challenge**

Women Win the Vote, by Joann A. Grote (Barbour & Company, ISBN 1-577-48452-5, 1998) **Challenge**

The Great Irish Potato Famine, by James S. Donnelly, Jr. (Sutton Publishing, ISBN 0-750-92632-5, 2001) **Teacher reference**

The Industrial Revolution, by James A. Corrick (Lucent Books, ISBN 1-560-06318-1, 1998) **Teacher reference**

Watching Nature: A Mid-Atlantic Natural History, by Mark S. Garland (Smithsonian Institution Press, ISBN 1-560-98742-1, 1997) **Teacher reference**

***Discovery Channel School* Videos**

Understanding: Cities Explore "The Big Apple" and four other great cities around the world, examining how they function, their history, and their evolution. (Item #717611, 52 minutes)

- To order Discovery Channel School videos, please call the following toll-free number: 1-888-892-3484.
- Free online lesson plans are available at **DiscoverySchool.com.**

Look for this symbol throughout the Teacher's Edition to find **Award-Winning Selections.** Additional book references are found throughout this unit.

The Northeast

UNIT 2

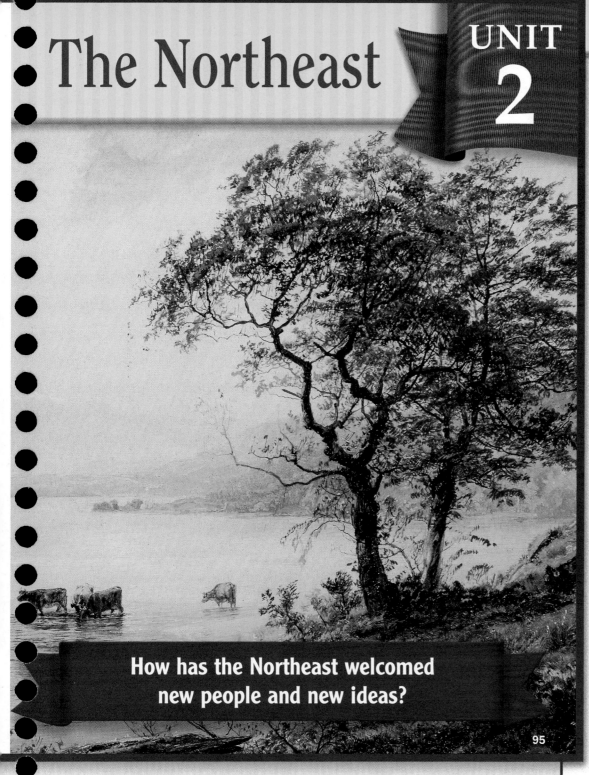

How has the Northeast welcomed new people and new ideas?

95

Practice and Extend

Hands-on Unit Project

✓ **Unit 2 Performance Assessment**

- The Unit Project, *On the Spot,* found on p. 156 is an ongoing performance assessment project to enrich students' learning throughout the unit.
- This project, which has students creating a documentary, may be started now or at any time during this unit of study.
- A performance assessment scoring guide is located on p. 156.

UNIT 2

The Northeast

Unit Overview

Niagara Falls, the woods in autumn, and Chesapeake Bay are three outstanding attractions in the Northeast. Both Native Americans and immigrants have made their homes in the Northeast, and women and industrialists from the region have made a great difference.

Unit Outline

Chapter 4 ***Land and Water in the Northeast*** pp. 102–123

Chapter 5 ***People of the Northeast*** pp. 124–151

Unit Question

- Have students read the question under the picture.
- To activate prior knowledge, ask students how new people and new ideas sometimes come to an area. Then ask them how new people and new ideas might be made to feel welcome.
- On chart paper have students write a list of states they think might be included in the Northeast.
- Next, have them brainstorm a preliminary list of new groups of people and new ideas that have come to the Northeast, even if the answers are only guesses.

✓**Portfolio Assessment** Keep this list to review with students at the end of the unit on p. 155.

Begin with a Primary Source

Objective

- Use primary sources to acquire information.

Resource

- Poster 3

Interpret a Primary Source

- Tell students that this primary source is a quotation from a book by Henry David Thoreau.
- Explain that *Walden* is a famous collection of writings in which the author stresses the importance of living simply and learning to exist in harmony with nature.
- Thoreau loved the natural world and was a careful observer of it. People still turn to his writings today for inspiration about nature and the environment.

✓**Portfolio Assessment** Remind students of the list they began on p. 95. As students read, have them make changes to the class list as necessary. Review the list at the end of the unit on p. 155.

Interpret Fine Art

- This rendering of a peaceful natural setting is called *New England Landscape* and was painted by Jasper Francis Cropsey.
- Explain that this painting portrays the lush countryside of the Northeast.
- Discuss what students think are the main elements of this painting. (Water, coastline, trees, sky)
- Ask students how this painting makes them feel about the area that is pictured. Discuss whether these feelings make the Northeast seem more attractive or less attractive to them and why.

UNIT 2

Begin with a Primary Source

96

Practice and Extend

SOCIAL STUDIES
Background

About the Primary Source

- The quotation from Henry David Thoreau's *Walden* focuses on the beauty of the Northeast in the fall.
- Thoreau named his book *Walden* after Walden Pond, a body of water near Concord, Massachusetts. In 1845 Thoreau leased some land near the pond and lived there in a cabin for two years, two months, and two days. During that time he wrote about the wonders of nature and people's relationship to it.
- Tell students that the land Thoreau leased was owned by the author's friend and mentor, Ralph Waldo Emerson. Have volunteers do research, write a brief description of Emerson, and share it with the class. Discuss what interests these two men might have shared. (Writing, nature, philosophy)

"Gradually from week to week the character of each tree came out...reflected in the smooth mirror of the lake."

—Henry David Thoreau, *Walden*

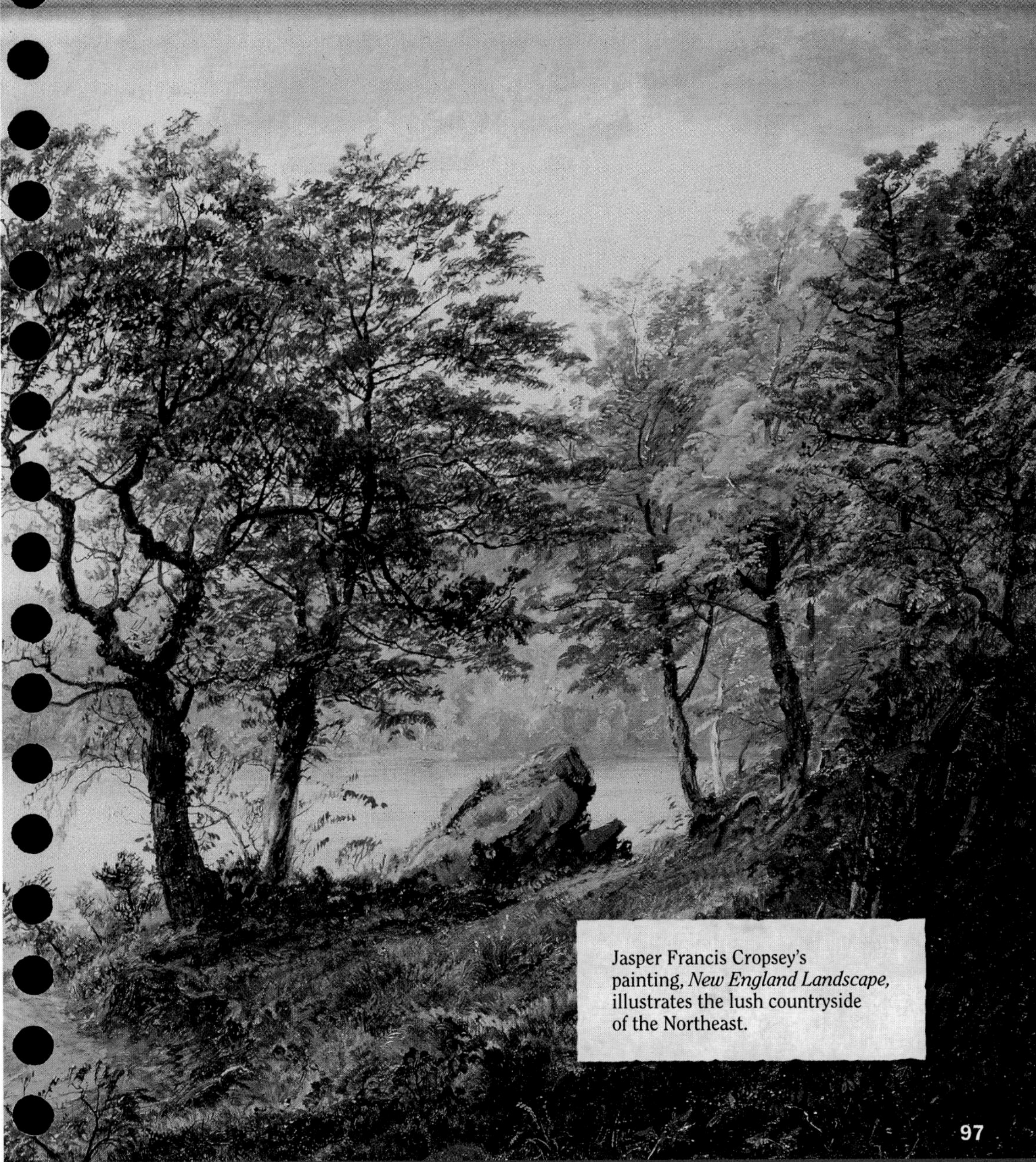

Jasper Francis Cropsey's painting, *New England Landscape*, illustrates the lush countryside of the Northeast.

97

WEB SITE
Technology

Students can learn more about Henry David Thoreau online by selecting the encyclopedia from *Social Studies Library* at **www.sfsocialstudies.com.**

Meet the Artist

- Born in 1823 on Staten Island in New York, Jasper Francis Cropsey suffered from ill health as a child. During periods when he was unable to attend school, the youngster taught himself to draw.
- Cropsey became devoted to painting autumn landscapes after taking a trip to London in 1856. The English, whose native trees do not turn vibrant colors in the fall, were fascinated by the artist's paintings of New England's fall foliage.
- Cropsey's paintings of fall colors were so foreign to the British that many doubted they were accurate. To prove that his paintings were true representations of nature, the artist began displaying preserved autumn leaves on pieces of cardboard next to his paintings.

Welcome to the Northeast

Objective

- Identify objects and places of interest in the Northeast.

Resource

- Poster 4

Research the Region

Each of the states featured on these pages is an important part of the Northeast region. Have students do research to find out the answers to the following questions.

- **What major rivers flow into the Chesapeake Bay?** The James, Rappahannock, Potomac, Patuxent, Susquehanna, Chester, Choptank, York, and Nanticoke
- **What is a square dance?** A dance in which four couples form a square and do complex dance moves commanded by a caller.
- **What are the most common shellfish caught in Narragansett Bay in Rhode Island?** Lobster and quahogs (hard-shelled clams)
- **A whale lamp is a lamp that burns whale oil. What else was whale oil traditionally used for? What new use for whale oil was found in the 1900s?** Traditionally: in soapmaking; 1900s: in margarines and cooking oils

Students may wish to write their own questions about places in this region for the rest of the class to answer.

UNIT 2

Welcome to the Northeast

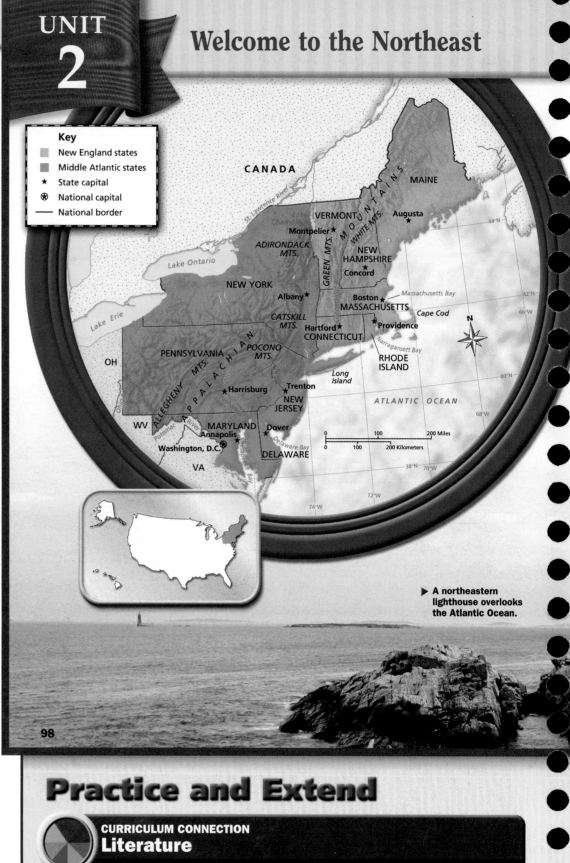

Key
- New England states
- Middle Atlantic states
- ★ State capital
- ⊛ National capital
- — National border

CANADA
MAINE
Augusta
VERMONT
Montpelier
NEW HAMPSHIRE
Concord
NEW YORK
Albany
MASSACHUSETTS
Boston
Massachusetts Bay
Cape Cod
Providence
RHODE ISLAND
Narragansett Bay
CONNECTICUT
Hartford
Long Island
PENNSYLVANIA
Harrisburg
NEW JERSEY
Trenton
DELAWARE
Dover
MARYLAND
Annapolis
Washington, D.C.
VA
WV
OH
Lake Ontario
Lake Erie
Lake Champlain
St. Lawrence River
ADIRONDACK MTS.
CATSKILL MTS.
POCONO MTS.
ALLEGHENY MTS.
APPALACHIAN MOUNTAINS
GREEN MTS.
WHITE MTS.
Potomac River
Delaware Bay
Chesapeake Bay
ATLANTIC OCEAN
N

▶ A northeastern lighthouse overlooks the Atlantic Ocean.

98

Practice and Extend

CURRICULUM CONNECTION
Literature

Read About the Region

Use the following selections to extend the content.

Square Dancing, by Mark Thomas (Children's Press, ISBN 0-516-23070-0, 2000) **Easy**

Rhode Island, by Kathleen Thompson (Raintree/Steck-Vaughn, ISBN 0-811-47466-6, 1996) **On-Level**

Where Did All the Water Go? by Carolyn Stearns (Tidewater Publishers, ISBN 0-870-33506-5, 1998) **Challenge**

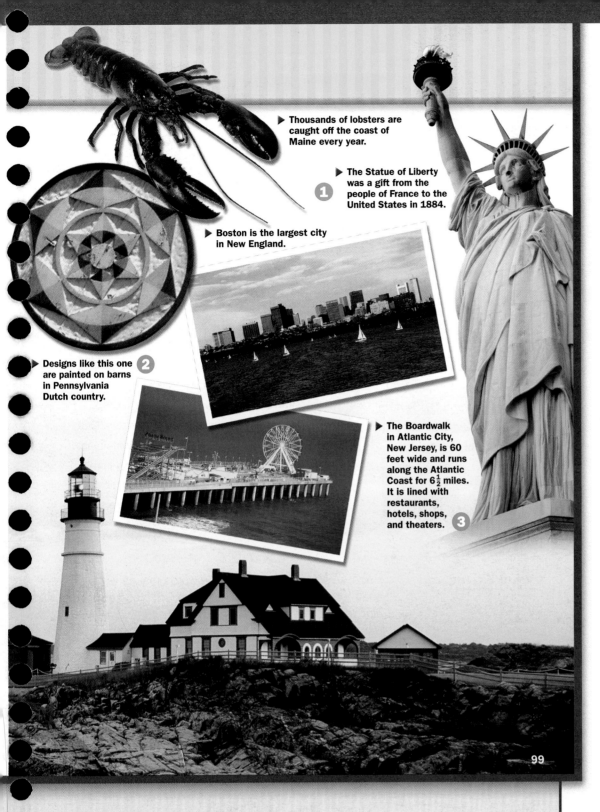

Thousands of lobsters are caught off the coast of Maine every year.

1 The Statue of Liberty was a gift from the people of France to the United States in 1884.

Boston is the largest city in New England.

Designs like this one are painted on barns in Pennsylvania Dutch country. 2

The Boardwalk in Atlantic City, New Jersey, is 60 feet wide and runs along the Atlantic Coast for $6\frac{1}{2}$ miles. It is lined with restaurants, hotels, shops, and theaters. 3

99

WEB SITE
Technology

Students can learn more about places in this unit by clicking on *Atlas* at **www.sfsocialstudies.com.**

Discuss the Region

Have students use the photos and captions to answer the following questions.

1 **When did the United States celebrate the Statue of Liberty's centennial?** 1984 Analyze Information

2 **What unusual artwork can be found in Pennsylvania Dutch country?** Artwork on barns Analyze Pictures

3 **Why do you think thousands of tourists each year flock to the Boardwalk in Atlantic City?** Possible answer: To enjoy the Atlantic coast and the many restaurants, hotels, shops, and theaters located there Make Inferences

Read About the States

The states shown here are discussed in the text on the following pages in Unit 2.

- New York, pp. 104–107, 113, 117, 129, 131–133, 138–139, 142–144, 146, 148–149
- Connecticut, p. 106
- Maine, pp. 106, 108
- Pennsylvania, pp. 106–108, 117, 130–131, 137, 143–147
- New Jersey, pp. 106, 108–109, 117, 119, 142, 144
- Vermont, pp. 106, 108, 114–115
- Massachusetts, pp. 106, 108, 113, 118–119, 131, 133, 143–144
- Maryland, pp. 106, 108, 117, 136, 143–144
- New Hampshire, pp. 106, 115
- Delaware, pp. 117, 119
- Rhode Island, pp. 127–128, 143

UNIT 2

Reading Social Studies

Sequence

Objective

- Analyze information by sequencing events.

Resource

- Workbook, p. 21

About the Unit Target Skill

- The target reading skill for this unit is Sequence.
- Students are introduced to the unit target skill here and are given an opportunity to practice it.
- Further opportunities to sequence are found throughout Unit 2.

1 Introduce and Motivate

Preview To activate prior knowledge, ask students for examples of a sequence of events from their everyday lives. (Possible answer: Each morning they wake up, rise from bed, brush their teeth and wash their face, get dressed, eat breakfast, and go to school.)

UNIT 2

The Northeast

Sequence

Sequence means the order in which things happen.

- Clue words such as *first, then, next,* and *finally* can help you figure out the sequence of events.
- Dates and times of day are other clues to the sequence of events.
- Some events take place at the same time. Clue words such as *meanwhile* or *during* signal this.

Read this paragraph. **First, then,** and **finally** have been highlighted to show the sequence of events.

The brilliant colors of autumn leaves in the Northeast attract visitors from all over the country. When leaves change color they follow a pattern. **First,** leaves lose their green color. **Then,** yellow and orange pigments begin to show through, and red and purple pigments form from sugar that is trapped in the leaves. **Finally,** the leaves turn brown and fall from the tree.

Word Exercise

Precise Words Using precise words makes writing clearer and more interesting. Precise words, such as *shot* and *plunged*, paint a more vivid picture than the word *moved*. Use a word web to find more precise and exciting words for your ideas.

moved
shot
plunged
raced
dashed
scurried

Practice and Extend

ACTIVATE PRIOR KNOWLEDGE

ESL Support

Demonstrate Sequence Have students demonstrate their understanding of clue words that signal a sequence.

Beginning Have students point out the sequencing clue words as you say groups of sentences aloud. For example, say *First,* Juan stands up. *Then* Juan sits down. *Finally,* Juan raises his hand. *While* Juan's hand is up, Maria stands up.

Intermediate Have students use sequencing clue words to give oral accounts of recent personal or classroom experiences.

Advanced Have students use sequencing clue words to write and illustrate a short how-to paragraph. Have students read their paragraphs aloud, emphasizing the clue words.

An Exciting Sequence of Events Near the Falls

Niagara Falls is located at the border of New York and Canada. A boat at the bottom of the falls, called the *Maid of the Mist,* carries tourists near the waterfall. The very first *Maid of the Mist* sailed in 1846.

Farther down the river from the falls are dangerous rapids (part of a river's course where the water rushes quickly). An exciting event happened here in 1861 when the *Maid of the Mist*'s owner sold the steamboat. The boat had to be taken through the rapids to its new owner.

Joel Robinson, the *Maid of the Mist*'s captain, set out at 3:00 P.M. on June 6, 1861. First, the boat shot into the rapids. Then, huge waves crashed over the boat and tore off its smokestack.

Meanwhile, observers on the shore watched the boat being tossed about by waves. When the boat plunged into a whirlpool, Robinson grabbed the wheel and steered the boat out of the whirling water. The boat hurtled into the Devil's Hole Rapids.

Finally, the *Maid of the Mist* made it safely to Lake Ontario. The entire trip had taken only seventeen minutes.

Use the reading strategy of sequence to answer questions 1 and 2. Then answer the vocabulary question.

1. What sequence of events took place between the time Robinson began his journey and the time his boat arrived in Lake Ontario?
2. What happened at the same time that waves were crashing over the boat? How do you know?
3. Look for the word *tore* in the reading selection. What word could you use to replace it in the sentence?

101

2 Teach and Discuss

- Point out that we use sequence all the time, for example, when we tell others about something that happened to us or when we describe a book or a television show.
- Have students read the sample paragraph on p. 100. Confirm that they can identify the purpose of the highlighted clue words.
- Then have students read the longer practice sample on p. 101 and answer the questions that follow.
- Ask students why, when studying geography, it is important to understand sequence. (To understand how a region might change over time)

Precise Words

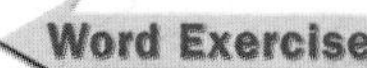

Students may say that the words *ripped, split, shredded,* and *pulled* could replace *tore* in the sentence. Have students explain why these words are more precise. Have students choose from two choices to complete each sentence below in the more precise way.

- Angela went or hurtled (hurtled) down the course ahead of the other runners.
- After the race, she gulped or drank (gulped) the glass of water greedily.

3 Close and Assess

Apply it!

1. (1) Boat shot into rapids, (2) huge waves crashed over boat, (3) waves tore off boat's smokestack, (4) boat plunged into whirlpool, (5) Robinson steered boat out of whirlpool, (6) boat hurtled into Devil's Hole Rapids, (7) boat made it safely to Lake Ontario
2. Observers on the shore watched the boat being tossed by the waves. The writer uses the word *meanwhile*.
3. Possible answers: ripped, split, shredded, pulled

Standardized Test Prep

- Use Workbook p. 21 to give students practice with standardized test format.
- Chapter and Unit Tests in the Assessment Book use standardized test format.
- Test-taking tips are contained in the front portion of the Assessment Book Teacher's Edition.

Also on Teacher Resources CD-ROM.

Workbook, p. 21

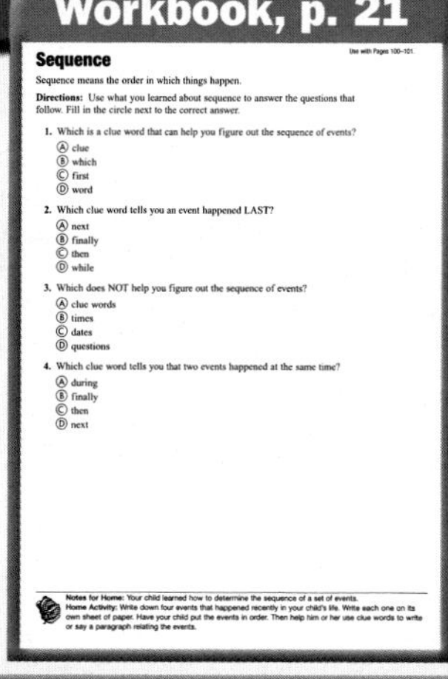

Sequence

Use with Pages 100–101.

Sequence means the order in which things happen.

Directions: Use what you learned about sequence to answer the questions that follow. Fill in the circle next to the correct answer.

1. Which is a clue word that can help you figure out the sequence of events?
   - Ⓐ clue
   - Ⓑ which
   - Ⓒ first
   - Ⓓ word
2. Which clue word tells you an event happened LAST?
   - Ⓐ next
   - Ⓑ finally
   - Ⓒ then
   - Ⓓ while
3. Which does NOT help you figure out the sequence of events?
   - Ⓐ clue words
   - Ⓑ times
   - Ⓒ dates
   - Ⓓ questions
4. Which clue word tells you that two events happened at the same time?
   - Ⓐ during
   - Ⓑ finally
   - Ⓒ then
   - Ⓓ next

Notes for Home: Your child learned how to determine the sequence of a set of events.
Home Activity: Write down four events that happened recently in your child's life. Write each one on its own sheet of paper. Have your child put the events in order. Then help him or her use clue words to write or say a paragraph relating the events.

CHAPTER 4

Chapter Planning Guide

Chapter 4 • Land and Water in the Northeast

Locating Places pp. 102–103

Lesson Titles	Pacing	Main Ideas
Lesson 1 **The Beautiful Northeast** pp. 104–109	3 days	• The Northeast region is one of incredible scenery and magnificent natural formations.
Chart and Graph Skills: Read a Cross-Section Diagram pp. 110–111		• Analyze and interpret a cross-section diagram.
Lesson 2 **Resources of the Northeast** pp. 112–115	1 day	• The Northeast produces products for the world to enjoy.
Lesson 3 **The Plentiful Sea** pp. 116–119	2 days	• Chesapeake Bay and other bays in the Northeast provide seafood for millions.
Here and There: Bay Life pp. 120–121		• Shark Bay in Australia is considered a living fossil and needs to be protected from overfishing and pollution.
✓ **Chapter 4 Review** pp. 122–123		

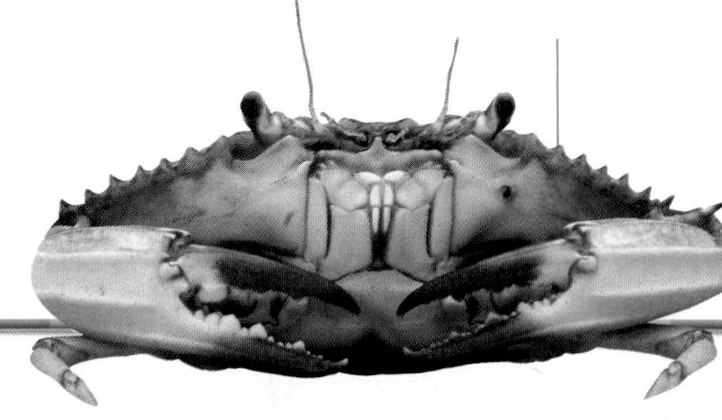

For decades watermen have harvested shellfish like this blue crab from the waters of Chesapeake Bay.

✓ **= Assessment Options**

The thundering waters of Niagara Falls provide hydroelectricity for Northeasterners and a spectacular sight for tourists from around the world.

Vocabulary	Resources	Meeting Individual Needs
glacier gorge hydropower hydroelectricity lighthouse peninsula	• Workbook, p. 23 • Transparencies 9, 36 • Every Student Learns Guide, pp. 38–41 • Quick Study, pp. 20–21	• ESL Support, TE p. 105 • Leveled Practice, TE p. 108
cross-section diagram reservoir	• Workbook, p. 24	• Leveled Practice, TE p. 110
vineyard bog sap mineral quarry	• Workbook, p. 25 • Transparencies 10, 37 • Every Student Learns Guide, pp. 42–45 • Quick Study, pp. 22–23	• Leveled Practice, TE p. 113 • ESL Support, TE p. 114
bay inlet watermen crab pot	• Workbook, p. 26 • Transparency 11 • Every Student Learns Guide, pp. 46–49 • Quick Study, pp. 24–25	• ESL Support, TE p. 117 • Leveled Practice, TE p. 118 • Learning Styles, TE p. 119
	✔Chapter 4 Content Test, Assessment Book, pp. 17–18 ✔Chapter 4 Skills Test, Assessment Book, pp. 19–20	✔Chapter 4 Performance Assessment, TE p. 122

Providing More Depth

Additional Resources

- Vocabulary Workbook and Cards
- Social Studies Plus! pp. 40–45
- Daily Activity Bank
- Big Book Atlas
- Student Atlas
- Outline Maps
- Desk Maps

Technology

- AudioText
- MindPoint® Quiz Show CD-ROM
- ExamView® Test Bank CD-ROM
- Teacher Resources CD-ROM
- Map Resources CD-ROM
- SFSuccessNet: iText (Pupil Edition online), iTE (Teacher's Edition online), Online Planner
- **www.sfsocialstudies.com** (Biographies, news, references, maps, and activities)

To establish guidelines for your students' safe and responsible use of the Internet, use the Scott Foresman Internet Guide.

Additional Internet Links

To find out more about:

- Chesapeake Bay Foundation, visit **www.cbf.org**
- Shark Bay, visit **www.sharkbay.org**
- Hydroelectric power, visit **www.nrel.gov**

Key Internet Search Terms

- Carnegie Corporation
- Vermont Maple Festival
- blue crabs

Workbook Support

Use the following Workbook pages to support content and skills development as you teach Chapter 4. You can also view and print Workbook pages from the Teacher Resources CD-ROM.

Workbook, p. 21

Use with Pages 100–101.

Sequence

Sequence means the order in which things happen.

Directions: Use what you learned about sequence to answer the questions that follow. Fill in the circle next to the correct answer.

1. Which is a clue word that can help you figure out the sequence of events?
- Ⓐ clue
- Ⓑ which
- ● first
- Ⓓ word

2. Which clue word tells you an event happened LAST?
- Ⓐ next
- ● finally
- Ⓒ then
- Ⓓ while

3. Which does NOT help you figure out the sequence of events?
- Ⓐ clue words
- Ⓑ times
- Ⓒ dates
- ● questions

4. Which clue word tells you that two events happened at the same time?
- ● during
- Ⓑ finally
- Ⓒ then
- Ⓓ next

Notes for Home: Your child learned how to determine the sequence of a set of events.
Home Activity: Write down four events that happened recently in your child's life. Write each one on its own sheet of paper. Have your child put the events in order. Then help him or her use clue words to write or say a paragraph relating the events.

Use with Pupil Edition, p. 101

Workbook, p. 22

Use with Chapter 4.

Vocabulary Preview

Directions: These are the vocabulary words from Chapter 4. How much do you know about these words? Write the number of the vocabulary word on the line next to its definition. You may use your glossary.

1. glacier
2. gorge
3. hydropower
4. hydroelectricity
5. lighthouse
6. peninsula
7. vineyard
8. bog
9. sap
10. mineral
11. quarry
12. bay
13. inlet
14. waterman
15. crab pot

Answer	Definition
2	**a.** deep, narrow valley, usually with a stream or river
8	**b.** area of soft, wet, spongy ground
15	**c.** a large wire cage with several sections
3	**d.** power that is produced by capturing the energy of flowing water
7	**e.** place where grapevines are planted
13	**f.** narrow opening in a coastline
10	**g.** material that was never alive and is found in the earth
11	**h.** place where stone is dug, cut, or blasted out for use in building
5	**i.** tower with bright lights that shine out over the water to guide ships
9	**j.** liquid that circulates through a plant carrying water and food
12	**k.** part of a sea or lake that cuts into a coastline
4	**l.** electricity produced by water
1	**m.** huge sheet of ice that covers land
6	**n.** piece of land almost surrounded by water, or extending far out into the water
14	**o.** person who fishes the bay

Notes for Home: Your child learned the vocabulary terms for Chapter 4.
Home Activity: Four of the terms from this chapter are compound nouns: *lighthouse, vineyard, waterman,* and *crab pot*. Discuss with your child how these words probably were first created.

Use with Pupil Edition, p. 102

Workbook, p. 23

Use with Pages 104–109.

Lesson 1: The Beautiful Northeast

The Northeast region is one of beautiful scenery and magnificent formations.

Directions: Use complete sentences to answer the questions below. You may use your textbook.

1. What caused the formation of Niagara Falls?

Glaciers that once covered the land began to melt, carving out the Great Lakes and the Niagara Gorge. The Niagara River plunges into the gorge, creating the Niagara Falls.

2. Why is the Niagara River important to millions of people in the Northeast?

There are hydropower plants on the Niagara River that capture the energy from the flowing water to produce hydroelectricity. Niagara is the largest producer of electricity in New York State, generating enough power to light 24 million 100-watt light bulbs at once.

3. What are the names of at least four mountain ranges located in the Northeast region? Where are they located?

Appalachian Mountain Range begins in Canada and extends to Alabama; Green Mountains run north and south through Vermont; White Mountains of New Hampshire extend partly into the western part of Maine; Catskill Mountains are about 2 hours north of New York City.

4. How is the coastline of Maine different from New Jersey's coastline?

Along the Maine coastline there are huge rocks and cliffs. The rocky coast is dotted with lighthouses. The New Jersey coastline is made up of sandy beaches.

Notes for Home: Your child learned about the different natural formations located in the Northeast region.
Home Activity: Suppose that your family is going to the Northeast to hike along the Appalachian Trail. With your child, use a map or an atlas to plan your route and discuss what items you will need to bring with you on your trip.

Use with Pupil Edition, p. 109

Workbook Support

Workbook, p. 24

Use with Pages 110–111.

Read a Cross-Section Diagram

A cross-section diagram shows you what you would see if you could cut through something and then look inside.

Directions: The steps to studying a cross-section diagram can be found in the box below. On the lines provided, write the steps in the order in which they should occur. You may use your textbook.

Think about the terms used in the diagram. Figure out how each part works. Gather information from the labels on the diagram. Look at the numbers or arrows on the diagram. Study each labeled part of the diagram.

Step 1: Gather information from the labels on the diagram.

Step 2: Study each labeled part of the diagram.

Step 3: Figure out how each part works.

Step 4: Look at the numbers or arrows on the diagram.

Step 5: Think about the terms used in the diagram.

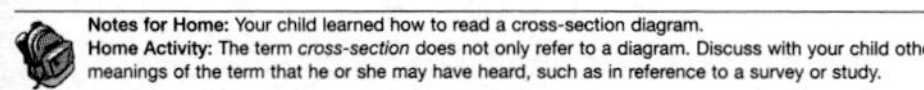

Notes for Home: Your child learned how to read a cross-section diagram.
Home Activity: The term *cross-section* does not only refer to a diagram. Discuss with your child other meanings of the term that he or she may have heard, such as in reference to a survey or study.

Use with Pupil Edition, p. 111

Workbook, p. 25

Use with Pages 112–115.

Lesson 2: Resources of the Northeast

The Northeast produces many products that people all over the world enjoy.

Directions: Suppose that you are planning a vacation to the Northeast to visit a friend or relative. Use the information from Lesson 2 to write that person a letter in which you describe some of the places you might visit, events you might attend, and the resources located there. Write your letter on the lines provided.

Dear ____________,

Answers will vary but should reflect an understanding of the products that are produced in the Northeast and the places where they are produced.

Sincerely yours,

Notes for Home: Your child learned about resources of the Northeast.
Home Activity: Discuss with your child how the resources described in the text are similar to or different from resources produced in your own region or community.

Use with Pupil Edition, p. 115

Workbook, p. 26

Use with Pages 116–119.

Lesson 3: The Plentiful Sea

Chesapeake Bay provides seafood for people around the country.

Directions: Complete the outline with information from this lesson. You may use your textbook.

Chesapeake Bay

I. **Great Shellfish Bay**
   - **A.** Got its name from the Native American word *Chesepiook*, which means Great Shellfish Bay
   - **B.** Rich in crabs, oysters, clams, other shellfish, and about two hundred different kinds of fish
   - **C.** Watermen
     1. Gather different kinds of seafood in different seasons
     2. Crabbers are watermen who use crab pots to capture crabs.

II. **Challenges to Chesapeake Bay**
   - **A.** Pollution
     1. Polluted soil washes into rivers that drain into the bay.
     2. Harms the natural habitat of the fish and shellfish
   - **B.** Overfishing
     1. Means taking oysters, crabs, and fish from the bay faster than they can be replaced
     2. Organization, Chesapeake Bay Foundation, educates people about the environment

Notes for Home: Your child learned about seafood found in Chesapeake Bay.
Home Activity: Making a living on the water can be very difficult, yet very rewarding. Discuss with your child the pros and cons of being a Chesapeake Bay waterman.

Use with Pupil Edition, p. 119

Workbook, p. 27

Use with Chapter 4.

Vocabulary Review

Directions: Write each term on the line beside its definition.

glacier	lighthouse	sap	inlet
gorge	peninsula	mineral	waterman
hydropower	vineyard	quarry	crab pot
hydroelectricity	bog	bay	

1. bay — part of a sea or lake that cuts into a coastline
2. quarry — place where stone is dug, cut, or blasted out for use in building
3. gorge — deep, narrow valley, usually with a stream or river
4. inlet — narrow opening in a coastline
5. mineral — material found in the earth that was never alive
6. bog — area of soft, wet, spongy ground
7. glacier — huge sheet of ice that covers land
8. waterman — person who fishes the Chesapeake Bay
9. sap — liquid that circulates through a plant carrying water and food
10. peninsula — piece of land almost surrounded by water, or extending far out into the water
11. crab pot — large wire cage that has several sections
12. vineyard — place where grapevines are planted
13. lighthouse — tower with bright lights that shine out over the water to guide ships
14. hydropower — power that is produced by capturing the energy of flowing water
15. hydroelectricity — electricity produced by water

Notes for Home: Your child learned the vocabulary terms for Chapter 4.
Home Activity: Write a sentence that uses one of the terms above. Leave a blank where the term would be. Have your child try to fill in the missing term. Repeat for other vocabulary terms from this chapter.

Workbook Vocabulary Review 27

Use with Pupil Edition, p. 123

Assessment Support

Use the following Assessment Book pages and The test maker to assess content and skills in Chapter 4. You can also view and print Assessment Book pages from the Teacher Resources CD-ROM.

Assessment Book, p. 17

Chapter 4 Test

Part 1: Content Test

Directions: Fill in the circle next to the correct answer.

Lesson Objective (1:1)

1. Between which two Great Lakes is Niagara Falls located?
   - ● Lakes Erie and Ontario
   - Ⓑ Lakes Huron and Erie
   - Ⓒ Lakes Michigan and Huron
   - Ⓓ Lakes Superior and Michigan

Lesson Objective (1:2)

2. Which is NOT a reason why Niagara Falls is important to the Northeast?
   - Ⓐ Much of the electricity in the region is produced by the falls.
   - ● The falls make the autumn leaves turn beautiful colors.
   - Ⓒ People can use the power of the falls to run machines.
   - Ⓓ Many tourists spend money visiting the beautiful falls each year.

Lesson Objective (1:5)

3. What is produced by hydropower plants on the Niagara River?
   - Ⓐ Niagara falls
   - Ⓑ deep, narrow valleys
   - ● hydroelectricity
   - Ⓓ natural gas

Lesson Objective (1:3)

4. Which mountain range does NOT make up part of the Appalachian Mountains?
   - ● Rocky Mountains
   - Ⓑ White Mountains
   - Ⓒ Green Mountains
   - Ⓓ Catskill Mountains

Lesson Objective (1:4)

5. Which of these Northeast states does NOT share a border with the Atlantic Ocean?
   - Ⓐ Delaware
   - Ⓑ New Jersey
   - Ⓒ Maine
   - ● Pennsylvania

Lesson Objective (2:3)

6. Which of the following is the largest of the Finger Lakes?
   - Ⓐ Lake Ontario
   - Ⓑ Lake Michigan
   - Ⓒ Lake Erie
   - ● Lake Seneca

Lesson Objective (2:2)

7. Why do grapes grow well in the Finger Lakes region?
   - Ⓐ The Finger Lakes are made up of swampy land, which is important for grape growth.
   - Ⓑ Grapevines are only planted in the freshwater of the Finger Lakes.
   - ● Warm air surrounding the Finger Lakes creates the right conditions for the grape's long growing season.
   - Ⓓ Grapes will only grow in areas having long winters and heavy snowfall.

Assessment Book — Unit 2, Chapter 4 Test **17**

Use with Pupil Edition, p. 122

Assessment Book, p. 18

Lesson Objective (2:4)

8. In which way is water NOT essential to the growth of cranberries?
   - Ⓐ In winter, water freezes over the bogs to protect the plants.
   - Ⓑ Water protects the plants against insects and disease in the spring.
   - ● Cranberry plants are placed 600 feet deep in one of the Finger Lakes.
   - Ⓓ In the fall, air pockets cause cranberries to rise when they are flooded.

Lesson Objective (2:1)

9. Which of the following is NOT a key step in maple syrup production?
   - Ⓐ Sap is emptied into a large barrel and taken to a sugar house.
   - Ⓑ A hole is drilled into a tree, and a spout is placed in the hole.
   - Ⓒ Sap is boiled until water evaporates and pure maple syrup remains.
   - ● Sap is ready to flow only when temperatures drop below freezing.

Lesson Objective (2:1)

10. Why does it take many hours to make maple syrup?
    - Ⓐ Sap used to make maple syrup must be flown to sugar houses in other countries.
    - ● About 40 gallons of sap are needed to produce one gallon of maple syrup.
    - Ⓒ Sap used to make maple syrup can only be found in rare oak trees.
    - Ⓓ Sap must be refrigerated for several days before it can be boiled.

Lesson Objective (3:3)

11. How do many families in the Chesapeake Bay area make a living?
    - Ⓐ making and selling crab pots
    - ● harvesting the sea
    - Ⓒ painting souvenirs for tourists
    - Ⓓ eating soft-shell crabs

Lesson Objective (3:1)

12. What are the people who fish Chesapeake Bay called?
    - Ⓐ keepers
    - ● watermen
    - Ⓒ crab pots
    - Ⓓ industries

Lesson Objective (3:2)

13. How does soil around Chesapeake Bay get polluted?
    - Ⓐ Some residents dump waste onto the land.
    - ● Some factories dump waste onto the land.
    - Ⓒ The bay area once was a public dumping ground.
    - Ⓓ The soil contains natural poisons.

Lesson Objective (3:2)

14. How does polluted soil get into Chesapeake Bay?
    - Ⓐ Factories dump their polluted soil directly into the bay.
    - Ⓑ Birds carry clumps of the soil over the bay and drop them.
    - ● Rain and snow wash the soil into rivers that drain into the bay.
    - Ⓓ People who visit the bay have polluted soil on their shoes.

Lesson Objective (3:4)

15. What is one way in which people have tried to help save the bay?
    - Ⓐ overfishing to decrease the fish population
    - Ⓑ visiting watermen at the bay and purchasing shellfish
    - Ⓒ keeping boats out of the bay at all times
    - ● creating the Chesapeake Bay Foundation to educate people about the environment

18 Unit 2, Chapter 4 Test — Assessment Book

Use with Pupil Edition, p. 122

Assessment Support

Assessment Book, p. 19

Part 2: Skills Test

Directions: Use complete sentences to answer questions 1–5. Use a separate sheet of paper if you need more space.

1. Write at least three details to support the following main idea: **Niagara River is important to people in the Northeast region. Main Idea and Details**

   Possible answers: Hydropower plants on the Niagara River capture the energy of the flowing water to run mills and machines; Niagara is the largest producer of electricity in New York State; Niagara generates enough power to light 24 million 100-watt light bulbs at once.

2. How are the Green Mountains and White Mountains alike? How are they different? **Compare and Contrast**

   Alike: Both make up part of the Appalachian Mountains, receive heavy snowfall, and have many ski resorts. Different: The Green Mountains are named for their evergreen forests and run through Vermont; the White Mountains are named for their snow-covered peaks and extend from New Hampshire into the western part of Maine.

3. Sequence the events in preparing a cranberry bog. **Sequence**

   The swampy land must be leveled and cleared. Then it is covered with sand for good drainage. New cranberry plants are then pressed into the sand in the bogs.

Assessment Book　　Unit 2, Chapter 4 Test　**19**

Use with Pupil Edition, p. 122

Assessment Book, p. 20

4. Suppose that you are a member of the Chesapeake Bay Foundation. What can you do to help end the pollution and overfishing of the bay? **Solve Problems**

   Students should apply the steps of the problem-solving process to devise a plan to end the pollution and overfishing of the bay.

Spile
Layer 4
Trunk
Collecting Bucket
Layer 3
Layer 2
Layer 1 (bark)
Roots

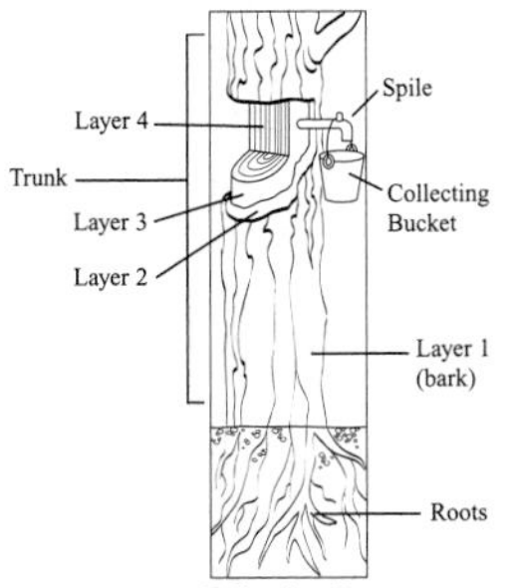

Collecting Sap

5. The diagram shows how sap is collected from a maple tree.
   a. From what part of the plant is the sap collected?

   trunk

   b. Into which layer of the tree does the spile go?

   layer 3

   c. How does the sap get from the tree to the bucket?

   The sap travels through the spile into the bucket.

Use with Pupil Edition, p. 122

CHAPTER 4

Land and Water in the Northeast

Chapter 4 Outline

- **Lesson 1, *The Beautiful Northeast,*** pp. 104–109
- **Chart and Graph Skills: *Read a Cross-Section Diagram,*** pp. 110–111
- **Lesson 2, *Resources of the Northeast,*** pp. 112–115
- **Lesson 3, *The Plentiful Sea,*** pp. 116–119
- **Here and There: *Bay Life,*** pp. 120–121

Resources

- Workbook, p. 22: Vocabulary Preview
- Vocabulary Cards
- Social Studies Plus!

Niagara Falls: Lesson 1

This picture shows just a portion of Niagara Falls. Ask students what they think they might hear, see, smell, and feel near the falls. (Possible answers: Rushing water, water crashing on rocks, spray from the waterfall)

St. Albans, Vermont: Lesson 2

This man is harvesting sap to make maple syrup. Ask students what they can tell about harvesting sap by looking at the picture. (The sap flows into buckets and then it is collected.)

Chesapeake Bay: Lesson 3

Crabs like the one in this picture are an important resource of Chesapeake Bay. Ask students what other types of sea life might be found in a bay. (Clams, fish)

CHAPTER 4

Land and Water in the Northeast

Lesson 1

Niagara Falls
Niagara Falls is a place of beauty and power.

1

Lesson 2

St. Albans, Vermont
The Northeast produces many products, such as maple syrup.

2

Lesson 3

Chesapeake Bay
Crabs and shellfish help support the economy of the Northeast region.

3

102

Practice and Extend

Vocabulary Preview

- Use Workbook p. 22 to help students preview the vocabulary words in this chapter.
- Use Vocabulary Cards to preview key concept words in this chapter.

Also on Teacher Resources CD-ROM.

Workbook, p. 22

Vocabulary Preview

Use with Chapter 4.

Directions: These are the vocabulary words from Chapter 4. How much do you know about these words? Write the number of the vocabulary word on the line next to its definition. You may use your glossary.

1. glacier
2. gorge
3. hydropower
4. hydroelectricity
5. lighthouse
6. peninsula
7. vineyard
8. bog
9. sap
10. mineral
11. quarry
12. bay
13. inlet
14. waterman
15. crab pot

_____ a. deep, narrow valley, usually with a stream or river
_____ b. area of soft, wet, spongy ground
_____ c. a large wire cage with several sections
_____ d. power that is produced by capturing the energy of flowing water
_____ e. place where grapevines are planted
_____ f. narrow opening in a coastline
_____ g. material that was never alive and is found in the earth
_____ h. place where stone is dug, cut, or blasted out for use in building
_____ i. tower with bright lights that shine out over the water to guide ships
_____ j. liquid that circulates through a plant carrying water and food
_____ k. part of a sea or lake that cuts into a coastline
_____ l. electricity produced by water
_____ m. huge sheet of ice that covers land
_____ n. piece of land almost surrounded by water, or extending far out into the water
_____ o. person who fishes the bay

Notes for Home: Your child learned the vocabulary terms for Chapter 4.
Home Activity: Four of the terms from this chapter are compound nouns: *lighthouse, vineyard, waterman,* and *crab pot.* Discuss with your child how these words probably were first created.

Locating Places

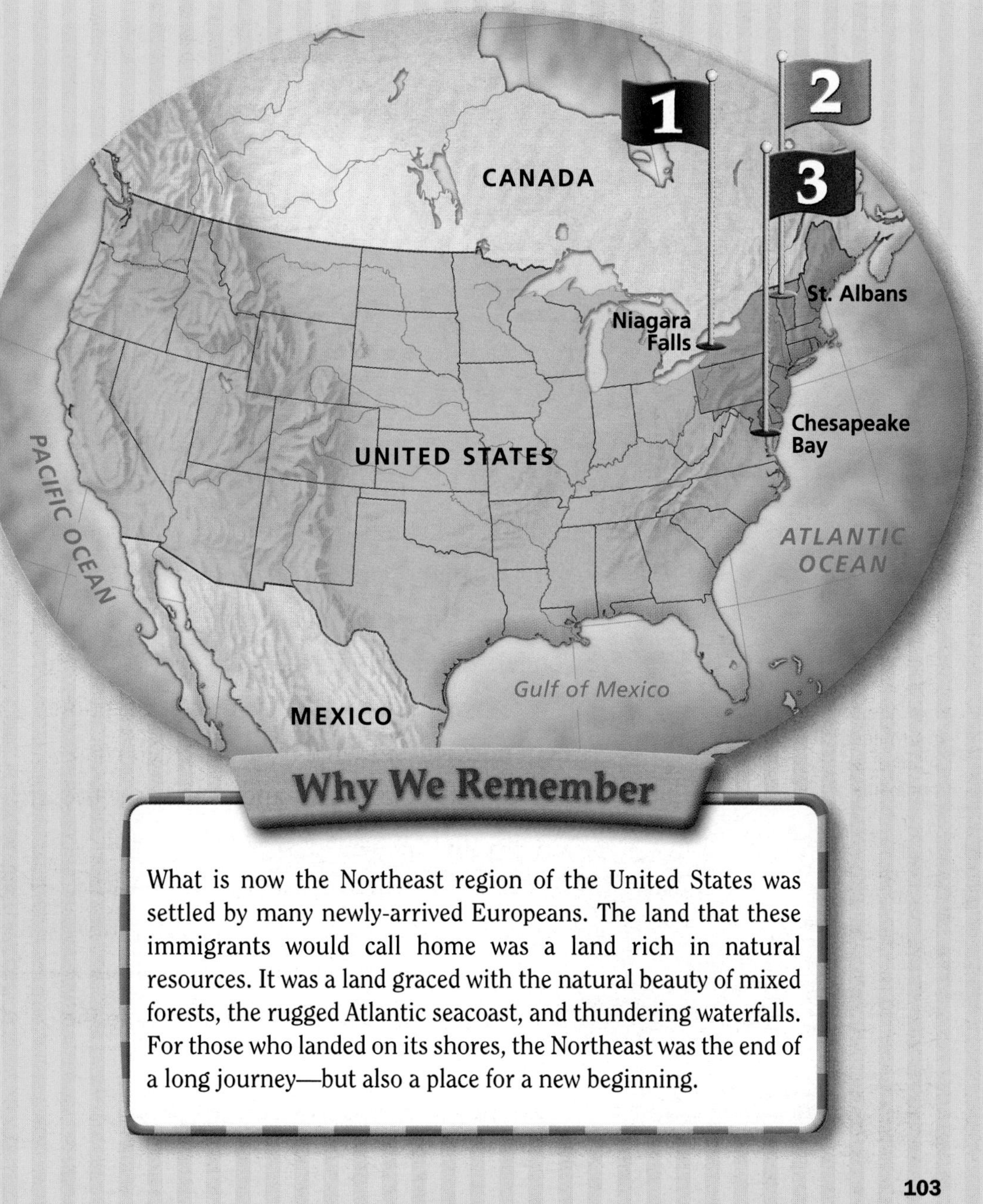

Why We Remember

What is now the Northeast region of the United States was settled by many newly-arrived Europeans. The land that these immigrants would call home was a land rich in natural resources. It was a land graced with the natural beauty of mixed forests, the rugged Atlantic seacoast, and thundering waterfalls. For those who landed on its shores, the Northeast was the end of a long journey—but also a place for a new beginning.

103

WEB SITE
Technology

You can learn more about Niagara Falls; St. Albans, Vermont; and Chesapeake Bay by clicking on *Atlas* at **www.sfsocialstudies.com.**

SOCIAL STUDIES STRAND
Geography

Mental Mapping On an outline map of the United States, have students color in the states that they think make up the Northeast Region. Students may label any cities or landforms of the Northeast that they know of. Discuss students' knowledge and/or impressions of the Northeast.

Locating Places

- Have students examine the pictures on p. 102 for Lessons 1, 2, and 3.
- Remind students that each picture is coded with both a number and a color to link it to a place on the map on p. 103.

Why We Remember

Have students read the "Why We Remember" paragraph on p. 103, and ask them why places in this chapter might be important to them. Have students consider how the climate and geography of the Northeast might have contributed to many European immigrants' decision to settle in the region. Encourage students to give specific examples.

The Beautiful Northeast

Objectives

- Identify the two Great Lakes between which Niagara Falls is located.
- Identify the two main features for which Niagara Falls is known.
- Identify the three main mountain ranges in the northeastern part of the Appalachian Mountains.
- Identify the two states in the Northeast that do not border the Atlantic Ocean.

Vocabulary

glacier, p. 105; **gorge,** p. 105; **hydropower,** p. 105; **hydroelectricity,** p. 105; **lighthouse,** p. 108; **peninsula,** p. 108

Resources

- Workbook, p. 23
- Transparency 9
- Every Student Learns Guide, pp. 38–41
- Quick Study, pp. 20–21

Quick Teaching Plan

If time is short, have students independently read each section of text in this lesson and write a one-sentence summary. Then have them compare summaries with a partner.

1 Introduce and Motivate

Preview To activate prior knowledge, ask students if they have ever seen a waterfall. Have volunteers describe how the falls looked and sounded and how the air felt near the falls. Tell students they will learn more about Niagara Falls as they read Lesson 1.

You Are There On a map of the United States, show students the location of Niagara Falls (North of Buffalo, New York, between Lake Ontario and Lake Erie, on the Canadian border). Ask students in what ways water might affect life in the Northeast.

LESSON 1

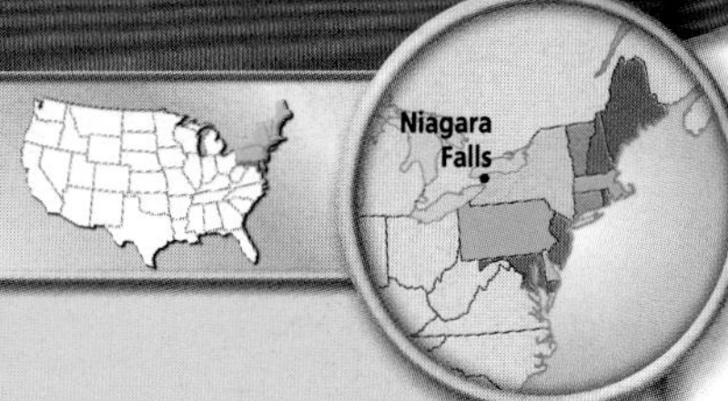

The Beautiful Northeast

PREVIEW

Focus on the Main Idea
The Northeast region is one of incredible scenery and magnificent natural formations.

PLACES
Niagara Falls
Appalachian Mountain Range
Green Mountains
White Mountains
Catskill Mountains
Acadia National Park

VOCABULARY
glacier
gorge
hydropower
hydroelectricity
lighthouse
peninsula

You Are There You are so excited! Your class is taking a trip to Niagara Falls with thirty students visiting from Madrid, Spain. You will spend part of the day at the American Falls. Later you will all cross the border into Canada to see the Canadian, or the Horseshoe, Falls too. The students tell you that before they left Spain, everyone told them to be sure to see Niagara Falls, that they were indeed one of the natural wonders of the world. As the bus comes within view of the American Falls, your teacher points them out. The students from Spain all rush to one side of the bus, and as they see the falls, there is a silence. This beautiful natural wonder that you grew up with now becomes even more meaningful!

Target Skill **Sequence** As you read, note the sequence of natural events that formed Niagara Falls.

▶ Binoculars help visitors get a closer look at Niagara Falls.

104

Practice and Extend

READING SKILL
Sequence

In the Lesson Review, students complete a graphic organizer like the one below. You may want to provide students with a copy of Transparency 9 to complete as they read the lesson.

Use Transparency 9

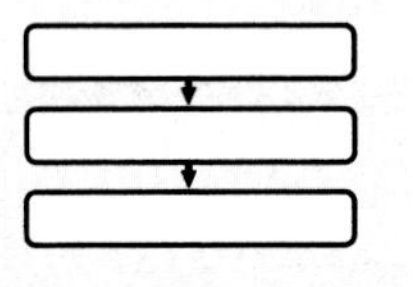

VOCABULARY
Related Word Study

Write the words *hydropower* and *hydroelectricity* on the board. Point to *hydro-* and tell students that this prefix means "water." Then have students define *power* and *electricity* in their own words. Next, tell students to read the definitions of these two words on page 105, and discuss how water fits into each definition. You may also ask students to guess what *hydrology* is. (science of water)

Niagara Falls

On the border of the United States and Canada between Lake Erie and Lake Ontario, two of the five Great Lakes, is one of the natural wonders of North America—**Niagara Falls.**

Many thousands of years ago, glaciers covered what we now call the Northeast. A **glacier** is a huge sheet of ice that covers land. About 12,000 years ago, as the ice began to melt, it carved out the Great Lakes and the Niagara Gorge. A **gorge** is a deep, 1 narrow valley, usually with a stream or river. At the Falls, the Niagara River plunges into this gorge, creating the site visited by millions of tourists throughout the year.

But the beauty of Niagara Falls is only part of its story. For hundreds of years, people have used hydropower to run mills and machines. **Hydropower** is power produced by capturing the energy of flowing water. Today, hydropower plants on the Niagara River take in water through power tunnels to produce hydroelectricity for millions of people. **Hydroelectricity** is electricity produced by water. Niagara is the largest producer of electricity in New York State, generating enough power to light 24 million 100-watt light bulbs at once! 2

REVIEW What sequence of events caused the formation of Niagara Falls? Sequence

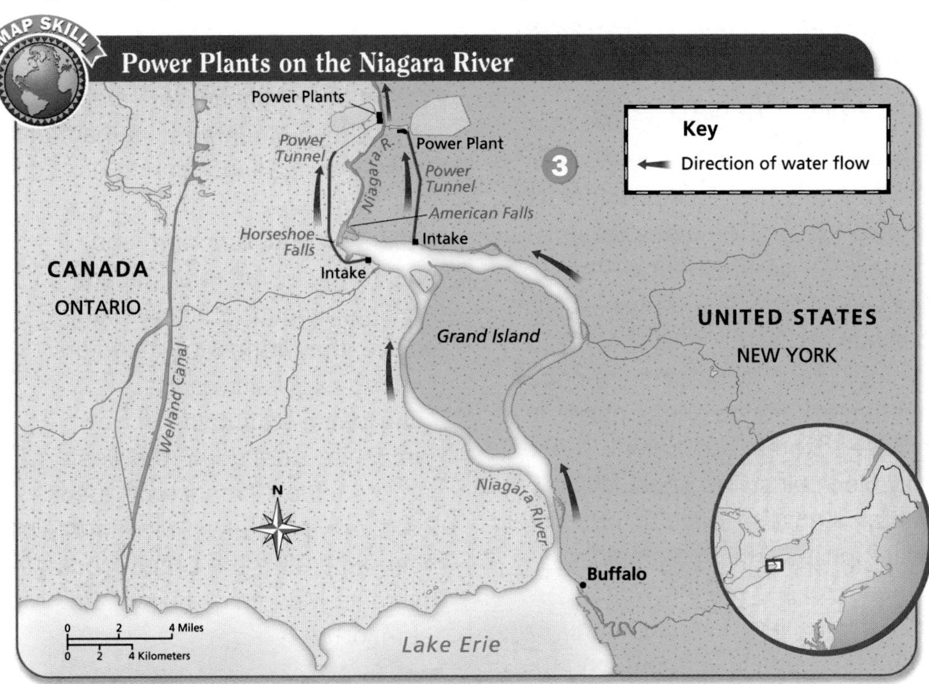

▶ Power plants on the Niagara River produce electricity for the United States and Canada.

MAP SKILL Understand Directions ***What direction does the Niagara River flow?***

105

2 Teach and Discuss

PAGE 105

Niagara Falls

Quick Summary Long ago, melting glaciers created Niagara Falls. Today, the falls attract thousands of tourists and produce hydroelectricity for the surrounding area.

1 What two geographic features were created long ago by melting glaciers? The Great Lakes and Niagara Gorge **Main Idea and Details**

2 What do you think might happen to New York's power supply if the Niagara River were to dry up? Possible answers: The amount of available hydropower would be reduced; New York would have to find another source of energy. **Predict**

✓ **REVIEW ANSWER** (1) Glaciers covered the Northeast, (2) ice began to melt, (3) melting ice carved out the Great Lakes and the Niagara Gorge, (4) the Niagara River plunged into the gorge. **Sequence**

Power Plants on the Niagara River

3 What special structures divert water from the Niagara River to power plants? Power tunnels **Interpret Maps**

MAP SKILL Answer North and west

EXTEND LANGUAGE

ESL Support

Examine Compound Nouns Help students explore different types of compound nouns.

Beginning Demonstrate three kinds of compound nouns: two words that act together, such as *ice cream*; a hyphenated word, such as *great-aunt*; and two words treated as one, such as *baseball*. Ask students to identify similar types of compound words in the text (e.g. *hydropower*, *cross-section*, and *hydroelectricity*).

Intermediate Ask students to explain in their own words the meanings of the compound nouns in the text on this page.

Advanced Have students use each of the compound nouns in the text in an original sentence. Have them illustrate one of their sentences and post it on the board for the class to see.

For additional ESL support, use Every Student Learns Guide, pp. 38–41.

CURRICULUM CONNECTION

Music

Listen to Niagara Falls

- Have students seek out a recording of Ferde Grofé's symphony *Niagara Suite*.
- Encourage students to listen for "Thunder of the Waves" in the first movement, the mood of tourists in "Honeymooners," and more water, a howling siren, and a riverboat horn in the last movement, "Power of Niagara."

The Mountains of the Northeast

Quick Summary The Appalachian Mountain Range, which includes the Green, White, and Catskill Mountains, and the Poconos and Adirondack Mountains, helps make the Northeast a beautiful place to enjoy sports, recreation, and day-to-day living.

FACT FILE The Appalachian Trail

4 **The Appalachian Trail runs through 14 states. Which of these states are part of the Northeast region?** Maine, New Hampshire, Vermont, Massachusetts, Connecticut, New York, New Jersey, Pennsylvania, Maryland
Apply Information

5 **Do you think Benton MacKaye's idea to create an Appalachian Trail was a success? Explain.** Possible answer: Yes; Today the Appalachian Trail is part of the National Parks System, and people volunteer to maintain the trail.
Evaluate

Ongoing Assessment

If... students have difficulty evaluating whether MacKaye's idea was successful or unsuccessful,	**then...** ask them what resulted from MacKaye's idea. Then ask them whether they think Mr. MacKaye probably was happy or upset with the way his idea turned out.

6 **How are the Appalachian Mountains related to the Green, White, and Catskill Mountains?** The Green, White, and Catskill Mountains all are part of the Appalachian Mountain Range.
Analyze Information

FACT FILE

The Appalachian Trail

- The Appalachian Trail is the footpath that runs along the ridge of the Appalachian Mountain Range in the eastern United States.
- The trail is about 2,160 miles long, and it passes through fourteen states: Maine, New Hampshire, Vermont, Massachusetts, Connecticut, New York, New Jersey, Pennsylvania, Maryland, West Virginia, Virginia, Tennessee, North
4 Carolina, and Georgia.
- The northernmost end of the trail is in Katahdin, Maine.
- The southernmost end of the trail is in Springer Mountain, Georgia.
- A man named Benton MacKaye had the idea for the Appalachian Trail. He thought hiking the trail would be a good getaway for city people.
- The Appalachian Trail is now part
of the National Park System, but it 5
is maintained by volunteers.

The Mountains of the Northeast

The Northeast is also known for its many mountains. The oldest chain of mountains in North America—the **Appalachian Mountain Range**—begins in Canada and extends all the way to Alabama. These mountains are one of the largest groups of mountains in the United States, second only to the Rocky Mountains. The Appalachian Mountain Range is made up of several smaller ranges. The three main Northeast ranges are the White Mountains in New Hampshire, the Green Mountains in Vermont, and the
Catskill Mountains in New York. 6

The **Green Mountains,** named for the forest of evergreens that covered the mountains when the first European settlers arrived, run north and south through Vermont. Because of the large amount of snowfall they receive, the Green Mountains are home to many ski resorts.

The **White Mountains** of New Hampshire extend into the western part of Maine. The snow-covered peaks may have given the mountains their name. Like the Green Mountains, the White Mountains have many ski resorts.

106

Practice and Extend

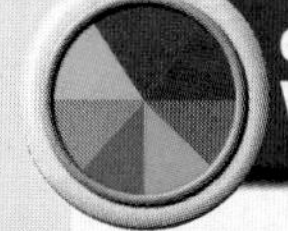

CURRICULUM CONNECTION
Writing

Create a Slide Show of the Appalachian Trail

- Show students the route of the Appalachian Trail on a map. Divide the trail into four equal sections.
- Divide the class into four groups, and assign each group one section of the trail.
- Have students in each group research the features of their assigned part of the trail. Have them use presentation software to create a slide show highlighting those features. (If presentation software is unavailable, have students use pictures from magazines or the Internet and write their narration on note cards.)
- Combine the groups' completed presentations to create a class slide show of the Appalachian Trail.

The **Catskill Mountains** are about two hours north of New York City. These mountains, carved by glaciers
7 thousands of years ago, make up one of the most beautiful areas in New York. The Catskills became famous in the 1800s as a setting for writers and painters. Today many vacationers there enjoy fishing, skiing, and other winter sports.

There are many other mountains in the Northeast, such as the Pocono Mountains in Pennsylvania and the Adirondack Mountains in New York. The Poconos are known for many spectacular waterfalls. These mountains are a popular spot for vacationers, especially in the fall when the autumn colors are at their peak.

▶ **A skier performs his jump in competition at Lake Placid.**

The Adirondack Mountains in New York have many beautiful lakes and resorts. One of the 8
most famous lakes, Lake Placid, is at the edge of the village of Lake Placid. The Winter Olympics were held here in 1932 and 1980.

REVIEW What would be the sequence of mountain ranges you might cross if you traveled from Maine southwest to Pennsylvania? Sequence

Literature and Social Studies

Stopping by Woods on a Snowy Evening

The beautiful landscape of the Northeast has often been the subject of literature. Robert Frost was a very popular poet who lived in and wrote about the Northeast. Here is part of one of his most famous poems.

Whose woods these are I think I know.
His house is in the village though;
He will not see me stopping here
To watch his woods fill up with snow.

. . .

The woods are lovely, dark, and deep,
But I have promises to keep,
And miles to go before I sleep,
And miles to go before I sleep. 9

Test Talk

Locate Key Words in the Question

7 **What do the Catskill Mountains have in common with Niagara Gorge?** Tell students "Key words such as *in common* tell you to look for similarities." Possible answers: Both were formed by glaciers; both are found in the Northeast. Compare and Contrast

8 **What is one important source of income in the Pocono Mountains and the Adirondack Mountains?** Possible answer: Tourism Draw Conclusions

✓ **REVIEW ANSWER** (1) White, (2) Green, (3) Adirondack, (4) Catskill, (5) Pocono Sequence

Literature and Social Studies

Have students read the two stanzas of Robert Frost's poem.

9 **Based on the poem, what are two words you might use to describe the Northeast in winter?** Possible answers: Peaceful, silent, beautiful, wooded, snowy, cold Express Ideas

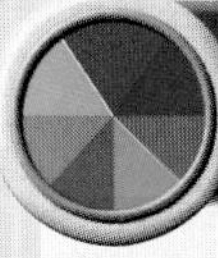

CURRICULUM CONNECTION
Drama

Present a Dramatic Reading

- Have students research all four stanzas of Robert Frost's "Stopping by Woods on a Snowy Evening."
- Divide the class into three groups, and ask one group to practice giving a dramatic reading of the poem. Have another group choose appropriate music to accompany the reading. Have the remaining group research or create appropriate pictures to illustrate the poem.
- Finally, have the groups combine their work to create a dramatic presentation.
- Videotape the finalized presentation, and discuss the dramatic reading as a class.

PAGES 108-109

The Northeast Coastline

Quick Summary From its rocky cliffs to its sandy beaches, the Atlantic coastline has a great effect on life in the Northeast region.

10 **Based on the text, what is common to all but two of the states in the Northeast region?** The Atlantic coast as a border Main Idea and Details

11 **What is a peninsula?** A piece of land almost surrounded by water, or extending far out into the water Main Idea and Details

12 **Why do you think lighthouses are more common along the Maine coastline than along the coast of New Jersey?** Possible answer: Because, unlike the sandy shores of New Jersey, the Maine coastline is rugged and rocky, which could be dangerous to ships at sea Make Inferences

The Northeast Coastline

The Northeast region's coastline differs greatly from place to place. All but two of the Northeast states—Pennsylvania and Vermont—share
10 their borders with the Atlantic Ocean. From the rocky coast of Maine to Chesapeake Bay, which is bordered by Maryland and Virginia, the Northeast Atlantic coastline is one of the most recognized in the world.

Maine is known for its beautiful shore on the Atlantic Ocean. The rocky coast is dotted with **lighthouses,** towers with bright lights that shine far out over the water to guide ships. Along the Maine coastline is **Acadia National Park,** the first U.S. National Park east of the Mississippi River. Huge rocks and cliffs make the Maine coastline a favorite of photographers and painters.

Cape Cod is one of Massachusetts' most interesting features. Cape Cod is a **peninsula,** a piece of land almost surrounded by water, or extending far
out into the water. The Cape, as it is 11
commonly known, is home to tourists during the warm summer months. Its location and climate have made it one of the most well-known fishing areas in the world.

Thousands of vacationers visit New Jersey's shore every year. Many come to enjoy the warm sandy beaches
on the Atlantic coast. All along the 12
beaches in the summer, vacationers play volleyball, swim in the warm waters of the Atlantic, or just gather to relax in the sun.

▶ Bass Harbor Head lighthouse on Mount Desert Island, Maine

Practice and Extend

MEETING INDIVIDUAL NEEDS
Leveled Practice

Write Home About the Northeast Help students write about the Northeast coastline as if they were tourists.

Easy Have students draw a picture of one part of the Northeast coastline on one side of an index card. On the other side of this "postcard," have them write a note about this area to someone they know. **Reteach**

On-Level Have students write a short letter to someone they know about their trip to one part of the Northeast coastline. **Extend**

Challenge Have students write a letter that includes both a description of their trip and facts they have learned about the geography of the Northeast coastline. **Enrich**

For a Lesson Summary, use Quick Study, p. 20.

From famous Atlantic City to beautiful Cape May, the New Jersey coastline is known as "the shore."

REVIEW If you took a boat ride from Maine to Maryland, what sequence of coastline sights might you see? Sequence

Summarize the Lesson

- **The Niagara Falls area provides not only a natural wonder but hydroelectricity for millions.**
- **The Appalachian Mountain Range, the oldest in North America, runs from Canada to Alabama and includes many smaller ranges in the Northeast.**
- **The coastline of the Northeast ranges from rocky cliffs to sandy beaches.**

Colorful, old houses such as this are common sights in Cape May, New Jersey.

LESSON 1 REVIEW

Check Facts and Main Idea

1. Sequence On a separate sheet of paper, copy the diagram below. Fill in sights you would like to see if you traveled south from the northern part of the Northeast region to its southern part.

Niagara Falls
↓
Responses will vary, but sights should be sequenced from north to south.
↓
(blank)

2. Niagara Falls is located between what two Great Lakes?
3. What are the three main Northeast mountain ranges in the Appalachian Mountains?
4. What two Northeast states do not share borders with the Atlantic Ocean?
5. **Critical Thinking:** ***Solve Problems*** The demand for electricity is always high. What could you and others do to reduce this demand? Use the word **hydropower** in your answer.

Link to Writing

Write a Poem Make a list of words that might describe the beauty and power of Niagara Falls. Use these words to write a poem about this natural wonder. Use the words **glacier** and **gorge** in your poem.

REVIEW ANSWER (1) Rocky cliffs and lighthouses in Maine, (2) Cape Cod peninsula in Massachussetts, (3) sandy beaches, Atlantic City, and Cape May in New Jersey
Sequence

3 Close and Assess

Summarize the Lesson

Ask students to review the three main points independently. Then have each student draw a picture to illustrate one of the points. Have students share and explain their drawings to the class.

LESSON 1 REVIEW

1. Sequence For possible answers, see the reduced pupil page.
2. Lake Erie and Lake Ontario
3. White, Green, and Catskill Mountains
4. Pennsylvania and Vermont
5. **Critical Thinking: *Solve Problems*** Possible answers: To reduce demand for electricity, including hydropower, turn off lights and appliances that are not in use; use the heater less in winter and the air conditioner less in summer

Link to Writing

Students' poems need not rhyme but should include the words *glacier* and *gorge,* as well as other words that describe their impressions of Niagara Falls.

CURRICULUM CONNECTION
Science

Analyze Ecological Threats

Have students research threats to the ecology of the Northeast coastline.

- Have students work in pairs to research one specific example of an environmental hazard or ecological threat to the wildlife, vegetation, land, or water of the Northeast coastline.
- Tell each pair to create a one- to two-minute presentation about the chosen threat and what is being done to correct it.
- Have students share their presentations with the class.

Workbook, p. 23

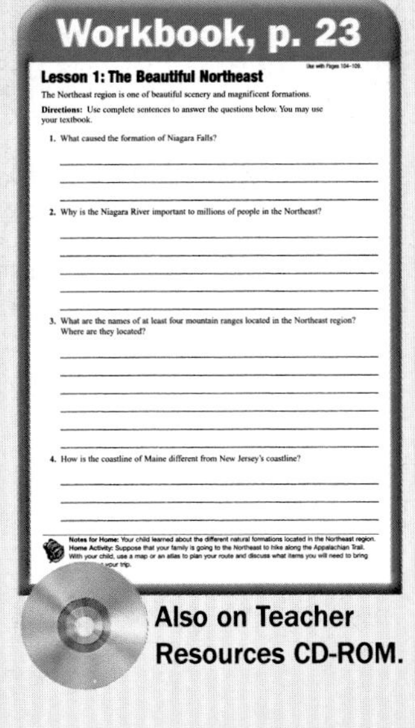
Lesson 1: The Beautiful Northeast

1. What caused the formation of Niagara Falls?
2. Why is the Niagara River important to millions of people in the Northeast?
3. What are the names of at least four mountain ranges located in the Northeast region? Where are they located?
4. How is the coastline of Maine different from New Jersey's coastline?

Also on Teacher Resources CD-ROM.

Chart and Graph Skills

Read a Cross-Section Diagram

Objective

- Describe the operations of a hydroelectric power plant.

Vocabulary

cross-section diagram, p. 110;
reservoir, p. 111

Resource

- Workbook, p. 24
- Transparency 36

1 Introduce and Motivate

What is a cross-section diagram? Discuss with students why engineers might use diagrams that show how complicated things work. Then have students read the **What?** section of text on p. 110 to help set the purpose of the lesson.

Why use cross-section diagrams? Have students read the **Why?** section of text on pp. 110–111. Help students "see" a cross-section of the dam and powerplant, first with the cut made from front to back, then from left to right.

2 Teach and Discuss

How is this skill used? Examine with students the diagram and labels on pp. 110–111.

- As students trace the flow of water in the diagram, explain that they should keep in mind the overall concept of where the water originally came from and where it ultimately is going.
- Have student volunteers relate the sequence aloud: "First the water enters here, then it moves here," and so on.
- Have students read the **How?** section of text on p. 111.

Chart and Graph Skills

Read a Cross-Section Diagram

What? A **cross-section diagram** is a drawing that shows you what you would see if you could cut through something and look inside. It may show how something works.

Why? Sometimes it's hard to imagine what something looks like or how it works simply by reading about it. You have to see it.

Look at the cross-section diagram of a dam and a hydroelectric power plant. The plant is similar to power plants on the Niagara River. The diagram shows parts that are inside the plant. With your finger, trace the path of water through the plant.

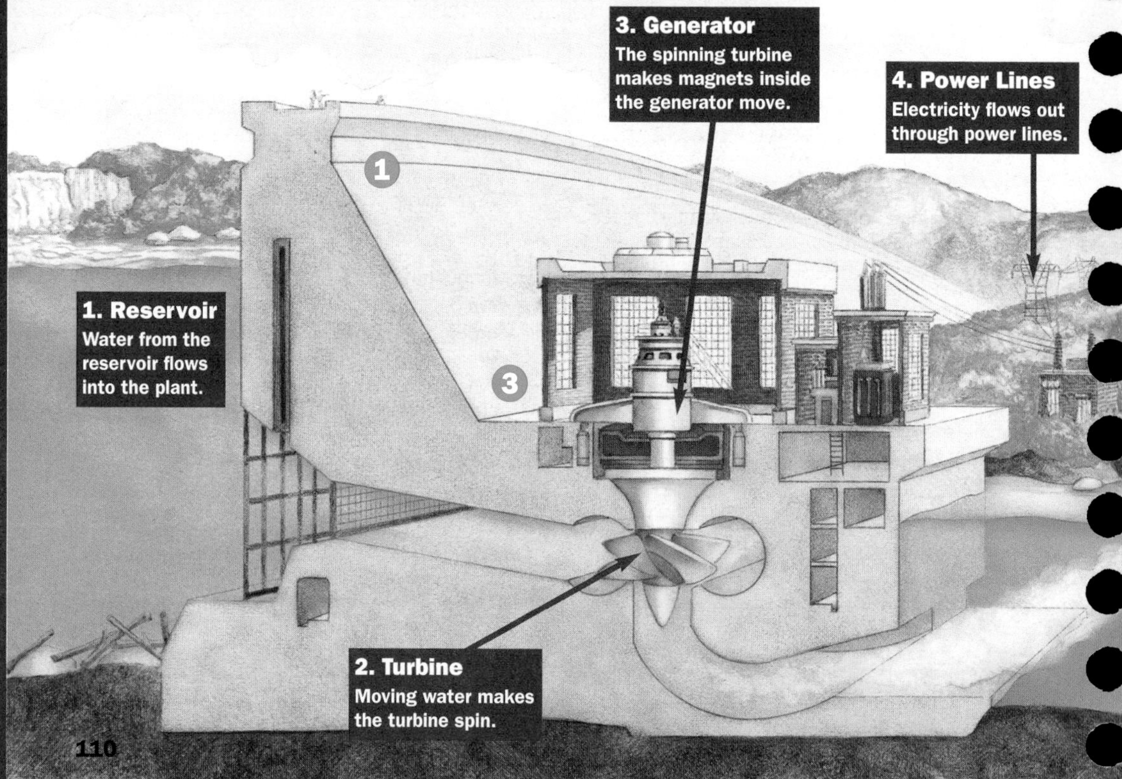
3. Generator
The spinning turbine makes magnets inside the generator move.
4. Power Lines
Electricity flows out through power lines.
1
1. Reservoir
Water from the reservoir flows into the plant.
3
2. Turbine
Moving water makes the turbine spin.
110

Practice and Extend

MEETING INDIVIDUAL NEEDS
Leveled Practice

Create a Cross-Section Diagram Help students create a cross-section diagram of their own.

Easy Have students draw a cross-section diagram of an apple, with the apple sliced either horizontally or vertically. **Reteach**

On-Level Have students research and draw a horizontal cross-section of a tree trunk. Tell students to be prepared to explain what their diagram shows and the significance of the tree's rings. **Extend**

Challenge Have students research and draw a cross-section diagram of a simple machine of their choice, such as a pencil sharpener, a coffee maker, or an audio speaker. **Enrich**

Moving water makes the power plant work. Find the reservoir (REZ er vwar) behind the power plant. A **reservoir** is a place that holds water. When water is released from the reservoir, it flows past a turbine (TER bin). The moving
2 water makes the turbine spin. The turbine is connected to the generator. In the generator, magnets move past coils of copper wire. This action produces electricity.

4

How? Study a cross-section diagram in steps. First, gather information from the labels you see on the diagram. Second, study each labeled part. Try to figure out how each part of the plant works. Third, look at the numbers that show the way water is converted into electricity. Note that the water pushes the turbine to move the generator.

Think of the terms that are used in this diagram. These terms can help you understand and remember how a hydroelectric power plant makes electricity.

Use the **cross-section diagram** to answer the questions.

1. What is a **reservoir?**
2. What happens when water is released from a reservoir?
3. How does a power plant use renewable resources?

111

1 **In what direction was the power plant "sliced" to create this cross-section?** Vertically Analyze Pictures

2 ***Turbine* comes from a Latin word that means "a spinning thing, a top." How does this relate to a turbine in a power plant?** Moving water causes the turbine to spin. Apply Information

Test Talk

Use Information from Graphics

3 **Does the water from the reservoir move through the turbine or the generator or both?** Tell students that labels can help them find the right answer. Ask students to look at the diagram to find the right answer. The turbine Analyze Pictures

4 **What do you think happens to water after it has passed through the power plant?** It is returned to the river downstream. Make Inferences

3 Close and Assess

Think and Apply

1. A place that holds water
2. It flows past the turbine and makes the turbine spin.
3. It creates energy from flowing water, and water is a renewable resource.

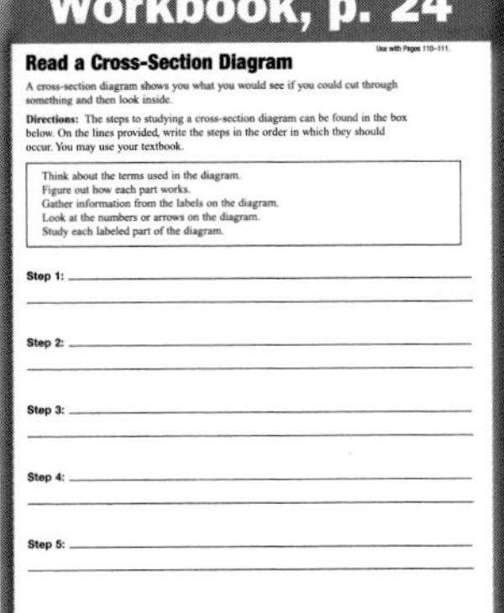

Workbook, p. 24

Use with Pages 110–111.

Read a Cross-Section Diagram

A cross-section diagram shows you what you would see if you could cut through something and then look inside.

Directions: The steps to studying a cross-section diagram can be found in the box below. On the lines provided, write the steps in the order in which they should occur. You may use your textbook.

Think about the terms used in the diagram.
Figure out how each part works.
Gather information from the labels on the diagram.
Look at the numbers or arrows on the diagram.
Study each labeled part of the diagram.

Step 1: ______

Step 2: ______

Step 3: ______

Step 4: ______

Step 5: ______

Notes for Home: Your child learned how to read a cross-section diagram.
Home Activity: The term *cross-section* does not only refer to a diagram. Discuss with your child other meanings of the term that he or she may have heard, such as in reference to a survey or study.

Also on Teacher Resources CD-ROM.

Decision Making

Use a Decision-Making Process

- Have students consider the following decision-making scenario. **Suppose you are told to make a cross-section diagram of a high-rise office building. Would you draw the building as though it were cut in half vertically or horizontally? Why?**
- Students should use the decision-making process at right to decide how to draw their diagram. For each step in the process, have students discuss and write about what must be considered as they make their decision.

1. **Identify a situation that requires a decision.**
2. **Gather information.**
3. **Identify options.**
4. **Predict consequences.**
5. **Take action to implement a decision.**

Resources of the Northeast

Objectives

- Identify key steps in the production of maple syrup.
- Explain why grapes grow well in certain areas of the Northeast.
- Identify the largest lake of the Finger Lakes.
- Explain why water is essential to the production and growth of cranberries.

Vocabulary

vineyard, p. 113; **bog,** p. 113; **sap,** p. 114; **mineral,** p. 115; **quarry,** p. 115

Resources

- Workbook, p. 25
- Transparency 10
- Every Student Learns Guide, pp. 42–45
- Quick Study, pp. 22–23

Quick Teaching Plan

If time is short, have students read the lesson independently and then take categorized notes.

- Tell students to cut out three outline shapes: a cluster of grapes or cranberries, a maple leaf, and a rock.
- Have students take notes about the lesson, writing each note on the shape to which it is most closely related.

1 Introduce and Motivate

Preview To activate prior knowledge, ask students what foods they enjoy that come from the Northeast. Tell them that they will learn more about the foods and other resources of the region as they read Lesson 2.

You Are There Ask students if they have ever picked grapes or any other type of fruit fresh from a vine or tree. Ask them what things they have to keep in mind when picking fresh fruit.

LESSON 2

Resources of the Northeast

PREVIEW

Focus on the Main Idea
The Northeast produces products for the world to enjoy.

PLACES
Lake Seneca
South Carver, Massachusetts
St. Albans, Vermont

VOCABULARY
vineyard
bog
sap
mineral
quarry

You Are There As your dad drives into the parking lot, you spot the beginning of the rows and rows of grapevines. You are so excited! Each year, you and your brothers have a contest to see who can pick the most grapes. Last year when you were here, your older brother won—he picked five more baskets than you did. This year, you're ready to win! It is so much fun to walk up and down all of the rows of the beautiful purple berries. The best part, though, is thinking of the grape jelly that your mom will make from all of the baskets and baskets of grapes. It's really hard work, but you'll have grape jelly all winter long!

Target Skill **Sequence** As you read, pay attention to the many steps it takes to grow and produce some products.

Practice and Extend

READING SKILL
Sequence

In the Lesson Review, students complete a graphic organizer like the one below. You may want to provide students with a copy of Transparency 10 to complete as they read the lesson.

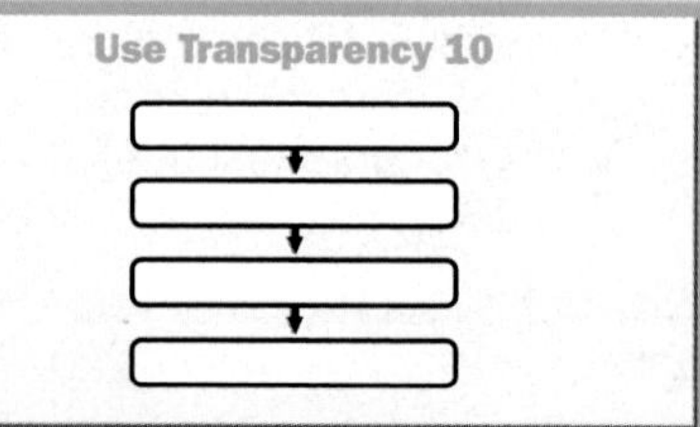

VOCABULARY
Individual Word Study

Have students read the definitions for *sap* and *bog* in the student text. Then write the following sentences on the board.

- She was pale and tired and looked like all the sap had run out of her.
- He is bogged in paperwork.

Discuss how students' understanding of the words' original meanings helps them understand the figurative uses. Ask if the figurative use helps them remember the original meaning.

Grapes and Cranberries

Grapes are just one of the many products of the Northeast. Grown in **vineyards,** places where grapevines are planted, thousands of tons of the large purple berries are produced every year.

The vineyards are usually found in hilly areas where the climate is right for the grape's long growing season,
1 which is often as long as 205 days.

Some of the largest vineyards in the Northeast are in New York, near Lake Erie, one of the Great Lakes, and in the Finger Lakes region, an area with several long, finger-shaped lakes. **Lake Seneca,** the largest of the Finger Lakes, is over 600 feet deep and never freezes. The warm air that surrounds the lake helps create just the right conditions for a plentiful grape production.

Another berry grown in the Northeast is the cranberry. Of the 1,000 cranberry farms in the United States, 500 of them are in Massachusetts. Most cranberries are grown in bogs. A **bog** is an area of soft, wet, spongy ground. To prepare a cranberry bog, swampy land must be
leveled and cleared. Then it is covered 2
with sand for good drainage. Finally, small, new cranberry plants are pressed into the sand.

As the plants grow, they form a covering over the bottom of the bog. In winter the bogs are covered with water that freezes and protects the plants. When spring arrives, the bogs are drained. They are once again covered with water to protect the plants against insects and disease.

As fall approaches, water becomes very important to the harvest. Since cranberries have small air pockets in the center, they rise when they are flooded. Raking the bog knocks the berries from their vines. They are then collected. Each year, the harvest is celebrated at the Annual Massachusetts Cranberry Harvest Festival in **South Carver, Massachusetts,** home to a cranberry
museum! 3

REVIEW What are steps used to prepare a cranberry bog? Sequence

▶ Raking a cranberry bog

2 Teach and Discuss

PAGE 113

Grapes and Cranberries

Quick Summary The climate and geography of the Northeast make it an excellent location for growing grapes and cranberries.

1 **Why are the hilly areas of the Northeast ideal for growing grapes?** The climate is right for the grape's long growing season. Main Idea and Details

2 **Which word do you think best describes much of the land in Massachusetts—*dry, mountainous,* or *swampy*? Why?** Swampy; Cranberry bogs are created on swampy land, and about half of all the cranberry farms in the United States are located in Massachusetts. Draw Conclusions

3 **How are cranberries harvested?** The area is flooded, which causes the cranberries to float, and the bog is raked to collect the berries. Main Idea and Details

✓ **REVIEW ANSWER** (1) Swampy land is cleared and leveled, (2) land is covered with sand for good drainage, (3) cranberry plants are pressed into the sand Sequence

MEETING INDIVIDUAL NEEDS
Leveled Practice

Report on Native Northeastern Crops Have students work together to report on three fruits native to the Northeast: Concord grapes, cranberries, and blueberries.

Easy Have students research and clip or draw pictures of Concord grapes, cranberries, and blueberries. **Reteach**

On-Level Divide students into three groups. Have each group research and indicate on a map of the Northeast where one of these fruits is grown. **Extend**

Challenge Divide students into three groups. Have each group research three interesting facts about one of the Northeastern fruits. **Enrich**

For a Lesson Summary, use Quick Study, p. 22.

SOCIAL STUDIES
Background

Native Americans and Cranberries

- Long before the Pilgrims arrived in New England, Native Americans mixed mashed cranberries with wild game to make pemmican, a form of preserved meat.
- They also used cranberries in cooking, as a dye, and to draw the poison from arrow wounds.

PAGES 114–115

Other Resources

Quick Summary The Northeast also is an important producer of maple syrup and minerals such as granite and marble.

4 **What role does sap play in the life of a plant?** The sap carries water and food through the plant. Main Idea and Details

5 **When is sap harvested from sugar maple trees?** In the spring Main Idea and Details

Test Talk

Use Information from the Text

6 **About how many gallons of sap are needed to create 20 gallons of maple syrup?** Tell students that a quantity such as *gallons* can help them find the right information to support their answer. Ask students to skim the text to find information about *gallons* of sap. About 800 Apply Information

7 **What kinds of activities are held at the Maple Festival in St. Albans, Vermont?** A parade, carnival rides, pancake breakfasts, food shows and demonstrations Main Idea and Details

Resources of the Northeast

8 **What generalization might you make when comparing where grapes are grown and where cranberries are grown in the Northeast?** Possible answer: Cranberries are grown along the coast, but grapes are grown farther inland. Generalize

MAP SKILL Answer Massachusetts, Rhode Island, New Jersey

Other Resources

Another famous Northeast product known around the world is maple syrup. Maple syrup is a sweet liquid made from the sap of sugar maple trees. **Sap** is the liquid that circulates through a plant carrying water and food. Since

4 a great many sugar maple trees grow in Vermont, more maple syrup is produced there than in any other state in the United States.

In order for the sap to flow, the weather in early spring must grow warmer and warmer until temperatures

5 rise above freezing. To get the sap, one or more holes are drilled into the tree. A spout, either metal or plastic, is then placed in the hole. The sap runs through the spout and into a bucket, which is then emptied into a large barrel and taken to a place called a sugar house. Some producers use what is known as a pipeline system where the sap flows through tubes.

At the sugar house, workers boil the sap. As the sap boils, water evaporates until pure maple syrup remains. This process takes many hours. About forty gallons of sap are

6 needed to produce one gallon of syrup!

▶ Beginning to collect sap

To celebrate Vermont's maple harvest, every year people from the area and around the world attend the Vermont Maple Festival in **St. Albans, Vermont.** Here visitors enjoy a parade, carnival rides, crafts, pancake breakfasts, and food shows, including maple candy-making demonstrations. 7

MAP SKILL

Resources of the Northeast

8

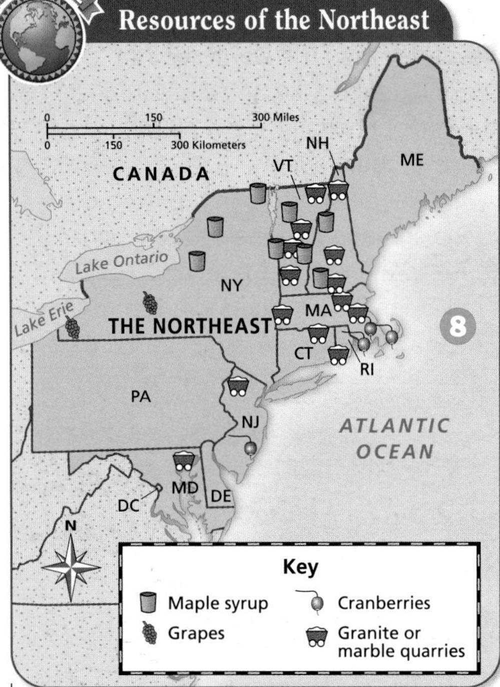

▶ Vermont, New Hampshire, and Massachusetts have many quarries.

MAP SKILL Use a Resource Map ***According to the map, what states grow cranberries?***

Practice and Extend

EXTEND LANGUAGE

ESL Support

Recognize Colors Help students learn words to describe maples and other northeastern trees in autumn.

Beginning Explain that maples and many other trees turn colors in the fall. On the chalkboard, write *green*, *yellow*, *orange*, *red*, *purple*, and *brown* and hold up an object of each color. Then hold up random objects and have students say the correct color.

Intermediate Have students go through old magazines and cut out pictures that illustrate the fall colors. Have them label each with an identifying phrase such as "a red coat."

Advanced Have students research the different stages a maple tree goes through in the autumn. For each stage, students should draw and color a maple leaf and write a descriptive sentence about it.

For additional ESL support, use Every Student Learns Guide, pp. 42–45.

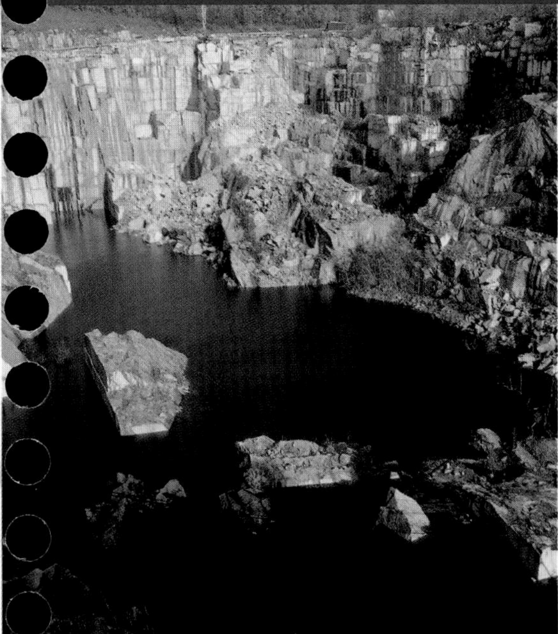

▶ A northeastern granite quarry

Minerals are also an important resource of the Northeast. A **mineral**
9 is a material that was never alive and is found in the earth. Most rocks, such as granite and marble, are combinations of minerals. New Hampshire, known as the Granite State, has many **quarries,** places where stone is dug, cut, or blasted out for use in building. The products from the quarries are often used in building construction. For example, marble from Vermont is in the Supreme Court Building in Washington, D.C.

REVIEW What has to happen for sap to start flowing in maple trees? *Cause and Effect*

Summarize the Lesson

- **Grapes and cranberries are two important products grown in the Northeast.**
- **Vermont is a leading producer of maple syrup.**
- **Minerals are an important resource of the Northeast.**

LESSON 2 REVIEW

Check Facts and Main Idea

1. Sequence On a separate sheet of paper, copy the chart below. Fill in the missing information to show the sequence of steps needed to produce maple syrup.

   - The days grow warmer.
   - ↓ A hole is drilled into the tree and a spout is attached.
   - ↓ **Sap** is collected in buckets.
   - ↓ Sap is boiled into maple syrup.

2. Why are **vineyards** able to grow in certain areas of the Northeast?
3. What is the name of the largest lake of the Finger Lakes?
4. Why is water important in the production of cranberries? Use the word **bog** in your answer.
5. **Critical Thinking:** ***Make Inferences*** Why are annual festivals in the Northeast so popular?

Link to Science

Give a Report Do research in the library or on the Internet to find out more about how sap nourishes trees and other plants. Gather your notes and present your report to the class.

115

CURRICULUM CONNECTION
Literature

Read About Northeastern Resources

Cranberries: Fruit of the Bogs, by Diane L. Burns (Lerner Publishing, ISBN 0-87614-964-6, 1994) **Easy**

Sugaring Time, by Kathryn Lasky (Aladdin, ISBN 0-689-71081-X, 1986) **On-Level**

The Maple Syrup Book, by Marilyn Linton (Kids Can Press, ISBN 0-919964-52-4, 1993) **Challenge**

Workbook, p. 25

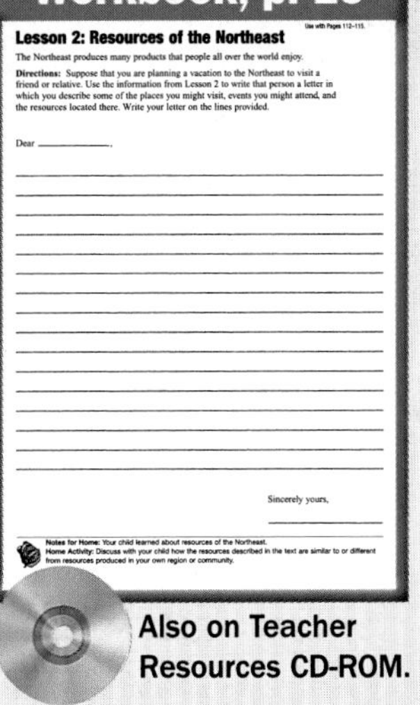

Lesson 2: Resources of the Northeast Use with Pages 112–115.

The Northeast produces many products that people all over the world enjoy.

Directions: Suppose that you are planning a vacation to the Northeast to visit a friend or relative. Use the information from Lesson 2 to write that person a letter in which you describe some of the places you might visit, events you might attend, and the resources located there. Write your letter on the lines provided.

Dear ______________,

Sincerely yours,

Notes for Home: Your child learned about resources of the Northeast.
Home Activity: Discuss with your child how the resources described in the text are similar to or different from resources produced in your own region or community.

Also on Teacher Resources CD-ROM.

9 **According to the text, how do minerals differ from the other natural resources you read about in this lesson?** Possible answer: Unlike grapes, cranberries, and maple trees, minerals were never alive. *Compare and Contrast*

Ongoing Assessment

If... students have difficulty making this comparison,	**then...** review with them the other resources studied in this lesson and ask what those three things have in common.

REVIEW ANSWER The weather must grow warmer and warmer until temperatures rise above freezing. *Cause and Effect*

3 Close and Assess

Summarize the Lesson

Ask students to review the three main points independently. Then have volunteers point out one fact about each point.

LESSON 2 REVIEW

1. **Sequence** For possible answers, see the reduced pupil page.
2. The climate is right for the grape's long growing season.
3. Lake Seneca
4. Water is an important part of the bog and it protects cranberry plants from harsh weather, insects, and disease. It is used to help farmers harvest the cranberries.
5. **Critical Thinking:** ***Make Inferences*** Possible answer: They provide an opportunity for people to come together and celebrate the natural resources of the Northeast.

Link to Science

Students' reports should provide some explanation of how sap moves through a plant and what nutritional products it delivers.

The Plentiful Sea

Objectives

- Define the name of the people who fish Chesapeake Bay.
- Explain how pollution from a factory gets into Chesapeake Bay.
- Explain why Chesapeake Bay is important to the Northeast.
- Describe actions a resident of the Chesapeake Bay area could take to help preserve the bay.

Vocabulary

bay, p. 117; **inlet,** p. 117; **watermen,** p. 117; **crab pot,** p. 117

Resources

- Workbook, p. 26
- Transparency 11
- Every Student Learns Guide, pp. 46–49
- Quick Study, pp. 24–25

Quick Teaching Plan

If time is short, have students write one question for each section in Lesson 3, exchange papers with a partner, answer the questions, and check their answers.

1 Introduce and Motivate

Preview To activate prior knowledge, ask students if they have ever eaten shellfish such as shrimp or crab. Ask them if shellfish live in their local waters. Tell students they will learn more about a place where shellfish are very important as they read Lesson 3.

You Are There Ask students if they have ever gone fishing, seen someone fish, or pretended to fish. Have them compare these experiences with the description they just read.

LESSON 3

PREVIEW

Focus on the Main Idea
Chesapeake Bay and other bays in the Northeast provide seafood for millions.

PLACES
Chesapeake Bay
Delaware Bay
Massachusetts Bay

VOCABULARY
bay
inlet
watermen
crab pot

The Plentiful Sea

You Are There The wind is blowing in your face as you smell the fresh salt air. Uncle Rob and Aunt Ellen have decided to take you fishing with them on Chesapeake Bay. They are watermen, the third generation in their family to follow this profession.

All day long you help them hook and pull their crab pots. The blue crabs you catch are amazing! You pass a sailboat and wave at the watermen on board. They are harvesting oysters with large nets. There are so many oysters in their catch!

As the sun starts to go down, you head toward the docks. It's been a long day. Uncle Rob pats you on the head. Aunt Ellen smiles. You have done well. They are very proud.

Sequence As you read, look for the sequence of events in the day of a waterman.

116

Practice and Extend

READING SKILL Sequence

In the Lesson Review, students complete a graphic organizer like the one below. You may want to provide students with a copy of Transparency 11 to complete as they read the lesson.

Use Transparency 11

VOCABULARY Related Word Study

Have students turn to the illustrated diagram of Geography Terms on page R16–17 of the Atlas at the back of their books. Have them identify the bay in the diagram. Point out the inlet on page R16 (it is not labeled, but is opposite the Island). Have students make a list of words that relate to water and discuss how the items described are related (for example, rivers flow into the bay; the ocean is bigger than a lake).

Great Shellfish Bay

Chesapeake Bay got its name from the Native American word *Chesepiook* (cheez PEE ook), which means "Great
1 Shellfish Bay." A **bay** is a part of a sea or lake that cuts into a coastline. Chesapeake Bay also has inlets that go into the shore. An **inlet** is a narrow opening in a coastline. An inlet is usually smaller than a bay.

Maryland surrounds part of Chesapeake Bay. Maryland is one of the Middle Atlantic states. Others are New York, New Jersey, Pennsylvania, and Delaware.

Chesapeake Bay is rich in crabs, oysters, clams, and other shellfish. About two hundred different kinds of fish live in the bay as well. Because of this abundance, many families in the Chesapeake Bay area earn their livings harvesting the sea. 2

The people who fish the bay are called **watermen.** These men and women gather different kinds of seafood in different seasons.

Watermen who catch crabs are called "crabbers." Crabbers fish for crabs in the summer using crab pots. As you can see from the above photo, a **crab pot** isn't really a pot at all—it is a large wire cage with several sections. Crabs can swim into the pot, but they cannot swim out of it.

To harvest crabs, a crabber pulls the crab pot into the fishing boat, empties the pot, and sorts the catch by size and type. Then the crabber takes the catch to market.

REVIEW How is a bay like an inlet? How are they different? Compare and Contrast

117

2 Teach and Discuss

PAGE 117

Great Shellfish Bay

Quick Summary Chesapeake Bay is rich in fish and shellfish and provides a living for the watermen who fish there.

Test Talk

Locate Key Words in the Text

1 **Why is *Chesapeake* a good name for this bay?** Have students skim the text to look for key words in the text that match key words in the question. The name comes from a Native American word that means "Great Shellfish Bay" and there are, indeed, many shellfish in the bay. **Apply Information**

2 **How does the availability of fish and shellfish affect many of the families in the bay area?** Many of the families make their livings harvesting the sea. **Cause and Effect**

✓ Ongoing Assessment

If... students have difficulty understanding the tie between fish and humans	**then...** ask what watermen and other people in the area depend on for their living.

✓ REVIEW ANSWER Alike: both are openings in a coastline; Different: an inlet is smaller than a bay. **Compare and Contrast**

ACCESS CONTENT
ESL Support

Identify Types of Shellfish Help students identify and create a poster of different types of shellfish.

Beginning Have students work in a group to draw or paste pictures of crabs, oysters, and clams on posterboard. For each one, create a semantic word web on the board and have students brainstorm descriptive characteristics.

Intermediate Have students transcribe the semantic webs into their notebooks and also insert their native language equivalents for as many words as they can.

Advanced Have students research several different species of shellfish found in Chesapeake Bay and create a semantic web for each one.

For additional ESL support, use Every Student Learns Guide, pp. 46–49.

Challenges to Chesapeake Bay

Quick Summary Pollution and overfishing threaten Chesapeake Bay, but the Chesapeake Bay Foundation is working to save it.

3 **How does pollution from factories end up in Chesapeake Bay?** Some factories around the bay dump waste onto the land, polluting the soil. When it rains or snows, the polluted soil washes into rivers that drain into the bay. Sequence

Decision Making

4 **What groups do you think should be involved in decisions about protecting Chesapeake Bay? Why?** Possible answers: Industries, area residents, watermen, other people concerned about the bay, and politicians; Most of these groups are directly affected by the health of the bay, and politicians could pass laws to protect the bay. Make Decisions

✓ **REVIEW ANSWER** Pollution, overfishing Main Idea and Details

Nantucket

5 **Why do you think there is no longer a whaling industry in Nantucket?** Possible answers: The whales were overfished and disappeared; today people want to protect whales rather than hunt them. Hypothesize

Challenges to Chesapeake Bay

Pollution of the land around Chesapeake Bay threatens the bay's fish and shellfish. Some factories around the bay dump waste onto the land, polluting the soil. When it rains or snows, the polluted soil washes into rivers that drain into the bay. 3

Pollution harms the natural habitat, making it difficult for fish and shellfish to reproduce. The result is a decrease in their numbers. However, pollution is not the only reason that fish and shellfish populations have become smaller.

Overfishing also challenges the balance of life in the bay. Overfishing means taking oysters, crabs, and fish from the bay faster than natural processes can replace them.

People are trying to stop pollution and overfishing. One organization, the Chesapeake Bay Foundation, is working to educate people about the environment. Its slogan is "Save the Bay!" 4

REVIEW List factors that harm the fish population of Chesapeake Bay. Main Idea and Details

Nantucket Historical Association

▶ A 40-foot whale skeleton at Nantucket's Whaling Museum

Then and Now

Nantucket

Between 1800 and 1840, Nantucket was known as the "Whaling Capital of the World." Whaling ships sailed from the island of Nantucket, off the coast of Massachusetts, to hunt whales. Today, there is no longer a whaling industry on Nantucket. But the Nantucket Historical Association's Whaling Museum contains many artifacts from this famous period in history. About 80,000 people visit the Whaling Museum each year.

5

118

Practice and Extend

MEETING INDIVIDUAL NEEDS

Leveled Practice

Analyze a Quotation Write the quotation at right on the board, and ask students to respond.

Easy Have students paraphrase and explain the quotation in their own words. **Reteach**

On-Level Have students read the quotation and then give examples of individual actions that might impact the bay either positively or negatively. **Extend**

Challenge Have students create a television public service announcement that conveys the basic message of the quotation. **Enrich**

For a Lesson Summary, use Quick Study, p. 24.

"If we want a clean, healthy bay that can sustain the biological diversity and be economically stable, we must identify, alter and, if possible, eliminate our own individual actions that impact the bay. People alter ecosystems. The solutions to problems threatening the Chesapeake Bay lie in the lifestyles we choose." Cited in a report by George Mason University of Virginia

Other Northeast Bays

▶ A fisherman off the coast of Massachusetts hauls in his catch of shrimp.

Chesapeake Bay is only one of many bays of the Northeast known for plentiful products from the sea. For example, north of Chesapeake Bay is **Delaware Bay.** It forms part of the border between New Jersey and Delaware. Oyster fishing is popular in this bay.

Farther north is **Massachusetts Bay.** It is near the city of Boston. Many other cities and towns around Massachusetts Bay serve as tourist,
6 fishing, and boating centers.

REVIEW Name other bays along the Northeast Atlantic coast, starting from the north. Sequence

Summarize the Lesson

- **Chesapeake Bay is one major bay of the Atlantic Ocean and a rich source of fish and shellfish.**
- **Pollution and overfishing challenge Chesapeake Bay.**
- **Several other bays are along the coast of the Northeast.**

LESSON 3 REVIEW

Check Facts and Main Ideas

1. Sequence On a separate sheet of paper, explain how pollution from a factory gets into Chesapeake Bay. Be sure to list the steps in the correct sequence.

Factories produce waste.
↓
Waste is dumped onto land.
↓
Polluted soil can wash into rivers.
↓
Rivers flow into the Bay.
↓
Pollution reaches the Bay.

2. What are the people who fish Chesapeake Bay called?
3. Why is Chesapeake Bay important to the Northeast region?
4. What is the purpose of the Chesapeake Bay Foundation?
5. **Critical Thinking:** ***Draw Conclusions*** What are some kinds of businesses that would grow near **bays?**

Link to Reading

Research Nantucket Go to the library or online and find information about the whaling industry on Nantucket in the early 1800s. Share what you learn with the class.

119

PAGE 119

Other Northeast Bays

Quick Summary Delaware Bay and Massachusetts Bay are two other bays important to the Northeast.

6 What is one feature that the bays of the Northeast have in common? Possible answer: They all are important sources of fish. Generalize

✓ **REVIEW ANSWER** (1) Massachusetts Bay, (2) Delaware Bay Sequence

3 Close and Assess

Summarize the Lesson

Have students read the three main points. Then have them draw a fish and write important facts from the lesson inside the shape.

✓ **LESSON 3 REVIEW**

1. Sequence For possible answers, see the reduced pupil page.
2. Watermen
3. It is an important source of fish and shellfish, which are important sources of income.
4. Possible answer: To educate people about the environment
5. **Critical Thinking: *Draw Conclusions*** Possible answers: Fish markets, restaurants, fishing supply stores, boat rentals, boat repair shops

Link to Reading

Encourage students to find a story about New England's whaling industry.

MEETING INDIVIDUAL NEEDS
Learning Styles

Explore "Keepers" Fishing laws state that a hard-shell crab must be at least 5 inches across before it can be harvested for market. Watermen have developed tools to identify which crabs are "keepers."

Kinesthetic Learning Have students create a keeper measuring tool from cardboard or posterboard.

Visual Learning Have students draw a life-sized picture of a blue crab that is large enough to be a keeper.

Musical Learning Have students develop a short jingle to help them remember how large a keeper crab must be.

Workbook, p. 26

Lesson 3: The Plentiful Sea

Also on Teacher Resources CD-ROM.

Bay Life

Objective

- Identify marine creatures native to Shark Bay.

1 Introduce and Motivate

Preview To activate prior knowledge, ask students to look at the map on p. 121 and explain why Shark Bay is called an inlet. Ask why it might be interesting to compare a bay in the United States with one on the other side of the world. (To see whether they have a similar ecology and face similar problems)

2 Teach and Discuss

1 **What ocean feeds into Shark Bay?**
Indian Ocean Interpret Maps

2 **How did Shark Bay get its name?**
Possible answers: Early settlers thought it was shaped like a shark; many sharks live in the bay.
Main Idea and Details

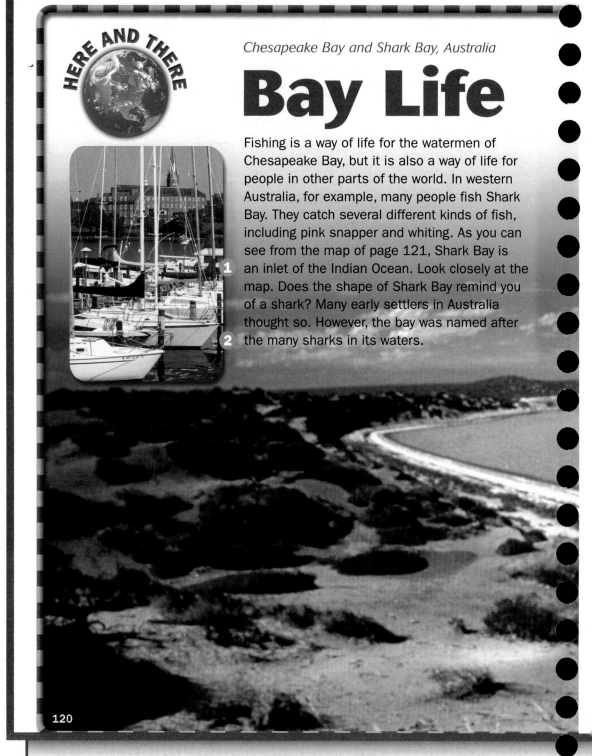

Chesapeake Bay and Shark Bay, Australia

Bay Life

Fishing is a way of life for the watermen of Chesapeake Bay, but it is also a way of life for people in other parts of the world. In western Australia, for example, many people fish Shark Bay. They catch several different kinds of fish, including pink snapper and whiting. As you can see from the map of page 121, Shark Bay is
1 an inlet of the Indian Ocean. Look closely at the map. Does the shape of Shark Bay remind you of a shark? Many early settlers in Australia thought so. However, the bay was named after
2 the many sharks in its waters.

120

Practice and Extend

SOCIAL STUDIES
Background

About Shark Bay

- Shark Bay is a World Heritage Area, part of a UNESCO program that seeks to conserve sites important to the world's cultural and natural heritage.
- Visitors to Shark Bay can see manta rays, turtles, and whales, and can interact with dolphins.
- The tiny living fossils in Shark Bay started growing thousands of years ago. Many have mineralized into mushroom-shaped towers called stromatolites.
- The shoreline of Shark Bay also is a rich environment, with more than 700 species of flowering plants.

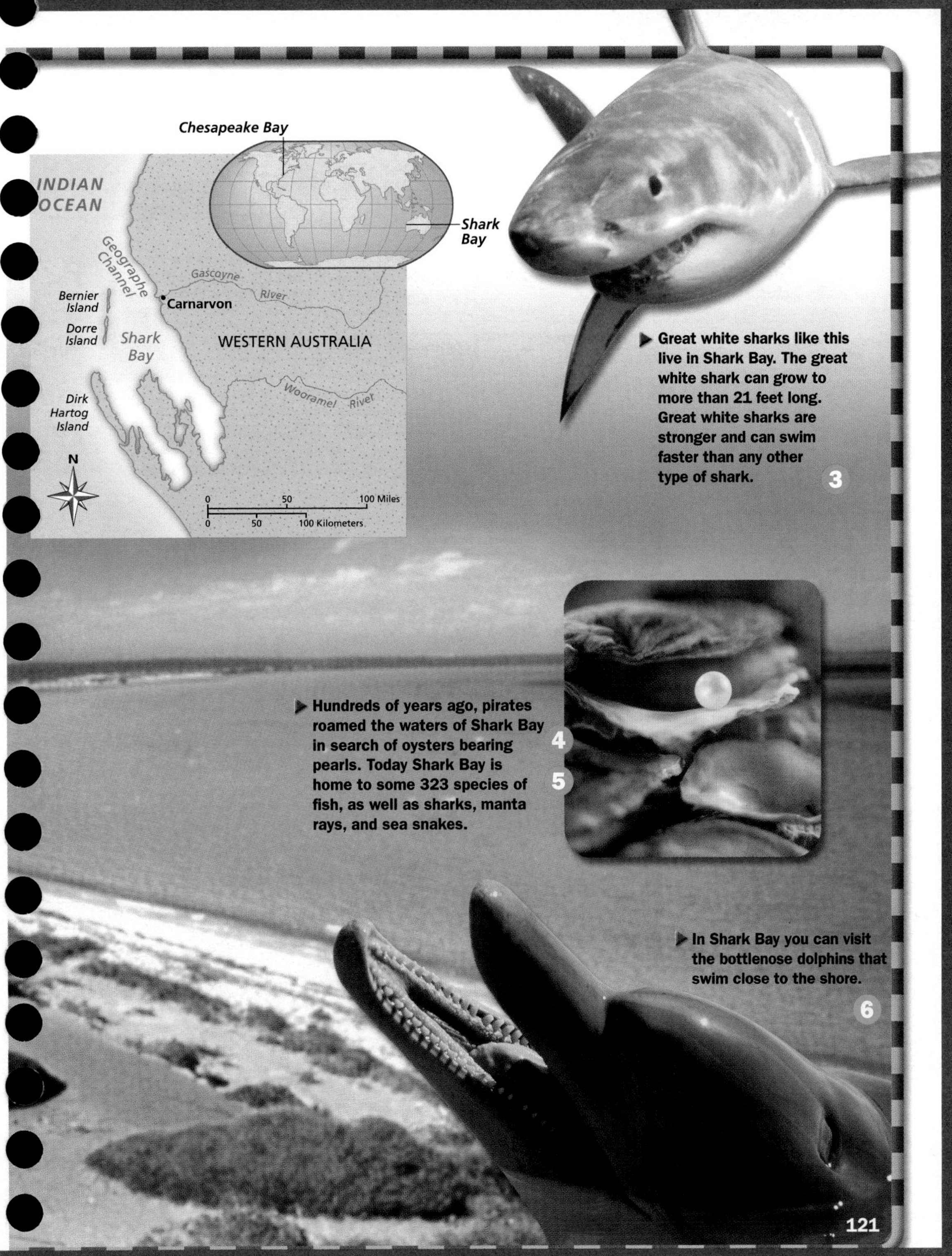

▶ Great white sharks like this live in Shark Bay. The great white shark can grow to more than 21 feet long. Great white sharks are stronger and can swim faster than any other type of shark. 3

▶ Hundreds of years ago, pirates roamed the waters of Shark Bay in search of oysters bearing pearls. Today Shark Bay is home to some 323 species of fish, as well as sharks, manta rays, and sea snakes. 4 5

▶ In Shark Bay you can visit the bottlenose dolphins that swim close to the shore. 6

121

3 **What makes the great white shark different from other species of sharks?** Great whites are stronger and can swim faster than any other type of shark. Main Idea and Details

4 **Why were pirates once drawn to Shark Bay?** They came to the bay in search of oysters bearing pearls. Main Idea and Details

5 **Why do you think bays often are popular fishing grounds?** Possible answers: Many different types of fish live in bays; they have a long shoreline from which people can fish and fishing boats can put out. Make Inferences

6 **Do you think Shark Bay is or is not important to the economy of Western Australia? Explain.** Possible answer: Important; Because many fish are caught in the bay and sold, and many tourists visit the bay Draw Conclusions

3 Close and Assess

- Discuss with students how Chesapeake Bay and Shark Bay are alike and different.
- Have students work in pairs to create a Venn diagram comparing and contrasting these two important bays.
- To aid memory, encourage students to create their Venn diagrams using relevant shapes, such as a crab for Chesapeake Bay and a shark for Shark Bay.

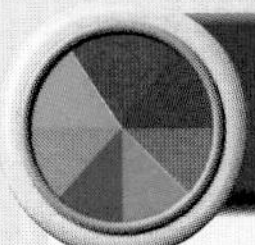

CURRICULUM CONNECTION Science

Explore Shark Bay

Have students research Shark Bay to complete one of the following projects.

- Describe dolphins' interaction with humans in Shark Bay.
- Report on one of the endangered species of the bay, such as the burrowing bettong.
- Create a chart of different species of mammals, birds, fish, or lizards in and around Shark Bay.

WEB SITE Technology

Students can find out more about Shark Bay and Chesapeake Bay by clicking on *Encyclopedia* at **www.sfsocialstudies.com.**

Resources

- Assessment Book, pp. 17–20
- Workbook, p. 27: Vocabulary Review

Chapter Summary

For possible answers, see the reduced student page.

Vocabulary

1. d, **2.** b, **3.** f, **4.** a, **5.** c, **6.** e

Places

Possible answers:

1. In addition to producing hydropower, Niagara Falls is a beautiful sight to see.
2. Next to the Rocky Mountains, the Appalachian Mountain Range is the largest group of mountains in the United States.
3. Lake Seneca is the largest of the Finger Lakes.
4. Every year the Vermont Maple Festival is held in St. Albans, Vermont.
5. Many watermen make a living by fishing the waters of Chesapeake Bay.

CHAPTER 4 Review

Chapter Summary

Sequence

On a separate sheet of paper, make a diagram like the one shown. Fill in the steps it takes to catch crabs and get them to market.

Waterman lowers crab pots into the bay.

Later the waterman pulls up the pots and takes out the crabs.

The crabs are sorted by size and type.

Crabs are taken to market and sold.

▶ A blue crab from Maryland

Vocabulary

1. **glacier** (p. 105)
2. **gorge** (p. 105)
3. **hydroelectricity** (p. 105)
4. **peninsula** (p. 108)
5. **bog** (p. 113)
6. **sap** (p. 114)

a. piece of land almost surrounded by water

b. a deep, narrow valley

c. soft, wet, spongy ground

d. a sheet of ice that covers land

e. liquid in a plant that carries water and food

f. electricity produced by water

Places

Write a sentence or two describing an important fact about each of the following places.

1. **Niagara Falls** (p. 105)
2. **Appalachian Mountain Range** (p. 106)
3. **Lake Seneca** (p. 113)
4. **St. Albans, Vermont** (p. 114)
5. **Chesapeake Bay** (p. 117)

Practice and Extend

Assessment Options

✓Chapter 4 Assessment

- Chapter 4 Content Test: Use Assessment Book, pp. 17–18.
- Chapter 4 Skills Test: Use Assessment Book, pp. 19–20.

Standardized Test Prep

- Chapter 4 Tests contain standardized test format.

✓Chapter 4 Performance Assessment

- Have students work in pairs to review information in this chapter.
- Have pairs portray a reporter and a person from one of the areas of the Northeast described in this chapter.
- Have them use an audiocassette recorder or videocamera to conduct a two-minute interview about the region. Share the recorded interviews with the class.
- Assess students' understanding of the Northeast region.

Facts and Main Ideas

Write your answers on a separate sheet of paper.

1. Why is Niagara Falls important for reasons other than its beauty?
2. How does the coastline of the Northeast change from Maine to New Jersey?
3. What does a waterman do?
4. **Main Idea** Describe three important geographic features of the Northeast.
5. **Main Idea** What are some foods that are grown or produced in the Northeast region?
6. **Main Idea** How do many people who live near Chesapeake Bay earn a living?
7. **Critical Thinking: *Evaluate*** Why is there a need for groups such as the Chesapeake Bay Foundation?

Write About the Region

1. **Write a journal entry** as a tourist visiting Niagara Falls for the first time. What are some of the things you notice about the waterfalls?
2. **Write an advertisement** for grape jelly made from grapes grown in the Finger Lakes region of New York. Create a brand name for your jelly. Use words in your ad that will convince the reader to buy your jelly.
3. **Write a letter to the editor** of a Chesapeake Bay area newspaper. State the problems that affect the bay. Explain the causes of the problems. Then suggest possible solutions.

Apply Skills

Read a Cross-Section Diagram

Look at the cross-section diagram of a grape. Then answer the questions.

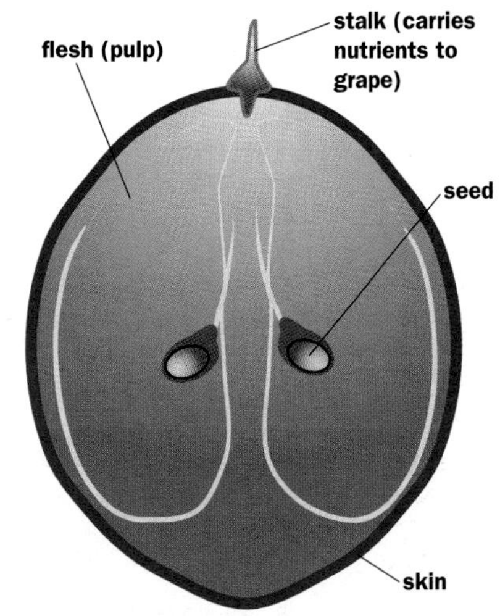

1. What is another word for the flesh of a grape?
2. What carries the nutrients to the grape?
3. Name the parts of a grape from the outside to the inside.

Internet Activity

To get help with vocabulary and places, select dictionary or encyclopedia from *Social Studies Library* at **www.sfsocialstudies.com.**

Hands-on Unit Project

Unit 2 Performance Assessment

- See p. 156 for information about using the Unit Project as a means of performance assessment.
- A scoring guide is provided on p. 156.

WEB SITE
Technology

For more information, students can select the dictionary or encyclopedia from *Social Studies Library* at **www.sfsocialstudies.com**.

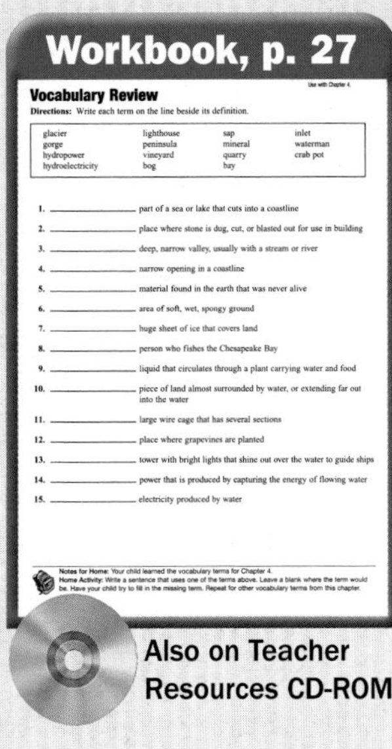

Workbook, p. 27

Use with Chapter 4.

Vocabulary Review

Directions: Write each term on the line beside its definition.

glacier	lighthouse	sap	inlet
gorge	peninsula	mineral	waterman
hydropower	vineyard	quarry	crab pot
hydroelectricity	bog	bay	

1. ______ part of a sea or lake that cuts into a coastline
2. ______ place where stone is dug, cut, or blasted out for use in building
3. ______ deep, narrow valley, usually with a stream or river
4. ______ narrow opening in a coastline
5. ______ material found in the earth that was never alive
6. ______ area of soft, wet, spongy ground
7. ______ huge sheet of ice that covers land
8. ______ person who fishes the Chesapeake Bay
9. ______ liquid that circulates through a plant carrying water and food
10. ______ piece of land almost surrounded by water, or extending far out into the water
11. ______ large wire cage that has several sections
12. ______ place where grapevines are planted
13. ______ tower with bright lights that shine out over the water to guide ships
14. ______ power that is produced by capturing the energy of flowing water
15. ______ electricity produced by water

Notes for Home: Your child learned the vocabulary terms for Chapter 4.
Home Activity: Write a sentence that uses one of the terms above. Leave a blank where the term would be. Have your child try to fill in the missing term. Repeat for other vocabulary terms from this chapter.

Also on Teacher Resources CD-ROM.

Facts and Main Ideas

1. Because of its ability to generate hydropower
2. It begins in Maine as rugged, rocky cliffs and then becomes sandy beaches in New Jersey.
3. A waterman fishes Chesapeake Bay.
4. Possible answers: The Appalachian Mountain Range, a part of which is located in the Northeast, is the second largest mountain range in the U.S.; Niagara Falls is a major tourist attraction; Chesapeake Bay provides seafood for the Northeast region.
5. Possible answers: Grapes, cranberries, maple syrup, blue crabs, oysters, fish, shellfish
6. By fishing
7. Possible answer: Without them, pollution and overfishing might devastate areas like Chesapeake Bay.

Write About the Region

1. Encourage students to use the illustrations in the chapter as they brainstorm details for their journal entries.
2. Encourage students to create an appealing name for their product and to emphasize the best qualities of grapes from the Northeast.
3. Advise students not only to discuss potential harm to the bay but also positive reasons for keeping the bay healthy.

Apply Skills

1. Pulp
2. Stalk
3. Stalk, skin, flesh, seed

CHAPTER 5

Chapter Planning Guide

Chapter 5 • People of the Northeast

Locating Places pp. 124–125

Lesson Titles	Pacing	Main Ideas
Lesson 1 **The Narragansett People** pp. 126–129	1 day	• The Narragansett lived in the Northeast region before European settlers came to North America.
Lesson 2 **The Land of New Beginnings** pp. 130–133 **Chart and Graph Skills: Use a Vertical Time Line** pp. 134–135	2 days	• The Northeast saw the beginnings of the American Revolution, the writing of our nation's Constitution, and the start of many new lives as immigrants arrived in the United States. • A vertical time line shows important events that happened over a period of time.
Lesson 3 **Taking a Stand** pp. 136–138 **Biography: Elizabeth Cady Stanton** p. 139 DK **Winning the Right to Vote** pp. 140–141	3 days	• The Northeast was the birthplace of the abolitionist movement and the women's rights movement. • Elizabeth Cady Stanton fought for the rights of all people. • People worked hard for many years to win women the right to vote.
Lesson 4 **Cities Grow and Change** pp. 142–146 **Biography: Andrew Carnegie** p. 147 **Citizen Heroes: Responsibility Capturing History** pp. 148–149	4 days	• Northeastern cities and their industries have grown and changed. • Andrew Carnegie brought the steel-making process to the U.S. and used his wealth to help others. • Volunteers stepped forward to help others in many ways after the attacks on September 11, 2001.

✓ **Chapter 5 Review**
pp. 150–151

✓ = **Assessment Options**

◀ **Elizabeth Cady Stanton helped organize the first women's rights convention in the United States.**

Although their lives were greatly changed by the arrival of European settlers, the Narragansett continue to observe many of their traditions today.

Vocabulary	Resources	Meeting Individual Needs
cooperation wigwam sachem reservation powwow confederacy	• Workbook, p. 29 • Transparency 10 • Every Student Learns Guide, pp. 50–53 • Quick Study, pp. 26–27	• ESL Support, TE p. 128 • Leveled Practice, TE p. 129
colony revolution vertical time line	• Workbook, p. 30 • Transparencies 11, 38 • Every Student Learns Guide, pp. 54–57 • Quick Study, pp. 28–29 • Workbook, p. 31	• ESL Support, TE p. 131 • Leveled Practice, TE p. 132 • Leveled Practice, TE p. 134
abolitionist slave convention	• Workbook, p. 32 • Transparency 14 • Every Student Learns Guide, pp. 58–61 • Quick Study, pp. 30–31 • Workbook, p. 33	• ESL Support, TE p. 137 • Leveled Practice, TE p. 138 • Learning Styles, TE p. 141
commerce import export diverse	• Workbook, p. 34 • Transparencies 15, 39 • Every Student Learns Guide, pp. 62–65 • Quick Study, pp. 32–33	• ESL Support, TE p. 143 • Leveled Practice, TE p. 145
	✔Chapter 5 Content Test, Assessment Book, pp. 21–22 ✔Chapter 5 Skills Test, Assessment Book, pp. 23–24	✔Chapter 5 Performance Assessment, TE p. 150

Providing More Depth

Additional Resources

- Vocabulary Workbook and Cards
- Social Studies Plus! pp.46-51
- Daily Activity Bank
- Big Book Atlas
- Student Atlas
- Outline Maps
- Desk Maps

Technology

- AudioText
- MindPoint® Quiz Show CD-ROM
- ExamView® Test Bank CD-ROM
- Teacher Resources CD-ROM
- Map Resources CD-ROM
- SFSuccessNet: iText (Pupil Edition online), iTE (Teacher's Edition online), Online Planner
- **www.sfsocialstudies.com** (Biographies, news, references, maps, and activities)

To establish guidelines for your students' safe and responsible use of the Internet, use the Scott Foresman Internet Guide.

Additional Internet Links

To find out more about:

- Declaration of Sentiments, visit **www.fordham.edu**
- Elizabeth Cady Stanton, visit **www.greatwomen.org**
- Alexander Graham Bell, visit **www.invent.org**

Key Internet Search Terms

- Narragansett people
- American Industrial Revolution
- Seneca Falls Convention

Workbook Support

Use the following Workbook pages to support content and skills development as you teach Chapter 5. You can also view and print Workbook pages from the Teacher Resources CD-ROM.

Workbook, p. 28

Vocabulary Preview

Use with Chapter 5.

Directions: These are the vocabulary words from Chapter 5. How much do you know about these words? Read each definition. Which word is defined? Fill in the circle next to the correct answer. You may use your glossary.

1. working together to get things done
   Ⓐ sachem Ⓑ convention Ⓒ import ● cooperation
2. varied
   Ⓐ reservation Ⓑ wigwam ● diverse Ⓓ slave
3. a fight to overthrow the government
   ● revolution Ⓑ export Ⓒ cooperation Ⓓ powwow
4. person who is owned as property by another person
   Ⓐ convention ● slave Ⓒ diverse Ⓓ import
5. a meeting held for a special purpose
   Ⓐ reservation Ⓑ sachem Ⓒ confederacy ● convention
6. an area of land set aside for Native Americans
   Ⓐ powwow ● reservation Ⓒ convention Ⓓ wigwam
7. item that is brought from abroad to be offered for sale
   ● import Ⓑ colony Ⓒ export Ⓓ abolitionist
8. chief of a Narragansett territory
   ● sachem Ⓑ abolitionist Ⓒ commerce Ⓓ wigwam
9. settlement of people who come from one country to live in another
   Ⓐ reservation Ⓑ diverse ● colony Ⓓ convention
10. union of groups, countries, or states
    Ⓐ cooperation ● confederacy Ⓒ sachem Ⓓ revolution
11. the buying and selling of goods between places
    Ⓐ export Ⓑ confederacy Ⓒ diverse ● commerce
12. festival of Native Americans
    ● powwow Ⓑ wigwam Ⓒ convention Ⓓ reservation

Notes for Home: Your child learned the vocabulary terms for Chapter 5.
Home Activity: Have your child use five of the vocabulary words correctly in a sentence.

28 Vocabulary Preview Workbook

Use with Pupil Edition, p. 124

Workbook, p. 29

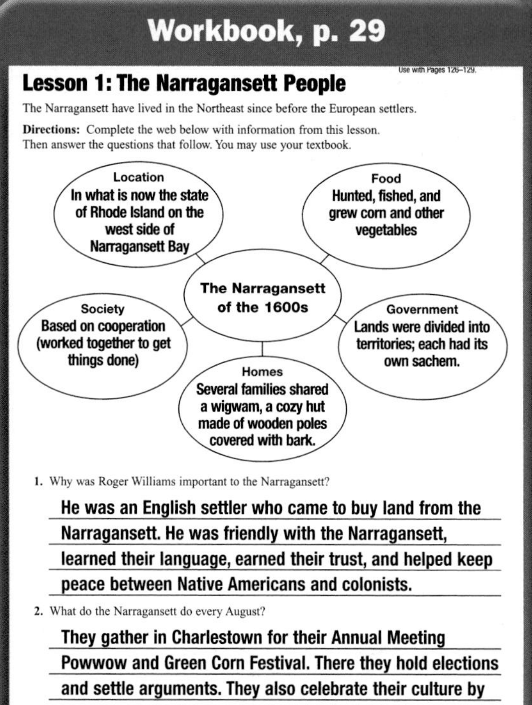

Lesson 1: The Narragansett People

Use with Pages 126–129.

The Narragansett have lived in the Northeast since before the European settlers.

Directions: Complete the web below with information from this lesson. Then answer the questions that follow. You may use your textbook.

The Narragansett of the 1600s
Location
In what is now the state of Rhode Island on the west side of Narragansett Bay
Food
Hunted, fished, and grew corn and other vegetables
Society
Based on cooperation (worked together to get things done)
Government
Lands were divided into territories; each had its own sachem.
Homes
Several families shared a wigwam, a cozy hut made of wooden poles covered with bark.

1. Why was Roger Williams important to the Narragansett?
   He was an English settler who came to buy land from the Narragansett. He was friendly with the Narragansett, learned their language, earned their trust, and helped keep peace between Native Americans and colonists.
2. What do the Narragansett do every August?
   They gather in Charlestown for their Annual Meeting Powwow and Green Corn Festival. There they hold elections and settle arguments. They also celebrate their culture by singing, dancing, and renewing old friendships.

Notes for Home: Your child learned about the history of the Narragansett.
Home Activity: Discuss with your child the idea of cooperation. How can he or she cooperate better with you and other family members? How does your family cooperate with others to meet your needs?

Use with Pupil Edition, p. 129

Workbook, p. 30

Lesson 2: The Land of New Beginnings

Use with Pages 130–133.

Directions: Complete the chart below with information from this lesson. You may use your textbook.

What caused the American Revolution to take place?	Colonies protested when they felt Great Britain was passing unjust laws and collecting taxes unfairly.
What became necessary when the U.S. won independence?	To form a government and write the Constitution
Why did immigrants come to the United States?	Find jobs; own their own land; escape hardships; find a better life
From where did immigrants come?	All around the world
Who are some immigrants that have contributed to the United States?	Alexander Graham Bell, Andrew Carnegie, Albert Einstein, Madeleine Albright

Notes for Home: Your child learned about the American Revolution and immigration to the United States.
Home Activity: Discuss with your child to explain why our country can be called the "land of new beginnings"?

30 Lesson Review Workbook

Use with Pupil Edition, p. 133

Workbook Support

Workbook, p. 31

Use with Pages 134–135.

Use a Vertical Time Line

A vertical time line shows events that happened over a period of time.

Directions: Complete the vertical time line below with information about the Narragansett. You may use your textbook. Information about the Narragansett can be found on pages 126–129.

Events in the History of the Narragansett

Dates	Events
1636	Roger Williams visits the Grand Sachem, Canonicus.
1675	Native Americans in Massachusetts attack the English settlers.
1880	The state of Rhode Island sells part of the Narragansett land.
1978	Rhode Island returns about 1,800 acres of land to the Narragansett.

Notes for Home: Your child learned how to use a vertical time line.
Home Activity: Work with your child to make a vertical time line of his or her life.

Use with Pupil Edition, p. 135

Workbook, p. 32

Use with Pages 136–138.

Lesson 3: Taking a Stand

People have worked for many years to win rights in the United States.

Directions: Complete the chart below with information that explains the importance of each person or place. You may use your textbook.

Person or Place	Importance?
Philadelphia, Pennsylvania	Where abolitionists met to form the American Anti-Slavery Society in 1833
William Lloyd Garrison	Abolitionist who published a newspaper called *The Liberator*
Frederick Douglass and Sojourner Truth	Speakers who worked for freedom for all people and convinced people to fight against slavery
Elizabeth Cady Stanton and Lucretia Mott	Organized the first women's rights convention in the United States
Seneca Falls, New York	Where the first U.S. women's rights convention was held in 1848
Susan B. Anthony	One of the leaders of the women's rights movement

Notes for Home: Your child learned about the abolitionist movement and the women's rights movement.
Home Activity: Discuss with your child the importance of having the right to vote. How might your child feel if, as an adult, he or she was denied the right to vote? Why?

Use with Pupil Edition, p. 138

Workbook, p. 33

Writing Prompt: The Right to Vote

In the United States, women did not have the right to vote in national elections before 1920. Many people thought this was unfair. They did many things to try to persuade others to help women gain the right to vote. Think about why it is important for citizens to vote. Write a paragraph persuading citizens that voting is important.

Answers will vary.

Notes for Home: Your child learned about women's voting rights.
Home Activity: With your child, discuss voting and the election process. Discuss why voting is an important responsibility of citizenship.

Use with Pupil Edition, p. 141

Workbook, p. 34

Use with Pages 142–146.

Lesson 4: Cities Grow and Change

Northeast cities and states have undergone many changes in their history.

Directions: Read the following phrases about Northeast cities and decide which state each one describes. For a city in Pennsylvania write *PA* in the blank; for a city in New York write *NY;* for a city in Massachusetts write *MA;* write *ALL* if it describes cities in all three states. You may use your textbook.

PA 1. Declaration of Independence and Constitution signed here
NY 2. location of the Empire State Building
ALL 3. began as a port where ocean-going ships docked
NY 4. became an important port on Lake Erie
ALL 5. became centers of industry
MA 6. location of Paul Revere's house and Bunker Hill
PA 7. once famous for its steel mills
PA 8. headquarters for robot-making factories
ALL 9. hub of commerce
NY 10. famous for its skyscrapers and its theater
MA 11. Freedom Trail winds past its historic sites
NY 12. harbor contains the Statue of Liberty
PA 13. passed laws to clean up the city in the mid-1900s
ALL 14. shipping and transportation are important
PA 15. plentiful resources included coal and limestone
ALL 16. center of banking, health care, and high-tech industries

Notes for Home: Your child learned about the history of Northeast cities and states.
Home Activity: With your child, discuss the attractions of Northeast cities today. What might your family enjoy on a visit to these cities?

Use with Pupil Edition, p. 146

Workbook, p. 35

Use with Chapter 5.

Vocabulary Review

Directions: Use the vocabulary words from Chapter 5 to complete the crossword puzzle.

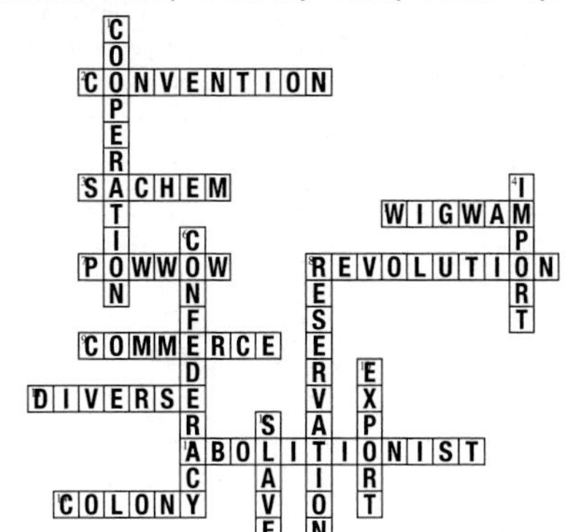

Across

2. meeting held for a special purpose
3. chief or "ruler" of a Narragansett territory
5. cozy hut made of wooden poles covered with bark
7. festival of Native Americans
8. a fight to overthrow the government
9. the buying and selling of goods between different places
11. varied
13. reformer who believed that slavery should be erased from the law of the land
14. settlement of people who come from one country to live in another

Down

1. working together to get things done
4. item that is brought from abroad to be offered for sale
6. union of groups, countries, or states
8. area of land set aside for Native Americans
10. item sent from one country to be sold in another country
12. person who is owned as property by another person

Notes for Home: Your child learned the vocabulary terms for Chapter 5.
Home Activity: Work with your child to write an original sentence using each of the terms above.

Use with Pupil Edition, p. 150

Workbook, p. 36

Unit 2 Project On the Spot

Discovery School

Directions: In a group, make a documentary about the experiences of early settlers or Native American groups in the Northeast.

1. We chose to make our documentary about the experiences of (✔ one):
___ Native Americans ___ European settlers
2. We included these topics:
___ geographic location ___ weather ___ landforms ___ homes ___ activities
___ foods available ___ other groups of people ___ other topics: ______
3. These are facts about the topics:
4. This is a description of our diorama or model:

Encourage students to reread sections of the textbook about the group they selected. Use maps to locate important geographical features.

✔ **Checklist for Students**
___ We chose a group to study.
___ We chose topics and wrote facts for the documentary.
___ We made a diorama or model.
___ We presented our documentary to the class.

Notes for Home: Your child learned about the experiences of early European settlers and Native Americans.
Home Activity: With your child, research the early settlers and Native Americans of your community or region. Discuss interesting facts about their experiences and their reasons for settling in the area in which you live.

Use with Pupil Edition, p. 156

Assessment Support

Use the following Assessment Book pages and The test maker to assess content and skills in Chapter 5 and Unit 2. You can also view and print Assessment Book pages from the Teacher Resources CD-ROM.

Assessment Book, p. 21

Chapter 5 Test

Part 1: Content Test

Directions: Fill in the circle next to the correct answer.

Lesson Objective (1:2)

1. What is a sachem?
   - (A) a meeting and festival
   - (B) a type of corn plant
   - (C) a cozy wooden hut
   - ● a Narragansett ruler

Lesson Objective (1:3)

2. How did Europeans use the iron axes and hoes, brass kettles, and other items they brought from Europe?
   - (A) to decorate their wigwams
   - (B) to give as gifts to the Native Americans
   - ● to trade with the Native Americans for animal furs
   - (D) to bury for later use

Lesson Objective (1:1)

3. Which did NOT occur once European settlers arrived in the Northeast?
   - (A) The Europeans and Native Americans traded goods.
   - (B) The Narragansett and the Europeans began to mistrust each other.
   - (C) Native Americans in Massachusetts attacked the English settlers.
   - ● The Europeans gave up the struggle and moved out of the Northeast.

Lesson Objective (1:4)

4. Which statement best describes the Iroquois Confederacy?
   - (A) It was made up of both Native Americans and Europeans.
   - ● It was the strongest Native American organization.
   - (C) Fifty women representatives made decisions for the Confederacy.
   - (D) The Confederacy disbanded in 1722.

Lesson Objective (2:1)

5. Which is NOT an event that led to the founding of the United States?
   - (A) The colonies protested England's laws and taxes.
   - (B) The American Revolution began in Lexington, Massachusetts.
   - ● The capital moved to Washington, D.C., in 1800.
   - (D) Colonial leaders met in Pennsylvania to write and sign the Declaration of Independence.

Lesson Objective (2:2)

6. Which of the following was the first capital of the United States?
   - (A) Washington, D.C.
   - (B) Jamestown
   - ● New York City
   - (D) Philadelphia

Lesson Objective (2:4)

7. Which is NOT a reason why immigrants came to the United States?
   - ● to protest England's rule
   - (B) to find jobs
   - (C) to own their own land
   - (D) to escape war or other hardships

Lesson Objective (2:3)

8. Through which Northeast port did most Europeans come to the United States?
   - (A) Philadelphia
   - (B) Pennsylvania
   - (C) Washington, D.C.
   - ● New York

Use with Pupil Edition, p. 150

Assessment Book, p. 22

Lesson Objective (3:1, 2)

9. Which of the following describes an abolitionist?
   - (A) person who fought for women's rights
   - ● reformer who believed slavery should be outlawed
   - (C) person who thought slaves should have no rights
   - (D) women's rights convention in 1848

Lesson Objective (3:3)

10. Which of the following leaders was an important women's rights reformer?
    - ● Elizabeth Cady Stanton
    - (B) William Lloyd Garrison
    - (C) Benjamin Franklin
    - (D) Alexander Graham Bell

Lesson Objective (3:4)

11. Which is a reason why women wanted the right to vote?
    - (A) They believed Frederick Douglass should be elected President.
    - (B) They believed women should no longer be owned as property by another person.
    - (C) They believed women should not have the same right to jobs as men.
    - ● They believed women should have the same rights as men, including the right to vote.

Lesson Objective (4:1)

12. Which Northeast city did NOT begin as a port where ocean-going ships docked?
    - ● Buffalo, New York
    - (B) New York City, New York
    - (C) Boston, Massachusetts
    - (D) Philadelphia, Pennsylvania

Lesson Objective (4:3)

13. How have Pittsburgh's industries changed over the years?
    - (A) The demand for steel has increased, causing Pittsburgh to find new ways to make it.
    - (B) The steel industry is still Pittsburgh's only industry.
    - ● Pittsburgh now has a diverse group of industries.
    - (D) Pittsburgh no longer is a center of health-care and environmental research.

Lesson Objective (4:2)

14. What do Philadelphia, New York City, and Boston have in common?
    - (A) All are important historic cities in the Midwest.
    - (B) These cities house the world's tallest buildings.
    - (C) Harbors in these cities welcomed immigrants to America.
    - ● Many tourists visit landmarks in these cities each year.

Lesson Objective (4:4)

15. How do people in the Northeast contribute to the economy of this region?
    - (A) They send pollution into the air.
    - (B) People travel to other regions to work.
    - ● They work, shop, and spend money.
    - (D) They travel the Freedom Trail.

Use with Pupil Edition, p. 150

Assessment Book, p. 23

Part 2: Skills Test

Directions: Use complete sentences to answer questions 1–5. Use a separate sheet of paper if you need more space.

1. How did life change for the Narragansett when they lost much of their native land to the Europeans? **Summarize**

   Because they lost their land, many Narragansett sided with or joined other Native American groups. Many were killed in battles that followed, and the Narragansett scattered. Some moved to Canada, while others remained on their lands even after much of their land had been sold.

2. What problems do you think an immigrant might face when moving to a new country? How might those problems be solved? **Solve Problems**

   Possible answer: Immigrants might face language and cultural barriers that could keep them from getting good jobs and progressing economically. Free or low-cost training might be provided to immigrants to help them adapt more successfully to American society.

3. Write at least three details to support the following main idea: **An important reform movement that grew in the Northeast was the abolitionist movement. Main Idea and Details**

   Possible answers: Abolitionists organized groups and published anti-slavery newspapers such as the *Liberator*; the American Anti-Slavery Society began in Philadelphia in 1833.

Use with Pupil Edition, p. 150

Assessment Book, p. 24

4. What events led to women winning the right to vote? Write them in the order in which they happened. **Sequence**

   In the 1800s reformers began to fight for women's rights. In 1848 Elizabeth Cady Stanton and Lucretia Mott organized the first U.S. women's rights convention in Seneca Falls, New York. Susan B. Anthony also began to lead the women's rights movement. In 1920 the Nineteenth Amendment to the Constitution gave women the right to vote.

5. Use the information in the paragraph to make a vertical timeline about Susan B. Anthony. **Use a Vertical Timeline**

   Susan B. Anthony was born on February 15, 1820, in Massachusetts. In 1845 she moved to New York, and the next year she began teaching. In 1857 Anthony went to a teacher's convention where she spoke about education for women. In 1869 she organized a convention in Washington, D.C. to discuss the right of women to vote. Anthony met with President Theodore Roosevelt in 1905. They talked about submitting an amendment to Congress that would give women the right to vote. The next year Susan B. Anthony died.

   Title: ______

   - 1820 **Susan B. Anthony is born.**
   - **1846 She begins teaching.**
   - **1857 Anthony speaks at a convention about education of women.**
   - **1869 Anthony organizes a convention to discuss the right of women to vote.**
   - **1905 Anthony meets with President Roosevelt about the right of women to vote.**
   - 1906 **Anthony dies.**

Use with Pupil Edition, p. 150

Assessment Support

Assessment Book, p. 25

Unit 2 Test

Part 1: Content Test

Directions: Fill in the circle next to the correct answer.

Lesson Objective (4–1:2)

1. Why is Niagara Falls important to the Northeast region?
   - Ⓐ It is one of Mexico's most spectacular natural wonders.
   - Ⓑ It provides drinking water for people in the West.
   - ● Thousands of tourists spend money to visit the breathtaking site.
   - Ⓓ It is a main mountain range located in the Appalachian Mountains.

Lesson Objective (4–1:4)

2. Which states in the Northeast do NOT share a border with the Atlantic Ocean?
   - ● Pennsylvania and Vermont
   - Ⓑ Maine and New Jersey
   - Ⓒ Delaware and Massachusetts
   - Ⓓ Maryland and New York

Lesson Objective (4–2:3)

3. Which of the following is the largest of the Finger Lakes?
   - Ⓐ Lake Erie
   - ● Lake Seneca
   - Ⓒ Lake Michigan
   - Ⓓ Lake Ontario

Lesson Objective (4–2:2)

4. Which is NOT a true statement about the Northeast?
   - ● The Finger Lakes are important in the production of cranberries.
   - Ⓑ The climate in the Northeast is good for the grape's long growing season.
   - Ⓒ Cranberries are grown in the bogs of the Northeast region.
   - Ⓓ More maple syrup is produced in Vermont than in any other U.S. state.

Lesson Objective (4–2:1)

5. What is the first key step in maple syrup production?
   - Ⓐ Boil the sap until the water evaporates and pure maple syrup remains.
   - Ⓑ Collect sap in buckets and transfer it to barrels.
   - ● Drill a hole into a tree and attach a spout.
   - Ⓓ Take the sap to a sugar house to be boiled.

Lesson Objective (4–3:1)

6. Which describes the group known as watermen?
   - Ⓐ men who play water sports
   - Ⓑ men and women who make a living from water sports
   - Ⓒ independent men who try to stop water pollution
   - ● men and women who fish the bay

Lesson Objective (4–3:2, 3, 4)

7. Which is NOT a true statement about the Chesapeake Bay area?
   - Ⓐ Chesapeake Bay is rich in crabs, oysters, clams, and other shellfish.
   - ● Most families in the area earn their livings in agriculture.
   - Ⓒ Some factories pollute the Chesapeake Bay by dumping waste onto the land around the bay.
   - Ⓓ The Chesapeake Bay Foundation was formed to educate people and save the bay.

Use with Pupil Edition, p. 154

Assessment Book, p. 26

Lesson Objective (5–1:1, 2, 3)

8. Which is NOT true about the Narragansett?
   - ● They moved to the Northeast after the European settlers.
   - Ⓑ Each of their territories was ruled by a sachem.
   - Ⓒ Rhode Island eventually returned land to the Narragansett reservation.
   - Ⓓ They traded furs to the Europeans for metal tools.

Lesson Objective (5–2:1)

9. Which event happened first in the founding of the United States?
   - ● England's North American colonies protested England's laws and taxes.
   - Ⓑ Delegates met in Philadelphia to write a constitution for the new government.
   - Ⓒ The first shots of the American Revolution were fired at Lexington, Massachusetts.
   - Ⓓ Colonial leaders met in Philadelphia to write the Declaration of Independence.

Lesson Objective (5–2:4)

10. What is one reason why immigrants came to the United States in the 1800s?
    - Ⓐ to help write the Constitution
    - Ⓑ to fight as paid soldiers in the American Revolution
    - ● to find new jobs and own land
    - Ⓓ to meet with colonial leaders in Philadelphia following the American Revolution

Lesson Objective (5–3:1, 2)

11. Which is NOT true about the reform movements that took place in the Northeast?
    - Ⓐ The Nineteenth Amendment gave women the right to vote in 1920.
    - Ⓑ Disagreements about slavery between Northern and Southern states led to the Civil War.
    - ● Frederick Douglass organized the first women's rights convention in Seneca Falls.
    - Ⓓ In 1865, the Thirteenth Amendment ended slavery in the United States.

Lesson Objective (5–3:3)

12. Why was Elizabeth Cady Stanton important to the women's rights movement?
    - Ⓐ She believed that only African American men should have the right to vote.
    - Ⓑ She convinced many people to fight against slavery.
    - Ⓒ She published a newspaper called *The Liberator.*
    - ● She helped organize the first women's rights convention.

Lesson Objective (5–4:1)

13. Why did northeastern cities develop around natural harbors?
    - ● Trade with Europe was very important.
    - Ⓑ Coal could only be found near oceans and rivers.
    - Ⓒ Northeastern cities wanted to develop around the Statue of Liberty.
    - Ⓓ The building of lighthouses was an important industry.

Use with Pupil Edition, p. 154

Assessment Book, p. 27

Lesson Objective (5–4:2)

14. Why are New York City, Boston, and Philadelphia important cities?
    - Ⓐ The steel industry is based here.
    - Ⓑ They are known for their seafood industry.
    - Ⓒ All were early capitals of the United States.
    - ● Famous landmarks attract visitors to these cities.

Lesson Objective (5–4:3, 4)

15. Which is NOT a major industry in Pittsburgh today?
    - Ⓐ factories that make robots
    - ● space exploration
    - Ⓒ health-care research
    - Ⓓ computer software companies

Part 2: Skills Test

Directions: Use complete sentences to answer questions 1–5. Use a separate sheet of paper if you need more space.

1. When and from where did most immigrants come to the United States in the 1800s and early 1900s? **Sequence**

   From 1820 to 1860, most immigrants were from Great Britain, Ireland, and Germany. From 1860 to 1890, many came from Scandinavia. From 1890 to 1910, many came from southern and eastern Europe.

2. Who do you think is more important in the history of the Northeast: Roger Williams or Elizabeth Cady Stanton? Why? **Express Ideas**

   Possible answers: Roger Williams is more important because he founded Rhode Island and helped keep the peace between the colonists and the Native Americans; Elizabeth Cady Stanton is more important because she made a major contribution to history by helping women win the right to vote.

Use with Pupil Edition, p. 154

Assessment Book, p. 28

3. How do the people and the economy of a city affect each other? **Cause and Effect**

   Citizens of a city help build the economy by working, living, and spending money in the city. In turn, a healthy economy makes the city a good place to live, work, and visit.

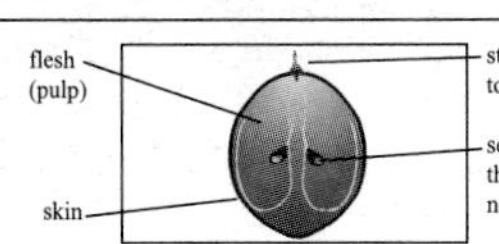

Grape Cross Section

4. Use the diagram to answer the questions. **Read a Cross-Section Diagram**
   - a. What does the diagram show? **the inside of a grape**
   - b. What is the name of the part that can grow into a new plant? **seed**
   - c. What surrounds the seed? **the flesh or pulp**

U.S. Capital Cities

- 1775
- 1776 The Declaration of Independence is signed
- 1787 The U.S. Constitution is written.
- 1789 New York City, New York, became the first capital of the United States
- 1790 Philadelphia became the second capital city.
- 1800 The capital moved to Washington, D.C.
- 1810

5. Use the timeline to answer the questions. **Use a Vertical Timeline**
   - a. In what year was the U.S. Constitution written? **1787**
   - b. How long after the Constitution was written was the first capital city named? **2 years**
   - c. How long was Philadelphia the capital of the United States? **1 year**

Use with Pupil Edition, p. 154

CHAPTER 5

People of the Northeast

Chapter 5 Outline

- **Lesson 1, *The Narragansett People,*** pp. 126–129
- **Lesson 2, *The Land of New Beginnings,*** pp. 130–133
- **Chart and Graph Skills: *Use a Vertical Time Line,*** pp. 134–135
- **Lesson 3, *Taking a Stand,*** pp. 136–138
- **Biography: *Elizabeth Cady Stanton,*** p. 139
- **Smithsonian Institution: *Winning the Right to Vote,*** pp. 140–141
- **Lesson 4, *Cities Grow and Change,*** pp. 142–146
- **Biography: *Andrew Carnegie,*** p. 147
- **Citizen Heroes: *Capturing History,*** pp. 148–149

Resources

- Workbook, p. 28: Vocabulary Preview
- Vocabulary Cards
- Social Studies Plus!

Charlestown, Rhode Island: Lesson 1

This picture shows the framework of a wigwam. Ask students why they think the Narragansett built wigwams. (For shelter)

Ellis Island, New York: Lesson 2

Thousands of immigrants like these came to the United States through Ellis Island. Ask students how these immigrants might have felt upon arriving at Ellis Island. (Excited, scared, hopeful)

Seneca Falls, New York: Lesson 3

These women met at Seneca Falls to discuss how to win their rights. Ask students what rights they think these women wanted. (The right to vote)

Pittsburgh, Pennsylvania: Lesson 4

This is a picture of Pittsburgh, which once was known as the "Steel City." Ask students to speculate about the reason for this nickname. (Pittsburgh produced huge amounts of steel.)

CHAPTER 5

People of the Northeast

Lesson 1

Charlestown, Rhode Island
The Narragansett meet European settlers.

1

Lesson 2

Ellis Island, New York
Many Europeans come to the United States to look for opportunities.

2

Lesson 3

Seneca Falls, New York
Women join together to win the right to vote.

3

Lesson 4

Pittsburgh, Pennsylvania
Pittsburgh becomes a center of industry in the Northeast region.

4

Practice and Extend

Vocabulary Preview

- Use Workbook p. 28 to help students preview the vocabulary words in this chapter.
- Use Vocabulary Cards to preview key concept words in this chapter.

Also on Teacher Resources CD-ROM.

Workbook, p. 28

Locating Places

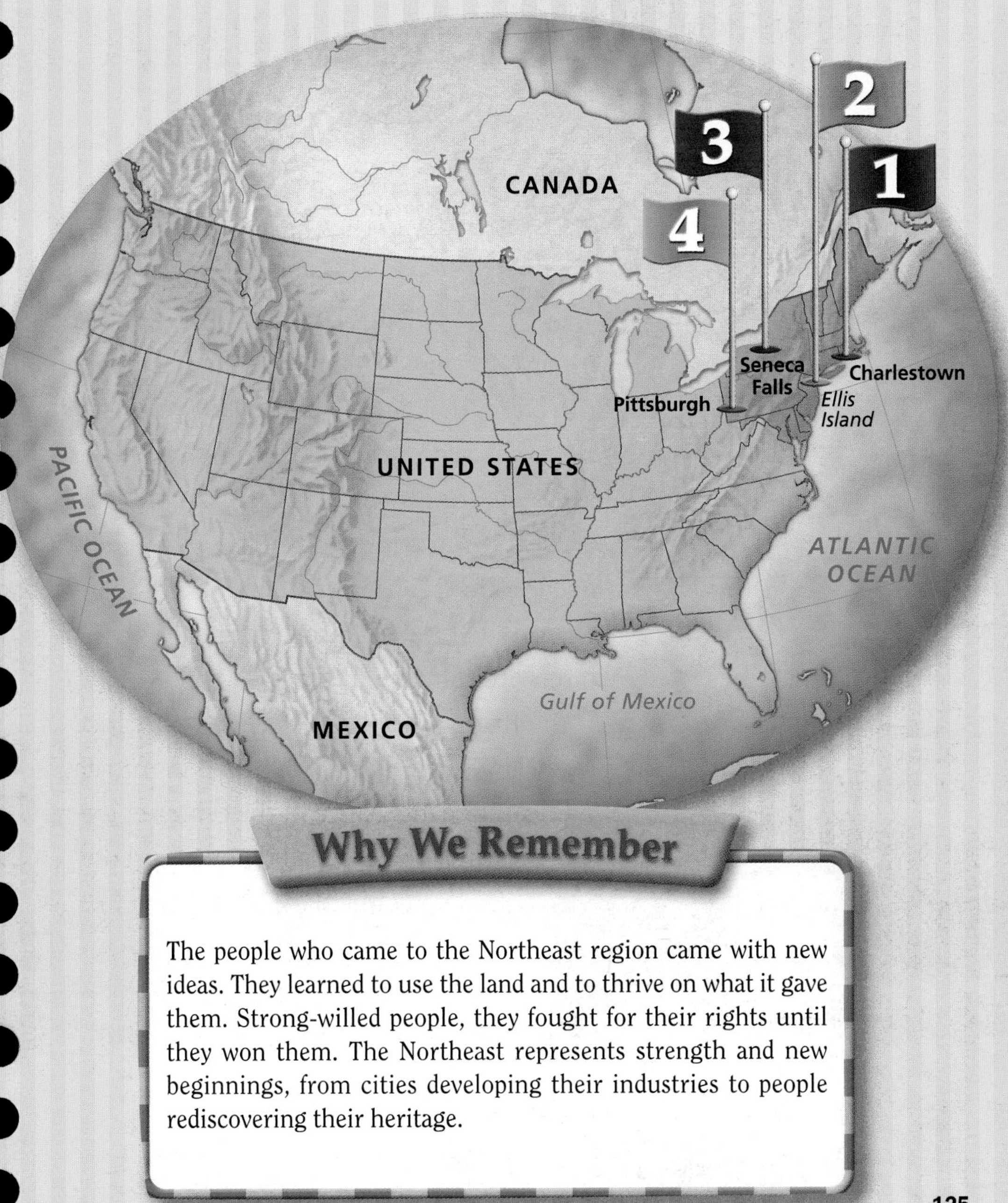

Why We Remember

The people who came to the Northeast region came with new ideas. They learned to use the land and to thrive on what it gave them. Strong-willed people, they fought for their rights until they won them. The Northeast represents strength and new beginnings, from cities developing their industries to people rediscovering their heritage.

125

WEB SITE
Technology

You can learn more about Charlestown, Rhode Island; Ellis Island, New York; Seneca Falls, New York; and Pittsburgh, Pennsylvania, by clicking on *Atlas* at **www.sfsocialstudies.com.**

SOCIAL STUDIES STRAND
Geography

Mental Mapping Ask students to picture in their minds the Atlantic Ocean with the continents of North America on one coast and Europe on the other coast. Discuss with students ways people can travel from one continent to another. Use this discussion to introduce the concept of immigration.

Locating Places

- Have students examine the pictures on p. 124 for Lessons 1, 2, 3, and 4.
- Remind students that each picture is coded with both a number and a color to link it to a place on the map on p. 125.

Why We Remember

Have students read the "Why We Remember" paragraph on p. 125, and ask why places in this chapter might be important to them. Ask students to speculate about why pursuing new ideas might take a strong will.

The Narragansett People

Objectives

- Describe key events that affected the Narragansett way of life once European settlers arrived.
- Define *sachem*.
- Describe what goods the Europeans and Native Americans traded.
- Explain why the Iroquois Confederacy was established.

Vocabulary

cooperation, p. 127; **wigwam,** p. 127; **sachem,** p. 127; **reservation,** p. 128; **powwow,** p. 128; **confederacy,** p. 129

Resources

- Workbook, p. 29
- Transparency 10
- Every Student Learns Guide, pp. 50–53
- Quick Study, pp. 26–27

Quick Teaching Plan

If time is short, have students read the lesson independently and record information about the Narragansett in a three-column chart labeled *Before European Contact, After European Contact,* and *Today*.

1 Introduce and Motivate

Preview To activate prior knowledge, ask students to tell who lived in the Northeast area before the colonists arrived. Tell students they will learn more about one group of Native Americans in the Northeast as they read Lesson 1.

You Are There The Narragansett and other Native American groups have lived in North America for many centuries. Ask students how this compares to other groups who settled in North America, such as the people in their own community.

LESSON 1

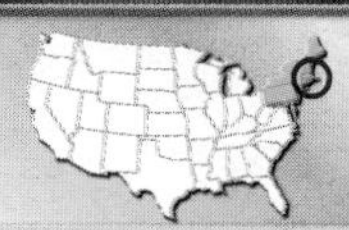

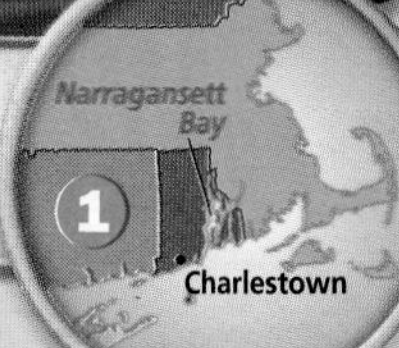

The Narragansett People

PREVIEW

Focus on the Main Idea
The Narragansett lived in the Northeast region before European settlers came to North America.

PLACE
Charlestown, Rhode Island

PEOPLE
Roger Williams
Canonicus

VOCABULARY
cooperation
wigwam
sachem
reservation
powwow
confederacy

You Are There You and your friend are visiting the Narragansett Indian Reservation during the group's Annual Meeting. You are standing in a field with a crowd of people, waiting for a dance to begin. You see a group of Narragansett men dressed in fringed leather pants and beaded necklaces. You ask a woman next to you how long the Narragansett have lived here. She tells you that Narragansett Indians have lived in this area for hundreds of years.

You turn toward the clearing as the dance begins. Three dancers dressed in fringed leather pants dance in the center of the clearing. You are glad that you had the chance to come to the reservation to see this joyful dance.

Sequence As you read, keep track of the order in which things happen.

▶ Narragansett chief

126

Practice and Extend

READING SKILL Sequence

In the Lesson Review, students complete a graphic organizer like the one below. You may want to provide students with a copy of Transparency 10 to complete as they read the lesson.

Use Transparency 10

VOCABULARY Related Word Study

Tell students that many words, including *wigwam, sachem,* and *powwow* come from Native American languages. List the following on the board: *toboggan, squash, tomato, barbecue, pecan, chipmunk, potato, moose, raccoon, skunk, llama, cashew, jaguar,* and *tapioca.*

Have students define any of the words that are familiar. If there is time, allow them to look up words and identify the Native American language from which it comes.

The Narragansett Way of Life

▶ A Narragansett wigwam made from tree bark and animal hides

For hundreds of years, the Narragansett (nair uh GAN sit) Indians lived in what is now the state of Rhode Island. They lived on the west side of Narragansett Bay. They hunted, fished, and grew corn and vegetables for food.

The Narragansett lived in a society that was based on **cooperation,** or working together to get things done. When a family needed a field cleared for planting vegetables, all of their
2 neighbors and friends helped. Several
3 families also shared a home. The Narragansett home was a **wigwam,** a cozy hut made of wooden poles covered with bark.

The Narragansett lands were divided up into a number of territories. Each territory had its own chief, or sachem. **Sachem** means "ruler."

The first Europeans to set foot on the Narragansett lands were Dutch, French, and English fishermen and fur traders. The traders brought goods such as iron axes and hoes and brass kettles. They traded these goods with the Narragansett in exchange for their animal furs. The Narragansett had used tools made of stone and shell. They were happy to use the stronger tools made of metal. The traders also brought glass beads and other attractive items.

REVIEW Describe how the Narragansett organized their government. Main Idea and Details

North Wind Picture Archives

127

SOCIAL STUDIES Background

About the Early Narragansett

- Archaeologists studying the Narragansett Bay area have found mounds of clam and oyster shells deposited by the Narragansett as well as broken pieces of pottery and arrowheads.
- Because of the Narragansett's emphasis on cooperation and generosity, murder and robbery were rare.
- The dead were buried with their knees drawn up to their chests and their faces turned toward the southwest. The Narragansett believed this was the direction of the afterworld.

2 Teach and Discuss

PAGE 127

The Narragansett Way of Life

Quick Summary Before the arrival of colonists, the Narragansett of Rhode Island had a society based on cooperation and ruled by sachems.

SOCIAL STUDIES STRAND
History

The name Narragansett is believed to mean "people of the small point."

1 Look at the map on p. 126. Why is *Narragansett* an especially good name for the people who lived in this area of the Northeast? The area in which they lived has a shoreline made up of many little points and bays. Interpret Maps

2 If a Narragansett family was unable to hunt, do you think it had to go without meat? Explain your reasoning. Possible answer: No; Because the society was based on cooperation, other families probably offered the family meat Make Inferences

✓ Ongoing Assessment

If... students have difficulty relating this scenario to the lesson,	**then...** ask them how the Narragansett solved other problems, such as clearing fields.

3 What might be some advantages and disadvantages of several families living together? Possible answers: Advantages: shared responsibilities, more collective skills; Disadvantages: little privacy, few personal possessions Draw Conclusions

✓ **REVIEW ANSWER** Narragansett lands were divided into territories. Each territory had its own chief, or sachem. Main Idea and Details

PAGE 128

Changes in the Narragansett Way of Life

Quick Summary English settler Roger Williams bought land for the Rhode Island colony in 1636 and treated the Narragansett fairly, but some other Europeans did not.

SOCIAL STUDIES STRAND
Citizenship

4 How did Roger Williams show his respect for the Narragansett? He was friendly, learned their language, and earned their trust. He also helped keep peace between the Native Americans and the colonists. Main Idea and Details

5 How do you think the Narragansett's reservation compared to the group's original homelands? Possible answer: The reservation probably was much smaller than the original homeland. Make Inferences

6 Where do the Narragansett hold their elections today? On their reservation, in Charlestown, Rhode Island Main Idea and Details

✓ **REVIEW ANSWER** Possible answer: The Europeans took away Narragansett lands and killed many Narragansett people, causing the group to scatter. Main Idea and Details

Changes in the Narragansett Way of Life

In 1636 an English settler named **Roger Williams** visited the Grand Sachem, **Canonicus.** Williams came to buy land from the Narragansett for a colony that was later called Rhode Island.

Williams was friendly with the Narragansett. He learned their language and earned their trust. He helped keep peace between the Native
4 Americans and the colonists.

At first, the two groups got along well. Gradually, though, the Narragansett and the Europeans began to mistrust each other. Some Europeans took part of the Narragansett's land. The Narragansett and other Native Americans tried to keep their land and their independence by resisting expansion of the Europeans.

In 1675 Native Americans in Massachusetts attacked the English settlers. Because the Narragansett were angry about losing their land, they sided with the other Native American groups. Many Narragansett were killed in battles that followed. The Narragansett scattered. Many moved to Canada or joined other Native American groups. Some Narragansett remained on their lands, even after the State of Rhode Island sold part of their land in 1880.

In 1978 Rhode Island returned about 1,800 acres of land to the Narragansett reservation. A **reservation** is an area of land set aside for Native Americans. Some Narragansett live on the reservation today. Other Narragansett live throughout the Northeast. 5

Every August, the Narragansett hold their Annual Meeting Powwow and Green Corn Festival on their reservation in **Charlestown,** Rhode Island. A **powwow** is a festival of Native Americans. The Narragansett's powwow is a time for dancing, singing, and renewing old friendships. During this meeting, they also hold elections and settle disputes. 6

REVIEW How did the Europeans change the way the Narragansett lived? Main Idea and Details

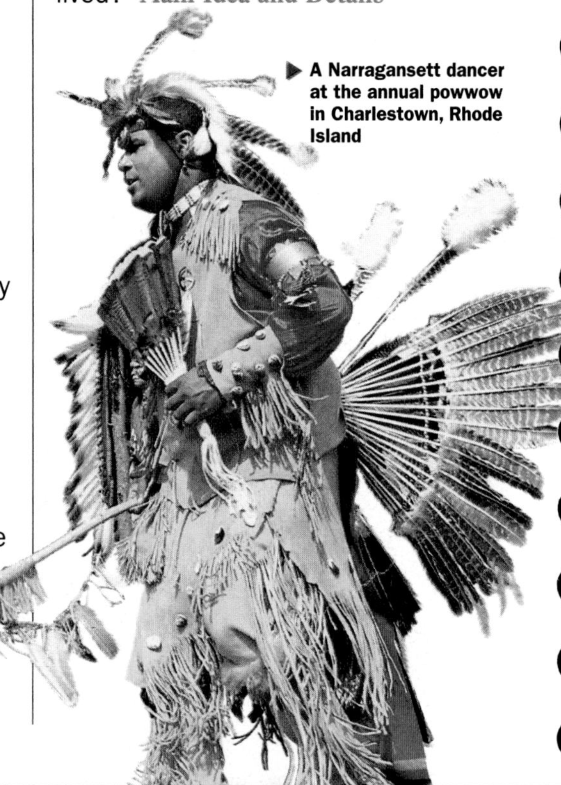

▶ A Narragansett dancer at the annual powwow in Charlestown, Rhode Island

128

Practice and Extend

CURRICULUM CONNECTION
Science

Research Diseases

- Explain that European settlers not only claimed land that belonged to the Narragansett, but they also introduced deadly diseases to the native peoples.
- Have students research some of the diseases the Europeans brought to the Americas, why Native Americans were so vulnerable to them, and what effect they had on the population.
- Have students write a brief report and present it to the class.

ESL
EXTEND LANGUAGE
ESL Support

Examine Double-Consonant Spellings Point out to students that the English language contains many words that have double consonants (all letters except vowels).

Beginning Explain that double consonants usually sound the same as their single counterparts—for example, *t* and *tt*. Write *bb, dd, gg, ll, mm, nn, pp, rr, ss,* and *tt* on the board and have volunteers pronounce each consonant pair.

Intermediate Have students list double-consonant words from p. 128 of the text and pronounce each word aloud.

Advanced Urge students to memorize the spellings of double-consonant words. Have students quiz each other on writing the double-consonant words on p. 128.

For additional ESL support, use Every Student Learns Guide, pp. 50–53.

▶ Iroquois boys in their traditional dress gather on the Onondaga Reservation in New York State.

Other Native Americans of the Northeast

The Iroquois Confederacy was the strongest Native American organization. A **confederacy** is a union of groups, countries, or states. Five Native American groups—the Seneca, Mohawk, Oneida, Onondaga, and Cayuga—had formed the Iroquois Confederacy by 1722. The groups selected fifty representatives who made up a Great Council. The representatives made decisions that affected the whole Confederacy. The Tuscarora later joined the Confederacy. 7

The Iroquois Confederacy still exists today. Great Council representatives meet on the Onondaga Reservation in New York State.

REVIEW How is the Iroquois Confederacy like the government of the United States? Draw Conclusions

Summarize the Lesson

- **Before Europeans arrived, the Narragansett lived in present-day Rhode Island.**
- **The Europeans changed the way the Narragansett lived.**
- **Five Native American groups formed the Iroquois Confederacy.**

LESSON 1 REVIEW

Check Facts and Main Ideas

1. Sequence On a separate sheet of paper, make a diagram like the one shown. Then fill in events that affected the Narragansett in the order they occurred.

The Narragansett lived in what is now the state of Rhode Island.

↓

Dutch, French, and English traders came.

↓

Narragansett sided with other Native Americans in fighting for their land.

↓

Every August, the Narragansett gather in Charlestown, Rhode Island, for a festive, two-day meeting.

2. What is a **sachem?**
3. What did the Europeans receive from the Native Americans in exchange for the goods they traded?
4. Describe the Iroquois **Confederacy.**
5. **Critical Thinking:** ***Draw Conclusions*** Why did five tribes decide to form the Iroquois Confederacy?

Link to Art

Draw a Poster Based on what you've read in this lesson, draw a poster showing the items that the Narragansett and Europeans traded.

MEETING INDIVIDUAL NEEDS
Leveled Practice

Demonstrate Cooperative Problem Solving
Help students demonstrate cooperation.

Easy Have pairs of students demonstrate how to decide who gets to read a book first when there is only one copy. **Reteach**

On-Level Have students demonstrate how a small group of students might decide who gets to sit where on a bus during a field trip. **Extend**

Challenge Have students demonstrate how the whole class might decide what to do with a $100 gift to the class. **Enrich**

For a Lesson Summary, use Quick Study, p. 26.

Workbook, p. 29

Lesson 1: The Narragansett People

Location, Food, The Narragansett of the 1600s, Society, Government, Homes

1. Why was Roger Williams important to the Narragansett?
2. What do the Narragansett do every August?

Also on Teacher Resources CD-ROM.

PAGE 129

Other Native Americans of the Northeast

Quick Summary The Iroquois Confederacy was and still is a powerful Native American organization that makes its home in the Northeast.

7 **What do members of the Great Council do for the Iroquois Confederacy?** Make decisions that affect the whole group Main Idea and Details

✓ **REVIEW ANSWER** Like the U.S. government, the Great Council is made up of representatives who act on behalf of the people. Draw Conclusions

3 Close and Assess

Summarize the Lesson

Have students review the three main points. Then have student pairs quiz each other on key terms from the lesson.

✓ LESSON 1 **REVIEW**

1. **Sequence** For possible answers, see the reduced pupil page.
2. A Narragansett chief
3. Animal furs
4. The strongest Native American organization; has a Great Council that makes decisions for the entire group
5. **Critical Thinking: *Draw Conclusions*** Possible answers: To increase their power; to become more unified; to make rules and laws more standardized

Link to Art

Students may want to do additional research to find out what kinds of animal furs the Iroquois traded.

The Land of New Beginnings

Objectives

- Identify events leading from colonization up to the founding of the United States.
- Identify cities in the Northeast that have been capitals of the United States.
- Identify the city in the Northeast where most European immigrants arrived in the 1800s.
- Explain why immigrants came to the United States.

Vocabulary

colony, p. 131; **revolution,** p. 131

Resources

- Workbook, p. 30
- Transparency 11
- Every Student Learns Guide, pp. 54–57
- Quick Study, pp. 28–29

Quick Teaching Plan

If time is short, have students use the time line at the top of the pupil page as a study tool.

- As students read each section independently, have them refer to the time line on this page.
- Tell students to be prepared to explain each item on the time line and to add other details from the lesson.

1 Introduce and Motivate

Preview To activate prior knowledge, ask students from what country the United States broke away when it decided to form its own government. Tell them that they will learn more about this new beginning as they read Lesson 2.

You Are There Explain that our country's founders wanted to create a government that was fair to all citizens. Ask students what kinds of challenges this goal might present.

LESSON 2

1770 1810 1850 1890

1776 The Declaration of Independence is signed.

1787 The U.S. Constitution is written.

1820 The first of several waves of immigration to the United States begins.

1892 Ellis Island immigration station opens.

The Land of New Beginnings

PREVIEW

Focus on the Main Idea
The Northeast saw the beginnings of the American Revolution, the writing of our nation's Constitution, and the start of many new lives as immigrants arrived in the United States.

PLACES
Plymouth, Massachusetts
Lexington, Massachusetts
Philadelphia, Pennsylvania
New York City, New York
Ellis Island

PEOPLE
John Adams
Benjamin Franklin
Alexander Graham Bell
Albert Einstein
Andrew Carnegie
Madeleine Albright

VOCABULARY
colony
revolution

EVENTS
American Revolution

You Are There It is a hot day in Philadelphia, and yet the windows and the shutters are closed. The meeting hall is very stuffy. Tempers are rising. The delegates are trying to write a constitution, or a plan of government. There are so many issues yet to be decided.

For example, should little Rhode Island have as many representatives in the government as big New York? There are fewer southern states than northern states. What about their say in the government? It is hard work, but eventually the delegates reach their decisions. The result is the United States Constitution. It begins "We, the People . . ."

Sequence As you read, note the order of events that led from the arrival of early colonists to the immigrants who come to the United States today.

130

Practice and Extend

READING SKILL
Sequence

In the Lesson Review, students complete a graphic organizer like the one below. You may want to provide students with a copy of Transparency 11 to complete as they read the lesson.

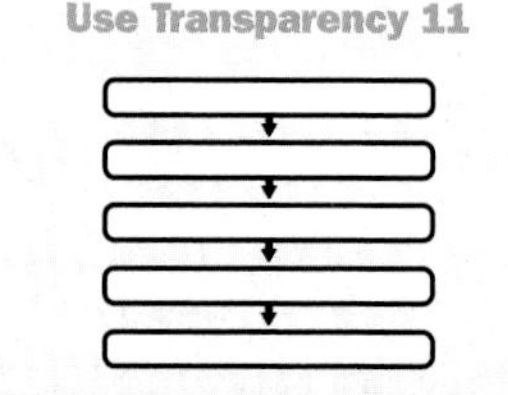

WEB SITE
Technology

- You can look up vocabulary words by clicking on *Social Studies Library* and selecting the dictionary at **www.sfsocialstudies.com.**
- Students can learn about current news by clicking on *Current Events* at **www.sfsocialstudies.com.**
- Explore other events that occurred on this day by clicking on *This Day in History* at **www.sfsocialstudies.com.**

A New Nation

The Constitution set up the government of our new nation. The Northeast played an important role in the beginning of this nation. One of the first English colonies in North America began at **Plymouth, Massachusetts,** in 1620. A **colony** is a settlement of people who come from one country to live in another. By the early 1700s there were thirteen American colonies.
1 Nine of them were in the Northeast.

All of the colonies protested when they felt that England was passing unjust laws and collecting taxes
2 unfairly. Some of the strongest protests came from the colony of Massachusetts. The first shots of the **American Revolution** were fired at **Lexington, Massachusetts,** a town near Boston. A **revolution** is a fight to overthrow the government. Shortly after that, colonial leaders met in **Philadelphia, Pennsylvania,** to write and sign the Declaration of Independence. This document was dated July 4, 1776, and it marked the beginning of the United States of America. **John Adams,** from Massachusetts, provided strong leadership in the writing of the document. Later as our nation's second president, his leadership skills were once again important.

After the United States won independence from England, it became necessary to form a government. In 1787 delegates met in Philadelphia to write the Constitution. **Benjamin Franklin** from Pennsylvania played an important role. He helped settle disputes between the states. At eighty-one, he had become a famous publisher, inventor, and statesman.

Before Washington, D.C., was built, our first two capitals were in the Northeast. **New York City, New York,** was our capital from 1789 to 1790. This is where George Washington took the oath of office and became our first president. In 1790 Philadelphia became our second capital city. The capital 3
moved to Washington, D.C., in 1800.

REVIEW What were some events that led to the development of the new nation? Sequence

▶ Working on the writing of the Declaration of Independence

131

ACCESS CONTENT
ESL Support

Locate Place Names on a Map Help students locate places associated with the birth of the United States.

Beginning Explain that the United States began in the Northeast. Call out the names of the thirteen colonies, and have students point to each on a map of the United States.

Intermediate Have students locate each of the thirteen colonies on an outline map of the United States. Have them shade the colonies that were part of the Northeast region in one color and the remaining colonies in a second color.

Advanced Have students find each city mentioned on p. 131 and mark it on an outline map of the United States.

For additional ESL support, use Every Student Learns Guide, pp. 54–57.

2 Teach and Discuss

PAGE 131

A New Nation

Quick Summary Nine of the thirteen original American colonies and the new U.S. government were based in the Northeast.

1 **How many of the original thirteen colonies were located in the Northeast?** Nine Main Idea and Details

2 **Why did the colonists decide to break ties with England?** They felt that England was passing unjust laws and collecting taxes unfairly. Main Idea and Details

3 **What role did Massachusetts play in the journey to U.S. independence? Pennsylvania?** Possible answers: Massachusetts: made strong protests against unjust laws and taxes, first shots of the American Revolution fired there; Pennsylvania: Declaration of Independence and Constitution written there, second U.S. capital located there Apply Information

Ongoing Assessment

If... students have difficulty describing what each state contributed to this effort,	**then...** have them review the text on this page and list what happened in each location.

✓ **REVIEW ANSWER** Possible answers: (1) Colonies were established, (2) colonies revolted against England, (3) colonial leaders wrote Declaration of Independence, (4) U.S. delegates wrote Constitution, (5) U.S. capital established at New York City, (6) capital moved to Philadelphia and then to Washington, D.C. Sequence

A Land of Promise

Quick Summary During the 1800s and early 1900s, huge numbers of people immigrated to the United States from different parts of Europe. Today immigrants continue to arrive in the U.S. from all parts of the world.

4 **For what reasons did immigrants come to the United States?** Possible answers: To get a job, to own their own land, to escape war or other hardships in their home countries, to find a better life **Main Idea and Details**

5 **Describe three major waves of immigration that occurred in the United States between 1820 and 1910.** 1820–1860: many immigrants from Great Britain, Ireland, and Germany; 1860–1890: immigrants from Scandinavia; 1890–1910: immigrants from southern and eastern Europe **Summarize**

6 **What did most European immigrants' journeys have in common?** Possible answer: They entered the United States through the port of New York. **Compare and Contrast**

7 **What is one way immigration has benefited the United States?** Possible answer: It has brought many valuable people and ideas to this country, including Alexander Graham Bell, Andrew Carnegie, Albert Einstein, and Madeleine Albright. **Cause and Effect**

A Land of Promise

Even before the American Revolution, the American colonies attracted many people from other nations. After the United States became a nation, many more immigrants came to start a new life in the new nation.

Why did they come? Some were looking for jobs. The growing cities and industries of the Northeast needed plenty of workers. Others wanted to own their own land. Still others hoped to escape war or other hardships in their countries of origin. All of them hoped to
4 find a better life in the United States.

Immigrants came to the United States from all around the world. Since the early 1800s, there have been several waves of immigration from Europe to the Northeast. From 1820 to 1860, most of the immigrants were from Great Britain, Ireland, and Germany. From 1860 to 1890, many of the immigrants came from Scandinavia, a region in northwestern Europe. Many Scandinavians moved westward and started family farms in the Midwest. From 1890 to 1910, many of the immigrants came from
5 southern and eastern Europe.

The Bettmann Archive

▶ The Ellis Island Registration Hall in 1915

Most European immigrants came to the United States through the port of New York. In 6
1892 the United States government opened a huge immigration station on **Ellis Island** in New York harbor. Inspectors there checked the immigrants' papers. They also checked to make sure the immigrants were in good health. By the time the immigration station was closed in 1954, more than 12 million immigrants had passed through the inspection station at Ellis Island. Then they began a new life in the United States.

Immigrants to the United States have contributed much to our nation. **Alexander Graham Bell,** the inventor of the telephone, was a Scottish immigrant. So was **Andrew Carnegie,** who introduced an important steel-making process to the United States. **Albert Einstein,** one of the world's most important scientists, immigrated to the United States from Germany. **Madeleine Albright,** the United States'
first female Secretary of State, was an 7
immigrant from eastern Europe.

Today immigrants continue to come to the United States from all parts of the world. Most immigrants are seeking a better way of life, just as the waves of

132

MEETING INDIVIDUAL NEEDS
Leveled Practice

Learn About Notable Immigrants Have students do research to find out more about notable immigrants.

Easy Have students use online or library resources to find one important accomplishment of one of the famous immigrants introduced on this page. **Reteach**

On-Level Have students research and write a paragraph about one of the immigrants discussed in this lesson. **Extend**

Challenge Have students research and write a one-page report about a famous immigrant from the lesson or another important immigrant to the United States. **Enrich**

For a Lesson Summary, use Quick Study, p. 28.

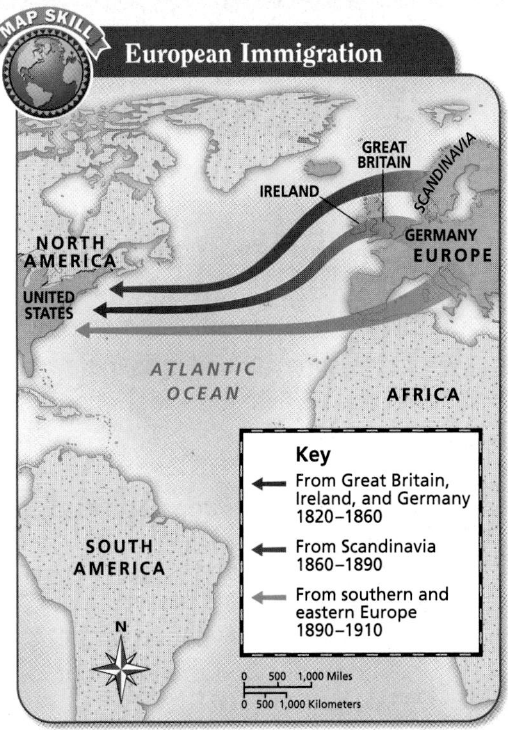

▶ Many immigrants came to the United States from Europe.

MAP SKILL Trace Movement on a Map ***How many years are represented by the three waves of immigration shown on the map?***

immigrants who came before them. In time many immigrants become citizens of the United States. They contribute to their communities in the Northeast and throughout our nation.

REVIEW Why would the United States set up an immigration station such as the one at Ellis Island? Draw Conclusions

Summarize the Lesson

- **1620** A colony was founded at Plymouth, Massachusetts.
- **1776** The Declaration of Independence was signed.
- **1787** The U.S. Constitution was written.
- **1820** The first of several waves of immigration to the United States began.
- **1892** Ellis Island immigration station was opened.

LESSON 2 REVIEW

Check Facts and Main Ideas

1. Sequence On a separate sheet of paper, fill in the sequence of events that led to the founding of the United States of America.

   - Colonies are founded in North America.
   - ↓ Colonists protest against England.
   - ↓ Declaration of Independence is written and signed.
   - ↓ The United States wins the American Revolution.
   - ↓ U.S. Constitution is written.

2. Where were the first shots of the American Revolution fired?
3. What two Northeastern cities were capitals of the United States before Washington, D.C.?
4. What are some reasons immigrants came to the United States?
5. **Critical Thinking:** ***Make Inferences*** Why do you think so many European immigrants first arrived in the Northeast region?

Link to Writing

Write a Letter Suppose that you are on a ship sailing from a nation in Europe to the United States in 1895. Write a letter to your friends back in your old home explaining what you are thinking and how you are feeling.

European Immigration

8 What ocean did the immigrants cross when traveling from Europe to the United States? The Atlantic Ocean Interpret Maps

MAP SKILL Answer 90 years

✓ **REVIEW ANSWER** To check immigrants' papers and to make sure people were in good health before entering the country Draw Conclusions

3 Close and Assess

Summarize the Lesson

Have students review the time line and add one important detail about each point.

✓ **LESSON 2 REVIEW**

1. **Sequence** For possible answers, see the reduced pupil page.
2. Lexington, Massachusetts
3. New York City, New York, and Philadelphia, Pennsylvania
4. To look for jobs, to own their own land, to escape war or other hardships, to find better lives

Test Talk

Write Your Answer to Score High

5. **Critical Thinking: *Make Inferences*** Students should make sure that their written answer is focused and has only details from the text that answer the question. Possible answer: Many European immigrants arrived in the Northeast because they traveled to the United States across the Atlantic Ocean and needed to go through the immigration station on Ellis Island.

Link to Writing

Students' letters should take into account the types of things an immigrant might expect to see, hear, and experience in the United States in 1895.

CURRICULUM CONNECTION
Drama

Present a Dramatization

- Explain to students that language barriers caused problems for many immigrants.
- Ask one student to play the role of a non-English speaker arriving at Ellis Island in 1900. (You may wish to choose a student who speaks another language for this role.)
- Have the other students portray immigration officials, police officers, ferry operators, employers, and other people with whom the immigrant might come into contact.
- Discuss changes that might make this experience easier for the immigrant.

Workbook, p. 30

Lesson 2: The Land of New Beginnings

What caused the American Revolution to take place?	
What became necessary when the U.S. won independence?	
Why did immigrants come to the United States?	
From where did immigrants come?	
Who are some immigrants that have contributed to the United States?	

Also on Teacher Resources CD-ROM.

Chart and Graph Skills

Use a Vertical Time Line

Objective

- Analyze a vertical time line to acquire information.

Vocabulary

vertical time line, p. 134

Resource

- Workbook, p. 31
- Transparency 38

1 Introduce and Motivate

What is a vertical time line? Ask students to tell how they think vertical time lines are similar to horizontal time lines. (Both list dates of events in sequence.) Then have students read the **What?** section of text on p. 134 to help set the purpose of the lesson.

Why use a vertical time line? Have students read the **Why?** section of text on p. 134. Ask students what advantage they think a vertical time line has over a paragraph. (Readers can see and compare information at a glance.)

2 Teach and Discuss

How is the skill used? Examine with students the time line on p. 135.

- Point out that the title of the time line identifies the subject.
- Make sure students realize that the vertical time line should be read from top to bottom.
- Have students read the **How?** section of text on p. 134.

Chart and Graph Skills

Use a Vertical Time Line

What? A **vertical time line** shows important events that happened over a period of time. The events are listed along a vertical line, or line that runs up and down.

Why? Sometimes it's difficult to keep track of events that you read about or to understand how the events may be related. A vertical time line lists important events and helps you see their relationship to each other.

How? Page 135 shows an example of a vertical time line. To use the time line, begin at the top and read down. As you read, try to understand how each event relates to the events around it. Also think about what was happening elsewhere in the world at the same time.

Think and Apply

To make sure you understand how to read a **vertical time line,** answer these questions.

1. The most inventions occurred between what years?
2. How many years passed between the invention of the automobile and the invention of the airplane?
3. After the invention of the locomotive, how many years passed without a major invention?

134

Practice and Extend

MEETING INDIVIDUAL NEEDS
Leveled Practice

Create a Vertical Time Line Help students create vertical time lines of their own lives.

Easy Have students divide their lives into three age groups—birth to three years, four to six years, and seven years to present. Tell them to record one key experience from each time period on their time line. **Reteach**

On-Level Have students create entries on their time lines for each year of their lives. **Extend**

Challenge Have students create entries in their time lines for each year of their lives. Then have students research one interesting U.S. or world event for each year and add these to their time lines. **Enrich**

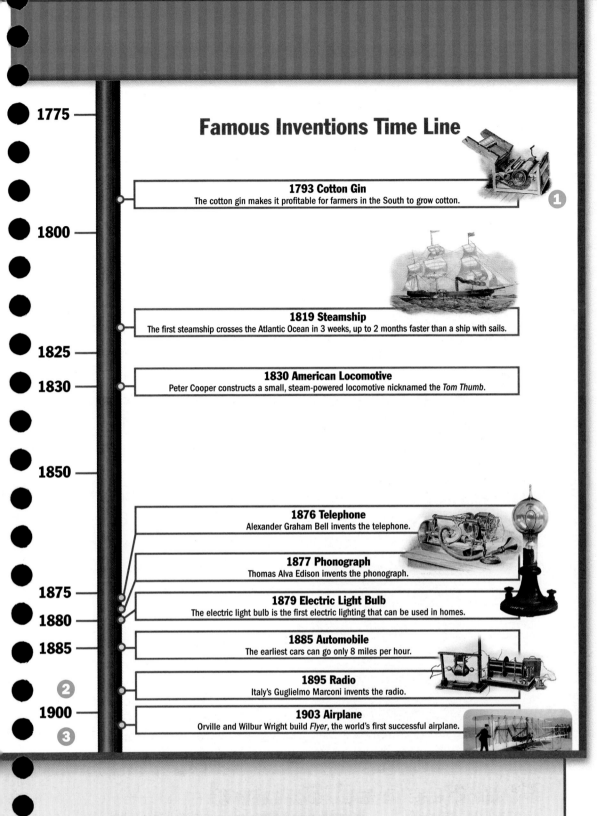

Famous Inventions Time Line

1775

1793 Cotton Gin
The cotton gin makes it profitable for farmers in the South to grow cotton. 1

1800

1819 Steamship
The first steamship crosses the Atlantic Ocean in 3 weeks, up to 2 months faster than a ship with sails.

1825

1830

1830 American Locomotive
Peter Cooper constructs a small, steam-powered locomotive nicknamed the *Tom Thumb*.

1850

1876 Telephone
Alexander Graham Bell invents the telephone.

1877 Phonograph
Thomas Alva Edison invents the phonograph.

1875

1879 Electric Light Bulb
The electric light bulb is the first electric lighting that can be used in homes.

1880

1885

1885 Automobile
The earliest cars can go only 8 miles per hour.

2

1895 Radio
Italy's Guglielmo Marconi invents the radio.

1900

1903 Airplane
Orville and Wilbur Wright build *Flyer*, the world's first successful airplane.

3

1. **Which of the entries describes an invention that occurred before 1800? What was the invention?** The first one; cotton gin **Interpret Time Lines**

2. **How many of the inventions on the time line were invented in the 1800s?** Seven inventions **Interpret Time Lines**

3. **How many years passed between the invention of the steamship and the invention of the airplane?** About 84 years **Interpret Time Lines**

3 Close and Assess

Think and Apply

1. 1875–1900
2. 18 years
3. 46 years

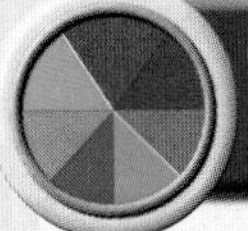

CURRICULUM CONNECTION
Math

Calculate Averages

- Have students create a vertical time line entitled *Number of Immigrants to the United States*.
- Have them plot the following dates and approximate numbers on their time lines: 1961–1970: 3,322,000; 1971–1980: 4,493,000; 1981–1990: 7,338,000; 1991–1995: 5,426,000.
- Ask students to calculate the average rate of immigration each year over the entire 35-year period (587,971) and have them explain trends in immigration over the charted period.

Workbook, p. 31

Use with Pages 134–135.

Use a Vertical Time Line

A vertical time line shows events that happened over a period of time.

Directions: Complete the vertical time line below with information about the Narragansett. You may use your textbook. Information about the Narragansett can be found on pages 126–129.

Events in the History of the Narragansett

Dates	Events
1636	
1675	
1880	
1978	

Notes for Home: Your child learned how to use a vertical time line.
Home Activity: Work with your child to make a vertical time line of his or her life.

Also on Teacher Resources CD-ROM.

Taking a Stand

Objectives

- Explain similarities and differences between the abolitionist movement and the women's rights movement.
- Explain the meaning of the word *abolitionist.*
- Identify important women's rights reformers.
- Explain why reformers fought to win voting rights for women.

Vocabulary

abolitionist, p. 137; **slave,** p. 137; **convention,** p. 138

Resources

- Workbook, p. 32
- Transparency 14
- Every Student Learns Guide, pp. 58–61
- Quick Study, pp. 30–31

Quick Teaching Plan

If time is short, have students read the lesson independently, focusing on main ideas.

- Have students write a one-sentence summary of each section of the lesson.

1 Introduce and Motivate

Preview To activate prior knowledge, ask students if they think all U.S. citizens have the same rights. Tell students they will learn more about the struggle for rights as they read Lesson 3.

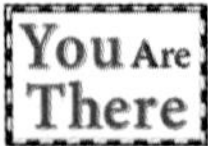

Ask students how they might feel if they were not allowed to learn how to read. Ask how it might affect their daily lives.

LESSON 3

1830	1855	1880	1905	1930

- **1833** American Anti-Slavery Society is formed.
- **1848** First women's rights convention in the United States is held.
- **1865** Thirteenth Amendment abolishes slavery in the United States.
- **1920** Nineteenth Amendment grants women the right to vote.

PREVIEW

Focus on the Main Idea
The Northeast was the birthplace of the abolitionist movement and the women's rights movement.

PLACES
Philadelphia, Pennsylvania
Seneca Falls, New York

PEOPLE
William Lloyd Garrison
Frederick Douglass
Sojourner Truth
Elizabeth Cady Stanton
Lucretia Mott
Susan B. Anthony

VOCABULARY
abolitionist
slave
convention

TERMS
Thirteenth Amendment
Nineteenth Amendment

Taking a Stand

You Are There The room is hushed. A tall, muscular man takes his place, front and center. His name is Frederick Douglass. As he begins to speak, you realize that his voice is as powerful as his body.

He tells the crowd that he was born into slavery in Maryland. He says that the wife of one of his owners taught him to read. He explains how he read about slavery and learned about freedom. He also speaks about beatings and punishment. He describes his escape to New York, disguised as a free sailor. He warns that even now, slave hunters could track him down and return him to his master.

Everyone in the crowd is moved by his story. They promise to take a stand against slavery.

▶ Frederick Douglass

The Granger Collection

Compare and Contrast As you read, think about the similarities and differences between the abolitionist movement and the women's rights movement.

136

Practice and Extend

READING SKILL
Compare and Contrast

In the Lesson Review, students complete a graphic organizer like the one below. You may want to provide students with a copy of Transparency 14 to complete as they read the lesson.

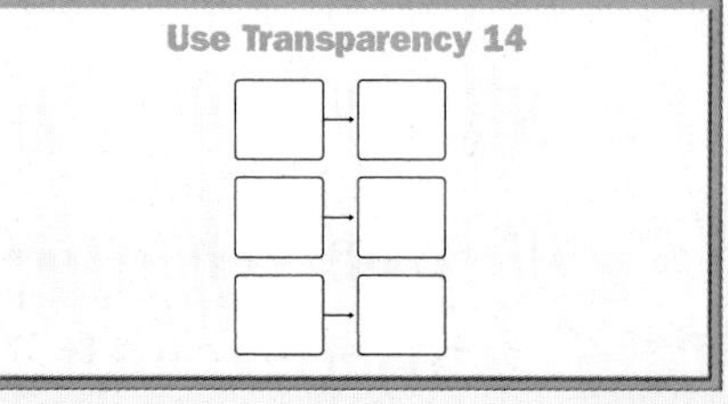

VOCABULARY
Individual Word Study

Ask students how the text defines *convention* (a meeting held for a special purpose). Tell students that another meaning of *convention* is "a rule based on common consent." Explain that *convention* comes from the Latin *convenire*, which means "to come together." Discuss how both meanings of *convention* have to do with groups of people coming together, either to meet together or in mental agreement.

The Abolitionists

During the 1800s, many reforms, or changes, took place in American society. Many of these reform movements began in the Northeast. One of the most important was the abolitionist movement. An **abolitionist** was a reformer who believed that slavery should be erased, or abolished, from the land.

Since the early days of the colonies, Africans had been captured and brought to the Americas to work as slaves on farms and in homes. A **slave** is a person who is owned as property by another person. A slave often has no rights and must do whatever his or her master wishes.

The Bettmann Archive

▶ Sojourner Truth

Some people spoke out against slavery. Even some people in the South, where slavery was widespread, were against it. The movement grew in the Northeast, however. Abolitionists organized groups and published newspapers against slavery. African Americans and whites joined together
1 to seek an end to slavery.

In **Philadelphia** in 1833, abolitionists met to form the American Anti-Slavery Society. One strong abolitionist, **William Lloyd Garrison,** published a newspaper called *The Liberator.* The word *liberator* means "one who brings freedom." Speakers such as **Frederick Douglass** and **Sojourner Truth** addressed abolitionist meetings and told about their lives as slaves. They convinced many people to fight against slavery. They also worked for freedom for all people.

Disagreements about slavery and other issues grew between Northern and Southern states. These tensions
led to the Civil War. In 1865, after this 2
war, the **Thirteenth Amendment** to the
Constitution made slavery illegal in the 3
United States.

REVIEW Why were Frederick Douglass and Sojourner Truth able to convince many people to join the abolitionist cause? Draw Conclusions

2 Teach and Discuss

PAGE 137

The Abolitionists

Quick Summary The struggle to abolish slavery continued through much of the 1800s and resulted in the Thirteenth Amendment, which made slavery illegal.

1 **How did the movement against slavery grow in the Northeast?** Abolitionists organized groups and published newspapers against slavery, and African Americans and whites joined together to seek an end to slavery. **Apply Information**

2 **What was one cause of the Civil War?** Possible answer: Growing tensions over slavery **Cause and Effect**

3 **What was the purpose of the Thirteenth Amendment?** It made slavery illegal in the United States. **Main Idea and Details**

✓ **REVIEW ANSWER** Possible answer: They were very convincing because they had actually experienced slavery firsthand. **Draw Conclusions**

EXTEND LANGUAGE
ESL Support

Identify the Meaning of *Right* Help students understand the correct meaning of the word *right* in this lesson.

Beginning Explain that, in this context, the word *right* means "something that everyone can do or have." Help students grasp this meaning by having them act out the right to vote, the right to assemble, and the right to speak out.

Intermediate Point out that in addition to meaning "something that everyone can do or have," the word *right* can mean "correct." Ask students to give examples of both of these uses.

Advanced Have students use a dictionary to discover even more uses of the word *right*. Have them write at least five sentences demonstrating these uses.

For additional ESL support, use Every Student Learns Guide, pp. 58–61.

PAGE 138

Votes for Women

Quick Summary Elizabeth Cady Stanton and others organized a convention in 1848 to demand rights for women.

4 Why do you think it took so long for women to gain the right to vote? Possible answer: Because it was difficult to persuade some men to share their political power with women **Point of View**

Ongoing Assessment

If... students have difficulty determining why women's suffrage was such a struggle,	**then...** ask them who had the power to change laws at that time and how those people might have felt about losing some of their power.

REVIEW ANSWER Seneca Falls, New York **Main Idea and Details**

3 Close and Assess

Summarize the Lesson

Have students review the time line. Then have them brainstorm similarities between the abolitionist movement and the women's rights movement.

LESSON 3 REVIEW

1. **Compare and Contrast** For possible answers, see the reduced pupil page.
2. Because they worked to abolish slavery
3. Possible answers: Elizabeth Cady Stanton/Lucretia Mott: organized first U.S. women's rights convention; Susan B. Anthony: a leader of women's rights movement
4. Possible answer: To have a voice in government
5. **Critical Thinking: *Make Inferences*** Possible answer: Both wanted to help people win their rights.

Link to Geography

Students may need guidance with their research.

Votes for Women

Before the 1900s, women in the United States did not have the same rights as men. For example, women did not have the right to vote. In the 1800s reformers began to fight for women's rights.

Elizabeth Cady Stanton and **Lucretia Mott** organized the first women's rights convention in the United States. A **convention** is a meeting held for a special purpose. The convention took place in 1848, in **Seneca Falls, New York.** **Susan B. Anthony** was one of the leaders of the women's rights movement.

▶ **Susan B. Anthony**

The struggle was long and hard. In 1920, seventy-two years after the Seneca Falls convention, the **Nineteenth Amendment** to the Constitution gave women the right to vote. 4

REVIEW Where was the first women's rights convention in the United States held? **Main Idea and Details**

Summarize the Lesson

- **1833** American Anti-Slavery Society was formed.
- **1848** First women's rights convention in the United States was held.
- **1865** Thirteenth Amendment abolished slavery in the United States.
- **1920** Nineteenth Amendment granted women the right to vote.

LESSON 3 REVIEW

Check Facts and Main Ideas

1. **Compare and Contrast** On a separate sheet of paper, list the similarities and differences between the abolitionist movement and the women's rights movement.

Similarities	Differences
Both were reform movements.	Abolitionists fought to end slavery.
Both fought for rights.	Women's rights movement fought for women's rights.
Frederick Douglass and Sojourner Truth worked for both.	Women didn't get the right to vote until 1920.

2. Why were the antislavery reformers called **abolitionists?**
3. Name two important women's rights reformers and state one fact about each.
4. Why did women fight for the right to vote?
5. **Critical Thinking: *Make Inferences*** Why might Frederick Douglass and Sojourner Truth work for both the abolitionist movement and the women's rights movement?

Link to Geography

Research a City Find Seneca Falls, New York, on a map. Use an encyclopedia or other resource to find out more about the history and geography of Seneca Falls. Present your findings in a report.

138

Practice and Extend

MEETING INDIVIDUAL NEEDS
Leveled Practice

Create a Graphic Organizer Help students organize information about the women's rights movement.

Easy Have students create a concept map of the women's rights movement. **Reteach**

On-Level Tell students to add one detail about each person or event in the organizer. **Extend**

Challenge Have students write a one-page report about one person or event listed in the organizer. **Enrich**

For a Lesson Summary, use Quick Study, p. 30.

Workbook, p. 32

Lesson 3: Taking a Stand

Person or Place	Importance?
Philadelphia, Pennsylvania	
William Lloyd Garrison	
Frederick Douglass and Sojourner Truth	
Elizabeth Cady Stanton and Lucretia Mott	
Seneca Falls, New York	
Susan B. Anthony	

Also on Teacher Resources CD-ROM.

Elizabeth Cady Stanton

1815–1902

Elizabeth Cady was born in Johnstown, New York. When Elizabeth was eleven years old, Eleazar, her only living brother, died. Elizabeth's father was very sad and said to her, "Oh, my daughter, I wish you were a boy!" From then on, Elizabeth tried to act as if she were her father's son. To her, acting like a man meant studying, learning as much as possible, and having courage. 1 2

Elizabeth read many books, including her father's law books. However, Elizabeth did not go to college. Most colleges did not accept 3 women then. She attended Troy Female Seminary in Troy, New York. At this school women received the same type of education that men received in college.

BIOFACT

Elizabeth tried wearing bloomers instead of long skirts.

Elizabeth fought for the rights of all people. When she was twenty-four years old, she married Henry B. Stanton. Her husband also worked for equal rights for all.

Learn from Biographies

How did Elizabeth Cady Stanton's childhood experiences help her prepare for her work as a leader of the women's rights movement?

For more information, go online to *Meet the People* at **www.sfsocialstudies.com.**

Curriculum Connection: Literature

Read Biographies Use the following selections to extend the content.

The Ballot Box Battle, by Emily Arnold McCully (Dragonfly, ISBN 0-679-89312-1, 1998) **Easy**

The Road to Seneca Falls, by Gwenyth Swain (Lerner, ISBN 1-57505-025-0, 1996) **On-Level**

Women's Rights and Nothing Less, by Lisa Frederiksen Bohannon (Morgan Reynolds, ISBN 1-883846-66-8, 2000) **Challenge**

Web Site: Technology

Students can find out more about Elizabeth Cady Stanton by going online and clicking on *Meet the People* at **www.sfsocialstudies.com.**

BIOGRAPHY

Elizabeth Cady Stanton

Objective

- Explain how Elizabeth Cady Stanton came to be involved in women's rights.

1 Introduce and Motivate

Preview To activate prior knowledge, ask students if they have ever spoken out against a rule they thought was wrong. Ask volunteers whether speaking out is a difficult thing to do and why.

2 Teach and Discuss

1 **Why might Elizabeth's father have wished she were a boy?** Possible answers: He wanted a son to become a lawyer and take over his practice; he saw that she was smart, but he also knew it would be a struggle for her to get a good education. **Point of View**

2 **How do you think many girls' attitudes today compare with Elizabeth's?** Possible answer: Many girls today agree that education and courage are important. **Compare and Contrast**

3 **What kept Elizabeth from going to college?** Most colleges at that time did not accept women. **Main Idea and Details**

3 Close and Assess

Learn from Biographies Answer

Possible answers: She knew that women needed equal rights because she had not been allowed to attend college or become a lawyer simply because she was a woman; Because she had studied law, she understood the importance of people's legal rights.

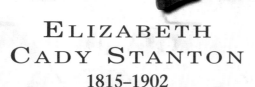

Dorling Kindersley

Winning the Right to Vote

Objective

- Use visual artifacts to acquire information.

Resource

- Workbook, p. 33

1 Introduce and Motivate

Preview To activate prior knowledge, ask students how they might feel if they were not allowed to vote for class officers or to determine a classroom activity.

2 Teach and Discuss

1 **How do you think protests and parades might have helped suffragists gain publicity?** Possible answer: Both types of events draw crowds and the attention of the public. They also might be written about in local newspapers. Draw Conclusions

2 **Do you think political buttons are a good way of attracting people to a cause? Explain.** Possible answer: Yes, because they let people know how others feel about a cause, and they encourage people to discuss the cause with others. Evaluate

DORLING KINDERSLEY EYEWITNESS BOOKS

Winning the Right to Vote

Women did not have the right to vote in the United States until 1920. For many years, people worked long and hard for women's suffrage—the right for women to vote. Here are some of the ways they tried to persuade others to join their fight.

Pro-suffrage buttons

2 3 **The Pro Faction and the Anti-Suffragists**
Women needed men to support suffage as well; without men's votes, the Nineteenth Amendment never would have passed in Congress. A nationwide political campaign produced buttons and other materials that supported the suffragists' cause. Anti-suffrage groups did the same.

MR. PRESIDENT HOW LONG MUST WOMEN WAIT FOR LIBERTY

Anti-suffrage buttons

1 **How Long Must Women Wait?**
In January 1917, the National Woman's Party began protesting in front of the White House. This angered Mrs. Wilson, the first lady, who nevertheless invited them to come in from the cold. They refused. The group was later arrested for protesting at the White House.

140

Practice and Extend

CURRICULUM CONNECTION
Writing

Create a Suffrage Time Line

- Have student pairs research the important people and events involved in the women's suffrage movement.
- Tell each student pair to create a vertical time line from the information they find.
- Encourage students to include pictures and other graphic elements in their time lines.

CURRICULUM CONNECTION
Art

Create a Protest Button

- As a class, discuss issues of unfairness facing students at your school or certain groups in the United States.
- Using the buttons on p. 141 as a guide, have students design a protest button. Explain that the button should provide a call to action or publicity for a related group.
- Have students cut out their buttons and glue them to cardboard circles. If you wish, have students attach tape or a safety pin to the back of the cardboard and allow them to wear their buttons in the classroom.
- Ask each student to explain his or her protest button.

Suffrage sash over armor

Marching On to Victory
Support for women's suffrage took many forms. This sheet music honored the suffragists of the world. The cover shows a suffrage herald who raises her trumpet to announce a new day.

4 **A Suffragist's Cape**
A suffragist wore this cape and sash in the early 1900s. Women suffagists wore this uniform to show their unity and gain publicity for their cause.

A March on Washington 1 5
Suffrage supporters held a parade in Washington, D.C., on March 3, 1913. The parade drew five to eight thousand marchers. This is the official program from that march.

141

3 **Why was the support of men necessary to pass the Nineteenth Amendment?** Only men had the right to vote in national elections. If they had not supported suffrage for women, this amendment never would have passed.
Cause and Effect

4 **What kinds of clothing do people wear today to support or promote causes?** People wear slogans on T-shirts, caps, jackets, and buttons.
Apply Information

SOCIAL STUDIES STRAND
Citizenship

5 **Were suffragist marchers displaying good citizenship when they marched in Washington D.C.? Explain.** Possible answer: Yes. Since they could not vote, they made their voices heard by marching in the nation's capital.
Draw Conclusions

3 Close and Assess

- Explain to students that organizations such as the National League of Women Voters and the National Organization for Women continue to fight for women's rights today.
- Discuss with students issues such as "equal pay for equal work" that face women in the United States today.
- Ask students how these current issues compare to the struggle for women's right to vote.

MEETING INDIVIDUAL NEEDS
Learning Styles

Celebrate Women's Achievements Help students do research to find out more about Elizabeth Cady Stanton, Lucretia Mott, and Susan B. Anthony.

Visual Learning Have students create a poster honoring one of these women.

Verbal Learning Have students role-play a meeting of these three women in which they discuss women's rights.

Linguistic Learning Have students prepare a written report discussing the background and work of one of these women and evaluating her contributions to the women's movement.

Workbook, p. 33

Writing Prompt: The Right to Vote

Also on Teacher Resources CD-ROM.

Cities Grow and Change

Objectives

- Explain why northeastern cities developed where they did.
- Identify and explain the importance of places that make tourism a major industry in northeastern cities.
- Describe how Pittsburgh's industries, like those of the other northeastern cities, have changed over the years.
- Describe the relationship between the people and the economies of northeastern cities.

Vocabulary

commerce, p. 143; **import,** p. 143; **export,** p. 143; **diverse,** p. 145

Resources

- Workbook, p. 34
- Transparency 15
- Every Student Learns Guide, pp. 62–65
- Quick Study, pp. 32–33

Quick Teaching Plan

If time is short, have students study the lesson in small groups.

- After reading the lesson independently, have each student write one question about the content of each section.
- Then have students gather into small groups and ask and answer the questions in their groups.

1 Introduce and Motivate

Preview To activate prior knowledge, ask students what they know about New York City. If any students have been there, have them share their impressions of the city. Tell students they will learn more about cities of the Northeast as they read Lesson 4.

You Are There Ask students to name other sights and activities associated with New York City.

LESSON 4

Cities Grow and Change

PREVIEW

Focus on the Main Idea
Northeastern cities and their industries have grown and changed.

PLACES
New York City, New York
Boston, Massachusetts
Philadelphia, Pennsylvania
Pittsburgh, Pennsylvania

VOCABULARY
commerce
import
export
diverse

You Are There You're excited. You're looking down from the observation deck of the Empire State Building. All of New York City is spread out before you. You spot Broadway, where you and your family saw a musical last night. In the distance you see New Jersey. Your sister finds the Brooklyn Bridge and you spot the Statue of Liberty out in the harbor.

There are more tall buildings than you've ever seen. Among the buildings, you see a big patch of green. It's Central Park—your next stop. There your family plans to see the zoo. And if there's time, you'll cross the street to see the dinosaurs at the American Museum of Natural History. There are so many different things to do in New York!

Cause and Effect As you read, note why the cities of the Northeast grew to be so important to commerce and industry.

142

Practice and Extend

READING SKILL
Cause and Effect

In the Lesson Review, students complete a graphic organizer like the one below. You may want to provide students with a copy of Transparency 15 to complete as they read the lesson.

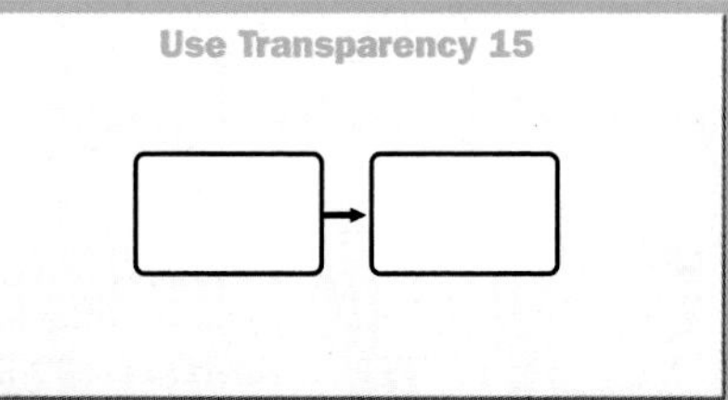

WEB SITE
Technology

- You can look up vocabulary words by clicking on *Social Studies Library* and selecting the dictionary at **www.sfsocialstudies.com.**
- Students can learn about current news by clicking on *Current Events* at **www.sfsocialstudies.com.**
- Explore other events that occurred on this day by clicking on *This Day in History* at **www.sfsocialstudies.com.**

Cities of the Northeast

The large cities of the Northeast are centers of culture, transportation, and commerce. **Commerce** is the buying and selling of goods, especially in large amounts between different places. The three largest cities—**New York City, New York; Boston, Massachusetts;** and **Philadelphia, Pennsylvania**—began as ports where ocean-going ships docked. Trade with Europe was very important to the early colonies, so cities grew up around
1 natural harbors. Providence, Rhode Island, and Baltimore, Maryland, are also important port cities.

Hulton Archive/Getty Images

▶ Workers unload merchandise from ships in New York City in the 1880s.

Merchants set up shop in port cities to sell imported goods. An **import** is an item that is brought from abroad to be offered for sale. Also, industries grew in port cities to make goods to export. An **export** is an item sent from one country to be sold in another
2 country. Stores and industries provided jobs and attracted people to the great port cities of the Northeast.

As the colonies spread westward, new cities grew beside rivers and canals. **Pittsburgh, Pennsylvania,** was founded at the point where three major rivers meet. Boats used these rivers to bring natural resources and raw materials to the industries that grew in Pittsburgh. After the Erie Canal was built, Buffalo, New York, became an important port on Lake Erie. The Erie Canal linked Lake Erie to the Hudson River and New York City. Because of good transportation and plentiful natural resources, many of the cities
of the Northeast became centers of 3
industry.

Shipping and transportation are still important to the cities of the Northeast. The region's cities have also become centers of banking, health care, and high-tech industries.

REVIEW Why did cities grow around natural harbors? Cause and Effect

143

PAGE 143

Cities of the Northeast

Quick Summary As industry developed in the colonies, cities grew up near harbors and rivers where goods could be easily transported.

1 **Which developed first, harbor cities such as New York City and Philadelphia or riverside cities such as Pittsburgh?** Harbor cities Sequence

2 **How do imports differ from exports?** Imports are brought from abroad to be offered for sale, whereas exports are sent from one country to be sold in another country. Compare and Contrast

✓ **Ongoing Assessment**

If... students have difficulty differentiating between imports and exports, **then...** have them review the meanings of the prefixes *im-* and *ex-*.

3 **Name two factors that helped cities of the Northeast develop into major centers of industry.** Transportation and plentiful natural resources
Main Idea and Details

✓ **REVIEW ANSWER** Trade with Europe was very important to the early colonies and ocean-going ships could dock in the harbors.
Cause and Effect

ESL

EXTEND LANGUAGE
ESL Support

Examine Prefixes Help students differentiate between words that use the prefixes *im-* and *ex-*.

Beginning Write *import* and *export* on the board and underline the prefixes *im-* and *ex-*. Have a volunteer read the definitions of both words from p. 143 or the glossary. Then ask students what they think each prefix means. (*im-:* in, *ex-:* out)

Intermediate Have students brainstorm other words that begin with the prefixes *im-* and *ex-*.

Advanced Have students research at least three other *im-* words and three other *ex-* words and use each in a written sentence.

For additional ESL support, use Every Student Learns Guide, pp. 62–65.

SOCIAL STUDIES STRAND
History

New York City The study of New York City may trigger a discussion about the attacks on the World Trade Center on September 11, 2001.

- Students may want to share memories and ask questions about these attacks.
- You may want to discuss how New York City is currently developing and changing.
- For suggestions about how to help children deal with fear and loss, see pages TR1–TR2 of this Teacher's Edition.

PAGE 144

City Landmarks

Quick Summary Each of the cities of the Northeast has its own personality and famous landmarks.

Map Adventure Answers

A. Southwest

B. Atlantic

C. Possible answer: The Boardwalk in Atlantic City and the Liberty Bell in Philadelphia; Because the cities are located near each other

D. Chesapeake Bay

SOCIAL STUDIES STRAND
Science • Technology

Students can take a virtual tour of the Freedom Trail at **www.thefreedomtrail.org.**

4 If you were to travel along the Freedom Trail, what historic sites might you see? The Public Gardens, Paul Revere's house, and Bunker Hill
Main Idea and Details

5 How do you think the residents of these cities feel about their local landmarks? Explain your reasoning. Possible answers: They probably feel proud of the landmarks; They have preserved the landmarks for many years and encourage tourists to visit them.
Express Ideas

✓ **REVIEW ANSWER** Possible answers: Philadelphia: Liberty Bell; Boston: Freedom Trail; Charlestown: Bunker Hill; New York City: Empire State Building
Main Idea and Details

Map Adventure

Northeastern Landmarks

A. You have ridden the swan boats in the Boston Commons. Now you want to visit the Liberty Bell in Philadelphia. In what direction would you travel?

B. If you walked on the Boardwalk in Atlantic City, New Jersey, what ocean would you see?

C. If you wanted to see two famous landmarks in one day, which might be the easiest to see in that time period? Why?

D. On what body of water is Baltimore?

City Landmarks

If you visit Philadelphia, you can see the Liberty Bell and walk through Independence Hall. The Declaration of Independence and the Constitution were both signed in this historic building.

Boston's Freedom Trail winds past the city's historic sites. It begins near the Public Gardens, with its lagoon and famous swan boats. It ends in the nearby city of Charlestown, near the top of Bunker Hill. It passes by Paul Revere's house and a number of other important historic places. 4

New York City is famous for its skyscrapers and its theater. The Empire State Building, built in 1931, is still one of the world's tallest buildings. The bright lights of Broadway attract theatergoers from all over the globe. Out in New York's harbor, the Statue of Liberty still welcomes newcomers to the United States. 5

REVIEW Name one landmark that tourists can visit in each of the cities named above.
Main Idea and Details

144

Practice and Extend

CURRICULUM CONNECTION
Writing

Write a Travel Itinerary

- Tell students to imagine that they have just won an all-expenses-paid trip to a northeastern city of their choice.
- Have them choose a city that they would like to visit and then research the different landmarks and attractions they might like to see on their trip.
- Tell students to map out a logical route between landmarks in the city. Then have them write a detailed itinerary for a two-day visit to that city. Encourage them to include visuals in their descriptions.
- Have students share their itineraries with the class.

Centers of Industry

The cities of the Northeast are centers of industry. The types of industries have changed over the years, however.

For example, Pittsburgh was once so famous for its steel mills that it was called the "Steel City." Coal and limestone, two important ingredients for making steel, were plentiful around
6 Pittsburgh. Iron ore was mined in the
7 Midwest and transported to the city. In
the 1870s, Andrew Carnegie brought a new steel-making process to Pittsburgh from England. Soon the city was supplying the world with steel for railroads, bridges, and, eventually, skyscrapers.

The steel industry brought money and jobs to Pittsburgh, but it also polluted the air. In fact, sometimes the air was so thick with smoke that the streetlights came on during the day. In the mid-1900s, the citizens of Pittsburgh passed laws to clean up the city. At the same time, the demand for steel was decreasing. The economy of Pittsburgh began to change.

Today, Pittsburgh boasts a **diverse,** or varied, group of industries. High-tech businesses such as computer software companies and factories that make robots have headquarters there. The city is also a center of health-care
and environmental research. 8

The story of Pittsburgh's changing economy is similar to that of other cities of the region. Northeastern cities are still centers of industry.

REVIEW What sequence of events led Pittsburgh to develop a diverse economy? Sequence

▶ **Present-day Pittsburgh**

PAGE 145

Centers of Industry

Quick Summary A plentiful supply of coal and limestone helped Pittsburgh became an important center for the steel industry. Today, the city boasts a diverse economy.

SOCIAL STUDIES STRAND
Science • Technology

Coal comes from fossilized plants. About 300 million years ago, tree-sized ferns, reeds, and other plants grew in the marshes that covered much of North America. Over time, these plants died and were covered with soil. Heavy pressure exerted on the plants turned them into coal.

6 **A large bed of coal lies under Pittsburgh. Based on the note above, what can you hypothesize about the landscape of the Pittsburgh area millions of years ago?** Marshes must have covered the area. **Hypothesize**

7 **What are three important ingredients for making steel?** Coal, limestone, iron ore **Main Idea and Details**

8 **What types of industries are found in Pittsburgh today?** High-tech businesses, health-care, and environmental research **Main Idea and Details**

✓ **REVIEW ANSWER** Citizens passed laws to clean up the city and the demand for steel decreased. Soon other industries moved in. **Sequence**

MEETING INDIVIDUAL NEEDS
Leveled Practice

Analyze a Viewpoint Write the following quotation on the board. Have students examine the speaker's viewpoint.

Easy Have students summarize the speaker's viewpoint in their own words. **Reteach**

On-Level Ask students to describe why they believe the speaker feels as he/she does. **Extend**

Challenge Ask students to present a speech in which they extend the viewpoint of the speaker. **Enrich**

For a Lesson Summary, use Quick Study, p. 32.

"It is in the best interest of the United States for coal to be recognized as an important energy resource for the 1990s and the twenty-first century."
From a report issued by the Illinois Clean Coal Institute

PAGE 146

Hubs of Commerce

Quick Summary The cities of the Northeast have become major centers of business that are important to the region's economy.

9 **What are the benefits of a healthy economy to an area?** It makes an area a good place to live, work, and visit. Main Idea and Details

✓ **REVIEW ANSWER** They provide many places to work, shop, and visit. Draw Conclusions

3 Close and Assess

Summarize the Lesson

Have students take turns reading the four main points. Then divide the class into teams, and see which team can add the most details to each point.

✓ **LESSON 4 REVIEW**

1. **Cause and Effect** For possible answers, see the reduced pupil page.
2. Cities grew up near harbors, rivers, and canals because they made the transportation and the import and export of trade goods possible.
3. Independence Hall: Declaration of Independence and Constitution were signed there; Freedom Trail: passes by many historic sites, such as Bunker Hill and Paul Revere's house; Empire State Building: one of the world's tallest buildings
4. Steel; High-tech businesses, health-care, and environmental research
5. **Critical Thinking: *Cause and Effect*** Possible answer: People create commerce through their businesses. A diverse group of businesses keeps a city's economy strong.

Link to Reading

Encourage students to choose different cities. If two or more students choose the same city, ask them to read different books.

▶ Crowded city streets have become a common sight.

Hubs of Commerce

Northeastern cities are hubs of commerce. Each day, millions of people go to these cities to work, to shop, and to enjoy themselves. Whether they are doing business on New York's Wall Street or assembling robots in Pittsburgh, citizens of the Northeast's cities help build the economy of the region. In turn, a healthy economy makes the cities of the Northeast good places to live and good places to visit. 9

REVIEW Why do cities attract a large number of workers? Draw Conclusions

Summarize the Lesson

- **Because trade was important, businesses and cities grew near places where transportation by water was easy.**
- **Northeastern cities have many important places to visit.**
- **Industries in Northeastern cities, such as Pittsburgh, have changed over the years.**
- **Northeastern cities are centers of commerce and good places to live or visit.**

LESSON 4 REVIEW

Check Fact and Main Idea

1. **Cause and Effect** On a separate sheet of paper, copy the diagram below and fill in the cause.

Cause	Effect
Trade was important.	Businesses and cities grew where transportation was easy.

2. How did trade and the need for good transportation affect where Northeastern cities grew? Use the words **import** and **export** in your answer.
3. Explain the importance of Philadelphia's Independence Hall, Boston's Freedom Trail, and New York City's Empire State Building.
4. What was once Pittsburgh's major industry? What are some of its important industries today?
5. **Critical Thinking: *Cause and Effect*** Describe how a city's people and its economy affect each other. Use the words **commerce** and **diverse** in your answer.

Link to Reading

Read About a City Choose one of the cities mentioned in this lesson. Then find and read a book about the city. Share what you learned about the city with classmates.

146

Practice and Extend

CURRICULUM CONNECTION
Writing

Write a Description

- Have students write a description of their own community.
- Before they begin writing, have students brainstorm a list of landmarks and other details and organize their thoughts on note cards.
- Remind students to state their overall impression as well as details that support it.
- Encourage students to work in pairs to edit and revise their work.

Workbook, p. 34

Lesson 4: Cities Grow and Change

Also on Teacher Resources CD-ROM.

Andrew Carnegie
1835–1919

Andrew Carnegie was born in Scotland. When he was twelve years old, his family moved to the United States and settled in Pittsburgh. Carnegie started working in a cotton factory and went to school at night.

Years later, after he started working for the Pennsylvania Railroad, Carnegie spent time in England. While there, he learned that the British made bridges from steel. He brought his knowledge of the British steel-making process to the United States and built steel and iron factories around Pittsburgh. He also formed the Carnegie Steel Company. 1

BIOFACT

Carnegie started out as a bobbin boy. He fed yarn into factory looms from bobbins like the ones here.

2 When Carnegie sold his company to the United States Steel Corporation, he became the richest person in the world. He then gave much of his time and money toward helping people.

Carnegie gave money to schools and to other institutions. He also paid for the building of libraries. His words are carved over the doors of the Carnegie Library in Pittsburgh: "Free to the People."

Learn from Biographies

Why do you think Andrew Carnegie built libraries?

For more information, go online to *Meet the People* at **www.sfsocialstudies.com.**

147

CURRICULUM CONNECTION
Art

Promote Libraries

- Have students create a poster encouraging people to use the public library in your community.
- Have students find out if the library has a motto. If so, tell them to incorporate it in their posters. If not, have students use the motto on the Carnegie Library: "Free to the People."
- Encourage students to donate their posters to the library.

WEB SITE
Technology

You can learn more about Andrew Carnegie by going online and clicking on *Meet the People* at **www.sfsocialstudies.com.**

Andrew Carnegie

Objective

- Explain key events that shaped Andrew Carnegie's life.

1 Introduce and Motivate

Preview To activate prior knowledge, ask students if they have ever traveled to a new home, school, or city where routine things were done differently. Ask volunteers what they learned from the experience.

2 Teach and Discuss

1 **How do you think Andrew Carnegie's childhood and adult life were similar? How were they different?** Possible answers: Similar: he worked hard as a child and as an adult; Different: as an adult, he had more money and was able to give time and money toward helping people. **Compare and Contrast**

2 **Once Carnegie sold his company, to what did he give his time and attention?** Helping people **Main Idea and Details**

3 Close and Assess

Learn from Biographies Answer

Possible answer: Carnegie valued education and reading; he wanted people to have access to the information and learning necessary to improve their lives.

Capturing History

Objective

- Describe how citizens of New York City have shown responsibility on and after September 11, 2001.

1 Introduce and Motivate

Preview To activate prior knowledge, ask students if they have ever helped out when someone was in distress. Have volunteers describe how they felt when they decided to help and how they felt after the incident was over.

2 Teach and Discuss

1 **Why do you think New York City police officers and firefighters have been called heroes?** Possible answer: They rushed into a very dangerous situation at the World Trade Center in order to help others. Express Ideas

SOCIAL STUDIES STRAND
Citizenship

2 **How did ordinary people show good citizenship after the attacks on September 11?** Possible answers: Many handed out food and water to rescue workers; they photographed or reported on the event. Summarize

3 **How do you think Ethan felt when he learned of the disaster at the World Trade Center?** Possible answers: Shocked, frightened, saddened Hypothesize

CITIZEN HEROES

Capturing History

The World Trade Center attacks on September 11, 2001, shocked and saddened the entire country. On that day, police and firefighters rushed to the burning World Trade Center towers to help people escape. Hundreds of other people volunteered their help at the scene of the disaster. 1

Police officers and firefighters came from all over New York City to the site of the Trade Towers. They were responding to their duty to help others during an emergency. On that day, they did their jobs under very difficult and dangerous conditions.

Volunteers took on responsibility for handing out food and water to the rescue workers. Other people photographed or reported on the collapse of the towers. 2 One photographer, named Ethan, was a senior at nearby Stuyvesant High School. Stuyvesant is located just four blocks north of the World Trade Center.

Ethan is a staff photographer for *The Spectator*, the Stuyvesant High School newspaper. While the towers were burning, Ethan left the school building to make a phone

▶ Ethan took photographs of the ruins of the World Trade Center, as well as people placing candles at memorials. He also photographed fellow students who came together to paint two giant murals honoring the victims and heroes of September 11, 2001.

148

Practice and Extend

CURRICULUM CONNECTION
Drama

Stage a Disaster Drill

- As a class, choose a specific type of emergency. Then divide the class into two groups, "victims" and helpers.
- Help the "victims" realistically depict injuries and other circumstances that might result from the chosen emergency.
- Have the helpers decide how best to assist the victims.
- Ask a scribe to note the helpers' actions in their proper sequence.

CURRICULUM CONNECTION
Art

Create an Emergency-Action Poster

- Have students use the notes taken during the disaster drill to create an emergency-action poster.
- As a class, edit the notes down to the three or four most important instructions.
- Then divide the class into small groups, and have each group create an illustrated poster.
- Display the posters in the classroom or school library.

call. As he walked, he saw one of the burning towers begin to fall. "I couldn't see the towers go down without doing something," he said. "I felt an obligation to take pictures of the towers, but felt guilty because of that obligation." 3

Later, Ethan talked with a family friend who is a professional photographer. Ethan told him that he felt guilty for taking pictures of a disaster in which so many people lost their lives. Ethan wrote about this conversation in a special edition of *The Spectator.* "I told him I was ashamed to be taking pictures, but he said that it was our responsibility. He told me that through our photographs, even more than our writing, the world would remember what happened on September 11, 2001." 4 5 6

Ethan could have chosen to stay home and avoid the destruction and sorrow that filled New York after the attacks. But he decided to go back with his camera to help record history.

Responsibility in Action

The people who took action on September 11, 2001, showed responsibility during a major emergency. However, it is also important to act responsibly in situations that don't involve emergencies. We all have things we should do every day. Just as the heroes of September 11 followed through on their responsibilities, it is important for us to follow through on the responsibilities we have to others. What are your responsibilities?

SOCIAL STUDIES
Background

About September 11, 2001

- The attacks of September 11, 2001, constituted the deadliest act of terrorism in the history of the United States to that date.
- In addition to the two airplanes that crashed into the twin towers of the World Trade Center, a third airliner crashed into the Pentagon near Washington, D.C., killing many civilians, military employees, and government workers.
- Citizen heroes on a fourth airliner may have overpowered terrorists and crashed the plane before it could hit a public target.
- Students may want to share thoughts and memories about the tragedies of September 11, 2001.
- For suggestions about how to help children deal with fear and loss, see pages TR1–TR2 of this Teacher's Edition.

4 **Why do you think Ethan felt obligated to take pictures of the tragedy?** Possible answer: It was his job as photographer for the school newspaper to take pictures of events that might affect students.
Draw Conclusions

5 **Why do you think Ethan's friend told him that people would remember the events of September 11 "through our photographs, even more than our writing"?** Possible answer: Sometimes pictures can convey a stronger, more memorable message than a written account of an event.
Analyze Primary Sources

6 **Why do you think it is important for people to remember the World Trade Center tragedy?** Possible answers: So they can take steps to prevent similar tragedies in the future; to remember the victims and heroes of the tragedy
Evaluate

3 Close and Assess

Responsibility in Action

Encourage students to have a discussion about a time when they have shown responsibility or times in everyday life when they could be more responsible.

CHAPTER 5 REVIEW

Resources

- Assessment Book, pp. 21–24
- Workbook, p. 35: Vocabulary Review

Chapter Summary

For possible answers, see the reduced pupil page.

Vocabulary

1. a, **2.** d, **3.** b, **4.** c, **5.** f, **6.** e

People

Possible answers:

1. Roger Williams was an English settler who bought land from the Narragansett to establish a colony. The colony was later called Rhode Island.
2. John Adams was the second President of the United States and provided strong leadership in the writing of the Declaration of Independence.
3. Benjamin Franklin was a newspaper publisher, inventor, and statesman.
4. William Lloyd Garrison was an abolitionist who published the newspaper *The Liberator*.
5. Susan B. Anthony was a leader in the women's rights movement.

CHAPTER 5 REVIEW

1620	1775	1800	1825

- **1620** Plymouth colony founded
- **1776** Declaration of Independence signed
- **1787** U.S. Constitution written
- **1820** European immigration continues
- **1833** American Anti-Slavery Society formed

Chapter Summary

Sequence

On a separate piece of paper, show the sequence of events that changed the population of the Northeast region.

The Narragansett and other Native American peoples lived in the Northeast.

↓

By the 1700s nine English colonies were established in the Northeast.

↓

From 1820 to 1860 many immigrants came to the United States from Great Britain, Ireland, and Germany.

↓

From 1860–1910, many immigrants came to the United States from Scandinavia, southern Europe, and eastern Europe.

Vocabulary

Match each word with the correct definition or description.

1. **sachem** (p. 127)
2. **confederacy** (p. 129)
3. **revolution** (p. 131)
4. **import** (p. 143)
5. **export** (p. 143)
6. **diverse** (p. 145)

a. a ruler
b. fight to overthrow a government
c. item brought from abroad to be sold
d. a union of groups, countries, or states
e. varied
f. item sent from one country to be sold in another

People

Write a sentence or two explaining why each of the following people was important.

1. **Roger Williams** (p. 128)
2. **John Adams** (p. 131)
3. **Benjamin Franklin** (p. 131)
4. **William Lloyd Garrison** (p. 137)
5. **Susan B. Anthony** (p. 138)

Practice and Extend

Assessment Options

✓ Chapter 5 Assessment

- Chapter 5 Content Test: Use Assessment Book, pp. 21–22.
- Chapter 5 Skills Test: Use Assessment Book, pp. 23–24.

Standardized Test Prep

- Chapter 5 Tests contain standardized test format.

✓ Chapter 5 Performance Assessment

- Have students create a vertical time line to review information in this chapter.
- Students can work in small groups and take turns adding information to the time line.
- Encourage students to discuss among themselves any questions that arise.
- Assess students' ability to accurately sequence the events from the chapter on the time line.

1850	1875	1900	1925

- **1848** First women's rights convention held in U.S.
- **1865** Thirteenth Amendment abolished slavery.
- **1892** Ellis Island immigration station opened.
- **1920** Nineteenth Amendment granted women the right to vote.

Facts and Main Ideas

1. In the 1600s the Narragansett people lived on land that is now what state?
2. In what year was the U.S. Constitution written?
3. **Main Idea** What caused changes in the lives of the Narragansett and other Native American peoples in the Northeast?
4. **Main Idea** What was the purpose of the American Revolution?
5. **Main Idea** Why are the Thirteenth and the Nineteenth Amendments important?
6. **Main Idea** What do the Northeast cities of New York, Boston, and Philadelphia have in common?
7. **Critical Thinking:** ***Make Inferences*** Why do you think that some cities that are not on water have grown in recent years?

Write About History

1. **Write a journal entry** telling which city in the Northeast you would like to visit.
2. **Write a letter** to a friend's older relative. Explain that you have been reading about when people immigrated to the United States. Ask about his or her ancestors.
3. **Write quiz questions** about the people, places, and events in this chapter. Exchange questions with a partner to review the chapter.

Apply Skills

Vertical Time Line

Look at the vertical time line below. Then answer the questions.

- **1815** Elizabeth Cady was born. (When she married, her name changed to Elizabeth Cady Stanton.)
- **1848** The Seneca Falls Convention was held.
- **1850** The first national convention of the women's movement was held.
- **1870** The 15th Amendment was passed, giving African American men the right to vote.
- **1878** The 19th Amendment was introduced to Congress.
- **1920** The 19th Amendment was ratified, giving women the right to vote.

1. In what year were African American men given the right to vote?
2. How many years passed between the Seneca Falls Convention and the passing of the 19th Amendment?
3. Using the dates on the time line, do you think that it is likely that Elizabeth Cady Stanton ever voted in an election?

Internet Activity

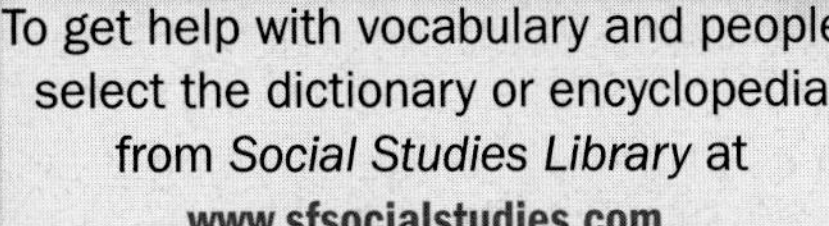

To get help with vocabulary and people, select the dictionary or encyclopedia from *Social Studies Library* at **www.sfsocialstudies.com.**

151

Hands-on Unit Project

✓ Unit 2 Performance Assessment

- See p. 156 for information about using the Unit Project as a means of performance assessment.
- A scoring guide is provided on p. 156.

WEB SITE Technology

Students can get help with vocabulary, people, and terms by going online and choosing the dictionary or encyclopedia from *Social Studies Library* at **www.sfsocialstudies.com.**

Workbook, p. 35

Vocabulary Review

Also on Teacher Resources CD-ROM.

Facts and Main Ideas

1. Rhode Island
2. 1787
3. The arrival of European settlers
4. To win the American colonies' independence from England
5. The Thirteenth Amendment made slavery illegal in the United States; the Nineteenth Amendment gave women the right to vote. They both provided rights to people who had previously been denied them.
6. All three began as ports where ocean-going ships docked.
7. Possible answer: Today, trade and transportation are not limited to areas near oceans or rivers. Trains, airplanes, and automobiles have allowed cities in other areas to thrive.

Write About History

1. You may wish to display a map of the United States for students to refer to when selecting a city.
2. Have students ask them about their experiences or their ancestors' experiences as immigrants.
3. Encourage students to formulate at least one question from each section of the text in the chapter.

Apply Skills

1. 1870
2. 72 years
3. No

Niagara

Objective

- Analyze the poem "Niagara," by Carl Sandburg.

1 Introduce and Motivate

Preview To activate prior knowledge, ask students if they have ever seen a waterfall. If they have, ask them what words they might use to describe the sound of a waterfall. List their suggestions on the board.

2 Teach and Discuss

1 **What do you think the "tumblers of the rapids" are?** Possible answer: The water rushing over rocks in the river Draw Conclusions

2 **To what does Sandburg compare the flow of the water over the rocks?** A fight Analyze Information

3 **How do you know that the water in this poem wins the fight?** Possible answers: The water foams with laughter; the water breaks free of the rocks and goes over the falls. Make Inferences

4 **What do you think Sandburg is describing with the words *growl, chutter, boom, muffle,* and *hoo hoi*?** Possible answer: The sound the water makes going over the falls and crashing into the pool at the bottom Make Inferences

UNIT 2 End with a Poem

NIAGARA

Carl Sandburg

Close your eyes and see if you can imagine Niagara Falls. Listen to the sound of the water as it rushes over the rocks.

1 The tumblers of the rapids go white, go green,
go changing over the gray, the brown, the rocks.
2 The fight of the water, the stones,
the fight makes a foam laughter
before the last look over the long slide
3 down the spread of a sheen in the straight fall.
Then the growl, the chutter,
down under the boom and the muffle,
4 the hoo hoi deep,
the hoo hoi down,
this is Niagara.

Practice and Extend

SOCIAL STUDIES
Background

About Carl Sandburg

- Carl Sandburg (1878–1967) started working when he was around eleven years old. Over time he worked as a porter in a barbershop, drove a milk truck, worked in a brickyard, and harvested wheat. Later, he served in the Spanish-American War, held political positions, and wrote for newspapers.
- Sandburg wrote biographies as well as poetry. He wrote a six-volume biography of Abraham Lincoln and a biography of photographer Edward Steichen, his brother-in-law. During his lifetime, he won the Pulitzer Prize for both poetry and biography.

Bridgeman Art Library

5 6

153

5 What changes do you think you might observe traveling down the Niagara River to the area pictured on pp. 152–153? Possible answer: Water begins flowing faster, river becomes louder, rapids appear **Hypothesize**

6 Judging from the picture on pp. 152–153, what adjectives might you use to describe Niagara Falls? Possible answers: Beautiful, dramatic, noisy, dangerous, spectacular, violent, giant **Analyze Pictures**

3 Close and Assess

Have students work in small groups to prepare a choral reading of "Niagara." Remind students that their voices should reflect the sounds of the waterfall and that their pacing affects those sounds.

CURRICULUM CONNECTION

Reading

Read Carl Sandburg's Work

- Encourage students to find and read "Smoke and Steel," a poem that celebrates steel workers.
- Alternatively, encourage students to seek out and report on one of Sandburg's books for children: *Rootabaga Stories, Rootabaga Pigeons, Rootabaga Country,* or *Potato Face*.

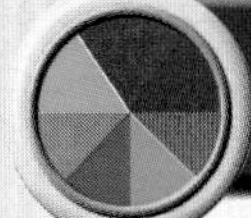

CURRICULUM CONNECTION

Music

Perform a Folk Song

- Carl Sandburg was a folk singer as well as a writer. He collected and published American folk songs in two volumes, *The American Songbag* and *New American Songbag*.
- Have students seek out one of these books, choose a song, and perform it for the class.

Resource

- Assessment Book, pp. 25–28

Main Ideas and Vocabulary

1. b, **2.** c, **3.** d, **4.** a

Test Talk

Locate Key Words in the Text
Use Main Ideas and Vocabulary, Question 2, to model the Test Talk strategy.

Make sure you understand the question.
Have students find key words. Students should finish the statement "I need to find out ...."

Find key words in the text.
Have students reread or skim the text to look for key words that will help them answer the question.

Vocabulary and People

Look for an understanding of each person and term in students' stories.

Apply Skills

- Students may wish to research online, in history books, or in other sources of information to help them add detail to their time lines.
- Encourage them to review *Use a Vertical Time Line* on pp. 134–135.

UNIT 2 Review

Test Talk

Find key words in the text.

Main Ideas and Vocabulary

TEST PREP

Read the passage below and use it to answer the questions that follow.

The Northeast region is beautiful. There are mountain ranges and miles of coastline. One of the most beautiful and famous landforms in the country is in this region—Niagara Falls. These waterfalls provide hydropower, or power produced by capturing the energy of running water.

When the English arrived in this region, the Narragansett and other Native Americans lived there. One of the English settlers, Roger Williams, was friendly with the Narragansett. In 1636 Williams went to the Grand Sachem, Canonicus, the ruler of the Narragansett, to buy land. The land became the colony of Rhode Island. Today the Narragansett have a reservation in Rhode Island.

People and places of the Northeast region played an important part in the founding of our country. The Declaration of Independence was signed in Philadelphia, Pennsylvania. John Adams, from Massachusetts, played an important role. The Constitution was also written there. Benjamin Franklin from Pennsylvania was an important representative. Also, the first two capitals of the new nation were in the Northeast—New York City and Philadelphia.

As the nation grew, many people immigrated to the United States to find a better life. Ellis Island in New York was the gateway for many of these immigrants. Some came for jobs. Others wanted to own their own land. Still others came to escape war or hard times.

The Northeast was also home to two important reform movements. One was the abolitionist movement. Abolitionists believed that slavery was wrong and should be ended. In 1865 the Thirteenth Amendment ended slavery. Another reform movement worked to give women the right to vote. In 1920 the Nineteenth Amendment gave women that right.

Port cities of the Northeast have grown into centers of commerce and industry. Rural areas produce products like cranberries, grapes, and maple syrup. Tourism is also a big business. People visit for the beauty of the Northeast as well as for its history.

1. In the passage, the word hydropower means
   A wetland
   B power produced by the energy of water
   C power produced by the energy of wind
   D an airplane that can float on water

2. According to the passage, one of the early capitals of the nation was in
   A Rhode Island
   B Massachusetts
   C Pennsylvania
   D Washington, D.C.

3. According to the passage, why did many immigrants come to the Northeast?
   A They were looking for adventure.
   B Everyone they knew was immigrating.
   C They wanted to come to a land where everyone was happy.
   D They were seeking a better life.

4. According to the passage, slavery was ended by
   A the Thirteenth Amendment
   B the Nineteenth Amendment
   C the Declaration of Independence
   D the U.S. Constitution

154

Practice and Extend

Assessment Options

✓Unit 2 Assessment

- Unit 2 Content Test: Use Assessment Book, pp. 25–26.
- Unit 2 Skills Test: Use Assessment Book, pp. 27–28.

Standardized Test Prep

- Unit 2 Tests contain standardized test format.

✓Unit 2 Performance Assessment

- See p. 156 for information about using the Unit Project as a means of performance assessment.
- A scoring guide for the Unit Project is provided in the teacher's notes on p. 156.

Test Talk

- Test Talk Practice Book

WEB SITE Technology

For more information, you can select the dictionary or encyclopedia from *Social Studies Library* at **www.sfsocialstudies.com.**

Vocabulary and People

Choose six of the vocabulary words and people. Then write a story that uses all six.

1. **slave** (p. 137)
2. **cooperation** (p. 127)
3. **powwow** (p. 128)
4. **convention** (p. 138)
5. **abolitionist** (p. 137)
6. **reservation** (p. 128)
7. **Frederick Douglass** (p. 137)
8. **Canonicus** (p. 128)
9. **William Lloyd Garrison** (p. 137)
10. **Elizabeth Cady Stanton** (p. 138)
11. **Sojourner Truth** (p. 137)

Apply Skills

Create a Poster Make a poster with a vertical time line. List several important events that you read about in this unit.

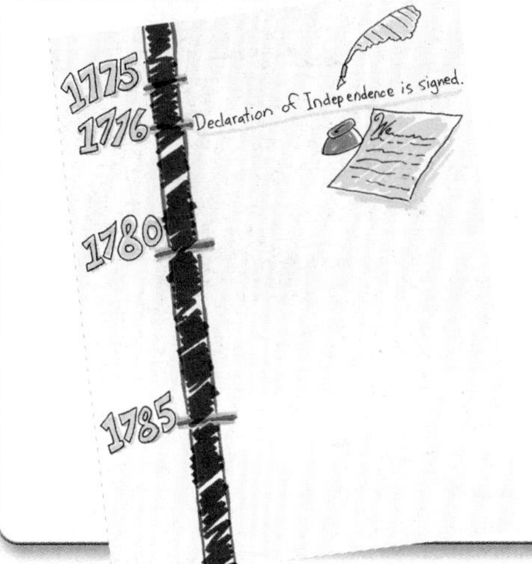

Write and Share

Write and Publish a Newspaper Many newsworthy events have taken place in the Northeast region over the history of the nation. Choose an event or a person and write a newspaper article telling about the occasion. Remember to include the important parts of a news story—who, what, where, when, why, and how. Write a catchy headline. Work with classmates to combine your news articles into a newspaper. Share the historical "news" with other classrooms in your school.

Read on Your Own

Look for books like these in the library.

155

Revisit the Unit Question

✓ Portfolio Assessment

- Have students look at the lists they compiled throughout Unit 2 of new ideas and groups of people that have been welcomed in the Northeast.
- Ask students to put a check mark beside each item they brainstormed before reading the unit.
- Have them highlight all the additional entries they added to their list while reading the unit.
- Have students write a summary stating whether they think these ideas and people still are closely tied to the Northeast and why.
- Have students add their lists and summaries to their Social Studies Portfolio.

Write and Share

- Encourage students to include pictures, charts, and other graphics with their articles.
- You may wish to have volunteers provide letters to the editor or political cartoons in lieu of articles to add variety.
- Encourage students to use desktop-publishing software to give their published newspaper a professional look.
- Use the following scoring guide.

✓ Assessment Scoring Guide

Write and Publish a Newspaper	
6	Article is clearly related to topic; has a compelling headline; answers the questions who, what, where, when, why, and how; and uses correct spelling and grammar.
5	Article is clearly related to topic, has a catchy headline, and answers all six vital questions accurately.
4	Article has a catchy headline, and is related to topic, but does not answer all six vital questions.
3	Article has an accurate headline and is generally related to topic, but does not answer all six vital questions.
2	Article has a headline, but is not clearly related to topic and does not answer all six vital questions.
1	Article does not have a suitable headline, is unrelated to topic, and answers few or none of the six vital questions.

If you require a 4-point rubric, adjust accordingly.

Read on Your Own

Have students prepare oral reports using the following books.

If Your Name Was Changed at Ellis Island, by Ellen Levine (Scholastic Trade, ISBN 0-590-43829-8, 1994) **Easy**

Eagle Song, by Joseph Bruchac (Puffin, ISBN 0-14-130169-4, 1999) **On-Level**

You Want Women to Vote, Lizzie Stanton? by Jean Fritz (PaperStar, ISBN 0-698-11764-6, 1999) **Challenge**

On the Spot

Objective

- Understand the experiences of Native Americans or early settlers in America.

Resource

- Workbook, p. 36

Materials

paper, pencils, shoeboxes or small cardboard boxes, construction paper, glue, twigs, leaves, grass, craft sticks, scissors, crayons, coloring materials

Follow This Procedure

- Divide the class into groups of four or five. Tell students they will be describing and modeling the experiences of Native Americans or settlers in America. Students should complete the descriptions and models as if they were preparing a documentary film.
- Help students choose different groups of Native Americans or settlers.
- Instruct students to write sentences about the Native Americans' or settlers' earliest observations and experiences.
- Students will construct a diorama or classroom model to show the settlement of their chosen group. They should include buildings and the physical setting of landforms, vegetation, and weather, if possible.
- Use the following scoring guide.

✓ Assessment Scoring Guide

On the Spot	
6	Uses elaborate details, accurate and clear information, and precise word choices
5	Uses accurate details and information and clear word choices
4	Uses some details, accurate information, and clear word choices
3	Uses some details, some inaccurate information, and mostly clear word choices
2	Uses few details, some inaccurate information, and vague word choices
1	Uses few or no details, inaccurate information, and incorrect word choices

If you require a 4-point rubric, adjust accordingly.

UNIT 2 Project

On the Spot

Life was often challenging for America's early settlers, as well as for Native American groups who had lived in the Northeast for hundreds of years. Make a documentary about their experiences.

1. **Form** a group and choose Native Americans or early European settlers who settled in the Northeast.
2. **Write** sentences about their experiences and observations. Include a variety of topics.
3. **Make** a diorama or model to show the environment and settlements. Include where they lived, other buildings, and the physical setting.
4. **Present** your documentary. Show the diorama or model to the class.

Internet Activity

Explore the Northeast on the Internet. Go to **www.sfsocialstudies.com/activities** and select your grade and unit.

156

Practice and Extend

Hands-on Unit Project

✓ Performance Assessment

- The Unit Project can also be used as a performance assessment activity.
- Use the scoring guide to assess each group's work.

WEB SITE

Technology

Students can launch the Internet Activity by clicking on *Grade 4, Unit 2* at **www.sfsocialstudies.com/activities.**

Workbook, p. 36

Unit 2 Project On the Spot

Directions: In a group, make a documentary about the experiences of early settlers or Native American groups in the Northeast.

1. We chose to make our documentary about the experiences of (✓ one):
   ___Native Americans ___European settlers
2. We included these topics:
   ___geographic location ___weather ___landforms ___homes ___activities
   ___foods available ___other groups of people ___other topics: ________
3. These are facts about the topics:
4. This is a description of our diorama or model:

✓ Checklist for Students

___ We chose a group to study.
___ We chose topics and wrote facts for the documentary.
___ We made a diorama or model.
___ We presented our documentary to the class.

Notes for Home: Your child learned about the experiences of early European settlers and Native Americans.
Home Activity: With your child, research the early settlers and Native Americans of your community or region. Discuss interesting facts about their experiences and their reasons for settling in the area

Also on Teacher Resources CD-ROM.

★ Unit 3 ★

Vocabulary Routines

The following examples of reading and vocabulary development strategies can be used to instruct students about unit vocabulary.

BEFORE READING

Individual Word Study

Student-Friendly Definitions Building student-friendly definitions helps students fully comprehend the meanings of new words in context, both for the lesson and for other reading and real-life situations. Guiding students to explain new words using their own terms makes vocabulary more accessible to them. First, have students characterize the new word by asking why we use the word and what we think of when we hear the word. If a word is unfamiliar, read a definition of the word or read the lesson sentence in which the word is highlighted in the text. Next, help students put what they know about the vocabulary word into their own words.

Let's look at the word **consensus.** *When do we use this word?* (We use it when we have many people and need to make a decision.) *What do you think of when you hear the word* **consensus?** *Do you think about people agreeing or disagreeing?* (agreeing) *So what is a good definition of* **consensus?** (A consensus is when a group of people agrees on something. The group comes to a consensus.)

DURING READING

Context Clues

Idea Completions Students may use a word in a sentence without actually knowing the meaning of the word. The sentence "Fossil fuels are important" does not fully demonstrate that a student knows what fossil fuels are. You can use the idea completions routine to provide students with sentence stems to build context for vocabulary words.

We've been reading about Earth and its resources. Let's talk about fossil fuel. Listen closely so you can finish the sentence. Coal is an important fossil fuel. Knowing what a fossil fuel is, I would expect to find coal... (in the earth).

AFTER READING

Related Word Study

Word Association This routine helps students make a connection between a familiar word or phrase and a new vocabulary word. List the vocabulary words for one or more lessons on the board. Then present a familiar word and ask students which vocabulary word goes best with the familiar word and why. Ask students to explain the association between each set of words.

Write *secede, segregate,* and *civil rights* on the board. *Which word on the board goes best with* **leaving?** *Why?* (*secede,* because states that seceded left the United States to form their own group) *Which word on the board goes best with* **apart?** *Why?* (*segregate,* because segregation keeps groups of people apart) *Which word on the board goes best with* **voting?** (*civil rights,* because one of the civil rights people in the United States have is the right to vote)

secede — apart
segregate
civil rights

08164

The Southeast

UNIT 3

Unit Planning Guide

Unit 3 • The Southeast

Begin with a Primary Source pp. 158–159

Welcome to the Southeast pp. 160–161

Reading Social Studies, Main Idea and Details pp. 162–163

Chapter Titles	Pacing	Main Ideas
Chapter 6 **The Land of the Southeast** pp. 164–183 ✓ **Chapter 6 Review** pp. 184–185	6 days	• The main areas of the Southeast region include the coastal plains, the Piedmont, and Appalachia. • The mild climates of the coastal areas of the Southeast bring many tourists, but the area has some natural hazards. • The Southeast is rich in different resources. These resources are used in different industries throughout the region.
Chapter 7 **People and Events That Shaped the Southeast** pp. 186–215 ✓ **Chapter 7 Review** pp. 216–217	12 days	• The Cherokee have contributed greatly to the history of the Southeast. • Exploration, settlements, agriculture, and slavery all shaped the early growth of the Southeast region. • The Civil War had a major impact on the history of the Southeast. • Cities in the Southeast are growing and changing.

End with a Song pp. 218–219

✓ **Unit 3 Review** pp. 220–221

✓ **Unit 3 Project** p. 222

✓ = **Assessment Options**

Coal is an important natural resource found in the Southeast.

Resources	Meeting Individual Needs
• Workbook, pp. 38–42 • Every Student Learns Guide, pp. 66–77 • Transparencies 1, 40–44 • Quick Study, pp. 34–39 • Workbook, p. 43 ✓Chapter 6 Content Test, Assessment Book, pp. 29–30 ✓Chapter 6 Skills Test, Assessment Book, pp. 31–32	• Leveled Practice, TE pp. 167, 174, 181 • ESL Support, TE pp. 168, 173, 179 • Learning Styles, TE p. 175 ✓Chapter 6 Performance Assessment, TE p. 184
• Workbook, pp. 44–49 • Every Student Learns Guide, pp. 78–93 • Transparencies 1, 45 • Quick Study, pp. 40–47 • Workbook, p. 50 ✓Chapter 7 Content Test, Assessment Book, pp. 33–34 ✓Chapter 7 Skills Test, Assessment Book, pp. 35–36	• ESL Support, TE pp. 189, 198, 205, 211 • Leveled Practice, TE pp. 191, 195, 204, 208, 212 • Learning Styles, TE p. 214 ✓Chapter 7 Performance Assessment, TE p. 216

This newspaper, published in 1828, was written in both Cherokee and English. The Cherokee did not develop a written language until the early 1800s.

Providing More Depth

Additional Resources

- Trade Books
- Family Activities
- Vocabulary Workbook and Cards
- Social Studies Plus! pp. 54–73
- Daily Activity Bank
- Read Alouds and Primary Sources pp. 35–51
- Big Book Atlas
- Student Atlas
- Outline Maps
- Desk Maps

Technology

- AudioText
- Video Field Trips: Exploring the Southeast
- Songs and Music
- Digital Learning CD-ROM Powered by KnowledgeBox (Video clips and activities)
- MindPoint® Quiz Show CD-ROM
- ExamView® Test Bank CD-ROM
- Colonial Williamsburg Primary Sources CD-ROM
- Teacher Resources CD-ROM
- Map Resources CD-ROM
- SF SuccessNet: iText (Pupil Edition online), iTE (Teacher's Edition online), Online Planner
- **www.sfsocialstudies.com** (Biographies, news, references, maps, and activities)

To establish guidelines for your students' safe and responsible use of the Internet, use the Scott Foresman Internet Guide.

Additional Internet Links

To find out more about:

- Key West, Florida, visit **www.keywestchamber.org**
- Dr. Martin Luther King, Jr., visit **www.thekingcenter.org**
- Rosa Parks, visit **www.greatwomen.org**

Unit 3 Objectives

Beginning of Unit 3

- Use primary sources to acquire information. (p. 158)
- Identify characteristics of the Southeast region of the United States. (p. 160)
- Analyze information by identifying the main idea and details. (p. 162)

Chapter 6

Lesson 1 Coastal Plains to the Mountains pp. 166–169

- Identify and describe major landforms in the Southeast.
- Explain how barrier islands are formed.
- Compare and contrast landform elevations in the Southeast.
- Explain how to use an elevation map. (p. 170)
- Use an elevation map to compare and contrast landform elevations in the Southeast. (p. 170)

Lesson 2 Sunlight and Storms pp. 172–175

- Describe the climate of the Southeast.
- Examine hurricanes in the Southeast.
- Explain the function of lighthouses.
- Explain how hurricanes form. (p. 176)
- Describe the effects of hurricanes. (p. 176)

Lesson 3 Wildlife and Resources pp. 178–183

- Describe the importance of protecting endangered species.
- Identify ways in which resources of the Southeast are used.
- Identify a renewable and a nonrenewable resource found in the Southeast.
- Explain why coal is an important resource in the Southeast.

Chapter 7

Lesson 1 The Cherokee pp. 188–192

- Describe how the Cherokee lived before Europeans came to North America.
- Evaluate how Cherokee culture changed after Europeans came to the Southeast.
- Identify the Trail of Tears and describe its impact on the Cherokee.
- Explain how the North Carolina Cherokee support themselves and keep their culture alive today.
- Describe Sequoyah's contributions in preserving Cherokee culture. (p. 193)

Lesson 2 Early History of the Southeast pp. 194–199

- Identify important explorers of the Southeast and the areas they explored.
- Locate the earliest European settlements in the Southeast.
- Identify early leaders from the Southeast and describe their contributions to the United States.
- Evaluate the impact of agriculture in the Southeast.
- Identify the contributions of Sarah and Angelina Grimké to the antislavery movement. (p. 200)

Lesson 3 The Nation Divided pp. 202–206

- Identify two causes of the Civil War.
- Explain the effects of the Civil War on the Southeast.
- Describe how the Southeast changed during Reconstruction.
- Analyze the development of the civil rights movement.
- Describe the contributions of Rosa Parks to the civil rights movement. (p. 207)
- Distinguish between fact and opinion. (p. 208)

Lesson 4 The Glittering Cities pp. 210–213

- Describe the first gold rush in the United States.
- Explain why Atlanta is an important transportation center.
- Identify the causes of growth in Southeastern cities.
- Compare and contrast a cultural celebration held in both Charleston, South Carolina, and Spoleto, Italy. (p. 214)

End of Unit 3

- Identify significant examples of music from the Southeast. (p. 218)
- Report a significant event in the history of your state. (p. 222)

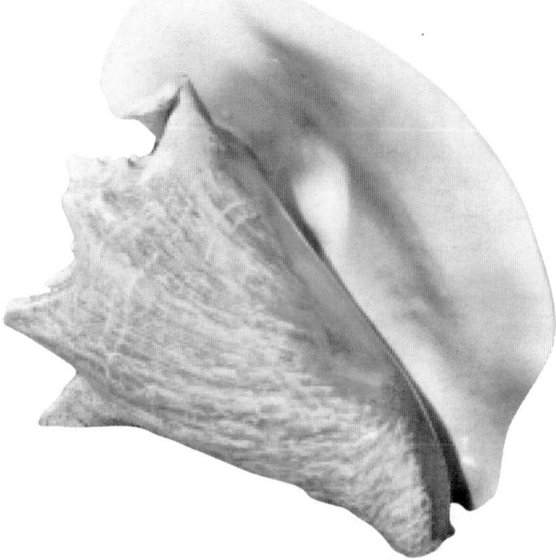

Each year, thousands of tourists flock to the beaches of the Southeast in search of beautiful seashells.

Assessment Options

✓ Formal Assessment

- **Lesson Reviews,** PE/TE pp. 169, 175, 183, 192, 199, 206, 213
- **Chapter Reviews,** PE/TE pp. 184–185, 216–217
- **Chapter Tests,** Assessment Book pp. 29–36
- **Unit Review,** PE/TE pp. 220–221
- **Unit Tests,** Assessment Book pp. 37–40
- **ExamView® Test Bank CD-ROM**

✓ Informal Assessment

- **Teacher's Edition Questions,** throughout Lessons and Features
- **Section Reviews,** PE/TE pp. 167, 169, 173, 175, 179–180, 182–183, 189–192, 195–199, 203–206, 211–213
- **Close and Assess,** TE pp. 163, 169, 171, 175, 177, 183, 192–193, 199, 201, 206–207, 209, 213, 215, 219

Ongoing Assessment

Ongoing Assessment is found throughout the Teacher's Edition lessons using an **If...then** model.

If = students' observable behavior,	**then =** reteaching and enrichment suggestions

✓ Portfolio Assessment

- **Portfolio Assessment,** TE pp. 157, 158, 221
- **Leveled Practice,** TE pp. 167, 174, 181, 191, 195, 204, 208, 212
- **Workbook,** pp. 37–51
- **Chapter Reviews: Write About It,** PE/TE pp. 185, 217
- **Unit Review: Apply Skills,** PE/TE p. 221
- **Curriculum Connection: Writing,** PE/TE pp. 192, 206, 213; TE pp. 169, 193, 197, 209

✓ Performance Assessment

- **Hands-on Unit Project** (Unit 3 Performance Assessment), TE pp. 157, 185, 217, 220, 222
- **Internet Activity,** PE/TE p. 222
- **Chapter 6 Performance Assessment,** TE p. 184
- **Chapter 7 Performance Assessment,** TE p. 216
- **Unit Review: Write and Share,** PE/TE p. 221
- **Scoring Guides,** TE pp. 221–222

Test Talk

Test-Taking Strategies

Understand the Question

- **Locate Key Words in the Question,** TE pp. 157, 179
- **Locate Key Words in the Text,** TE p. 204

Understand the Answer

- **Choose the Right Answer,** PE/TE p. 220
- **Use Information from the Text,** TE p. 191
- **Use Information from Graphics,** TE p. 171
- **Write Your Answer to Score High,** TE p. 169

For additional practice, use the Test Talk Practice Book.

Featured Strategy

Choose the Right Answer

Students will:

- Narrow the answer choices and rule out choices they know are wrong.
- Choose the best answer.

PE/TE p. 220

Curriculum Connections

Integrating Your Day

The lessons, skills, and features of Unit 3 provide many opportunities to make connections between social studies and other areas of the elementary curriculum.

Social Studies

READING

Reading Skill—Main Idea and Details, PE/TE pp. 162–163, 166, 172, 178, 188, 194, 202, 210

Lesson Review—Main Idea and Details, PE/TE pp. 169, 175, 183, 192, 199, 206, 213

Link to Reading, PE/TE p. 199

WRITING

Describe the Appalachian Trail, TE p. 169

Link to Writing, PE/TE pp. 192, 206, 213

Write in Cherokee, TE p. 193

Write About Monticello, TE p. 197

Write an Advertisement, TE p. 209

MATH

Calculate Differences in Elevation, TE p. 171

Calculate Percentages, TE p. 196

LITERATURE

Read About the Region, TE p. 160

Read About Coal Mining, TE p. 183

Read Biographies, TE pp. 197, 207

Read About Civil Rights, TE p. 206

SCIENCE

Create a Chart of Bayou Life, TE p. 159

Link to Science, PE/TE pp. 169, 175

Learn More About Hurricanes, TE p. 176

Explore the Forest, TE p. 182

Comparing Temperatures, TE p. 215

MUSIC / DRAMA

Perform Monologues, TE p. 176

Sell Southeastern Produce, TE p. 180

Link to Music, PE/TE p. 183

Present a Skit, TE p. 199

Write a Song, TE p. 213

Write a Sea Shanty, TE p. 219

ART

Create an Elevation Map, TE p. 170

Design a Stamp, TE p. 192

Make a Political Poster, TE p. 201

Look for this symbol throughout the Teacher's Edition to find **Curriculum Connections.**

Professional Development

Making Social Studies Meaningful

by M. Gail Hickey, Ed.D.
Indiana University-Purdue University at Fort Wayne

The study of people, places, and human-environment interactions assists students as they create their spatial views and geographic perspectives of the world beyond their personal locations. Students need knowledge, skills, and understanding to answer questions such as *Where are things located?* and *Why are they located where they are?*

- *The text on p. 191 of the Pupil Edition discusses the relocation of the Cherokee to Indian Territory (Oklahoma) and to what eventually became the Qualla Boundary in North Carolina. Discuss with students why some of the Cherokee refused to move west to Indian Territory.*
- Social studies learning and literacy skills are enhanced, and students experience more personal connections, when writing and speaking activities are woven into the social studies curriculum. Stories and storytelling are linked to the development of literacy. Children learn sequencing and structure by listening to and telling stories.
- *The Link to Writing on p. 192 of the Pupil Edition asks students to write a poem from the viewpoint of a member of a Cherokee village hundreds of years ago. This requires students to sequence their ideas as they describe the physical, emotional, and historical aspects of their lives.*
- Quality children's literature can supplement and enrich social studies textbook content. Many topics that capture students' interest cannot be covered in depth by textbooks. Children's literature offers teachers a way to broaden coverage of selected topics.
- *On p. 207 of the Teacher's Edition, a list of children's books on Rosa Parks and the civil rights movement provides additional resources to students who would like to learn more about this historic struggle than is provided on pp. 206–207 of the Pupil Edition.*

ESL Support

by Jim Cummins, Ph.D.
University of Toronto

In Unit 3, you can use the following fundamental strategy to help ESL students access social studies content.

Access Content

Good teaching strategies can help reduce the cognitive and linguistic load of academic text. Similarly, relating the content and themes of the social studies text to what students already know can minimize the cultural loading of the text and lower cultural barriers.

We should constantly search for ways to link the academic content with what students already know or what is familiar to them from their family or cultural experiences. In addition to making cultural connections, use visuals and dramatize. Teachers and students can draw pictures, maps, and diagrams to clarify concepts and meaning. Students' attention can also be drawn to the importance of context and picture clues in the texts they are reading.

The following examples in the Teacher's Edition will help you access content for your ESL students:

- ***Examine Word Meanings** on p. 168 uses actual samples of different types of soil to introduce vocabulary and then has students use the words in sentences related to the geography of the Southeast.*
- ***Explore Climate** on p. 173 uses oral and visual descriptions to help students relate word meanings to the concept of climate.*
- ***Identify Species** on p. 179 has students relate pictures of animals to new vocabulary as they practice pronunciation and elaboration.*

Read Aloud

Hurricane

A hurricane is brewing
In the waters to the east.
The raging winds and waters
Threaten man and beast.
The warm tropical temperatures
Cooled by an ocean breeze
Have turned into a hurricane
Uprooting homes and trees.
Everything is flying,
And water floods the shore.
Whatever has happened to
The climate of before?

Read Alouds and Primary Sources

- *Read Alouds and Primary Sources* contains additional selections to be used with Unit 3.

Bibliography

Mathew Brady: Civil War Photographer, by Elizabeth Van Steenwyk (Franklin Watts, ISBN 0-531-20264-X, 1997) **Easy**

Thomas Jefferson: A Picture Book Biography, by James Cross Giblin (Scholastic Trade, ISBN 0-590-44838-2, 1994) **Easy**

The Trail of Tears, by Joseph Bruchac (Random House, ISBN 0-679-89052-1, 1999) **Easy**

The Boys' War: Confederate and Union Soldiers Talk About the Civil War, by Jim Murphy (Clarion Books, ISBN 0-395-66412-8, 1993) **On-Level** ***Golden Kite Award***

The Day Martin Luther King, Jr., Was Shot: A Photo History of the Civil Rights Movement, by Jim Haskins (Scholastic, Inc., ISBN 0-590-43661-9, 1992) **On-Level**

Tom Jefferson: Third President of the United States, by Helen Albee Monsell (Aladdin Paperbacks, ISBN 0-689-71347-9, 1989) **On-Level**

Dancing Drum: A Cherokee Legend, by Terri Cohlene (Troll Associates, ISBN 0-8167-2362-1, 1990) **Challenge**

Growing Up in a Holler in the Mountains: An Appalachian Childhood, by Karen Gravelle (Franklin Watts, ISBN 0-531-11452-X, 1997) **Challenge**

Now Is Your Time! The African-American Struggle for Freedom, by Walter Dean Myers (HarperCollins Juvenile Books, ISBN 0-06-446120-3, 1992) **Challenge** ***ALA Notable Book, Coretta Scott King Award***

The Education of Little Tree, by Forrest Carter, (University of New Mexico Press, ISBN 0-8263-2809-1, 2001) **Teacher reference** ***American Bestsellers Book of the Year***

Why We Can't Wait, by Martin Luther King, Jr. (Signet Classic, ISBN 0-451-52753-4, 2000) **Teacher reference**

***Discovery Channel School* Videos**

Native Americans This video shows how Native American groups were affected by the arrival of European settlers. (Item #745299, 52 minutes)

- To order *Discovery Channel School* videos, please call the following toll-free number: 1-888-892-3484.
- Free online lesson plans are available at **DiscoverySchool.com.**

Look for this symbol throughout the Teacher's Edition to find **Award-Winning Selections.** Additional book references are found throughout this unit.

The Southeast

UNIT 3

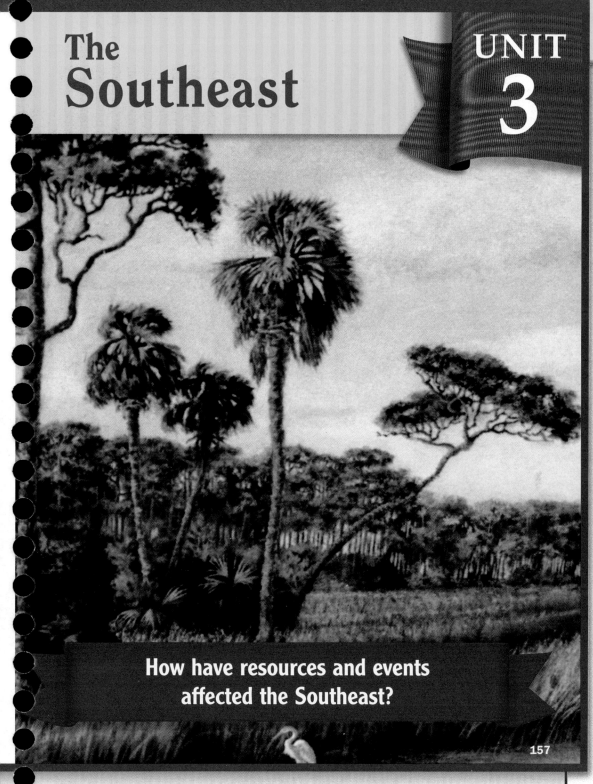

How have resources and events affected the Southeast?

157

Practice and Extend

Hands-on Unit Project

✓ **Unit 3 Performance Assessment**

- The Unit Project, *This Just In,* found on p. 222, is an ongoing performance assessment project to enrich students' learning throughout the unit.
- This project, which has students holding a historical news conference, may be started now or at any time during this unit of study.
- A performance assessment scoring guide is located on p. 222.

The Southeast

Unit Overview

In early times, the land, climate, and resources of the Southeast appealed to the Cherokee and, later, to early settlers. These features continue to draw people to the region today. Fighting over this area during the Civil War had an enormous impact on the Southeast.

Unit Outline

Chapter 6 *The Land of the Southeast* pp. 164–185

Chapter 7 *People and Events That Shaped the Southeast* pp. 186–217

Unit Question

Test Talk

Locate Key Words in the Question

- Have students read the question under the picture on p. 157. Have students ask themselves, "Who or what is this question about?" Tell students that the words that tell *who* or *what* the question is about are key words.
- To activate prior knowledge, have students identify the resources suggested by the picture. (Trees, water, land, sunshine, and so on)
- Have students brainstorm a list of preliminary answers to the question, even if the answers are only guesses. Write their ideas on chart paper.

✓ **Portfolio Assessment** Keep this list to review with students at the end of the unit on p. 221.

Begin with a Primary Source

Objective

- Use primary sources to acquire information.

Resource

- Poster 5

Interpret a Primary Source

- Tell students that this primary source is a quotation from American poet Henry Wadsworth Longfellow.
- Tell students that Longfellow's *Evangeline* is based on the true story of French Acadians who were expelled by the British in 1755 from what is now Nova Scotia. In the poem, the Acadian orphan Evangeline is separated from her love, Gabriel. After searching for some time, she eventually finds him on his deathbed.
- In addition to his picturesque descriptions of the Southeast, Longfellow vividly describes the mistreatment of the Acadian people by the British.

1 **Based on the quote, how do you think Longfellow felt about the Southeast?** Possible answer: He felt it was a beautiful land with many natural resources. Analyze Primary Sources

✓**Portfolio Assessment** Remind students of the list of ideas they began on p. 157. As students read the unit, have them revise the class list. Review the list at the end of the unit on p. 221.

UNIT 3

Begin with a Primary Source

158

Practice and Extend

SOCIAL STUDIES **Background**

About the Primary Source

- *Evangeline* was first published in 1847 while Longfellow was working as a professor at Harvard University.
- Longfellow was among the first American authors to write about the American people, environment, and history. Until his time, works of literature, art, and music were not taken seriously unless they came from Europe.
- Today the state of Louisiana maintains the Longfellow-Evangeline Memorial State Commemorative Area along the Bayou Teche. There, visitors can learn about the Acadian people and the legend of Evangeline and Gabriel.

"Beautiful is the land, with its prairies and forests of fruit-trees;
Under the feet a garden of flowers . . ." 1

—Henry Wadsworth Longfellow, describing the banks of a Southeastern bayou in his poem *Evangeline*.

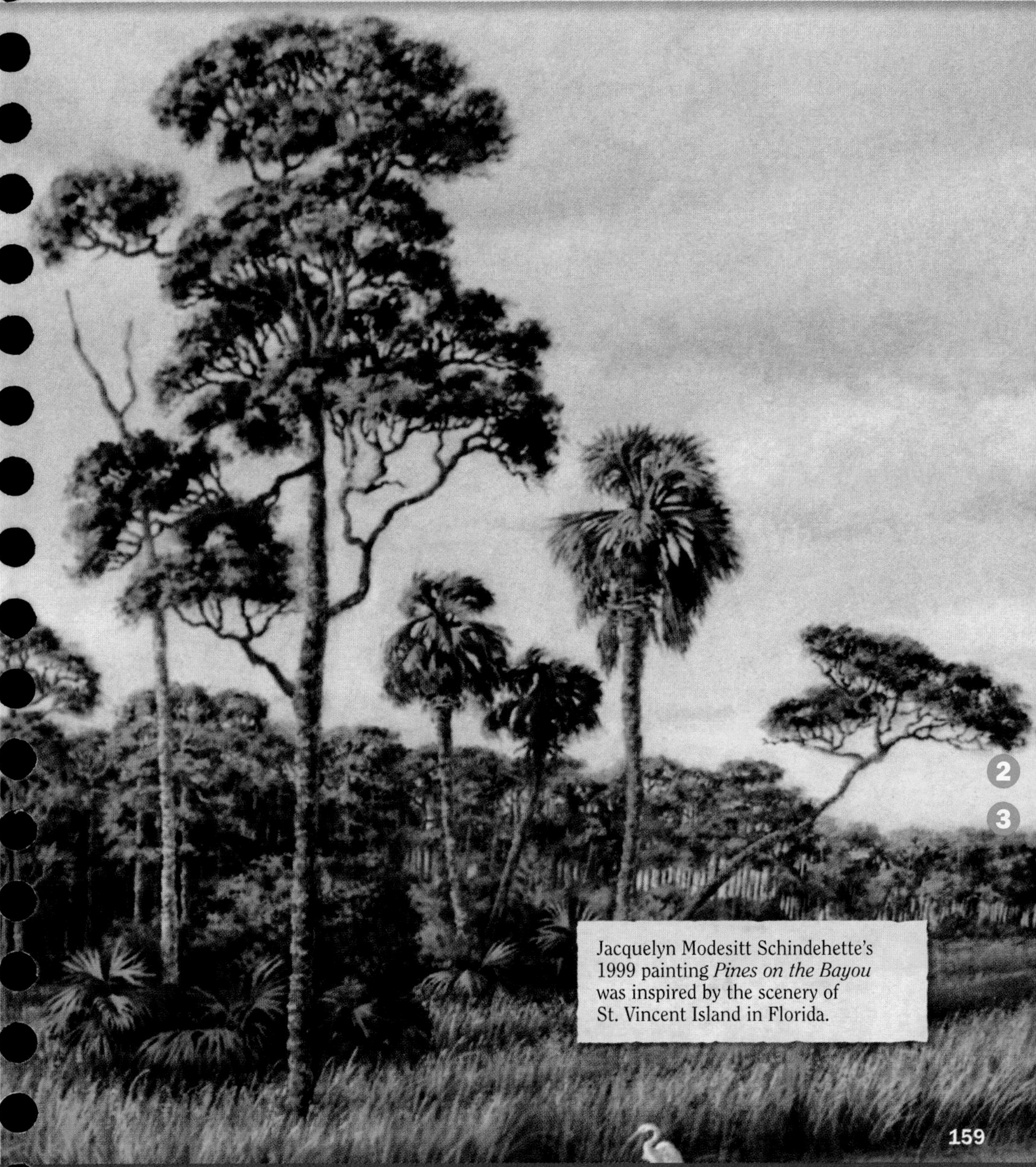

Jacquelyn Modesitt Schindehette's 1999 painting *Pines on the Bayou* was inspired by the scenery of St. Vincent Island in Florida.

159

Interpret Fine Art

- Explain that St. Vincent Island, the landscape that inspired this painting, lies off the coast of the Florida Panhandle, near the city of Apalachicola.
- Point out that St. Vincent Island not only is a place of unusual beauty, but it also is a national wildlife refuge and an important breeding ground for loggerhead turtles.

Meet the Artist

- Tell students that Floridian Jacquelyn Modesitt Schindehette has been recognized throughout her home state for depicting the unique beauty of Florida's backcountry.
- Explain that Schindehette's paintings strive to show the beauty of Florida beyond its well-known beaches.
- Among the regional characteristics featured in Schindehette's paintings are wild egrets, cranes, and ibis as well as giant oaks, pines, and cypress.

2 **Judging from this painting, what do you think the word *bayou* means?** Possible answer: A type of marshy stream found in the southeast
Analyze Pictures

3 **How is the landscape in this painting similar to and different from that of a Florida beach?** Possible answers: Similar: both feature water and a coastline; Different: a beach is sandy with fewer trees and less vegetation
Compare and Contrast

CURRICULUM CONNECTION
Science

Create a Chart of Bayou Life

- Tell students that the bayous and swamps of the Southeast contain some of the most unique plant and animal life in the United States.
- Have students work with a partner to research at least four types of plant life or animal life found in these environments. Suggest that they use the Internet or classroom and library resources for their research.
- Have students combine their data in a class chart of bayou life. Display the chart on a classroom bulletin board.

Welcome to the Southeast

Objective

- Identify characteristics of the Southeast region of the United States.

Resource

- Poster 6

Research the Region

Each of the resources and places featured on these pages is an important part of the Southeast region. Have students do research to find out the answers to the following questions.

- ***Magnolia grandiflora* is the most widely recognized type of magnolia. What are the common names of some other magnolias of the Southeast?** Possible answers: Sweet bay, umbrella tree, cucumber tree
- **What is the most serious threat to manatees in Florida waterways?** Boat propellers
- **The Southeastern state of Georgia is known for its important agriculture. What famous Georgia farmer became president of the United States?** Jimmy Carter
- **Novaculite, a type of rock found in Arkansas, is used to make whetstones of very high quality. What is a whetstone?** A stone used for sharpening tools
- **When was Florida acquired by the United States? When did it become a state?** 1821; 1845

Students may wish to write their own questions about resources or places in this region for the rest of the class to answer.

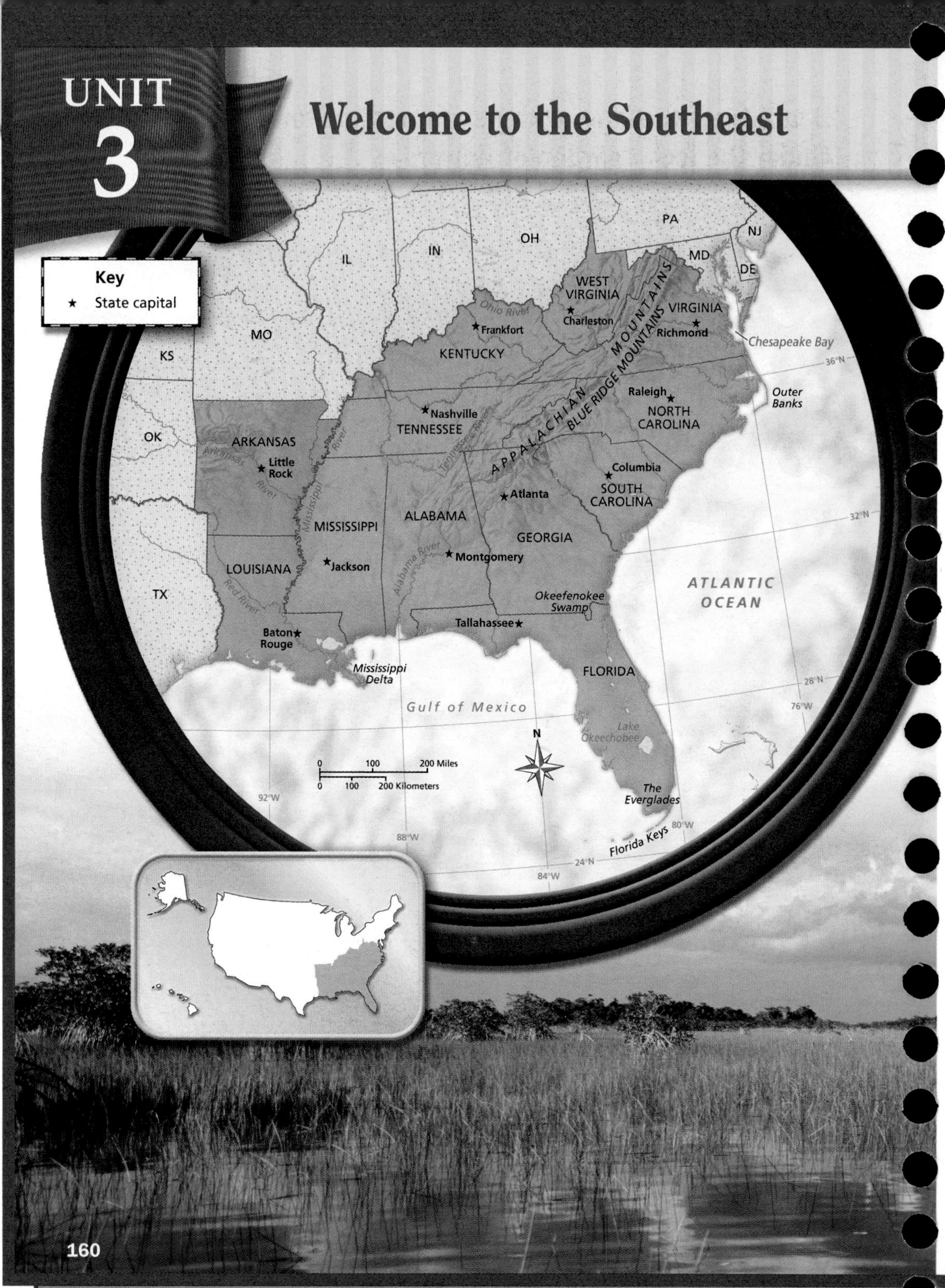

UNIT 3

Welcome to the Southeast

160

Practice and Extend

CURRICULUM CONNECTION
Literature

Read About the Region

Use the following selections to extend the content.

Manatee Blues, by Laurie Halse Anderson (Pleasant Company Publications, ISBN 1-58485-049-3, 2000) **Easy**

Georgia, by Nancy Robinson Masters (Children's Press, ISBN 0-516-20685-0, 1999) **On-Level**

Jammin' on the Avenue: Going to New Orleans, by Whitney Stewart (Four Corners Publishing, ISBN 1-893577-06-6, 2001) **Challenge**

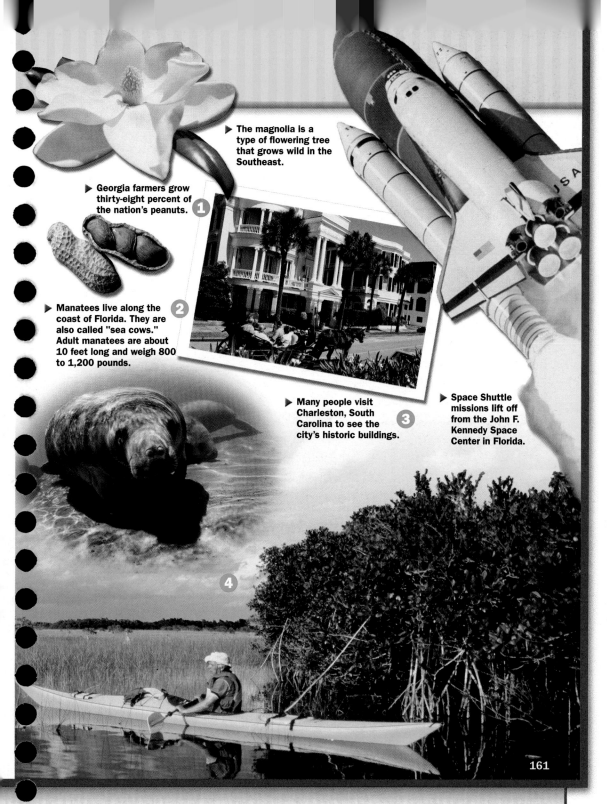

▶ The magnolia is a type of flowering tree that grows wild in the Southeast.

▶ Georgia farmers grow thirty-eight percent of the nation's peanuts. 1

▶ Manatees live along the coast of Florida. They are also called "sea cows." Adult manatees are about 10 feet long and weigh 800 to 1,200 pounds. 2

▶ Many people visit Charleston, South Carolina to see the city's historic buildings. 3

▶ Space Shuttle missions lift off from the John F. Kennedy Space Center in Florida.

4

161

WEB SITE
Technology

Students can learn more about the places in this unit by clicking on *Atlas* at **www.sfsocialstudies.com.**

Discuss the Region

Have students use the pictures and captions to answer the following questions.

1 **Many people think of peaches when they think of Georgia, but what other crop is associated with that state?** Peanuts **Main Idea and Details**

2 **Why do you think manatees also are known as "sea cows"?** Possible answer: Because they are so large **Draw Conclusions**

3 **How is the history of Charleston, South Carolina, continuing to affect that city's economy?** Many people visit the city to see its historic buildings. **Main Idea and Details**

4 **According to the picture, what covers at least a portion of the land of the Southeast region?** Possible answers: Water, swamps, wetlands **Analyze Pictures**

Read About the Region

The states mentioned here are discussed in the text on the following pages in Unit 3.

- South Carolina, pp. 167, 169, 173, 181, 195, 197, 200–201, 203, 212, 214
- North Carolina, pp. 167, 169, 173, 181, 191, 195, 196, 198, 213
- Virginia, pp. 167, 169, 173, 181, 196–197
- Georgia, pp. 169, 173, 180–181, 195, 206, 210–212
- West Virginia, pp. 169, 181, 183
- Kentucky, pp. 169, 181, 183, 198
- Tennessee, pp. 169, 181, 195, 198
- Alabama, pp. 169, 173, 181, 195, 207
- Mississippi, pp. 173, 181
- Florida, pp. 173, 179–181, 195–196, 212
- Louisiana, pp. 173, 180–181
- Arkansas, pp. 180, 181

UNIT 3

Reading Social Studies

Main Idea and Details

Objective

Analyze information by identifying the main idea and details.

Resource

- Workbook, p. 37

About the Unit Target Skill

- The target reading skill for this unit is Main Idea and Details.
- Students are introduced to the unit target skill here and are given an opportunity to practice it.
- Further opportunities to practice identifying the main idea and details are found throughout Unit 3.

1 Introduce and Motivate

Preview To activate prior knowledge, ask a student volunteer to tell the class the main idea of a well-known story such as a fairy tale or a tall tale. Have other students provide details to support the main idea in that story.

UNIT 3

The Southeast

Main Idea and Details

Main Idea

Detail Detail Detail

Learning to find the main idea and details will help you understand what you read.

- A main idea is the most important thought in the paragraph or passage.
- The supporting details give more information about the main idea.

Read this paragraph. The **main idea** and **supporting details** have been highlighted.

The Mississippi River is one of the longest and deepest rivers in the world. In some places, it is more than 400 feet deep, which is equal to the height of a building that is 40 stories high. It starts at Lake Itasca in Minnesota and goes south to the Gulf of Mexico, a distance of 2,350 miles.

Word Exercise

Context Clues Sometimes you can use clues from the text and what you already know to figure out the meaning of an unfamiliar word. Look at the sentence below and try to determine the meaning of the word *deposits*.

They made *deposits* at the bank and watched their accounts grow.

Context Clues	+	What I already know	=	What I think *deposits* means
•The deposits took place at the bank. •Their accounts grew.		Banks hold money for people.		Money that people put into the bank

Practice and Extend

ACTIVATE PRIOR KNOWLEDGE

ESL Support

Classify Details Have students develop a main idea and details to describe their own community.

Beginning On the board, write two main ideas about your community and read them aloud. Then state various details and have students classify each under the correct main idea.

Intermediate Have students brainstorm additional details to write under the two main ideas above. Write their ideas in outline form under each main idea.

Advanced Have students choose one of the main ideas on the board and develop the idea and two of its details into a paragraph describing the community.

The Big River

The Mississippi River affects the land and people of the Southeast. It is the largest river in the United States. It is wide—a mile and a half across in some places. It curves back and forth on its long journey like a big ribbon.

As the Mississippi approaches the Gulf of Mexico, its waters fan out into smaller, marshy rivers. These marshy rivers are called bayous (BEYE yooz). As the Mississippi flows south, it carries dirt, sand, and mud. These materials are deposited at the mouth of the river, the place where the river flows into the Gulf of Mexico. Over thousands of years, land has been built up by these deposits. This rich, flat land is called a delta. The delta of the Mississippi River juts out into the Gulf of Mexico. It covers thousands of square miles.

The Mississippi River is also a water highway. Native Americans used it as a main trade route. Today, the river is still a major route for ships and barges loaded with many different goods. One of the nation's busiest ports is located on the Mississippi. It is called the Port of South Louisiana. New Orleans and Baton Rouge, Louisiana, and Memphis, Tennessee, are some other Mississippi River ports.

Use the reading strategy of main idea and details to answer questions 1 and 2. Then answer the vocabulary question.

1. Which sentence is the main idea of the whole passage?
2. What details tell how the Mississippi delta was formed?
3. Find the word *deposits* in the reading selection. From the other words in that paragraph, what does *deposits* mean? Use a dictionary to check your definition.

Standardized Test Prep

- Use Workbook p. 37 to give students practice with standardized test format.
- Chapter and Unit Tests in the Assessment Book use standardized test format.
- Test-taking tips are contained in the front portion of the Assessment Book Teacher's Edition.

Also on Teacher Resources CD-ROM.

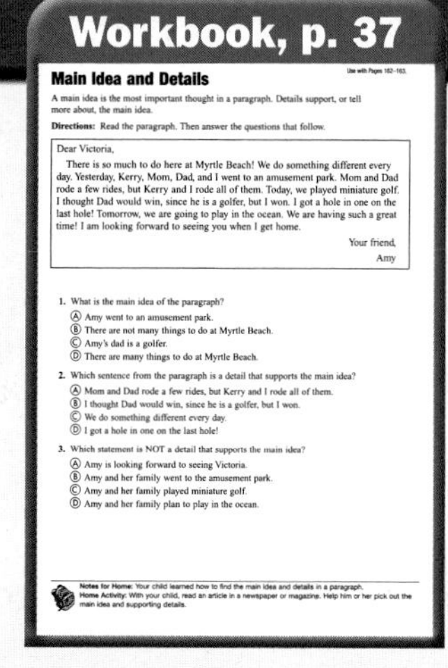

Workbook, p. 37

Main Idea and Details

Use with Pages 162–163.

A main idea is the most important thought in a paragraph. Details support, or tell more about, the main idea.

Directions: Read the paragraph. Then answer the questions that follow.

Dear Victoria,

There is so much to do here at Myrtle Beach! We do something different every day. Yesterday, Kerry, Mom, Dad, and I went to an amusement park. Mom and Dad rode a few rides, but Kerry and I rode all of them. Today, we played miniature golf. I thought Dad would win, since he is a golfer, but I won. I got a hole in one on the last hole! Tomorrow, we are going to play in the ocean. We are having such a great time! I am looking forward to seeing you when I get home.

Your friend,
Amy

1. What is the main idea of the paragraph?
   Ⓐ Amy went to an amusement park.
   Ⓑ There are not many things to do at Myrtle Beach.
   Ⓒ Amy's dad is a golfer.
   Ⓓ There are many things to do at Myrtle Beach.
2. Which sentence from the paragraph is a detail that supports the main idea?
   Ⓐ Mom and Dad rode a few rides, but Kerry and I rode all of them.
   Ⓑ I thought Dad would win, since he is a golfer, but I won.
   Ⓒ We do something different every day.
   Ⓓ I got a hole in one on the last hole!
3. Which statement is NOT a detail that supports the main idea?
   Ⓐ Amy is looking forward to seeing Victoria.
   Ⓑ Amy and her family went to the amusement park.
   Ⓒ Amy and her family played miniature golf.
   Ⓓ Amy and her family plan to play in the ocean.

Notes for Home: Your child learned how to find the main idea and details in a paragraph.
Home Activity: With your child, read an article in a newspaper or magazine. Help him or her pick out the main idea and supporting details.

2 Teach and Discuss

- Have students read the bulleted items on p. 162. Explain that many paragraphs include a sentence that expresses the main idea. Tell students that this often is the first or last sentence in the paragraph. The supporting details usually appear in the remaining sentences.
- Have students read the sample paragraph on p. 162. Have them explain how the details, highlighted in yellow, support the main idea.
- Then have students read the longer practice sample on p. 163 and answer the questions that follow it.
- Ask students why, when studying geography, it is important to understand the main idea and details. (The main idea paints a general picture of a geographical region, but the details help you know what makes that region special.)

Context Clues

Be sure that students understand that *deposits* means "layers of matter that build up over time." Discuss how this is related to the meaning of deposits in banks.

3 Close and Assess

Apply it!

1. The Mississippi River affects the land and people of the Southeast.
2. As the Mississippi flows south, it carries dirt, sand, and mud. These materials are deposited at the mouth of the river. Land has been built up by these deposits. This land is called a delta.
3. *Deposits* means "layers of matter that build up over time."

CHAPTER 6

Chapter Planning Guide

Chapter 6 • The Land of the Southeast

Locating Places pp. 164–165

Lesson Titles	Pacing	Main Ideas
Lesson 1 **Coastal Plains to the Mountains** pp. 166–169	2 days	• The main areas of the Southeast region include the coastal plains, the Piedmont, and Appalachia.
Map and Globe Skills: Read Elevation Maps pp. 170–171		• Elevation maps show how high land rises above sea level.
Lesson 2 **Sunlight and Storms** pp. 172–175	2 days	• The mild climates of the coastal areas of the Southeast bring many tourists, but the area has some natural hazards.
DK **Hurricanes** pp. 176–177		• Hurricanes can cause many different types of damage to Southeastern coastlines.
Lesson 3 **Wildlife and Resources** pp. 178–183	2 days	• The Southeast is rich in different resources. These resources are used in different industries throughout the region.
✓ **Chapter 6 Review** pp. 184–185		

Once an endangered species, alligators have made a comeback in the Florida Everglades.

✓ = **Assessment Options**

At the fall line, the rivers of the Southeast tumble toward the Atlantic Ocean in the form of beautiful waterfalls.

Vocabulary	Resources	Meeting Individual Needs
barrier islands wetlands fall line sea level	• Workbook, p. 39 • Transparencies 1, 40, 41 • Every Student Learns Guide, pp. 66–69 • Quick Study, pp. 34–35 • Workbook, p. 40	• Leveled Practice, TE p. 167 • ESL Support, TE p. 168
key hurricane hurricane season	• Workbook, p. 41 • Transparencies 1, 42, 43 • Every Student Learns Guide, pp. 70–73 • Quick Study, pp. 36–37	• ESL Support, TE p. 173 • Leveled Practice, TE p. 174 • Learning Styles, TE p. 175
endangered species extinct pulp fossil fuel	• Workbook, p. 42 • Transparencies 1, 44, 45 • Every Student Learns Guide, pp. 74–77 • Quick Study, pp. 38–39	• ESL Support, TE p. 179 • Leveled Practice, TE p. 181
	✔Chapter 6 Content Test, Assessment Book, pp. 29–30 ✔Chapter 6 Skills Test, Assessment Book, pp. 31–32	✔Chapter 6 Performance Assessment, TE p. 184

Providing More Depth

Additional Resources

- Vocabulary Workbook and Cards
- Social Studies Plus! pp. 62–67
- Daily Activity Bank
- Big Book Atlas
- Student Atlas
- Outline Maps
- Desk Maps

Technology

- AudioText
- MindPoint® Quiz Show CD-ROM
- ExamView® Test Bank CD-ROM
- Teacher Resources CD-ROM
- Map Resources CD-ROM
- SFSuccessNet: iText (Pupil Edition online), iTE (Teacher's Edition online), Online Planner
- **www.sfsocialstudies.com** (Biographies, news, references, maps, and activities)

To establish guidelines for your students' safe and responsible use of the Internet, use the Scott Foresman Internet Guide.

Additional Internet Links

To find out more about:

- Endangered species, visit **www.worldwildlife.org**
- Everglades National Park, visit **www.nps.gov**
- Hurricanes, visit **www.miamisci.org**

Key Internet Search Terms

- Dismal Swamp
- Appalachian Mountains
- Key West, Florida

Workbook Support

Use the following Workbook pages to support content and skills development as you teach Chapter 6. You can also view and print Workbook pages from the Teacher Resources CD-ROM.

Workbook, p. 37

Use with Pages 162–163.

Main Idea and Details

A main idea is the most important thought in a paragraph. Details support, or tell more about, the main idea.

Directions: Read the paragraph. Then answer the questions that follow.

Dear Victoria,

There is so much to do here at Myrtle Beach! We do something different every day. Yesterday, Kerry, Mom, Dad, and I went to an amusement park. Mom and Dad rode a few rides, but Kerry and I rode all of them. Today, we played miniature golf. I thought Dad would win, since he is a golfer, but I won. I got a hole in one on the last hole! Tomorrow, we are going to play in the ocean. We are having such a great time! I am looking forward to seeing you when I get home.

Your friend,
Amy

1. What is the main idea of the paragraph?
   - Ⓐ Amy went to an amusement park.
   - Ⓑ There are not many things to do at Myrtle Beach.
   - Ⓒ Amy's dad is a golfer.
   - ● There are many things to do at Myrtle Beach.
2. Which sentence from the paragraph is a detail that supports the main idea?
   - Ⓐ Mom and Dad rode a few rides, but Kerry and I rode all of them.
   - Ⓑ I thought Dad would win, since he is a golfer, but I won.
   - ● We do something different every day.
   - Ⓓ I got a hole in one on the last hole!
3. Which statement is NOT a detail that supports the main idea?
   - ● Amy is looking forward to seeing Victoria.
   - Ⓑ Amy and her family went to the amusement park.
   - Ⓒ Amy and her family played miniature golf.
   - Ⓓ Amy and her family plan to play in the ocean.

Notes for Home: Your child learned how to find the main idea and details in a paragraph.
Home Activity: With your child, read an article in a newspaper or magazine. Help him or her pick out the main idea and supporting details.

Use with Pupil Edition, p. 163

Workbook, p. 38

Use with Chapter 6.

Vocabulary Preview

Directions: Choose the vocabulary word from the box that best completes each sentence. Write the word on the line provided. You may use your glossary.

barrier islands	hurricane	extinct
wetlands	hurricane season	pulp
fall line	endangered species	fossil fuel
key		

1. A(n) **hurricane** is a violent storm that forms over the ocean.
2. A(n) **fossil fuel** is a material that is formed in the earth from the remains of plants or animals.
3. The **fall line** is a line that marks the boundary between the Piedmont and the coastal plains.
4. A low island is a(n) **key**.
5. Islands formed from deposits of sand and mud are **barrier islands**.
6. **Pulp** is a combination of ground-up wood chips, water, and chemicals.
7. Lands that are at times covered with water are **wetlands**.
8. A kind of animal or plant that is thought to be in danger of dying out is a(n) **endangered species**.
9. The period from June until the beginning of November when hurricanes usually occur is called the **hurricane season**.
10. About a dozen kinds of animals that live in the Everglades are in danger of becoming **extinct**, or no longer existing.

Notes for Home: Your child learned the vocabulary terms for Chapter 6.
Home Activity: With your child, make flash cards of the vocabulary terms. Illustrate a term on one side of the card and write its definition on the other side. As you show your child each picture, have him or her spell and define the corresponding term.

38 Vocabulary Preview Workbook

Use with Pupil Edition, p. 164

Workbook, p. 39

Use with Pages 166–169.

Lesson 1: Coastal Plains to the Mountains

Directions: Read the following statements. Then write *T* (True) or *F* (False) on the line before each statement. If the answer is false, correct the underlined term or terms to make the statement true. You may use your textbook.

T 1. Most of the states of the Southeast lie along the Atlantic coast, the coast of the Gulf of Mexico, or both.

F 2. Off the shore are groups of long, low streams.
(barrier) islands

F 3. The Outer Coastal Plain is very hilly and has a very high elevation.
flat, low

T 4. Swamps, bogs, and marshes are different kinds of wetlands.

F 5. The soil of the Piedmont is sandy.
coastal plains

F 6. The Blue Ridge marks the boundary between the Piedmont and the coastal plains.
fall line

T 7. The Appalachian Mountains are rugged and steep, with narrow valleys.

T 8. Mount Mitchell in North Carolina is the highest peak east of the Mississippi River.

F 9. Appalachia is known for its rich natural resources, such as steep valleys.
coal

Notes for Home: Your child learned about the coastal plains and the mountains in the Southeast.
Home Activity: With your child, look in an encyclopedia, a magazine, or online to find a picture of a place in the Southeast. Together, discuss in which part of the Southeast you think the picture was taken. Ask your child to point out characteristics that led him or her to this conclusion.

Workbook Lesson Review 39

Use with Pupil Edition, p. 169

Workbook Support

Workbook, p. 40

Use with Pages 170–171.

Read Elevation Maps

Directions: Fill in the blanks with information about the elevation map below. You may use your textbook for additional information.

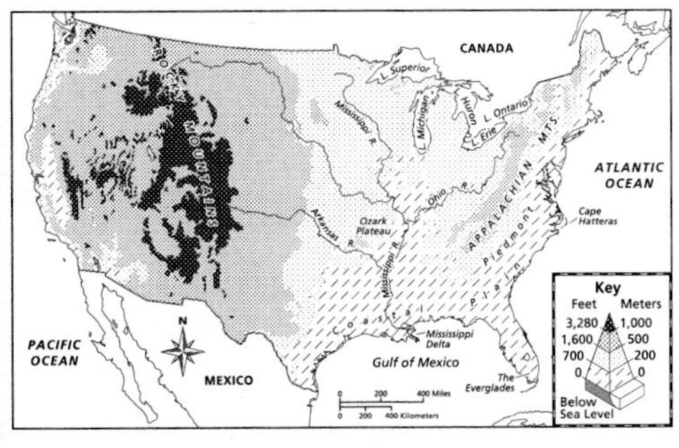

1. To read an elevation map, first look at the map **key**.
2. This elevation maps uses **shading or patterns** to show elevation.
3. Elevation is the height above **sea level**.
4. A place that is at sea level is at the same **height** as the surface of the ocean's water.
5. Most of the Southeast is at what elevation range? **0–1,600 feet above sea level**
6. What is the elevation range of the highest part of the Appalachian Mountains?
   1,600–3,280 feet above sea level
7. The state of Florida is entirely at what elevation range?
   0–700 feet above sea level

Notes for Home: Your child learned how to read elevation maps.
Home Activity: With your child, use the map above to find the elevation of one of the physical features such as the Coastal Plain. Have your child explain how he or she used the map key to find this elevation.

40 Map and Globe Skills Workbook

Use with Pupil Edition, p. 171

Workbook, p. 41

Use with Pages 172–175.

Lesson 2: Sunlight and Storms

Directions: Answer the following questions on the lines provided. You may use your textbook.

1. What is Key West?
   Possible answers: An island off the southern coast of Florida; one of the Florida Keys
2. Describe the climate of Florida.
   Possible answers: Mild and sunny; the northern part gets cool in winter, and the southern part usually stays warm in winter; summers are hot and humid.
3. What is a hurricane?
   a violent storm with strong, circular winds and heavy rains that forms over the ocean
4. How can a hurricane affect communities in its path?
   Possible answer: Its strong winds can send large objects flying, uproot trees, and damage buildings, and its huge waves can cause flooding.
5. Why were lighthouses originally built?
   to help sailors avoid the rocky coastlines and to warn them of dangerous rocks and currents
6. Are lighthouses as important today as they once were? Explain.
   Possible answer: No; Sailors now use other tools to help them find their way, so many lighthouses are no longer working. However, people still enjoy visiting them.

Notes for Home: Your child learned about the climate of the Southeast.
Home Activity: Have your child draw a lighthouse or examine a picture of a lighthouse. Together, discuss why lighthouses were designed to look the way they do.

Workbook Lesson Review 41

Use with Pupil Edition, p. 175

Workbook, p. 42

Use with Pages 176–183.

Lesson 3: Wildlife and Resources

Directions: The first column of the chart below lists some of the wildlife and resources found in the Southeast. Complete the chart by writing at least one specific part of the Southeast in which each can be found.

Wildlife and Resources	Where Is It Found?
alligator	**Possible answers: swamps, canals, and lakes in Florida and other parts of Southeast**
Florida panther	**Florida Everglades**
black bear	**Appalachian Mountains**
deer	**Possible answers: Appalachian Mountains, coastal plain, Piedmont**
oranges, grapefruits, lemons, limes	**Possible answers: coastal plains, Florida**
peanuts	**Possible answers: coastal plains, Georgia, Alabama, North Carolina, Virginia**
rice	**Possible answers: coastal plains, Arkansas, Louisiana, Mississippi**
coal	**Possible answers: Appalachia, Kentucky, West Virginia**

Notes for Home: Your child learned about the wildlife and resources of the Southeast.
Home Activity: With your child, examine food resources from the Southeast, such as peanuts, rice, and citrus fruits, and discuss how your family and community depend on these resources.

Use with Pupil Edition, p. 183

Workbook, p. 43

Use with Chapter 6.

Vocabulary Review

Directions: Write the letter of the correct definition beside each vocabulary term. You may use your textbook.

d 1. hurricane season
e 2. pulp
a 3. barrier islands
i 4. extinct
c 5. fossil fuel
g 6. wetlands
j 7. endangered species
b 8. fall line
h 9. hurricane
f 10. key

a. islands formed from deposits of sand and mud
b. marks the boundary between the Piedmont and the coastal plains
c. fuel that is formed in the earth from the remains of plants or animals
d. period from June to the beginning of November when hurricanes usually occur
e. combination of ground-up wood chips, water, and chemicals
f. low island
g. lands that are at times covered with water
h. violent storm that forms over the ocean
i. no longer existing
j. kind of animal or plant that is thought to be dying out

Notes for Home: Your child learned the vocabulary terms for Chapter 6.
Home Activity: Call out the vocabulary terms to your child in random order. As you say each term, have your child spell it and use it in an original sentence.

Use with Pupil Edition, p. 185

Assessment Support

Use the following Assessment Book pages and TestWorks to assess content and skills in Chapter 6. You can also view and print Assessment Book pages from the Teacher Resources CD-ROM.

Assessment Book, p. 29

Chapter 6 Test

Part 1: Content Test

Directions: Fill in the circle next to the correct answer.

Lesson Objective (1:1)

1. Which of these landforms is NOT found in the Southeast?
   - Ⓐ beaches
   - Ⓑ wetlands
   - Ⓒ mountains
   - ● deserts

Lesson Objective (1:2)

2. How are barrier islands formed?
   - Ⓐ As animals dig their burrows along the shore, the sand is piled up, hardens, and becomes islands.
   - Ⓑ People who live along the shore pile sand and gravel in the shallow water to make islands on which to live.
   - ● Sediment is deposited by ocean waves, currents, and rivers into shallow areas off the coast.
   - Ⓓ Volcanoes deep under the water erupt, spewing lava upward where it hardens and forms islands.

Lesson Objective (1:1)

3. Which of the following is an area that is very flat, has a very low elevation, and has different kinds of wetlands?
   - Ⓐ Appalachian Mountains
   - ● Outer Coastal Plain
   - Ⓒ Gulf of Mexico
   - Ⓓ Inner Coastal Plain

Lesson Objective (1:3)

4. How is the Inner Coastal Plain different from the Outer Coastal Plain?
   - ● The Inner Coastal Plain's elevation is higher.
   - Ⓑ The Inner Coastal Plain's elevation is lower.
   - Ⓒ The Inner Coastal Plain has more wetlands.
   - Ⓓ The Inner Coastal Plain is flatter.

Lesson Objective (1:3)

5. Which of the following has the highest elevation?
   - ● Appalachian Mountains
   - Ⓑ Piedmont
   - Ⓒ Inner Coastal Plain
   - Ⓓ fall line

Lesson Objective (2:1)

6. How might you describe the weather of the Florida Keys?
   - Ⓐ cold and snowy
   - Ⓑ hot and dry
   - Ⓒ cold and rainy
   - ● mild and sunny

Lesson Objective (2:1)

7. Which word best describes the climates of the states in the coastal plains?
   - ● warm
   - Ⓑ cool
   - Ⓒ cold
   - Ⓓ hot

Use with Pupil Edition, p. 184

Assessment Book, p. 30

Lesson Objective (2:2)

8. Which of the following best describes the characteristics of a hurricane?
   - Ⓐ strong winds that move in a zigzag pattern along with misty rain
   - Ⓑ heavy snowfall along with very strong, straight-line winds
   - Ⓒ heavy rains along with light breezes
   - ● strong winds that move in a circular path along with heavy rains

Lesson Objective (2:2)

9. What time of year is hurricane season in the Southeast?
   - Ⓐ from December 31 until late January
   - Ⓑ from November until the end of June
   - ● from June until the beginning of November
   - Ⓓ from March 15 until the middle of June

Lesson Objective (2:3)

10. Why did people build lighthouses along the coasts of the Southeast?
    - Ⓐ People wanted tourists to come and visit their coastal communities.
    - ● Lighthouses helped sailors avoid the rocky coastlines.
    - Ⓒ There were not enough streetlights to keep the roads lighted.
    - Ⓓ Children who could see the lighthouses would not be afraid of the dark.

Lesson Objective (3:1)

11. Which of the following animals makes its home in the swamps of the Southeast?
    - Ⓐ moose
    - Ⓑ bear
    - ● alligator
    - Ⓓ giraffe

Lesson Objective (3:2)

12. Which is NOT a major crop of the Southeast?
    - Ⓐ soybeans
    - ● bananas
    - Ⓒ peanuts
    - Ⓓ oranges

Lesson Objective (3:2)

13. Which Southeast state is a major producer of rice?
    - ● Arkansas
    - Ⓑ Florida
    - Ⓒ Alabama
    - Ⓓ Virginia

Lesson Objective (3:3)

14. Which is NOT a product of the Southeast logging industry?
    - Ⓐ paper
    - ● juice
    - Ⓒ boards
    - Ⓓ furniture

Lesson Objective (3:4)

15. Which Southeastern resource do many power plants burn to run their generators?
    - Ⓐ pulp
    - Ⓑ paper
    - ● coal
    - Ⓓ wood

30 Unit 3, Chapter 6 Test Assessment Book

Use with Pupil Edition, p. 184

Assessment Support

Assessment Book, p. 31

Part 2: Skills Test

Directions: Use complete sentences to answer questions 1–5. Use a separate sheet of paper if you need more space.

1. Compare and contrast the coastal plains and the Piedmont. **Compare and Contrast**

   Similar: the coastal plains and the Piedmont are both found in the Southeast. Different: the coastal plains are flat and have a low elevation. The soil there is sandy. The Piedmont is an area of rolling hills and valleys. Its elevation is higher and the soil there is rich and feels like clay.

2. Write three details you would include for the following main idea: **Hurricane season in the Southeast can be dangerous and costly. Main Idea and Details**

   Possible answer: Hurricane winds can be strong enough to send large objects flying. They can uproot trees and damage buildings. Huge waves can cause flooding.

3. Why did the alligator become endangered? Is it still endangered? Explain. **Summarize**

   Great numbers of alligators were hunted for food or for their hides. By 1967, the alligator had become an endangered species, and a law was passed making it illegal to hunt alligators. By 1987 the alligator had made a comeback, and it is no longer endangered.

Use with Pupil Edition, p. 184

Assessment Book, p. 32

4. What products from the Southeast do you use most? Explain. **Express Ideas**

   Possible answer: I drink orange juice and eat oranges, I eat peanuts and rice, and I use paper in school.

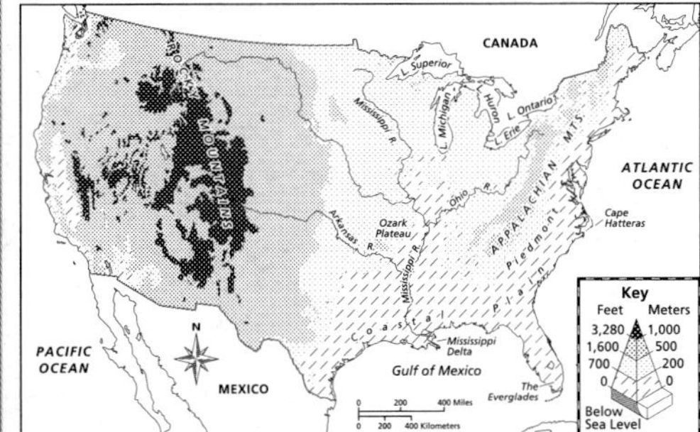

Elevations of the United States

5. Use the map to answer the questions. **Read Elevation Maps.**

   a. What do the different shades on the map represent?

   The shades show how high above sea level different parts of the United States are.

   b. What can you learn from this map about the state of Florida?

   The map shows that Florida is at an elevation of 0 to 700 feet (0–200 meters) above sea level.

   c. How does the area around the Great Lakes differ from the area of the Rocky Mountains?

   The area around the Great Lakes has an elevation range of 700–1,600 feet (200–500 meters). The elevation of the Rocky Mountains is higher—above 3,280 feet (1,000 meters).

Use with Pupil Edition, p. 184

CHAPTER 6

The Land of the Southeast

Chapter 6 Outline

- **Lesson 1, *Coastal Plains to the Mountains,*** pp. 166–169
- **Map and Globe Skills: *Read Elevation Maps,*** pp. 170–171
- **Lesson 2, *Sunlight and Storms,*** pp. 172–175
- DK ***Hurricanes,*** pp. 176–177
- **Lesson 3, *Wildlife and Resources,*** pp. 178–183

Resources

- Workbook, p. 38: Vocabulary Preview
- Vocabulary Cards
- Social Studies Plus!

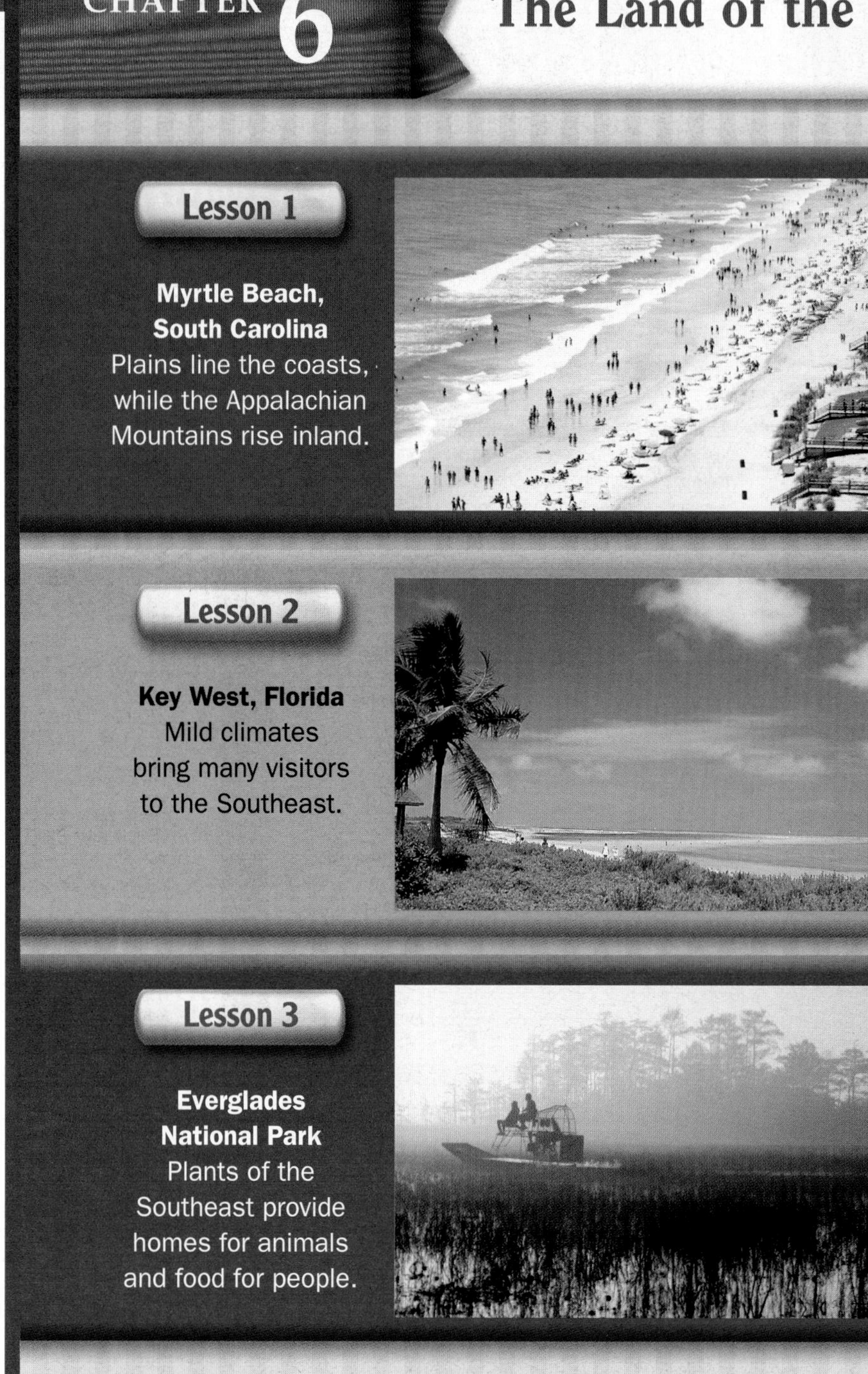

CHAPTER 6 The Land of the Southeast

Lesson 1

Myrtle Beach, South Carolina
Plains line the coasts, while the Appalachian Mountains rise inland.

Lesson 2

Key West, Florida
Mild climates bring many visitors to the Southeast.

Lesson 3

Everglades National Park
Plants of the Southeast provide homes for animals and food for people.

164

Myrtle Beach, South Carolina: Lesson 1

The picture shows crowds of tourists at Myrtle Beach. Ask students how they think beaches contribute to the economy of a region. (Possible answer: They attract people who spend money in nearby shops, hotels, and restaurants.)

Key West, Florida: Lesson 2

Ask students what they can observe about Key West by looking at the picture. (Possible answers: Key West is sunny with ocean beaches; it looks like a great place for outdoor activities.)

Everglades National Park: Lesson 3

Ask students what types of animals might live in the pictured environment. (Possible answers: Fish, snakes, alligators, birds, insects)

Practice and Extend

Vocabulary Preview

- Use Workbook p. 38 to help students preview the vocabulary words in this chapter.
- Use Vocabulary Cards to preview key concept words in this chapter.

Also on Teacher Resources CD-ROM.

Workbook, p. 38

Vocabulary Preview Use with Chapter 6.

Directions: Choose the vocabulary word from the box that best completes each sentence. Write the word on the line provided. You may use your glossary.

barrier islands	hurricane	extinct
wetlands	hurricane season	pulp
fall line	endangered species	fossil fuel
key		

1. A(n) ____________ is a violent storm that forms over the ocean.
2. A(n) ____________ is a material that is formed in the earth from the remains of plants or animals.
3. The ____________ is a line that marks the boundary between the Piedmont and the coastal plains.
4. A low island is a(n) ____________.
5. Islands formed from deposits of sand and mud are ____________.
6. ____________ is a combination of ground-up wood chips, water, and chemicals.
7. Lands that are at times covered with water are ____________.
8. A kind of animal or plant that is thought to be in danger of dying out is a(n) ____________.
9. The period from June until the beginning of November when hurricanes usually occur is called the ____________.
10. About a dozen kinds of animals that live in the Everglades are in danger of becoming ____________, or no longer existing.

Notes for Home: Your child learned the vocabulary terms for Chapter 6.
Home Activity: With your child, make flash cards of the vocabulary terms. Illustrate a term on one side of the card and write its definition on the other side. As you show your child each picture, have him or her spell and define the corresponding term.

Locating Places

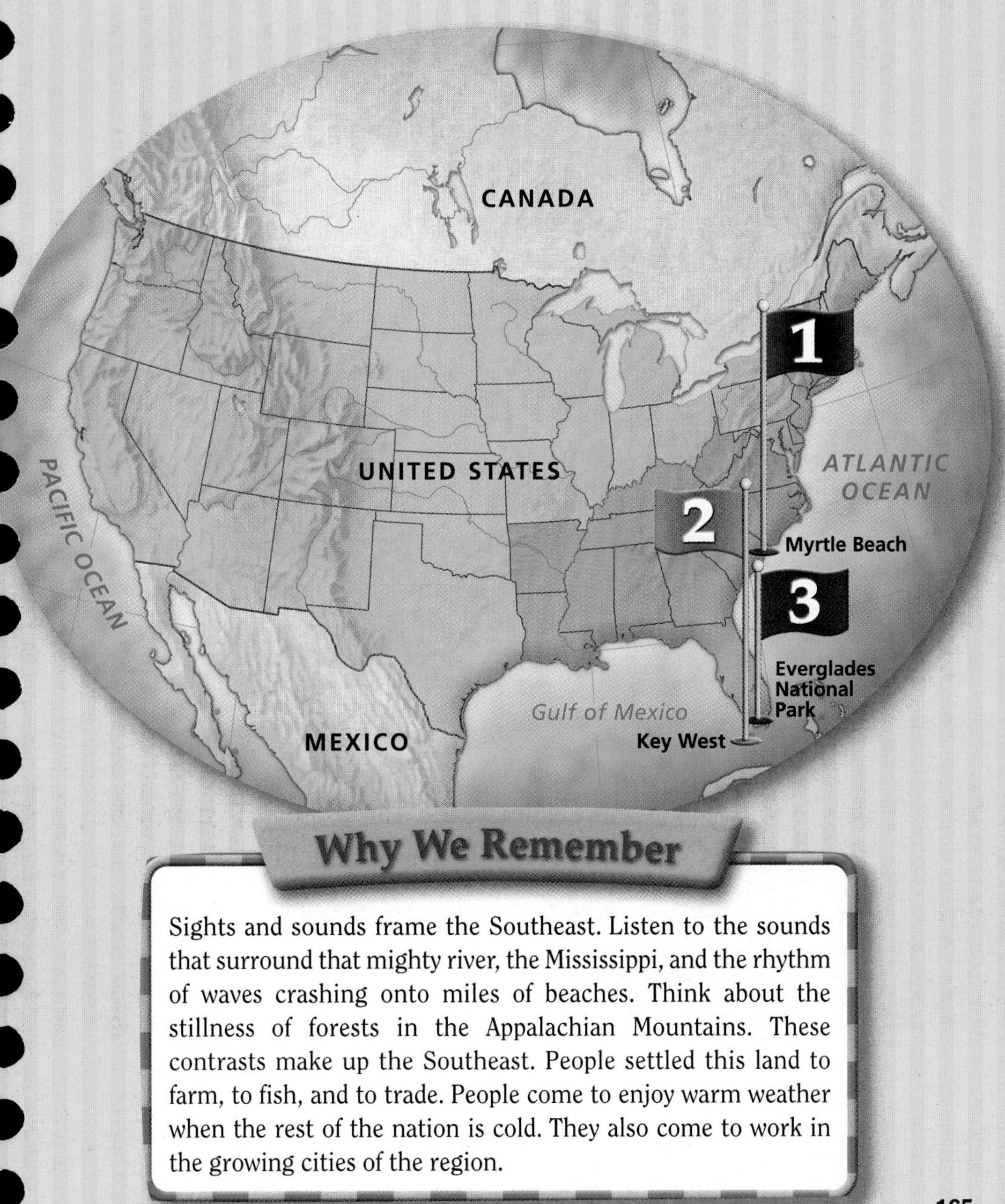

Why We Remember

Sights and sounds frame the Southeast. Listen to the sounds that surround that mighty river, the Mississippi, and the rhythm of waves crashing onto miles of beaches. Think about the stillness of forests in the Appalachian Mountains. These contrasts make up the Southeast. People settled this land to farm, to fish, and to trade. People come to enjoy warm weather when the rest of the nation is cold. They also come to work in the growing cities of the region.

WEB SITE
Technology

You can learn more about Myrtle Beach, South Carolina; Key West, Florida; and Everglades National Park by clicking on *Atlas* at **www.sfsocialstudies.com.**

SOCIAL STUDIES STRAND
Geography

Mental Mapping On an outline map of the United States, have students color in the states that they think make up the Southeast Region. Students may label any cities or landforms of the Southeast that they know of. Discuss students' knowledge and/or impressions of the Southeast.

Locating Places

- Have students examine the pictures shown on p. 164 for Lessons 1, 2, and 3.
- Remind students that each picture is coded with both a number and a color to link it to a place on the map on p. 165.

Why We Remember

Have students read the "Why We Remember" paragraph on p. 165. Ask them why places in this chapter might be important to them. Have students list some natural sights and sounds of the Southeast. Then have them list human-made sights and sounds of the region. Finally, ask students to speculate about how people have changed the environment of the Southeast. (Possible answer: The natural beauty of many beaches, forests, and mountains has been changed by the presence of roads, people, and businesses, and many forms of wildlife have been displaced.)

Coastal Plains to the Mountains

Objectives
- Identify and describe major landforms in the Southeast.
- Explain how barrier islands are formed.
- Compare and contrast landform elevations in the Southeast.

Vocabulary
barrier islands, p. 167; **wetlands,** p. 167; **fall line,** p. 168

Resources
- Workbook, p. 39
- Transparency 1
- Every Student Learns Guide, pp. 66–69
- Quick Study, pp. 34–35

Quick Teaching Plan

If time is short, have students create visual notes about Southeastern landforms.
- Tell students to draw a line that gradually slopes downward from left to right.
- Have students read the lesson independently and then add these labels to their drawing: *mountains, Piedmont, fall line, Inner Coastal Plain, Outer Coastal Plain, wetlands,* and *barrier island.*

1 Introduce and Motivate

Preview To activate prior knowledge, invite students who have been to a beach to describe the experience. Tell students they will learn more about beaches and other landforms in this lesson.

You Are There Have students brainstorm activities that often take place on or near beaches. Discuss with students how people can keep these activities from harming the beach environment.

LESSON 1

Coastal Plains to the Mountains

PREVIEW

Focus on the Main Idea
The main areas of the Southeast region include the coastal plains, the Piedmont, and Appalachia.

PLACES
Myrtle Beach, South Carolina
Outer Coastal Plain
Inner Coastal Plain
Piedmont
Appalachia

VOCABULARY
barrier islands
wetlands
fall line

You Are There You've waited a long time for this vacation trip. The drive from Atlanta to Myrtle Beach took many hours, but you didn't mind. You're excited about seeing the Atlantic Ocean. You've never seen an ocean before!

After you put your suitcases in your hotel room, your family heads off for the beach. Your mother puts sun block lotion all over your back, and then you run to the shore. Waves roll toward you as you put your toes into the cold ocean water. As you bend over to pick up some pretty seashells, you feel a hand grabbing yours. "Come on, Pal," your father says. "Just hold my hand. I'll show you how to dive into these waves!"

Main Idea and Details As you read, notice how the Southeast region changes as you travel from the seacoast to the mountains.

166

Practice and Extend

READING SKILL Main Idea/Details

In the Lesson Review, students complete a graphic organizer like the one below. You may want to provide students with a copy of Transparency 1 to complete as they read the lesson.

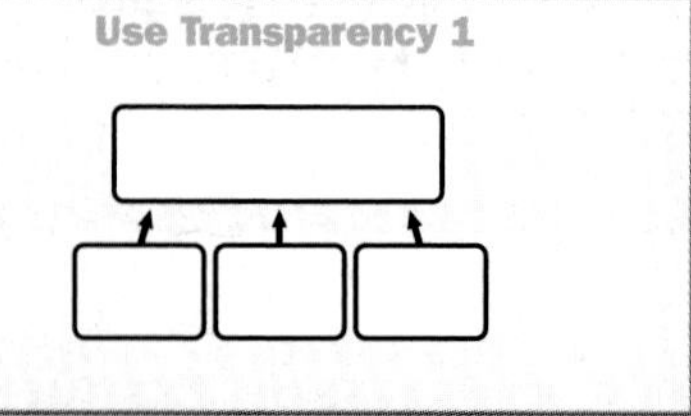

VOCABULARY Individual Word Study

Remind students that examining the smaller words that make up a compound word can help them understand and remember the meaning of the compound word. Ask students what *barrier* means ("something that stands in the way"). Discuss how a barrier island is a kind of island that forms a barrier around something else. Repeat this process with *wetlands* and *fall line*, making sure that students understand that a fall line is a stretch of land where rivers fall.

Along the Coasts

Most of the states of the Southeast lie along the Atlantic coast, the coast of the Gulf of Mexico, or both. Beaches, such as **Myrtle Beach** in South Carolina, line some of the shore.

Off the shore are groups of long, low islands. Thousands of years ago, when glaciers began to melt, the rising waters of the ocean deposited sediment, material such as sand and mud left by a glacier, into shallow areas
1 off the coast. These islands, known as **barrier islands,** were formed over thousands of years as more and more sediment was deposited by ocean waves, currents, and mainland rivers.

Inland from the shore is an area known as the **Outer Coastal Plain.** This area is very flat and has very low elevation.

The Outer Coastal Plain has different kinds of wetlands. **Wetlands** are lands that are at times covered with water.
Swamps, bogs, and marshes are kinds 2
of wetlands. A huge swamp, the Dismal Swamp, is between Virginia and North Carolina.

Farther inland is the **Inner Coastal Plain.** The elevation here is slightly
higher than in the Outer Coastal Plain. 3

REVIEW How does the land change as you move inland from the coast? Main Idea and Details

MAP SKILL States and Landforms of the Southeast 4

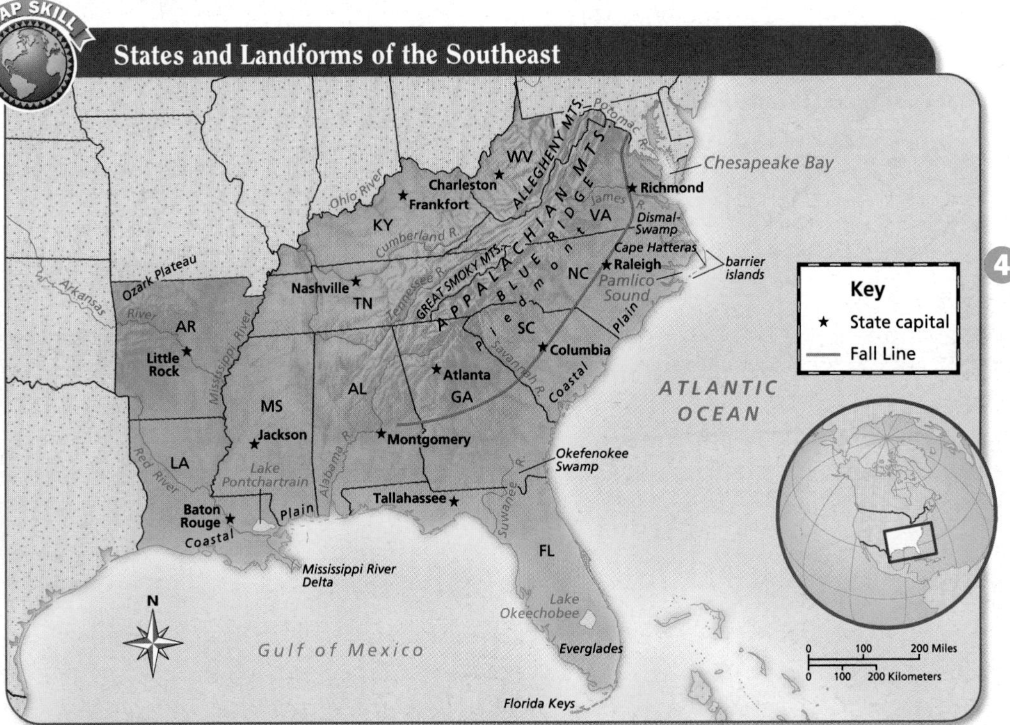

▶ The Southeast has plains, mountain ranges, rivers, and lakes.

MAP SKILL Understanding Continents and Oceans ***In what body of water are the barrier islands?***

Teach and Discuss

PAGE 167

Along the Coasts

Quick Summary Barrier islands lie off the shores of parts of the Southeast. Onshore, beaches and wetlands give way to the low, flat Outer Coastal Plain and the somewhat higher Inner Coastal Plain.

1 **Describe how the barrier islands were formed.** Thousands of years ago, glaciers melted, causing sediment material to be deposited off the coast. As more and more sediment was deposited by ocean and river activity, the islands were formed. Summarize

✓ Ongoing Assessment

If... students have difficulty describing how the barrier islands formed,	**then...** discuss with students how a build-up of sediment over many years can form an island.

2 **What kinds of wetlands are found in the Outer Coastal Plain of the Southeast?** Swamps, bogs, and marshes Main Idea and Details

3 **Which has a higher elevation, the Outer Coastal Plain or the Inner Coastal Plain?** Inner Coastal Plain Compare and Contrast

✓ **REVIEW ANSWER** The elevation increases. Main Idea and Details

States and Landforms of the Southeast

Point out the relationships of the different landforms of the Southeast.

4 **The barrier islands shown on this map are located off the coast of what state?** North Carolina Interpret Maps

MAP SKILL Answer Atlantic Ocean

MEETING INDIVIDUAL NEEDS
Leveled Practice

Differentiate Among Wetlands Ask students to differentiate among the various wetlands that characterize parts of the Southeast region.

Easy Have students look up the words *swamp, bog,* and *marsh* in a dictionary and write each definition on a separate index card. **Reteach**

On-Level Have students choose one of the wetlands above and find a picture of it. Have them describe their chosen wetlands and match the picture with a definition card. **Extend**

Challenge Have students create a poster including the pictures and definitions of the three kinds of Southeastern wetlands and the types of wildlife that live in each. **Enrich**

For a Lesson Summary, use Quick Study, p. 34.

PAGES 168–169

Toward the Mountains

Quick Summary Moving inland from the coastal plains, the fall line marks the beginning of the Piedmont. These rolling hills lead even farther inland to the Appalachian Mountains.

5 **What does the word *piedmont* mean?** Foot of the mountain
Main Idea and Details

SOCIAL STUDIES STRAND
History

As the Europeans were settling North America, they began traveling inland along the rivers. Cities such as Baltimore, Maryland; Washington, D.C.; and Richmond, Virginia, sprang up along the fall line because settlers could not easily move people and supplies upriver beyond that area.

6 **Why do you think the Piedmont was a good place for people to settle?** The soil of the Piedmont is rich and good for farming. Draw Conclusions

Toward the Mountains

An area of rolling hills and beautiful valleys lies inland from the coastal plains. This area is known as the
5 **Piedmont.** The word *piedmont* means "foot of the mountain." Its elevation is higher than that of the coastal plains.

The soil of the Piedmont is different from the sandy soil of the coastal plains. Piedmont soil is dark brown or reddish and feels like clay. It is very
6 rich soil and can be good farmland.

Many rivers flow through the Piedmont toward the Atlantic Ocean. The rivers tumble through waterfalls from the higher Piedmont to the lower coastal plains. On a map the waterfalls seem to be arranged in a line. This line is called the **fall line.** The fall line

▶ The Callasaja Falls tumble down the fall line between the Piedmont and the coastal plains of North Carolina.

▶ The hilly landscape of the Piedmont

168

Practice and Extend

ACCESS CONTENT
ESL Support

Examine Word Meanings Help students learn more about the geography of the Southeast by examining its different soils.

Beginning Show students examples of sandy, claylike, and rocky soils. Invite students to touch each different type of soil as you name it and tell where it is found in the Southeast.

Intermediate Demonstrate for students the relationship between the noun/adjective pairs *sand/sandy, clay/claylike,* and *rock/rocky.* Help students use each in a sentence.

Advanced Write the soil types *sandy, claylike,* and *rocky* in one column on the board and the landforms *beach, farmland,* and *mountain* in a second column. Ask students to match the words from each column and use each word pair in a sentence.

For additional ESL support, use Every Student Learns Guide, pp. 66–69.

marks the boundary between the Piedmont and the coastal plains.

Rising above the Piedmont is part of the Appalachian Mountain Range. The Appalachians in this area are rugged and steep, with narrow valleys. Farms in this area tend to be small.

The Blue Ridge Mountains are a chain that forms part of the eastern edge of the Appalachians. Mount Mitchell in North Carolina is in this chain. It is the highest peak east of the Mississippi River. The Great Smoky Mountains form part of the western edge of the Appalachians.

One area in and around the Appalachian Mountains is known as **Appalachia.** This area is known for its rich natural resources, such as coal, and
7 its dense forests. Most of Appalachia lies in the Southeast region. Virginia, West Virginia, Kentucky, North Carolina, South Carolina, Tennessee, Georgia, and Alabama all include parts of Appalachia.

REVIEW What areas lie inland from the coastal plains?
Main Idea and Details

Summarize the Lesson

- **Beaches and wetlands line the shores of the Southeast region.**
- **The elevation of the land increases as you go farther inland from the coast.**
- **The fall line is the border between the coastal plains and the Piedmont.**
- **The Appalachian Mountains extend through the Southeast region.**

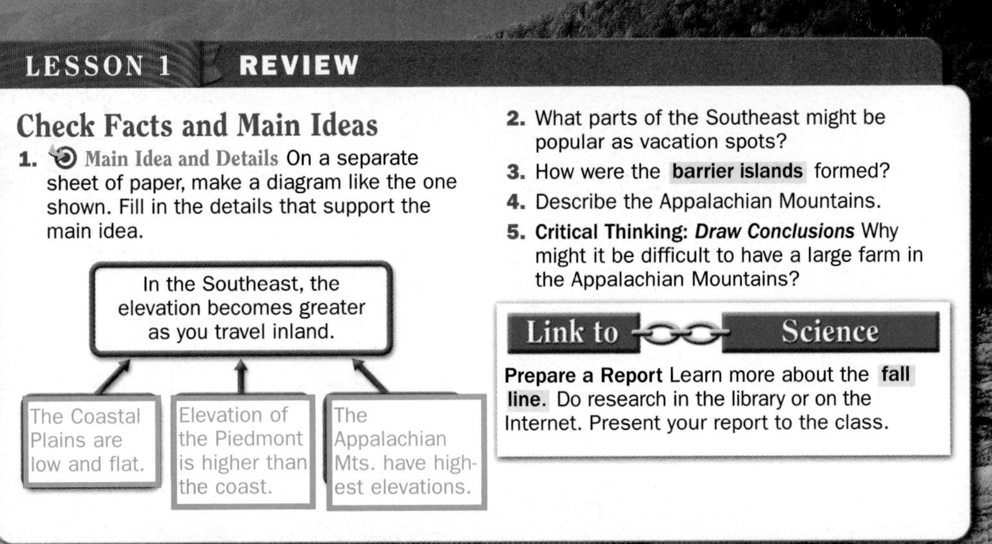

LESSON 1 **REVIEW**

Check Facts and Main Ideas

1. Main Idea and Details On a separate sheet of paper, make a diagram like the one shown. Fill in the details that support the main idea.

In the Southeast, the elevation becomes greater as you travel inland.
The Coastal Plains are low and flat.
Elevation of the Piedmont is higher than the coast.
The Appalachian Mts. have highest elevations.

2. What parts of the Southeast might be popular as vacation spots?
3. How were the **barrier islands** formed?
4. Describe the Appalachian Mountains.
5. **Critical Thinking:** ***Draw Conclusions*** Why might it be difficult to have a large farm in the Appalachian Mountains?

Link to Science

Prepare a Report Learn more about the **fall line.** Do research in the library or on the Internet. Present your report to the class.

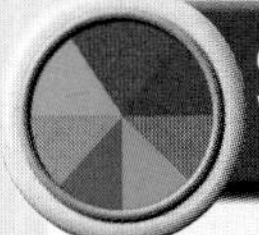

CURRICULUM CONNECTION
Writing

Describe the Appalachian Trail

- Have students use online or library resources to research facts about the Appalachian Trail, a 2,167-mile footpath along the crests and valleys of the Appalachian Mountains.
- Tell students to use these facts in a story, poem, or essay celebrating the trail and the Southeast region.

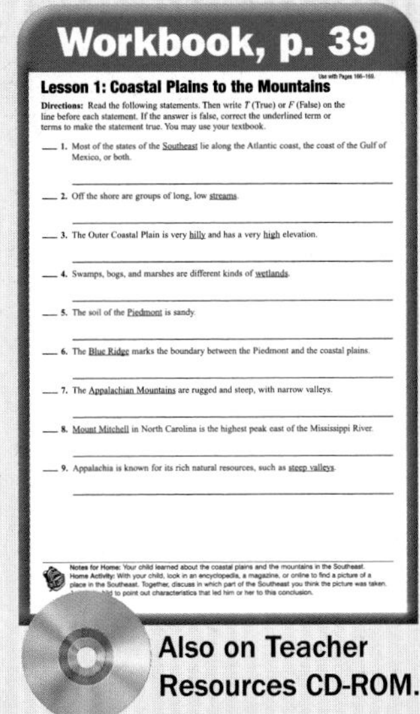

Workbook, p. 39

Use with Pages 166–169.

Lesson 1: Coastal Plains to the Mountains

Directions: Read the following statements. Then write *T* (True) or *F* (False) on the line before each statement. If the answer is false, correct the underlined term or terms to make the statement true. You may use your textbook.

___ 1. Most of the states of the Southeast lie along the Atlantic coast, the coast of the Gulf of Mexico, or both.

___ 2. Off the shore are groups of long, low streams.

___ 3. The Outer Coastal Plain is very hilly and has a very high elevation.

___ 4. Swamps, bogs, and marshes are different kinds of wetlands.

___ 5. The soil of the Piedmont is sandy.

___ 6. The Blue Ridge marks the boundary between the Piedmont and the coastal plains.

___ 7. The Appalachian Mountains are rugged and steep, with narrow valleys.

___ 8. Mount Mitchell in North Carolina is the highest peak east of the Mississippi River.

___ 9. Appalachia is known for its rich natural resources, such as steep valleys.

Notes for Home: Your child learned about the coastal plains and the mountains in the Southeast.
Home Activity: With your child, look in an encyclopedia, a magazine, or online to find a picture of a place in the Southeast. Together, discuss in which part of the Southeast you think the picture was taken. ... to point out characteristics that led him or her to this conclusion.

Also on Teacher Resources CD-ROM.

7 What kinds of natural resources would you find in Appalachia? Coal, forests Main Idea and Details

✓ **REVIEW ANSWER** The Piedmont, Appalachian Mountains, and Appalachia Main Idea and Details

3 Close and Assess

Summarize the Lesson

Have student volunteers read the four main points aloud. As they read, have the remaining students point to each described area on the map on p. 167 of their textbook.

✓ LESSON 1 **REVIEW**

1. **Main Idea and Details** For possible answers, see the reduced pupil page.
2. Possible answers: Beaches, mountains, the fall line

Test Talk

Write Your Answer to Score High

3. Students should make sure that their written answer is focused and has only details from the text that answer the question. As glaciers melted, streams and rivers carried sand and gravel away from the land and deposited them in the shallow waters off the coast to form islands.

4. Rugged and steep, with narrow valleys and small farms
5. **Critical Thinking:** ***Draw Conclusions*** Possible answer: It might be difficult to plant and maintain crops on the steep, rugged mountainsides.

Link to Science

Reports should include interesting details about the fall line.

Map and Globe Skills

Read Elevation Maps

Objectives

- Explain how to use an elevation map.
- Use an elevation map to compare and contrast landform elevations in the Southeast.

Vocabulary

elevation map p. 170; **sea level,** p. 170

Resources

- Workbook, p. 40
- Transparency 41

1 Introduce and Motivate

What is an elevation map? Ask students how hikers might use information about elevations when planning a hiking trip. (Possible answer: It might help them judge how difficult it will be to hike a certain area and to estimate how long it will take.) Then have students read the **What?** section of text on p. 170 to help set the purpose of the lesson.

Why use elevation maps? Have students read the **Why?** section of text on p. 171. Ask them to describe what an elevation map of your city, state, or region might look like and why.

Map and Globe Skills

Read Elevation Maps

What? Maps help you locate different places and find out about a region. Different kinds of maps can show you different kinds of things. An **elevation map** shows you how high the land is. Elevation is height above **sea level.** A place that is at sea level is at the same height as the surface of the ocean's water.

This elevation map uses color to show elevation. The map below uses color to show the average height of the land across the Southeast. It also gives the elevations of some mountains.

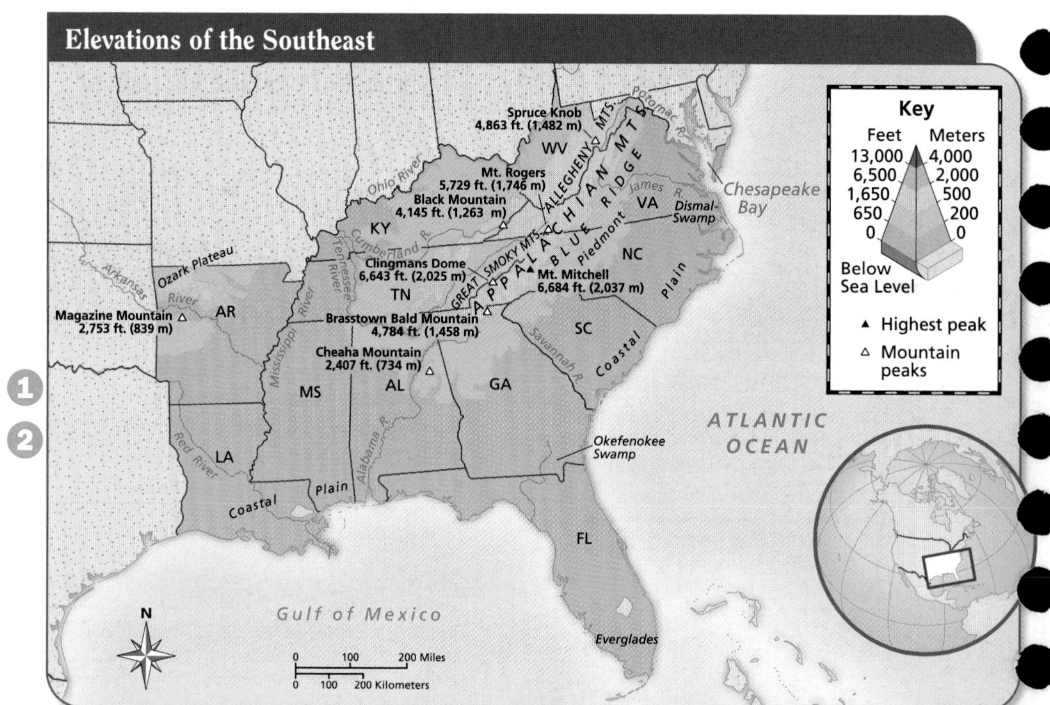

1

2

Practice and Extend

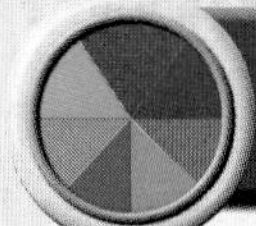

CURRICULUM CONNECTION
Art

Create an Elevation Map

- Have students use an atlas or the Internet to find an elevation map of your state.
- Tell students to draw the elevation map, assigning specific colors to each elevation range.
- Next, have them add symbols to their maps for cities, important landmarks, historical attractions, recreational areas, lakes, and rivers.
- Display students' completed maps in the classroom.

SOCIAL STUDIES STRAND
Geography

The following map resources are available:

- Big Book Atlas
- Student Atlas
- Outline Maps
- Desk Maps
- Map Resources CD-ROM

WEB SITE
Technology

Students can find out more by clicking on *Atlas* at **www.sfsocialstudies.com.** Help students identify key search terms.

For more information, go online to the *Atlas* at **www.sfsocialstudies.com.**

Why? Elevation maps can help you locate important landmarks. They can show you the location of important features in a region and help you better understand what that region is like.

How? To read an elevation map, first (3) look at the map key. Notice that there are numbers next to each color on the (4) map key. The numbers show the range of elevation that each color represents. Notice that on the elevation map on page 170, dark green represents the lowest elevations. The range for dark green is between 0 and 650 feet above sea level.

Think and Apply

1. What is the elevation range of the coastal plain that borders the Atlantic Ocean? that borders the Gulf of Mexico?
2. Based on the **elevation map**, what is the name of the highest elevation range? Explain how you know.
3. What is the difference in elevation in feet between Mt. Mitchell and Magazine Mountain?

▶ The view from Magazine Mountain, the highest point in the Boston Mountains of Arkansas.

171

2 Teach and Discuss

How is this skill used? Examine with students the elevation map on p. 170.

- Point out that the different colors on the map show different elevations of landforms in the Southeast region of the United States.
- Have students read the **How?** section of text on p. 171.

1 Look at the map on p. 170. Which has a higher average elevation, Virginia or Mississippi? Virginia Interpret Maps

2 Look again at the map on p. 170. Which has a lower elevation, the Piedmont or the Ozark Plateau? Piedmont Interpret Maps

3 When using an elevation map, what is the first thing you should do? Look at the map key Sequence

Test Talk

Use Information from Graphics

4 What do the colors represent on the elevation map on p. 170? What do the numbers represent? Tell students to go back and look at the key on the map to find the right answer. Different elevation ranges; number of feet above sea level Interpret Maps

3 Close and Assess

Think and Apply

1. 0 to 650 feet; 0 to 650 feet
2. The Appalachian mountain range, including the Great Smoky Mountains and the Allegheny Mountains; because the color key shows that 6,500 feet to 13,000 feet is the highest range on this map
3. 3,931 feet

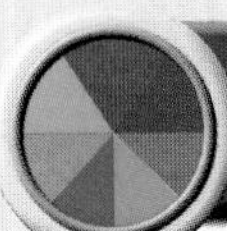

CURRICULUM CONNECTION
Math

Calculate Differences in Elevation

- Write the following mean elevations on the board: *Raleigh, North Carolina: 434 ft.; Knoxville, Tennessee: 936 ft.; Atlanta, Georgia: 1,035 ft.; Montgomery, Alabama: 160 ft.; Tallahassee, Florida: 55 ft.*
- Have students find the difference in elevation between the two highest cities on the list (99 ft.; 1,035 – 936) and between the highest and lowest cities on the list (980 ft.; 1,035 – 55).
- Ask students what mathematical operation they used to find their answers. (Subtraction)

Workbook, p. 40

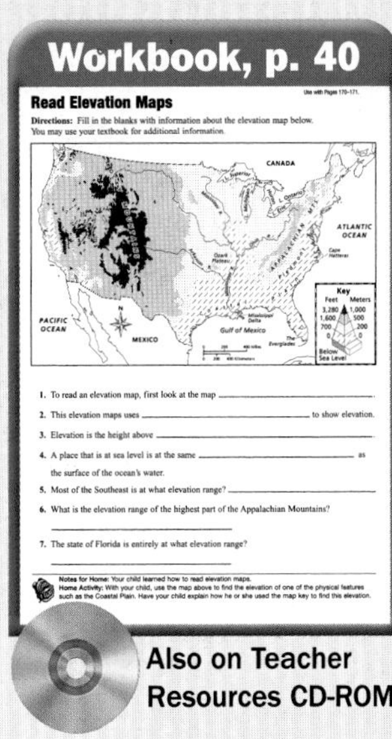

Use with Pages 170–171.

Read Elevation Maps

Directions: Fill in the blanks with information about the elevation map below. You may use your textbook for additional information.

1. To read an elevation map, first look at the map ______.
2. This elevation maps uses ______ to show elevation.
3. Elevation is the height above ______.
4. A place that is at sea level is at the same ______ as the surface of the ocean's water.
5. Most of the Southeast is at what elevation range? ______
6. What is the elevation range of the highest part of the Appalachian Mountains? ______
7. The state of Florida is entirely at what elevation range? ______

Notes for Home: Your child learned how to read elevation maps.
Home Activity: With your child, use the map above to find the elevation of one of the physical features such as the Coastal Plain. Have your child explain how he or she used the map key to find this elevation.

Also on Teacher Resources CD-ROM.

Sunlight and Storms

Objectives

- Describe the climate of the Southeast.
- Examine hurricanes in the Southeast.
- Explain the function of lighthouses.

Vocabulary

key, p. 173; **hurricane,** p. 174; **hurricane season,** p. 174

Resources

- Workbook, p. 41
- Transparency 1
- Every Student Learns Guide, pp. 70–73
- Quick Study, pp. 36–37

Quick Teaching Plan

If time is short, have students list the pros and cons of the climate of the Southeast.

- Have students create a T-chart with the headings *Pros* and *Cons.*
- As students read the lesson, have them complete the chart with details about the climate of the Southeast.

1 Introduce and Motivate

Preview To activate prior knowledge, ask volunteers to describe a typical winter day in their region. If students live in a southern state, discuss why some people from colder climates come to their area in the winter. Tell students that in Lesson 2, they will learn more about the climate of the Southeast.

You Are There Point out that outdoor sports such as deep-sea fishing play a large role in the economy of areas with warm climates. Have students brainstorm how the scene described could bring money into an area's economy.

LESSON 2

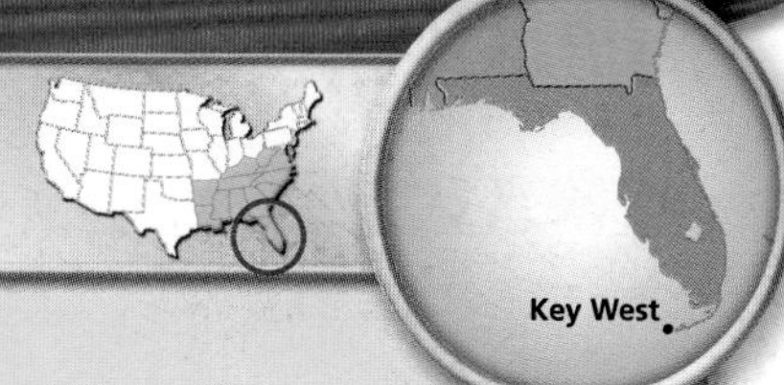

PREVIEW

Focus on the Main Idea
The mild climates of the coastal areas of the Southeast bring many tourists, but the area has some natural hazards.

PLACES
Key West, Florida
Florida Keys

VOCABULARY
key
hurricane
hurricane season

Sunlight and Storms

You Are There The little boat is bobbing up and down and from side to side. It's hard to hold onto the fishing pole because your safety vest is so big. It's December, but you feel warm. The sun is bright and the winds are gentle.

Just yesterday, you were wearing boots, mittens, and a heavy jacket. It was snowing in Boston, and the winds almost blew you down. You helped your father shovel snow.

Now, your father is helping you hold your fishing pole. You feel very lucky to be in Key West, Florida. December here is not at all like it is in Boston. You can see why so many people like to come here, especially in the winter. Now, if only you could catch a really big fish!

Main Idea and Details As you read, find the details about the different climates of the Southeast.

172

Practice and Extend

READING SKILL Main Idea/Details

In the Lesson Review, students complete a graphic organizer like the one below. You may want to provide students with a copy of Transparency 1 to complete as they read the lesson.

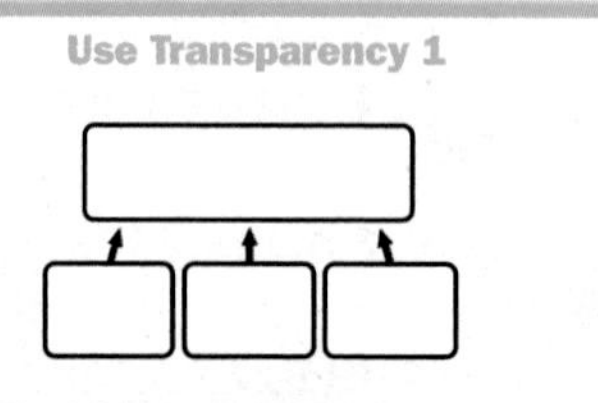

VOCABULARY Related Word Study

Explain that **homonyms** are words that sound alike and are spelled alike, but have different meanings and word origins. *Key* in the lesson comes from *cayo*, a word that was adopted by Spanish explorers from a term they learned from the native people of the Caribbean islands. Context can help students recognize when a familiar definition doesn't work, and can often provide clues to meaning. Point out that the dictionary has separate listings for the different types of keys.

Enjoying the Climate

Key West, an island off the southern coast of Florida, is one of a chain of islands called the **Florida Keys**. A **key** is a low island.

1 Mild, sunny weather attracts many tourists to Florida in winter. The northern part of the state gets cool in winter—in the 50 degree range. The southern part usually stays warm—in the 70 degree range. In the summer, though, all of Florida is hot and humid. Cool ocean or gulf breezes make the coastal beaches good places to visit in the summer!

Louisiana, Mississippi, and Alabama also have hot, humid climates in the summer. Louisiana is also one of the rainiest states. The average yearly rainfall there is 57 inches.

States in the coastal plains—Georgia, South Carolina, North Carolina, and Virginia—have warm climates most of the year. When you get into the Appalachian Mountains, however, the temperature drops. Snow 2
falls in the mountains in winter.

REVIEW How does the climate of the Southeast change as you move north? **Main Idea and Details**

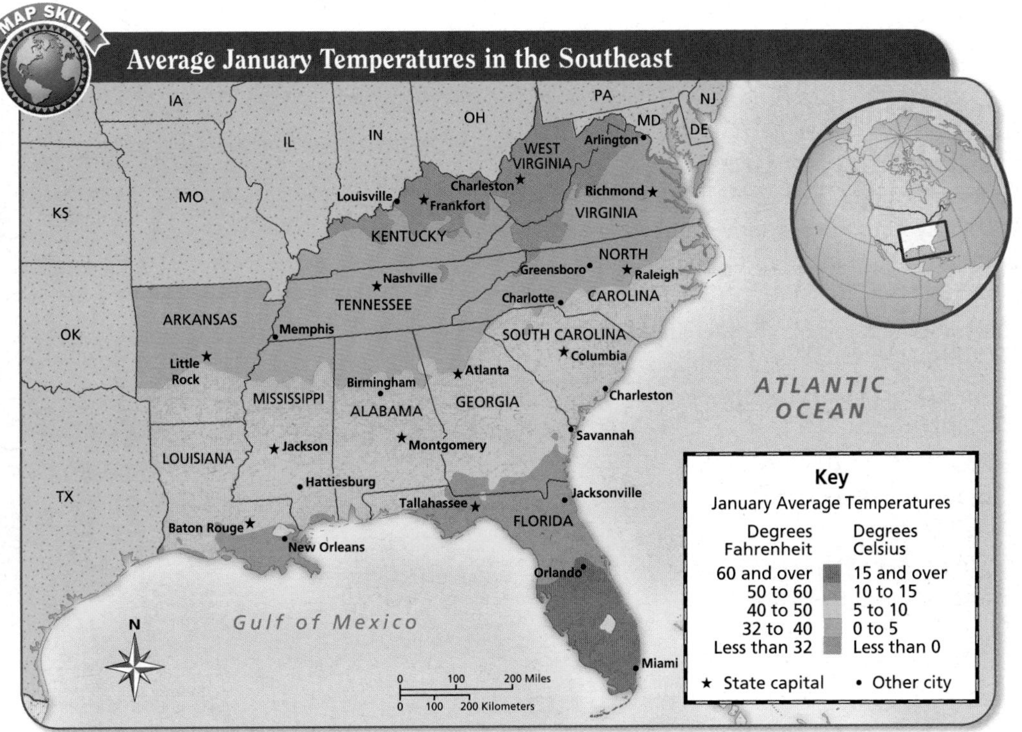

▶ **In January, the Southeast is usually warmer than many other parts of the United States.**

MAP SKILL **Use Intermediate Directions** ***In what direction would you travel from Savannah, Georgia to Atlanta, Georgia?***

ESL Support

ACCESS CONTENT

Explore Climate Help students learn words related to climate.

Beginning Write the words *climate, tropical, temperate,* and *arctic* on the board and display pictures related to each. Ask students to point to the correct word as you ask questions such as "Where do palm trees grow?"

Intermediate Show students the words and pictures above, and ask students to identify the climate of a different region or country.

Advanced Have students give a brief oral description of each type of climate pictured above.

For additional ESL support, use Every Student Learns Guide, pp. 70–73.

2 Teach and Discuss

PAGE 173

Enjoying the Climate

Quick Summary Southern Florida and the Florida Keys have a tropical climate. Northern Florida and its neighboring states have a more temperate, or mild, climate.

SOCIAL STUDIES STRAND
Geography

The John Pennekamp Coral Reef State Park, along the eastern coast of Key Largo, was the first underwater park in the United States. It protects the largest living coral reefs in North America.

1 **Why might tourists want to visit southern Florida during the winter?** Possible answers: To enjoy the warm weather and participate in outdoor activities **Draw Conclusions**

2 **Why do you think the Appalachian Mountains receive snow in the winter when so much of the Southeast region is warm?** The elevation is much higher. **Draw Conclusions**

✓ **REVIEW ANSWER** Along the southern part of Florida and the Florida Keys, the climate is hot and humid. Farther north, the climate is temperate. Inland toward the mountains, the climate is cooler. **Main Idea and Details**

Average January Temperatures in the Southeast

Point out the shading on the map and the corresponding map key that denotes different temperatures in the Southeast.

Which state in the Southeast has the coldest average temperature in January? West Virginia **Interpret Maps**

MAP SKILL Answer Northwest

Watch Out!

Quick Summary Weather forecasters help people prepare for bad weather such as severe storms and hurricanes. Lighthouses were originally built to warn sailors of other hazards.

Decision Making

3 **What factors should people consider when they are deciding whether to live along the Southeast coast?** Possible answer: The pleasant climate and beauty of the coast as well as the danger of hurricanes and the rocky shorelines Make Decisions

✓ Ongoing Assessment

If... students have difficulty recognizing that this is a two-part question,	then... break the question up by asking "What is a reason for living near the coast? What is a reason not to live there?"

4 **How does a hurricane cause destruction?** Its strong winds can uproot trees and damage buildings, and it creates huge waves that can cause flooding. Main Idea and Details

Map Adventure Answers

1. Route 12; **2.** Atlantic Ocean;
3. A car and a ferry; Southwest;
4. Pamlico Sound

Watch Out!

People in the Southeast enjoy mild weather much of the time, but sometimes the weather can be
3 dangerous. Hurricanes sometimes occur along the Atlantic and Gulf coasts. A **hurricane** is a violent storm that forms over the ocean. Its strong winds move in a circular path. Along with the winds are very heavy rains. A hurricane smashing into the coast can be very destructive.

Hurricane winds can be strong enough to send large objects flying. They can uproot trees and damage buildings. The huge waves pound the shore and often cause flooding. 4

Hurricanes mainly occur from June until the end of November. This time of year is known as **hurricane season.** Weather forecasters have the equipment and technology to help them figure out the path that a hurricane will most likely take. This information helps people prepare for hurricanes and move to safety. People usually move inland, away from the coast.

The rocky shorelines are another hazard of the coastal areas. Long ago, as in the Northeast, people built lighthouses to

Map Adventure

Visiting Lighthouses

Take a trip along the outer coast of North Carolina to visit some famous lighthouses. Use the map to plan your trip.

1. Your first stop is the Bodie Island Lighthouse. What road will take you to the Cape Hatteras Lighthouse?
2. What body of water is to the east of the Cape Hatteras Lighthouse?
3. What types of transportation take you to the Ocracoke Lighthouse from the Cape Hatteras Lighthouse? In what direction would you be traveling?
4. What body of water is to the north of the Ocracoke Lighthouse?

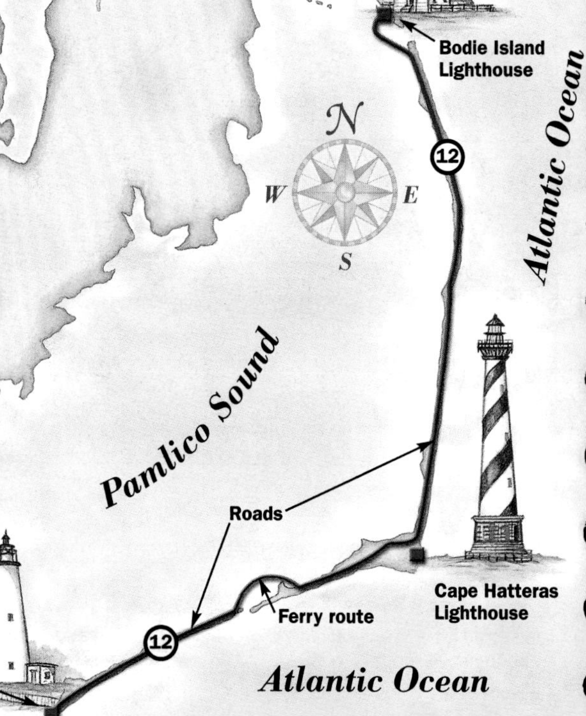

174

Practice and Extend

MEETING INDIVIDUAL NEEDS
Leveled Practice

Report on Storms Have students deliver an oral report on destructive storms.

Easy Have students research and report on five facts about hurricanes. **Reteach**

On-Level Have students use an almanac, the Internet, or other sources to research the most destructive hurricane in U.S. history. Have them report their findings orally. **Extend**

Challenge Have students prepare and deliver an oral report comparing and contrasting hurricanes, tornadoes, cyclones, and blizzards. **Enrich**

For a Lesson Summary, use Quick Study, p. 36.

help sailors avoid the rocky coastlines. The lighthouses warned the sailors of dangerous rocks and currents along the Southeast coast. The strong lights were very bright, and many could be seen as far as twenty miles out to sea. Lighthouses were built in different shapes and colors. In the daytime, sailors could tell where they were because they could recognize the lighthouses. At night, each lighthouse had a light using a special pattern. This helped sailors know which lighthouse they were near. 5 6

Sailors now use other tools and technology to help them find their way. Many lighthouses are no longer working, but people still enjoy visiting these colorful buildings. 7

REVIEW What are some natural hazards of living near the coast in the Southeast? Main Idea and Details

Summarize the Lesson

- **The mild climates of the Southeast attract many tourists.**
- **Hurricanes are dangerous storms that can strike coastal areas.**
- **Lighthouses were built to warn sailors about rocky shores and also to help sailors determine their location.**

▶ **The Bodie Island Lighthouse is near the coast of North Carolina.**

LESSON 2 **REVIEW**

Check Facts and Main Ideas

1. Main Idea and Details On a separate sheet of paper, draw a diagram like the one shown. Fill in some details that support the main idea.

Many tourists visit the Southeast, especially from November to June.

Temperatures are warm in the winter.	People might not visit during the hurricane season.	Tourists can find many things to do.

2. When do **hurricanes** usually occur?
3. Why are hurricanes dangerous?
4. Why were lighthouses built?
5. **Critical Thinking:** ***Make Inferences*** Why is living near the Southeast coast both good and bad?

Link to Science

Learn about Hurricanes Use reference materials to learn what causes hurricanes. Find out why they are more likely to occur at certain times of the year. Prepare a brief report and present it to the class.

175

MEETING INDIVIDUAL NEEDS
Learning Styles

Explore Lighthouses Using their individual learning styles, students learn more about lighthouses.

Kinesthetic Learning Have students use cardboard, construction paper, or other classroom materials to build a model lighthouse.

Visual Learning Have students create an illustrated map, like the one on p. 174, showing lighthouses in another portion of the Southeast.

Logical Learning Have students research and explain what was used as a light source in early lighthouses and what is used today.

Workbook, p. 41

Lesson 2: Sunlight and Storms

Also on Teacher Resources CD-ROM.

5 **What purpose did lighthouses originally serve?** To help sailors avoid the rocky coastlines, to warn them about dangerous rocks and currents, and to help them tell where they were Main Idea and Details

6 **In what two ways did lighthouses provide information to sailors?** Through their different shapes and colors and through a light that flashes in a special pattern Apply Information

7 **What purpose do many lighthouses serve today?** People enjoy visiting them. Main Idea and Details

✓ **REVIEW ANSWER** Hurricanes can occur; shorelines can be rocky, with dangerous currents. Main Idea and Details

3 Close and Assess

Summarize the Lesson

Have students take turns reading the three main points. As each point is read, work together as a class to add details and brainstorm examples.

✓ LESSON 2 **REVIEW**

1. **Main Idea and Details** For possible answers, see the reduced pupil page.
2. Hurricane season usually lasts from June until the end of November.
3. Winds can be strong enough to damage trees and buildings, and huge waves can cause flooding.
4. To help sailors avoid rocky coastlines and to warn them about dangerous rocks and currents
5. **Critical Thinking: *Make Inferences*** Possible answer: The coast has nice weather and beautiful beaches, but it also can be hit by dangerous storms.

Link to Science

Students' research should reveal that hurricanes often are formed when storms over warm ocean waters gain intensity and wind speed. Hurricanes usually occur between June and November because that is when the Atlantic waters are warmest.

Dorling Kindersley

Hurricanes

Objectives

- Explain how hurricanes form.
- Describe the effects of hurricanes.

1 Introduce and Motivate

- Tell students that one drawback of living along the coast of the Southeast in the United States is a recurring threat of hurricanes.
- Before students read these pages, have them brainstorm and list reasons hurricanes might present a danger to people living or working near a coastline. Tell students they will learn more about the dangers of hurricanes as they read these pages.
- Students will revise their lists as part of the assessment for these pages.

2 Teach and Discuss

1 **Why might a forecast of "high seas" be important to a fisherman?** High seas are stormy seas with dangerous waves that can sink a ship or leave it stranded. Apply Information

2 **Does a hurricane usually increase or decrease coastal erosion? Explain.** Increase; A hurricane can create waves and stormy seas that dissolve rock and break off parts of cliffs along the coastline. Main Idea and Details

DORLING KINDERSLEY EYEWITNESS BOOK

Hurricanes

The sea covers about two-thirds of our planet. Strong winds constantly disturb the surface of the oceans, producing waves that break as they reach the shore. During severe storms, particularly hurricanes, winds push seawater high onto the shore. Areas close to the shore can become flooded. At high tides, the risk of serious flooding during storms increases. People living on the coast are not the only ones who are at risk. Ships can sink in stormy weather, leaving passengers and crew members stranded in dangerous waters.

1 **In Deep Water**
High seas are stormy seas with dangerous waves that can sink a ship or leave it stranded. Air-sea rescue helicopters rush to the aid of survivors. The helicopters hover above the sea while a rescuer is lowered on a winch to lift the survivors clear of the water.

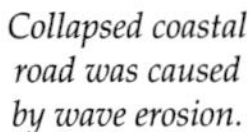

A rescuer is lowered to the sea by a search and rescue helicopter.

2 **Tearing Along**
Crashing waves damage the coastlines. The waves dissolve pieces of rock and break off parts of cliffs. As the sea becomes stormier and its level becomes higher, the erosion becomes greater.

Collapsed coastal road was caused by wave erosion.

3 **Stormy Sea**
When Hurricane Hugo hit the West Indies and southeastern United States in 1989, it produced a sudden surge 6 feet (2 m) high in open water. This wall of water rose to 18 feet (6 m) in some places. The sudden and dramatic rise in sea level when a hurricane reaches land is caused by low air pressure at the storm's center.

176

Practice and Extend

CURRICULUM CONNECTION
Drama

Perform Monologues

- Have students use the Internet or other resources to find a news description of a historical or recent hurricane.
- Ask students to write and present a first-person monologue from the point of view of someone who experienced the hurricane, such as a local resident, a police officer, the city's mayor, or a reporter.

CURRICULUM CONNECTION
Science

Learn More About Hurricanes

- Have students use the Internet or library resources to find out more about the science of hurricanes or accounts of actual storms, such as the Galveston hurricane of 1900 or Hurricane Hugo.
- Have students create a poster illustrating their findings. Encourage them to include pictures, accurate labels, and explanations of important information on their posters.

Wall of Water

An ocean wave begins as wind blows across the sea's surface, making the water swing up and down, and back and forth. When the wave nears the shore, where the sea becomes shallower, the movement is broken, and the water topples over, forming a breaker. Huge breakers, such as this one, are sometimes called "dumpers." They send water crashing in all directions if they hit the shore. 4

This huge wave is on the verge of breaking.

177

3 **What can cause a sudden and dramatic rise in sea level when a hurricane reaches land?** Low air pressure at the storm's center
Main Idea and Details

4 **How can huge breakers called "dumpers" contribute to the erosion of a shore?** They send water crashing in all directions when they hit the shore, which can wash away parts of the shoreline. **Draw Conclusions**

3 Close and Assess

- Encourage students to use the Internet and print resources to learn more about hurricanes.
- Ask students to revise the lists they created earlier of dangers that hurricanes present to people living and working along a coastline. Have students discuss what they learned about hurricanes from the pictures on these pages.

SOCIAL STUDIES
Background

About Hurricanes

- Hurricanes appear on radar as a large, swirling mass of clouds. In the Northern Hemisphere, hurricanes rotate in a counterclockwise direction around a center point known as the "eye" of the storm.
- A hurricane is a severe tropical storm. To be classified as a hurricane, a tropical storm's winds must exceed 64 knots, or 74 miles per hour.
- Hurricanes are classified into five categories according to wind speed. A Category One hurricane has winds of 74 to 95 miles per hour. The most devastating hurricanes are Category Five storms, with winds in excess of 155 miles per hour.
- The most destructive hurricane in recent U.S. history was Hurricane Andrew in 1992, which caused about $26.5 billion in damage to southern Florida and south-central Louisiana.

Wildlife and Resources

Objectives

- Describe the importance of protecting endangered species.
- Identify ways in which resources of the Southeast are used.
- Identify a renewable and a nonrenewable resource found in the Southeast.
- Explain why coal is an important resource in the Southeast.

Vocabulary

endangered species, p. 179; **extinct,** p. 179; **pulp,** p. 182; **fossil fuel,** p. 183

Resources

- Workbook, p. 42
- Transparency 1
- Every Student Learns Guide, pp. 74–77
- Quick Study, pp. 38–39

Quick Teaching Plan

If time is short, have students set up a three-column chart with the headings *Animal, Vegetable,* and *Mineral* and take notes in the chart as they read the lesson independently.

1 Introduce and Motivate

Preview To activate prior knowledge, ask students to identify the animal pictured on p. 178. (alligator) If some students incorrectly identify the reptile as a crocodile, explain that an alligator has a wider, shorter snout than a crocodile. Tell students that in Lesson 3 they will be reading more about animals and other resources of the Southeast.

You Are There Ask students how they might act if they saw an alligator up close in the wild. Discuss with students why it might be important to preserve the diverse wildlife habitat of the Florida Everglades.

LESSON 3

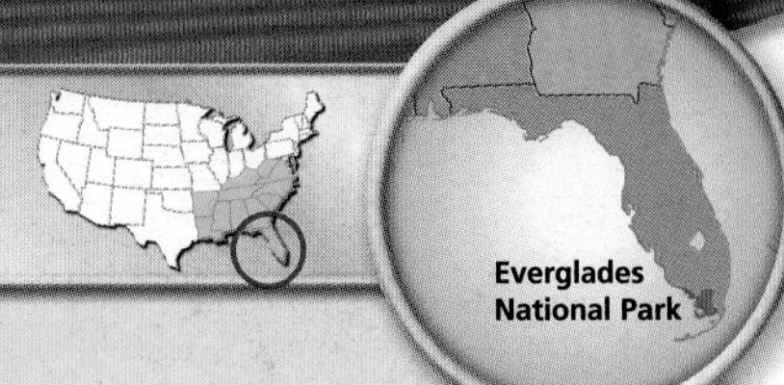

Wildlife and Resources

PREVIEW

Focus on the Main Idea
The Southeast is rich in different resources. These resources are used in different industries throughout the region.

PLACES
Everglades National Park

VOCABULARY
endangered species
extinct
pulp
fossil fuel

You Are There You and your family are riding in a boat through the Everglades. Your boat glides underneath cypress trees and past high grasses. Suddenly, something moves in the water. Seconds later, you hear an enormous splash! You look out over the water. You see only a pair of eyes looking back at you from the surface. The eyes come nearer and nearer as the creature swims closer to your boat. You see its long, low head first, and then you stare in fascination as you recognize it as an alligator.

Your mom tells you that alligators have lived in the Everglades for hundreds of years!

Main Idea and Details As you read, look for details that describe the resources of the Southeast.

178

Practice and Extend

READING SKILL
Main Idea/Details

In the Lesson Review, students complete a graphic organizer like the one below. You may want to provide students with a copy of Transparency 1 to complete as they read the lesson.

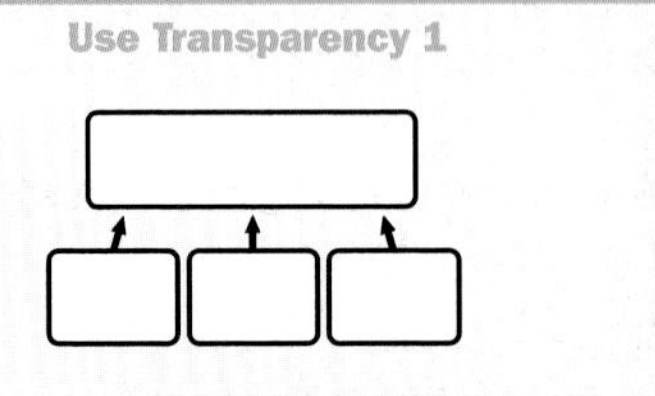

VOCABULARY
Context Clues

Discuss the terms *endangered species* and *extinct.* Have students review the definitions of these words in the text. Then ask students to think of times in their own lives when they have read, heard about, or discussed endangered species or extinct animals. Help students list examples of extinct animals, such as dinosaurs, dodos, and mammoths. Then discuss endangered species, such as blue whales, humpback whales, and Florida panthers.

Fins, Feathers, and Fur

If you visit a swamp in the Southeast, you may see alligators. In Florida many alligators live in swamps, canals, and lakes. But alligators were not always so common in Florida and other parts of the Southeast. In the 1960s many alligators were hunted for food or for their hides. By 1967 the alligator became an endangered species. An **endangered species** is a kind of animal or plant that is thought to be in danger of becoming **extinct,** or no longer existing.

After 1967 it was against the law to
1 hunt alligators. The numbers of alligators slowly grew. By 1987 alligators had made a comeback. The United States Fish and Wildlife Service took the alligator off the list of endangered species.

Many other animals, including herons, turtles, and fish, can be found in the wetlands of the Southeast. The **Everglades National Park,** a huge area of wetlands in southern Florida, is
home to about 600 different kinds of 2
birds and other animals. About a dozen kinds of animals that live in the Everglades, including the Florida panther and the manatee, are endangered.

The Coastal Plain and Piedmont are also home to a wide variety of animals, such as deer and birds. In the Appalachian Mountains, black bears, deer, and other animals live in the forests.

REVIEW How have certain laws affected the number of alligators? Cause and Effect

Literature and Social Studies

The Yearling

Marjorie Kinnan Rawlings wrote this famous novel about farm life in central Florida in the late 1800s. In the passage below, a 12-year-old boy named Jody finds a young deer, a one-year-old fawn, known as a yearling, in the forest.

Under a scrub palmetto he was able to make out a track, pointed and dainty as the mark of a ground-dove. He crawled past the palmetto.

Movement directly in front of him startled him so that he tumbled backward. The fawn lifted its face to his. It turned its head with a wide, wondering motion and shook [scared] him through with the stare of its liquid eyes. It was quivering [shaking]. It made no effort to rise or run. Jody could not trust himself to move. 3

He whispered, "It's me."

The fawn lifted its nose, scenting [smelling] him. He reached out one hand and laid it on the soft neck.

ACCESS CONTENT
ESL Support

Identify Species Help students learn about different species of animals.

Beginning Show students pictures of the animals discussed on p. 179: alligator, heron, turtle, fish, panther, manatee, deer, and black bear. Help students pronounce the name of each animal as you show its picture.

Intermediate Tape the animal pictures to the board in one column and write the animal names in another column. Have students match each animal to its name.

Advanced Have students work in pairs to create an illustrated poster of these animals. Have students tell one detail about one of the animals as they share their posters with the class.

For additional ESL support, use Every Student Learns Guide, pp. 74–77.

2 Teach and Discuss

PAGE 179

Fins, Feathers, and Fur

Quick Summary The Southeast is home to many types of animals, some of which are endangered species. The Florida Everglades is especially rich in wildlife.

SOCIAL STUDIES STRAND
History

The word *alligator* comes from the Spanish words *el lagarto,* meaning "the lizard."

1 **How did the alligator become an endangered species? How did the species make a comeback?** Too many alligators were hunted for food or for their hides; A law made it illegal to hunt alligators. Cause and Effect

2 **About how many different kinds of birds and other animals live in the Everglades National Park?** About 600 different kinds
Main Idea and Details

✓ **REVIEW ANSWER** Laws against hunting alligators have kept the species from dying out. Cause and Effect

Literature and Social Studies

Have students read the selection from *The Yearling* by Marjorie Kinnan Rawlings.

Test Talk

Locate Key Words in the Question

3 **Based on the passage and what you know about wild animals, what do you predict will be the central conflict, or problem, that Jody will face?** Tell students, "A key word such as *predict* tells you to write what you think will happen based on the information in the passage." Possible answer: Whether to keep the deer as a pet or to let it remain a wild animal Predict

PAGE 180

Harvesting a Bumper Crop

Quick Summary The Southeast is an important agricultural region, made possible by good farmland, a long growing season, warm temperatures, and plenty of rain.

4 **What vegetable is grown more than any other crop in the Southeast?** Soybeans Main Idea and Details

5 **The Southeast leads the nation in production of some crops. What are two of these crops?** Possible answers: Peanuts and rice Apply Information

Ongoing Assessment

If... students have trouble identifying two crops,	**then...** ask them which states produce the most peanuts and the most rice, and where these states are located.

6 **Do you think the increasing importance of manufacturing and other industries is a positive change for the Southeast? Why or why not?** Possible answers: Yes; It may be risky to base an area's economy entirely on a single industry. Evaluate

REVIEW ANSWER The coastal plains have good farmland, warm temperatures, plenty of rain, and a long growing season. Main Idea and Details

▶ Orange grove near Orlando, Florida

Harvesting a Bumper Crop

In addition to forests and swamps, the coastal plains of the Southeast contain wide stretches of good farmland. Land for farming is a valuable resource. Farming has been an important industry ever since the first settlers came to the Southeast. Today, the major crops of the region include cotton, corn, peanuts, rice, oranges, and soybeans. Soybeans
4 are used to make vegetable oil and food for livestock. They also can be made into many other healthful foods.

The coastal plains have warm temperatures and plenty of rain, which makes this area excellent for farming. Most parts of the Southeast coastal plains have a long growing season, the time of year when it is warm enough for crops to grow. A long growing season makes it possible to grow crops like cotton, peanuts, and sugar cane. These crops cannot grow well in colder regions.

Citrus fruits, such as oranges, lemons, limes, and grapefruits, grow well in Florida because of the long growing season. Throughout the state nearly 107 million trees produce citrus fruits. Many of them are shipped to colder regions of the United States.

Directly to the north of Florida, Georgia produces more peanuts than any other state. Farms sometimes produce more than 1.5 billion pounds of peanuts a year.

Rice is also a major product of the Southeast. In fact, the Southeast produces more rice than any other part of the United States. Arkansas and Louisiana are two major producers of
rice. One-third of the rice harvested in 5
the United States is grown in Arkansas.

The agriculture industry is very important in the Southeast. Agriculture was the basis of the Southeast region's economy until the mid-1900s. However, since then manufacturing and other industries have also become important in the region.

REVIEW Why is the Southeast 6
a good region for agriculture? Main Idea and Details

Practice and Extend

CURRICULUM CONNECTION
Music

Sell Southeastern Produce

- Have students work in small groups to write an advertising jingle for a particular southeastern crop, such as soybeans, Florida oranges, or Georgia peanuts.
- Tell students to edit and revise their jingles so that they last 10–12 seconds.
- Have one group member introduce the product and the remaining group members sing or chant the jingle as you record them on audiotape.

Decision Making

Use a Decision-Making Process

- Have students consider the following decision-making scenario: **Suppose you are a new farmer in the Southeast region. The location of your farm makes it suitable to grow a number of different crops.**
- Students should use the decision-making process to decide which crops they would plant. For each step in the process, have students work in small groups to discuss and write about what must be considered as they make their decision. Write the steps on the board, or read them aloud.

1. **Identify a situation that requires a decision.**
2. **Gather information.**
3. **Identify options.**
4. **Predict consequences.**
5. **Take action to implement a decision.**

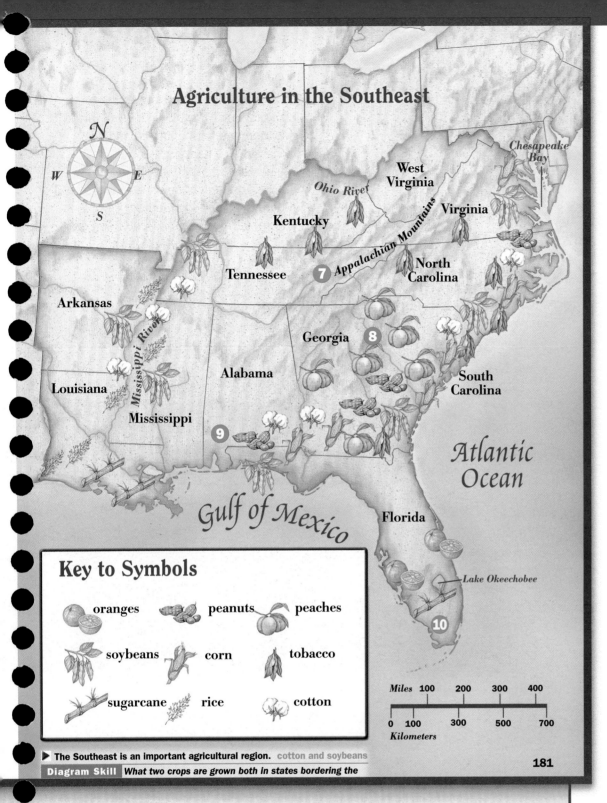

Agriculture in the Southeast

N W E S

Chesapeake Bay
West Virginia
Ohio River
Virginia
Kentucky
Appalachian Mountains
Tennessee
7
North Carolina
Arkansas
Mississippi River
Georgia
8
Alabama
South Carolina
Louisiana
Mississippi
9
Atlantic Ocean
Gulf of Mexico
Florida
Lake Okeechobee
10

Key to Symbols

oranges, peanuts, peaches, soybeans, corn, tobacco, sugarcane, rice, cotton

Miles 100 200 300 400
0 100 300 500 700
Kilometers

▶ **The Southeast is an important agricultural region.** cotton and soybeans

Diagram Skill *What two crops are grown both in states bordering the*

181

7 Why do you think few agricultural products are produced in the Appalachian Mountains? Possible answers: Because the land is steep and rugged; because the high elevation and cool climate make it difficult to grow crops **Draw Conclusions**

8 In which two states are most of the Southeast region's peaches grown? Georgia and South Carolina **Interpret Maps**

9 In which states are most of the region's peanuts grown? Virginia, North Carolina, Georgia, Alabama **Interpret Maps**

10 According to the map, what agricultural product do Louisiana and Florida have in common? Sugarcane **Interpret Maps**

Diagram Skill Answer Cotton and soybeans

MEETING INDIVIDUAL NEEDS

Leveled Practice

Report on Modern Farming Have students report on an important crop of the Southeast.

Easy Have students use one source, such as the Internet or an encyclopedia, and write a paragraph describing the growing process and uses of one southeastern crop. **Reteach**

On-Level Have students use at least two sources to prepare a two-paragraph report on how one crop is grown and how much of the U.S. supply comes from the Southeast. **Extend**

Challenge Have students use at least two sources to prepare a report on how one crop is grown, as well as any problems (such as pests) or controversies (such as the use of insecticides) associated with this crop. **Enrich**

For a Lesson Summary, use Quick Study, p. 38.

PAGE 182

Valuable Trees

Quick Summary Trees are an important resource in the Southeast, supporting the lumber, furniture, and paper industries.

11 **Name two goods that are made from trees.** Furniture and paper
Main Idea and Details

SOCIAL STUDIES STRAND
Economics

The Southeast is home to several different kinds of forests. These forests are a valuable resource for the logging industry. However, they also provide a habitat for many different kinds of plants and animals.

12 **How can the logging industry help preserve forests while still harvesting trees?** Possible answer: By practicing reforestation Solve Problems

✓ **REVIEW ANSWER** The wood from trees can be made into many different products, and trees provide homes for animals and the oxygen we breathe.
Main Idea and Details

Valuable Trees

Trees are another important resource of the Southeast. Some farmers in the Southeast grow and harvest trees, just like other crops.

Trees are also harvested from the pine forests of the coastal plains and parts of Appalachia. The trees are used to make boards for the lumber industry. They are also used for other wood products, such as furniture. Some trees are made into **pulp,** a combination of ground-up wood chips,
11 water, and chemicals. Pulp is used in the production of paper. The book you are reading right now is made from pulp!

Trees are also important to the environment. They help cool the earth, provide homes for animals, and give off oxygen we need to breathe. So that we always have enough trees, companies replant new trees where others have been harvested. This is
known as reforestation. It guarantees 12
that we will always have this very important renewable resource.

REVIEW Why are trees valuable?
Main Idea and Details

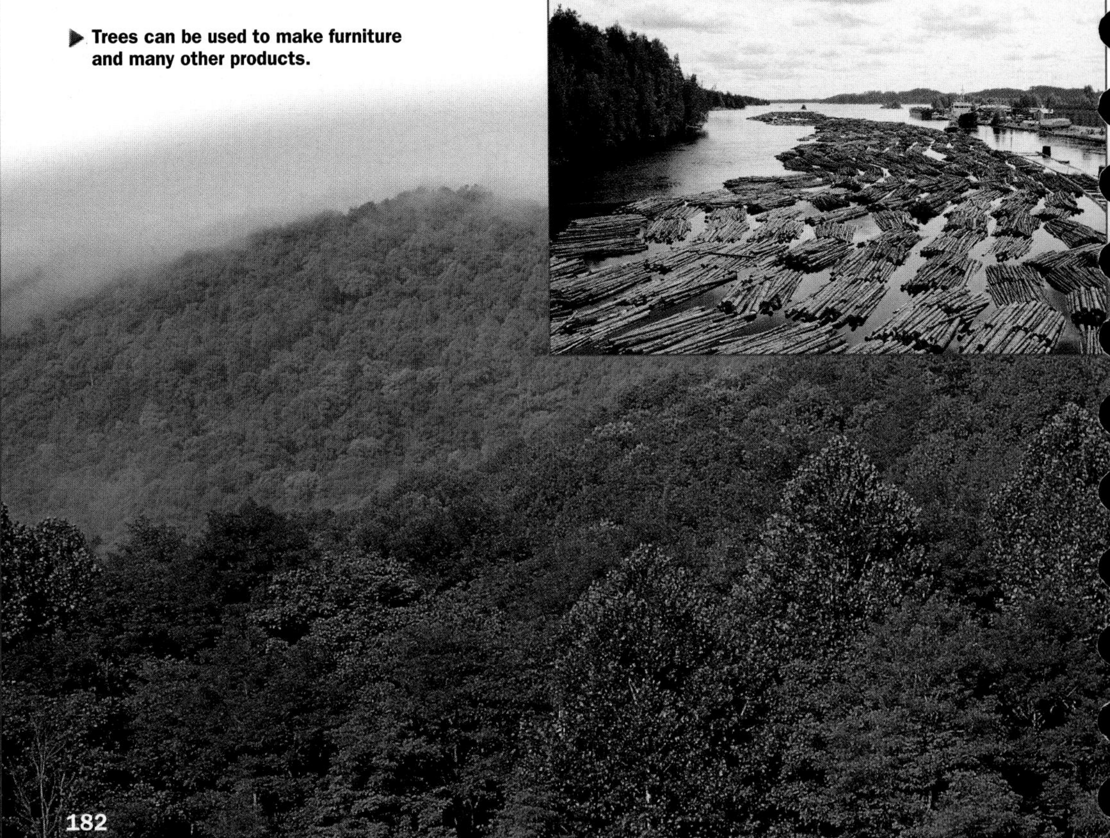

▶ Trees can be used to make furniture and many other products.

182

Practice and Extend

CURRICULUM CONNECTION
Science

Explore the Forest

- Many species of trees grow in the Great Smoky Mountains National Park. This unique collection of trees is called the Appalachian Cove Forest.
- Tell students to research the Appalachian Cove Forest to discover what species of trees grow there and why the area is so rich in plant life.
- Have students share their findings as a class.

SOCIAL STUDIES
Background

Possible Misconceptions

- Logging companies do not always own the lands on which trees are harvested. About 70 percent of commercial logging forests are on privately owned land, about 20 percent are on federal land, and about 10 percent are on state or local government land.
- Logging companies do not simply cut down trees and then move on. They almost always plant new trees to replace the mature trees that they cut down.

Coal Mining in the Southeast

Trees are a resource that grow high into the air. Deep underground, there is another resource that is important in the Southeast. This nonrenewable resource is a black fossil fuel called coal. A **fossil fuel** is a fuel that is formed in the earth from the remains of plants or animals. Coal forms over millions of years. Coal is found in some parts of Appalachia, including parts of Kentucky and West Virginia. Many electric power plants burn coal to run their generators. Chemicals made from coal are used to produce nylon, paints, plastics, aspirin, and many other products. 13

REVIEW What is coal used for? Main Idea and Details

▶ A piece of coal

Summarize the Lesson

- The Southeast is home to many different types of animals.
- Some crops grow in the warm climate of the Southeast that cannot grow in colder regions of the United States.
- In some areas of the Southeast, trees are grown as crops.
- Coal mining is important to the Appalachian economy.

LESSON 3 REVIEW

Check Facts and Main Ideas

1. Main Idea and Details On a separate sheet of paper, make a diagram like the one shown. Fill in the diagram with two more details that support the main idea.

   The resources of the Southeast are used in many ways.
   - Trees are used to make lumber, paper, and furniture.
   - Farmland is used to grow crops.
   - Coal is used for electric power.

2. Name a renewable and a nonrenewable resource found in the Southeast.
3. Why is coal an important resource? Use the term **fossil fuel** in your answer.
4. What have you eaten in the past week that might have been grown in the Southeast?
5. **Critical Thinking:** *Draw Conclusions* Why is it important to protect **endangered species?**

Link to Music

Find a Song Many folk songs have been written about coal mining. Find one or think of one you know. Write down the words. If your song mentions a specific place, find that place on a map. Share your song and its meaning with your classmates.

183

CURRICULUM CONNECTION
Literature

Read About Coal Mining

Together in Pinecone Patch, by Thomas F. Yezerski (Farrar, Straus & Giroux, ISBN 0-374-37647-6, 1998) **Easy**

Boy of the Deeps, by Ian Wallace (Dorling Kindersley Publishing, ISBN 0-7894-2569-6, 1999) **On-Level**

Growing Up in Coal Country, by Susan Campbell Bartoletti (Houghton Mifflin, ISBN 0-395-77847-6, 1996) **Challenge** ***ALA Notable Book, Jane Addams Book Award***

Workbook, p. 42

Lesson 3: Wildlife and Resources Use with Pages 178–183.

Directions: The first column of the chart below lists some of the wildlife and resources found in the Southeast. Complete the chart by writing at least one specific part of the Southeast in which each can be found.

Wildlife and Resources	Where Is It Found?
alligator	
Florida panther	
black bear	
deer	
oranges, grapefruits, lemons, limes	
peanuts	
rice	
coal	

Notes for Home: Your child learned about the wildlife and resources of the Southeast.
Home Activity: With your child, examine food resources from the Southeast, such as peanuts, rice, and citrus fruits, and discuss how your family and community depend on these resources.

Also on Teacher Resources CD-ROM.

Coal Mining in the Southeast

Quick Summary Coal, used as a fuel for electric power plants and as a source of chemicals for many everyday products, is another important resource in the Southeast.

13 **How are trees and coal similar resources? How are they different?** Possible answers: Similar: both are natural resources; both are important to the economy of the Southeast; Different: trees grow high in the air, while coal is found deep underground; trees are a renewable resource, while coal is nonrenewable. **Compare and Contrast**

✓ **REVIEW ANSWER** Coal is used for fuel or to produce nylon, paints, plastics, aspirin, and many other products. **Main Idea and Details**

3 Close and Assess

Summarize the Lesson

Have students create a short quiz using the four main points. Then have them exchange papers and answer each other's questions.

✓ **LESSON 3 REVIEW**

1. **Main Idea and Details** For possible answers, see the reduced pupil page.
2. Renewable: trees; nonrenewable: coal
3. This fossil fuel can be used for fuel and to produce many other products.
4. Possible answers: Corn, peanuts, rice, oranges
5. **Critical Thinking: *Draw Conclusions*** Because the species may become extinct without protection

Link to Music

Students' answers will depend on the songs they choose. Possible answers: *Coal Miner's Daughter* mentions Butcher Holler, Kentucky; it is about the economic hardships and personal rewards of being part of a hard-working coal miner's family.

Resources

- Assessment Book, pp. 29–32
- Workbook, p. 43: Vocabulary Review

Chapter Summary

For possible answers, see the reduced pupil page.

Vocabulary

Possible answers:

1. Wetlands, lands that are at times covered with water, can be found throughout the Southeast.
2. Many beautiful waterfalls mark the fall line between the Piedmont and the coastal plains.
3. Key West is a low island, or key, off the southern coast of Florida.
4. Many Southeastern states have suffered the effects of hurricanes, violent storms that form over the ocean.
5. The alligator is an animal of the Southeast that once was in danger of becoming extinct.
6. Trees from southeastern forests are ground into a pulp, a combination of wood chips, water, and chemicals, which is used to make paper.
7. Coal is a type of fossil fuel found in the Southeast.

Places

1. Everglades National Park
2. Piedmont
3. Appalachia

CHAPTER 6 Review

Chapter Summary

Main Idea and Details

On a separate sheet of paper, make a diagram like the one shown. Fill in details that support the main idea.

The Southeast has many different types of land.

- Along the coast are coastal plains.
- The Piedmont is inland from the plains.
- Barrier islands lie offshore.

Vocabulary

For each vocabulary word, write a sentence that defines or shows what the word means. Show how the word relates to the Southeast region.

1. **wetlands** (p. 167)
2. **fall line** (p. 168)
3. **key** (p. 173)
4. **hurricane** (p. 174)
5. **extinct** (p. 179)
6. **pulp** (p. 182)
7. **fossil fuel** (p. 183)

Places

Complete the sentences by filling in the correct place from the list below.

Piedmont (p. 168)
Appalachia (p. 169)
Everglades National Park (p. 179)

1. __________ is a huge area of wetlands in southern Florida.
2. The __________ is an area of rolling hills and valleys inland from the coastal plain.
3. One area around the Appalachian Mountains is called __________.

184

Practice and Extend

Assessment Options

✓ Chapter 6 Assessment

- Chapter 6 Content Test: Use Assessment Book, pp. 29–30.
- Chapter 6 Skills Test: Use Assessment Book, pp. 31–32.

Standardized Test Prep

- Chapter 6 Tests contain standardized test format.

✓ Chapter 6 Performance Assessment

- Have students work in pairs to review information in this chapter.
- Tell students to make a three-column chart labeled *Landforms, Climate,* and *Resources.*
- Have students take turns writing notes from this chapter in the appropriate column.
- Assess students' understanding of important details from the chapter.

Facts and Main Ideas

1. What areas of the Southeast contain large stretches of good farmland?
2. What is a hurricane and where do hurricanes form?
3. Which area of the Southeast has a warmer climate, the mountains or the coastal plains?
4. **Main Idea** What are some differences between the Inner Coastal Plain, Outer Coastal Plain, Piedmont, and mountains of the Southeast?
5. **Main Idea** Which states in the Southeast have warm climates most of the year?
6. **Main Idea** What are some important resources of the Southeast coastal plain? of Appalachia?
7. **Critical Thinking: *Evaluate*** If you moved to the Southeast, which area or state would you choose to live in? Why?

Internet Activity

To get help with vocabulary and places, select the dictionary or encyclopedia from *Social Studies Library* at **www.sfsocialstudies.com.**

Write About Geography

1. **Write a poem** that tells about one of the geographic features of the Southeast.
2. **Write a television newscast** about a hurricane that is offshore from the Southeast region. Describe the hurricane, including its wind speed and where it is heading. Tell people in that area what they should do to stay safe during the hurricane.
3. **Write a Letter** If you took a trip to the Everglades in Florida, you would see many different kinds of plants and animals. Write a letter to a friend describing several different plants and animals that you see.

Apply Skills

Using Elevation Maps

Study the map below. Then answer the questions.

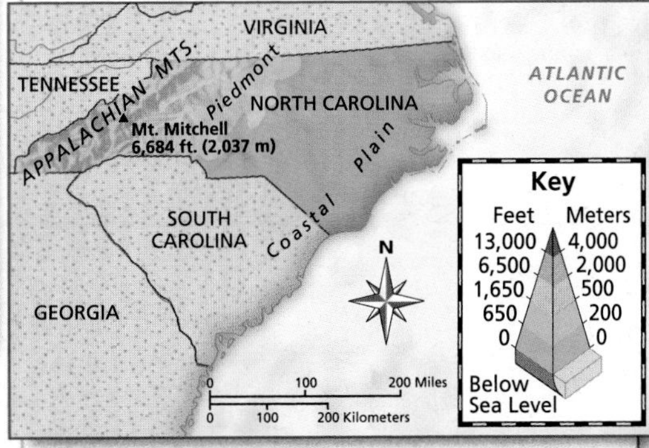

1. What does this map show?
2. Which part of North Carolina has the highest elevation?
3. What is the elevation range in feet in the Piedmont region?

Hands-on Unit Project

Unit 3 Performance Assessment

- See p. 222 for information about using the Unit Project as a means of performance assessment.
- A scoring guide is provided on p. 222.

WEB SITE Technology

For more information, students can select the dictionary or encyclopedia from *Social Studies Library* at **www.sfsocialstudies.com.**

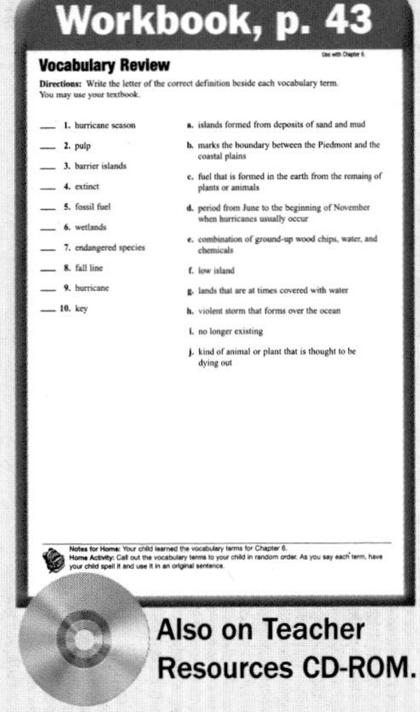

Workbook, p. 43

Use with Chapter 6

Vocabulary Review

Directions: Write the letter of the correct definition beside each vocabulary term. You may use your textbook.

___ 1. hurricane season	a. islands formed from deposits of sand and mud
___ 2. pulp	b. marks the boundary between the Piedmont and the coastal plains
___ 3. barrier islands	c. fuel that is formed in the earth from the remains of plants or animals
___ 4. extinct	d. period from June to the beginning of November when hurricanes usually occur
___ 5. fossil fuel	e. combination of ground-up wood chips, water, and chemicals
___ 6. wetlands	f. low island
___ 7. endangered species	g. lands that are at times covered with water
___ 8. fall line	h. violent storm that forms over the ocean
___ 9. hurricane	i. no longer existing
___ 10. key	j. kind of animal or plant that is thought to be dying out

Notes for Home: Your child learned the vocabulary terms for Chapter 6.
Home Activity: Call out the vocabulary terms to your child in random order. As you say each term, have your child spell it and use it in an original sentence.

Also on Teacher Resources CD-ROM.

Facts and Main Ideas

1. The coastal plains and the Piedmont
2. A strong storm that forms over the ocean
3. The coastal plains
4. Possible answers: As you progress from the Outer Coastal Plain to the Inner Coastal Plain to the Piedmont and the mountains, elevations increase and temperatures get lower; the Outer Coastal Plain has wetlands, and the Inner Coastal Plain and the Piedmont have good farmland.
5. Florida, Louisiana, Mississippi, and Alabama
6. Coastal plain—farmland; Appalachia—coal and trees
7. Possible answer: I would live near the Florida Everglades because there are so many interesting plants and animals there.

Write About Geography

1. Tell students that their poems do not have to rhyme but should contain descriptive information about the feature they choose.
2. You may wish to have students present their newscasts orally, sitting at a table that represents the anchor desk.
3. Encourage students to use a travel guide, an encyclopedia, or the Internet to identify actual plants and animals of the Everglades.

Apply Skills

1. Elevations of North Carolina
2. The Appalachian Mountains
3. 650 feet to 1,650 feet

CHAPTER 7

Chapter Planning Guide

Chapter 7 • People and Events That Shaped the Southeast

Locating Places pp. 186–187

Lesson Titles	Pacing	Main Ideas
Lesson 1 **The Cherokee** pp. 188–192 **Biography: Sequoyah** p. 193	3 days	• The Cherokee have contributed greatly to the history of the Southeast. • Sequoyah developed a writing system for the Cherokee.
Lesson 2 **Early History of the Southeast** pp. 194–199 **Citizen Heroes: Courage Speaking Out** pp. 200–201	3 days	• Exploration, settlements, agriculture, and slavery all shaped the early growth of the Southeast region. • Sarah and Angelina Grimké were abolitionists who wrote and spoke against slavery.
Lesson 3 **The Nation Divided** pp. 202–206 **Biography: Rosa Parks** p. 207 **Thinking Skills: Identify Fact and Opinion** pp. 208–209	4 days	• The Civil War had a major impact on the history of the Southeast. • Rosa Parks worked for the fair treatment of African Americans. • By identifying fact and opinion, people can determine what is true about a subject.
Lesson 4 **The Glittering Cities** pp. 210–213 **Here and There: Spoleto Festival of Two Worlds** pp. 214–215	2 days	• Cities in the Southeast are growing and changing. • The Spoleto Festival of Two Worlds is an art festival celebrated in Spoleto, Italy, and Charleston, South Carolina.

✓ **Chapter 7 Review**
pp. 216–217

◀ **This bugle was used in the Civil War, a war that had a devastating effect on the Southeast.**

✓ **= Assessment Options**

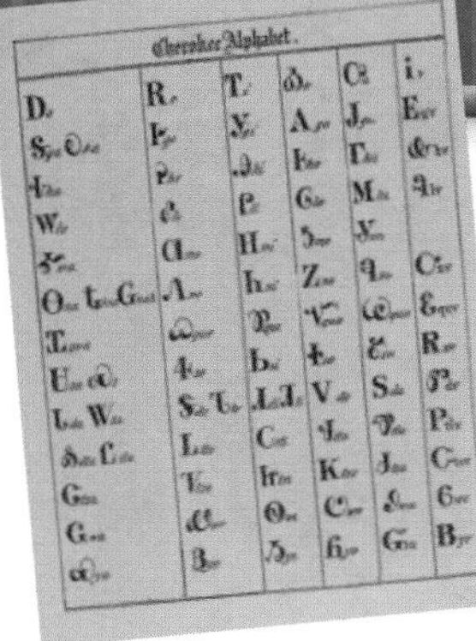

Sequoyah developed a symbol for each of the 85 syllables in the Cherokee language. His writing system was adopted by Cherokee leaders in 1821.

Vocabulary	Resources	Meeting Individual Needs
consensus Trail of Tears	• Workbook, p. 45 • Transparency 1 • Every Student Learns Guide, pp. 78–81 • Quick Study, pp. 40–41	• ESL Support, TE p. 189 • Leveled Practice, TE p. 191
pioneer backwoodsman plantation	• Workbook, p. 46 • Transparency 1 • Every Student Learns Guide, pp. 82–85 • Quick Study, pp. 42–43	• Leveled Practice, TE p. 195 • ESL Support, TE p. 198
Civil War Union Confederacy secede Reconstruction civil rights segregate boycott	• Workbook, p. 47 • Transparency 1 • Every Student Learns Guide, pp. 86–89 • Quick Study, pp. 44–45 • Workbook, p. 48	• Leveled Practice, TE p. 204 • ESL Support, TE p. 205 • Leveled Practice, TE p. 208
gold rush public transportation system	• Workbook, p. 49 • Transparencies 1, 45 • Every Student Learns Guide, pp. 90–93 • Quick Study, pp. 46–47	• ESL Support, TE p. 211 • Leveled Practice, TE p. 212 • Learning Styles, TE p. 214
	✔Chapter 7 Content Test, Assessment Book, pp. 33–34 ✔Chapter 7 Skills Test, Assessment Book, pp. 35–36	✔Chapter 7 Performance Assessment, TE p. 216

Providing More Depth

Additional Resources

- Vocabulary Workbook and Cards
- Social Studies Plus! pp. 68–73
- Daily Activity Bank
- Big Book Atlas
- Student Atlas
- Outline Maps
- Desk Maps

Technology

- AudioText
- MindPoint® Quiz Show CD-ROM
- ExamView® Test Bank CD-ROM
- Teacher Resources CD-ROM
- Map Resources CD-ROM
- SFSuccessNet: iText (Pupil Edition online), iTE (Teacher's Edition online), Online Planner
- **www.sfsocialstudies.com** (Biographies, news, references, maps, and activities)

To establish guidelines for your students' safe and responsible use of the Internet, use the Scott Foresman Internet Guide.

Additional Internet Links

To find out more about:

- The Cherokee Nation, visit **www.cherokee.org**
- Monticello, visit **www.monticello.org**
- The Civil War, visit **www.civilwar.org**

Key Internet Search Terms

- Jamestown, Virginia
- Dr. Martin Luther King, Jr.
- Rosa Parks

Workbook Support

Use the following Workbook pages to support content and skills development as you teach Chapter 7. You can also view and print Workbook pages from the Teacher Resources CD-ROM.

Workbook, p. 44

Use with Chapter 7.

Vocabulary Preview

Directions: Circle the word that best completes each sentence. You may use your glossary.

1. A system of trains and buses that carry many people through a city is a (Trail of Tears, public transportation system).
2. Many Southern states decided to (secede, consensus), or pull out, from the United States when Abraham Lincoln won the presidency.
3. The Cherokee's journey from the Southeast to what is now Oklahoma is known as the (Reconstruction, Trail of Tears).
4. (Pioneers, Civil rights) include the right to vote and to have the protection of the law.
5. In the past, you might have expected to find slaves on a (plantation, segregation) in the Southeast.
6. A (backwoodsman, pioneer) is a person who lived in a forest far away from towns.
7. The Northern states in the Civil War were called the (Union, Confederacy).
8. The Southern states in the Civil War formed a group called the (Union, Confederacy).
9. A person who settled in a part of a country and prepared it for others was a (slave, pioneer).
10. The (Civil War, civil rights) began in 1861 and pitted U.S. citizens against each other.
11. The separation of black people and white people in public places is called (segregation, Confederacy).
12. Before making a decision, the Cherokee first had to reach a (Civil War, consensus).
13. (Segregation, Reconstruction) was the period of time after the Civil War when the South's buildings and economy were rebuilt.
14. In 1828 people rushed to Dahlonega, Georgia, during the first (gold rush, plantation) in the United States.

Notes for Home: Your child learned the vocabulary terms for Chapter 7.
Home Activity: Use the vocabulary terms to create a crossword puzzle for your child. Use the definitions as clues for each term in the puzzle.

44 Vocabulary Preview — Workbook

Use with Pupil Edition, p. 186

Workbook, p. 45

Use with Pages 188–192.

Lesson 1: The Cherokee

Directions: Read each of the following phrases. Number them from 1 (earliest) to 8 (most recent) to show the order in which they occurred.

8 The United States government forced the Cherokee to give up their land and move to what is now Oklahoma.
3 Many Cherokee and other Native Americans became ill with diseases the Europeans brought.
4 Traders and other settlers began moving onto Cherokee land.
1 The Cherokee made their homes in the mountains of southern Appalachia.
5 The United States government tried to end conflicts between the Cherokee and settlers.
6 The Cherokee formed their own government and wrote a constitution that was similar to the United States Constitution.
2 Spanish explorers traveled through the Southeast.
7 Gold was discovered on Cherokee land.

Directions: Answer the following questions on the lines provided.

1. What did Sequoyah contribute to the Cherokee? How was his contribution beneficial to others?
   He made up an alphabet for the Cherokee language. With it, many Cherokee could learn how to read and write in their own language.
2. How was the Cherokee constitution similar to the U.S. Constitution?
   The Cherokee constitution established a senate and a house of representatives, and it stated that a head chief would be elected once every four years.

Notes for Home: Your child learned about the Cherokee in the Southeast.
Home Activity: With your child, discuss how settlers and the Cherokee might have found a more constructive way to resolve their conflicts over land. Ask your child how he or she might apply this principle to conflicts in his or her own life.

Use with Pupil Edition, p. 192

Workbook, p. 46

Use with Pages 194–199.

Lesson 2: Early History of the Southeast

Directions: The box below contains the names of people and places that were very important to the early history of the Southeast. Match one name from the box with each label on the time line. You may use your textbook.

George Washington	Hernando de Soto	St. Augustine
Andrew Jackson	Roanoke Island	Juan Ponce de León
Jamestown, Virginia	Thomas Jefferson	Robert de La Salle

Time line 1450–1850:

- 1492 — Christopher Columbus sailed to the New World.
- 1513 — **Juan Ponce de León** believed Native American stories about the fountain of youth and set out to find it.
- 1539 — **Hernando de Soto** was an explorer who landed in Florida while searching for gold.
- 1565 — **St. Augustine** was the first permanent European settlement in what is now the United States.
- 1587 — **Roanoke Island** was the location of John White's colony. It later became known as the "Lost Colony."
- 1607 — **Jamestown, Virginia** was the first successful English colony in North America.
- 1682 — **Robert de La Salle** was the first European to sail down the Mississippi River to the Gulf of Mexico.
- 1776 — American Revolution began. **Thomas Jefferson** was the author of the Declaration of Independence.
- 1789 — **George Washington** was known for his honesty, bravery, dedication, and service to his country. He became the first President of the United States.
- 1829 — **Andrew Jackson** was the President who appealed to the common people.

Notes for Home: Your child learned about the early history of the Southeast.
Home Activity: With your child, discuss what each of the early explorers of the Southeast originally set out to do. Did the explorers achieve their goals? What did they accomplish?

46 Lesson Review — Workbook

Use with Pupil Edition, p. 199

Workbook, p. 47

Use with Pages 202–206.

Lesson 3: The Nation Divided

Directions: Read each phrase below. Then decide whether the phrase refers to the North or the South during the Civil War. If it refers to the North, write an *N* on the line beside the statement. If it refers to the South, write an *S*. If it refers to both, write a *B*. You may use your textbook.

S 1. location of Fort Sumter
B 2. fought over Fort Sumter
N 3. called itself the Union
S 4. formed the Confederate States of America
B 5. had strong opinions about slavery
S 6. thought that each state should have more control over what its citizens could do
N 7. thought that the national government should have more power
S 8. seceded from the United States
N 9. did not want slavery to be allowed in the new states added to the nation
S 10. thought slavery should be allowed in the new states
S 11. surrendered after four years of fighting
N 12. won the war
B 13. suffered the loss of many lives during the war
S 14. one in four soldiers died in the war
S 15. underwent Reconstruction after the Civil War
S 16. enforced "Jim Crow" laws
B 17. tried to return their lives to normal after the war
B 18. did not allow slavery after the war

Notes for Home: Your child learned about the Civil War and its effects on the Southeast.
Home Activity: With your child, discuss how the United States would be affected if the North and South went to war today. How might your family be affected?

Use with Pupil Edition, p. 206

Workbook Support

Workbook, p. 48

Use with Pages 208–209.

Identify Fact and Opinion

A *fact* is a statement that can be checked and proved to be true. An *opinion* tells about personal feelings and cannot be proved to be true or false.

Directions: Read the following paragraph. Then answer the questions about facts and opinions.

> Today is December 2, 1862. Mother, Father, and I have been in Washington, D.C., for almost one week now. We are very lucky to be here right now. Washington, D.C., must be the busiest city in the world! Yesterday, President Lincoln sent Congress a State of the Union Address. Father took me with him to listen as the address was read. It was amazing! In the address, the President said that if his new plan is passed, it will shorten the war. I think that would be wonderful.

1. What are two facts from the paragraph? How do you know these are facts?
   Possible answers: Today is December 2, 1862. Yesterday, President Lincoln sent Congress a State of the Union Address. I know these are facts because they can be proved to be true.
2. What are two opinions from the paragraph? How do you know these are opinions?
   Possible answers: We are very lucky to be here right now. It was amazing! I know these are opinions because they cannot be proved to be true or false.

Notes for Home: Your child learned to distinguish between fact and opinion.
Home Activity: With your child, find a newspaper or magazine article about a current event. Discuss which parts of the article are facts and which parts are opinions.

Use with Pupil Edition, p. 209

Workbook, p. 49

Use with Pages 210–213.

Lesson 4: The Glittering Cities

Directions: Use the terms in the box to complete each sentence with information from Lesson 4. You may use your textbook.

Dahlonega	Southeast	Triangle Region
Dahlonega Courthouse	Myrtle Beach	Raleigh
Atlanta	Naples	Durham
railroad center	Orlando	Chapel Hill
	Charleston	

1. The cities of the **Southeast** are among the fastest growing in the United States. These cities include **Myrtle Beach**, South Carolina, and **Naples** and **Orlando**, Florida.
2. Atlanta started as a **railroad center** in 1837.
3. A fast-growing center for research in medicine, computers, and other industries is the **Triangle Region** of North Carolina.
4. The **Dahlonega Courthouse** is made of bricks that contain gold.
5. In **Charleston**, South Carolina, you can go to the South Carolina Aquarium and see plants and animals from all areas of the state.
6. The dome of Georgia's state capitol in **Atlanta** is made partially from gold that the people of Dahlonega gave to the state.
7. The Triangle Region of North Carolina is made up of the cities of **Raleigh**, **Durham**, and **Chapel Hill**.
8. In 1828, gold was found in **Dahlonega**, a town in a mountain area in northern Georgia.

Notes for Home: Your child learned about the growing cities of the Southeast.
Home Activity: With your child, review the reasons for population growth in the Southeast. Then discuss what features might attract people to your city or community.

Workbook Lesson Review **49**

Use with Pupil Edition, p. 213

Workbook, p. 50

Use with Chapter 7.

Vocabulary Review

Directions: Write the definition of each vocabulary term below on the lines provided. You may use your glossary.

1. consensus **method of decision-making in which the issues are debated until all can come to agreement**
2. Trail of Tears **Cherokee's forced journey to Oklahoma**
3. pioneer **person who settled in a part of a country and prepared it for others**
4. backwoodsman **person living in a forest far away from towns**
5. plantation **a large farm**
6. slave **a person who is held against his or her will and forced to work without pay**
7. Civil War **the war between the Union and the Confederacy that began in the United States in 1861**
8. Union **Northern states in the Civil War**
9. Confederacy **group of Southern states in the Civil War**
10. secede **to pull out**
11. Reconstruction **rebuilding of the South after the Civil War**
12. civil rights **right to vote and to have protection of the law**
13. segregation **separation of blacks from whites in public places**
14. gold rush **period of time when towns quickly filled with people searching for gold**
15. public transportation system **system of trains and buses that carry people through a city**

Notes for Home: Your child learned the vocabulary terms for Chapter 7.
Home Activity: With your child, make flash cards of the vocabulary terms by writing the term on one side of an index card and the definition on the other side. Then show your child one side of each card and have him or her supply the missing word or definition.

50 Vocabulary Review Workbook

Use with Pupil Edition, p. 216

Workbook, p. 51

Unit 3 Project This Just In

Directions: Hold a classroom press conference about an important event in your state's history.

1. Our historic event is ________.
2. My role in the news conference (✔ one): ___government official ___expert ___news reporter ___eyewitness ___event participant
3. These are the most important details of the event:
   #1 ________
   #2 ________
   Outcome: ________
4. These are questions and answers about the event:
   Question: ________
   Answer: ________
   Question: ________
   Answer: ________
5. This is a description of our poster: ________

You may wish to have students write a script for their press conference and rehearse it before presenting it to the class.

✔ Checklist for Students

- ____ We chose a historic event.
- ____ We assigned roles for the press conference.
- ____ We wrote details of the event.
- ____ We wrote questions and answers.
- ____ We made a poster to announce the event.
- ____ We presented our press conference.

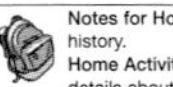

Notes for Home: Your child learned how to report breaking news about an important event in your state's history.
Home Activity: With your child, watch a local or national press conference or news program. Discuss details about the reported events, roles of the participants in the program, and features included in the visuals used.

Use with Pupil Edition, p. 222

Assessment Support

Use the following Assessment Book pages and TestWorks to assess content and skills in Chapter 7 and Unit 3. You can also view and print Assessment Book pages from the Teacher Resources CD-ROM.

Assessment Book, p. 33

Chapter 7 Test

Part 1: Content Test

Directions: Fill in the circle next to the correct answer.

Lesson Objective (1:1, 2)

1. How was Cherokee culture before the Europeans arrived different from Cherokee culture after the Europeans arrived?
   - Ⓐ Before the Europeans arrived, the Cherokee were sick with many diseases.
   - ● Before the Europeans arrived, the Cherokee hunted much of their food.
   - Ⓒ Before the Europeans arrived, the Cherokee traded skins and furs to make a living.
   - Ⓓ Before the Europeans arrived, the Cherokee went to school to learn English.

Lesson Objective (1:3)

2. Who forced the Cherokee to give up their land and travel west on a journey called the Trail of Tears?
   - ● the U.S. government
   - Ⓑ European settlers
   - Ⓒ the Cherokee government
   - Ⓓ George Washington

Lesson Objective (1:4)

3. Which is NOT a major business run by the North Carolina Cherokee today?
   - Ⓐ shops for tourists
   - Ⓑ lumber industry
   - Ⓒ artworks and crafts
   - ● cotton farming

Lesson Objective (2:1)

4. Where did Juan Ponce de León explore?
   - Ⓐ Arkansas
   - Ⓑ Georgia
   - ● Florida
   - Ⓓ Alabama

Lesson Objective (2:2)

5. Which was the first permanent European settlement in the area that is now the United States?
   - Ⓐ the French colony of New Orleans in present-day Louisiana
   - Ⓑ the English colony of Jamestown in present-day Virginia
   - Ⓒ the English colony of Roanoke Island in present-day North Carolina
   - ● the Spanish colony of St. Augustine in present-day Florida

Lesson Objective (2:3)

6. Which of these Southeasterners was NOT President of the United States?
   - Ⓐ George Washington
   - ● John White
   - Ⓒ Andrew Jackson
   - Ⓓ Thomas Jefferson

Lesson Objective (2:4)

7. Which industry helped people in the Southeast become rich and powerful?
   - ● agriculture
   - Ⓑ exploration
   - Ⓒ tourism
   - Ⓓ religion

Use with Pupil Edition, p. 216

Assessment Book, p. 34

Lesson Objective (3:1)

8. Which is one cause of the Civil War?
   - Ⓐ The people of Charleston had built an army and wanted to test their soldiers' skills in battle.
   - Ⓑ No one could decide whether to name the country the United States or the Confederate States.
   - ● The two sides disagreed about how much authority the national government should have.
   - Ⓓ Neither side wanted to move and relocate to the new areas being settled in the West.

Lesson Objective (3:2)

9. Which was NOT an effect of the Civil War on the Southeast?
   - Ⓐ One in four Confederate soldiers died in the war.
   - ● African Americans lost all civil rights.
   - Ⓒ Many cities had been burned down in the war.
   - Ⓓ Slavery became illegal in the United States.

Lesson Objective (3:2, 3)

10. Which of the following did NOT occur in the Southeast during Reconstruction?
   - Ⓐ Farmers began planting crops again.
   - Ⓑ The government established the Freedmen's Bureau to help former slaves.
   - Ⓒ Rail lines were repaired.
   - ● Diseases spread through army camps.

Lesson Objective (3:4)

11. Who was the main leader of the civil rights movement in the 1950s and 1960s?
   - Ⓐ Davy Crockett
   - Ⓑ Jim Crow
   - ● Dr. Martin Luther King, Jr.
   - Ⓓ Harriet Beecher Stowe

Lesson Objective (4:2)

12. Where was the first gold rush in the United States?
   - Ⓐ Raleigh, North Carolina
   - Ⓑ Orlando, Florida
   - ● Dahlonega, Georgia
   - Ⓓ Charleston, South Carolina

Lesson Objective (4:3)

13. Which is NOT a major mode of transportation that runs through Atlanta?
   - Ⓐ planes
   - ● barges
   - Ⓒ trains
   - Ⓓ buses

Lesson Objective (4:1, 4)

14. What is one reason why cities in the Southeast are growing quickly?
   - Ⓐ A gold rush is happening there.
   - Ⓑ The climate is cold, but dry.
   - ● Many people are moving there from colder northern climates.
   - Ⓓ The beautiful Rocky Mountains are there.

Lesson Objective (4:1, 4)

15. Which is NOT a reason why many people have moved to Chapel Hill, North Carolina?
   - ● It has an aquarium in its harbor.
   - Ⓑ It is a center of medical research.
   - Ⓒ It is close to two other major cities.
   - Ⓓ It is home to many businesses.

Use with Pupil Edition, p. 216

Assessment Book, p. 35

Part 2: Skills Test

Directions: Use complete sentences to answer questions 1–5. Use a separate sheet of paper if you need more space.

1. The Cherokee governed by consensus. Do you think that coming to a consensus is a good way to make decisions? Why or why not? What problems might you face with this method of decision making? **Evaluate**

   Possible answers: Yes; Because everyone has a say in major decisions; It probably takes a long time to reach a consensus, and sometimes it may be impossible.

2. Write three details to support the following main idea: **Many Cherokee changed to fit in with the surrounding culture. Main Idea and Details**

   Possible answers: Many Cherokee built large farms. They went to school to learn English. They also learned how to read and write in their own language.

3. What character traits would be important for an explorer to have? Do you think a pioneer would need those same traits? Why or why not? **Express Ideas**

   Possible answers: Adventurous, brave, and curious; Yes; Because he or she is moving to a land where few people have lived before

Use with Pupil Edition, p. 216

Assessment Book, p. 36

4. Suppose a state today has a disagreement with the other 49 states. Do you think the state should secede from the United States? Why or why not? What other methods could the state use to solve its problem? **Solve Problems**

   Possible answers: No; Because the Civil War showed that seceding results in great damage to the country; The state could have its senators and representatives in Washington, D.C., try to compromise with the other states.

5. Suppose you could visit either Charleston, South Carolina, or Atlanta, Georgia. Which would you choose? Why? **Express Ideas**

   Possible answers: Charleston; I would like to see the beautiful old buildings there and visit the South Carolina Aquarium.

Use with Pupil Edition, p. 216

Assessment Support

Assessment Book, p. 37

Unit 3 Test

Part 1: Content Test

Directions: Fill in the circle next to the correct answer.

Lesson Objective (6–1:1, 2, 3)

1. Which is NOT true about the geography of the Southeast?
   - Ⓐ The coastal plains of the Southeast have many kinds of wetlands.
   - ● As you move inland from the coast, the elevation of the land gets lower.
   - Ⓒ There is an area of rolling hills and valleys known as the Piedmont.
   - Ⓓ Barrier islands are formed from sand that has been deposited near the shore.

Lesson Objective (6–2:1)

2. How would you describe the climate of the Southeast?
   - Ⓐ The coastal plains are cool, and the mountain areas are warm.
   - Ⓑ Hurricanes pose a danger to the region from November until May.
   - Ⓒ The few storms in the region never produce damage.
   - ● Most of the region is warm and sunny with plenty of rain.

Lesson Objective (6–2:3)

3. Which is NOT a function of lighthouses?
   - ● to light amusement parks
   - Ⓑ to help sailors avoid the rocky coastlines
   - Ⓒ to warn sailors of dangerous rocks and currents
   - Ⓓ to serve as tourist attractions

Lesson Objective (6–3:1, 2, 3, 4)

4. Which is NOT true about the Southeast?
   - Ⓐ Logging and coal mining are important industries in the region.
   - Ⓑ About a dozen kinds of animals that live in the Everglades are endangered.
   - ● Rice is primarily grown in the states of Arkansas and North Carolina.
   - Ⓓ Paper and furniture are made from trees harvested in the region.

Lesson Objective (7–1:1, 2, 3)

5. Which of the following best describes the Cherokee?
   - ● They once farmed, hunted, fished, and gathered for a living.
   - Ⓑ They passed many deadly diseases to the Europeans.
   - Ⓒ Their language is the oldest written language in the world.
   - Ⓓ Although the Cherokee were sad, none died on the Trail of Tears.

Lesson Objective (7–2:1, 2)

6. Which is NOT true about the Spanish in the Southeast?
   - Ⓐ Juan Ponce de León explored what is now the state of Florida.
   - Ⓑ St. Augustine was the first permanent European settlement in what is now the United States.
   - ● Louisiana was named by La Salle in honor of the king of Spain.
   - Ⓓ Hernando de Soto searched for gold through much of the region.

Use with Pupil Edition, p. 220

Assessment Book, p. 38

Lesson Objective (7–2:3)

7. What is important about Daniel Boone?
   - Ⓐ He was the leader of the Colonial forces in the Revolutionary War.
   - ● He developed the Wilderness Road, a route followed by many pioneers traveling west.
   - Ⓒ He was the author of the Declaration of Independence and was one of our country's founders.
   - Ⓓ He was a Tennessee congressman and defender of the Alamo.

Lesson Objective (7–2:4)

8. Which crop was NOT a major crop grown on Southeastern plantations?
   - ● wheat
   - Ⓑ rice
   - Ⓒ cotton
   - Ⓓ tobacco

Lesson Objective (7–3:1)

9. Which is one reason why the Civil War began?
   - Ⓐ Eleven Northern states seceded from the United States.
   - Ⓑ Southerners did not want slavery in the Southeast region.
   - Ⓒ Many Southerners wanted their states to have less power.
   - ● Northerners did not want slavery in the new states added to the nation.

Lesson Objective (7–3:2, 3)

10. Which did NOT happen during Reconstruction?
    - Ⓐ Farmers plowed their overgrown fields and planted crops.
    - ● Many people died from wounds or diseases in army camps.
    - Ⓒ Factories, homes, and other buildings were rebuilt and repaired.
    - Ⓓ Southern states were readmitted to the United States.

Lesson Objective (7–3:4)

11. Which was largely the result of the protests led by Dr. Martin Luther King, Jr.?
    - ● Civil Rights Act of 1964
    - Ⓑ Declaration of Independence
    - Ⓒ Thirteenth Amendment
    - Ⓓ United States Constitution

Lesson Objective (7–4:2)

12. What was found in Dahlonega, Georgia, in 1828?
    - Ⓐ oil
    - ● gold
    - Ⓒ iron
    - Ⓓ coal

Lesson Objective (7–4:3)

13. What caused Atlanta to grow and prosper after 1837?
    - Ⓐ It was a center of communications and finance.
    - Ⓑ People in search of gold moved to the area.
    - ● It was the western end of a new railroad line.
    - Ⓓ People moved there to work in the aquarium.

Lesson Objective (7–4:1, 4)

14. Why is Myrtle Beach, South Carolina, one of the fastest growing cities in the country?
    - Ⓐ People enjoy going there to snow ski and mountain bike.
    - Ⓑ It is a part of the Triangle Region, a center for research.
    - ● It has a warm climate, and many jobs are available there.
    - Ⓓ People travel there to visit the South Carolina Aquarium.

Use with Pupil Edition, p. 220

Assessment Book, p. 39

Lesson Objective (7–4:4)

15. Which city did NOT develop because of growth in medical research and computers in the Triangle Region?
    - Ⓐ Raleigh
    - Ⓑ Chapel Hill
    - ● Orlando
    - Ⓓ Durham

Part 2: Skills Test

Directions: Use complete sentences to answer questions 1–5. Use a separate sheet of paper if you need more space.

1. Would you rather visit Florida in July or in December? Explain your reasoning. **Apply Information**

   Possible answer: I would rather visit Florida in December because July is during hurricane season. Also, it is very cold in December where I live, and I might like to get away to someplace warmer.

2. Compare and contrast the logging and coal mining industries in the Southeast. **Compare and Contrast**

   Possible answer: Alike: both industries can be found in the Appalachians. Different: the logging industry relies on trees, a renewable resource. The mining industry relies on coal, a nonrenewable resource. The logging industry produces wood and pulp. The coal mining industry produces coal, which is used for chemicals to make products such as nylon, paints, plastics, and aspirin.

Use with Pupil Edition, p. 220

Assessment Book, p. 40

3. Write three details to support the following main idea: **Many early leaders of the United States were born in the Southeast. Main Idea and Details**

   Possible answers: George Washington, the country's first President, was born in Virginia. Presidents Thomas Jefferson and James Madison also were born in Virginia. President Andrew Jackson was born in South Carolina.

4. Do you think the Southeast's greatest gift to the United States has been its people, its products, or something else? Explain. **Evaluate**

   Possible answer: Its people; Many important U.S. leaders were born there. Also, the pioneers and backwoodsmen who were born there helped expand the country.

Elevations of the Southeast

5. Use the map to answer the questions. **Read Elevation Maps**
   a. What can you learn from the map about the areas that are shaded the darkest?

   The darkest areas are the highest—between 6,500 and 13,000 feet (2,000–4,000 meters).

   b. What is the highest peak in the Appalachian Mountains. How do you know?

   The dark triangle tells me that the highest peak is Mt. Mitchell.

   c. What is the difference in elevation in feet between Spruce Knob and Black Mountain?

   219 feet

Use with Pupil Edition, p. 220

CHAPTER 7

People and Events That Shaped the Southeast

Chapter 7 Outline

- **Lesson 1, *The Cherokee,*** pp. 188–192
- **Biography: *Sequoyah,*** p. 193
- **Lesson 2, *Early History of the Southeast,*** pp. 194–199
- **Citizen Heroes: *Speaking Out,*** pp. 200–201
- **Lesson 3, *The Nation Divided,*** pp. 202–206
- **Biography: *Rosa Parks,*** p. 207
- **Thinking Skills: *Identify Fact and Opinion,*** pp. 208–209
- **Lesson 4, *The Glittering Cities,*** pp. 210–213
- **Here and There: *Spoleto Festival of Two Worlds,*** pp. 214–215

Resources

- Workbook, p. 44: Vocabulary Preview
- Vocabulary Cards
- Social Studies Plus!

Qualla Boundary, North Carolina: Lesson 1

This picture shows some of the land in the Qualla Boundary Cherokee reservation. Ask students what types of natural resources might be found on this reservation.

St. Augustine, Florida: Lesson 2

This picture shows a Spanish fort built at St. Augustine in the 1500s. Ask students why Spanish settlers might have wanted to build a fort.

Charleston, South Carolina: Lesson 3

A battle at Fort Sumter in Charleston, South Carolina, started the Civil War. Ask students to describe the fort shown in the picture.

Atlanta, Georgia: Lesson 4

Atlanta, Georgia, has become a center of business and culture in the Southeast. Have students compare Atlanta to their own community.

CHAPTER 7

People and Events That Shaped the Southeast

Lesson 1

Qualla Boundary, North Carolina
The Cherokee way of life changes after Europeans arrive.

1

Lesson 2

St. Augustine, Florida
The Spanish build the first permanent European settlement.

2

Lesson 3

Charleston, South Carolina
Events starting at Fort Sumter change the whole Southeast.

3

Lesson 4

Atlanta, Georgia
Cities in the Southeast grow quickly.

4

186

Practice and Extend

Vocabulary Preview

- Use Workbook p. 44 to help students preview the vocabulary words in this chapter.
- Use Vocabulary Cards to preview key concept words in this chapter.

Also on Teacher Resources CD-ROM.

Workbook, p. 44

Vocabulary Preview

Locating Places

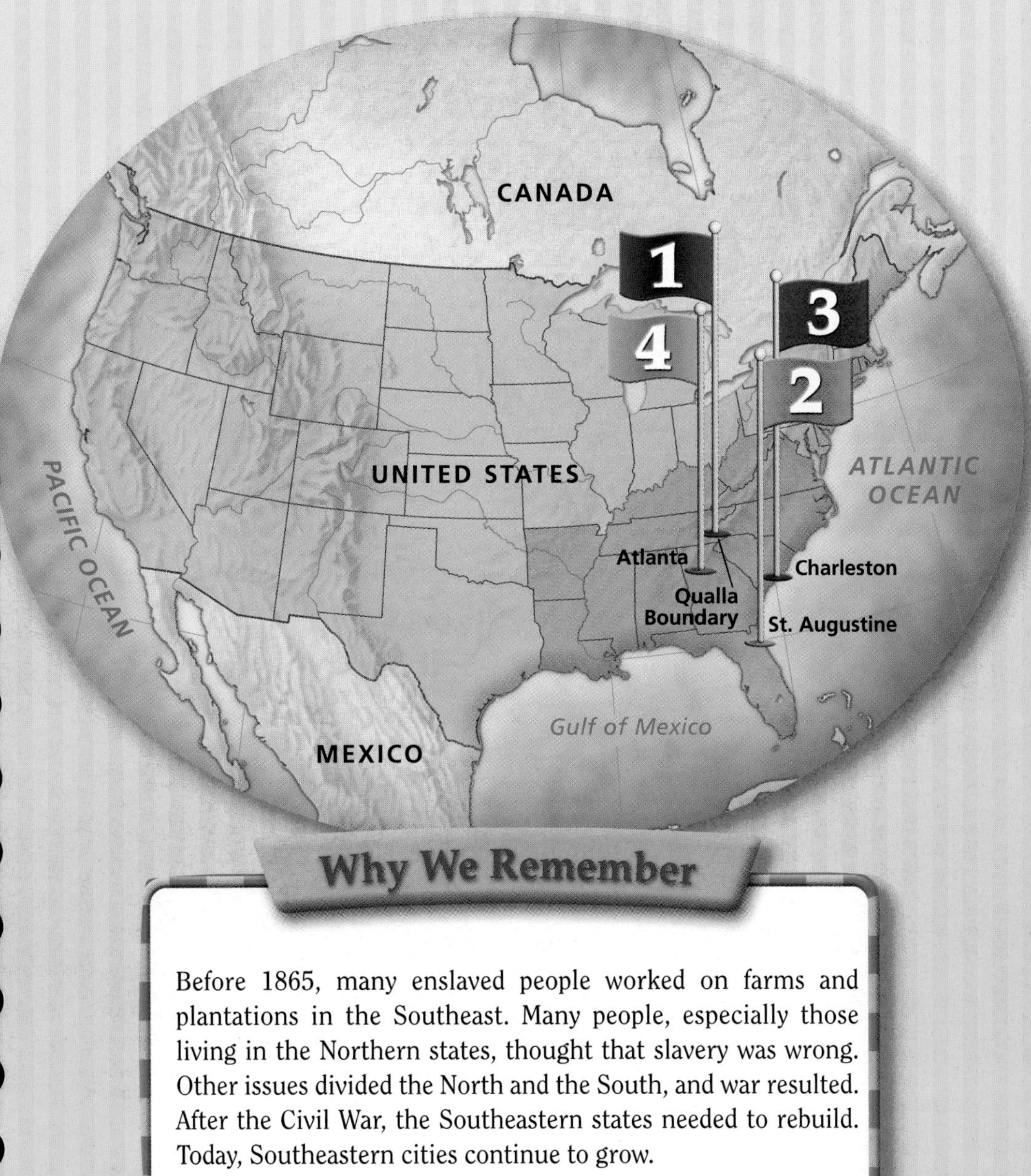

Why We Remember

Before 1865, many enslaved people worked on farms and plantations in the Southeast. Many people, especially those living in the Northern states, thought that slavery was wrong. Other issues divided the North and the South, and war resulted. After the Civil War, the Southeastern states needed to rebuild. Today, Southeastern cities continue to grow.

187

Locating Places

- Have students examine the pictures shown on p. 186 for Lessons 1, 2, 3, and 4.
- Remind students that each picture is coded with both a number and a color to link it to a place on the map on p. 187.

Why We Remember

Have students read the "Why We Remember" paragraph on p. 187, and ask them how things that affect the Southeast might also affect the entire United States. Have them consider how the Southeast continues to grow and change today.

WEB SITE
Technology

You can learn more about Qualla Boundary, North Carolina; St. Augustine, Florida; Charleston, South Carolina; and Atlanta, Georgia, by clicking on *Atlas* at **www.sfsocialstudies.com.**

SOCIAL STUDIES STRAND
Geography

Mental Mapping Divide students into four groups. Assign each group a separate state from the Southeast, for example, Florida, Louisiana, Virginia, and Georgia. Have groups brainstorm about the climate and resources of their assigned states, including how the geography of the state affects these issues. Groups then share their findings with the class as a whole.

The Cherokee

Objectives

- Describe how the Cherokee lived before Europeans came to North America.
- Evaluate how Cherokee culture changed after Europeans came to the Southeast.
- Identify the Trail of Tears and describe its impact on the Cherokee.
- Explain how the North Carolina Cherokee support themselves and keep their culture alive today.

Vocabulary

consensus, p. 189; **Trail of Tears,** p. 191

Resources

- Workbook, p. 45
- Transparency 1
- Every Student Learns Guide, pp. 78–81
- Quick Study, pp. 40–41

Quick Teaching Plan

If time is short, have students read the lesson independently, then make an illustrated time line of the Cherokee people from before the arrival of Europeans to today.

- Visuals should show changes in the Cherokee way of life and important historical events.
- Have students tape their pictures in order across a classroom wall to create a time line.

1 Introduce and Motivate

Preview Ask students to describe languages other than English that they have heard spoken in the United States. Tell students they will learn more about an alphabet invented by the Cherokee in the Southeast as they read Lesson 1.

You Are There Ask students to describe times when they have seen other alphabets, or writing that uses characters other than those used in English.

LESSON 1

1500 | 1700 | 1900

1500s First European explorers travel through the Southeast region.

1700s The Cherokee begin trading with Europeans.

1838–1839 The Cherokee are forced to leave the Southeast on the Trail of Tears.

Qualla Boundary

The Cherokee

PREVIEW

Focus on the Main Idea
The Cherokee have contributed greatly to the history of the Southeast.

PLACES
Qualla Boundary, North Carolina

PEOPLE
George Washington
Sequoyah

VOCABULARY
consensus
Trail of Tears

You Are There You walk up the path to the front door of the school. Once inside the building, you go to the front desk and check in. You ask the woman at the desk if your first-grade teacher is still here. She points down the hallway and says, "Yes. She is at the end of the hall."

Quietly you walk down the hall and look into the classroom. On the wall is a poster of the Cherokee alphabet. The children are all sitting in a circle on the carpet. As you walk into the classroom, they start singing a song—a welcome song in Cherokee. How wonderful that your ancient language survives!

North Wind Picture Archives

▶ Cherokee alphabet

Main Idea and Details (Target Skill)
As you read, notice events and changes that affected the Cherokee and how the Cherokee responded to them.

Practice and Extend

READING SKILL
Main Idea/Details

In the Lesson Review, students complete a graphic organizer like the one below. You may want to provide students with a copy of Transparency 1 to complete as they read the lesson.

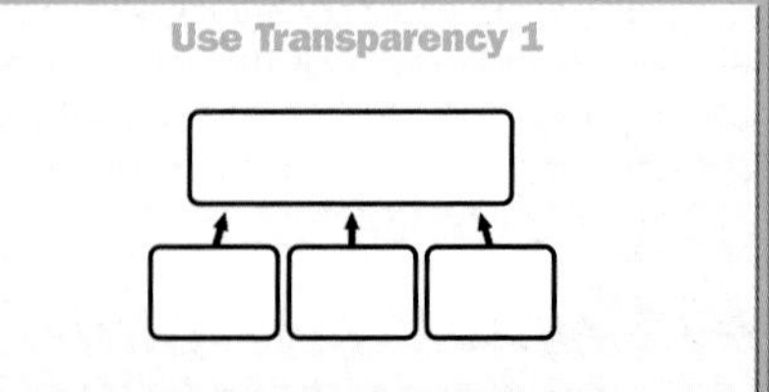

VOCABULARY
Related Word Study

Tell students that, most of the time, when they see the prefix *con-* or *com-*, it means "with" or "together." For example, *compress* means "press together," and, as mentioned on p. 136, *convention* means "to come together." Here, *con-* is combined with the Latin *sentire*, "to feel or think." Ask students how "to think or feel together" relates to the definition of *consensus*.

Early Cherokee Culture

Hundreds of years ago, the Cherokee made their homes in the mountains of southern Appalachia. They lived in villages. They farmed in family units on land in their villages. They grew corn, squash, beans, and other crops. They hunted in the forests. Cherokee hunters traveled for hundreds of miles through shared territory that no single group claimed but many used. They trapped rabbits and shot deer with bow and arrow. They also hunted wild turkeys and bears and fished in the region's many streams, rivers, and lakes. They gathered wild fruits and nuts. The land provided many resources that they used. 1

▶ The Cherokee made spoons like these to use in cooking.

In the summer, the Cherokee lived in rectangular houses. In the winter, they lived in smaller, warmer round huts. Their huts had thick walls made of clay and poles. The center of the Cherokee village was a large meeting house. There, the villagers gathered to celebrate religious holidays and to make important decisions. All adults in the village could express their thoughts about issues. The Cherokee debated issues until all could come to agreement. This method of decision-making is called **consensus.** 2

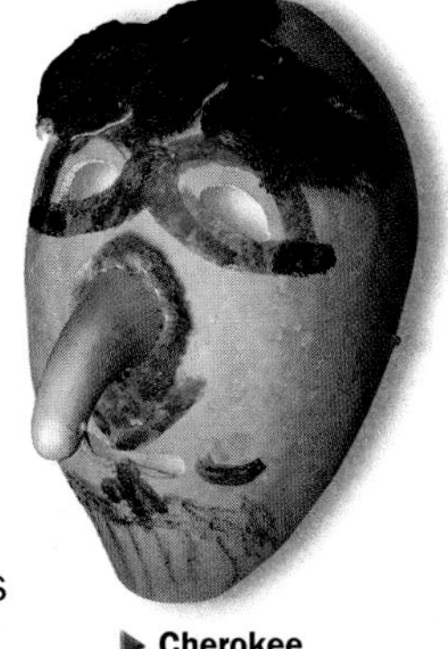

▶ Cherokee dance mask

REVIEW How did the Cherokee make their living? What were their villages like? Main Idea and Details

▶ In this model of a Cherokee village, the large building is the meeting house.

189

EXTEND LANGUAGE

ESL Support

Examine Word Meanings Explain that *consensus* comes from the same root word as *consent*, meaning "to agree" or "agreement."

Beginning Ask students yes-or-no questions about activities that they might or might not want to do and have them vote by a show of hands. After each vote, have students point out whether or not there is a consensus.

Intermediate Have student volunteers use the word *consensus* to explain why the result of each vote is or is not a consensus.

Advanced Ask students to describe the difference between consensus and majority vote. Ask students to explain whether it is easier to make a decision by consensus or by majority vote and why.

For additional ESL support, use Every Student Learns Guide, pp. 78–81.

Teach and Discuss

PAGE 189

Early Cherokee Culture

Quick Summary Years ago, the Cherokee lived in villages in southern Appalachia. They were farmers, hunters, trappers, and gatherers. All adults in a village helped make decisions about important issues.

1 **What types of resources might the Cherokee have looked for when choosing a location for a village?** Possible answers: Rich soil for farming, forests with abundant wildlife for hunting, a stream, river, or lake for fishing, and a location where wild fruits and nuts were nearby Make Inferences

SOCIAL STUDIES STRAND

Government

Point out that today elections in the United States are decided by a majority vote. U.S. citizens eighteen years and older have the right to vote in elections.

2 **How was the Cherokee way of deciding issues similar to our election process today? How was it different?** Possible answers: Similar: all adults who were members of the group had a voice in making decisions; Different: the Cherokee made decisions by consensus, meaning all the adults had to agree. Today we determine elections by a majority vote. Compare and Contrast

✓ **Ongoing Assessment**

If... students do not understand similarities and differences between a consensus and a majority vote,	**then...** have students vote on several issues. Have students determine whether the voting results are a majority vote or a consensus.

✓ **REVIEW ANSWER** The Cherokee grew crops, hunted, trapped, fished, and gathered fruits and nuts; Cherokee villages had a large meeting house in the center, surrounded by large, rectangular houses for use in the summer and round huts made of clay and poles for use in the winter. Main Idea and Details

PAGE 190

Changes in Cherokee Culture

Quick Summary The Cherokee's way of life changed after the arrival of European explorers and settlers. In the mid-1700s, the Cherokee were forced to move westward, and in the late 1700s, the federal government urged them to learn English and become farmers.

3 **What effect did Spanish explorers have on Native Americans in the Southeast?** Possible answer: They brought many new diseases that made the Native Americans ill. Cause and Effect

4 **What goods did Europeans and the Cherokee trade?** The Europeans traded goods such as knives, hoes, guns, cloth, and beads for the Cherokee's deerskins and furs. Apply Information

SOCIAL STUDIES STRAND
History

Gold was discovered in northern Georgia in 1828. This discovery created greater pressure for the Cherokee to leave their lands.

5 **Why were the Cherokee forced to move westward?** To ease conflicts between the Cherokee and settlers Main Idea and Details

6 **Who was Sequoyah?** A Cherokee man who developed an alphabet for the Cherokee language. With the new alphabet, many Cherokee learned to read and write in their own language. Main Idea and Details

✓ **REVIEW ANSWER** Many Cherokee were forced to move westward. Many of those who remained became farmers, built large farms, and learned to speak English. They also learned how to read and write in their own language. Main Idea and Details

Changes in Cherokee Culture

Life for the Cherokee began to change when Europeans first came to the region. In the early 1500s, Spanish explorers traveled through the
3 Southeast. Some explorers had diseases that were new to North America. Many Cherokee and other Native Americans became ill with the new diseases.

The first Europeans to settle on Cherokee land were traders. They brought goods such as knives, hoes, guns, cloth, and beads to trade for the
4 Native Americans' deerskins and furs. By the mid-1700s, this trade was very important.

Around the same time, conflicts grew between the settlers and the Native
5 Americans. The Cherokee were forced to give up land and to move westward, away from the settlers.

In the late 1700s, the newly formed United States government tried to help end these conflicts. President **George Washington** encouraged the Cherokee to stop hunting and to focus more on farming instead. The government gave the Cherokee horses, plows, and other farm tools. They hoped that the Cherokee would change to fit in with the surrounding culture.

Many Cherokee took up Washington's offer. They built large farms. They went to school to learn English. They also learned how to read and write in their own language. A Cherokee man named
Sequoyah made up an alphabet for the 6
Cherokee language. He was one of the few people to ever develop an alphabet on his own. With the new alphabet, many Cherokee learned how to read and write in their own language.

Although many Cherokee took up new ideas and changed their ways of life, it did not end conflicts with the settlers and government.

REVIEW What changes occurred in Cherokee culture after the Europeans came? Main Idea and Details

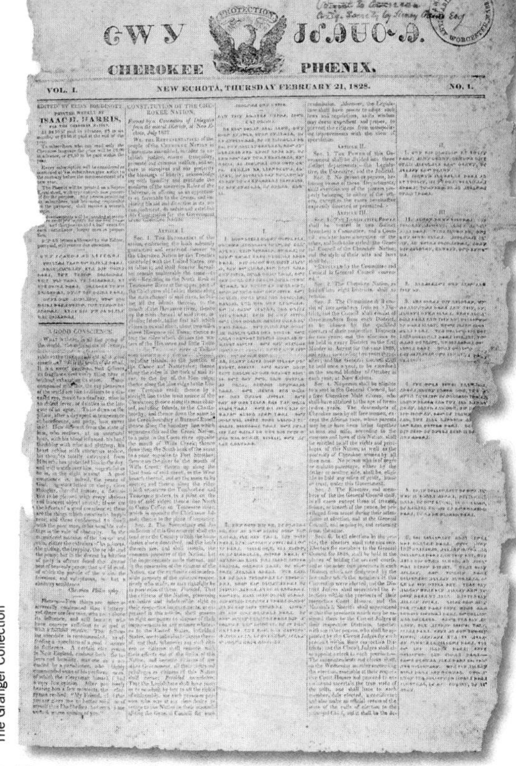
CHEROKEE PHŒNIX.
VOL. I. NEW ECHOTA, THURSDAY FEBRUARY 21, 1828. NO. 1.

The Granger Collection

▶ The *Cherokee Phoenix* newspaper was written in both Cherokee and English. This copy is from February 21, 1828.

190

Practice and Extend

SOCIAL STUDIES
Background

About the Cherokee

- Spanish explorer Hernando de Soto's expedition first encountered the Cherokee in 1540.
- In the mid-1700s, smallpox, probably introduced to the region by European explorers, killed almost half of the Cherokee.
- Sequoyah was born in Loudon County, Tennessee. During his life, he was a hunter, trader, and skilled silver craftsman.
- Sequoia National Park and the giant sequoia tree were named after Sequoyah. *Sequoia* is the Latin spelling of his name.
- The state of Georgia has acknowledged its Native American heritage by naming the Cherokee rose as the state flower.

The Cherokee Leave Their Lands

After the American Revolution, settlers continued to try to gain control of Cherokee land. In the early 1800s, the Cherokee decided that forming a new government would help them hold onto their land. They wrote a constitution in 1827. It stated that the land belonged
7 to the Cherokee nation.

The Cherokee constitution was similar to the United States Constitution in many ways. The Cherokee constitution stated that a head chief would be elected once every four years. The constitution also established a senate and a house of representatives.

After gold was discovered on Cherokee land in 1828, settlers were even more determined to force the Cherokee off their lands. In the 1830s, the United States government ordered the Native American groups of the region, including the Cherokee, to give up their land. The Native American groups would occupy new territory west of the Mississippi River. American soldiers forced the Cherokee families to move west to what is now Oklahoma. Forced to walk hundreds of miles without enough food or warm clothing,
8 thousands of Cherokee died. Their journey came to be called the **Trail of Tears.**

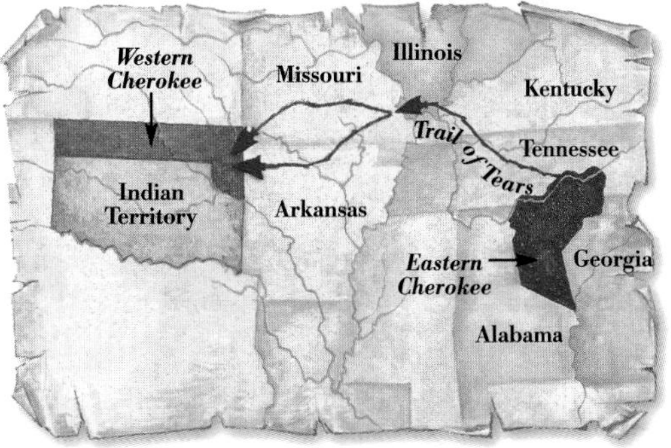

▶ **The Trail of Tears led from Tennessee to what is now Oklahoma.**

The Cherokee who traveled to Oklahoma became known as the Western Cherokee. However, some Cherokee stayed in the Southeast. Several hundred Cherokee bought land together in a mountainous part of North Carolina. A few simply hid in the mountains when soldiers came to round them up. All of these people came to be known as the Eastern Cherokee. Together, the Western and Eastern Cherokee are now the largest Native American group in the United States.

Today, the Eastern Cherokee number more than 11,000. Many live on **Qualla** 9
Boundary, a Cherokee reservation in western North Carolina.

REVIEW How was the Cherokee constitution similar to the U.S. Constitution? **Compare and Contrast**

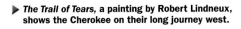

▶ ***The Trail of Tears,*** **a painting by Robert Lindneux, shows the Cherokee on their long journey west.**

PAGE 191

The Cherokee Leave Their Lands

Quick Summary The Cherokee tried to protect their lands by forming their own government. But in the 1830s, the United States government forced them to move west to what is now Oklahoma.

7 **Why did the Cherokee decide to form a new government and write a constitution?** They thought that it would help them hold onto their land.
Main Idea and Details

Test Talk

Use Information from the Text

8 **Why do you think the Cherokee's journey westward was called the Trail of Tears?** Have students make notes about details from the text that answer the question. Students should reread the question and ask themselves, "Do I have enough information to answer the question?" If details are missing, have them go back to the text. Possible answers: Because the Cherokee were being forced to leave their home; because they were tired, cold, and hungry; and because so many Cherokee died during the journey **Draw Conclusions**

9 **Where do many of the Eastern Cherokee live today?** On Qualla Boundary, a Cherokee reservation in western North Carolina
Main Idea and Details

✓ **REVIEW ANSWER** The Cherokee Constitution stated that a head official would be elected once every four years, and it established a senate and house of representatives. **Compare and Contrast**

MEETING INDIVIDUAL NEEDS
Leveled Practice

Identify Cause and Effect Ask students to describe the causes and effects of the Trail of Tears.

Easy Have students create a cause-and-effect graphic organizer or chart about the Trail of Tears. **Reteach**

On-Level Have students write a paragraph summarizing the causes and effects of the Trail of Tears. **Extend**

Challenge Have students research and write a report on the Cherokee in Oklahoma after the Trail of Tears. **Enrich**

For a Lesson Summary, use Quick Study, p. 40.

PAGE 192

The North Carolina Cherokee

Quick Summary Today the Cherokee in North Carolina run businesses and sell artworks and crafts. To keep their culture alive, they teach the Cherokee language.

10 **How are Cherokee speakers trying to keep their language alive?** Possible answer: Some elementary teachers are now teaching the Cherokee language in school. Main Idea and Details

✓ **REVIEW ANSWER** They sell their arts and crafts in stores across the country, and, to keep their language alive, Cherokee speakers and teachers teach the language. Main Idea and Details

3 Close and Assess

Summarize the Lesson

Have students read the four main points and add a sentence to each to add more details to each main idea.

✓ LESSON 1 **REVIEW**

1. **Main Idea and Details** For possible answers, see the reduced pupil page.
2. The Cherokee farmed, hunted, fished, trapped, and gathered before Europeans came to the region. Village decisions were made by consensus, or agreement.
3. After European settlers arrived, the Cherokee traded more. Then they were encouraged to do more farming. Now the Cherokee run businesses and sell artworks and crafts.
4. The Cherokee suffered greatly, and thousands died while traveling west.
5. **Critical Thinking: *Draw Conclusions*** Possible answer: Having a written language allows written records to be kept.

Link to Writing

Poems should include appropriate details about Cherokee village life.

The North Carolina Cherokee

The Cherokee who remained in the Southeast found new ways to support themselves and keep their culture alive. Today, many Cherokee artists belong to an organization called Qualla. They make artworks and crafts that are sold in stores across the country. The Cherokee also run a number of businesses, including a lumber business and shops for tourists.

Some Cherokee leaders fear that their language is dying out. Many Cherokee in their fifties and younger can speak only a few phrases. To keep the language alive, Cherokee speakers have begun to lead special classes in Cherokee school.

Recently, elementary school teachers began teaching the Cherokee language to their students for at least twenty minutes a day. Now, many people are learning the Cherokee language. 10

▶ Mask made by a Qualla artist

REVIEW How do the Eastern Cherokee keep their culture strong? Main Idea and Details

Summarize the Lesson

- **Before 1500s** Cherokee followed their traditional lifestyle.
- **1500s** Europeans came to the Southeast.
- **1830s** Cherokee were forced to move off their land and go west.
- **Today** Many Eastern Cherokee live in the Southeast.

LESSON 1 **REVIEW**

Check Facts and Main Ideas

1. Main Idea and Details On a separate sheet of paper, make a diagram like the one shown. Fill in the diagram with two more details that support the main idea.

Life for the Cherokee changed when Europeans came to the Southeast region.

- Many Cherokee died of diseases that Europeans brought.
- U.S. government convinced the Cherokee to do more farming.
- The Cherokee were forced to move west.

2. What was the Cherokee culture like before Europeans came to the region? Use the word **consensus** in your answer.
3. How has work changed for the Cherokee people?
4. Why was the Cherokee journey to Oklahoma called the **Trail of Tears?**
5. **Critical Thinking:** ***Draw Conclusions*** How might developing a written language change a culture?

Link to Writing

Write a Poem What if you had lived in a Cherokee village hundreds of years ago? Write a poem about life in the village.

192

Practice and Extend

CURRICULUM CONNECTION
Art

Design a Stamp

- Tell students to suppose that the United States Postal Service is issuing a new series of stamps to honor Native Americans.
- Have students create a postage stamp to honor the Cherokee. Encourage students to use a variety of art materials to create their designs.
- Have students display their completed stamps and explain to the class what their designs represent.

Workbook, p. 45

Lesson 1: The Cherokee

Also on Teacher Resources CD-ROM.

Sequoyah

1763?–1843

Some Cherokee thought that white people had magic powers—reading and writing. Sequoyah disagreed. Sequoyah could not read. But he did not think that the marks on paper were special charms. He thought they stood for words. Sequoyah was determined to find a way to write the Cherokee language. He hoped that reading and writing would help Native Americans develop a stronger government and gain more respect. 1

Sequoyah began working on his writing system for the Cherokee language in 1809. At first, he made up a symbol for each word. Sequoyah decided that working with sounds would be easier than using a separate symbol for every word. He based his alphabet not on single sounds but on
2 syllables. Sequoyah made up a symbol for each of the
3 85 syllables in the Cherokee language. This system is called a *syllabary* after the syllables that the letters represent. Cherokee leaders officially adopted the writing system in 1821. This written language made it possible for the Cherokee to start their own newspaper, *The Cherokee Phoenix*. Sequoyah's syllabary is still used today.

BIOFACT

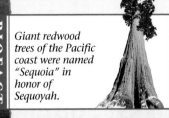

Giant redwood trees of the Pacific coast were named "Sequoia" in honor of Sequoyah.

Learn from Biographies

How could Sequoyah's writing system help the Cherokee keep their traditions and culture?

For more information, go online to *Meet the People* at **www.sfsocialstudies.com.**

193

CURRICULUM CONNECTION
Writing

Write in Cherokee

- Hand out a copy of the Cherokee syllabary and explain how it works. The syllabary can be found at **www.sequoyahmuseum.org.**
- Have students attempt to write Sequoyah's name using the syllabary.

WEB SITE
Technology

Students can find out more about Sequoyah by clicking on *Meet the People* at **www.sfsocialstudies.com.**

Sequoyah

Objective

- Describe Sequoyah's contributions in preserving Cherokee culture.

1 Introduce and Motivate

Preview To activate prior knowledge, have students recite the alphabet. Tell students that they will read more about the creator of the Cherokee alphabet.

2 Teach and Discuss

1 **Why did Sequoyah want to invent a writing system for the Cherokee language?** He hoped that reading and writing would help the Cherokee develop a stronger government and gain more respect. Main Idea and Details

2 **How are the Cherokee syllabary and the English alphabet similar? How are they different?** Possible answers: Similar: both are used to write words; Different: the English alphabet has 26 letters, and letters can have more than one sound. The Cherokee syllabary has 85 symbols, and each symbol stands for one syllable. Compare and Contrast

3 **Describe the steps Sequoyah followed in trying to develop a writing system for the Cherokee.** He made up a symbol for each word, decided that working with sounds would be easier, and then based the alphabet on the 85 syllables in the Cherokee language. Sequence

3 Close and Assess

Learn from Biographies Answer

Possible answer: It allowed the Cherokee to create a written account of their history and traditions so that future generations could read them.

Early History of the Southeast

Objectives

- Identify important explorers of the Southeast and the areas they explored.
- Locate the earliest European settlements in the Southeast.
- Identify early leaders from the Southeast and describe their contributions to the United States.
- Evaluate the impact of agriculture in the Southeast.

Vocabulary

pioneer, p. 198; **backwoodsman,** p. 198; **plantation,** p. 198

Resources

- Workbook, p. 46
- Transparency 1
- Every Student Learns Guide, pp. 82–85
- Quick Study, pp. 42–43

Quick Teaching Plan

If time is short, have students read the lesson independently, then make a set of flashcards summarizing the early history of the Southeast.

- Have each student draw or write a historical event on an index card.
- Collect and shuffle the cards.
- Have the class arrange the cards in chronological order.

1 Introduce and Motivate

Preview Ask students what they know about early explorers of North America. Tell students they will learn more about the history and settlement of the Southeast as they read Lesson 2.

You Are There Have students suppose that they are one of the soldiers in the story. Ask them if they would have wanted to join the expedition and to give reasons for going or staying behind.

LESSON 2

1565 — 1765

- 1565 Spanish build St. Augustine, Florida.
- 1587 British start a colony on Roanoke Island, Virginia.
- 1607 British start a colony at Jamestown, Virginia.
- 1776 American colonies declare independence from Britain.

PREVIEW

Focus on the Main Idea
Exploration, settlements, agriculture, and slavery all shaped the early growth of the Southeast region.

PLACES
St. Augustine, Florida
Roanoke Island
Jamestown, Virginia
Monticello

PEOPLE
Juan Ponce de León
Hernando de Soto
Robert La Salle
Thomas Jefferson
James Madison
Andrew Jackson

VOCABULARY
pioneer
backwoodsman
plantation

Early History of the Southeast

You Are There The year is 1513. You are sitting with a group of Spanish soldiers around a crackling campfire in Puerto Rico. One soldier is telling stories he heard from the native people of Puerto Rico. "Across the sea, there is an island called Bimini, where the fountain of youth flows. Anyone who drinks from this fountain will stay young forever," he says.

The other soldiers are clearly interested in the tale. The leader of the group rises to his feet and says, "I propose an expedition to search for Bimini. Who is with me?" Several soldiers rise to their feet, and you step forward, shouting "Aye!" with the soldiers. You feel ready to face the dangers of exploring a land you know nothing about.

▶ Juan Ponce de León led an expedition to a land he named Florida.

Main Idea and Details As you read, notice how European settlements in the Southeast region developed over time.

Practice and Extend

READING SKILL
Main Idea/Details

In the Lesson Review, students complete a graphic organizer like the one below. You may want to provide students with a copy of Transparency 1 to complete as they read the lesson.

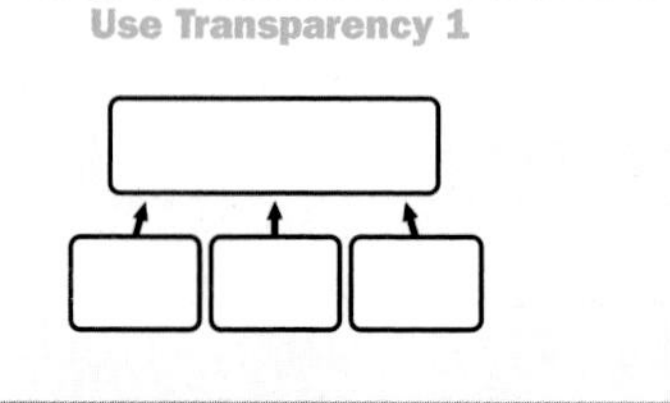

VOCABULARY
Context Clues

Have students read the definitions in the lesson of *pioneer, backwoodsman, plantation,* and *slave,* then assess their understanding by asking them questions such as the following:

- Who might work on a plantation, a pioneer or a slave? (slave)
- What tools would a backwoodsman use? (ax, saw, hunting trap, rope)

Guide students to correct definitions, if necessary.

The Explorers

The Spanish governor of Puerto Rico, **Juan Ponce de León,** believed the Native Americans' stories about the fountain of youth. He set sail to find the island of Bimini in 1513. Ponce de León sailed to the eastern shore of present-day Florida. He mistakenly believed it to be the island of Bimini. He named the land "Florida" because he first saw the land on Easter Sunday, which in Spanish is *Pascua Florida*, or "flowery Easter." He claimed the land for Spain. He was the first European to explore Florida, but he never found the fountain of youth.

Another Spanish explorer, **Hernando de Soto,** landed in Florida in
1 1539. He was searching for gold. He explored a large area of what was to become the Southeastern United States, including present-day Georgia, the Carolinas, Tennessee, and Alabama. He was the first European to see the Mississippi River, but he never found any gold.

The first European to sail down the Mississippi River and reach the Gulf of Mexico was French explorer **Robert La Salle.** In 1682 La Salle headed an expedition that sailed through the Great Lakes and down the Mississippi. When he reached the end of the Mississippi, La Salle claimed the Mississippi River valley (the land surrounding all the rivers that flow into the Mississippi) for his king, Louis XIV of France. In honor of the king, La Salle named the region Louisiana. 3

▶ Robert La Salle

MAP SKILL

Where Explorers Traveled

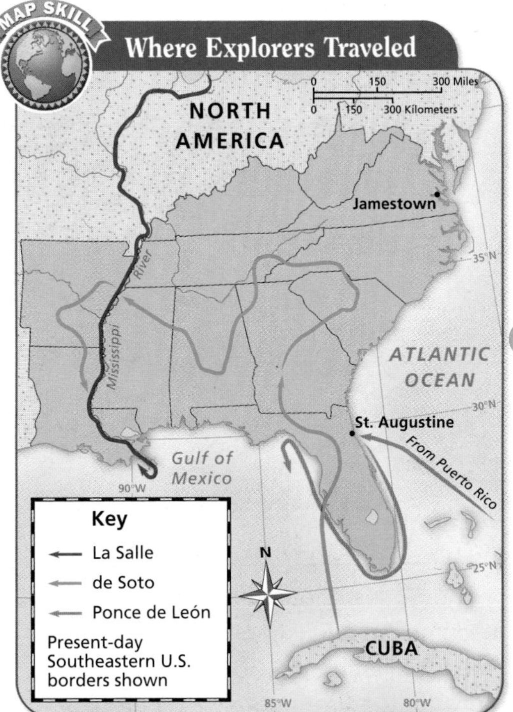

2

▶ Explorers from Spain and France traveled through the Southeast.

MAP SKILL **Movement** ***Which explorer went north and west and crossed the Mississippi River?***

REVIEW Who were the major explorers of the Southeast?
Main Idea and Details

2 Teach and Discuss

PAGE 195

The Explorers

Quick Summary Juan Ponce de León and Hernando de Soto claimed for Spain the land they explored in what is now the Southeast. Robert La Salle claimed the Mississippi River valley for France, naming the region *Louisiana*.

1 **Did Juan Ponce de León and Hernando de Soto have the same goals for their expeditions?** No; De León was looking for the fountain of youth; De Soto was searching for gold.
Compare and Contrast

MAP SKILL

Where Explorers Traveled

2 **Which explorers' routes crossed each other? Where did this occur?** De Soto and La Salle, the Mississippi River; De León and De Soto, on the coast of Florida **Interpret Maps**

MAP SKILL Answer De Soto

3 **How did Louisiana get its name?** La Salle named the region in honor of Louis XIV, the king of France.
Main Idea and Details

✓ **REVIEW ANSWER** Juan Ponce de León explored Florida. Hernando de Soto explored what is now Florida, Georgia, the Carolinas, Tennessee, Alabama, and Mississippi. He was the first European to see the Mississippi River. La Salle sailed through the Great Lakes and all the way down the Mississippi River.
Main Idea and Details

MEETING INDIVIDUAL NEEDS

Leveled Practice

Describe the Explorers' Routes Ask students to describe the routes the explorers took.

Easy Have students work in pairs to create and complete a four-column chart with the headings *Explorer, Country, Date,* and *Places Explored*. **Reteach**

On-Level Have students work with a partner and take turns using the map on p. 195 to describe the explorers' routes. Have partners describe the explorer with whom they would most like to have traveled. Students' descriptions should include reasons and details. **Extend**

Challenge Have each student research and write a one-page report about one of the explorers. Tell them to describe the expedition from the explorer's viewpoint, including the reasons for the expedition, the explorer's experiences, and the results of his travels. **Enrich**

For a Lesson Summary, use Quick Study, p. 42.

PAGE 196

Settlers Come to the Southeast

Quick Summary In 1565 the Spanish established St. Augustine, the first permanent European settlement in the United States. The first successful English colony was founded in Jamestown, Virginia, in 1607.

SOCIAL STUDIES STRAND
Geography

As a class, locate St. Augustine, Roanoke Island, and Jamestown on a map.

4 **For what reasons might people visit St. Augustine?** Possible answers: It was the first permanent European settlement in what is now the United States; the Castillo de San Marcos, the largest remaining Spanish structure in the United States, is there. Make Inferences

5 **For how long did English settlers establish a colony on Roanoke Island?** Three years or fewer Analyze Information

6 **What was the effect of Jamestown's success?** The English founded more colonies up and down the Atlantic coast. Cause and Effect

✓ **REVIEW ANSWER** St. Augustine, Florida—Spain; Roanoke Island, North Carolina—England; Jamestown, Virginia—England
Main Idea and Details

▶ The Castillo de San Marcos in St. Augustine, Florida

Settlers Come to the Southeast

The Spanish founded a city that became **St. Augustine** on the east coast of Florida in 1565. This city
4 became the first permanent European settlement in any area that is now part of the United States. The Spanish built a fort there called the Castillo de San Marcos. They built the fort to protect themselves against attacks. Today, this enormous stone fort is the largest remaining Spanish structure in the United States.

A famous colony in the Southeast is called the "Lost Colony." In 1587 a group of about 100 settlers sailed from England to establish a colony in North America. They arrived on **Roanoke Island** in what is now North Carolina. Their leader, John White, left the colony to go to England for more supplies.
5 When White returned to Roanoke in 1590, the colony had disappeared. The only clue left was the word "CROATOAN" carved on a fence post. No one has ever found out what happened to the lost colony.

The first successful British colony in North America was **Jamestown, Virginia.** In 1607 a group of 105 settlers landed on an area of marshy land on the James River in Virginia. The land turned out to be a breeding ground for diseases. Many settlers became ill and died. The nearby Powhatan Indians offered the colonists food and helped them survive.

The success of Jamestown led to the 6
founding of more colonies up and down the Atlantic coast. The Southeast became home to the oldest English settlements in North America.

REVIEW Name the early colonies of the Southeast and the countries that founded them. Main Idea and Details

196

Practice and Extend

FAST FACTS

- **St. Augustine** has the oldest wooden schoolhouse in the United States. It became the first coeducational school (a school for both boys and girls) in 1788.
- English explorer Sir Walter Raleigh called the **Roanoke Island** colony *Virginia* and that name was given to the first child born there. Virginia Dare was the first English child born in what is now the United States.
- **Jamestown** and the James River were named in honor of King James I of England.

CURRICULUM CONNECTION
Math

Calculate Percentages

- Write the following list of the first ten U.S. Presidents and the states of their birth on the board: Washington, VA; John Adams, MA; Jefferson, VA; Madison, VA; Monroe, VA; John Q. Adams, MA; Jackson, SC; Van Buren, NY; Harrison, VA; and Tyler, VA.
- Have students calculate the percentage of these Presidents that were born in the Southeast (70 percent) and the percentage that were born in Virginia (60 percent).

Building the Nation

Many early leaders of the United States were born in the Southeast. George Washington, who was born in Virginia in 1732, led the Colonial forces against the British army in the Revolutionary War. Some important battles of the Revolutionary War were fought in the Southeast.

George Washington became the first President of the United States in 1789. Washington is known for his
7 honesty, bravery, dedication, and service to his country. As the "Father of His Country," he set an example for other presidents to follow.

Another leader of the Revolutionary War was **Thomas Jefferson,** the author of the Declaration of Independence. In this document, the American colonies declared themselves free and independent from Great Britain in 1776.

Jefferson was born in Virginia in 1743, and became President of the United States in 1801. As president, he doubled the size of the United States when he purchased the Louisiana Territory from France. He designed his home, **Monticello,** which is in Virginia.

Another famous Virginian, **James Madison,** is often called the "Father of the Constitution." Madison was one of the leaders of the Constitutional Convention of 1787. Here, political leaders met to write the Constitution of the United States. In 1809 Madison became the fourth President of the United States.

Andrew Jackson, who became president in 1829, was the first president to be born in poverty. Jackson was born in South Carolina in 1767. Jackson received wide support from ordinary working people who believed that he understood their needs.

REVIEW What major contributions did four early presidents from the Southeast make to the nation? Main Idea and Details

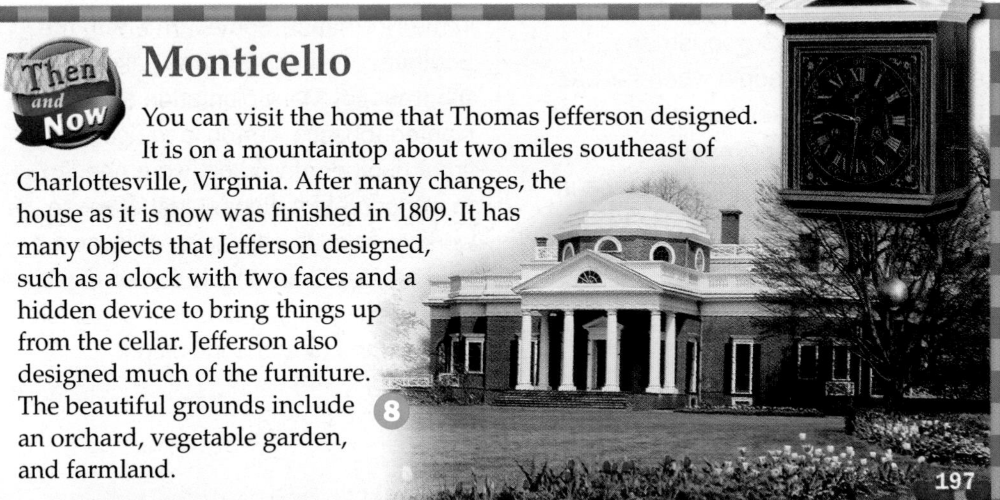

Then and Now — Monticello

You can visit the home that Thomas Jefferson designed. It is on a mountaintop about two miles southeast of Charlottesville, Virginia. After many changes, the house as it is now was finished in 1809. It has many objects that Jefferson designed, such as a clock with two faces and a hidden device to bring things up from the cellar. Jefferson also designed much of the furniture. The beautiful grounds include
8 an orchard, vegetable garden, and farmland.

197

PAGE 197

Building the Nation

Quick Summary Many of the early Presidents of the United States, such as George Washington, Thomas Jefferson, and Andrew Jackson, were born in the Southeast.

7 **Why do you think George Washington was elected the first President of the United States?** Possible answers: He was a leader and hero of the Revolutionary War; he was known for his honesty, bravery, dedication, and service to his country. **Apply Information**

✓ **REVIEW ANSWER** George Washington led the country to victory in the Revolutionary War, was the first President of the United States, and set an example for other Presidents to follow; Thomas Jefferson wrote the Declaration of Independence and purchased the Louisiana Territory from France; James Madison helped write the Constitution; Andrew Jackson supported the needs of ordinary working people. **Main Idea and Details**

Then and Now — Monticello

Have students study the photo of Monticello and read the accompanying text.

8 **How is Monticello different from a typical home today?** Possible answers: It is larger, with extensive grounds, including an orchard and farmland; many houses today are built on smaller plots of land. **Compare and Contrast**

CURRICULUM CONNECTION — Literature

Read Biographies Use the following selections to extend the content.

Thomas Jefferson, by Lucia Raatma (Compass Point Books, ISBN 0-7565-0070-2, 2001) **Easy**

Monticello, by Leonard Everett Fisher (Holiday House, ISBN 0-8234-1406-X, 1996) **On-Level**

George Washington, by Wendie C. Old (Enslow Publishers, ISBN 0-89490-832-4, 1997) **Challenge**

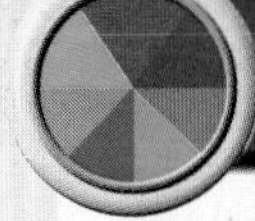

CURRICULUM CONNECTION — Writing

Write About Monticello

- Have students go online to **www.monticello.org** and take a virtual tour of Monticello and its grounds or experience a day in the life of Thomas Jefferson.
- Have students write five interesting facts that they learn on their tour.
- Have students report their findings to the class.

PAGE 198

Pioneers and Backwoodsmen

Quick Summary Daniel Boone was a legendary pioneer who explored Kentucky. David Crockett was a famous backwoodsman who became a congressman for Tennessee.

9 **Why might pioneers and backwoodsmen have become popular figures in stories and songs?** Possible answer: People may have admired their ability to settle, often alone, in parts of the country far away from towns.
Cause and Effect

✓ **REVIEW ANSWER** Boone explored Kentucky and developed the Wilderness Road used by pioneers traveling west. Crockett was a skilled soldier and scout and became a successful congressman for Tennessee. He died defending the Alamo. Main Idea and Details

PAGES 198–199

Farmers and Plantations

Quick Summary Some farmers in the Southeast developed large tobacco, cotton, and rice plantations. Plantation owners often used slaves to work in the fields.

10 **What caused the spread of slavery in the Southeast?** Some settlers built large plantations that required a great number of workers. Most of these workers were African slaves.
Cause and Effect

Pioneers and Backwoodsmen

American settlers moving west created their own folklore and legends. Pioneers and backwoodsmen became popular figures in stories and songs of the day. A **pioneer** was a person who settled in a part of the country and prepared it for others. A **backwoodsman**
9 was a person who lived in forests far away from towns.

Daniel Boone was a pioneer. He explored Kentucky and developed the Wilderness Road, a route followed by many pioneers traveling west. Daniel Boone was born in Pennsylvania in 1734. As a teenager, he moved to North Carolina with his family.

David, also known as "Davy," Crockett, was born in the backwoods of Tennessee in 1786. He was a skilled hunter, soldier, scout, and humorist. This backwoodsman surprised many people when he was elected a Tennessee congressman in 1827. He was a successful and popular leader. After leaving office in 1835, he moved to Texas. He was killed in 1836 while fighting at the Alamo, a battle fought in Texas.

REVIEW What contributions did Daniel Boone and David Crockett make to the region? Main Idea and Details

The Burstein Collection

▶ David "Davy" Crockett

Farmers and Plantations

Settlers who came to farm the Southeast's coastal plains were able to build large farms. This is because the land is flat, not hilly and rocky like land in the Northeast. Some farmers in the Southeast built large farms called **plantations.** Many plantation owners planted tobacco, cotton, and rice. A great number of workers were needed to work on plantations. Most of these workers were African slaves. Slaves are 10
held against their will and forced to work without pay. A slave is usually considered to be owned by someone else.

198

Practice and Extend

EXTEND LANGUAGE
ESL Support

Conceptualize Word Meanings Explore the meaning of *backwoodsman*.

Beginning Have students draw a picture showing a scene from the life of a backwoodsman.

Intermediate Ask students to describe why some people might have enjoyed being backwoodsmen. Students' descriptions should show an understanding of the life of a backwoodsman.

Advanced Have students construct a word web with *Davy Crockett, backwoodsman* in the center. Four spokes radiating from the center should contain the words *hunter*, *soldier*, *scout*, and *humorist*. Ask students to add spokes defining these words, using dictionaries to find definitions.

For additional ESL Support, use Every Student Learns Guide, pp. 82–85.

▶ Boone Hall Plantation near Charleston, South Carolina

By 1776 slaves made up close to half the population in some states. Many Southerners owned slaves who worked in the cotton fields. Farmers who had the largest plantations and the most slaves planted the largest crops. These farmers grew rich growing cotton and became very powerful. 11

REVIEW How does the farmland in the Southeast compare with farmland in the Northeast? Compare and Contrast

Summarize the Lesson

- **1500s to 1600s** Explorers from Spain and France traveled through the Southeast.
- **1607** British colony was started at Jamestown, Virginia.
- **1700s** Plantations grew.
- **1776** American colonies declared independence from Great Britain.

LESSON 2 REVIEW

Check Facts and Main Ideas

1. Main Idea and Details On a separate sheet of paper, make a diagram like the one shown. Fill in the diagram with two more details that support the main idea.

Early leaders from the Southeast have made major contributions to the nation.

President Jefferson bought territory from France.

Washington led the colonists in the Revolutionary War.

Madison was one of the leaders of the Constitutional Convention of 1787.

2. What areas did Juan Ponce de León, Hernando de Soto, and Robert La Salle explore?
3. When was the first permanent European settlement founded in North America, and what was its name?
4. Why were some farmers able to build huge farms called **plantations** in the Southeast?
5. **Critical Thinking:** ***Point of View*** Of all the qualities listed for George Washington, which one do you think is most important for a president to have? Why?

Link to Reading

Read About Plantations Find a book in the library that describes life on a plantation. Report to your class about what you read.

199

11 **How did slavery affect the people of the Southeast?** Possible answers: It deprived enslaved persons of their freedom; it helped plantation owners grow rich. Cause and Effect

✓ **REVIEW ANSWER** The farmland in the Southeast is flat. The farmland in the Northeast is hilly and rocky. Compare and Contrast

3 Close and Assess

Summarize the Lesson

Have students read the main points and then work in groups to play a guessing game using events, people, and other examples from this lesson. For example, one student might say, "I am thinking of a French explorer," and other students apply information from the lesson to respond.

✓ LESSON 2 REVIEW

1. **Main Idea and Details** For possible answers, see the reduced pupil page.
2. Juan Ponce de León explored Florida; Hernando de Soto explored Florida, Georgia, the Carolinas, Tennessee, Alabama and Mississippi; Robert La Salle explored the Great Lakes region and down the Mississippi.
3. The settlement, founded in 1565, was named St. Augustine.
4. The land is flat.
5. **Critical Thinking: *Point of View*** Possible answers: Honesty, bravery, dedication, or service to country; students should support their choice with logical reasoning.

Link to Reading

Reports might include a description of how plantation owners and slaves lived and how their work was done.

CURRICULUM CONNECTION
Drama

Present a Skit

- Have students work in small groups to research and write a three-minute skit on the life of Daniel Boone or David Crockett.
- Tell students that they may try to summarize the person's life, portray an important event, or portray a typical day in the life of their chosen person.
- Have students present their skits for the class. If possible, videotape the skits for the class to review.

Workbook, p. 46

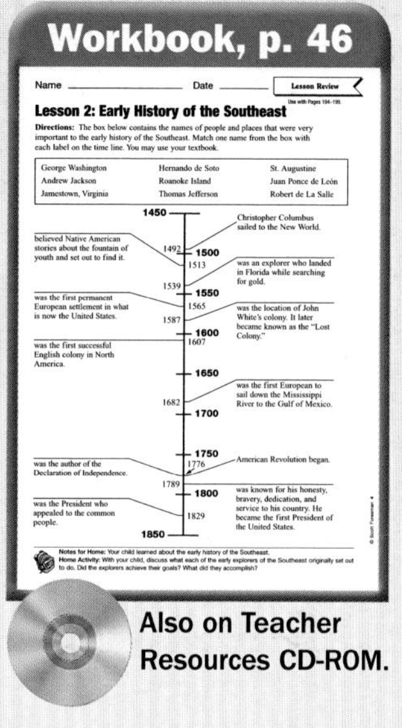

Also on Teacher Resources CD-ROM.

CITIZEN HEROES

Speaking Out

Objective

- Identify the contributions of Sarah and Angelina Grimké to the antislavery movement.

1 Introduce and Motivate

Preview To activate prior knowledge, ask students to describe an experience in which they or someone they know spoke out against something they believed was wrong.

2 Teach and Discuss

SOCIAL STUDIES STRAND
Citizenship

Sometimes standing up for a belief that you think is right takes courage.

1 **How do you think Sarah and Angelina Grimké showed courage?** They spoke out against slavery and tried to get it abolished. Evaluate

2 **How did the Grimké sisters try to change people's views about slavery?** Possible answers: Angelina wrote a letter to a newspaper supporting abolition; they wrote booklets that were sent to women across the South and to religious leaders in the Southeast urging others to speak out against slavery and support the Abolitionists. Main Idea and Details

CITIZEN HEROES

Speaking Out

Have you ever stood up for a belief you thought was right, even though other people said you were wrong? In the 1830s, sisters Sarah and Angelina Grimké had the courage to speak out against slavery. Even though their words made it dangerous for them, the sisters continued speaking and writing against slavery.

Before 1850, some people who lived in the Southeast believed that slavery should be ended, or abolished. People who wanted to abolish slavery were called Abolitionists. **Sarah and Angelina Grimké** (GRIM-kee) were Abolitionists who grew up in Charleston, South Carolina. Sarah visited Philadelphia, Pennsylvania, where she met people who were opposed to slavery. After several visits, Sarah decided to leave her home permanently in 1821. Her sister followed her in 1829. Angelina wrote a letter supporting abolition that was printed in an Abolitionist newspaper.
From then on, the sisters were 1
deeply involved in the antislavery movement.

▶ Angelina Grimké

In 1836 Angelina wrote an antislavery booklet that was sent to women across the South.

200

Practice and Extend

Decision Making

Use a Decision-Making Process

- Have students consider the following decision-making scenario: **Suppose you are against an issue that some other people support. How might you go about persuading people to change their view? What methods and tools might you use today?**
- Students should use a decision-making process to decide what to do. For each step in the process, have students work in small groups to discuss and write about what must be considered. Write these steps on the board or read them aloud.

1. **Identify a situation that requires a decision.**
2. **Gather information.**
3. **Identify options.**
4. **Predict consequences.**
5. **Take action to implement a decision.**

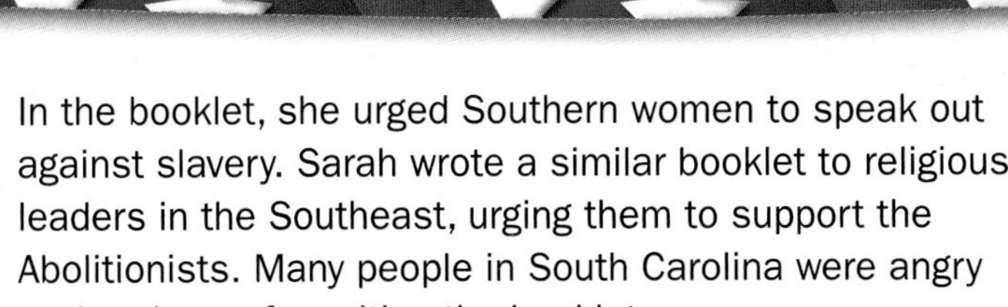

In the booklet, she urged Southern women to speak out against slavery. Sarah wrote a similar booklet to religious 2 leaders in the Southeast, urging them to support the Abolitionists. Many people in South Carolina were angry 3 at the sisters for writing the booklets.

The Grimké sisters were among the first women to give speeches in public in the United States. Many people paid attention to the sisters' words, in part because the sisters were wealthy Southerners speaking out against slavery. Sarah, Angelina, and Angelina's husband, Theodore Dwight Weld, wrote a booklet, *Slavery as It Is: Testimony of a Thousand Witnesses*, in 1839. Harriet Beecher Stowe, a writer and Abolitionist, was said to have based parts of her novel, *Uncle Tom's Cabin*, on this booklet. Abolitionists like Weld, Stowe, and the Grimké sisters gradually convinced many people that slavery was wrong. The Grimké sisters lived to see their dreams made reality when slavery ended in 1865.

▶ Sarah Grimké

Courage in Action

Research other people who have stood up for what they believed, even when they were criticized for their beliefs. You may choose important figures in history or people from the present day who are not well-known. What beliefs did they stand up for? How did they respond to people who attacked their beliefs?

201

3 **Why do you think many people in South Carolina were angry at the Grimké sisters?** Possible answers: Many people there owned slaves and did not want slavery to be abolished; they supported slavery and did not want the Grimké sisters to persuade people to make it illegal. Make Inferences

3 Close and Assess

Courage in Action

- Students' choices of people will vary. Possible historical figures might include Dr. Martin Luther King, Jr., Frederick Douglass, or Horace Greeley.
- Possible beliefs might relate to civil rights or human rights.
- Encourage students to share the results of their research with the class. Ask them to compare and contrast the actions of the different people they researched.

SOCIAL STUDIES Background

About Abolitionists

- The Grimkés' family owned slaves and a plantation in South Carolina.
- The sisters were also among the earliest crusaders for equal rights for women.
- Published in 1852, Harriet Beecher Stowe's book *Uncle Tom's Cabin* contained an antislavery message that influenced many people.

CURRICULUM CONNECTION Art

Make a Political Poster

- Tell students that the Grimké sisters belonged to the American Anti-Slavery Society, which was founded in 1833.
- Have students research the society (search for *American Anti-Slavery Society* at **usinfo.state.gov**) and create a poster from that time period urging people to join the society or to come to a meeting. Encourage students to use visuals in their posters.
- Discuss the accuracy of the posters and display them in the classroom.

The Nation Divided

Objectives

- Identify two causes of the Civil War.
- Explain the effects of the Civil War on the Southeast.
- Describe how the Southeast changed during Reconstruction.
- Analyze the development of the civil rights movement.

Vocabulary

Civil War, p. 203; **Union,** p. 203; **Confederacy,** p. 203; **secede,** p. 203; **Reconstruction,** p. 205; **civil rights,** p. 205; **segregate,** p. 205

Resources

- Workbook, p. 47
- Transparency 1
- Every Student Learns Guide, pp. 86–89
- Quick Study, pp. 44–45

Quick Teaching Plan

If time is short, have students make a cause-and-effect chart of the Civil War.

- Have students fill in their charts as they read the lesson independently.
- Have students compare their charts and fill in any missing details.

1 Introduce and Motivate

Preview To activate prior knowledge, ask students what types of problems can arise when people disagree on an issue. Explain that during the 1800s, the country became divided over the issues of slavery and states' rights. Tell students they will learn more about these issues, the Civil War, and the civil rights movement as they read Lesson 3.

You Are There Ask students what Lucy is describing in the letter. (The battle at Fort Sumter in Charleston) Then have them predict what might happen next. (The battle at Fort Sumter marked the beginning of the Civil War.)

LESSON 3

Charleston

1860 — 1880

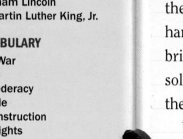

1861 The Civil War begins.

1865 The Civil War ends.

1877 Reconstruction ends.

PREVIEW

Focus on the Main Idea
The Civil War had a major impact on the history of the Southeast.

PLACES
Charleston, South Carolina

PEOPLE
Abraham Lincoln
Dr. Martin Luther King, Jr.

VOCABULARY
Civil War
Union
Confederacy
secede
Reconstruction
civil rights
segregate

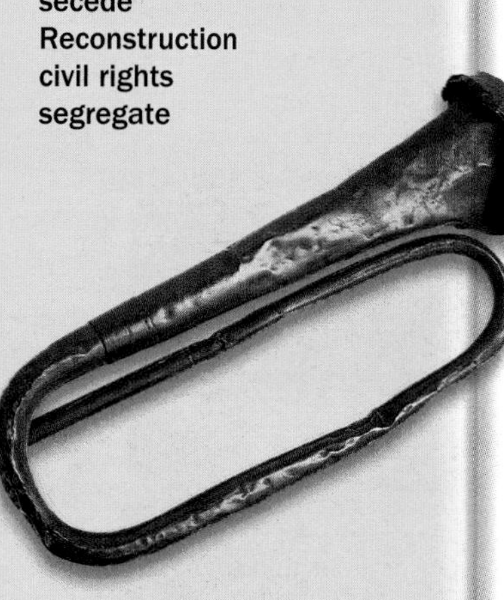

▶ A bugle used by soldiers in the Civil War.

The Nation Divided

You Are There Dear Mary,

We've known for a long time that a war could break out. But I didn't think that it would happen here in Charleston. As you may have heard, there was shooting at Fort Sumter in our harbor. We heard that a Union ship was bringing food and supplies to the Union soldiers there. Our Southern soldiers attacked the fort before the supply ship arrived.

We could see the whole battle from the city. People clapped whenever a shell blew up near the fort. We were happy when the soldiers at the fort surrendered. No one was killed. I hope nothing worse happens.

Your loving cousin,
Lucy

Main Idea and Details As you read, note why the Civil War was important in the history of the Southeast region.

Practice and Extend

READING SKILL
Main Idea/Details

In the Lesson Review, students complete a graphic organizer like the one below. You may want to provide students with a copy of Transparency 1 to complete as they read the lesson.

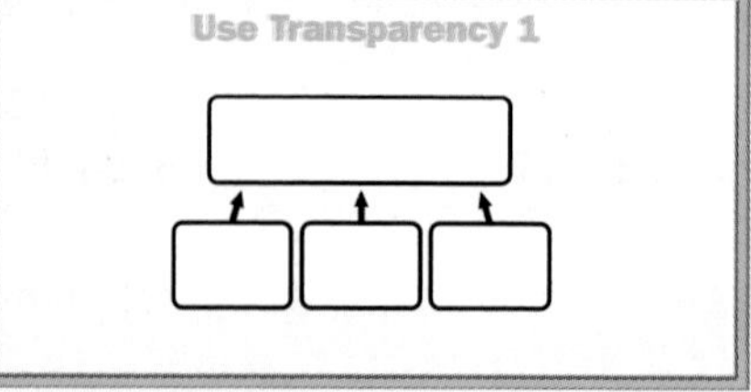

VOCABULARY
Word Exercise

Students may think that "Civil War" and "civil rights" represent completely unrelated uses of *civil*. Explain that *civil* comes from the Latin *civis*, which means "citizen." *Civil* means "having to do with citizens" or "occurring among citizens of one community." Discuss how these definitions of *civil* help students understand both of the vocabulary terms. You may also wish to introduce "civil defense" and "civil liberty," to further deepen students' understanding.

The Civil War

Many people of **Charleston, South Carolina,** were excited by the battle at Fort Sumter. They were ready for war.

The **Civil War** began in 1861 and lasted for four years. It is called a civil war because it was a war between two groups in one country. On one side were the Northern states, called the **Union.** They continued to call themselves the United States of America.

On the other side were the Southern states, called the Confederate States of America, or the **Confederacy.** A confederacy is a group of countries or states. Because the war set Northern states against Southern states, some
1 people call the Civil War the "War Between the States."

Slavery was one important issue of the Civil War. Northerners and Southerners argued over whether slavery should be allowed in the new states added to the nation. Northerners did not want slavery to expand. Southerners thought they had a right to bring slaves as their property.

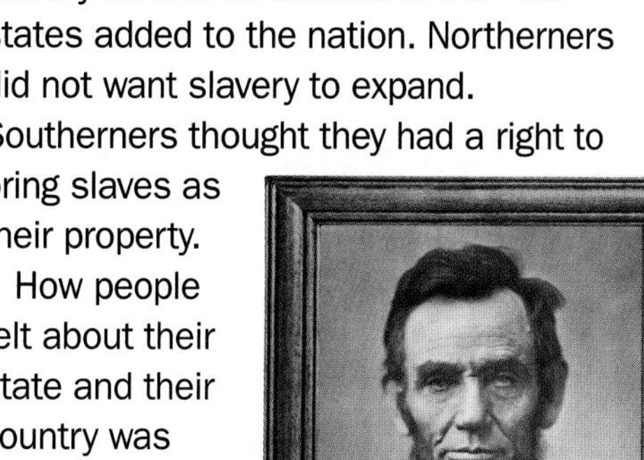

Abraham Lincoln

How people felt about their state and their country was another important issue. Many Southerners thought that each state should have more control over what its citizens could do. Many Northerners thought that the national government should have more power.

Abraham Lincoln, who was running for president in 1860, agreed with these Northerners. When he won, seven Southern states **seceded,** or pulled out, of the United States. They thought that Lincoln would work against the Southern states and might even pass laws to abolish slavery. In time, four 2
more states seceded. These eleven states formed their own country, called the Confederate States of America.

REVIEW Summarize some reasons the Civil War began. Summarize

North Wind Picture Archive

People of Charleston watched the battle at Fort Sumter in 1861.

2 Teach and Discuss

PAGE 203

The Civil War

Quick Summary Disagreements over states' rights and slavery eventually led to a civil war between Northern and Southern states.

1 **Why was the Civil War also known as the "War Between the States"?** Because the war set Northern states against Southern states Main Idea and Details

SOCIAL STUDIES STRAND
Government

A federal government is one in which power is shared by the national and state governments. The Southern states believed that state governments should have sovereignty regarding what was best for the people.

2 **Which group seceded from the United States—the Union or the Confederacy? Why did these states secede?** Confederacy; Possible answer: Because many Southerners believed each state should have more control over what its citizens could do Summarize

Ongoing Assessment

If... students have difficulty determining which group seceded,

then... help them create a mnemonic by pointing out the similarity between the words *union* and *united.* The *Union* remained in the *United* States, while the Confederacy seceded.

REVIEW ANSWER Possible answers: Southerners and Northerners disagreed about whether states or the national government should have the most say about what citizens could do. Many Southerners wanted to allow slavery in the new states added to the nation, but many Northerners did not want slavery to expand. Summarize

FYI SOCIAL STUDIES
Background

About the Confederacy and the Union

- In 1861, the Confederacy was comprised of Virginia, North Carolina, South Carolina, Georgia, Florida, Tennessee, Alabama, Mississippi, Arkansas, Louisiana, and Texas.
- Jefferson Davis became the President of the Confederate States of America. Abraham Lincoln was President of the United States during the Civil War.
- The capital of the Confederacy was Richmond, Virginia, only about 100 miles from Washington, D.C., the capital of the United States.

PAGE 204

The Civil War's Effects on the Southeast

Quick Summary The Civil War caused great destruction in the South, and many Northerners and Southerners died. After the war, the Thirteenth Amendment made slavery illegal in the United States.

SOCIAL STUDIES STRAND
History

General Sherman's war tactics in his campaign through Georgia included "total war." His men were ordered to destroy any industrial or civilian property that could help the South continue fighting. Railroad tracks, barns, houses and fields were stripped, burned, or destroyed.

3 **The bridge in this photograph was destroyed during the Civil War. What effect do you think the destruction of the bridge had on daily life in that area?** Possible answer: Travel in the area probably was more difficult. Analyze Pictures

Test Talk

Locate Key Words in the Text

4 **What was the final event of the Civil War?** Have students decide where they will look for the answer. Ask students if the answer is *right there* or if they have to *think* and *search* for it. Students should be able to find the answer in one place—the first sentence of the second paragraph of text. The surrender of the South Main Idea and Details

5 **What was an important result of the Civil War?** Slavery was made illegal in the United States. Apply Information

✓ **REVIEW ANSWER** Many people died. Cities were burned down. Factories and farms were destroyed. Summarize

3

▶ This field and bridge in Virginia were left in ruins after the Civil War.

The Civil War's Effects on the Southeast

The Civil War was a time of great suffering. Confederate soldiers who fought in the war often had little food. Many people died from wounds or diseases that spread through army camps.

4 After four years of fighting, the South surrendered. Many soldiers returned home to find only ruins. During the war, cities had been burned down and factories had been destroyed. Farms had been burned and trampled.

The war did not just change the South physically. It also changed Southern society. One in four Confederate soldiers died in the war. Many families lost sons or fathers or both. Life was sad and difficult for many people.

The greatest change in the South came with the end of slavery. After the end of the Civil War, in 1865, the United States government passed the Thirteenth Amendment to the United States Constitution. This amendment made slavery illegal in the United States. Former slaves became new American citizens. 5

REVIEW Why was the Civil War a time of great suffering for people in the Southeast? Summarize

204

Practice and Extend

MEETING INDIVIDUAL NEEDS
Leveled Practice

Describe the Civil War's Effects Have students describe the effects of the Civil War on the Southeast.

Easy Have students list the Civil War's effects on the people and the land of the Southeast. **Reteach**

On-Level Have students use encyclopedias and research online to find and make copies of pictures showing the aftermath of the Civil War in the Southeast. Tell them to write captions for the pictures and create a collage of the effects of the Civil War on the Southeast. **Extend**

Challenge Have students research and write a three-paragraph report describing the effects of General William T. Sherman's "march to the sea" in 1864. **Enrich**

For a Lesson Summary, use Quick Study, p. 44.

Rebuilding the Region

Slowly, the South began to recover from the war. **Reconstruction** is the period of time after the Civil War when the South's buildings and its economy were rebuilt. Reconstruction lasted from 1865 to 1877. Farmers again plowed their overgrown fields and planted crops. Factory owners rebuilt their factories. Rail lines were repaired. The government established the Freedmen's Bureau in 1865. For a time it provided food, clothing, and medical care to former slaves. The Bureau also built more than 1,000 schools for African Americans.

During Reconstruction, Southern states were readmitted to the United States government. To rejoin the United States, each Southern state had to promise African Americans their **civil rights.** Civil rights include the right to vote and to have the protection of the law. 6

Many former slaves remained on the farms of landowners. Because many had few skills for other jobs and no land of their own to farm, most former slaves lived in poverty. Many landowners tried to keep African Americans in a condition very close to slavery. After 1877 many Southeastern states enforced "Jim Crow" laws. 7 These laws separated black people from white people on buses, in schools, and in other public places. 8 This separation is known as **segregation.**

REVIEW How did the Southeast change during Reconstruction?
 Main Idea and Details

The Granger Collection

▶ The Freedmen's Bureau set up schools like this one for newly-freed African Americans. This school was in Richmond, Virginia.

205

PAGE 205

Rebuilding the Region

Quick Summary After the Civil War, the South entered a period of Reconstruction as it tried to rebuild its economy. At the end of Reconstruction in 1877, "Jim Crow" laws enforced the segregation of African Americans and whites in the South.

6 **What are two examples of civil rights?** Possible answers: The rights to vote and to have the protection of the law  Main Idea and Details

SOCIAL STUDIES STRAND
Culture

Point out that many African Americans in South Carolina, Georgia, Alabama, Mississippi, and Louisiana could not read in 1870. This made it difficult for many of them to learn new skills and get good jobs.

7 **After African Americans in the South gained their freedom, what other problems did they face?** Possible answer: Many remained on the farms of white landowners, lived in poverty, and remained in a condition very close to slavery because of "Jim Crow" laws and because they had few job skills and no land of their own to farm. Summarize

SOCIAL STUDIES STRAND
History

Although African Americans gained a number of rights during Reconstruction, as Southern Democrats began to regain their power in the 1870s, new laws were passed that again restricted the rights of African Americans.

8 **What were "Jim Crow" laws?** Laws that segregated African Americans and whites on public transportation, in schools, and in other public places Main Idea and Details

✓ **REVIEW ANSWER** Possible answers: Farms were replanted and factories and railroads were rebuilt. All states that had seceded were readmitted to the Union. African Americans were promised their civil rights but many continued to live in poverty. Main Idea and Details

EXTEND LANGUAGE
ESL Support

Examine Word Meanings As students study Reconstruction, have them explore the prefix *re-*, which means "again."

Beginning Model and ask students to repeat the word *reconstruction.* Have students find other words on this page that have the prefix *re-* and explain their meanings. (*rebuilt:* built again or repaired; *readmitted:* admitted again; *rejoin:* join again)

Intermediate Ask students to use a dictionary to find four other words with the prefix *re-*. Have them share the definitions with the class.

Advanced Invite students to name some synonyms for *reconstruction* (*rebuilding, restoration*). Then ask volunteers to use the term *reconstruction* in a sentence.

For additional ESL support, use Every Student Learns Guide, pp. 86–89.

PAGE 206

The Civil Rights Movement

Quick Summary Dr. Martin Luther King, Jr., led the civil rights movement in the 1950s and 1960s. The Civil Rights Act of 1964 ended legal segregation.

Primary Source

In *Stride Toward Freedom,* by Martin Luther King, Jr.

9 **Describe King's views about nonviolence and civil rights.** King stated that nonviolent resistance was the best way to win the fight for civil rights. Summarize

✓ **REVIEW ANSWER** They used nonviolent protests. Main Idea and Details

3 Close and Assess

Summarize the Lesson

Have students write true-or-false sentences using the information in the four points on the time line and then use the sentences to review the lesson.

✓ **LESSON 3 REVIEW**

1. Main Idea and Details For possible answers, see the reduced pupil page.
2. Slavery, the rights of states
3. North: national government should have more power; South: states should have more control.
4. By providing food, clothing, education, and medical care to former slaves
5. **Critical Thinking: *Draw Conclusions*** The act ended legal segregation in schools and public places, making it possible for all people to be treated more fairly.

Link to Writing

Reports should describe King's life and contribution to the civil rights movement, and should use the terms "civil rights" and "segregation" correctly.

The Civil Rights Movement

In the 1950s and 1960s, many people began to work for civil rights. An important leader of the civil rights movement was **Dr. Martin Luther King, Jr.** He was born in Atlanta, Georgia. He spoke out against segregation and other kinds of unfair treatment.

Dr. King urged people to protest unfair treatment without violence. He
9 believed that nonviolent protest was a powerful way to win the fight for civil rights. Dr. King said,

> *". . . nonviolent resistance is the most potent [strongest] weapon available to oppressed [treated unjustly] people in their struggle for freedom."*

Many people agreed with Dr. King. A new law was written and Congress passed the Civil Rights Act of 1964. According to this law, segregation in schools and other public places was no longer allowed.

REVIEW How did Dr. King and his followers protest segregation? Main Idea and Details

Summarize the Lesson

- **1861** The Civil War began.
- **1865** The Civil War ended.
- **1865–1877** The South began to rebuild during Reconstruction.
- **1964** Congress passed the Civil Rights Act of 1964.

▶ Dr. Martin Luther King, Jr.

LESSON 3 REVIEW

Check Facts and Main Ideas

1. Main Idea and Details On a separate sheet of paper, fill in the diagram with details that support the main idea.

The Civil War had a major impact on the land and people of the Southeast.		
Farms and factories were destroyed.	Slavery ended.	One in three of the South's soldiers died.

2. What were two conflicts between North and South that led to the **Civil War**?
3. Compare the Northern and the Southern pre-Civil War view of state governments and their importance.
4. How did the Freedmen's Bureau help former slaves during **Reconstruction?**
5. **Critical Thinking: *Draw Conclusions*** Why was the Civil Rights Act of 1964 important for everyone in the United States?

Link to Writing

Write a Book Report Look in the library for a book about Dr. Martin Luther King, Jr. After you read the book, write a short book report. Use the words **civil rights** and **segregation** in your answer. Share your report with the class.

206

Practice and Extend

CURRICULUM CONNECTION
Literature

Read About Civil Rights

Young Rosa Parks: A Civil Rights Heroine, by Anne Benjamin (Troll Associates, ISBN 0-8167-3775-4, 1997) **Easy**

Let It Shine: Stories of Black Women Freedom Fighters, by Andrea Davis Pinkney (Gulliver Books, ISBN 0-15-201005-X, 2000) **On-Level** ***Coretta Scott King Honor Book***

Freedom's Children: Young Civil Rights Activists Tell Their Own Stories, by Ellen Levine (Puffin, ISBN 0-698-11870-7, 2000) **Challenge** ***Jane Addams Book Award***

Workbook, p. 47

Lesson 3: The Nation Divided Use with Pages 202–206.

Directions: Read each phrase below. Then decide whether the phrase refers to the North or the South during the Civil War. If it refers to the North, write an *N* on the line beside the statement. If it refers to the South, write an *S*. If it refers to both, write a *B*. You may use your textbook.

___ 1. location of Fort Sumter
___ 2. fought over Fort Sumter
___ 3. called itself the Union
___ 4. formed the Confederate States of America
___ 5. had strong opinions about slavery
___ 6. thought that each state should have more control over what its citizens could do
___ 7. thought that the national government should have more power
___ 8. seceded from the United States
___ 9. did not want slavery to be allowed in the new states added to the nation
___ 10. thought slavery should be allowed in the new states
___ 11. surrendered after four years of fighting
___ 12. won the war
___ 13. suffered the loss of many lives during the war
___ 14. one in four soldiers died in the war
___ 15. underwent Reconstruction after the Civil War
___ 16. enforced "Jim Crow" laws
___ 17. tried to return their lives to normal after the war
___ 18. did not allow slavery after the war

Notes for Home: Your child learned about the Civil War and its effects on the Southeast.
Home Activity: With your child, discuss how the United States would be affected if the North and South went to war today. How might your family be affected?

Also on Teacher Resources CD-ROM.

Rosa Parks 1913–

Rosa Parks grew up in a small town in Alabama. During that time in the South, many whites treated blacks unfairly. Rosa Parks' family taught her to be proud of herself and her culture. Rosa Parks said about her mother:

". . . she believed in freedom and equality for people, and did not have the notion that we were supposed to live as we did."

BIOFACT
Montgomery, Alabama has named a street in honor of Rosa Parks.

When Rosa Parks became an adult, she lived in Montgomery, Alabama. There she worked to get fair treatment for African Americans. She joined (1) the National Association for the Advancement of Colored People (NAACP). The NAACP is an organization that works for the fair treatment of African Americans and other minority groups. Rosa Parks became secretary of the NAACP.

During the 1950s, many African Americans in the South did not like the way they were treated on city buses. When Rosa Parks was arrested in 1955 for refusing to give up her seat to a white man, a bus boycott began. A **boycott** is the policy of refusing to buy something as a form of protest. (2) After the boycott succeeded, Rosa Parks became famous for her action.

Learn from Biographies

What did Rosa Parks learn during her childhood that might have inspired her to fight segregation?

For more information, go online to *Meet the People* at **www.sfsocialstudies.com.**

207

Rosa Parks

Objective

- Describe the contributions of Rosa Parks to the civil rights movement.

Vocabulary

boycott, p. 207

1 Introduce and Motivate

Preview To activate prior knowledge, ask students if they have ever heard of a protest. Have student volunteers describe examples of protests. Tell students they will learn how one woman helped make the United States a fairer place in which to live.

2 Teach and Discuss

SOCIAL STUDIES STRAND
Citizenship

(1) **How did Rosa Parks demonstrate good citizenship?** She worked to get fair treatment for African Americans. Analyze Information

(2) **During the boycott many people of different races refused to ride the buses, even though this made it hard for them to get around. Why do you think they made this sacrifice?** Possible answer: They believed people should be treated fairly and equally. Evaluate

3 Close and Assess

Learn from Biographies Answer

Possible answers: From her mother, she learned to be proud of herself and her culture and to believe in freedom and equality.

CURRICULUM CONNECTION
Literature

Read Biographies

I Am Rosa Parks, by Rosa Parks (Puffin, ISBN 0-14-130710-2, 1999) **Easy**

Rosa Parks: From the Back of the Bus to the Front of a Movement, by Camilla Wilson (Scholastic Paperbacks, ISBN 0-439-16330-7, 2001) **On-Level**

Rosa Parks: My Story, by Rosa Parks (Puffin, ISBN 0-14-130120-1, 1999) **Challenge**
ALA Notable Book

WEB SITE
Technology

Students can find out more about Rosa Parks by clicking on *Meet the People* at **www.sfsocialstudies.com.**

Thinking Skills

Identify Fact and Opinion

Objective

- Distinguish between fact and opinion.

Vocabulary

fact, p. 208; **opinion,** p. 208

Resource

- Workbook, p. 48

1 Introduce and Motivate

What are facts and opinions? To activate prior knowledge, ask students for examples of facts and opinions from TV commercials. Then have students read the **What?** section of text on p. 208 to help set the purpose of the lesson.

Why identify facts and opinions? Have students read the **Why?** section of the text on p. 208. Ask students to give some examples of facts and opinions related to current events.

2 Teach and Discuss

How is this skill used? Examine with students the diary entry on p. 208.

- Point out that historical events, dates, and many statistics are facts because they can be proven. Conclusions, theories, and interpretations of events are opinions.
- Explain that what a person thinks about a subject is not a fact; it is an opinion.
- Have students read the **How?** section of text on p. 209.

Thinking Skills

Identify Fact and Opinion

1 **What?** A **fact** is a statement that can be checked. It can be proved to be true. An **opinion** tells about personal feelings. It cannot be proved to be true or false.

Why? Facts and opinions help you understand the world. However, you need to be able to tell the difference between facts and opinions.

2 Writers often combine facts and opinions. They may use facts to support their opinions. They may also use opinions to make a story lively or to persuade others.

Suppose you found a diary with the following page written by a young man who lived in Georgia during the 1860s. In 1864 his family was forced to leave their farm when the Union army advanced through Georgia. They stayed with relatives until the Civil War was over. When the family returned, the young man wrote about what they found.

Our farm stood directly in the way of the Union troops advancing from Atlanta to Savannah in 1864. When we heard about the army's approach, my family left the farm to stay with our relatives in Columbus, 120 miles away. My mother, sister, and I made the journey back to our farm in May of 1865. When we arrived, it was wonderful to see that our house was still standing. Where a field of corn had stretched to the horizon, there was a sea of burned stalks. The field of vegetables that I had planted was trampled with what looked like hundreds of footprints. In my opinion, our land was ruined.

My mother was silent until now. "We'll plant again," she said, looking around. "We'll put in another crop of corn and maybe some peach trees." I felt better as I thought about the new crops we could plant. "Peaches are the best fruit in the world," I said.

208

Practice and Extend

MEETING INDIVIDUAL NEEDS
Leveled Practice

Identify Fact and Opinion Ask students to identify opinions found in the "You Are There" selections at the beginning of each lesson in Chapter 7 (pp. 188, 194, 202, 210).

Easy Have students copy the "You Are There" text from one lesson onto a sheet of paper and highlight the opinions in color. **Reteach**

On-Level Have students copy the "You Are There" text from two lessons onto a sheet of paper. Students should highlight in color the opinions contained on those pages. **Extend**

Challenge Have students list the opinions found in all of the "You Are There" text in Chapter 7. **Enrich**

How? To tell the difference between a fact and an opinion, follow these steps.

- First, read the diary entry on page 208.
- Then, ask yourself, "What statements can be proved to be true?" These statements are facts. You can use reference sources such as encyclopedias, almanacs, and maps to check facts. The first sentence of the entry is a fact. Historical records would show that the farm stood between Atlanta and Savannah.
- Ask yourself, "What statements cannot be proved to be true or  false?" These statements are opinions. Sometimes statements of opinion begin with clues such as *I believe* or *In my opinion.* Opinions are also signaled by words such as *wonderful, horrible, best,* and *worst*.

Think and Apply

1. What is an example of another **fact** from the passage on page 208? What is one way to prove that this fact is true?
2. What is an example of an **opinion** from the passage? What words signal the opinion?
3. How does reading for facts and opinions help you to understand the passage?

209

1. **What is the main difference between a fact and an opinion?** A fact can be proved to be true. An opinion tells about personal feelings and cannot be proven true or false.
Main Idea and Details

2. **Do you think a biography would contain facts, opinions, or both? Explain.** Possible answers: Probably both; it would contain facts about the person's life, but it also might contain the opinions of the author.
Apply Information

3. **What steps are involved in identifying facts and opinions in written material?** Read all the material; ask, "What statements can be proved to be true?"; ask, "What statements cannot be proved to be true or false?" Sequence

3 Close and Assess

Think and Apply

1. Possible answers: The distance from the writer's town to Columbus is 120 miles; by checking a map
2. Possible answers: It was wonderful to see that the house was still standing; *wonderful*; Peaches are the best fruit in the world; *best*
3. Possible answer: The facts tell you about the destruction of the South during the Civil War. The opinions tell you how the destruction affected the people who lived in the Southeast.

CURRICULUM CONNECTION
Writing

Write an Advertisement

- Explain to students that advertisements often use strongly stated opinions to attempt to persuade people to buy a product or service.
- Have student pairs write an advertisement for a product of their choice. Tell them to use both facts and opinions in their ads.
- Listen to the ads as a class. Then have students identify the facts and opinions in each ad.

Workbook, p. 48

Identify Fact and Opinion

Use with Pages 208–209.

A *fact* is a statement that can be checked and proved to be true. An *opinion* tells about personal feelings and cannot be proved to be true or false.

Directions: Read the following paragraph. Then answer the questions about facts and opinions.

Today is December 2, 1862. Mother, Father, and I have been in Washington, D.C., for almost one week now. We are very lucky to be here right now. Washington, D.C., must be the busiest city in the world! Yesterday, President Lincoln sent Congress a State of the Union Address. Father took me with him to listen as the address was read. It was amazing! In the address, the President said that if his new plan is passed, it will shorten the war. I think that would be wonderful.

1. What are two facts from the paragraph? How do you know these are facts?
2. What are two opinions from the paragraph? How do you know these are opinions?

Notes for Home: Your child learned to distinguish between fact and opinion.
Home Activity: With your child, find a newspaper or magazine article about a current event. Discuss which parts of the article are facts and which parts are opinions.

Also on Teacher Resources CD-ROM.

The Glittering Cities

Objectives

- Describe the first gold rush in the United States.
- Explain why Atlanta is an important transportation center.
- Identify the causes of growth in Southeastern cities.

Vocabulary

gold rush, p. 211;
public transportation system, p. 212

Resources

- Workbook, p. 49
- Transparency 1
- Every Student Learns Guide, pp. 90–93
- Quick Study, pp. 46–47

Quick Teaching Plan

If time is short, have students make a two-column chart with the headings *Atlanta* and *Triangle Region.*

- On the left side of the chart, tell students to label the rows *Major Industries* and *Changes.*
- Have students complete the chart as they read the lesson.

1 Introduce and Motivate

Preview To activate prior knowledge, ask students to name some large cities in the Southeast and to locate them on a map. Tell students they will learn more about Atlanta and other cities in the Southeast as they read Lesson 4.

You Are There Ask students if they have ever been to Atlanta. Encourage volunteers to share their experiences with the class. If no one has visited Atlanta, then ask students which attractions mentioned in the text they might like to see and why.

LESSON 4

PREVIEW

Focus on the Main Idea
Cities in the Southeast are growing and changing.

PLACES
Dahlonega, Georgia
Atlanta, Georgia

VOCABULARY
gold rush
public transportation system

The Glittering Cities

You Are There It's so bright! Even though the sun is not shining directly on it, the golden dome looks as if it's all lit up. You're looking out the window at the Georgia State Capitol as the train pulls into the station. You're riding a MARTA train through Atlanta. You've just been to Centennial Olympic Park in downtown Atlanta. You're glad that the train runs above the ground here so that you can see the beautiful dome. Later, you'll get back on the train to go to the Dr. Martin Luther King, Jr., National Historic Site.

It's your first visit to Atlanta. There's so much to do and see!

Main Idea and Details As you read, look for details that describe Atlanta.

▶ Georgia State Capitol, Atlanta, Georgia

210

Practice and Extend

READING SKILL
Main Idea/Details

In the Lesson Review, students complete a graphic organizer like the one below. You may want to provide students with a copy of Transparency 1 to complete as they read the lesson.

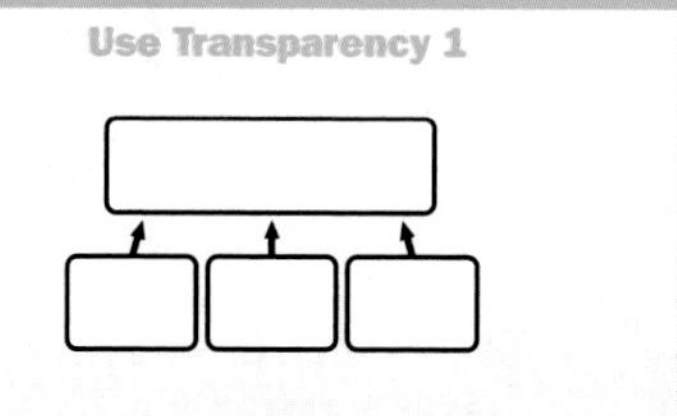

VOCABULARY
Individual Word Study

Help students work through the meanings of "gold rush" and "public transportation system" by breaking the terms down into parts. Discuss how *rush* helps us understand the reaction people had to the discovery of gold. Then talk about how *public* and *system* help describe the type of transportation being discussed in the lesson.

The Golden Dome

In 1828 gold was found in **Dahlonega,** a town in a mountain area in northern Georgia. The first **gold rush** in the United States started
1 soon afterward. People rushed to Dahlonega to look for gold. The town quickly filled with people mining and panning for gold. If you go to Dahlonega, you can visit the Dahlonega Courthouse. The Courthouse was made with bricks that contain gold.

The dome of the state capitol in **Atlanta** gleams with gold from Georgia that the people of Dahlonega gave to the state. The Georgia State Capitol was modeled after the United States
2 Capitol in Washington D.C. The Georgia Capitol has a Georgia Hall of Fame, with pictures of governors and other famous Georgians. The building also contains the State Museum of Science and Industry.

Before the Civil War, Atlanta was an important city in the Southeast. During the war, the city was destroyed. After
the war, Atlanta was rebuilt, and soon 3
became an important city again. It became the capital of Georgia in 1868, after the Civil War. The new capitol building was dedicated on July 4, 1889.

REVIEW What is the source of the gold that covers the dome of the Georgia State Capitol?
Main Idea and Details

▶ A street in Atlanta after the Civil War

211

EXTEND LANGUAGE
ESL Support

Understand Compound Nouns Identify and understand compound nouns such as *courthouse.*

Beginning Have students review Lesson 4 for other compound nouns. Ask students what they think compound nouns are and have them explain why they are used.

Intermediate Ask students to locate other compound nouns in Chapter 7. Once they have made a list, ask them to write definitions for the compound nouns.

Advanced Ask students to make a list of compound nouns not found in their textbook. Have them write and share their definitions with the class.

For additional ESL support, use Every Student Learns Guide, pp. 90–93.

2 Teach and Discuss

PAGE 211

The Golden Dome

Quick Summary Gold was discovered in Dahlonega, Georgia, in 1828, setting off the first gold rush in the United States. Today, gold from Dahlonega covers the dome of Georgia's State Capitol in Atlanta.

SOCIAL STUDIES STRAND
Geography

Point out the location of Dahlonega, Georgia, on a map. Tell students that *Dahlonega* means "yellow money," "precious metal," or "yellow metal" in Cherokee. Remind students that Dahlonega was located in Cherokee territory at that time.

1 **Why did the town of Dahlonega grow quickly?** After gold was discovered there, many people rushed to Dahlonega to look for gold. Draw Conclusions

2 **The Georgia State Capitol was modeled after what building in Washington, D.C.?** United States Capitol
Main Idea and Details

3 **Even though Georgia is one of the original 13 colonies, there are few very old buildings in Atlanta. Why do you think this is true?** During the Civil War, many of the city's buildings were destroyed. After the war new buildings were built. Apply Information

✓ **REVIEW ANSWER** The people of Dahlonega gave the state gold from Georgia. Main Idea and Details

PAGE 212

Getting Around

Quick Summary Railroads helped Atlanta grow. Today the city is a major transportation center.

4 **What effect did the railroad have on Atlanta?** It helped the city grow and prosper. **Cause and Effect**

✓ **REVIEW ANSWER** When many people can ride together in a bus or on a train instead of driving separately in cars, less fuel is used. **Draw Conclusions**

PAGES 212–213

The Growing Cities

Quick Summary A warm climate and good job opportunities attract people to cities in the Southeast, which causes these cities to grow.

5 **How are Orlando and Atlanta alike?** Possible answers: Alike: both are in the Southeast, are growing, have a warm climate, and have good job opportunities. **Compare and Contrast**

✓ **Ongoing Assessment**

If... students have difficulty comparing Atlanta and Orlando, **then...** have them make a list of the characteristics of Orlando that are described in the text. Have students put check marks next to the characteristics that also apply to Atlanta.

Getting Around

Atlanta started as a railroad center in 1837. It was the western end of a new
4 railroad line. As the railroad grew, Atlanta also grew and prospered. Trains carried goods, especially cotton, to the cities in the North. Atlanta is a center of transportation today. It is still a railroad center, and many major highways pass through it. Atlanta's airport is one of the busiest in the United States.

Like many other large cities, Atlanta has a public transportation system to take people to work or to other places. A **public transportation system** is made up of of trains and buses that carry many people through a city. Public transportation helps cut down on automobile traffic. Atlanta's public transportation system is called MARTA, which stands for Metropolitan Atlanta Rapid Transit Authority.

REVIEW How do public transportation systems save fuel? **Draw Conclusions**

▶ **MARTA trains carry people around Atlanta.**

The Growing Cities

Cities in the Southeast are growing. Many people are moving to the South from colder climates in the North. Atlanta is growing quickly. Shiny new buildings are going up all over town. New industries are moving into Atlanta. People are moving here for the jobs that the industries provide. Because Atlanta is the state capital, many people who work for the state government live in Atlanta.

Communications is a major industry in Atlanta. Television stations broadcast all over the world from Atlanta. Financial centers, such as banks and insurance companies, have their headquarters in the city too.

Other Southeastern cities are also among the fastest growing in the United States. Among these cities are Myrtle Beach, South Carolina, and the cities of Naples and Orlando in Florida. The warm climate and the availability of jobs in these cities encourage
people to move there. 5

Charleston, South Carolina, is another growing city. This city has many beautiful old buildings. Near its harbor is the South Carolina Aquarium. There you can see plants and animals from all areas of the state.

212

Practice and Extend

MEETING INDIVIDUAL NEEDS

Leveled Practice

Create a Brochure Ask students to create a brochure to persuade people to move to a city in the Southeast.

Easy Have students use encyclopedias or the Internet to find pictures of one of the cities, and its attractions, industries, and forms of transportation mentioned in this lesson. Have them paste the pictures onto a blank sheet of paper folded into thirds to form a standard brochure. Students should describe the pictures they find. **Reteach**

On-Level Have students complete the assignment described above, and ask them to write captions to describe the visuals pasted into the brochures. **Extend**

Challenge Have students complete the assignment described above, then ask them to research, write, and add four interesting facts about the Southeast to complete the brochure. **Enrich**

For a Lesson Summary, use Quick Study, p. 46.

▶ The Rocky Reef exhibit at the South Carolina Aquarium in Charleston, South Carolina

Photograph by Eric Horan

Another fast-growing area is called the Triangle Region of North Carolina. This area includes the cities of Raleigh, Durham, and Chapel Hill. This area is a center for research in medicine, computers, and many other industries. It is also important as a center for business and education.

Many cities in the Southeast lead the country in population growth. The region is well-known not only for its warm climate and beautiful beaches, but also for its growing economy and industries.

REVIEW What are some reasons why people are moving into cities in the Southeast? Main Idea and Details

Summarize the Lesson

- **The Georgia State Capitol has a dome covered with gold that came from mines in Georgia.**
- **Atlanta started as a railroad center, and now has a public transportation system to move people throughout the city.**
- **Atlanta and many other cities in the Southeast are growing.**

LESSON 4 REVIEW

Check Facts and Main Ideas

1. Main Idea and Details On a separate sheet of paper, make a diagram like the one shown. Fill in the main idea and some facts to support it.

Atlanta and other cities in the Southeast are growing quickly.

- Many people in Atlanta work for the state government.
- Industries are moving into cities in the Southeast.
- Warm climates in the Southeast draw people from colder places.

2. Where was the first **gold rush** in the United States?
3. How has transportation affected Atlanta?
4. In what way is Atlanta a center of industry?
5. **Critical Thinking:** ***Fact and Opinion*** A friend says, "The Southeast is the best part of the country to live in." Is this a fact or an opinion? How can you tell?

Link to  **Writing**

Write a Comparison In what ways are Atlanta and the other cities in the lesson like your home town? In what ways are they different? Make a chart that shows the ways that your hometown compares with one of them.

213

✓ **REVIEW ANSWER** Possible answers: Warm climate, job opportunities
Main Idea and Details

3 Close and Assess

Summarize the Lesson

Have students add details to support each of the bulleted main ideas.

✓ **LESSON 4 REVIEW**

1. **Main Idea and Details** For possible answers, see the reduced pupil page.
2. Dahlonega, Georgia
3. Atlanta started as a railroad center. Highways and airports have helped the city to grow and prosper. A public transportation system—MARTA—helps cut down on automobile traffic.
4. Possible answers: New industries are moving into Atlanta. It is a major center for the communications and finance industries.
5. **Critical Thinking: *Fact and Opinion*** An opinion, because the word *best* is used, and the statement cannot be proved to be true or false

Link to Writing

Charts should compare students' home town with one of the cities mentioned in the lesson. Students might compare such features as geography, climate, history, attractions, transportation, and industry.

CURRICULUM CONNECTION
Music

Write a Song

- Divide the class into small groups and have each group choose one major city of the Southeast.
- Have students in each group research, write, and perform a short song or jingle about their chosen city.
- Have audience members identify the facts and opinions in each group's song or jingle.

Workbook, p. 49

Lesson 4: The Glittering Cities

Also on Teacher Resources CD-ROM.

Spoleto Festival of Two Worlds

Objective

- Compare and contrast a cultural celebration held in both Charleston, South Carolina, and Spoleto, Italy.

1 Introduce and Motivate

Preview To activate prior knowledge, ask students if they have ever been to a festival. Have volunteers share their experiences with the class. Then tell them that, each year, the people of Charleston, South Carolina, hold a festival in cooperation with the people of Spoleto, Italy. The celebration is called the Spoleto Festival of Two Worlds.

2 Teach and Discuss

1 **Would you classify the Spoleto Festival as a historical, cultural, or patriotic festival? Why?** Possible answers: Cultural; Because the festival focuses on dance, music, theater, opera, and visual arts Categorize

2 **Who founded the Spoleto Festival of Two Worlds?** Gian Carlo Menotti

 Main Idea and Details

3 **How do you think Charleston and Spoleto benefit from this festival?** Possible answers: It allows both communities to share their culture with others; people enjoy the performances; it brings money into both communities. Draw Conclusions

Spoleto Festival —of— Two Worlds

▶ A poster from the festival in Italy

Every summer, a music festival is celebrated in two countries. Charleston, South Carolina, in the United States and Spoleto in Italy, come alive with dance, music, theater, opera,
1 and visual art. The Spoleto Festival of Two 4
Worlds is a festival founded by Italian-born
2 composer Gian Carlo Menotti. People from all around the world come to both Spoleto
3 and Charleston to enjoy the festival events. 5

▶ If you visit Charleston in late May and early June, you might see puppet shows, circuses, jazz bands, or chamber music concerts.

▶ A dancer at the Spoleto Festival in Charleston

214

Practice and Extend

MEETING INDIVIDUAL NEEDS
Learning Styles

Study Italian Culture Using individual learning styles, students learn about different aspects of Italian culture.

Visual Learning Have students create a bulletin board with drawings or pictures of Italian art, inventions and inventors, buildings, foods, and geographic features.

Auditory/Verbal Learning Have students use the Internet to research some simple words and phrases in Italian. Allow them to work in pairs to learn these words and phrases.

Musical Learning Explain that opera is a popular pastime for many people in Italy and the United States. Have students listen to a brief portion of an Italian opera, such as *Rigoletto* or *La Traviata* by Giuseppe Verdi.

A cathedral stands in the middle of Spoleto, Italy. The cathedral's colorful windows and mosaics are a beautiful background for the festival.

215

SOCIAL STUDIES STRAND
Culture

4 **What cultural similarities might you find between these two festivals? What cultural differences might you expect to find?** Possible answers: Similar: both celebrate with dance, music, theater, opera, and visual arts; Different: people at the festivals probably would speak different languages. Some art and performances might differ. The events would take place in different settings. **Compare and Contrast**

5 **Would you rather go to the Spoleto Festival of Two Worlds in Charleston or in Italy? Why?** Possible answers: Italy; Because it is in a different country, and I could experience a different culture; Charleston; Because it is closer to where I live **Evaluate**

3 Close and Assess

- Ask students to tell which part of the festivals they would most enjoy and to explain why.
- Have small groups devise a new festival event they think would be appreciated in both cities.

CURRICULUM CONNECTION
Science

Comparing Temperatures

- Have students reread pp. 214–215 and note when the Spoleto Festival is held in South Carolina. Have students do research to find when it is held in Italy.
- Have students research the average temperature in both locations during those periods.
- Tell students to create a double bar graph of the average temperatures during the two festivals.

WEB SITE
Technology

Students can find out more about places on these pages by clicking on *Atlas* at **www.sfsocialstudies.com.**

Resources

- Assessment Book, pp. 33–36
- Workbook, p. 50: Vocabulary Review

Chapter Summary

For possible answers, see the reduced pupil page.

Vocabulary

1. d, **2.** a, **3.** b, **4.** e, **5.** c

People and Places

Possible answers:

1. As the first President of the United States, George Washington tried to encourage the Cherokee, then living in the Southeast, to stop hunting and to focus on farming.
2. Sequoyah developed a writing system for the Cherokee, who were then living in the Southeast.
3. The Eastern Cherokee refused to leave the Southeast. Today many of them live on Qualla Boundary in North Carolina.
4. A group of English colonists who settled on Roanoke Island mysteriously disappeared between 1587 and 1590.
5. The first successful British colony in North America was at Jamestown, Virginia.
6. The Civil War began at Fort Sumter, which is located in the harbor of Charleston, South Carolina.
7. Born in Atlanta, Georgia, a city in the Southeast, Dr. Martin Luther King, Jr., was the main leader of the civil rights movement.
8. When gold was found in Dahlonega, Georgia, people rushed to the Southeast in search of riches.

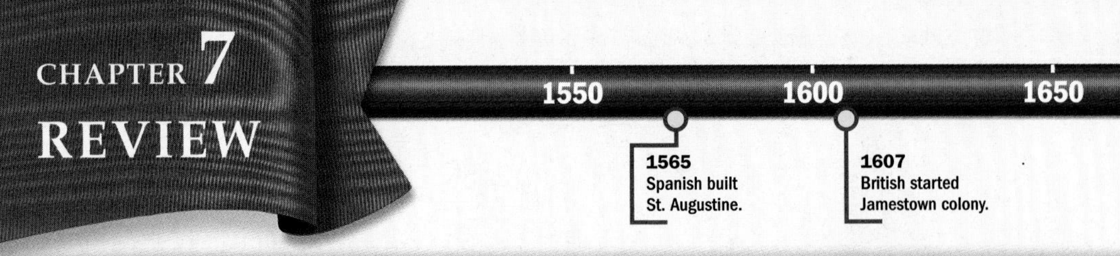
CHAPTER 7
REVIEW
1550
1600
1650
1565
Spanish built
St. Augustine.
1607
British started
Jamestown colony.

Chapter Summary

Target Skill

Main Idea and Details

On a separate sheet of paper, make a diagram like the one shown. Fill in details that support the main idea.

▶ A Cherokee water drum

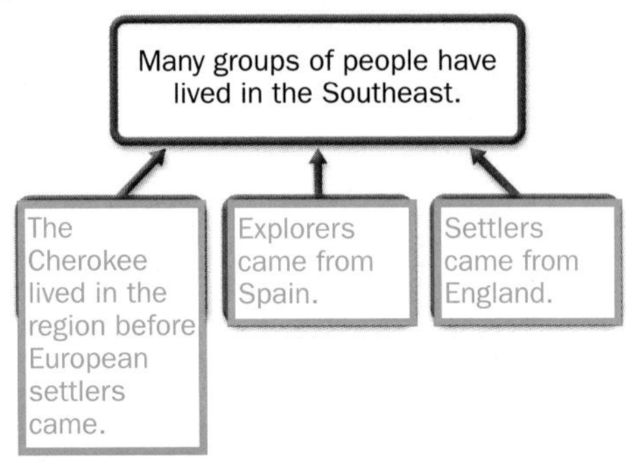
Many groups of people have lived in the Southeast.
The Cherokee lived in the region before European settlers came.
Explorers came from Spain.
Settlers came from England.

Vocabulary

Match each word with the correct definition or description.

1. **plantation** (p. 198)
2. **consensus** (p. 189)
3. **secede** (p. 203)
4. **civil rights** (p. 205)
5. **segregate** (p. 205)

a. a method of decision-making in which all people agree
b. pull out of
c. to separate people by race
d. a very large farm
e. the right to vote and to have protection of the law

People and Places

Tell how each of the following was important in the Southeast region.

1. **George Washington** (p. 190)
2. **Sequoyah** (p. 190)
3. **Qualla Boundary** (p. 191)
4. **Roanoke Island** (p. 196)
5. **Jamestown, Virginia** (p. 196)
6. **Charleston, South Carolina** (p. 203)
7. **Dr. Martin Luther King, Jr.** (p. 206)
8. **Dahlonega, Georgia** (p. 211)

216

Practice and Extend

Assessment Options

✓ Chapter 7 Assessment

- Chapter 7 Content Test: Use Assessment Book, pp. 33–34.
- Chapter 7 Skills Test: Use Assessment Book, pp. 35–36.

Standardized Test Prep

- Chapter 7 Tests contain standardized test format.

✓ Chapter 7 Performance Assessment

- Have students work in groups to compete in an "information bee" about the Southeast.
- Divide the class into two groups. Then have both groups write three original questions (with answers) for each lesson in Chapter 7.
- Have the teams take turns asking their questions to the other team. If a team answers incorrectly, the opposing team gets to continue asking questions. The first team to ask all its questions is the winner.

1700
1750
1800
1850
1900
1700s Cherokee traded with Europeans.
1776 American colonies declared independence.
1838 Cherokee were forced to move.
1861–1865 Civil War

Facts and Main Ideas

1. **Time Line** How many years passed between the American colonies declaring independence and the start of the Civil War?
2. **Main Idea** What issues did Northerners and Southerners disagree about that caused them to go to war?
3. **Main Idea** Compare the Cherokee lifestyle before and after the Europeans came.
4. **Main Idea** How did Jamestown's success affect the settlement of North America?
5. **Main Idea** Name several growing cities of the Southeast and explain what is attracting people to these cities.
6. **Critical Thinking: *Evaluate*** What was the most important event in the history of the Southeast region? Give two or more reasons.

Write About History

1. **Write a Story** Suppose that you are a colonist living in Jamestown. Write a short story about your life in the colony. Describe the colony and what kind of work you do.
2. **Write a travel brochure** about Atlanta. Use the information in Lesson 4 to help you write your description.
3. **Make a time line** about the Civil War and Reconstruction or about the exploration and settlement of the Southeast. Show six or more key events. Illustrate your time line.

1860 Abraham Lincoln is elected President of the United States.
1861 The Civil War begins with the Battle at Fort Sumter.

Apply Skills

Identify Facts and Opinions

Read the advertisement. Then answer the questions.

Come to Jamestown!
Jamestown is the first successful English colony in North America! You will enjoy the beautiful Virginia landscape. The food in Jamestown is the best in North America.

1. **List a sentence** that contains a fact.
2. **List two sentences** that contain opinions.
3. What words are clues that these two sentences are opinions?

Internet Activity

To get help with vocabulary, people, and places, select the dictionary or encyclopedia from *Social Studies Library* at **www.sfsocialstudies.com.**

Hands-on Unit Project

Unit 3 Performance Assessment

- See p. 222 for information about using the Unit Project as a means of performance assessment.
- A scoring guide is provided on p. 222.

WEB SITE Technology

For more information, students can select the dictionary or encyclopedia from *Social Studies Library* at **www.sfsocialstudies.com.**

Workbook, p. 50

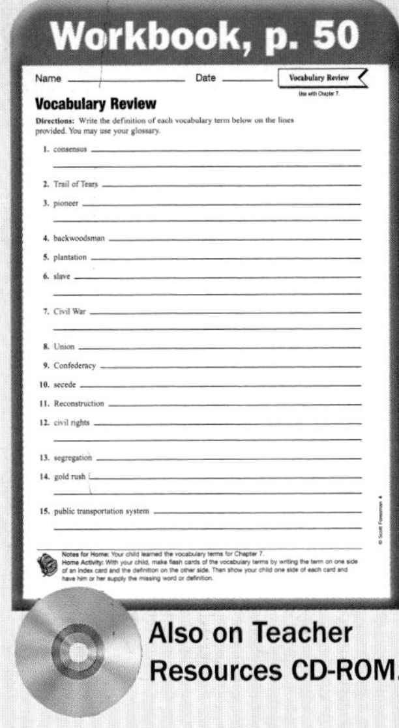
Vocabulary Review
1. consensus
2. Trail of Tears
3. pioneer
4. backwoodsman
5. plantation
6. slave
7. Civil War
8. Union
9. Confederacy
10. secede
11. Reconstruction
12. civil rights
13. segregation
14. gold rush
15. public transportation system

Also on Teacher Resources CD-ROM.

Facts and Main Ideas

1. About 85 years
2. Slavery and the amount of power the national government should have, as opposed to how much control the states should have
3. Before: The Cherokee lived in villages, made decisions by consensus, hunted freely, and spoke the Cherokee language; After: Many gave up hunting for farming and were forced to move to Oklahoma on the Trail of Tears, and they developed a written language
4. Its success encouraged more settlement and led to the founding of more colonies along the Atlantic Coast.
5. Possible answers: Atlanta, Georgia; Myrtle Beach and Charleston, South Carolina; Naples and Orlando, Florida; People are attracted to the warm climate and availability of jobs.
6. Possible answer: the Civil War; it led to the Thirteenth Amendment and the civil rights movement.

Apply Skills

1. Jamestown is the first successful English colony in North America!
2. You will enjoy the beautiful Virginia landscape. The food in Jamestown is the best in North America.
3. beautiful; best

Write About History

1. Stories should accurately describe life in Jamestown and a job that a colonist might have held during that time period.
2. Encourage students to include interesting visuals and persuasive language in their brochures to persuade readers to visit Atlanta.
3. Students' time lines should include at least six separate events, accurate dates, and correct sequencing.

Shenandoah

Objective

- Identify significant examples of music from the Southeast.

Resource

- Transparency 45

1 Introduce and Motivate

Preview To activate prior knowledge, ask students if a song has ever reminded them of a specific place, person, or time in their life. Explain that long ago people sang the song "Shenandoah" to remind themselves of the Shenandoah Valley and their home in the Southeast.

2 Teach and Discuss

1 **Do you think shanties made people's work easier? Why or why not?** Possible answers: Yes; because they took people's minds off of work; they helped people bond over a shared memory; they reminded people that there was a better life waiting for them at home
Draw Conclusions

Shenandoah

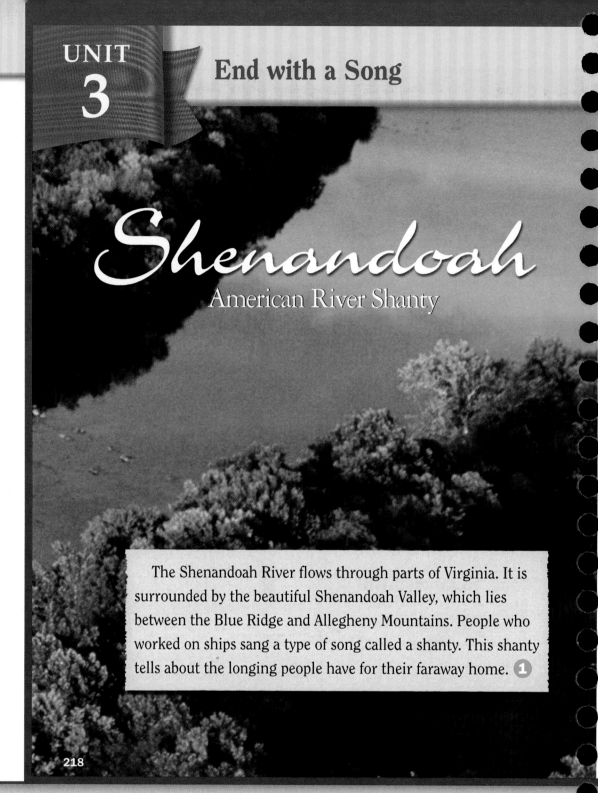

American River Shanty

The Shenandoah River flows through parts of Virginia. It is surrounded by the beautiful Shenandoah Valley, which lies between the Blue Ridge and Allegheny Mountains. People who worked on ships sang a type of song called a shanty. This shanty tells about the longing people have for their faraway home. 1

Practice and Extend

SOCIAL STUDIES
Background

"Shenandoah"

- Although no one knows who wrote the original "Shenandoah" or when it was written, the song is believed to date as far back as the 1820s.
- "Shenandoah" has been known by many names, including "Shennydore," "The Wide Missouri," "The Wild Mizzourye," "Rolling River," and "World of Misery—Solid Fa's." "Solid Fa's" began as a West Indian rowing shanty and is believed to date back farther than any other version.
- The Shenandoah Valley is one of the most beautiful areas of the Southeast. Today it is home to Shenandoah National Park, which covers approximately 200,000 acres of wilderness.

AUDIO CD
Technology

Play the CD, *Songs and Music,* to listen to "Shenandoah."

Shenandoah

Capstan Sea Shanty

Call—Shantyman

1. Oh, Shen - an - doah, I long to hear you, ___
2. Oh, Shen - an - doah, I'm bound to leave you, ___
3. 'Tis sev'n long years since last I saw you, ___
4. When first I took a ram - bling no - tion ___

Response—Crew

And ___ see ___ you roll - in' riv - er, ___
A - way ___ you roll - in' riv - er, ___
And ___ heard ___ you roll - in' riv - er, ___
To ___ leave ___ you roll - in' riv - er, ___

Call—Shantyman

Oh, Shen - an - doah, I long to hear you, ___
Oh, Shen - an - doah, I'll not de - ceive you, ___
'Tis sev'n long years since last I saw you, ___
To sail a - cross the brin - y o - cean, ___

Response—Crew

A - way, ___ I'm bound a - way, 'Cross the wide ___ Mis-sou - ri.

2 3 4

219

2 **What do you think the word *sev'n* means in the song? Why do you think it is written this way?** Seven; *Sev'n* is a one-syllable word that fits better in the song than the two-syllable word *seven*. **Analyze Information**

3 **What do you think the songwriter means by "the wide Missouri"?** The Missouri River **Make Inferences**

4 **Read the words to the song. What words refer to the sea? What rivers are mentioned?** Briny ocean; Shenandoah River, Missouri River **Analyze Information**

3 Close and Assess

- Have small groups of students write another verse to the song that relates to the area where they live.
- Have students copy their verses onto a master sheet.
- Copy and distribute the new verses to the class, and sing them together.

CURRICULUM CONNECTION
Music

Write a Sea Shanty

- Tell students to suppose they are sailors far from home during the early 1800s. Photography has not yet been invented, so they must rely on memories and vivid descriptions to picture their home far away.
- Have students work in small groups to write and perform a sea shanty about their home, community, state, or region.

UNIT 3 Review

Resource

- Assessment Book, pp. 37–40

Main Ideas and Vocabulary

1. c, **2.** a, **3.** a, **4.** a

Test Talk

Choose the Right Answer

Use Main Ideas and Vocabulary, Question 3, to model the Test Talk strategy.

Narrow the answer choices.
Tell students to read each answer choice carefully. Students should rule out any choice that they know is wrong.

Choose the best answer.
After students mark their answer choice, tell them to check their answer by comparing it with the text.

People and Places

1. The Florida Keys is a chain of low islands.
2. Ponce de León claimed Florida for Spain.
3. Robert La Salle sailed down the Mississippi to a region he named Louisiana.
4. St. Augustine, Florida, was settled in 1565.
5. Monticello was Thomas Jefferson's home.
6. James Madison was our fourth President.

UNIT 3 Review

Test Talk

Narrow the answer choices. Rule out answers you know are wrong.

Main Ideas and Vocabulary

TEST PREP

Read the passage below and use it to answer the questions that follow.

The Southeast region has three main landforms: the flat <u>coastal plains</u> located along or near the coast, the rolling hills and valleys of the Piedmont, and the rugged mountains. The warm climate and plentiful water supply of the coastal plains and Piedmont make the lands well-suited for farming. Farming has always been important to the economy of the Southeast. Native Americans first raised corn and other crops there. In the late 1700s, European settlers started growing large amounts of cotton in the region. Many plantation owners in the Southeast had slaves to work in their fields.

At the close of the Civil War in 1865, slavery was abolished across the nation. Many of the freed slaves chose to remain on the farms of the white landowners.

Some of these landowners denied African American workers their civil rights. After Reconstruction ended in 1877, many southern states passed laws that segregated black people and white people in public places.

These laws lasted through the first half of the 20th century. In the 1950s, more African Americans began to speak out against <u>segregation</u> laws. Their protests grew into the Civil Rights Movement. Dr. Martin Luther King, Jr. was an important leader of the Civil Rights Movement in the 1950s and 1960s. He urged his followers to use nonviolent methods of protest. Eventually, the protests resulted in the passage of the Civil Rights Act of 1964. This act ended segregation laws throughout the United States.

1 What are the coastal plains?
- **A** rugged and steep lands near a river
- **B** rolling hills and valleys at the foot of a mountain
- **C** flat land that begins near the ocean
- **D** vast forests

2 When did people in the Southeast begin growing large amounts of cotton?
- **A** in the 1700s
- **B** after 1865
- **C** during the 1940s
- **D** during the 1960s

3 In this passage, <u>segregation</u> means
- **A** separation based on race
- **B** the act of isolating someone based on religion
- **C** the act of giving individuals special rights and privileges
- **D** the coming together of different cultures

4 After the Civil War, African Americans in the Southeast were promised their civil rights. However, they did not always receive their full rights. How many years passed between the end of the Civil War and the passage of the Civil Rights Act?
- **A** 99 years
- **B** 85 years
- **C** 12 years
- **D** 150 years

220

Practice and Extend

Assessment Options

✔ Unit 3 Assessment
- Unit 3 Content Test: Use Assessment Book, pp. 37–38.
- Unit 3 Skills Test: Use Assessment Book, pp. 39–40.

Standardized Test Prep
- Unit 3 Tests contain standardized test format.

✔ Unit 3 Performance Assessment
- See p. 222 for information about using the Unit Project as a means of Performance Assessment.
- A scoring guide is provided on p. 222.

Test Talk
- Test Talk Practice Book

WEB SITE Technology

For more information, you can select the dictionary or encyclopedia from *Social Studies Library* at **www.sfsocialstudies.com.**

People and Places

For each word, write a sentence that defines or shows what the word means and relate it to the Southeast region.

1. **Florida Keys** (p. 173)
2. **Ponce de León** (p. 195)
3. **Robert La Salle** (p. 195)
4. **St. Augustine, Florida** (p. 196)
5. **Monticello** (p. 197)
6. **James Madison** (p. 197)

Write and Share

Write a Scene About the Southeast As a class, write a dramatic scene about a historic event that occurred in the Southeast. With the entire class, choose the event that your scene will be about. Then, divide into four groups. One group will write the dialogue (the conversation between different characters). Another group will edit the dialogue. A third group will write descriptions of the different scenery, furniture, and props needed for the scene. A fourth group can add the scenery and prop descriptions where they belong. Perform your scene for another class.

Apply Skills

Identify Facts and Opinions

Read a newspaper article about a person, place, or event in the Southeast. Use two different colored highlighters. Mark facts in one color. Mark opinions in the second color. Make a key to label the colors you use. Then share your article with a classmate. Discuss any disagreements you have about which statements are facts and which are opinions.

Why Georgia's Capital Is Booming

Atlanta, Georgia is one of the fastest-growing urban areas in the United States. Darla Evans, who lives in Atlanta, says, "I believe Atlanta is one of the most beautiful cities in the United States. We have many flowering trees, mild winter weather, and the best baseball team in the country."

Read on Your Own

Look for books like these in the library.

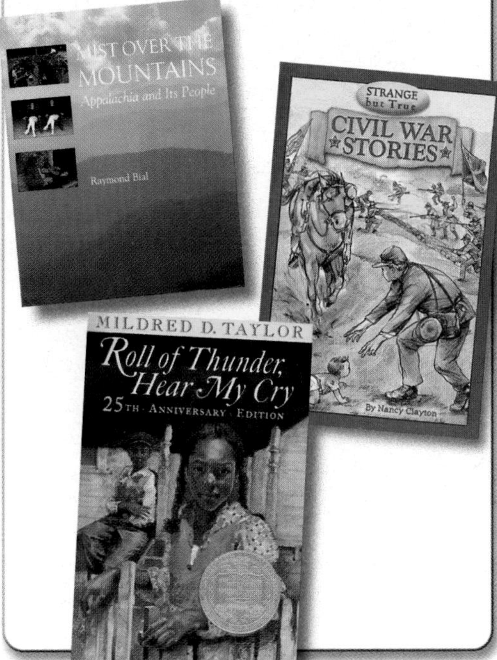

221

Revisit the Unit Question

✓Portfolio Assessment

- Have students look at the class list they created on p. 157 of how resources and events have affected the Southeast.
- Then have students look at the lists they revised throughout Unit 3.
- Ask students to compare these two lists.
- Have students write a summary expressing how their own ideas have changed regarding the effects of resources and events on the Southeast.
- Have students add these lists and summaries to their Social Studies Portfolio.

Apply Skills

- Have students find articles that have two or more paragraphs.
- You may wish to have students look in newspapers or on Internet sites.
- Use the following scoring guide.

✓ Assessment Scoring Guide

Identify Facts and Opinions	
6	Correctly identifies all facts and opinions and includes a coded key
5	Correctly identifies all facts and opinions and includes a key
4	Correctly identifies most facts and opinions and includes a key
3	Correctly identifies most facts and opinions but does not include a key
2	Identifies only a few facts and opinions and does not include a key
1	Cannot identify facts and opinions and does not include a key

If you require a 4-point rubric, adjust accordingly.

Write and Share

- Remind students that their scene should be historically accurate. Have students research people, their manner of speech, and the types of scenery one might have observed in the Southeast at that time.
- Assign students roles in the scene and have them rehearse their parts thoroughly before performing the scene for another class.

Read on Your Own

Have students prepare oral reports using the following books.

Mist Over the Mountains: Appalachia and Its People, by Raymond Bial (Houghton Mifflin, ISBN 0-395-73569-6, 1997) **Easy**

Strange But True Civil War Stories, by Nancy Clayton (Lowell House Juvenile Books, ISBN 0-737-30110-4, 1999) **On-Level**

Roll of Thunder, Hear My Cry, by Mildred D. Taylor (Puffin, ISBN 0-140-38451-0, 1997) **Challenge** ***Newbery Medal***

Unit Project

This Just In

Objective

- Report a significant event in the history of your state.

Resource

- Workbook, p. 51

Materials

paper, pencils, posterboard or large sheets of paper, paints, crayons, and other coloring materials

Follow This Procedure

- Tell students they will report an event in the history of their state as if they were participating in a news conference.
- Brainstorm with students important events from this unit. Have the class choose an event.
- Help students assign roles. Have students write questions, answers, and other statements, such as an eyewitness's account of the event, including what, where, and when it occurred; who was involved; and any consequences.
- Students may also bring in or make props that represent the event, such as tools, hats, uniforms, microphones, etc.
- Have the students hold their news conference.
- Use the following scoring guide.

✓ Assessment Scoring Guide

This Just In	
6	Uses clear, detailed descriptions; accurate and complete information; and precise word choices
5	Uses detailed descriptions; clear, complete information; and appropriate word choices
4	Uses several details; clear, complete information; and appropriate word choices
3	Uses several details, nearly complete information, and appropriate word choices
2	Uses few details, incomplete information, and vague word choices
1	Uses few details, almost no information, and incorrect word choices

If you require a 4-point rubric, adjust accordingly.

This Just In

Report breaking news in your state's history.

1. **Choose** an important event in your state's history.
2. **Choose** roles to play for a press conference about the event: government officials or experts, news reporters, eyewitnesses, and other participants.
3. **Research** the event, focusing on one or two important details of the event. Work together to write questions and answers about the event.
4. **Create** a poster that a TV news station might use to announce breaking news about an event.
5. **Hold** your press conference as a class activity.

Internet Activity

Learn more about the United States. Go to **www.sfsocialstudies.com/activities** and select your grade and unit.

222

Practice and Extend

Hands-on Unit Project

✓ Performance Assessment

- The Unit Project can also be used as a performance assessment activity.
- Use the scoring guide to assess each group's work.

WEB SITE

Technology

Students can launch the Internet Activity by clicking on *Grade 4, Unit 3* at **www.sfsocialstudies.com/activities.**

Workbook, p. 51

Also on Teacher Resources CD-ROM.

★ Unit 4 ★

Vocabulary Routines

The following examples of reading and vocabulary development strategies can be used to instruct students about unit vocabulary.

BEFORE READING

Related Word Study

Word Relationships Exploring the relationships and associations of new vocabulary can help students learn to organize information and retain word meaning. Encouraging students to think about other words that relate to words they are learning will help them make connections and remember the new words. Content-area word mapping can be achieved through the use of graphic organizers such as the one shown.

Draw a box and divide it into four squares. Write **mission** *and* **trading post** *in two of the squares. Ask: What do you think of when I say* **mission?** *(priests, church, teach) Write students' answers in the box next to mission. Then ask: What do you think of when I say* **trading post?** *(fur trade, goods, buy and sell, tools) Write students' answers in the box next to trading post.*

If **mission** *or* **trading post** *is unfamiliar to students, read the lesson sentences in which these words are highlighted in the text. Discuss with students how both* **mission** *and* **trading post** *are places, but how different things happened at each of these places.*

Mission	• teach • church • teach
Trading Post	• goods • buy and sell • tools

DURING READING

Individual Word Study

Examples and Non-Examples When students encounter a new word as they read, draw a circle on the board and describe things that are examples and non-examples of the word. Ask students if the things you are describing belong inside the circle (examples) or outside (non-example). Have students explain their reasoning.

We have just been reading what a **hub** *is. Remember that a* **hub** *is a center of activity.* Draw a circle on the board. *I'm going to describe some places. If you think a place I describe* is *a hub, tell me to write it inside the circle. If you think a place I describe is* not *a hub, tell me to write it outside the circle. A city that has many roads and railroad lines running through it.* (inside) *A small town that is way off in the mountains by itself.* (outside) *A city on a river that is visited by many boats with goods to trade.* (inside)

AFTER READING

Context Clues

Act It Out When learning new vocabulary, it is helpful to use the words being learned in speech and in writing. Encouraging students to perform a creative skit will give them practice in speaking unfamiliar words and confidence in using words that might not be part of their everyday life. The example here shows how vocabulary can be incorporated into creative play.

After reading the selection on pp. 232–237, ask students to use their own words to define the vocabulary terms *waterway, canal, lock,* and *barge.* Then break students into small groups and say, *I want each group to create a short skit about traveling down a canal and through a lock on a barge. Be sure to use your new vocabulary words in the skit. In ten minutes, you will perform your short skits in front of the class.*

08164

The Midwest

UNIT 4

UNIT 4

Unit Planning Guide

Unit 4 • The Midwest

Begin with a Primary Source pp. 224–225

Welcome to the Midwest pp. 226–227

Reading Social Studies, Cause and Effect pp. 228–229

Chapter Titles	Pacing	Main Ideas
Chapter 8 **Water and Land of the Midwest** pp. 230–251 ✓ **Chapter 8 Review** pp. 252–253	7 days	• The Great Lakes link the Midwest region to the Gulf of Mexico and to the Atlantic Ocean. • Erosion has shaped the South Dakota Badlands. • The Midwest is one of the world's leading farming regions.
Chapter 9 **People of the Midwest** pp. 254–283 ✓ **Chapter 9 Review** pp. 284–285	12 days	• The Ojibwa have maintained important cultural traditions and have contributed to the culture of the Midwest. • European settlement in the Great Lakes region and the Mississippi valley began with the fur trade. Many of the region's cities and towns began as fur trading centers. • Many settlers came to the Midwest in the 1800s to farm the land. • The Midwest has been a trade and transportation hub, from long ago to the present.

End with a Song pp. 286–287

✓ **Unit 4 Review** pp. 288–289

✓ **Unit 4 Project** p. 290

✓ = Assessment Options

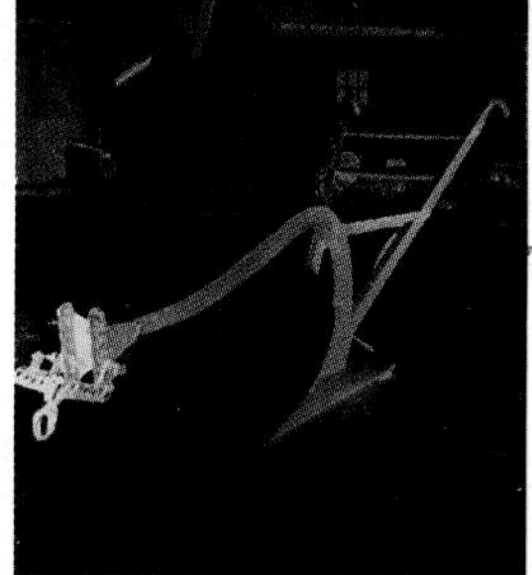

The development of the steel plow made farming easier.

Resources	Meeting Individual Needs
• Workbook, pp. 53–57 • Every Student Learns Guide, pp. 94–105 • Transparencies 20, 46–48 • Quick Study, pp. 48–53 • Workbook, p. 58 ✓ Chapter 8 Content Test, Assessment Book, pp. 41–42 ✓ Chapter 8 Skills Test, Assessment Book, pp. 43–44	• Leveled Practice, TE pp. 233, 240, 243, 247 • ESL Support, TE pp. 234, 244, 249 • Learning Styles, TE p. 245 ✓ Chapter 8 Performance Assessment, TE p. 252
• Workbook, pp. 59–65 • Every Student Learns Guide, pp. 106–121 • Transparencies 20, 49–52 • Quick Study, pp. 54–61 • Workbook, p. 66 ✓ Chapter 9 Content Test, Assessment Book, pp. 45–46 ✓ Chapter 9 Skills Test, Assessment Book, pp. 47–48	• ESL Support, TE pp. 257, 265, 267, 269, 279 • Leveled Practice, TE pp. 259, 263, 266, 270, 280 • Learning Styles, TE pp. 261, 281 ✓ Chapter 9 Performance Assessment, TE p. 284

Today farmers in the Midwest use giant machines to harvest their crops.

Providing More Depth

Additional Resources

- Trade Books
- Family Activities
- Vocabulary Workbook and Cards
- Social Studies Plus! pp. 76–95
- Daily Activity Bank
- Read Alouds and Primary Sources pp. 52–68
- Big Book Atlas
- Student Atlas
- Outline Maps
- Desk Maps

Technology

- AudioText
- Video Field Trips: Exploring the Midwest
- Songs and Music
- Digital Learning CD-ROM Powered by KnowledgeBox (Video clips and activities)
- MindPoint® Quiz Show CD-ROM
- ExamView® Test Bank CD-ROM
- Colonial Williamsburg Primary Sources CD-ROM
- Teacher Resources CD-ROM
- Map Resources CD-ROM
- SF SuccessNet: iText (Pupil Edition online), iTE (Teacher's Edition online), Online Planner
- **www.sfsocialstudies.com** (Biographies, news, references, maps, and activities)

To establish guidelines for your students' safe and responsible use of the Internet, use the Scott Foresman Internet Guide.

Additional Internet Links

To find out more about:

- Badlands National Park, visit **www.nps.gov**
- The Dust Bowl, visit **www.pbs.org**

Unit 4 Objectives

Beginning of Unit 4

- Use primary sources to acquire information. (p. 224)
- Describe selected aspects of states in the Midwest. (p. 226)
- Analyze information by identifying cause-and-effect relationships. (p. 228)

Chapter 8

Lesson 1 A Route to the Sea pp. 232–237

- Explain how the Great Lakes were formed.
- Describe how the Great Lakes are connected to the Atlantic Ocean.
- Define the words *waterway, canal, lock,* and *barge.*
- Explain why the flow of the Chicago River was changed.
- Explain the advantages of shipping by water.
- Describe the effect of zebra mussels on the freshwater lakes in the Midwest. (p. 238)
- Use bar graphs to compare information. (p. 240)

Lesson 2 The Badlands of South Dakota pp. 242–245

- Describe the landscape and climate of the Badlands 67 million years ago.
- Define *erosion* and describe the way it changes the land.
- Define *prairie* and describe the types of life that live there.
- Explain why the climate of the Badlands changed.

Lesson 3 Bountiful Midwestern Farms pp. 246–249

- Explain why the Midwest is an important agricultural region.
- Explain why some farmers irrigate their crops.
- Identify the rainfall in the Midwest and explain how it affects the growth of crops.
- List ten crops grown in the Midwest.
- Identify some crops grown in the Central Plains and the Great Plains.
- Describe the differences between farming methods in Thailand and those in the Midwest. (p. 250)
- Compare the importance of the rice crop in Thailand to the importance of the corn crop in the Midwest. (p. 250)

Chapter 9

Lesson 1 The Ojibwa pp. 256–259

- Describe early Ojibwa culture.
- Describe the ways Ojibwa culture has changed since the mid-1600s.
- Explain the purpose of the American Indian Center and Joseph Podlasek's role in developing respect within the Native American community. (p. 260)
- Describe what Joseph Podlasek has done for the Ojibwa community. (p. 260)
- Use a search engine to find information on the Internet. (p. 262)

Lesson 2 The Fur Trade pp. 264–266

- Describe why the French came to the Midwest in the 1600s.
- Identify the roles of Louis Jolliet and Jacques Marquette in the fur trade.
- Explain the role fur trading played in the development of towns in the Midwest.
- Explain the role that Jean Baptiste Point Du Sable played in trade. (p. 267)
- Identify the importance of trade in meeting countries' needs and wants. (p. 268)
- Explain the impact of trade in early America. (p. 268)

Lesson 3 Building Farms pp. 270–274

- Explain some events that forced Native American tribes in the Midwest to give up their land.
- Compare and contrast a home built out of sod and one built out of logs.
- Explain the difficulties settlers faced in farming the land and their ultimate success.
- Describe the causes and long-term effects of farming the prairie, including the Dust Bowl.
- Explain how John Deere became an entrepreneur. (p. 275)

Lesson 4 Hub of the Nation pp. 276–282

- Describe Cahokia as the early trading center of the Midwest.
- Identify the goals of the Lewis and Clark expedition.
- Identify the role of the steamboat in shipping.
- Describe the advantages of railroads as compared to steamboats.
- Explain the role the government played in developing superhighways that became the interstate highway system.
- Explain the effect of steamboats on Mark Twain's career. (p. 283)

End of Unit 4

- Analyze the meaning of the work song "I've Been Working on the Railroad." (p. 286)
- Understand that people have more than one point of view about events. (p. 290)

Assessment Options

✓ Formal Assessment

- **Lesson Reviews,** PE/TE pp. 237, 245, 249, 259, 266, 274, 282
- **Chapter Reviews,** PE/TE pp. 252–253, 284–285
- **Chapter Tests,** Assessment Book pp. 41–48
- **Unit Review,** PE/TE pp. 288–289
- **Unit Tests,** Assessment Book pp. 49–52
- **ExamView® Test Bank CD-ROM**

✓ Informal Assessment

- **Teacher's Edition Questions,** throughout Lessons and Features
- **Section Reviews,** PE/TE pp. 233, 235, 237, 243–245, 247–249, 257, 259, 265–266, 271–274, 277–278, 280–282
- **Close and Assess,** TE pp. 229, 237, 239, 241, 245, 249, 251, 259, 261, 263, 266–267, 269, 274–275, 282–283, 287

Ongoing Assessment

Ongoing Assessment is found throughout the Teacher's Edition lessons using an **If...then** model.

If = students' observable behavior, **then =** reteaching and enrichment suggestions

✓ Portfolio Assessment

- **Portfolio Assessment,** TE pp. 223, 224, 289
- **Leveled Practice,** TE pp. 233, 240, 243, 247, 259, 263, 266, 272, 280
- **Workbook,** pp. 52–67
- **Chapter Reviews: Write About It,** PE/TE pp. 253, 285
- **Unit Review: Apply Skills,** PE/TE p. 289
- **Curriculum Connection: Writing,** PE/TE pp. 249, 266, 282; TE pp. 235, 273

✓ Performance Assessment

- **Hands-on Unit Project** (Unit 4 Performance Assessment), TE pp. 223, 253, 285, 288, 290
- **Internet Activity,** PE/TE p. 290
- **Chapter 8 Performance Assessment,** TE p. 252
- **Chapter 9 Performance Assessment,** TE p. 284
- **Unit Review: Write and Share,** PE/TE p. 289
- **Scoring Guides,** TE pp. 289–290

Test Talk

Test-Taking Strategies

Understand the Question

- **Locate Key Words in the Question,** TE p. 280
- **Locate Key Words in the Text,** TE p. 239

Understand the Answer

- **Choose the Right Answer,** Test Talk Practice Book
- **Use Information from the Text,** PE/TE p. 288
- **Use Information from Graphics,** TE p. 235
- **Write Your Answer to Score High,** TE p. 259

For additional practice, use the Test Talk Practice Book.

Featured Strategy

Use Information from the Text

Students will:

- Decide where they will look for the answer and make notes about details from the text.
- Use information from the text, then look back at the question and the text to make sure they have the right answer.

PE/TE p. 288

Curriculum Connections

Integrating Your Day

The lessons, skills, and features of Unit 4 provide many opportunities to make connections between social studies and other areas of the elementary curriculum.

Social Studies

READING

Reading Skill—Cause and Effect, PE/TE pp. 228–229, 232, 242, 246, 256, 264, 270, 276

Lesson Review—Cause and Effect, PE/TE pp. 237, 245, 249, 259, 266, 274, 282

WRITING

Write for Information, TE p. 235

Link to Writing, PE/TE pp. 249, 266, 282

Write a Diary Entry, TE p. 273

MATH

Make a Bar Graph, TE p. 248

Link to Mathematics, PE/TE p. 259

Make Calculations, TE p. 283

SCIENCE

Link to Science, PE/TE pp. 237, 245

Compare Precipitation, TE p. 248

Identify Uses for Rice, TE p. 251

Learn More About Wild Rice, TE p. 257

Research Sacagawea on the Internet, TE p. 278

LITERATURE

Read About the Region, TE p. 226

Read Literature, TE p. 273

MUSIC / DRAMA

Discover Traditional Music, TE p. 258

Explore Dust Bowl Songs, TE p. 274

ART

Draw a Picture of the Midwest, TE p. 225

Link to Art, PE/TE p. 274

Look for this symbol throughout the Teacher's Edition to find **Curriculum Connections.**

Professional Development

The Role of Women in America's History

by Carol Berkin, Ph.D.
The City University of New York

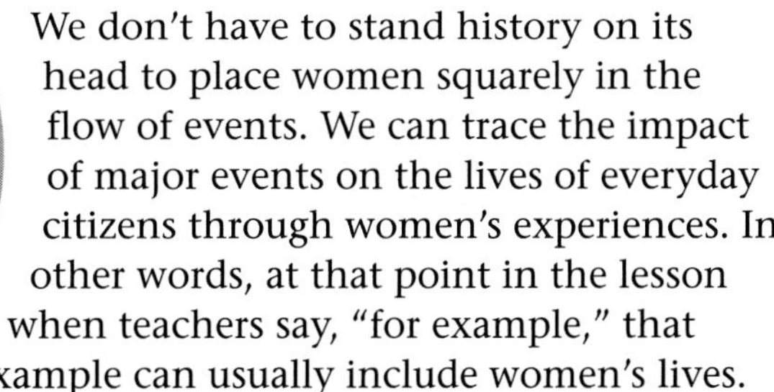

We don't have to stand history on its head to place women squarely in the flow of events. We can trace the impact of major events on the lives of everyday citizens through women's experiences. In other words, at that point in the lesson when teachers say, "for example," that example can usually include women's lives.

One frequently asked question in the social studies classroom is "How do we get students interested in history?" The answer lies, in part, in efforts to make history a mirror in which to discover the past. Educators, authors, and publishers across the country have made a commitment to reflect a past that portrays both women and men as active agents in shaping the society around them.

The following activities in the Teacher's Edition spotlight the contributions of women to American history. In Unit 4 these women speak to us through their works, accomplishments, contributions, and legacies.

- *On p. 242 of the Pupil Edition, students are introduced to Sue Hendrickson, the scientist who discovered one of the most complete* Tyrannosaurus rex *fossils ever found.*
- *On p. 273 of the Teacher's Edition, students are provided with a list of literature resources to expand their knowledge of Laura Ingalls Wilder. Wilder's writing is highlighted on the corresponding Pupil Edition page.*
- *On p. 278 of the Teacher's Edition, students conduct online research to answer specific questions and examine the life and accomplishments of Sacagawea.*

ESL Support

by Jim Cummins, Ph.D.
University of Toronto

In Unit 4 you can use the following fundamental strategy to help ESL students expand their language abilities.

Extend Language

Academic language proficiency does not automatically develop from conversational fluency in English, direct instruction, or language practice. Students must read academic language. Teachers can help by systematically exploring how academic language works.

Academic language includes many abstract words seldom used in conversation. Teachers can help students to understand their meaning and structure and to apply the words in relevant contexts. This helps students understand how words in general work. With practice they can apply this understanding when they write or speak.

The following examples in the Teacher's Edition will help you extend the language abilities of ESL students:

- ***Compare and Contrast a Waterway and a Seaway*** *on p. 234 has students distinguish between the words* waterway *and* seaway *by applying them in relevant context.*
- ***Explore Alternate Word Meanings*** *on p. 265 has students explore the nontraditional uses of* up *and* down *in the text and apply these meanings to other concrete situations.*
- ***Explore Multiple Meanings*** *on p. 271 has students examine multiple meanings of the word* reservation *and apply the term in the context of Native American reservations.*

Read Aloud

The Midwest
by Victoria Kruse

Flat, dry and grassy,
With scarcely a bush or tree,
The Great and Central Plains
Stretch far as the eye can see.
Farmers grow their crops
Across the fields so fair.
If you munch on corn or wheat,
It may have come from there!
Rivers cross the land nearby,
And railroads top the rest,
In case you ever want to see
The vast lands called *Midwest*.

Read Alouds and Primary Sources

- *Read Alouds and Primary Sources* contains additional selections to be used with Unit 4.

Bibliography

I Have Heard of a Land, by Joyce Carol Thomas (HarperTrophy, ISBN 0-06-443617-9, 2000) **Easy** ***ALA Notable Book, Coretta Scott King Honor Book***

The Messenger of Spring: A Chippewa/Ojibwa Legend, by C. J. Taylor (Tundra Books, ISBN 0-88776-413-4, 1997) **Easy**

The Story of Jumping Mouse, by John Steptoe (William Morrow, ISBN 0-688-08740-X, 1989) **Easy** ***Caldecott Honor Book***

The Big Rivers: The Missouri, the Mississippi, and the Ohio, by Bruce Hiscock (Atheneum, ISBN 0-689-80871-2, 1997) **On-Level**

Children of the Dust Bowl: The True Story of the School at Weedpath Camp, by Jerry Stanley (Crown Publishing, ISBN 0-517-88094-6, 1993) **On-Level**

Grandpa's John Deere Tractors, by Roy Harrington (American Society of Agricultural Engineers, ISBN 0-929355-81-4, 1996) **On-Level**

Caddie Woodlawn, by Carol Ryrie Brink (Aladdin Paperbacks, ISBN 0-689-81521-2, 1997) **Challenge** ***Newbery Honor Book***

Lewis and Clark for Kids: Their Journey of Discovery with 21 Activities, by Janis Herbert (Chicago Review Press, ISBN 1-55652-374-2, 2000) **Challenge**

Sarah, Plain and Tall, by Patricia MacLachlan (HarperTrophy, ISBN 0-06-447149-7, 1996) **Challenge** ***Newbery Medal Winner, ALA Notable Book***

Cahokia: City of the Sun, by Claudia G. Mink (Cahokia Mounds Museum Society, ISBN 1-881563-00-6, 1992) **Teacher reference**

Meeting the Neighbors: Sketches of Life on the Northern Prairie, by W. Scott Olsen (North Star Press of St. Cloud, ISBN 0-878-39080-4, 1993) **Teacher reference**

Look for this symbol throughout the Teacher's Edition to find **Award-Winning Selections.** Additional book references are suggested throughout this unit.

The Midwest

UNIT 4

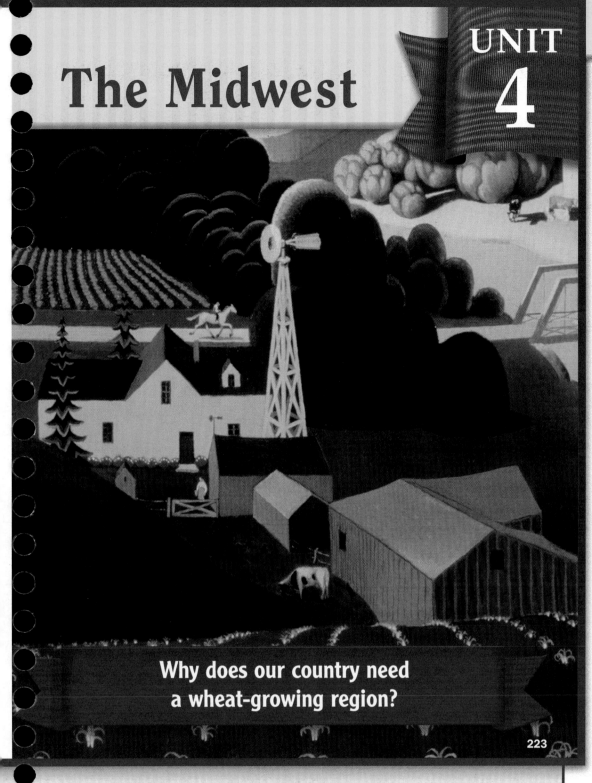

Why does our country need a wheat-growing region?

223

Practice and Extend

Hands-on Unit Project

✓ Unit 4 Performance Assessment

- The Unit Project, *Point of View,* found on p. 290, is an ongoing performance assessment project to enrich students' learning throughout the unit.
- This project, which has students debating two sides of a topic covered in this unit, may be started now or at any time during this unit of study.
- A performance assessment scoring guide is located on p. 290.

The Midwest

Unit Overview

The Midwest region of the United States is rich in natural resources. It has abundant waterways, fertile farmlands, and a rich culture. It has been home to many different peoples.

Unit Outline

Chapter 8 ***Water and Land in the Midwest*** pp. 230–253

Chapter 9 ***People of the Midwest*** pp. 254–285

Unit Question

- Have students read the question under the picture.
- Explain that the Midwest is sometimes referred to as "America's Bread Basket" because the region produces so much wheat.
- Ask students where the Midwest region of our country is located. (In the middle of the United States) Connect the syllable *mid-* with *middle* and *Midwest*.
- Have students brainstorm how a major wheat-growing region like the Midwest might affect the United States. Encourage them to consider such aspects as the economy, transportation, and technology. List their answers on the board.

✓**Portfolio Assessment** Keep this list to review with students at the end of the unit on p. 289.

Begin with a Primary Source

Objective

- Use primary sources to acquire information.

Resource

- Poster 7

Interpret a Primary Source

- Tell students that this primary source is a quotation from the poem "America, the Beautiful," by Katharine Lee Bates, an English professor from Massachusetts.
- Explain that Bates wrote the poem while visiting Colorado in the summer of 1893. At summer's end, she joined a party traveling to Pikes Peak. Upon reaching the summit, Bates was inspired to write four verses of what would later be referred to as the country's unofficial second national anthem.

✓**Portfolio Assessment** Remind students of the list they began of the effects of having a major wheat-growing region in the United States (see p. 223). As students read, have them revise or add to the class list. Review the list at the end of the unit on p. 289.

Interpret Art

- Ask students how they think this painting relates to the quote by Katharine Lee Bates.
- Point out the rolling fields of crops in the foreground and in the upper center of the painting. Ask students what types of crops might appear as "amber waves of grain." (Wheat)
- Ask students what types of landforms they see in this painting. (hills, river)

UNIT 4

Begin with a Primary Source

224

Practice and Extend

About the Primary Source

- "America, the Beautiful," was first published on July 4, 1895, in the weekly journal *The Congregationalist.*
- Over time "America, the Beautiful" has been set to many different melodies. Today, it almost always is sung to the tune of Samuel A. Ward's "Materna."
- In 1926 many people pushed to make "America, the Beautiful" the national anthem of the United States. However, in 1931, President Herbert Hoover chose "The Star-Spangled Banner" as the official anthem.

"O beautiful for spacious skies, for amber waves of grain . . ."

—from "America, the Beautiful," written by Katharine Lee Bates in 1893

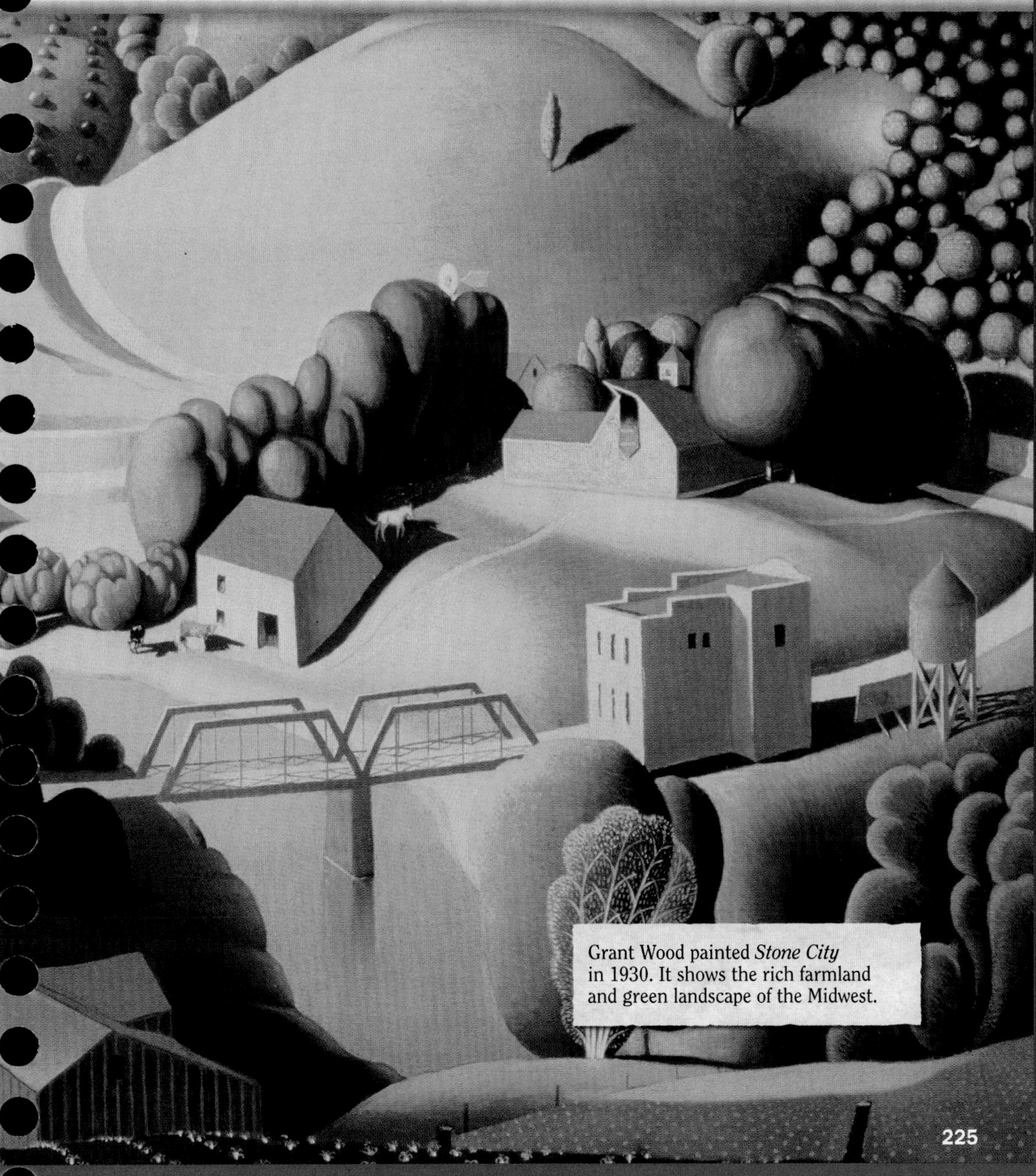

Grant Wood painted *Stone City* in 1930. It shows the rich farmland and green landscape of the Midwest.

225

CURRICULUM CONNECTION

Art

Draw a Picture of the Midwest

- Grant Wood is famous for his portrayals of the American Midwest in paintings such as *Stone City, American Gothic, Breaking the Prairie, Fall Plowing,* and *Young Corn.*
- Using the Internet or library resources, research Wood's and other artists' paintings of the Midwest. Consider how these paintings are similar and how they are different.
- After analyzing the paintings, create your own drawing or painting of the region. Be sure to include details in your artwork that reflect the land, people, and/or resources of the Midwest.

Meet the Artist

- Tell students that the title of this painting is *Stone City.* It was painted in 1930 by American artist Grant Wood (1891–1942).
- Tell them that Wood ran an artists' school in the real Stone City, in east central Iowa, during the summers of 1932 and 1933. The river in the center of the painting is the Wapsipinicon River.
- Explain to students that Stone City grew up around three large, successful limestone quarries. However, the invention of Portland cement caused the local limestone business to decline. Wood's painting shows the community after it had returned to simple farmland.
- Ask students if they can find the old quarry in the painting. (Upper left, just above the rows of dark trees)
- Point out that Wood painted *Stone City* the same year that he created another important painting of the Midwest, *American Gothic. American Gothic,* which also portrays life in the Midwest, has been called the most famous American painting of all time.

Welcome to the Midwest

Objective

- Describe selected aspects of states in the Midwest.

Resource

- Poster 8

Research the Region

Each of the states featured on these pages is part of the Midwest region. Have students use online or library resources to research the answers to the following questions.

- **What is the state motto of Minnesota?** *L'Etoile du Nord,* or "Star of the North"
- **What does North Dakota's Natural Heritage Inventory do?** It keeps track of important species and habitats in the state.
- **What interesting fossil was found in 1922 near Wellfleet, Nebraska?** The world's largest fossil elephant
- **Which President of the United States came from Indiana?** Benjamin Harrison
- **What is the Missouri state animal?** Mule
- **What does *Illinois* mean in the Algonquian language?** "Tribe of superior men"

Students may wish to write their own questions about the states listed on these pages for the rest of the class to answer.

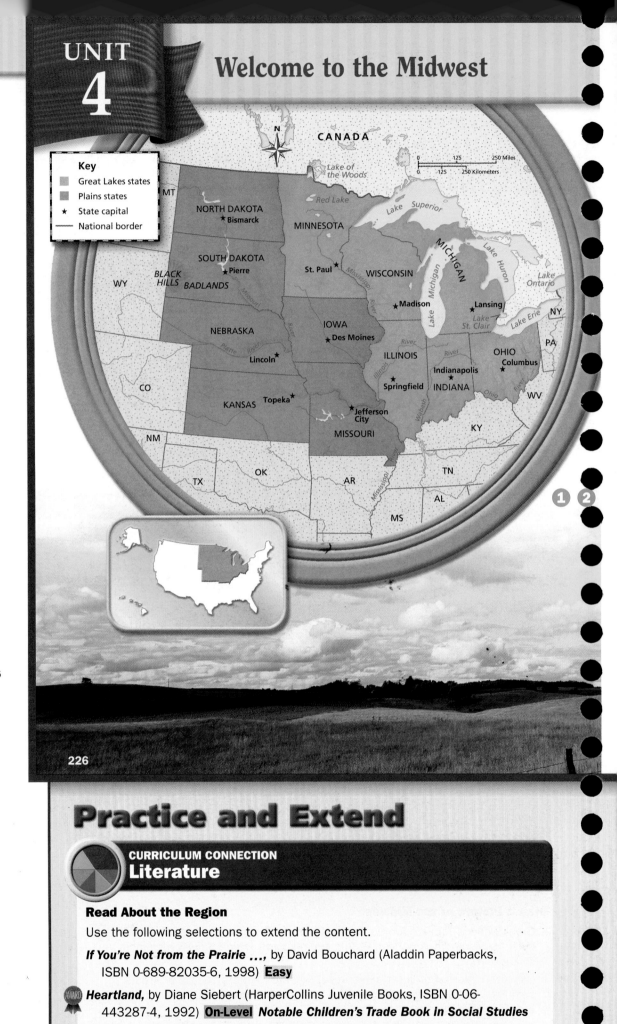

UNIT 4

Welcome to the Midwest

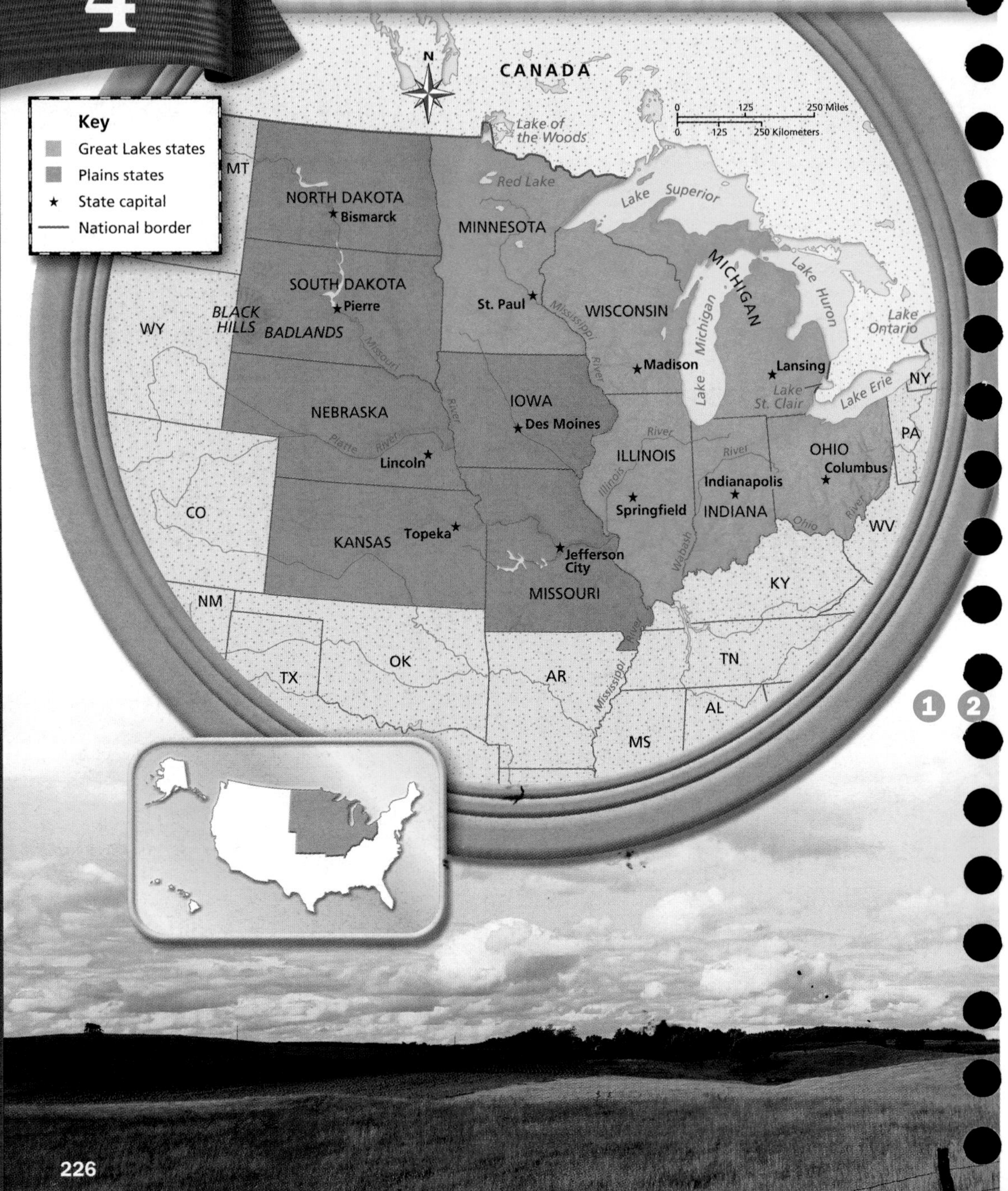

226

Practice and Extend

CURRICULUM CONNECTION
Literature

Read About the Region

Use the following selections to extend the content.

If You're Not from the Prairie ..., by David Bouchard (Aladdin Paperbacks, ISBN 0-689-82035-6, 1998) **Easy**

AWARD ***Heartland,*** by Diane Siebert (HarperCollins Juvenile Books, ISBN 0-06-443287-4, 1992) **On-Level** ***Notable Children's Trade Book in Social Studies***

My Face to the Wind: The Diary of Sarah Jane Price, a Prairie Teacher, Broken Bow, Nebraska, 1881, by Jim Murphy (Scholastic Trade, ISBN 0-590-43810-7, 2001) **Challenge**

Thousands of people enjoy sailing on the Great lakes every year.

Sculptor Gutzon Borglum spent more than 14 years carving the faces of four United States Presidents on Mt. Rushmore in South Dakota.

3 Nearly half of the corn grown in the United States is grown in Iowa, Illinois, Indiana, and Ohio.

The 630-foot Gateway Arch in St. Louis, Missouri, is the nation's tallest monument. It is a monument to the spirit of western pioneers.

The moose is Minnesota's largest animal. Moose can grow to be 6 1/2 feet high at the shoulder.

An old schoolhouse sits on the prairie in the Midwest.

227

WEB SITE
Technology

Students can learn more about places in this unit by clicking on *Atlas* at **www.sfsocialstudies.com.**

Discuss the Region

Have students use the pictures and captions to answer the following questions.

1 **What generalization can you make about where a state capital is located within the state?** Many state capitals are located in the center of the state.
Draw Conclusions

2 **Which two rivers form part of the southern border of the Midwest region?** The Mississippi and Ohio Rivers
Interpret Maps

3 **Which states produce nearly half of all corn in the United States?** Iowa, Illinois, Indiana, and Ohio
Main Idea and Details

Read About the Region

The Midwestern states shown here are discussed in the text on the following pages in Unit 4.

- Illinois, pp. 230–232, 234–235, 237, 242, 246, 258, 260, 266–267, 275–277, 276–277, 280–281
- Indiana, p. 231
- Iowa, pp. 254, 270–271, 274
- Kansas, pp. 259, 275
- Michigan, pp. 249, 254, 257, 259, 265–267
- Minnesota, pp. 254, 257–259
- Missouri, pp. 231, 237, 254, 276–278, 280–281
- Nebraska, pp. 246–247, 258
- North Dakota, p. 258
- South Dakota, pp. 242–247, 258
- Wisconsin, pp. 231, 249, 257, 259, 260, 265, 267

UNIT 4

Reading Social Studies

Cause and Effect

Objective

- Analyze information by identifying cause-and-effect relationships.

Resource

- Workbook, p. 52

About the Unit Target Skill

- The target reading skill for this unit is Cause and Effect.
- Students are introduced to the unit target skill here and are given an opportunity to practice it.
- Further opportunities to use cause and effect are found throughout Unit 4.

1 Introduce and Motivate

Preview To activate prior knowledge, ask students for examples of cause and effect from previous units of this textbook. (Examples: Distance from equator affects climate; amount of water used for hydropower along Niagara River affects energy supply)

UNIT 4

Reading Social Studies

The Midwest

Cause and Effect

Finding causes and effects can help you understand what you read.

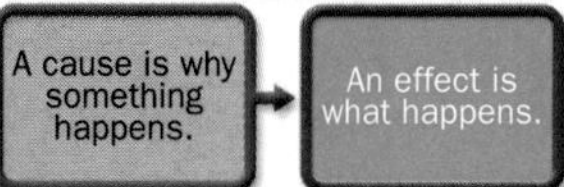

- Sometimes writers use clue words such as *so, since,* or *because* to signal cause and effect.
- An effect can have more than one cause.
- One cause can have many effects, as in the paragraph below.

Read the following paragraph. **Causes** and **effects** have been highlighted.

A tornado is a type of violent storm that sometimes happens in the Midwest. Tornadoes are sometimes called "twisters" because their winds spin around in a whirling funnel-shaped cloud. Tornadoes are dangerous because they can cause serious damage. Effects of tornadoes include destroyed buildings, uprooted trees, and objects as large as trucks being thrown in the air.

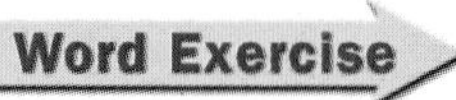

Comparatives The passage describes the Midwestern plains as flat. The word *flat* is an adjective that means "smooth and even." Doubling the *t* and add *-er* forms the word *flatter*, which means "more smooth and even." Adding the *-est* ending forms *flattest*, which means "the most smooth and even."

Word	More	Most
flat	flatter	flattest

Practice and Extend

ACTIVATE PRIOR KNOWLEDGE

ESL Support

Apply Cause-and-Effect Structures Have students use cause-and-effect sentences to write about the climate of their region.

Beginning On the board, draw simple pictures to convey a cause-and-effect relationship, such as a sun and a wilted flower. Then explain the relationship using the word *because*. For example, "Because it doesn't rain much here in the summer, we need to water outdoor plants." Help students identify the cause and the effect in each relationship.

Intermediate Have students work in small groups to act out one cause-and-effect sentence for each of the clue words: *because, so,* and *since*.

Advanced Have students write sentences demonstrating cause and effect. Then have students make graphic organizers showing a cause leading to one or more effects.

Causes and Effects of the Rainfall Patterns in the Midwest

The Midwest region stretches from the state of Ohio at the east to the states of the Dakotas, Nebraska, and Kansas at the west. The patterns of rainfall vary across the Midwest. The western part of the region is much drier than the central and eastern parts are.

What causes this difference? The dry weather of the western Midwest is caused by the presence of mountain ranges to the west of the region. Because weather in the United States generally moves from west to east, much of the moisture in the air from the Pacific Ocean falls as rain on the western slopes of the Sierra Nevada and the Rocky Mountains. By the time the air gets to the eastern slopes, it is very dry. That is why the flat, Midwestern plains on the eastern side of the Rocky Mountains get so little rain.

The dry climate of the western plains affects the types of crops grown there. Farmers plant wheat and other products that do not need much water.

The central and eastern plains of the Midwest receive more rain. This is because moist air from the Gulf of Mexico flows northward. This moist air brings rain to the central and eastern parts of the Midwest.

Apply it!

Use the reading strategy of cause and effect to answer questions 1 and 2. Then answer the vocabulary question.

1. What causes the western part of the Midwest to be dry?
2. What effect does the lack of rainfall have on the farmers of the western plains?
3. In the reading selection, find the word *dry* and the comparative form *drier*. What word means "most dry"?

Standardized Test Prep

- Use Workbook p. 52 to give students practice with standardized test format.
- Chapter and Unit Tests in the Assessment Book use standardized test format.
- Test-taking tips are contained in the front portion of the Assessment Book Teacher's Edition.

Also on Teacher Resources CD-ROM.

Workbook, p. 52

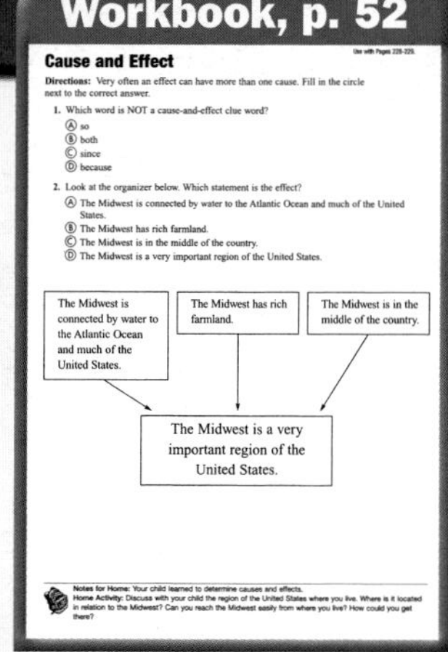

Cause and Effect

Use with Pages 228–229.

Directions: Very often an effect can have more than one cause. Fill in the circle next to the correct answer.

1. Which word is NOT a cause-and-effect clue word?
   Ⓐ so
   Ⓑ both
   Ⓒ since
   Ⓓ because
2. Look at the organizer below. Which statement is the effect?
   Ⓐ The Midwest is connected by water to the Atlantic Ocean and much of the United States.
   Ⓑ The Midwest has rich farmland.
   Ⓒ The Midwest is in the middle of the country.
   Ⓓ The Midwest is a very important region of the United States.

The Midwest is connected by water to the Atlantic Ocean and much of the United States.
The Midwest has rich farmland.
The Midwest is in the middle of the country.
The Midwest is a very important region of the United States.

Notes for Home: Your child learned to determine causes and effects.
Home Activity: Discuss with your child the region of the United States where you live. Where is it located in relation to the Midwest? Can you reach the Midwest easily from where you live? How could you get there?

2 Teach and Discuss

- Explain that an effect (what happens) has a cause (a reason). As students read, have them look for clue words such as *so, since,* or *because* to find causes and effects. Point out that some sentences have no clue words signaling cause and effect.
- Have students read the sample paragraph on p. 228. Confirm that they can identify the cause in the sentence highlighted in blue and the effect in the sentence highlighted in yellow.
- Then have students read the longer practice sample on p. 229 and answer the questions that follow.
- Ask students why, when studying social studies, it is important to understand causes and effects. (We need to know why something happens and how one action can lead to another.)

Discovering Comparatives

Word Exercise

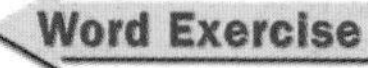

Positives, comparatives, and superlatives show different degrees of an adjective. Have students create a chart like the one below and use it to show the different forms of the word *dry*.

(Word)	More	Most
dry	drier	driest

Encourage students to chart other adjectives, such as *happy, sad, fast,* and *slow,* and use them in a sentence. Explain that comparatives and superlatives are also often created by adding *more* or *most* to the adjective, as in *more beautiful* and *most beautiful*.

3 Close and Assess

Apply it!

1. The mountain ranges to the west of the region
2. They must raise crops that grow well in a dry climate.
3. Driest

CHAPTER 8

Chapter Planning Guide

Chapter 8 • Water and Land of the Midwest

Locating Places pp. 230–231

Lesson Titles	Pacing	Main Ideas
Lesson 1 **A Route to the Sea** pp. 232–237 **Issues and Viewpoints: Zebra Mussel Invasion** pp. 238–239 **Chart and Graph Skills: Compare Line and Bar Graphs** pp. 240–241	4 days	• The Great Lakes link the Midwest region to the Gulf of Mexico and to the Atlantic Ocean. • The spread of zebra mussels is causing problems and posing challenges. • Bar graphs are used to compare the amounts of different things.
Lesson 2 **The Badlands of South Dakota** pp. 242–245	1 day	• Erosion has shaped the South Dakota Badlands.
Lesson 3 **Bountiful Midwestern Farms** pp. 246–249 **Here and There: United States and Thailand: Big Farms and Little Farms** pp. 250–251	2 days	• The Midwest is one of the world's leading farming regions. • The Thai rice crop and the midwestern corn crop are both important to their regions.
✓ **Chapter 8 Review** pp. 252–253		

Dinosaurs once roamed the area that is now the Badlands of South Dakota.

✓ **= Assessment Options**

◀ **Zebra mussels have a black and white striped shell.**

Vocabulary	Resources	Meeting Individual Needs
waterway **canal** **lock** **barge** **line graph** **bar graph**	• Workbook, p. 54 • Transparencies 20, 46–48 • Every Student Learns Guide, pp. 94–97 • Quick Study, pp. 48–49	• Leveled Practice, TE p. 233 • ESL Support, TE p. 234
	• Workbook, p. 55	• Leveled Practice, TE p. 240
badlands **erosion** **prairie**	• Workbook, p. 56 • Transparency 20 • Every Student Learns Guide, pp. 98–101 • Quick Study, pp. 50–51	• Leveled Practice, TE p. 243 • ESL Support, TE p. 244 • Learning Styles, TE p. 245
crop rotation **irrigation**	• Workbook, p. 57 • Transparencies 20, 49 • Every Student Learns Guide, pp. 102–105 • Quick Study, pp. 52–53	• Leveled Practice, TE p. 247 • ESL Support, TE p. 249
	✔ Chapter 8 Content Test, Assessment Book, pp. 41–42 ✔ Chapter 8 Skills Test, Assessment Book, pp. 43–44	✔ Chapter 8 Performance Assessment, TE p. 252

Providing More Depth

Additional Resources

- Vocabulary Workbook and Cards
- Social Studies Plus! pp. 84–89
- Daily Activity Bank
- Big Book Atlas
- Student Atlas
- Outline Maps
- Desk Maps

Technology

- AudioText
- MindPoint® Quiz Show CD-ROM
- ExamView® Test Bank CD-ROM
- Teacher Resources CD-ROM
- Map Resources CD-ROM
- SFSuccessNet: iText (Pupil Edition online), iTE (Teacher's Edition online), Online Planner
- **www.sfsocialstudies.com** (Biographies, news, references, maps, and activities)

To establish guidelines for your students' safe and responsible use of the Internet, use the Scott Foresman Internet Guide.

Additional Internet Links

To find out more about:

- Zebra mussels, select *Mollusks* at **nas.er.usgs.gov**
- Rice, visit **www.asiarice.org**
- The Corn Palace, visit **www.cornpalace.org**

Key Internet Search Terms

- glacier
- Chicago River
- fossils

Workbook Support

Use the following Workbook pages to support content and skills development as you teach Chapter 8. You can also view and print Workbook pages from the Teacher Resources CD-ROM.

Workbook, p. 52

Use with Pages 228–229.

Cause and Effect

Directions: Very often an effect can have more than one cause. Fill in the circle next to the correct answer.

1. Which word is NOT a cause-and-effect clue word?
   - Ⓐ so
   - ● both
   - Ⓒ since
   - Ⓓ because
2. Look at the organizer below. Which statement is the effect?
   - Ⓐ The Midwest is connected by water to the Atlantic Ocean and much of the United States.
   - Ⓑ The Midwest has rich farmland.
   - Ⓒ The Midwest is in the middle of the country.
   - ● The Midwest is a very important region of the United States.

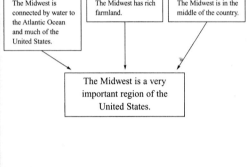

The Midwest is connected by water to the Atlantic Ocean and much of the United States. | The Midwest has rich farmland. | The Midwest is in the middle of the country.

→ The Midwest is a very important region of the United States.

Notes for Home: Your child learned to determine causes and effects.
Home Activity: Discuss with your child the region of the United States where you live. Where is it located in relation to the Midwest? Can you reach the Midwest easily from where you live? How could you get there?

Use with Pupil Edition, p. 229

Workbook, p. 53

Use with Chapter 8.

Vocabulary Preview

Directions: These are the vocabulary words from Chapter 8. How much do you know about them? Write the letter of each word's definition on the line at left. You may use your glossary.

Answer	Word	Definition
d	1. waterway	a. region of dry hills and sharp cliffs formed of crumbling rock
g	2. canal	b. flat-bottomed boat
i	3. lock	c. area where grasses grow well, but trees are rare
b	4. barge	d. system of rivers, lakes, and canals through which many ships travel
a	5. badlands	e. process of bringing water to farms to spray over fields
h	6. erosion	f. the planting of different crops in different years
c	7. prairie	g. waterway that has been dug across land for ships to go through
f	8. crop rotation	h. process by which water and wind wear away rock
e	9. irrigation	i. gated part of a canal or a river

Notes for Home: Your child learned the vocabulary terms for Chapter 8.
Home Activity: Discuss with your child any *canals, badlands,* or *prairies* you may have visited or seen in pictures, on television, or in movies.

Use with Pupil Edition, p. 230

Workbook, p. 54

Use with Pages 232–237.

Lesson 1: A Route to the Sea

The Great Lakes connect the Midwest region to other waterways around the world.

Directions: Use the waterways from this lesson to complete each sentence. Then answer the questions that follow. You may use your textbook.

1. The Great Lakes include Lake **Huron**, Lake **Ontario**, Lake **Michigan**, Lake **Erie**, and Lake **Superior**.
2. The **Illinois Waterway** connects Lake Michigan to the largest river in the United States. That river is the **Mississippi** River.
3. The **St. Lawrence Seaway** links the Great Lakes with the **St. Lawrence** River. That river flows into the **Atlantic** Ocean.
4. Many of the goods from the Midwest travel by barge and boat from the Great Lakes to the **Atlantic** Ocean.

Directions: Answer the following questions on the lines provided.

5. What are the disadvantages of shipping goods by barge?
   Barges are slow. Some things cannot be shipped by barge because they might spoil or take too long to reach the customer.
6. What are the advantages of shipping goods by barge?
   Barges move large or heavy products long distances at a much lower cost than trucks or trains. They also require less maintenance and use less fuel.

Notes for Home: Your child learned how waterways allow the goods of the Midwest to be sent all over the world.
Home Activity: Help your child map the Illinois Waterway. Have him or her list the bodies of water in order from west to east.

54 Lesson Review Workbook

Use with Pupil Edition, p. 237

Workbook Support

Workbook, p. 55

Compare Line and Bar Graphs

Use with Pages 240–241.

Line graphs show changes over time. Bar graphs also can show changes over time, or they can compare amounts.

Directions: Read the information in the box and create a line or bar graph to show the facts in a clear, simple picture. Choose the type of graph that best displays this type of information.

Farming is very important to many Midwestern states. Illinois is one state in which many different crops are grown. The following figures give the approximate number of Illinois farms that grew certain crops in a recent year: corn (for grain), 46,000; hay (along with silage and field seeds), 10,000; oats, 2,000; soybeans, 47,000; wheat, 15,000.

Title: **Number of Illinois Farms That Grow Certain Crops**

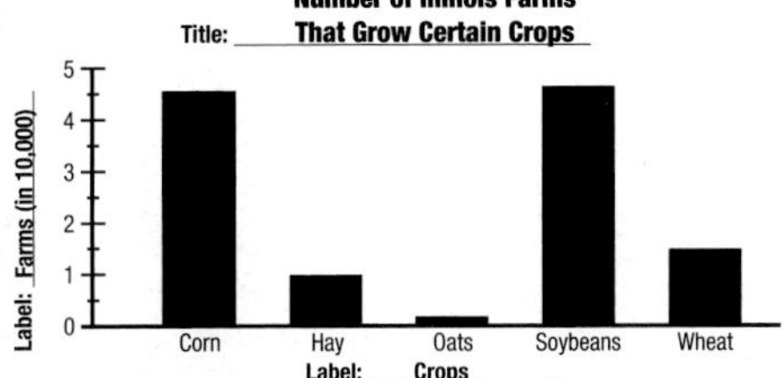

Directions: Answer the following questions about the graph you created.

1. What type of graph did you use to show the information? Why?
   Possible answer: Bar graph; Bar graphs help you compare amounts.
2. What information did you plot on the y axis?
   Possible answer: The number of farms
3. What information did you plot on the x axis?
   Possible answer: The different crops

Notes for Home: Your child learned how to use line graphs and bar graphs.
Home Activity: Ask your child to think about the number of hours he or she spends each day on various activities, such as going to school, playing, and helping at home. Help your child create a line or bar graph to illustrate that information.

Use with Pupil Edition, p. 241

Workbook, p. 56

Lesson 2: The Badlands of South Dakota

Use with Pages 242–245.

Many years of erosion have created the Badlands of South Dakota. The changes that have taken place there have been dramatic.

Directions: Write a description of the Badlands in each of the boxes below. Include information about the types of plants and animals that have lived there. You may use your textbook.

Millions of Years Ago	Changes That Occurred Over Time
Broad rivers flowed through a lush, green plain. Many plants and animals, such as dinosaurs, lived there. The climate was warmer and more humid than today.	The climate became cooler and less humid. The Rocky Mountains and the Black Hills rose to the west and caused the climate to change even more by blocking the rain to the region. Rivers, wind, and rain carved the landscape.

Today
There are dry hills and sharp cliffs formed of crumbling rock. Birds, reptiles, and insects live there, as do mammals such as prairie dogs and porcupines. A prairie surrounds the badlands. Cattle and sheep graze there.

Notes for Home: Your child learned about the changes in the landscape that created the Badlands of South Dakota.
Home Activity: Discuss with your child how this type of landscape, *badlands*, might have received its name.

Use with Pupil Edition, p. 245

Workbook, p. 57

Lesson 3: Bountiful Midwestern Farms

Use with Pages 246–249.

The Midwest is an important farming region for the United States and the rest of the world.

Directions: Complete the chart with information about the many crops of the Midwest region. You may use your textbook.

Crop	Where Is It Grown?	Why Is It Grown There?
Wheat	Great Plains	Does not need much rain
Sunflowers	Great Plains	Do not need much rain
Corn	Central Plains, Great Plains	Needs rain; gets nutrients from soybeans grown there
Soybeans	Central Plains, Great Plains	Need much rain; add nutrients to the land so corn can grow well
Oats	Great Plains	Do not need much rain
Barley	Great Plains	Does not need much rain
Hogs	Central Plains, Great Plains	They eat the corn that is grown there.
Cattle	Great Plains	They eat the grain that is grown there.

Notes for Home: Your child learned about the variety of crops and livestock grown in the Midwest region of the United States.
Home Activity: Discuss the products your family uses that might have come from crops grown in the Midwest.

Workbook Lesson Review 57

Use with Pupil Edition, p. 249

Workbook, p. 58

Vocabulary Review

Use with Chapter 8.

Directions: Use the clues from the chapter to complete the crossword puzzle.

waterway	lock	badlands	prairie	irrigation
canal	barge	erosion	crop rotation	

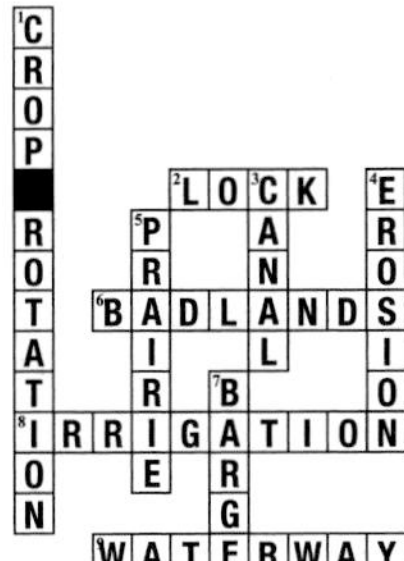

Across

2. gated part of a canal or river
6. region of dry hills and sharp cliffs formed of crumbling rock
8. process of bringing water to farms to spray over fields
9. system of rivers, lakes, and canals through which many ships travel

Down

1. the planting of different crops in different years
3. waterway that has been dug across land for ships to go through
4. process by which water and wind wear away rock
5. area where grasses grow well, but trees are rare
7. flat-bottomed boat

Notes for Home: Your child learned the vocabulary terms for Chapter 8.
Home Activity: Choose a few of the vocabulary words for your child to use in original sentences.

Use with Pupil Edition, p. 252

Assessment Support

Use the following Assessment Book pages and The test maker to assess content and skills in Chapter 8. You can also view and print Assessment Book pages from the Teacher Resources CD-ROM.

Assessment Book, p. 41

Chapter 8

Part 1: Content Test

Directions: Fill in the circle next to the correct answer.

Lesson Objective (1:1)

1. Which of the following was created by the melting of Ice Age glaciers?
   - Ⓐ thick sheets of ice
   - ● Great Lakes
   - Ⓒ Earth's climate
   - Ⓓ Midwest region

Lesson Objective (1:3)

2. Which of the following describes a canal?
   - Ⓐ flat-bottomed boat that carries goods
   - Ⓑ prehistoric period when the earth was covered with ice
   - Ⓒ gated part of a river that raises or lowers the water level
   - ● waterway dug across land for ships to go through

Lesson Objective (1:2)

3. Which of the following connects the Great Lakes to the Atlantic Ocean?
   - ● St. Lawrence Seaway and St. Lawrence River
   - Ⓑ Illinois Waterway and Illinois River
   - Ⓒ Mississippi River
   - Ⓓ Chicago River

Lesson Objective (1:4)

4. Why did engineers change the flow of the Chicago River?
   - ● to connect Lake Michigan to the Mississippi River
   - Ⓑ to connect Lake Huron to the Atlantic Ocean
   - Ⓒ to connect the St. Lawrence River to the Chicago River
   - Ⓓ to connect the Chicago River to Lake Huron

Lesson Objective (1:3)

5. Which of these is a flat-bottomed boat that transports goods?
   - Ⓐ canal
   - Ⓑ lock
   - ● barge
   - Ⓓ glacier

Lesson Objective (1:5)

6. What is one advantage of shipping goods by barge?
   - Ⓐ It is very fast.
   - Ⓑ It uses a lot of fuel.
   - Ⓒ It allows food to spoil.
   - ● It costs less than other methods.

Lesson Objective (2:1)

7. Which of the following describes the badlands millions of years ago?
   - Ⓐ Rivers, wind, and rain carved the land.
   - Ⓑ There were dry hills and sharp, rocky cliffs.
   - ● Rivers flowed through a lush, green plain.
   - Ⓓ The land was filled with jagged rocks and steep canyons.

Use with Pupil Edition, p. 252

Assessment Book, p. 42

Lesson Objective (2:4)

8. Which is one reason why the climate of the badlands became cooler and less humid?
   - Ⓐ Dinosaurs once lived and roamed there, killing the green plants.
   - Ⓑ Rivers flowed through the lush, green plain.
   - ● Mountain ranges rose and blocked rain that once fell there.
   - Ⓓ The last Ice Age began.

Lesson Objective (2:2)

9. What is erosion?
   - Ⓐ a region of dry hills and sharp cliffs formed of crumbling rock
   - ● the process by which water and wind wear away rock
   - Ⓒ one of the richest fossil beds in the world
   - Ⓓ the region of southwestern South Dakota

Lesson Objective (2:3)

10. Which of the following would you probably NOT see on a prairie?
    - ● trees
    - Ⓑ grasses
    - Ⓒ sheep
    - Ⓓ cattle

Lesson Objective (3:1)

11. Which is NOT a reason why the Midwest is an important agricultural region?
    - Ⓐ The growing season is long.
    - ● All the farms grow the same type of crop.
    - Ⓒ The summers are warm.
    - Ⓓ The soil is deep and rich.

Lesson Objective (3:3)

12. Why is the area of the Central Plains known as the Corn Belt?
    - Ⓐ Farmers there wear belts made out of corn.
    - ● It gets enough rain so that corn grows well there.
    - Ⓒ It gets very little rain so that corn grows well there.
    - Ⓓ Farmers there grow soybeans as well as corn.

Lesson Objective (3:4)

13. Which is NOT one of the main crops grown in the Midwest?
    - Ⓐ corn
    - ● cotton
    - Ⓒ soybeans
    - Ⓓ wheat

Lesson Objective (3:2)

14. How does irrigation help farmers?
    - ● It allows them to bring water from rivers or from underground to spray over their crops.
    - Ⓑ It allows them to see the current prices of crops on a sign.
    - Ⓒ It allows them to plant oats and wheat, which add nutrients to the soil.
    - Ⓓ It allows them to switch between two crops on one field.

Lesson Objective (3:5)

15. Which of the following is a very important product of Wisconsin?
    - ● milk and dairy products
    - Ⓑ farm machinery
    - Ⓒ wheat
    - Ⓓ cotton

Use with Pupil Edition, p. 252

Assessment Support

Assessment Book, p. 43

Part 2: Skills Test

Directions: Use complete sentences to answer questions 1–5. Use a separate sheet of paper if you need more space.

1. How are the St. Lawrence Seaway and the Illinois Waterway alike? How are they different? **Compare and Contrast**

   Alike: both are waterways that link the Great Lakes with a river that flows into an ocean. They consist of rivers, lakes, and canals. Different: the St. Lawrence Seaway links the Great Lakes with the St. Lawrence River, which flows into the Atlantic Ocean. The Illinois Waterway links Lake Michigan to the Mississippi River, which flows into the Gulf of Mexico.

2. Suppose that the canal connecting the Chicago River to the Illinois River had never been built. How would it affect the shipment of goods around the country? What effect might it have on the trucking and railroad industries? **Cause and Effect**

   If the canal had not been built, ships would have no way to get from Lake Michigan to the Mississippi River or vice versa. The shipping industry would lose business because there are no other waterways that travel that far south or connect the Midwest to the Gulf of Mexico. The trucking and rail industries would have much more business.

3. Would you like to visit Badlands National Park? Why or why not? **Express Ideas**

   Answers should include an understanding of the climate and landscape of the area.

Use with Pupil Edition, p. 252

Assessment Book, p. 44

4. A large amount of milk and many different dairy products are produced in Wisconsin. What do you think the land of Wisconsin is like? Why? What crops do you think are important to dairy farmers? **Draw Conclusions**

   Possible answers: The land in Wisconsin is probably flat and open so that the dairy cows can roam freely on it. Grasses and other grains probably grow well there. Dairy farmers probably need crops of oats, corn, and other grains that their cattle like to eat.

5. Use the bar graph to answer the questions. **Compare Line and Bar Graphs**

   a. Which lake received the most precipitation in October 2002? Which received the least?

   Lake Superior received the most—4.1 inches. Lake Erie received the least—1.9 inches.

   b. How could you show on the same graph the precipitation for each lake in November, 2002?

   I could add a second bar for each lake in a color different from the October bar to show the November precipitation.

   c. Could a line graph be used to show this information? Explain your answer.

   No, a line graph shows change over time. The information in the bar graph does not show change over time. It compares the amount of precipitation among the Great Lakes.

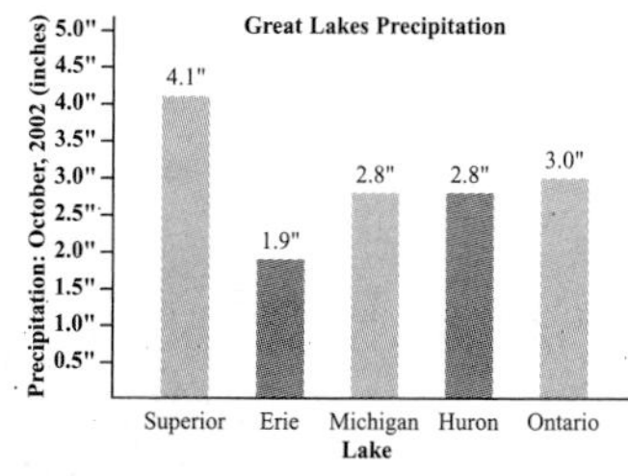

Use with Pupil Edition, p. 252

CHAPTER 8

Water and Land of the Midwest

Chapter 8 Outline

- **Lesson 1, *A Route to the Sea,*** pp. 232–237
- **Issues and Viewpoints: *Zebra Mussel Invasion,*** pp. 238–239
- **Chart and Graph Skills: *Compare Line and Bar Graphs,*** pp. 240–241
- **Lesson 2, *The Badlands of South Dakota,*** pp. 242–245
- **Lesson 3, *Bountiful Midwestern Farms,*** pp. 246–249
- **Here and There: *United States and Thailand: Big Farms and Little Farms,*** pp. 250–251

Resources

- Workbook, p. 53: Vocabulary Preview
- Vocabulary Cards
- Social Studies Plus!

Lake Huron: Lesson 1

Ask students to describe the scene and suggest why the Illinois Waterway might be important to the Midwest. (Possible answer: Many goods are shipped on it.)

Badlands National Park: Lesson 2

This picture shows the rugged landscape of Badlands National Park in South Dakota. Ask students what words come to mind when they look at the picture. (Possible answers: Barren, treeless, rugged)

Hoopeston, Illinois: Lesson 3

The Midwest is famous for its farms. Ask students to try to identify the crop being grown on the farm in this picture. (Corn)

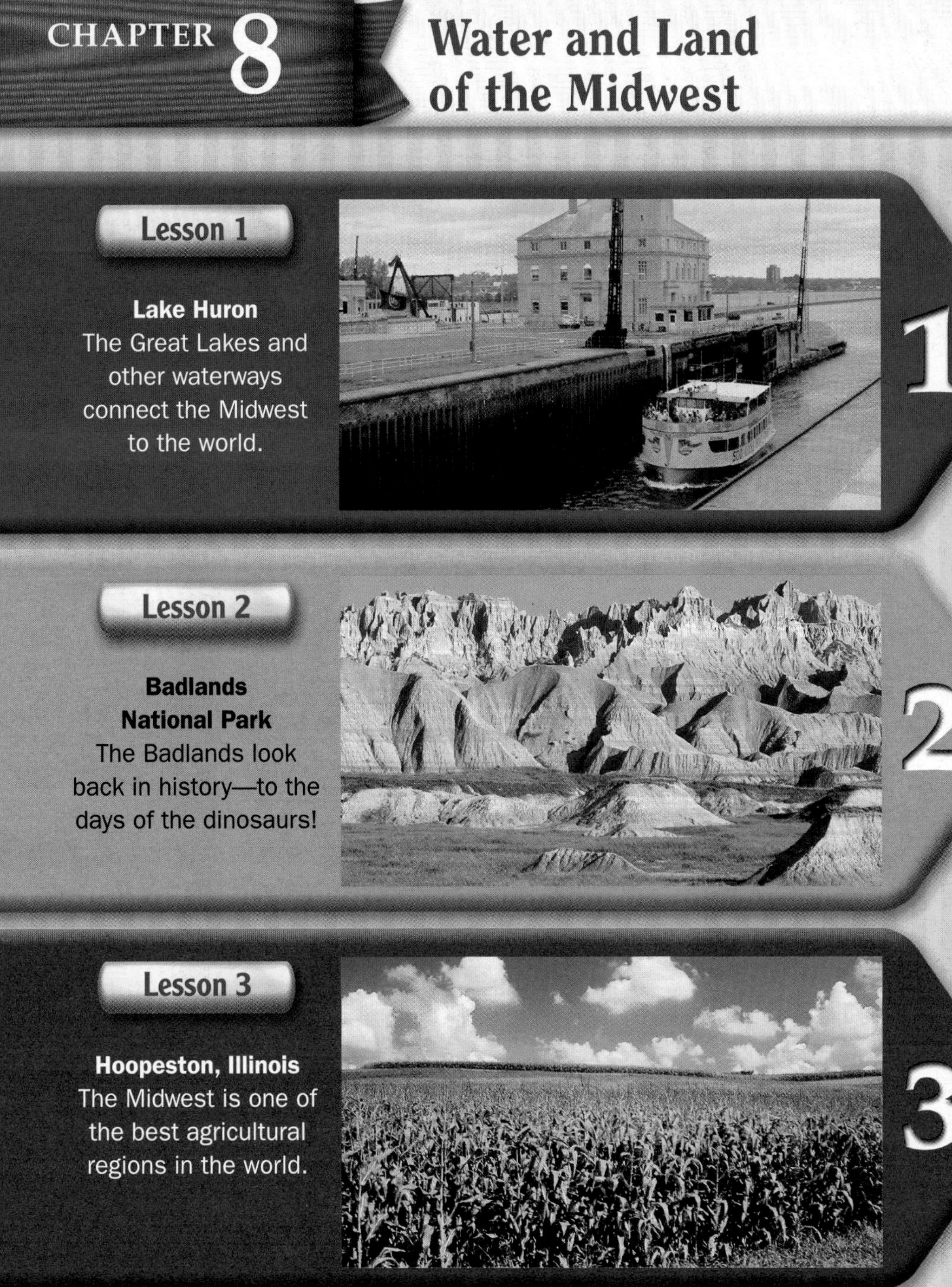

CHAPTER 8
Water and Land of the Midwest
Lesson 1
Lake Huron
The Great Lakes and other waterways connect the Midwest to the world.
1
Lesson 2
Badlands National Park
The Badlands look back in history—to the days of the dinosaurs!
2
Lesson 3
Hoopeston, Illinois
The Midwest is one of the best agricultural regions in the world.
3
230

Practice and Extend

Vocabulary Preview

- Use Workbook p. 53 to help students preview the vocabulary words in this chapter.
- Use Vocabulary Cards to preview key concept words in this chapter.

Also on Teacher Resources CD-ROM.

Workbook, p. 53

Use with Chapter 8.

Vocabulary Preview

Directions: These are the vocabulary words from Chapter 8. How much do you know about them? Write the letter of each word's definition on the line at left. You may use your glossary.

____ 1. waterway		a. region of dry hills and sharp cliffs formed of crumbling rock
____ 2. canal		b. flat-bottomed boat
____ 3. lock		c. area where grasses grow well, but trees are rare
____ 4. barge		d. system of rivers, lakes, and canals through which many ships travel
____ 5. badlands		e. process of bringing water to farms to spray over fields
____ 6. erosion		f. the planting of different crops in different years
____ 7. prairie		g. waterway that has been dug across land for ships to go through
____ 8. crop rotation		h. process by which water and wind wear away rock
____ 9. irrigation		i. gated part of a canal or a river

Notes for Home: Your child learned the vocabulary terms for Chapter 8.
Home Activity: Discuss with your child any canals, *badlands*, or *prairies* you may have visited or seen in pictures, on television, or in movies.

Locating Places

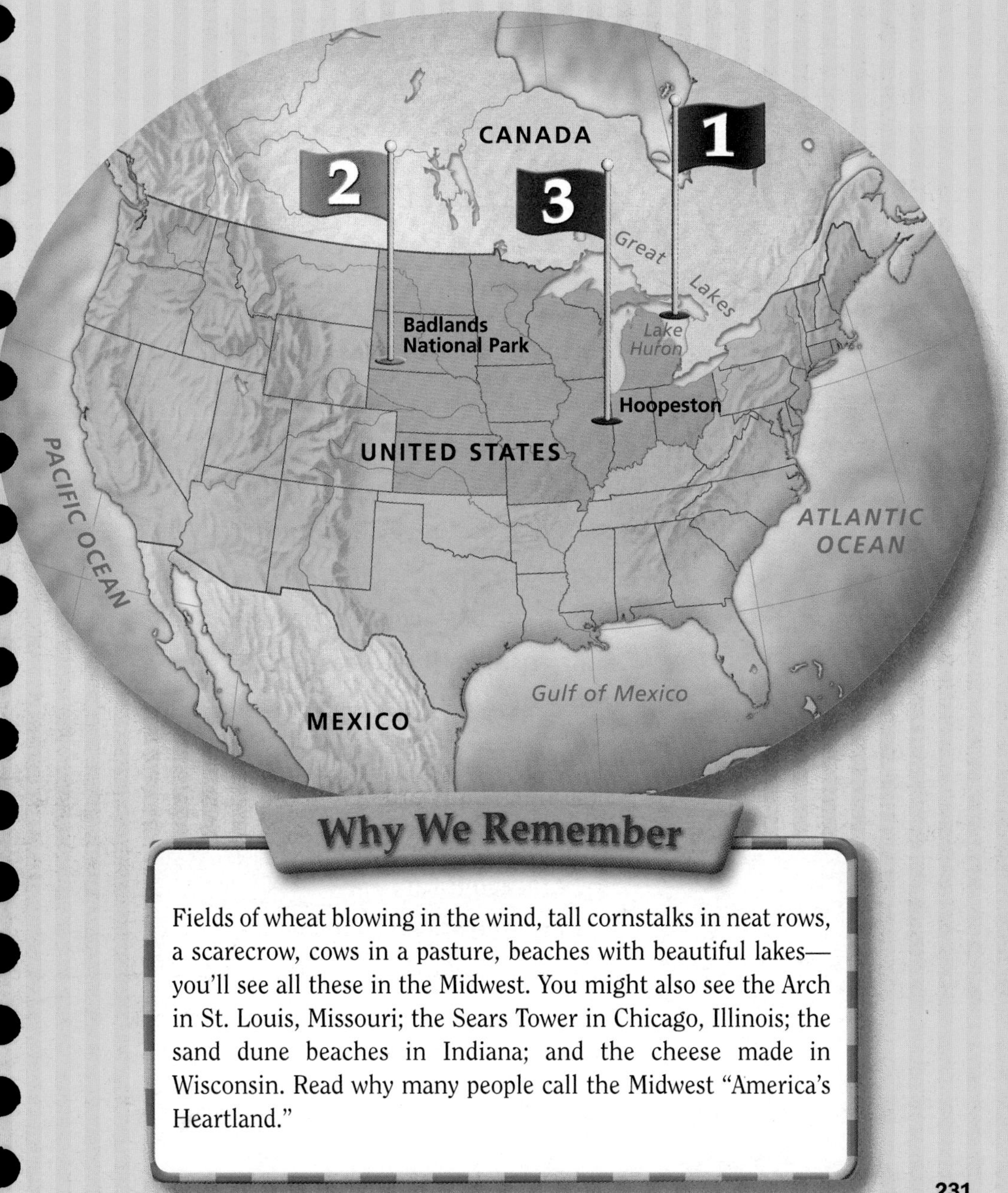

Why We Remember

Fields of wheat blowing in the wind, tall cornstalks in neat rows, a scarecrow, cows in a pasture, beaches with beautiful lakes—you'll see all these in the Midwest. You might also see the Arch in St. Louis, Missouri; the Sears Tower in Chicago, Illinois; the sand dune beaches in Indiana; and the cheese made in Wisconsin. Read why many people call the Midwest "America's Heartland."

231

WEB SITE
Technology

You can learn more about Lake Huron, Badlands National Park, and Hoopeston, Illinois, by clicking on *Atlas* at **www.sfsocialstudies.com.**

SOCIAL STUDIES STRAND
Geography

Mental Mapping On an outline map of the United States, have students color in the states that they think make up the Midwest Region. Students may label any cities or landforms of the Midwest that they know of. Discuss students' knowledge and/or impressions of the Midwest.

Locating Places

- Have students examine the pictures on p. 230 for Lessons 1, 2, and 3.
- Remind students that each picture is coded with both a number and a color to link it to a place on the map on p. 231.

Why We Remember

Have students read the "Why We Remember" paragraph on p. 231 and ask them why places in this chapter might be important to them. Have them consider how places in the Midwest could have an effect on their lives.

A Route to the Sea

Objectives

- Explain how the Great Lakes were formed.
- Describe how the Great Lakes are connected to the Atlantic Ocean.
- Define the words *waterway, canal, lock,* and *barge*.
- Explain why the flow of the Chicago River was changed.
- Explain the advantages of shipping by water.

Vocabulary

waterway, p. 234; **canal,** p. 234; **lock,** p. 234; **barge,** p. 236

Resources

- Workbook, p. 54
- Transparency 20
- Every Student Learns Guide, pp. 94–97
- Quick Study, pp. 48–49

Quick Teaching Plan

If time is short, have students read the lesson independently and make a list of each body of water named in the lesson.

- Have students list the features waterways have in common.
- Have students list ways in which waterways are different.

1 Introduce and Motivate

Preview To activate prior knowledge, ask students to name some lakes or rivers they have visited and tell how they are used. Tell students they will learn about the Great Lakes and other waterways as they read Lesson 1.

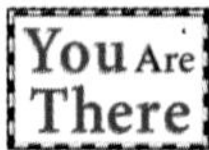

Ask students if they have ever been through a canal. Have volunteers describe the canal they went through and what the experience was like.

LESSON 1

PREVIEW

Focus on the Main Idea
The Great Lakes link the Midwest region to the Gulf of Mexico and to the Atlantic Ocean.

PLACES
The Great Lakes
Illinois Waterway
Mississippi River
St. Lawrence Seaway

VOCABULARY
waterway
canal
lock
barge

A Route to the Sea

You Are There You are riding on a boat in the Chicago River. You are going to go through the locks into Lake Michigan. Your teacher explains that locks are gated parts of a canal or river. She says that the gates could be closed at each end separately to raise or lower the water level. You stop. You see the gate close behind you. The boat is trapped in this little area. As you look over the side of the boat, you see the water rising. The water rises until the boat is at Lake Michigan level. The gate opens and the boat moves forward. As you look behind, you see the Chicago River lock closing. You are on Lake Michigan now!

Cause and Effect As you read, look for the effects the glaciers had on the formation of the Great Lakes.

232

Practice and Extend

READING SKILL
Cause and Effect

In the Lesson Review, students complete a graphic organizer like the one below. You may want to provide students with a copy of Transparency 20 to complete as they read the lesson.

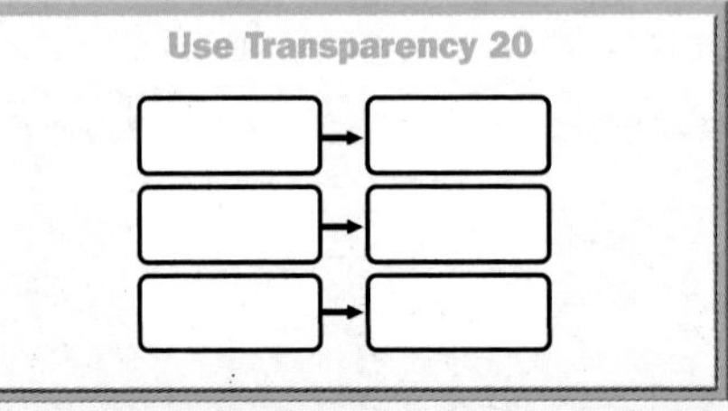

VOCABULARY
Individual Word Study

Reviewing a familiar meaning of a word may help students understand the word's meaning in a different context. Have students read the definition of *lock* on p. 234. Ask what another meaning of *lock* is. (a device for keeping something closed). Ask students to look at the illustration on p. 235 and think about how "keeping something closed" might help them remember this kind of lock. (The lock keeps the ship closed in until the water level is right. The lock locks the ship in.)

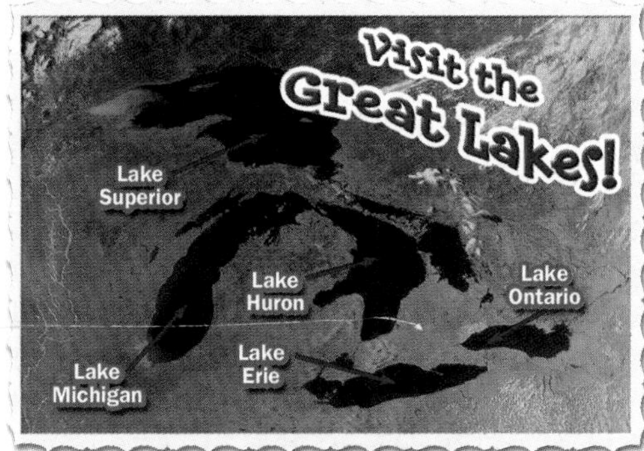

The History of the Great Lakes

The states of the Midwest that are near the Great Lakes are called the Great Lakes states. The **Great Lakes** are Lake Ontario, Lake Erie, Lake Huron, Lake Michigan, and Lake
1 Superior. The Lakes are connected to each other. The Great Lakes are the
2 largest group of freshwater lakes in the world. They contain about one-fifth of the world's freshwater—water that is not salty. They are so large that they appear to be seas. In most places, you cannot see the opposite shore.

The Great Lakes were formed many thousands of years ago during the last Ice Age. At that time, much of North America was covered by thick sheets of ice called glaciers. Movement of the glaciers caused deep pits to form in the Earth. As the Ice Age ended, the glaciers melted. The melting water of the glaciers filled the pits, forming the Great Lakes. 3

REVIEW What happened at the end of the last Ice Age that caused the Great Lakes to form? Cause and Effect

▶ Lake Michigan is a huge, deep lake. It was formed when glaciers melted and moved.

233

2 Teach and Discuss

PAGE 233

The History of the Great Lakes

Quick Summary The Great Lakes were formed by Ice Age glaciers.

1 **What are the names of the five Great Lakes?** Lake Ontario, Lake Erie, Lake Huron, Lake Michigan, Lake Superior **Main Idea and Details**

2 **How do the Great Lakes compare to other groups of freshwater lakes?** They are the largest group. **Compare and Contrast**

3 **What do you think caused the glaciers in North America to melt?** Possible answer: The Earth was getting warmer. **Hypothesize**

Ongoing Assessment

If... students have difficulty forming a hypothesis about how the glaciers melted,	**then...** set an ice cube in the sun to melt. Tell students that the melting cube represents the melting glaciers.

REVIEW ANSWER The glaciers melted, filling deep pits in the earth's surface with water. **Cause and Effect**

MEETING INDIVIDUAL NEEDS
Leveled Practice

Identify the Great Lakes Help students remember the names and locations of the Great Lakes.

Easy Teach students the memory device HOMES (Huron, Ontario, Michigan, Erie, Superior) to help them recall the five Great Lakes. **Reteach**

On-Level Have students point to each of the Great Lakes in order as they name them according to the HOMES memory device. **Extend**

Challenge Have students invent a new memory device to help them name the Great Lakes in order from west to east or east to west. **Enrich**

For a Lesson Summary, use Quick Study, p. 48.

PAGES 234–235

Connecting the Midwest to the World

Quick Summary Canals and natural waterways link the Midwest with the rest of the world.

4 **What is a waterway?** A system of rivers, lakes, and canals through which many ships travel **Main Idea and Details**

5 **Why do you think it might be necessary to dig a canal?** Possible answer: To allow ships to travel where there is no natural waterway **Draw Conclusions**

6 **How does a lock differ from a waterway?** A lock is a part of a waterway with gates that are used to raise or lower ships. **Compare and Contrast**

7 **How was the Chicago River connected to the Illinois River?** A canal was dug. **Main Idea and Details**

MAP SKILL

Waterways Connect Regions

Point out that many states are linked by the St. Lawrence Seaway, the Great Lakes, the Illinois Waterway, and the Mississippi River.

8 **What two countries are linked by the Great Lakes and other waterways?** The United States and Canada **Main Idea and Details**

MAP SKILL Answer Through Lake Michigan, Lake Huron, and Lake Erie

Connecting the Midwest to the World

The Great Lakes are part of a system that links the Midwest with the rest of the world. The system forms a **waterway,** which consists of rivers, lakes, and canals through which many
4 ships travel. A **canal** is one kind of
5 waterway that has been dug across land for ships to go through. The **Illinois Waterway** connects Lake Michigan to the **Mississippi River.** This waterway consists of several rivers and canals. The Mississippi River flows into the Gulf of Mexico.

Another waterway, the **St. Lawrence Seaway,** links the Great Lakes with the St. Lawrence River. The St. Lawrence River flows into the Atlantic Ocean.

Some parts of waterways are at higher or lower levels than other parts. Locks were built so that ships could be raised or lowered to a different level. A **lock** is a gated part of a canal or river. Between the gates, water can be let in 6
or out to raise or lower the water level.

The Chicago River originally flowed into Lake Michigan. Engineers dug a canal to connect the Chicago River to the Illinois River, which flows into the 7
Mississippi. The canal and locks forced

MAP SKILL

8

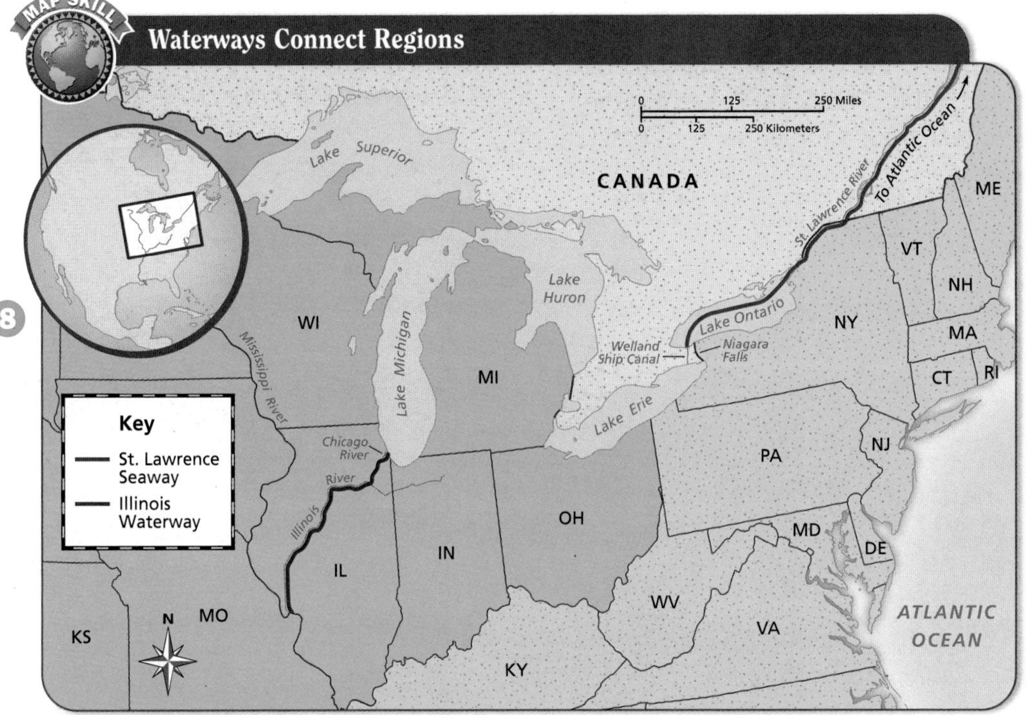

▶ The Great Lakes, rivers, and canals combine to form a large network of water routes.

MAP SKILL Using Routes *What route would goods take if they are shipped by water from Chicago to New York state?*

Practice and Extend

EXTEND LANGUAGE

ESL Support

Compare and Contrast a Waterway and a Seaway Help students understand the similarities and differences between a waterway and a seaway.

Beginning Explain that the word *waterway* means a body of water through which a boat can navigate. The word *seaway* means a type of waterway that is deep enough for oceangoing ships. On a classroom map of the United States, have student volunteers use a finger to trace the Illinois Waterway and the St. Lawrence Seaway.

Intermediate Have students brainstorm a list of different types of boats and ships and then tell which ones would need to travel by seaway to move inland.

Advanced Have students name different waterways or seaways in their state or region. Then have them write a paragraph describing what they might see while traveling along a local waterway or the Illinois waterway.

For additional ESL support, use Every Student Learns Guide, pp. 94–97.

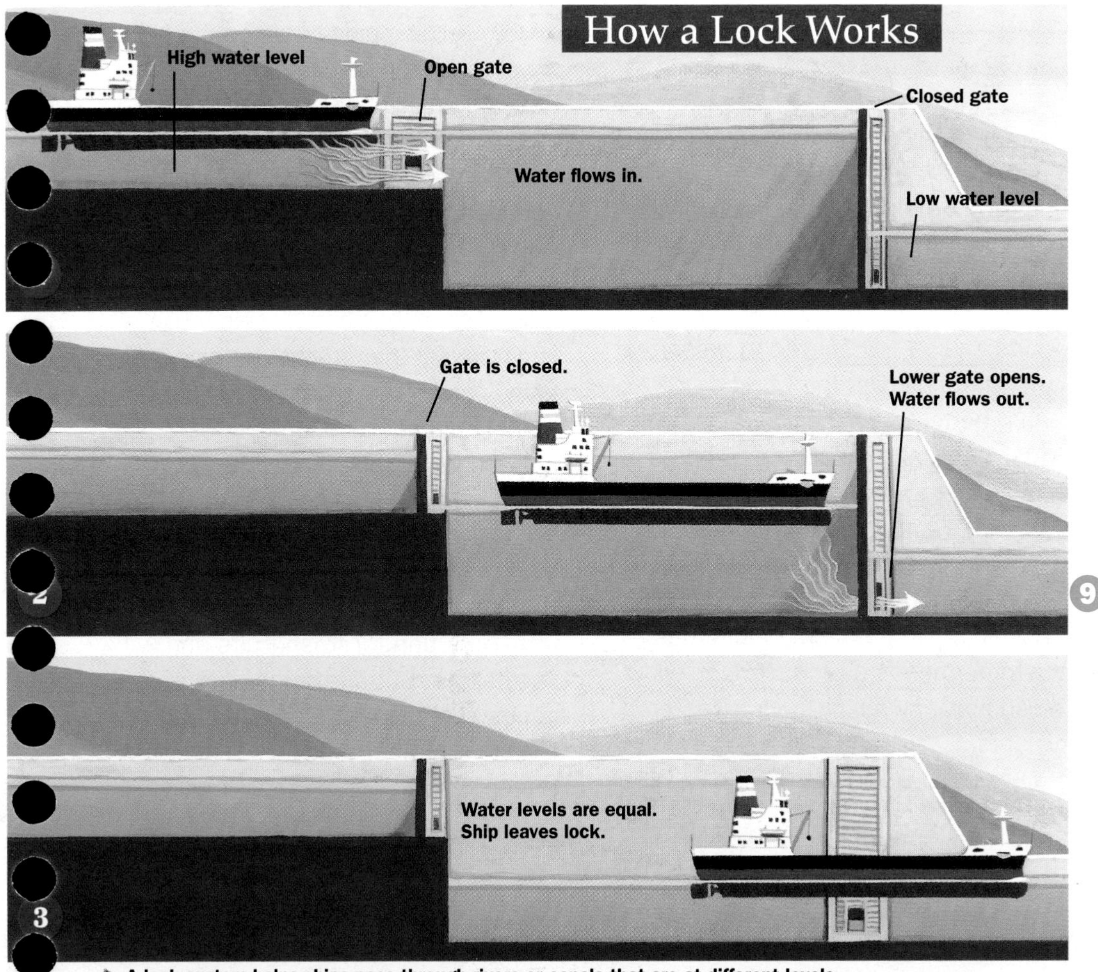
How a Lock Works
High water level
Open gate
Closed gate
Water flows in.
Low water level
Gate is closed.
Lower gate opens. Water flows out.
Water levels are equal. Ship leaves lock.
3

▶ A lock system helps ships pass through rivers or canals that are at different levels.

9

the Chicago River to flow backwards so that it would link Lake Michigan to the Mississippi. Engineers solved the problem of how to let boats travel from Lake Michigan to the Mississippi River.

The builders of the St. Lawrence Seaway, however, faced a different problem. Boats could not use the Niagara River to get from Lake Erie to Lake Ontario. Boats could not travel through Niagara Falls. So engineers designed the Welland Ship Canal between the two lakes. The St. Lawrence Seaway has a number of other canals and locks as well. These canals and locks make the seaway a smooth passageway to the ocean. 10

REVIEW What effect did changing the flow of the Chicago River have on transporting goods from Lake Michigan? Cause and Effect

235

CURRICULUM CONNECTION
Writing

Write for Information

- Tell students to write a letter to the engineers of the St. Lawrence Seaway asking for information about the history of the waterway.
- Have students brainstorm questions and organize their thoughts on note cards.
- Have students write their letters neatly and exchange them with a classmate.
- Have students research answers to their classmates' queries.
- Review students' research as a class.

Test Talk

Use Information from Graphics

9 **During which stage is the ship completely inside the lock?** Tell students to use details from the picture to support their answer. Stage 2
Apply Information

10 **What waterways make it possible for ships to travel from Lake Erie to Lake Ontario and finally to the Atlantic Ocean?** Welland Ship Canal, St. Lawrence Seaway Sequence

✓ **REVIEW ANSWER** It made it easier to transport goods to and from Lake Michigan by linking Lake Michigan to the Mississippi River. Cause and Effect

PAGES 236–237

To Ship Over Land or Water?

11 **What is one way some Midwest products are transported?** Possible answer: By boat or barge
Main Idea and Details

12 **Sometimes canals are shallow. Why do you think barges are often used in canals?** Flat-bottomed barges can move more easily in shallow canals.
Draw Conclusions

13 **What is one disadvantage of shipping by water?** Possible answer: It is slow. Analyze Information

14 **What kinds of goods should not be shipped by barge?** Possible answer: Foods that spoil quickly, such as milk, meat, and some fruits and vegetables
Draw Conclusions

15 **Of the three ways to transport goods described in the text, which is cheapest?** Transporting by barge
Apply Information

To Ship Over Land or Water?

Many of the goods from the Midwest
11 are shipped by boat and by barge. A
12 **barge** is a flat-bottomed boat. Barges
and boats transport goods through the Great Lakes and on rivers that eventually flow into the Atlantic Ocean. Then, the goods can be transferred to ships that carry them all over the world.

Is it better to transport goods by water or by land? Shipping by barge has advantages and disadvantages.
13 One disadvantage is that barges are
slow, averaging only six miles per hour. Since food can spoil, it is not usually
14 shipped by barge. Also, sometimes a
customer needs a product right away, so shipping by rail or truck is faster.

However, shipping by water has a big advantage. Barges can move large or heavy products long distances at a much lower cost than trucks or trains can. Barges use less fuel to ship the
same amount of product than trucks or 15
trains do. Barges also do not require as much maintenance as trucks or trains.

In addition, barges can ship much larger freight than trucks or trains. A barge can move 15 times more material than a railroad car, and about 60 times more material than a truck. Coal and metals are often shipped on barges.

However, barges cannot provide door-to-door shipping the way trucks can. Trucks are the main method of transportation for fresh fruits and vegetables. But if a farmer is shipping goods across great distances, then a train is the most efficient means of transportation.

▶ Tugboats push or pull barges. Sometimes, several barges are connected together.

236

Practice and Extend

FAST FACTS

- About 60 percent of the freight that is transported on the waterways of the United States is carried on the Mississippi River.
- About 460 million tons of freight are shipped on the Mississippi River every year.
- Agricultural products, coal, and steel products make up most of the freight shipped on the Mississippi River.

▶ Freight train

Trains can carry much heavier loads than trucks can, and at faster speeds. Freight trains can travel at 75 miles per hour, while trucks travel at up to 65 miles per hour, depending on the speed limits of different highways. Barges travel much more slowly than trucks or trains.

Several cities in the Midwest are major transportation centers. Trains and trucks transport more freight through Chicago, Illinois, than through any other city in the nation. Ships and barges dock in St. Louis, Missouri, one of the busiest port cities on the
16 Mississippi River.

As you can see, shipping by water has advantages and disadvantages. It is up to the person in charge of shipping a product to decide if shipping by water is the best method of sending the product.

REVIEW What are some of the positive effects of shipping by water? Cause and Effect

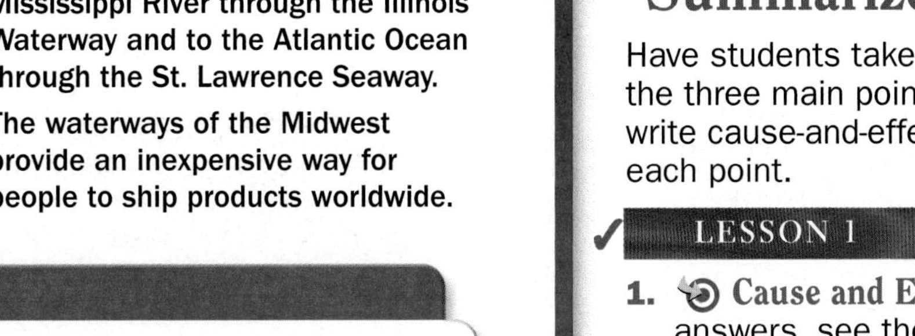

Summarize the Lesson

- **The Great Lakes formed thousands of years ago from glaciers carving channels in the land and then filling them with melted ice.**
- **The Great Lakes are linked to the Mississippi River through the Illinois Waterway and to the Atlantic Ocean through the St. Lawrence Seaway.**
- **The waterways of the Midwest provide an inexpensive way for people to ship products worldwide.**

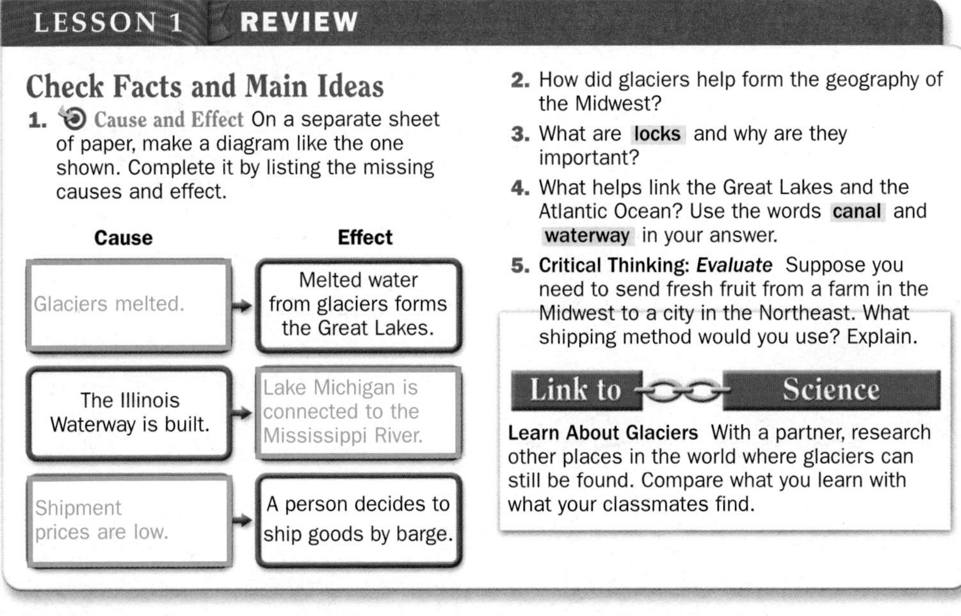

LESSON 1 REVIEW

Check Facts and Main Ideas

1. Cause and Effect On a separate sheet of paper, make a diagram like the one shown. Complete it by listing the missing causes and effect.

Cause		Effect
Glaciers melted.	→	Melted water from glaciers forms the Great Lakes.
The Illinois Waterway is built.	→	Lake Michigan is connected to the Mississippi River.
Shipment prices are low.	→	A person decides to ship goods by barge.

2. How did glaciers help form the geography of the Midwest?
3. What are **locks** and why are they important?
4. What helps link the Great Lakes and the Atlantic Ocean? Use the words **canal** and **waterway** in your answer.
5. **Critical Thinking:** ***Evaluate*** Suppose you need to send fresh fruit from a farm in the Midwest to a city in the Northeast. What shipping method would you use? Explain.

Link to Science

Learn About Glaciers With a partner, research other places in the world where glaciers can still be found. Compare what you learn with what your classmates find.

16 What are two major transportation centers in the Midwest? Possible answers: Chicago, Illinois; St. Louis, Missouri Apply Information

✓ **REVIEW ANSWER** Lower cost because barges are easy to maintain, carry large loads, and use less fuel Cause and Effect

3 Close and Assess

Summarize the Lesson

Have students take turns reading aloud the three main points. Then have them write cause-and-effect sentences for each point.

✓ **LESSON 1 REVIEW**

1. **Cause and Effect** For possible answers, see the reduced pupil page.
2. Glaciers carved out areas that filled with water and became the Great Lakes.
3. Locks are gated sections of a canal or river that can open or close to change water levels.
4. A system of canals and waterways, including the St. Lawrence Seaway
5. **Critical Thinking: *Evaluate*** Possible answer: Train; Because trains can travel at fast speeds; since fresh fruit can spoil, it needs to travel quickly.

Link to Science

Students should use print or online resources to research glaciers.

Workbook, p. 54

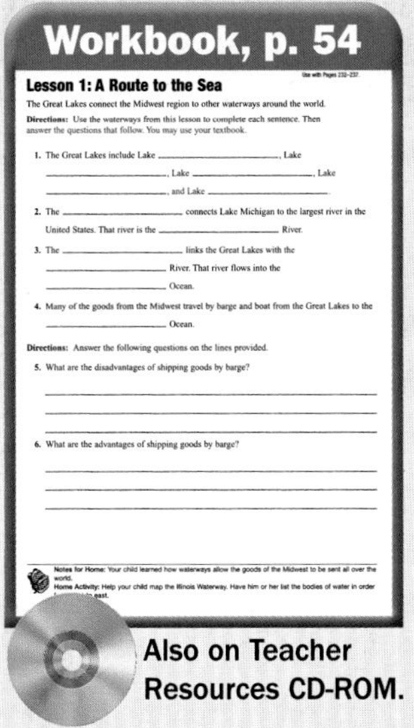

Use with Pages 232–237.

Lesson 1: A Route to the Sea

The Great Lakes connect the Midwest region to other waterways around the world.

Directions: Use the waterways from this lesson to complete each sentence. Then answer the questions that follow. You may use your textbook.

1. The Great Lakes include Lake ______, Lake ______, Lake ______, Lake ______, and Lake ______.
2. The ______ connects Lake Michigan to the largest river in the United States. That river is the ______ River.
3. The ______ links the Great Lakes with the ______ River. That river flows into the ______ Ocean.
4. Many of the goods from the Midwest travel by barge and boat from the Great Lakes to the ______ Ocean.

Directions: Answer the following questions on the lines provided.

5. What are the disadvantages of shipping goods by barge?
6. What are the advantages of shipping goods by barge?

Notes for Home: Your child learned how waterways allow the goods of the Midwest to be sent all over the world.
Home Activity: Help your child map the Illinois Waterway. Have him or her list the bodies of water in order

Also on Teacher Resources CD-ROM.

Zebra Mussel Invasion

Objective

- Describe the effect of zebra mussels on the freshwater lakes in the Midwest.

1 Introduce and Motivate

Preview To activate prior knowledge, ask students to name some kinds of animals that live in lakes and rivers. Ask them what might happen to a lake or river if the population of one kind of animal living there increased rapidly.

Tell students that in this section they are going to learn about a kind of animal—a shellfish called the zebra mussel—that is creating problems for the Great Lakes area and other parts of the United States.

2 Teach and Discuss

1 **When and how did zebra mussels arrive in the United States?** Probably in 1986; by traveling from Europe across the Atlantic Ocean in a ship
Main Idea and Details

2 **How do zebra mussels negatively affect the Great Lakes area?** They can starve out native fish, clog the water intake pipes, and upset the ecosystem of the waters. Cause and Effect

Issues and Viewpoints

ZEBRA MUSSEL INVASION

International trade on the waterways of the Midwest is great for the region's economy. However, it can bring with it a problem that is difficult to solve!

In 1988, a new type of shellfish was discovered in the waters of Lake Erie. This creature is called the zebra mussel, because it has a dark and light striped shell.

Where on Earth did they come from? Zebra mussels are native to Europe and Asia. They arrived in the United States undetected, probably in 1986. Zebra mussels 1 traveled across the Atlantic Ocean in European ships.

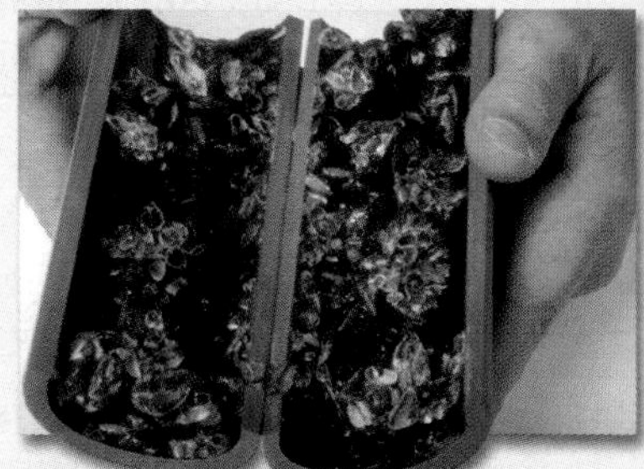
Zebra mussels clog the inside of water pipes.

Adult zebra mussels attach to hard surfaces, including boat hulls, water pipes, and the rocky bottom of lakes and rivers. They grow rapidly in thick colonies. There can be 500,000 zebra mussels in an area smaller than your teacher's desk.

These small creatures can cause big problems. They can eat most of the small plants floating in the water, leaving no food for the fish. They can cause the deaths of many larger clams. The mussels also clog the 2 water intake pipes in many cities along the Great Lakes. 3 Yet, when they are in the water for a long period of time, they filter the water and make it clearer.

238

Practice and Extend

SOCIAL STUDIES Background

The Zebra Mussel

- Zebra mussels are native to the Balkans, Poland, and the Ukraine.
- By 2000, zebra mussels had spread to the Atlantic Ocean on the east; to the Missouri River on the west; into Ontario and Quebec, Canada, on the north; and to the Gulf of Mexico on the south.
- Zebra mussels grow to about 2 inches in size; they feed on tiny, microscopic organisms called plankton.
- Zebra mussels have a variety of predators, including several species of fish, ducks, and raccoons.

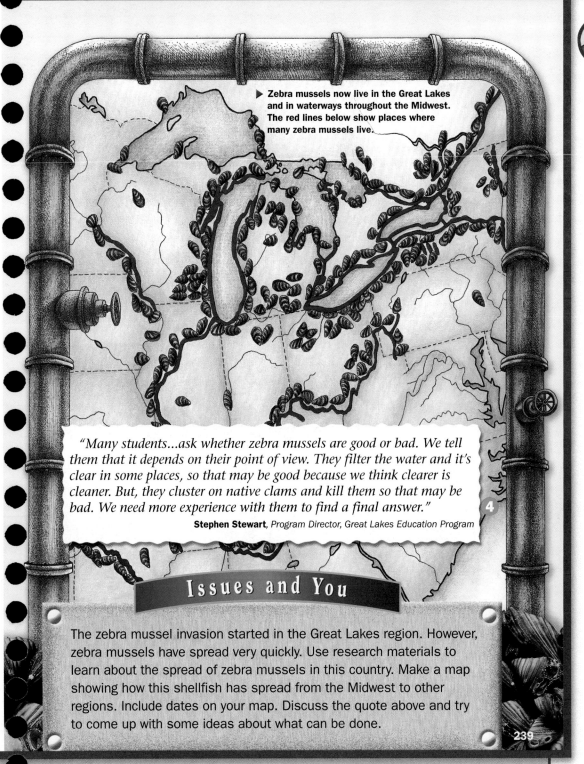

▶ Zebra mussels now live in the Great Lakes and in waterways throughout the Midwest. The red lines below show places where many zebra mussels live.

"Many students...ask whether zebra mussels are good or bad. We tell them that it depends on their point of view. They filter the water and it's clear in some places, so that may be good because we think clearer is cleaner. But, they cluster on native clams and kill them so that may be bad. We need more experience with them to find a final answer." 4

Stephen Stewart, *Program Director, Great Lakes Education Program*

Issues and You

The zebra mussel invasion started in the Great Lakes region. However, zebra mussels have spread very quickly. Use research materials to learn about the spread of zebra mussels in this country. Make a map showing how this shellfish has spread from the Midwest to other regions. Include dates on your map. Discuss the quote above and try to come up with some ideas about what can be done.

239

WEB SITE
Technology

Have students go online to **www.nsf.gov** to learn more about zebra mussels.

Test Talk

Locate Key Words in the Text

3 **What positive effect can zebra mussels have on water?** Have students locate key words in the text that match key words in the question. They filter water and make it clearer. **Main Idea and Details**

4 **Do you think zebra mussels are more helpful or harmful to the Great Lakes? Why?** Possible answers: More harmful; They can wipe out entire species of clams and clog the pipes that supply cities with water; More helpful: They make the water clearer and perhaps cleaner. **Evaluate**

3 Close and Assess

Issues and You

- Have students work in pairs to find information on the Internet. Have them record the information they find by printing it or copying it on paper.
- Provide students with an outline map of the United States on which to work. Instruct them to create a map legend that explains the colors and symbols they use on the map.

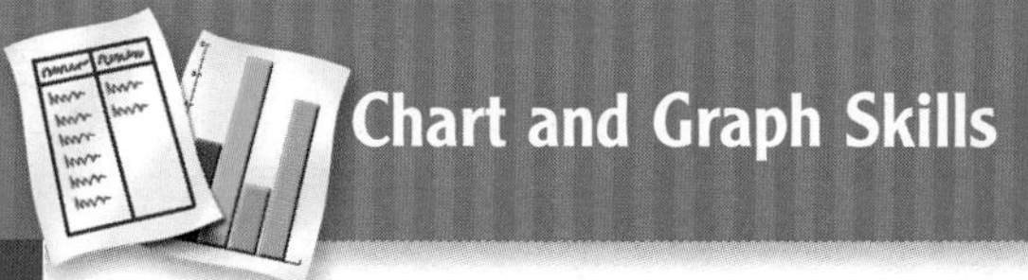

Compare Line and Bar Graphs

Objective

- Use bar graphs to compare information.

Vocabulary

line graph, p. 240; **bar graph,** p. 240

Resources

- Workbook, p. 55
- Transparency 48

1 Introduce and Motivate

What is a bar graph? Tell students to suppose that they want to find out how many siblings each student in the class has. Ask them how they might show this information. Then have students read the **What?** section of text on pp. 240–241 to help set the purpose of this lesson.

Why use bar graphs? Have students read the **Why?** section of text on p. 241. Then have them examine the bar graphs on pp. 240–241. Ask them how they can tell immediately which state, Michigan or Missouri, had the highest population in 1900. (By looking at the tallest or the longest bar on the graph)

2 Teach and Discuss

How is this skill used? Examine with students the bar graphs on pp. 240–241 and work through the example in the text.

- Ask students what information is compared in the graphs. (The populations of Illinois, Michigan and Missouri)
- Have students read the **How?** section of text on p. 241.

Chart and Graph Skills

Compare Line and Bar Graphs

What? A graph is a special kind of picture. It shows and compares information. Two common kinds of graphs are line graphs and bar graphs.

A **line graph** can show how something has changed over time. A line on the graph goes up or down to show these changes. For example, the line on the line graph below shows how the population of Illinois changed from 1850 to 2000.

A **bar graph** can also show how something changes over time.
1 The bar graph below shows the same information as the line graph.

Line Graph

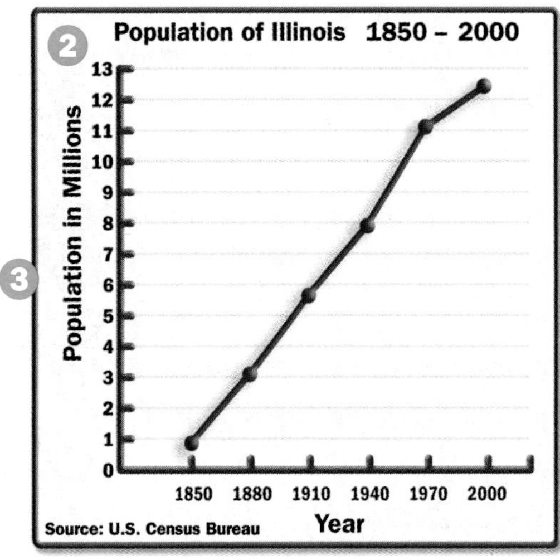

Bar Graph

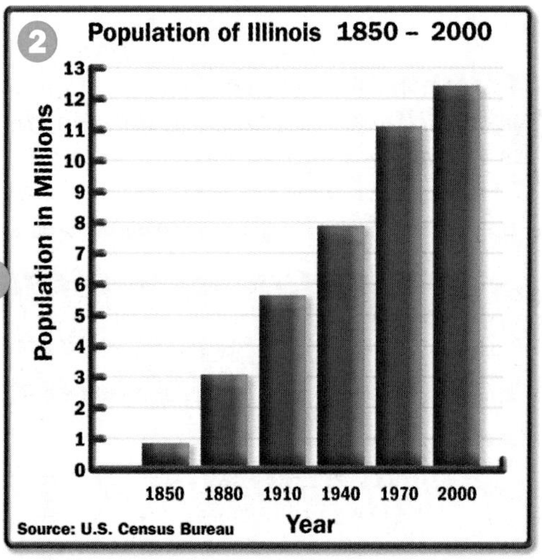

Population of Illinois 1850 – 2000

Population in Millions: 0–13

Year: 1850, 1880, 1910, 1940, 1970, 2000

Source: U.S. Census Bureau

240

Practice and Extend

MEETING INDIVIDUAL NEEDS

Leveled Practice

Make a Bar Graph Have students make bar graphs to compare information.

Easy Provide students with the average monthly high temperatures over a one-year period for Minneapolis, Minnesota, a city in the Midwest. (Jan.: 21.7°F; Feb.: 25.9°F; Mar.: 38.5°F; Apr.: 55.8°F; May: 68.4°F; Jun.: 77.7°F; Jul.: 83.1°F; Aug.: 80.4°F; Sept.: 71.2°F; Oct.: 58.8°F; Nov.: 40.3°F; Dec. 27°F) Work with students to create a bar graph that compares these temperatures. **Reteach**

On-Level Have students research and graph the actual monthly high temperatures for a city in the Midwest over a one-year period. **Extend**

Challenge Have students research and graph the actual monthly high and low temperatures for a city in the Midwest over a one-year period. **Enrich**

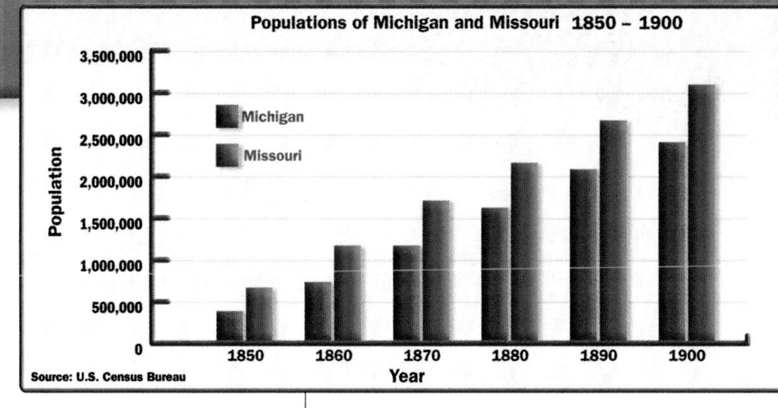

A bar graph can also be used to compare amounts. This bar graph compares the populations of Michigan and Missouri from 1850 to 1900.

Why? Line graphs and bar graphs show facts in a clear, simple picture. They help you find information quickly and easily. They also help you compare information. Choose the type of graph for the information you want to show.

How? Always read the title of a graph and the labels on the graph. This information tells you what the graph is showing.

Look at the line graph on page 240. The dates at the bottom tell you when the population was measured. The numbers at the left show the number of people living in Illinois. Each dot stands for the total number of people living in Illinois in a given year. Did the population of Illinois grow slowly or quickly from 1880 to 1940?

Look at the bar graph on page 240. It shows another way of presenting the same information that is in the line graph. How is this bar graph different from the line graph? Now look at the bar graph above. How is it different from the bar graph on page 240?

Think and Apply

1. Would you choose a **bar graph** or a **line graph** to show changes in your height each year since your birth? Why?
2. Suppose you wanted to compare the number of workers in two Illinois industries. What kind of graph would best show that information?
3. Look at the graphs on page 240. In which 30-year period did the population of Illinois change the fastest? How did you find the answer?

Workbook, p. 55

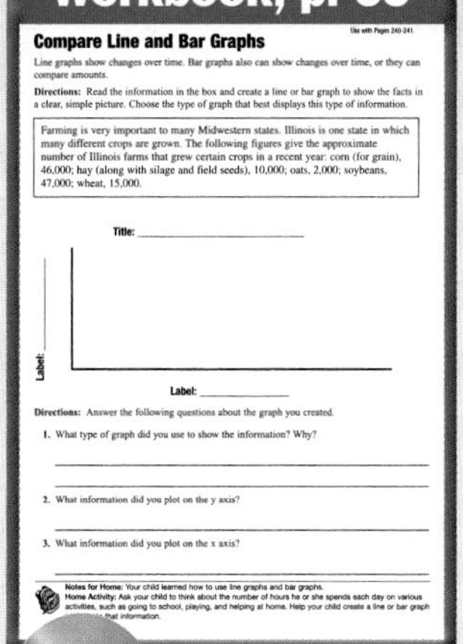

Compare Line and Bar Graphs

Also on Teacher Resources CD-ROM.

1 What kinds of information do you think bar graphs can help you compare? Possible answer: Many kinds of numerical comparisons, such as populations of states, ages, temperatures, distances, and heights
Draw Conclusions

2 What is the title of the graphs on p. 240? Population of Illinois 1850–2000
Main Idea and Details

3 What do the numbers on the side of the graphs show? Population in Millions
Interpret Graphs

3 Close and Assess

Think and Apply

1. Possible answer: Line graph; it shows how something has changed over time.
2. Bar graph
3. 1940–1970, Possible answer: I compared the increases in the heights of the bars in the bar graph.

The Badlands of South Dakota

Objectives

- Describe the landscape and climate of the Badlands 67 million years ago.
- Define *erosion* and describe the way it changes the land.
- Define *prairie* and describe the types of life that live there.
- Explain why the climate of the Badlands changed.

Vocabulary

badlands, p. 243; **erosion,** p. 244; **prairie,** p. 245

Resources

- Workbook, p. 56
- Transparency 20
- Every Student Learns Guide, pp. 98–101
- Quick Study, pp. 50–51

Quick Teaching Plan

If time is short, have students compare the landscape and climate of the Badlands 67 million years ago and today.

- Have students make a two-column chart and label the columns *67 Million Years Ago* and *Today*.
- Have them include two rows labeled *Landscape* and *Climate.*
- Have students complete the chart as they read the lesson independently.

1 Introduce and Motivate

Preview To activate prior knowledge, ask students to locate South Dakota on a map of the United States. Have students speculate why the region they will be studying is called the *Badlands.*

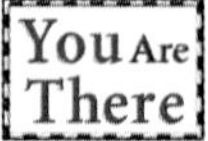

Ask students to describe how they think Sue Hendrickson felt when she discovered the fossil.

LESSON 2

The Badlands of South Dakota

PREVIEW

Focus on the Main Idea
Erosion has shaped the South Dakota Badlands.

PLACES
Badlands National Park

PEOPLE
Sue Hendrickson

VOCABULARY
badlands
erosion
prairie

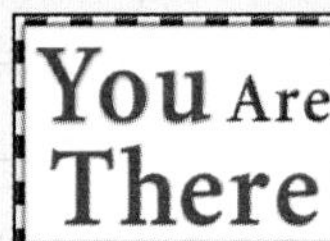

You ride a horse down a trail that winds between sand-colored hills. You and your family are riding with a group through the rock formations of the South Dakota Badlands. You were excited when you learned you were coming here because you wanted to look for fossils along the rocky trails.

Your guide says, "Many dinosaur fossils have been found in these hills. A scientist named Sue Hendrickson discovered one of the most complete *Tyrannosaurus rex* fossils ever found. The fossil was named 'Sue' in her honor." Perhaps you are about to make an incredible discovery of your own!

▶ Sue Hendrickson and the *Tyrannosaurus* skull

Cause and Effect As you read, look for the ways that the South Dakota Badlands have changed over time and some of the causes of these changes.

Practice and Extend

READING SKILL
Cause and Effect

In the Lesson Review, students complete a graphic organizer like the one below. You may want to provide students with a copy of Transparency 20 to complete as they read the lesson.

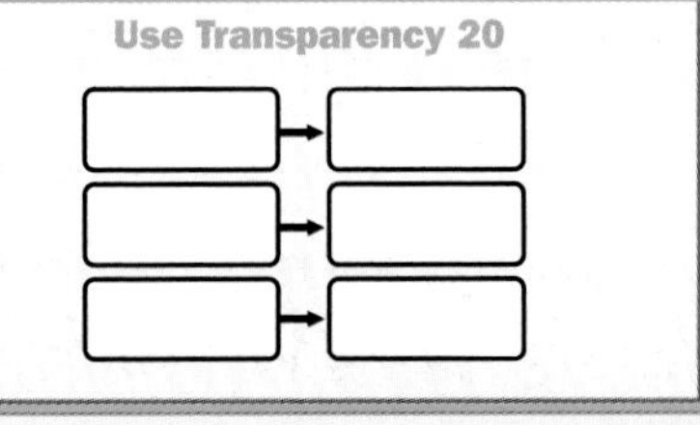

VOCABULARY
Related Word Study

Explain that *erosion* is what you get when something is eroded. These words come from the Latin *ex-*, "away" and *rodere*, "to gnaw." Have students read the definition for *erosion* on p. 244 and discuss how the Latin relates to the definition. Write the word *corrode* on the board. Ask students what they know about the word based on the origin of *erode*. (it involves something being eaten away) Relate that *corrode* does mean being eaten away, generally by chemicals.

Changes in the Badlands

The Great Lakes states are one part of the Midwest. Another part is known as the Great Plains. The badlands are in the Great Plains.

Sue Hendrickson found her famous fossil in the badlands of South Dakota. **Badlands** are regions of dry hills and sharp cliffs formed of crumbling rock. The badlands of western South Dakota are among the most beautiful landscapes in the United States.

Let's travel back in time to when *Tyrannosaurus rex* roamed this region, very long ago. There were no badlands then. Instead, broad rivers flowed through a lush, green plain. Many plants and animals lived on the plain. 1 The climate was warmer and more humid than it is today.

Over millions of years, the climate became cooler and less humid. The Rocky Mountains and the Black Hills rose to the west. These mountains affected the region's climate. They blocked some of the rain that once fell 2 on the region. Over the next millions of years, the land began to change. Rivers, wind, and rain carved the landscape we see today.

REVIEW How did the climate of this region change? Cause and Effect

▶ The *Tyrannosaurus rex* named "Sue" is on display at the Field Museum in Chicago.

243

2 Teach and Discuss

PAGE 243

Changes in the Badlands

Quick Summary The badlands of South Dakota, which have changed over many years, are among the most beautiful landscapes of the United States.

1 **What kind of landscape was found in the badlands area during the time of the dinosaurs?** The region was made up of lush, green plains with rivers.
Main Idea and Details

Ongoing Assessment

If... students have difficulty understanding how badlands could have once been green and lush,	**then...** ask students to describe the landscape of a warm and humid area.

2 **How did the Rocky Mountains and the Black Hills cause the climate of the area that is now the Badlands to change?** The mountains blocked some of the rain that fell on the region.
Cause and Effect

✓ **REVIEW ANSWER** It became cooler and less humid.
Cause and Effect

SOCIAL STUDIES
Background

Badlands

- There are badlands located in the Great Plains and on the Colorado Plateau in the United States and in southern Alberta in Canada.
- The South Dakota Badlands cover about 340 square miles and stretch 100 miles east and west.
- French-Canadian trappers, who described a part of southwestern South Dakota as "the bad lands to cross," first applied the term *badland* to the area.

MEETING INDIVIDUAL NEEDS
Leveled Practice

Compare the Badlands Then and Now Have students compare today's badlands with the area millions of years ago.

Easy Have students do research to find a picture of badlands today and a picture of a place they think has a climate similar to that of badlands millions of years ago.

On-Level Tell students to create a cause-and-effect chart showing what caused changes to the climate and landscape of the area that today is the badlands.

Challenge Ask students to describe a typical animal that lives in the badlands today and a typical animal that may have lived in the area millions of years ago.

For a Lesson Summary, use Quick Study, p. 50.

PAGE 244

Shaping the Land

Quick Summary Erosion has shaped the landscape of the Badlands, and continually uncovers fossils today.

Primary Source

3 **Do you think the quotation on p. 244 accurately describes the picture of the Badlands on that page? Explain.** Possible answer: Yes; the formations do seem to have gigantic domes and bizarre features. **Analyze Primary Sources**

4 **What two elements cause erosion?** Water, wind **Main Idea and Details**

5 **If the Badlands continue to erode, what do you think might happen to the landforms shown in the picture?** Possible answer: They might eventually wear away to nothing. **Predict**

6 **How does erosion help uncover fossils in the Badlands?** Water and wind wear away the rock, exposing fossils buried in it. **Main Idea and Details**

✓ **REVIEW ANSWER** Erosion shapes the land by wearing away rock. **Main Idea and Details**

▶ A part of Badlands National Park 5

Shaping the Land

Badlands National Park, in southwestern South Dakota, has the dry hills and cliffs typical of the area. In fact, these badlands are called the Badlands, with a capital *B* because they are a national park. Wind and water have carved its soft rock into sharp ridges and other fantastic shapes. An artist once described them as

> 3 *A city in ruins . . . containing a palace crowned with gigantic domes and monuments of the most fantastic and bizarre architecture.*

But how did they get that way?

Erosion shaped the Badlands. 4 **Erosion** is the wearing away of rock by water and wind. In the Badlands of South Dakota, most rock layers are fairly soft and crumbly. The rivers that flow through the region cut easily through the rock. Sand flung by the wind wears away cliff faces. Rain also washes the rock away. One big thunderstorm can erode so much rock that you can see a change in the landscape after the storm! This is how the steep canyons and jagged formations were shaped. They are still being formed. They erode an average of one inch per year.

Erosion continually uncovers fossils in the Badlands. The South Dakota Badlands are famous not only for dinosaur fossils, but for many other fossils as well. In fact, the area has one of the richest fossil beds in the world. 6

REVIEW What does erosion do to the land? **Main Idea and Details**

244

Practice and Extend

ACCESS CONTENT

ESL Support

Identify Main Idea and Details Students identify the main idea and details in the information about the Badlands.

Beginning Use the picture on p. 244, along with simple language and gestures, to explain the formation of the Badlands. Review key words such as *dry hills, sharp cliffs,* and *jagged ridges.*

Intermediate Have students write a simple paragraph summarizing the formation of the Badlands. Ask them to circle the main idea and underline the details.

Advanced Have students suppose they are in the Badlands of South Dakota. Have them write a narrative paragraph describing what they see. The first sentence should state the main idea. The other sentences should supply the supporting details.

For additional ESL support, use Every Student Learns Guide, pp. 98–101.

Life in the Badlands

You may think that the Badlands look too rocky and dry for anything to live there. However, it is home to many animals. Birds nest in the craggy rocks. Reptiles and insects live there along with mammals, such as prairie dogs and porcupines.

A prairie surrounds the Badlands. A **prairie** is an area where grasses
7 grow well, but trees are rare. A prairie gets much less rain than regions where forests are found. Huge herds of bison, which are often called buffalo, once grazed on the mixed-grass prairie around the Badlands. Native American people, such as the Lakota and Arikara, used to hunt bison here. Today, cattle and sheep graze on this land.

▶ Bison

REVIEW Why might the prairie be better for farming than the badlands? Draw Conclusions

Summarize the Lesson

- **The climate of the Badlands was once much warmer and more humid than it is today.**
- **Erosion shapes the landforms of the Badlands and exposes the fossils there.**
- **Many animals live in the Badlands and on the nearby prairie.**

LESSON 2 REVIEW

Check Facts and Main Ideas

1. Cause and Effect Make a diagram like the one shown. Complete it by listing the missing causes of events in the Badlands.

Cause	Effect
Mountains blocked rain that fell on the region.	The climate became cooler and less humid.
Rivers, wind, and rain caused changes to the land.	A new landscape was carved.
Erosion continually uncovers fossils in the Badlands.	Many fossils found in South Dakota.

2. What was the climate of western South Dakota like when dinosaurs lived there?
3. What caused the climate of the **badlands** to change?
4. How does **erosion** shape the South Dakota badlands?
5. **Critical Thinking: *Decision Making*** Your classmates need to decide about digging up fossils in the Badlands. Do you think that people should remove fossils found in the Badlands? Why? Use the decision-making steps listed on page H3.

Link to Science

Make a Mural Find out about the animals that are native to the **prairie.** Make a mural or bulletin-board display to share what you learned.

PAGE 245

Life in the Badlands

Quick Summary The Badlands and the prairie that surrounds it are home to many animals and plants.

7 **Why do few trees grow near the Badlands?** Because there is not enough rain Draw Conclusions

✓ **REVIEW ANSWER** The land is flatter, there is more rainfall, grasses grow there. Draw Conclusions

3 Close and Assess

Summarize the Lesson

Have students take turns reading aloud the three main points. Ask them to draw a picture to illustrate the climate, landforms, and animal life in the Badlands.

✓ **LESSON 2 REVIEW**

1. **Cause and Effect** For possible answers, see the reduced pupil page.
2. It was warmer and more humid.
3. The Black Hills and Rocky Mountains rose to the west, blocking the rain.
4. By wearing away rock
5. **Critical Thinking: *Decision Making*** Possible answers: Fossils should be removed only by scientists for research or display; anyone who wants to collect fossils should be able to if they get the landowner's permission; fossils should remain where they are as part of the region's history.

Link to Science

Murals or bulletin-board displays should include prairie animals such as bison, coyotes, badgers, jack rabbits, prairie dogs, grouse, quail, hawks, and grasshoppers.

MEETING INDIVIDUAL NEEDS
Learning Styles

Describe the Badlands Using their individual learning styles, have students present information about the Badlands.

Verbal Learning Have students prepare a short speech to encourage tourists to visit Badlands National Park.

Musical Learning Ask students to write lyrics to a popular melody to describe one aspect of the Badlands that they consider impressive.

Visual Learning Have students draw a diagram to illustrate how the Badlands were formed.

Workbook, p. 56

Lesson 2: The Badlands of South Dakota

Millions of Years Ago	Changes That Occurred Over Time

Today

Also on Teacher Resources CD-ROM.

Bountiful Midwestern Farms

Objectives

- Explain why the Midwest is an important agricultural region.
- Explain why some farmers irrigate their crops.
- Identify the rainfall in the Midwest and explain how it affects the growth of crops.
- List ten crops grown in the Midwest.
- Identify some crops grown in the Central Plains and the Great Plains.

Vocabulary

crop rotation, p. 248; **irrigation,** p. 248

Resources

- Workbook, p. 57
- Transparency 20
- Every Student Learns Guide, pp. 102–105
- Quick Study, pp. 52–53

Quick Teaching Plan

If time is short, have pairs of students draw two spider maps—one of the climate and another of the agricultural products of the Central Plains and the Great Plains.

- Ask student pairs to take turns writing details on each leg of the map.
- Review students' maps as a class.

LESSON 3

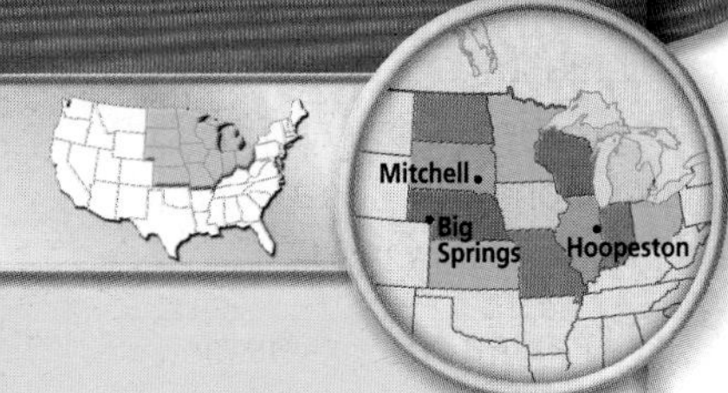

PREVIEW

Focus on the Main Idea
The Midwest is one of the world's leading farming regions.

PLACES
Mitchell, South Dakota
Big Springs, Nebraska
Hoopeston, Illinois
Great Plains
Central Plains

VOCABULARY
crop rotation
irrigation

Bountiful Midwestern Farms

You Are There

Dear Mary Beth,

I'm so glad my family saw the Corn Palace on our trip to South Dakota. The walls are covered with colorful pictures. And guess what? They are made from corncobs, bundles of wheat, stalks of prairie grass, and kernels of grain! I wonder if any of the crops we grow in Big Springs ever make it onto the walls of the Corn Palace. Maybe some of the corn you grow in Hoopeston is part of the mural!

Your friend,
Cathy

Cause and Effect As you read, look for facts that explain why the Midwest is an important farming region.

1 Introduce and Motivate

Preview To activate prior knowledge, ask volunteers to share a time when they drove by or visited farmlands. Ask them what crops were being grown on the farms. Tell students they will learn what crops farmers raise in the Midwest.

You Are There Ask students what the murals in the Corn Palace show. Ask them to identify the agricultural products used to make the mural. (Corncobs, bundles of wheat, stalks of grass, kernels of grain)

Practice and Extend

READING SKILL
Cause and Effect

In the Lesson Review, students complete a graphic organizer like the one below. You may want to provide students with a copy of Transparency 20 to complete as they read the lesson.

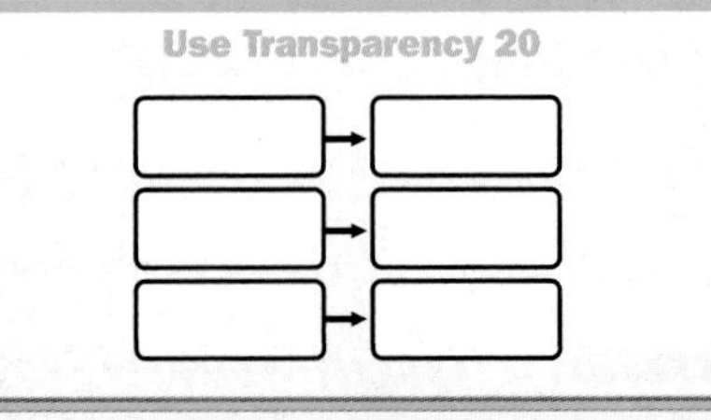

VOCABULARY
Context Clues

Have students locate and read the definitions for the vocabulary words. Then use the examples below or create your own in order to help students learn and practice new vocabulary.

The land becomes exhausted if the same crop is grown year after year. Because of this, farmers use _____. (crop rotation)

It does not rain often enough here to grow crops, but _____ will make farming possible. (irrigation)

The Rich Farmland

The Corn Palace is in **Mitchell, South Dakota.** It was built to show how important agriculture is to the Midwest. The Midwest is one of the world's most important agricultural regions. The soil is very rich and deep.
1 Rainfall is also plentiful. The growing season is long and summers are warm.

Midwestern farms produce crops that are used for food and many other products. Not all farms in the Midwest grow the same type of crops.

For example, Cathy's family lives on a farm near **Big Springs, Nebraska.** They grow wheat and sunflowers. Cathy's friend, Mary Beth, lives on a farm near **Hoopeston, Illinois.** Her family grows corn and soybeans. Both farms are in the Midwest.

The reason why these farms grow different crops has to do with water. The map shows how much rain falls on different parts of the country. Find Big Springs on the map. It is in an area called the **Great Plains.** How much rain does it receive each year? Now find Hoopeston. It is in the **Central Plains.** Which area receives more rain? How do you think rainfall affects the crops grown in each area? 2

REVIEW Why is the Midwest an important agricultural region?
Main Idea and Details

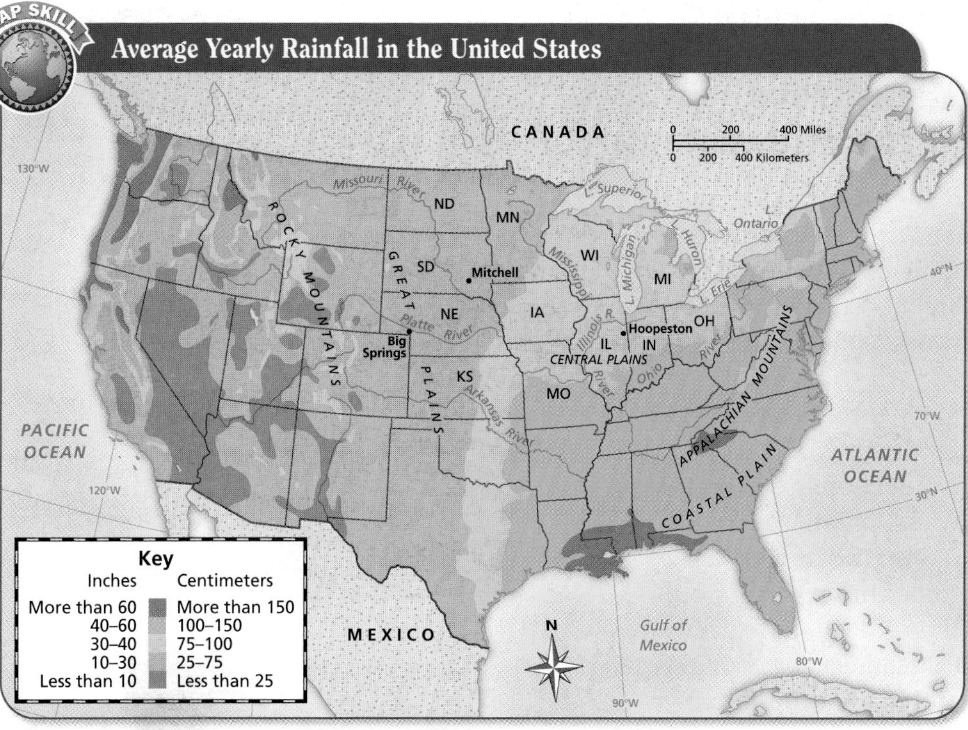

▶ **Compare the amounts of rain in the Great Plains and in the Central Plains.**

MAP SKILL Use Map Key ***About how many inches of rain fall each year in Hoopeston?***

2 Teach and Discuss

PAGE 247

The Rich Farmland

Quick Summary Rich soil and a long growing season make the Midwest an important agricultural region.

1 **Why was the Corn Palace built?** To show the importance of agriculture to the Midwest Main Idea and Details

2 **Why do farms on the Great Plains and on the Central Plains grow different types of crops?** Because they receive different amounts of rainfall, influencing what types of crops grow best
Apply Information

✓ **REVIEW ANSWER** Rich and deep soil, long growing season
Main Idea and Details

Average Yearly Rainfall in the United States

- Point out that the average yearly rainfall is varied throughout the United States.
- Ask students which region has the most varied rainfalls in the United States. (The West)

MAP SKILL Answer About 30–40 inches

MEETING INDIVIDUAL NEEDS
Leveled Practice

Analyze Precipitation Levels Have students analyze the effects of different levels of precipitation.

Easy Have students find their home state on the map on this page and identify the average yearly precipitation for the state. Ask them how they know.

On-Level Tell students to find their hometown's approximate location on the map on this page. Then have them explain in writing how precipitation levels are different 400 miles east or west of their location.

Challenge Ask students to research the area of the Midwest once known as the Dust Bowl and mark it on an outline map of the Midwest. Then have them explain how changes in precipitation helped create the Dust Bowl.

For a Lesson Summary, use Quick Study, p. 52.

SOCIAL STUDIES
Background

Corn Palace

- Each year the murals in the Corn Palace are stripped down and new murals are created.
- Local artists design the murals, which illustrate aspects of life in South Dakota.
- Thousands of bushels of crops, including corn, bluegrass, and wheat, are used to create the murals.
- The Corn Palace is used as a community center, hosting events such as sports and stage shows.

PAGE 248

The Central Plains and the Great Plains

Quick Summary The amount of rainfall in the Central Plains makes corn and soybeans the most important crops grown there. Irrigation allows farms on the Great Plains to produce a large variety of crops.

3 **Describe the practice of crop rotation.** The planting of different crops in different years Main Idea and Details

4 **How do farmers on the Great Plains get water for their crops?** Using irrigation with water from rainfall, rivers, or from deep underground Main Idea and Details

✓ **REVIEW ANSWER** More types of crops can be grown. Cause and Effect

FACT FILE

Main Crops of the Midwest

5 **Which crops can be used to make alcohol for fuel?** Corn and wheat Interpret Charts

The Central Plains and the Great Plains

The farmland of the Central Plains is known as the Corn Belt. This area gets plenty of rain, which is ideal for growing corn. Farmers of the Corn Belt often switch between two crops. They plant corn one year and soybeans the next year. The soybean plants add materials to the soil that the corn plants need in order to grow well. The planting of different crops in different years is called **crop rotation.** Corn and soybeans are important crops on the Central Plains. 3

The Great Plains does not get as much rain as the Central Plains does. Crops that do not require much rainfall include wheat, oats, and barley. Sunflowers also grow well in this area.

Today, farmers on the Great Plains are able to grow crops that need more water—such as corn and soybeans. The farmers bring water to their farms and spray it over their fields. This process is called **irrigation.** The water comes from rivers or from deep underground. 4

REVIEW What effect has irrigation had on the Great Plains? Cause and Effect

FACT FILE

Main Crops of the Midwest

The wheat, corn, and soybeans that farmers grow in the Midwest are made into foods for people all over the world. Parts of these plants are made into many other products as well.

The kernels of the wheat plant are ground up into flour. Here are some things made from flour: bread, pasta, cereals, cakes, crackers, cookies, and many other foods.

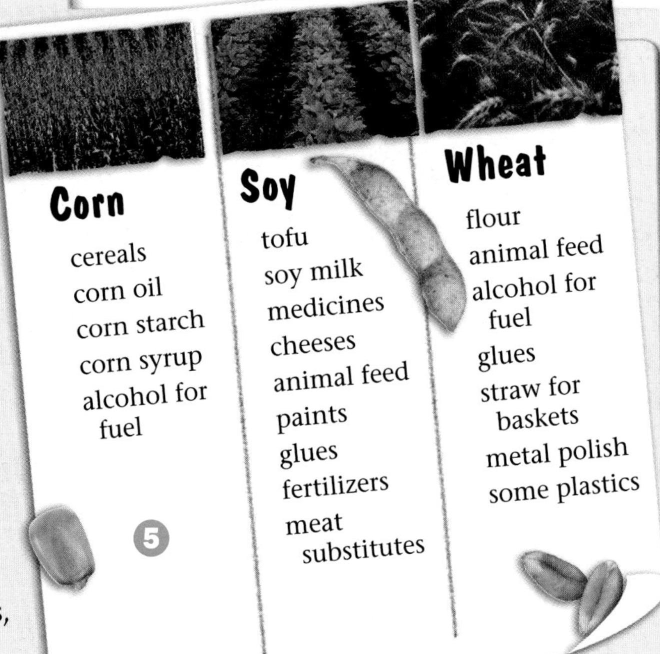

Corn	Soy	Wheat
cereals	tofu	flour
corn oil	soy milk	animal feed
corn starch	medicines	alcohol for fuel
corn syrup	cheeses	glues
alcohol for fuel	animal feed	straw for baskets
	paints	metal polish
	glues	some plastics
	fertilizers	
	meat substitutes	

5

248

Practice and Extend

CURRICULUM CONNECTION
Science

Compare Precipitation

- Have students go online to learn more about the precipitation differences between the Central Plains and the Great Plains.
- Have them find, print, and compare the average monthly precipitation for Big Springs, Nebraska, and Hoopeston, Illinois.
- Ask students to draw conclusions from their findings.

CURRICULUM CONNECTION
Math

Make a Bar Graph

- Have students complete the Science Curriculum Connection on this page.
- Ask students to work in pairs. Have one student create a bar graph showing average monthly precipitation in Big Springs and the other student show average monthly precipitation in Hoopeston.
- Have students compare their bar graphs and discuss the differences in precipitation.

Other Crops of the Midwest

Besides corn, soybeans, and wheat, many other farm products come from the Midwest. The region is a leading hog producer. Corn-fed hogs provide pork and ham. Michigan has acres of apple, cherry, peach, and plum orchards, and fields of blueberries, grapes, and strawberries. Milk and dairy products are very important to Wisconsin's economy.

Some of the nation's largest cattle ranches are on the wide-open spaces of the Great Plains. The grain-fed cattle of the Midwest provide top-quality beef. 6

REVIEW List ten different farm products that come from the Midwest. Main Idea and Supporting Details

Summarize the Lesson

- **Rich soil and a long growing season help make the Midwest an important agricultural region.**
- **Corn and soybeans are two main crops grown on the Central Plains. Wheat and other grains are main crops grown on the Great Plains.**
- **Irrigation has made it possible for farmers on the Great Plains to grow more types of crops.**

▶ **Farmers grow many kinds of fruits in the Midwest.**

LESSON 3 REVIEW

Check Facts and Main Ideas

1. Cause and Effect Make a diagram like the one shown. Complete it by listing the missing causes and effect.

Cause		Effect
The Midwest has rich, deep soil and a long growing season.	→	The Midwest is an important agricultural region.
Corn grows well where rainfall is plentiful.	→	The Central Plains are called the Corn Belt.
The Great Plains does not get as much rainfall as the Central Plains.	→	Farmers on the Great Plains use irrigation.

2. Why are soybeans an important crop in the Central Plains?
3. Name two crops grown on the Central Plains and two major crops grown on the Great Plains. Use the term **crop rotation** in your answer.
4. How has **irrigation** changed farming on the Great Plains?
5. **Critical Thinking:** ***Evaluate*** Is the Corn Belt a good name for the Central Plains? Why or why not?

Link to Writing

Write a Journal Find a book about farming in the Midwest. Based on the book, write a series of journal entries about daily life on a farm.

249

Other Crops of the Midwest

Quick Summary The Midwest produces a wide variety of crops.

6 What is one advantage of raising corn-fed hogs and grain-fed cattle in the Midwest? The food they eat is easily available because it is grown in the Midwest. Draw Conclusions

Ongoing Assessment

If... students have difficulty understanding why the food for these animals is easily found in the Midwest,	**then...** have students review what types of crops are grown in the Midwest.

REVIEW ANSWER Possible answers: Apples, barley, beef, blueberries, cheese, cherries, corn, ham, milk and other dairy products, peaches, plums, pork, soybeans, strawberries, and wheat Main Idea and Details

3 Close and Assess

Summarize the Lesson

Ask volunteers to use three blank transparencies, illustrating one point per sheet. Layer the transparencies to create a comprehensive picture of Midwest farmlands.

LESSON 3 REVIEW

1. **Cause and Effect** For possible answers, see the reduced pupil page.
2. Soybean plants add materials to the soil that other crops need.
3. Central Plains crop rotation: corn, soybeans; Great Plains crop rotation: wheat, sunflowers
4. A greater variety of crops can be grown.
5. **Critical Thinking: *Evaluate*** Possible answer: Yes; Because corn has always been a main crop there

Link to Writing

Encourage students to write from a first-person perspective.

ACTIVATE PRIOR KNOWLEDGE
ESL Support

Work with New Words Discuss crops grown in other places and practice the English names for the crops.

Beginning Have students describe crops from other countries. Write the English name for each crop and help students practice saying each aloud.

Intermediate Have students draw pictures of crops grown in other countries. Then have them brainstorm the English name for each crop and write each name.

Advanced Have students write a paragraph about the farming practices of another country. Have students share their paragraphs with the class.

For additional ESL support, use Every Student Learns Guide, pp. 102–105.

Workbook, p. 57

Lesson 3: Bountiful Midwestern Farms

Crop	Where Is It Grown?	Why Is It Grown There?
Wheat		
Sunflowers		
Corn		
Soybeans		
Oats		
Barley		
Hogs		
Cattle		

Also on Teacher Resources CD-ROM.

United States and Thailand: Big Farms and Little Farms

Objectives

- Describe the differences between farming methods in Thailand and those in the Midwest.
- Compare the importance of the rice crop in Thailand to the importance of the corn crop in the Midwest.

1 Introduce and Motivate

Preview To activate prior knowledge, ask students to make a list of recent meals they have had that included rice. Ask them how they think rice is grown.

2 Teach and Discuss

SOCIAL STUDIES STRAND
Economics

Thailand is the sixth largest producer of rice in the world. The country consumes approximately 60 percent of the rice locally and exports approximately 40 percent to countries worldwide.

1 **What is a major crop of Thailand?** Rice Main Idea and Details

2 **How does the size of rice farms in Thailand compare to the size of corn farms in the Midwest?** Thai rice farms are usually much smaller than farms in the Midwest. Compare and Contrast

3 **How do farmers in Thailand harvest rice?** By hand, with a sickle or knife Main Idea and Details

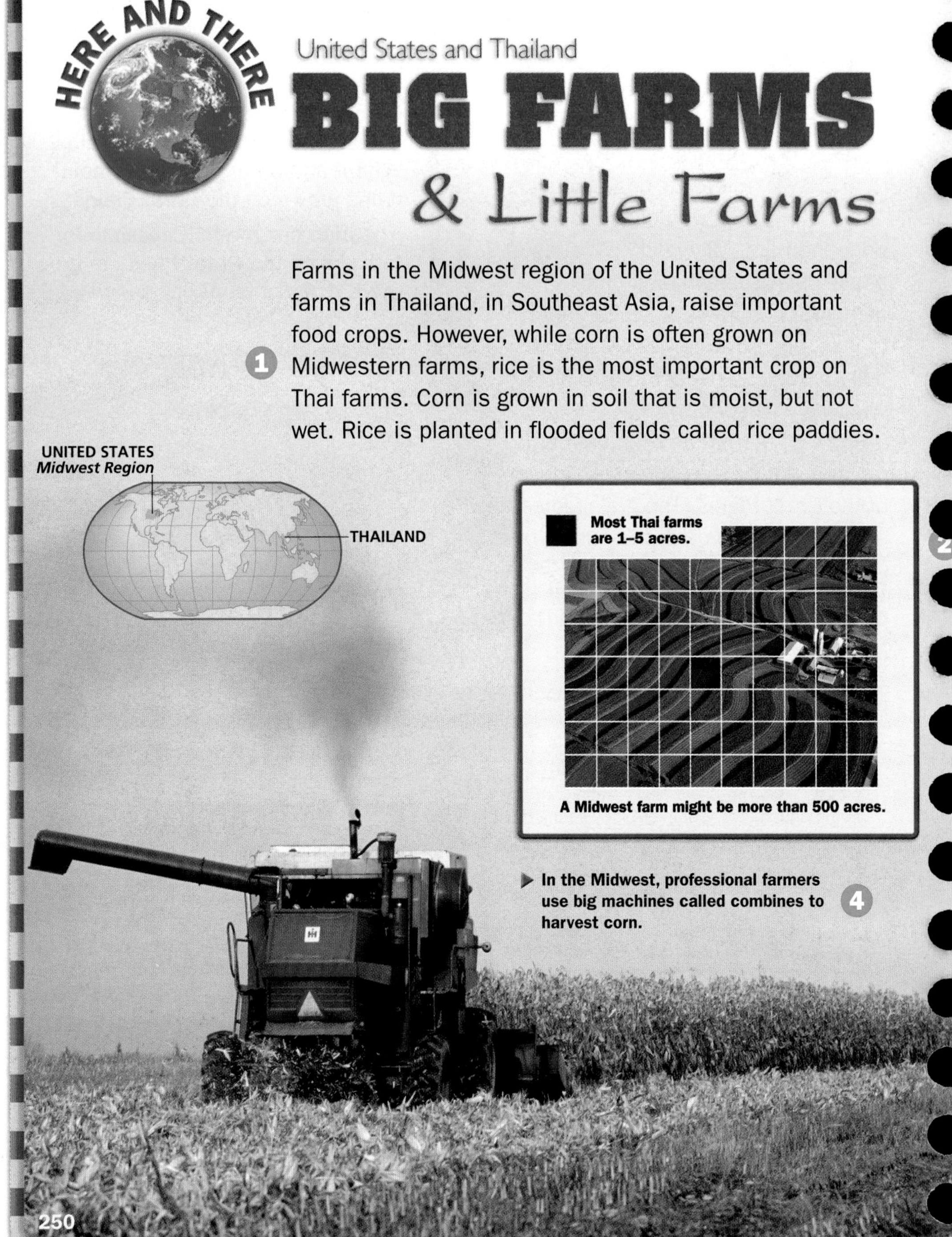

HERE AND THERE
United States and Thailand
BIG FARMS
& Little Farms
Farms in the Midwest region of the United States and farms in Thailand, in Southeast Asia, raise important food crops. However, while corn is often grown on 1 Midwestern farms, rice is the most important crop on Thai farms. Corn is grown in soil that is moist, but not wet. Rice is planted in flooded fields called rice paddies.
UNITED STATES
Midwest Region
THAILAND
Most Thai farms are 1–5 acres.
A Midwest farm might be more than 500 acres.
2
In the Midwest, professional farmers use big machines called combines to harvest corn. 4
250

Practice and Extend

FAST FACTS

- Six states—Arkansas, California, Louisiana, Mississippi, Missouri, and Texas—produce 99 percent of all rice grown in the United States.
- Arkansas produces the most rice.
- On average, people in the United States each eat about 26.5 pounds of rice per year.

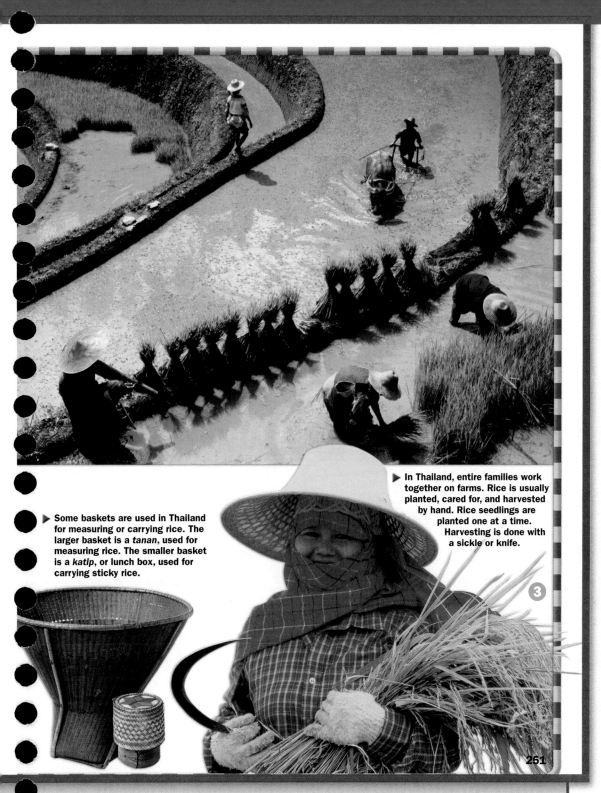

Some baskets are used in Thailand for measuring or carrying rice. The larger basket is a *tanan*, used for measuring rice. The smaller basket is a *katip*, or lunch box, used for carrying sticky rice.

In Thailand, entire families work together on farms. Rice is usually planted, cared for, and harvested by hand. Rice seedlings are planted one at a time. Harvesting is done with a sickle or knife.

3

251

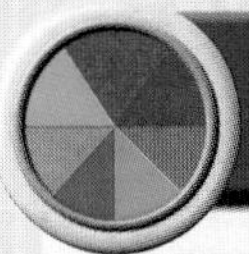

CURRICULUM CONNECTION
Science

Identify Uses for Rice

- Ask students to use library or online resources to find out the various uses of rice.
- Have them work in small groups to gather their information.
- Ask each group to present its findings in a captioned poster.
- Display completed posters in the classroom and discuss the uses of rice.

SOCIAL STUDIES
Background

Geography of Rice Growing

Here and There describes rice farming in Thailand. While displaying a world map, tell students that more than 100 countries around the world produce rice.

- Rice is grown on every continent except Antarctica.
- People in Asia, Africa, Latin America, and the Caribbean depend on rice for 35–80 percent of their daily caloric intake.

4 **Most farmers in the United States use machines to help them plant and harvest crops. How does using machines affect the amount of land a farmer is capable of farming?** Machines make it possible for a farmer to farm more land. Make Inferences

3 Close and Assess

Corn production in the Midwest and rice production in Thailand are alike and different in many ways. Have students analyze these similarities and differences by creating a comparison chart.

- Have students create a two-column chart on a sheet of paper.
- Tell them to label the columns *Alike* and *Different*.
- Have students complete the chart with information from the text.

CHAPTER 8 REVIEW

Resources

- Assessment Book, pp. 41–44
- Workbook, p. 58: Vocabulary Review

Chapter Summary

For possible answers, see the reduced pupil page.

Vocabulary

Sentences will vary but should reflect an understanding of the meaning of each word.

Places

Possible answers:

1. The Great Lakes include Lake Huron, Lake Ontario, Lake Michigan, Lake Erie, and Lake Superior. All but Lake Ontario lie at least partially in the Midwest. Lake Ontario lies in the Northeast and in Canada. The Great Lakes connect the Midwest to the world through waterways.
2. The Mississippi River is the nation's largest river. It runs north and south through the Midwest. It provides a waterway to the Gulf of Mexico.
3. The Illinois Waterway consists of rivers and canals. It is located in Illinois. It connects Lake Michigan to the Mississippi River.
4. The St. Lawrence Seaway is a large waterway. It is located along the path of the Great Lakes and into Canada. It links the Great Lakes with Canada's St. Lawrence River, which flows into the Atlantic Ocean.
5. The Badlands National Park is a region of dry hills and sharp cliffs formed from crumbling rocks. This region is located in western South Dakota. Many fossils are found there.
6. The Central Plains is an area of the Midwest that gets plenty of rain, which makes it ideal for growing corn and soybeans.

CHAPTER 8 Review

Chapter Summary

Cause and Effect

On a separate sheet of paper, fill in the effects related to the causes.

Cause	Effect
The temperature of the Earth rises at the end of the Ice Age.	The glaciers melt.
Sand is flung by the wind against cliff faces.	The sand erodes the cliff faces and carves them into different shapes.
Soybean plants add necessary materials to the soil.	Corn plants can grow well the following year.

▶ The Badlands

Vocabulary

For each vocabulary word, write a sentence that defines or shows what the word means.

1. **barge** (p. 236)
2. **canal** (p. 234)
3. **lock** (p. 234)
4. **waterway** (p. 234)
5. **badlands** (p. 243)
6. **erosion** (p. 244)
7. **prairie** (p. 245)
8. **crop rotation** (p. 248)
9. **irrigation** (p. 248)

Places

Describe each place, tell where it is located, and why it is important in the Midwest region.

1. **The Great Lakes** (p. 233)
2. **Mississippi River** (p. 234)
3. **Illinois Waterway** (p. 234)
4. **St. Lawrence Seaway** (p. 234)
5. **Badlands National Park** (p. 244)
6. **The Central Plains** (p. 247)

252

Practice and Extend

Assessment Options

✓ Chapter 8 Assessment

- Chapter 8 Content Test: Use Assessment Book, pp. 41–42.
- Chapter 8 Skills Test: Use Assessment Book, pp. 43–44.

Standardized Test Prep

- Chapter 8 Tests contain standardized test format.

✓ Chapter 8 Performance Assessment

- Have students work in groups to create a crossword puzzle of the places in each lesson of Chapter 8.
- You might have students limit the number of places to six, with three across and three down.
- Assess students' understanding of the places in Chapter 8 by observing them as they work on the crossword puzzle.

Facts and Main Ideas

Write your answers on a separate sheet of paper.

1. How did the Great Lakes form?
2. How did erosion shape the South Dakota Badlands?
3. What factors make the central Midwest a rich agricultural region?
4. **Main Idea** Describe the waterway that connects the Midwest with the Atlantic Ocean.
5. **Main Idea** What part of the Midwest has rich fossil beds?
6. **Main Idea** Name two Midwest states and crops they produce other than corn and soybeans.
7. **Critical Thinking:** ***Make Generalizations*** The central Midwest has many large cities. Based on what you have learned about the Midwest, give a reason why cities have flourished in this part of the region.

Write About Economics

1. **Write a story** using what you have learned about different types of transportation for getting goods to market. Tell why you chose this route.
2. **Write a radio advertisement** encouraging tourism in the Midwest.
3. **Write a journal** describing how you plan to transport a Midwestern farmer's soybeans to market.

Sending Beans to Market

Julie wonders, "How should I send my soybeans to Chicago? By truck or by train?"

Apply Skills

Using Graphs

Study the bar graph below. Then answer the questions.

1. What does this bar graph show?
2. Of the three Midwestern states shown—Illinois, Indiana, and Kansas—which one had the largest population in the year 2000? in the year 1990?
3. About how many people lived in Illinois in the year 2000?

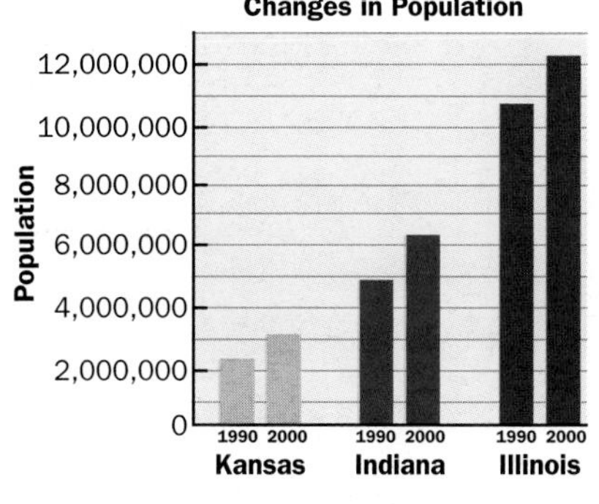

Internet Activity

To get help with vocabulary and terms, select the dictionary or encyclopedia from *Social Studies Library* at **www.sfsocialstudies.com.**

Hands-on Unit Project

✓ **Unit 4 Performance Assessment**

- See p. 290 for information about using the Unit Project as a means of performance assessment.
- A scoring guide is provided on p. 290.

WEB SITE Technology

For more information, students can select the dictionary or encyclopedia from *Social Studies Library* at **www.sfsocialstudies.com.**

Workbook, p. 58

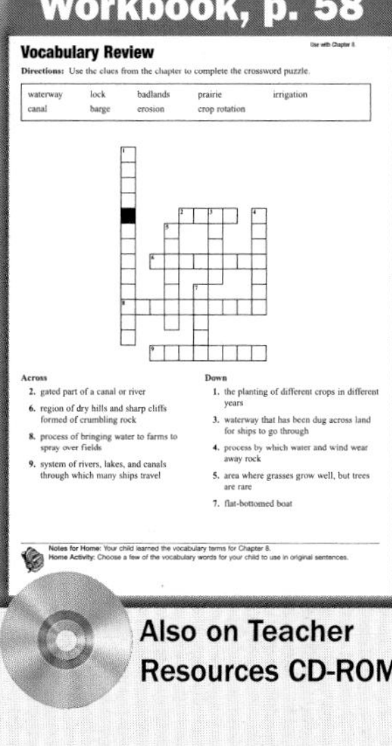

Also on Teacher Resources CD-ROM.

Facts and Main Ideas

1. Movement of glaciers caused deep pits to form. As the Ice Age ended, the glaciers melted. The melting water filled the pits, forming the Great Lakes.
2. Water and wind wore away rock.
3. It has rich soil and a long growing season.
4. The Welland Ship Canal connects Lake Erie and Lake Ontario. The St. Lawrence Seaway then uses canals, locks, and the St. Lawrence River to connect Lake Ontario to the Atlantic Ocean.
5. The Badlands
6. Possible answers: Nebraska—wheat and sunflowers; Michigan—apples, cherries, peaches, plums, blueberries, grapes, strawberries; Wisconsin—milk and other dairy products
7. Possible answers: The cities are hubs of many different types of transportation for getting goods to market.

Write About Economics

1. Students might draw a sketch of the route to accompany their story.
2. Students' advertisements should include reasons for tourists to visit, such as seeing the Corn Palace.
3. Encourage students to share their journal entries with the class.

Apply Skills

1. Changes in population for three Midwestern states
2. Illinois; Illinois
3. About 12,000,000

CHAPTER 9

Chapter Planning Guide

Chapter 9 • People of the Midwest

Locating Places pp. 254–255

Lesson Titles	Pacing	Main Ideas
Lesson 1 **The Ojibwa** pp. 256–259 **Citizen Heroes: Respect** **Keeping a Culture Strong** pp. 260–261 **Research and Writing Skills: Use a Search Engine on the Internet** pp. 262–263	3 days	• The Ojibwa have maintained important cultural traditions and have contributed to the culture of the Midwest. • Joseph Podlasek teaches Native Americans how to move successfully from reservations to cities. • The Internet is an excellent tool for research.
Lesson 2 **The Fur Trade** pp. 264–266 **Biography: Jean Baptiste Point Du Sable** p. 267 **Colonial Williamsburg: Trading for Goods** pp. 268–269	4 days	• European settlement in the Great Lakes region and the Mississippi valley began with the fur trade. Many of the region's cities and towns began as fur trading centers. • Jean Baptiste Point Du Sable established a successful trading post that caused Chicago to grow. • The fur trade was important to Native American, British, and French traders.
Lesson 3 **Building Farms** pp. 270–274 **Biography: John Deere** p. 275	2 days	• Many people came to the Midwest in the 1800s to farm the land. • John Deere invented a new type of plow that made farming easier.
Lesson 4 **Hub of the Nation** pp. 276–282 **Biography: Mark Twain** p. 283	3 days	• The Midwest has been a trade and transportation hub from long ago to the present. • Mark Twain, whose real name was Samuel Langhorne Clemens, was one of America's most popular writers.

✓ **Chapter 9 Review**
pp. 284–285

✓ = **Assessment Options**

For hundreds of years, the Ojibwa have used canoes to travel on Midwestern waterways.

Vocabulary	Resources	Meeting Individual Needs
fur trade research Internet search engine	• Workbook, p. 60 • Transparency 20 • Every Student Learns Guide, pp. 106–109 • Quick Study, pp. 54–55	• ESL Support, TE p. 257 • Leveled Practice, TE p. 259 • Learning Styles, TE p. 261
	• Workbook, p. 61	• Leveled Practice, TE p. 263
mission trading post	• Workbook, p. 62 • Transparencies 20, 50 • Every Student Learns Guide, pp. 110–113	• ESL Support, TE p. 265 • Leveled Practice, TE p. 266
	• Quick Study, pp. 56–57 • Workbook, p. 63	• ESL Support, TE p. 267
sod drought Dust Bowl blacksmith	• Workbook, p. 64 • Transparency 20 • Every Student Learns Guide, pp. 114–117 • Quick Study, pp. 58–59	• ESL Support, TE p. 271 • Leveled Practice, TE p. 272
mound steamboat hub transcontinental railroad Interstate highway system	• Workbook, p. 65 • Transparencies 20, 51, 52 • Every Student Learns Guide, pp. 118–121 • Quick Study, pp. 60–61	• ESL Support, TE p. 279 • Leveled Practice, TE p. 280 • Learning Styles, TE p. 281
	✔ Chapter 9 Content Test, Assessment Book, pp. 45–46 ✔ Chapter 9 Skills Test, Assessment Book, pp. 47–48	✔ Chapter 9 Performance Assessment, TE p. 284

Providing More Depth

Additional Resources

- Vocabulary Workbook and Cards
- Social Studies Plus! pp. 90–95
- Daily Activity Bank
- Big Book Atlas
- Student Atlas
- Outline Maps
- Desk Maps

Technology

- AudioText
- MindPoint® Quiz Show CD-ROM
- ExamView® Test Bank CD-ROM
- Teacher Resources CD-ROM
- Map Resources CD-ROM
- SFSuccessNet: iText (Pupil Edition online), iTE (Teacher's Edition online), Online Planner
- **www.sfsocialstudies.com** (Biographies, news, references, maps, and activities)

To establish guidelines for your students' safe and responsible use of the Internet, use the Scott Foresman Internet Guide.

Additional Internet Links

To find out more about:

- The fur trade, visit **www.furtrade.org**
- The American Indian Center, visit **www.aic-chicago.org**
- John Deere, visit **www.invent.org**

Key Internet Search Terms

- St. Lawrence River
- Cahokia Mounds
- Louis Jolliet

Workbook Support

Use the following Workbook pages to support content and skills development as you teach Chapter 9. You can also view and print Workbook pages from the Teacher Resources CD-ROM.

Workbook, p. 59

Use with Chapter 9.

Vocabulary Preview

Directions: These are the vocabulary words from Chapter 9. How much do you know about these words? Write each word on the line provided beside its definition. You may use your glossary.

fur trade	sod	mound	transcontinental railroad
mission	drought	steamboat	interstate highway system
trading post	Dust Bowl	hub	

1. **sod** grass, roots, and dirt that form the ground's top layer
2. **interstate highway system** set of wide, fast, interconnecting highways to link the states
3. **fur trade** the exchange of animal skins for other goods, such as cloth, guns, and knives
4. **steamboat** boat powered by a steam engine
5. **drought** time of little rain
6. **transcontinental railroad** rail line that crosses the entire country
7. **mission** settlement set up by a religious group to teach its religion and to help the people of an area.
8. **Dust Bowl** area in the Midwest and Southwest that suffered the most during the drought in the 1930s
9. **hub** center of activity
10. **trading post** type of store at which goods are traded
11. **mound** pile of earth or stones

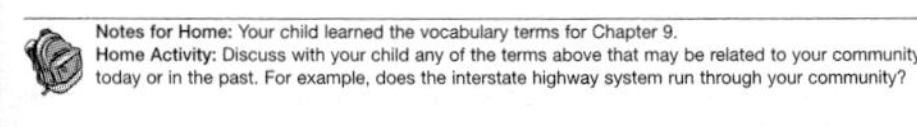

Notes for Home: Your child learned the vocabulary terms for Chapter 9.
Home Activity: Discuss with your child any of the terms above that may be related to your community today or in the past. For example, does the interstate highway system run through your community?

Workbook — Vocabulary Preview **59**

Use with Pupil Edition, p. 254

Workbook, p. 60

Use with Pages 256–259.

Lesson 1: The Ojibwa

The Ojibwa have been an important part of the culture of the Midwest for many years.

Directions: Write details about the Ojibwa in each box of the idea web below. You may use your textbook.

Ojibwa

Location: Early: Atlantic coast; Later: Duluth, Minnesota, Milwaukee, Wisconsin, and Mt. Pleasant, Michigan; Today: northern Great Lakes region

Activities/Fun: participating in traditional ceremonies, making traditional crafts (Students may include hunting, fishing, and canoeing.)

Food: hunting, fishing, gathering wild rice and berries, growing a few vegetables

Travel: birchbark canoes

Earning a Living: trapping and trading, hunting and fishing, making traditional crafts, working in cities

Notes for Home: Your child learned about the history of the Ojibwa.
Home Activity: Find out which Native American groups live or have lived near your community. Discuss with your child how these groups' cultures have influenced life in your community.

Use with Pupil Edition, p. 259

Workbook, p. 61

Use with Pages 262-263.

Use a Search Engine on the Internet

A search engine is a good tool to help you find information on the Internet. Using keywords allows you to narrow your search. Suppose that you are given the assignments that follow. Which keywords would you choose to research your task?

Directions: Circle the letter of the keyword or words that would best help you find information for each project below.

1. Plan an Ojibwa celebration for your classmates.
   a. Ojibwa (b.) Ojibwa celebration c. classmates
2. Write a paragraph about the northern Great Lakes region.
   a. paragraph b. northern regions (c.) northern Great Lakes region
3. Draw a map showing the Native American reservations in the United States.
   (a.) U.S. reservations b. draw a map c. maps
4. Make a model of an Ojibwa birchbark canoe.
   a. make a canoe b. birchbark models (c.) Ojibwa culture and travel
5. Write a report about the American Indian Movement.
   (a.) American Indian Movement b. writing c. report

Directions: Suppose you need to research the Midwest for a social studies presentation on this region. You plan to use a search engine to help you find information. On the lines below, list keywords you might use to research your task.

Midwest — **farmland**

Central United States — **(specific state names)**

Students' answers may vary from the possible answers shown here. Accept all reasonable responses.

Notes for Home: Your child learned how to use a search engine on the Internet.
Home Activity: Does your child have access to the Internet at home, at school, or at a local library? Discuss any rules you have for your child's Internet use.

Use with Pupil Edition, p. 263

Workbook Support

Workbook, p. 62

Use with Pages 264–266.

Lesson 2: The Fur Trade

Many of the cities and towns of the Midwest began because of the fur trade.

Directions: Sequence the following events in the history of the fur trade in the order in which they took place. Number the events from 1 (earliest) to 10 (most recent). You may use your textbook.

2 The French came to the Midwest.

5 Marquette and Jolliet returned north to a mission at Green Bay.

7 The French began building forts and using them as trading posts.

1 The Ojibwa settled in the Midwest.

3 Native Americans and the French began trapping beaver, mink, and otter.

8 Native Americans began to settle and farm around the French forts.

4 Jacques Marquette and Louis Jolliet traveled from Mackinaw in present-day Michigan to the Mississippi River.

6 Jolliet settled as a fur trader in Sault Sainte Marie.

9 Communities began to grow around the French forts.

10 Sault St. Marie and Chicago grew into major cities.

Directions: On a separate sheet of paper, trace the map on page 265 of your textbook. Label the rivers and waterways mentioned in Lesson 2. Highlight Marquette and Jolliet's journey on your map.

Notes for Home: Your child learned about the history of fur trade in the Midwest.
Home Activity: Trapping animals and wearing clothing made of animal fur are controversies today. Discuss with your child the advantages and disadvantages of fur trapping and trading as an industry.

Use with Pupil Edition, p. 266

Workbook, p. 63

Use with Pages 268–269.

Writing Prompt: Trading Long Ago and Today

Long ago, the English traded with Native Americans for furs. Trading helped both groups get the things they needed. Today, people still trade to get the things they need or want. Draw a picture of something you have traded and what you received in return. Write two sentences telling why you decided to make the trade.

Drawings will vary.

Answers will vary.

Notes for Home: Your child learned about trading in colonial times.
Home Activity: With your child, discuss the ways in which trading helps people get the things they need or want.

Use with Pupil Edition, p. 269

Workbook, p. 64

Use with Pages 268–272.

Lesson 3: Building Farms

As settlers began to farm in the Midwest, the land changed.

Directions: Use complete sentences to answer the questions that follow. You may use your textbook.

1. What happened to the Native Americans who had once lived in Wapello County?
   The U.S. government forced them to sell their land and move to reservations farther west.
2. How did the American settlers in the Midwest claim their land?
   They hammered a wooden stake into each of the four corners of the area they were claiming.
3. Describe the two types of Midwestern farmhouses in the 1800s.
   Most Midwestern farmhouses had only one room. Log cabins were made from the trees the farmers cut from their own land. Sod houses were built on the prairies. They were made of the grass, roots, and dirt that form the top layer of the ground. The sod was cut into bricks for walls and made into strips for the roof.
4. What were the advantages and disadvantages of a sod house?
   Sod houses were warm in the winter and cool in the summer. However, because they were made of dirt, they were hard to keep clean.
5. Why was John Deere important to Midwestern farmers?
   John Deere made a new steel plow. It allowed farmers to more easily prepare the land on the prairies for farming.

Notes for Home: Your child learned about the beginnings of farming in the Midwest.
Home Activity: Discuss with your child the challenges faced by the Native Americans and the early farmers who lived in the Midwest. What character traits might have been important for both of these groups to have?

Use with Pupil Edition, p. 274

Workbook, p. 65

Use with Pages 276–282.

Lesson 4: Hub of the Nation

The Midwest has long been a center of trade and transportation for the United States.

Directions: Complete the chart with details from the lesson that support each main idea. You may use your textbook.

Main Idea	Supporting Details
Cahokia was once a key trading center in the Midwest.	**It was close to three major rivers. Traders shipped copper, lead, and bison bones. Southern traders shipped shells, jewelry, and pottery.**
President Thomas Jefferson wanted to expand trade.	**Jefferson wanted to connect St. Louis with the Northeast, Southeast, and West. He sent Lewis and Clark to find an easy route to the Pacific Ocean.**
One of the main reasons that St. Louis grew quickly was the invention of steamboats.	**Steamboats were bigger and faster than human-powered boats. The rivers of the Midwest became highways, carrying cargo and passengers.**
Chicago began to rival St. Louis as the center of trade in the Midwest.	**The completion of the Erie Canal drew business to Chicago. Railroad lines attracted more people there.**
The interstate highway system is very important to the United States.	**Freight and passengers travel on the highways. The interstate highway system links the states. Most things we buy are shipped on trucks.**

Notes for Home: Your child learned how the Midwest has served as the hub of the United States throughout much of our nation's history.
Home Activity: Look at a highway map of the United States. Which highways that pass through or nearby your community lead to the Midwest?

Use with Pupil Edition, p. 282

Workbook, p. 66

Use with Chapter 9.

Vocabulary Review

Directions: Draw a picture to represent each of the vocabulary terms below. Then write the definition of each word on the lines that follow.

1. fur trade **the exchange of animal skins for other goods, such as cloth, guns, and knives**
2. mission **settlement set up by a religious group to teach its religion and to help the people of an area**
3. sod **grass, roots, and dirt that form the ground's top layer**
4. mound **pile of earth or stones**
5. transcontinental railroad **rail line that crosses the entire country**
6. interstate highway system **set of wide, fast, interconnecting highways to link the states**

Notes for Home: Your child learned the vocabulary terms for Chapter 9.
Home Activity: With your child, take turns using each of the vocabulary words from Chapter 9 in an original sentence.

Use with Pupil Edition, p. 285

Workbook, p. 67

Unit 4 Project Point of View

Directions: In a group, debate two sides of an event or topic in your state's history.

1. Our debate topic is ______.
2. Here are two points of view and facts to support each side:
   Pro: ______
   Facts: ______
   Con: ______
   Facts: ______
3. ______ will give the Pro argument.
4. ______ will give the Con argument.
5. The class chose the ______ argument as the best presentation.

You may wish to approve students' debate topics before they research facts to support their points of view.

Checklist for Students
- ____ We chose a topic to debate.
- ____ We identified two sides of the topic.
- ____ We wrote facts to support two sides of the topic.
- ____ We decided who will argue each side.
- ____ We held our debate for the class.

Notes for Home: Your child learned how to defend a point of view.
Home Activity: Identify a topic of interest at home and two opposing points of view. With your child, debate the issue to support your position. Which side of the discussion presents the best supporting information?

Use with Pupil Edition, p. 290

Assessment Support

Use the following Assessment Book pages and The test maker to assess content and skills in Chapter 9 and Unit 4. You can also view and print Assessment Book pages from the Teacher Resources CD-ROM.

Assessment Book, p. 45

Chapter 9

Part 1: Content Test

Directions: Fill in the circle next to the correct answer.

Lesson Objective (1:1)

1. Which of the following does NOT describe the early Ojibwa way of life?
   - ● They lived on fertile land and grew most of their vegetables.
   - Ⓑ Birchbark canoes were their main method of transportation.
   - Ⓒ They traveled through the northern Great Lakes region to gather food.
   - Ⓓ They grew only a small amount of vegetables.

Lesson Objective (1:1, 2)

2. What do the Ojibwa of today have in common with the early Ojibwa?
   - Ⓐ They still live on reservations and travel mainly by birchbark canoe.
   - Ⓑ Many have left the northern Great Lakes region to live in cities.
   - Ⓒ They still live in Minneapolis, Minnesota, and teach others how to work in the cities.
   - ● They still live, hunt, and fish in the northern Great Lakes region.

Lesson Objective (2:1, 2)

3. Fur trading posts were set up along Midwest rivers and lakes following the route of which two explorers?
   - Ⓐ Podlasek and Jolliet
   - Ⓑ Marquette and Chicago
   - Ⓒ Sault St. Marie and Wisconsin
   - ● Jolliet and Marquette

Lesson Objective (2:3)

4. Which two major Midwestern cities began as forts or trading posts?
   - ● Chicago and Sault St. Marie
   - Ⓑ Mackinaw and Green Bay
   - Ⓒ Marquette and Jolliet
   - Ⓓ Minneapolis and Duluth

Lesson Objective (2:3)

5. Which is NOT an effect of fur trading on the Midwest?
   - Ⓐ Trading posts were set up where fur traders settled.
   - ● People left the Midwest in search of furs.
   - Ⓒ Native Americans settled at the forts to farm and sell crops.
   - Ⓓ Communities and major cities grew around the forts.

Lesson Objective (3:1, 2)

6. Which is NOT something the Midwestern pioneers did when they first arrived in the Midwest?
   - Ⓐ started farms
   - Ⓑ rushed in to claim the land
   - Ⓒ built houses
   - ● lived peacefully with the Native American groups in the region

Lesson Objective (3:3)

7. What was one disadvantage of homes built out of sod?
   - ● They were hard to keep clean.
   - Ⓑ They were warm in the winter.
   - Ⓒ They were cool in the summer.
   - Ⓓ They were made of trees.

Use with Pupil Edition, p. 284

Assessment Book, p. 46

Lesson Objective (3:4)

8. Which problem did John Deere help Midwest farmers solve?
   - Ⓐ There was little water on the prairie.
   - ● The tough prairie sod was hard to plow.
   - Ⓒ The people had limited access to railroads.
   - Ⓓ There were many tree stumps on the land.

Lesson Objective (3:5)

9. What can happen to farmland during times of drought?
   - Ⓐ It can become richer and more fertile.
   - Ⓑ It can produce many different crops.
   - ● It can turn to dust and blow away.
   - Ⓓ It can wash away with the rainfall.

Lesson Objective (4:1)

10. Which does NOT describe Cahokia, the ancient Midwest trading center?
    - Ⓐ Mounds were used for burial sites and ceremonies.
    - ● Trade goods could not be shipped to and from there.
    - Ⓒ It was close to the junction of three rivers.
    - Ⓓ It was a meeting place of many cultures.

Lesson Objective (4:2)

11. Why did President Thomas Jefferson want to find a water route to the West?
    - Ⓐ to force Native American groups to leave
    - Ⓑ to swim to the Pacific
    - Ⓒ to sail to the Atlantic
    - ● to expand trade

Lesson Objective (4:2)

12. What is one thing that Lewis and Clark did NOT do?
    - Ⓐ They went in search of a water route from the Midwest to the Pacific Ocean.
    - ● They discovered an easy water route from the Midwest to the Pacific Ocean.
    - Ⓒ They asked Native Americans to trade with pioneers.
    - Ⓓ They set out on their expedition from an area near St. Louis.

Lesson Objective (4:3)

13. How did steamboats help farmers in the early 1800s?
    - ● They could ship their grain by boat to markets in St. Louis.
    - Ⓑ They could raise their cattle on huge steamboats.
    - Ⓒ They could irrigate their land with water from the boats.
    - Ⓓ They could grow crops near the ports where the boats stopped.

Lesson Objective (4:5)

14. What was one advantage of shipping by rail instead of by steamboat?
    - Ⓐ Trains could not run along the rails in cold weather.
    - Ⓑ Trains were only built along a waterway.
    - ● Rail lines could be built almost anywhere.
    - Ⓓ Shipping by rail was slower than by steamboat.

46 Unit 4, Chapter 9 Test Assessment Book

Use with Pupil Edition, p. 284

Assessment Book, p. 47

Lesson Objective (4:4)

15. What did the U.S. government begin to build in the 1950s?
    - Ⓐ Illinois Waterway
    - Ⓑ transcontinental railroad
    - ● interstate highway system
    - Ⓓ two-lane country roads

Part 2: Skills Test

Directions: Use complete sentences to answer questions 1–5. Use a separate sheet of paper if you need more space.

1. How did the fur trade change Ojibwa culture? **Cause and Effect**

   The Ojibwa began to spend more time trapping and trading. They no longer produced everything they wanted or needed. They were able to trade skins for items they wanted from the Europeans.

2. How is the Ojibwa way of life today similar to their early way of life? How is it different? **Compare and Contrast**

   Similar: many Ojibwa still live in the northern Great Lakes region. Some still hunt and fish and make traditional crafts. Different: some live on reservations. Many have left the reservations to live and work in cities.

3. What are two details to support the following main idea? **Midwestern farmhouses in the 1800s were small and simple. Main Idea and Details**

   Possible answers: Midwestern farmhouses usually had only one room; many were log cabins, made of trees cut down by the farmers themselves; many were made of sod.

Assessment Book Unit 4, Chapter 9 Test 47

Use with Pupil Edition, p. 284

Assessment Book, p. 48

4. What inventions and developments helped the Midwest to become a hub of transportation and trade? Explain. **Express Ideas**

   Possible answers: Because the Midwest is centrally located, its waterways, rail lines, and highways made it a hub for transportation and trade. The steamboat could carry tons of cargo, turning rivers into major highways. Rail lines connected the Midwest to the entire country. The interstate highway system linked all the states.

5. What type of person might choose to be an early explorer, like Louis Jolliet or William Clark? What character traits do you think would be important to an explorer? Why? **Generalize**

   Answers should reflect an understanding of early explorers, the conditions under which they explored, and traits suited for rugged and dangerous environments.

Use with Pupil Edition, p. 284

Assessment Support

Assessment Book, p. 49

Unit 4

Part 1: Content Test

Directions: Fill in the circle next to the correct answer.

Lesson Objective (8–1:1)

1. How were the Great Lakes formed?
- Ⓐ by volcano eruptions
- Ⓑ by wind and water erosion
- Ⓒ by engineers who designed them
- ● by melting glaciers

Lesson Objective (8–1:2, 3)

2. What did engineers build to make a smooth passageway from the Great Lakes to the Atlantic Ocean?
- Ⓐ barges and waterways on the St. Lawrence River
- ● canals and locks on the St. Lawrence Seaway
- Ⓒ locks and canals on the Illinois River
- Ⓓ bridges on the Chicago River

Lesson Objective (8–1:5)

3. Why was it important to connect the Great Lakes with the Mississippi River?
- Ⓐ Shipping goods by water is very fast.
- Ⓑ Goods can be shipped by rail at low cost.
- Ⓒ Shipping goods by truck is very slow.
- ● Goods can be shipped by water at low cost.

Lesson Objective (8–2:1)

4. How are today's badlands different from the same area millions of years ago?
- Ⓐ Today rivers flow through a lush, green plain near the badlands.
- Ⓑ Today the climate of the badlands is warm and humid.
- ● Today the badlands are made up of dry hills and sharp cliffs.
- Ⓓ Today the region is surrounded by prairies full of trees.

Lesson Objective (8–3:1, 2, 3, 5)

5. Which of these is NOT a reason why Great Plains farmers are able to grow corn and soybeans?
- Ⓐ The soil is rich and deep.
- ● It rains often there.
- Ⓒ Farmers irrigate the land.
- Ⓓ The growing season is long.

Lesson Objective (9–1:1)

6. Which present-day city is NOT one at which the Ojibwa settled?
- Ⓐ Duluth, Minnesota
- Ⓑ Milwaukee, Wisconsin
- Ⓒ Mt. Pleasant, Michigan
- ● Chicago, Illinois

Lesson Objective (9–1:1, 2)

7. How has Ojibwa culture changed since the 1600s?
- Ⓐ Today many Ojibwa hunt to earn a living.
- Ⓑ Today many Ojibwa fish to earn a living.
- ● Today some Ojibwa live on reservations.
- Ⓓ Today many Ojibwa live near the Great Lakes.

Use with Pupil Edition, p. 288

Assessment Book, p. 50

Lesson Objective (9–2:1, 2)

8. Why did the fur trade develop in the Midwest?
- Ⓐ Jean Baptiste Point Du Sable was born there.
- Ⓑ The Ottawa, Ojibwa, and Huron tribes explored there.
- Ⓒ Louis Jolliet and Jacques Marquette were born there.
- ● Louis Jolliet and Jacques Marquette explored there.

Lesson Objective (9–2:3, 4)

9. What major Midwestern city began as Jean Baptiste Point Du Sable's trading post?
- ● Chicago
- Ⓑ Detroit
- Ⓒ Sault St. Marie
- Ⓓ Green Bay

Lesson Objective (9–3:1)

10. Which is NOT a cause of the land rushes in the Midwest in the 1800s?
- Ⓐ Thousands of settlers wanted to move there to start farms.
- Ⓑ Years of suffering had weakened many Native American groups.
- ● Farmers overused the land and it turned to dust.
- Ⓓ European pioneers continued pushing westward.

Lesson Objective (9–3:3, 4, 5, 6)

11. Which of these was a positive development of early farming in the Midwest?
- Ⓐ Because of drought and the overuse of the land, the soil turned to dust and many farms failed.
- ● John Deere made a new steel plow to make turning the prairies into farmland much easier.
- Ⓒ Settlers had to chop down trees and dig up stumps to clear fields for farming.
- Ⓓ Many farmers lived in homes made of sod, or the grass, roots, and dirt from the ground's top layer.

Lesson Objective (9–4:1)

12. Which is NOT a reason why Cahokia was a key trading center in the ancient Midwest?
- Ⓐ It was close to the junction of three rivers.
- ● Some mounds were platforms for homes.
- Ⓒ Thousands of people may have gathered there for festivals and markets.
- Ⓓ It was a meeting place for many cultures.

Lesson Objective (9–4:2)

13. Which city did President Jefferson hope would become the Gateway to the West?
- ● St. Louis
- Ⓑ Chicago
- Ⓒ Minneapolis
- Ⓓ Green Bay

Use with Pupil Edition, p. 288

Assessment Book, p. 51

Lesson Objective (9–4:2)

14. Which was NOT a goal of the Lewis and Clark expedition?
- Ⓐ expand fur trade
- Ⓑ find a river flowing to the Pacific Ocean
- Ⓒ learn about land and peoples of the West
- ● find a water route to the Atlantic Ocean

Lesson Objective (9–4:3, 4, 5)

15. Which form of transportation did NOT help the Midwest become the hub of the nation?
- Ⓐ interstate highways
- ● airplanes
- Ⓒ steamboats
- Ⓓ railroads

Part 2: Skills Test

Directions: Use complete sentences to answer questions 1–5. Use a separate sheet of paper if you need more space.

1. Would you rather live in the badlands region of South Dakota today or millions of years ago? Why? **Express Ideas**

Answers should include an understanding of how the badlands region has changed over time.

2. Suppose you are an early French fur trapper in the Midwest. What kinds of problems might you find after moving there? How might you solve these problems? **Solve Problems**

Problems faced might include a language barrier and other cultural differences with Native American groups, missing your family and home, or competition from other trappers; solutions should reflect logical thinking.

Use with Pupil Edition, p. 288

Assessment Book, p. 52

3. How do you think the Midwest might be different today if the government had not forced many Native Americans to move to reservations? **Predict**

Answers should include an understanding of the interactions between Native Americans and settlers during the settling of the Midwest.

4. What opinions do you have about the Midwest region? Would you like to live there? Do you think it is an important region of our country? Write two statements of opinion and two facts about the Midwest. **Fact and Opinion**

Answers should include an understanding of the Midwest region and the differences between fact and opinion.

5. Study the graph and then answer the questions. **Compare Line and Bar Graphs**

a. How many farms were in Nebraska in 1997?

51,454 farms

b. What does the graph tell you about the size of farms in Wisconsin from 1982 until 1997? How does that compare to the same period for Nebraska?

The farms in both Wisconsin and Nebraska got smaller from 1982 until 1997.

c. Could you show the same information from this graph on a bar graph?

Yes, you could use the same labels and then use different colored bars for each state.

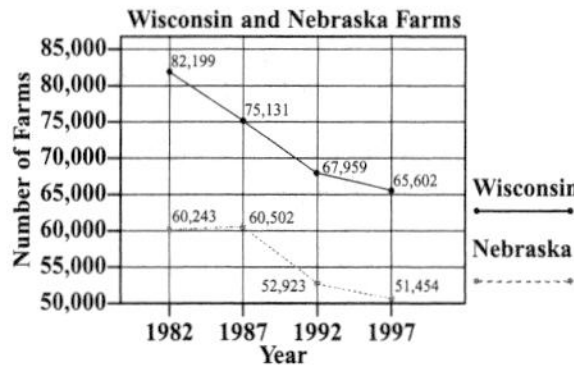

Use with Pupil Edition, p. 288

CHAPTER 9

People of the Midwest

Chapter 9 Outline

- **Lesson 1, *The Ojibwa,*** pp. 256–259
- **Citizen Heroes: *Keeping a Culture Strong,*** pp. 260–261
- **Research and Writing Skills: *Use a Search Engine on the Internet,*** pp. 262–263
- **Lesson 2, *The Fur Trade,*** pp. 264–266
- **Biography: *Jean Baptiste Point Du Sable,*** p. 267
- **Colonial Williamsburg: *Trading for Goods,*** p. 268–269
- **Lesson 3, *Building Farms,*** pp. 270–274
- **Biography: *John Deere,*** p. 275
- **Lesson 4, *Hub of the Nation,*** pp. 276–282
- **Biography: *Mark Twain,*** p. 283

Resources

- Workbook, p. 59: Vocabulary Preview
- Vocabulary Cards
- Social Studies Plus!

Duluth, Minnesota: Lesson 1

Ask students to describe the scene in the picture and suggest what advantages a lakeside village might offer Native Americans in the 1600s. (Easy access to transportation on water)

Sault Sainte Marie, Michigan: Lesson 2

This is a picture of a fort built in Michigan in the 1700s. Ask students why French traders might have built forts. (To protect themselves)

Wapello, Iowa: Lesson 3

Ask students to identify the kind of home shown in this picture. (House of sod)

St. Louis, Missouri: Lesson 4

Ask students what they can observe as differences between the early settlements (see pictures 2 and 3 on this page) and modern St. Louis, as shown here. (The buildings and structures are taller.)

CHAPTER 9 People of the Midwest

Lesson 1

Duluth, Minnesota
The Ojibwa settle near the Great Lakes.

1

Lesson 2

Sault Sainte Marie, Michigan
The French trade with Native Americans.

2

Lesson 3

Wapello County, Iowa
Settlers rush to claim land.

3

Lesson 4

St. Louis, Missouri
The Gateway Arch celebrates the western growth of the United States.

4

Practice and Extend

Vocabulary Preview

- Use Workbook p. 59 to help students preview the vocabulary words in this chapter.
- Use Vocabulary Cards to preview key concept words in this chapter.

Also on Teacher Resources CD-ROM.

Workbook, p. 59

Use with Chapter 9.

Vocabulary Preview

Directions: These are the vocabulary words from Chapter 9. How much do you know about these words? Write each word on the line provided beside its definition. You may use your glossary.

fur trade	sod	mound	transcontinental railroad
mission	drought	steamboat	interstate highway system
trading post	Dust Bowl	hub	

1. ________ grass, roots, and dirt that form the ground's top layer
2. ________ set of wide, fast, interconnecting highways to link the states
3. ________ the exchange of animal skins for other goods, such as cloth, guns, and knives
4. ________ boat powered by a steam engine
5. ________ time of little rain
6. ________ rail line that crosses the entire country
7. ________ settlement set up by a religious group to teach its religion and to help the people of an area.
8. ________ area in the Midwest and Southwest that suffered the most during the drought in the 1930s
9. ________ center of activity
10. ________ type of store at which goods are traded
11. ________ pile of earth or stones

Notes for Home: Your child learned the vocabulary terms for Chapter 9.
Home Activity: Discuss with your child any of the terms above that may be related to your community today or in the past. For example, does the interstate highway system run through your community?

Locating Places

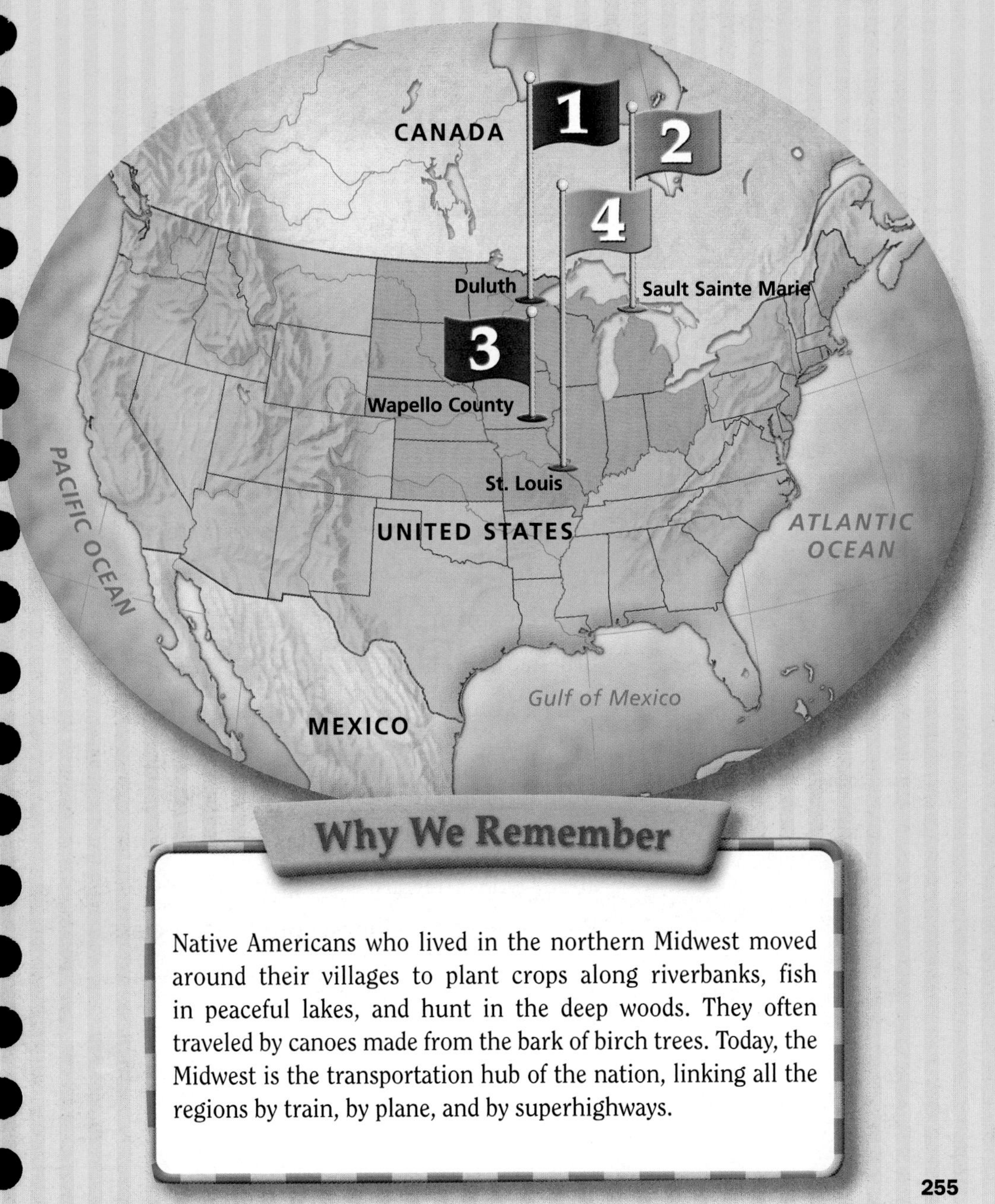

Why We Remember

Native Americans who lived in the northern Midwest moved around their villages to plant crops along riverbanks, fish in peaceful lakes, and hunt in the deep woods. They often traveled by canoes made from the bark of birch trees. Today, the Midwest is the transportation hub of the nation, linking all the regions by train, by plane, and by superhighways.

255

Locating Places

- Have students examine the pictures shown on p. 254 for Lessons 1, 2, 3, and 4.
- Remind students that each picture is coded with both a number and a color to link it to a place on the map on p. 255.

Why We Remember

Have students read the "Why We Remember" paragraph on p. 255 and ask why places in this chapter might be important. Have them consider why the Midwest is a place that invites movement.

WEB SITE
Technology

You can learn more about Duluth, Minnesota; Sault Sainte Marie, Michigan; Wapello, Iowa; and St. Louis, Missouri by clicking on *Atlas* at **www.sfsocialstudies.com.**

SOCIAL STUDIES STRAND
Geography

Mental Mapping Have students name the state in the Midwest that they would most like to visit and draw an outline map of it from memory. Ask students to share their maps with the class and tell why they would like to visit the state.

The Ojibwa

Objectives

- Describe early Ojibwa culture.
- Describe the ways Ojibwa culture has changed since the mid-1600s.

Vocabulary

fur trade, p. 258

Resources

- Workbook, p. 60
- Transparency 20
- Every Student Learns Guide, pp. 106–109
- Quick Study, pp. 54–55

Quick Teaching Plan

If time is short, have students make a Venn diagram to compare and contrast the Ojibwa of the past with the Ojibwa of the present.

- Have students compare common features in the overlapping area of the circles.
- Have them contrast details in the non-overlapping parts of the circles.

1 Introduce and Motivate

Preview To activate prior knowledge, ask students to list ways that people preserve and celebrate their culture. Ask why this might be an important thing to do. Tell students they will learn more about ways to keep a culture strong as they read Lesson 1.

You Are There Ask students if they have ever been to an event celebrating a specific culture. Have volunteers describe what the event was like.

LESSON 1

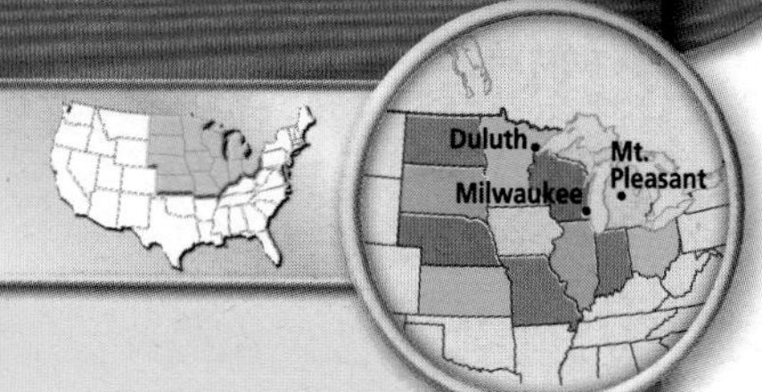

The Ojibwa

PREVIEW

Focus on the Main Idea
The Ojibwa have maintained important cultural traditions and have contributed to the culture of the Midwest.

PLACES
Duluth, Minnesota
Milwaukee, Wisconsin
Mt. Pleasant, Michigan

VOCABULARY
fur trade

▶ Ojibwa Talking Stick

You Are There Today your friend Ron, an Ojibwa, has brought his talking stick to class. You and your classmates are sitting in a circle while Ron speaks. He says that the Ojibwa use the talking stick to make sure that each person in a group has a chance to express his or her thoughts. Whoever holds the stick has the right to talk. Everyone else has to show respect and remain silent. When the speaker is finished talking, he or she passes the stick on.

The students in your class decide to use the talking stick to talk about what they wish were different in the world. You enjoy listening to your classmates and thinking about what they are saying. You decide to ask Ron more about Ojibwa culture after class.

Cause and Effect As you read, think about the effects the Europeans had on the changing ways of the Ojibwa.

256

Practice and Extend

READING SKILL
Cause and Effect

In the Lesson Review, students complete a graphic organizer like the one below. You may want to provide students with a copy of Transparency 20 to complete as they read the lesson.

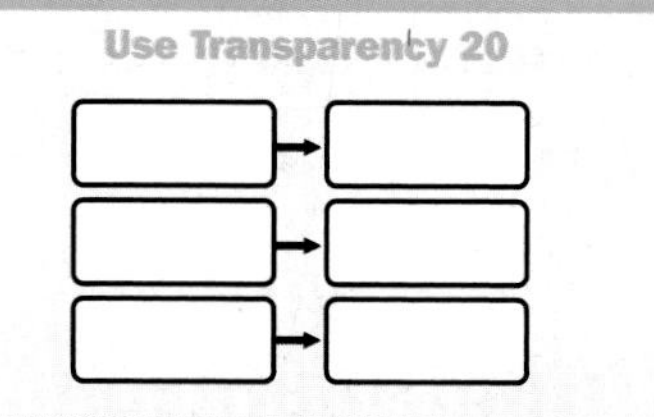

VOCABULARY
Context Clues

Relate to students that the meaning of *trade* includes buying and selling, as well as the exchange of goods that one usually associates with the word. Lead them to realize that the use of money is simply a standardized way of exchanging work or goods for other work or goods. Discuss the places in which we see the word *trade* today, such as the North American Free Trade Agreement or trading ball players between clubs.

Early Ojibwa Culture

The Ojibwa (oh JIB way) lived along the coast of the Atlantic Ocean. Centuries ago, they decided to move westward. They traveled along the St. Lawrence River and other rivers and lakes in what is now Canada. By 1641 they had reached the northern Great Lakes region. They settled in the present-day cities of **Duluth, Minnesota; Milwaukee, Wisconsin;** and **Mt. Pleasant, Michigan.**

The new Ojibwa homeland was covered with thick forests. The hunting was excellent. Fish from the region's many lakes and rivers were another plentiful source of food. The Ojibwa also gathered wild rice and berries from the forests, marshes, and waterways. In most of the region, they grew only a small amount of vegetables. The forests were too thick, the summers were too short, and the soil was not rich enough for much farming. 1

The Ojibwa had to travel widely to hunt, fish, and gather food. They traveled through the northern Great Lakes region in canoes made from the bark of birch trees. These lightweight, 2 durable boats would later become a main method of transportation for 3 European traders.

REVIEW Why did the Ojibwa rely on fish, game, and wild rice instead of farming as their main sources of food? **Main Idea and Details**

▶ This historic photo shows an Ojibwa couple carrying a birchbark canoe ashore in Minnesota.

257

CURRICULUM CONNECTION
Science

Learn More About Wild Rice

- Have students use library or online resources to compare the rice they read about in Chapter 8 with wild rice.
- Ask students to find out which animals feed on wild rice. (Waterfowl and other birds that seek shelter in wild rice stands eat it.)

BUILD BACKGROUND
ESL Support

Locate Place Names

Beginning On an outline map of the United States, have students locate and label the places discussed in this lesson.

Intermediate Ask students to write original sentences that use place names from the lesson.

Advanced Have students write a paragraph describing one of the places from the lesson.

For additional ESL support, use Every Student Learns Guide, pp. 106–109.

2 Teach and Discuss

PAGE 257

Early Ojibwa Culture

Quick Summary Centuries ago the Ojibwa moved from the Atlantic Coast to the northern Great Lakes region, where they lived by hunting, fishing, and gathering.

1 **How did the Ojibwa use the natural resources of their new homeland?** Trees for homes and canoes; forests for hunting; lakes and rivers for food, water, and transportation **Draw Conclusions**

2 **Summarize the importance of the birchbark canoes to the Ojibwa.** The light, durable canoes were used by the Ojibwa to travel in order to hunt, fish and gather food. They also became an important method of transportation for European traders. **Summarize**

SOCIAL STUDIES STRAND
Culture

Some Native American tribes made a food called pemmican, a mixture of meat, berries, and a large amount of fat, dried into cakes. It was a high-energy food that was convenient for travelers.

3 **Why would the Ojibwa need a special food for traveling? What kinds of foods today are similar to pemmican?** They traveled very often and needed a convenient, easy food to take with them. Possible answers: Jerky, trail mixes, energy bars **Compare and Contrast**

✓ **Ongoing Assessment**

If... students have difficulty comparing pemmican to a food today,	**then...** ask what special, long-lasting dried foods appeal to campers, hikers, and athletes.

✓ **REVIEW ANSWER** Farming was difficult, with thick forests, short summers (short growing seasons), and poor soil. Wild rice was available to be gathered. Fish and game were plentiful. **Main Idea and Details**

PAGES 258–259

Native Americans of the Midwest Today

Quick Summary While many Native Americans still live on reservations, some choose to live in cities.

4 **Why did the Ojibwa spend more time trapping after the European fur traders arrived?** To obtain skins to trade, in addition to those they needed for their own use Cause and Effect

5 **What advantages and disadvantages did the fur trade bring to the Ojibwa?** They traded furs and obtained a broader range of goods, but they were no longer self-sufficient. Evaluate

6 **Some Native Americans grow up on reservations and later move to cities. Why might some of them find a place like the American Indian Center helpful?** Possible answer: Their lives on reservations might not have prepared them to live in cities. Make Inferences

Native Americans of the Midwest Today

In the mid-1600s, Europeans first came to the northern Great Lakes region where the Ojibwa lived. The Europeans traded cloth, guns, and knives for skins
4 from beavers trapped by the Ojibwa. This **fur trade** changed Ojibwa culture. The Ojibwa started to spend more time trapping and trading than they had done before. They no longer produced
5 everything they wanted and needed.

Today, many Ojibwa still live in the northern Great Lakes region. Some live on reservations. These reservations resulted from treaties, or agreements that the Ojibwa made with the United States government. Some Ojibwa still hunt and fish and make traditional crafts. Many have also left the reservation and have gone to live and work in cities. Centers like the American Indian Center in Chicago, Illinois, offer technology training for Native Americans. The
6 centers also teach the skills of different trades.

The Sioux (SOO) Indians also live on the Great Plains. The Sioux belong to several different groups: Lakota, Nakota, and Dakota. Today, many Sioux live on reservations in several Midwestern states. They live in South Dakota, North Dakota, Minnesota, and Nebraska.

Some Sioux live in cities, such as Minneapolis and St. Paul in Minnesota. Many Sioux who live in cities keep their ties to their culture by visiting the reservations for special occasions, such as traditional ceremonies. Many urban Sioux also take part in Native American cultural activities at urban social centers.

▶ **This Ojibwa boy is wearing a traditional costume.**

258

Practice and Extend

ISSUES AND VIEWPOINTS
Critical Thinking

Analyze a Viewpoint

- Ojibwa preserve their traditions by teaching their traditions in school. At Lac Courte Oreilles Ojibwa Community College, located on an Ojibwa reservation in Wisconsin, students study science and computers, but they also build birchbark canoes.
- The following quotation is from Marilyn Benton, a professor at the college. Read it to students and ask them to discuss the school's point of view about knowledge and culture.

  "Identity requires knowledge of the past. So our mission at the college is to teach the traditional language and culture in order to restore the identity."

  (cited in *Contemporary Education* by David McGrath)

CURRICULUM CONNECTION
Music

Discover Traditional Music

- Have students use online or library resources to research the role of music in Native American ceremonies.
- Have students find, download, and share with the class a video or sound file of music from a Native American ceremony.

▶ Ojibwa harvesting wild rice

Other Native Americans who live in the Midwest include the Ottawa and the Potawatomi. Originally, these groups are thought to have come with the Ojibwa from the Atlantic coast to the Great Lakes region. The Ottawa and the Potawatomi supported themselves like the Ojibwa by hunting, fishing, and gathering wild rice. They also grew corn on their farmland. Today, some Ottawa and Potawatomi still live in the Midwest. Some Ottawa live in Michigan. Some Potawatomi live in Kansas, Michigan, and Wisconsin.

7

REVIEW Name one way that the Sioux and Ojibwa have continued to follow their traditions. Main Idea and Details

Summarize the Lesson

- **The Ojibwa live in the northern Great Lakes region.**
- **Hundreds of years ago, the Ojibwa adapted to life in the region by hunting, fishing, and gathering wild rice and other plants.**
- **Many Ojibwa and other Native American tribes still live in the Midwest.**

LESSON 1 REVIEW

Check Facts and Main Ideas

1. Cause and Effect On a separate sheet of paper, list the effect that goes with the appropriate cause and the cause that goes with the appropriate effect.

Cause	Effect
The soil in the northern Great Lakes region was poor.	The Ojibwa grew only a small amount of vegetables.
The Europeans traded cloth, guns, and knives for animal skins.	The Ojibwa started to spend more time trapping.
The Ojibwa made treaties with the U.S. government.	The Ojibwa still live in the Northern Great Lakes region.

2. Describe the places where the Ojibwa traveled before the Europeans came to the Great Lakes region.
3. What is one way that Ojibwa use of the land changed after Europeans came to the region? Use the term **fur trade** in your answer.
4. How do some Native Americans help other Native Americans today?
5. **Critical Thinking:** ***Point of View*** What special relationship do the Ojibwa have with the United States government?

Link to Mathematics

Make a Bar Graph Find out the population of the Ojibwa in the four different midwestern states where most Ojibwa live: Michigan, Wisconsin, Minnesota, and North Dakota. Make a bar graph that shows the Ojibwa population of these states.

259

7 In what ways were the early Ottawa and Potawatomi similar to the Ojibwa? Both the Ottawa and the Potawatomi hunted, fished, and gathered rice to support themselves like the Ojibwa. Compare and Contrast

✓ **REVIEW ANSWER** Many Sioux visit reservations for traditional ceremonies; some Ojibwa still make traditional crafts. Main Idea and Details

3 Close and Assess

Summarize the Lesson

Have students take turns reading aloud the three main points. Have them write phrases on sentence strips, then join them to make cause-and-effect sentences illustrating each point.

✓ **LESSON 1 REVIEW**

1. Cause and Effect For possible answers, see the reduced pupil page.
2. The Ojibwa traveled along the St. Lawrence River and other rivers and lakes in the northern Great Lakes region.

Test Talk

Write Your Answer to Score High

3. Ask students to reread their answer to make sure they described the Ojibwa *after* the Europeans arrived. The Ojibwa spent more time trapping and fur trading. They no longer produced everything themselves.

4. They set up organizations and build places such as the American Indian Center to teach the skills of different trades.
5. **Critical Thinking: *Point of View*** Possible answer: Some Ojibwa live on reservations that resulted from treaties made with the U.S. government.

Link to Mathematics

Students should use print or online resources to research their answers.

MEETING INDIVIDUAL NEEDS
Leveled Practice

Identify Ojibwa Crafts Ask students to find out more about Ojibwa crafts.

Easy Have students analyze the picture of a canoe shown in this lesson. Ask them why canoes might have been important to the Ojibwa. **Reteach**

On-Level Have students analyze the picture of a birchbark canoe in this lesson and research how it was made. **Extend**

Challenge Have students work in groups to research how birchbark canoes are made. Then have them write step-by-step instructions for making a birchbark canoe. **Enrich**

For a Lesson Summary, use Quick Study, p. 54.

Workbook, p. 60

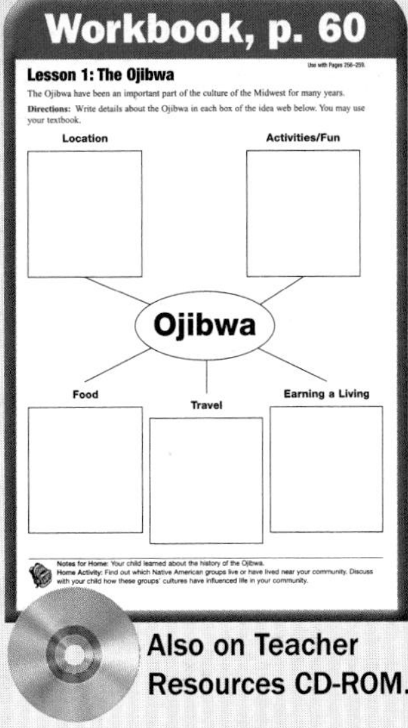

Also on Teacher Resources CD-ROM.

Keeping a Culture Strong

Objectives

- Explain the purpose of the American Indian Center and Joseph Podlasek's role in developing respect within the Native American community.
- Describe what Joseph Podlasek has done for the Ojibwa community.

1 Introduce and Motivate

Preview To activate prior knowledge, ask students to describe the services and facilities they think community centers offer.

2 Teach and Discuss

1 How was Joseph Podlasek's first experience at the American Indian Center similar to those of his ancestors who engaged in the fur trade? He traded his services for other services from the center much like his ancestors traded furs for other goods. Generalize

SOCIAL STUDIES STRAND
Citizenship

Good citizens play active roles in their communities by respecting the needs of the community and contributing to its goals.

2 How did Joseph Podlasek show his respect for the community? He wanted to contribute to the community by offering his own services, by becoming the center's director, by helping other Native Americans, and by developing a program for students. Summarize

CITIZEN HEROES

Keeping a Culture Strong

How do you make a community stronger? One way is by celebrating holidays and other events together. Joseph Podlasek, an Ojibwa, works hard to keep his community and its culture strong.

Joseph Podlasek's mother, a member of the Ojibwa from the Lac Courte Oreilles (La COO TOO Ray) Reservation in Wisconsin, had always taught him to respect his Native American roots. In 1989, when Joseph was looking for a new career, he turned to the American Indian Center for help. The organization allowed him to use his construction skills in exchange for taking courses 1 in a computer technology program. Joseph then began a life-long journey teaching people to respect his culture.

Joseph Podlasek is now the Executive Director of the American Indian Center. The American Indian Center has become a symbol of Chicago's American Indian community. The center promotes the well-being, education, and business of Chicago's Native American community. The Center also teaches people about the culture of the Ojibwa and other Native Americans.

Practice and Extend

Problem Solving

Use a Problem-Solving Process

- Have students consider the following problem-solving scenario. **Suppose you want to make a contribution to your community. Consider what you could do and how you could persuade your parents or other adults to help you get started.**
- Students should use the following problem-solving process to deal with the scenario. For each step in the process, have students work in small groups to discuss and write about what must be considered as they solve the problem. Then have students compare their solution with that of Joseph Podlasek.

1. **Identify a problem.**
2. **Gather information.**
3. **List and consider options.**
4. **Consider advantages and disadvantages.**
5. **Choose and implement a solution.**
6. **Evaluate the effectiveness of the solution.**

BUILDING CITIZENSHIP

Caring
Respect
Responsibility
Fairness
Honesty
Courage

The American Indian Center has a program for students in Illinois. The program includes storytelling, drumming, and other traditions. But most important of all, students learn about the talking stick. People pass the talking stick around a circle. A person who receives the stick may speak. Everyone else is silent, showing respect to the speaker. Many students who visit the American Indian Center make a talking stick to take home. 2

Joseph Podlasek enjoys working at the center because of what it has taught him.

"It is about going full circle and giving back to the community. I was taught that if and when possible, you should provide back to the community that has helped you grow." 3 4

Respect in Action

Show how people in the community can teach and demonstrate respect for their cultures.

Primary Source

From a December 2000 interview with a Scott Foresman editor

3 Based on the quotation, why do you think Joseph Podlasek works at the American Indian Center? Possible answer: He wants to give back to his community. **Analyze Primary Sources**

4 Do you agree that it is important for people to give back to their community? Why? Possible answers: Yes; Because it makes the community stronger; to repay the community for helping a person grow **Express Ideas**

3 Close and Assess

Respect in Action

- Encourage students to make a class list of ways people can demonstrate their respect for a community and teach it to others.
- Have students share ways children can show respect for their community. (Volunteer, support events, read about local current events, learn more about the community and its traditions)

MEETING INDIVIDUAL NEEDS
Learning Styles

Use a Talking Stick Using their individual learning styles, students practice one of Joseph Podlasek's communication techniques.

Kinesthetic Learning Have students make a talking stick.

Social Learning Have students use a talking stick to discuss a current school or community issue.

Auditory Learning Have students listen to the group using the talking stick and then comment on whether the technique was effective.

Use a Search Engine on the Internet

Objective

- Use a search engine to find information on the Internet.

Vocabulary

research, p. 262; **Internet,** p. 262; **search engine,** p. 262

Resource

- Workbook, p. 61

1 Introduce and Motivate

What is a search engine? Ask students how people today might use computers to gather information. Then have students read the **What?** section of text on p. 262 to help set the purpose of the lesson.

Why use a search engine? Have students read the **Why?** section of text on p. 262. Ask them if they believe online magazines and newspapers will someday replace paper ones.

2 Teach and Discuss

How is this skill used? Examine with students the illustrations about using a search engine on pp. 262–263.

- Have students restate in their own words how a search engine works.
- If you have a classroom computer with Internet access, demonstrate the use of a search engine. Guide students through an evaluation of the results.
- Give students some practice with choosing keywords. For example, ask them what keywords might be useful if they want to find out more about Ojibwa culture today. (Ojibwa Nation, Ojibwa reservations, or Ojibwa culture)
- Have students read the **How?** section of text on p. 263.

Research and Writing Skills

Use a Search Engine on the Internet

What? You can find out more about a topic by doing **research.** One place to find lots of research information is on the Internet. The **Internet** is a huge network of computers. It contains many World Wide Web (Web) sites. One of the quickest ways to find information on the Internet is to use a search engine. A **search engine** is a special Web site that locates other Web sites that can provide information on the topic you are researching.

Why? A search engine can provide links to Web sites from all over the world. The search engine usually gives you the title of the Web site and a little information about it. From the search engine, you can choose a link to find out more about the topic you are researching.

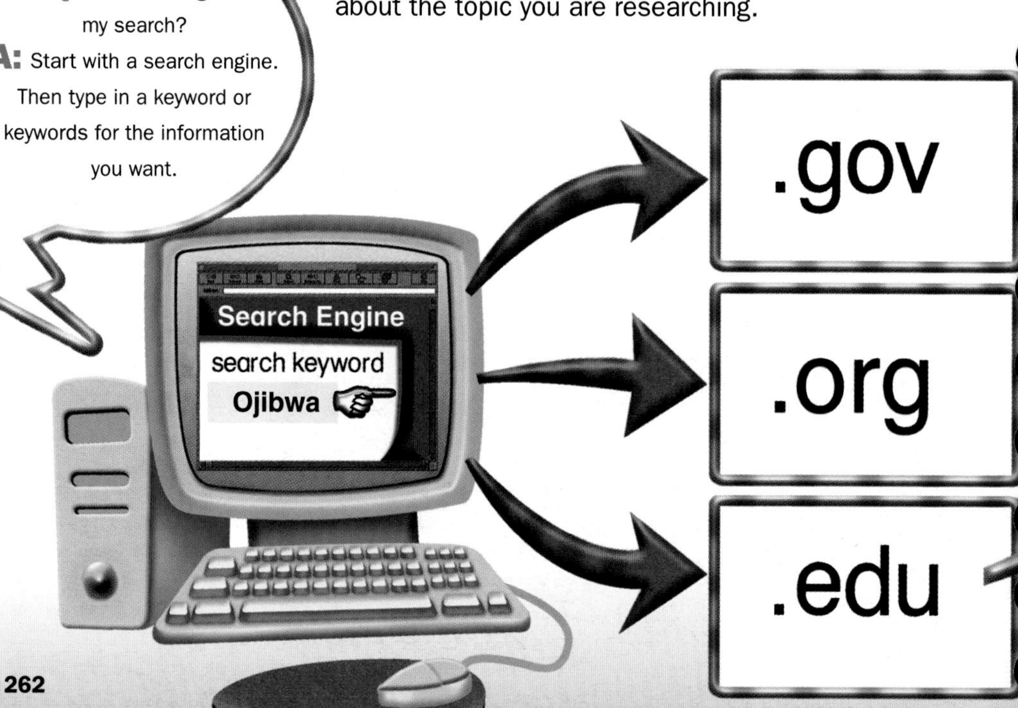
Q: How do I begin my search?
A: Start with a search engine. Then type in a keyword or keywords for the information you want.
Search Engine
search keyword
Ojibwa
.gov
.org
.edu

262

Practice and Extend

FYI SOCIAL STUDIES
Background

The Internet

- The search engine and Web sites modeled on pp. 262–263 are for demonstration only; they are not active sites on the World Wide Web.
- Each entry highlights information on your topic. If you click on the underlined phrase, your computer will link you to that Web site.
- The last line of the entry gives the Web address (URL).
- You often get the most reliable information from online encyclopedias and from Web sources that end with *.gov* or *.edu.*

Current Events

- Have students choose a current event of interest to them, determine likely keywords, and use a search engine to find information about their topic.
- Ask students to work in small groups to evaluate the results of their search and decide which sources are most useful and reliable.

How? To use a search engine, follow these steps.

1 • First, select a search engine. A teacher or librarian can help you choose a search engine that will best help you conduct your search.

• Next, type in a keyword or two. A keyword is a word or phrase related to your topic, such as "Ojibwa." Then click on "Search." You may have to experiment with different words and phrases. If you need help, click on "Help" or "Search Tips."

2 • If your search brings no results, try another keyword, or ask for help from someone with Internet experience.

3 • Check the facts you find on the Internet with another source such as an encyclopedia.

Think and Apply

1. What is one way that the **Internet** can be a useful **research** tool?
2. What words or phrases would you type in a **search engine** to begin a search of Native Americans in the Midwest?
3. How would you choose which sites to visit from the list that appears on a search engine?

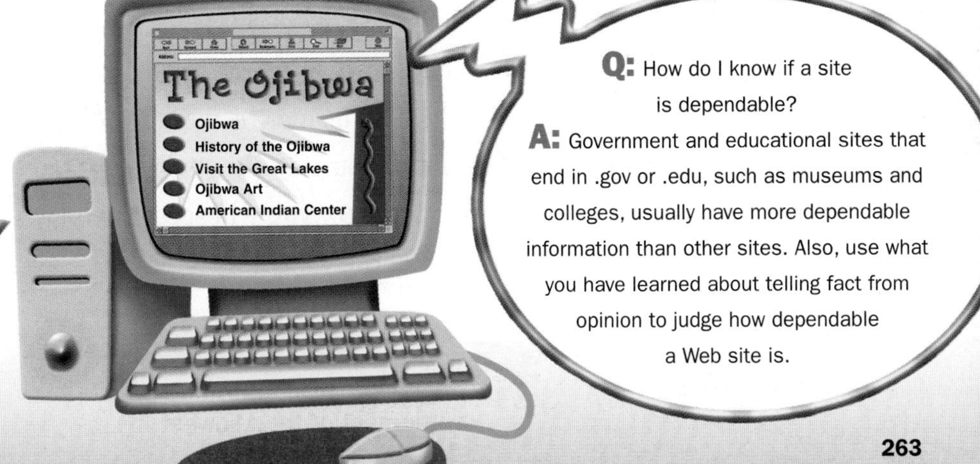

The Ojibwa
Ojibwa
History of the Ojibwa
Visit the Great Lakes
Ojibwa Art
American Indian Center
Q: How do I know if a site is dependable?
A: Government and educational sites that end in .gov or .edu, such as museums and colleges, usually have more dependable information than other sites. Also, use what you have learned about telling fact from opinion to judge how dependable a Web site is.

263

1 **What is the first step in using a search engine?** Select a search engine. Sequence

2 **Name one thing you could do if your search produces no results.** Try a new search word. Main Idea and Details

3 **How can you make sure that you have found dependable information?** Possible answer: Check the information with another source. Main Idea and Details

3 Close and Assess

Think and Apply

1. It can provide current information on many topics.
2. Possible answers: Native Americans, Ojibwa, Chippewa
3. Possible answer: Read the brief information about the Web sites

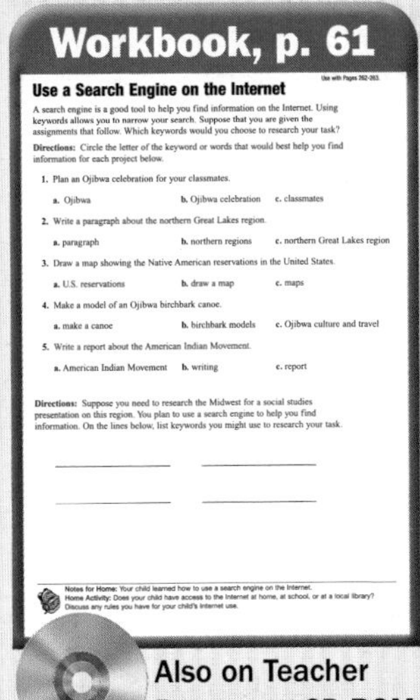
Workbook, p. 61

Use with Pages 262–263.

Use a Search Engine on the Internet

A search engine is a good tool to help you find information on the Internet. Using keywords allows you to narrow your search. Suppose that you are given the assignments that follow. Which keywords would you choose to research your task?

Directions: Circle the letter of the keyword or words that would best help you find information for each project below.

1. Plan an Ojibwa celebration for your classmates.
   a. Ojibwa b. Ojibwa celebration c. classmates
2. Write a paragraph about the northern Great Lakes region.
   a. paragraph b. northern regions c. northern Great Lakes region
3. Draw a map showing the Native American reservations in the United States.
   a. U.S. reservations b. draw a map c. maps
4. Make a model of an Ojibwa birchbark canoe.
   a. make a canoe b. birchbark models c. Ojibwa culture and travel
5. Write a report about the American Indian Movement.
   a. American Indian Movement b. writing c. report

Directions: Suppose you need to research the Midwest for a social studies presentation on this region. You plan to use a search engine to help you find information. On the lines below, list keywords you might use to research your task.

Notes for Home: Your child learned how to use a search engine on the Internet.
Home Activity: Does your child have access to the Internet at home, at school, or at a local library? Discuss any rules you have for your child's Internet use.

Also on Teacher Resources CD-ROM.

MEETING INDIVIDUAL NEEDS

Leveled Practice

Use a Search Engine Students use a search engine to identify Native American groups in the Midwest.

Easy Have students use a search engine and the keywords *Native American*, *Ojibwa*, and *Chippewa* to find two sources of information for each topic. **Reteach**

On-Level Have students use a search engine to find one source of information about the Ojibwa in the seventeenth century and another source about the same group today. **Extend**

Challenge Have students type in eight to ten keywords for Native American groups in the Midwest. Ask them to evaluate the usefulness of a search engine. **Enrich**

The Fur Trade

Objectives

- Describe why the French came to the Midwest in the 1600s.
- Identify the roles of Louis Jolliet and Jacques Marquette in the fur trade.
- Explain the role fur trading played in the development of towns in the Midwest.

Vocabulary

mission, p. 265; **trading post,** p. 266

Resources

- Workbook, p. 62
- Transparency 20
- Every Student Learns Guide, pp. 110–113
- Quick Study, pp. 56–57

Quick Teaching Plan

If time is short, have students take notes on a time line.

- First have students copy the time line dates on the top of p. 264 into their notebooks.
- Have students read the lesson independently.
- As they read, ask them to add appropriate dates or details to their time lines.

1 Introduce and Motivate

Preview To activate prior knowledge, ask students what clothing is made from today. Explain that, in the past, people used more fur for clothing. Tell students they will learn more about the early North American fur trade in this lesson.

You Are There Ask students if they have ever ridden in a boat. Have volunteers describe the experience. Have students compare a canoe or rowboat with a motorboat or large ship. Remind students that there were no motors during this time.

LESSON 2

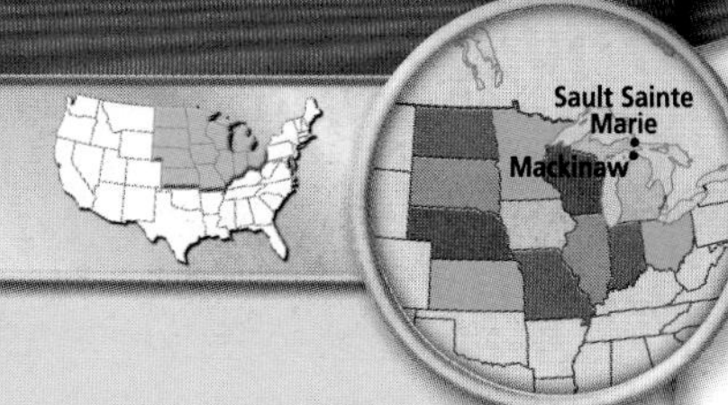

1650		1700		1750
Middle 1600s French fur traders come to the Midwest.	**1673** Marquette and Jolliet explore midwestern waterways.	**1680s** The French build forts as trading posts.	**1700s** Settlements grow around the French forts.	

PREVIEW

Focus on the Main Idea
European settlement in the Great Lakes region and the Mississippi valley began with the fur trade. Many of the region's cities and towns began as fur trading centers.

PEOPLE
Jacques Marquette
Louis Jolliet
Jean Baptiste Point du Sable

PLACES
Mackinaw, Michigan
Sault Sainte Marie, Michigan

VOCABULARY
mission
trading post

The Fur Trade

You Are There You are a trapper. Today you leave on your journey down river. Two young Ojibwa men will be your guides. You are taking beaver and fox furs to trade. The Ojibwa have provided you with sturdy birchbark canoes. They have given you corn and smoked meat to eat on your journey. You have traded metal tools for their goods. As you travel down the rivers you will watch the beauty of the spring flowers blooming and the trees budding. It will be a long journey but you are excited because you know you will see many new things along the way.

▶ Top hat made from beaver fur

Cause and Effect As you read, look for ways that the fur trade affected the settlement of the Midwest.

264

Practice and Extend

READING SKILL
Cause and Effect

In the Lesson Review, students complete a graphic organizer like the one below. You may want to provide students with a copy of Transparency 20 to complete as they read the lesson.

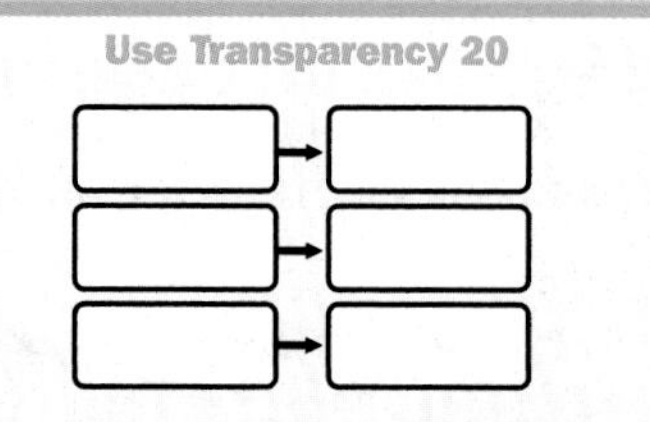

VOCABULARY
Related Word Study

The word *mission* comes from the Latin *mittere*, which means "to send, let go." When a person is on a mission, they have been sent on a special errand. In the text, a mission is the building where people on a mission do their work. Other words that come from *mittere* include *commit, emissary, emission, message, missile, missive, permission,* and *transmission*. Have students discuss how the meanings of these words relate to *mittere*, looking up their definitions as necessary.

The Fur Trade in the Midwest

The French were the first Europeans to come to the Midwest. They came in the mid-1600s in search of furs. The French and the Native Americans trapped and skinned beaver, mink, and otter. The animal furs were very valuable. Europeans used the furs to make coats and hats.

In 1673 a French priest and explorer, **Jacques Marquette,** and a French Canadian, **Louis Jolliet,** explored areas of the Midwest. They traveled in birchbark canoes from Michilimackinac **(Mackinaw)** in present-day Michigan, across Lake Michigan, and down river to the Mississippi River. On their return journey, they followed the Illinois River to a place near present-day Chicago. They stopped at a mission on Green Bay in present-day Wisconsin. A **mission** is a settlement set up by a religious group to teach their religion and to help the people of an area. Marquette stayed at the mission. 1
Jolliet continued on to **Sault Sainte Marie, Michigan.** Trace Marquette and Jolliet's journey on the map. 2

REVIEW Why did the French trap animals for their furs?
Main Idea and Details

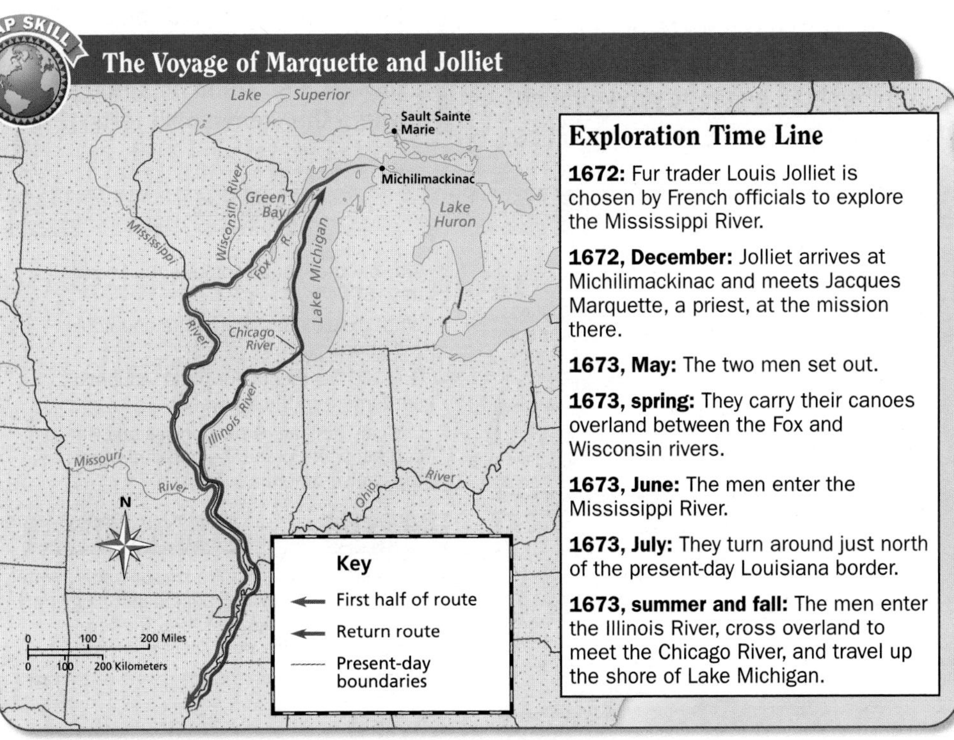
MAP SKILL
The Voyage of Marquette and Jolliet
Lake Superior
Sault Sainte Marie
Michilimackinac
Green Bay
Wisconsin River
Fox R.
Lake Michigan
Lake Huron
Mississippi River
Chicago River
Illinois River
Missouri River
Ohio River
N
0 100 200 Miles
0 100 200 Kilometers
Key
First half of route
Return route
Present-day boundaries
Exploration Time Line
1672: Fur trader Louis Jolliet is chosen by French officials to explore the Mississippi River.
1672, December: Jolliet arrives at Michilimackinac and meets Jacques Marquette, a priest, at the mission there.
1673, May: The two men set out.
1673, spring: They carry their canoes overland between the Fox and Wisconsin rivers.
1673, June: The men enter the Mississippi River.
1673, July: They turn around just north of the present-day Louisiana border.
1673, summer and fall: The men enter the Illinois River, cross overland to meet the Chicago River, and travel up the shore of Lake Michigan.
3

▶ **Marquette and Jolliet explored areas around rivers of the Midwest.**

MAP SKILL Intermediate Direction ***In what direction did the explorers travel along the Fox River?***

2 Teach and Discuss

PAGE 265

The Fur Trade in the Midwest

Quick Summary By the mid-1600s, French fur traders and explorers were traveling and trading throughout the Midwest.

1 **What personal qualities do you think Marquette and Jolliet needed to make their journey?** Possible answers: A spirit of adventure, courage, strength, flexibility, ingenuity, ability to learn other languages **Make Inferences**

✓ **Ongoing Assessment**

If... students have difficulty identifying qualities,	**then...** ask them to consider that these men had few supplies and little protection and did not speak the local languages.

Decision Making

2 **Marquette and Jolliet eventually settled in two different places. Today, how do people decide where to live?** Possible answers: Climate; cost of housing; nearness to family and schools; availability of jobs
Make Decisions

✓ **REVIEW ANSWER** The furs were very valuable in Europe. **Main Idea and Details**

The Voyage of Marquette and Jolliet

3 **According to the map, Marquette and Jolliet traveled mainly in what direction on the first half of their trip? the return trip?** South; north
Interpret Maps

MAP SKILL Answer Southwest

EXTEND LANGUAGE
ESL Support

Explore Alternate Word Meanings Have students analyze the nontraditional uses of *up* and *down* in the text.

Beginning Explain to students the meanings of "*up* river" (toward the river's source) and "*down* river" (toward the mouth of the river). Have them trace with a finger routes up river and down river on the map on this page.

Intermediate Have students brainstorm other similar uses of *up* and *down*. (Up North, down South, upstream, downstream, upstate, downtown, and so on)

Advanced Discuss with students which would be more difficult, traveling up river or down river. (Up river, because it requires going against the current)

For additional ESL support, use Every Student Learns Guide, pp. 110–113.

PAGE 266

Trade Grows at French Forts

Quick Summary Communities grew up around French forts that were set up as trading posts.

4 What was the original purpose of the forts built by the French? What happened later in the areas around the forts? Trading posts; communities began to grow *Make Inferences*

✓ **REVIEW ANSWER** Forts were built. Trade occurred. People settled nearby. Communities grew around the forts. Some communities grew into cities. *Sequence*

3 Close and Assess

Summarize the Lesson

Have students take turns reading aloud the three main points. Then have them draw a strip-picture story to illustrate the sequence of events in the fur trade.

✓ LESSON 2 **REVIEW**

1. **Cause and Effect** For possible answers, see the reduced pupil page.
2. To trade for furs
3. They explored the Great Lakes region and the Mississippi River valley.
4. People settled around forts that the French had set up as trading posts. Some of these settlements grew into cities.
5. **Critical Thinking: *Draw Conclusions*** Possible answers: Help: Native Americans could trade with the Europeans; Hurt: Native Americans and Europeans may have had conflicts over land

Link to Writing

Students should include specific details in their letters, as well as the correctly used terms “trading post” and “mission.”

Trade Grows at French Forts

▶ Cannon at a French trading post

Where Marquette and Jolliet traveled, French fur traders soon followed. They built many forts in the Midwest, setting them up as trading posts. A **trading post** is a sort of store at which goods are bought and sold. The traders exchanged tools for fur from the Native Americans.

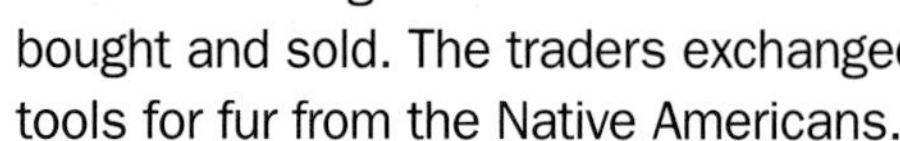

The Ottawa, Ojibwa, and Huron tribes brought furs to trade at the forts. Some Native Americans settled at the forts as well. In places where the soil was good, they farmed. They sold their extra crops to the traders at the nearby forts. They also made canoes.

4 Communities began to grow around the forts. Many of these communities eventually grew into major cities. Sault Sainte Marie and Chicago are two Midwestern cities that began as forts or trading posts. On the next page you can read how **Jean Baptiste Point Du Sable's** trading post became the city of Chicago.

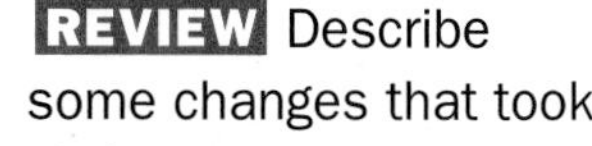

REVIEW Describe some changes that took place as French fur traders came to the Midwest. *Sequence*

Summarize the Lesson

- **middle 1600s** Fur traders from France came to the Midwest.
- **1673** Marquette and Jolliet explored waterways.
- **Today** Cities stand on some sites where the French built forts.

LESSON 2 **REVIEW**

Check Facts and Main Ideas

1. **Cause and Effect** Make a diagram like the one shown. Fill in the cause and effects.

Cause	Effect
The French came to the Midwest to trade furs.	They set up forts as trading posts.
Forts were set up for fur trade.	People came to trade and then settled at the forts.
Communities grew around the forts.	Many communities became major cities.

2. Why did the French come to the Midwest in the 1600s?
3. What did Jacques Marquette and Louis Jolliet do?
4. How did the French fur trade influence the settlement of the Midwest?
5. **Critical Thinking: *Draw Conclusions*** How did contact with Europeans both help and hurt the Native Americans?

Link to Writing

Write a Letter You are a French fur trader. Write a letter to your family in France describing your life at a fort in the Midwest. Use the terms **mission** and **trading post** in your letter.

Practice and Extend

MEETING INDIVIDUAL NEEDS
Leveled Practice

Create a Poster Ask students to use online or library resources to create posters about beavers.

Easy Have students draw a picture of beavers and list basic beaver characteristics. **Reteach**

On-Level Have students research and create a poster showing how beaver skins were used in the fur trade. **Extend**

Challenge Have students research and create a poster showing why and when beaver populations declined and what their status is today. **Enrich**

For a Lesson Summary, use Quick Study, p. 56.

Workbook, p. 62

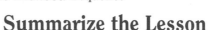

Lesson 2: The Fur Trade

Also on Teacher Resources CD-ROM.

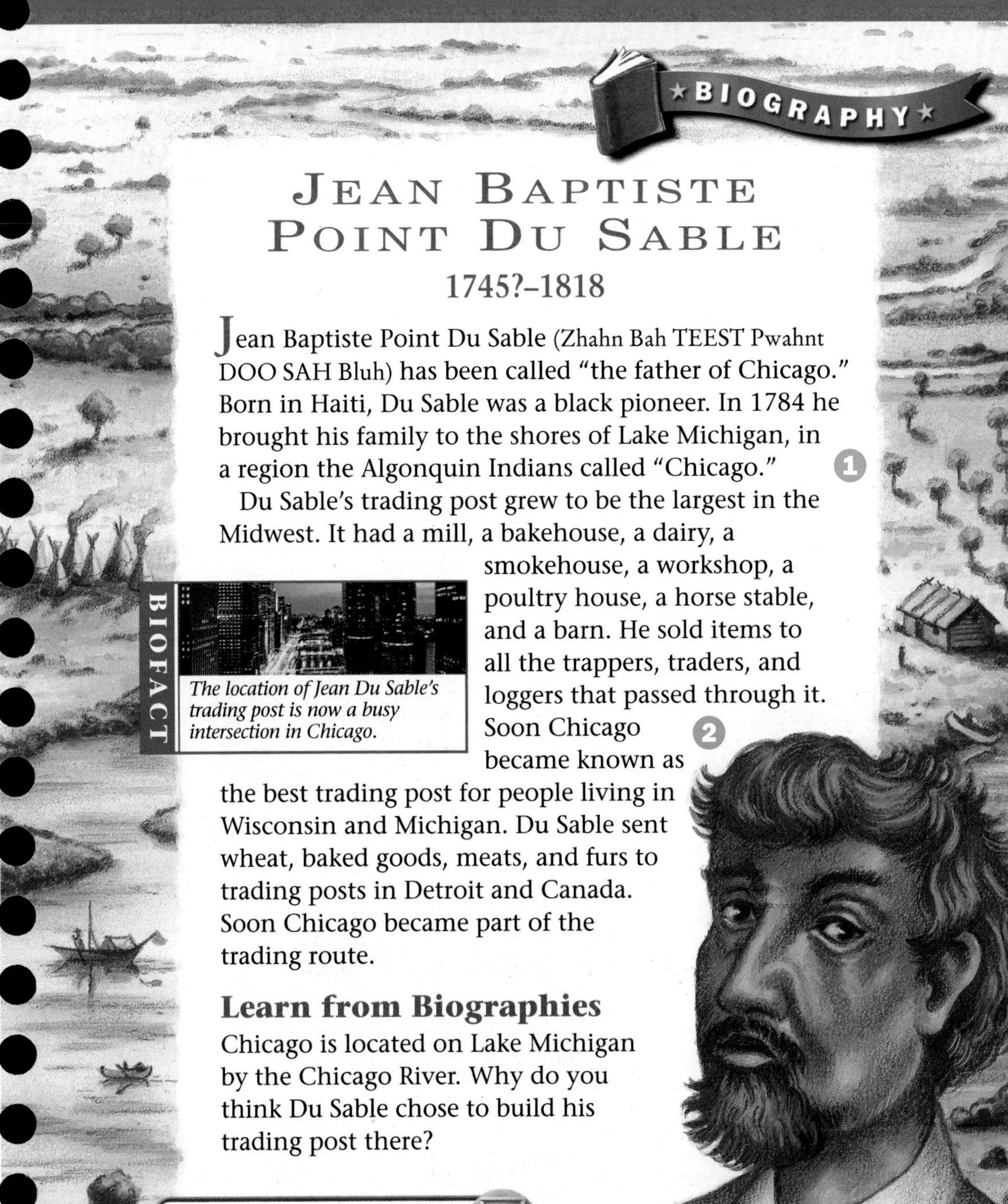

Jean Baptiste Point Du Sable

1745?–1818

Jean Baptiste Point Du Sable (Zhahn Bah TEEST Pwahnt DOO SAH Bluh) has been called "the father of Chicago." Born in Haiti, Du Sable was a black pioneer. In 1784 he brought his family to the shores of Lake Michigan, in a region the Algonquin Indians called "Chicago." 1

Du Sable's trading post grew to be the largest in the Midwest. It had a mill, a bakehouse, a dairy, a smokehouse, a workshop, a poultry house, a horse stable, and a barn. He sold items to all the trappers, traders, and loggers that passed through it. Soon Chicago 2 became known as the best trading post for people living in Wisconsin and Michigan. Du Sable sent wheat, baked goods, meats, and furs to trading posts in Detroit and Canada. Soon Chicago became part of the trading route.

BIOFACT

The location of Jean Du Sable's trading post is now a busy intersection in Chicago.

Learn from Biographies

Chicago is located on Lake Michigan by the Chicago River. Why do you think Du Sable chose to build his trading post there?

For more information, go online to *Meet the People* at **www.sfsocialstudies.com.**

267

Jean Baptiste Point Du Sable

Objective

- Explain the role that Jean Baptiste Point Du Sable played in trade.

1 Introduce and Motivate

Preview To activate prior knowledge, ask students how they think a person might come to be regarded as the father or mother of a city. (By founding a community that grew into a city or by playing a key role in a city's early development) Tell the class they will be reading about such a person.

2 Teach and Discuss

1 **Why is Du Sable considered "the father of Chicago"?** Because the trading post that he established attracted a great deal of business to the area that grew into Chicago Draw Conclusions

2 **Why did Du Sable's trading post become well known?** Because it offered so many goods and services to so many different people Cause and Effect

3 Close and Assess

Learn from Biographies Answer

Possible answers: Water access (to both the Mississippi River and the Great Lakes/St. Lawrence River) made trade easier; fish were available for food; good water supply

ACTIVATE PRIOR KNOWLEDGE

ESL Support

Relate to Personal Experience

Beginning Du Sable's father was from France. His mother was from Haiti. Have students tell where their families are from and what languages they speak at home.

Intermediate On a map, show students the places where Du Sable's parents lived. Have students write two sentences to tell where their families have lived.

Advanced Have students research the number of languages spoken in their own school and community.

WEB SITE

Technology

Students can find out more about Jean Baptiste Point Du Sable by going online and clicking on *Meet the People* at **www.sfsocialstudies.com.**

Trading for Goods

Objectives

- Identify the importance of trade in meeting countries' needs and wants.
- Explain the impact of trade in early America.

1 Introduce and Motivate

- Explain to students that Spain, France, and England colonized North America. In addition to land, they wanted natural resources that were not available in Europe.
- Explain to students that when European explorers failed to find riches such as gold or silver, they turned their attention to something almost as valuable: beaver fur. Native Americans traded these furs for a variety of European goods.
- Write the following categories on the board: *natural resources, manufactured goods,* and *produce.* Ask students to identify items the United States imports and assign each item to a category.

2 Teach and Discuss

H SOCIAL STUDIES STRAND
History

English, French, and Spanish Flags
These flags represent the three European countries that explored and competed for land and resources in North America in the 1700s. Ask students if they can identify the North American countries that were colonized by England, France, and Spain. Explain to students that European influences can still be seen in these countries, including language, culture, and place names.

Trading for Goods

European countries explored North America looking for wealth. Many searched for gold. Although the French and English did not find gold, they found something almost as valuable: beaver fur.

British flag

French flag

Spanish flag

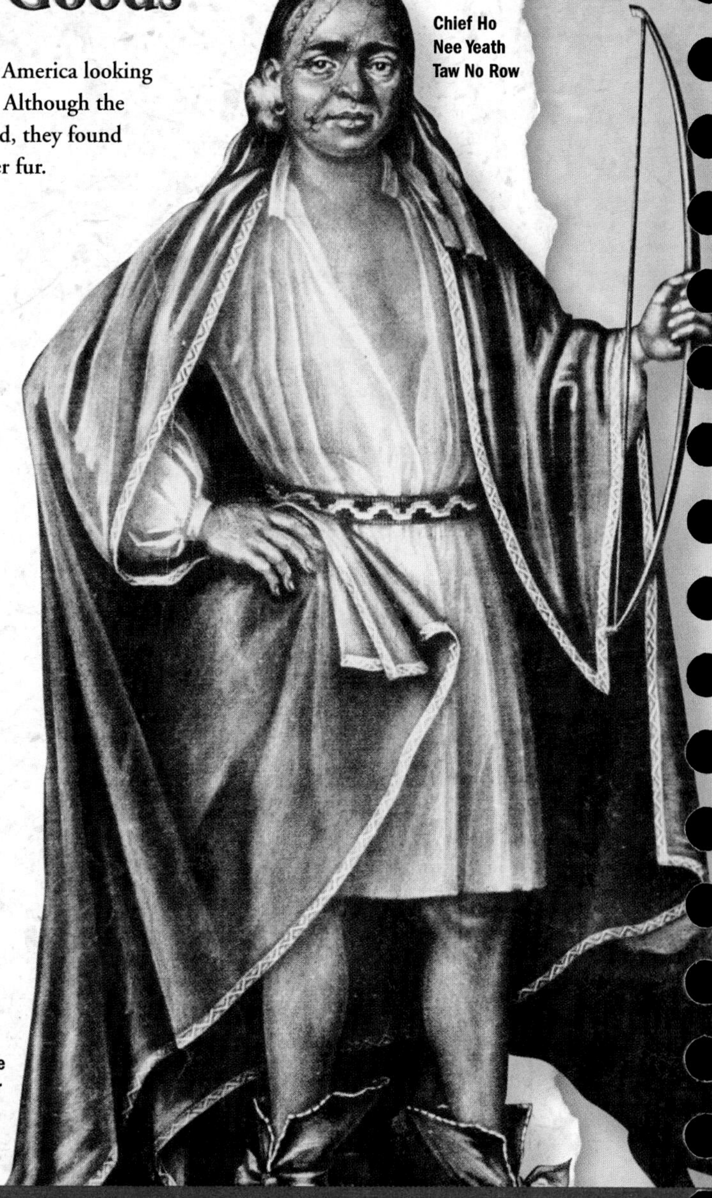

Chief Ho Nee Yeath Taw No Row

By 1750, the English had steady trade with some Native American nations. But the Iroquois, who traded with the French, handled most of the beaver fur. This helped the French control most of the fur trade. The conflict for control of the trade eventually helped lead to war between the French and English.

268

Practice and Extend

SOCIAL STUDIES
Background

International Trade *Dr. William E. White, Colonial Williamsburg Historian*

- No country is self-sufficient. We all want and need items that are not available in our own country. To get those items, we trade, or exchange, items that are plentiful in our country for items we want and need from other countries.
- Early European explorers, such as Marco Polo, found silk and spices in Asia. In the Americas, Europeans found natural resources such as silver, gold, wood, minerals, crops, and animal furs.
- An important by-product of trade is the sharing of cultures. In colonial America, Native Americans began using European tools and clothing. European colonists adopted Native American agricultural practices by growing corn and tobacco.

North America in 1750

- Disputed areas
- French claim
- English claim
- Spanish claim
- Unclaimed land

Why did the English want to control the fur trade? Fur was extremely valuable. People in Europe were willing to pay a lot of money for the furs.

Benjamin Franklin

Beaver fur was used to make expensive felt hats in Europe. In exchange for furs, the Native Americans got valuable items including cloth and metal products such as cooking kettles and knives. It was an important trade for both Native Americans and Europeans.

Countries today still trade for goods from other places. Many things you use come from these places. Explore your classroom or home. What products come from other countries?

269

- **Engraving: "Ho Nee Yeath Taw No Row, King of the Generethgarich"** This portrait of an Iroquois chief was engraved by John Verelst in London, England, in 1710. Native Americans traded materials such as beaver fur and food. Europeans traded manufactured goods, including iron tools, guns, cooking kettles, and clothing, such as the shirt and wool blanket worn by this Iroquois chief. Ask students if they know from what materials Native Americans made their traditional clothing.
- **Engraving of a beaver** This illustration appeared in a French book, *Etats-Unis D'Amerique (The United States of America),* written by M. Roux de Rochelle in 1837. Europeans used beaver fur to make fashionable fur felt hats. Ask students to discuss what kinds things people wear today to be fashionable.
- **Engraving of Benjamin Franklin** and **a beaver felt hat** This engraving of Benjamin Franklin was made by John Martin Will in France in 1777. Franklin is dressed in a fur-trimmed coat and a fur cap. This man's cocked hat was made in England, ca. 1750–1790, from American beaver fur and was worn by Josiah Bartlett, one of the signers of the Declaration of Independence.

3 Close and Assess

- Review with students why control of the fur trade was important to English and French colonists.
- Have students make a list of the classroom items and the countries from which they were imported by examining labels and tags for manufacturing information. Once students have made their list, have them categorize items by type and rank these items to identify which of the items are needs and which items are wants.

C SOCIAL STUDIES Culture

- Explain to students that when we trade with another country we learn about, and sometimes adopt, elements of that country's culture. Food is an excellent example of this kind of exchange.
- Ask students to list food items that come from other countries and discuss where they those foods might be found in their community.
- Have students create an "International Menu" featuring foods from around the world.

Workbook, p. 63

Also on Teacher Resources CD-ROM.

Building Farms

Objectives

- Explain some events that forced Native American tribes in the Midwest to give up their land.
- Compare and contrast a home built out of sod and one built out of logs.
- Explain the difficulties settlers faced in farming the land and their ultimate success.
- Describe the causes and long-term effects of farming the prairie, including the Dust Bowl.

Vocabulary

sod, p. 272; **drought,** p. 274; **Dust Bowl,** p. 274

Resources

- Workbook, p. 64
- Transparency 20
- Every Student Learns Guide, pp. 114–117
- Quick Study, pp. 58–59

Quick Teaching Plan

If time is short, have students create illustrated notes.

- After students read the lesson independently, have them draw two simple, captioned pictures summarizing the information in this lesson.
- Have students share their illustrations and captions with the class.

LESSON 3

PREVIEW

Focus on the Main Idea
Many settlers came to the Midwest in the 1800s to farm the land.

PEOPLE
John Deere

VOCABULARY
sod
drought
Dust Bowl

PLACE
Wapello County, Iowa

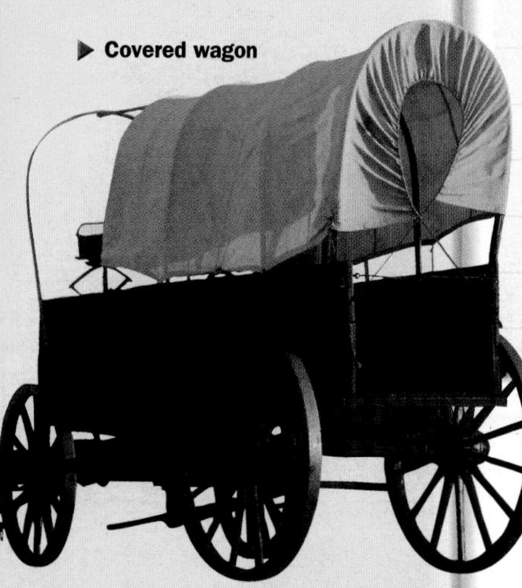

▶ Covered wagon

Building Farms

You Are There You stand tense and waiting with your family. In the darkness of the night, the flicker of torches lights up the faces of hundreds of others in the crowd around you. A man near you cracks a joke, and people break into quiet laughter. A mother sings softly to soothe a whimpering baby. Your father pulls out his pocket watch. It will be just a few minutes now.

When the cannon fires, you and everyone around you will run forward to stake claims on the land. The date is May 1, 1843. The place is Wapello County, Iowa. You are part of a land rush. People enter an area at the same time to claim land for homes, farms, and businesses. Your family is among the first white settlers in this part of the state.

Cause and Effect As you read, look for ways that pioneer farmers changed the natural landscape of the Midwest.

270

1 Introduce and Motivate

Preview To activate prior knowledge, ask students if they have ever helped plant a garden. Tell students that Lesson 3 will explain how settlers began farming the Midwest.

Ask students to picture themselves in the scene on May 1, 1843, and to describe the emotions they feel.

Practice and Extend

READING SKILL
Cause and Effect

In the Lesson Review, students complete a graphic organizer like the one below. You may want to provide students with a copy of Transparency 20 to complete as they read the lesson.

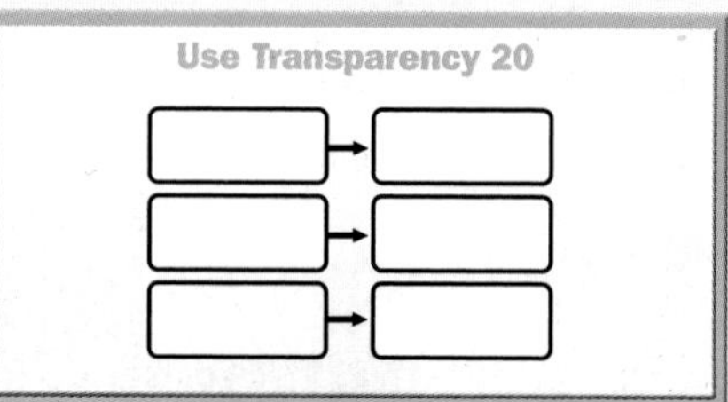

VOCABULARY
Related Word Study

Have students brainstorm and use thesauruses and dictionaries to come up with synonyms and near-synonyms for *sod* (*land, turf, soil, earth, field*). Discuss why some of them are closer in meaning to *sod* than others. (*Turf,* like *sod,* includes the upper part of the ground—grass and roots—while *earth* refers only to the dirt part of the ground.) Discuss when to use *sod* in a sentence and when these synonyms could be used.

Before the Settlers

The settlers of **Wapello County** were not rushing forward onto empty land. For many centuries, Native Americans had lived in this part of Iowa.

Some Native American groups of the Midwest had farmed. Others had hunted bison, or buffalo, that roamed the prairies. Still others had combined farming and bison hunting. Each group had claimed a particular area as its homeland. Throughout the 1600s and 1700s, the Europeans who had settled on the East Coast had been moving westward.

By the early 1800s, centuries of suffering had weakened many Native American groups. Then settlers started coming by the thousands to the Midwest. The United States forced Native Americans to sell their land to (1) the government and move to reservations farther west. (2) Once the Native Americans left, pioneers rushed in to claim the land.

REVIEW What were some factors that led some Native American groups in the Midwest to lose their land? Main Idea and Details

▶ This painting shows settlers racing for their piece of land during a land rush.

271

EXTEND LANGUAGE
ESL Support

Explore Multiple Meanings Help students explore different meanings for the word *reservation* and apply it to Native American reservations.

Beginning Give students two meanings for the word *reservation* (land set aside for Native Americans, an agreement to set aside a seat in a restaurant or a room in a hotel). Ask students to act out each meaning.

Intermediate Have students write sentences using each meaning of *reservation*.

Advanced Ask student pairs to research a Native American reservation that still exists today. Have them share their findings with the class.

For additional ESL support, use Every Student Learns Guide, pp. 114–117.

2 Teach and Discuss

PAGE 271

Before the Settlers

Quick Summary Many Native Americans of the Midwest were displaced as a result of government policy and settlement patterns.

1 **How did the westward movement of European settlers affect Native Americans in the Midwest?** Many Native Americans were forced to sell their land and move to reservations farther west. Cause and Effect

2 **Why would the United States government force Native Americans to move?** To make room for settlers from the East Make Inferences

✓ **REVIEW ANSWER** Government policies Main Ideas and Details

PAGE 272

Starting a Farm, Building a Home

Quick Summary Settlers in the Midwest started farms and built houses.

3 **How did some settlers get land in the United States in the 1800s?** By placing stakes in the ground to mark their claim to land Main Idea and Details

4 **What do you think it would be like for a whole family to live in one room?** Possible answers: Little privacy; always someone around to help; difficult to keep things tidy Express Ideas

5 **Why were sod houses practical homes on the prairie?** They were made of readily available materials, and they suited the climate. Draw Conclusions

Ongoing Assessment

If... students have difficulty analyzing sod as a building material,	**then...** ask them to create a mental picture of the treeless prairie and of conditions in summer and winter.

REVIEW ANSWER Possible answer: Sod homes were formed by stacking bricks made of thick prairie sod, with sod strips for the roof; log cabins were built using trees. Compare and Contrast

Starting a Farm, Building a Home

Almost all of the settlers who came to the Midwest in the early 1800s built farms. First, a settler claimed land by hammering a wooden stake into each of the four corners of the area. Then, 3 the family built their home.

Midwestern farmhouses in the 1800s were small and simple. Most had a single room about the size of a 4 modern living room. Most were log cabins, made of trees the farmers cut on their own land. However, some parts of the Midwest had very few trees. These regions were prairies. A prairie is a grassland that stretches for miles and miles. Many pioneers who settled on the prairie built homes out of **sod.** Sod is made of the grass, roots, and dirt that forms the ground's top layer. Settlers cut the prairie sod into thick bricks, stacking them to form walls. They rolled out sod strips to cover the roof.

Sod houses were warm in the winter and cool in the summer. But sod 5 houses were small and hard to keep clean. Most families moved into wooden houses as soon as they could.

REVIEW Contrast the two main types of homes that Midwestern pioneers built. Compare and Contrast

▶ Some families lived in houses made of sod, such as the one pictured below.

272

Practice and Extend

SOCIAL STUDIES Background

The Homestead Act

- The opening up of Midwestern and Western lands to settlers was called the Homestead Movement.
- In 1862 President Abraham Lincoln signed the Homestead Act, which gave individuals 160 acres of free land if they lived and worked on it for at least five years.
- By 1900, about 600,000 homesteaders had claimed more than 80 million acres of public land.

MEETING INDIVIDUAL NEEDS Leveled Practice

Plan a Prairie Homestead Have students analyze what type of homestead to build on a Midwestern farm settlement.

Easy Have students choose a Midwestern state and then explain what type of home they might build there and why. **Reteach**

On-Level Ask students to create a layout for a Midwestern prairie house. Remind students that these homes usually were quite small, focusing more on practicality than luxury. **Extend**

Challenge Have students create a layout for an entire prairie farm. Tell them to include a house, livestock area, places for crops, storage areas, and any other areas or structures that would have been important to a Midwestern farm family. **Enrich**

For a Lesson Summary, use Quick Study, p. 58.

Farming in the Midwest

In some parts of the Midwest, farming the land was easy. In many river valleys, Native Americans had already cleared the land for farm fields. The settlers who took over only had to plant their own corn. In most places, farmers had to clear the land before they could plant. It took a lot of hard work to chop down trees and dig up the stumps to make a field. 6

On the Banks of Plum Creek

Laura Ingalls Wilder wrote books about life on Midwest farms in the 1800s. Many stories came from her family's experiences. This is a part of one book.

Laura went . . . into the dugout. It was one room, all white. The earth walls had been smoothed and whitewashed. The earth floor was smooth and hard.

When Ma and Mary stood in the doorway the light went dim. There was a small greased-paper window beside the door. But the wall was so thick that the light from the window stayed near the window.

That front wall was built of sod. Mr. Hanson had dug out his house, and then he had cut long strips of prairie sod and laid them on top of one another, to make the front wall. It was a good, thick wall with not one crack in it. No cold could get through that wall. 8

▶ Farmers in the Midwest in the 1800s used horse-drawn plows like this one.

In still other places, Midwestern farmers had to plow up the tough prairie sod. In the early 1800s this was not easy. The plows of the time had great difficulty breaking through the tangled prairie grass roots. In the 1850s farmers could get a new steel plow made by **John Deere.** Then, farming on the prairies became easier. 7

Many farmers raised cattle, pigs, and chickens. They made money by selling the animals or the milk or eggs the animals produced. In the early 1800s, farmers close to the Mississippi and other big rivers and lakes could ship farm products to the cities of the Northeast and the Southeast. In the mid-1800s, railroads were built across the Midwest. The region quickly became a center of farming and shipping, supplying the nation with food.

REVIEW What challenges did Midwestern settlers face and how could they overcome these challenges? Main Idea and Details

273

PAGE 273

Farming in the Midwest

Quick Summary As settlers began farming and sending their products to other cities, the Midwest quickly became a center of farming and shipping.

6 **Why did the farmers who settled in river valleys have an easier time growing crops?** Many times, Native Americans had already cleared the land for farm fields. **Main Idea and Details**

7 **How were the Midwestern prairies made into farmland?** Settlers plowed the prairies to prepare the land for farming. **Cause and Effect**

Literature and Social Studies

Read aloud the selection as students read along silently.

8 **Do you think the dugout on the banks of Plum Creek sounds like a place where you might like to live? Why or why not?** Possible answer: No; Because there was very little light inside; Yes; Because it was clean and warm **Analyze Information**

✓ **REVIEW ANSWER** Clearing and plowing land and transporting products to market. New plows made plowing prairie soil easier. New rail lines made shipping easier. **Main Idea and Details**

CURRICULUM CONNECTION Literature

Read Literature

Pioneer Girl: The Story of Laura Ingalls Wilder, by William Anderson (HarperTrophy, ISBN 0-064-46234-X, 2000) **Easy**

Laura's Album: A Remembrance Scrapbook of Laura Ingalls Wilder, by William Anderson (HarperCollins, ISBN 0-060-27842-0, 1998) **On-Level**

Laura Ingalls Wilder: A Biography, by William Anderson (HarperCollins, ISBN 0-064-46103-3, 1995) **Challenge**

CURRICULUM CONNECTION Writing

Write a Diary Entry

- Have students use their imaginations as well as details from the text, illustrations, and the literature selection to write their own diary entry from the point of view of a child living on the prairie in the 1800s.
- Suggest that students draw sketches to accompany their diary entries.

PAGE 274

Using Farm Land

Quick Summary The experience of the Dust Bowl led to better farming methods.

SOCIAL STUDIES STRAND
Citizenship

Many farmers take responsibility for caring for their land so that future farmers will have good land.

9 **How do farmers protect their farmland?** By plowing and planting in curves, using crop rotation, and allowing prairie grasses to grow back
Apply Information

✓ **REVIEW ANSWER** They farmed the land in a harmful way.
Cause and Effect

Close and Assess

Summarize the Lesson

Have students read aloud the main points. Then have them present short skits to act out these points.

✓ **LESSON 3 REVIEW**

1. Cause and Effect For possible answers, see the reduced pupil page.
2. Possible answer: Government policies forced them to sell their land and move.
3. Those with trees on their land built log cabins. Prairie farmers had few trees, so they usually built their houses from sod.
4. Advances helped the economy grow. Steel plow: easier for farmers to plow the prairies and grow more crops; Rail lines: easier to transport crops and other products
5. **Critical Thinking: *Draw Conclusions*** Possible answers: Trade farm products for building supplies, borrow money, use materials from the land

Link to Art

Murals should include details from all periods.

Using Farm Land

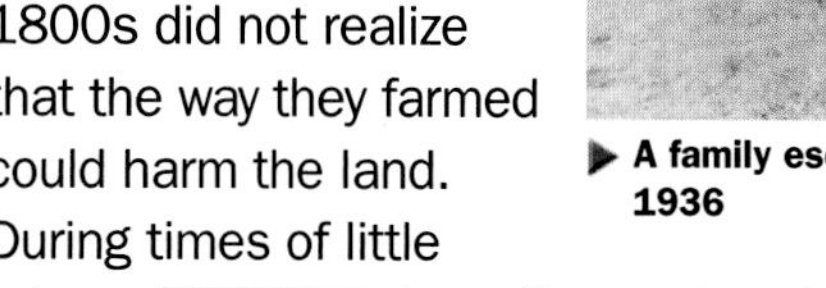

▶ A family escaping from the Dust Bowl, 1936

Farmers who came to the Midwest in the 1800s did not realize that the way they farmed could harm the land. During times of little rain, or **drought,** the soil turned to dust and blew away in huge dust storms.

Years of drought struck the Midwest in the 1930s. Farmers suffered greatly. The area became known as the **Dust Bowl.** Soil from the Dust Bowl darkened the skies for weeks and even blew as far as the East Coast.

Today, farmers plow and plant in curves to help stop soil from washing or blowing away. They plant different crops to help keep the soil fertile. In some areas, they have let the prairie grasses grow back. 9

REVIEW What did farmers do that contributed to the cause of the Dust Bowl? Cause and Effect

Summarize the Lesson

- In the 1800s thousands of settlers came to the Midwest to start farms.
- Midwestern farmers cleared the land, plowed it, and built homes.
- Improved farm equipment allowed Midwestern farmers to become important food producers.
- Midwestern farmers learned better ways to farm the land.

LESSON 3 REVIEW

Check Facts and Main Ideas

1. Cause and Effect Make a diagram like the one shown below. Complete it by listing the missing cause and effects.

Cause	Effect
Many settlers moved west, looking for opportunities.	Farms grew throughout the Midwest.
The pioneer family would build a house and begin farming.	After crops grew, farmers could feed and raise livestock.
Farmers didn't realize they could harm the land.	The **Dust Bowl** developed.

2. What affected Native Americans in the Midwest from the 1600s to the early 1800s?
3. What kind of houses did the pioneers build and why?
4. What effect did advances in technology in the mid-1800s have on the economy of the Midwest?
5. **Critical Thinking:** ***Draw Conclusions*** In the early and mid-1800s, money was scarce in the Midwest. What could a family with little money do to buy what they needed?

Link to Art

Make a Mural With a partner, design a mural that shows the history of the Midwest from the 1600s to the 1800s.

274

Practice and Extend

CURRICULUM CONNECTION
Music

Explore Dust Bowl Songs

- Woody Guthrie (1912–1967) was a famous folk singer whose works included the Dust Bowl ballads "So Long It's Been Good to Know Ya" and "I Ain't Got No Home."
- Have students find and listen to one of Guthrie's Dust Bowl songs.
- Ask students what the words say about that period of time.

Workbook, p. 64

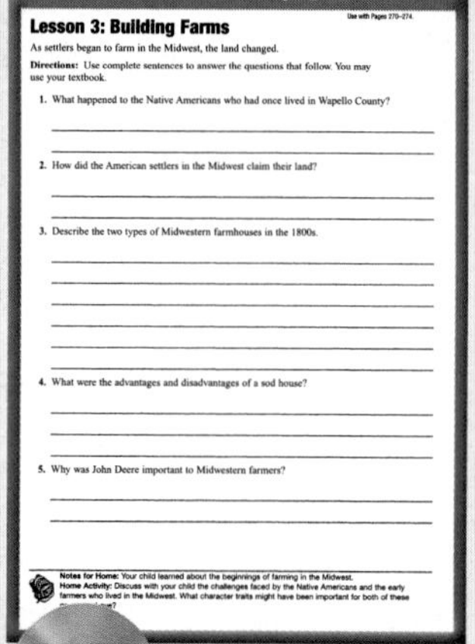

Use with Pages 270–274.

Lesson 3: Building Farms

As settlers began to farm in the Midwest, the land changed.

Directions: Use complete sentences to answer the questions that follow. You may use your textbook.

1. What happened to the Native Americans who had once lived in Wapello County?
2. How did the American settlers in the Midwest claim their land?
3. Describe the two types of Midwestern farmhouses in the 1800s.
4. What were the advantages and disadvantages of a sod house?
5. Why was John Deere important to Midwestern farmers?

Notes for Home: Your child learned about the beginnings of farming in the Midwest.
Home Activity: Discuss with your child the challenges faced by the Native Americans and the early farmers who lived in the Midwest. What character traits might have been important for both of these

Also on Teacher Resources CD-ROM.

John Deere

1804–1886

John Deere was a blacksmith who moved to Illinois from Vermont. A blacksmith is a craftsperson who makes and repairs metal items such as horseshoes and tools for working in the fields. The farmers in Illinois were always bringing in their iron plows for sharpening. Farmers complained that the thick clay soil stuck to the blade and made it dull. They couldn't plow more than a few furrows before they had to stop and clean the blade. 1

BIOFACT

To use John Deere's plow, the farmer walked behind it, holding the reins of the horse.

That gave Deere an idea. Deere used a broken steel saw to make the blade for his new plow. It worked much better than the old iron plow blades. John Deere was soon in the plow-making business. He called his steel plow the "Self-Polisher" because it stayed clean as it plowed the soil.

John Deere was an entrepreneur. An entrepreneur is someone who organizes and manages a new business. Today the company that John Deere founded is one of the 2 largest manufacturers of farm equipment in the world.

Learn from Biographies

How did Deere use problem-solving skills to improve the plow?

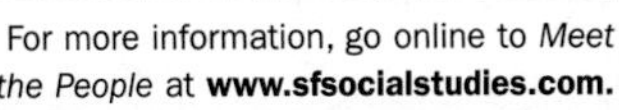

For more information, go online to *Meet the People* at **www.sfsocialstudies.com.**

275

John Deere

Objective

- Explain how John Deere became an entrepreneur.

Vocabulary

blacksmith, p. 275

1 Introduce and Motivate

Preview To activate prior knowledge, ask students what they know about life on a farm. Tell students that modern farms use many types of farm equipment. One type is a plow.

2 Teach and Discuss

SOCIAL STUDIES STRAND
Citizenship

Tell students that some community workers supply goods, such as plows. Other members of the community, such as teachers, provide services.

1 **What role did blacksmiths play in early pioneer communities?** They made and repaired metal items (such as horseshoes) and tools. Apply Information

2 **How was John Deere a successful entrepreneur?** He started a business manufacturing a new type of plow. The company he started is still in business today. Apply Information

3 Close and Assess

Learn from Biographies Answer

Farmers were complaining that iron plows were difficult to use, so Deere made a better plow blade from a broken steel saw.

SOCIAL STUDIES
Background

About John Deere

- John Deere invented his steel plow in 1837. The following year, he opened a business to produce and market it.
- In the 1960s and 1970s, John Deere's company began making tractors, seeders, and harvesting equipment.
- By the late twentieth century, five generations of the Deere family had been involved with the company John Deere began over 150 years earlier.

WEB SITE
Technology

Students can find out more about John Deere by going online and clicking on *Meet the People* at **www.sfsocialstudies.com.**

Hub of the Nation

Objectives

- Describe Cahokia as the early trading center of the Midwest.
- Identify the goals of the Lewis and Clark expedition.
- Identify the role of the steamboat in shipping.
- Describe the advantages of railroads as compared to steamboats.
- Explain the role the government played in developing superhighways that became the interstate highway system.

Vocabulary

mound, p. 277; **steamboat,** p. 280; **hub,** p. 280; **transcontinental railroad,** p. 281; **Interstate highway system,** p. 282

Resources

- Workbook, p. 65
- Transparency 20
- Every Student Learns Guide, pp. 118–121
- Quick Study, pp. 60–61

Quick Teaching Plan

If time is short, have students read the lesson and compare forms of transportation in the Midwest.

- Have students draw a three-column chart labeled *Waterways, Railroads,* and *Highways*.
- Have students note the history and the advantages and disadvantages of each kind of transportation in the chart.

1 Introduce and Motivate

Preview To activate prior knowledge, ask students to describe distinctive structures—such as the Gateway Arch in St. Louis—in some cities in the Midwest. Tell students that they will learn more about the growth of Midwestern cities in Lesson 4.

You Are There Have students describe what it might be like to look down on a city from a great height, such as from the top of the Arch.

LESSON 4

1800 1850 1900 1950

1804 Lewis and Clark Expedition begins.

1869 Transcontinental Railroad is completed.

1950s Interstate highway system is built.

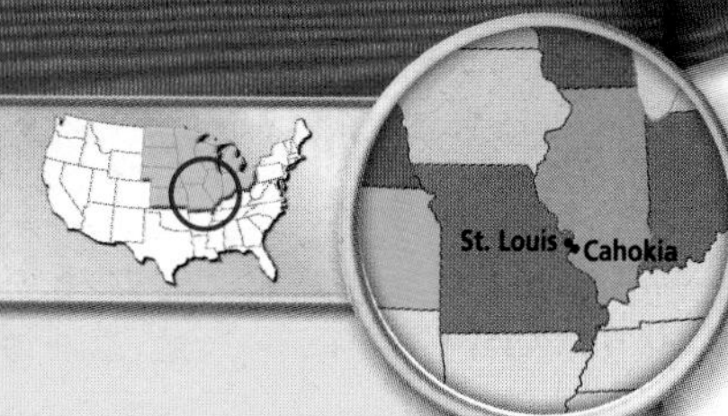

PREVIEW

Focus on the Main Idea
The Midwest has been a trade and transportation hub, from long ago to the present.

PLACES
St. Louis, Missouri
Cahokia, Illinois

PEOPLE
Meriwether Lewis
William Clark

VOCABULARY
mound
steamboat
hub
transcontinental railroad
Interstate highway system

Hub of the Nation

You Are There The tram ride is an exciting one, taking you up a steep, curved path to the top of the Arch. With each upward yank of cables, the round car twists and turns as it climbs the arch. When you get out of the tram, the view amazes you. You can see so many things! Barges that look like toys travel down the silver strip of the Mississippi River. You feel the slight sway of the Arch in the wind. Outside the other window you see the stadium. The guide announces that the tram is about to leave. You and two others pile into the egg-shaped car. As it cranks and juts forward, you smile at the thought that you were at the top of the Gateway Arch in St. Louis!

Cause and Effect As you read, look for events that caused the Midwest to become an important center for trade and transportation.

276

Practice and Extend

READING SKILL Cause and Effect

In the Lesson Review, students complete a graphic organizer like the one below. You may want to provide students with a copy of Transparency 20 to complete as they read the lesson.

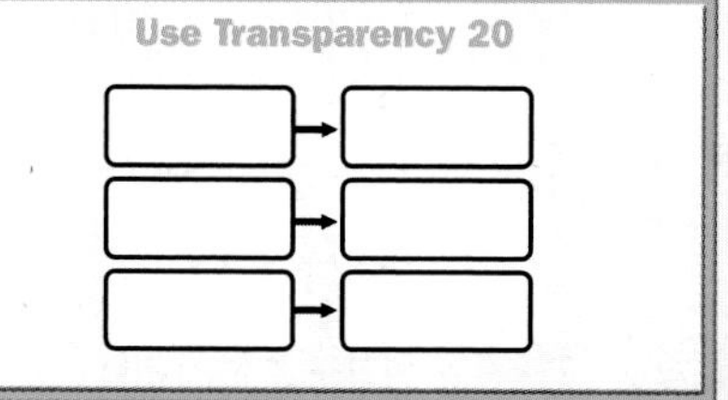

VOCABULARY Individual Word Study

The prefix *inter-* often means "between, among" Ask what *inter-state* means (between or among states) Invite students to locate another *inter-* word on p. 282 *(interconnecting)*. Have students define this word. (connecting between) Repeat the first part of this activity with the term *transcontinental,* telling students that the prefix *trans-* often means "across" or "through," and having them guess what *transatlantic* means. (across the Atlantic Ocean)

Cahokia

You can visit Monks Mound near Cahokia, Illinois. When Cahokia was at its peak, around A.D. 1100, about 20,000 people might have lived there. Archaeologists continue to dig up more of the mounds to learn about life in this ancient city. 1

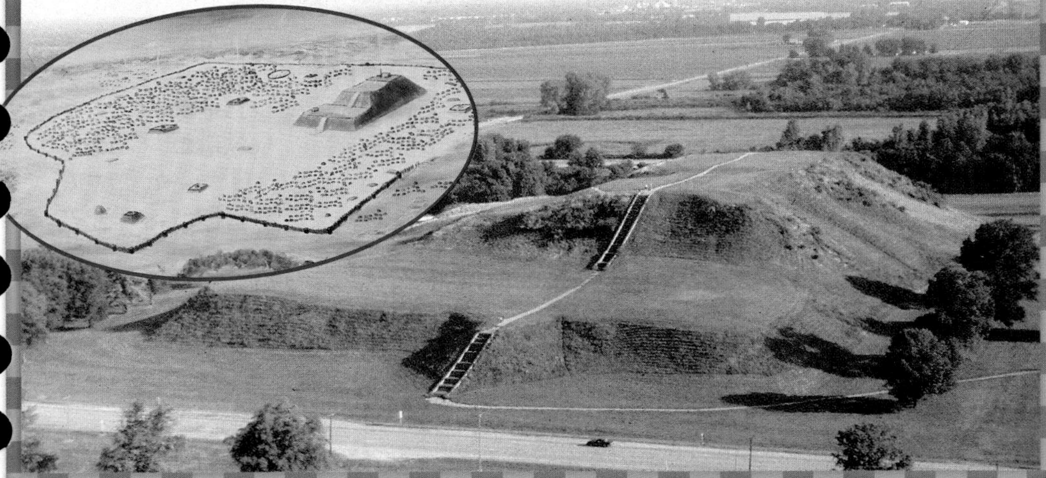

Cahokia: Early Trade Center of the Midwest

If you are in the **St. Louis** area, you can spot them. The mounds were built by Native Americans who lived in the area more than 1,000 years ago. A **mound** is a pile of earth or stones. Some mounds were burial sites for important people. Other mounds were platforms where important members of the community built their homes. Still other mounds probably were places where ceremonies were held. 2

The biggest of these mounds is in Cahokia Mounds State Park in Illinois. Called Monks Mound, it is the largest structure built by any group of Native Americans north of Mexico. Monks Mound towered over a huge plaza. Thousands of people gathered at the **Cahokia** plaza for festivals and perhaps for markets.

Cahokia was once a key trading center in the Midwest. It was close to the junction of three rivers—the Illinois, the Missouri, and the Mississippi. Traders from the Great Lakes area and from the western plains shipped copper, lead, and bison bones on these rivers to Cahokia. Southern traders in the Mississippi valley shipped shells, jewelry, and pottery to Cahokia. With its widespread trade, Cahokia was a meeting place of many cultures.

REVIEW What caused Cahokia to be a key trade center? Cause and Effect

277

FYI SOCIAL STUDIES Background

Cahokia Mounds

- Native American mounds can be found in the shape of circles, octagons, and zigzagging snakes. At Cahokia, builders also constructed four-sided pyramids similar to the stone ones built by the Maya in Mexico.
- Monks Mound is 100 feet high, built up in four levels. Archaeologists think the residents built it by carrying dirt in baskets on their back. On top of the mound was a building 50 feet high.
- At Cahokia, a circle of 48 poles was used as a calendar. When the eastern pole, a pole in the center, and the front of Monks Mound lined up with the rising sun, it marked the equinox, the day in spring and fall when night and day are about the same length (around March 21 and September 22).

2 Teach and Discuss

PAGE 277

Cahokia: Early Trade Center of the Midwest

Quick Summary Large mounds made over 1,000 years ago reveal that Cahokia, in Illinois, was once a large, important trading center for many cultures.

Cahokia

1 **Why might digging up the mounds near Cahokia, Illinois, help archaeologists learn about life there?** They might find objects people used in everyday life, which could help archaeologists understand how the people lived. Make Inferences

2 **Why do you think the tops of mounds may have been reserved for important people and buildings?** Possible answer: Being up high or "on top" shows a sense of importance. Hypothesize

✓ **REVIEW ANSWER** It was close to the junction of three rivers that were used for shipping goods: the Illinois, the Missouri, and the Mississippi. Cause and Effect

PAGE 278

A Gateway to the West

Quick Summary Sent by President Thomas Jefferson, Lewis and Clark explored the Missouri River to find a route to the Pacific.

3 **Describe the route that Jefferson hoped might connect St. Louis with the West.** Up the Missouri River to its source and then on a nearby westward-flowing river to the Pacific Ocean
Main Idea and Details

SOCIAL STUDIES STRAND
Science • Technology

Lewis and Clark wrote about their expedition in journals, in which they recorded information about the land and the rivers they saw, the plants and the animals they found, and the people they met.

4 **What might have been some of the difficulties Lewis and Clark faced on their journey?** Possible answers: Sickness, cold, rain, finding food, traveling unknown lands, not knowing the language of the local people
Hypothesize

REVIEW ANSWER To find a westward-flowing river near the source of the Missouri that would take them to the Pacific Ocean; to expand fur trade
Main Idea and Details

A Gateway to the West

Native Americans were not the only people who used the area near present-day St. Louis as a center for trade. The French set up a fur-trade center there in the 1700s.

In the early 1800s, the United States bought the area from the French. Thomas Jefferson, who was the United States President at the time, wanted to expand trade. He also wanted to learn about the land and peoples of the West. He wanted to see if St. Louis could connect the Midwest not only with the Northeast and the Southeast, but with the West as well. He sent two explorers, **Meriwether Lewis** and **William Clark,** on an expedition to travel up the Missouri River to its source. Jefferson hoped that once they reached the source of this eastward-flowing river, Lewis and Clark would find a nearby river flowing westward all the way to the Pacific Ocean. With a water route to the
3 Pacific Ocean, the United States could expand the fur trade. He asked Lewis and Clark to keep a record of their trip.

Lewis and Clark set out on their expedition from the area near St. Louis in 1804. On their way up the Missouri River, they met many different Native American groups. They tried to get each group to promise to trade with pioneers. They asked for advice on routes to the Pacific. Lewis and Clark had many adventures, as shown on the map on the facing page. However, they learned that there was no direct water route connecting the Midwest with the
Pacific Ocean. 4

REVIEW What were two main goals of the Lewis and Clark expedition?
Main Idea and Details

▶ A page from Lewis's journal with his drawing of a sage grouse

▶ William Clark

▶ Meriwether Lewis

278

Practice and Extend

SOCIAL STUDIES
Background

Lewis and Clark Expedition

- There were about 40 members of Lewis and Clark's expedition, including people who were knowledgeable about plants, animals, weather, the sign language used by some Native American tribes, gun repair, and handling boats.
- The expedition suffered from hunger, accidents, and illness, plus attacks by grizzly bears and rattlesnakes. However, only one person died during the journey.

CURRICULUM CONNECTION
Science

Research Sacagawea on the Internet

Tell students that Lewis and Clark were accompanied on their expedition by a young Native American woman named Sacagawea. Then have them use the Internet to answer the following questions about Sacagawea's life.

- To which Native American group was Sacagawea born? With which group did she live as a young woman? Why?
- Why did Lewis and Clark think it was important to include Sacagawea in their expedition?
- In what ways did Sacagawea help Lewis and Clark?
- Why do you think the United States placed Sacagawea's image on a coin?
- Who was "Pomp"? What happened to him after Sacagawea's death?

Map Adventure

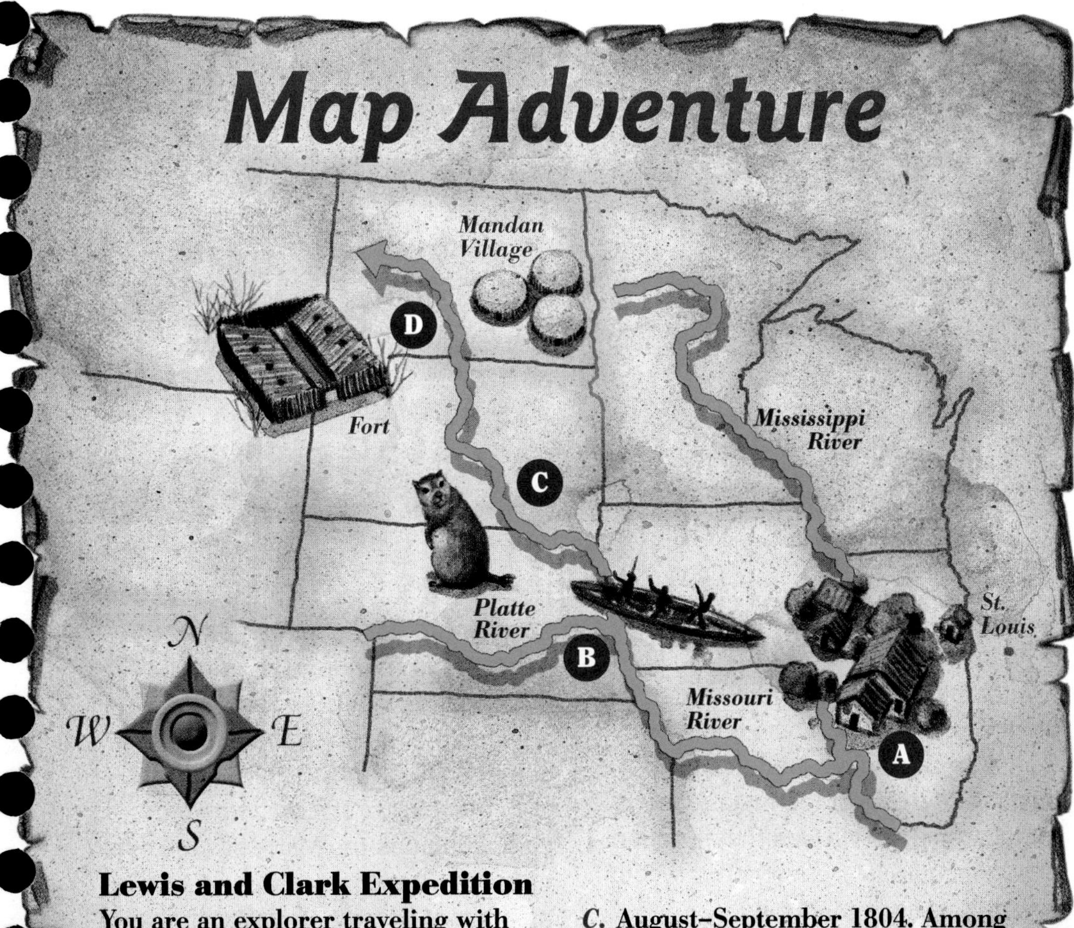

Lewis and Clark Expedition

You are an explorer traveling with Lewis and Clark. You have never been this far west before.

You will experience new things as you travel through territory that will some day form part of the Midwest. The following questions match locations on the map.

A. May 1804. You leave your camp near St. Louis to begin your up-river journey. What two rivers meet near the site of your camp?

B. July 1804. Your party reaches the Platte River. In what direction is St. Louis?

C. August–September 1804. Among the different animals you see are prairie dogs, which Lewis calls "barking squirrels." In what direction are you traveling?

D. October–November 1804. You encounter a grizzly bear. Two weeks later you feel the weather turning cold. Winter is coming. You help the party set up a fort by a Mandan Indian village. You will stay here until spring of 1805. In what direction will you go to return to St. Louis? 5 6

279

ACCESS CONTENT

ESL Support

Orient Yourself Help students understand the meanings of directional words.

Beginning Place signs indicating *North, South, East,* and *West* on the walls of the classroom. Have students point to the correct direction as you cue each aloud.

Intermediate Draw two intersecting lines on the board, with the ends labeled *North, West, South,* and *East*. Have students take turns coming to the board to draw a check mark in the correct quadrant as you say the words *northwest, southwest, northeast,* and *southeast*.

Advanced Ask students to create an illustrated compass rose with the main and secondary directions labeled. Have them orient their compass to the north and then point to the correct cardinal direction as you cue them aloud.

For additional ESL support, use Every Student Learns Guide, pp. 118–121.

Map Adventure

Have students look at the map of the Lewis and Clark expedition. Have the class trace the movement of the expedition up the Missouri River, from point A to point B to point C to point D.

5 **How long were the explorers traveling before they settled in at the fort for the winter?** About five or six months **Analyze Pictures**

6 **Why do you think the expedition stayed at the fort for the winter?** Possible answers: The rivers may have been frozen, making travel difficult. They may have felt that it was too cold and dangerous to camp. **Make Inferences**

***Map Adventure* Answers**

A. Missouri River and Mississippi River

B. East

C. Northwest

D. Southeast

PAGE 280

Steamboats Chug Upstream

Quick Summary Steamboats carrying cargo and passengers caused St. Louis to grow, and the completion of the Erie Canal stimulated growth in Chicago.

7 **Name an advantage that steamboats had over human-powered boats.** Possible answers: Bigger, faster **Compare and Contrast**

Ongoing Assessment

If... students have difficulty making the comparison between a steamboat and a human-powered boat, **then...** ask what limitations a person might face while rowing a boat (Gets tired, cannot pull much weight, can go fast only for a limited time)

8 **Why is a river sometimes called a highway?** It, too, can carry many passengers and cargo. **Apply Information**

Test Talk

Locate Key Words in the Question

9 **What is similar about the growth of St. Louis and Chicago during the 1830s?** Help students recognize that the key word *similar* in the question tells them to look for traits that are alike. Possible answer: Both hub cities grew in response to improved transportation. **Compare and Contrast**

REVIEW ANSWER The steamboat led to increased shipping and transportation, which caused St. Louis to grow. **Cause and Effect**

A steamboat race on the Mississippi River in the early 1800s

Steamboats Chug Upstream

Within fifteen years of the Lewis and Clark expedition, St. Louis had grown from a small trading post into a bustling city. One of the main reasons for this rapid growth was the invention of steamboats. A **steamboat** is a boat powered by a steam engine.

7 Steamboats were bigger and faster than human-powered boats. By the 1820s, steamboats carrying tons of cargo and hundreds of passengers chugged up rivers at speeds as fast as 10 miles per hour. In the 1820s, that was very fast. Such steamboats turned the great rivers of the Midwest into
8 major highways.

In the first three decades of the 1800s, the fur trade held the biggest share of St. Louis's shipping business. However, the steady stream of settlers coming into the region or heading westward from there also made business grow quickly. Farmers shipped their grain by steamboat to sell in markets in St. Louis.

By the 1830s St. Louis ran into competition as the Midwest's main hub of transportation and trade. A **hub** is a center of activity. Chicago, on the banks of Lake Michigan, became a strong rival. The completion of the Erie Canal, which connected the Great Lakes with the Hudson River in New York, drew business to Chicago. In time, the building of railroad lines across the United States would further increase competition between St. Louis and Chicago. 9

REVIEW How did the invention of steamboats affect the city of St. Louis? **Cause and Effect**

280

Practice and Extend

MEETING INDIVIDUAL NEEDS
Leveled Practice

Create a Display Trains still are an important form of transportation. Have students create a two-panel "Then and Now" display.

Easy Have students find pictures and write a brief description (length, number of passengers) comparing passenger trains in the nineteenth century and today. Have them post their information on a "Then and Now" display. **Reteach**

On-Level Have students write "Then" advertisements and "Now" advertisements inviting people to travel by train. Add these to the display. **Extend**

Challenge Have students research improvements in trains over the past 200 years and add this information to the display. **Enrich**

For a Lesson Summary, use Quick Study, p. 60.

Railroads Crisscross the Nation

By the mid-1800s the steamboat was no longer the most modern form of transportation. Railroads had several advantages over water transportation. Rail lines could be built almost anywhere. Weather also did not affect train travel as much as it did travel on steamboats. Ice generally
10 would not keep the trains from running. But ice-clogged rivers stopped steamboat traffic for months during Midwestern winters.

In the 1860s the United States government decided to help build a **transcontinental railroad.** Such a rail 11
line would cross the entire country. While the Civil War was raging, Congress planned a northern route for the railroad. 12
Since Chicago was farther north, it became a more important rail center than St. Louis. In 1869 the transcontinental railroad was completed.

Railroads remained important for travel and trade for almost a century. But by the middle 1900s, cars and trucks had taken over as the main form of transportation in the United States.

REVIEW How did the Civil War affect transportation decisions made at that time? Cause and Effect

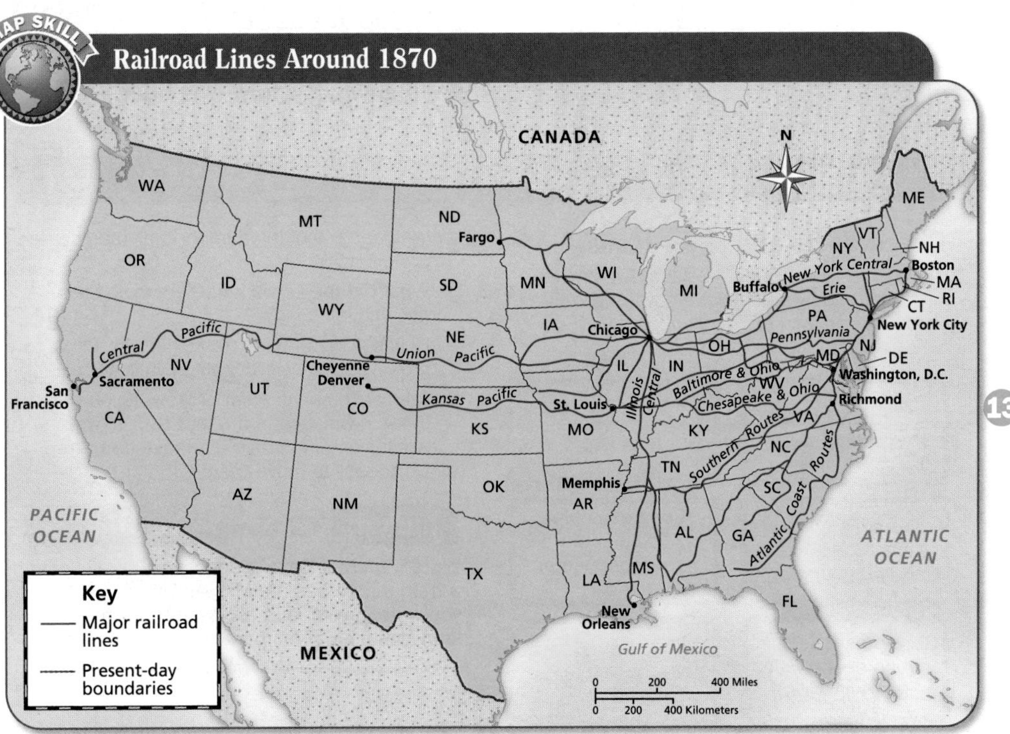

▶ **In 1869 the transcontinental railroad was completed.** 13

MAP SKILL Use a Transportation Map ***What rail lines would you have taken to go from Chicago to Sacramento?***

281

PAGE 281

Railroads Crisscross the Nation

Quick Summary In the mid- to late 1800s, railroads expanded and became an important means of travel and trade.

10 **Compared to boats, what advantages do trains offer?** They can go almost anywhere and in almost any weather. Main Idea and Details

11 **Why do you think the government might be interested in building a transcontinental railroad?** Possible answers: To link the country; to help carry goods; to help the economy Draw Conclusions

Problem Solving

12 **To build the transcontinental railroad, workers began at both ends. What problem might this plan solve? What problem might it cause?** Problem solved: Long time needed to lay all the track (Building from both ends was faster than building from one end.); Possible problem caused: The two sets of tracks might not meet correctly. (Builders were careful to avoid this problem.) Solve Problems

✓ **REVIEW ANSWER** A northern route was chosen because the Southern states had pulled out of the government. Cause and Effect

Railroad Lines About 1870

Point out to students that many of the state boundaries on the map did not yet exist in the 1800s.

13 **How did rail travel in the East differ from rail travel in the West during the late 1800s? Why?** There were many more available routes in the East and only one rail line that reached all the way to the West Coast; the West was not yet as heavily settled as the East. Interpret Maps

MAP SKILL Answer Union Pacific and Central Pacific

MEETING INDIVIDUAL NEEDS
Learning Styles

Ride the Rails Students use their individual learning styles to explore the transcontinental railroad.

Visual Learning Have students do research to trace the route of the first transcontinental railroad. Then they should make an outline map of the United States, shade in mountains and major rivers, trace the route, and locate Promontory Point, Utah, where the two ends met in 1869, with a symbol.

Logical Learning Have students find out how long the first transcontinental railroad was and how long it took to build. Then have students calculate the average length of rail laid each day.

Individual Learning Have students research and then report to the class on passenger rail service in the United States today.

Superhighways Span the States

Quick Summary The government began improving roads in the early 1900s and decided to create the Interstate highway system in the 1950s.

SOCIAL STUDIES STRAND
Government

Land travel in the days before cars and trucks was on foot, on horseback, or in horse-drawn wagons.

14 **Why did the U.S. government decide to link the states by roads?** To improve freight transportation, to transport people, to improve trade **Summarize**

✓ **REVIEW ANSWER** Most things we buy are shipped by truck over the interstate highways. Cause and Effect

Close and Assess

Summarize the Lesson

Have students take turns reading aloud the points on the time line. Have them add details under each event.

✓ **LESSON 4 REVIEW**

1. Cause and Effect For possible answers, see the reduced pupil page.
2. It was near the junction of three important rivers used for trade.
3. Learned that there was no direct water route from the Midwest to the Pacific Ocean; met different Native Americans
4. Many people heading west on steamboats traveled through St. Louis, which was a hub for trade and travel.
5. **Critical Thinking: *Point of View*** Possible answers: Hub of trade and transportation; exciting, big city with people of different cultures

Link to Writing

Student journals should include the term "transcontinental railroad" and details of their imaginary trip.

Superhighways Span the States

In the early 1900s automobiles began to catch on in the United States. People liked being able to travel when they wanted to instead of following a railroad schedule. However, there were few good roads.

The government started building better roads for automobiles in the early 1900s. By the 1950s the government decided that the nation needed a set of wide, fast, interconnecting highways to link all the states. They
14 built the **Interstate highway system,** commonly called superhighways.

Interstate highways carry freight as well as car passengers. Most of the things that we buy are now shipped by truck over the interstate highways. Because of the Midwest's central location, its highways are important for trade.

REVIEW What effect did the building of interstate highways have on shipping? Cause and Effect

Summarize the Lesson

- **More than 1,000 years ago** Native Americans built mounds at Cahokia.
- **1804** Lewis and Clark set out to find a water route to the Pacific Ocean.
- **1820s** Steamboats carried trade on rivers in the Midwest.
- **1869** A transcontinental railroad was built.
- **1950s** The Interstate highway system was built.

LESSON 4 REVIEW

Check Facts and Main Ideas

1. Cause and Effect Make a diagram like the one shown. Complete it by filling in the cause and effects.

Cause	Effect
Steamboats were invented.	Goods and passengers travel on rivers.
Railroads are faster and more reliable than steamboats.	Congress helps to build the transcontinental railroad.
Government decides nation needs wide, fast highways.	The interstate highway system is built.

2. Why was Cahokia an important trade center around 1100?
3. What did the Lewis and Clark expedition accomplish?
4. How did **steamboat** traffic help St. Louis to grow? Use the word **hub** in your answer.
5. **Critical Thinking: *Point of View*** If you were living in Chicago in the mid-1800s, why would you encourage a relative from the Northeast to move there?

Link to Writing

Write a Journal Entry Suppose you are taking a train trip across the Midwest. What would you write in your journal? Use the term **transcontinental railroad** in your journal entry.

282

Practice and Extend

ISSUES AND VIEWPOINTS
Critical Thinking

The government helps automobile owners by building and maintaining roads. It helps rail passengers by supporting some rail lines. Ask: **What if there were not enough money for both?** Write the arguments below on the board. Ask students which they find more persuasive.

Supporters of Roads
- Most families have cars, so the government should meet their needs.
- Trucks can carry important freight, so they need good roads.

Supporters of Railways
- Many people rely on trains to travel to and from work.
- Trains carry many passengers at once, reducing pollution.

Workbook, p. 65

Lesson 4: Hub of the Nation

Main Idea	Supporting Details
Cahokia was once a key trading center in the Midwest.	
President Thomas Jefferson wanted to expand trade.	
One of the main reasons that St. Louis grew quickly was the invention of steamboats.	
Chicago began to rival St. Louis as the center of trade in the Midwest.	
The interstate highway system is very important to the United States.	

Also on Teacher Resources CD-ROM.

Mark Twain

1835–1910

Mark Twain's real name was Samuel Langhorne Clemens. Mark Twain was one of America's most popular writers. He grew up in the small, riverfront town of Hannibal, Missouri. According to Twain, life in Hannibal centered on the steamboats that visited daily. Twain's love of the great river began when he took a trip downstream, intending to go to South America.

BIOFACT

Halley's Comet appeared in 1835, the year that Mark Twain was born. The next time it appeared was 1910, the year that Twain died.

Twain started his career in writing when he worked as a printer's assistant. His first story was about life on the Mississippi.

However, Twain longed to work on the steamboats. In 1859 he became a steamboat pilot and worked on the river for another two years. Twain's years on the (1) Mississippi gave him many stories to tell. It also gave (2) him his pen name. On the riverboats the crew measured the depth of the water using a rope with flags. When someone shouted, "Mark one," the rope went down to its first mark. At this measurement, the water was six feet deep. At "mark twain" the rope was at its second mark. "Mark Twain," or twelve feet, meant the water was deep enough for riverboats to travel safely. Samuel Clemens took this riverboat cry as his name. It represented his love for the Mississippi and the riverboats.

Learn from Biographies

In what ways did working on a steamboat help Twain in the career he later chose as a writer?

For more information go online to *Meet the People* at **www.sfsocialstudies.com.**

283

CURRICULUM CONNECTION
Math

Make Calculations

Ask students to make these calculations.

- Twain means "two." How deep is mark twain? (12 feet)
- How deep is a river at a point that is mark four? (24 feet deep)

WEB SITE
Technology

Students can find out more about Mark Twain by going online and clicking on *Meet the People* at **www.sfsocialstudies.com.**

Mark Twain

Objective

- Explain the effect of steamboats on Mark Twain's career.

1 Introduce and Motivate

Preview To activate prior knowledge, ask students if they have read or seen *Huckleberry Finn* or *Tom Sawyer.* Tell students they will read about the author of these stories. Ask why it is interesting to learn about writers' lives. (To see if their writing is based on their lives)

2 Teach and Discuss

(1) **How did Mark Twain use his experiences in his writing?** He grew up on the Mississippi, so he knew a lot about the river. He used this knowledge in his stories. Apply Information

SOCIAL STUDIES STRAND
Geography

A pilot directs a vehicle's movements. Steamboat pilot Mark Twain wrote that he needed to learn the river's course by heart.

(2) **Why is it important for a pilot to know a course by heart?** To get safely around curves or shallow spots in the river and to travel in the fog and at night Make Inferences

3 Close and Assess

Learn from Biographies Answer

He wrote about his experiences in many stories, and he also got his pen name from his time on the riverboats.

CHAPTER 9
REVIEW

Resources

- Assessment Book, pp. 45–48
- Workbook, p. 66: Vocabulary Review

Chapter Summary

For possible answers, see the reduced pupil page.

Vocabulary

1. d, **2.** e, **3.** a, **4.** b, **5.** c

People

Possible answers:

1. Jacques Marquette was a French priest and explorer who helped develop the fur trade.

2. Jean Baptiste Point Du Sable was a French Haitian settler who built a trading post in a place that grew to become Chicago.

3. John Deere was a blacksmith from Vermont who invented the steel plow.

4. Meriwether Lewis was an explorer who searched for a water route from the Midwest to the Pacific Ocean.

5. Mark Twain was a popular American writer who described life along the Mississippi River.

CHAPTER 9
REVIEW

1800 · 1810 · 1820

1804 Lewis and Clark expedition began.

1820s Steamboats travel on rivers.

Chapter Summary

Cause and Effect

Make a diagram like the one shown at the right. Complete the empty boxes.

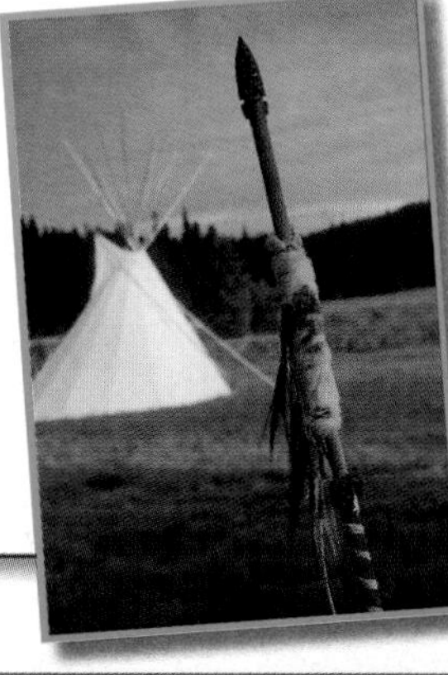

▶ Ojibwa hunting tools

Cause	Effect
In the Ojibwa homeland, forests were too thick for farming.	The Ojibwa's main food source was from hunting and fishing.
Wood was not available on the prairie.	Farmers used available materials such as sod to build homes.
Interstate highways are built.	People and freight move more easily.

Vocabulary

Match each word with the correct definition or description.

1. **mission** (p. 265)
2. **sod** (p. 270)
3. **drought** (p. 272)
4. **transcontinental railroad** (p. 281)
5. **interstate highway system** (p. 282)

a. little precipitation over a long period
b. rail lines that cross the country
c. roads that link all states
d. a settlement set up by a religious group
e. earth materials used for building

People

Describe each person, and tell why each has been important in the Midwest region.

1. **Jacques Marquette** (p. 265)
2. **Jean Baptiste Point Du Sable** (p. 266)
3. **John Deere** (p. 273)
4. **Meriwether Lewis** (p. 278)
5. **Mark Twain** (p. 283)

284

Practice and Extend

Assessment Options

✓ Chapter 9 Assessment

- Chapter 9 Content Test: Use Assessment Book, pp. 45–46.
- Chapter 9 Skills Test: Use Assessment Book, pp. 47–48.

Standardized Test Prep

- Chapter 9 Tests contain standardized test format.

✓ Chapter 9 Performance Assessment

- Have students work in small groups to review events in time. Provide each group with a large piece of paper.
- Students should make four large circles on the paper, one labeled *1600s,* one labeled *1700s,* one labeled *1800s,* and one labeled *1900s*. Students should take turns adding a detail from this chapter to the appropriate circle.
- Observe students as they work; if necessary, have them review the lesson for details.

1830 | 1840 | 1850 | 1860 | 1870

1843 Wapello County land rush

1869 Transcontinental railroad was completed.

Facts and Main Ideas

Write your answers on a separate sheet of paper.

1. How did the Ojibwa of the 1600s adapt to living in the northern Great Lakes region?
2. **Main Idea** Why was the fur trade very important to the Midwest?
3. **Main Idea** What was the result of special treaties the Ojibwa had with the United States government?
4. **Main Idea** Why were Cahokia and St. Louis good places for trade?
5. What advances in technology and transportation in the mid-1800s helped Midwestern farmers be successful?
6. **Time Line** About how many years were there between the Lewis and Clark expedition and the Wapello County land rush in Iowa?
7. **Critical Thinking:** ***Make Generalizations*** How can the Midwest be called the "Hub of the Country"?

Write About History

1. **Write an advertisement** for your favorite form of transportation. Include pictures and a slogan or a plan for a videotape.
2. **Write a diary entry** telling what it was like for someone your age to live in the Midwest some time long ago. You might be a member of a Native American family or a member of a pioneer family.
3. **Write a story** from the point of view of a railroad worker living in what is today South Dakota, near the Missouri River. Describe the changes you hope to see in the area after the tracks are laid.

Apply Skills

Using a Search Engine

Look at the following list to be used to search the Web for information:

- Samuel L. Clemens
- Hannibal, Missouri
- Steamboats
- Famous American writers

1. What is this research probably about?
2. What other words and phrases might you add to the list? Why?
3. Would you be more likely to find the information you want at a .gov, .com, or .edu site? Why?

Create your own list of search terms for another topic in the chapter.

Internet Activity

To get help with vocabulary, people, and terms, select the dictionary or encyclopedia from *Social Studies Library* at **www.sfsocialstudies.com.**

285

Hands-on Unit Project

✓ Unit 4 Performance Assessment

- See p. 290 for information about using the Unit Project as a means of performance assessment.
- A scoring guide is provided on p. 290.

WEB SITE Technology

For more information, students can select the dictionary or encyclopedia from *Social Studies Library* at **www.sfsocialstudies.com.**

Workbook, p. 66

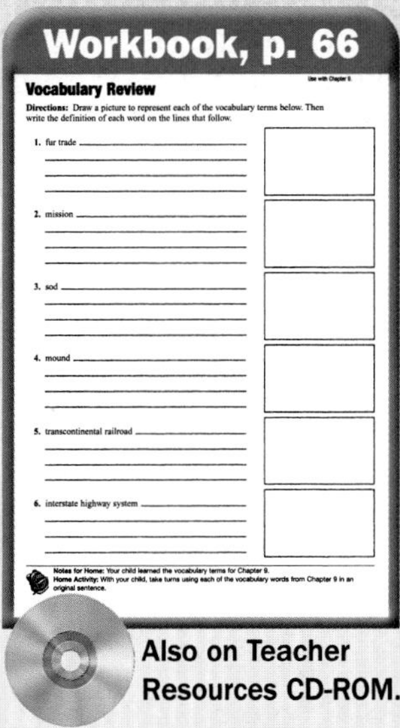

Vocabulary Review

1. fur trade
2. mission
3. sod
4. mound
5. transcontinental railroad
6. interstate highway system

Also on Teacher Resources CD-ROM.

Facts and Main Ideas

1. By hunting and fishing and traveling by canoe
2. It established a relationship between Native Americans and the French.
3. Reservations were set up for them in the Great Lakes area.
4. They were in excellent locations near several major rivers.
5. Steamboat, plow, railroad
6. About 39 years
7. Possible answers: Because the Midwest is accessible by boats, trains, cars, and airplanes; much trade and business goes through the Midwest.

Write About History

1. Encourage students working on print ads to feature a prominent slogan and to add supporting details in smaller letters. Point out to students planning a videotape that the subject matter lends itself to motion.
2. Students need not write diary entries for every day. Instead, encourage them to choose significant days such as holidays or birthdays and a few representative days from each season.
3. Students' stories might tell of growth in population, modernization, and replacement of forests and unsettled areas with housing, roads, and railroad tracks.

Apply Skills

1. Mark Twain
2. Mark Twain; Tom Sawyer; Mississippi River; These also have to do with the subject.
3. Possible answer: .edu; because schools throughout the United States teach about Mark Twain

I've Been Working on the Railroad

Objective

- Analyze the meaning of the work song "I've Been Working on the Railroad."

Resource

- Transparency 52

1 Introduce and Motivate

Preview To activate prior knowledge, hum the tune or sing the melody. Many students will be familiar with this song. Have volunteers sing aloud, using the words to prompt any memory lapses.

2 Teach and Discuss

1 **How do you think rhythmic songs like this one might have helped railroad workers do their job?** Possible answers: The rhythm may have provided a steady beat for hammering or digging; rhythmic singing may have helped them pass the time or keep their spirits up.
Draw Conclusions

UNIT 4 End with a Song

I've Been Working on the Railroad

1 People came from many countries to build the railroads that cross the United States. In the 1800s men worked to the rhythm of this song as they laid the first railroad tracks.

Work Song from the United States

Ⓐ *With a swing*

2 I've been work-ing on the rail - road, All the live-long day;
I've been work-ing on the rail - road, Just to pass the time a - way.
3 Don't you hear the whis-tle blow - ing? Rise up so ear-ly in the morn.
Don't you hear the cap-tain shout - ing: "Di - nah, blow your horn!"

286

Practice and Extend

SOCIAL STUDIES
Background

"I've Been Working on the Railroad"

- The origins of the tune are not known, but it may have come from an African American song or a song sung by Irish work gangs in the Old West.
- The first two verses are original. "Dinah" and "Someone's in the kitchen" were added later.
- *Dinah* possibly refers to a locomotive engine or a woman. A horn blowing was the signal for railroad workers to break for lunch.

AUDIO CD
Technology

Play the CD *Songs and Music* to listen to "I've Been Working on the Railroad."

287

2 Who is the "I" of the song? A railroad worker **Draw Conclusions**

3 What do you think the whistle signals? The beginning of the workday **Make Inferences**

3 Close and Assess

- Have students discuss ways to perform this song. Students who play musical instruments may be interested in playing the song for the class.
- Tell students that, throughout history, workers have sung rhythmic songs like this one to make their work easier. As a class, think of other groups that are well-known for their use of rhythmic songs or chants.
- Sing "I've Been Working on the Railroad" as a class. While students are singing, have them pantomime using a shovel or sledgehammer in time to the music.

ESL

BUILD BACKGROUND

ESL Support

Interpret a Song Students analyze and practice singing a familiar American tune.

Beginning Act out the lyrics as you speak them. Have children hum the tune and pantomime to accompany you.

Intermediate Explain the meaning of each line as students repeat the lyrics after you. Rehearse the song in small groups, then act out blowing the horn, the captain shouting, and the strumming banjo.

Advanced Have groups of students perform the song as a musical play.

Resource

- Assessment Book, pp. 49–52

Main Ideas and Vocabulary

1. b, **2.** c, **3.** a, **4.** d

Test Talk

Use Information from the Text
Use Main Ideas and Vocabulary, Question 3, to model the Test Talk strategy.

Decide where you will look for the answer.
Have students make notes about details from the text that answer the question.

Use information from the text.
Have students check their notes, then ask themselves, "Do I have the right information?" Have students look back at the question and the text to make sure they have the right answer.

UNIT 4 Review

Test Talk

Look for details to support your answer.

Main Ideas and Vocabulary

TEST PREP

Read the passage below and use it to answer the questions that follow.

The Midwest region is at the center of the United States. Its waterways connect the Midwest to the rest of the United States and to the world.

In the 1700s the French came to the Midwest region. The French also used the waterways for trade. They built fur-trading posts on the rivers. These trading posts grew into large cities.

In the early and mid-1800s, many people traveled on waterways as they settled in the Midwest. However, in the 1900s, automobiles began to catch on in America. People liked being able to travel when they wanted to instead of following a railroad schedule. Soon the Interstate highway system was developed.

The Midwest has served as a center, or hub, of transportation. In the early 1800s steamboats brought traffic to the region's many rivers and lakes. In the mid-1800s railroads became the most popular form of transportation. Trains from the Northeast and Southeast regions connected to trains going westward. Today the vast superhighways carry traffic across the country.

1. According to the passage, which became large cities?
   - **A** Native American hunting grounds
   - **B** French fur-trading posts
   - **C** farms beside the Great Lakes
   - **D** railroad repair yards

2. In the passage the phrase Interstate highway system means
   - **A** a large road
   - **B** transportation
   - **C** a set of roads that connect states
   - **D** traffic jams

3. The passage as a whole illustrates
   - **A** how the Midwest became a transportation hub
   - **B** how the Midwest became popular
   - **C** why people chose to move to the Midwest
   - **D** why wheels also have hubs

4. In the passage the word superhighways means
   - **A** the waterways of the Midwest
   - **B** the Midwest's central locations
   - **C** unpaved roads
   - **D** large roads that carry goods and people across the country

288

Practice and Extend

Assessment Options

✓ Unit 4 Assessment

- Unit 4 Content Test: Use Assessment Book, pp. 49–50.
- Unit 4 Skills Test: Use Assessment Book, pp. 51–52.

Standardized Test Prep

- Unit 4 Tests contain standardized test format.

✓ Unit 4 Performance Assessment

- See p. 290 for information about using the Unit Project as a means of performance assessment.
- A scoring guide for the Unit 4 Project is provided in the teacher's notes on p. 290.

Test Talk

- Test Talk Practice Book

WEB SITE
Technology

For more information, you can select the dictionary or encyclopedia from *Social Studies Library* at **www.sfsocialstudies.com.**

People and Places

Match each person or term with its description.

1. **Illinois Waterway** (p. 234)
2. **Cahokia** (p. 277)
3. **Louis Jolliet** (p. 265)
4. **Jean Baptiste Point Du Sable** (p. 267)
5. **William Clark** (p. 278)

a. canoed down the Mississippi River to claim land for France

b. traveled the Missouri River

c. connects Lake Michigan to Mississippi River

d. built a trading post in area that became Chicago

e. ancient city that was a center of trade

Apply Skills

Make a Bar Graph There is an Arts Camp located in Michigan. Students from all over the United States attend this camp. With the following data, create a bar graph showing how many students come from each state:

The number of students ranges from 0–400.

73 from Florida
225 from Illinois
50 from Indiana
350 from Michigan
60 from New York
140 from Ohio

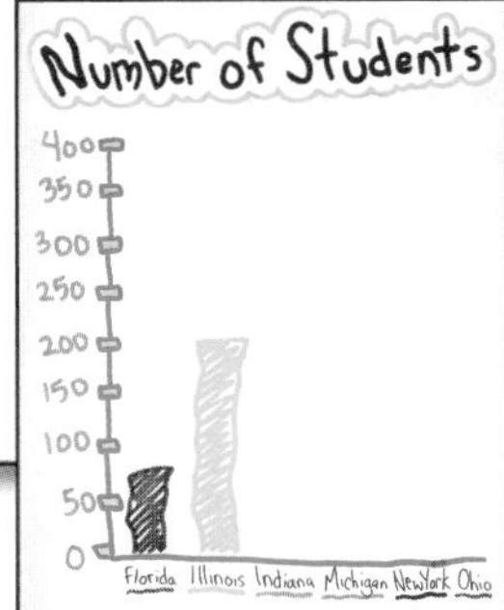

Write and Share

Write a Poem As a class write a poem about how the Midwest has changed from the 1600s to the present. Divide up the centuries and form small groups to write a stanza about each time division. Decide whether or not you want your poem to rhyme. After all the groups have finished writing their stanzas, get together with the other groups and read your stanzas in time order.

Read on Your Own

Look for books like these in the library:

289

Revisit the Unit Question

✓ Portfolio Assessment

- Have students look at the lists that they compiled throughout Unit 4 of advantages midwesterners enjoy.
- Ask students to write a summary expressing whether they would like to live in the Midwest and why or why not.
- Have students add their lists and summaries to their Social Studies Portfolio.

People and Places

1. c, **2.** e, **3.** a, **4.** d, **5.** b

Apply Skills

- Analyze the sample bar graph with students, reviewing how it is constructed and read.
- Help students decide what scale they should use.
- Use the following scoring guide.

✓ Assessment Scoring Guide

Make a Bar Graph	
6	Graph is clear, readable, and accurate with correctly proportioned bars.
5	Graph is clear, readable, and mostly accurate. One bar may not be entirely proportional.
4	Graph is generally clear, readable, and accurate. Two bars may not be entirely proportional.
3	Graph is generally clear and accurate. Bars may not be entirely proportional.
2	Graph lacks clarity or accuracy. At least one bar has errors.
1	Graph lacks clarity and accuracy. Two or more bars have errors.

If you prefer a 4-point rubric, adjust accordingly.

Write and Share

- If possible, keep groups small so that each student contributes directly.
- Encourage students to read their stanzas aloud within the group. Hearing the poem can help them identify and fix errors.

Read on Your Own

Have students prepare oral reports, using the following books.

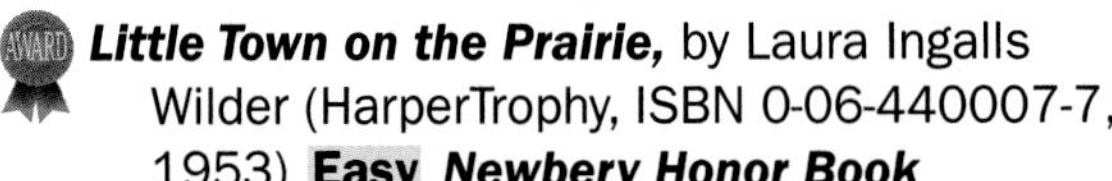

Little Town on the Prairie, by Laura Ingalls Wilder (HarperTrophy, ISBN 0-06-440007-7, 1953) **Easy** ***Newbery Honor Book***

One Nation, Many Tribes, by Kathleen Krull (Viking Penguin, ISBN 0-140-36522-2, 1999) **On-Level**

The Adventures of Tom Sawyer, by Mark Twain (Viking Children's Books, ISBN 0-670-86985-6, 1996) **Challenge**

Unit Project

Point of View

Objective
- Understand that people have more than one point of view about events.

Resource
- Workbook, p. 67

Materials
pencils, paper, additional reference materials if necessary

Follow This Procedure
- Explain that students will debate an issue that was important to the history of a state in the Midwest.
- Brainstorm a list of issues with students and write them on the board.
- Group students into teams. Have each team summarize for their issue.
- Brainstorm definitions of factual evidence with students, and discuss how to gather it. Explain that, even if students present a point of view they don't agree with, they must present it in a convincing fashion.
- Allow students time to gather facts. Encourage students to be prepared to argue against the opposing side.
- Choose a student to be the moderator and make sure that students have equal time presenting their positions.
- Have students conduct their debate before the class. Each team should present their point of view as well as argue against the opposing side.
- Use the following scoring guide.

✓Assessment Scoring Guide

	Point of View
6	Finds and presents many accurate facts and information to support clear point of view
5	Finds and presents accurate facts and information to support point of view
4	Finds and presents facts and information to support point of view
3	Finds and presents several facts and some information to support point of view
2	Finds and presents few facts and little information to weakly support point of view
1	Presents few or no facts and inaccurate information, or does not support point of view at all

If you require a 4-point rubric, adjust accordingly.

UNIT 4 Project

Point of View

People often have different ideas about one topic. Take sides and discuss different points of view.

1 Form a group. Choose a topic covered in this unit that was important to your state's history. Write a sentence about your topic.

2 Find two sides of the topic. Write sentences with facts that support each side.

3 Decide who will argue each side.

4 Debate your topic for the class.

Internet Activity

Explore the Midwest on the Internet. Go to **www.sfsocialstudies.com/activities** and select your grade and unit.

290

Practice and Extend

Hands-on Unit Project

✓Performance Assessment
- The Unit Project can also be used as a performance assessment activity.
- Use the scoring guide to assess each group's work.

WEB SITE
Technology

Students can launch the Internet Activity by clicking on *Grade 4, Unit 4* at **www.sfsocialstudies.com/activities.**

Workbook, p. 67

Unit 4 Project **Point of View**

Directions: In a group, debate two sides of an event or topic in your state's history.

1. Our debate topic is ______
2. Here are two points of view and facts to support each side:

Pro: ______

Facts: ______

Con: ______

Facts: ______

3. ______ will give the Pro argument.
4. ______ will give the Con argument.
5. The class chose the ______ argument as the best presentation.

✓Checklist for Students
- ____ We chose a topic to debate.
- ____ We identified two sides of the topic.
- ____ We wrote facts to support two sides of the topic.
- ____ We decided who will argue each side.
- ____ We held our debate for the class.

Notes for Home: Your child learned how to defend a point of view.
Home Activity: Identify a topic of interest at home and two opposing points of view. With your child, debate the issue to support your position. Which side of the discussion presents the best supporting

Also on Teacher Resources CD-ROM.

★ Unit 5 ★

Vocabulary Routines

The following examples of reading and vocabulary development strategies can be used to instruct students about unit vocabulary.

BEFORE READING

Individual Word Study

Creating Sentences Students will be better prepared to read about a new topic if they have had the opportunity to think about key terms before reading. Having students create sentences that use an unfamiliar new concept in combination with related words that they already know well helps students assess their knowledge and engage more fully with a new topic. Before students read a new lesson, select a key term and write it on the board. Beside it, write a number of familiar words that might appear in a sentence with the key term. Then assign partners and have students work together to write one or more sentences using both the new word and some of the familiar words.

I've written the word homestead *on the board because it's an important concept in the lesson we're about to read. At one time, the United States government gave land to settlers who would live on the land and raise crops. This land was called a homestead. Here are some words that are related to homestead.* (Write *settler, land, farm, crops, fences, live, own,* and *fields.*) *I want you and your partner and write one or more sentences using* homestead *with any of these other words. Then we can share some of your ideas.*

homestead
I own this homestead. I put a fence around my land.

DURING READING

Context Clues

Have You Ever Having students use newly learned words to describe their own experiences or thoughts will help them understand that there is a place for these new terms in their own vocabulary. The routine shown below can be used with vocabulary terms throughout the unit, directly after a new term has been encountered. Allow as much discussion as time permits.

Think about the word arid. *Have you ever visited an arid climate? What sorts of climates have you seen in movies, television, and cartoons? Have any of these shown a scene that takes place in an arid climate? Have you ever read a book that described an arid climate? Think of a sentence that describes a scene that you watched or read about that is set in an arid place. Use the word* arid *in your sentence.*

AFTER READING

Related Word Study

Picture This Assign pairs of students a Unit 5 vocabulary word (for example, *vaquero* or *missionary*) or group of words (possible combinations might include *adobe* with *pueblo* or *gusher* with *refinery*). Have a collection of books and magazines that students can go through to find images that might be used to illustrate each word. Students can also use the Internet or encyclopedias. Once students find some images, have them write a paragraph explaining how the images relate to the word or words. Then have students share with the class what they found.

I want you and your partner to talk about the words you have been assigned. Find where they are used in the book. This will help you to remember why we have learned them. Then go through the books and magazines, or use the Internet or encyclopedias, and find pictures that show something about what your words mean. Work together and write a paragraph explaining how the pictures relate to the meaning of your word. Then you will share the pictures with the class and tell us what the picture shows about your word's meaning.

The Southwest

UNIT 5

Unit Planning Guide

Unit 5 • The Southwest

Begin with a Primary Source pp. 292–293

Welcome to the Southwest pp. 294–295

Target Skill **Reading Social Studies, Draw Conclusions** pp. 296–297

Chapter Titles	Pacing	Main Ideas
Chapter 10 **Land and Resources of the Southwest** pp. 298–319 ✓ **Chapter 10 Review** pp. 320–321	8 days	• The Grand Canyon dazzles visitors with its size and beauty. • The Southwest climate can vary greatly. It is dry in some places and moist in others. • The Southwest is a region of discovery and research.
Chapter 11 **The People of the Southwest** pp. 322–351 ✓ **Chapter 11 Review** pp. 352–353	12 days	• The Navajo have lived in the Southwest for centuries. • Explorers and missionaries brought a Spanish presence to the Southwest. • The cattle industry boomed in the Southwest in the 1800s. The cowboys who herded cattle became part of our nation's lore. • High temperatures and a shortage of water can make living in the desert a challenge.

End with Literature pp. 354–355

✓ **Unit 5 Review** pp. 356–357

✓ **Unit 5 Project** p. 358

✓ = **Assessment Options**

The Grand Canyon is a "natural treasure" of the Southwest. It was made a national park in 1919.

Resources	Meeting Individual Needs
• Workbook, pp. 69–73 • Every Student Learns Guide, pp. 122–133 • Transparencies 23, 53 • Quick Study, pp. 62–67 • Workbook, p. 74 ✓Chapter 10 Content Test, Assessment Book, pp. 53–54 ✓Chapter 10 Skills Test, Assessment Book, pp. 55–56	• Leveled Practice, TE pp. 301, 311, 316 • ESL Support, TE pp. 302, 306, 309, 317, 318 • Learning Styles, TE p. 310 ✓Chapter 10 Performance Assessment, TE p. 320
• Workbook, pp. 75–81 • Every Student Learns Guide, pp. 134–149 • Transparencies 18, 23, 54–56 • Quick Study, pp. 68–75 • Workbook, p. 82 ✓Chapter 11 Content Test, Assessment Book, pp. 57–58 ✓Chapter 11 Skills Test, Assessment Book, pp. 59–60	• Leveled Practice, TE pp. 325, 334, 343, 347 • ESL Support, TE pp. 327, 335, 336, 341, 348 • Learning Styles, TE p. 350 ✓Chapter 11 Performance Assessment, TE p. 352

The Navajo, who lived in the Southwest long before European settlers, have long been known for their extraordinary craftsmanship.

Providing More Depth

Additional Resources

- Trade Books
- Family Activities
- Vocabulary Workbook and Cards
- Social Studies Plus! pp. 98–117
- Daily Activity Bank
- Read Alouds and Primary Sources pp. 69–85
- Big Book Atlas
- Student Atlas
- Outline Maps
- Desk Maps

Technology

- AudioText
- Video Field Trips: Exploring the Southwest
- Songs and Music
- Digital Learning CD-ROM Powered by KnowledgeBox (Video clips and activities)
- MindPoint® Quiz Show CD-ROM
- ExamView® Test Bank CD-ROM
- Teacher Resources CD-ROM
- Map Resources CD-ROM
- SF SuccessNet: iText (Pupil Edition online), iTE (Teacher's Edition online), Online Planner
- **www.sfsocialstudies.com** (Biographies, news, references, maps, and activities)

To establish guidelines for your students' safe and responsible use of the Internet, use the Scott Foresman Internet Guide.

Additional Internet Links

To find out more about:

- John Wesley Powell, visit **www.powellmuseum.org**
- Willis Haviland Carrier, visit **www.invent.org**
- Kit Carson, visit **www.pbs.org**

Unit 5 Objectives

Beginning of Unit 5

- Use primary sources to acquire information. (p. 292)
- Describe selected aspects of states in the Southwest. (p. 294)
- Interpret print and visual material by drawing conclusions. (p. 296)

Chapter 10

Lesson 1 A Land of Canyons
pp. 300–304

- Describe how the Grand Canyon was carved out by erosion caused by the Colorado River.
- Describe how erosion by water, wind, and sand continues to shape the Grand Canyon.
- Explain that the Grand Canyon is a magnificent landform that provides beauty and adventure.
- Explain why the Grand Canyon has been made a national park.
- Interpret print and visual material by drawing conclusions.
- Identify the contributions of early explorers of the Southwest, such as John Wesley Powell. (p. 305)
- Interpret information by making generalizations. (p. 306)

Lesson 2 Climates in the Southwest
pp. 308–311

- Describe different climates found in the Southwest.
- Describe how the saguaro has adapted to a desert climate.
- Explain why the saguaro is important to desert animals.
- Compare and contrast climates and vegetation in different regions of the world. (p. 312)

Lesson 3 Oil and Technology
pp. 314–317

- Identify a nonrenewable natural resource in the Southwest.
- Describe how the technology of the Southwest has impacted the United States.
- Identify the technological contributions of women such as Jerrie Cobb. (p. 318)
- Identify an example of a person who shows caring. (p. 318)

Chapter 11

Lesson 1 The Navajo pp. 324–328

- Describe the early culture of the Navajo people.
- Describe "The Long Walk."
- Explain how the Navajo Council governs the Navajo Nation.
- Identify the contributions of significant individuals, such as Henry Chee Dodge. (p. 329)
- Use primary and secondary sources to acquire information. (p. 330)

Lesson 2 Spanish Influence
pp. 332–337

- Describe Spanish influence in the Southwest.
- Describe the effects missionaries had on some Native Americans.

Lesson 3 Ranches and Drivers
pp. 338–343

- Explain how cattle raising helped the economy of the Southwest develop.
- Describe the roles of cowboys and cowgirls in the Southwest.
- Identify the route of the Chisholm Trail and explain the role it played in the cattle trade.
- Contrast ranching in the Southwest in the past with ranching in the present.
- Describe life on ranches and cattle trails. (p. 344)
- Explain how the work of cowboys and cowgirls has changed over time. (p. 344)

Lesson 4 Living in the Desert
pp. 346–348

- Explain how irrigation has affected the economy of the Southwest.
- Describe how air conditioning has impacted the economy of the Southwest.
- Identify the technological contributions of inventors such as Willis Haviland Carrier. (p. 349)
- Identify the historical significance of Route 66 to the Southwest. (p. 350)

End of Unit 5

- Describe the tasks that cowhands perform. (p. 354)
- Infer that skills become more developed as a person matures. (p. 354)
- Understand that products and businesses contribute to a state's economy. (p. 358)

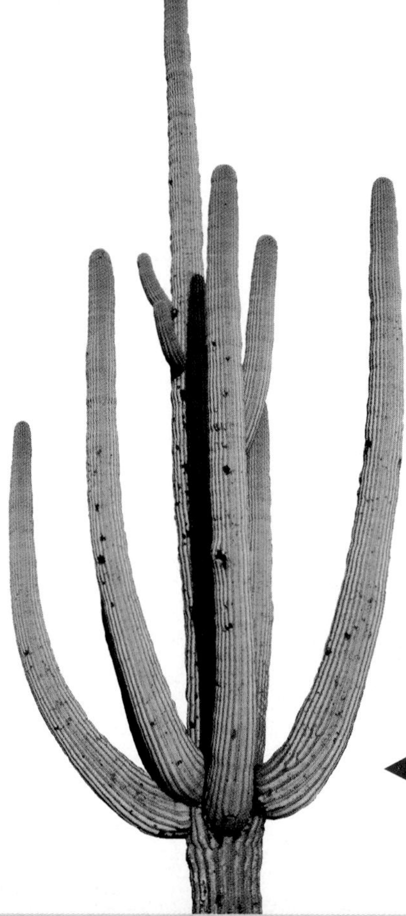

The giant saguaro cactus has become a symbol of the Southwest.

Assessment Options

✓ Formal Assessment

- **Lesson Reviews,** PE/TE pp. 304, 311, 317, 328, 337, 343, 348
- **Chapter Reviews,** PE/TE pp. 320–321, 352–353
- **Chapter Tests,** Assessment Book pp. 53–60
- **Unit Review**, PE/TE pp. 356–357
- **Unit Tests,** Assessment Book, pp. 61–64
- **ExamView® Test Bank CD-ROM** (test-generator software)

✓ Informal Assessment

- **Teacher's Edition Questions,** throughout Lessons and Features
- **Section Reviews,** PE/TE pp. 301, 303–304, 309, 311, 315, 317, 325, 327–328, 333, 335, 337, 339–341, 343, 347–348
- **Close and Assess,** TE pp. 297, 304–305, 307, 311, 313, 317, 319, 328–329, 331, 337, 343, 345, 348–349, 351, 355

Ongoing Assessment

Ongoing Assessment is found throughout the Teacher's Edition lessons using an **If...then** model.

If = students' observable behavior, **then =** reteaching and enrichment suggestions

✓ Portfolio Assessment

- **Portfolio Assessment,** TE pp. 291, 292, 357
- **Leveled Practice,** TE pp. 301, 311, 316, 325, 334, 343, 347
- **Workbook Pages,** pp. 68–83
- **Chapter Reviews: Write About It,** PE/TE pp. 321, 353
- **Unit Review: Apply Skills,** PE/TE p. 357
- **Curriculum Connection: Writing,** PE/TE pp. 311, 337, 343; TE pp. 293, 340, 355

✓ Performance Assessment

- **Hands-on Unit Project** (Unit 5 Performance Assessment), TE pp. 291, 321, 353, 358
- **Internet Activity,** PE p. 358
- **Chapter 10 Performance Assessment,** TE p. 320
- **Chapter 11 Performance Assessment,** TE p. 352
- **Unit Review: Write and Share,** PE/TE p. 357
- **Scoring Guides,** TE pp. 357–358

Test Talk

Test-Taking Strategies

Understand the Question

- **Locate Key Words in the Question,** TE p. 316
- **Locate Key Words in the Text,** TE p. 302

Understand the Answer

- **Choose the Right Answer,** Test Talk Practice Book
- **Use Information from the Text,** TE p. 340
- **Use Information from Graphics,** PE/TE p. 356, TE p. 309
- **Write Your Answer to Score High,** TE p. 345

For additional practice, use the Test Talk Practice Book.

Featured Strategy

Use Information from Graphics

Students will:

- Understand the question and form a statement that begins "I need to find out . . ."
- Skim the graphics to find the right information to support their answer.

PE/TE p. 356, **TE** p. 309

Curriculum Connections

Integrating Your Day

The lessons, skills, and features of Unit 5 provide many opportunities to make connections between social studies and other areas of the elementary curriculum.

Social Studies

READING

Reading Skill—Draw Conclusions, PE/TE pp. 296–297, 300, 308, 314, 332, 338

Lesson Review—Draw Conclusions, PE/TE pp. 304, 311, 317, 337, 343

WRITING

Write an Exploration Journal, TE p. 293

Link to Writing, PE/TE pp. 311, 337, 343

"Ride 'em, Cowboy!" TE p. 340

Write a Poem, TE p. 355

SCIENCE

Link to Science, PE/TE pp. 304, 317, 348

Investigate Tallow, TE p. 339

ART

Use Perspective, TE p. 293

Research Canyon Activities, TE p. 307

Link to Art, PE/TE p. 328

Explore Spanish Architecture, TE p. 337

MUSIC / DRAMA

Hear the Grand Canyon, TE p. 304

Write and Perform a Play, TE p. 329

"Git Along, Little Dogie," TE p. 340

LITERATURE

Read About the Southwest, TE p. 294

Read Biographies, TE p. 305

Read About Unusual Plants, TE p. 312

Read About Ranching, TE p. 345

MATH

Create a Bar Graph, TE p. 309

Multiply and Divide, TE p. 339

Look for this symbol throughout the Teacher's Edition to find **Curriculum Connections.**

Professional Development

Real-World Knowledge and Authentic Assessment

by James B. Kracht, Ph.D.
Texas A&M University

Assessment provides information about how well students have achieved the goals set forth in the curriculum.

Traditional assessments such as quizzes, tests, and standardized achievement-styled tests can be used to identify mastery of factual information and determine a student's ability to comprehend, analyze, and apply information. *Test-taking strategies and a variety of assessment options for Unit 5 are outlined on p. 291e of the Teacher's Edition. On pp. 297, 320, 352, and 356, content, skills, and standardized tests identify traditional assessment opportunities by chapter and by unit.*

Authentic assessments are based on real-world tasks and require students to do things or solve problems faced by adults in their daily lives. *On p. 349 of the Teacher's Edition, students are asked to use problem solving to find ways to conserve energy when using air conditioning.*

Portfolio assessments are purposeful collections of student work that provide evidence of how well students meet curricular standards. *On pp. 291, 292, and 357 of the Teacher's Edition, students are directed to compile lists of geographic, cultural, and economic features that might encourage people to visit or move to the Southwest, then form a generalization about these features, and finally add these generalizations to their Social Studies portfolio.*

Performance tasks actively involve students in applying their knowledge to produce a product or a performance. *The Hands-on Unit Project, noted on pp. 291, 321, 353, and 358 of the Teacher's Edition, has students creating an infomercial about a product or business.*

ESL Support

by Jim Cummins, Ph.D.
University of Toronto

In Unit 5, you can use the following fundamental strategy to help ESL students access content.

Access Content

We can support students' learning by modifying the input itself. There is general agreement among applied linguists that sufficient *comprehensible input* is necessary for acquisition of a second or third language. Exposure itself is not enough—it must be exposure that learners can understand. Furthermore, the input should contain structures that are a little beyond what the learner already knows.

The Use of Visuals

There is a lot of truth to the expression "A picture is worth a thousand words." Visuals enable students to "see" a basic concept much more effectively than through words alone. Once students have the concept, they are much more likely to be able to figure out the meaning of the words we use to talk about it.

The Role of Student Identity

Equally important in accessing content is the motivation and sense of ownership that students bring to the task. If social studies is to become more than just a set of inert facts, we need to find ways to make the content relevant to students' lives. The challenge is to link the social realities and history of society to students' personal realities and histories.

The following examples in the Teacher's Edition will help you empower ESL students to access content:

- ***Identify Electronic Products** on p. 317 uses illustrations to help English Language Learners identify and understand different technologies.*
- ***Use Context and Picture Clues** on p. 327 uses visual cues to help students understand concepts developed in the text.*

Read Aloud

Flashback
by Rebecca Salinas

I looked upon the ol' Southwest
From where I could see the best.
I witnessed Coronado
And his fading golden dreams.
I saw the brave vaqueros
Drive the cattle teams.
I watched the missionaries
Teaching Navajos a trade.
I saw Spindletop shoot crude,
From which oil's made.
Yes, the past played out before me
As I stood on the edge of history.

Definitions

- *vaquero:* Spanish cowboy
- *missionary:* person who works to advance a religion

Read Alouds and Primary Sources

- *Read Alouds and Primary Sources* contains additional selections to be used with Unit 5.

Bibliography

The Legend of the African Bao-Bab Tree, by Bobbie Dooley Hunter (Africa World Press, ISBN 0-86543-422-0, 1994) **Easy**

Pecos Bill, by Steven Kellogg (HarperCollins Children's Book Group, ISBN 0-688-05871-X, 1986) **Easy** ***Land of Enchantment Book Award***

The Unbreakable Code, by Sara Hoagland Hunter (Northland Publishing, ISBN 0-87358-638-7, 1996) **Easy**

Calamity Jane, by Calamity Jane (Applewoods Books, ISBN 1-55709-369-5, 1997) **On-Level**

The Colorado River, by Carol B. Rawlins (Franklin Watts, ISBN 0-531-16421-7, 2000) **On-Level**

A Right Fine Life: Kit Carson on the Santa Fe Trail, by Andrew Glass (Holiday House, ISBN 0-8234-1326-8, 1997) **On-Level**

Annie Oakley, by Ellen Wilson (Simon & Schuster, ISBN 0-689-71346-0, 1989) **Challenge**

Get Along, Little Dogies: The Chisholm Trail Diary of Hallie Lou Wells, by Lisa Waller Rogers (Texas Tech University Press, ISBN 0-89672-448-4, 2001) **Challenge**

In Search of the Grand Canyon: Down the Colorado with John Wesley Powell, by Mary Ann Fraser (Henry Holt & Company, ISBN 0-8050-5543-6, 1997) **Challenge**

Business Builders in Oil, by Nathan Aaseng (Oliver Press, ISBN 1-881508-56-0, 2000) **Teacher reference**

Cowboys in the Old West, by Gail B. Stewart (Lucent Books, ISBN 1-56006-077-8, 1995) **Teacher reference**

***Discovery Channel School* Video**

The Battle of the Alamo This video uses recent footage of the fort along with historic artwork from American hero David Crockett to re-create the Battle of the Alamo. (Item #715870, 52 minutes)

- To order *Discovery Channel School* videos, please call the following toll-free number: 1-888-892-3484.
- Free online lesson plans are available at **DiscoverySchool.com.**

Look for this symbol throughout the Teacher's Edition to find **Award-Winning Selections.** Additional book references are suggested throughout this unit.

The Southwest

UNIT 5

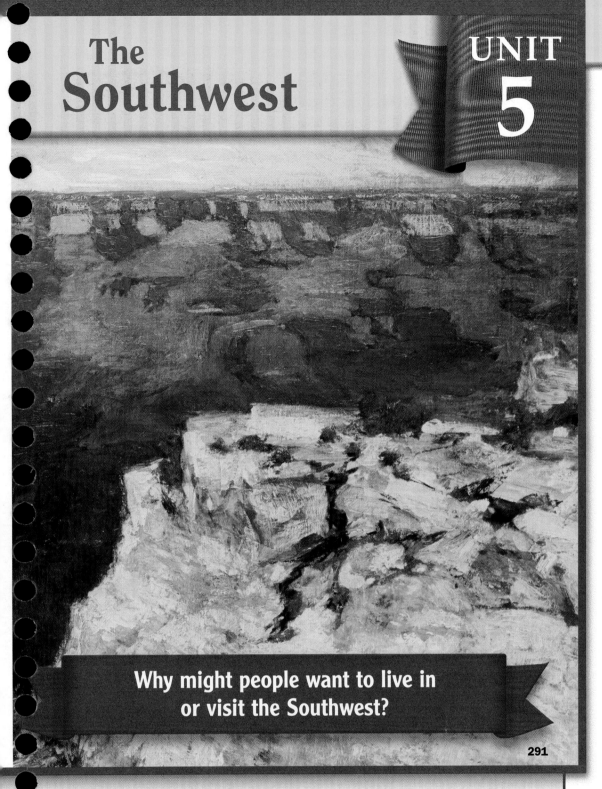

Why might people want to live in or visit the Southwest?

291

Practice and Extend

Hands-on Unit Project

✓ **Unit 5 Performance Assessment**

- The Unit Project, *Ad Sales,* found on p. 358, is an ongoing performance assessment project to enrich students' learning throughout the unit.
- This project, which has students creating an infomercial, may be started now or at any time during this unit of study.
- A performance assessment scoring guide is located on p. 358.

UNIT 5

The Southwest

Unit Overview

Home to deserts, canyons, and oil fields, the Southwest has attracted people since ancient times. These people have had an enormous impact on the region, which continues to grow today.

Unit Outline

Chapter 10 ***Land and Resources of the Southwest*** pp. 298–321

Chapter 11 ***The People of the Southwest*** pp. 322–353

Unit Question

- Have students read the question under the painting.
- To activate prior knowledge, review the word *Southwest* with students.
- Write responses on the board as students brainstorm a list of geographical, cultural, or economic reasons people might enjoy living in or visiting the Southwest, such as the warm, dry climate, the broad prairies, or the Grand Canyon.
- Have students copy the list onto a sheet of paper.

✓**Portfolio Assessment** Keep this list to review with students at the end of the unit on p. 357.

UNIT 5

Begin with a Primary Source

Objective
- Use primary sources to acquire information.

Resource
- Poster 9

Interpret a Primary Source

- Tell students that this primary source is a quotation from President Theodore Roosevelt, speaking about the Grand Canyon.

1 Theodore Roosevelt often is referred to as the first conservationist president. Do you think the quotation supports this idea? Why or why not? Possible answer: Yes; Because he is urging people to keep, or conserve, the Grand Canyon for all who come after them **Analyze Primary Sources**

✓**Portfolio Assessment** Remind students of their list of things that might make people want to live in or visit the Southwest (see p. 291). As students read Unit 5, have them add to the class list. Review the list at the end of the unit on p. 357.

Interpret Fine Art

- Have students discuss what they can tell about the Grand Canyon by viewing the painting.
- Remind students that a painting is a two-dimensional picture drawn on a flat surface. As a class, discuss how Edward Potthast has created the illusion of depth in his painting. (Through the use of perspective, shadow, and highlights)
- Show students a photo of the Grand Canyon that depicts a similar scene. Ask them which they like better, the photo or the painting and why.

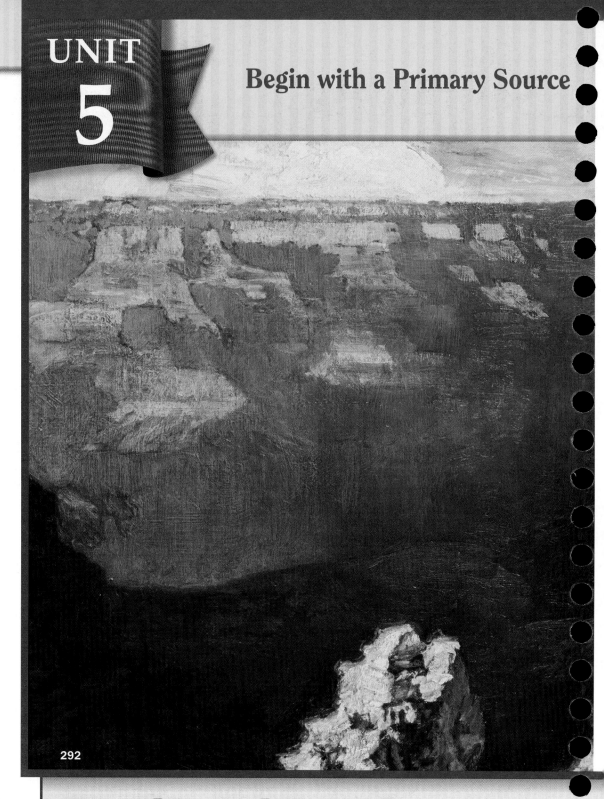

UNIT 5

Begin with a Primary Source

Practice and Extend

SOCIAL STUDIES Background

About the Primary Source
- The primary source above—the quotation by President Theodore Roosevelt—was stated by Roosevelt during a speech he made at the Grand Canyon on May 6, 1903.
- Theodore Roosevelt first visited the Grand Canyon in 1903 with world-famous wilderness explorer, writer, and naturalist John Muir.
- Concerned with preserving our nation's "national treasures" for the future, Roosevelt created 16 national monuments, 51 wildlife refuges, and 5 new national parks, including the Petrified Forest, Crater Lake, and Mesa Verde.
- Congress changed the status of the Grand Canyon from monument to national park in 1919, after Roosevelt's death.

"... keep it for your children, your children's children, and for all who come after you ..." 1

—President Theodore Roosevelt, May 6, 1903, on his first visit to the Grand Canyon.

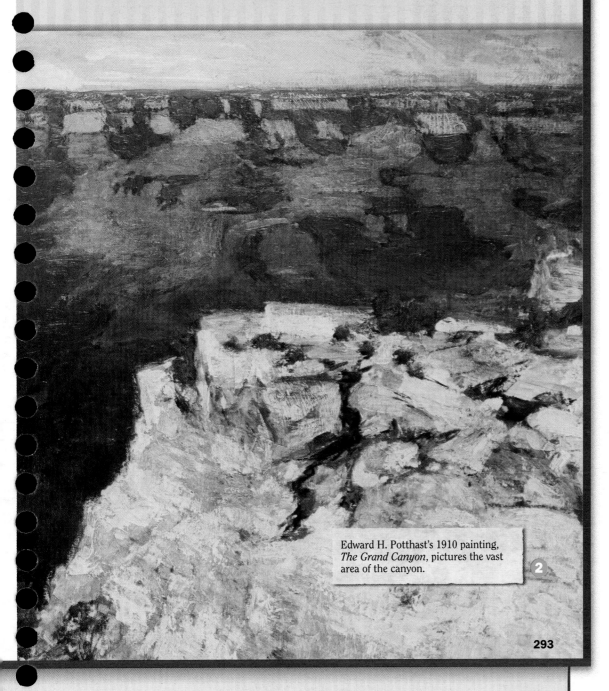

Edward H. Potthast's 1910 painting, *The Grand Canyon*, pictures the vast area of the canyon. 2

Meet the Artist

- Tell students that Edward Potthast was the son of German immigrants who settled in Cincinnati, Ohio. His first exposure to art and painting was through the Saturday art classes he attended when he was a teenager.
- As an adult, Potthast worked as a freelance artist for publications such as *Harper's Magazine*. These magazines sometimes sent him west to paint what he saw there.
- Potthast's first glimpse of the Grand Canyon was in 1910, when he and four other artists were selected to depict the Southwestern marvel for the Santa Fe Railway.
- Later in life, Potthast founded a special organization called the Society of Men Who Paint the West.

2 **What about the painting gives you an idea of the enormous size of the Grand Canyon?** Possible answers: The canyon stretches as far as you can see in the distance; the more distant canyon walls are less detailed than the ones in the foreground, giving the illusion that they are very far away. **Analyze Pictures**

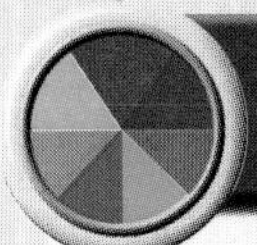

CURRICULUM CONNECTION Writing

Write an Exploration Journal

- Tell students to imagine that they are among the first people to explore the Grand Canyon.
- Have them write at least three journal entries describing a fictitious trip to the bottom of the canyon.
- Encourage students to use descriptive language and to illustrate their journal entries to convey the amazing things they see.

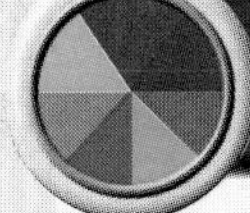

CURRICULUM CONNECTION Art

Use Perspective

- Point out to students that this painting shows a perspective from the top of the canyon looking down.
- As a class, brainstorm how the picture might look different if the perspective were looking up from the canyon floor or a birds-eye view from midway down in the canyon.
- Have students choose one of these perspectives and draw or paint a picture from that viewpoint.

UNIT 5

Welcome to the Southwest

Objective

- Describe selected aspects of states in the Southwest.

Resource

- Poster 10

Research the Region

Each of the states featured on these pages is part of the Southwest region. Have students do research to find out the answers to the following questions.

- **What is the origin of the state name *Texas*?** It is a pronunciation of the Native American word *tejas,* meaning "friends" or "allies."
- **What was the Long Walk to Bosque Redondo?** Possible answer: Because of clashes between Native Americans and settlers in the 1860s, the U.S. military forced Navajo people to walk 300 miles from their home in Fort Defiance, New Mexico, to a barren area of New Mexico.
- **How did the wood in the Petrified Forest become petrified?** Branches and logs from an ancient forest were buried by ash from volcanoes. Minerals in the ash crystallized as quartz within the wood. Other minerals also mixed in, creating the brilliant colors visible in petrified wood.
- **People interested in bats often head to Texas because it has the largest bat colony in the world (about 20 million bats) and the largest colony in a city (about 1.5 million bats). Where are these two colonies?** Bracken Cave, near San Antonio, and in Austin under a bridge

Students may wish to write their own questions about places in this region for the rest of the class to answer.

UNIT 5

Welcome to the Southwest

Key
★ State capital
—— National border

WY
NE
UT
CO
KS
MO
ROCKY MOUNTAINS
Lake Powell
Lake Mead
NV
GRAND CANYON
Santa Fe
OKLAHOMA
Oklahoma City
AR
CA
ARIZONA
NEW MEXICO
Red River
Lake Texoma
Phoenix
Gila River
SONORAN DESERT
TEXAS
Colorado River
Brazos River
Pecos River
Rio Grande
LA
Austin
MEXICO
Gulf of California
Gulf of Mexico
N
0 125 250 Miles
0 125 250 Kilometers

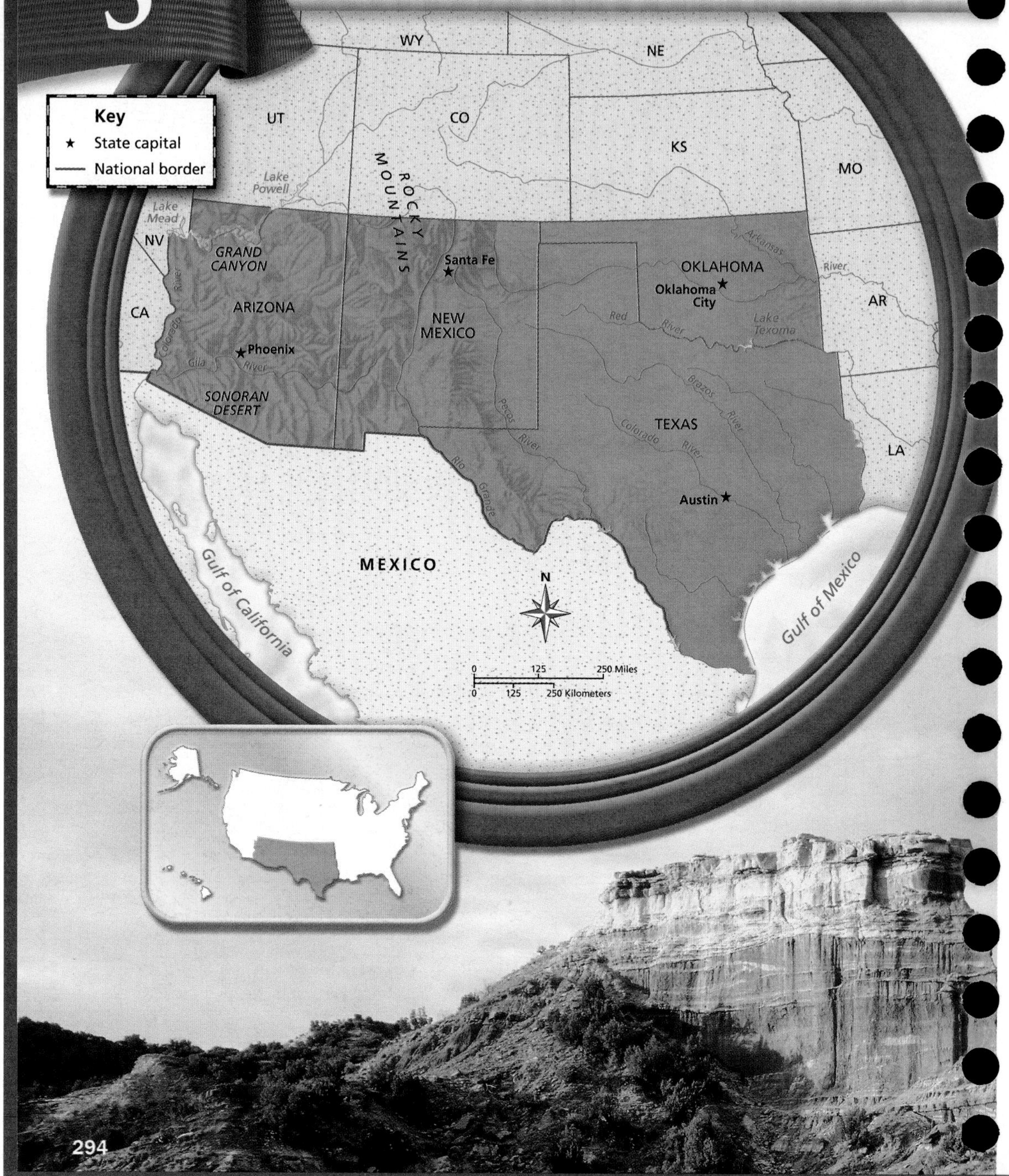

294

Practice and Extend

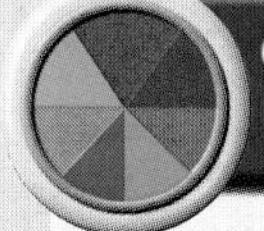

CURRICULUM CONNECTION
Literature

Read About the Southwest

Use the following selections to extend the content.

The Navajos: A First Americans Book, by Virginia Driving Hawk Sneve (Holiday House, ISBN 0-8234-1168-0, 1993) **Easy**

Valleys and Canyons, by Larry Dane Brimner (Children's Press, ISBN 0-516-27193-8, 2001) **On-Level**

The Deserts of the Southwest, by Maria Mudd Ruth (Marshall Cavendish Corp., ISBN 0-7614-0899-1, 1999) **Challenge**

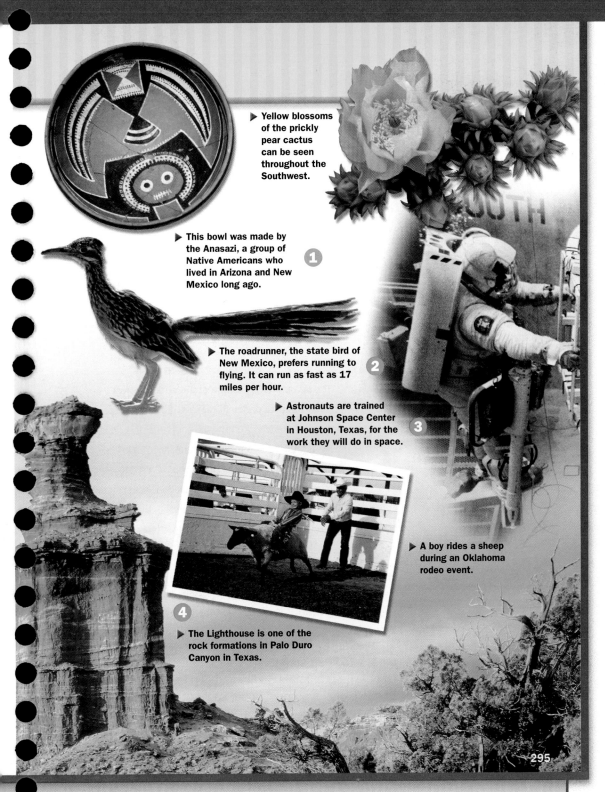

▶ Yellow blossoms of the prickly pear cactus can be seen throughout the Southwest.

▶ This bowl was made by the Anasazi, a group of Native Americans who lived in Arizona and New Mexico long ago. 1

▶ The roadrunner, the state bird of New Mexico, prefers running to flying. It can run as fast as 17 miles per hour. 2

▶ Astronauts are trained at Johnson Space Center in Houston, Texas, for the work they will do in space. 3

▶ A boy rides a sheep during an Oklahoma rodeo event.

4 ▶ The Lighthouse is one of the rock formations in Palo Duro Canyon in Texas.

295

Discuss the Region

Have students use the pictures and captions to answer the following questions.

1 **Which parts of the Southwest did the Anasazi call home?** Arizona and New Mexico Main Idea and Details

2 **How do you think the roadrunner got its name?** Possible answers: It can run very fast; it prefers running to flying. Make Inferences

3 **Why is Houston, Texas, important to the U.S. space program?** Astronauts are trained at Johnson Space Center in Houston for the work they will do in space. Main Idea and Details

4 **Why do you think the pictured rock formation is called the Lighthouse?** Possible answers: It is shaped like a lighthouse; like a lighthouse, it can be seen clearly for many miles. Analyze Pictures

Read About the States

The states shown here are discussed in the text on the following pages in Unit 5.

- Arizona, pp. 295, 298, 300–305, 309–310, 312, 316, 322, 324–328, 333–334, 346–347
- New Mexico, pp. 295, 309, 311, 316, 322, 326–328, 333–334, 336–337, 347
- Oklahoma, pp. 295, 309, 317–318, 341
- Texas, pp. 295, 298, 309, 314–315, 317, 322, 334–335, 338–341, 343, 344–345, 348

WEB SITE
Technology

Students can learn more about places in this unit by clicking on *Atlas* at **www.sfsocialstudies.com.**

Reading Social Studies

Draw Conclusions

Objective

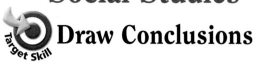

- Interpret print and visual material by drawing conclusions.

Resource

- Workbook, p. 68

About the Unit Target Skill

- The target reading skill for this unit is Draw Conclusions.
- Students are introduced to the unit target skill here and are given an opportunity to practice it.
- Further opportunities to draw conclusions are found throughout Unit 5.

1 Introduce and Motivate

Preview To activate prior knowledge, ask students for examples of conclusions they have drawn from Unit 4 of this textbook. (Possible answers: The Badlands of South Dakota have changed drastically over time due to the effects of wind and water; parts of the Midwest were called the Dust Bowl because droughts had turned the soil to dust.)

UNIT 5

Reading Social Studies

The Southwest

Draw Conclusions

Details → Conclusion
Details → Conclusion

Authors do not always tell you everything. Instead, they may give you a few details about what happens and expect you to draw conclusions.

- A conclusion is a decision you reach after you think about details that you have read.
- You can use the details and what you already know about a subject to draw conclusions about it.

Read the paragraph at the right. The **conclusion** was reached from the **details** in the paragraph.

The Grand Canyon is one of the nation's most popular national parks. In the year 2000, almost 5 million people visited the park. Most of them drove there in their cars, but the park does not have many roads or parking spaces. This combination caused traffic jams. Park managers concluded that they must find a better way for tourists to travel in the park.

Word Exercise

Inferring Meaning Sometimes the same word can be used as two different parts of speech. Knowing the meaning of the word when it is used as one part of speech can help you understand the meaning of the word when it is used as another part of speech. For example, the verb *preserve* means to keep something safe. Sometimes, people create a place where animals and plants can be kept safe. The name of this place is a noun, and if you remembered what it means to **preserve** something, you would know exactly what this place was for as soon as you heard its name. It's called a **preserve.**

296

Practice and Extend

ACTIVATE PRIOR KNOWLEDGE

ESL Support

Practice Drawing Conclusions Have students draw conclusions about where they live.

Beginning Work with students to list words that describe their community. Then have students use the listed words to draw a conclusion about their community, such as "It is hot and dry" or "It is a crowded city."

Intermediate Tell students that they draw conclusions every day. Ask students what they might conclude if people in line at a movie theater suddenly walked away and the ticket-taker closed the window. Elicit that they might conclude that the movie was sold out. Ask students for other examples.

Advanced Start students off with a conclusion about your area, such as "My community is a good place to live." Then have students list details that support this conclusion.

Draw Conclusions About the Grand Canyon

After Major John Wesley Powell explored the Grand Canyon and wrote reports about his trip, many people became interested in this natural wonder. Miners came to search for minerals. Tourists came to see the wonders Powell had written about. Some miners found that there was more wealth in guiding tourists than in digging for minerals.

In 1882, the United States government began a movement to protect the canyon. A bill was introduced in Congress to make the Grand Canyon a national park. It took more than thirty years for the Grand Canyon to win this honor. In the meantime, the area became the Grand Canyon Forest Preserve. Mining and cutting trees for lumber were still allowed.

In 1903, President Theodore Roosevelt visited the Grand Canyon. He was impressed by its beauty. He said, "Leave it as it is. . . . keep it for your children, your children's children, and for all who come after you as one of the great sights which every American . . . should see." In 1908, the Grand Canyon became a national monument. Then, in 1919, part of the Grand Canyon became a national park.

Use the reading strategy of drawing conclusions to answer questions 1 and 2. Then answer the vocabulary question.

1. Why did the government make the Grand Canyon a national park?
2. Do you think that the Grand Canyon should have been made a national park? Why or why not?
3. What does the name "Grand Canyon Forest Preserve" mean? How can you tell?

Standardized Test Prep

TEST PREP

- Use Workbook p. 68 to give students practice with standardized test format.
- Chapter and Unit Tests in the Assessment Book use standardized test format.
- Test-taking tips are contained in the front portion of the Assessment Book Teacher's Edition.

Also on Teacher Resources CD-ROM.

Workbook, p. 68

Draw Conclusions

Use with Pages 296–297.

A conclusion is a decision you reach after you think about certain facts or details.

Directions: Read the facts. Answer the questions that follow. Fill in the circle next to the correct answer.

1. The Grand Canyon is a national park. There are many trails to hike on and activities to do there. There also are many hotels and restaurants located near the Grand Canyon. On the basis of these facts, what conclusion can you draw about the Grand Canyon?
   - Ⓐ The Anasazi lived on the Colorado Plateau.
   - Ⓑ The Grand Canyon was formed by erosion.
   - Ⓒ The Havasupai still live at the bottom of the canyon.
   - Ⓓ Many people visit the Grand Canyon each year.
2. The saguaro is a special cactus. It can only be found in the Sonoran Desert. This desert is located in Saguaro National Park in Arizona, where the climate is hot and dry. What conclusion can you draw about the saguaro on the basis of these facts?
   - Ⓐ The saguaro does not need much water to live.
   - Ⓑ The saguaro grows from a tiny, black seed.
   - Ⓒ The saguaro has become a symbol of the Southwest.
   - Ⓓ The saguaro can grow to over 40 feet tall.
3. Pattillo Higgins saw gas bubbles in a stream near Spindletop Hill in Texas. He thought that if there was gas underground, there might be oil, too. He tried to drill for oil at Spindletop. What conclusion can you draw about Pattillo Higgins on the basis of these facts?
   - Ⓐ He did not find oil at Spindletop.
   - Ⓑ He was a famous geologist.
   - Ⓒ He was a smart and curious man.
   - Ⓓ He liked to fish in streams.

Notes for Home: Your child learned to draw conclusions from a set of facts.
Home Activity: Share with your child a set of facts about activities that various family members enjoy. Help your child draw conclusions based on those facts.

2 Teach and Discuss

- Draw students' attention to the bulleted items on p. 296.
- Have students read the sample paragraph on p. 296. Make sure they can state why the sentences highlighted in yellow are the facts that support the conclusion.
- Then have students read the longer practice sample on p. 297 and answer the questions that follow.
- Ask students why, when studying geography, it is important to be able to draw conclusions. (It is helpful to have a "big picture" in mind when we think about an area. That big picture is the conclusion we draw.)

Inferring Meaning

Students should be able to say that "Grand Canyon Forest Preserve" means a place in the Grand Canyon where forests are protected in some way. Remind students that if they don't understand what a word means right away, they can see if they are familiar with its meaning when it is used as a different part of speech.

3 Close and Assess

Apply it!

1. Possible answers: Because the government thought that the wonder and beauty of the park should be preserved
2. Possible answers: Yes, because it preserved the park for future generations. No, because it was an unnecessary use of government money. Accept any answer that is supported by a valid reason.
3. Possible answer: A place set aside for nature, because it was a first step to protecting the canyon.

CHAPTER 10

Chapter Planning Guide

Chapter 10 • Land and Resources of the Southwest

Locating Places pp. 298–299

Lesson Titles	Pacing	Main Ideas
Lesson 1 **A Land of Canyons** pp. 300–304	4 days	• The Grand Canyon dazzles visitors with its size and beauty.
Biography: John Wesley Powell p. 305		• John Wesley Powell was an early explorer of the Grand Canyon.
Thinking Skills: Make Generalizations pp. 306–307		• Making generalizations helps explain the big picture and makes it easier to remember facts.
Lesson 2 **Climates in the Southwest** pp. 308–311	2 days	• The Southwest climate can vary greatly. It is dry in some places and moist in others.
Here and There: Giant Plants pp. 312–313		• Giant plants grow in many places in the world.
Lesson 3 **Oil and Technology** pp. 314–317	2 days	• The Southwest is a region of discovery and research.
Citizen Heroes: Caring Flying to Help pp. 318–319		• Jerrie Cobb once dreamed of traveling in space, but instead used her talents to help people in need.
✓ **Chapter 10 Review** pp. 320–321		

◀ **John Wesley Powell led the first scientific expedition through the Grand Canyon.**

✓ = **Assessment Options**

The roadrunner is the state bird of New Mexico.

Vocabulary	Resources	Meeting Individual Needs
adobe pueblo generalization	• Workbook, p. 70 • Transparency 23 • Every Student Learns Guide, pp. 122–125 • Quick Study, pp. 62–63 • Workbook, p. 71	• Leveled Practice, TE p. 301 • ESL Support, TE p. 302 • ESL Support, TE p. 306
arid savanna	• Workbook, p. 72 • Transparencies 23, 53 • Every Student Learns Guide, pp. 126–129 • Quick Study, pp. 64–65	• ESL Support, TE p. 309 • Learning Styles, TE p. 310 • Leveled Practice, TE p. 311
gusher refinery	• Workbook, p. 73 • Transparency 23 • Every Student Learns Guide, pp. 130–133 • Quick Study, pp. 66–67	• Leveled Practice, TE p. 316 • ESL Support, TE p. 317 • ESL Support, TE p. 318
	✓ Chapter 10 Content Test, Assessment Book, pp. 53–54 ✓ Chapter 10 Skills Test, Assessment Book, pp. 55–56	✓ Chapter 10 Performance Assessment, TE p. 320

Providing More Depth

Additional Resources

- Vocabulary Workbook and Cards
- Social Studies Plus! pp. 106–111
- Daily Activity Bank
- Big Book Atlas
- Student Atlas
- Outline Maps
- Desk Maps

Technology

- AudioText
- MindPoint® Quiz Show CD-ROM
- ExamView® Test Bank CD-ROM
- Teacher Resources CD-ROM
- Map Resources CD-ROM
- SFSuccessNet: iText (Pupil Edition online), iTE (Teacher's Edition online), Online Planner
- **www.sfsocialstudies.com** (Biographies, news, references, maps, and activities)

To establish guidelines for your students' safe and responsible use of the Internet, use the Scott Foresman Internet Guide.

Additional Internet Links

To find out more about:

- The Grand Canyon, visit **www.grandcanyon.org**
- Spindletop, visit **www.aapg.org**
- Very Large Array, visit **www.nrao.edu**

Key Internet Search Terms

- Jerrie Cobb
- Saguaro National Park
- Havasupai Reservation

Workbook Support

Use the following Workbook pages to support content and skills development as you teach Chapter 10. You can also view and print Workbook pages from the Teacher Resources CD-ROM.

Workbook, p. 68

Use with Pages 296–297.

Draw Conclusions

A conclusion is a decision you reach after you think about certain facts or details.

Directions: Read the facts. Answer the questions that follow. Fill in the circle next to the correct answer.

1. The Grand Canyon is a national park. There are many trails to hike on and activities to do there. There also are many hotels and restaurants located near the Grand Canyon. On the basis of these facts, what conclusion can you draw about the Grand Canyon?
   - Ⓐ The Anasazi lived on the Colorado Plateau.
   - Ⓑ The Grand Canyon was formed by erosion.
   - Ⓒ The Havasupai still live at the bottom of the canyon.
   - ● Many people visit the Grand Canyon each year.
2. The saguaro is a special cactus. It can only be found in the Sonoran Desert. This desert is located in Saguaro National Park in Arizona, where the climate is hot and dry. What conclusion can you draw about the saguaro on the basis of these facts?
   - ● The saguaro does not need much water to live.
   - Ⓑ The saguaro grows from a tiny, black seed.
   - Ⓒ The saguaro has become a symbol of the Southwest.
   - Ⓓ The saguaro can grow to over 40 feet tall.
3. Pattillo Higgins saw gas bubbles in a stream near Spindletop Hill in Texas. He thought that if there was gas underground, there might be oil, too. He tried to drill for oil at Spindletop. What conclusion can you draw about Pattillo Higgins on the basis of these facts?
   - Ⓐ He did not find oil at Spindletop.
   - Ⓑ He was a famous geologist.
   - ● He was a smart and curious man.
   - Ⓓ He liked to fish in streams.

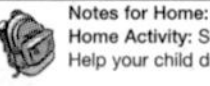

Notes for Home: Your child learned to draw conclusions from a set of facts.
Home Activity: Share with your child a set of facts about activities that various family members enjoy. Help your child draw conclusions based on those facts.

Use with Pupil Edition, p. 297

Workbook, p. 69

Use with Chapter 10.

Vocabulary Preview

Directions: These are the vocabulary words from Chapter 10. How much do you know about these words? Write the number of each term on the line next to its definition. You may use your glossary.

1. adobe
2. pueblo
3. arid
4. savanna
5. gusher
6. refinery

5 a. an oil well that produces a large amount of oil
3 b. a climate that is dry, but is not a desert climate
6 c. a factory that separates crude oil into different groups of chemicals
1 d. mud brick
2 e. "village" in Spanish
4 f. a grassy plain on which few trees grow, with a hot and seasonally dry climate

Directions: Write the vocabulary word that best completes each sentence. Write the word on the line provided.

7. Some parts of the Southwest have an **arid** climate because these areas might go a long time without rain.
8. The separation of crude oil into different groups of chemicals happens at an oil **refinery**.

Notes for Home: Your child learned the vocabulary terms for Chapter 10.
Home Activity: Discuss the term *landform* with your child. Share examples of landforms from your community and the surrounding area.

Use with Pupil Edition, p. 298

Workbook, p. 70

Use with Pages 300–304.

Lesson 1: A Land of Canyons

The Grand Canyon is one of the most amazing landforms in the United States.

Directions: Suppose that you are going to write an article about the Grand Canyon for your school newspaper. Complete the chart below to help you get started. You may use your textbook.

The Grand Canyon

HOW was it formed?	Through erosion caused by the Colorado River, rainwater, melting glaciers and wind
WHO first lived there? WHAT were their lives like?	The Anasazi; they made baskets and pots, built roads, farmed, and built adobe and cliff dwellings.
WHO still lives there?	Native Americans such as the Havasupai and Pueblo peoples
WHO explored there?	Captain García López de Cárdenas, twelve soldiers, and Major John Wesley Powell
WHO helped it become a tourist attraction? HOW?	Miners gave tours; President Theodore Roosevelt wanted to preserve its beauty; in 1919 part of it became a national park.
WHAT can you do there today?	You can walk along the rim of the canyon to see the view, hike into the canyon on trails, learn about its wildlife and earth science, explore the site of a Native American village, and listen to ranger talks.

Notes for Home: Your child learned about the history of the Grand Canyon.
Home Activity: Has your family ever visited a national park? Perhaps you have been to the Grand Canyon. Discuss with your child any national parks that you have visited or would like to visit.

Use with Pupil Edition, p. 304

Workbook Support

Workbook, p. 71

Use with Pages 306–307.

Make Generalizations

A generalization is a statement that applies to many examples. It explains how many facts have one idea in common.

Directions: Read the following journal entries from a student who recently visited the Grand Canyon. Answer the questions below. Fill in the circle next to the correct answer.

> Saturday, July 9
> Mom and I left our apartment in Phoenix at 8 A.M. The drive seemed to take forever! When we arrived at the South Rim around noon, I was stunned by the canyon's magnificent views. The temperature was a hot 90 degrees!
>
> Sunday, July 10
> Today we took a mule ride down into the canyon. We could have also hiked or taken a helicopter to reach the bottom. The mule ride led us to the Colorado River at the canyon's floor. We saw people riding rafts on the river. We also saw campers trout fishing in it. The temperature really cooled off at dusk.
>
> Monday, July 11
> After spending the night at Phantom Ranch, a lodge on the canyon floor, we explored the site of an ancient Native American village. A park ranger then took us on a tour to learn about the different types of wildlife in the canyon.

1. Which of the following statements is a true generalization?
   - Ⓐ Mom and I left our apartment at 8 A.M.
   - ● There are several ways to reach the floor of the Grand Canyon.
   - Ⓒ We arrived at the South Rim by noon.
   - Ⓓ We saw campers trout fishing in the Colorado River.
2. Which of the following statements is a true generalization?
   - Ⓐ On Saturday, the temperature was a hot 90 degrees.
   - Ⓑ On Sunday, the temperature really cooled off at dusk.
   - ● The temperature varies in the Grand Canyon.
   - Ⓓ We explored the site of an ancient Native American village.
3. Write a generalization based on the following facts. Write your answer on the lines provided.
   - Phantom Ranch is located at the bottom of the Grand Canyon.
   - An ancient Native American village is located at the bottom of the Grand Canyon.
   - Park rangers give tour guides at the bottom of the Grand Canyon.

   Possible answer: There are many sites and things to explore at the bottom of the Grand Canyon.

Notes for Home: Your child learned how to make generalizations.
Home Activity: With your child, take turns inventing sentences that begin with "Generally," or "Generally speaking."

Workbook — Thinking Skills 71

Use with Pupil Edition, p. 307

Workbook, p. 72

Use with Pages 308–311.

Lesson 2: Climates in the Southwest

Much of the Southwest has a hot, dry climate.

Directions: Using information from this lesson, circle the term in parentheses that best completes each sentence. You may use your textbook.

1. A desert is an area that gets less than (**ten**, five) inches of rain each year.
2. Some parts of the Southwest have an (**arid**, icy) climate but are not deserts.
3. The eastern part of (Colorado, **Texas**) has a hot, humid climate.
4. (**Oklahoma**, New Mexico) can sometimes have a humid and windy climate.
5. Thunderstorms, blizzards, and tornadoes are caused when (wet, **cold**) and warm air masses meet.
6. Thunderstorms, blizzards, and (**tornadoes**, hurricanes) are possible in Oklahoma.
7. The saguaro is a kind of cactus that grows naturally in the (**Sonoran Desert**, Central Plain).
8. The saguaro's white, night-blooming blossom is (Oklahoma's, **Arizona's**) state flower.
9. To grow big and strong, the saguaro spreads its (**roots**, flowers) to drink in the rainwater.
10. The cactus can store enough (food, **water**) to keep alive through long, dry periods.
11. The saguaro provides shelter for desert (plants, **animals**).
12. Some trees grow in a savanna, but most of the plants growing here are (cactuses, **grasses**).
13. Piñon pines and junipers grow in the (**savannas**, deserts) of the Southwest.

Notes for Home: Your child learned about the climates of the Southwest region.
Home Activity: Discuss with your child the climate of your community. How is it similar to or different from the climates in the Southwest region?

72 Lesson Review — Workbook

Use with Pupil Edition, p. 311

Workbook, p. 73

Use with Pages 314–317.

Lesson 3: Oil and Technology

For many years, the Southwest has been a leader in research and discovery.

Directions: Complete the outline with information from this lesson. You may use your textbook.

Research and Discovery in the Southwest

I. The Discovery of Oil
   - A. Many people went to **Texas** in search of oil and natural gas.
   - B. **Beaumont** became an important oil town.
   - C. Pattillo Higgins
     1. was a businessman and **scientist**.
     2. thought there might be **oil** beneath **Spindletop**.
     3. hired **Anthony Lucas** to drill the gusher.
   - D. Oil
     1. comes out of the ground as a thick, black liquid called **crude oil**.
     2. is separated in a **refinery**.
     3. can be used in products such as **gasoline**, **airplane fuel**, **medicines**, **clothing fibers**, **detergents**, **lubricants**, and **asphalt**.
     4. is a **nonrenewable** resource, or one that cannot be replaced by nature.

II. Technology in the Southwest
   - A. Arizona companies manufacture **electronic equipment**, **aircraft**, **space vehicles**, and **missiles**.
   - B. **New Mexico**'s researchers study medicine, genetics, and telecommunications.
   - C. Texas companies make **computers**, **radios**, **calculators**, and **electronic equipment**.
   - D. **Oklahoma** companies assist the electronic, aviation, and space industries.

Notes for Home: Your child learned about some of the research and discoveries that have taken place in the Southwest.
Home Activity: Many products are made from oil. Which of the products listed and pictured in your child's textbook do you use? Do you know of any others that your family uses? Discuss these with your child.

Use with Pupil Edition, p. 317

Workbook, p. 74

Use with Chapter 10.

Vocabulary Review

Directions: Use each of the vocabulary terms from Chapter 10 in a sentence. Write the sentences on the lines provided. You may use your glossary.

1. adobe

   Answers will vary but should reflect an understanding of the meaning of each vocabulary term.
2. pueblo
3. arid
4. savanna
5. refinery
6. gusher

Notes for Home: Your child learned the vocabulary terms for Chapter 10.
Home Activity: Choose one of the terms from this chapter. Take turns with your child using the term in a sentence. See how many sentences you can create!

Use with Pupil Edition, p. 321

Assessment Support

Use the following Assessment Book pages and TestWorks to assess content and skills in Chapter 10. You can also view and print Assessment Book pages from the Teacher Resources CD-ROM.

Assessment Book, p. 53

Chapter 10 Test

Part 1: Content Test

Directions: Fill in the circle next to the correct answer.

Lesson Objective (1:1)

1. Which river wore away rock and helped carve out the Grand Canyon?
   - Ⓐ Platte River
   - Ⓑ Arkansas River
   - Ⓒ Mississippi River
   - ● Colorado River

Lesson Objective (1:2)

2. Why are the formations in the Grand Canyon always changing?
   - Ⓐ Visitors help carve out the canyon.
   - ● Erosion takes place all the time.
   - Ⓒ The canyon is a national park.
   - Ⓓ Miners still look for lead there.

Lesson Objective (1:2)

3. Which of the following is NOT a cause of the canyon's continued erosion?
   - Ⓐ gravel and sand
   - Ⓑ water from the river
   - ● melting and moving glaciers
   - Ⓓ wind

Lesson Objective (1:4)

4. Which is one reason why the Grand Canyon was made a national park?
   - ● President Roosevelt wanted to preserve its beauty.
   - Ⓑ Visitors wanted to float down the Colorado River.
   - Ⓒ Miners wanted to search the canyon for valuable minerals.
   - Ⓓ Native Americans still live there.

Lesson Objective (1:3)

5. Which is NOT a reason that people might visit the Grand Canyon today?
   - Ⓐ Visitors can walk along the canyon's edge.
   - Ⓑ Park rangers can tell visitors about the wildlife of the canyon.
   - ● Visitors can see the gold from the rim of the canyon.
   - Ⓓ It is exciting to hike into the canyon on one of the trails.

Lesson Objective (2:1)

6. Which is true about the climate of the Southwest?
   - Ⓐ The region gets much snowfall.
   - Ⓑ The entire region is a desert.
   - Ⓒ The climate is the same in all areas of the region.
   - ● It has a varied climate with different temperatures and precipitation.

Lesson Objective (2:1)

7. Which of the following climates can NOT be found in the Southwest?
   - Ⓐ arid
   - Ⓑ hot and humid
   - Ⓒ humid and windy
   - ● dry and snowy

Use with Pupil Edition, p. 320

Assessment Book, p. 54

Lesson Objective (2:1)

8. What is a desert?
   - ● an area that gets less than 10 inches of rain each year
   - Ⓑ an area with wetlands and forests along a coastline
   - Ⓒ an area with a warm, humid, subtropical climate
   - Ⓓ an area where warm and cold air masses often meet

Lesson Objective (2:2)

9. Which is NOT a way that the saguaro has adapted to little rainfall?
   - Ⓐ It spreads its long, shallow roots to drink the rainwater.
   - Ⓑ Its ribbed trunk and branches expand to store water.
   - ● It has white, night-blooming blossoms.
   - Ⓓ It can store enough water to live through long, dry periods.

Lesson Objective (2:3)

10. Which is a way that the saguaro helps desert wildlife?
    - ● Saguaros provide shelter for many animals.
    - Ⓑ Many birds live in holes near saguaros.
    - Ⓒ Animals eat the saguaros.
    - Ⓓ The saguaro spreads its roots to drink rainwater.

Lesson Objective (3:1)

11. What does it mean when a resource is nonrenewable?
    - Ⓐ It cannot be separated in a refinery.
    - Ⓑ It cannot be used by human beings.
    - ● It cannot be replaced by nature.
    - Ⓓ It cannot be found on Earth.

Lesson Objective (3:1)

12. Which of these is a nonrenewable resource found in the Southwest?
    - Ⓐ saguaro
    - Ⓑ snow
    - Ⓒ piñon pines
    - ● oil

Lesson Objective (3:2)

13. Which is NOT a technology industry that exists in the Southwest?
    - ● canyon erosion
    - Ⓑ aircraft and missile manufacturing
    - Ⓒ computer, radio, and calculator production
    - Ⓓ space industry

Lesson Objective (3:2)

14. Which Southwest state has laboratories that develop military resources and study nuclear energy?
    - Ⓐ Texas
    - ● New Mexico
    - Ⓒ Arizona
    - Ⓓ Oklahoma

Lesson Objective (3:2)

15. What is the Very Large Array?
    - Ⓐ a medical center located in Houston, Texas
    - Ⓑ the largest producer of electronics
    - Ⓒ an aeronautics center that was built by the FAA
    - ● one of the world's largest radio observatories

Use with Pupil Edition, p. 320

Assessment Support

Assessment Book, p. 55

Part 2: Skills Test

Directions: Use complete sentences to answer questions 1–5. Use a separate sheet of paper if you need more space.

1. Describe how erosion formed the Grand Canyon. **Cause and Effect**

   The Colorado River carried sand, gravel, and boulders that helped cut the canyon. Rainwater continues to dissolve certain kinds of rock, causing it to wear away. Also, sand is picked up by the wind and blown against the canyon's walls, wearing away the surface of the rock.

2. Some of the early miners in the Grand Canyon decided to stop mining because they could make more money from tourism. In what ways do you think the miners could earn money from tourists? **Make Inferences**

   Possible answers: They could charge admission to see the canyon, charter tours to the bottom of the canyon, lead sightseeing tours, and sell souvenirs.

3. What are at least two details to support the following main idea? **The Southwest is a region of varied climates. Main Idea and Details**

   Answers should include two of the following: Much of the Southwest is desert; some parts have an arid climate but are not deserts; the climates in Texas vary greatly; some parts of Texas are hot and humid, and other parts are hot and dry; Oklahoma sometimes has a humid and windy climate, and it can experience thunderstorms, blizzards, or tornadoes.

Use with Pupil Edition, p. 320

Assessment Book, p. 56

4. Why should people conserve oil? What would happen if the world ran out of oil? **Draw Conclusions**

   Answers should reflect an understanding that oil is a nonrenewable resource and that many important products come from oil.

5. What type of technology is common in the Southwest? Why do you think this is true? **Categorize**

   Much of the technology in the Southwest is related to space and aeronautics. Possible answer: The Southwest has a lot of open land, which allows clear views of the sky and allows space shuttles and airplanes to easily land, take off, and be tested.

Use with Pupil Edition, p. 320

CHAPTER 10

Land and Resources of the Southwest

Chapter 10 Outline

- **Lesson 1, *A Land of Canyons,*** pp. 300–304
- **Biography: *John Wesley Powell,*** p. 305
- **Thinking Skills: *Make Generalizations,*** pp. 306–307
- **Lesson 2, *Climates in the Southwest,*** pp. 308–311
- **Here and There: *Giant Plants,*** pp. 312–313
- **Lesson 3, *Oil and Technology,*** pp. 314–317
- **Citizen Heroes: *Flying to Help,*** pp. 318–319

Resources

- Workbook, p. 69: Vocabulary Preview
- Vocabulary Cards
- Social Studies Plus!

Grand Canyon National Park, Arizona: Lesson 1

Ask students what words they might use to describe the Grand Canyon. (Possible answers: Deep, rocky, massive)

Saguaro National Park, Arizona: Lesson 2

Ask students to draw conclusions about how a saguaro is adapted to desert life. (Possible answer: A saguaro requires very little water in order to survive.)

Beaumont, Texas: Lesson 3

Ask students to describe the picture. Then ask how the discovery of oil in Texas might have affected the economy of the region. (Possible answer: Many people may have come to the area to find oil.)

CHAPTER 10

Land and Resources of the Southwest

Lesson 1

Grand Canyon National Park, Arizona
The Grand Canyon is a landform of great beauty and history.

1

Lesson 2

Saguaro National Park, Arizona
The saguaro cactus is adapted to desert life.

2

Lesson 3

Beaumont, Texas
The Southwest has rich resources and cutting-edge technology.

3

Practice and Extend

Vocabulary Preview

- Use Workbook p. 69 to help students preview the vocabulary words in this chapter.
- Use Vocabulary Cards to preview key concept words in this chapter.

Also on Teacher Resources CD-ROM.

Workbook, p. 69

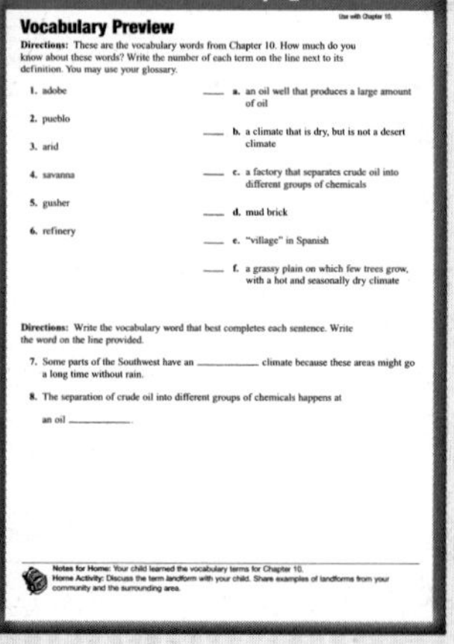

Vocabulary Preview — Use with Chapter 10.

Directions: These are the vocabulary words from Chapter 10. How much do you know about these words? Write the number of each term on the line next to its definition. You may use your glossary.

1. adobe
2. pueblo
3. arid
4. savanna
5. gusher
6. refinery

___ a. an oil well that produces a large amount of oil
___ b. a climate that is dry, but is not a desert climate
___ c. a factory that separates crude oil into different groups of chemicals
___ d. mud brick
___ e. "village" in Spanish
___ f. a grassy plain on which few trees grow, with a hot and seasonally dry climate

Directions: Write the vocabulary word that best completes each sentence. Write the word on the line provided.

7. Some parts of the Southwest have an ________ climate because these areas might go a long time without rain.
8. The separation of crude oil into different groups of chemicals happens at an oil ________.

Notes for Home: Your child learned the vocabulary terms for Chapter 10.
Home Activity: Discuss the term *landform* with your child. Share examples of landforms from your community and the surrounding area.

Locating Places

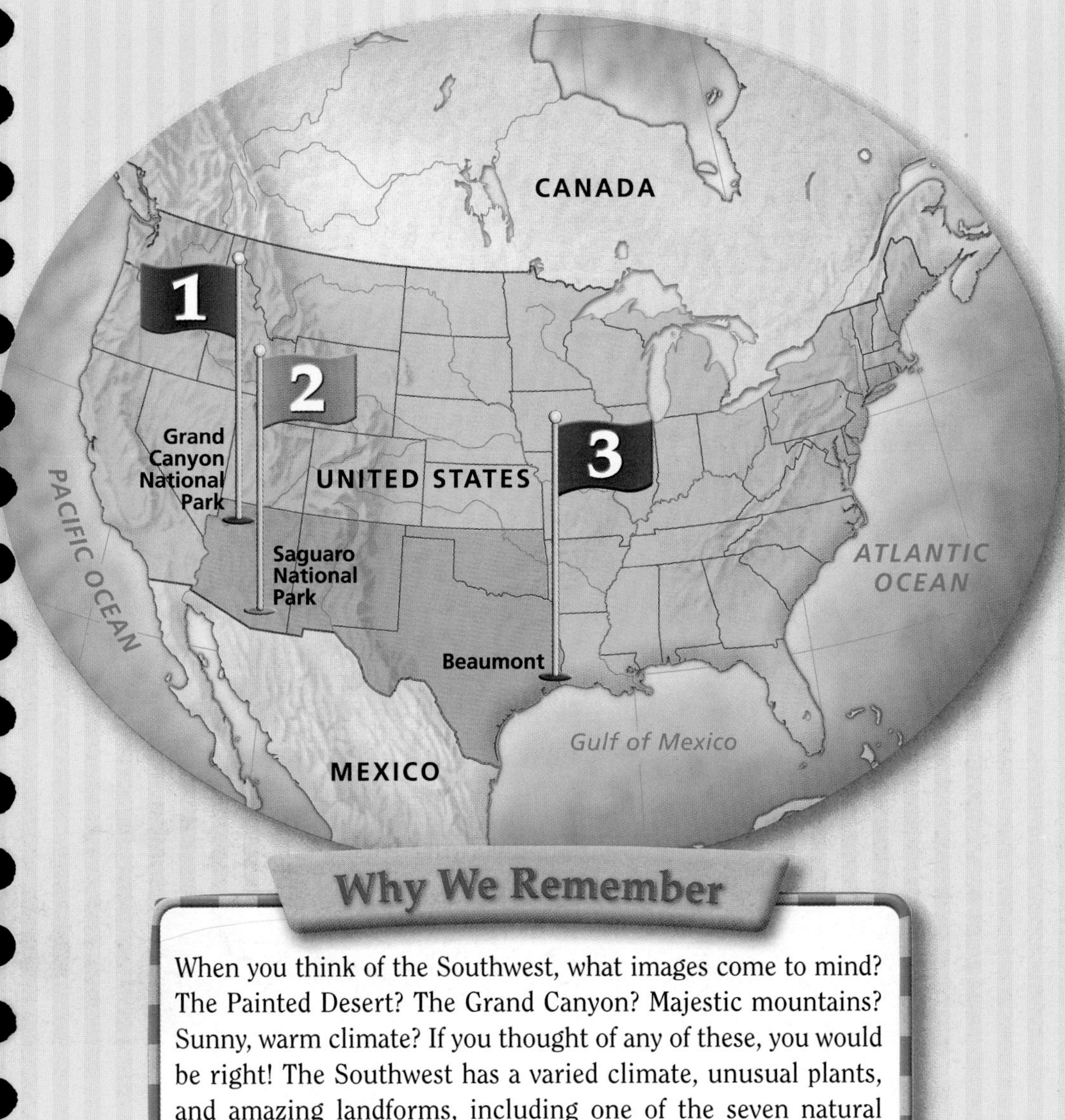

Why We Remember

When you think of the Southwest, what images come to mind? The Painted Desert? The Grand Canyon? Majestic mountains? Sunny, warm climate? If you thought of any of these, you would be right! The Southwest has a varied climate, unusual plants, and amazing landforms, including one of the seven natural wonders of the world—the Grand Canyon. It also has state-of-the-art technology and much more. Turn the page and find out just what the Southwest has to offer.

299

Locating Places

- Have students examine the pictures on p. 298 for Lessons 1, 2, and 3.
- Remind students that each picture is coded with both a number and a color to link it to a place on the map on p. 299.

Why We Remember

Have students read the "Why We Remember" paragraph on p. 299 and ask why places in this chapter might be important to them. Have students consider their current perceptions of the Southwest and possible new information suggested by the text.

WEB SITE
Technology

You can learn more about the Grand Canyon National Park, Arizona; Saguaro National Park, Arizona; and Beaumont, Texas, by clicking on *Atlas* at **www.sfsocialstudies.com.**

SOCIAL STUDIES STRAND
Geography

Mental Mapping On an outline map of the United States, have students color in the states that they think make up the Southwest Region. Students may label any cities or landforms of the Southwest that they know of. Discuss students' knowledge and/or impressions of the Southwest.

A Land of Canyons

Objectives

- Describe how the Grand Canyon was carved out by erosion caused by the Colorado River.
- Describe how erosion by water, wind, and sand continues to shape the Grand Canyon.
- Explain that the Grand Canyon is a magnificent landform that provides beauty and adventure.
- Explain why the Grand Canyon has been made a national park.
- Interpret print and visual material by drawing conclusions.

Vocabulary

adobe, p. 302; **pueblo,** p. 302

Resources

- Workbook, p. 70
- Transparency 23
- Every Student Learns Guide, pp. 122–125
- Quick Study, pp. 62–63

Quick Teaching Plan

If time is short, have students create a categorized list of notes.

- Tell students to list the three subheads found in the text for Lesson 1.
- Have them list, under each subhead, important terms or names from that section of text.
- Have students write brief notes about each entry in their lists.

1 Introduce and Motivate

Preview To activate prior knowledge, ask students what they know about canyons. Tell students they will be reading more about how the Grand Canyon was formed, the role it has played in history, and what it is like today.

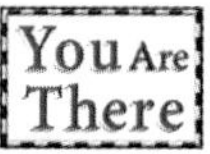

Ask students if they have ever been to the Grand Canyon. Have volunteers describe what they did in the park and what the experience was like.

LESSON 1

PREVIEW

Focus on the Main Idea
The Grand Canyon dazzles visitors with its size and beauty.

PLACES
Grand Canyon National Park

PEOPLE
García López de Cárdenas
Francisco Vásquez de Coronado
John Wesley Powell
Theodore Roosevelt

VOCABULARY
adobe
pueblo

A Land of Canyons

You Are There Finally, you are going hiking in the Grand Canyon. You can feel the excitement as your guide signals the beginning of your adventure down Bright Angel Trail. As you look down you think, "I'd better watch my step, or I might find myself down there faster than I planned." On the rim, two mule deer pass by. Out from behind a fallen boulder some rock squirrels chase one another. Overhead a beautiful butterfly flits through the air. Below you in the canyon, some jet black ravens roll and tumble like acrobats. What an adventure this is going to be!

▶ Binoculars

Draw Conclusions As you read, draw conclusions about why the Grand Canyon attracts so many tourists.

300

Practice and Extend

READING SKILL
Draw Conclusions

In the Lesson Review, students complete a graphic organizer like the one below. You may want to provide students with a copy of Transparency 23 to complete as they read the lesson.

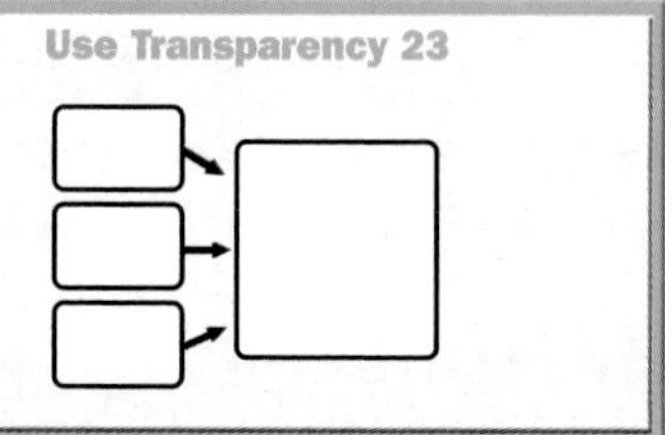

VOCABULARY
Individual Word Study

Tell students that the Spanish word *pueblo* means not only "village," but also "nation, people." This Spanish word developed from the Latin word *populus* (meaning "people"), as did the English words *people, popular,* and *population*. Students know from the text that Spanish explorers used *pueblo* to describe the type of village in which certain Native Americans lived. However, these explorers also named the Pueblo peoples after the impressive villages in which they lived.

The Role of Erosion

Scientists still don't know exactly how the Grand Canyon was formed. What they do know is that erosion played a part in it. This gradual process of wearing away soil and rock can be caused by gravel and sand, by water from rushing rivers, by rainwater, by melting and moving glaciers, and even by the wind.

Many scientists think that the rushing water of the Colorado River helped dissolve and wear away the rock of the Grand Canyon. The sand, gravel, and boulders carried by the river most likely
1 helped cut the canyon as well.
Rainwater also causes erosion by dissolving certain kinds of rock, such as limestone, causing it to wear away.

Wind may also play a part in the canyon's continued erosion. Sand is often picked up by wind and blown against the canyon's walls. If you have felt sand, you know how sharp its edges can be. Blowing sand can wear
away the surface of the rock. 2

Because erosion takes place all the time, the Grand Canyon may never
stop changing. However, these 3
changes happen very slowly—over thousands of years. Hikers and visitors may never see any changes at all.

REVIEW How might the canyon continue to change because of erosion? Draw Conclusions

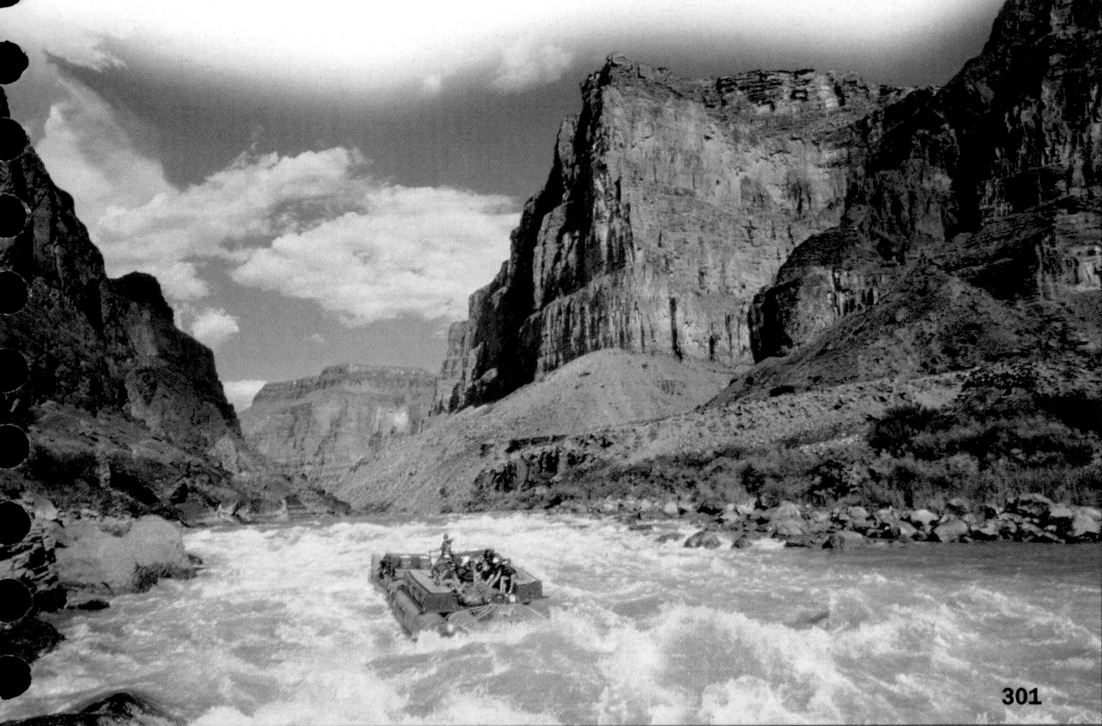

▶ **Rafting through the Grand Canyon on the Colorado River is an exciting experience. The river's swift waters helped carve the canyon.**

301

2 Teach and Discuss

PAGE 301

The Role of Erosion

Quick Summary Erosion caused by the Colorado River and wind-blown sand, along with other factors, created the Grand Canyon.

1 **What erosion "tools" are carried by the Colorado River?** Sand, gravel, and boulders **Main Idea and Details**

2 **Would you expect wind erosion to create sharp or smooth edges on the rock walls of the Grand Canyon? Why?** Smooth; Because the rock is worn away slowly **Analyze Pictures**

3 **Was the canyon always as deep as it is today?** No; long ago, before the land eroded, the canyon must have been much shallower. **Make Inferences**

✓ **Ongoing Assessment**

If... students have difficulty theorizing about the past,	**then...** remind them that *erosion* means "a wearing away" and have them visualize what it was that was wearing away.

✓ **REVIEW ANSWER** Blowing sand and other factors may continue to wear away the surface of the rock, making the canyon deeper and wider. **Draw Conclusions**

MEETING INDIVIDUAL NEEDS
Leveled Practice

Experiment with Erosion Help students understand the process of erosion.

Easy Have students devise a simple experiment to demonstrate erosion by wind and by water. For example, they could allow a fan to blow over a pile of sand or trickle water down one side of a pile of dirt. **Reteach**

On-Level Have students write a paragraph explaining how erosion by wind or water occurs. **Extend**

Challenge Have students find and photocopy diagrams or other illustrations of the process of wind and water erosion. Have students display these in the classroom and explain them to their classmates. **Enrich**

For a Lesson Summary, use Quick Study, p. 62.

People and the Canyon

Quick Summary Native Americans have lived in the Grand Canyon for centuries. Europeans first explored the area in 1540.

Test Talk

Locate Key Words in the Text

4 The Anasazi had many skills. What facts support this conclusion? Have students locate key words in the text that match key words in the question. They made baskets and pottery, built pueblos and roads, and developed irrigation systems. **Analyze Information**

SOCIAL STUDIES STRAND
Culture

Point out that the pueblos of the Southwest traditionally were carved into cliffs or built of sandstone or adobe. They blended in with their surroundings.

5 Why might Native Americans have carved their homes into cliffs or built houses of adobe? Possible answers: They used available materials; they wanted to be hidden from outsiders. **Draw Conclusions**

6 Why would it be incorrect to say a European explorer "discovered" the Grand Canyon? Native Americans lived in the canyon for hundreds of years before the Europeans arrived in 1540. **Draw Conclusions**

People and the Canyon

For centuries, people have hunted, farmed, and lived around the Grand Canyon. Scientists have found artifacts in the canyon that are more than 3,000 years old.

Hundreds of years ago, people we call the Anasazi (ah nuh SAH zee) lived in the Southwest and as far north as Colorado. Some lived near the Grand Canyon. *Anasazi* means "ancient ones" in the Navajo language.

The Anasazi were skilled basket
4 makers and potters. They also built networks of roads. Anasazi farmers built irrigation systems to bring water to their crops.

Some Anasazi homes were one- or
5 two-story houses of **adobe,** or mud brick. The Anasazi also built large, apartment-like homes on cliffs. These cliff dwellings had many rooms and housed many families.

Native Americans still live in the canyon area today. Some, such as the Pueblo peoples, may be the descendants of the Anasazi. **Pueblo** means "village" in Spanish. Some Pueblo still live in villages of adobe homes similar to those of the Anasazi.

The Havasupai (hah vah SOO peye) live in Havasu Canyon, a part of the Grand Canyon. *Havasupai* means "people of the blue-green water." There are no roads to their reservation, only hiking and mule trails. Even so, tourists hike or ride in to see the beautiful waterfalls and blue-green pools along Havasu Creek.

▶ Anasazi buildings within Grand Canyon

Spanish explorer Captain **García López de Cárdenas** (CAR deh nas) and a small band of soldiers were the first Europeans to see the Grand Canyon. Their leader, **Francisco Vásquez de Coronado,** explored the Southwest in search of gold. He had heard rumors of a great river that flowed through a golden canyon. Coronado sent Cárdenas and the soldiers to see if the rumors were true. In 1540, they found
the river and the canyon, but no gold. 6

There was not much interest in the Grand Canyon until 1869, when Major **John Wesley Powell** explored it. He made a dangerous trip by boat down the Colorado River and through the canyon. His report led others to want to see this natural wonder. Powell was the first to call it the "Grand Canyon."

Practice and Extend

EXTEND LANGUAGE
ESL Support

Explore Compound Words Help students explore compound words such as *butterfly* and *overhead*.

Beginning Have students separate compound words into their component parts. Students should draw a picture to represent each part, forming a compound word "rebus." Then have students find other compound words in the lesson (*rainwater, limestone, network, waterfall, breathtaking, wildlife*) and create rebuses for those words.

Intermediate Have students write compound words on index cards and then cut apart the cards to form separate words. Students should mix the cards together, exchange them with classmates, and have classmates re-create the words.

Advanced Ask students to invent a new compound word about the Southwest region, using what they have learned in this lesson.

For additional ESL support, use Every Student Learns Guide, pp. 122–125.

In the 1880s, miners came to the canyon in search of zinc, copper, lead, and other minerals, but the steep canyon walls made mining difficult. At the same time, tourists came to see the Grand Canyon. Some miners began taking tourists into the canyon. They charged for the tour.

In 1903, President **Theodore Roosevelt** visited the Grand Canyon. He wanted to preserve its beauty for years to come. In 1919, part of the Grand Canyon became a national park. 7

REVIEW Why did Spanish explorers come to the Grand Canyon?
Draw Conclusions

FACT FILE

Grand Canyon Facts

- The Grand Canyon is about 277 miles long and about 6,000 feet deep at its deepest point. That is the height of four Sears Towers. 8
- At its widest point, the Grand Canyon is more than 18 miles wide. 9
- At the South Rim the average temperature in July is 69°F. In the same month, the average temperature on the canyon floor is 92°F.

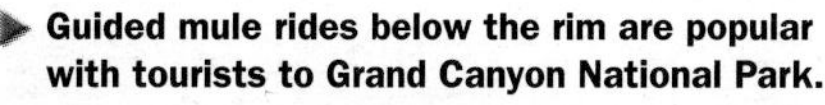

▶ Guided mule rides below the rim are popular with tourists to Grand Canyon National Park.

303

7 **Today we consider the Grand Canyon a national treasure. Why is our view different from that of the early Spanish explorers?** Possible answer: The Spanish explorers were seeking gold. Today people value the beauty of the environment. Point of View

✓ **REVIEW ANSWER** They were searching for gold. Draw Conclusions

FACT FILE

Grand Canyon Facts

8 **Which do you think would give you a grander view of your surroundings, standing at the top of the Sears Tower or the top of the Grand Canyon? Why?** Possible answer: The Grand Canyon; Because it is about 4 times taller than the Sears Tower. Draw Conclusions

9 **Which is greatest, the Grand Canyon's depth, width, or length? Explain.** Its length; It is about 277 miles long, but it is "only" 6,000 feet deep at its deepest point and 18 miles wide at its widest point. Analyze Information

FYI SOCIAL STUDIES Background

About the Grand Canyon

- People have slowed erosion in much of the Grand Canyon. The Colorado River used to carry about 500,000 tons of mud and sand a day down the canyon. After the Glen Canyon Dam was completed in the 1960s, that material was reduced to less than 100,000 tons a day. The lake created behind the dam, Lake Powell, absorbs the rest of the sediment.
- Hard stone does not erode as fast as softer stone such as limestone. As the softer stones wore away, they left behind mountains of harder stone rising from the floor of the canyon.
- The layers visible in the canyon walls reveal many years of the Earth's geologic history.

PAGE 304

Visiting the Grand Canyon

Quick Summary Once used for mining, the Grand Canyon is now protected as a national park.

Problem Solving

10 **The many visitors to the Grand Canyon create problems of traffic, noise, and smog. How might park managers deal with these problems?** Possible answers: Limit the number of visitors or cars; limit noisy planes; reduce the causes of air pollution
Solve Problems

✓ **REVIEW ANSWER** Possible answers: See the view; hike in the canyon; explore Native American villages
Draw Conclusions

3 Close and Assess

Summarize the Lesson

Have students take turns reading the three main points. Then have them write two sentences explaining the points.

✓ LESSON 1 **REVIEW**

1. **Draw Conclusions** For possible answers, see the reduced pupil page.
2. Possible answers: A vast canyon in the Southwest; To see its beauty, to hike its trails, or to learn more about its wildlife, and Native American heritage
3. At least partially by erosion
4. It continues to gradually change the canyon.
5. **Critical Thinking:** ***Predict*** Possible answer: The canyon's wildlife and Native American artifacts and even the canyon itself might have been damaged.

Link to Science

Students' research may reveal information about various mountains, hills, or rock formations found throughout the world.

Visiting the Grand Canyon

If you visit **Grand Canyon National Park,** you can walk along the rim of the canyon to see the breathtaking view. You can hike into the canyon on one of the trails. Park rangers can tell you about the wildlife and earth science of the canyon. You can also explore the
10 site of a Native American village.

REVIEW Why do people want to visit the Grand Canyon? Draw Conclusions

Summarize the Lesson

- **The Grand Canyon is a magnificent landform.**
- **Erosion carved out and is still carving the features of the canyon.**
- **Native Americans, Spanish explorers, miners, and tourists have played a part in the history of the Grand Canyon.**

LESSON 1 **REVIEW**

Check Facts and Main Ideas

1. Draw Conclusions On a separate sheet of paper, write a conclusion about people living in the Grand Canyon from the details given.

Details
- Scientists have found artifacts in the canyon that are over 3,000 years old.
- The Anasazi lived in and near the Grand Canyon hundreds of years ago.
- Native Americans live in the canyon area today.

Conclusion
People have lived in the canyon for thousands of years.

2. What is the Grand Canyon and why do so many people travel to the Grand Canyon each year?
3. How might the Grand Canyon have been formed?
4. How does erosion affect the Grand Canyon today?
5. **Critical Thinking:** ***Predict*** How might the Grand Canyon be different today if the Grand Canyon National Park had not been formed?

Link to Science

Do Research About Erosion Erosion can help create beautiful landforms, such as the Grand Canyon. It can also wear away topsoil needed for growing crops. Find out about other landforms that may have been shaped by erosion. Share your findings with classmates.

304

Practice and Extend

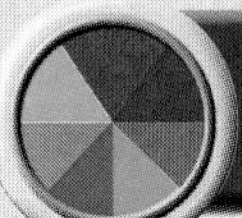

CURRICULUM CONNECTION
Music

Hear the Grand Canyon
- Have students find and listen to a recording of Ferde Grofé's *Grand Canyon Suite* (1931).
- Ask students to explain how each of the five movements ("Sunrise," "Painted Desert," "On the Trail," "Sunset," and "Cloudburst") fits their mental image of the canyon.

Workbook, p. 70

Lesson 1: A Land of Canyons

The Grand Canyon is one of the most amazing landforms in the United States.

Directions: Suppose that you are going to write an article about the Grand Canyon for your school newspaper. Complete the chart below to help you get started. You may use your textbook.

The Grand Canyon

HOW was it formed?	
WHO first lived there? WHAT were their lives like?	
WHO still lives there?	
WHO explored there?	
WHO helped it become a tourist attraction? HOW?	
WHAT can you do there today?	

Also on Teacher Resources CD-ROM.

John Wesley Powell 1834–1902

The year was 1869. Major John Wesley Powell gathered nine brave men and four sturdy boats to take a trip through nearly 1 a thousand miles of canyons.

Powell had lost part of his right arm in the Civil War, but that didn't stop him. This journey had been a lifelong dream of this college professor and geologist. On May 24, 1869, Powell and his crew set off on the Green River in Wyoming.

BIOFACT

A chair was tied to Powell's boat so that he could see ahead and signal the other boats.

Nearly two months into the trip, the crew reached the place where the Green River meets the Colorado River in Utah. The Colorado River is rough with many dangerous rapids as it passes through the Grand Canyon.

By August 29, 1869, Powell and his crew had braved the danger and traveled through the Grand Canyon! Powell made the first scientific exploration of the Grand Canyon. His account of the canyon sparked interest in this awe-inspiring landform. In a report about his trip he wrote,

> ***"The Grand Canyon is a land of song. . . . This is the music of waters."*** 2

Learn from Biographies

Powell was a scientist who kept a detailed journal of his trip. How do you think this journal influenced people?

For more information, go online to *Meet the People* **www.sfsocialstudies.com.**

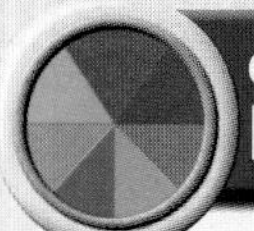

CURRICULUM CONNECTION
Literature

Read Biographies

Exploring the Earth with John Wesley Powell, by Michael Elsohn Ross (Carolrhoda Books, ISBN 1-57505-254-7, 2000) **Easy**

The Diary of John Wesley Powell, by John Wesley Powell (Benchmark Books, ISBN 0-7614-1013-9, 2000) **On-Level**

John Wesley Powell: Explorer of Grand Canyon, by Roger A. Bruns (Enslow Publishers, ISBN 0-89490-783-2, 1997) **Challenge**

WEB SITE
Technology

Students can find out more about John Wesley Powell by going online and clicking on *Meet the People* at **www.sfsocialstudies.com.**

★BIOGRAPHY★

John Wesley Powell

Objective

- Identify the contributions of early explorers of the Southwest such as John Wesley Powell.

1 Introduce and Motivate

Preview To activate prior knowledge, ask students to review what they learned about Major Powell in Lesson 1. Tell them they will learn about how this professor of geology explored the Grand Canyon.

2 Teach and Discuss

- Point out to students that Powell's team encountered treacherous waters, had to navigate the river in bad weather and at night, and faced unknown dangers on shore.
- Ask students what part of the trip would have been scariest to them or most interesting.

1 **Judging from the text, what words might be used to describe Major Powell?** Possible answers: Brave, curious, adventurous, determined, clever
Draw Conclusions

2 **Why might Powell have called the Grand Canyon "a land of song"?** Possible answers: He was thinking of the sound of the river; his own heart was singing when he saw it.
Make Inferences

3 Close and Assess

Learn from Biographies Answer

Possible answer: The descriptions in his journal may have inspired other people to visit the canyon.

Make Generalizations

Objective

- Interpret information by making generalizations.

Vocabulary

generalization, p. 306

Resource

- Workbook, p. 71

1 Introduce and Motivate

What is a generalization? Ask students how historians draw conclusions about the past. (They study many details to form a general conclusion.) Then have students read the **What?** section of text on p. 306 to help set the purpose of this lesson.

Why make generalizations? Have students read the **Why?** section of text on p. 307. Ask them why a teacher might make generalizations about students' grades in a school. (To determine whether students, as a group, are learning or whether a specific teaching method is working)

2 Teach and Discuss

How is the skill used? Examine with students the paragraph and analysis on p. 307.

- Point out that sometimes an author will provide a generalization, as in the last sentence of the example. In this case, readers must judge whether or not the generalization is valid.
- Tell students that sometimes an author will provide examples or details, and it is up to readers to make the generalization.

Thinking Skills

Make Generalizations

What? A **generalization** is a statement that applies to many examples. It explains how many facts have one idea in common. Sometimes, clue words such as *all, most, some, none,* and *many* signal the use of a generalization.

In Lesson 1, you learned these facts:

Peoples of the Grand Canyon	What they did there
Anasazi	Lived and farmed
Spanish Explorers	Looked for gold
John Wesley Powell	Explored

From these statements of fact, you can form this generalization:

Many different people have lived in or explored the Grand Canyon.

▶ **Anasazi cliff dwellings**

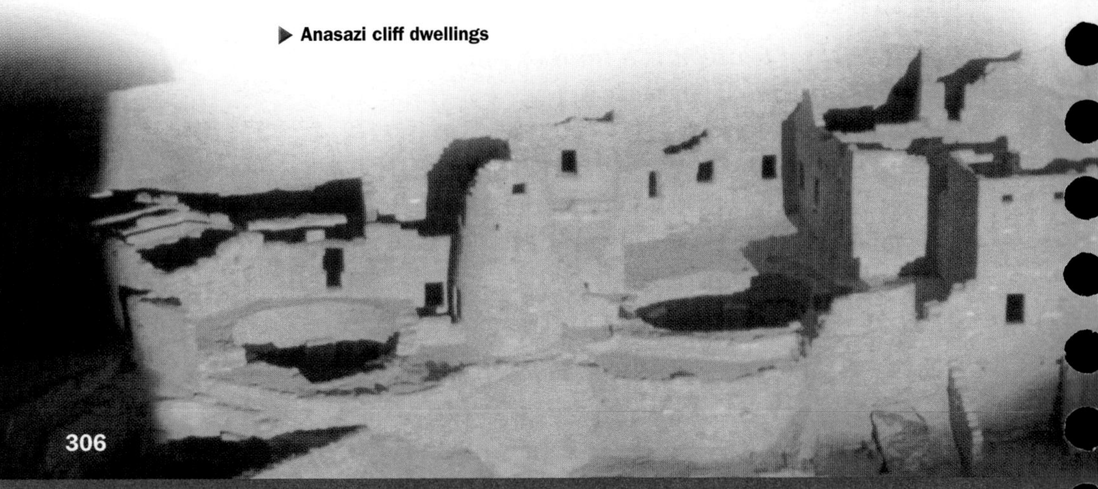

306

Practice and Extend

EXTEND LANGUAGE

ESL Support

Examine a Verb/Noun Connection Help students explore the noun-forming suffix *-ation*.

Beginning On the board show students how the English language may use the suffix *-ation* to make a noun from a verb, such as with *generalize, generalization; explain, explanation; inform, information.*

Intermediate Have students scan other pages of this textbook to find additional examples of *-ation* nouns.

Advanced Have students write sentences using verbs and the nouns that can be formed by adding *-ation*.

Why? Generalizations help you see the big picture. They make it easier for you to remember many facts. They help you understand new information.

How? To make a generalization, you need to identify the topic and gather facts about it. Then you figure out what these facts have in common. Finally, you make one statement that is true for all the information.

This passage is about tourists and the Grand Canyon:

> There are six lodges and three campgrounds on the South Rim of the Grand Canyon. Two main roads lead into the South Rim, which is open year-round. Only one road leads to the tourist area on the North Rim, which has only one lodge and one campground. Because of snow, the North Rim is closed from late autumn until mid-spring. Most tourists to the Grand Canyon visit the South Rim. 1 2 3

The last sentence of the paragraph is a generalization. Based on the information, it is a valid generalization—one that is supported by facts.

Think and Apply

Based on the paragraph about the Grand Canyon at left, which of the following statements are valid **generalizations** and which are not valid? Why?

1. The South Rim of the Grand Canyon is more beautiful than the North Rim.
2. There is more traffic at the South Rim.
3. Park rangers would rather work at the North Rim.

307

- Tell students that generalizations often are signaled by a clue word such as *all, most, many, usually,* or *generally*.
- Have students read the **How?** section of text on p. 307.

1 **In the passage, what generalization is made about tourism at the Grand Canyon?** Most tourists to the Grand Canyon visit the South Rim. **Generalize**

2 **What word or words signal the generalization in the passage?** Most **Analyze Information**

3 **What facts support the generalization in the passage?** There are more roads leading to the South Rim than to the North Rim, there are more lodges and campgrounds on the South Rim than on the North Rim, and the North Rim is closed from late autumn until mid-spring. **Main Idea and Details**

3 Close and Assess

Think and Apply

1. Not valid; Not supported by information in the paragraph
2. Valid; Paragraph states that most tourists visit the South Rim
3. Not valid; Not supported by information in the paragraph

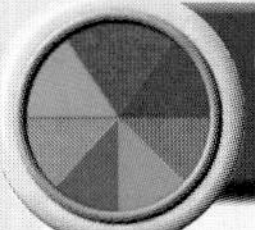

CURRICULUM CONNECTION
Art

Research Canyon Activities

- Have students work in small groups to research the different activities available to tourists on the South Rim and the North Rim of the Grand Canyon.
- Have each group create a poster to illustrate its findings.

Workbook, p. 71

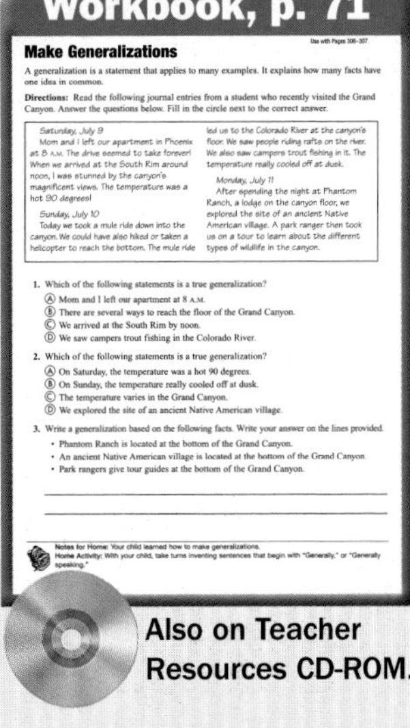

Make Generalizations Use with Pages 306–307

A generalization is a statement that applies to many examples. It explains how many facts have one idea in common.

Directions: Read the following journal entries from a student who recently visited the Grand Canyon. Answer the questions below. Fill in the circle next to the correct answer.

Saturday, July 9
Mom and I left our apartment in Phoenix at 8 A.M. The drive seemed to take forever! When we arrived at the South Rim around noon, I was stunned by the canyon's magnificent views. The temperature was a hot 90 degrees!

Sunday, July 10
Today we took a mule ride down into the canyon. We could have also hiked or taken a helicopter to reach the bottom. The mule ride led us to the Colorado River at the canyon's floor. We saw people riding rafts on the river. We also saw campers trout fishing in it. The temperature really cooled off at dusk.

Monday, July 11
After spending the night at Phantom Ranch, a lodge on the canyon floor, we explored the site of an ancient Native American village. A park ranger then took us on a tour to learn about the different types of wildlife in the canyon.

1. Which of the following statements is a true generalization?
   - Ⓐ Mom and I left our apartment at 8 A.M.
   - Ⓑ There are several ways to reach the floor of the Grand Canyon.
   - Ⓒ We arrived at the South Rim by noon.
   - Ⓓ We saw campers trout fishing in the Colorado River.
2. Which of the following statements is a true generalization?
   - Ⓐ On Saturday, the temperature was a hot 90 degrees.
   - Ⓑ On Sunday, the temperature really cooled off at dusk.
   - Ⓒ The temperature varies in the Grand Canyon.
   - Ⓓ We explored the site of an ancient Native American village.
3. Write a generalization based on the following facts. Write your answer on the lines provided.
   - Phantom Ranch is located at the bottom of the Grand Canyon.
   - An ancient Native American village is located at the bottom of the Grand Canyon.
   - Park rangers give tour guides at the bottom of the Grand Canyon.

Notes for Home: Your child learned how to make generalizations.
Home Activity: With your child, take turns inventing sentences that begin with "Generally," or "Generally speaking."

Also on Teacher Resources CD-ROM.

Climates in the Southwest

Objectives
- Describe different climates found in the Southwest.
- Describe how the saguaro has adapted to a desert climate.
- Explain why the saguaro is important to desert animals.

Vocabulary

arid, p. 309; **savanna,** p. 310

Resources
- Workbook, p. 72
- Transparency 23
- Every Student Learns Guide, pp. 126–129
- Quick Study, pp. 64–65

Quick Teaching Plan

If time is short, have students create a climate scale.
- Tell students to draw a horizontal line labeled *desert* on the left, *arid* in the center, and *humid* on the right.
- As students read the lesson independently, have them chart the climate of each place mentioned in the lesson by writing the name of each place above the climate scale in the appropriate position.

1 Introduce and Motivate

Preview To activate prior knowledge, ask students what type of climate they imagine when they think of the Southwest. Tell students they will learn more about the climate of the Southwest as they read Lesson 2.

You Are There Ask students to speculate about the answers to the questions raised in the text on this page.

LESSON 2

Climates in the Southwest

PREVIEW

Focus on the Main Idea
The Southwest climate can vary greatly. It is dry in some places and moist in others.

PLACES
Sonoran Desert
Saguaro National Park

VOCABULARY
arid
savanna

You Are There You are walking outside on a hot summer day. You are wearing a hat, but you can still feel the sun beating down on your head. You think, "Whew, it's really hot! But I'm not sweating." Even the air around you feels dry. You take out your water bottle and take a long drink. That cool water tastes good!

You look around and see plants growing here. You wonder, "Where did that squirrel come from?" You notice birds flitting from one cactus to another. You think, "How can living things survive in such a hot, dry climate? Where do they get the water they need to live?"

▶ The tiny elf owl may nest in a hole in the trunk of a saguaro cactus.

Draw Conclusions As you read, draw some conclusions about living in a climate that is hot and dry.

308

Practice and Extend

READING SKILL
Draw Conclusions

In the Lesson Review, students complete a graphic organizer like the one below. You may want to provide students with a copy of Transparency 23 to complete as they read the lesson.

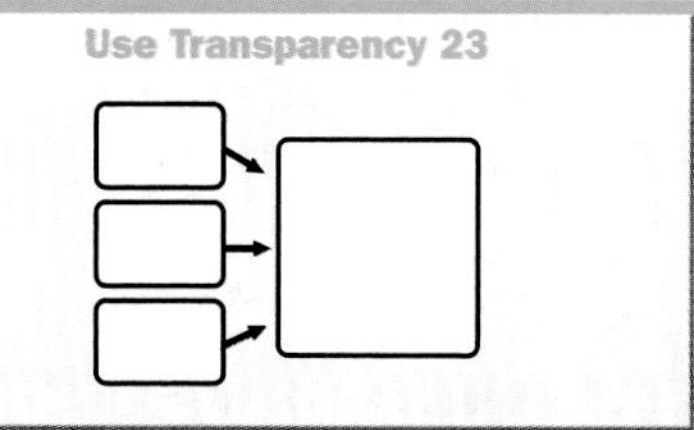

VOCABULARY
Individual Word Study

Savanna came to English from Spanish *(sabana)*. Spanish explorers adopted the word from the language of the Taino, a native people they encountered in the Caribbean. Their word, *zabana*, described a region with which the Spanish were not familiar. Another Taino word that came into English through Spanish describes a bed that is hung by ropes between two trees. The Spanish is *hamaca*—can students guess the English word? *(hammock)*

A Region of Varied Climates

The Southwest region has a variety of climates with wide differences in temperature and precipitation. Some parts of the Southwest are deserts. Remember, a desert is an area that gets less than ten inches of rain each year. The rains may come in heavy downpours, but they don't last long.

Some parts of the Southwest have an **arid** climate. They are dry, but are not deserts. For example, parts of Arizona, Oklahoma, New Mexico, and
1 Texas receive more than ten inches of rain each year, but they are still very dry. These areas might go for a long time without rain.

Because Texas is so large, the state has several types of climate. The eastern part of Texas has a hot, humid climate. Western Texas is also hot, but it is usually dry. 2

Oklahoma sometimes has humid and windy weather. When cold and warm air masses meet over the state, Oklahoma can experience thunderstorms, blizzards, or tornadoes.

REVIEW How would you describe the climate of the Southwest? Main Idea and Details

MAP SKILL

Average Temperatures in the Southwest During May 3

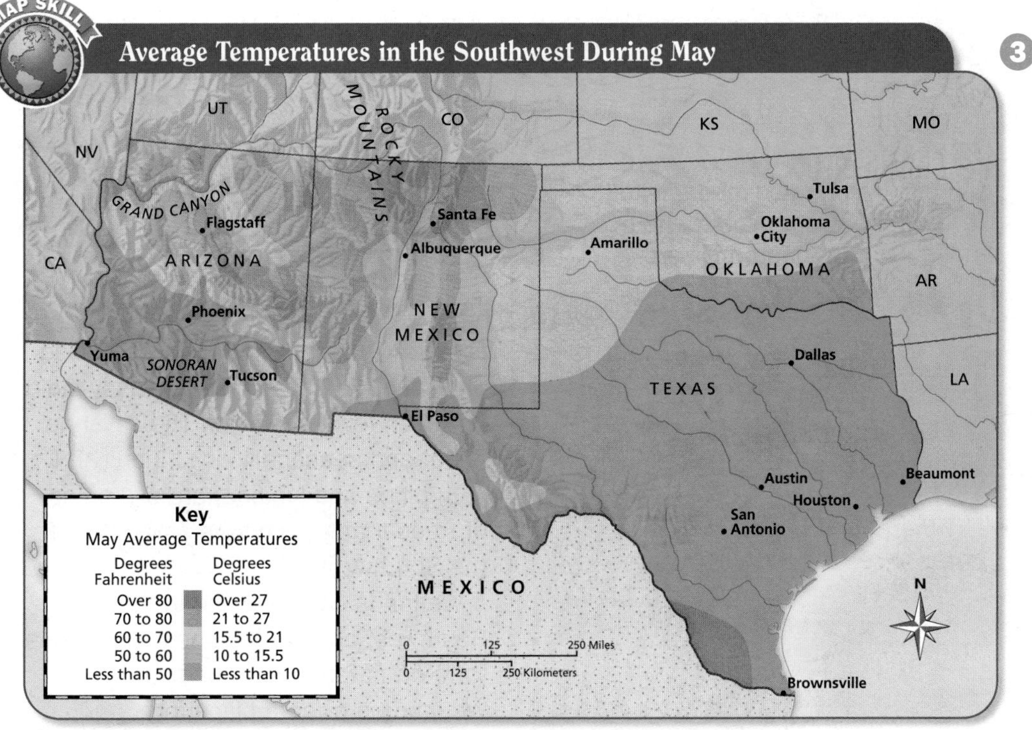

▶ Temperatures in the Southwest vary greatly during the month of May.

MAP SKILL Use a Climate Map ***What Southwestern state has the highest average temperatures in May? Which states in the Southwest have the lowest average temperature in May?*** New Mexico and Arizona

309

Teach and Discuss

PAGE 309

A Region of Varied Climates

Quick Summary Some of the Southwest is desert or other arid land, but some parts are humid.

1 **How does rainfall in desert areas of the Southwest compare to rainfall in arid areas of the Southwest?** Desert: less than 10 inches; Arid: more than 10 inches but still very dry
Compare and Contrast

✓ **Ongoing Assessment**

If... students have difficulty distinguishing between desert areas and arid areas, **then...** have them find the definition of each term in the text.

2 **What generalization does the author make about the climate of West Texas?** It is usually dry. Generalize

✓ **REVIEW ANSWER** Possible answer: It is varied; it is dry in some places, but humid in others. Main Idea and Details

MAP SKILL

Average Temperatures in the Southwest During May

Test Talk

Use Information from Graphics

3 **On average, which city is coolest in May—Phoenix, Dallas, or Tulsa?** Tell students to use details from the map to support their answer. Tulsa Interpret Maps

MAP SKILL Answer Texas; New Mexico or Arizona

ACCESS CONTENT

ESL Support

Describe Climate Describe the climates of different locations.

Beginning Ask students to brainstorm a web of words describing climate.

Intermediate Ask students to create a Venn diagram comparing the climate of their community to the climate of the Southwest.

Advanced Have students make a Venn diagram like the one described above and then write a narrative based on their diagram.

For additional ESL support, use Every Student Learns Guide, pp. 126–129.

CURRICULUM CONNECTION

Math

Create a Bar Graph

- Have students consult an almanac or online resources to research the average rainfall in at least six cities in different parts of the United States, including the Southwest.
- Have students create a bar graph to present their data.

PAGES 310–311

Plants of the Southwest

Quick Summary Saguaros are well adapted to their desert habitat. Other types of plants and animals live in Southwestern savannas and wetlands.

Literature and Social Studies

4 **What scientific reason might explain how saguaro seeds were spread throughout the desert?** Possible answer: Birds and other wildlife ate the seeds and spread them around. Hypothesize

5 **How do saguaros take in and store water?** Long, shallow roots take in water. The saguaro's body expands as water is taken in. Main Idea and Details

6 **In what ways is the saguaro important to wildlife in the desert?** It provides shelter for many forms of wildlife. Main Idea and Details

Plants of the Southwest

The saguaro (sa WAR oh) is a kind of cactus that grows naturally in the **Sonoran Desert,** which stretches through Arizona, parts of Mexico, and southern California. This cactus is the symbol of the Southwest. Its white, night-blooming blossom is Arizona's state flower. You can see many of these spectacular plants in **Saguaro National Park** near Tucson, Arizona.

▶ Saguaro in the Sonoran Desert

The saguaro is well suited for living in the desert. To grow big and strong, the saguaro spreads its long, shallow roots to drink in the rainwater. Its ribbed trunk and branches expand to store water. The saguaro can store enough water to stay alive through long, dry periods. 5

The saguaro's relationship with desert animals is good for all. The saguaro provides shelter for gila woodpeckers, elf owls, bluebirds, warblers, cactus wrens, wood rats, and lizards. Many animals return the favor by eating insects that could cause disease and destroy the saguaro. 6

Other types of plants grow in a climate region of the Southwest called a savanna. A **savanna** is a grassy plain on which few trees grow. The savanna is hot and seasonally dry. Piñon (PIN yon) pines and junipers are examples of trees that grow on the savannas of the Southwest.

Wetlands can be found in the Southwest as well. Marshes sometimes form on flat land surrounding rivers. Wetlands provide a place for water birds such as ducks and cranes.

Literature and Social Studies

The Desert Is Theirs

Byrd Baylor collected folktales from the Southwest. Here is part of a poem based on a tale told by the Papago people who live in the Sonoran Desert.

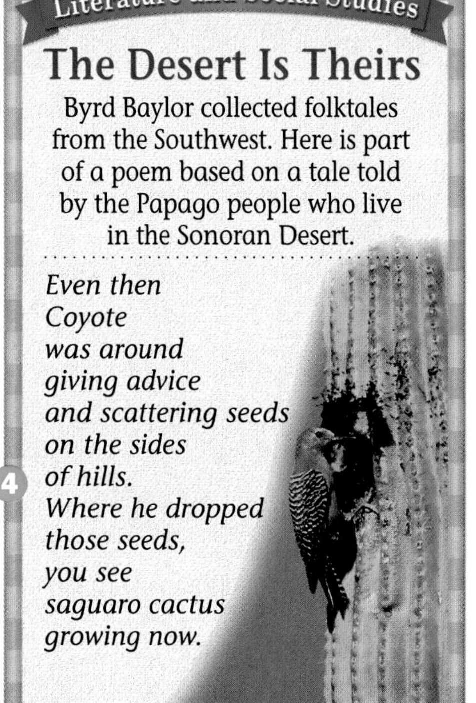

Even then
Coyote
was around
giving advice
and scattering seeds
on the sides
4 *of hills.*
Where he dropped
those seeds,
you see
saguaro cactus
growing now.

310

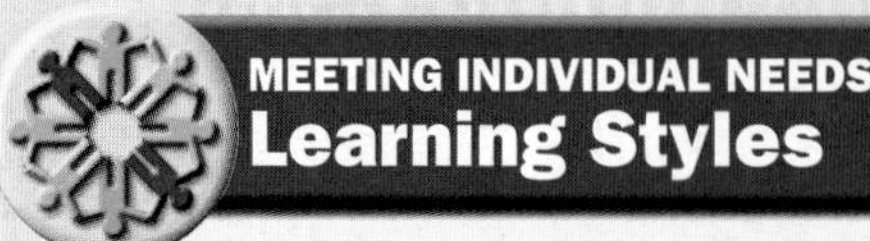

MEETING INDIVIDUAL NEEDS

Learning Styles

Demonstrate the Value of the Saguaro Using their individual learning styles, students learn more about the saguaro.

Kinesthetic Learning Have students use an old, dried sponge to model how a saguaro absorbs and stores water.

Visual Learning Have students find or create a chart that shows animals, including birds, that use the saguaro.

Verbal Learning Have students research and report to the class why the saguaro is considered a keystone species—that is, one that is crucial to the desert ecosystem.

▶ A Southwestern Savanna

▶ Wetlands in Bosque del Apache National Wildlife Refuge in New Mexico

Marsh plants include reeds, grasses, and wild grains.

REVIEW Name three types of plants that grow in the Southwest. Main Idea and Details

Summarize the Lesson

- **Much of the Southwest has an arid climate, but not all of the region is desert.**
- **The saguaro is a cactus that is well suited to growing in the Sonoran Desert of the Southwest.**

LESSON 2 REVIEW

Check Facts and Main Ideas

1. Draw Conclusions Make a diagram like the one shown. Draw a conclusion about the saguaro from the facts given in the diagram.

Details

- Its roots spread wide to drink in rainwater.
- Its trunk and branches expand to store water.
- Animals help the saguaro by eating harmful insects.

Conclusion

The saguaro is adapted to living in the desert.

2. How does the climate of the Southwest vary?
3. In what area of the Southwest do the saguaro grow?
4. Describe a **savanna.**
5. **Critical Thinking:** ***Make Generalizations*** What do plants and animals of the Southwest have in common?

Link to Writing

Describe the Climate Write a postcard to a friend describing the climate of the Southwest. On the front of the postcard, draw a picture to show what the Southwest is like. Use the word **arid** in your postcard message.

311

✓ **REVIEW ANSWER** Possible answers: Saguaro cactus, piñon pines, junipers, reeds **Main Idea and Details**

3 Close and Assess

Summarize the Lesson

Have students read the two main points. Then have them discuss how the climate of the Southwest is similar to and different from the climates of other regions in the United States and how the saguaro cactus is adapted to the climate of the Southwest.

✓ **LESSON 2 REVIEW**

1. **Draw Conclusions** For possible answers, see the reduced pupil page.
2. Some of the Southwest has a dry climate, but parts of Texas have a hot, humid climate. Parts of Oklahoma are also humid and windy.
3. In the Sonoran Desert
4. A hot, seasonally dry grassy plain on which few trees grow
5. **Critical Thinking: *Make Generalizations*** Possible answer: Both are adapted to the varied climate of the Southwest

Link to Writing

Answers will vary but should reflect an understanding of the climate of the Southwest. Postcards should include the word *arid,* used correctly.

MEETING INDIVIDUAL NEEDS

Leveled Practice

Write About Climate Have students demonstrate their understanding of the climate of the Southwest.

Easy Have students draw a poster of the climate of the Southwest. Have them add sentences describing what is shown on the poster. **Reteach**

On-Level Have students write a brief letter to someone in the Northeast, Southeast, or Midwest describing how the climate in one area of the Southwest differs from the climate in his or her region. **Extend**

Challenge Have students write and illustrate a travel brochure describing the climate of the Southwest. **Enrich**

For a Lesson Summary, use Quick Study, p. 64.

Workbook, p. 72

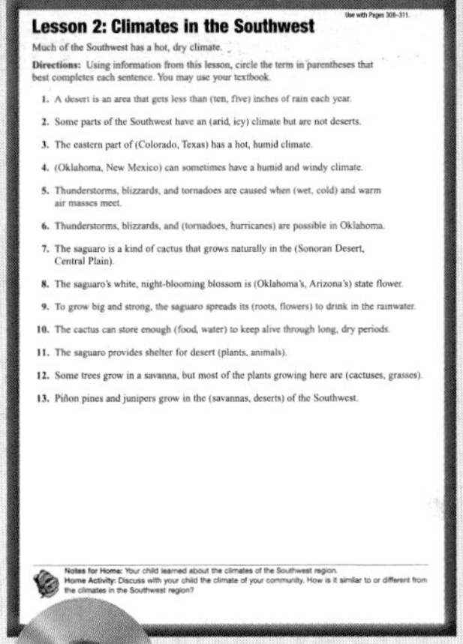

Lesson 2: Climates in the Southwest

Also on Teacher Resources CD-ROM.

Giant Plants

Objective

- Compare and contrast climates and vegetation in different regions of the world.

1 Introduce and Motivate

Preview To activate prior knowledge, ask students to name the types of trees that grow in your area. Tell them they will read about an unusual tree that grows in Africa.

Have students make a concept web of the information they learn about the baobab tree.

2 Teach and Discuss

Tell students that just as the saguaro is a symbol of the American Southwest, the baobab tree is a symbol of the African savanna.

1 **How do you think the climate of the African savanna compares with the climate of the Southwest?** Possible answer: It probably is similar to some arid parts of the Southwest but different from the humid parts. Make Inferences

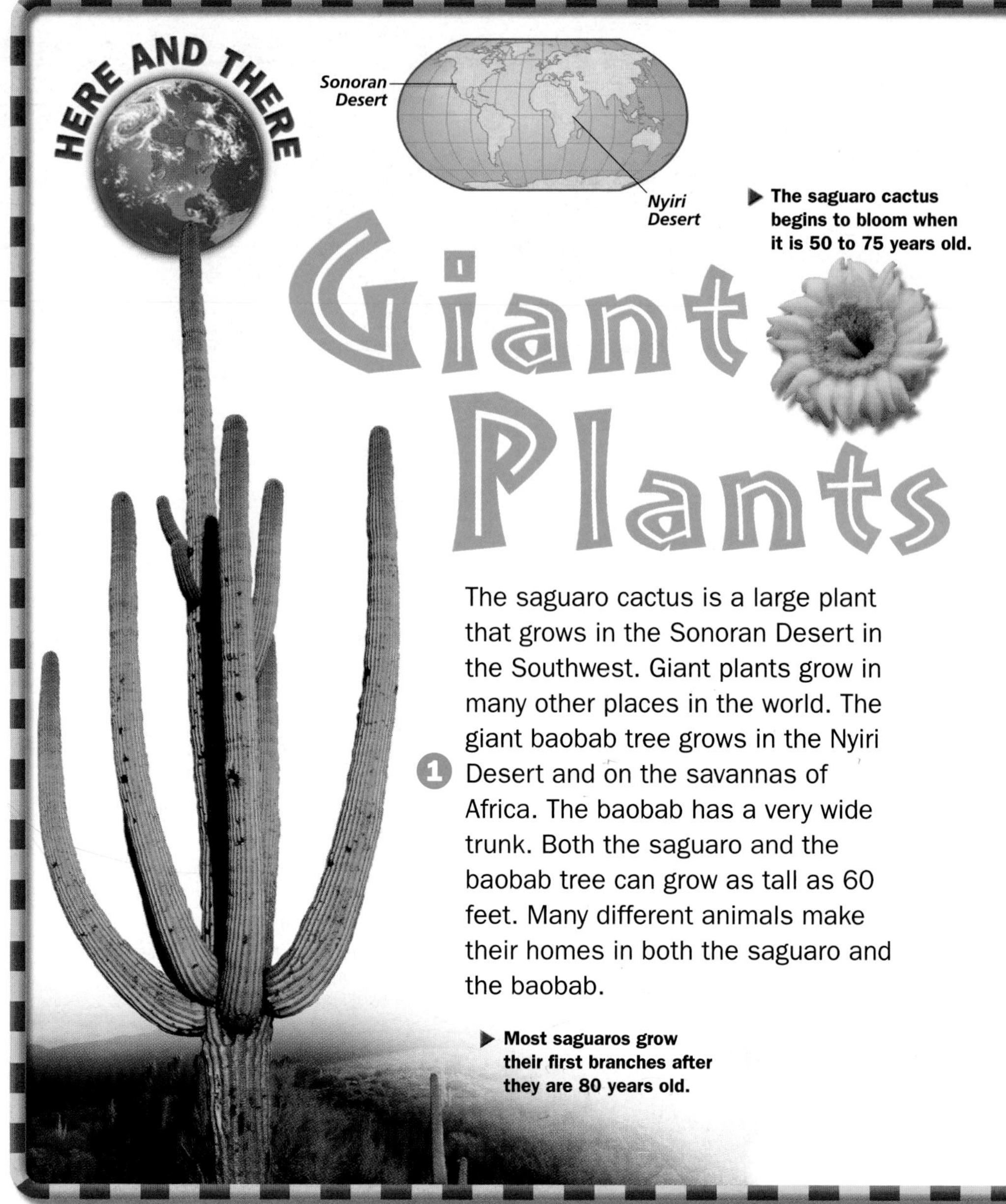

▶ The saguaro cactus begins to bloom when it is 50 to 75 years old.

The saguaro cactus is a large plant that grows in the Sonoran Desert in the Southwest. Giant plants grow in many other places in the world. The giant baobab tree grows in the Nyiri 1 Desert and on the savannas of Africa. The baobab has a very wide trunk. Both the saguaro and the baobab tree can grow as tall as 60 feet. Many different animals make their homes in both the saguaro and the baobab.

▶ Most saguaros grow their first branches after they are 80 years old.

Big Hug for a Big Tree It would take about 15 students touching hands to go all around the trunk of an average baobab.

312

Practice and Extend

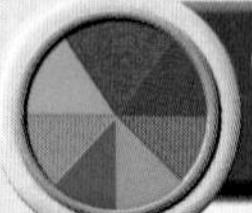

CURRICULUM CONNECTION Literature

Read About Unusual Plants Encourage students to read more about the important plants of a region.

Here Is the African Savanna, by Madeleine Dunphy (Hyperion Press, ISBN 0-78680-162-X, 1999) **Easy**

Tree of Life: The World of the African Baobab, by Barbara Bash (Sierra Club Books for Children, ISBN 1-57805-086-3, 2002) **On-Level**

Desert Giant: The World of the Saguaro Cactus, by Barbara Bash (Sierra Club Books for Children, ISBN 1-57805-085-5, 2002) **Challenge**

WEB SITE Technology

Students can find out more about places on these pages by clicking on *Atlas* at **www.sfsocialstudies.com.**

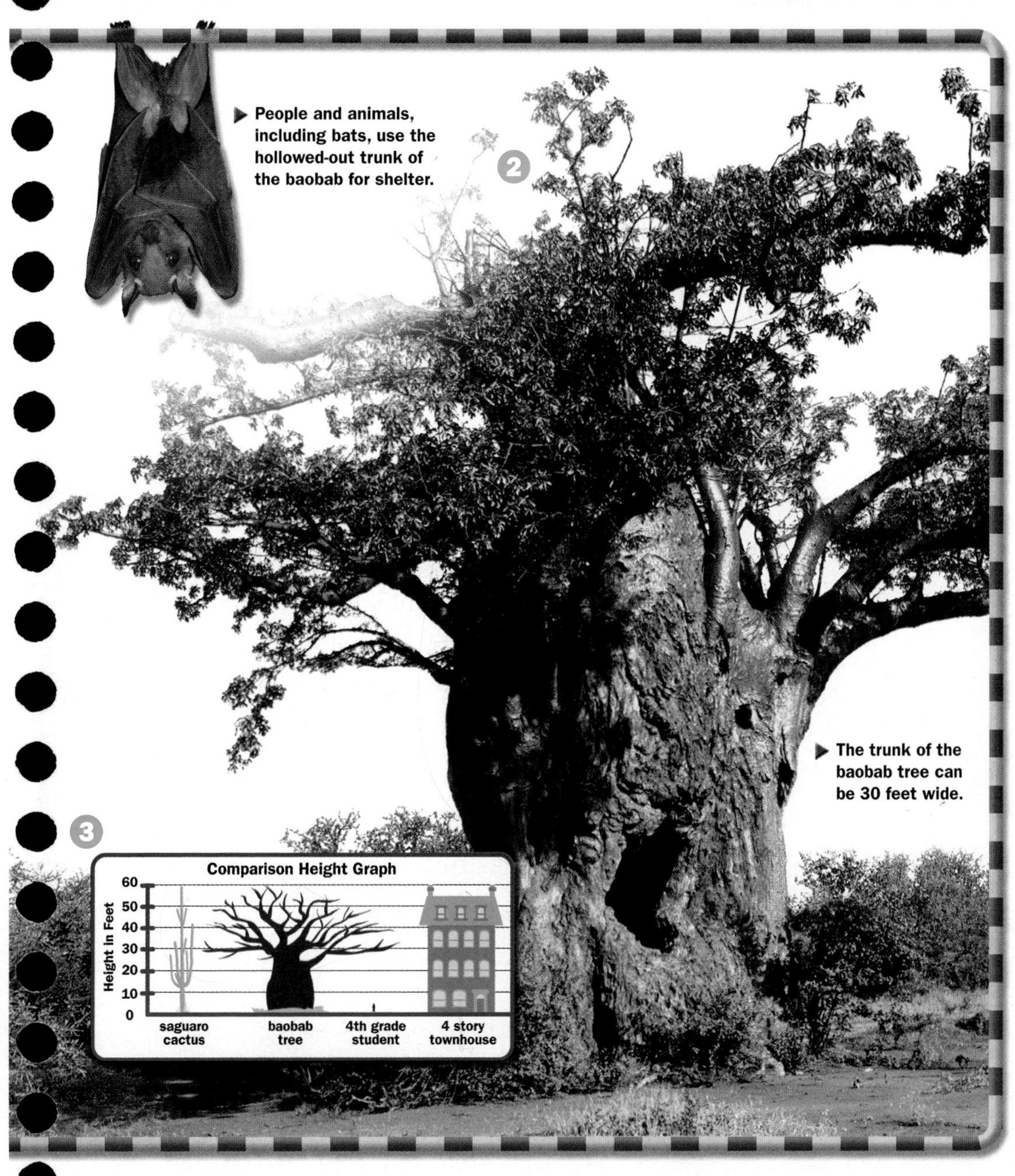

People and animals, including bats, use the hollowed-out trunk of the baobab for shelter.

The trunk of the baobab tree can be 30 feet wide.

SOCIAL STUDIES STRAND

Science • Technology

In addition to serving human needs, the baobab also provides shelter and food for many birds and animals.

2 **What generalization can you make about the baobab and the saguaro?** Both the baobab and the saguaro are important to the wildlife in their regions. Generalize

3 **According to the graph on p. 313, the African baobab and the saguaro cactus can grow to the height of a building of what size?** A four-story townhouse Interpret Graphs

3 Close and Assess

- Encourage students to learn more about the baobab tree and other plants that grow on the African savanna.
- Ask students to add to the concept webs they began earlier. Have students discuss what they learned about the baobab tree from these pages.

SOCIAL STUDIES

Background

About the Baobab

- The flowers of the baobab appear at the end of the dry season. The petals are white, the stamens are purple and fluffy-looking, and the flower is about 7 inches long.
- The flowers hang down on long stalks. They are pollinated by bats gathering nectar.
- Baboons eat the fruit of the baobab. Giraffes eat its leaves.

Oil and Technology

Objectives

- Identify a nonrenewable natural resource in the Southwest.
- Describe how the technology of the Southwest has impacted the United States.

Vocabulary

gusher, p. 315; **refinery,** p. 315

Resources

- Workbook, p. 73
- Transparency 23
- Every Student Learns Guide, pp. 130–133
- Quick Study, pp. 66–67

Quick Teaching Plan

If time is short, have students create note frames to help them remember important information from the lesson.

- Tell students to draw outlines of both an oil well and a large radio antenna. Students may wish to use the pictures in the text as models.
- Have students fill in the outlines with notes containing information about oil or technology in the Southwest.

1 Introduce and Motivate

Preview To activate prior knowledge, ask students if they know where the gasoline that powers most school buses and cars comes from. Tell students that they will read about crude oil, oil processing, and products made from oil in Lesson 3.

You Are There Ask students why they think crude oil is sometimes called "black gold." Ask students to predict what they think happened to the population of Texas as a result of the discovery of oil.

LESSON 3

Preview

Focus on the Main Idea
The Southwest is a region of discovery and research.

PLACES
Beaumont, Texas
Albuquerque, New Mexico
Los Alamos, New Mexico
Houston, Texas

PEOPLE
Pattillo Higgins
Anthony Lucas

VOCABULARY
gusher
refinery

Oil and Technology

You Are There It's 10:30 in the morning on January 10, 1901. You're watching a crew drilling on Spindletop Hill near Beaumont, Texas. All of a sudden the earth begins to rumble. All at once, mud begins gushing from the ground! Drilling string and pieces of equipment fly high into the air. Then comes the oil! Everyone runs for cover. Safe at last, but covered with oil, the drillers rejoice. "We have struck 'black gold'!"

▶ Gusher at Spindletop

Draw Conclusions As you read, draw conclusions about how oil and technology play an important role in the economy of the Southwest.

314

Practice and Extend

READING SKILL
Draw Conclusions

In the Lesson Review, students complete a graphic organizer like the one below. You may want to provide students with a copy of Transparency 23 to complete as they read the lesson.

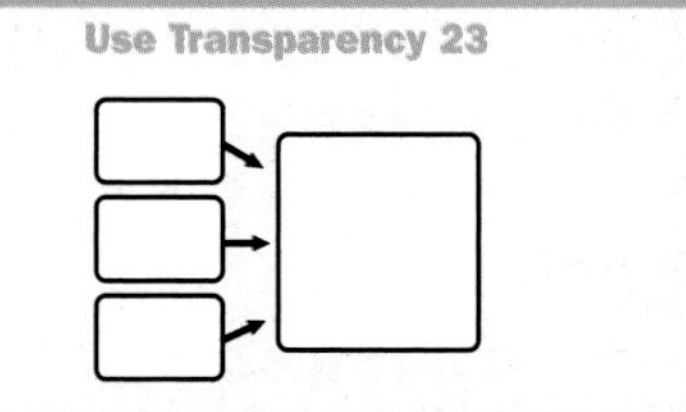

VOCABULARY
Context Clues

Use the questions below or create your own to help students practice new vocabulary. Encourage students to draw upon their own knowledge in answering questions.

- Which happens in a **refinery**: oil is pumped out of the ground or oil is separated into different chemicals? (oil is separated into different chemicals)
- Which kind of well is a **gusher**: a well that has dried up or a well that spouts a lot of oil? (a well that spouts a lot of oil)

Using Oil

The gusher at Spindletop had an effect on Texas history. A **gusher** is an oil well that produces a large amount of oil. After the gusher at Spindletop many people came to Texas in search of oil and natural gas. By 1902, more than 500 Texas companies were doing business in **Beaumont** and other
1 Texas towns.

Pattillo Higgins, a businessman and scientist, thought that there might be oil beneath Spindletop. He saw signs that there might be natural gas in the area. He thought if there was underground gas, there might also be oil. Higgins hired **Anthony Lucas,** a mining engineer, to drill at Spindletop. Lucas's crew drilled the gusher.

Oil comes out of the ground in the form of a thick, black liquid called crude oil. This liquid must be separated, or refined, into different groups of chemicals. The factory that does this separation is called a **refinery.** From the refinery the chemicals go to other factories to be made into many different products.

Oil is a natural resource, and it is nonrenewable. A nonrenewable resource is one that cannot be replaced by nature. 2

REVIEW Using details from this page, draw a conclusion about the importance of oil. Draw Conclusions

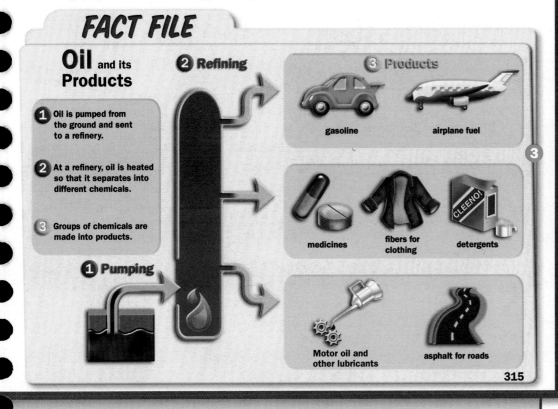

FACT FILE

Oil and its Products 3

1 Oil is pumped from the ground and sent to a refinery.

2 At a refinery, oil is heated so that it separates into different chemicals.

3 Groups of chemicals are made into products.

1 Pumping

2 Refining

3 Products

gasoline

airplane fuel

medicines

fibers for clothing

detergents

CLEENO!

Motor oil and other lubricants

asphalt for roads

315

ISSUES AND VIEWPOINTS
Critical Thinking

Analyze Different Viewpoints Write the lists below on the board or read them aloud. Ask students to add their own opinions to the debate.

Argument to Increase Supply

- Americans have a high standard of living that they want to maintain. Therefore, they need large supplies of energy.
- The United States has unused supplies of oil, gas, and coal, and should tap into these to meet people's growing needs.

Argument to Decrease Demand

- If Americans adapt their lifestyles to use less energy, they will not need to tap into additional supplies of oil and other resources.
- Some untapped energy resources are located in places such as wildlife refuges and offshore in important fish habitats. In these areas drilling or mining could harm the environment.

PAGE 315

Using Oil

Quick Summary Oil is a nonrenewable resource with many uses.

SOCIAL STUDIES STRAND
Economics

The natural resources of an area can affect the economy of an area because many people may be involved in harvesting, processing, or selling those resources.

1 **What effect did the discovery of oil have on Texas?** Many people came to Texas, and businesses grew there. Cause and Effect

SOCIAL STUDIES STRAND
Science • Technology

Like oil, some water comes from deep caverns created long ago. However, water in lakes and streams usually is replaced by rain.

2 **Of the two sources of water mentioned above, which is nonrenewable? What must people using lake water be careful about?** Water from deep caverns is nonrenewable; People using lake water must be careful not to use more than can be replaced by normal rainfall. Apply Information

✓ **REVIEW ANSWER** Possible answer: Oil is an important nonrenewable resource. Draw Conclusions

FACT FILE

Oil and Its Products

3 **Name at least three products that are made from oil after it is refined into chemicals.** Possible answers: Gasoline, detergents, and asphalt Analyze Pictures

PAGES 316–317

Technology in the Southwest

Quick Summary Technology, including electronics, aeronautics, and radio astronomy, plays an important role in the Southwest.

Test Talk

Locate Key Words in the Question

4 **What generalization can you make about the importance of technology to the Southwest?** Tell students "A key word such as *generalization* tells you to look for a broad, overall statement." Technology is an important part of the Southwest's economy. **Generalize**

5 **What kind of workforce do you think would be most useful to industries that deal with technology?** A well-educated workforce that has strong skills in math and science **Draw Conclusions**

Technology in the Southwest

The oil industry is important to the economy of the Southwest. Technology is another important part of the Southwestern economy. 4

Arizona factories manufacture electronic equipment, aircraft, space vehicles, and missiles. You can see some of these products at the Pima Air and Space Museum near Tucson.

Companies in New Mexico make computer chips and computers. Researchers study telecommunications, medicine, and genetics. At the Sandia National Laboratories in **Albuquerque,** workers develop military resources. Scientists in **Los Alamos** study nuclear energy. Astronomers from around the world receive information about space from one of the world's largest radio observatories, the Very Large Array in the desert of central New Mexico. The observatory has 27 radio antennas that allow scientists to view objects in space. 5

▶ Pima Air and Space Museum

▶ Radio telescopes at the Very Large Array

316

Practice and Extend

MEETING INDIVIDUAL NEEDS
Leveled Practice

Map the Technology of the Southwest Have students practice map skills by mapping information from this section.

Easy Have students find the location of several of the places mentioned on this page and mark them on an outline map of the Southwest. **Reteach**

On-Level Have students mark locations on an outline map, as described above. Then have them research what each facility does and write a one- or two-sentence summary of each on the map. **Extend**

Challenge Have students mark locations on an outline map, as described above. Then have them present an oral report on how one or more of the facilities has affected its local community. **Enrich**

For a Lesson Summary, use Quick Study, p. 66.

6 Texas industries make computers, radios, calculators, and electronic equipment. Texas is also home to the Johnson Space Center in **Houston.** Scientists and engineers at the Johnson Space Center manage space flights and conduct research.

Oklahoma companies assist the electronic, aviation, and space industries. Many NASA astronauts train at Vance Air Force Base in Oklahoma.

REVIEW How does technology in the Southwest affect people all over the world? Draw Conclusions

Summarize the Lesson

- **Oil is a nonrenewable natural resource found in the Southwest.**
- **Technology is important to the economy of the Southwest.**

▶ **This jet, the SR-71 Blackbird, is one of the fastest planes in the world.**

LESSON 3 REVIEW

Check Facts and Main Ideas

1. Draw Conclusions On a separate sheet of paper, complete the chart about the importance of oil to the development of the Southwest.

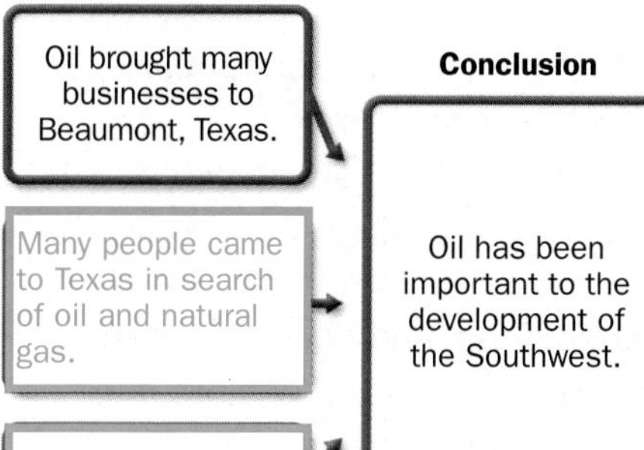

Details
Oil brought many businesses to Beaumont, Texas.
Many people came to Texas in search of oil and natural gas.
Many different products are made from oil.
Conclusion
Oil has been important to the development of the Southwest.

2. Why is oil called a nonrenewable natural resource?
3. Name one technology industry for each state in the Southwest.
4. How has technology in the Southwest helped the rest of the United States?
5. **Critical Thinking:** ***Evaluate*** How have the lives of the people of the Southwest been affected by the discovery of oil? Use the words **gusher** and **refinery** in your answer.

Link to Science

Conserve Resources Research different types of nonrenewable resources and ways to conserve their use. Make a poster showing ways to conserve a nonrenewable resource.

ACCESS CONTENT
ESL Support

Identify Electronic Products Help students identify products mentioned in this lesson.

Beginning Ask students to find examples in the school of a computer, a radio, and a calculator. Explain that these products are related to technology.

Intermediate Have students orally describe what they see in the illustrations in this lesson. Ask what these items all have in common.

Advanced Have students write brief sentences describing what a computer, a radio, a calculator, and an antenna do.

For additional ESL support, use Every Student Learns Guide, pp. 130–133.

Workbook, p. 73

Lesson 3: Oil and Technology

Also on Teacher Resources CD-ROM.

6 **What kinds of electronic equipment are produced in Texas?** Computers, radios, calculators Main Idea and Details

✓ **REVIEW ANSWER** Possible answer: It provides them with equipment and information to expand their knowledge and perform tasks better. Draw Conclusions

3 Close and Assess

Summarize the Lesson

Have students read the two main points. Then have them create a five-question quiz about the content of this lesson, exchange with a partner, and answer each other's quizzes.

✓ **LESSON 3 REVIEW**

1. Draw Conclusions For possible answers, see the reduced pupil page.
2. Because it cannot be replaced by nature
3. Possible answers: Arizona—aerospace industry; New Mexico—computer industry; Texas—electronics industry; Oklahoma—aerospace industry
4. Possible answer: The United States benefits from technological advances developed in the Southwest.
5. **Critical Thinking: *Evaluate*** Starting with the gushers, oil has led to the growth of refineries, new businesses, and jobs. These, in turn, have given people an alternative to farming and improved the economy.

Link to Science

Students' posters will vary but should reflect an understanding of realistic conservation methods.

Flying to Help

Objectives

- Identify the technological contributions of women such as Jerrie Cobb.
- Identify an example of a person who shows caring.

1 Introduce and Motivate

Preview To activate prior knowledge, ask students what goals they are passionate about pursuing.

2 Teach and Discuss

1 **Was Jerrie Cobb qualified to become an astronaut? Explain.** Yes; she passed all the tests.
Draw Conclusions

SOCIAL STUDIES STRAND
Citizenship

2 **How can citizens care for others?** Possible answer: By using their skills to help others Main Idea and Details

CITIZEN HEROES

Flying to Help

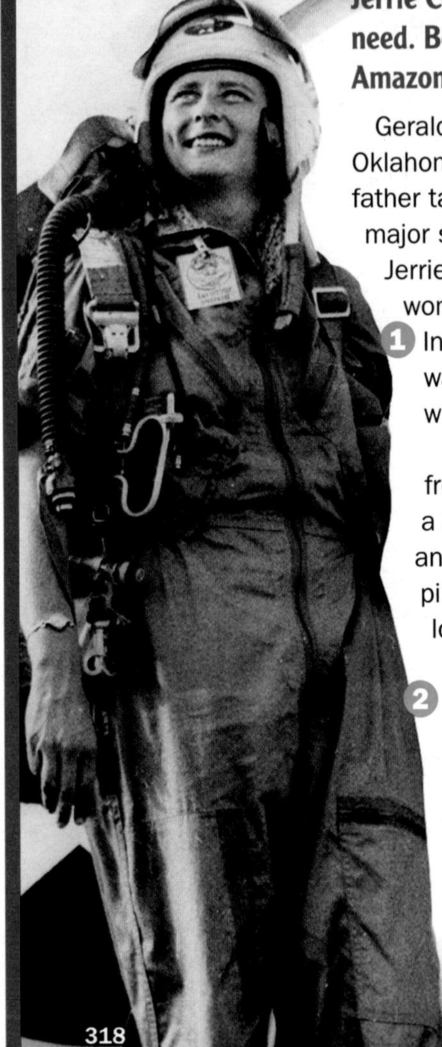

When her dream of flying in space didn't come true, Jerrie Cobb decided to use her skills to help others in need. Because Jerrie Cobb cared, many people in the Amazon rain forest lead healthier lives.

Geraldyn (Jerrie) Cobb was born in 1931 in Norman, Oklahoma. When she was only twelve years old, her father taught her to fly a plane. After Project Mercury, a major space project, was announced in 1958 by NASA, Jerrie was chosen to take physical tests to compare women's and men's abilities to become astronauts. 1 In 1960, Jerrie easily passed the 75 tests and was named one of the participants in the women's astronaut training program.

A change in the rules, however, kept Jerrie Cobb from her dream of going into space. NASA made a rule that astronauts must be military jet pilots and at that time only men could be military jet pilots. So the 13 women chosen for *Mercury 13* lost their chance to go into space.

Jerrie was discouraged, but she decided to use 2 her skill as a pilot to help others. She knew that the people of the Amazon rain forest needed medicine, clothes, food, and doctors. For more than 35 years, Jerrie has flown doctors and supplies into this South American rain forest.

318

Practice and Extend

EXTEND LANGUAGE
ESL Support

Examine Word Roots Help students explore words based on the root *astro-* meaning "star" or "space."

Beginning Show students a picture of an astronaut in space and an astronomer using a telescope. (The word *astronomer* appears on p. 316.) Have students pantomime each term as you point to its picture.

Intermediate Have students look up the roots of the words *astronaut* and *astronomer*. Encourage students to use this information as a memory aid.

Advanced Have students explain the different jobs that an astronaut and an astronomer do.

BUILDING CITIZENSHIP

Caring

Respect

Responsibility

Fairness

Honesty

Courage

Cobb's plane takes her to parts of the Amazon rain forest that cannot be reached on foot or by car.

Her flights have helped more than 6 million people living in parts of Brazil, Colombia, Bolivia, Peru, Venezuela, and Ecuador. Because of her caring efforts, Jerrie Cobb was nominated for a Nobel Peace Prize. 3

Jerrie Cobb organized this project on her own. Her work in the Amazon has given her a new dream. She hopes to go on a mission to study the Amazon from space one day.

Caring in Action

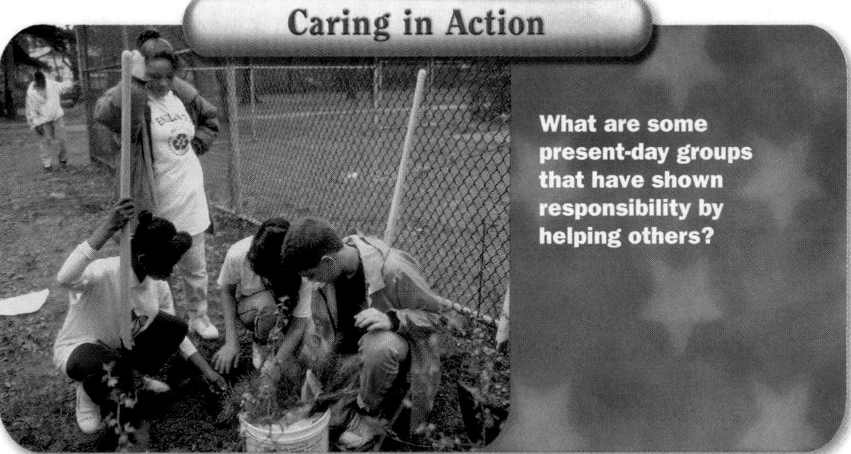

What are some present-day groups that have shown responsibility by helping others?

3 Some observers say Jerrie Cobb "flew hope" to the people of the Amazon. Do you agree? Possible answer: Yes, because she brought things the people needed to have hope for tomorrow Evaluate

Ongoing Assessment

If... students have difficulty understanding how a person can bring hope to others,

then... ask them to consider what the people's lives might be like without the food, clothes, and medicine Cobb brings in.

3 Close and Assess

Caring in Action

Encourage students to identify local, national, and international organizations in their answer.

ISSUES AND VIEWPOINTS

Critical Thinking

- Jerrie Cobb was born in 1931. In an interview in 1998, she said her current goal was to become the oldest woman in space.
- Write the following quote on the board and ask students to discuss whether a person's age should affect his or her dreams.

"You can't give up a dream that you feel is really your destiny."

People Weekly, Oct. 19, 1998

WEB SITE

Technology

Students can find out more about Jerrie Cobb by clicking on *Meet the People* at **www.sfsocialstudies.com.**

SOCIAL STUDIES STRAND

History

Women in Space

- Have students do research and create a poster celebrating the women who have made it into space.
- Among the women they might include are Russian cosmonaut Valentina Tereshkova, the first woman in space; Sally Ride, the first American woman in space; Mae Jemison, the first African American woman in space; and mission specialist Judith Resnik.

Resources

- Assessment Book, pp. 53–56
- Workbook, p. 74: Vocabulary Review

Chapter Summary

For possible answers, see the reduced pupil page.

Vocabulary

1. b, **2.** c, **3.** e, **4.** a, **5.** d

People and Places

Possible answers:

1. Captain García López de Cárdenas and his Spanish soldiers were the first Europeans to see the Grand Canyon.
2. In 1869, Major John Wesley Powell explored the Grand Canyon.
3. President Theodore Roosevelt made the Grand Canyon a national monument.
4. The Sonoran Desert is the only place where the saguaro cactus grows naturally.
5. Beaumont, Texas, is near where the Spindletop Oil Field was discovered in 1901.
6. Pattillo Higgins realized there might be oil at Spindletop when he saw signs that there might be natural gas in the area.

CHAPTER 10 Review

Chapter Summary

Draw Conclusions

On a separate sheet of paper, fill in three details that would lead you to draw this conclusion about the Southwest.

Details

- The Southwest has canyons, rivers, deserts and savannas.
- The Southwest has oil and minerals.
- The Southwest is a center of technology.

Conclusion

The Southwest has many natural resources.

Vocabulary

Match each word with the correct definition or description.

1. **adobe** (p. 302)
2. **pueblo** (p. 302)
3. **arid** (p. 309)
4. **savanna** (p. 310)
5. **refinery** (p. 315)

a. grassy area with little rainfall
b. mud brick
c. village
d. a factory where crude oil is separated
e. dry

People and Places

Write a sentence explaining why each of the following people or places is important to the Southwest. You may use two or more people or places in one sentence.

1. **García López de Cárdenas** (p. 302)
2. **John Wesley Powell** (p. 302)
3. **Theodore Roosevelt** (p. 303)
4. **Sonoran Desert** (p. 310)
5. **Beaumont, Texas** (p. 315)
6. **Pattillo Higgins** (p. 315)

320

Practice and Extend

Assessment Options

✓ Chapter 10 Assessment

- Chapter 10 Content Test: Use Assessment Book, pp. 53–54.
- Chapter 10 Skills Test: Use Assessment Book, pp. 55–56.

Standardized Test Prep

- Chapter 10 Tests contain standardized test format.

✓ Chapter 10 Performance Assessment

- Have students work in small groups to review information in this chapter by analyzing the pictures.
- Have students take turns describing the significance of each picture and explaining the related facts, places, or people.
- Assess students' understanding of the chapter content by monitoring their descriptions. If they have trouble identifying the significance of a picture, ask a question relating to the picture.

Facts and Main Ideas

1. Why was Major John Wesley Powell important to the history of the Grand Canyon?
2. How does the arid climate of the Southwest affect the kinds of plants that grow there?
3. How was oil found at Spindletop?
4. **Main Idea** How has erosion affected the Grand Canyon?
5. **Main Idea** Describe three types of climate you might find in the Southwest.
6. **Main Idea** Name four technology industries found in the Southwest.
7. **Critical Thinking:** ***Cause and Effect*** How did the discovery of oil affect the development of the Southwest?

Apply Skills

Make Generalizations

Read the paragraph below. Which numbered statement is a generalization?

> The saguaro cactus is well suited to grow in the desert. The saguaro has long, shallow roots that take in water quickly when it rains. Saguaros have ribbed trunks and branches that expand as water is taken in. The cactus can store huge amounts of water that keep the plant alive during dry periods.

1. The saguaro cactus is well suited to grow in the desert.
2. The cactus can store huge amounts of water.
3. Saguaros have ribbed trunks and branches.

Write About Geography

1. **Write a diary entry** about a day at the Grand Canyon.
2. **Write a report** describing ways to conserve oil and reasons for doing so.
3. **Write a newspaper article** describing the plants and animals of the Southwest.

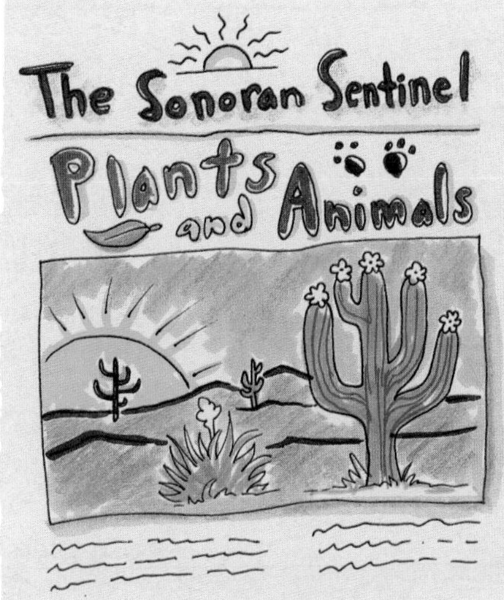

Internet Activity

To get help with vocabulary, people, and places, select dictionary or encyclopedia from *Social Studies Library* at **www.sfsocialstudies.com.**

321

Facts and Main Ideas

1. His reports led others to explore and study the canyon area.
2. Many plants that grow there, such as the saguaro, store and conserve water and are otherwise adapted to the dry climate.
3. People spotted clues to its existence and drilled to find it.
4. Erosion has gradually worn away rock to create a deep canyon, and it continues to shape the canyon today.
5. Some areas are deserts, receiving less than 10 inches of rain per year. Other areas are arid but not quite as dry as a desert. Still other areas are hot and humid, which can be very uncomfortable.
6. Possible answer: Aerospace, computer, electronics, defense
7. Possible answer: After oil was discovered at Spindletop, many people came to the Southwest in search of oil and natural gas.

Apply Skills

Statement 1 is a generalization.

Write About Geography

1. Encourage students to use the pictures in the chapter to help them provide descriptive details.
2. Encourage students to develop easy and practical ways for companies and individuals to conserve oil.
3. Encourage students to use Internet and library resources to research information for their article.

Hands-on Unit Project

✓ **Unit 5 Performance Assessment**

- See p. 358 for information about using the Unit Project as a means of performance assessment.
- A scoring guide is provided on p. 358.

WEB SITE
Technology

For more information, students can select the dictionary or encyclopedia from *Social Studies Library* at **www.sfsocialstudies.com.**

Workbook, p. 74

Vocabulary Review

Also on Teachers Resources CD-ROM.

CHAPTER 11

Chapter Planning Guide

Chapter 11 • The People of the Southwest

Locating Places pp. 322–323

Lesson Titles	Pacing	Main Ideas
Lesson 1 **The Navajo** pp. 324–328	4 days	• The Navajo have lived in the Southwest for centuries.
Biography: Henry Chee Dodge p. 329		• Henry Chee Dodge was a leader as well as a representative and interpreter for the Navajo people.
Research and Writing Skills: Identify Primary and Secondary Sources pp. 330–331		• Primary and secondary sources help to provide information about events from different points of view.
Lesson 2 **Spanish Influence** pp. 332–337	2 days	• Explorers and missionaries brought a Spanish presence to the Southwest.
Lesson 3 **Ranches and Drivers** pp. 338–343	3 days	• The cattle industry boomed in the Southwest in the 1800s. The cowboys who herded cattle became part of our nation's lore.
DK **Cowboys and Cowgirls** pp. 344–345		• Cowboys and cowgirls have been a colorful part of southwestern life.
Lesson 4 **Living in the Desert** pp. 346–348	3 days	• High temperatures and a shortage of water can make living in the desert a challenge.
Biography: Willis Haviland Carrier p. 349		• Willis Haviland Carrier developed an air-conditioning system that controlled both temperature and humidity.
Issues and Viewpoints: Save "America's Main Street"? pp. 350–351		• Route 66 was once a major highway in the United States.
✓ **Chapter 11 Review** pp. 352–353		

The influence of Spanish and Mexican culture can be seen throughout the Southwest.

✓ **= Assessment Options**

Henry Chee Dodge served as the first chairman of the Navajo Tribal Council and worked with the U.S. Military Navajo Code Talkers during World War II.

Vocabulary	Resources	Meeting Individual Needs
hogan primary source secondary source	• Workbook, p. 76 • Transparency 18 • Every Student Learns Guide, pp. 134–137 • Quick Study, pp. 68–69 • Workbook, p. 77	• Leveled Practice, TE p. 325 • ESL Support, TE p. 327
viceroy missionary vaquero	• Workbook, p. 78 • Transparencies 23, 54, 55 • Every Student Learns Guide, pp. 138–141 • Quick Study, pp. 70–71	• Leveled Practice, TE p. 334 • ESL Support, TE pp. 335, 336
tallow homestead	• Workbook, p. 79 • Transparencies 23, 56 • Every Student Learns Guide, pp. 142–145 • Quick Study, pp. 72–73 • Workbook, p. 80	• ESL Support, TE p. 341 • Leveled Practice, TE p. 343
aqueduct	• Workbook, p. 81 • Transparency 18 • Every Student Learns Guide, pp. 146–149 • Quick Study, pp. 74–75	• Leveled Practice, TE p. 347 • ESL Support, TE p. 348 • Learning Styles, TE p. 350
	✔ Chapter 11 Content Test, Assessment Book, pp. 57–58 ✔ Chapter 11 Skills Test, Assessment Book, pp. 59–60	✔ Chapter 11 Performance Assessment, TE p. 352

Providing More Depth

Additional Resources

- Vocabulary Workbook and Cards
- Social Studies Plus! pp. 112–117
- Daily Activity Bank
- Big Book Atlas
- Student Atlas
- Outline Maps
- Desk Maps

Technology

- AudioText
- MindPoint® Quiz Show CD-ROM
- ExamView® Test Bank CD-ROM
- Teacher Resources CD-ROM
- Map Resources CD-ROM
- SFSuccessNet: iText (Pupil Edition online), iTE (Teacher's Edition online), Online Planner
- **www.sfsocialstudies.com** (Biographies, news, references, maps, and activities)

To establish guidelines for your students' safe and responsible use of the Internet, use the Scott Foresman Internet Guide.

Additional Internet Links

To find out more about:

- Route 66, visit **www.rt66nm.org**
- Cowboys, visit **www.westfolk.org**
- Navajo Code Talkers, visit **www.navajocentral.org**

Key Internet Search Terms

- Navajo Long Walk
- Francisco Vásquez de Coronado
- Sonoran Desert

Workbook Support

Use the following Workbook pages to support content and skills development as you teach Chapter 11. You can also view and print Workbook pages from the Teacher Resources CD-ROM.

Workbook, p. 75

Use with Chapter 11.

Vocabulary Preview

Directions: These are the vocabulary words from Chapter 11. How much do you know about these words? Write each word in the space beside its meaning. You may use your glossary.

hogan	missionary	tallow	aqueduct
viceroy	vaquero	homestead	

1. **viceroy** governor
2. **vaquero** Spanish cowboy
3. **hogan** one-room home of the Navajo
4. **aqueduct** trench or pipe used to bring water from a distance
5. **tallow** fat of cattle used for candles and soap
6. **missionary** person who is sent by a religious organization into other parts of the world to spread its beliefs
7. **homestead** land given to a settler

Directions: Use the following vocabulary words in an original sentence. Write your sentences on the lines provided.

8. hogan ______________________
9. tallow ______________________

Notes for Home: Your child learned the vocabulary terms for Chapter 11.
Home Activity: Even today, aqueducts carry water to some communities. From where does your community receive its water supply? Discuss this with your child.

Use with Pupil Edition, p. 322

Workbook, p. 76

Use with Pages 324–328.

Lesson 1: The Navajo

The Navajo have lived in and been an important part of the Southwest for centuries.

Directions: Write the number for each term on the line next to its definition or description.

1. Diné	**5.** Bosque Redondo	**8.** Henry Chee Dodge
2. hogan	**6.** "The Long Walk"	**9.** Navajo Nation
3. Kit Carson	**7.** Navajo Tribal Council	**10.** Window Rock
4. Fort Canby		

9 the largest Native American group in the United States
5 area in New Mexico to which the Navajo were forced to walk three hundred miles
2 home made of logs and covered with a thick layer of soil
4 army post in Arizona to which the Navajo were ordered to move
10 in Arizona; the Navajo capital
3 a soldier who was ordered by the U.S. government to stop conflicts between the Navajo and the white settlers in New Mexico
1 "the people;" what Navajo people called themselves before European settlers came to North America
8 first chairman of the Navajo Tribal Council
6 the 300-mile journey to Bosque Redondo along which many Navajo died
7 made the first written system of Navajo laws

Notes for Home: Your child learned about the history of the Navajo.
Home Activity: Discuss "The Long Walk" of the Navajo with your child. Together, brainstorm a list of reasons how the journey got its name.

76 Lesson Review Workbook

Use with Pupil Edition, p. 328

Workbook, p. 77

Use with Pages 330–331.

Identify Primary and Secondary Sources

As you research a particular topic, you can use primary and secondary sources for different purposes.

Directions: Read the descriptions below. Write whether each source is *primary* or *secondary* on the lines provided.

1. You have found an article in a magazine about life at the Grand Canyon written by a Havasupai. Is the article a primary or secondary source? **primary**
2. You are reading a biography of John Wesley Powell written by a historian. Is the book a primary or secondary source? **secondary**
3. You have discovered a newspaper article describing a tornado in Oklahoma. It was written by an eyewitness to the storm. Is the article a primary or secondary source? **primary**
4. You have found a letter written by Pattillo Higgins about his search for oil. Is the letter a primary or secondary source? **primary**
5. You are reading the section in your social studies textbook about Jerrie Cobb. Is the section a primary or secondary source? **secondary**
6. You read an editorial in your newspaper written by a Navajo Native American. Is the editorial a primary or secondary source? **primary**
7. You found a biography about Henry Chee Dodge. Is it a primary or secondary source? **secondary**

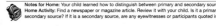

Notes for Home: Your child learned how to distinguish between primary and secondary sources.
Home Activity: Find a newspaper or magazine article. Review it with your child. Is it a primary or secondary source? If it is a secondary source, are any eyewitnesses or participants quoted in it?

Use with Pupil Edition, p. 331

Workbook Support

Workbook, p. 78

Use with Pages 332–337.

Lesson 2: Spanish Influence

The Spanish established their presence in the Southwest many years ago.

Directions: Complete the charts below with information from the lesson. You may use your textbook.

Spanish Influence in the Southwest

Francisco Vásquez de Coronado:	
WHAT was his goal?	**To find the "Cities of Gold" and claim them for Spain**
WHAT did he really do?	**He searched for the mythical city of "Quivira."**
WHAT happened when he went back to Mexico later?	**He reported that there was no gold, and the expedition was labeled a failure.**

Missionaries:	
WHAT were their goals?	**To claim land and make Christians of the Native Americans**
WHAT did they really do?	**Possible answer: They taught the Native Americans many things; they built missions; some treated the Native Americans cruelly; some protected the Native Americans from other Spaniards, who were cruel.**
WHAT happened later?	**Pueblos grew around the missions; some pueblos governed themselves; some Spanish mission churches still stand.**

Notes for Home: Your child learned about Spanish influence in the Southwest United States.
Home Activity: Look at a map of the Southwest region, either in your child's textbook or in another source. Point out to your child places with Spanish names, such as *Santa Fe, New Mexico,* and *San Antonio, Texas*. Discuss with your child other Spanish place names.

Use with Pupil Edition, p. 337

Workbook, p. 79

Use with Pages 338–343.

Lesson 3: Ranches and Drivers

Cattle ranches can be found throughout the Southwest region.

Directions: Using information from this lesson, select a term in the box to complete each sentence. You may use your textbook.

Montana	tallow	Annie Oakley	Mexican
meat	Kansas	King	Philip Armour

1. Early Texas settlers raised cattle to use as **meat** for their families.
2. The **tallow** of the cattle was used for candles and soap.
3. In 1870 **Philip Armour** started a meat-packing industry in Chicago.
4. Cattle became important not only to the Southwest but also to northern states, such as **Montana** and the Dakotas.
5. In South Texas, many cowboys were of **Mexican** descent.
6. **Annie Oakley** and Calamity Jane were famous cowgirls who performed in wild-west shows.
7. Many ranchers drove their cattle from Texas all the way to **Kansas** on the Chisholm Trail.
8. The **King** Ranch spreads over 800,000 acres and is larger than the state of Rhode Island.

Notes for Home: Your child learned about ranching in the Southwest.
Home Activity: Discuss with your child the importance of cattle ranching to families in your town. Also discuss the dairy industry.

Use with Pupil Edition, p. 343

Workbook, p. 80

Writing Prompt: Cowboys and Cowgirls

Driving cattle was an important and difficult job in the "Wild West." Think about what you have read about the cowboys and cowgirls of today and long ago. Write a paragraph about how modern cowhands' jobs are similar to and different from those of cowhands long ago.

Answers will vary.

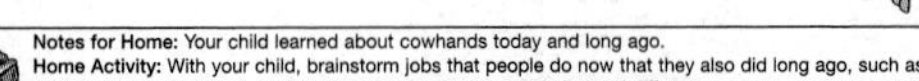

Notes for Home: Your child learned about cowhands today and long ago.
Home Activity: With your child, brainstorm jobs that people do now that they also did long ago, such as doctor or cook. Discuss how jobs today and long ago are similar and different.

Use with Pupil Edition, p. 345

Workbook, p. 81

Use with Pages 346–348.

Lesson 4: Living in the Desert

Even though most of Arizona is a desert, large cities have been built there.

Directions: Suppose that you live in Phoenix, Arizona. Write a letter to a friend or family member who lives in another region. Describe life in the desert. Include information about inventions that have improved desert living. You may use your textbook.

Dear ____________,

Answers should reflect an understanding of the impact of irrigation and air conditioning on life in the Southwest desert.

Sincerely yours,

Notes for Home: Your child learned about living in a desert region.
Home Activity: Discuss air conditioning with your child. Does your family have it at home? If so, discuss the need to conserve energy by keeping the thermostat at a reasonable setting. If not, brainstorm with your child ways your family can keep cool during warm weather.

Use with Pupil Edition, p. 348

Workbook, p. 82

Use with Chapter 11.

Vocabulary Review

Directions: Use the vocabulary words from Chapter 11 to complete the crossword puzzle.

											1 H	O	G	A	N
					2 M						O				
					I			3 V			M				
					S			4 A	Q	U	E	D	U	C	T
					S			Q			S				
					I			U			T				
5 V	I	C	E	R	O	Y		E			E				
					N			R			A				
				6 T	A	L	L	O	W		D				
					R										
					Y										

Across

1. one-room home of the Navajo
4. trench or pipe used to bring water from a distance
5. governor
6. fat of cattle used for candles and soap

Down

1. land given to a settler
2. person who is sent by a religious organization into other parts of the world to spread its beliefs
3. Spanish cowboy

Notes for Home: Your child learned the vocabulary terms for Chapter 11.
Home Activity: Some of the terms from this chapter come directly from other languages. For example, the word *aqueduct* comes from Latin. Have your child find the chapter vocabulary term that is in Spanish. Discuss with your child why the word for the first cowboys is Spanish.

Use with Pupil Edition, p. 353

Workbook, p. 83

Unit 5 Project Ad Sales

Discovery School

Directions: In a group, make an infomercial to sell a product or business that helps your state's economy.

1. Our product or business is ____________.
2. These are facts about our product or business:
3. We wrote a script for our infomercial, including these topics:
   ____ history ____ value or importance ____ cost
   ____ success stories ____ how it helps our state's economy
4. We made a poster or banner to use in our infomercial. This is the slogan we used in our advertisement:

You may wish to show students examples of advertisements and discuss how persuasion is used to sell products and services.

Checklist for Students

- ____ We chose a product or business.
- ____ We wrote facts about the product or business.
- ____ We wrote an infomercial script.
- ____ We made an advertisement on a poster or banner.
- ____ We presented our infomercial to the class.

Notes for Home: Your child made an infomercial to advertise a product or business.
Home Activity: With your child, make a chart of local businesses and the products and services they provide to your community. Discuss different ways in which businesses advertise their products to the community.

Use with Pupil Edition, p. 358

Assessment Support

Use the following Assessment Book pages and The test maker to assess content and skills in Chapter 11 and Unit 5. You can also view and print Assessment Book pages from the Teacher Resources CD-ROM.

Assessment Book, p. 57

Chapter 11 Test

Part 1: Content Test

Directions: Fill in the circle next to the correct answer.

Lesson Objective (1:1)

1. Which is true about the Navajo hogans?
   - ● They were made of poles that were covered with a layer of soil and bark.
   - Ⓑ They were built so that their doors faced west—toward the rising sun.
   - Ⓒ They were considered sacred houses even after the owner died.
   - Ⓓ They were blessed with the pollen of the soybean plant.

Lesson Objective (1:2)

2. What was the destination of the Navajo on "The Long Walk"?
   - Ⓐ Fort Defiance
   - Ⓑ Santa Fe
   - ● Bosque Redondo
   - Ⓓ Fort Wingate

Lesson Objective (1:2)

3. Which of these is NOT true about "The Long Walk"?
   - Ⓐ The walk covered 300 miles.
   - Ⓑ Many Navajo died during the walk.
   - ● The Navajo found plenty of food, clothing, and homes at the end of the walk.
   - Ⓓ The Navajo found poor soil and unsafe water at the end of their walk.

Lesson Objective (1:3)

4. Which describes the Navajo Tribal Council today?
   - Ⓐ Its council members meet with its chairman, Henry Chee Dodge.
   - Ⓑ It has 12 alternates who are elected by the Navajo people.
   - ● It has council members and a chairperson who are elected every four years.
   - Ⓓ It has 12 delegates who meet with the Secretary of the Interior.

Lesson Objective (2:2)

5. Which of these was NOT a purpose of the Spanish missions?
   - Ⓐ to make Christians of the Native Americans
   - Ⓑ to support itself by raising crops and livestock
   - ● to provide a place for Native American rituals
   - Ⓓ to claim land

Lesson Objective (2:2)

6. What is one way that Spanish missions helped the Native Americans?
   - Ⓐ Some gave the Native Americans money to buy their own houses and food.
   - ● Some protected the Native Americans from their enemies.
   - Ⓒ They set up reservations where the Native Americans could live with their families.
   - Ⓓ They built hogans so that the Native Americans could perform their rituals.

Use with Pupil Edition, p. 352

Assessment Book, p. 58

Lesson Objective (2:1)

7. Which of these was NOT brought to the Southwest by the Spanish?
   - Ⓐ cattle ranching
   - Ⓑ Mexican and Spanish foods
   - ● hogan building
   - Ⓓ Spanish language

Lesson Objective (2:1)

8. Which of these cultures has the most influence in the Southwest today?
   - ● Spanish
   - Ⓑ French
   - Ⓒ German
   - Ⓓ Italian

Lesson Objective (3:1)

9. How did Philip Armour help the cattle industry grow in the Southwest?
   - Ⓐ He was the first person to round up and brand wild longhorns in the Southwest.
   - Ⓑ He brought cattle from Spain to Texas, and the cattle were left behind when he and other missionaries left.
   - ● He started a meat-packing industry in Chicago that helped the market for beef grow.
   - Ⓓ He developed a way to use the hides, horns, hooves, and tallow of the cattle for different products.

Lesson Objective (3:3)

10. Why did Texas cowboys need an easy way to get their cattle to Kansas?
    - Ⓐ Kansas had much more open grazing land for the cattle than Texas did.
    - Ⓑ People living in Kansas enjoyed eating beef much more than the people of Texas.
    - ● The cattle could be sent to meat-packing plants from the railroad towns in Kansas.
    - Ⓓ The people of Texas did not allow cattle to be raised or sold within the state's borders.

Lesson Objective (3:2)

11. Which was NOT a job of the cowboys in the Southwest?
    - ● building missions
    - Ⓑ training horses
    - Ⓒ guarding cattle
    - Ⓓ driving cattle

Lesson Objective (3:3)

12. Where did the Chisholm Trail begin?
    - Ⓐ Houston, Texas
    - ● San Antonio, Texas
    - Ⓒ Ellsworth, Kansas
    - Ⓓ Santa Fe, New Mexico

Lesson Objective (3:4)

13. Which is NOT a way that ranching in the Southwest today is different from ranching in the past?
    - Ⓐ Ranchers raise crops to feed the animals.
    - Ⓑ The animals drink mainly from water wells, so they don't have to travel far.
    - ● Open range grasslands are available for shared grazing.
    - Ⓓ Many ranchers fence their land to keep cattle from wandering off.

Use with Pupil Edition, p. 352

Assessment Book, p. 59

Lesson Objective (4:1)

14. How has irrigation changed Arizona?
    - Ⓐ Rain falls in Arizona much more often now.
    - Ⓑ Cacti, such as the saguaro, can grow there now.
    - Ⓒ Most of Arizona now has become a hot, dry desert.
    - ● Land that once was dry is now rich farmland.

Lesson Objective (4:2)

15. How has air conditioning affected the Southwest?
    - Ⓐ Humidity is added to the dry Southwest air.
    - Ⓑ It freezes the water in the air around businesses and homes.
    - ● The heat of the Southwest is more bearable for businesses and families there.
    - Ⓓ Many factories close in the hot summer months.

Part 2: Skills Test

Directions: Use complete sentences to answer questions 1–5. Use a separate sheet of paper if you need more space.

1. How do you think the Navajo people felt after making "The Long Walk"? How do you think they felt when they saw their new homeland? Why? **Draw Conclusions**

   Possible answer: The Navajo probably had mixed feelings. They probably were happy to be finished walking and to have made it alive to Bosque Redondo. They probably also were sad for the people they lost on the way. After they saw that their new home had bad soil and water, the people probably felt sad, scared, frustrated, or even angry.

2. Why do you think the Navajo Tribal Council made a system of written rules? **Make Inferences**

   Possible answer: Rules help them to govern a large number of people. All the people can read the rules and know what is expected of them, and the rules can be handed down to the next generation.

Assessment Book   Unit 5, Chapter 11 Test 59

Use with Pupil Edition, p. 352

Assessment Book, p. 60

3. What are the main events of Coronado's search for the Cities of Gold? Write them in the order that they happened. **Sequence**

   In 1540 the viceroy sent Coronado to find the golden cities. He came upon a Zuñi pueblo and saw that the walls were not gold. Coronado then sent search parties in different directions. The groups found the Grand Canyon, the Gulf of California, and Pueblo villages in what is now New Mexico. Coronado's group looked for a mythical city of riches but found no gold. They went back to Mexico and reported that there was no gold.

4. Why do you think pueblos grew up around the Spanish missions in the Southwest? **Make Inferences**

   Possible answers: Some Native Americans who lived at the mission married and built homes near there. Eventually, pueblos grew there. Also, each mission was a center of activity for the area. Many missions had farms and ranches, a good water supply, and mills. It was natural for people to be drawn to the area.

5. What effect did the Chisholm Trail have on cattle ranching in Texas? **Cause and Effect**

   Possible answers: Cattle ranching in Texas grew because of the Chisholm Trail. Cowboys had a way to take their cattle to Kansas to sell them to meat-packing plants. The Chisholm Trail may have decreased cattle ranching in Texas, too. Some cowboys who learned of open grazing land closer to Kansas and the Midwest may have decided to move to another location along the trail.

Use with Pupil Edition, p. 352

Assessment Support

Assessment Book, p. 61

Unit 5 Test

Part 1: Content Test

Directions: Fill in the circle next to the correct answer.

Lesson Objective (10–1:1)

1. Which river carried the sand, gravel, and boulders that helped shape the Grand Canyon?
   - Ⓐ Platte River
   - ● Colorado River
   - Ⓒ Mississippi River
   - Ⓓ Arkansas River

Lesson Objective (10–1:2)

2. What is the name of the process that formed the Grand Canyon and continues to shape it today?
   - Ⓐ irrigation
   - Ⓑ resource
   - ● erosion
   - Ⓓ tourism

Lesson Objective (10–2:1, 2)

3. How is the saguaro able to survive in Arizona's climate?
   - ● Most of Arizona is a desert, and the saguaro is able to store huge amounts of water.
   - Ⓑ Arizona gets more than 10 inches of rain each year, and the saguaro is waterproof.
   - Ⓒ Arizona's climate is subtropical, and the saguaro produces beautiful flowers.
   - Ⓓ Arizona gets many inches of snowfall each year, and the saguaro is able to stay warm.

Lesson Objective (10–3:1)

4. Why is oil considered a nonrenewable resource?
   - Ⓐ It comes out of the ground in the form of a thick black liquid.
   - Ⓑ It was discovered on Spindletop Hill.
   - Ⓒ It has to be separated into different products.
   - ● It is a resource that cannot be replaced by nature.

Lesson Objective (10–3:2)

5. Which is NOT a technology industry located in New Mexico?
   - Ⓐ genetics
   - Ⓑ telecommunications
   - Ⓒ nuclear energy
   - ● space vehicles and missiles

Lesson Objective (10–3:2)

6. In which state is the Johnson Space Center located?
   - Ⓐ Oklahoma
   - Ⓑ Arizona
   - ● Texas
   - Ⓓ New Mexico

Lesson Objective (11–1:1)

7. How were the people in the early Navajo culture organized?
   - Ⓐ in groups of neighbors
   - Ⓑ in a large tribal council
   - ● in groups of relatives
   - Ⓓ in a council with many members

Use with Pupil Edition, p. 356

Assessment Book, p. 62

Lesson Objective (11–1:2)

8. What was "The Long Walk"?
   - Ⓐ the effort of Colonel Kit Carson to stop settlers' raids on the Navajo
   - ● the trip made by the Navajo from Fort Defiance to Bosque Redondo
   - Ⓒ the destruction of the Navajo crops and livestock by the government
   - Ⓒ the reservation the government created for the Navajo people

Lesson Objective (11–1:3)

9. Why was the Navajo Tribal Council formed?
   - Ⓐ establish the Navajo capital in Arizona
   - ● make agreements over oil drilling on Navajo land
   - Ⓒ collect food and clothing from the government
   - Ⓓ build schools for the Navajo

Lesson Objective (11–2:1, 2)

10. Who built the Spanish-style churches that can still be seen in the Southwest?
    - ● Spanish missionaries
    - Ⓑ Francisco Vásquez de Coronado
    - Ⓒ Pattillo Higgins
    - Ⓓ Navajo Council members

Lesson Objective (11–3:3)

11. Why did the Chisholm Trail lead to Kansas?
    - ● Kansas had railroad towns from which cattle could be sent to meat-packing plants.
    - Ⓑ Kansas had many ranches where cowboys could rest on their way to the meat-packing plants.
    - Ⓒ Cattle could drink water and wallow in the mud of Kansas's seven rivers.
    - Ⓓ There was no charge for cattle driven into Kansas nor for the grass the cattle ate there.

Lesson Objective (11–3:1)

12. How did the Native Americans and Mexicans in Texas help the cattle industry grow?
    - Ⓐ They enjoyed eating beef more than anyone else.
    - ● They showed newer settlers how to be cowboys.
    - Ⓒ They invested heavily in raising beef.
    - Ⓓ They brought their music, food, and language to the region.

Lesson Objective (11–3:2)

13. Which of these was NOT a famous cowgirl who performed in wild-west shows?
    - Ⓐ Calamity Jane
    - Ⓑ Martha Canary
    - ● Jesse Chisholm
    - Ⓓ Annie Oakley

Lesson Objective (11–4:1)

14. What practice has made the desert of Arizona a more inviting place to live?
    - Ⓐ erosion
    - ● irrigation
    - Ⓒ meat packing
    - Ⓓ landscaping

Lesson Objective (11–4:2)

15. What is important about the Milam Building in San Antonio, Texas?
    - Ⓐ It was once the tallest building in San Antonio.
    - Ⓑ It was where Carrier invented air conditioning.
    - Ⓒ It was the first office building in the Southwest.
    - ● It was the first high-rise air-conditioned office building.

Use with Pupil Edition, p. 356

Assessment Book, p. 63

Part 2: Skills Test

Directions: Use complete sentences to answer questions 1–5. Use a separate sheet of paper if you need more space.

1. Why do you think the Grand Canyon is considered one of the seven natural wonders of the world? **Draw Conclusions**

   Possible answer: The canyon is a huge landform, about 277 miles long and 6,000 feet deep. There is not another like it in the world. It also is very beautiful. Because it was formed by erosion, it is very interesting to study.

2. Describe the climate of the Southwest? **Main Idea and Details**

   The Southwest has a variety of climates. Some parts have an arid climate, and others are deserts. Texas has several climates. The eastern part is hot and humid, and the western part is hot and dry. Oklahoma sometimes has humid and windy weather and can experience thunderstorms, blizzards, or tornadoes.

3. Suppose you were lost in the Sonoran Desert. What problems might you face? How might you solve those problems? **Solve Problems**

   Accept all reasonable answers. Possible answer: I would get very hot, thirsty, and hungry. Because water is scarce in a desert, I would have to find water in the cacti, and I could eat the cacti for food. To keep cool, I could sit beneath the huge saguaro or look for another shelter. Because the Sonoran Desert is in a national park, I could look for an official building and a park ranger for help.

Assessment Book — Unit 5 Test 63

Use with Pupil Edition, p. 356

Assessment Book, p. 64

4. Which state in the Southwest region do you think has the best chance for a strong economic future? Why? **Apply Information**

   Accept all reasonable answers. Some students may select Texas because of its technology industry.

5. What are two ways the Southwest region might be different if the Spanish had never settled there? **Hypothesize**

   Answers may include: Places might not have Spanish names, such as Santa Fe and San Antonio. The region might not have cattle, Spanish-style churches, or other buildings. People might have found other ways to make money and other foods to eat. Cowboys and cowgirls might not be a part of the Southwest.

Use with Pupil Edition, p. 356

CHAPTER 11

The People of the Southwest

Chapter 11 Outline

- **Lesson 1, *The Navajo,*** pp. 324–328
- **Biography: *Henry Chee Dodge,*** p. 329
- **Research and Writing Skills: *Identify Primary and Secondary Sources,*** pp. 330–331
- **Lesson 2, *Spanish Influence,*** pp. 332–337
- **Lesson 3, *Ranches and Drivers,*** pp. 338–343
- **Dorling Kindersley: *Cowboys and Cowgirls,*** pp. 344–345
- **Lesson 4, *Living in the Desert,*** pp. 346–348
- **Biography: *Willis Haviland Carrier,*** p. 349
- **Issues and Viewpoints: *Save "America's Main Street"?*** pp. 350–351

Resources

- Workbook, p. 75: Vocabulary Preview
- Vocabulary Cards
- Social Studies Plus!

Window Rock, Arizona: Lesson 1

Ask students what they think might have created this unusual rock formation. (Possible answers: Weathering; erosion)

Santa Fe, New Mexico: Lesson 2

Ask students how they think early Spanish settlements in New Mexico might have differed from the city shown in the picture. (Early Spanish settlements in New Mexico were smaller and based around missions.)

King Ranch, Texas: Lesson 3

Ask students why a ranch might include buildings like the one shown. (Possible answer: To house workers)

Tucson, Arizona: Lesson 4

Ask students what they think the weather might be like in a desert city like Tucson. (Possible answer: Warm and sunny)

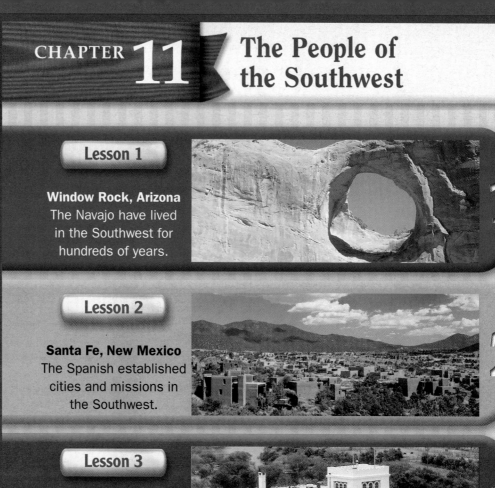

CHAPTER 11

The People of the Southwest

Lesson 1

Window Rock, Arizona
The Navajo have lived in the Southwest for hundreds of years.

1

Lesson 2

Santa Fe, New Mexico
The Spanish established cities and missions in the Southwest.

2

Lesson 3

King Ranch, Texas
Cattle ranches became legendary in the Southwest.

3

Lesson 4

Tucson, Arizona
Cities in the desert are growing quickly.

4

Practice and Extend

Vocabulary Preview

- Use Workbook p. 75 to help students preview the vocabulary words in this chapter.
- Use Vocabulary Cards to preview key concept words in this chapter.

Also on Teacher Resources CD-ROM.

Workbook, p. 75

Vocabulary Preview

Directions: These are the vocabulary words from Chapter 11. How much do you know about these words? Write each word in the space beside its meaning. You may use your glossary.

hogan	missionary	tallow	aqueduct
viceroy	vaquero	homestead	

1. ________ governor
2. ________ Spanish cowboy
3. ________ one-room home of the Navajo
4. ________ trench or pipe used to bring water from a distance
5. ________ fat of cattle used for candles and soap
6. ________ person who is sent by a religious organization into other parts of the world to spread its beliefs
7. ________ land given to a settler

Directions: Use the following vocabulary words in an original sentence. Write your sentences on the lines provided.

8. hogan ________
9. tallow ________

Notes for Home: Your child learned the vocabulary terms for Chapter 11.
Home Activity: Even today, aqueducts carry water to some communities. From where does your community receive its water supply? Discuss this with your child.

Locating Places

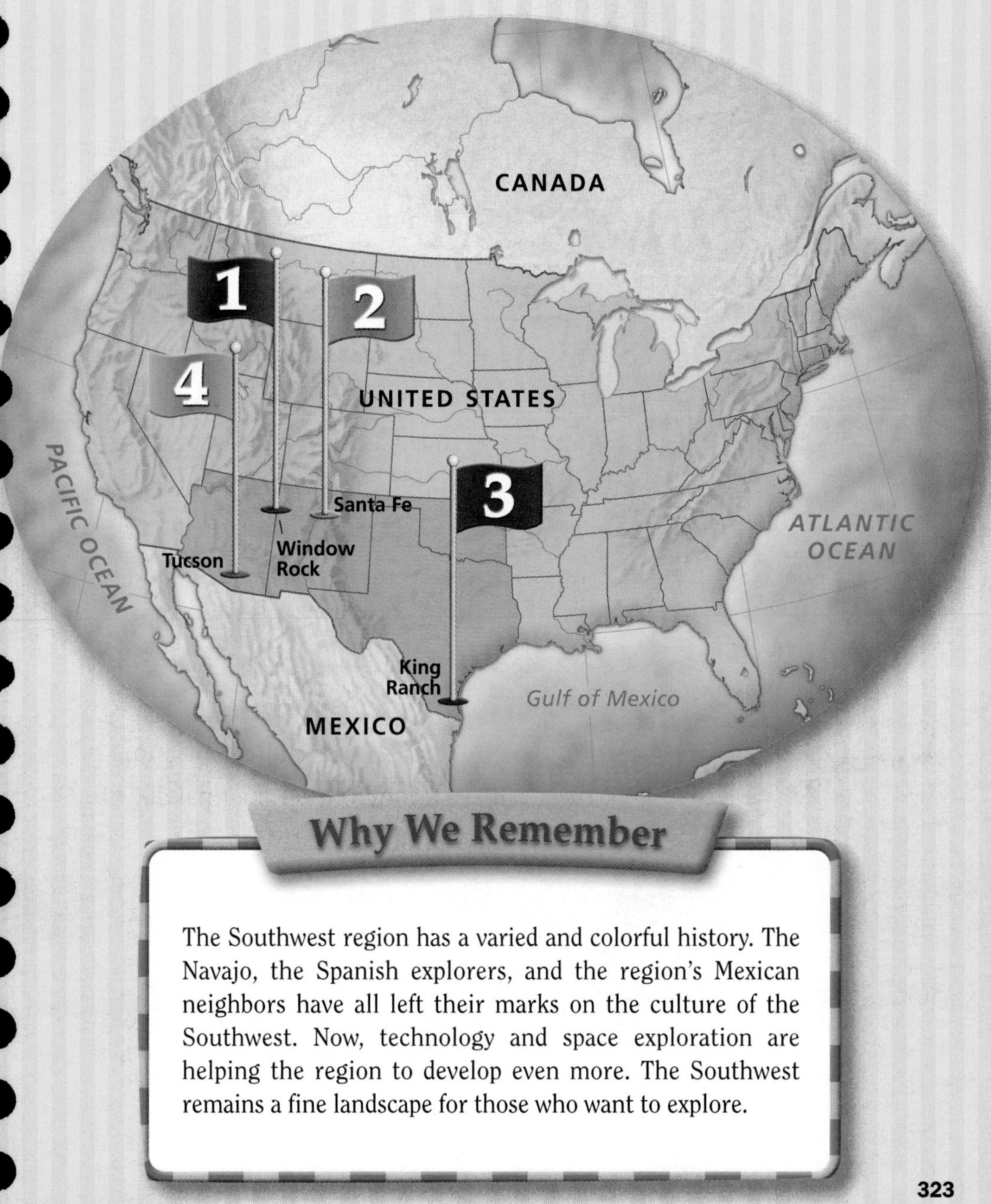

Why We Remember

The Southwest region has a varied and colorful history. The Navajo, the Spanish explorers, and the region's Mexican neighbors have all left their marks on the culture of the Southwest. Now, technology and space exploration are helping the region to develop even more. The Southwest remains a fine landscape for those who want to explore.

323

WEB SITE

Technology

You can learn more about Window Rock, Arizona; Santa Fe, New Mexico; King Ranch, Texas; and Tucson, Arizona, by clicking on *Atlas* at **www.sfsocialstudies.com.**

SOCIAL STUDIES STRAND

Geography

Mental Mapping Have students picture in their minds where the country of Mexico is in relation to the states of the Southwest Region. Discuss with students how this relationship has affected the culture of the Southwest.

Locating Places

- Have students examine the pictures on p. 322 for Lessons 1, 2, 3, and 4.
- Remind students that each picture is coded with both a number and a color to link it to a place on the map on p. 323.

Why We Remember

Have students read the "Why We Remember" paragraph on p. 323 and ask whether they identify the Southwest more by its cultural heritage or by its recent technological history. As a class, discuss why one time period might be more memorable than another when it comes to the history of a region.

The Navajo

Objectives

- Describe the early culture of the Navajo people.
- Describe "The Long Walk."
- Explain how the Navajo Council governs the Navajo Nation.

Vocabulary

hogan, p. 325

Resources

- Workbook, p. 76
- Transparency 18
- Every Student Learns Guide, pp. 134–137
- Quick Study, pp. 68–69

Quick Teaching Plan

If time is short, have students create a chart showing key information in this lesson.

- Have students divide the chart into three sections: *Early Days, 1800s,* and *Today.* Then have students take notes about each of these time periods as they read the lesson independently.
- Have students create a journal entry describing an event or an experience from one time period on the chart.

1 Introduce and Motivate

Preview To activate prior knowledge, ask students what they know about the Navajo. Some students may be familiar with Navajo jewelry or blankets. Tell students they will learn more about the early days of the Navajo and Navajo life today as they read Lesson 1.

You Are There Ask students how the Navajo Nation Fair is similar to or different from other fairs they have attended, read about, or seen on television.

LESSON 1

1850 1900 1950

1864 The Long Walk

1868 Navajo sign a treaty with the United States government.

1923 Navajo Tribal Council is formed.

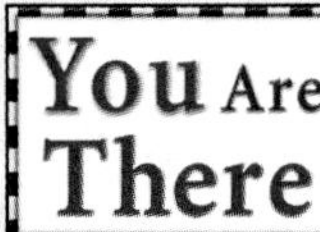

The Navajo

PREVIEW

Focus on the Main Idea
The Navajo have lived in the Southwest for centuries.

PLACES
Fort Canby, Arizona
Bosque Redondo, New Mexico
Window Rock, Arizona

PEOPLE
Kit Carson
Henry Chee Dodge

VOCABULARY
hogan

EVENTS
The Long Walk

You Are There You've spent the day wandering around the fairgrounds, sampling frybread and barbecue and watching artists make beautiful jewelry. Then you spent some time at the rodeo, cheering on the riders. Now it is evening, time for dancing. You watch the dancers make their way across the floor. Their movements are graceful and full of purpose. The Navajo dance, then the Apache. Now a Pueblo group appears. You want to know more about these dances. Perhaps you can learn about the meaning of these dances tomorrow, on the final day of the Navajo Nation Fair.

Cause and Effect As you read, think about the way the lives of the Navajo have changed over the years. Look for information about what caused these changes.

324

Practice and Extend

READING SKILL
Cause and Effect

In the Lesson Review, students complete a graphic organizer like the one below. You may want to provide students with a copy of Transparency 18 to complete as they read the lesson.

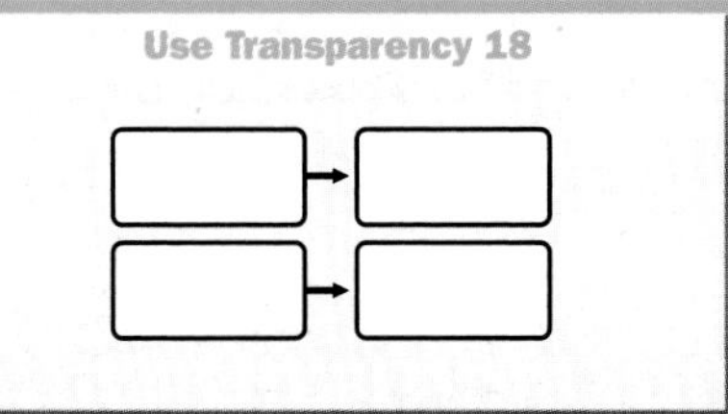

VOCABULARY
Related Word Study

Have students review the paragraph about hogans on p. 325. Then have them review the information about Anasazi dwellings on p. 302. Have them create a chart that compares and contrasts Navajo and Anasazi dwellings. (Answers could include that Anasazi dwellings are made of adobe, some are large and built on cliffs; some have many rooms. Navajo dwellings are called hogans, they are made of soil, bark, stone, adobe or wood; they have one room; the door faces east.)

Early Culture

When European explorers came to North America, the Navajo (NAH vah hoh) lived in the hot, dry land of the Southwest. They did not call themselves *Navajo*. They called themselves *Diné* (Din NAY), which means "the people."

The Navajo were mainly hunters and gatherers, but they learned farming, pottery making, and basket weaving from the Pueblo, who lived nearby.

The Navajo lived in homes called **hogans.** Usually, a hogan had only one room. The frame of the hogan was made of logs, which were covered with a thick layer of soil. Later, hogans were made of stone, adobe, or wood.
1 The door of a hogan would always face east, toward the rising sun.

The Navajo got sheep and horses from the Spanish colonists who settled in the area. Raising sheep became very important to the Navajo. The Navajo used the sheep for food and wool. 2

The Navajo were organized into clans, or family groups. Each clan had a leader, but there was no main Navajo leader. When white settlers came, the U.S. government made a treaty with the Navajo, but only a few clans knew about the treaty. This led to conflict. 3

▶ **Navajo blankets are skillfully woven and highly prized.**

▶ **A Navajo hogan in Arizona**

REVIEW What are some ways that the Navajo culture was influenced by the Pueblo? Main Idea and Details

2 Teach and Discuss

PAGE 325

Early Culture

Quick Summary Many Navajo live in the Southwest. Some of their ways of living changed after Spanish colonists arrived in the region.

1 **How did the early Navajo use natural resources in their everyday lives?** Possible answers: Hunted and gathered food resources; farmed the land; made pottery; wove baskets; built homes from wood, soil, bark, stone and adobe **Summarize**

2 **What role did sheep play in Navajo life after Spanish colonists arrived?** They used the sheep for food and wool. **Main Idea and Details**

3 **Why do you think there were conflicts after the U.S. government made a treaty with the Navajo?** Possible answers: Not all the clans knew about the treaty; not all the clans may have agreed with the treaty. **Draw Conclusions**

✓ **REVIEW ANSWER** The Navajo learned farming, pottery making, and basket weaving from the Pueblo. **Main Idea and Details**

MEETING INDIVIDUAL NEEDS
Leveled Practice

Explore a Ritual Help students go online to learn more about sand painting, a part of some Navajo ceremonies.

Easy Have students use encyclopedias or go online to find pictures of Navajo sand painting and display them in the classroom. **Reteach**

On-Level Have students use encyclopedias or go online to research how Navajo sand painting is done. Ask students to write several paragraphs giving a summary or a description of sand painting. **Extend**

Challenge Have students research and explain the purpose of sand painting and describe how it relates to Navajo ceremonies. **Enrich**

For a Lesson Summary, use Quick Study, p. 68.

PAGES 326–327

The Long Walk

Quick Summary In the 1860s the Navajo were driven from their homes and forced to walk to Bosque Redondo, a dry area with poor soil. Later in the decade, after signing a treaty with the U.S. government, the Navajo were allowed to return home.

4 Why did the Navajo go to Fort Canby in the 1860s? Their crops and homes had been destroyed and their animals had been taken away, so they needed food and shelter. Cause and Effect

MAP SKILL: The Long Walk

Have students use the map to answer the following questions.

What rivers did the Navajo cross during the Long Walk? (Rio Grande, Pecos River)

Through which present-day deserted town did the Navajo travel during the Long Walk? (Los Pinos)

MAP SKILL Answer About 150 miles

SOCIAL STUDIES STRAND History

Kit Carson was a highly regarded hunter, guide, and soldier, but he also was considered by many to be fair and sympathetic to Native Americans. He has been honored with place names such as Carson City, the capital of Nevada, and Fort Carson, in Colorado.

5 After the Long Walk, how do you think the Navajo remembered Kit Carson? Why? Possible answer: With sadness or bitterness; he destroyed their crops and homes, forcing them to leave their homeland Point of View

The Long Walk

In 1863, a soldier named **Kit Carson** was ordered by the U.S. government to stop the conflicts between the Navajo and the white settlers in New Mexico. First, Colonel Kit Carson and his men destroyed Navajo crops and hogans. Then, they took the Navajo's animals. The Navajo were left with little food and without a safe place to live. Carson ordered the Navajo to leave their land and move to the army post at **Fort Canby,** now known as Fort Defiance, in Arizona.

▶ Kit Carson

In 1864, many Navajo arrived at Fort Canby. The soldiers gave the Navajo food and blankets. However, in order to prevent further conflict with the Navajo, the army pushed them farther east.

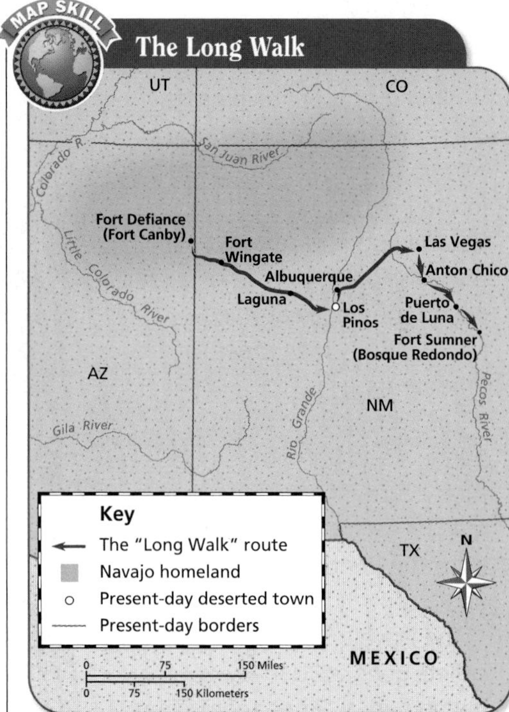

▶ The Long Walk covered almost 300 miles.

MAP SKILL Use Map Scale *About how far was Fort Canby from Los Pinos?*

The Navajo were forced to walk 300 miles to an area known as **Bosque Redondo** (BOHS kay ray DON doh).

Practice and Extend

ISSUES AND VIEWPOINTS Critical Thinking

Discuss the Long Walk

Navajo writer Johnny Rustywire tells the story of a ten-year-old orphan girl forced into The Long Walk. Read the quotation to students and have them discuss the following questions:

- How might people have felt before they learned they could go back to their homeland?
- How did the Navajo show feelings about their homeland?

"The next day they were told they could return home, and it was as if the whole of them were lifted by the wind and they walked every way they could . . . they began to sing old songs and walk with sore feet, and hunger . . . did not stop them."

From the story "Althabah, a Young Navajo Girl, and the Long Walk of 1868," by Johnny Rustywire

Bosque Redondo was near Fort Sumner, in eastern New Mexico. It was a very difficult journey. Many Navajo died along the way. Their journey
5 became known as **"The Long Walk."**

The soil at Bosque Redondo was poor for growing crops. The water was not safe to drink. Clothing and blankets were scarce. Many more
6 Navajo became sick and died.

Finally, in 1868, the U.S. government decided to allow the Navajo to return home. The Navajo signed a treaty with the government. They would live on a reservation of 3.5 million acres that included their old lands. In return, the Navajo promised to end their conflict with the white settlers. The government promised to build schools for the Navajo and to give them sheep to herd. The Navajo returned to rebuild their homes and their lives. 7

REVIEW Why was life at Bosque Redondo difficult for the Navajo? Main Idea and Details

The Navajo Tribal Council

In 1923 oil and minerals were discovered on the Navajo reservation. The Navajo Tribal Council was formed to make agreements over drilling for oil and digging for minerals on Navajo land. The council made the first written system of Navajo laws. **Henry Chee Dodge** was the first chairman of the Navajo Tribal Council. 8

The Navajo are now officially called the Navajo Nation. The Navajo capital is in **Window Rock, Arizona.** Today, the Navajo Tribal Council is the largest tribal government body in the United States. The council members and a chairperson are elected every four years. The Council meets often in Window Rock to make decisions for its people. 9

REVIEW How did the discovery of oil and minerals on their land affect the Navajo? Cause and Effect

▶ Navajo wait to receive coupons for food at Fort Sumner after the Long Walk.

327

ACCESS CONTENT

ESL Support

Use Context and Picture Clues Use aids to help students understand concrete concepts mentioned in this lesson.

Beginning Show students examples or draw pictures of items such as pottery, baskets, soil, bark, adobe, wool, sheep, or blankets. Ask questions like "Which item keeps you warm in bed?" and have students point to the correct item or picture. Repeat the word for that item aloud.

Intermediate Have pairs of students write simple sentences about these items, each with the word for the item omitted. Then have partners exchange papers and fill in the blanks.

Advanced Ask students to provide simple definitions or descriptions of each item or picture while their classmates listen.

For additional ESL support, use Every Student Learns Guide, pp. 134–137.

6 **How do you think the Navajo felt when they first arrived at Bosque Redondo?** Possible answers: Disappointed, angry, tired, hungry Express Ideas

7 **How do you think the Long Walk and the return walk were similar and different?** It was a difficult journey both ways, but whereas the journey to Bosque Redondo was marked by despair, the journey home probably was filled with joy and hope. Compare and Contrast

✓ **Ongoing Assessment**

If... students have difficulty comparing and contrasting the two journeys, **then...** ask them first to compare the physical journeys and then to contrast how people might have felt emotionally on each journey.

✓ **REVIEW ANSWER** The soil was poor for growing crops. The water was not safe to drink. Clothing and blankets were scarce. Main Idea and Details

PAGE 327

The Navajo Tribal Council

Quick Summary After oil and minerals were discovered on the Navajo reservation in 1923, the Navajo Tribal Council was formed to develop laws to govern the Navajo Nation.

8 **Do you think it was necessary for the Navajo to form the Tribal Council? Why or why not?** Possible answer: Yes; The Navajo needed leaders to defend their land and interests after oil and minerals were found on the Navajo reservation Draw Conclusions

9 **How is the Navajo Tribal Council similar to the U.S. government?** It has representatives who are elected by the people. Compare and Contrast

✓ **REVIEW ANSWER** It led them to form the Navajo Tribal Council. Cause and Effect

Navajo Life Today

Quick Summary Today, many members of Navajo Nation live on the Navajo reservation, where they work to preserve their way of life.

10 **Why do you think a member of the Navajo Nation might choose to live on the Navajo reservation?** Possible answer: Because he or she would be exposed to more of the Navajo culture and would have more opportunities to play a role in Navajo politics, business, and religion **Draw Conclusions**

✓ **REVIEW ANSWER** Possible answers: They continue to teach their language, some still live in hogans, and they still conduct Navajo ceremonies. **Main Idea and Details**

3 Close and Assess

Summarize the Lesson

Have students take turns reading the time line. As each point on the time line is read, have volunteers add one detail relating to that concept.

✓ **LESSON 1 REVIEW**

1. **Cause and Effect** For possible answers, see the reduced pupil page.
2. The people lived in hogans, hunted, farmed, and made pottery and baskets.
3. Many ceremonies are still performed. Hogans are still important. The Navajo language is taught.
4. They are elected every four years.
5. **Critical Thinking: *Evaluate*** Accept any reasonable answer. Possible answer: Yes; it is better for the Navajo Nation to be ruled by its own people because they understand the needs and ways of the Navajo.

Link to Art

Encourage students to base their artwork on research and facts.

Navajo Life Today

The Navajo Nation is the largest Native American group in the United States. Many Navajo live on the reservation, which covers parts of
10 Arizona, New Mexico, and Utah.

The Navajo continue to keep much of their traditional culture. Even though many young people speak only English, the Navajo language is taught in schools on the reservation. Many Navajo families still live in hogans and work together in agriculture. Both men and women play an important role in Navajo politics, business, and religion.

▶ Navajo shepherds

Navajo culture includes many ceremonies. Some of the ceremonies are for curing sickness. Others teach the history of the people and their responsibility to the Navajo Nation. The Navajo also respect nature and aim to "walk in beauty" always.

REVIEW What are some ways that the Navajo keep their traditional culture? **Main Idea and Details**

Summarize the Lesson

- **1864** The Navajo were forced to walk 300 miles to New Mexico.
- **1868** The Navajo were allowed to return to their land.
- **1923** The Navajo Tribal Council was formed.
- **Today** The Navajo Nation is the largest Native American group in the United States.

LESSON 1 REVIEW

Check Facts and Main Ideas

1. **Cause and Effect** On a separate sheet of paper, make a chart like the one shown. Fill in the missing causes of the events listed.

Cause	Effect
The government ordered Kit Carson to stop the conflicts between the Navajo and the settlers.	Soldiers destroyed Navajo crops and hogans and took Navajo animals.
The government wanted to prevent further conflicts between settlers and the Navajo.	The army forced the Navajo to go on The Long Walk.

2. What was the early Navajo culture like? Use the word **hogan** in your answer.
3. How is Navajo culture today similar to the early Navajo culture?
4. How are the members of the Navajo Tribal Council chosen?
5. **Critical Thinking: *Evaluate*** Do you think it is better for the Navajo people to be governed by the Navajo Tribal Council rather than by laws made by people outside the Navajo Nation? Why or why not?

Link to Art

Draw a Picture The Navajo people use materials from their land and their animals to create art. Research types of Navajo art. Tell about one type of Navajo art and draw pictures to show it.

328

Practice and Extend

SOCIAL STUDIES Background

About the Navajo Reservation

- For many years, most teaching at the Navajo Rough Rock Demonstration School was done in the Navajo language of Dine. English was the second language at the school.
- Window Rock, the Navajo capital, has many stores, a tribal museum, a research library, and a zoo.
- Since 1931, Canyon de Chelly has been a national monument. At the base of cliffs and in caves are dwellings built in ancient times, and in the bottomland are modern homes and farms built by the Navajo.

Workbook, p. 76

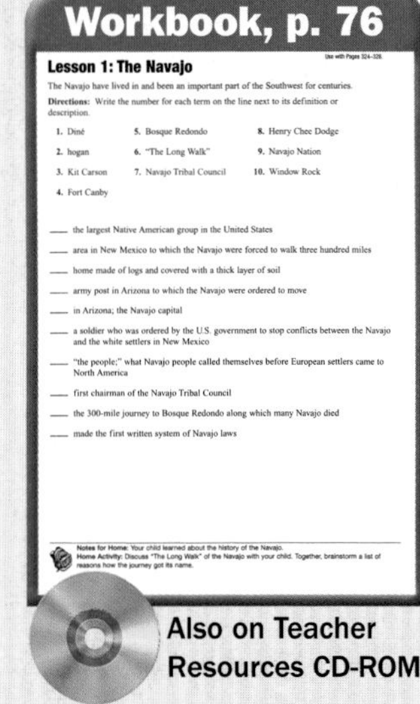

Lesson 1: The Navajo Use with Pages 324–328.

The Navajo have lived in and been an important part of the Southwest for centuries.

Directions: Write the number for each term on the line next to its definition or description.

1. Diné
2. hogan
3. Kit Carson
4. Fort Canby
5. Bosque Redondo
6. "The Long Walk"
7. Navajo Tribal Council
8. Henry Chee Dodge
9. Navajo Nation
10. Window Rock

____ the largest Native American group in the United States
____ area in New Mexico to which the Navajo were forced to walk three hundred miles
____ home made of logs and covered with a thick layer of soil
____ army post in Arizona to which the Navajo were ordered to move
____ in Arizona; the Navajo capital
____ a soldier who was ordered by the U.S. government to stop conflicts between the Navajo and the white settlers in New Mexico
____ "the people;" what Navajo people called themselves before European settlers came to North America
____ first chairman of the Navajo Tribal Council
____ the 300-mile journey to Bosque Redondo along which many Navajo died
____ made the first written system of Navajo laws

Notes for Home: Your child learned about the history of the Navajo.
Home Activity: Discuss "The Long Walk" of the Navajo with your child. Together, brainstorm a list of reasons how the journey got its name.

Also on Teacher Resources CD-ROM.

Henry Chee Dodge *1857–1947*

Henry Chee Dodge faced many hardships as a child. Both his Navajo mother and Mexican father died when Chee was very young. At age six he was forced to march with his people on The Long Walk. 1

After the U.S. government allowed the Navajo to return home in 1868, Chee Dodge learned to speak English. He soon began to interpret for the U.S. agents governing the Navajo. Later, he worked to keep peace between his people and the government agents. When the first Navajo Tribal Council was formed in 1923, Chee Dodge became chairman. He served until 1928. 2 In 1942, Chee Dodge was once again elected tribal chairman. In 1945, Henry Chee Dodge was awarded the Silver Achievement Medal from the Indian Council Fire. In his acceptance speech he said,

> ***"The greatest of all Indian needs is education."***

BIOFACT *Before the U.S. government reduced Navajo livestock herds in the 1930s, Chee Dodge owned a flock of sheep so large that it took two months to shear them all.*

Learn from Biographies

How do you think Henry Chee Dodge's experiences helped prepare him to be chairman of the Navajo Tribal Council?

For more information, go online to *Meet the People* at **www.sfsocialstudies.com.**

329

Henry Chee Dodge

Objective

- Identify the contributions of significant individuals such as Henry Chee Dodge.

1 Introduce and Motivate

Preview To activate prior knowledge, explore students' understanding of what it is to be an orphan. Tell students they will be reading about an orphan who grew up to be an honored leader.

2 Teach and Discuss

1 **What do you think the Long Walk might have been like for Henry Chee Dodge?** Because he was young and both his parents were dead, it might have been even more difficult and terrifying for him than for the adults. **Apply Information**

2 **What responsibilities do you think would be involved in being the first chairman of such an important organization?** Possible answer: The first chairman would have to provide leadership while rules and methods were being developed. **Make Inferences**

3 Close and Assess

Learn from Biographies Answer

Possible answer: His years as an interpreter may have helped him learn to deal effectively with others and to be a good listener.

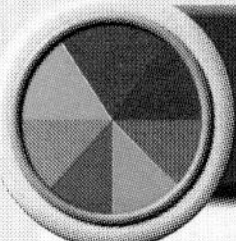

CURRICULUM CONNECTION
Drama

Write and Perform a Play

- Divide the class into three groups to write and perform a three-act play about the life of Henry Chee Dodge.
- Assign each group a different part of Chee's life to portray in a two- to three-minute script.
- When the scripts are complete, have all three groups perform their acts in sequence.

WEB SITE
Technology

Students can find out more about Henry Chee Dodge by going online and clicking on *Meet the People* at **www.sfsocialstudies.com.**

Research and Writing Skills

Identify Primary and Secondary Sources

Objective

- Use primary and secondary sources to acquire information.

Vocabulary

primary source, p. 330;
secondary source, p. 330

Resource

- Workbook, p. 77

1 Introduce and Motivate

What are primary and secondary sources? Ask students why historians would be interested in people's accounts of an event. Also ask why a reader might appreciate a summary of that event. Then have students read the **What?** section of text on p. 330 to help set the purpose of the lesson.

Why use primary and secondary sources? Have students read the **Why?** section of text on p. 331. Ask whether this textbook is a primary or a secondary source. (secondary source) Point out that textbooks often include examples of primary sources.

Research and Writing Skills

Identify Primary and Secondary Sources

What? A **primary source** is an eyewitness account or observation. Primary sources can be letters, diaries, documents, speeches, interviews, quotations, and even photographs and newspaper interviews.

A **secondary source** is a secondhand account of history. Writers of secondary sources collect information about a person, place, or event from different sources. Then they organize that information and present it in their own way. History textbooks and articles in encyclopedias and newspapers are examples of secondary sources.

In this primary source quotation, a Navajo Code Talker describes an experience during World War II. Navajo Code Talkers worked with the U.S. Marines from 1942 to 1945. They sent secret radio messages in
1 Navajo. The enemy was never able to decode these messages.

> **"One experience that stands out in my memory is being on combat patrol in Okinawa in Japan. Our patrol was pinned down for two days—the antenna of my radio was shot off, but I was able to get a message through [in code] for**
> 2 **reinforcements."**
>
> **Roy O. Hawthorne, Kin lichii'nii Clan**

The description below tells about the same event as a reporter might write in a newspaper article. The article would be a secondary source.

> Those Marines were able to get themselves out of many difficult situations using their Navajo words as a code language in voice (radio and wire) transmission. For instance, a combat patrol in Okinawa got a message asking for reinforcements through in code
> 3 in the middle of fighting.

330

Practice and Extend

SOCIAL STUDIES
Background

About the Navajo Code Talkers

- The idea of using Navajo as a code came from Philip Johnston. He grew up on a Navajo reservation and learned to speak the Navajo language fluently. Also, as a veteran of World War I, he knew the value of codes.
- For many years after the war, no one knew about the Navajo Code Talkers because the Navy wanted to keep the code secret. Today, however, an exhibit at the Pentagon honors their contribution, and their story has been told in the motion picture *Windtalkers*.
- The 29 original Code Talkers of World War II, along with their families, were honored with a ceremony at the White House on July 26, 2001. Each Code Talker or his family was presented with the Congressional Gold Medal.

WEB SITE
Technology

Students can learn more about Navajo Code Talkers by going online and selecting the encyclopedia from *Social Studies Library* at **www.sfsocialstudies.com.**

Why? As you study, you can use primary and secondary sources for different purposes.

Primary sources can give you information about how real people thought, felt, or acted at a particular time and place.

Secondary sources help show how people have come to understand an event that took place in the past.

How? To tell if something is a primary source or a secondary source, consider the following:

In a primary source, the writer is a part of the action described, or an eyewitness to it. The writer may say, "I saw this," or "we did that." In the example on page 330, Roy O. Hawthorne describes his own feelings and actions. It is clear from his words that he was present.

Secondary sources are written by someone who did not see the events firsthand. The writer is not part of the events described. Instead, he or she describes what took place.

Both primary and secondary sources are useful. They can provide a different point of view of the same information.

Think and Apply

1. Suppose you wanted to read the words of a soldier in a war. Would you look for a **primary source** or a **secondary source**? Explain.
2. If you need a single source to tell you about all of the events leading up to a certain battle, what kind of source might be most helpful? Explain.
3. In which type of source is the writer also a part of the scene?

▶ Navajo Code Talkers

331

2 Teach and Discuss

How is the skill used? Examine with students the examples and analysis on p. 330.

- Point out that words and terms such as *in my memory, our,* and *I* provide clues that the first example is a primary source.
- Tell students that a secondary source can provide background to help readers understand a historical event.
- Have students read the **How?** section of text on p. 331.

H SOCIAL STUDIES STRAND
History

Navajo was used as a code because it was not a written language, because it is an extremely difficult language to learn, and because so few people spoke it.

1 **Why do you think the Navajo code was effective?** Possible answer: The enemy did not speak Navajo, so it was never able to decode the messages. Make Inferences

2 **What can you assume about the skills of the person Mr. Hawthorne was trying to contact?** That person must have also been a speaker of Navajo. Make Inferences

3 **How do you think Mr. Hawthorne knew his message got through?** Possible answers: He got a response message; the reinforcements indeed arrived. Hypothesize

3 Close and Assess

Think and Apply

1. A primary source; I would want to find a description by a person who was actually present at that time
2. A secondary source; Because it can give a broader overview of an event and show how people have come to understand that event over time
3. A primary source

FAST FACTS

- Navajo Code Talkers used a true code, based on the first letter of the English translation of Navajo words.
- A few whole words were also used. *Besh-lo,* "iron fish," meant "submarine," for example, and *dah-he-tih-hi,* "hummingbird," meant "fighter plane."

Workbook, p. 77

Identify Primary and Secondary Sources

Use with Pages 330–331.

As you research a particular topic, you can use primary and secondary sources for different purposes.

Directions: Read the descriptions below. Write whether each source is *primary* or *secondary* on the lines provided.

1. You have found an article in a magazine about life at the Grand Canyon written by a Havasupai. Is the article a primary or secondary source? ____________
2. You are reading a biography of John Wesley Powell written by a historian. Is the book a primary or secondary source? ____________
3. You have discovered a newspaper article describing a tornado in Oklahoma. It was written by an eyewitness to the storm. Is the article a primary or secondary source? ____________
4. You have found a letter written by Pattillo Higgins about his search for oil. Is the letter a primary or secondary source? ____________
5. You are reading the section in your social studies textbook about Jerrie Cobb. Is the section a primary or secondary source? ____________
6. You read an editorial in your newspaper written by a Navajo Native American. Is the editorial a primary or secondary source? ____________
7. You found a biography about Henry Chee Dodge. Is it a primary or secondary source? ____________

Notes for Home: Your child learned how to distinguish between primary and secondary sources.
Home Activity: Find a newspaper or magazine article. Review it with your child. Is it a primary or secondary source? If it is a secondary source, are any eyewitnesses or participants quoted in it?

Also on Teacher Resources CD-ROM.

Spanish Influence

Objectives

- Describe Spanish influence in the Southwest.
- Describe the effects missionaries had on some Native Americans.

Vocabulary

viceroy, p. 333; **missionary,** p. 334; **vaquero,** p. 336

Resources

- Workbook, p. 78
- Transparency 23
- Every Student Learns Guide, pp. 138–141
- Quick Study, pp. 70–71

Quick Teaching Plan

If time is short, have students conduct a question-and-answer session with each other.

- Tell students to read the lesson independently and prepare one question for each section in the lesson.
- Have pairs of students ask and answer each other's questions.

1 Introduce and Motivate

Preview To activate prior knowledge, ask students if they have ever seen a glint of gold—fool's gold, perhaps—in an oddly shaped stone. Ask students the meaning of the saying "All that glitters is not gold." Tell students they will learn more about the lure of gold as they read Lesson 2.

You Are There Ask students who they think is speaking in the passage. (Someone participating in an early Spanish expedition to the Southwest) Have them explain their reasoning. (The picture shows a Spanish helmet.)

LESSON 2

1540 Coronado sets off to find the "Cities of Gold."

1610 City of Santa Fe is founded.

1687 Father Kino founds missions in Arizona.

1720 Mission San José is established in San Antonio, Texas.

Spanish Influence

PREVIEW

Focus on the Main Idea
Explorers and missionaries brought a Spanish presence to the Southwest.

PLACES
San Antonio, Texas
Santa Fe, New Mexico

PEOPLE
Father Eusebio Kino

VOCABULARY
viceroy
missionary
vaquero

You Are There It has been a long journey. It seems as if you've been walking for years, searching for gold. You haven't found any yet.

When you started this expedition, you were sure that you would find cities of gold. After all, eyewitnesses said they had seen them, glistening in the desert sun. But when you got there, every "golden city" you came upon was only a town of mud and brick. This time, though, you know there must be treasure ahead.

You're making your way toward the grand city of Quivira. Your guide has been there. He has seen its riches! You only hope it is but a few more days' walk.

▶ Spanish soldiers wore helmets similar to this one on their expeditions in North America.

Draw Conclusions As you read, think about the effects that the Spanish had on life in the Southwest.

332

Practice and Extend

READING SKILL
Draw Conclusions

In the Lesson Review, students complete a graphic organizer like the one below. You may want to provide students with a copy of Transparency 23 to complete as they read the lesson.

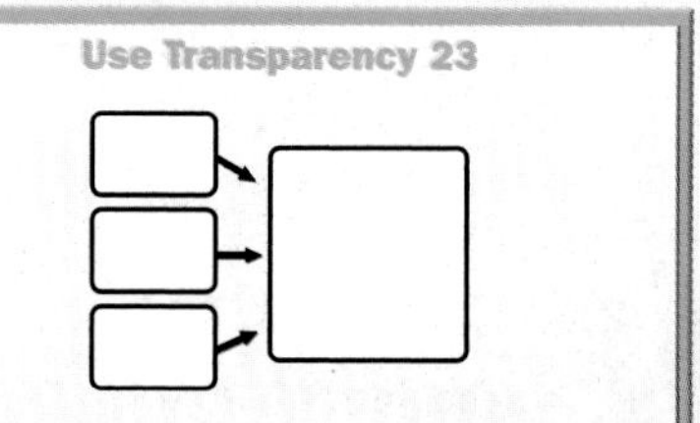

VOCABULARY
Individual Word Study

The word *viceroy* is made up of the Latin *vice*, which means "in the place of," and the French *roi*, "king". A viceroy is a leader who acts as a deputy of a king. Explain that this *vice* is related to the English prefix *vice-*, which means "substitute, deputy or next in rank." So the Vice-president is the leader who is next in rank to the President, and who can take over when the President is absent. Students may also see this prefix in such terms as *vice-principal* or *vice-admiral*.

Coronado and His Search

One of Spain's purposes for sending explorers to the Americas was to find gold. When the **viceroy**, or governor, of Mexico heard reports of "Cities of Gold" to the north, he wanted to claim them for Spain. The cities were said to have ". . . walls of gold blocks, gates studded with precious jewels, and streets paved with
1 silver. . . . "

In 1540, the viceroy sent Francisco Vásquez de Coronado to
2 search for Cíbola, the golden cities.

On his journey, Coronado saw a Zuñi pueblo near the present-day border of New Mexico and Arizona. The walls that were supposed to be gold were merely adobe shining in the desert sun. But Coronado did not give up.

Coronado sent search parties in different directions. You have read about the group that went west. They became the first Europeans to see the Grand Canyon. Another group came upon the Gulf of California. A group that went east explored Pueblo villages on the Rio
3 Grande in what is now New Mexico.

Meanwhile, Coronado's party had heard about a mythical city of riches called "Quivira." They traveled as far as present-day Kansas, but they found no gold. They found only herds of buffalo and Native American villages.

Coronado returned to Mexico and reported that there was no gold. His expedition was labeled a failure.

Coronado's Expedition

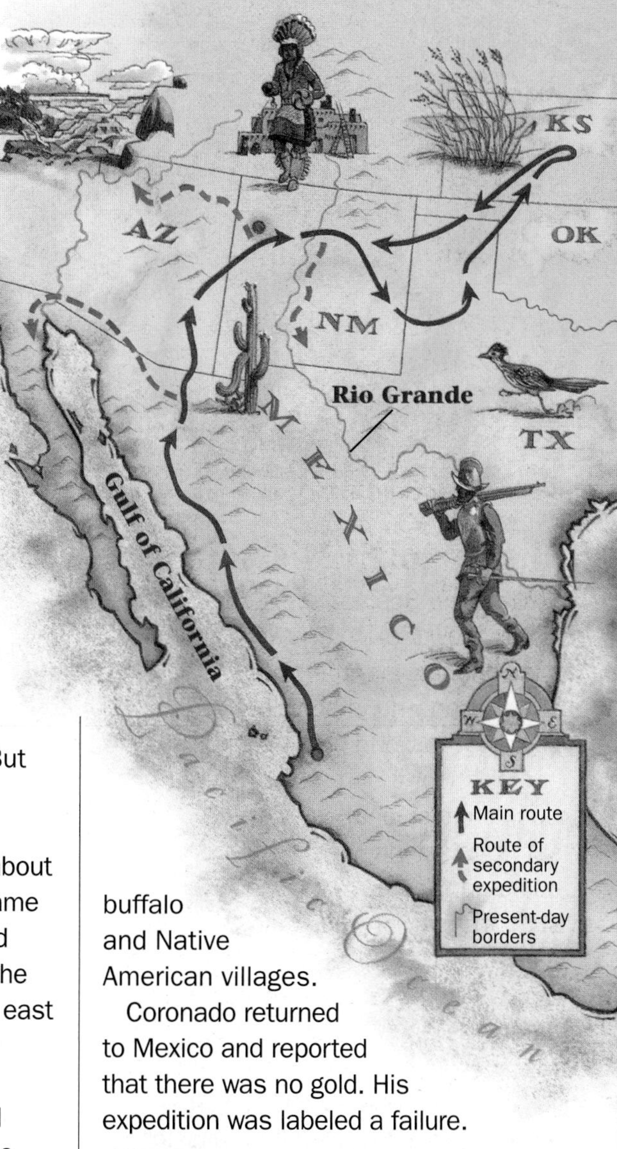

REVIEW What did Coronado and his explorers find on their journey instead of gold? **Main Idea and Details**

2 Teach and Discuss

PAGE 333

Coronado and His Search

Quick Summary Searching for "Cities of Gold," Spanish explorers under Coronado explored the Southwest.

1 **Why might the descriptions of "Cities of Gold" lure people to the Southwest?** Possible answers: Curiosity about such a place, a desire to get rich **Cause and Effect**

2 **What do you think might have happened if Coronado had found gold?** Possible answers: The gold would have been brought back to Mexico. Even more Spaniards would have come to the area. **Hypothesize**

3 **Do you agree that Coronado's expedition was a failure? Why or why not?** Possible answers: Yes, they did not find what they were looking for; No, the expedition led the first Europeans to see such wonders as the Grand Canyon, the Gulf of California, and the pueblo villages of the Southwest. **Evaluate**

✓ **REVIEW ANSWER** Possible answers: The Grand Canyon, the Gulf of California, buffalo, Native American villages **Main Idea and Details**

FYI SOCIAL STUDIES Background

About the Cities of Gold

- Reports of the Seven Golden Cities of Cíbola originated with a Spanish explorer who was shipwrecked off Florida and subsequently wandered through the Southwest.
- Great Bend, Kansas, grew up on the supposed site of Quivira. Omaha, Nebraska, crowns a king and queen of Quivira in an annual celebration.
- Another explorer who searched for Quivira was Juan de Oñate, who founded the colony of New Mexico for Spain in 1598. Oñate was cruel to both settlers and Native Americans and was later exiled from the colony for his crimes.

PAGES 334–335

Spanish Missions

Quick Summary Spanish missions were established in the Southwest to make Christians of Native Americans, teach them farming and crafts, and make them subjects of Spain.

4 **Were all parts of a Spanish mission enclosed by protective walls? Explain.** No; The crops, animals, and some of the work areas needed more room, so they remained outside the mission walls. Analyze Pictures

5 **What did the animals and the crops provide for the mission?** Possible answers: Food, leather, wool, transportation, and other materials that could be used in daily life Apply Information

6 **Why do you think it was important to enclose the missions with thick walls and locking gates?** Possible answer: To keep the people and the goods inside the mission safe Draw Conclusions

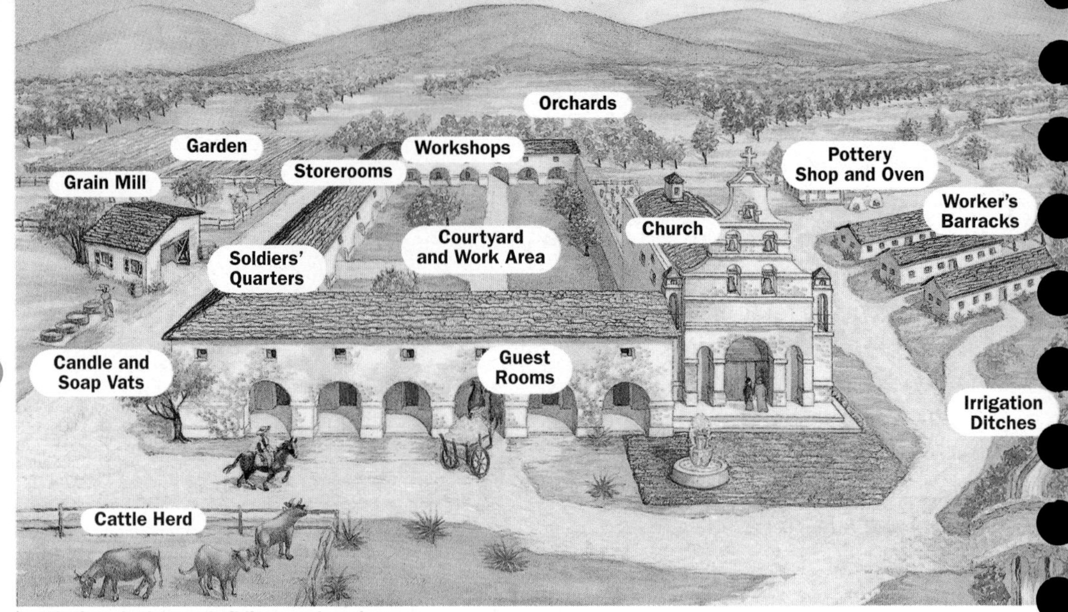

4

▶ Missions had many buildings and work areas.

Spanish Missions

When the Spanish moved into what is now New Mexico, they brought missionaries with them. A **missionary** is a person who is sent into other parts of the world by a religious organization to spread its beliefs. Spanish missionaries in the Southwest set up missions, which were their headquarters. Each mission tried to support itself by raising cows, pigs, and sheep. Mission farms also raised crops such as corn, beans, fruit, and
5 pumpkins.

Over time the missions spread into Texas and Arizona. In 1687, **Father Eusebio Kino** founded three missions in present-day Arizona, where he taught Native American Pima and Yuma people for 25 years. He was kind to the Native Americans and they were devoted to him. One of his missions, Mission Dolores, which was in Sonora, Mexico, had a ranch with cattle and sheep, wheat and corn fields, and orchards. It even had a water-powered mill so the people who lived there could grind their own grain.

Mission San José in **San Antonio, Texas,** was established in 1720. It was so beautiful that it was called "Queen of the Missions." Most missions were enclosed by stone and mud walls with wooden gates that could be locked. 6
They had buildings for the missionaries, offices, and a church. Missions also had rooms for Native Americans and others who lived there.

The purposes of missions were to claim land and to make Christians of the Native Americans.

Practice and Extend

MEETING INDIVIDUAL NEEDS
Leveled Practice

Visit a Mission Help students explore what mission life was like in the Southwest.

Easy Have students work together to draw and label a simple floor plan for an enclosed mission that includes a church, areas for people to gather and eat, sleeping quarters, work rooms, offices, and barns. Point out to students that buildings often were clustered near the walls of the mission, leaving the central area open. **Reteach**

On-Level Have students research a more complete description of an actual mission and its surrounding settlement and draw a detailed layout to reflect their findings. **Extend**

Challenge Have students research the layout of a Spanish mission and its surrounding settlement and build a model to reflect their findings. **Enrich**

For a Lesson Summary, use Quick Study, p. 70.

The Spanish government supported the missions because they wanted the Native Americans to become good citizens and loyal subjects of the king of Spain. The Spanish also saw the Native Americans as laborers. Most Native Americans who lived at the missions were put to work farming, making leather goods, spinning yarn, and weaving cloth.

Native Americans were persuaded to enter the mission in exchange for food and protection from enemies. Sometimes, however, they were forced to live and work at the missions. Some Spanish viceroys treated Native Americans cruelly. But some missionaries were kind to the Native Americans and protected them from people who mistreated them. 7

Some Native Americans who lived at the mission married and built homes near there. In time, pueblos grew up around missions. The mission priests allowed the pueblos to govern themselves with some supervision from the missionaries. 8

REVIEW Why were Spanish missions started in the Southwest? Draw Conclusions

"Remember the Alamo!"

Then and Now

The Alamo is one of five Spanish missions in San Antonio, Texas. Its real name is Mission San Antonio de Valero. It was built in 1718, when Texas was still part of Mexico. In 1836, a band of Texas settlers used the mission as a fort to fight for independence from Mexico. All the Texas solders were killed. Soon after, Texas won its independence with the rally cry "Remember the Alamo!" 9

Today, the Alamo is a historical site. Other missions are part of the San Antonio Mission National Historical Park. Some, such as Mission San José, are still active places of worship.

▶ **Only the chapel remains of the mission that the Texans used as a fort.**

335

7 Native Americans probably had a very mixed opinion of the Spaniards. Why? They might have appreciated kind treatment, new technologies, and learning new trades, but they might have resented any cruelty and injustice. Express Ideas

8 How are the Spanish missions similar to the French trading posts you read about in Chapter 9? Possible answers: Both offered Native Americans security and a settled way of life. Towns sometimes grew up around both types of settlements. Compare and Contrast

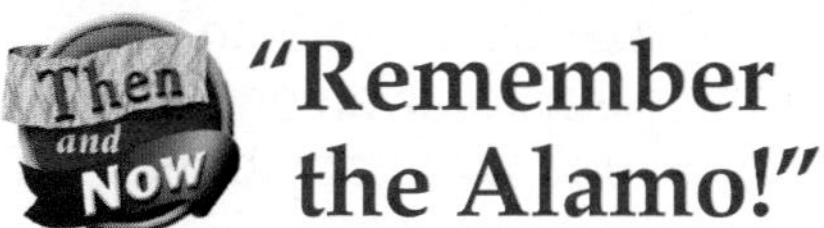

Ongoing Assessment

If... students have difficulty making this comparison, **then...** have them skim Lesson 2 of Chapter 9 to review information about French trading posts.

REVIEW ANSWER Possible answers: To claim land, to make Christians of the Native Americans, to teach them farming and other trades, and to make them subjects of Spain Draw Conclusions

Then and Now "Remember the Alamo!"

SOCIAL STUDIES STRAND
History

Alamo is a Spanish word that means "cottonwood." The mission was named this because it stood in a grove of cottonwood trees. In 1835 Texas volunteers took over the Alamo and used it as a fort.

9 In what way is it *not* surprising that a mission could become a fort? It was built partly for protection, with strong walls. Draw Conclusions

EXTEND LANGUAGE
ESL Support

Analyze Hyphenated Adjectives Help students analyze hyphenated terms used in descriptions.

Beginning Introduce the concept by showing students a *full-color* illustration and a *black-and-white* photo. Write *full-color* and *black-and-white* on the board and explain that they are examples of hyphenated describing words. Help them to find the words *present-day* and *water-powered* in the text on p. 334.

Intermediate Have students use the example words and the hyphenated words in the text to write sentences.

Advanced Have students find additional examples of hyphenated descriptive words in the chapter and explain them to their classmates, e.g., *Spanish-style* (p. 336).

For additional ESL support, use Every Student Learns Guide, pp. 138–141.

PAGES 336–337

Influence of Spanish and Mexican Culture

Quick Summary Spanish culture influenced the architecture, lifestyle, and language of the Southwest. Mexican culture also has influenced the Southwest.

SOCIAL STUDIES STRAND
Culture

Many of the dishes we think of as Spanish foods were influenced by Native Americans. Chili, for example, often uses Native American beans, and the word comes from an Indian word. When meat is added to the dish, we also add the Spanish phrase for "with meat." The result is a dish known as *chili con carne*.

10 **What are some Mexican and Spanish foods enjoyed in the Southwest and elsewhere?** Possible answers: Tortillas, tamales **Categorize**

11 **How are *Cinco de Mayo* and *Diez y Seis de Septiembre* alike? How are they different?** Alike: Both are Mexican festivals, both celebrate overcoming a European power, both are named after specific dates; Different: They are celebrated at different times of the year, *Cinco de Mayo* celebrates a military victory while *Diez y Seis* celebrates Mexico's independence from Spain. **Compare and Contrast**

12 **What is a *vaquero*?** A Spanish cowboy **Main Idea and Details**

Influence of Spanish and Mexican Culture

The influence of Spanish and Mexican culture can be seen throughout the Southwest. Some of the Spanish mission churches are still standing. By 1610, the Spanish had founded **Santa Fe,** the capital of present-day New Mexico. Santa Fe is the oldest center of government in the United States. Today many Spanish-style buildings can be seen in the Southwest.

The culture of Native Americans from the Southwest and Mexico influenced the culture of the region. Mexican and Spanish foods are popular in the
10 Southwest. Bright western clothing and lively music are a result of Mexican influence.

Many people in the Southwest celebrate two important festivals that have their roots in Mexico. The first, *Cinco de Mayo,* celebrates a Mexican victory against French forces at Puebla, Mexico, in 1862. The second, Mexican Independence Day, is also known as *Diez y Seis de Septiembre* (September 16). The festival celebrates Mexico's
independence from Spain. 11

Modern ranches also reflect the influence of Spanish culture. The Spanish were the first to bring cattle to the region. They started the cattle ranches of the Southwest. Spanish
cowboys, called **vaqueros,** handed 12
down the skills used by modern cowboys—herding cattle, roping, branding, rounding up herds, and riding on trail drives.

▶ A dancer twirls at a Cinco de Mayo celebration.

336

Practice and Extend

EXTEND LANGUAGE
ESL Support

Learn About Spanish Influences on English After they read p. 337, help students create a poster illustrating Spanish words that have become part of the English language.

Beginning Have students display a poster with pictures of a corral, a lasso, and a ranch. Have them label each picture.

Intermediate Have students add labeled pictures of other Spanish words that have become part of the English language, such as *pueblo, plaza, adobe, burro, fiesta,* and *canyon.*

Advanced Have students add Spanish place names such as *Los Angeles, San Antonio, Eldorado,* and *Rio Grande,* and provide literal translations of each.

For additional ESL support, use Every Student Learns Guide, pp. 138–141.

Even the language of the Southwest uses many Spanish words. The wooden pen for cattle and horses is called by the Spanish name *corral*. The ropes used to capture steers and horses are called *lassos. Ranch* comes from the Spanish word *rancho.* Many people in the Southwest speak both
13 English and Spanish.

REVIEW How did Spanish settlers affect cattle ranching in the Southwest? Cause and Effect

Summarize the Lesson

- **1540** Coronado set off in search of gold.
- **1610** City of Santa Fe was founded.
- **1687** Father Kino founded missions in Arizona.
- **1720** Mission San José was established in San Antonio.
- **Today** Spanish influences can be seen throughout the Southwest.

▶ Santa Fe, New Mexico

LESSON 2 REVIEW

Check Facts and Main Ideas

1. Draw Conclusions On a separate sheet of paper, fill in a conclusion about Coronado's exploration from the facts given.

Details

- Coronado came to find the "Cities of Gold."
- He did not find any gold.
- He did not find anything of value to the **viceroy.**

Conclusion

His mission was thought to be a failure.

2. What parts of the Southwest did Coronado's soldiers explore?
3. How did the Spanish missions affect the settlement of the Southwest?
4. How is Spanish influence still seen in the Southwest?
5. **Critical Thinking:** *Recognize Point of View* Why did some Native Americans resist living at missions? How did their point of view differ from those who lived at missions willingly?

Link to Writing

Write a Travel Brochure Do some research to learn about a Spanish mission in the Southwest that is still open to visitors. Write a travel brochure to tell tourists about interesting things to do and see at the mission. Be sure to draw some pictures for your brochure. Use the term **missionary** in your brochure.

337

13 **Why might knowing two or more languages be useful?** Possible answers: You could communicate with more people; knowing a language can help a person better understand a culture. Evaluate

✓ **REVIEW ANSWER** They started the cattle ranches of the Southwest and handed down skills such as roping, branding, herding cattle, and riding on trail drives. Cause and Effect

3 Close and Assess

Summarize the Lesson

Have students read the time line. Then have them take turns naming specific examples of Spanish and Mexican influence in the Southwest today.

✓ **LESSON 2 REVIEW**

1. Draw Conclusions For possible answers, see the reduced pupil page.
2. They explored the Grand Canyon, the Gulf of California, and pueblo villages in what is now New Mexico.
3. Possible answer: Native Americans and others living at the missions began building settlements around the missions.
4. Possible answers: In architecture, food, festivals, clothing, ranches, and so on
5. **Critical Thinking: *Recognize Point of View*** Possible answer: Some probably did not want the Spanish to invade their lands or influence their culture; others probably wanted to learn new skills and ideas from the Spanish and wanted the protection a mission could provide.

Link to Writing

Encourage students to research activities at Spanish missions in the Southwest and present the information in their brochures. Brochures should include the word *missionary,* used correctly.

CURRICULUM CONNECTION Art

Explore Spanish Architecture

- Have students create a two-part collage that illustrates historic Spanish architecture and contemporary Spanish-style architecture in the Southwest.
- Ask students to describe some of the features of this architecture, such as the thick walls, recessed windows, arched windows and doorways, and tile roofs.

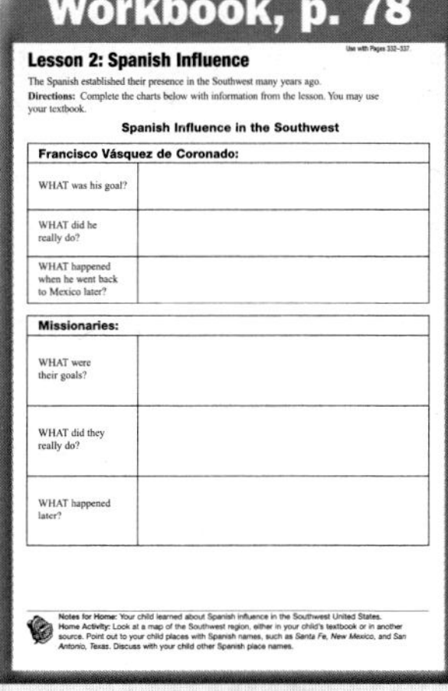

Workbook, p. 78

Use with Pages 332–337.

Lesson 2: Spanish Influence

The Spanish established their presence in the Southwest many years ago.

Directions: Complete the charts below with information from the lesson. You may use your textbook.

Spanish Influence in the Southwest

Francisco Vásquez de Coronado:	
WHAT was his goal?	
WHAT did he really do?	
WHAT happened when he went back to Mexico later?	

Missionaries:	
WHAT were their goals?	
WHAT did they really do?	
WHAT happened later?	

Notes for Home: Your child learned about Spanish influence in the Southwest United States.
Home Activity: Look at a map of the Southwest region, either in your child's textbook or in another source. Point out to your child places with Spanish names, such as *Santa Fe, New Mexico,* and *San Antonio, Texas.* Discuss with your child other Spanish place names.

Also on Teacher Resources CD-ROM.

LESSON 3 Pages 338–343

Ranches and Drivers

Objectives

- Explain how cattle raising helped the economy of the Southwest develop.
- Describe the roles of cowboys and cowgirls in the Southwest.
- Identify the route of the Chisholm Trail and explain the role it played in the cattle trade.
- Contrast ranching in the Southwest in the past with ranching in the present.

Vocabulary

tallow, p. 339; **homestead,** p. 342

Resources

- Workbook, p. 79
- Transparency 23
- Every Student Learns Guide, pp. 142–145
- Quick Study, pp. 72–73

Quick Teaching Plan

If time is short, have students create a "cattle drive" of facts.

- Have students work in small groups to draw and cut out four outlines of cattle. Tell the groups to record one key idea from each section of the lesson on a separate cutout.
- Post the groups' cattle in a horizontal line on the bulletin board.

1 Introduce and Motivate

Preview Ask students if they have ever ridden a horse or what they think it might be like. Tell students they will learn about cowhands who often spent more than twelve hours a day on horseback as they read Lesson 3.

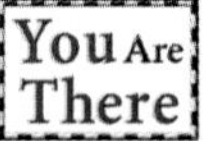

Ask students which season(s) might be best for driving cattle on the Chisholm Trail and why. (Possible answer: Summer and fall because the trail would be drier, weather would be more pleasant, and rivers might be lower and easier to cross)

LESSON 3

1850 1875 1900

- 1853 King Ranch is established.
- 1865 Jesse Chisholm blazes a cattle trail.
- 1870 Philip Armour starts a meat packing industry.
- 1890 The open range is closed.

San Antonio
King Ranch

PREVIEW

Focus on the Main Idea
The cattle industry boomed in the Southwest in the 1800s. The cowboys who herded cattle became part of our nation's lore.

PLACES
San Antonio, Texas
King Ranch

PEOPLE
Philip Armour
Annie Oakley
Calamity Jane (Martha Canary)
Jesse Chisholm

VOCABULARY
tallow
homestead

TERMS
Chisholm Trail

▶ A cowhand's spur

Ranches and Drivers

You Are There It is June of 1872. You and your team are driving a herd of about 3,000 cattle from Texas to Abilene, Kansas. You still have hundreds of miles to go on the dusty Chisholm Trail. You can't drive the cattle too fast or they will lose weight, so you cover only about 15 miles a day. It will take about six weeks to get to Abilene. The work is hard and the days are long. The sun beats down on your hat. The kerchief you wear over your face protects you from breathing in dust. At night you sleep on the ground in your bedroll. You can't wait to get to a hot bath and a soft bed!

Draw Conclusions As you read, draw your own conclusions about why ranching became such an important industry in the Southwest.

338

Practice and Extend

READING SKILL
Draw Conclusions

In the Lesson Review, students complete a graphic organizer like the one below. You may want to provide students with a copy of Transparency 23 to complete as they read the lesson.

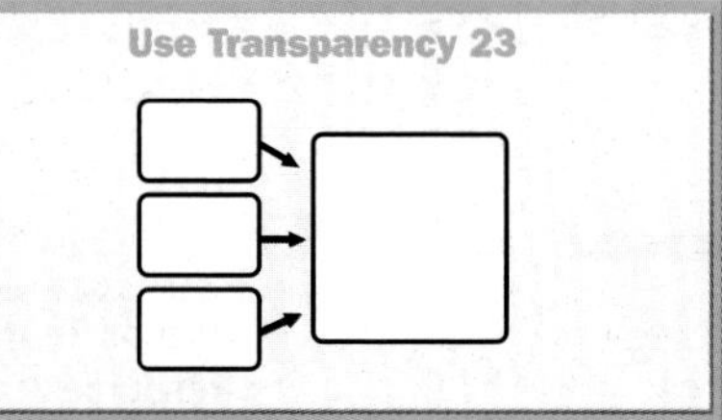

VOCABULARY
Context Clues

Have students review the information about homesteads on p. 342 and make a list of phrases that describe a homestead (fenced in, used to farm crops, bought from the government, etc.). Ask students to share their phrases and collect them on the board. Then tell students that you will name some things, and students should tell you whether or not they would expect to see these things on a homestead: horse (yes); post office (no); wheat fields (yes); train (no); house (yes), and so on.

Cattle Country

1 The Spanish missionaries and soldiers brought cattle to Texas. When the missionaries withdrew, they left the cattle behind. As a result, settlers moving to Texas found thousands of wild cattle roaming the grasslands.

The early settlers raised cattle to use as meat for their families. They used cattle for other purposes too. For example, cattle hides were used for leather, and horns and hooves were made into buckles and buttons. The **tallow,** or fat, of the cattle was used for candles and soap. Some settlers sold a few cattle to people in nearby towns.

During the Civil War, **Philip Armour** sold beef to the army. Then in 1870, Armour started a meat-packing industry in Chicago. Business people in Texas thought that the market for beef would grow. The possibility of large profits attracted people from the East and overseas to invest in raising beef. Suddenly raising cattle became a booming business. 2

Texas farmers and ranchers coming home from the Civil War began rounding up the wild cattle. They grazed them on grasslands until they were large enough to sell. Since there was no railroad connection in Texas yet, they took cattle to railroad towns in Kansas and Missouri. There the cattle were loaded onto freight cars headed for meat-packing plants in Kansas City or Chicago.

As the market for beef grew, cattle ranching spread northward out of Texas. Before long, not only the Southwest, but also the northern plains states as far north as Montana and the Dakotas were cattle country. The northern plains that once were grazing land for buffalo were filled with cattle. 3

REVIEW How was cattle raising introduced into Texas? Main Idea and Details

▶ A cattle drive in the Southwest

339

2 Teach and Discuss

PAGE 339

Cattle Country

Quick Summary Settlers in the Southwest raised cattle. Over time, the cattle industry expanded.

1 **In what way did the Spaniards affect the cattle business in the Southwest?** Spanish missionaries and soldiers brought cattle to the region. Cattle that they left behind formed the basis for the wild cattle that later settlers to Texas found. Main Idea and Details

2 **How were cattle in the Southwest similar to gold in California?** Both attracted settlers and businesspeople, and both created wealth. Compare and Contrast

Decision Making

Before the arrival of Europeans, somewhere between 30 and 60 million buffalo roamed the West. By 1900 there were fewer than 1,000 left. Today there are about 150,000 buffalo in the West and Midwest. However, some farmers fear that buffalo can spread disease to cattle. In an effort to protect their cattle and their livelihoods, some ranchers kill buffalo that wander off protected lands onto ranch lands.

3 **How do you think the interests of ranchers and those who are interested in preserving buffalo could best be served?** Accept any reasonable answer but encourage decisions based on compromise. Make Decisions

✓ **REVIEW ANSWER** Possible answer: Spanish missionaries and soldiers brought cattle to Texas and raised them. Main Idea and Details

CURRICULUM CONNECTION
Science

Investigate Tallow

- Have one group of students report to the class on how tallow is used to make soap. Students also should report on soaps not made from tallow.
- Have another group of students report on how tallow is used to make candles. Ask them to explain what materials other than tallow can be used to make candles.

CURRICULUM CONNECTION
Math

Multiply and Divide Have students perform these calculations:

- If a cattle drive covers about 15 miles a day and takes 8 weeks to complete, how long is the journey? (840 miles)
- If 12 people are driving 3,000 cattle, each person would be responsible for about how many animals? (250, but point out to students that each person watched over the whole herd, not just a specific portion)

Cowboys and Cowgirls

Quick Summary Many different types of people worked as cowhands. Cowhands worked hard training horses and herding cattle.

4 **In South Texas how did new settlers learn how to be cowboys?** The vaqueros of South Texas taught the newer settlers to be cowboys. Main Idea and Details

Test Talk

Use Information from the Text

5 **Why might books and movies present cowboy life as being more exciting than it really was?** Have students make notes about details from the text that answer the question and then use their own reasoning skills to fill in any missing details. Possible answer: To make it seem more interesting; presenting the routine life of a real cowhand might attract few readers or moviegoers. Hypothesize

6 **Do you think most cowgirls led lives as glamorous as Annie Oakley's or Calamity Jane's? Explain.** Possible answer: No; their lives were likely filled with hard work. Make Inferences

✓ **REVIEW ANSWER** Possible answers: Cowboys trained horses and herded cattle. Cowhands worked long hours, slept on the ground, and rarely carried guns. Main Idea and Details

Calamity Jane, 1901

Cowboys and Cowgirls

Many different types of people worked on ranches training horses and herding cattle. After the Civil War many freed slaves hired on as cowhands. Native Americans and European settlers also worked as cowhands.

In South Texas, where some ranches were owned by Mexican families, many cowboys were of Mexican descent. In fact, the Mexican vaqueros of South Texas taught the newer settlers how to be cowboys. 4

Native American cowboy, c. 1907

The life of the cowboy shown today in books, movies, songs, and on TV was far from real life. Cowhands rarely fought Native Americans. They worked long hours. They often spent more than twelve hours a day on horseback. On trail drives the cowhands took turns guarding the cattle throughout the night. Cowhands slept on the ground and rarely carried guns. 5

Cowgirls were also a part of the old West. Only a few women went on cattle drives. The most famous cowgirls took part in rodeos and wild-west shows. **Annie Oakley** was a sharpshooter who had her own show. **Calamity Jane,** whose real name was Martha Canary, was also a famous cowgirl. She performed shooting displays in wild-west shows. 6

REVIEW What was the life of a real cowhand like? Main Idea and Details

340

Practice and Extend

CURRICULUM CONNECTION Writing

"Ride 'em, Cowboy!"

- Have students find a description of a Wild West show such as the show staged by Buffalo Bill Cody.
- Next, have students prepare a radio script narrating each act as a play-by-play announcer describing a live performance.
- Have students produce their radio show, including sound effects to represent the performance and the audience.

CURRICULUM CONNECTION Music

"Git Along, Little Dogie"

- Tell students there is a rich tradition of songs associated with the cowboy. Have students research and perform one of these songs and then define some of the "cowboy" terms used in the song. For example, a *dogie* is a motherless calf.
- Alternatively, have students find and listen to the soundtrack of a western movie or TV program and comment on the mood it creates.

The Chisholm Trail

In 1865 **Jesse Chisholm,** (CHIZ uhm), a trader who was part Native American, blazed, or marked, a trail
7 from **San Antonio, Texas,** to Abilene, Kansas. As railroad lines were extended, the trail also went to Ellsworth, Kansas, and other cities.

The **Chisholm Trail** went through Indian Territory (now Oklahoma). Some Native American groups charged a toll of ten cents a head for cattle driven through their land. They also charged a grazing fee for the grass the cattle ate along the way. The toll on the Chisholm Trail could be paid with a head or two of cattle. Many ranchers began using this trail.

While the rivers along the trail provided water, they were also hazards. The cattle were afraid of water and had to be forced to cross rivers. After heavy rains some cattle were swept away by swiftly running rivers. At times the cattle got stuck in mud or quicksand along the rivers. Getting the cattle across the rivers was a difficult and dangerous job for the cowboys. 8

REVIEW Why did ranchers like the Chisholm Trail? *Main Idea and Details*

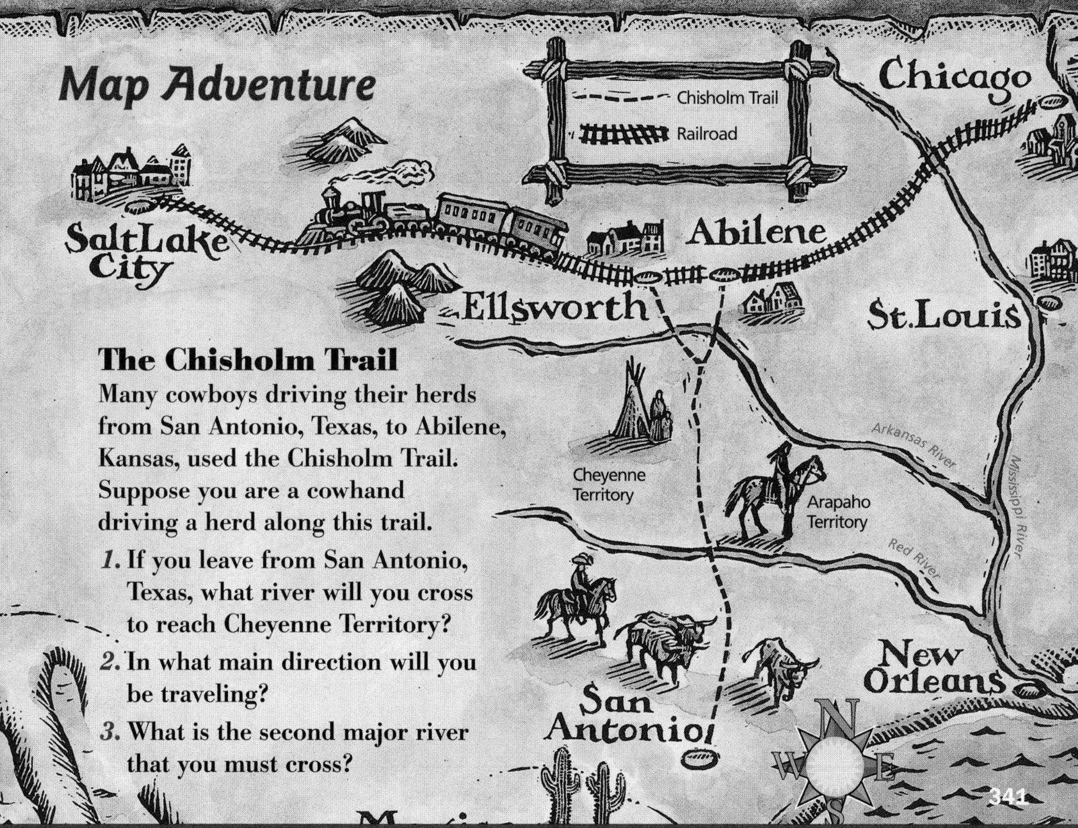

The Chisholm Trail
Many cowboys driving their herds from San Antonio, Texas, to Abilene, Kansas, used the Chisholm Trail. Suppose you are a cowhand driving a herd along this trail.

1. If you leave from San Antonio, Texas, what river will you cross to reach Cheyenne Territory?
2. In what main direction will you be traveling?
3. What is the second major river that you must cross?

ESL Support
ACTIVATE PRIOR KNOWLEDGE

Apply a Concept Help students understand the concept of a toll, such as the toll charged by Native American groups for cattle driven through their land.

Beginning Set up a "toll booth" at the door of the classroom. Provide students with counters or buttons with which to pay a toll when entering the classroom.

Intermediate Have students explain in simple terms what a *toll road*, a *toll bridge*, and a *toll booth* are.

Advanced Have students explain how the toll described in the text benefitted both Native American groups and ranchers.

For additional ESL support, use Every Student Learns Guide, pp. 142–145.

The Chisholm Trail

Quick Summary After Jesse Chisholm blazed the Chisholm Trail in 1865, ranchers used the trail to drive cattle from Texas to railroad lines in Kansas.

Decision Making

7 **What are some decisions that might need to be made when blazing a trail?** Possible answers: Where to find water, where to cross a river, how to get around obstacles, how to avoid unfriendly territories **Make Decisions**

Ongoing Assessment

If... students have difficulty visualizing the blazing of a trail, **then...** have students who have hiked in unfamiliar places describe their experiences.

8 **What advantages did a river crossing offer during a cattle drive? What disadvantages?** Possible answers: Advantages: Water for the cattle to drink; Disadvantages: The danger of drowning or getting stuck in mud and the difficulty of getting across **Main Idea and Details**

REVIEW ANSWER Possible answer: They could pay the toll with a head or two of cattle. **Main Idea and Details**

***Map Adventure* Answers**

1. Red River
2. North
3. Arkansas River

PAGES 342–343

How Ranching Influenced the Southwest

Quick Summary Open-range grazing ended as railroads expanded, homesteaders arrived, and cattle ranchers built fences.

9 **What brought an end to the cattle drives of the 1800s?** The spread of more railroads through the Southwest decreased the distance from the ranches to the railroads. Summarize

10 **What agreement did settlers make with the government when they bought a homestead?** They agreed to live on the land and raise crops. Analyze Information

SOCIAL STUDIES STRAND
Science • Technology

Barbed wire was invented in the 1860s, and a machine to make it was developed in the 1870s. By 1890 this technology had changed the open range into fenced pastures.

11 **Why might settlers and ranchers need a material like barbed wire to fence large sections of prairie land?** Possible answer: To keep cattle and other animals from wandering off Cause and Effect

Some settlers to the Southwest built houses of sod on their homesteads.

How Ranching Influenced the Southwest

As more railroads were built in the Southwest, the distance from the ranches to the railroads became shorter and shorter. The days of long
9 cattle drives were over. Cowhands now worked in different jobs on the ranches.

By 1890 ranchers could no longer graze their cattle on the open range. This was partly due to the increasing number of settlers who were moving to the Southwest. The U.S. government granted land to settlers for a few dollars if they would live on the land and raise
crops. The land given to a settler was 10
called a **homestead.** To keep animals out of their fields, homesteaders fenced their land. Cattle ranchers also began to fence their land to keep their animals from wandering off. As a result, the
grasslands were no longer available for 11
shared grazing.

Ranchers began to decrease the size of their herds to a number that could graze on their land. At the same time, they began to raise crops to feed their animals during the winter. The ranchers also began to drill water wells so their animals didn't have to travel a long way to drink.

Practice and Extend

SOCIAL STUDIES STRAND
Culture

Ranch Houses

- Have students note the shape and size of the sod house pictured on this page.
- Tell students that, as homesteaders abandoned their sod houses, they often built more permanent, small, wood-framed homes with one or two rooms. Rooms were added to these houses as families grew or settlers became more prosperous.
- This resulted in houses that were generally single-level, with rooms laid end to end.
- The design of these old ranch houses gave rise to the style of housing that became popular throughout the United States during the second half of the twentieth century.

Some large ranches still remain in the Southwest. Among them is the **King Ranch.** It was established in 1853 and it is still in business. This ranch spreads over 800,000 acres in South Texas. It is larger than the state of Rhode Island. The King Ranch is also used for scientific studies of cattle and cattle diseases. 12

▶ **King Ranch is about 250 square miles larger than Rhode Island.**

REVIEW How did fences affect cattle ranching in the Southwest?
Draw Conclusions

Summarize the Lesson

- **1853** King Ranch was founded.
- **1865** Jesse Chisholm blazed a cattle trail.
- **1870** Philip Armour started a meat-packing company.
- **1890** The open range was closed.

LESSON 3 REVIEW

Check Facts and Main Ideas

1. Draw Conclusions On a separate sheet of paper, fill in a conclusion that you can draw about ranching from the facts given.

Details
- Cattle provided food and other necessities for early settlers.
- Cowhands made their living working with cattle.
- Philip Armour sold beef and started a meat-packing industry.

Conclusion
Cattle provided food and jobs for many people.

2. How did cattle raising help develop the economy of the Southwest?
3. How did ranching change when the open range was closed?
4. How have cowhands become part of the lore of our nation?
5. **Critical Thinking:** ***Solve Problems*** How did the Chisholm Trail solve the problem of getting cattle to the railroad towns?

Link to Writing

Write a Story Write a story about a day in the life of a cowboy or cowgirl. Do some research to find out more about their lives. Tell about what they wore, what they ate, and what they did. Use the words **tallow** and **homestead** in your story.

MEETING INDIVIDUAL NEEDS
Leveled Practice

Surf for Ranches Help students use the Internet to learn more about modern ranching.

Easy Have students find the Web site of a Southwestern ranch and write a description of the kinds of information the site includes. **Reteach**

On-Level Have students find Web sites for two ranches and compare in writing the types of information the sites provide. **Extend**

Challenge Have students browse several Web sites and prepare a written report on a topic of their choice that relates to modern ranching. **Enrich**

For a Lesson Summary, use Quick Study, p. 72.

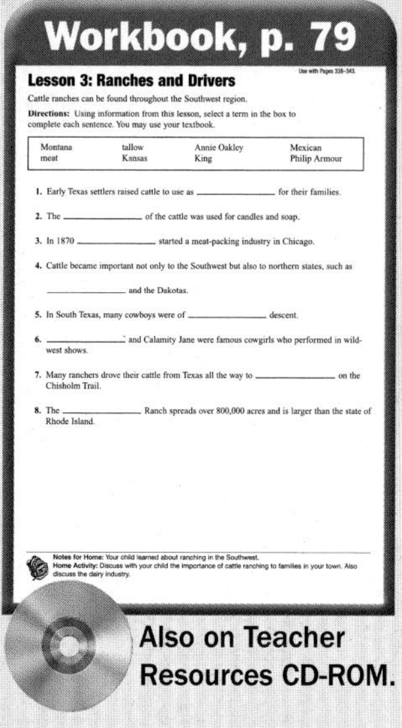

Workbook, p. 79

Use with Pages 338–343.

Lesson 3: Ranches and Drivers

Cattle ranches can be found throughout the Southwest region.

Directions: Using information from this lesson, select a term in the box to complete each sentence. You may use your textbook.

Montana	tallow	Annie Oakley	Mexican
meat	Kansas	King	Philip Armour

1. Early Texas settlers raised cattle to use as ____________ for their families.
2. The ____________ of the cattle was used for candles and soap.
3. In 1870 ____________ started a meat-packing industry in Chicago.
4. Cattle became important not only to the Southwest but also to northern states, such as ____________ and the Dakotas.
5. In South Texas, many cowboys were of ____________ descent.
6. ____________ and Calamity Jane were famous cowgirls who performed in wild-west shows.
7. Many ranchers drove their cattle from Texas all the way to ____________ on the Chisholm Trail.
8. The ____________ Ranch spreads over 800,000 acres and is larger than the state of Rhode Island.

Notes for Home: Your child learned about ranching in the Southwest.
Home Activity: Discuss with your child the importance of cattle ranching to families in your town. Also discuss the dairy industry.

Also on Teacher Resources CD-ROM.

12 **Besides the daily functions of a ranch, what other types of activities are conducted at King Ranch?** Scientific studies of cattle and cattle diseases
Main Idea and Details

✓ **REVIEW ANSWER** Grasslands were no longer available for shared grazing, so herds had to be smaller.
Draw Conclusions

3 Close and Assess

Summarize the Lesson

Have students take turns reading the time line. Then have them discuss how raising cattle has affected the Southwest region of the United States.

✓ **LESSON 3 REVIEW**

1. Draw Conclusions For possible answers, see the reduced pupil page.
2. The possibility of large profits attracted people from the East and overseas to invest in raising beef. Raising cattle became a booming business.
3. Herds became smaller and were kept in fenced pastures. Ranchers began to raise crops and drill wells to feed and water their cattle.
4. Songs, stories, movies, and television shows celebrate their work.
5. **Critical Thinking: *Solve Problems*** The Chisholm Trail provided a route north from Texas to Ellsworth and Abilene, Kansas. By paying a toll, ranchers were able to drive their cattle through Indian Territory.

Link to Writing

Ideas in students' stories should be supported with facts and should depict a realistic situation. Stories should include the words *tallow* and *homestead,* used correctly.

Cowboys and Cowgirls

Objectives

- Describe life on ranches and cattle trails.
- Explain how the work of cowboys and cowgirls has changed over time.

Resource

- Workbook, p. 80

1 Introduce and Motivate

- Tell students that the cattle industry represents a large part of the history, culture, and economy of the Southwest.
- Before students read these pages, have them list everything they think of when they hear the words *cowboy* and *cowgirl*. Tell students to classify the items into these categories: *clothing*, *duties*, *famous cowboys/cowgirls*, and *miscellaneous*.
- Students will refer to these lists as part of the assessment for these pages.

2 Teach and Discuss

① **How was Annie Oakley's job different from Margaret Borland's? Would you call both of them cowgirls?** Oakley performed with a gun; Borland raised, sold, and drove cattle. Possible answer: No, Oakley did not work on a ranch. Draw Conclusions

② **How has the role of the cowgirl changed since the 1800s?** Possible answer: It is more common to see women perform the duties of a cowhand than it was when people still rode the range. Compare and Contrast

DORLING KINDERSLEY EYEWITNESS BOOK

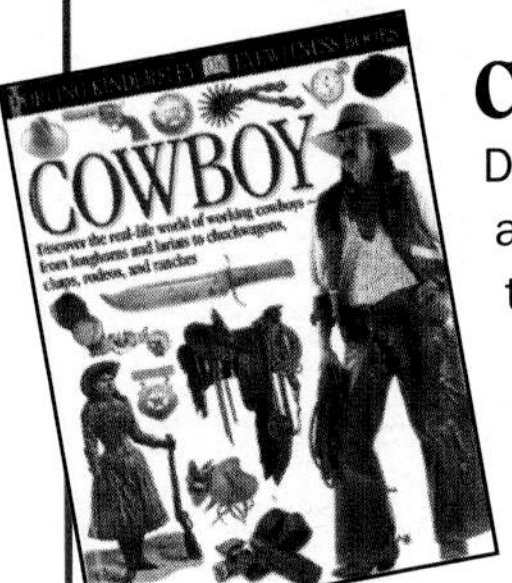

Cowboys and Cowgirls

Driving cattle to the railroads required courage and energy, and most cowboys took pride in their work. This work attracted people who were independent and who relied on themselves. During the days of the cattle trails, very few women could be called "cowgirls." Still, some women raised and sold cattle. One, Margaret Borland, even led a cattle drive. Today you can see cowgirls and cowboys as they compete in rodeos. They use roping and riding skills that were useful years ago on the cattle trails. ①

Flying the Texas Flag
The birthplace of American ranching, Texas was an important part of the "Wild West."

The powerful mustang—an ideal cow pony

Skillful Lady
Although very few women rode the range, in recent years women have proven that they can ride as skillfully as men. This rodeo cowgirl is competing in a demonstration of range skills. ②

A light touch of the rein to the horse's neck guides the horse around the barrel.

Silver concha

North American cowboy wearing batwing chaps

344

Practice and Extend

FYI SOCIAL STUDIES
Background

About Ranchers and Cowhands

- Most ranchers branded their cattle because unbranded longhorn cattle, or mavericks, were free for the taking. The name *maverick* comes from Texas politician and rancher Sam Maverick, who allowed his unbranded cattle to wander the plains freely.
- Driving an average herd of 3,000 cattle from the ranch to the railroads required a dozen cowhands, a herd of spare horses, a cook, and a chuck wagon stocked with about one month's worth of food.
- Ranchers paid little to have their cattle driven north from Texas. As a result, cowhands on the drive only earned about $15–$20 a month plus food.
- On the trail, cowhands typically ate simple meals of beans, cornbread, molasses, beef, coffee, and some wild game.

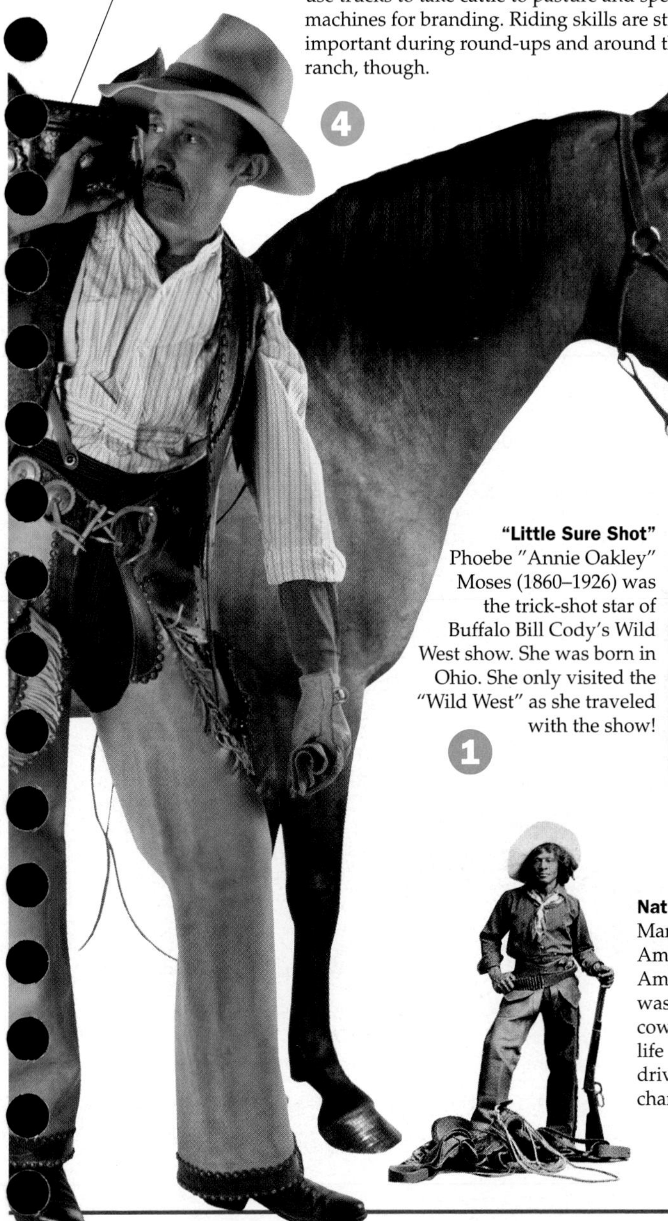

California A-fork style saddle, c. 1870

The Famous North American Cowboy
North American cowboys are world famous because of their role in the fabled "Wild West." The truth is that their work was hard. Cattle drives were long, and cowboys were not paid very much. The work could be boring, and it was sometimes dangerous. Modern cowboys use trucks to take cattle to pasture and special machines for branding. Riding skills are still important during round-ups and around the ranch, though.

Charros and Vaqueros
Cattle ranching in the Western Hemisphere began in Mexico. Landowners, called *charros,* and their working cowboys, the *vaqueros,* developed the skills later used by cowboys in the western United States.

Poster advertising the amazing feats of marksmanship exhibited by Annie Oakley in Buffalo Bill's Wild West show

"Little Sure Shot"
Phoebe "Annie Oakley" Moses (1860–1926) was the trick-shot star of Buffalo Bill Cody's Wild West show. She was born in Ohio. She only visited the "Wild West" as she traveled with the show!

Nat Love
Many cowboys were African Americans, Mexicans, or Native Americans. Nat Love (1854–1921) was a famous African American cowboy. He wrote a book about his life as a cowboy. In addition to driving cattle, he was a rodeo champion and a crack shot.

345

3 Has life for a cowhand become easier since the days of the old West? How can you tell? Possible answer: Yes, modern machines and transportation means less of the work is done by hand or on horseback. **Draw Conclusions**

4 How can you tell that the North American cowboy borrowed ideas for equipment from the vaquero? Possible answers: They both used saddles, large hats, chaps, and boots. **Analyze Pictures**

SOCIAL STUDIES STRAND
Culture

Point out that the original vaqueros were considered rough and rowdy and were sometimes tolerated only because of their skills as horseback riders.

5 Why would the work of a cowboy or vaquero appeal to someone considered to be rough and rowdy? Possible answers: Ranch work was rough and physical, and cowboys and vaqueros could ride freely over large areas without many rules or restriction. **Make Inferences**

3 Close and Assess

- Have students refer to the lists they created earlier. Ask: Were any of these ideas about cowboys and cowgirls discussed on pp. 344–345?
- Tell students to research more about cowboys and cowgirls in the Southwest. Then have them draw a line through every misconception on their list.
- Have students add information to their categories based on their research and what they read on these pages.

CURRICULUM CONNECTION
Literature

Read About Ranching in the Old Southwest
Use the following selections to extend the content.

Cowboys & the Trappings of the Old West, by William Manns, Elizabeth Clair Flood (Zon International Publishing Co., ISBN 0-939-54913-1, 1997) **Easy**

In the Days of the Vaqueros: America's First True Cowboys, by Russell Freedman (Clarion Books, ISBN 0-395-96788-0, 2001) **On-Level**

Richard King: Texas Cattle Rancher, by Carl R. Green, William R. Sanford (Enslow Publishers, ISBN 0-894-90673-9, 1997) **Challenge**

Workbook, p. 80

Also on Teacher Resources CD-ROM.

Test Talk

Write Your Answer to Score High

- Using their corrected lists as a guide, have students write a paragraph explaining whether or not they would have liked to have been a rancher or cowhand in the old Southwest and why.
- Tell students to use details from the text to support their written answer. Students should make sure that their answer is correct, complete, and detailed.

Living in the Desert

Objectives

- Explain how irrigation has affected the economy of the Southwest.
- Describe how air conditioning has impacted the economy of the Southwest.

Vocabulary

aqueduct, p. 347

Resources

- Workbook, p. 81
- Transparency 18
- Every Student Learns Guide, pp. 146–149
- Quick Study, pp. 74–75

Quick Teaching Plan

If time is short, have students create a two-column problem-solving chart and complete the chart as they independently read the lesson.

- In the first column, have students identify the key problem discussed in each section.
- In the second column, have students identify a solution to each problem.

1 Introduce and Motivate

Preview To activate prior knowledge, ask students to review what they learned about the Southwestern desert in Chapter 10. Tell students they will learn about life in the Southwestern desert as they read Lesson 4.

You Are There Ask students to compare and contrast the setting in the passage to their own communities. If your community is in a desert area, invite students to offer additional details to the description. If not, have students contrast their community to that of a desert.

LESSON 4

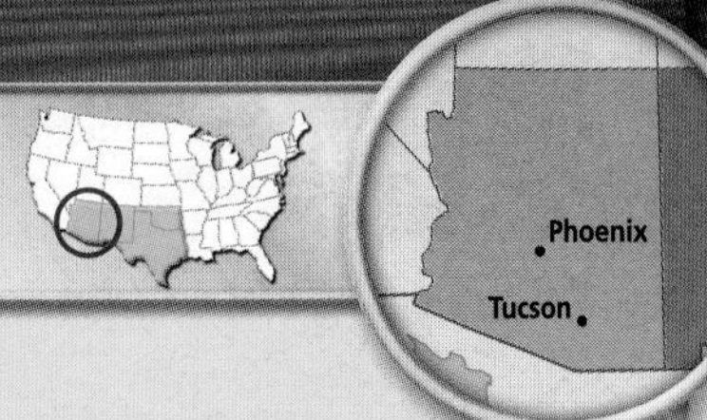

1900 | 1925 | 1950 | 1975

1911 Willis Carrier develops a useful air-conditioning system.

1928 Air-conditioned Milam Building is completed.

1960 California State Water Project begins.

PREVIEW

Focus on the Main Idea
High temperatures and a shortage of water can make living in the desert a challenge.

PLACES
Phoenix, Arizona
Tucson, Arizona

PEOPLE
Willis Haviland Carrier

VOCABULARY
aqueduct

Living in the Desert

You Are There You step outside your home near Tucson, Arizona, in the Sonoran Desert. It is a warm autumn day. A lizard scurries across the stones that cover the ground. A few prickly-pear and barrel cacti grow in the yard. So do a few small mesquite trees. It can get very hot during the summer, and it doesn't rain much. Still, everywhere you look you can see beautiful mountains. Sometimes there is snow on their peaks. The sky is almost always a clear blue, with not a cloud to be seen!

◄ Western Banded Gecko

Cause and Effect As you read, think about what effects a dry climate has on a region.

346

Practice and Extend

READING SKILL
Cause and Effect

In the Lesson Review, students complete a graphic organizer like the one below. You may want to provide students with a copy of Transparency 18 to complete as they read the lesson.

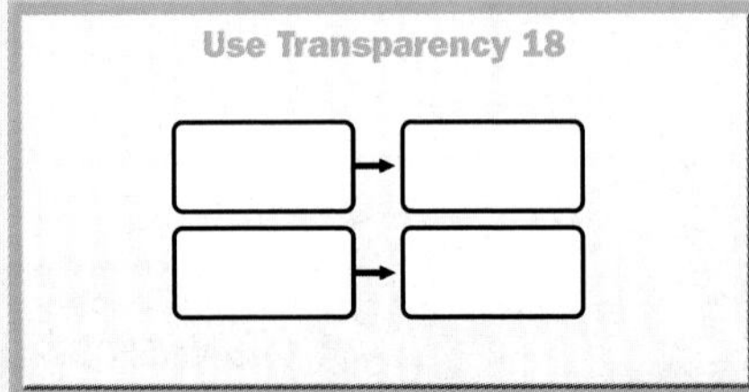

WEB SITE
Technology

- You can look up vocabulary words by clicking on *Social Studies Library* and selecting the dictionary at **www.sfsocialstudies.com.**
- Students can learn about current news by clicking on *Current Events* at **www.sfsocialstudies.com.**
- Explore other events that occurred on this day by clicking on *This Day in History* at **www.sfsocialstudies.com.**

Irrigation

The Sonoran Desert in Arizona gets only about 8 to 10 inches of rainfall a year. About half of that comes in the rainy months from July to September. In order to raise crops, people have to find other sources of water. Before Europeans came to Arizona, some Native Americans dug irrigation canals and built aqueducts to get water for their crops. An **aqueduct** is a trench or pipe
1 used to bring water from a distance.

Today, there are dams and reservoirs in Arizona, especially in the **Phoenix** area. These reservoirs store water for various valleys and regions. In 1960, the California State Water Project was designed to bring water to Southern California. It provided funds for an aqueduct on the Colorado River. This aqueduct also carries water to the regions around Phoenix and **Tucson.**

Because of irrigation, some of the dry land of the Southwest has become rich farmland. Farms in Arizona provide fresh vegetables, citrus fruit, apples, peaches, and pecans. Another important crop is cotton. The long growing season in Arizona makes the
2 farms very productive.

The use of irrigation has also made
3 the desert a more inviting place to live.

MAP SKILL

Dams in the Phoenix Area

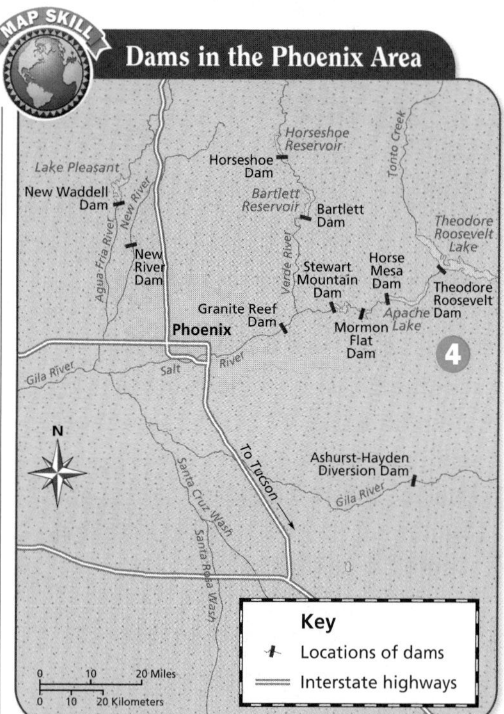

▶ Dams control the flow of water from reservoirs.

MAP SKILL **Human-Environment Interaction**
How have people controlled the movement of river water in the Southwest?

Phoenix, Tucson, and other desert cities are growing communities. In the last 40 years, Arizona's population has increased almost four times over.

REVIEW Would the population of Arizona be able to grow as quickly without a good irrigation system? Draw Conclusions

▶ Irrigation helps crops grow in New Mexico.

347

2 Teach and Discuss

PAGE 347

Irrigation

Quick Summary Irrigation helps crops grow in the desert.

1 **How are aqueducts used in irrigation?** They bring water to crops from a distance. **Main Idea and Details**

2 **What is one major advantage and one major disadvantage of farming in Arizona?** Possible answers: Advantage: long growing season; Disadvantage: need to bring water to the crops **Evaluate**

3 **How would Arizona be different today without irrigation?** Possible answers: Far less farming; fewer people living there; many farmlands would still look like desert **Draw Conclusions**

MAP SKILL

Dams in the Phoenix Area

4 **Which river in the Phoenix area has five dams?** The Salt River **Interpret Maps**

MAP SKILL Answer People have built dams to control the movement of river water in the Southwest.

✓ **REVIEW ANSWER** Possible answer: Probably not because irrigation allows agriculture, which creates jobs, which brings more people to the area **Draw Conclusions**

MEETING INDIVIDUAL NEEDS
Leveled Practice

Investigate Water Use Help students develop a mental picture of how the Southwest gets water.

Easy Have students use an encyclopedia or go online to find pictures of a dam, a reservoir, an aqueduct, and an irrigation canal. Discuss with students how each works. **Reteach**

On-Level Have students use an encyclopedia or go online to find pictures and descriptions of a dam, a reservoir, an aqueduct, and an irrigation canal and explain in writing how each works. **Extend**

Challenge Have students investigate and report on a specific dam, reservoir, aqueduct, or irrigation canal in the Southwest, explaining when it was built and why. **Enrich**

For a Lesson Summary, use Quick Study, p. 74.

PAGE 348

Air Conditioning

5 **San Antonio is located near the Gulf of Mexico in a very warm and humid part of Texas. Why might air conditioning be particularly important in San Antonio?** Air conditioning reduces humidity and cools air temperature, making living conditions much more comfortable. **Apply Information**

Ongoing Assessment

If... students cannot decide why people in San Antonio would need air conditioning,	**then...** have them review how air conditioning works.

✓ **REVIEW ANSWER** It has made living and doing business in the desert more comfortable, and therefore it has stimulated growth. **Cause and Effect**

3 Close and Assess

Summarize the Lesson

Have students read the time line. Then have them speculate about how people's lives would be different in the Southwest without irrigation and air conditioning.

✓ **LESSON 4 REVIEW**

1. **Cause and Effect** For possible answers, see the reduced pupil page.
2. Aqueducts and irrigation have turned parts of the desert into farmland.
3. Willis Haviland Carrier
4. By air conditioning their homes and businesses and by bringing in water through canals and aqueducts
5. **Critical Thinking: *Point of View*** Amusement park owners might expect business to be good. Farmers might fear for the survival of their crops.

Link to Science

Students' research should reveal that the energy in flowing water is harnessed as hydroelectric power.

▶ Carrier's air-cooling system, 1922

Air Conditioning

Although air conditioning was invented in New York, the growth of air conditioning made it possible for businesses and people to thrive in the Southwest. In 1911, **Willis Haviland Carrier** developed a useful air-conditioning system. This system cooled the air temperature and lowered humidity, or moisture in the air, at the same time.

Many factories and businesses depend on air conditioning to keep their machines and workers cool. The first high-rise air-conditioned office building, the Milam Building, was opened in San Antonio, Texas, in 1928.

Today air conditioning is common in homes and offices. It has made the heat of the Southwest easier to bear. 5

REVIEW What effect did the invention of air conditioning have on businesses in hot climates? **Cause and Effect**

Summarize the Lesson

- **1911** Willis H. Carrier developed a useful air-conditioning system.
- **1928** The air-conditioned Milam Building was competed in San Antonio, Texas.
- **1960** The California State Water Project began.

LESSON 4 REVIEW

Check Facts and Main Ideas

1. **Cause and Effect** On a separate sheet of paper, fill in the missing causes of the effects shown below.

Cause		Effect
Irrigation, dams, and reservoirs brought water to the desert.	→	Farms and cities in Arizona grew.
Air conditioning was invented.	→	People could live more comfortably in hot climates.

2. How has irrigation changed the desert in Arizona? Use the word **aqueduct** in your answer.
3. Who developed a useful air-conditioning system?
4. How have people in desert communities been able to overcome the heat and lack of plentiful water?
5. **Critical Thinking: *Point of View*** How might an amusement park owner and a farmer view a hot, sunny day differently?

Link to Science

Learn About Dams Find out how dams can be used to make electric power. Draw a diagram to show how this process works.

348

Practice and Extend

EXTEND LANGUAGE
ESL Support

Practice Pronunciations Help students correctly pronounce *humid* and other words beginning with *hu-*.

- Write *humid* and *humidity* on the board.
- Have student volunteers pronounce each word as you write the phonetic pronunciations beside each (HYOO mid, hyoo MID i tee).
- Ask student volunteers to brainstorm other *hu-* words with similar pronunciations (*humility, human, huge,* and so on).

For additional ESL support, use Every Student Learns Guide, pp. 146–149.

Workbook, p. 81

Lesson 4: Living in the Desert

Also on Teacher Resources CD-ROM.

Willis Haviland Carrier *1876–1950*

Willis Haviland Carrier, "the king of cool," helped develop modern air-conditioning. Carrier studied the temperature and humidity of air. In 1911 he developed the basic equations scientists use to understand how temperature and humidity are related. He started a company to make air-conditioning systems.

BIOFACT

A pasta maker once asked Carrier to find a way to dry 5 tons of wet macaroni.

Carrier also studied people. Carrier reasoned that for people to be comfortable, both temperature and humidity must be controlled. Carrier invented ways to control ① both temperature and humidity. People found air-conditioned air to be comfortable and refreshing!

At first, air-conditioning was used in some factories where controlling temperature and humidity was necessary. In time, theater owners began to install air-conditioners. They hoped to attract customers during hot weather. Soon more businesses got air-conditioning.

Today many homes and cars are air-conditioned. Even some schools are air-conditioned.

Learn from Biographies

Why is Carrier known as the "the king of cool"?

For more information, go online to *Meet the People* at **www.sfsocialstudies.com.**

349

Willis Haviland Carrier

Objective

- Identify the technological contributions of inventors such as Willis Haviland Carrier.

1 Introduce and Motivate

Preview To activate prior knowledge, ask students when and where they most appreciate air conditioning.

Ask students why it is important to learn about the invention of new technologies. (It reminds us of our dependence on science and technology.)

2 Teach and Discuss

① **What two things was Carrier trying to control?** Temperature, humidity **Main Idea and Details**

3 Close and Assess

Learn from Biographies Answer

Because he helped develop modern air conditioning

Problem Solving

Use a Problem-Solving Process

- Have students consider this statement and question: **Air conditioning is a great benefit, but it also uses a great deal of energy. How can we reduce the energy we use for air conditioning?**
- Have students work in small groups and use the problem-solving process at right. Have each group present its findings in a two- to three-minute oral report.

1. **Identify a problem.**
2. **Gather information.**
3. **List and consider options.**
4. **Consider advantages and disadvantages.**
5. **Choose and implement a solution.**
6. **Evaluate the effectiveness of the solution.**

WEB SITE
Technology

Students can find out more about Willis Haviland Carrier by going online and clicking on *Meet the People* at **www.sfsocialstudies.com.**

Save "America's Main Street"?

Objective

- Identify the historical significance of Route 66 to the Southwest.

1 Introduce and Motivate

Preview To introduce the idea of historic preservation, remind students of historic buildings in your community or state that have been preserved.

To activate prior knowledge, ask students what other historic roads or routes they have read about in their textbook. (Chisholm Trail, route followed by Lewis and Clark)

2 Teach and Discuss

1 **What city lies at the east end of Route 66? the west end?** East: Chicago, Illinois; West: Santa Monica, California **Analyze Information**

2 **Do you think that a road, like a building, can have historical value? Why? Do you think it is a good idea to save Route 66?** Possible answer: Yes, because it may have allowed people to more easily visit or migrate to new places; Possible answers: Yes, because it brought new businesses and people to the Southwest; No, because it is too expensive to preserve **Evaluate**

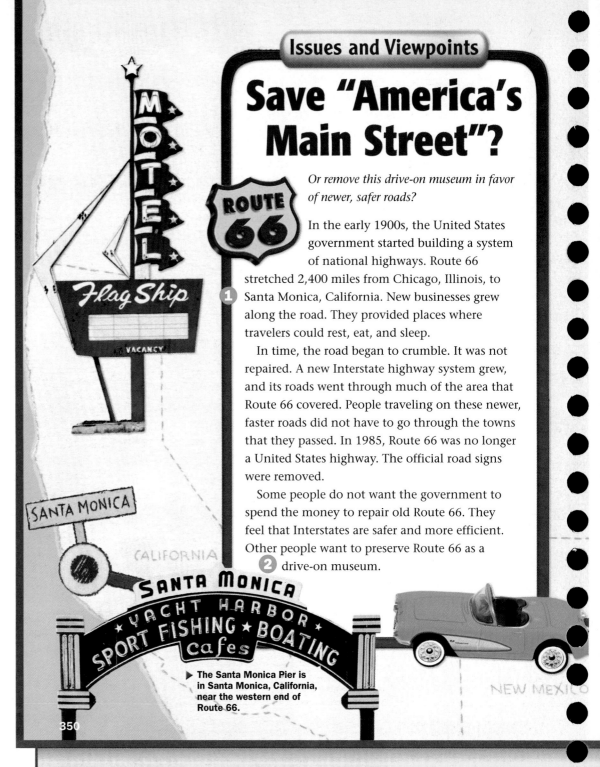

Issues and Viewpoints

Save "America's Main Street"?

Or remove this drive-on museum in favor of newer, safer roads?

In the early 1900s, the United States government started building a system of national highways. Route 66 stretched 2,400 miles from Chicago, Illinois, to
1 Santa Monica, California. New businesses grew along the road. They provided places where travelers could rest, eat, and sleep.

In time, the road began to crumble. It was not repaired. A new Interstate highway system grew, and its roads went through much of the area that Route 66 covered. People traveling on these newer, faster roads did not have to go through the towns that they passed. In 1985, Route 66 was no longer a United States highway. The official road signs were removed.

Some people do not want the government to spend the money to repair old Route 66. They feel that Interstates are safer and more efficient. Other people want to preserve Route 66 as a
2 drive-on museum.

The Santa Monica Pier is in Santa Monica, California, near the western end of Route 66.

350

Practice and Extend

MEETING INDIVIDUAL NEEDS

Learning Styles

Explore Route 66 Using their individual learning styles, students deepen their awareness of Route 66.

Logical Learning Have students research the approximate length of Route 66 and which interstate highways replaced it.

Visual Learning Have students create a map of Route 66, researching and illustrating some key attractions along the route.

Auditory Learning Have students find and perform a song or tell a story that mentions Route 66.

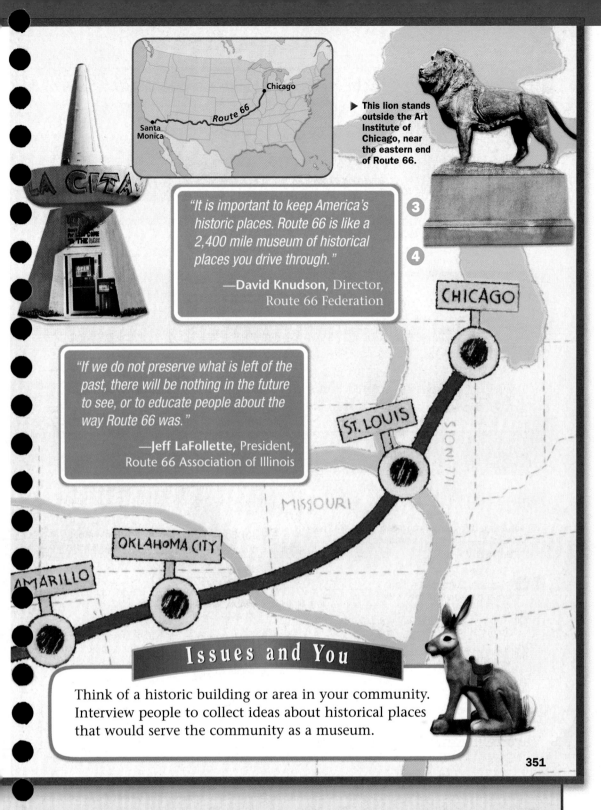

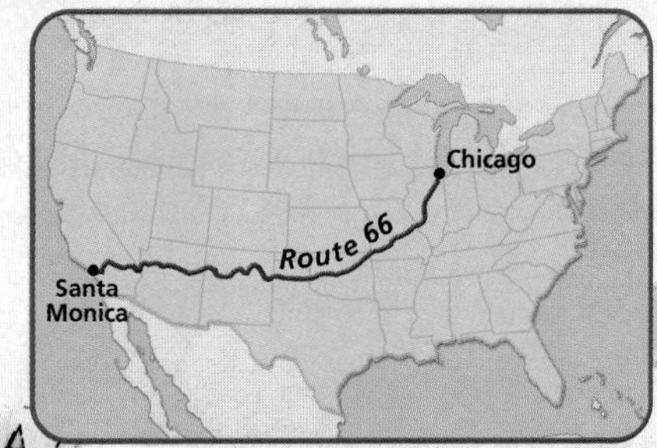

▶ This lion stands outside the Art Institute of Chicago, near the eastern end of Route 66.

"It is important to keep America's historic places. Route 66 is like a 2,400 mile museum of historical places you drive through." 3 4

—**David Knudson,** Director, Route 66 Federation

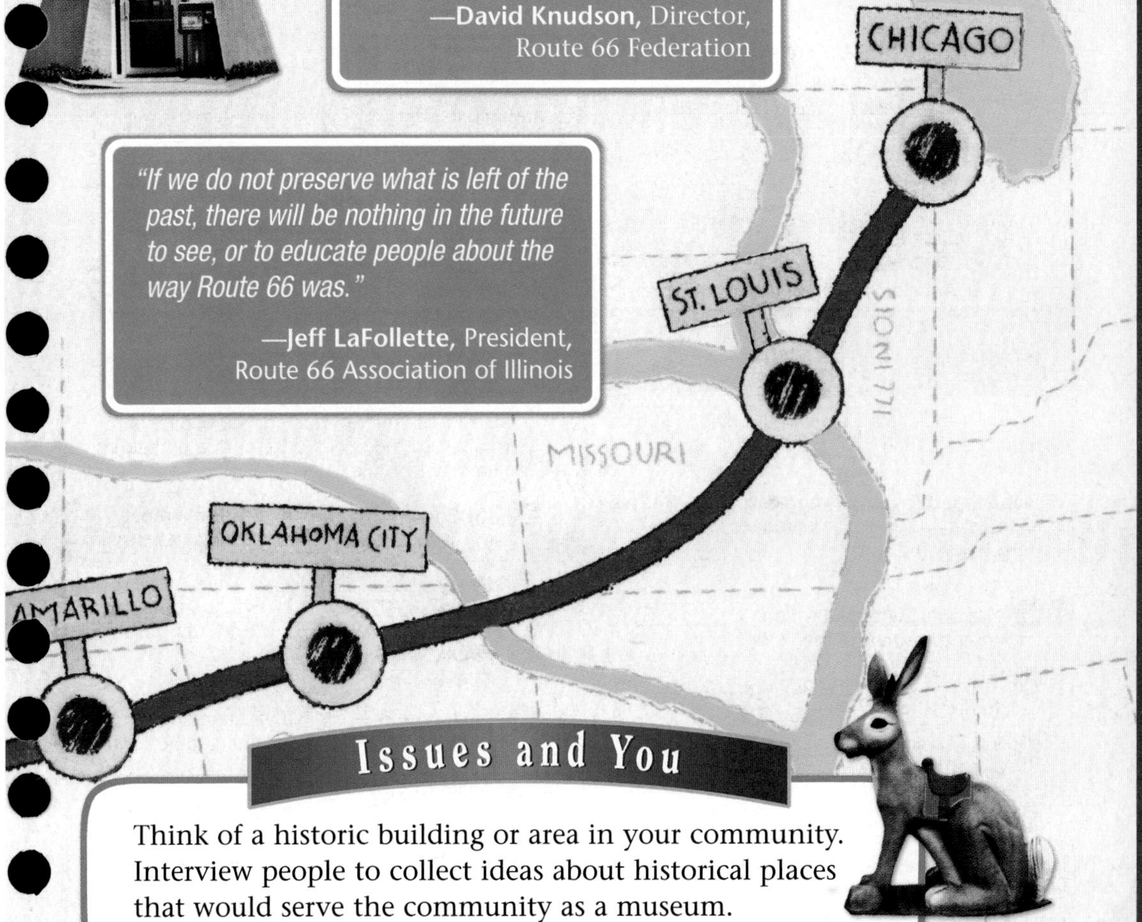

"If we do not preserve what is left of the past, there will be nothing in the future to see, or to educate people about the way Route 66 was."

—**Jeff LaFollette,** President, Route 66 Association of Illinois

Issues and You

Think of a historic building or area in your community. Interview people to collect ideas about historical places that would serve the community as a museum.

3 **What opinions does David Knudson state?** It is important to keep America's historic places. Route 66 is like a museum you drive through. **Fact and Opinion**

4 **To what does Knudson compare Route 66?** A 2,400-mile museum of historical places **Analyze Primary Sources**

3 Close and Assess

Issues and You

- Have students prepare interview questions such as "What is the oldest building in this area?" or "Do you know of interesting historic events that happened in a building around here?"
- Ask one group of students to interview community or school officials about this topic. Have another group interview family members or long-term residents of the community. Encourage students to seek out senior citizens to interview about the area's historic buildings.
- Have students take pictures of the buildings named in their interviews, write captions on cards, and create a bulletin-board display of historic sites in your community.

SOCIAL STUDIES Background

About the National Register of Historic Places

- Since 1966, about 73,000 historically or culturally significant areas, buildings, and objects have been listed in the National Register of Historic Places. Route 66 is among them.
- Being listed is a confirmation of a property's importance and makes it eligible for grants and tax benefits.

WEB SITE Technology

For more information, students can select the dictionary or encyclopedia from *Social Studies Library* at **www.sfsocialstudies.com.**

CHAPTER 11 REVIEW

Resources

- Assessment Book, pp. 57–60
- Workbook, p. 82: Vocabulary Review

Chapter Summary

For possible answers, see the reduced pupil page.

Vocabulary

1. missionary

2. aqueduct

3. viceroy

4. hogan

5. homestead

People and Terms

1. f, **2.** e, **3.** c, **4.** a, **5.** d, **6.** b

CHAPTER 11 REVIEW

1675 — 1725

1687 Father Kino founded missions in Arizona.

Chapter Summary

Draw Conclusions

On a separate sheet of paper, make a chart like the one shown. Draw a conclusion from the details listed.

Details

- The Navajo follow many of the same customs today as long ago.
- Many missions built by the Spanish are still standing.
- Modern cowboys dress and work very much like Spanish vaqueros.

Conclusion

Many influences shaped the Southwest.

▶ **A traditional Navajo hogan**

Vocabulary

Use the words listed to fill in the blanks in the sentences below.

hogan (p. 325)
viceroy (p. 333)
missionary (p. 334)
homestead (p. 342)
aqueduct (p. 347)

1. A religious group may send a _________ to another part of the world.
2. Water is carried through an _________ for irrigation.
3. The _________ of Mexico wanted to claim land for Spain.
4. A Navajo home is called a _________.
5. Settlers paid just a few dollars for land called a _________.

People and Terms

Match the number of each of the people or terms in Column 1 with a letter of a phrase in Column 2.

1. **Kit Carson** (p. 326)
2. **Henry Chee Dodge** (p. 327)
3. **Father Eusebio Kino** (p. 334)
4. **Philip Armour** (p. 339)
5. **Annie Oakley** (p. 340)
6. **Chisholm Trail** (p. 341)

a. Started a meat-packing industry in Chicago

b. Extended from Texas to Kansas

c. A missionary

d. A sharpshooter who had her own wild-west show

e. First chairman of the Navajo Tribal Council

f. Forced the Navajo from their land

352

Practice and Extend

Assessment Options

✓ Chapter 11 Assessment

- Chapter 11 Content Test: Use Assessment Book, pp. 57–58.
- Chapter 11 Skills Test: Use Assessment Book, pp. 59–60.

Standardized Test Prep

- Chapter 11 Tests contain standardized test format.

✓ Chapter 11 Performance Assessment

- Have students create a two-column chart. Have them entitle the chart *The Southwest* and label the columns *Then* and *Now*.
- Under *Then,* have students list at least three characteristics of the Southwest before 1900.
- Under *Now,* have them list at least three characteristics of the Southwest after 2000.
- Have students write one paragraph in which they compare and contrast their lists.
- Assess students' understanding of changes in the lives of people in the Southwest region over time.

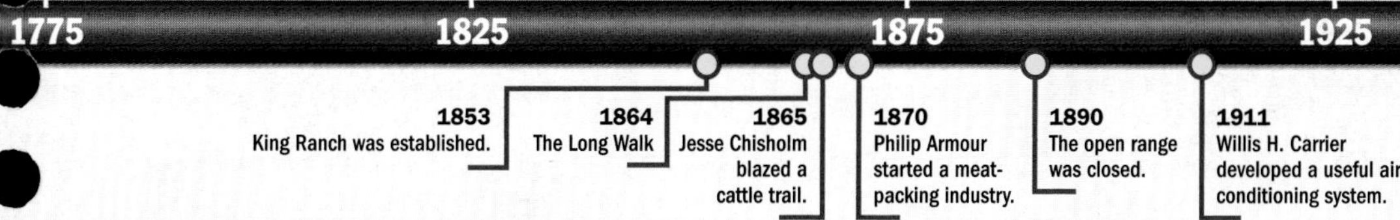
1775
1825
1875
1925
1853 King Ranch was established.
1864 The Long Walk
1865 Jesse Chisholm blazed a cattle trail.
1870 Philip Armour started a meat-packing industry.
1890 The open range was closed.
1911 Willis H. Carrier developed a useful air-conditioning system.

Facts and Main Ideas

1. How did cattle raising get started in Texas?
2. **Time Line** How many years passed between the blazing of the Chisholm Trail and the closing of the open range?
3. **Main Idea** Describe modern Navajo culture.
4. **Main Idea** How did missions help establish a Spanish presence in the Southwest?
5. **Main Idea** How have the cowboy and cowgirl been a part of our nation's lore?
6. **Main Idea** Why is the Southwest a fast-growing region today?
7. **Critical Thinking:** ***Fact or Opinion*** Which of the following statements are fact and which are opinion?
   a. Colonel Kit Carson captured the Navajo and held them prisoner for four years.
   b. It was not fair for Spanish missionaries to offer food and protection to Native Americans in exchange for work.
   c. Irrigation turned dry desert land into productive fields.

Write About History

1. **Write a skit** about a day in the life of a cowboy or cowgirl.
2. **Write a TV commercial** about interesting places to visit in the Southwest.
3. **Write a magazine article** in which you tell how different the Southwest region would be without air conditioning.

Internet Activity

To get help with vocabulary, people, and terms, select the dictionary or encyclopedia from *Social Studies Library* at **www.sfsocialstudies.com.**

Apply Skills

Identify Primary Sources

Read the primary source below. It is Coronado's description of a Native American pueblo in the Southwest from a report he made to a Spanish viceroy. Then answer the questions.

> "In this place where I am now lodged there are perhaps 200 houses, all surrounded by a wall, and it seems to me that with the other houses, which are not so surrounded, there might be altogether 500 families."

1. How do you know that this is a primary source?
2. What is the purpose of this document?
3. What is the main idea of this primary source?

353

Hand-on Unit Project

✓ Unit 5 Performance Assessment

- See p. 358 for information about using the Unit Project as a means of performance assessment.
- A scoring guide is provided on p. 358.

WEB SITE Technology

For more information, students can select the dictionary or encyclopedia from *Social Studies Library* at **www.sfsocialstudies.com.**

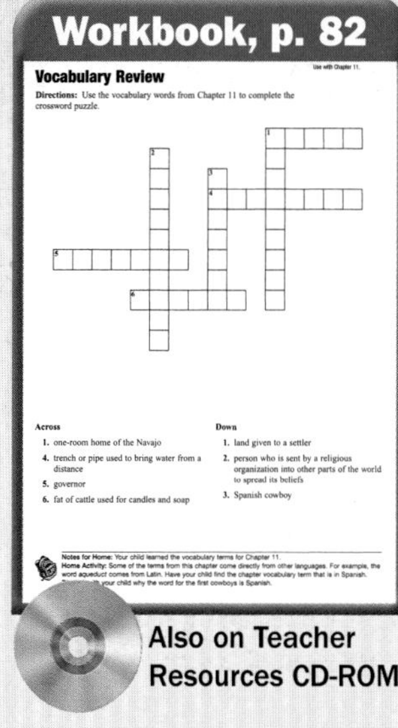

Workbook, p. 82

Vocabulary Review Use with Chapter 11.

Directions: Use the vocabulary words from Chapter 11 to complete the crossword puzzle.

Across

1. one-room home of the Navajo
4. trench or pipe used to bring water from a distance
5. governor
6. fat of cattle used for candles and soap

Down

1. land given to a settler
2. person who is sent by a religious organization into other parts of the world to spread its beliefs
3. Spanish cowboy

Notes for Home: Your child learned the vocabulary terms for Chapter 11.
Home Activity: Some of the terms from this chapter come directly from other languages. For example, the word aqueduct comes from Latin. Have your child find the chapter vocabulary term that is in Spanish. ... your child why the word for the first cowboys is Spanish.

Also on Teacher Resources CD-ROM.

Facts and Main Ideas

1. Spanish missionaries brought cattle to Texas and left the cattle behind when they withdrew.
2. About 25 years
3. Religion and traditional ceremonies are still important. Some of the Navajo still live in hogans. The Navajo language is still spoken and taught in schools.
4. Possible answer: Many of the churches, buildings, and settlements first established by the missions or near missions still exist today, and many elements of Spanish culture still influence life in the Southwest.
5. They have inspired many books, movies, TV shows, and songs.
6. Irrigation and air conditioning have made living in the desert more comfortable, so many people have moved to the Southwest.
7. **a.** Fact, **b.** Opinion, **c.** Fact

Write About History

1. Encourage students to plan their skits around a problem a cowboy or cowgirl might face.
2. Remind students that their scripts must include at least a description of the visual part of the commercial.
3. As students are planning their work, encourage them to list facts and opinions they will use. Suggest that they consider describing both the positive and negative effects of air conditioning.

Apply Skills

1. It uses words such as "I" and "me."
2. Possible answer: To let the viceroy know about how many people live in the pueblo.
3. Possible answer: Many people live in this pueblo.

Cowboy Country

Objectives

- Describe the tasks that cowhands perform.
- Infer that skills become more developed as a person matures.

1 Introduce and Motivate

Preview To activate prior knowledge, remind students that being a cowhand usually involves hard work, long hours, and low pay. Discuss what students have learned about real-life cowhands. Point out that most real cowhands bear little resemblance to those portrayed in books and movies. You also may wish to have students review the *Ranchers and Cowhands* feature on pp. 344–345.

2 Teach and Discuss

1 **Why do you think a cowboy's eyes and ears are "working all the time"?** Possible answers: To keep the cowboy aware of everything going on around him; to help him detect problems with the herd Apply Information

2 **Why do you think the author says "you don't need to be a vet" to treat some of the cattle's injuries and illnesses?** Possible answers: Because some medical treatments are fairly routine; because it would be too time-consuming and expensive to call a vet every time an animal needed to be treated for a minor ailment
Draw Conclusions

SOCIAL STUDIES SKILLS
Citizenship

3 **How does the author's concern about his neighbor's bull show good citizenship?** By helping his neighbor locate and retrieve the bull, the author has taken steps to solve a problem for someone else. Make Inferences

UNIT 5 End with Literature

Cowboy Country

BY ANN HERBERT SCOTT

Cowboy Country is a book that tells about the life of a cowboy, or *buckaroo*. Here is a part of the book that describes some of the things that a good buckaroo needs to learn.

Illustration by Ted Lewin

You think you'd like to learn to cowboy?
Then you'll need to watch and listen.
Most cowboys don't say much
1 but their eyes and ears are working all the time.
See that old cow lying on her side in the willows?
She may be asleep, but on the other hand
she could have run a thorn into her hoof.
Let's check her out. Right here by my saddle
I carry a kit for doctoring.
2 You don't need to be a vet
to give a sick calf a shot
or swab out a cut or treat a cow for worms.

See that bull over by the boulder?
I think he belongs to our neighbors
3 over beyond Lone Mountain.
Let's check his brand.

Practice and Extend

SOCIAL STUDIES
Background

Branding Cattle

- Branding cattle has been done for many years. Spanish ranchers first introduced brands to the Southwest in 1762. Texas began registering individual brands in 1848.
- Many brands include letters that have been modified in some way. For example, an *S* leaning to one side is called a "tumbling *S*." An *A* lying on its side is a "lazy *A*."
- Some brands involve putting extra marks on a letter to make it unique. A letter with short, curved marks at the top is said to be "flying." A half circle below a letter means it is "rocking." Some letters are also marked with bars, chains, stripes, or slashes.

They trucked that critter all the way from Canada.
I know they wouldn't want to lose him now.

Do the cattle all look the same to you?
Well, they're just as different as people are
when you take the care to know them. 4
If you've seen western movies
or watched cowboys on TV,
you might guess it's bronc riding
and roping snorting steers that makes a top hand.
Well, you'd guess wrong.

Of course, any good buckaroo needs to know
how to handle a rough pony and slip a slick noose,
but it's reading cows that makes a good cowboy—
knowing what an old cow is thinking
before she knows herself. It takes years 5
to learn that—maybe a lifetime—
but you're starting young,
and you've got lots of time. 6

355

4 According to the author, why do the cows all look different to a cowboy? Because the cowboy has taken care to know them **Main Idea and Details**

5 Why might it be helpful for a cowboy to "know what an old cow is thinking before she knows herself"? Possible answer: So he can anticipate her actions and take steps to keep her safe and out of trouble **Draw Conclusions**

6 Why might it take a long time for a cowboy to learn how to "read" cows? Possible answer: Because he needs to experience all the different ways cows react in a variety of situations **Make Inferences**

3 Close and Assess

- Tell students that a cowboy's work can be both exciting and very routine.
- Have students create a two-column chart on a sheet of paper and label the columns *Pros* and *Cons*.
- Then, in the appropriate columns, have them list the best and worst things about being a cowboy.
- When the lists are complete, discuss how students' different opinions affected their lists.

CURRICULUM CONNECTION

Writing

Write a Poem

- Tell students to review the information about cowhands found on these two pages and elsewhere in Unit 5. As they review the text, have them note important facts and descriptive words about cowhands and cowhand life.
- Have students use their notes to write a poem about cowhands in the Southwest. Tell them that they may focus on cowhands in the past or the present.
- Have students illustrate their poems and share them with the class.

UNIT 5 Review

Resource

- Assessment Book, pp. 61–64

Main Ideas and Vocabulary

1. d, **2.** c, **3.** a, **4.** b

Test Talk

Use Information from Graphics
Use Main Ideas and Vocabulary, Question 3, to model the Test Talk strategy.

Understand the question.
Have students identify the information in the passage that relates to the question. Then have them finish the statement "I need to find out ...."

Use information from graphics.
Ask students to skim the picture to find the right information to support their answer.

People

Be sure that students include at least one factually correct detail about each person and that the paragraph is coherent overall.

UNIT 5 Review

Test Talk

Use the picture to help you find the answers.

Main Ideas and Vocabulary

TEST PREP

Read the passage below and use it to answer the questions that follow.

Spanish explorer Francisco Vásquez de Coronado explored a large part of the Southwest in search of "Cities of Gold." He found only adobe pueblos. His explorations were labeled as failures.

When Spanish missionaries came to the Southwest, they brought cattle. Cattle ranching became an important part of the economy of the region. The American cowboy became a part of our nation's lore.

Later, the discovery of oil in the Southwest brought more jobs to the region. Oil brought wealth to people who came to invest in that resource.

The Navajo are one of the largest Native American groups in the United States. They also are ruled by one of the largest tribal councils. The Navajo have kept many of their old traditions.

Many people visit the Southwest to enjoy its beautiful landforms. Others come to see plants such as the saguaro cacti that grow only in the Sonoran Desert. Saguaro grow to be 60 feet tall. They are 80 years old before they begin to grow branches.

Much of the Southwest has an arid climate, but it is not all desert. Parts of the Southwest get a lot of rain and even have wetlands. Until the 1900s, heat and lack of water in the desert regions kept the population low. With the advances of irrigation and air conditioning, life in the desert became more comfortable. New businesses and the growth of technology have allowed desert cities to grow quickly.

1. Why did Coronado explore the Southwest?
   - **A** He wanted to make Christians of the Navajo.
   - **B** He was searching for the Grand Canyon.
   - **C** He wanted to claim land.
   - **D** He was looking for the "Cities of Gold."

2. In the passage, the word *pueblos* means—
   - **A** Native American group
   - **B** gold mines
   - **C** villages
   - **D** cattle ranches

3. According to this passage, the cactus pictured must be at least how many years old?
   - **A** 80
   - **B** 3
   - **C** 25
   - **D** 60

4. In the passage, the word *arid* means—
   - **A** regional
   - **B** dry
   - **C** ranch land
   - **D** irrigated

▶ Saguaro cactus

356

Practice and Extend

Assessment Options

✓ Unit 5 Assessment

- Unit 5 Content Test: Use Assessment Book, pp. 61–62.
- Unit 5 Skills Test: Use Assessment Book, pp. 63–64.

Standardized Test Prep

- Unit 5 Tests contain standardized test format.

✓ Unit 5 Performance Assessment

- See p. 358 for information about using the Unit Project as a means of Performance Assessment.
- A scoring guide for the Unit 5 Project is provided in the teacher's notes on p. 358.

Test Talk

- Test Talk Practice Book

WEB SITE Technology

For more information, students can select the dictionary or encyclopedia from *Social Studies Library* at **www.sfsocialstudies.com.**

People

Choose five of the people listed below and use them in a paragraph about the Southwest Region.

García López de Cárdenas (p. 302)

John Wesley Powell (p. 302)

Theodore Roosevelt (p. 303)

Pattillo Higgins (p. 315)

Kit Carson (p. 326)

Henry Chee Dodge (p. 327)

Father Eusebio Kino (p. 334)

Philip Armour (p. 339)

Annie Oakley (p. 340)

Calamity Jane (p. 340)

Jesse Chisholm (p. 341)

Willis Haviland Carrier (p. 348)

Apply Skills

Create a Primary Source Guide About Your Community Write a three-paragraph description of a favorite community event or a favorite place in your community. With classmates, bind your descriptions into a book to create a primary source guide about your community.

Write and Share

Write and Perform a Skit With a group of classmates, write a skit about cattle ranching, cowboys, and cowgirls. Include examples that show how real lives of cowhands were different from what might be shown in a movie. Choose classmates to play each of the parts in the skit. Make costumes and perform the skit for another class.

Read on Your Own

Look for books like these in your library.

357

Revisit the Unit Question

✓Portfolio Assessment

- Have students look at their brainstormed list of things people might find attractive about the Southwest.
- Divide the class into small groups, one for each lesson of this unit. Have each group describe a geographic, cultural, or economic feature mentioned in their lesson.
- Have students use their lists and descriptions to write a one-paragraph generalization about what the Southwest has to offer to residents and visitors.
- Have students add these lists and generalizations to their Social Studies Portfolio.

Apply Skills

- You may wish to have students work in small groups with each group highlighting a different event or place.
- Encourage students to first decide what main idea they want their guide to convey. That decision will guide their choice of visual images and text.

Write and Share

- If possible, create groups that include students with different kinds of skills so that each has something unique to contribute.
- Use the following score guide.

✓Assessment Scoring Guide

Write and Perform a Skit	
6	Skit has clear beginning, middle, and end. Costumes and music, if any, are well done and appropriate. Actors convey appropriate tone.
5	Skit has clear beginning, middle, and end. Actors generally convey appropriate tone.
4	Skit has one major flaw. It lacks coherence, good staging, or acting skill.
3	Skit has two major flaws and lacks coherence, good staging, or acting skill.
2	Skit has more than two major flaws, such as poor ending, inconsistent staging, or lack of practiced actors.
1	Skit does not tell coherent story, has little or no staging, and seems unrefined.

If you prefer a 4-point rubric, adjust accordingly.

Read on Your Own

Have students prepare oral reports using the following books.

Cowboys: Roundup on an American Ranch, by Joan Anderson (Scholastic Trade, ISBN 0-590-48424-9, 1996) **Easy**

Anasazi, by Leonard Everett Fisher (Atheneum, ISBN 0-689-80737-6, 1997) **On-Level**

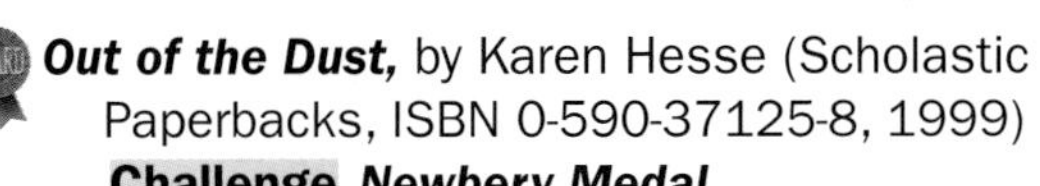
Out of the Dust, by Karen Hesse (Scholastic Paperbacks, ISBN 0-590-37125-8, 1999) **Challenge** ***Newbery Medal***

Unit Project

Ad Sales

Objective

- Understand that products and businesses contribute to a state's economy.

Resource

- Workbook, p. 83

Materials

poster board or large sheets of paper, pencils, markers

Follow This Procedure

- Tell students that they will write a script and an infomercial about a product or business.
- Encourage students to prepare a list of facts to include in the infomercial.
- Direct students in making banners or posters for the products or businesses.
- Invite each student group to present its infomercial to the class.
- Discuss how products or businesses contribute to your state's economy.
- Use the following scoring guide.

✓ Assessment Scoring Guide

	Ad Sales
6	Uses accurate content, many vivid details, precise word choices, and solid examples
5	Uses accurate content, many details, clear word choices, and solid examples
4	Uses accurate content, several details, clear word choices, and some examples
3	Uses mostly accurate content, several details, appropriate word choices, and some examples
2	Uses mostly inaccurate content, few details, vague word choices, and few examples
1	Uses inaccurate content, few or no details, incorrect word choices, and no examples

If you require a 4-point rubric, adjust accordingly.

Ad Sales

Healthy businesses are good for your state's economy. Make your own infomercial about a product or a business.

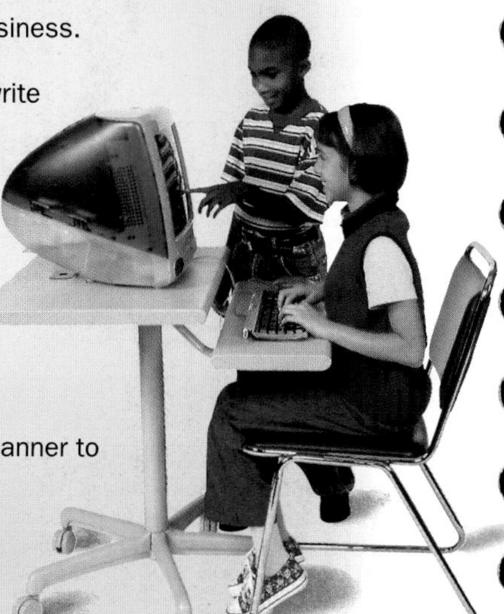

1 **Form** a group. Choose a product or a business.

2 **Research** the product or business and write a list of facts about it.

3 **Write** a script for an infomercial about the product or business. Include the value and cost, as well as the history of the product or business. Give examples of its successes. Tell how it contributes to your state's economy.

4 **Make** an advertisement on a poster or banner to use in your infomercial.

5 **Present** your infomercial to the class.

Explore the Southwest on the Internet. Go to **www.sfsocialstudies.com/activities** and select your grade and unit.

358

Practice and Extend

Hands-on Unit Project

✓ Performance Assessment

- The Unit Project can also be used as a performance assessment activity.
- Use the scoring guide to assess each group's work.

WEB SITE Technology

Students can launch the Internet Activity by clicking on *Grade 4, Unit 5* at **www.sfsocialstudies.com/activities.**

Workbook, p. 83

Also on Teacher Resources CD-ROM.

★ Unit 6 ★

Vocabulary Routines

The following examples of reading and vocabulary development strategies can be used to instruct students about unit vocabulary.

BEFORE READING

Individual Word Study

K-W-L Use a K-W-L chart to build background for unit vocabulary words. Ask students what they already Know **(K)** about the word. This is particularly helpful in clearing up any misconceptions they might have about the meaning of a particular vocabulary word. Have students ask questions about What they would like to learn **(W)** about the word. Revisit the chart after reading, and fill in what children have Learned **(L)** about the word.

Let's take a look at the word **volcano.** *What do you already know about volcanoes?* (They are mountains that blow up.) *Have you ever seen a photograph of a volcano? What does it look like?* (It looks like a mountain, except there is fire and smoke coming out of it.) *What are some things you would like to learn about volcanoes?* (What makes volcanoes erupt? Where are volcanoes located?)

DURING READING

Context Clues

Apply That Word At the end of each page, stop briefly and encourage students to think about how a new word relates to something they have seen or done in their own lives. By applying the vocabulary word, students increase their chances of recalling the word and retaining its meaning. You can use this technique with any of the unit vocabulary, as shown in the example below:

When it is snowing and icy outside, you could say, "The weather outside is **frigid.**" *If you forgot your gloves on a very cold day, you might say, "My hands feel* **frigid.**" *What other sentences could you make with the word* **frigid?** (My lunch was *frigid* after I put it in the refrigerator. I didn't want to swim in the *frigid* water.)

AFTER READING

Related Word Study

Compare and Contrast Chart After students have finished reading a lesson, select pairs of related words and have students create a chart comparing and contrasting the words. This routine helps students become aware of similarities and differences between related vocabulary words. After filling out a chart such as the one shown at right, students should write a paragraph comparing and contrasting the two terms. Other terms that could be compared and contrasted include *geyser* and *volcano* from Chapter 12, Lesson 1.

Let's compare and contrast **boom town** *and* **ghost town.** *Help me list pairs of related points in this chart.* (Both are towns. Boom towns grow quickly while ghost towns are deserted. Boom towns are full of miners and merchants while ghost towns are empty except for visiting tourists. Boom towns can turn into ghost towns. Ghost towns used to be boom towns.) *Now, use the information in our chart to write a paragraph comparing and contrasting boom towns and ghost towns.*

Boom town	Ghost town
• Is a town • Grows quickly • Full of miners and merchants • Could turn into a ghost town	• Is a town • Is deserted • Empty except for visiting tourists • Used to be a boom town

The West

UNIT 6

Unit Planning Guide

Unit 6 • The West

Begin with a Primary Source pp. 360–361

Welcome to the West pp. 362–363

Reading Social Studies, Compare and Contrast pp. 364–365

Chapter Titles	Pacing	Main Ideas
Chapter 12 **The Land of the West** pp. 366–389 ✓ **Chapter 12 Review** pp. 390–391	9 days	• Many parts of the West are mountainous. • The climate in different areas of the West varies greatly. • The West is rich in natural resources.
Chapter 13 **Living in the West** pp. 392–417 ✓ **Chapter 13 Review** pp. 418–419	9 days	• The Tlingit live in the northern part of the West. • Explorers from Spain and settlers seeking gold helped shape the West. • Cities in the West have many different kinds of businesses and attractions.

End with a Song pp. 420–421

✓ **Unit 6 Review** pp. 422–423

✓ **Unit 6 Project** p. 424

✓ = **Assessment Options**

The Bird of Paradise is one of the many beautiful flowers that thrive in Hawaii's tropical climate.

Resources	Meeting Individual Needs
• Workbook, pp. 85–89 • Every Student Learns Guide, pp. 150–161 • Transparencies 6, 14, 57–60 • Quick Study, pp. 76–81 • Workbook, p. 90 ✔ Chapter 12 Content Test, Assessment Book, pp. 65–66 ✔ Chapter 12 Skills Test, Assessment Book, pp. 67–68	• ESL Support, TE pp. 370, 379, 385 • Leveled Practice, TE pp. 372, 377, 381, 386 • Learning Styles, TE p. 387 ✔ Chapter 12 Performance Assessment, TE p. 390
• Workbook, pp. 91–95 • Every Student Learns Guide, pp. 162–173 • Transparencies 6, 14, 23, 61–64 • Quick Study, pp. 82–87 • Workbook, p. 96 ✔ Chapter 13 Content Test, Assessment Book, pp. 69–70 ✔ Chapter 13 Skills Test, Assessment Book, pp. 71–72	• ESL Support, TE pp. 396, 403, 414 • Leveled Practice, TE pp. 397, 402, 412 • Learning Styles, TE p. 398 ✔ Chapter 13 Performance Assessment, TE p. 418

Chilkat blankets like this one use symbols to tell stories of Tlingit life.

Providing More Depth

Additional Resources

- Trade Books
- Family Activities
- Vocabulary Workbook and Cards
- Social Studies Plus! pp. 120–139
- Daily Activity Bank
- Read Alouds and Primary Sources pp. 86–102
- Big Book Atlas
- Student Atlas
- Outline Maps
- Desk Maps

Technology

- AudioText
- Video Field Trips: The Mountain States
- Songs and Music
- Digital Learning CD-ROM Powered by KnowledgeBox (Video clips and activities)
- MindPoint® Quiz Show CD-ROM
- ExamView® Test Bank CD-ROM
- Teacher Resources CD-ROM
- Map Resources CD-ROM
- SF SuccessNet: iText (Pupil Edition online), iTE (Teacher's Edition online), Online Planner
- **www.sfsocialstudies.com** (Biographies, news, references, maps, and activities)

To establish guidelines for your students' safe and responsible use of the Internet, use the Scott Foresman Internet Guide.

Additional Internet Links

To find out more about:

- Rocky Mountain National Park, visit **www.nps.gov**
- Seattle, Washington, visit **www.ci.seattle.wa.us**
- Salt Lake City, Utah, visit **www.saltlake.org**

Unit 6 Objectives

Beginning of Unit 6

- Use primary sources to acquire information. (p. 360)
- Identify the physical characteristics of the West. (p. 362)
- Analyze printed information by comparing and contrasting. (p. 364)

Chapter 12

Lesson 1 A Land of Mountains pp. 368–373

- Identify the largest system of mountains in the United States.
- Compare and contrast mountain ranges of the West.
- Identify mountain ranges in the West and tell where they are located.
- Compare geysers to volcanoes.
- Compare and contrast different kinds of volcanoes. (p. 374)
- Use notes and outlines to organize information. (p. 376)

Lesson 2 Climates in the West pp. 378–383

- Compare and contrast the climates of Hawaii and California.
- Name the different climates of the West and give an example of each.
- Identify states in the West with extreme weather.
- Explain how the rain shadow works.
- Compare and contrast the amount of precipitation that falls on the east and west sides of the Cascade Range.

Lesson 3 Resources of the West pp. 384–388

- Identify some resources of the West.
- Identify places where agricultural products are grown in the West.
- Locate areas of the West that have important fishing industries.
- Explain how people benefit from the resources of the West.
- Describe an agricultural contribution of Seth Lewelling to the economy of the region. (p. 389)

Chapter 13

Lesson 1 The Tlingit pp. 394–397

- Write a summary of traditional Tlingit life.
- Describe how the Tlingit make use of natural resources.
- Compare and contrast Tlingit potlatches held in the past and today.
- List details of modern Tlingit life.
- Analyze cultural symbols and traditions of the Haida, the Moche, and the Incas. (p. 398)

Lesson 2 Exploration and Growth pp. 400–406

- Draw a conclusion about changes in the West in the 1800s.
- Explain why various groups explored the West.
- Describe the Gold Rush of 1848 and explain how it affected the West.
- Explain how a boom town might become a ghost town.
- Explain when and how various territories of the West gained statehood.
- Identify important inventors such as Levi Strauss and describe their accomplishments. (p. 407)
- Use latitude and longitude to find locations on maps and globes. (p. 408)

Lesson 3 Business and Pleasure pp. 410–415

- Compare and contrast the cities of Los Angeles and Salt Lake City.
- Name some of the industries found in Los Angeles, Seattle, and Salt Lake City.
- Explain how climate can affect tourism in selected western cities.
- Identify products that the United States exports to and imports from the Pacific Rim countries.
- Identify individuals such as Thomas Bradley who exemplify good citizenship. (p. 416)

End of Unit 6

- Identify geographic locations in songs. (p. 420)
- Identify historical events in songs. (p. 420)
- Explain how examples of music reflect the times in which they were written. (p. 420)
- Describe a current event in your state and make a prediction about the future. (p. 424)

The tallest trees in the United States are California's giant redwoods. ▶

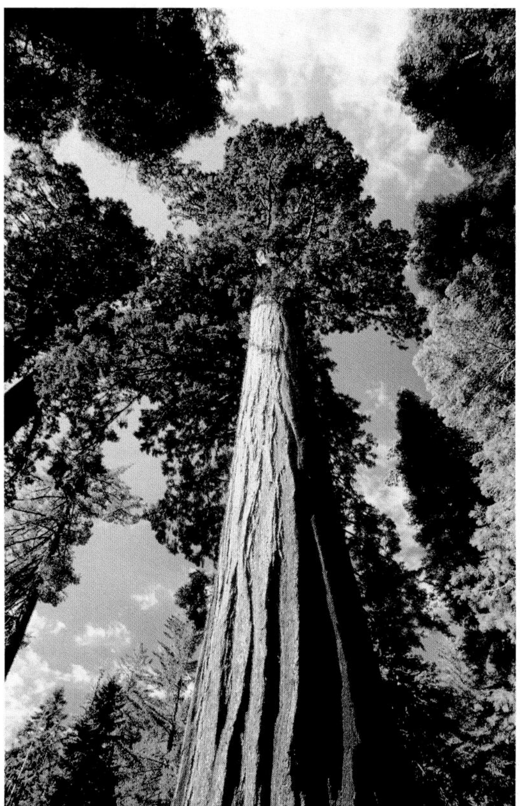

Assessment Options

✓ Formal Assessment

- **Lesson Reviews,** PE/TE pp. 373, 383, 388, 397, 406, 415
- **Chapter Reviews,** PE/TE pp. 390–391, 418–419
- **Chapter Tests,** Assessment Book, pp. 65–72
- **Unit Review,** PE/TE pp. 422–423
- **Unit Tests,** Assessment Book, pp. 73–76
- **ExamView® Test Bank CD-ROM** (test-generator software)

✓ Informal Assessment

- **Teacher's Edition Questions,** throughout Lessons and Features
- **Section Reviews,** PE/TE pp. 369, 371, 373, 379, 381, 383, 385–386, 388, 395–397, 401, 402, 403–406, 411–412, 414–415
- **Close and Assess,** TE pp. 365, 373, 375, 377, 383, 388–389, 397, 399, 406–407, 409, 415, 417, 421

Ongoing Assessment

Ongoing Assessment is found throughout the Teacher's Edition lessons using an **If...then** model.

If = students' observable behavior,	**then =** reteaching and enrichment suggestions

✓ Portfolio Assessment

- **Portfolio Assessment,** TE pp. 359, 360, 423
- **Leveled Practice,** TE pp. 372, 377, 381, 386, 397, 402, 412
- **Workbook Pages,** pp. 84–97
- **Chapter Review: Write About It,** PE/TE pp. 391, 419
- **Unit Review: Apply Skills,** PE/TE p. 423
- **Curriculum Connection: Writing** PE/TE p. 415; TE pp. 388, 417

✓ Performance Assessment

- **Hands-on Unit Project** (Unit 6 Performance Assessment), TE pp. 359, 391, 419, 422, 424
- **Internet Activity,** PE p. 424
- **Chapter 12 Performance Assessment,** TE p. 390
- **Chapter 13 Performance Assessment,** TE p. 418
- **Unit Review: Write and Share,** PE/TE p. 423
- **Scoring Guides,** TE pp. 423–424

Test Talk

Test-Taking Strategies

Understand the Question

- **Locate Key Words in the Question,** TE p. 370
- **Locate Key Words in the Text,** TE p. 386

Understand the Answer

- **Choose the Right Answer,** Test Talk Practice Book
- **Use Information from the Text,** TE pp. 382, 411
- **Use Information from Graphics,** TE pp. 372, 403
- **Write Your Answer to Score High,** PE p. 423; TE p. 422

For additional practice, use the Test Talk Practice Book.

Featured Strategy

Write Your Answer to Score High

Students will:

- Make sure their answer is correct.
- Make sure their answer is complete.
- Make sure their answer is focused.

PE p. 423; **TE** p. 422

Curriculum Connections

Integrating Your Day

The lessons, skills, and features of Unit 6 provide many opportunities to make connections between social studies and other areas of the elementary curriculum.

Social Studies

READING

Reading Skill—Compare and Contrast, PE/TE pp. 364–365, 368, 378, 410

Lesson Review—Compare and Contrast, PE/TE pp. 373, 383, 415

Link to Reading, PE/TE p. 388

WRITING

Write a Personal Essay, TE p. 388

Link to Writing, PE/TE p. 415

Write a Story About Unfairness, TE p. 417

SCIENCE

Explore Mountain Plants, TE p. 369

Examine How Lava Flows, TE p. 375

Link to Science, PE/TE p. 383

Investigate Engineering, TE p. 416

ART

Illustrate a Community, TE p. 383

Draw a Totem Pole, TE p. 395

Link to Art, PE/TE p. 397

Trace a Route on a Map, TE p. 421

MUSIC / DRAMA

Give a Dramatic Reading, TE p. 369

Listen to Rain, TE p. 382

Sing a Ballad, TE p. 395

Evaluate a Wild West Drama, TE p. 404

Link to Music, PE/TE p. 406

LITERATURE

Read About the West, TE p. 362

Read About Mountains and Geysers, TE p. 373

Read About Masks, TE p. 399

MATH

Create a Bar Graph, TE p. 382

Analyze the Cost of Alaska, TE p. 405

Create a Local Fact File, TE p. 413

Look for this symbol throughout the Teacher's Edition to find **Curriculum Connections.**

Professional Development

Economics in the Elementary Classroom

by Bonnie Meszaros, Ph.D.
University of Delaware

Today's children will face many economic issues as adults. In the ordinary business of life, they will decide what to buy, what careers to pursue, and how much of their income they should spend and how much to save. They will need to comprehend the impact that various news events, such as the closing of a major manufacturing plant, may have on their lives. Adults without some understanding of economics will find many of these issues complex and confusing.

Young children need to be taught important economic concepts in developmentally appropriate ways. Strategies include identifying students' misconceptions, replacing misconceptions with factually correct ideas, using teacher-directed feedback and student practice to apply foundation skills, providing opportunities for experienced-based instruction, allowing students to verbalize economic ideas, and integrating economics across the curriculum and into daily life.

On p. 412 of the Teacher's Edition, students are asked to examine resources held by different cities in the West. After considering the economic value of a natural resource such as the Great Salt Lake, students analyze the value of a human-made resource such as the software industry.

On p. 414 of the Pupil Edition, students read about how the United States engages in international trade with Pacific Rim countries. Discuss with students how international trade benefits the economy of the United States.

ESL Support

by Jim Cummins, Ph.D.
University of Toronto

Extend Language

The following strategy can help ESL students harvest the academic language they encounter in Unit 6 and apply prior knowledge of word structure and meaning to analyze more complex, content-specific language.

Nominalization

When students know some of the rules or conventions of how academic words are formed, it helps them extend their vocabulary. It helps students figure out the meanings of individual words and understand how to form different parts of speech from those words. A central aspect of academic language is understanding nominalization, the process of forming abstract nouns from verbs and adjectives.

Word Derivations

Another way to extend academic language is to demystify the meanings of the roots of many words of Latin and Greek origin. Students discover and learn to apply rules that govern words derived from Greek and Latin to English and Spanish. They can explore particular words by brainstorming as a group; by looking up words in a dictionary, encyclopedia, or thesaurus; or by asking more linguistically proficient learners for help.

The following examples in the Teacher's Edition will help you extend language for ESL students.

***Examine Different Forms of Adjectives** on p. 379 helps students use the positive, comparative, and superlative forms of adjectives.*

***Examine Root Words** on p. 414 has students explore the meaning of the root* port *and derive other words with the root.*

Read Aloud

Totem Pole

Standing tall above the tribe
Looking out both far and wide.
Animals painted bright
Watch the western countryside.
The busy Tlingit
Down below
Have planned a potlatch,
Many will come and go.
Oh, the life of a totem pole.

◀ **Tlingit totem pole**

Read Alouds and Primary Sources

- *Read Alouds and Primary Sources* contains additional selections to be used with Unit 6.

Bibliography

Mountain Town, by Bonnie Geisert (Houghton Mifflin Co., ISBN 0-395-95390-1, 2000) **Easy**
Parents' Choice Gold Award

Nine for California, by Sonia Levitin (Orchard Books, ISBN 0-531-07176-6, 2000) **Easy**

The Wave of the Sea-Wolf, by David Wisniewski (Houghton Mifflin Co., ISBN 0-395-96892-5, 1999) **Easy**

Buried Treasures of the Rocky Mountain West: Legends of Lost Mines, Train Robbery Gold, Caves of Forgotten Riches, and Indians' Buried Silver, by W. C. Jameson (August House Publications, ISBN 0-87483-272-1, 1993) **On-Level**

Glaciers, by John Ewart Gordon (Voyageur Press, ISBN 0-89658-559-X, 2001) **On-Level**

Seeds of Hope: The Gold Rush Diary of Susanna Fairchild, California Territory, 1849, by Kristiana Gregory (Scholastic Trade, ISBN 0-590-51157-2, 2001) **On-Level**

Cloud: Wild Stallion of the Rockies, by Ginger Kathrens (BowTie Press, ISBN 1-889540-70-6, 2001) **Challenge**

The Eagle's Shadow, by Nora Martin (Scholastic Trade, ISBN 0-590-36087-6, 1997) **Challenge**

Lost in Death Valley: The True Story of Four Families in California's Gold Rush, by Connie Goldsmith (Twenty First Century Books, ISBN 0-7613-1915-8, 2001) **Challenge**

The Tlingit: An Introduction to Their Culture & History, by Wallace M. Olson (Heritage Research, ISBN 0-965-90090-8, 1997) **Teacher reference**

The World Rushed In: The California Gold Rush Experience, by J. S. Holliday (University of Oklahoma Press, ISBN 0-8061-3464-X, 2002) **Teacher reference**

The Yellowstone Story: A History of Our First National Park, by Aubrey L. Haines (University Press of Colorado, ISBN 0-87081-390-0, 1996) **Teacher reference**

***Discovery Channel School* Videos**

How the West Was Lost Explore Native Americans' struggle to maintain their lands, lives, and cultures as settlers began moving west. (Item #716233, 52 minutes)

- To order *Discovery Channel School* videos, please call the following toll-free number: 1-888-892-3484.
- Free online lesson plans are available at **DiscoverySchool.com.**

Look for this symbol throughout the Teacher's Edition to find **Award-Winning Selections.** Additional book references are found throughout this unit.

The West

UNIT 6

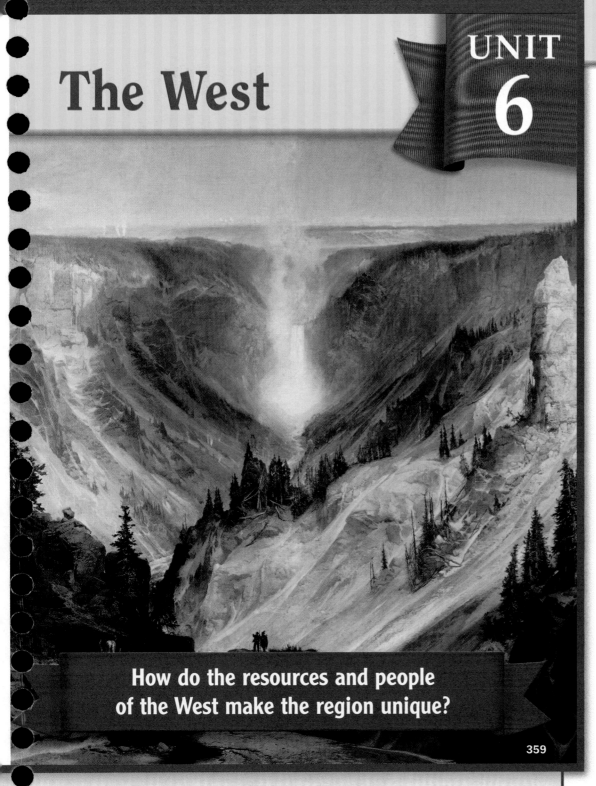

How do the resources and people of the West make the region unique?

359

Practice and Extend

Hands-on Unit Project

✓ Unit 6 Performance Assessment

- The Unit Project, *Great State,* found on p. 424, is an ongoing performance assessment project to enrich students' learning throughout the unit.
- This project, which has students creating a booklet that shows what is great about their state, may be started now or at any time during this unit of study.
- A performance assessment scoring guide is located on p. 424.

The West

Unit Overview

The West has rich and varied landforms, climates, and resources. Native Americans have long lived in the West. The region also has attracted explorers, missionaries, fortune seekers, farmers, business people, and tourists.

Unit Outline

Chapter 12 *The Land of the West*
pp. 366–391

Chapter 13 *Living in the West*
pp. 392–419

Unit Question

- Have students read the question under the picture.
- To activate prior knowledge, ask what other natural resources and human resources students have read about in this textbook and how they affect life in different regions.
- On chart paper, have students brainstorm a list of preliminary answers to the unit question.

✓ Portfolio Assessment Keep this list to review with students at the end of the unit on p. 423.

Begin with a Primary Source

Objective

- Use primary sources to acquire information.

Resource

- Poster 11

Interpret a Primary Source

- Tell students that this primary source is a quotation from John Muir, a famous and influential naturalist and conservationist. Muir is often called the "Father of Our National Park System."
- The primary source is from Muir's book *Our National Parks.* The book brought Muir to the attention of President Theodore Roosevelt. Roosevelt and Muir worked together to help establish a number of important conservation programs.

✓**Portfolio Assessment** Remind students of the list of ideas they began on p. 359. As students read the unit, have them make changes to the class list. Review the list at the end of the unit on p. 423.

Interpret Art

- Tell students that Thomas Moran painted *The Grand Canyon of the Yellowstone* in 1872 after participating in a government-sponsored expedition to the Yellowstone area.
- Point out that the original painting measures a full 7 feet by 12 feet (about 2.1 m by 3.7 m). To help students understand the scale of the painting, have them compare it to a chalkboard or another classroom object of about the same size.
- Challenge students to find the small group of people depicted in the painting. Ask them why they think Moran included people in his painting of the canyon.

UNIT 6

Begin with a Primary Source

360

Practice and Extend

SOCIAL STUDIES
Background

About the Primary Source

- In *Our National Parks,* Muir describes in vivid details the natural beauty of the West. About Yellowstone, he says "the scenery is wild enough to awaken the dead."
- Through his books and articles, Muir was instrumental in the formation of Yosemite, Sequoia, Mount Rainier, Petrified Forest, and Grand Canyon National Parks.
- After recovering from a terrible eye injury, Muir dedicated his life to observing as much of nature as possible. He walked 1,000 miles from Indiana to Florida. He later traveled to many other places around the world.

"Climb the mountains. . . . Nature's peace will flow into you as sunshine flows into trees."

—John Muir, from *Our National Parks*, 1901

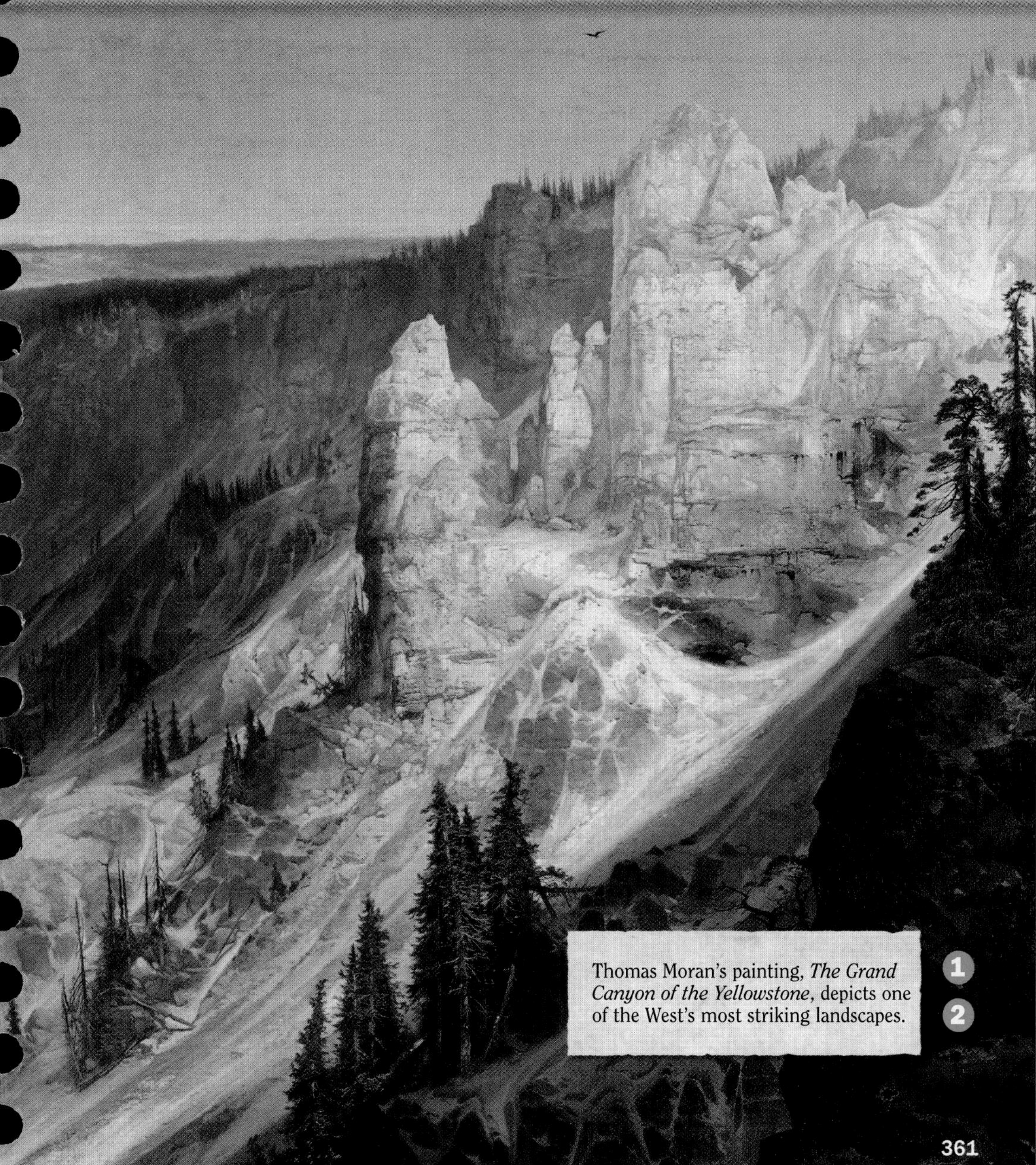

Thomas Moran's painting, *The Grand Canyon of the Yellowstone*, depicts one of the West's most striking landscapes. 1 2

361

Meet the Artist

- Tell students that Thomas Moran was born in England in 1837 and, as a child, moved to the United States with his family. He became a self-taught artist, never pursuing a formal education in painting.
- The turning point in Moran's career occurred in 1871, when he joined geologist Ferdinand V. Hayden on an expedition to Yellowstone. Hayden had been commissioned by the government to map and measure the region. Moran was invited, along with photographer William Henry Jackson, to document the area through pictures.
- Moran's journey was funded in part by the directors of the Northern Pacific Railroad. They believed that the artist's paintings of Yellowstone would attract crowds of tourists to the relatively unknown region.

1 **Why might paintings such as *The Grand Canyon of the Yellowstone* have encouraged early tourists to travel to Yellowstone and other parts of the West?** Possible answer: They portray the region as a beautiful and strikingly unusual wilderness. Draw Conclusions

2 **Why do you think Moran chose to create such a large painting of the Yellowstone canyon?** Possible answer: He was trying to convey the grand scale of the canyon walls, waterfall, and the landscape of the West itself. Draw Conclusions

SOCIAL STUDIES
Background

About the Painting

- Moran's watercolor sketches from the 1871 expedition became the first color images of Yellowstone ever seen in the East. They played a major role in persuading Congress to preserve Yellowstone as a national park.
- Moran later used these rough sketches to create detailed landscape paintings such as the one shown here.
- *The Grand Canyon of the Yellowstone* became the first American landscape painted by an American artist ever purchased by the U.S. government. Moran was paid $10,000, and the painting was displayed in the U.S. Capitol.

WEB SITE
Technology

Students can learn more about John Muir online by selecting the encyclopedia from the *Social Studies Library* at **www.sfsocialstudies.com.**

UNIT 6

Welcome to the West

Objective

- Identify the physical characteristics of the West.

Resource

- Poster 12

Research the Region

Each of the states featured on these pages is an important part of the West. Have students use online or library resources to research the answers to the following questions.

- **Which western state has more glaciers than the other 47 contiguous states combined?** Washington
- **The highest and lowest points in the continental United States are both located in California. What are these two points?** Highest: Mount Whitney; Lowest: Bad Water in Death Valley
- **About one-third of which state lies in the Arctic Circle?** Alaska
- **What is the deepest lake in the United States? In what state is it located?** Crater Lake; Oregon
- **Which western state leads the country in coal production? in oil production?** Wyoming; Alaska

Students may wish to write their own questions about these places for the rest of the class to answer.

UNIT 6

Welcome to the West

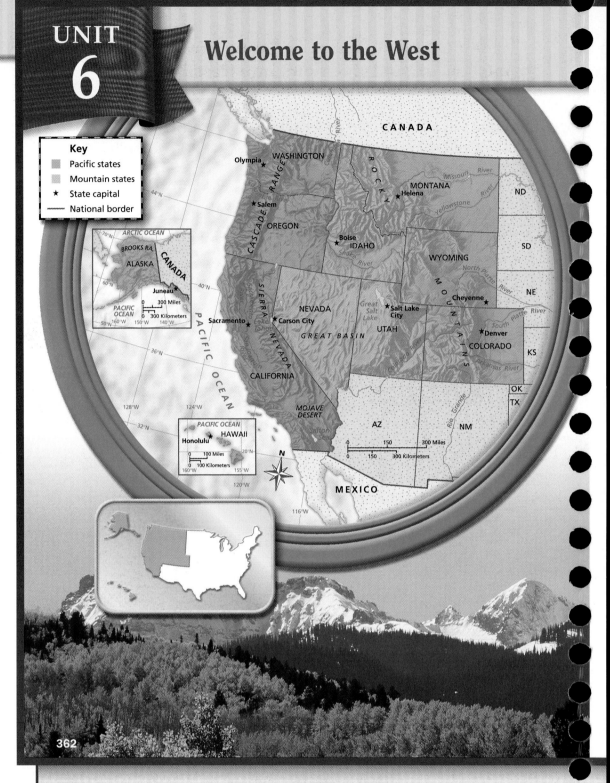

Key
- Pacific states
- Mountain states
- ★ State capital
- —— National border

362

Practice and Extend

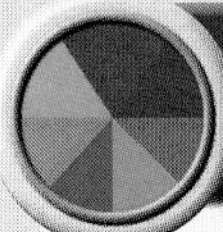

CURRICULUM CONNECTION
Literature

Read About the West

Use the following books to extend the content.

Giant Sequoia Trees, by Ginger Wadsworth (Lerner Publications Company, ISBN 0-8225-3001-5, 1995) **Easy**

The American West, Brian Williams, ed. (World Book, Inc., ISBN 0-7166-1805-2, 1997) **On-Level**

The Hoover Dam: The Story of Hard Times, Tough People and the Taming of a Wild River, by Elizabeth Mann (Mikaya Press, ISBN 1-931414-02-5, 2003) **Challenge**

▶ Sea otters live in the Pacific Ocean off the Northwest coast of the United States. Sea otters eat and sleep while floating on their backs.

1 ▶ Most of the pineapples that are grown in the United States are grown in Hawaii.

2 ▶ The Hoover Dam was built on the Colorado River on the border of Nevada and Arizona. Workers used more than 5 million barrels of concrete to build the dam.

3 ▶ The Golden Gate bridge links San Francisco to Marin County, California. At 8,981 feet long, it is one of the longest suspension bridges in the world.

4 ▶ The Rocky Mountains are the largest system of mountain ranges in North America. In the United States, the Rockies stretch across New Mexico, Colorado, Utah, Wyoming, Idaho, Montana, Washington, and Alaska.

▶ This redwood tree grows in California. Redwoods are the tallest trees in the United States. They can grow to a height of 350 feet and can live to be 2,000 years old.

WEB SITE
Technology

Students can learn more about places in this unit by clicking on *Atlas* at **www.sfsocialstudies.com.**

Discuss the Region

Have students use the photos and captions to answer the following questions.

1 **Name one valuable crop grown in Hawaii.** Possible answer: Pineapple **Summarize**

2 **Which river is home to the Hoover Dam?** Colorado River **Main Idea and Details**

3 **What two locations are linked by the Golden Gate Bridge?** San Francisco and Marin County, California **Main Idea and Details**

4 **The Rocky Mountains stretch across the West and into the Southwest. Which of the eight states named in the text is located in the Southwest region?** New Mexico **Analyze Information**

Read About the States

The states shown here are discussed in the text on the following pages in Unit 6.

- Colorado, pp. 368–369, 379, 382, 386, 403, 405
- Montana, pp. 369–370, 379, 386, 404–405
- Wyoming, pp. 369–371, 379, 381, 386, 404–405
- Alaska, pp. 369, 372, 378–379, 385–386, 394–398, 401, 405
- Idaho, pp. 369–370, 379–380, 385–386, 405
- Utah, pp. 369, 380–381, 386, 404–405, 412–413
- Hawaii, pp. 372–373, 375, 380, 382, 385–386, 405–406, 414
- Washington, pp. 372, 374–375, 379–380, 382, 385–386, 401, 405, 412–414
- California, pp. 372, 380, 382, 385–386, 400–405, 407, 410–411, 413–414, 416–417
- Nevada, pp. 372, 380, 386, 403–405
- Oregon, pp. 372, 380, 385, 389, 401, 405

UNIT 6

Reading Social Studies

Compare and Contrast

Objective

Analyze printed information by comparing and contrasting.

Resource

- Workbook, p. 84

About the Unit Target Skill

- The target reading skill for this unit is Compare and Contrast.
- Students are introduced to the unit target skill here and are given an opportunity to practice it.
- Further opportunities to compare and contrast are found throughout Unit 6.

1 Introduce and Motivate

Preview To activate prior knowledge, ask students for examples of comparing and contrasting that they have read in previous units of this textbook. (Example: In Unit 5, students compared and contrasted the climates and vegetation in different regions of the world.)

UNIT 6

The West

Compare and Contrast

Features that are alike

Features that are different

To **compare** is to tell how two or more things are alike. To **contrast** is to tell how two or more things are different.

- Clue words such as *similar* and *as,* show comparisons.
- Clue words such as *different* and *but* show contrasts.
- Sometimes authors do not use clue words. Readers must make comparisons for themselves.

Read the paragraph. The sentences that **compare** and **contrast** have been highlighted.

Hawaii and southern California are alike in some ways, but are different in other ways. Both are warm and sunny much of the time. However, Hawaii has some areas that receive a great deal of rain. Unlike those places, southern California has desert areas that are very dry.

Word Exercise

Using Antonyms to Build Context An **antonym** is a word that means the opposite of another word. Learning both a word and its antonym can help you understand the word. You may be confused to read, "These volcanic mountains are also old, but many are still active." In this case, *active* means "acting or working"—active volcanoes erupt regularly. An antonym of *active* is *dormant*. *Dormant* means "asleep." A dormant volcano has not erupted in a very long time.

364

Practice and Extend

ACTIVATE PRIOR KNOWLEDGE

ESL Support

Demonstrate Comparing and Contrasting Have students compare and contrast other communities with their current community.

Beginning Using gestures and pictures as appropriate, ask students questions comparing and contrasting other communities with their current community. For example, ask, "Is (community name) bigger, smaller, or about the same size as this community? Are the sizes of the two communities similar or different?"

Intermediate Have students use a similarities and differences chart to identify two similarities and two differences between their community and another community. Then have pairs of students share their ideas with one another.

Advanced Have students make a Venn diagram comparing and contrasting one other community with their community. Then have students present their diagram to the class.

Not All Mountains Are the Same

There are a number of mountain ranges in the West. Two of these ranges are the Rocky Mountains and the Cascade Range. The Rocky Mountains extend more than 3,000 miles through the United States and Canada, but the Cascade Mountains cover a smaller distance, 700 miles, from northern California to British Columbia in Canada.

Most of the Rocky Mountains' peaks were formed millions of years ago during a huge shift in the Earth's crust. Over time, this shift created the mountains. Unlike most of the Rocky Mountains, many of the mountains in the Cascade Range are volcanoes. These volcanic mountains are also old, but many are still active. Mount St. Helens, one of the Cascade's most famous volcanoes, erupted in 1980.

Rainfall is heavy in the Cascade Range. Some parts get more than 100 inches of rainfall each year! The range takes its name from the cascades, or waterfalls, that can be seen in the area. Visitors to the Cascades, like those who go to the Rocky Mountains, can enjoy many different activities, including hiking and camping.

Use the reading strategy of comparing and contrasting to answer questions 1 and 2. Then answer the vocabulary question.

1. In what ways are the Cascade Range and the Rocky Mountains alike? Give examples from the passage that support your answer.
2. How do the two ranges of mountains differ from one another? What clue words are used in the passage to show contrast?
3. Look at the sentence that reads, "Over time, this shift created the mountains." What word is an antonym for *created*? How does the meaning of the sentence change if you replace *created* with this word?

Standardized Test Prep

- Use Workbook p. 84 to give students practice with standardized test format.
- Chapter and Unit Tests in the Assessment Book use standardized test format.
- Test-taking tips are contained in the front portion of the Assessment Book Teacher's Edition.

Also on Teacher Resources CD-ROM.

Workbook, p. 84

Compare and Contrast — Use with Pages 364–365.

Comparisons and contrasts often are used to tell how two or more things are alike and different.

Directions: Read the passage and use the reading strategy of compare and contrast to answer the questions below. Fill in the circle next to the correct answer.

There are many national parks in the United States. Two of them are Yellowstone National Park and Yosemite National Park. Yellowstone covers more than 2.2 million acres in parts of Idaho, Wyoming, and Montana. Yosemite covers more than 760,000 acres in an area of California called the Sierra Nevada.

Yellowstone and Yosemite are both known for their waterfalls, meadows, and forests. The forests of Yosemite also include hundreds of giant sequoias, the world's largest living trees. Yellowstone has thousands of hot springs and geysers. A famous geyser, Old Faithful, is one of Yellowstone's biggest attractions.

Yosemite is famous for El Capitan, the largest single rock on earth. Rock climbers travel from all over the world to try to climb it. El Capitan was left standing when glaciers swept through the land long ago. In fact, much of both parks was formed when glaciers carved through sections of rock and covered the land. When the glaciers melted, the water formed lakes and valleys throughout the land.

1. How does Yosemite differ from Yellowstone?
   Ⓐ Yosemite has waterfalls, forests, and meadows.
   Ⓑ The forests of Yosemite include sequoias.
   Ⓒ Much of Yosemite was formed by glaciers.
   Ⓓ Yosemite has thousands of hot springs and geysers.
2. In what ways are the two parks alike?
   Ⓐ Both parks cover more than 2.2 million acres of land.
   Ⓑ Rock climbers travel from all over the world to try to climb El Capitan.
   Ⓒ Both parks have thousands of hot springs and geysers.
   Ⓓ Much of both parks was formed by glaciers.

Notes for Home: Your child learned how to compare and contrast printed information.
Home Activity: Help your child compare and contrast weekday activities and weekend activities. How do your child's weekdays compare and contrast with weekends?

2 Teach and Discuss

- Draw students' attention to the bulleted points on p. 364. Point out that we compare and contrast things all the time, including places, foods, books, and other everyday things.
- Have students read the sample paragraph on p. 364. Confirm that they can recognize the similarity identified in the second sentence and the differences identified in the third and fourth sentences. Emphasize the clue word in each sentence.
- Then have students read the longer practice sample on p. 365 and answer the questions that follow. Be sure students support their answers with examples from the text.
- Ask students why, when studying geography, it is important to be able to compare and contrast. (It is both helpful and interesting to know how regions—or areas within one region—are similar and different.)

Antonyms

Be sure students understand that some words have multiple meanings, and that an antonym should match the meaning of the word in a particular context. A good antonym for *created* in this case is *destroyed*. Discuss the fact that mountains can be both made and broken back down.

3 Close and Assess

Apply it!

1. Both are in the West. Both are partly in the United States and partly in Canada. Visitors to both can enjoy a variety of activities.
2. The Rocky Mountains are longer than the Cascades. The Rockies were formed during a shift in Earth's crust. Many mountains in the Cascade Range are volcanoes. *Unlike* is a clue word.
3. *Destroyed;* It makes the sentence mean the opposite of what it does now.

CHAPTER 12

Chapter Planning Guide

Chapter 12 • The Land of the West

Locating Places pp. 366–367

Lesson Titles	Pacing	Main Ideas
Lesson 1 **A Land of Mountains** pp. 368–373 DK **When a Mountain Explodes** pp. 374–375 **Research and Writing Skills: Take Notes and Write Outlines** pp. 376–377	4 days	• Many parts of the West are mountainous. • In a volcanic eruption, hot magma from inside Earth moves to Earth's surface. • Notes and outlines help organize information.
Lesson 2 **Climates in the West** pp. 378–383	2 days	• The climate in different areas of the West varies greatly.
Lesson 3 **Resources of the West** pp. 384–388 **Biography: Seth Lewelling** p. 389	3 days	• The West is rich in natural resources. • Seth Lewelling and Ah Bing developed the Bing cherry.
✓ **Chapter 12 Review** pp. 390–391		

The varied climates of the West allow farmers to grow a variety of valuable crops, such as these apples from Washington state.

✓ = Assessment Options

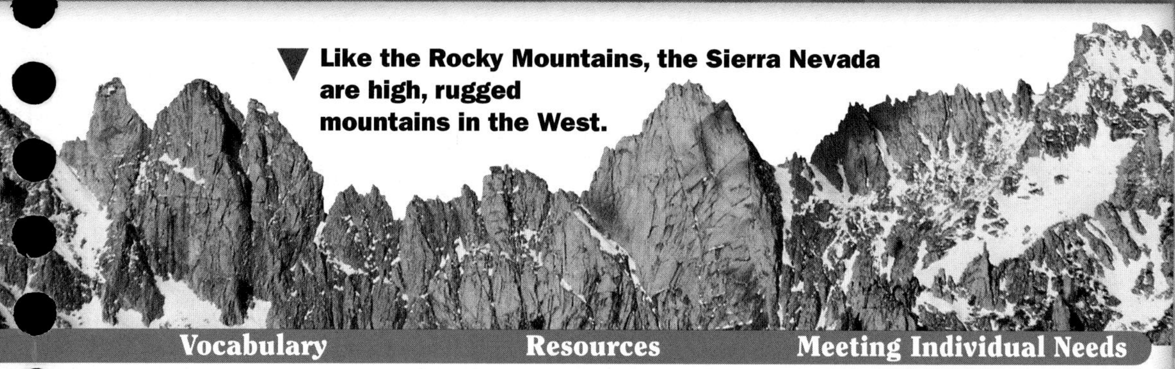
Like the Rocky Mountains, the Sierra Nevada are high, rugged mountains in the West.

Vocabulary	Resources	Meeting Individual Needs
timberline geyser magma volcano lava	• Workbook, p. 86 • Transparencies 14, 57 • Every Student Learns Guide, pp. 150–153 • Quick Study, pp. 76–77	• ESL Support, TE p. 370 • Leveled Practice, TE p. 372
notes outline	• Workbook, p. 87	• Leveled Practice. TE p. 377
tundra frigid rain shadow	• Workbook, p. 88 • Transparencies 14, 58, 59 • Every Student Learns Guide, pp. 154–157 • Quick Study, pp. 78–79	• ESL Support, TE p. 379 • Leveled Practice, TE p. 381
greenhouse livestock reforest	• Workbook, p. 89 • Transparencies 6, 60 • Every Student Learns Guide, pp. 158–161 • Quick Study, pp. 80–81	• ESL Support, TE p. 385 • Leveled Practice, TE p. 386 • Learning Styles, TE p. 387
	✓Chapter 12 Content Test, Assessment Book, pp. 65–66 ✓Chapter 12 Skills Test, Assessment Book, pp. 67–68	✓Chapter 12 Performance Assessment, TE p. 390

Providing More Depth

Additional Resources

- Vocabulary Workbook and Cards
- Social Studies Plus! pp. 128–133
- Daily Activity Bank
- Big Book Atlas
- Student Atlas
- Outline Maps
- Desk Maps

Technology

- AudioText
- MindPoint® Quiz Show CD-ROM
- ExamView® Test Bank CD-ROM
- Teacher Resources CD-ROM
- Map Resources CD-ROM
- SFSuccessNet: iText (Pupil Edition online), iTE (Teacher's Edition online), Online Planner
- **www.sfsocialstudies.com** (Biographies, news, references, maps, and activities)

To establish guidelines for your students' safe and responsible use of the Internet, use the Scott Foresman Internet Guide.

Additional Internet Links

To find out more about:

- Continental Divide Trail, visit **www.cdtrail.org**
- Yellowstone National Park, visit **www.nps.gov**
- Alaska, visit **www.state.ak.us**

Key Internet Search Terms

- Mt. McKinley
- Death Valley
- Mount Waialeale

Workbook Support

Use the following Workbook pages to support content and skills development as you teach Chapter 12. You can also view and print Workbook pages from the Teacher Resources CD-ROM.

Workbook, p. 84

Use with Pages 364–365.

Compare and Contrast

Comparisons and contrasts often are used to tell how two or more things are alike and different.

Directions: Read the passage and use the reading strategy of compare and contrast to answer the questions below. Fill in the circle next to the correct answer.

There are many national parks in the United States. Two of them are Yellowstone National Park and Yosemite National Park. Yellowstone covers more than 2.2 million acres in parts of Idaho, Wyoming, and Montana. Yosemite covers more than 760,000 acres in an area of California called the Sierra Nevada.

Yellowstone and Yosemite are both known for their waterfalls, meadows, and forests. The forests of Yosemite also include hundreds of giant sequoias, the world's largest living trees. Yellowstone has thousands of hot springs and geysers. A famous geyser, Old Faithful, is one of Yellowstone's biggest attractions.

Yosemite is famous for El Capitan, the largest single rock on earth. Rock climbers travel from all over the world to try to climb it. El Capitan was left standing when glaciers swept through the land long ago. In fact, much of both parks was formed when glaciers carved through sections of rock and covered the land. When the glaciers melted, the water formed lakes and valleys throughout the land.

1. How does Yosemite differ from Yellowstone?
   - Ⓐ Yosemite has waterfalls, forests, and meadows.
   - ● The forests of Yosemite include sequoias.
   - Ⓒ Much of Yosemite was formed by glaciers.
   - Ⓓ Yosemite has thousands of hot springs and geysers.
2. In what ways are the two parks alike?
   - Ⓐ Both parks cover more than 2.2 million acres of land.
   - Ⓑ Rock climbers travel from all over the world to try to climb El Capitan.
   - Ⓒ Both parks have thousands of hot springs and geysers.
   - ● Much of both parks was formed by glaciers.

Notes for Home: Your child learned how to compare and contrast printed information.
Home Activity: Help your child compare and contrast weekday activities and weekend activities. How do your child's weekdays compare and contrast with weekends?

Use with Pupil Edition, p. 364

Workbook, p. 85

Use with Chapter 12.

Vocabulary Preview

Directions: Match each vocabulary term in the box to its meaning. Write the vocabulary term on the line provided. You may use your glossary.

timber line	lava	rain shadow
geyser	tundra	greenhouse
magma	frigid	livestock
volcano		reforest

1. **livestock** animals that are raised on farms and ranches
2. **lava** form of molten rock that rises and flows on Earth's surface
3. **geyser** type of hot spring that erupts, shooting hot water into the air
4. **tundra** cold, flat area where trees cannot grow
5. **volcano** mountain with an opening through which ash, gas, and lava are forced
6. **timber line** place on a mountain above which no trees can grow
7. **greenhouse** enclosed structure that allows light to enter and keeps heat and moisture from escaping
8. **frigid** very cold
9. **reforest** process of planting new trees to replace those that have been cut
10. **rain shadow** condition of dryness that occurs on the eastern side of high coastal mountains
11. **magma** large mass of molten rock within the ground that provides heat for geysers and hot springs

Notes for Home: Your child learned the vocabulary terms for Chapter 12.
Home Activity: With your child, make flash cards of the vocabulary terms. Have your child illustrate the term on one side of the card and write the term on the other side. As you show your child each picture, have him or her identify and define the corresponding term.

Use with Pupil Edition, p. 366

Workbook, p. 86

Use with Pages 368–373.

Lesson 1: A Land of Mountains

Many people visit the Rocky Mountains and Yellowstone National Park to see their beauty and landscape.

Directions: Complete the chart with information from this lesson. Then answer the questions that follow. You may use your textbook.

	Rocky Mountains	Yellowstone National Park
What Is It?	Largest system of mountains in North America	Oldest national park in the world
Where Is It Located?	From New Mexico north through Canada and into Alaska	Northwest corner of Wyoming and parts of Idaho and Montana
What Is Its Size?	350 miles wide in some places and more than 3,000 miles in length	More than 2.2 million acres
What Are Its Features?	Mountains with forests, valleys, and wildlife; rivers on east and west	Mountains, canyons, forests, waterfalls, lakes, and wildlife
What Are Its Attractions?	Pikes Peak; sports such as skiing, mountain climbing, and hiking	Natural attractions; hot springs and geysers; Old Faithful.

1. What are some of the animals that live in the mountains? In which areas of the mountains do they live?

   Mountain goats and bighorn sheep live above the timber line; bears, mountain lions, elk, and mink live in the forests; chipmunks, coyotes, moose, and many types of fish live in the valleys and streams.

2. What are some other mountain ranges located in the western United States?

   Possible answers: Sierra Nevada, Olympic Mountains, Cascade Range, and Aleutian Range

Notes for Home: Your child learned about mountain ranges and national parks located in the West region of the United States.
Home Activity: With your child, find out more about the Rocky Mountains or Yellowstone National Park. Use information from the lesson to help you make a list of things to do and sights to see there.

Use with Pupil Edition, p. 373

Workbook Support

Workbook, p. 87

Use with Pages 376–377.

Take Notes and Write Outlines

Taking notes can help you remember what you have read. Notes are bits of information you write in your own words. An outline is a way of organizing important information.

Directions: Read the paragraph below and take notes by writing important facts and details on the note card. Then use your notes to complete the outline.

Glacier

A glacier is a moving mass of ice that can survive for many years. Glaciers are formed in regions of high snowfall and freezing temperatures. With each new snowstorm, layers of snow build. The snow becomes compacted under the weight of each new layer. The layers slowly grow together to form a thickened mass of ice. As the ice gets thicker, it begins to move. The great weight of glacier ice causes it to flow down mountains, through valleys, across plains, and spread into the sea. Glaciers transform and reshape the landscape.

Note Card

Glacier

- **Moving mass of ice**
- **Regions of snowfall and freezing temperatures**
- **Layers of snow grow together and move**
- **Weight causes it to flow into valleys, plains, and seas**

Outline

Glacier

I. What is a glacier?
- A. **moving mass of ice**
- B. can survive for many years

II. How is a glacier formed?
- A. layers of snow build
- B. **snow becomes compacted under weight of layers**
- C. layers grow together to form mass of ice

III. What happens to a glacier?
- A. ice thickens and begins to move
- B. **flows into valleys, plains, and seas and transforms landscape**

Notes for Home: Your child learned how to take notes and make an outline.
Home Activity: With your child, take notes on a newspaper or magazine article of your choice. Then organize your notes in an outline. How are your notes and outline alike and different?

Use with Pupil Edition, p. 377

Workbook, p. 88

Use with Pages 378–383.

Lesson 2: Climates in the West

Directions: Read the following statements. Then write *T* (True) or *F* (False) on the line before each statement. If the answer is false, correct the underlined term or terms to make the statement true. You may use your textbook.

F 1. Of all the areas in the United States, parts of Hawaii have some of the coldest temperatures.
Alaska

F 2. At 20,320 feet, Death Valley is the highest peak in North America.
Mount McKinley

T 3. Some parts of California and Hawaii very rarely have temperatures that drop below freezing.

F 4. California is such a large state that it has the same climate in its different areas.
a variety of climates

F 5. Plants in the Great Basin need large amounts of water to survive.
small

T 6. Many areas in the West are made up of tundra, tropics, or deserts.

F 7. Rainier Paradise Ranger Station in Washington receives fewer than two inches of rain each year.
Death Valley, California

F 8. Mount McKinley is the wettest place on Earth, with an average annual rainfall on the mountain of 460 inches.
Mount Waialeale

T 9. The reason for differences in precipitation between western and eastern sides of the Cascade Mountains is an effect called the rain shadow.

Notes for Home: Your child learned about variations in the climates of the West.
Home Activity: With your child, compare and contrast the climate in which you live with the different climates in the West. Which climate in the West is most similar to the region in which you live?

Use with Pupil Edition, p. 383

Workbook, p. 89

Use with Pages 384–388.

Lesson 3: Resources of the West

Directions: The first column of the chart below lists products that are produced in the West. Complete the second column of the chart by writing the state of the West that matches each description. You may use your textbook.

Agricultural Products	States
Producer of the widest variety of fruits, vegetables, and nuts	**California**
Grows barley, oats, hay, and potatoes in a harsh climate	**Alaska**
Biggest producer of potatoes in U.S.	**Idaho**
Produces sugarcane, pineapples, macadamia nuts, and coffee in a tropical climate	**Hawaii**
Famous for its apples but also grows cherries, pears, and potatoes	**Washington**
More than 880 million dollars a year made in catching cod, flounder, salmon, crab, and shrimp	**Alaska**
Swordfish and tuna caught off the coast of the islands	**Hawaii**

Notes for Home: Your child learned about food and other products provided by the West.
Home Activity: With your child, discuss how different states in the West are able to produce the resources for which they are known. How do climate and location affect what they are able to produce?

Use with Pupil Edition, p. 388

Workbook, p. 90

Use with Chapter 12.

Vocabulary Review

Directions: Circle the vocabulary term that best completes each sentence. You may use your textbook.

1. Because the climate in most of Alaska is harsh, plants grown there often are grown in a (rain shadow, **greenhouse**).
2. A (glacier, **tundra**) is a cold, flat land area where trees cannot grow, and where some people enjoy cross-country skiing.
3. Areas east of the Cascade Mountains receive much less rain than other areas of the mountain because of an effect called the (**rain shadow**, timber line).
4. A large mass of molten rock, or (lava, **magma**), still lies beneath the surface of Yellowstone and provides heat for the park's geysers and hot springs.
5. Old Faithful, the most famous (greenhouse, **geyser**) at Yellowstone, erupts about every 45 to 110 minutes, sending a stream of boiling water into the air.
6. Because wood is an important part of our daily lives, timber companies usually (**reforest**, tundra) areas where they have cut the trees.
7. Cattle, sheep, and pigs are examples of (timber line, **livestock**), or animals that are raised on farms and ranches.
8. No trees can grow above the (volcano, **timber line**) of a mountain because temperatures are too cold.
9. When a volcano erupts, a form of molten rock called (**lava**, magma) comes out of the opening.
10. States such as Washington and Montana are accustomed to very cold, or (glacier, **frigid**), winter temperatures and heavy snowfall.
11. A (**volcano**, geyser) is a type of mountain that has an opening through which ash, gas, and lava are forced.

Notes for Home: Your child learned the vocabulary terms for Chapter 12.
Home Activity: Create a crossword puzzle of the vocabulary terms in this chapter, using the definitions as clues for each term. Have your child complete the puzzle.

Use with Pupil Edition, p. 391

Assessment Support

Use the following Assessment Book pages and TestWorks to assess content and skills in Chapter 12. You can also view and print Assessment Book pages from the Teacher Resources CD-ROM.

Assessment Book, p. 65

Chapter 12 Test

Part 1: Content Test

Directions: Fill in the circle next to the correct answer.

Lesson Objective (1:1)

1. Which of the following describes the Rocky Mountains?
- Ⓐ system of mountains with very little wildlife and few trees
- Ⓑ small chain of mountains located in the eastern United States
- ● largest system of mountains in the United States
- Ⓓ old, low mountains located in a desert region

Lesson Objective (1:4)

2. How are volcanoes similar to geysers?
- Ⓐ They are caused by heated groundwater that rises to the surface.
- Ⓑ Both can be seen at Yellowstone.
- ● Both are heated by magma and erupt.
- Ⓓ They erupt every 45 to 110 minutes.

Lesson Objective (1:2)

3. How are the Rockies like some of the other mountain ranges in the United States?
- Ⓐ They are 350 miles wide and run over 3,000 miles in length.
- Ⓑ They have a peak in the east called Pikes Peak.
- Ⓒ They share the Continental Divide.
- ● They have high, rugged mountains with many peaks.

Lesson Objective (1:3)

4. Which is NOT a mountain range that is located in the West?
- Ⓐ Cascade Range
- Ⓑ Sierra Nevada
- Ⓒ Olympic Mountains
- ● Appalachian Mountains

Lesson Objective (1:5)

5. Which of the following mountain ranges does NOT have a volcano?
- ● Sierra Nevada
- Ⓑ Cascade Range
- Ⓒ Aleutian Range
- Ⓓ Mount Kilauea

Lesson Objective (2:2, 3)

6. Which western state has very cold winter temperatures?
- ● Alaska
- Ⓑ California
- Ⓒ Hawaii
- Ⓓ Nevada

Lesson Objective (2:1)

7. How is the climate of Hawaii similar to the climate of California?
- Ⓐ It rains less in Hawaii than in California.
- Ⓑ It is colder in Hawaii and California than in most states.
- Ⓒ Hawaii and California have frigid winter temperatures.
- ● Temperatures in parts of California and Hawaii rarely drop below freezing.

Lesson Objective (2:2)

8. Which of the following describes the climate in the Great Basin?
- Ⓐ hot, sunny, and rainy
- Ⓑ cold, cloudy, and snowy
- Ⓒ hot, sunny, and dry
- ● mild, cloudy, and rainy

Use with Pupil Edition, p. 390

Assessment Book, p. 66

Lesson Objective (2:3)

9. In which state is the wettest place on Earth located?
- ● Hawaii
- Ⓑ Oregon
- Ⓒ Alaska
- Ⓓ Utah

Lesson Objective (2:4, 5)

10. Which side of the Cascade Range receives more rain as a result of the rain shadow?
- Ⓐ eastern
- Ⓑ northern
- Ⓒ southern
- ● western

Lesson Objective (3:2)

11. Which state of the West produces the widest variety of fruits, vegetables, and nuts?
- ● California
- Ⓑ Colorado
- Ⓒ Wyoming
- Ⓓ Alaska

Lesson Objective (3:1, 2)

12. Which western state is the biggest producer of potatoes in the United States?
- ● Idaho
- Ⓑ Washington
- Ⓒ Colorado
- Ⓓ New Mexico

Lesson Objective (3:3)

13. Which of these western states includes fish as a major source of income?
- Ⓐ Idaho
- Ⓑ Montana
- ● Hawaii
- Ⓓ Nevada

Lesson Objective (3:3)

14. How are Alaska and Hawaii alike?
- Ⓐ They both mainly grow plants in greenhouses.
- Ⓑ They both have cold, snowy climates.
- ● They both have major fishing industries.
- Ⓓ They are both producers of tropical flowers.

Lesson Objective (3:4)

15. Which is a product provided by the timber industry from which people benefit?
- Ⓐ wheat
- Ⓑ flounder
- Ⓒ potatoes
- ● paper

Use with Pupil Edition, p. 390

Assessment Support

Assessment Book, p. 67

Part 2: Skills Test

Directions: Use complete sentences to answer questions 1–5. Use a separate sheet of paper if you need more space.

1. How are rivers on the east side of the Continental Divide different from those on the west side? **Compare and Contrast**

   Rivers on the east side of the Continental Divide flow toward the east into the Atlantic Ocean or the Gulf of Mexico. Those on the west side flow west toward the Pacific Ocean.

2. What is the timber line, and how does it affect where animals live? **Cause and Effect**

   The timber line is the place above which no trees can grow because temperatures are too cold. Much of this area is covered with snow year-round. Some animals cannot live above the timber line because there is not enough food, and it is too cold for them.

3. Why might the climate of Montana attract some visitors and not others? **Draw Conclusions**

   The climate of Montana is frigid in the winter with heavy snowfall. People who participate in winter sports may enjoy visiting there. Others who do not enjoy cold weather might not visit Montana.

Use with Pupil Edition, p. 390

Assessment Book, p. 68

4. Which three details might you include in a summary about agricultural products from California? **Summarize**

   Possible answer: Many farms are located in California's Central Valley. California produces many types of fruit, such as grapes and strawberries. California also produces a variety of vegetables and nuts.

5. List three products created, grown, or raised in the West in each of these categories: **Vegetables, Fruit, Livestock, Fish, Timber. Categorize**

   Possible answers: Vegetables: broccoli, potatoes, sugarbeets; Fruit: apples, grapes, strawberries; Livestock: cattle (beef), sheep, pigs (pork); Fish: salmon, swordfish, tuna, cod; Timber: houses, furniture, paper

Use with Pupil Edition, p. 390

CHAPTER 12

The Land of the West

Chapter 12 Outline

- **Lesson 1, *A Land of Mountains,*** pp. 368–373
- DK ***When a Mountain Explodes,*** pp. 374–375
- **Research and Writing Skills: *Take Notes and Write Outlines,*** pp. 376–377
- **Lesson 2, *Climates in the West,*** pp. 378–383
- **Lesson 3, *Resources of the West,*** pp. 384–388
- **Biography: *Seth Lewelling,*** p. 389

Resources

- Workbook, p. 85: Vocabulary Preview
- Vocabulary Cards
- Social Studies Plus!

The Rocky Mountains: Lesson 1

This picture shows some of the beautiful scenery found in the Rocky Mountains. Ask students why they think people like to vacation in the Rockies. (Possible answers: The scenery is beautiful; there are many places to camp, explore, hike, and fish.)

The Great Basin: Lesson 2

The Great Basin gets very hot on summer days. How do you think this affects vegetation in the area? (Possible answer: Few plants can grow there.)

California's Central Valley: Lesson 3

Ask students to compare the climate of California's Central Valley with that of Barrow, Alaska. (The climate of the Central Valley is warmer.)

CHAPTER 12

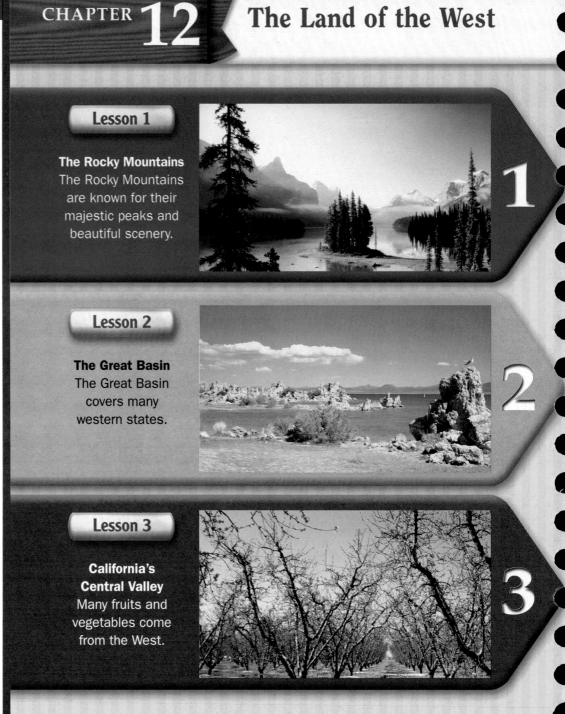

The Land of the West

Lesson 1

The Rocky Mountains
The Rocky Mountains are known for their majestic peaks and beautiful scenery.

1

Lesson 2

The Great Basin
The Great Basin covers many western states.

2

Lesson 3

California's Central Valley
Many fruits and vegetables come from the West.

3

366

Practice and Extend

Vocabulary Preview

- Use Workbook p. 85 to help students preview the vocabulary words in this chapter.
- Use Vocabulary Cards to preview key concept words in this chapter.

Also on Teacher Resources CD-ROM.

Workbook, p. 85

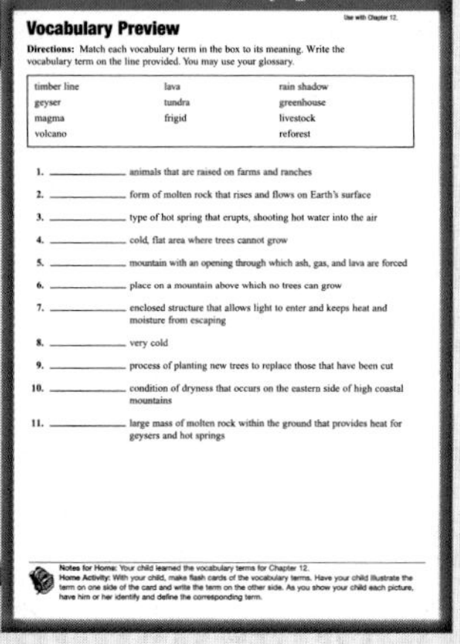

Vocabulary Preview

Use with Chapter 12.

Directions: Match each vocabulary term in the box to its meaning. Write the vocabulary term on the line provided. You may use your glossary.

timber line	lava	rain shadow
geyser	tundra	greenhouse
magma	frigid	livestock
volcano		reforest

1. ______ animals that are raised on farms and ranches
2. ______ form of molten rock that rises and flows on Earth's surface
3. ______ type of hot spring that erupts, shooting hot water into the air
4. ______ cold, flat area where trees cannot grow
5. ______ mountain with an opening through which ash, gas, and lava are forced
6. ______ place on a mountain above which no trees can grow
7. ______ enclosed structure that allows light to enter and keeps heat and moisture from escaping
8. ______ very cold
9. ______ process of planting new trees to replace those that have been cut
10. ______ condition of dryness that occurs on the eastern side of high coastal mountains
11. ______ large mass of molten rock within the ground that provides heat for geysers and hot springs

Notes for Home: Your child learned the vocabulary terms for Chapter 12.
Home Activity: With your child, make flash cards of the vocabulary terms. Have your child illustrate the term on one side of the card and write the term on the other side. As you show your child each picture, have him or her identify and define the corresponding term.

Locating Places

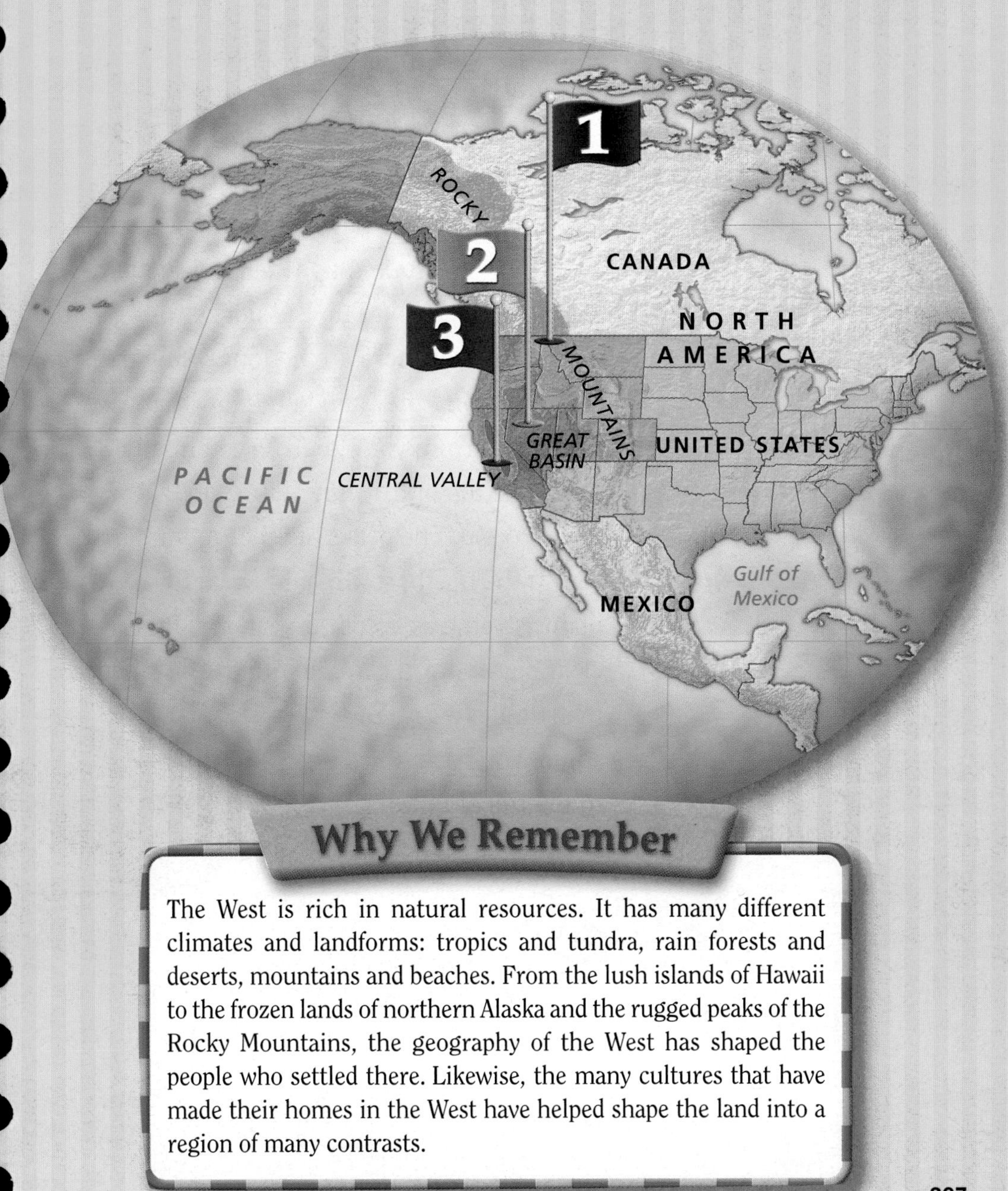

Why We Remember

The West is rich in natural resources. It has many different climates and landforms: tropics and tundra, rain forests and deserts, mountains and beaches. From the lush islands of Hawaii to the frozen lands of northern Alaska and the rugged peaks of the Rocky Mountains, the geography of the West has shaped the people who settled there. Likewise, the many cultures that have made their homes in the West have helped shape the land into a region of many contrasts.

367

WEB SITE
Technology

You can learn more about the Rocky Mountains, the Great Basin, and California's Central Valley by clicking on *Atlas* at **www.sfsocialstudies.com.**

SOCIAL STUDIES STRAND
Geography

Mental Mapping On an outline map of the United States, have students color in the states that they think make up the West Region. Students may label any cities or landforms of the West that they know of. Discuss students' knowledge and/or impressions of the West.

Locating Places

- Have students examine the pictures shown on p. 366 for Lessons 1, 2, and 3.
- Remind students that each picture is coded with both a number and a color to link it to a place on the map on p. 367.

Why We Remember

Have students read the "Why We Remember" paragraph on p. 367 and ask what overall impression the paragraph gives them about the West. (Possible answer: Its resources, climate, landforms, people, and cultures are varied.)

A Land of Mountains

Objectives

- Identify the largest system of mountains in the United States.
- Compare and contrast mountain ranges of the West.
- Identify mountain ranges in the West and tell where they are located.
- Compare geysers to volcanoes.

Vocabulary

timberline, p. 369; **geyser,** p. 370; **magma,** p. 370; **volcano,** p. 372; **lava,** p. 372

Resources

- Workbook, p. 86
- Transparency 14
- Every Student Learns Guide, pp. 150–153
- Quick Study, pp. 76–77

Quick Teaching Plan

If time is short, have students work in groups of three to review key ideas.

- Ask students to read the lesson independently. Have them write one question from each section on the front of an index card and write the answer on the back.
- Have groups ask and answer the questions, discussing any questions that they answer incorrectly.

1 Introduce and Motivate

Preview To activate prior knowledge, ask volunteers to explain how traveling in the mountains is different from traveling on flat ground. If no one has traveled in the mountains, ask students how they think it would differ from traveling around their hometown. Tell students that they will learn more about the mountains of the West as they read Lesson 1.

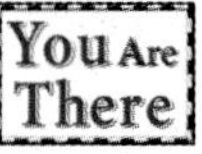

Discuss with students why people might work hard to climb to the summit of a mountain.

LESSON 1

PREVIEW

Focus on the Main Idea
Many parts of the West are mountainous.

PLACES
Rocky Mountains
Continental Divide
Yellowstone National Park

VOCABULARY
timberline
geyser
magma
volcano
lava

A Land of Mountains

You Are There You have been hiking uphill for a long time. Now you are so far up the side of the mountain that there are no longer any trees growing along the trail. You know that you are not far from your goal. As you finally reach the top of the mountain, you take a look around. The peaks of other mountains rise to the north, south, and west. To the east, plains stretch as far as you can see. It is a clear day and you can see into the distance many miles away. You smile. You have hiked to the top of Pikes Peak!

Compare and Contrast
As you read, look for ways that the mountain ranges of the West are alike and different.

Practice and Extend

READING SKILL
Compare/Contrast

In the Lesson Review, students complete a graphic organizer like the one below. You may want to provide students with a copy of Transparency 14 to complete as they read the lesson.

VOCABULARY
Context Clues

Point out to students that the words *magma, volcano,* and *lava* can be used together in the same context. Based on the descriptions and illustrations contained in this lesson and the information on page 374, have students draw labeled diagrams of what magma, a volcano, and lava look like together. Below the diagram, have students write sentences using at least two of the words, such as, **The lava flows out of the volcano.**

The Rocky Mountains

Pikes Peak, in Colorado, is one of the most famous peaks in the Rocky Mountains. The **Rocky Mountains** are the largest mountain system in North America. The "Rockies," as they are often called, are made up of a number of smaller ranges. Together, these ranges extend more than 3,000 miles from New Mexico north through Canada and into Alaska. In some places the Rockies are 350 miles wide. The highest peaks in the Rockies rise more than 14,000 feet above sea level. The Rocky Mountain states include Colorado, Utah, Wyoming, Idaho, and Montana.

The **Continental Divide** is an imaginary line that runs along the crest of the Rocky Mountains. Rivers on the east side of this line flow toward the Atlantic Ocean or the Gulf of Mexico. Rivers on the west side flow
1 west toward the Pacific Ocean.

Most of the Rocky Mountains are covered with forests. However, most trees will not grow above a certain elevation. This line of elevation is called the **timberline.** Many Rocky Mountain peaks rise above the timberline. Most of these high peaks are covered with snow year-round.

Many animals live in the Rocky Mountains. The forests are home to black bears and grizzly bears, mountain lions, elk, mink, and many other creatures. Chipmunks, coyotes, and moose live in mountain valleys, and fish are plentiful in mountain streams. Even above the timberline, mountain goats 2 and bighorn sheep make their homes.

The people who live in the Rocky Mountain states make use of the area's many natural resources such as minerals, ranch lands, and timber. Tourism is also important to the Rocky Mountain economy. Many people visit the Rockies every year to hike, ski, 3 climb mountains, and enjoy the scenery.

▶ Elk

REVIEW What is different about the Rocky Mountains below the timberline and above the timberline?
Compare and Contrast

369

2 Teach and Discuss

PAGE 369

The Rocky Mountains

Quick Summary The Rocky Mountains, the largest mountain system in North America, are home to many types of plants and animals. Natural resources and tourism are important to the economy of the area.

1 **What is the Continental Divide?** It is an imaginary line along the top of the Rockies that separates the country's eastward-flowing rivers from its westward-flowing rivers. Main Idea and Details

2 **What are some animals that live above the timberline?** Possible answers: Mountain goats, sheep
Main Idea and Details

3 **Name some activities visitors to the Rocky Mountains might enjoy.** Possible answers: Hiking, skiing, mountain climbing, viewing the scenery
Main Idea and Details

✓ **REVIEW ANSWER** Unlike the area below the timberline, the area above the timberline has few trees and high peaks that are snow-covered year round.
Compare and Contrast

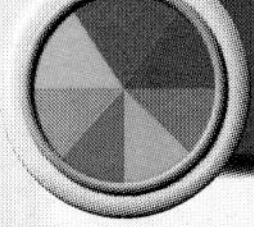

CURRICULUM CONNECTION
Science

Explore Mountain Plants

Mountains can support distinct communities of plants. Have students research and report answers to the following questions:

- Why do few trees grow above the timberline? (Too little air and water, low temperatures, high winds)
- What adaptations allow plants to live above the timberline? (Small leaves and low growth to protect against strong winds; summer blooms to protect against late-spring and early-fall frosts)

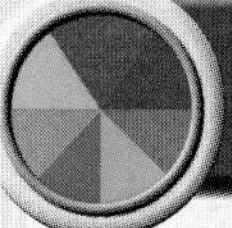

CURRICULUM CONNECTION
Drama

Give a Dramatic Reading

Have students perform a dramatic reading of a poem.

- Have students research a poem that describes the Rocky Mountains or another U.S. mountain or mountain range.
- Have students give a dramatic reading of the poem.
- Ask the audience (the class) how the poem makes them feel about the specific mountain or mountain range.

PAGES 370–371

Yellowstone National Park

Quick Summary Yellowstone National Park is the oldest national park in the world. The geysers, hot springs, and wildlife draw many tourists to the park.

4 **In what three western states can you find Yellowstone National Park?** Wyoming, Idaho, and Montana Main Idea and Details

Test Talk

Locate Key Words in the Question

5 ***Geyser* is an Icelandic word that means "gusher." Is *gusher* a good synonym for *geyser*? Explain.** Help students recognize that the key word *synonym* in the question refers to words that have similar meanings. Yes; Because, in a geyser, water gushes out of the Earth Apply Information

6 **If you watch Old Faithful for 150 minutes, what is the least number of times you would see it erupt? the greatest number of times?** One; Three Apply Information

Yellowstone National Park

Yellowstone National Park is the oldest national park in the world. It was established in 1872. The park covers more than 2.2 million acres of the northwest corner of Wyoming, and
4 includes parts of Idaho and Montana. Yellowstone is famous for its many natural attractions, such as mountains, canyons, waterfalls, lakes, forests, and wildlife.

By far, Yellowstone's most popular points of interest are its geysers and hot springs. A hot spring is a pool of water heated by forces beneath Earth's surface. A **geyser** is a type of hot spring that erupts, shooting hot water
5 into the air. There are more than 10,000 hot springs and geysers in Yellowstone. One of the most famous geysers in the park is Old Faithful,
6 which erupts every 45 to 110 minutes. Each time Old Faithful erupts, it sends a stream of boiling water more than a hundred feet into the air.

Why does Yellowstone have so many geysers and hot springs? Part of the park is located over a "hot spot" in Earth's crust. According to scientists, a hot spot occurs where **magma**, or molten rock, lies close to Earth's surface rather than deep underground. This magma heats groundwater that rises to the surface, causing geysers and hot springs. 7

Yellowstone National Park is also a place where wildlife can roam free. No one may hunt animals within the park, although fishing is allowed. As a result, many animals native to the West live within the boundaries of the park. Bison, which are also called buffalo, are plentiful in the park. Elk and moose also live within the park. Black bears, grizzly bears, and wolves are among the animals wildlife 8

▶ Bison and other animals graze near hot springs during Yellowstone's winter.

370

Practice and Extend

ACCESS CONTENT
ESL Support

Review Essential Vocabulary Help students review nouns that name features at Yellowstone: *mountain, canyon, waterfall, lake, forest, meadow, hot spring,* and *geyser.*

Beginning Write the above nouns on the board. Ask questions such as "Which word names a body of water?" and have students say the word and point to its picture on these or other pages in their textbook.

Intermediate Have students create an illustrated poster that includes all of the above features. Have them label each picture with its correct name and definition. Encourage them to share their poster with a classmate.

Advanced Have students create a multiple-choice vocabulary quiz using the features above. Allow them to exchange papers with a partner and then complete the quizzes and discuss the results.

For additional ESL support, use Every Student Learns Guide, pp. 150–153.

▶ Forests in Yellowstone are still recovering from fires in 1988.

watchers come to Yellowstone to view.

In 1988, a large portion of the park was burned in a series of wildfires. Although many acres of forests were burned, by the next year the forests
9 were showing signs of new growth. The fires and the forests' recovery have given firefighters and scientists a chance to study the effects of wildfire in the West.

REVIEW What is the difference between a geyser and a hot spring? Compare and Contrast

371

7 What heats the water in Yellowstone's geysers and hot springs? Underground magma Main Idea and Details

8 Name six types of wildlife that attract tourists to Yellowstone. Bison (buffalo), elk, moose, black bears, grizzly bears, and wolves Main Idea and Details

9 How are forests able to recover after wildfires? Possible answer: They start to grow back on their own. Draw Conclusions

Ongoing Assessment

If... students have difficulty understanding how a forest can renew itself, **then...** ask them how a single tree can lead to the growth of many new trees.

REVIEW ANSWER A geyser is a type of hot spring, but it is different from other types of hot springs in that a geyser spouts hot water into the air. Compare and Contrast

ISSUES AND VIEWPOINTS

Critical Thinking

Analyze Different Viewpoints

- In the late 1800s and early 1900s, the federal government paid a bounty on wolves. The last wolf living in Yellowstone National Park was killed in 1926.
- In 1995 wolves from Canada were reintroduced to Yellowstone, but their presence is still controversial.
- Read students the quotation at right from a Yellowstone official. Have students discuss the points of view it expresses as well as their own opinions.

"Some ranchers say, 'Look, it's people or wolves, not both.' I think we're at a point now with ... [our understanding of] biology in the United States that we can do better. It's not black or white. We can have both."

Cited on CNN, November 12, 1997

PAGES 372–373

Western Mountain Ranges

Quick Summary Mountain ranges in the West include the Rocky Mountains, the Sierra Nevada, the Olympic Mountains, the Cascade Range, the Aleutian Range, and the mountains of Hawaii.

10 **What kind of landforms are the Rocky Mountains, the Aleutians, the Cascades, the Sierra Nevada, and the Olympic Mountains?** Mountain ranges Categorize

11 **Name three mountain ranges that have volcanoes.** Cascade Range, Aleutian Range, and the mountains of Hawaii Main Idea and Details

Elevations in the West

Test Talk

Use Information from Graphics

12 **Which are farther west, the Rocky Mountains or the various volcanic mountains of the United States?** Tell students to use details from the map to support their answer. The volcanic mountains Analyze Maps

MAP SKILL **Answer** California

Western Mountain Ranges

The Rocky Mountains are not the only mountains in the West. Some mountain ranges, such as the Sierra Nevada, which extends through eastern California and western Nevada, are similar to the Rockies. They are high, rugged mountains with several peaks that rise higher than 14,000 feet above sea level. Other western ranges, such as Washington's Olympic Mountains, lie along the Pacific coast.

Still other western mountain ranges, such as the Cascade Range in Washington, Oregon, and northern California, and the Aleutian Range in 10
Alaska, have volcanoes. A **volcano** is a mountain with an opening through which ash, gas, and lava are forced. **Lava,** like magma, is molten rock. Magma that rises and flows on Earth's surface is called lava.

All the mountains of Hawaii are volcanoes. This chain of islands formed as volcanoes rose from the 11

MAP SKILL **Elevations in the West**

12

▶ **The West has the highest and lowest elevations in North America.**

MAP SKILL Use an Elevation Map ***What state has the greatest difference in elevation?***

Practice and Extend

MEETING INDIVIDUAL NEEDS
Leveled Practice

Compare Mountain Ranges Students make posters comparing mountain ranges.

Easy Have students make a poster showing pictures of the Rocky Mountains and the Appalachian Mountains. **Reteach**

On-Level Have students create a poster comparing features of the Rocky Mountains and the Appalachian Mountains. **Extend**

Challenge Ask students to create a poster-sized chart comparing the age, height, and extent of the Rocky Mountains, Aleutians, Sierra Nevada, and Olympic Mountains. **Enrich**

For a Lesson Summary, use Quick Study, p. 76.

ocean floor. Hawaii's Mount Kilauea is one of the world's most active volcanoes.

REVIEW How are the Sierra Nevada and the Cascade Range alike? How are they different? Compare and Contrast

Summarize the Lesson

- The Rockies are a large system of mountains that support many kinds of plants and animals.
- Attractions at Yellowstone National Park include geysers, hot springs, and lots of wildlife.
- The West has a variety of mountain ranges.

▶ Craggy peaks in the Sierra Nevada

LESSON 1 REVIEW

Check Facts and Main Ideas

1. Compare and Contrast On a separate sheet of paper, make a chart to compare and contrast the Rocky Mountains and the Sierra Nevada. Tell how they are similar and how they are different.

Similarities	Differences
Both are ranges of high, rugged mountains. Both have peaks more than 14,000 feet high.	The Rockies are a bigger range and span many states; the Sierra Nevada are a smaller range and are located in California and Nevada.

2. Which mountain system is the largest in the United States?
3. How are **geysers** similar to **volcanoes?**
4. Name some of the states in the West where mountains are located.
5. **Critical Thinking:** ***Make Inferences*** Why are a great many national parks located in the West?

Link to Geography

Find the Geysers Use reference materials to learn where geysers can be found on Earth besides Yellowstone National Park. Give a report that tells what these locations have in common besides geysers.

373

✓ **REVIEW ANSWER** Alike: both are mountain ranges, are located in the West, and are partly in California; Different: the Cascade Range has volcanoes, but the Sierra Nevada does not Compare and Contrast

3 Close and Assess

Summarize the Lesson

Call on volunteers to read each main point aloud and then ask the rest of the class to provide details about each.

✓ **LESSON 1 REVIEW**

1. **Compare and Contrast** For possible answers, see the reduced pupil page.
2. Rocky Mountains
3. Both geysers and volcanoes erupt hot materials.
4. Possible answers: Alaska, Colorado, California, Hawaii, Idaho, Nevada, Utah, Washington, Wyoming
5. **Critical Thinking: *Make Inferences*** Possible answer: The West has many scenic landforms such as mountain ranges and volcanoes that people feel should be protected and preserved.

Link to Geography

Reports should include at least two locations other than Yellowstone and should describe what is common to all the locations, such as climate or landforms.

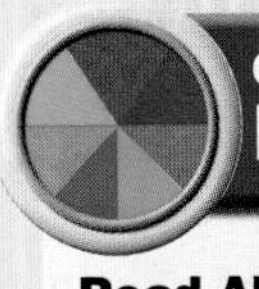

CURRICULUM CONNECTION
Literature

Read About Mountains and Geysers

Earth Dance: How Volcanoes, Earthquakes, Tidal Waves and Geysers Shake Our Restless Planet, by Cynthia Pratt Nicolson (Kids Can Press, ISBN 1-55074-155-1, 1997) **Easy**

Geysers: When Earth Roars, by Roy A. Gallant (Franklin Watts, ISBN 0-531-15838-1, 1998) **On-Level**

In the Heart of the Rockies, by G. A. Henty (Lost Classics Book Company, ISBN 1-890623-08-3, 1998) **Challenge**

Workbook, p. 86

Lesson 1: A Land of Mountains

	Rocky Mountains	Yellowstone National Park
What Is It?		
Where Is It Located?		
What Is Its Size?		
What Are Its Features?		
What Are Its Attractions?		

Also on Teacher Resources CD-ROM.

Dorling Kindersley

When a Mountain Explodes

Objective

- Compare and contrast different kinds of volcanoes.

1 Introduce and Motivate

To activate prior knowledge, ask students to name a specific volcano or a place that has volcanoes.

- Tell students that two volcanoes have erupted in the United States in recent years.
- Before students read these pages, have them draw a picture of an erupting volcano.
- Tell students they will learn more about volcanic eruptions as they read these pages.
- Students will add to their pictures later as part of the assessment for these pages.

2 Teach and Discuss

1 **In a volcanic eruption, what happens before the lava moves down the mountain?** Magma gathers in a magma chamber and powerful forces push magma, ash, and gases upward. Sequence

2 **How are magma and lava alike? How are they different?** Alike: both are melted rock; Different: magma is melted rock under Earth's surface. Lava is magma after it has erupted onto Earth's surface. Compare and Contrast

DORLING KINDERSLEY EYEWITNESS BOOK

When a Mountain Explodes

A volcano is a mountain that forms from material from deep inside Earth. Different kinds of volcanoes erupt in different ways. But when all volcanoes erupt, hot material from inside Earth moves to Earth's surface. This hot, melted rock material is known as magma. An active volcano is one that is erupting or might erupt. After a volcano erupts, it may remain dormant. A dormant volcano is one that has not erupted in recent times. Mount St. Helens in Washington had not erupted for 123 years. Then, in 1980, it erupted in a huge explosion. The sound of the explosion was heard 200 miles away.

Sleeping Giant
Mount St. Helens is in the Cascade mountain range. Before it erupted on May 18, 1980, Mount St. Helens was a popular vacation place. It was surrounded by peaceful forests and lakes.

Mount St. Helens Erupting
After two months of small earthquakes, the hot magma deep inside the volcano began to explode. This picture was taken 38 seconds after the first explosion started. The side of the mountain gave way, and a cloud of ash and gas blew into the sky.

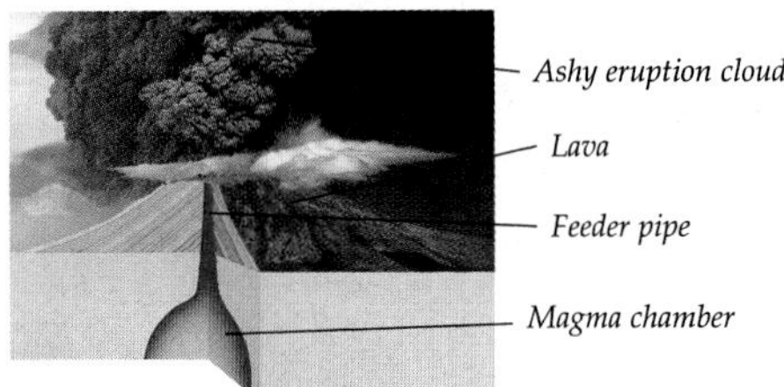

Inside the Volcano 1
Magma gathered far underground in a magma chamber. Powerful forces pushed the magma upward through the feeder pipe. Then magma, ash, and gases were pushed upward and erupted on the surface. Magma that erupts onto Earth's surface is called lava. 2 3

Four Seconds Later...
The cloud of ash grows with newly erupted material. The new material quickly rolls over the rock that had been blown from the side of the mountain.

374

Practice and Extend

SOCIAL STUDIES
Background

About Mount St. Helens

- When Mount St. Helens erupted, a giant hole formed on the north side of the mountain, spewing stone, ash, poisonous gas, and other debris for a 20-mile radius.
- The Mount St. Helens eruption flattened and buried 230 square miles of vegetation in the surrounding area. It also killed 65 people and large populations of elk, deer, bear, coyote, and other wildlife.
- Although the Mount St. Helens eruption was extremely powerful, it was much smaller than the one at Krakatoa, Indonesia, in 1883. The explosion at Krakatoa is believed to have been 26 times as powerful as the most powerful hydrogen bomb. Scientists say the sound of the explosion could be heard over one-thirteenth of Earth's surface.

Cascade Volcano
Mount Rainier is another volcano in the Cascade Mountains, the group that includes Mount St. Helens. Mount Rainier erupted last in the 1840s.

Mauna Loa Erupts
All the islands of Hawaii grew as volcanoes. Mauna Loa is an active volcano on the island of Hawaii. Mauna Loa erupts as a fire fountain. Lava streams down its side.

Flowing Lava
Lava like this in Hawaii erupts more slowly than at Mount St. Helens. It moves slowly down the mountain. Even so, the lava is very hot. This picture was taken at night, when you can easily see the red glow of the hot, melted rock.

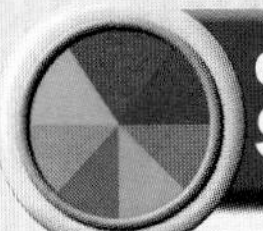

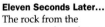

4 **Eleven Seconds Later...**
The rock from the mountainside is almost completely covered by ash. Huge chunks of rock have been thrown out from the ash cloud.

375

3 **Although different kinds of volcanoes erupt in different ways, what do all the eruptions have in common?** Magma moves from inside Earth to Earth's surface. **Main Idea and Details**

4 **How can a volcanic eruption damage the surrounding area?** Rock, ash, and lava can cover the surrounding area. **Draw Conclusions**

3 Close and Assess

- Encourage students to use the Internet, encyclopedias, or other sources to learn more about volcanoes in the United States and other parts of the world.
- Ask students to add to their pictures of volcanic eruptions that they began earlier. Have them show how a volcano can affect the surrounding environment, labeling important parts of their drawings.

CURRICULUM CONNECTION
Science

Examine How Lava Flows
- Have students work in small groups to create a volcano out of modeling clay. Tell them to leave a hollow cone in the center of their volcano.
- Tell students to fill the cone of their volcano half full of baking soda.
- Provide each group with 2–3 cups of plain, white vinegar with a few drops of red food coloring added. Then have students slowly pour the vinegar into the volcano.
- As the mixture "erupts," have groups analyze how lava flowing from a real volcano might affect area vegetation and wildlife.
- **Caution** Have students wear cover goggles while doing this activity. Instruct them to wash their hands thoroughly when finished.
- Because this activity can be messy, consider doing it outdoors, if appropriate. Otherwise have students do the activity in plastic tubs on the floor.

Take Notes and Write Outlines

Objective
- Use notes and outlines to organize information.

Vocabulary

notes, p. 376; **outline,** p. 376

Resource
- Workbook, p. 87

1 Introduce and Motivate

What are notes and outlines? To activate prior knowledge, ask students what newspaper reporters do at an event they are covering. (Possible answers: Observe, listen, take notes) Point out that most of the news stories we read, see, and hear every day come from the notes reporters take when they are covering an event. Explain that some reporters use an outline to organize their ideas and facts before they write an article. Then have students read the **What?** section of text on p. 376 to help set the purpose of the lesson.

Why use notes and outlines? Have students read the **Why?** section of text on p. 376. Then ask them to identify everyday situations in which notes or an outline might be helpful. (Possible answers: When taking a telephone message, when writing a report)

2 Teach and Discuss

How is the skill used? Examine with students the outline on p. 377.

- Point out that this example is based on an encyclopedia entry, a source frequently used by students.
- Explain that the encyclopedia entry could be in a book or on a screen—the principles of note-taking and outlining remain the same.
- Have students read the **How?** section of text on p. 376.

Research and Writing Skills

Take Notes and Write Outlines

What? **Notes** are bits of information you write in your own words. An **outline** is a framework for organizing information. It lets you see main ideas and details at a glance.

Why? Taking notes helps you remember what you have read. You can use your notes to make an outline. Taking notes and making an outline are useful ways to study for a test or prepare a report.

How? Follow these steps to take notes and write an outline.
- As you read, look for main ideas and important details. Write each main idea as a heading. Use the note card on page 377 as an example.
- Write important facts and details below the heading. Use your own words. You do not need to use complete sentences. Be sure to write the title of the source, the author's name, the publication date, and the page number where you found the information. 1
- Sort your note cards into an order that makes sense. Then use your cards to write an outline.
- Follow the example of the outline on page 377. Write the main ideas from your cards next to Roman numerals. Then write important facts about those ideas next to a capital letter below the main idea. 2

Think and Apply

1. What is the source of the information on the note card on page 377?
2. What important fact can be written next to *B* under Roman numeral *I* in the outline on page 377?
3. How can taking **notes** and creating an **outline** help you prepare for a test?

376

Practice and Extend

SOCIAL STUDIES
Background

About Volcanoes
- Not all volcanoes are cone-shaped. Shield volcanoes like Mauna Loa in Hawaii look like a curved shield resting on the ground. Other volcanoes create plateaus or steep ridges.
- A volcanic explosion can kill many people, but many more can die from related causes. In 1815, a volcano in Indonesia killed about 10,000 people, but 82,000 more died later from disease and famine related to the blast.
- Volcanoes can damage property also. One study estimates that volcanoes cause about $100 million in property damage each year worldwide.
- Volcanoes do good as well as harm. Over time volcanic ash can become rich soil.

Volcano A volcano is an opening in Earth's crust through which lava, hot gas, and rocks erupt. A volcano forms when melted rock from deep within Earth blasts upward through the surface. Volcanoes are often cone-shaped mountains. The cone is caused by the buildup of lava and other materials released from inside the volcano during eruptions. It takes thousands of years to form.

Encyclopedia One 712

Description of a volcano

- a hole in Earth's surface
- lava, hot gas, and pieces of rock erupt through the hole
- volcanoes—often cone-shaped mountains

Encyclopedia One, Michael Matthews, 2002, p. 712

Volcanoes

I. Description of a volcano
   A. A volcano is an opening in Earth's surface.
   B. ______________________
   C. Volcanoes are often mountains. (3)

II. How volcanoes form
   A. Melted rock deep within Earth erupts from an opening in Earth's surface.
   B. Lava, hot gas, and rocks come out.
   C. The buildup of these materials over thousands of years forms a cone-shaped mountain.

377

(1) **When taking notes, what types of information should you write on each sheet of paper or note card?** Main idea, important facts and details, title of source, author's name, publication date, page number where information was found **Summarize**

(2) **What kind of information is recorded next to capital letters on an outline?** Important facts **Categorize**

(3) **In the *Volcanoes* outline on p. 377, how many main ideas did the outline writer identify? What are they?** Two; *Description of a volcano* and *How volcanoes form* **Analyze Information**

3 Close and Assess

Think and Apply

1. *Encyclopedia One*
2. Lava, hot gas, and pieces of rock erupt through the hole.
3. Doing so helps you remember what you have read and helps you organize your information.

MEETING INDIVIDUAL NEEDS

Leveled Practice

Practice Note-Taking and Outlining Have students take notes and outline a report on a current event.

Easy Have students take notes on and outline three paragraphs of a newspaper or magazine article. **Reteach**

On-Level Have students take notes on and outline a five- to ten-paragraph newspaper or magazine article. **Extend**

Challenge Have students find two or three magazine or newspaper articles on the same topic, take notes on both, and create one master outline from the information. **Enrich**

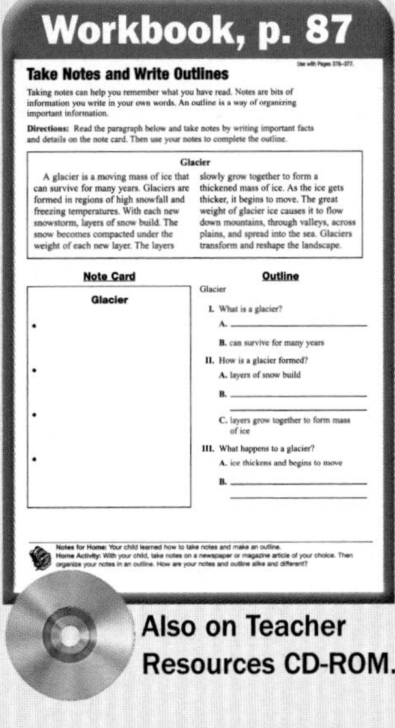

Workbook, p. 87

Use with Pages 376–377.

Take Notes and Write Outlines

Taking notes can help you remember what you have read. Notes are bits of information you write in your own words. An outline is a way of organizing important information.

Directions: Read the paragraph below and take notes by writing important facts and details on the note card. Then use your notes to complete the outline.

Glacier

A glacier is a moving mass of ice that can survive for many years. Glaciers are formed in regions of high snowfall and freezing temperatures. With each new snowstorm, layers of snow build. The snow becomes compacted under the weight of each new layer. The layers slowly grow together to form a thickened mass of ice. As the ice gets thicker, it begins to move. The great weight of glacier ice causes it to flow down mountains, through valleys, across plains, and spread into the sea. Glaciers transform and reshape the landscape.

Note Card

Glacier

-
-
-
-

Outline

Glacier

I. What is a glacier?
   A. ______________
   B. can survive for many years
II. How is a glacier formed?
   A. layers of snow build
   B. ______________
   C. layers grow together to form mass of ice
III. What happens to a glacier?
   A. ice thickens and begins to move
   B. ______________

Notes for Home: Your child learned how to take notes and make an outline.
Home Activity: With your child, take notes on a newspaper or magazine article of your choice. Then organize your notes in an outline. How are your notes and outline alike and different?

Also on Teacher Resources CD-ROM.

Climates in the West

Objectives

- Compare and contrast the climates of Hawaii and California.
- Name the different climates of the West and give an example of each.
- Identify states in the West with extreme weather.
- Explain how the rain shadow works.
- Compare and contrast the amount of precipitation that falls on the east and west sides of the Cascade Range.

Vocabulary

tundra, p. 379; **frigid,** p. 379; **rain shadow,** p. 382

Resources

- Workbook, p. 88
- Transparency 14
- Every Student Learns Guide, pp. 154–157
- Quick Study, pp. 78–79

Quick Teaching Plan

If time is short, have students copy the list of important places and vocabulary on this page and write a short description or definition of each term.

1 Introduce and Motivate

Preview To activate prior knowledge, ask students if they have ever read about a dogsled race or seen one on television. Explain that one famous dogsled race is the Iditarod in Alaska. Tell students they will learn more about Alaska and other areas of the West as they read Lesson 2.

You Are There To give students a sense of the length of the Iditarod, have them cut a length of string equal to 1,000 miles on a map of your region. Tell them to pin one end of the string to your city and rotate the string to see what lies within a 1,000-mile radius of your city.

LESSON 2

Climates in the West

PREVIEW

Focus on the Main Idea
The climate in different areas of the West varies greatly.

PLACES
Mount McKinley, Alaska
Death Valley, California
Great Basin
Mount Waialeale, Hawaii
Cascade Range

VOCABULARY
tundra
frigid
rain shadow

You Are There It's below zero and the wind is blowing across the frozen tundra. You and your team of dogs are waiting at the starting line of the Iditarod (eye DIT uh rod). This race is the most famous dogsled race in the world. You will race for more than a thousand miles between Anchorage and Nome, Alaska.

You hear the announcer yell, "Go!" The dogs dash forward and your sled flies from the starting line. The cold air stings your face as your sled picks up speed. The crowd by the side of the trail cheers as you ride off into the Alaskan wilderness.

Compare and Contrast As you read, look for places in the West that have the same or different climates.

▶ Iditarod teams take 10 to 17 days to complete the race.

Practice and Extend

READING SKILL
Compare/Contrast

In the Lesson Review, students complete a graphic organizer like the one below. You may want to provide students with a copy of Transparency 14 to complete as they read the lesson.

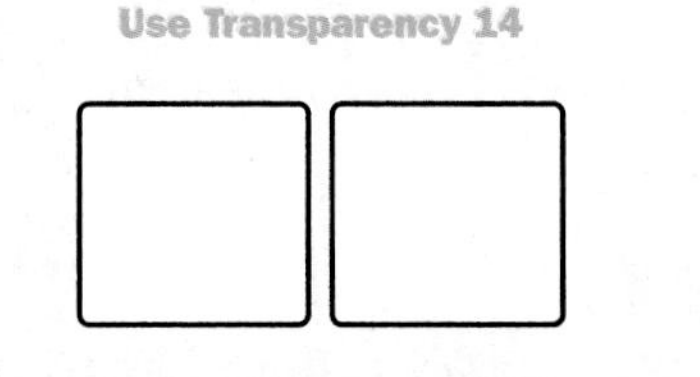

VOCABULARY
Related Word Study

Have students read the definition of *frigid* on page 379. Then explain that *frigid* comes from the Latin *frigere*, which means "to be cold." Ask students if they can think of other words that might come from this Latin word *(refrigerator, refrigerate).* Tell students that *frigid* can be used to describe a cold climate, but it can also be used to describe a cold feeling or manner, as in "the stranger received a frigid greeting."

Mt. McKinley, also known as Denali, is the tallest mountain in North America.

The Frosty North

Many areas of the western region of the United States have very cold winter temperatures. The tundra in Alaska, where the Iditarod is held, is one of these places. A **tundra** is a cold, flat area where trees cannot grow. 1

Think about these Alaskan temperatures, and you will understand how cold it really is there. In Barrow, Alaska, in the northern part of the state, the average temperature in February is –11°F. The record low temperature was recorded on January 23, 1971. On that day in Prospect Creek, Alaska, the temperature dropped to –80°F—80 degrees below zero. 2 To understand how cold this is, remember that water freezes at 32°F *above* zero.

Not all of Alaska has these **frigid**—or very cold—temperatures. Parts of southern Alaska have temperatures that range between 28°F and 55°F during the whole year. 3

Some of the other states in the West also have cold winter temperatures. Idaho, Montana, Wyoming, Colorado, and parts of Washington have wintry temperatures and heavy snowfall. For example, the average temperature in January in Idaho is only 23°F.

The cold, snowy weather in parts of the West attracts thousands of tourists each year. People enjoy winter sports. They downhill ski and snowboard in the mountains. Other winter activities that people enjoy are cross-country skiing, snowshoeing, dog sledding, and ice fishing. 4

Tourists also enjoy the scenery, such as Alaska's majestic **Mount McKinley.** It is the highest peak in North America at 20,320 feet. 5 Its peak is covered with snow year-round.

REVIEW How does the temperature in Alaska differ from the northern part of the state to the southern part? Compare and Contrast

379

2 Teach and Discuss

PAGE 379

The Frosty North

Quick Summary Alaska and some other northern states have very cold winters.

1 **What is a tundra?** A cold, flat area where trees cannot grow
Main Idea and Details

2 **What was the lowest temperature ever recorded in Alaska?** –80°F
Main Idea and Details

3 **Tell students that on a warm summer day in southern Alaska, the temperature may reach only 55°F. Compare a warm summer day in your area to a warm summer day in Alaska.** Possible answer: It is usually over 85° in my area—thirty degrees warmer than in Alaska. Compare and Contrast

4 **Compare the winter activities described on this page with winter activities in your area.** Possible answer: Because it usually does not freeze in my area, I cannot do activities like those described in the book, but I can go biking and hiking. Compare and Contrast

5 **What is the highest mountain in North America? What is its height?** Mt. McKinley; 20,320 feet
Main Idea and Details

✓ **REVIEW ANSWER** The northern part of Alaska generally is colder than the southern part of the state.
Compare and Contrast

ESL — EXTEND LANGUAGE: ESL Support

Examine Different Forms of Adjectives Help students use the positive, comparative, and superlative forms of adjectives.

Beginning Have students pantomime the concepts of *cold, colder,* and *coldest* and *high, higher,* and *highest.*

Intermediate Have students provide the comparative and superlative forms of other adjectives, such as *warm* and *low*.

Advanced Demonstrate how to form the comparative and superlative forms of adjectives that undergo spelling changes (e.g., *rainy*) or require the use of *more* and *most* (e.g., *comfortable*). Have students supply the altered forms of other adjectives, such as *sunny, cloudy,* and *frigid.*

For additional ESL support, use Every Student Learns Guide, pp. 154–157.

A Region of Many Climates

Quick Summary In addition to cold areas, the West also has tropics, deserts, and rain forests.

6 **Contrast the climate of the northern parts of the West with the climates of southern California and Hawaii.** Unlike the cold temperatures in northern areas, temperatures in most of southern California and Hawaii rarely drop below freezing.
Compare and Contrast

7 **What are two characteristics of a tropical climate?** Warm, wet weather
Draw Conclusions

8 **What type of climate does Death Valley have?** Desert Main Idea and Details

A Region of Many Climates

Unlike the wintry areas of the northern part of the region, parts of the West have warm weather throughout the year. Temperatures in some parts of California and Hawaii, for example, rarely drop below
6 freezing—even in the middle of winter!

Hawaii has a tropical climate. People who live there and visitors all enjoy the
7 warm, wet climate of Hawaii year-round. The islands have tropical rain forests, where the plants grow large and full.

California is such a large state that it has a variety of climates. Overall, though, California has two main seasons—the rainy season in the winter and the dry season in the summer. Temperatures in southern California are warm all year. Temperatures in northern California are cool in the winter, but rarely below freezing. Winter weather does come to parts of California—freezing temperatures and snow can be found in the mountains in winter.

Yet another climate can be found in California. There are deserts in southern California in the interior of the state. **Death Valley** is a desert area in southern California. 8

▶ A tropical rain forest in Hawaii

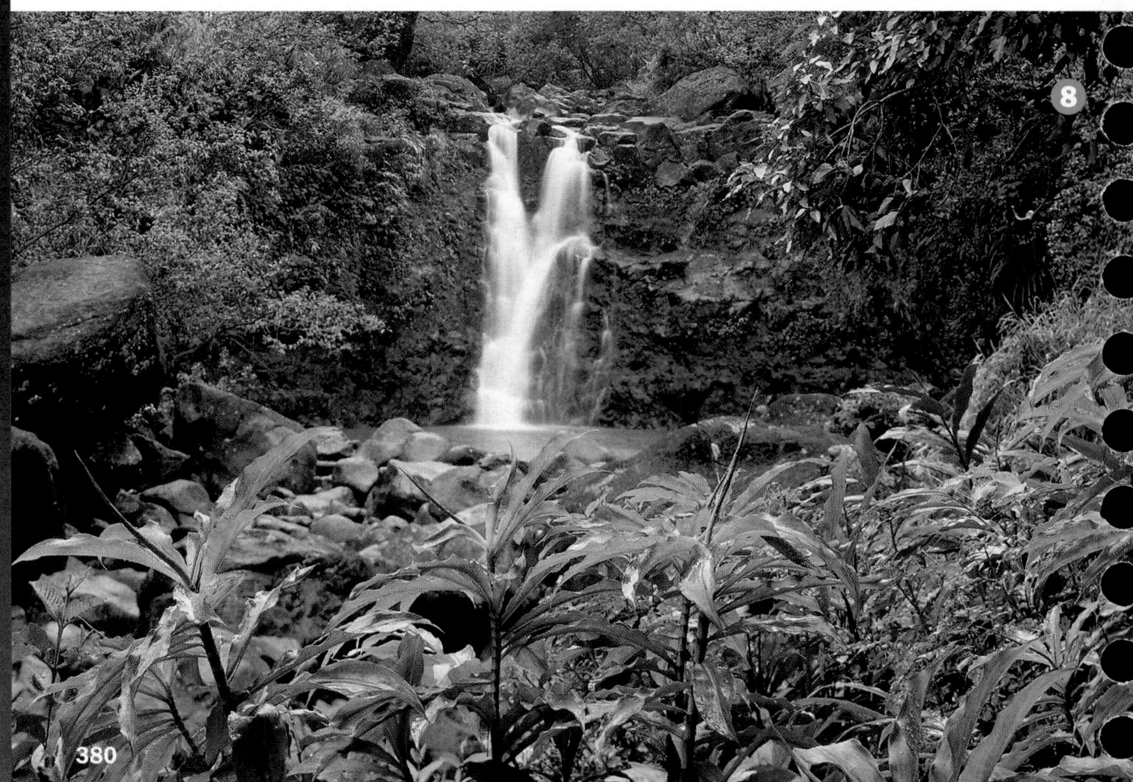

380

Practice and Extend

Decision Making

Use a Decision-Making Process

- Have students consider the following decision-making scenario: **Suppose you are working for a company that is planning to relocate your team to either southern California or Alaska. Your team must come to a consensus on where you will live and work.**
- Students should use the following decision-making process to choose the team's new home. For each step in the process, have students work in small groups to discuss and write about what must be considered as they make their decision. Write the steps above on the board or read them aloud.

1. **Identify a situation that requires a decision.**
2. **Gather information.**
3. **Identify options.**
4. **Predict consequences.**
5. **Take action to implement a decision.**

Death Valley is actually part of the **Great Basin,** a desert region in the West that includes most of Nevada and parts of Oregon, Utah, Idaho, and Wyoming. The word basin usually means "a wide, shallow bowl for holding liquids." The reason that this part of the country is called a basin is that the water from its streams drains into the area instead of into rivers that lead to an ocean. One place the water drains into in the Great Basin is the Great Salt Lake in Utah. 9 10

The Great Basin gets very hot on summer days. There are few trees. The desert shrubs that grow there need only small amounts of water to survive.

▶ **The Great Salt Lake is the largest inland body of salt water in the Western Hemisphere.**

REVIEW Name one way in which Hawaii and the Great Basin are similar and one way in which they are different. Compare and Contrast

MAP SKILL Average January Temperatures in the West

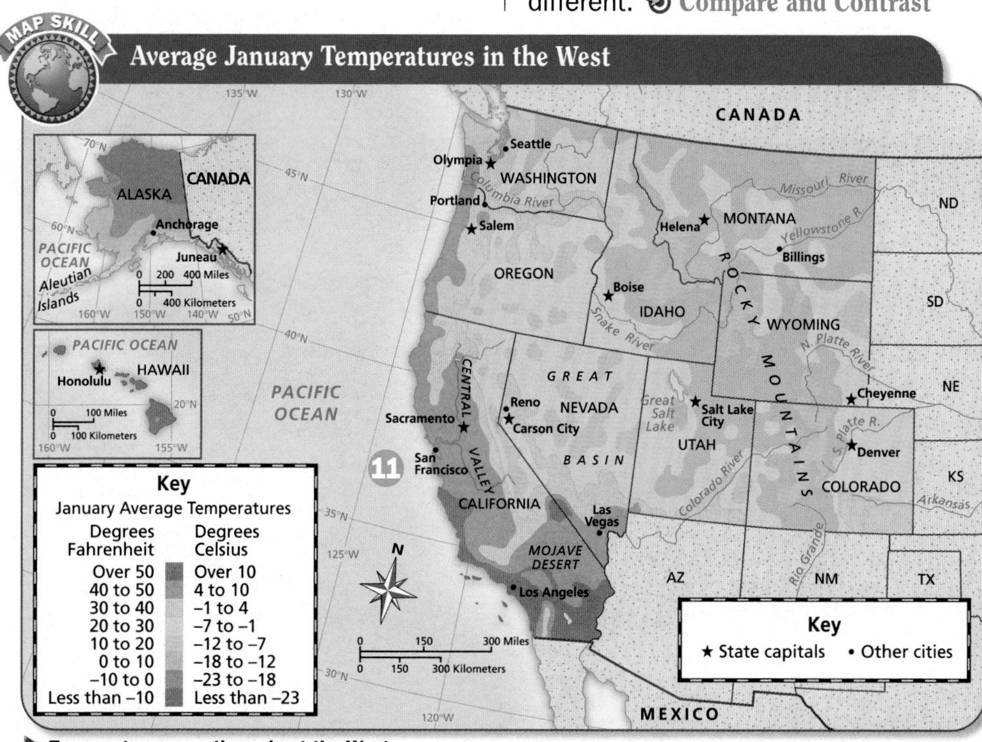

▶ **Temperatures vary throughout the West.**

MAP SKILL Using Map Key ***Which state has the greatest variation in temperature as shown on the map?***

381

9 In which states is the Great Basin located? Nevada, Oregon, Utah, Idaho, Wyoming **Main Idea and Details**

10 How do streams in the Great Basin area differ from streams in other parts of North America? Unlike other streams, streams in the Great Basin area do not drain into rivers that lead to an ocean. **Compare and Contrast**

✓ **REVIEW ANSWER** Similar: both have warm days; Different: parts of Hawaii have tropical rain forests, whereas there are very few trees in the Great Basin. **Compare and Contrast**

MAP SKILL Average January Temperatures in the West

11 Which is usually colder in January—Sacramento, California, or Helena, Montana? Helena, Montana **Analyze Maps**

MAP SKILL Answer Alaska

MEETING INDIVIDUAL NEEDS Leveled Practice

Explore Climate Have students prepare a presentation on climate.

Easy Have students work in pairs to create a three-section collage illustrating tropical, desert, and frigid climates. **Reteach**

On-Level Ask students to work in pairs to write a brief descriptive caption for each section of their classmates' collages. **Extend**

Challenge Have students use a map or globe to explain each illustrated climate in terms of latitude and/or altitude. **Enrich**

For a Lesson Summary, use Quick Study, p. 78.

PAGES 382–383

Let It Rain . . . and Snow!

Quick Summary The West is a region of weather contrasts. Both very dry and very wet areas are found in the West.

Test Talk

Use Information from the Text

12 **What do Rainier Paradise Ranger Station in Washington; Silver Lake, Colorado; and Mt. Waialeale, Hawaii, have in common?** Tell students that specific place names can help them find the right information to support their answer. Ask students to skim the text to find the place names that will support their answer. All three have experienced great amounts of precipitation. Generalize

Ongoing Assessment

If...students fail to see how these areas are similar, **then...**point out that the *-est* words *largest, largest,* and *wettest* indicate that each place received a great amount of something.

13 **Why is it so rainy on the western side of the Cascade Mountains?** Warm winds from the Pacific Ocean push clouds up the western side of the mountains. As the clouds move higher, they become cooler and drop their moisture as rain. Cause and Effect

Let It Rain . . . and Snow!

Precipitation in the West varies greatly. On average, fewer than two inches of rain fall each year in Death Valley, California. In fact, from October 3, 1912, to November 8, 1914, part of Death Valley had no precipitation at all. That is more than two years without rain!

However, the West is also known for record snowfalls. One of the largest snowfalls in one year was recorded at Rainier Paradise Ranger Station in Washington in the early 1970s. In one year, 1,122 inches of snow fell! Silver Lake, Colorado, has experienced one of the largest snowfalls in a 24-hour period—76 inches. That is more than six feet of snow in one day!

Some parts of the West are very rainy. The wettest place on Earth is **Mount Waialeale** (wah ya lee AH lee) in Hawaii. The average yearly rainfall on the mountain is 460 inches, or more than 38 feet of water. 12

Parts of Washington are also very wet. The high mountains in the **Cascade Range** greatly affect the surrounding area. West of the Cascades, in much of the Olympic Peninsula of Washington, precipitation averages more than 135 inches—or more than 11 feet—per year.

In contrast, areas east of the Cascades receive much less rain. For example, Yakima, Washington, receives less than eight inches of rain per year.

The reason for this difference is an effect called the **rain shadow.** Winds

The Cascade Rain Shadow

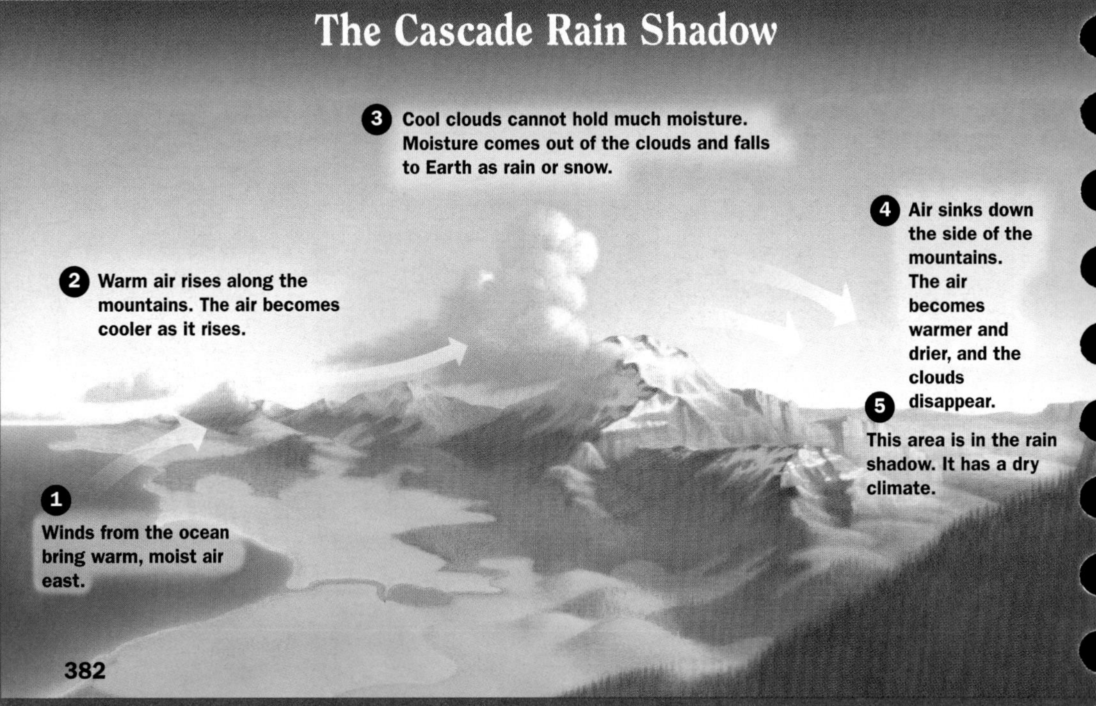

1 Winds from the ocean bring warm, moist air east.
2 Warm air rises along the mountains. The air becomes cooler as it rises.
3 Cool clouds cannot hold much moisture. Moisture comes out of the clouds and falls to Earth as rain or snow.
4 Air sinks down the side of the mountains. The air becomes warmer and drier, and the clouds disappear.
5 This area is in the rain shadow. It has a dry climate.
382

Practice and Extend

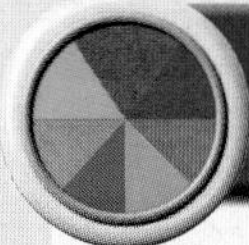

CURRICULUM CONNECTION Math

Create a Bar Graph

Have students create a vertical bar graph comparing annual rainfall in Death Valley, California; Mt. Waialeale, Hawaii; the Olympic Peninsula of Washington; and Yakima, Washington.

- Have students determine an appropriate scale for their bars.
- Students may want to design the graph to look like a rain gauge.
- Have students conduct research to find the annual rainfall in your area and include that data in a fifth bar.

CURRICULUM CONNECTION Music

Listen to Rain

Have students explore the natural "music" created by rain.

- Bring to class a tape, audio CD, or online recording of rainfall, widely available as relaxation music.
- Have students listen to the different tracks on the recording and choose their favorite selection.
- Ask students to explain the reasons for their choices, including how the selection makes them feel and how it compares to other types of music.

from the Pacific Ocean bring warm, moist air east. This warm air rises and forms clouds. The winds push the clouds up against the mountains. As
13 the clouds rise, they become cooler. Cool air cannot hold as much moisture as warm air, so much of the water falls back to Earth as rain or snow on the western side of the mountains. By the time the clouds have passed to the eastern side of the mountains, they carry very little moisture. Therefore, the eastern side of the Cascade Range receives less rain than the western 14 side. The land east of the Cascades lies in the rain shadow.

REVIEW Why might the West be known as a region of weather contrasts? Main Idea and Details

Summarize the Lesson

- **Though many areas of Alaska are very cold, some parts of the state have much milder climates.**
- **The West has areas that are warm and tropical year-round.**
- **The West is home to the wettest and driest places in the nation.**

▶ **Tropical flowers, such as this Bird of Paradise, thrive in Hawaii's warm climate.**

LESSON 2 REVIEW

Check Facts and Main Ideas

1. Compare and Contrast On a separate sheet of paper, make a chart like the one below. List similarities and differences in the climates of Hawaii and California.

Similarities	Differences
Both can be warm. Both can get a lot of rain in places.	Hawaii is warm and humid, California is usually dry when it's warm. California has a more varied climate.

2. Which state experienced one of the largest snowfalls in one year?
3. Explain how the **rain shadow** works.
4. Name three different climates in the West, and give an example of each.
5. **Critical Thinking:** *Point of View* Think about living in Barrow, Alaska. What do you think would be different from the way that you live now? What advantages are there to living in such a cold climate?

Link to Science

Learn About Plants With a partner, do research in the library or on the Internet to find out more about plants that live on the **tundra.** Present what you learned to the class.

383

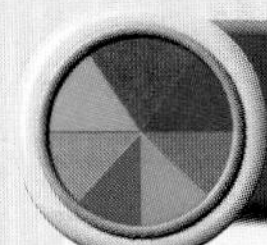

CURRICULUM CONNECTION
Art

Illustrate a Community

Climate affects which plants and animals live in an area.

- Have students choose the Alaskan tundra, an area of southern California near the ocean, Hawaii, the Great Basin, the short grass prairie of Montana, or the rain forests of the Northwest.
- Have students use a field guide or other resource to find out what types of plants and animals live in their chosen area.
- Have students create a labeled poster to illustrate their findings.

Workbook, p. 88

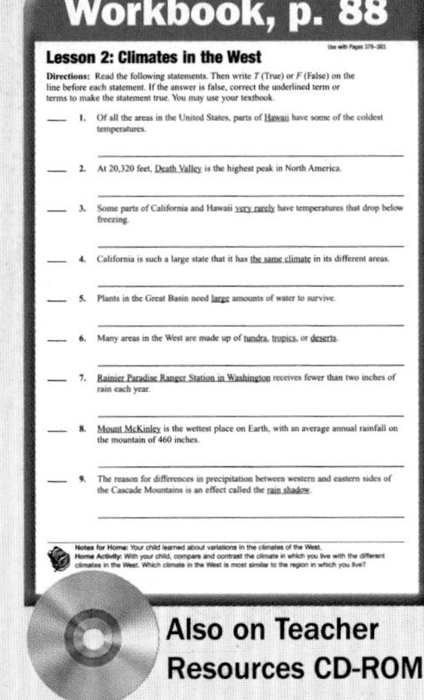

Lesson 2: Climates in the West

Use with Pages 378–383.

Directions: Read the following statements. Then write *T* (True) or *F* (False) on the line before each statement. If the answer is false, correct the underlined term or terms to make the statement true. You may use your textbook.

___ 1. Of all the areas in the United States, parts of Hawaii have some of the coldest temperatures.

___ 2. At 20,320 feet, Death Valley is the highest peak in North America.

___ 3. Some parts of California and Hawaii very rarely have temperatures that drop below freezing.

___ 4. California is such a large state that it has the same climate in its different areas.

___ 5. Plants in the Great Basin need large amounts of water to survive.

___ 6. Many areas in the West are made up of tundra, tropics, or deserts.

___ 7. Rainier Paradise Ranger Station in Washington receives fewer than two inches of rain each year.

___ 8. Mount McKinley is the wettest place on Earth, with an average annual rainfall on the mountain of 460 inches.

___ 9. The reason for differences in precipitation between western and eastern sides of the Cascade Mountains is an effect called the rain shadow.

Notes for Home: Your child learned about variations in the climates of the West.
Home Activity: With your child, compare and contrast the climate in which you live with the different climates in the West. Which climate in the West is most similar to the region in which you live?

Also on Teacher Resources CD-ROM.

14 What type of climate is created on the eastern side of the Cascades as the result of the rain-shadow effect?
Dry Summarize

✓ **REVIEW ANSWER** Because there are so many different types of weather; Different areas of the West have different climates. Very dry and very wet places are located in the West. In the Cascade Range, the western slopes are wet, while the eastern slopes are dry. Main Idea and Details

3 Close and Assess

Summarize the Lesson

Have students take turns reading the three main points. Then have students identify the places in the West to which each statement refers.

✓ **LESSON 2 REVIEW**

1. **Compare and Contrast** For possible answers, see the reduced pupil page.
2. Washington
3. The rain shadow in the Cascade Range happens when winds from the Pacific Ocean bring warm, moist air east. The air rises up and forms clouds. Winds push the clouds up the mountains. As the clouds get higher, they become cooler and much of the water falls back to earth. When the clouds pass over the mountain, there is very little moisture left, so the eastern side is drier.
4. Possible answers: Cold—Alaska, tropical—Hawaii, desert—Death Valley
5. **Critical Thinking:** ***Point of View*** Students should base their answers on information drawn from the lesson and knowledge of their home climate.

Link to Science

Encourage students to consult more than one source—an encyclopedia and a field guide, for instance.

Resources of the West

Objectives

- Identify some resources of the West.
- Identify places where agricultural products are grown in the West.
- Locate areas of the West that have important fishing industries.
- Explain how people benefit from the resources of the West.

Vocabulary

greenhouse, p. 385; **livestock,** p. 386; **reforest,** p. 388

Resources

- Workbook, p. 89
- Transparency 6
- Every Student Learns Guide, pp. 158–161
- Quick Study, pp. 80–81

Quick Teaching Plan

If time is short, have students create illustrated notes for this lesson.

- Have students draw a horizontal line across a sheet of paper and label the top *West* and the bottom *Individual States.*
- Tell students to read the lesson and draw a picture of each product mentioned. Explain that, if a product is general to the region, they should draw the picture above the line. If a product is related to a specific state, they should draw it below the line and label it with the state name.

1 Introduce and Motivate

Preview To activate prior knowledge, have students express whether they prefer red or green, sweet or tart apples. Tell students they will read more about apples and other resources of the West as they read Lesson 3.

You Are There Ask students to explain why some people might want to buy fresh apples at a roadside stand or a pick-your-own orchard rather than at a grocery store.

LESSON 3

PREVIEW

Focus on the Main Idea
The West is rich in natural resources.

PLACES
Willamette Valley, Oregon
Central Valley, California

VOCABULARY
greenhouse
livestock
reforest

Resources of the West

You Are There The summer is over and the coolness of autumn has begun to turn the leaves gold and brown. You head for the tree that is filled with the largest apples in the orchard. You sling a canvas bag over one shoulder and climb a ladder up to the tree's branches. You reach out and pick an apple. This is just the first of many apples you'll harvest today, but this one's not going in the bag. You smile and put this apple in your pocket so that you can enjoy it later. You know it will taste wonderful. You are so lucky that your parents own this apple orchard.

Summarize As you read, think of ways to summarize what you have learned about the wide variety of resources in the West.

384

Practice and Extend

READING SKILL Summarize

In the Lesson Review, students complete a graphic organizer like the one below. You may want to provide students with a copy of Transparency 6 to complete as they read the lesson.

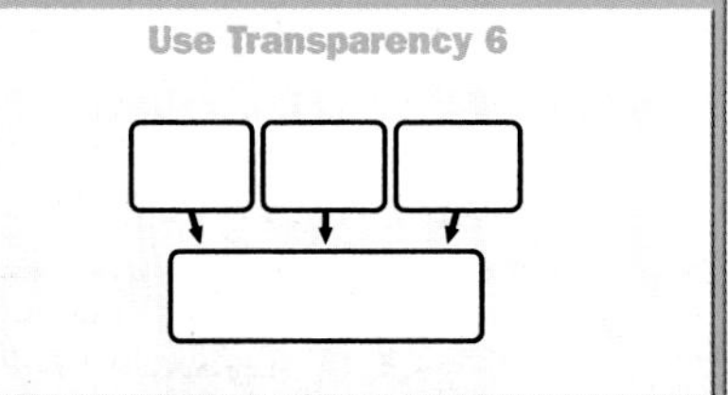

VOCABULARY Individual Word Study

Point out that livestock can be broken down into *live* and *stock*. Ask students what *stock* is (a supply of something). Discuss how *livestock* is the supply of live animals raised on a farm. Then talk about idioms that use the word *stock*, such as "in stock" (ready for use or sale), "out of stock" (no longer on hand), "take stock" (to find out how much stock one has on hand, or examine), and "take stock in" (take an interest in).

▶ Apples are harvested from late August to early November.

The Plentiful West

Apples are one of the many agricultural products of the West. Apples do not grow in all parts of the West, however. Like most crops, they grow where the climate and land are best for their growth. 1

The eastern part of Washington is famous for the many types of apples that are grown there. Cherries, pears, and potatoes are also grown in Washington. The biggest producer of potatoes in the United States, though, is Idaho. Oregon's **Willamette Valley** farms grow many types of berries and a wide variety of vegetables.

The state that produces the widest variety of fruits, vegetables, and nuts is California. Many farms are in the **Central Valley.** This huge area lies between the California Coastal Range to the west and the Sierra Nevada to the east. Among the fruits grown there are grapes, strawberries, peaches, plums, and melons.

Some Alaskan crops are barley, oats, hay, and potatoes. The harsh climate in parts of Alaska will not support many types of plants. Some Alaskan crops are grown in greenhouses. 2 A **greenhouse** is an enclosed structure that allows light to enter and keeps heat and moisture from escaping. 3

Hawaii's tropical climate is good for growing sugarcane and pineapples. Other Hawaiian crops are macadamia nuts and coffee.

REVIEW How would you compare the agricultural products of California and Alaska? Compare and Contrast

Literature and Social Studies

This type of short poem is a haiku. The word *haiku* comes from Japanese words meaning "joke" and "poem."

Ripening Cherries

by Florence Vilén

Ripening cherries,
who is the first to take them,
a hand or a beak? 4

2 Teach and Discuss

PAGE 385

The Plentiful West

Quick Summary A wide range of crops is grown in the West.

1 **How does the climate of the West affect the range of agricultural products produced there?** Most crops grow where the climate and land are best for their growth. The West has a wide variety of climates, so many different crops can be produced in their ideal climates. **Cause and Effect**

2 **Identify five crops you enjoy that can be grown in the West.** Possible answers: Apples, cherries, grapes, melons, peaches, pineapples, potatoes, strawberries **Express Ideas**

3 **Why are greenhouses particularly useful in Alaska?** Possible answer: They provide heat and light and protect plants from the harsh climate. **Evaluate**

✓ **REVIEW ANSWER** California produces a wide variety of fruits, vegetables, and nuts, while Alaska only produces a few types of crops. **Compare and Contrast**

Literature and Social Studies

4 **Haiku, a type of poetry that began in Japan, usually has 17 syllables and centers on an image in nature. How does this haiku fit that pattern?** The three lines of the poem have a total of 17 syllables (5, 7, and 5), and it refers to cherries, which are a product of nature. **Apply Information**

EXTEND LANGUAGE
ESL Support

Identify Agricultural Products Help students learn the names of many of the agricultural products of the West.

Beginning Have students work together to find pictures of as many of the products from the text as possible to create a bulletin board display. Encourage a discussion about the products. Have each student label at least one picture.

Intermediate Have students work in pairs to create a four-column chart labeled *Trees, Vines, Low-Growing Plants,* and *Grains* and list at least three products from the West that fit each category. Allow students to refer to the pictures from the "Beginning" activity as a reference.

Advanced Have each student choose a product from the display and give a brief oral report on how it is grown and used.

For additional ESL support, use Every Student Learns Guide, pp. 158–161.

PAGE 386

Not Just Fruits and Vegetables

Quick Summary Livestock, fish, greenhouse products, and minerals are some important products of the West.

Test Talk

Locate Key Words in the Text

5 Why do you think the fishing industries in Alaska and Hawaii focus on different species of fish? Have students look back in the text. Ask: Is the answer *right there*, or do you have to *combine what you know with what the author tells you?* Possible answer: The very different climates of the two states affect water temperature and which fish live in each place. **Make Inferences**

6 What products other than fruits and vegetables are important to the West? Livestock, fish and shellfish, greenhouse products, and mineral resources **Summarize**

✓ **REVIEW ANSWER** Both have large fishing industries. **Compare and Contrast**

Not Just Fruits and Vegetables

The West produces more than just fruits, vegetables, grains, and nuts. In some western states, livestock are the main source of income from agriculture. **Livestock** are animals that are raised on farms and ranches. Cattle, sheep, and pigs are examples of livestock. Montana, Idaho, Colorado, Washington, Wyoming, Alaska, and Utah all include beef cattle as one of their main sources of income. Nevada, Utah, and Montana also produce sheep and sheep products such as wool. Milk is produced in states around the region as well.

The fishing industry is very important to the economy of some Western states. In Alaska the yearly fish catch is valued at more than a billion dollars. Workers catch cod, flounder, salmon, and halibut, among other types of fish. Shellfish, such as crab and shrimp, are also important to Alaska's economy. Hawaii also has a large fishing industry. Swordfish and tuna are
5 caught off the coast of Hawaii.

▶ Fishing for salmon

In addition to the many food products that are grown in the West, many states grow flowers, plants, and bushes to be sold in plant and flower shops. These are often referred to as greenhouse products because they are generally grown in a greenhouse.

The West is also known for its wealth of mineral resources. Alaska and California produce oil. Coal, gold, and lead are three minerals mined in Colorado. Gold, silver, and copper, among other minerals, are mined in Nevada and Utah. 6

REVIEW Name one way in which Alaska and Hawaii are similar. **Compare and Contrast**

▶ Cattle are one kind of livestock.

386

Practice and Extend

MEETING INDIVIDUAL NEEDS
Leveled Practice

Learn About Salmon Have groups of students create a three-section written report on salmon, with each group contributing a different section of information.

Easy Have students report on the life cycle of salmon. Encourage them to include pictures or diagrams. **Reteach**

On-Level Have students explain why some western species of salmon have become endangered. Encourage them to include pictures of each endangered species. **Extend**

Challenge Have students describe what steps are being taken to save endangered salmon and what controversies have arisen because of those efforts. **Enrich**

For a Lesson Summary, use Quick Study, p. 80.

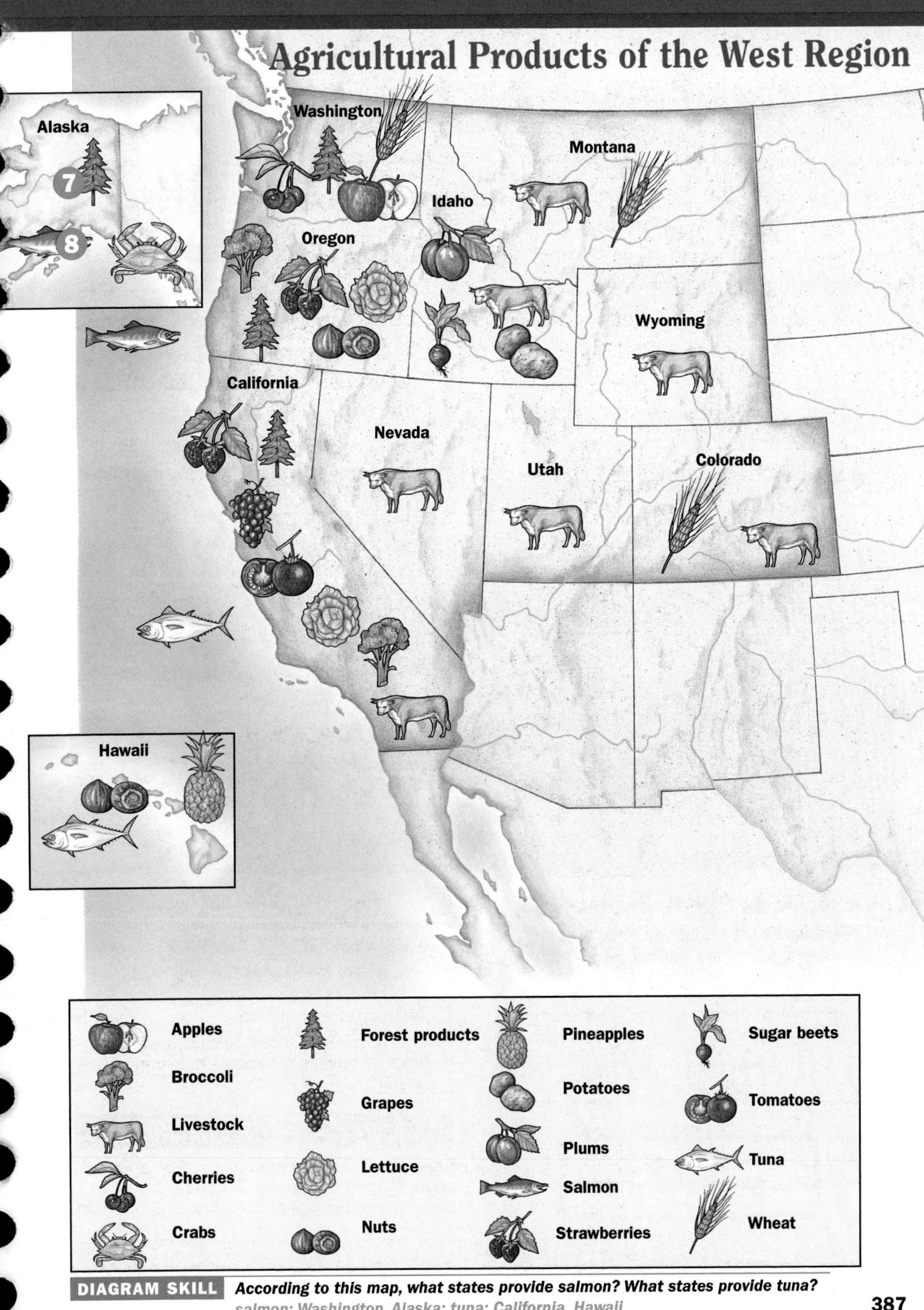

DIAGRAM SKILL ***According to this map, what states provide salmon? What states provide tuna?***
salmon: Washington, Alaska; tuna: California, Hawaii

387

7 Suppose you were moving to the West and wanted to get a job in an agricultural industry. What type of job might you find in Montana? in Alaska? Possible answers: Montana: a job in the cattle or wheat industries; Alaska: a job in the crab, fishing, or forest-products industries **Interpret Maps**

SOCIAL STUDIES STRAND
Economics

Prices of goods usually are determined by supply and demand. Generally, the more there is of a product, the lower its price to consumers.

8 According to the map, where in the West might the price of apples be lowest? of potatoes? Washington; Idaho **Interpret Maps**

DIAGRAM SKILL Answer salmon: Washington, Alaska; tuna: California, Hawaii

MEETING INDIVIDUAL NEEDS
Learning Styles

Explore Agriculture Using their individual learning styles, students learn more about the business of agriculture.

Auditory Learning Have students interview a local farmer, nursery manager, or flower shop owner about the pros and cons of that person's job. Tell students to report their findings to the class.

Logical Learning Have students analyze the map on this page and then state three conclusions that can be drawn from it. Have students justify their conclusions.

Kinesthetic Learning Have students work in pairs to create clay models of the agricultural products produced in a specific western state.

Trees, Please

Quick Summary The timber industry is an important industry in the West.

9 **How do timber companies ensure that their source of trees doesn't run out?** They reforest, or plant new trees to replace the ones they cut. Main Idea and Details

✓ **Ongoing Assessment**

If...	then...
If...students do not understand what it means to *reforest,*	**then...**review with them the meaning of the prefix *re–*.

✓ **REVIEW ANSWER** Possible answer: Because wood is a valuable resource Main Idea and Details

3 Close and Assess

Summarize the Lesson

Have students take turns reading the three main points. If you used the Quick Teaching Plan on p. 384, have students use their drawings to cite examples for each summary point.

✓ **LESSON 3 REVIEW**

1. **Summarize** For possible answers, see the reduced pupil page.
2. Central Valley
3. Possible answer: Fishing
4. Possible answer: People eat livestock and other agricultural products from the West and use wood products from the West. Lumber companies reforest to keep a steady supply of wood.
5. **Critical Thinking: *Draw Conclusions*** Answers should reflect logical thinking and an understanding of the recycling process.

Link to Reading

Encourage students to take notes on their reading and create an outline to organize information for their oral report.

Trees, Please

Wood, also known as timber, and wood products are also produced in certain parts of the West. The timber industry is important to the region. We use wood to build many things, such as houses and furniture. We also use wood products when we clean up a spill with a paper towel or read a book. Paper is a wood product. Wood is a very important part of our everyday lives.

Because wood is such a valuable resource, timber companies usually **reforest,** or plant new trees to replace the ones they cut.

REVIEW Why do timber companies reforest? Main Idea and Details 9

Summarize the Lesson

- **The West produces a wide variety of fruits, vegetables, grains, and nuts.**
- **Raising livestock, fishing, and mining are important industries in the West.**
- **The timber industry in the West provides a variety of wood products.**

LESSON 3 REVIEW

Check Facts and Main Ideas

1. **Summarize** On a separate sheet of paper, draw the following diagram. Fill in the boxes with examples to support the summary in the bottom box.

The West produces many agricultural products. | The West is rich in mineral resources. | The West is rich in timber.

The West has many varied resources.

2. What place in California produces a wide variety of fruits, vegetables, and nuts?
3. Name one of Alaska's important industries.
4. How do people benefit from the resources of the West? Use the terms **livestock** and **reforest** in your answer.
5. **Critical Thinking: *Draw Conclusions*** How does recycling newspapers help conserve timber?

Link to Reading

Read About the Timber Industry Find an article about the timber industry in the West and share it with the class.

388

Practice and Extend

CURRICULUM CONNECTION
Writing

Write a Personal Essay Have students write a personal essay about trees.

- Explain that students may focus their essay on an actual tree, a kind of tree, a specific forest, or a more general topic such as forests or conservation.
- Encourage students to express a point of view and to support their thesis with facts and descriptive details based on research and observation.

Workbook, p. 89

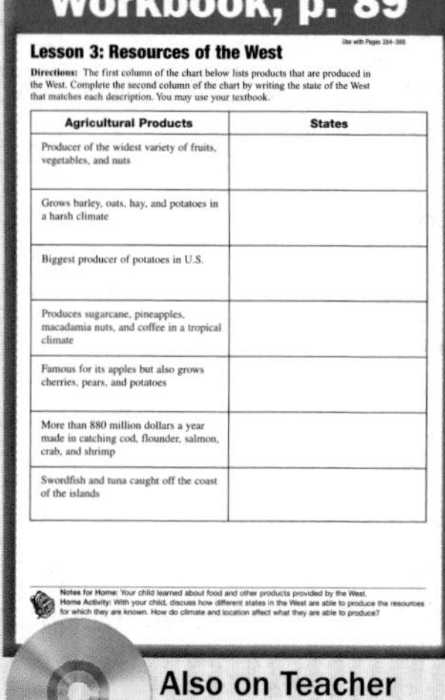

Lesson 3: Resources of the West Use with Pages 384–388.

Directions: The first column of the chart below lists products that are produced in the West. Complete the second column of the chart by writing the state of the West that matches each description. You may use your textbook.

Agricultural Products	States
Producer of the widest variety of fruits, vegetables, and nuts	
Grows barley, oats, hay, and potatoes in a harsh climate	
Biggest producer of potatoes in U.S.	
Produces sugarcane, pineapples, macadamia nuts, and coffee in a tropical climate	
Famous for its apples but also grows cherries, pears, and potatoes	
More than 880 million dollars a year made in catching cod, flounder, salmon, crab, and shrimp	
Swordfish and tuna caught off the coast of the islands	

Notes for Home: Your child learned about food and other products provided by the West.
Home Activity: With your child, discuss how different states in the West are able to produce the resources for which they are known. How do climate and location affect what they are able to produce?

Also on Teacher Resources CD-ROM.

Seth Lewelling

1820–1896

Seth Lewelling was born in 1820 in Randolph County, North Carolina. In 1850 Lewelling moved to Milwaukie, Oregon, and joined his brother in his plant nursery.

The Lewelling nursery was successful. Ah Bing, a farmer from China, was hired as a supervisor. He managed a team of workers. In time the nursery had 18,000 small plants to sell.

BIOFACT

The first trees in Lewelling's nursery traveled with the family over the Oregon Trail.

Lewelling and Bing became friends. Both men knew how to develop new varieties of plants. They both understood that farmers wanted to sell as much fruit as they could. Fruit that could be shipped a long way and still taste good was important. 1

In time, Lewelling and Bing developed a large, dark cherry that had a sweet taste. It remained crisp even when shipped a long 2 way. Lewelling named it the Bing cherry in honor of Ah Bing. Today more people in the United States eat Bing cherries than any other variety.

Learn from Biographies

Popular varieties of apples and grapes were also developed at the Lewelling nursery. Why do you think the nursery was successful in developing new fruits?

For more information, go online to *Meet the People* at **www.sfsocialstudies.com.**

389

BIOGRAPHY

Seth Lewelling

Objective

- Describe an agricultural contribution of Seth Lewelling to the economy of the region.

1 Introduce and Motivate

Preview To activate prior knowledge, ask students if they have ever eaten cherries. Ask what foods they like that are made with cherries.

2 Teach and Discuss

- Explain that many of the fruits, vegetables, and grains we enjoy today have been developed by people who experimented with plants that grow naturally.
- Tell students that Lewelling and Bing developed the most popular cherry in the United States, the Bing cherry.

1 **Why do you think it was important to develop a cherry that could be shipped a long way and still taste good?** Possible answer: So they could be shipped to markets all across the country
Draw Conclusions

2 **What facts do you think Lewelling and Bing considered when deciding if their new type of cherry was a success? What opinions do you think they considered?** Possible answers: Facts: whether the cherry could be shipped a long way and remain crisp; Opinions: the appearance and taste of the cherry
Fact and Opinion

3 Close and Assess

Learn from Biographies Answer

Lewelling and Bing knew how to develop new varieties of plants. Also, they thought carefully about what would ship well.

SOCIAL STUDIES
Background

About Cherries

- Many different species of the genus *Prunus*—which includes cherries, plums, apricots, and almonds—grow in cool areas of the Northern Hemisphere.
- Fruits within the genus *Prunus* have bony, stonelike seeds covered by fruit flesh and an outer peel or skin.
- Some cherry trees are grown for decoration rather than for their fruit, and the wild black cherry, a native North American tree, is valuable for making furniture.

WEB SITE
Technology

Students can find out more about Seth Lewelling by clicking on *Meet the People* at **www.sfsocialstudies.com.**

Resources

- Assessment Book, pp. 65–68
- Workbook, p. 90: Vocabulary Review

Chapter Summary

For possible answers, see the reduced pupil page.

Vocabulary

Possible answers:

1. No trees grow above the timberline of the Rocky Mountains.
2. A geyser is like a volcano because it spews hot material into the air.
3. Once magma reaches Earth's surface, it is called lava.
4. Trees will not grow on the Alaskan tundra.
5. Very little rain falls on the eastern side of the Cascades because of the rain shadow.
6. Many people raise livestock on their ranches in the West.

Places

1. The Rocky Mountains
2. Continental Divide
3. Yellowstone National Park
4. The Great Basin
5. Mount Waialeale in Hawaii

CHAPTER 12 Review

Chapter Summary

Compare and Contrast

On a separate sheet of paper, make a chart and label it like the one shown. List at least one similarity and three differences between the Rocky Mountains and desert areas of the West.

Similarities	Differences
They both extend over several states.	The mountains have a timberline. Desert areas get very little precipitation. Rocky Mountains are very high, but the desert is low.

▶ Rocky Mountains

Vocabulary

Use each word in a sentence that explains the meaning of the word.

1. **timberline** (p. 369)
2. **geyser** (p. 370)
3. **magma** (p. 370)
4. **tundra** (p. 379)
5. **rain shadow** (p. 382)
6. **livestock** (p. 386)

Places

Fill in the blanks with the place that best completes the sentence.

1. ____________ form the largest system of mountains in North America. (p. 369)
2. Rivers to the east of the ____________ flow toward the Atlantic Ocean. (p. 369)
3. The oldest national park in the world is ____________. (p. 370)
4. A large desert region that covers many western states is ____________. (p. 380)
5. ____________ is the wettest place in the world. (p. 382)

390

Practice and Extend

Assessment Options

✓Chapter 12 Assessment

- Chapter 12 Content Test: Use Assessment Book, pp. 65–66.
- Chapter 12 Skills Test: Use Assessment Book, pp. 67–68.

Standardized Test Prep

- Chapter 12 Tests contain standardized test format.

✓Chapter 12 Performance Assessment

- Have students work in small groups to review information in this chapter.
- Tell students to make a three-column chart labeled *Mountains, Climates,* and *Products.*
- Have students take turns adding notes from this chapter to the appropriate columns of their chart.

Facts and Main Ideas

1. What two nations do the Rocky Mountains extend through?
2. Describe two of the landforms in Yellowstone National Park.
3. Name two valleys in the West that produce many fruits and vegetables.
4. **Main Idea** Name three mountain ranges in the West.
5. **Main Idea** Why is the land on the eastern side of the Cascade Range drier than land on the western side?
6. **Main Idea** Describe the agriculture of the West.
7. **Critical Thinking: *Draw Conclusions*** Why are greenhouses important in Alaska?

Write About Geography

1. **Write a journal entry** about a trip to Yellowstone National Park. The entry might involve an animal or a landform.
2. **Write a poem** about climbing a mountain in the Rocky Mountains. Describe what you see and how you feel.
3. **Write an advertisement** for a tour company that takes people through the West. Describe three places where you would take visitors.

Apply Skills

Write Notes and Outlines

Read the following outline. Then answer the questions.

I. Farm products of the West
   A. Fruit
   B. Vegetables
   C. Livestock
II. Metal ores of the West
   A. Copper
   B. Gold
   C. Silver

1. What title would you give this outline?
2. Would a note card's information about apples fit into this outline? If so, where?
3. How might you use this outline?

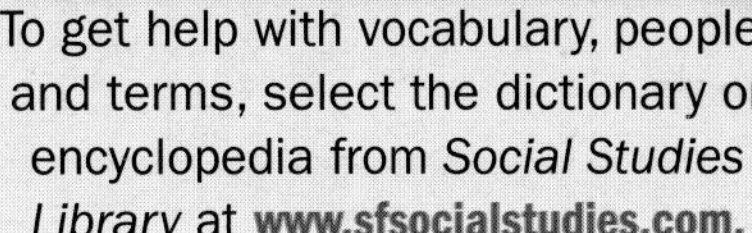

Internet Activity

To get help with vocabulary, people, and terms, select the dictionary or encyclopedia from *Social Studies Library* at **www.sfsocialstudies.com.**

391

Hands-on Unit Project

✓ Unit 6 Performance Assessment

- See p. 424 for information about using the Unit Project as a means of performance assessment.
- A scoring guide is provided on p. 424.

WEB SITE Technology

For more information, students can select the dictionary or encyclopedia from *Social Studies Library* at **www.sfsocialstudies.com.**

Workbook, p. 90

Vocabulary Review

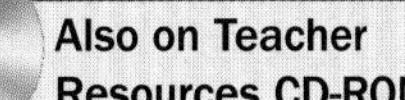

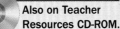

Also on Teacher Resources CD-ROM.

Facts and Main Ideas

Possible answers:

1. Canada, United States
2. Geysers in Yellowstone National Park erupt with steaming water heated by magma under the surface of the park. Yellowstone also has canyons and mountains.
3. Willamette Valley, Central Valley
4. Possible answers: Rocky Mountains, Aleutians, Sierra Nevada
5. The rain shadow effect causes the land on the eastern side of the Cascades to be drier.
6. Many different fruits and vegetables are grown in the West. The states of the West also produce nuts and grains. In some western states, raising livestock is the main source of income from agriculture.
7. The climate in Alaska is too harsh for many crops to be raised outdoors, but plants can be grown in greenhouses.

Write About Geography

1. Encourage students to use the textbook to find details they can use in their journal entries.
2. Encourage students to supplement their research with information from the textbook. Also encourage students to reexamine the photographs in Lesson 1 for inspiration.
3. Have students include a picture from a magazine or their own artwork with the text of their ad.

Apply Skills

1. Possible answer: *Products of the West*
2. Yes; Under *I.*, under *A. Fruit*
3. Possible answer: To guide the writing of a report or a speech on products of the West.

CHAPTER 13

Chapter Planning Guide

Chapter 13 • Living in the West

Locating Places pp. 392–393

Lesson Titles	Pacing	Main Ideas
Lesson 1 **The Tlingit** pp. 394–397	2 days	• The Tlingit live in the northern part of the West.
Here and There: Masks Tell a Story pp. 398–399		• Many different groups create masks for special purposes.
Lesson 2 **Exploration and Growth** pp. 400–406	4 days	• Explorers from Spain and settlers seeking gold helped shape the West.
Biography: Levi Strauss p. 407		• Levi Strauss, the inventor of blue jeans, was a fair employer who donated money for charity and education.
Map and Globe Skills: Understand Latitude and Longitude pp. 408–409		• Lines of latitude and longitude are used to determine location.
Lesson 3 **Business and Pleasure** pp. 410–415	3 days	• Cities in the West have many different kinds of businesses and attractions.
Citizen Heroes: Fairness Building a City pp. 416–417		• Thomas Bradley promoted fairness in Los Angeles and helped develop the Los Angeles Metro Rail system.
✓ **Chapter 13 Review** pp. 418–419		

◀ **Moviemaking is a major industry in California.**

✓ **= Assessment Options**

◀ **The Tlingit used wood from the surrounding forests to carve elaborate images.**

Vocabulary	Resources	Meeting Individual Needs
totem pole potlatch	• Workbook, p. 92 • Transparency 6 • Every Student Learns Guide, pp. 162–165 • Quick Study, pp. 82–83	• ESL Support, TE p. 396 • Leveled Practice, TE p. 397 • Learning Styles, TE p. 398
prospector boom town ghost town latitude parallel equator Northern Hemisphere Southern Hemisphere longitude meridian prime meridian	• Workbook, p. 93 • Transparencies 23, 61–63 • Every Student Learns Guide, pp. 166–169 • Quick Study, pp. 84–85 • Workbook, p. 94	• Leveled Practice, TE p. 402 • ESL Support, TE p. 403
computer software international trade	• Workbook, p. 95 • Transparencies 14, 64 • Every Student Learns Guide, pp. 170–173 • Quick Study, pp. 86–87	• Leveled Practice, TE p. 412 • ESL Support, TE p. 414
	✔ Chapter 13 Content Test, Assessment Book, pp. 69–70 ✔ Chapter 13 Skills Test, Assessment Book, pp. 71–72	✔ Chapter 13 Performance Assessment, TE p. 418

Providing More Depth

Additional Resources

- Vocabulary Workbook and Cards
- Social Studies Plus! pp. 134–139
- Daily Activity Bank
- Big Book Atlas
- Student Atlas
- Outline Maps
- Desk Maps

Technology

- AudioText
- MindPoint® Quiz Show CD-ROM
- ExamView® Test Bank CD-ROM
- Teacher Resources CD-ROM
- Map Resources CD-ROM
- SFSuccessNet: iText (Pupil Edition online), iTE (Teacher's Edition online), Online Planner
- **www.sfsocialstudies.com** (Biographies, news, references, maps, and activities)

To establish guidelines for your students' safe and responsible use of the Internet, use the Scott Foresman Internet Guide.

Additional Internet Links

To find out more about:

- The Tlingit, visit **www.tlingit-haida.org**
- California Gold Rush, visit **www.museumca.org**
- Los Angeles, California, visit **www.lacity.org**

Key Internet Search Terms

- Levi Strauss
- Seattle, Washington
- Salt Lake City, Utah

Workbook Support

Use the following Workbook pages to support content and skills development as you teach Chapter 13. You can also view and print Workbook pages from the Teacher Resources CD-ROM.

Workbook, p. 91

Use with Chapter 13.

Vocabulary Preview

Directions: Match each vocabulary term on the left with its definition on the right. Write the letter of the definition on the line beside the term. You may use your textbook.

Answer	Term	Definition
e	1. totem pole	a. feast often held to celebrate important events in a family's life
a	2. potlatch	b. programs that help computers run certain functions
g	3. prospector	c. fast-growing town located near the discovery of gold, silver or other valuable metal ore
c	4. boom town	d. trade between different countries
f	5. ghost town	e. tall post carved with images of people and animals
b	6. computer software	f. town that was deserted once the metal ore in the area was mined
d	7. international trade	g. person who searches for valuable minerals

Directions: Imagine you are a prospector heading toward California in search of gold. Write a diary entry in which you describe your experiences on your journey to California. Use the terms *prospector, boom town,* and *ghost town* in your entry.

Students should include the three vocabulary words and information from the chapter in their diary entries.

Notes for Home: Your child learned the vocabulary terms for Chapter 13.
Home Activity: With your child, make a list of products you have at home and, by reading the labels, identify the countries in which they were made. Discuss international trade and some of the goods that are exchanged between countries.

Use with Pupil Edition, p. 392

Workbook, p. 92

Use with Pages 394–397.

Lesson 1: The Tlingit

Directions: Use the terms in the box to complete each sentence with information from Lesson 1. Write the word on the line provided. You may use your textbook.

logging	money	gifts
fishing	Chilkat	trading network
potlatch	Sealaska Corporation	totem pole
Tlingit	household goods	

1. The **Tlingit** are a group of Native Americans who live along the southeastern coast of Alaska and the northern coast of British Columbia.
2. A Tlingit family often placed a **totem pole**, carved with images of people or animals, outside their home.
3. The Tlingit had a large **trading network** with other tribes through which they bought and sold canoes, copper, baskets, and other goods.
4. One of the most prized Tlingit products is a **Chilkat** blanket, which is woven from the dyed wool of mountain goats and sheep.
5. A Native American might hold a **potlatch** to celebrate an important event such as a wedding, birth, or death.
6. During a traditional potlatch, the host gave **gifts** such as canoes, blankets, and other goods to each guest.
7. The gifts given at today's potlatches often include **money** and **household goods**.
8. Today many Tlingit make their living by **logging** or **fishing**.
9. The **Sealaska Corporation** makes sure the Tlingit and other Native Americans will have enough money and land in the future.

Notes for Home: Your child learned about Native Americans called the Tlingit.
Home Activity: With your child, discuss what types of events occur at a traditional potlatch. Discuss reasons a potlatch might be held, the gifts that might be given, and the activities that might occur at a potlatch.

Use with Pupil Edition, p. 397

Workbook, p. 93

Use with Pages 400–406.

Lesson 2: Exploration and Growth

Directions: Sequence the events in the order in which they took place by numbering them from 1 (earliest) to 13 (most recent). You may use your textbook.

Answer	Event
6	1. The California Gold Rush begins.
11	2. Gold is found in Alaska.
1	3. Juan Rodríguez Cabrillo is probably the first European to see the coast of California.
3	4. American settlers travel to the West to claim California.
13	5. Hawaii becomes a state.
8	6. The Gold Rush ends, and many boom towns become ghost towns.
5	7. John Sutter and John Marshall discover gold in California, and word of the discovery gets out.
9	8. The cattle driving boom in the West begins.
4	9. The United States defeats Mexico, and Mexico is forced to give up California.
12	10. Alaska becomes a state.
7	11. Population in California soars, and businesses boom.
10	12. Russia sells Alaska to the United States for about two cents an acre.
2	13. The Franciscans build 21 missions in California.

Notes for Home: Your child learned about the history of the West.
Home Activity: With your child, discuss how the discovery of gold and other resources changed the West. How do these discoveries still affect the United States today?

Workbook — Lesson Review **93**

Use with Pupil Edition, p. 406

Workbook Support

Workbook, p. 94

Understand Latitude and Longitude

Use with Pages 408–409.

Directions: Use the terms in the box to complete each sentence. Write the terms on the line provided.

latitude	Northern Hemisphere	meridian	equator
parallel	Southern Hemisphere	prime meridian	longitude

1. Longitude is measured in degrees east and west of the **prime meridian**.
2. Each **parallel**, or line of latitude, is always the same distance apart from another.
3. The equator splits the Earth into two halves, called the **Northern Hemisphere** and the **Southern Hemisphere**.
4. A line that extends north and south is a line of **longitude**.
5. A line that extends east and west is a line of **latitude**.
6. Another name for a line of longitude is **meridian**.
7. The **equator** is the imaginary line, labeled 0° latitude, that divides Earth into two halves.

Directions: Answer the following questions on the lines provided. You may use your textbook.

8. What do lines of latitude and longitude form on globes and maps? **grid**
9. If a city is located on a line of latitude labeled 40°N, is it located in the Northern Hemisphere or Southern Hemisphere? **Northern Hemisphere**
10. How does someone locate a place on a map by using its lines of latitude and longitude? **Find the latitude line with that label. Run your finger along that line until it crosses the correctly labeled line of longitude. This is the location on the map.**

Notes for Home: Your child learned to use latitude and longitude to locate places on a map.
Home Activity: With your child, use the atlas map of the United States to find the approximate location of your city and other large cities in the United States.

Use with Pupil Edition, p. 409

Workbook, p. 95

Lesson 3: Business and Pleasure

Use with Pages 410–415.

Directions: Classify each term or phrase by writing it in one of the city boxes below.

computer software, ships, jet airplanes	pleasant climate	second largest city in the United States
entertainment industry	California	skiing and winter sports
named after Great Salt Lake	high-tech companies	Space Needle
mining industry	Utah	movies and television shows
Washington	north of California	next to mountains

Los Angeles
1. entertainment industry
2. pleasant climate
3. California
4. second largest city in the United States
5. movies and television shows

Seattle
1. computer software, ships, jet airplanes
2. Washington
3. high-tech companies
4. Space Needle
5. north of California

Salt Lake City
1. named after Great Salt Lake
2. mining industry
3. Utah
4. next to mountains
5. skiing and winter sports

Notes for Home: Your child learned about businesses and attractions of cities in the West.
Home Activity: With your child, locate Los Angeles, Seattle, and Salt Lake City on a United States map. Then make a Venn diagram to compare and contrast the climate, attractions, and businesses located in these cities.

Use with Pupil Edition, p. 415

Workbook, p. 96

Vocabulary Review

Use with Chapter 13.

Directions: The underlined vocabulary terms below have been misplaced so that each appears in the wrong sentence. Write each term on the line beside the sentence in which it actually belongs. You may use your textbook.

prospector 1. A potlatch was a person looking for gold.
international trade 2. Trade between the United States and countries that border the Pacific Ocean is called computer software.
boom town 3. A town that sprang up due to the discovery of gold or silver in the area was called a ghost town.
totem pole 4. The figures on a prospector are carved and often brightly painted with images of people and animals.
potlatch 5. A totem pole is a traditional feast held by some Native Americans to celebrate important events in a family's life.
ghost town 6. A town often became a boom town once an area was mined and the town was deserted.
computer software 7. Many high-tech companies that make international trade are located in Seattle, Washington.

Directions: In the box on the left, draw a picture of an 1800s boom town in the West. Then, in the box on the right, draw a picture to show what a boom town might have looked like when it became a ghost town.

Boom Town	Ghost Town

Notes for Home: Your child learned the vocabulary terms for Chapter 13.
Home Activity: With your child, practice saying, spelling, and using these vocabulary terms in correct contexts.

Use with Pupil Edition, p. 419

Workbook, p. 97

Discovery SCHOOL

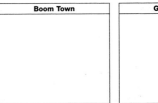

Unit 6 Project Great State

Directions: In a group, prepare a booklet that shows what's great about your state today—and what will be great in the future.

1. Our current event is ______.
2. This is a description of the current event: ______
3. This is our prediction of what will happen in the future: ______
4. This is a description of the pictures we will include in our booklet:
   1st picture: ______
   2nd picture: ______
   3rd picture: ______
   4th picture: ______

Gather relevant resources, such as recent newspapers or magazines, from your school or local library to assist groups in selecting and researching a current event.

Checklist for Students
- ____ We chose a current event about our state.
- ____ We wrote a paragraph about the current event.
- ____ We wrote predictions about the future.
- ____ We illustrated the current event.
- ____ We shared our booklet with the class.

Notes for Home: Your child learned about current events in your state.
Home Activity: With your child, discuss some events that occurred in the past in your state. Share details about the event, and discuss how the event has affected your state today.

Use with Pupil Edition, p. 424

Assessment Support

Use the following Assessment Book pages and The test maker to assess content and skills in Chapter 13 and Unit 6. You can also view and print Assessment Book pages from the Teacher Resources CD-ROM.

Assessment Book, p. 69

Chapter 13 Test

Part 1: Content Test

Directions: Fill in the circle next to the correct answer.

Lesson Objective (1:1)

1. Which of the following is NOT an example of the traditional Tlingit way of life?
   - Ⓐ During the summer they lived in small wooden homes near hunting and fishing grounds.
   - Ⓑ The designs of totem poles and Chilkat blankets told stories.
   - Ⓒ They carved wooden canoes for hunting and fishing.
   - ● They did not communicate with other tribes.

Lesson Objective (1:2)

2. Which is NOT a way in which the Tlingit used the natural resources in their region?
   - ● They celebrated important events in their lives.
   - Ⓑ They built homes from large planks of wood.
   - Ⓒ They fished for salmon.
   - Ⓓ They hunted deer and seals.

Lesson Objective (1:3)

3. Why do the Tlingit hold potlatches?
   - Ⓐ demonstrate Tlingit dances to tourists
   - Ⓑ teach children how to hunt and fish
   - Ⓒ show products of the Tlingit craftspeople
   - ● celebrate important events in a family's life

Lesson Objective (1:3)

4. How are potlatches today different from potlatches held in the past?
   - ● Today's gifts often include money and household goods.
   - Ⓑ The host provides food for the guests to eat.
   - Ⓒ The host and honored guests made speeches.
   - Ⓓ People participate in dancing.

Lesson Objective (1:4)

5. How are the lives of some Tlingit today similar to the lives of their ancestors?
   - Ⓐ They earn money in the logging industry.
   - ● They live on the same land.
   - Ⓒ They live in villages of modern homes.
   - Ⓓ They are part of the Sealaska Corporation.

Lesson Objective (2:2)

6. Why did people explore the West?
   - Ⓐ to hunt in the Appalachian Mountains
   - Ⓑ to find a way to reach the Mississippi River
   - ● to find riches
   - Ⓓ to become Catholic

Lesson Objective (2:1, 3)

7. How did the Gold Rush of 1849 change San Francisco?
   - Ⓐ It became a ghost town.
   - ● It grew into a large city.
   - Ⓒ It was named the state capital.
   - Ⓓ Businesses boarded up their windows and closed.

Assessment Book Unit 6, Chapter 13 Test **69**

Use with Pupil Edition, p. 418

Assessment Book, p. 70

Lesson Objective (2:4)

8. What might have occurred to cause a boom town to become a ghost town?
   - ● A boom town was deserted once the area was mined.
   - Ⓑ Businesses became successful and the town grew.
   - Ⓒ Ghost towns sprang up wherever gold was discovered.
   - Ⓓ Cattle drives took over the boom towns.

Lesson Objective (2:1)

9. What changes occurred in the West to give the "Wild West" its name?
   - Ⓐ William "Buffalo Bill" Cody formed a popular theater show known as the "Wild West."
   - ● Colorful and often violent characters in boom towns and "cow towns" created a lasting legend.
   - Ⓒ Herds of horses, cows, and other animals were allowed to roam wild throughout the region.
   - Ⓓ Once gold was discovered in Alaska, thousands of Californians rushed to claim it.

Lesson Objective (2:5)

10. Which of the following statements about the West is NOT true?
    - Ⓐ Alaska and Hawaii joined the Union in the same year.
    - Ⓑ The Western territories became states between 1850 and 1959.
    - Ⓒ The United States purchased Alaska for about two cents an acre.
    - ● Alaska was the fiftieth state to enter the Union.

Lesson Objective (3:3)

11. Why is Los Angeles a popular place to visit and live?
    - ● The area has a sunny, pleasant climate.
    - Ⓑ Tourism is not an important industry.
    - Ⓒ Los Angeles is the largest city in the United States.
    - Ⓓ Excellent fruits and vegetables are grown nearby.

Lesson Objective (3:2)

12. Which of the following is an important industry in Seattle?
    - Ⓐ entertainment
    - Ⓑ mining
    - Ⓒ salt
    - ● computer software

Lesson Objective (3:1)

13. How does tourism in Salt Lake City differ from tourism in Los Angeles?
    - ● In Salt Lake City, tourists enjoy winter sports, such as skiing.
    - Ⓑ Salt Lake City does not attract many tourists to its area.
    - Ⓒ Tourism is a very important industry in Salt Lake City.
    - Ⓓ In Salt Lake City, tourists visit beaches and amusement parks.

Lesson Objective (3:4)

14. Which of the following products is NOT imported to the United States from Pacific Rim countries?
    - ● timber
    - Ⓑ cars
    - Ⓒ clothing
    - Ⓓ electronic equipment

Use with Pupil Edition, p. 418

Assessment Book, p. 71

Lesson Objective (3:4)

15. From which country does the United States import many automobiles?
    - Ⓐ Australia
    - Ⓑ China
    - Ⓒ Malaysia
    - ● Japan

Part 2: Skills Test

Directions: Use complete sentences to answer questions 1–5. Use a separate sheet of paper if you need more space.

1. Compare and contrast traditional Tlingit potlatches with modern potlatches. **Compare and Contrast**

   Same: potlatches celebrate important events in the life of a family. Traditions are a part of modern potlatches. Different: traditional potlatches often lasted as long as 12 days, and the gifts were often canoes and blankets. Today potlatches are often held on weekends, and gifts include cash or household goods.

2. Why do you think many Tlingit have begun to learn more about the culture of their ancestors? Why would a culture's past be important for its future? **Make Inferences**

   Possible answers: Many Tlingit want to teach their traditions to their children. If the people of a culture do not pass on its traditions, that culture may disappear.

Use with Pupil Edition, p. 418

Assessment Book, p. 72

3. Summarize how, when, and by whom missions were set up in what is today southern California. **Summarize**

   In the late 1700s Father Junípero Serra left his mission to set up the first California mission in 1769. By 1823 the Franciscans had built 21 missions in California. These missions served both Native Americans and Spanish settlers.

4. What were two effects of the California Gold Rush? **Cause and Effect**

   Possible answer: Towns sprang up throughout the West wherever gold was discovered. Many businesses also grew to support the population in the new boom towns.

5. Why do countries conduct international trade? **Draw Conclusions**

   Countries trade with one another to buy or sell resources, goods, or services their people want or need.

Use with Pupil Edition, p. 418

Assessment Support

Assessment Book, p. 73

Unit 6 Test

Part 1: Content Test

Directions: Fill in the circle next to the correct answer.

Lesson Objective (12–1:1, 3)

1. Which is true about the Rocky Mountains?
   - ● Many types of animals, such as goats and minks, live there.
   - Ⓑ They are the smallest system of mountains in the United States.
   - Ⓒ Very few trees and almost no flowers grow there.
   - Ⓓ Visitors cannot ski or hike.

Lesson Objective (12–1:4)

2. Which of these are Yellowstone's most popular points of interest?
   - ● geysers
   - Ⓑ mountains
   - Ⓒ meadows
   - Ⓓ glaciers

Lesson Objective (12–2:1, 2)

3. How are the climates of Hawaii and California similar?
   - ● It is warm and sunny in most of both states.
   - Ⓑ Temperatures rarely rise above the freezing level.
   - Ⓒ Areas of both states have freezing temperatures and snow in the winter.
   - Ⓓ Both states are drier than the Great Basin region of the West.

Lesson Objective (12–2:3)

4. Which of these areas receives less than 2 inches of rainfall each year?
   - Ⓐ Yakima, Washington
   - ● Death Valley, California
   - Ⓒ Mount Waialeale, Hawaii
   - Ⓓ Olympic Peninsula, Washington

Lesson Objective (12–3:1, 2)

5. For which product is Washington most famous
   - Ⓐ apricots
   - Ⓑ sheep
   - Ⓒ fish
   - ● apples

Lesson Objective (12–3:1)

6. Which product from the West is used to make furniture and paper?
   - Ⓐ livestock
   - Ⓑ shellfish
   - ● timber
   - Ⓓ grains

Lesson Objective (13–1:1)

7. Which is NOT an example of the traditional Tlingit way of life?
   - Ⓐ They built homes out of large planks of wood.
   - Ⓑ They fished for salmon and hunted deer.
   - Ⓒ They traded goods with other Native Americans.
   - ● They sold totem poles and Chilkat blankets to tourists.

Lesson Objective (13–1:1, 2)

8. Which has been one of the most prized Tlingit products for many years?
   - Ⓐ totem pole
   - Ⓑ potlatch mask
   - Ⓒ Tlingit home
   - ● Chilkat blanket

Use with Pupil Edition, p. 422

Assessment Book, p. 74

Lesson Objective (13–1:1, 3)

9. Which is one reason why a Tlingit family would hold a potlatch?
   - Ⓐ celebrate a winning football team
   - Ⓑ teach neighbors about the family's history
   - ● celebrate a daughter's wedding
   - Ⓓ place a new totem pole by their door

Lesson Objective (13–1:3, 4)

10. How are modern Tlingit potlatches similar to traditional potlatches?
    - Ⓐ Gifts often include cash and household goods.
    - ● Potlatches include speeches, dancing, and feasting.
    - Ⓒ Potlatches can last up to 12 days.
    - Ⓓ Guests attend potlatches on the weekends so as not to miss work.

Lesson Objective (13–2:1, 3)

11. Why did many people rush to the West in the late 1840s?
    - ● seek their fortunes in gold
    - Ⓑ set up Catholic missions
    - Ⓒ build fur-trading posts
    - Ⓓ claim land for Mexico

Lesson Objective (13–2:1, 4)

12. What negative effect did boom towns have on California?
    - Ⓐ Boom towns grew into large cities.
    - Ⓑ New businesses were in great demand.
    - Ⓒ People made their way to California using different means of transportation.
    - ● Boom towns attracted often violent characters and rarely had good police departments.

Lesson Objective (13–2:1, 5)

13. Why did the United States purchase Alaska from Russia?
    - Ⓐ They thought gold might be discovered there.
    - ● They thought that fur trapping in Alaska would help the United States.
    - Ⓒ Oil deposits were discovered there.
    - Ⓓ There were important United States military bases there.

Lesson Objective (13–3:1, 2)

14. Which of these describes Los Angeles?
    - Ⓐ a city with a cool climate and many high-tech companies
    - Ⓑ a city in the Rockies where winter sports are very popular
    - ● a city with a sunny, pleasant climate and beautiful beaches
    - Ⓓ a city whose main industry is mining

Lesson Objective (13–3:4)

15. Which of these products is NOT imported to the United States from Pacific Rim countries?
    - ● milk
    - Ⓑ cars
    - Ⓒ electronics
    - Ⓓ meat

Use with Pupil Edition, p. 422

Assessment Book, p. 75

Part 2: Skills Test

Directions: Use complete sentences to answer questions 1–5. Use a separate sheet of paper if you need more space.

1. Which three details might you include in a summary of Yellowstone National Park? **Summarize**

   Possible answer: It is the oldest national park in the world. It is located in Wyoming, Idaho, and Montana. It is famous for many natural attractions, such as the geyser Old Faithful.

2. Compare and contrast a tundra with a desert. **Compare and Contrast**

   Same: both describe different types of land with limited vegetation. Trees cannot grow in a tundra, and only certain types of plants can grow in a desert. Different: a tundra is a cold, flat area. A desert is usually dry and warm.

3. Why do you think Sutter and Marshall tried to keep their gold discovery a secret? Why might it have been difficult for them to do so? **Hypothesize**

   Possible answer: Sutter and Marshall may have wanted to keep all the fortune for themselves.

Assessment Book   Unit 6 Test **75**

Use with Pupil Edition, p. 422

Assessment Book, p. 76

4. How did boom towns become ghost towns? Write the events in the order in which they happened. **Sequence**

   A boom town sprang up wherever gold, silver, or other valuable metal ore was discovered. As prospectors moved to the area, new businesses were needed. When the metal ore was mined, people moved away. Businesses were unable to survive without the booming population, and they eventually closed.

5. What effect did the rapid growth of boom towns have on California? **Cause and Effect**

   Possible answer: Many people rushed to California in search of gold, causing towns to grow quickly. Because towns grew so quickly, many of them had problems, such as no system of law enforcement.

Use with Pupil Edition, p. 422

CHAPTER 13

Living in the West

Chapter 13 Outline

- **Lesson 1, *The Tlingit,*** pp. 394–397
- **Here and There: *Masks Tell a Story,*** pp. 398–399
- **Lesson 2, *Exploration and Growth,*** pp. 400–406
- **Biography: *Levi Strauss,*** p. 407
- **Map and Globe Skills: *Understand Latitude and Longitude,*** pp. 408–409
- **Lesson 3, *Business and Pleasure,*** pp. 410–415
- **Citizen Heroes: *Building a City,*** pp. 416–417

Resources

- Workbook, p. 91: Vocabulary Preview
- Vocabulary Cards
- Social Studies Plus!

Tlingit Cultural Region: Lesson 1

As this picture shows, the Tlingit carved wooden canoes to use in their daily lives. Ask students how they think the Tlingit have used these canoes. (To travel and fish)

Sutter's Mill, California: Lesson 2

The discovery of gold at Sutter's Mill, California, brought a flood of fortune-seekers to the West. Ask students what they can tell about the life of a gold prospector from the picture. (Life was not easy for a prospector)

Los Angeles, California: Lesson 3

Ask students what images come to mind when they think of Los Angeles. Then ask them to look at the picture. How does the picture support or contradict their mental images of Los Angeles? (Many movies are made in Los Angeles.)

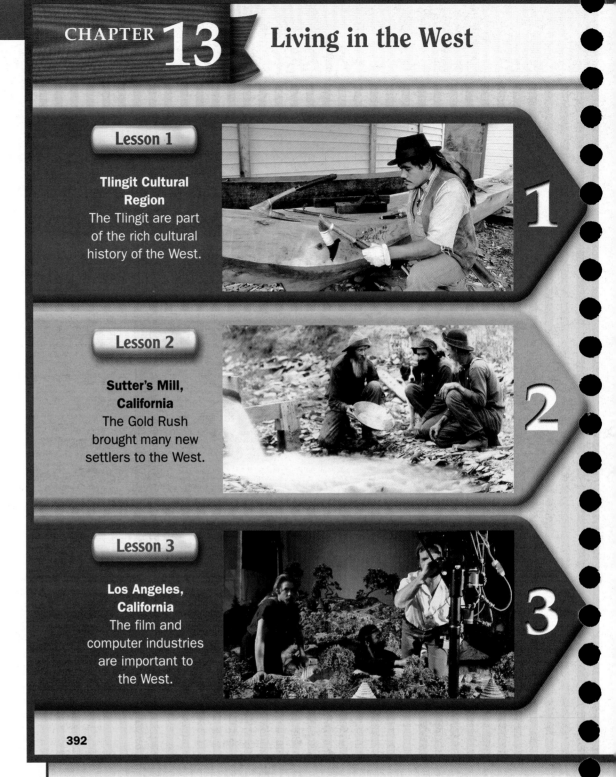

CHAPTER 13 **Living in the West**

Lesson 1

Tlingit Cultural Region
The Tlingit are part of the rich cultural history of the West.

1

Lesson 2

Sutter's Mill, California
The Gold Rush brought many new settlers to the West.

2

Lesson 3

Los Angeles, California
The film and computer industries are important to the West.

3

392

Practice and Extend

Vocabulary Preview

- Use Workbook p. 91 to help students preview the vocabulary words in this chapter.
- Use Vocabulary Cards to preview key concept words in this chapter.

Also on Teacher Resources CD-ROM.

Workbook, p. 91

Vocabulary Preview Use with Chapter 13.

Directions: Match each vocabulary term on the left with its definition on the right. Write the letter of the definition on the line beside the term. You may use your textbook.

____ 1. totem pole
____ 2. potlatch
____ 3. prospector
____ 4. boom town
____ 5. ghost town
____ 6. computer software
____ 7. international trade

a. feast often held to celebrate important events in a family's life
b. programs that help computers run certain functions
c. fast-growing town located near the discovery of gold, silver or other valuable metal ore
d. trade between different countries
e. tall post carved with images of people and animals
f. town that was deserted once the metal ore in the area was mined
g. person who searches for valuable minerals

Directions: Imagine you are a prospector heading toward California in search of gold. Write a diary entry in which you describe your experiences on your journey to California. Use the terms *prospector, boom town,* and *ghost town* in your entry.

Notes for Home: Your child learned the vocabulary terms for Chapter 13.
Home Activity: With your child, make a list of products you have at home and, by reading the labels, identify the countries in which they were made. Discuss international trade and some of the goods that are exchanged between countries.

Locating Places

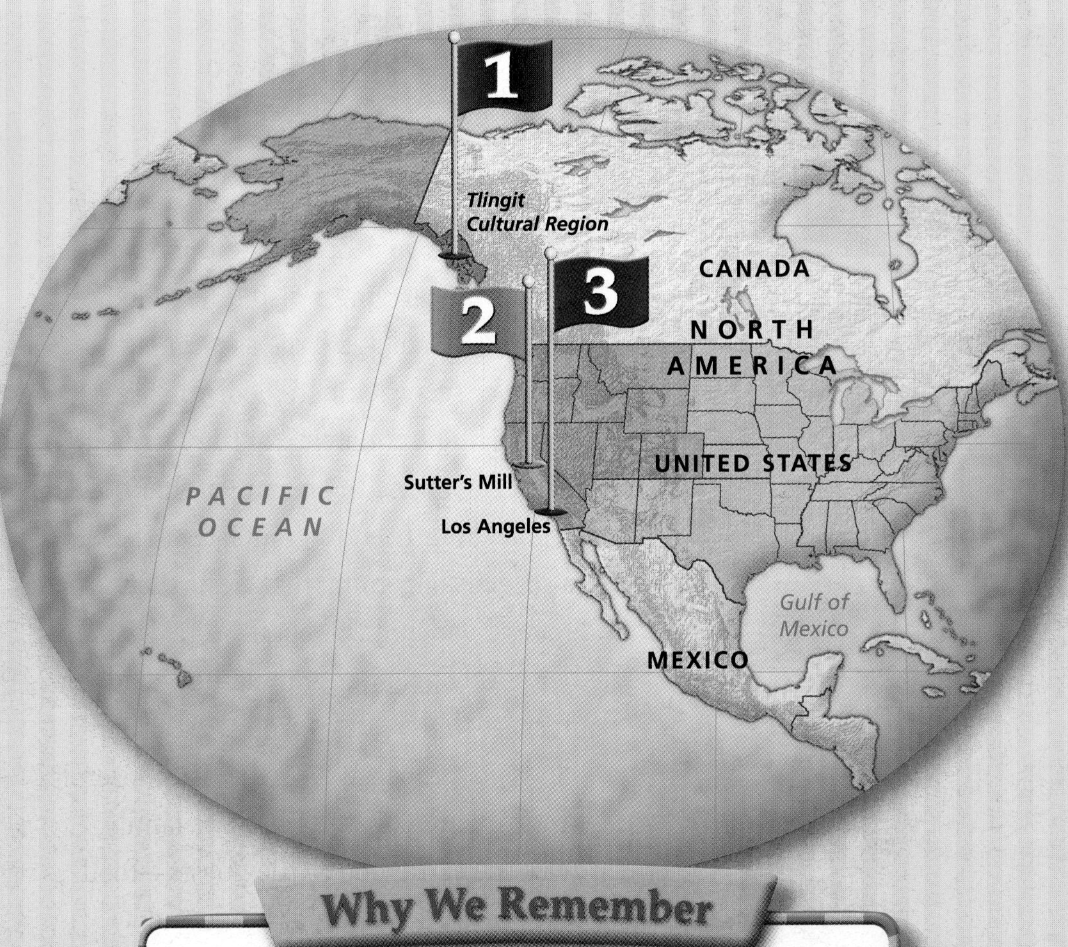

Why We Remember

People have long been attracted to the West because of its rich resources. People have lived in the West for thousands of years. Even before the Gold Rush, Americans were traveling west for rich farmland and living space. Then the Gold Rush brought thousands of people from all over the world. Many stayed even after most of the gold was gone, and more have since arrived. All the people of the West, past and present, have aided the development of the culture and economy of the United States.

393

Locating Places

- Have students examine the pictures shown on p. 392 for Lessons 1, 2, and 3.
- Remind students that each picture is coded with both a number and a color to link it to a place on the map on p. 393.

Why We Remember

Have students read the "Why We Remember" paragraph on p. 393 and ask why places in this chapter might be important to them. Have students consider how both natural resources and people have influenced the history of the West.

WEB SITE Technology

You can learn more about the Tlingit Cultural Region; Sutter's Mill, California; and Los Angeles, California, by clicking on *Atlas* at **www.sfsocialstudies.com.**

SOCIAL STUDIES STRAND Geography

Mental Mapping Have students picture in their minds the states that make up the West Region, including Alaska and Hawaii. Ask students what makes Alaska and Hawaii a part of the West. Extend discussion to include cultural relationships as well as geographical ones.

The Tlingit

Objectives

- Write a summary of traditional Tlingit life.
- Describe how the Tlingit make use of natural resources.
- Compare and contrast Tlingit potlatches held in the past and today.
- List details of modern Tlingit life.

Vocabulary

totem pole, p. 395; **potlatch,** p. 396

Resources

- Workbook, p. 92
- Transparency 6
- Every Student Learns Guide, pp. 162–165
- Quick Study, pp. 82–83

Quick Teaching Plan

If time is short, have students record information from the lesson in a compare-and-contrast chart.

- As they read the lesson, have students focus on the traditional and modern ways of the Tlingit.
- Have students use their charts to record similarities and differences between the Tlingit's lives in the past and in the present.

1 Introduce and Motivate

Preview To ac[...] invite volunteer[...] parties they ha[...] enjoyed firstha[...] family reunion.

You Are There Ask s[...] is like[...] Ask h[...] other tradition[...] birthday party[...] gathering. (Un[...] gatherings, th[...] party also is g[...]

Nebraska /
Nicholas Hudson

LESSON 1

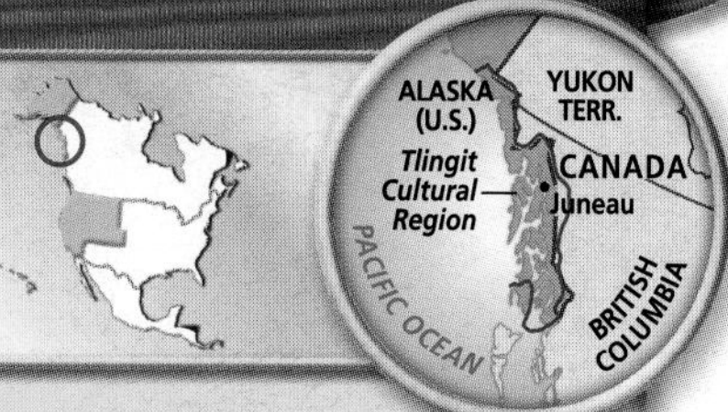

PREVIEW

Focus on the Main Idea
The Tlingit live in the northern part of the West.

PLACES
Tlingit Cultural Region
Juneau, Alaska

VOCABULARY
totem pole
potlatch

▶ Tlingit wood carving

The Tlingit

You Are There Two people enter the room carrying a dish full of food that's as large as a canoe. You've never seen so much food! You are a guest at a Tlingit potlatch. Your best friend's family is celebrating the raising of their new totem pole. Your friend's grandfather rises to give a speech welcoming his guests. Soon the singing and dancing will begin. Your friend and her family help her grandfather hand out presents to the guests. Your best friend hands you a special gift. She has chosen it just for you. After the feast, the family gives the extra food to the guests—food that everyone will eat at home and remember this celebration.

Summarize As you read, think of ways to summarize what you have learned about the Tlingit.

Practice and Extend

[...]ING SKILL
[...]mmarize

[...]e Lesson Review, students [...]plete a graphic organizer like [...]ne below. You may want to [...]de students with a copy of [...]sparency 6 to complete as they [...] the lesson.

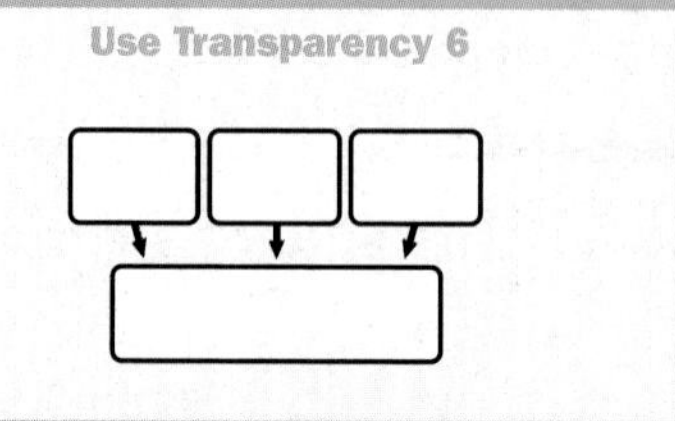
Use Transparency 6

VOCABULARY
Individual Word Study

The word *totem* comes from the Ojibwa word *do-daim,* which means "clan" or "village" (the village being where a family or clan lived together). An animal, bird, fish, plant, or other natural object may be taken as the emblem, or totem, of the family or group. Images of a group's totems often are important articles of decoration. In some groups, totem images are combined on a totem pole. The totem pole tells the story of the background of the family that created it.

Tlingit Traditions

The Tlingit (KLINHNG it) are Native Americans who live along the southeastern coast of Alaska and the northern coast of British Columbia in Canada. This area makes up the **Tlingit cultural region.** The influence of Tlingit culture is strong throughout this area.

This region is rich in natural resources. Vast forests grow there, and fish and game are plentiful. For hundreds of years the Tlingit made good use of these resources. They fished for salmon and hunted deer and seals. They used large planks of wood to build large homes. The Tlingit often carved figures into the doorways of their homes. Tlingit families often placed totem poles outside their homes as well, and some Tlingit families still follow this tradition. A **totem pole** is a tall post carved with the images of
1 people and animals. These images are often brightly painted. They often represent the history of the family.

The Tlingit lived in these homes during winter. During the warmer months, they moved to smaller wooden homes near hunting and fishing grounds. They carved wooden canoes for fishing and hunting.

Because game and fish were so plentiful, the Tlingit were able to spend time making and trading goods such as canoes, blankets, copper tools and ornaments, baskets, and seal oil. They had 2 a large trading network with other Native Americans. Sometimes they bought goods from one group to trade with another.

One of the most prized Tlingit products, even today, is the Chilkat (CHILL kat) blanket. It was traditionally woven from the dyed wool of mountain goats and sheep. These colorful blankets have detailed designs of shapes and animals. Just as a 3 totem pole might tell the story of a family, the designs on a Chilkat blanket tell stories too.

REVIEW Whom did the Tlingit trade with, and what did they trade? Main Idea and Details

▶ A Tlingit totem pole

395

2 Teach and Discuss

PAGE 395

Tlingit Traditions

Quick Summary The Tlingit lived by hunting and fishing, but also developed a large trading network. Among their cultural traditions are creating totem poles and blankets to record their family history.

1 **Besides using it as a hunting ground, how else did the Tlingit make use of the forest?** Possible answers: They used the wood for houses, canoes, and totem poles. Apply Information

2 **Why were the Tlingit able to spend time making and trading goods?** Because game and fish were plentiful, the Tlingit didn't need to spend as much time hunting for food. Cause and Effect

✓ **Ongoing Assessment**

If... students have difficulty explaining this relationship, **then...** ask what the Tlingit would have to spend their time doing if game and fish were *not* plentiful.

3 **What kinds of images are used in totem poles and Chilkat blankets?** Images of people, shapes, and animals Main Idea and Details

✓ **REVIEW ANSWER** They traded crafts, copper, baskets, oil, and other goods with other Native Americans. They sometimes traded goods they had bought from another group. Main Idea and Details

CURRICULUM CONNECTION
Art

Draw a Totem Pole

- Have students research and share pictures of Native American totem poles.
- Then have students draw a totem pole that celebrates their school, city, or state.
- Invite students to explain why they chose the images they included in their drawings.

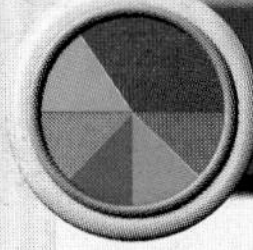

CURRICULUM CONNECTION
Music

Sing a Ballad

- Tell students that just as a totem pole or a blanket can tell a story, a ballad is a poem or song that tells a story.
- Play a recording of a ballad for the class, or have students write their own ballads.
- Have students sing or read examples of ballads, and then have the class summarize the story each ballad tells.

PAGE 396

The Potlatch

Quick Summary The Tlingit potlatch is a celebratory feast at which speeches, dances, feasting, and gift-giving were and continue to be important features.

4 **How might a family show its importance during a potlatch?** By inviting more guests, giving more and bigger gifts, offering more food, and having the potlatch last longer than other potlatches Make Inferences

5 **How might the host of a potlatch show generosity even to people who could not attend?** By providing so much food that guests might take some home to share with others Apply Information

6 **How are potlatches today similar to and different from potlatches of long ago?** Similar: both include speeches, dancing, feasting, and gift-giving; Different: the potlatches of long ago often lasted longer; the host today may give different kinds of gifts to the guests.  Compare and Contrast

✓ **REVIEW ANSWER** Speeches, dancing, feasting, and gift-giving Summarize

▶ Guests at a potlatch often perform traditional dances.

The Potlatch

A **potlatch** is a feast held to celebrate important events such as a wedding, a birth, or a death. A potlatch also shows a family's importance to the community. Sometimes more than a hundred guests will attend a potlatch. Many northwestern Native Americans, including the Tlingit, hold potlatches. This tradition has been practiced since long before Europeans came to this region.

During a potlatch long ago, the host gave gifts such as canoes, blankets, and other goods to each of the guests. The host and honored guests made speeches. People put on carved masks and participated in traditional dances.

The host also tried to provide much more food than the guests could eat during the feast, which could last up to
4 twelve days. Often, guests took food home so that they could share the host's generosity with others. 5

The potlatch is still an important part of the Tlingit culture. Speeches, dancing, feasting, and gift-giving are still important parts of a modern potlatch, although today's gifts often include money and household goods. Many modern potlatches are held during the weekend so that guests do not have to miss work or school. 6

REVIEW What types of events occur at a potlatch? Summarize

▶ Chilkat blanket

396

Practice and Extend

ACTIVATE PRIOR KNOWLEDGE
ESL Support

Compare Traditional Celebrations Have students compare a potlatch with a celebration of their culture.

Beginning Display a picture of a birthday party, and ask students to pantomime and/or use simple phrases to describe how the event is celebrated in their culture. Do the same with other events.

Intermediate Have students take turns describing how a specific event is celebrated in their family. If there is a related song in their native language, encourage them to share it with the class.

Advanced Have students contribute to a class anthology of celebrations by creating a page describing and illustrating their favorite family tradition.

For additional ESL support, use Every Student Learns Guide, pp. 162–165.

The Tlingit Today

Some Tlingit live on the same land their families have lived on for centuries. Many Tlingit make their living by logging or fishing. They live in modern villages and combine their
7 traditions with everyday modern life.

The Tlingit and Haida (HEYE duh), another Native American group, have formed the Central Council of the Tlingit and Haida Indian Tribes of Alaska. The council governs the Tlingit and Haida people. It meets in **Juneau, Alaska.**

Also, the Tlingit and other Native Americans have formed a company called the Sealaska Corporation. This corporation builds new buildings for the Tlingit and protects Tlingit property. The corporation makes sure the Tlingit and others will have enough money and land in the future.

REVIEW What is the purpose of the Sealaska Corporation?
Main Idea and Details

Summarize the Lesson

- **The Tlingit make use of the plentiful natural resources of their region.**
- **Potlatch ceremonies involve a feast, speeches, dancing, and gift-giving.**
- **Today, the Tlingit combine tradition with everyday modern life.**

LESSON 1 REVIEW

Check Facts and Main Ideas

1. **Summarize** Use the details below to write a summary about the Tlingit.

carved totem poles	wove Chilkat blankets	traded in the Northwest

↓

The Tlingit were skilled craftspeople and traders.

2. How did the Tlingit make use of natural resources?
3. How are modern **potlatches** like potlatches long ago? How are they different?
4. Give three details about the Tlingit today.
5. **Critical Thinking:** ***Make Inferences*** Why do you think the host of a potlatch gives so many gifts?

Link to Art

Create a Sculpture You read that **totem poles** tell the history of Tlingit families. Use clay to create a sculpture that tells something about you or your family. Share its meaning with your classmates.

397

PAGE 397

The Tlingit Today

Quick Summary Today, the Tlingit combine traditional and modern ways. They and other Native Americans have formed the Sealaska Corporation which helps protect and develop their interests.

7 **What traditions do the Tlingit carry on today?** Many Tlingit still make their living by fishing and using the resources of the surrounding forests.
Main Idea and Details

✓ **REVIEW ANSWER** To make sure the Tlingit and others will have enough money and land in the future
Main Idea and Details

3 Close and Assess

Summarize the Lesson

Have students take turns reading the three main points. For the first and third points, ask students to give examples. For the second point, ask students to identify the purpose.

✓ **LESSON 1 REVIEW**

1. **Summarize** For possible answers, see the reduced pupil page.
2. They hunted, fished, and used the trees around them to build homes, totem poles, and other items.
3. Alike: both have speeches, dancing, feasting, and gift-giving; Different: gifts today include cash and household goods. Gifts long ago included canoes and blankets. Long ago, a potlatch lasted up to 12 days. Today it usually lasts a weekend.
4. Possible answers: They log or fish; they combine traditions with modern life; they have formed a company called the Sealaska Corporation.
5. **Critical Thinking: *Make Inferences*** Possible answer: To show the family's importance to the community

Link to Art

You may want students to write a paragraph to accompany their sculptures.

MEETING INDIVIDUAL NEEDS
Leveled Practice

Use the Internet for Research Have students use the Internet to find out more about the Tlingit and the Sealaska Corporation.

Easy Have students find one site and prepare a summary report on its contents. **Reteach**

On-Level Have students find two sites and compare and contrast the information they provide. **Extend**

Challenge Have students find at least three sites and evaluate their comparative value for research purposes. **Enrich**

For a Lesson Summary, use Quick Study, p. 82.

Workbook, p. 92

Lesson 1: The Tlingit — Use with Pages 394–397.

Directions: Use the terms in the box to complete each sentence with information from Lesson 1. Write the word on the line provided. You may use your textbook.

logging	money	gifts
fishing	Chilkat	trading network
potlatch	Sealaska Corporation	totem pole
Tlingit	household goods	

1. The ______ are a group of Native Americans who live along the southeastern coast of Alaska and the northern coast of British Columbia.
2. A Tlingit family often placed a ______, carved with images of people or animals, outside their home.
3. The Tlingit had a large ______ with other tribes through which they bought and sold canoes, copper, baskets, and other goods.
4. One of the most prized Tlingit products is a ______ blanket, which is woven from the dyed wool of mountain goats and sheep.
5. A Native American might hold a ______ to celebrate an important event such as a wedding, birth, or death.
6. During a traditional potlatch, the host gave ______ such as canoes, blankets, and other goods to each guest.
7. The gifts given at today's potlatches often include ______ and ______.
8. Today many Tlingit make their living by ______ or ______.
9. The ______ makes sure the Tlingit and other Native Americans will have enough money and land in the future.

Notes for Home: Your child learned about Native Americans called the Tlingit.
Home Activity: With your child, discuss what types of events occur at a traditional potlatch. Discuss reasons a potlatch might be held, the gifts that might be given, and the activities that might occur at a

Also on Teacher Resources CD-ROM.

Masks Tell a Story

Objective

- Analyze cultural symbols and traditions of the Haida, the Moche, and the Incas.

1 Introduce and Motivate

Preview To activate prior knowledge, ask students if they have ever worn a mask. Ask those who have to describe the mask and the experience. Then, as a class, discuss why masks are worn on certain occasions.

2 Teach and Discuss

SOCIAL STUDIES STRAND
Culture

A *symbol* is an object or image that stands for something else. An oak tree, for example, is often used as a symbol of strength. Masks often symbolize human qualities or mythical characters.

1 **What do you think some of the masks on pp. 398 and 399 symbolize?** Possible answers: Religious characters, characters from stories, famous people, animals Make Inferences

2 **Why did the Haida and Inca create masks?** To wear during ceremonies and festivals; to place on the deceased before they were buried Main Idea and Details

SOCIAL STUDIES STRAND
Science • Technology

Copper was one of the first metals used by ancient peoples. Because copper is easy to shape, it was used to make tools and weapons as well as some ornamental objects.

3 **Why do you think some masks were made from copper?** Possible answers: It was an available material; it was easy to work with Draw Conclusions

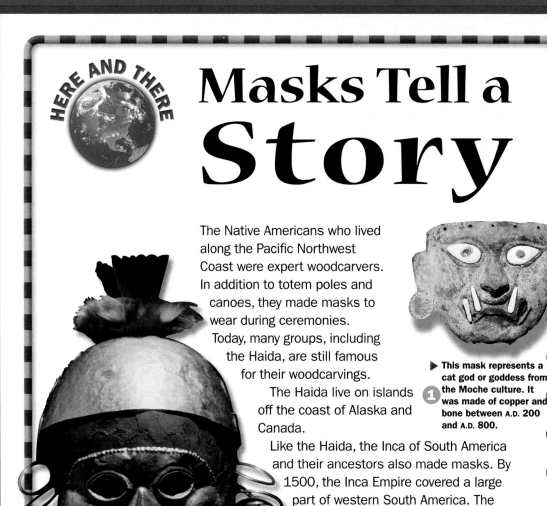

Masks Tell a Story

The Native Americans who lived along the Pacific Northwest Coast were expert woodcarvers. In addition to totem poles and canoes, they made masks to wear during ceremonies. Today, many groups, including the Haida, are still famous for their woodcarvings. The Haida live on islands off the coast of Alaska and Canada.

Like the Haida, the Inca of South America and their ancestors also made masks. By 1500, the Inca Empire covered a large part of western South America. The Inca wore masks during festivals. They also placed masks on the deceased before they were buried. Each mask had a special meaning. 2 Before the Inca formed their empire, many cultures existed in the area. One of the cultures, called Moche, was well-known for its crafts and artwork, including masks.

1 ▶ This mask represents a cat god or goddess from the Moche culture. It was made of copper and bone between A.D. 200 and A.D. 800.

3 ▶ This Inca warrior's mask is made of gold. It was made before Columbus came to the Americas. The Inca worked with metals such as gold, copper, and silver.

398

Practice and Extend

MEETING INDIVIDUAL NEEDS
Learning Styles

Explore Symbols Using their individual learning styles, students learn more about symbols.

Visual Learning Have students brainstorm a list of symbols that many people would recognize, such as a flag to symbolize a nation or a red rose to symbolize love. Have students gather pictures of as many of the listed symbols as possible.

Verbal Learning Have students bring in an object that they feel has symbolic value. Have them explain their reasoning.

Linguistic Learning Have students write a short poem or story that is built around a specific symbol and its meaning.

▶ This Haida mask can be worn closed or open. When the mask is closed, it represents an eagle, or thunderbird. When it is open, it represents the moon. The head in the center of the mask has real human hair. The mask is opened by pulling cords. The Haida wore masks in ceremonial dances and in performances during potlatches. Many Haida masks represent spirits. 5

399

4 **As shown in the pictures, what other materials besides copper did the Haida and the Inca use to make masks?** Possible answers: Wood, cord, hair, gold, and other metals **Analyze Pictures**

5 **How might a mask help the Haida tell a story about their history?** Possible answer: The mask might represent a specific person, animal, or spirit, or it might represent a force of nature that affected the Haida. **Hypothesize**

3 Close and Assess

Ask each student to create a mask, using a paper bag, markers, construction paper, and other classroom materials. Tell students their masks should represent a personal hero or a fictitious character.

CURRICULUM CONNECTION
Literature

Read About Masks

Cut and Make Mexican Masks, by A. G. Smith and Josie Hazen (Dover Publications, ISBN 0-486-28794-7, 1995) **Easy**

Northwest Coast Indian Punch-Out Masks, by A. G. Smith and Josie Hazen (Dover Publications, ISBN 0-486-29055-7, 1996) **On-Level**

Masks Tell Stories, by Carol Gelber (Millbrook Press, ISBN 1-56294-224-7, 1993) **Challenge**

WEB SITE
Technology

For more information about the Tlingit and the Inca, you can select the dictionary or encyclopedia from *Social Studies Library* at **www.sfsocialstudies.com.**

Exploration and Growth

Objectives

- Draw a conclusion about changes in the West in the 1800s.
- Explain why various groups explored the West.
- Describe the Gold Rush of 1848 and explain how it affected the West.
- Explain how a boom town might become a ghost town.
- Explain when and how various territories of the West gained statehood.

Vocabulary

prospector, p. 402; **boom town,** p. 403; **ghost town,** p. 403

Resources

- Workbook, p. 93
- Transparency 23
- Every Student Learns Guide, pp. 166–169
- Quick Study, pp. 84–85

Quick Teaching Plan

If time is short, have students copy the time line on p. 400, leaving extra space between the items shown. Then have them read the lesson and record additional dates and events.

1 Introduce and Motivate

Preview To activate prior knowledge, have students review what they learned about Spanish exploration in the Southwest in Chapter 11. Tell students they will read more about exploration of the West as they read Lesson 2.

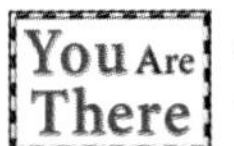

As a class, brainstorm a list of valuable products that are made or grown in the West. Then ask students, *Even if Cabrillo's expedition had found no gold or silver in the West, would you think the expedition was a success?*

LESSON 2

1760	1860	1960
1769 Father Serra builds the first California mission.	**1848** Gold is discovered at Sutter's Mill in California.	**1959** Alaska and Hawaii become states.

Exploration and Growth

PREVIEW

Focus on the Main Idea
Explorers from Spain and settlers seeking gold helped shape the West.

PLACES
American River
Sutter's Mill
San Francisco, California

PEOPLE
Juan Rodríguez Cabrillo
Junípero Serra
John Sutter
James Marshall
Levi Strauss

VOCABULARY
prospector
boom town
ghost town

EVENTS
Gold Rush

▶ Statue of Juan Rodríguez Cabrillo

You Are There It's 1542. Juan Rodríguez Cabrillo, a Portuguese explorer for Spain, sets sail from the west coast of New Spain, or Mexico. You're part of his crew. Cabrillo's ship is on a northerly course. He plans to explore the Pacific coast in search of riches and a water passage that connects the Pacific and Atlantic Oceans.

You don't know what to expect. You hope that the voyage will be successful. You've left your family to join Cabrillo. You have no idea what you will find. You walk the deck of the ship dreaming about finding lots of silver and gold.

Draw Conclusions As you read, think about how the discovery of gold and other resources changed the West.

400

Practice and Extend

READING SKILL
Draw Conclusions

In the Lesson Review, students complete a graphic organizer like the one below. You may want to provide students with a copy of Transparency 23 to complete as they read the lesson.

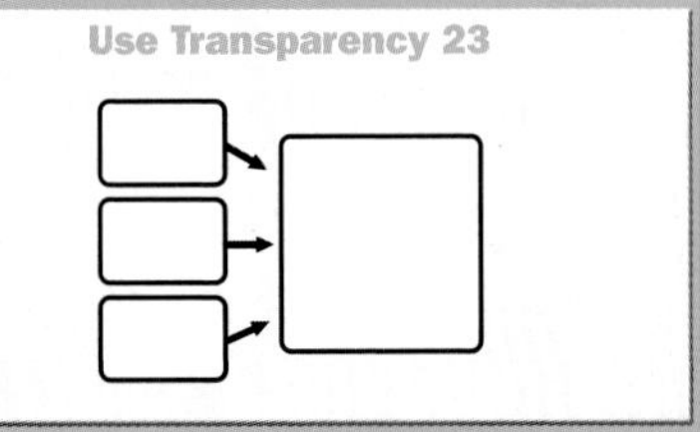

VOCABULARY
Related Word Study

Tell students that the word *prospector* comes from the Latin *prospectus*, which breaks down into the prefix *pro-* (forward) and the word *specere* (to look). Discuss how a prospector might be looking forward, in a way. Other words that come from *prospectus* include *prospect* and *prospective*. Other words that come from *specere* include *spectacles* and *inspect*. Have students look up some of these words and discuss their relationships to the Latin roots.

Exploring the West

Juan Rodríguez Cabrillo [kah BREE oh] was probably the first European to see the coast of what is now California. The Spanish sent other explorers north along the coast of California as well. Some of these explorers suggested that Spain should send colonists to settle in the new land.

When the Spanish settled in an area, they often established Roman Catholic missions. A Franciscan priest, Father **Junípero Serra** [hoo NEE peh roh SAIR rah], decided to leave his mission to set up a mission in what is today California. Father Serra built the first California mission in 1769. That mission was the beginning of the city
1 of San Diego.

By 1823 the Franciscans had built 21 missions in California. The missions served both Spanish settlers and Native Americans. Several California cities, such as Santa Barbara and San Francisco, began as
2 missions.

Explorers from other lands also traveled throughout the West. In 1812 Russians built a fur-trading post at Fort Ross, north of San Francisco. Russians also claimed much of Alaska. The British built fur-trading posts along the Pacific coast in what are today Oregon and Washington.

In 1841 the first of many wagon trains brought American settlers to the West. The United States wanted California to become an American territory. Mexico was now free of Spanish rule and owned the territory but refused to sell the land. In 1846 war started between Mexico and the United States over several areas of land in the West and Southwest. The United States won the war in 1848. 4
Mexico was forced to give up California along with some of its other territories in North America.

REVIEW What brought explorers from many different countries to the West Coast? *Draw Conclusions*

MAP SKILL

Claims to the Pacific Coast in the Early 1800s

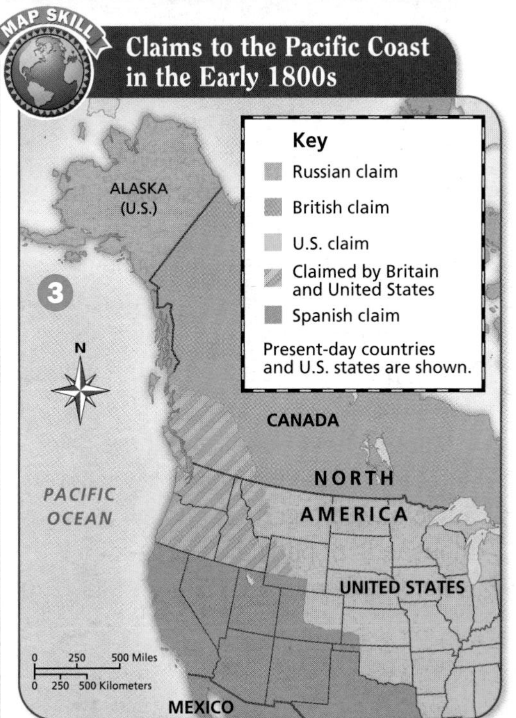

▶ **Many countries claimed parts of the West.**

MAP SKILL Use Map Key ***What modern states lie in the area claimed by both Britain and the United States?***

SOCIAL STUDIES
Background

About the Exploration of the West Coast

- During his 1602 voyage, Vizcaíno gave names to a number of important California locations, including San Diego, Santa Catalina Island, Santa Barbara, and Monterey Bay.
- The land north of California along the West Coast remained unexplored until after 1750.
- The United States and Great Britain settled the boundary between the United States and Canada in the Northwest in 1846. In 1848 Congress established the Oregon Territory and in 1853 divided off the Washington Territory, which included parts of present-day Idaho and Montana.

2 Teach and Discuss

PAGE 401

Exploring the West

Quick Summary Spain explored and established colonies and missions in California. Soon other Europeans and Americans began settling the region. Mexico laid claim to the territory until war forced Mexico to give up California and other lands to the United States.

1 **How did Spain establish claims in the West?** Spain sent colonists to settle there, and Franciscan priests set up missions. **Summarize**

2 **What is similar about the origins of San Diego and San Francisco?** Both started as Spanish missions.
 **Compare and Contrast**

MAP SKILL
Claims to the Pacific Coast in the Early 1800s

3 **In the early 1800s, which country claimed the northernmost part of what is now the United States?** Russia
Interpret Maps

MAP SKILL Answer Washington, Oregon, Idaho, Montana, Wyoming

4 **What was the cause of the war between Mexico and the United States in the 1840s?** Mexico wanted to keep its territory in the West and Southwest, but the United States wanted to claim those lands. **Cause and Effect**

✓ **REVIEW ANSWER** They were searching for land, natural resources, and riches. **Draw Conclusions**

PAGES 402–403

Gold!

Quick Summary The discovery of gold at Sutter's Mill led to the California Gold Rush of 1848. Many prospectors poured into the area. Some of the boom towns that resulted grew into cities, but many became ghost towns.

5 What was James Marshall doing when he discovered gold? He was building a mill along the American River. Main Idea and Details

6 What did Marshall and Sutter plan to do about the discovery of gold at Sutter's Mill? What actually happened? They planned to keep the gold a secret, but the word got out, and thousands of people rushed to California. Main Idea and Details

Decision Making

7 Suppose you and your family are planning to make the trip west to take part in the Gold Rush. Considering where you live now, would you decide to travel over land or by sea? Explain. Possible answer: Because my family lives in New York, near the ocean, we would travel by sea. Make Decisions

8 How might the *California* have benefited from the discovery of a northwest water passage? Possible answer: It would have been able to take a shorter, more direct route to California, saving time and money. Draw Conclusions

Map Adventure **Answers**

1. Southeast
2. Atlantic Ocean and Pacific Ocean
3. Four stops

Gold!

In 1839 a Swiss immigrant named **John Sutter** moved to California. He settled on land in the foothills of the Sierra Nevada. In January 1848, **James Marshall** was busy building a mill for Sutter along the **American River.** Marshall saw something shiny in the water as it passed by the mill. It
5 was gold!

Marshall told Sutter about the gold, and they decided to keep the discovery a secret. Word got out, though. Soon thousands of people were headed
6 toward California and **Sutter's Mill.** The California **Gold Rush** was on!

Prospectors came from all over the world hoping to find gold in California. A **prospector** is someone who searches for valuable minerals. Some came overland from the eastern United States. This was a long and dangerous trip. Some traveled by sea from the East Coast to the West Coast. At that time, the shortest sea route was a 15,000-mile journey around South America to the small port of **San Francisco** on the California coast. Prospectors even sailed across the Pacific Ocean from China. Any way the

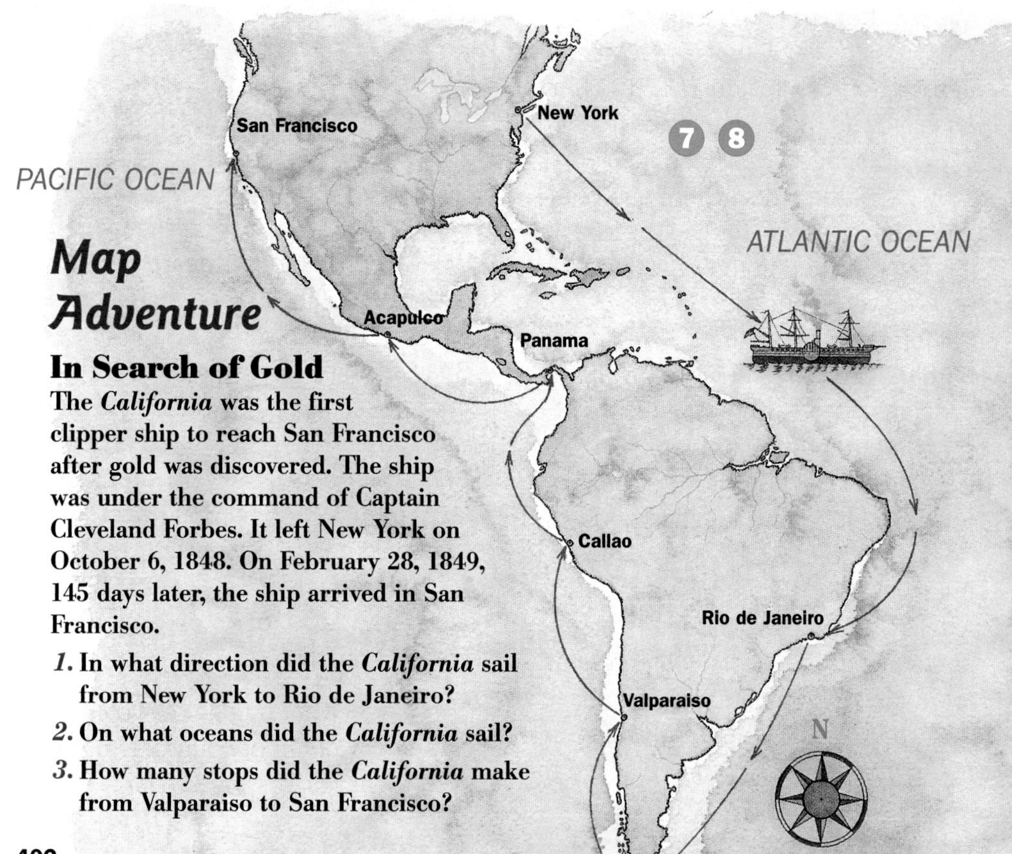

Map Adventure

In Search of Gold

The *California* was the first clipper ship to reach San Francisco after gold was discovered. The ship was under the command of Captain Cleveland Forbes. It left New York on October 6, 1848. On February 28, 1849, 145 days later, the ship arrived in San Francisco.

1. **In what direction did the *California* sail from New York to Rio de Janeiro?**
2. **On what oceans did the *California* sail?**
3. **How many stops did the *California* make from Valparaiso to San Francisco?**

Practice and Extend

MEETING INDIVIDUAL NEEDS

Leveled Practice

Discover Gold! Help students find out more about gold.

Easy Have students find pictures of both ancient and modern objects made of gold. **Reteach**

On-Level Have students interview a jeweler or conduct other research to find out the differences in 10-, 14-, and 18-carat gold. **Extend**

Challenge Have students research why the United States government owns a quantity of gold and where this government-owned gold is stored. **Enrich**

For a Lesson Summary, use Quick Study, p. 84.

prospectors traveled, the journey took a long time. Most gold-seekers didn't get to California until 1849. That is how they got the name "forty-niners."

San Francisco had a good harbor. It was the closest port to the California gold fields. Many forty-niners passed through the city. By 1849 the tiny port had grown into a big city with a population of 100,000. San Francisco was not the only city that boomed
9 because of the Gold Rush.

Wherever gold, silver, or other valuable metal ore was discovered, **boom towns** grew quickly. Miners came and so did merchants. Merchants built businesses to provide goods and services for the miners. In fact, many merchants became wealthier from the gold rush than the miners did. One of the most successful of these merchants was **Levi Strauss.** He made canvas tents for the miners until he realized that they needed sturdy pairs of pants. He made a fortune sewing and selling denim jeans.

Prospectors found valuable metal ore throughout the West. More towns, such as Denver, Colorado, and Carson City, Nevada, became boom towns.

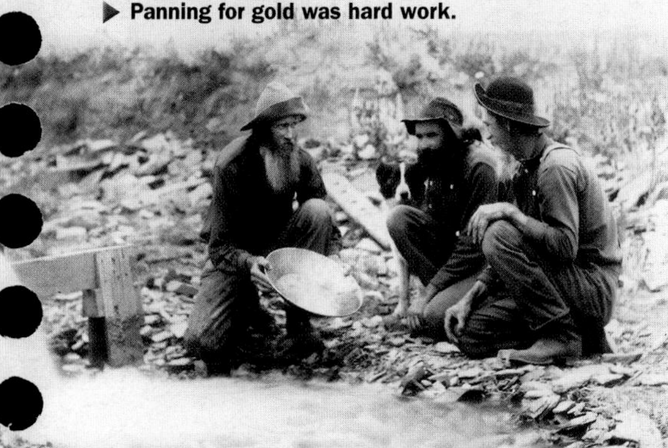

▶ Panning for gold was hard work.

MAP SKILL

Gold Rush Claims

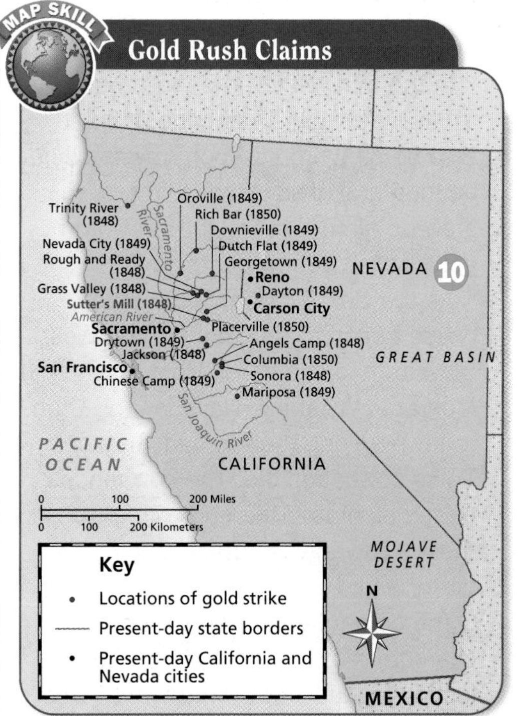

▶ Gold was found in many locations in the Sierra Nevada and foothills.

MAP SKILL **Use Map Scale** ***About how far is Mariposa from Trinity River?***

In time, a railroad was built across North America, linking the East and West Coasts. Traveling west by train was shorter and easier than sailing or traveling by wagon. More people moved to the West. Some cities, many of them along railroad lines, continued to grow. But once the metal ore was mined from an area, many boom towns were deserted. They became **ghost towns.** Today tourists can visit ghost towns throughout the West.

REVIEW Why did some merchants become wealthier than the gold miners? **Draw Conclusions**

403

SOCIAL STUDIES STRAND

Economics

Gold is used in telephones, computers, and satellites. Gold also is used in the aerospace industry to coat the face shields of spacesuits. Gold is a metal of choice for technology because it is easy to mold into tiny shapes and will not corrode or be destroyed by chemical reactions.

9 **Even before gold was used for technology, many people considered it very valuable. How can you tell that gold was considered very valuable during the Gold Rush?** Many thousands of people travelled from all over the world seeking gold. **Draw Conclusions**

Gold Rush Claims

Test Talk

Use Information from Graphics

10 **Which of the gold strike locations was not in the present-day state of California? What present-day cities are located near this site?** Have students skim the map to look for key words or symbols that will help them answer the question. Dayton; Reno and Carson City **Interpret Maps**

MAP SKILL **Answer** About 300 miles

✓ **REVIEW ANSWER** Possible answer: Because they provided products and services for the many thousands of miners **Draw Conclusions**

ACCESS CONTENT

ESL Support

Explore the Concept of Boom Towns

Beginning Explain that as a verb, *boom* can mean "to make a loud, deep noise" or "to grow fast." Connect this to the concept of a "boom town." Help students create a word web describing a boom town.

Intermediate Have pairs of students create a Venn diagram showing the relationship between boom towns and ghost towns. Encourage discussion.

Advanced Have small groups of students write and perform a skit as though they were prospectors living in a boom town.

For additional ESL support, use Every Student Learns Guide, pp. 166–169.

The Wild West

Quick Summary The Wild West was characterized by the rowdiness of boom towns and cow towns. Among the colorful figures of the era was "Buffalo Bill" Cody, who formed a famous touring show.

11 **What two events caused growth in the West? Which came first?** The Gold Rush and cattle drives; Gold Rush
Make Inferences

12 **Why do you think the cowhands often celebrated at the end of a cattle drive?** Possible answer: Because they had completed a long and difficult drive, and they wanted to have fun
Draw Conclusions

Ongoing Assessment

If... students do not understand why cowhands might have wanted to celebrate,	**then...** ask them how it feels to finish a long and difficult task, and what they might want to do after successfully completing it.

REVIEW ANSWER Many boom towns had colorful and often violent characters, but did not have good police departments. Cowboys celebrated noisily in cow towns at the end of cattle drives. Main Idea and Details

Bodie, California

13 **What factors caused the population of Bodie, California, to decline?** Most of the gold and silver had been mined, and fires occurred, destroying much of the town. Cause and Effect

The Wild West

In the mid-1800s, the West was new territory to most Americans. It could also be dangerous. Boom towns could be loud and rowdy places. Towns that grew up almost overnight rarely had good police departments.

As the Gold Rush ended, cattle
11 drives began to take hold in the West. Cowhands drove herds from ranches in Montana, Wyoming, Nevada, and Utah to towns along the railroad, just as Texas cowhands did. The cowhands often celebrated the end of the trail in these "cow towns." They could get
12 pretty wild.

The colorful and often violent characters of the West created a lasting legend—the "Wild West." One of the most famous characters was William "Buffalo Bill" Cody. In 1883 Cody formed a famous traveling show called "Buffalo Bill's Wild West." It featured trick riding and rifle-shooting, western wildlife, and more.

▶ Advertisement for "Buffalo Bill's Wild West" show

By the 1890s, the "Wild West" had been tamed. Through songs, stories, and movies, however, the legend still lives on.

REVIEW Why was the West called the "Wild West"? Main Idea and Details

Bodie, California

Bodie, California is one of the best-preserved ghost towns in the West. A large gold and silver strike in 1877 brought mines and mills to the town. By 1880 Bodie was a boom town with more than 10,000 people and 2,000 buildings.

In only a few years, most of the gold and silver had been mined. By 1882 miners had moved on to other boom towns. In later years, fires destroyed much of Bodie. Only 170 original buildings still stand.

▶ Bodie, California, present day

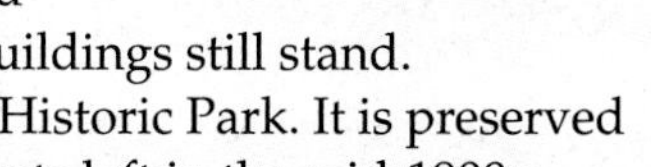

13 Today Bodie is a California State Historic Park. It is preserved much as it was when the last residents left in the mid-1900s.

404

Practice and Extend

CURRICULUM CONNECTION
Drama

Evaluate a Wild West Drama

- Have students watch a portion of a movie or television show set during the time of the Wild West (such as *Bonanza, Rawhide,* or *Gunsmoke*).
- Tell students to choose one scene from the program that seems to provide a realistic picture of the Wild West and one that seems false or exaggerated.
- Ask students to describe the scenes they chose and explain their reasoning.

WEB SITE
Technology

Students can find out more about Bodie, California, by clicking on *Atlas* at **www.sfsocialstudies.com.**

The Territories of the West Become States

State	Entry Date	Order	Flag	State	Entry Date	Order	Flag
California	Sept. 9, 1850	31st		Idaho	July 3, 1890	43rd	
Oregon	Feb. 14, 1859	33rd		Wyoming	July 10, 1890	44th	
Nevada	Oct. 31, 1864	36th		Utah	Jan. 4, 1896	45th	
Colorado	Aug. 1, 1876	38th		Alaska	Jan. 3, 1959	49th	14
Montana	Nov. 8, 1889	41st		Hawaii	Aug. 21, 1959	50th	15
Washington	Nov. 11, 1889	42nd					16

▶ Some western territories were among the last territories to become states.

CHART SKILL Use a Table *Name one of the three pairs of states that gained statehood in the same years.*

Statehood for Alaska

The territories of the West became states between 1850 and 1959. Look at the chart above. You will notice that the last two territories to become states, Alaska and Hawaii, are both in the West and became states in the same year.

Alaska was once a territory claimed by the country of Russia. The Russians used the territory mainly for fur trading. In 1867 Russia sold Alaska to the United States for a little more than $7 million, or about two cents an acre. The United States hoped that fur trapping in Alaska would help the United States' economy. Alaska had even more natural resources, however.

In the 1880s and 1890s, gold was discovered in parts of Alaska and Canada. Then, just as in California, thousands of people rushed to the area. The cities of Juneau and Fairbanks grew quickly.

During World War II, military bases in Alaska were an important line of defense for the United States. Airfields and highways built during the war helped boost transportation and business development after the war. Alaska became a state in 1959. In 1968 vast oil deposits were discovered on the coast of the Arctic Ocean in Alaska. An 800-mile-long pipeline was 17 built to bring the oil to Valdez, where it could be loaded onto ships and transported to ports around the world.

REVIEW Was the United States purchase of Alaska a good idea? Explain your answer. Draw Conclusions

405

CURRICULUM CONNECTION
Math

Analyze the Cost of Alaska

- Have students divide $7 million by 2 cents to calculate the approximate size of Alaska in acres. (7,000,000 ÷ .02 = 350,000,000 acres)
- Next, have them research the size of one acre and compare it to the size of a familiar object such as a building or parking lot.
- As a class, discuss whether the Alaska purchase was a good value and tell why or why not.

PAGE 405

Statehood for Alaska

Quick Summary Russia sold Alaska to the United States in 1867. The discovery of gold and oil brought people to the territory and boosted the economy.

14 **How many states were admitted to the Union *between* the admission of Wyoming and Alaska? How many of these were western states?** Four; One
Sequence

15 **Which of the western territories became states before the twentieth century?** All but Alaska and Hawaii
Analyze Information

16 **How many years passed between the first western territory's gaining statehood and the last?** 109 years
Analyze Information

CHART SKILL Answer Possible answers: Montana and Washington in 1889, Idaho and Wyoming in 1890, Alaska and Hawaii in 1959

17 **What have been three major sources of wealth in Alaska's history?** Furs, gold, and oil Summarize

✓ **REVIEW ANSWER** Possible answer: Yes; because Alaska has many valuable natural resources Draw Conclusions

United States even before it became a state? It was important because of its crops and the military base at Pearl Harbor. **Summarize**

✓ **REVIEW ANSWER** Alike: both had resources the United States wanted, both were important militarily; Different: the United States bought Alaska **Compare and Contrast**

3 Close and Assess

Summarize the Lesson

Have students take turns reading the three important events. Then ask volunteers to identify events from the lesson that happened before and after these dates.

✓ **LESSON 2 REVIEW**

1. **Draw Conclusions** For possible answers, see the reduced pupil page.
2. They were looking for land, natural resources, and riches.
3. The Gold Rush was a rush of people to California in search of gold. It caused boom towns to spring up and led to the settlement of much of the West.
4. Once a boom town's economic opportunities faded, the people moved away, leaving a ghost town.
5. **Critical Thinking: *Make Generalizations*** The territories of the West joined the Union between 1850 and 1959; Territories applied for statehood.

Link to Music

Students may find songs on the Internet or in the library. Students also may want to sing a few of the songs in pairs or small groups.

Hawaii Becomes a State

Hawaii is a chain of islands in the Pacific Ocean. In 1900 the United States made Hawaii a territory. Hawaiian farms produced sugarcane and pineapples for export to the United States mainland.

18 The United States also built ports and military bases on the islands. A major base was built at Pearl Harbor. In December 1941, Japanese warplanes attacked Pearl Harbor. This brought the United States into World War II. Hawaiians had discussed statehood even before World War II. After the war ended, Hawaiians again asked for statehood. Finally, in 1959 Hawaii became the fiftieth state.

REVIEW How were the paths to statehood alike and different for Alaska and Hawaii? **Compare and Contrast**

Summarize the Lesson

- **1769** Father Serra built the first California mission.
- **1848** Gold was discovered at Sutter's Mill in California.
- **1959** Alaska and Hawaii became states.

▶ **A lei, or garland of flowers, is a gift of welcome in Hawaii.**

LESSON 2 REVIEW

Check Facts and Main Ideas

1. **Draw Conclusions** Copy the diagram below on a separate sheet of paper. Fill in the details that would lead to the given conclusion.

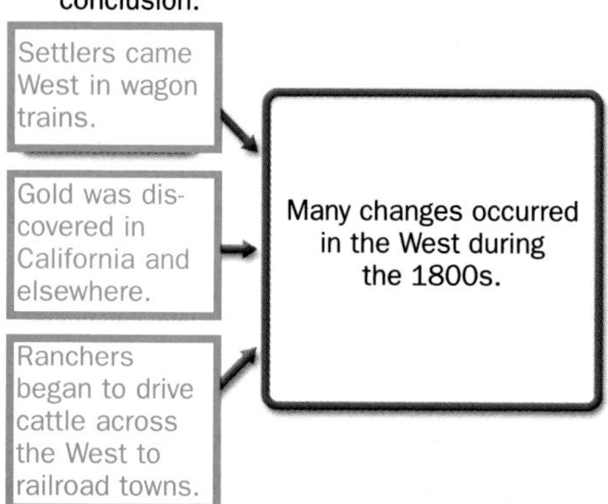

Settlers came West in wagon trains.
Gold was discovered in California and elsewhere.
Ranchers began to drive cattle across the West to railroad towns.
Many changes occurred in the West during the 1800s.

2. Why did people begin to explore the West?
3. What was the California Gold Rush and how did it change the West?
4. Why did some **boomtowns** become **ghost towns?**
5. **Critical Thinking:** ***Make Generalizations*** When and how did some territories in the West become states?

Link to Music

Find a Song of the Wild West Many songs were written about life in the Wild West. Some have become famous and are still sung today. Find a song and share with your class what the song tells you about life in the Wild West.

406

Practice and Extend

SOCIAL STUDIES Background

About Alaska and Hawaii

- The Seward Peninsula of Alaska is named for Secretary of State William Seward who negotiated the purchase of Alaska. At the time, many people considered the Alaskan land useless. They nicknamed the area "Seward's Folly" and "Seward's Icebox."
- Liliuokalani, the first queen to rule Hawaii, opposed the U.S. takeover of the islands. She gave up her throne to avoid a bloody war with the United States.

Workbook, p. 93

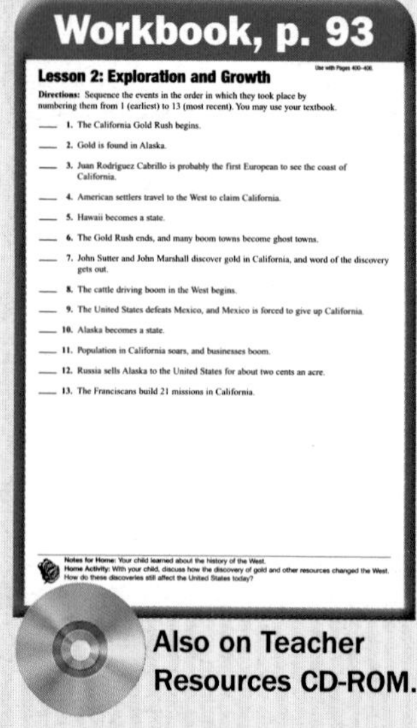

Also on Teacher Resources CD-ROM.

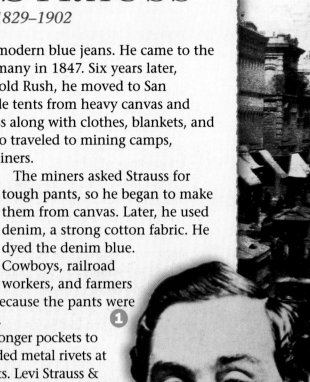

Levi Strauss

1829–1902

Levi Strauss invented modern blue jeans. He came to the United States from Germany in 1847. Six years later, during the California Gold Rush, he moved to San Francisco. There he made tents from heavy canvas and sold them at his business along with clothes, blankets, and household items. He also traveled to mining camps, selling these goods to miners.

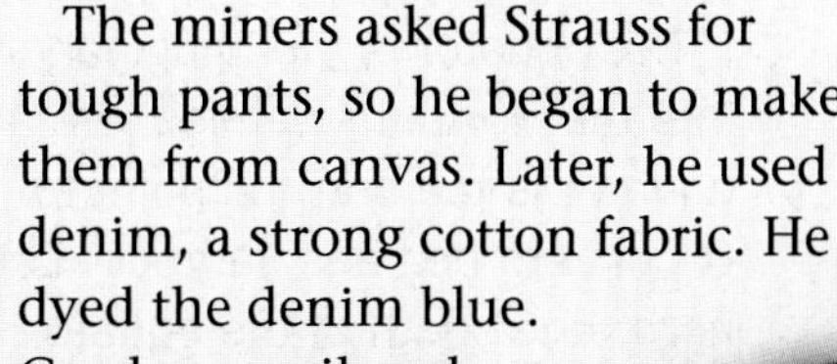

BIOFACT

The descendants of the family of Levi Strauss still own and run the company he founded, Levi Strauss & Company.

The miners asked Strauss for tough pants, so he began to make them from canvas. Later, he used denim, a strong cotton fabric. He dyed the denim blue. Cowboys, railroad workers, and farmers bought his blue pants because the pants were comfortable and strong. 1

The miners wanted stronger pockets to hold tools, so Strauss added metal rivets at the corners of the pockets. Levi Strauss & Company, the business he founded, still makes blue denim pants with riveted pockets.

Strauss was very successful. His pants were inexpensive, but Strauss paid his workers a good wage. Strauss donated generously to charities and gave scholarships for students. The business he began is now about 150 years old and remains successful.

Learn from Biographies

Why was Levi Strauss successful?

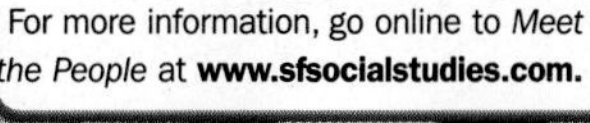

For more information, go online to *Meet the People* at **www.sfsocialstudies.com.**

Levi Strauss

Objective

- Identify important inventors such as Levi Strauss and describe their accomplishments.

1 Introduce and Motivate

Preview To activate prior knowledge, ask students which lasts longer and protects their legs better when they are working or playing outdoors—dress pants, shorts, a skirt, or blue jeans.

2 Teach and Discuss

- Explain that the Gold Rush not only caused growth in the mining industry but also in a great number of related businesses and industries, such as Levi Strauss's business.
- Discuss how Levi Strauss's invention has benefited other people besides gold miners.

1 **Why do you think miners needed inexpensive pants made out of tough cloth?** Possible answers: Most probably did not earn much money; They worked in rocky areas that could rip or wear holes in their pants. Tougher cloth would make their pants last longer and would better protect their legs. **Draw Conclusions**

3 Close and Assess

Learn from Biographies Answer

Possible answers: He met consumers' needs by producing inexpensive, strong, comfortable pants for miners, railroad workers, farmers, and cowboys; he gave back to his community.

SOCIAL STUDIES Background

About Blue Jeans

- Jeans were originally called "waist overalls."
- Blue jeans were originally sewn with orange thread to match the copper rivets used by Levi Strauss.
- U.S.-made jeans are popular in Japan. They were first introduced to Japan by the president of the Osaki Clothes Company. Mr. Osaki rode from door to door on his bicycle selling imported jeans.

WEB SITE Technology

Students can find out more about Levi Strauss by clicking on *Meet the People* at **www.sfsocialstudies.com.**

Understand Latitude and Longitude

Objective

- Use latitude and longitude to find locations on maps and globes.

Vocabulary

latitude, p. 408; **parallel,** p. 408; **equator,** p. 408; **Northern Hemisphere,** p. 408; **Southern Hemisphere,** p. 408; **longitude,** p. 409; **meridian,** p. 409; **prime meridian,** p. 409

Resource

- Workbook, p. 94
- Transparency 63

1 Introduce and Motivate

What are latitude and longitude? Display a map or globe that shows lines of latitude and longitude. Point to the lines and ask students to speculate on their purpose. Then have students read the **What?** section of text on p. 408 to help set the purpose of the lesson.

Why identify latitude and longitude? Have students read the **Why?** section of text on p. 409. Then ask students why knowing latitude and longitude might be especially important for someone piloting a ship on the ocean. (Because there are few landmarks at sea)

2 Teach and Discuss

How is this skill used?

- Circulate among students to be sure they are correctly relating the information in the text to the pictures of the globe on p. 408 and the map on p. 409.
- Have students read the **How?** section of text on p. 409.
- Be sure students can correctly identify Boise as the city at the indicated point.

Understand Latitude and Longitude

What? Lines of **latitude** (LAT i tood) extend east and west. They are lines drawn on a map or globe that are used to determine how far north or south of the equator a place is located. Lines of latitude are also called parallels. They are always the
1 same distance apart from one another. The globe on the left shows lines of latitude.

The equator is the imaginary line of latitude that divides Earth into the Northern Hemisphere and the Southern Hemisphere. The equator is the starting point for measuring latitude. It is labeled 0°, or zero degrees, latitude. Latitude is measured in degrees both north and south of the equator.

Find the equator on the globe on the left. Notice that the lines of latitude north of the equator are marked with an *N*. The lines that are south of the equator are marked with an *S*. The North
2 Pole is 90°N and the South Pole is 90°S.

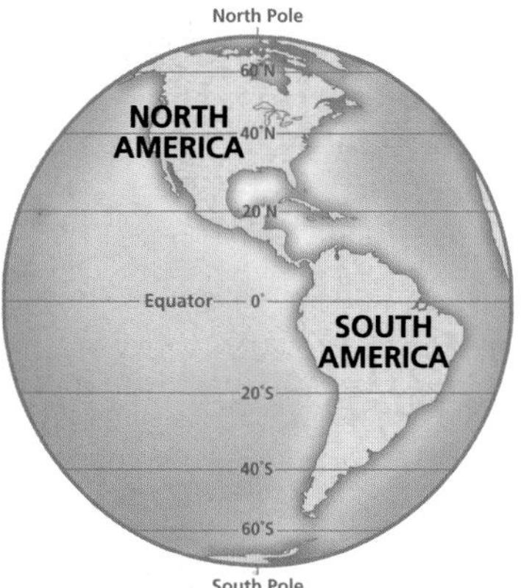

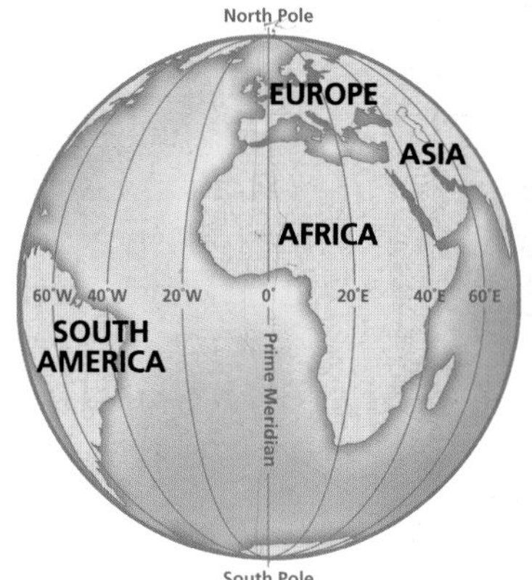

Practice and Extend

SOCIAL STUDIES
Background

About Latitude and Longitude

- Each degree of latitude spans about 69 miles. However, this distance varies slightly because the Earth is not uniformly curved. Degrees of longitude are about 69 miles apart at the equator, but the lines meet at the poles.
- The instrument used to determine latitude and longitude is a sextant, which measures the angle between the horizon and a heavenly body—the sun, the moon, or a star.
- By the sixteenth century, it was known that longitude could be measured by comparing the local time to some standard time—but a truly accurate clock was not available until the eighteenth century. To help students understand how time relates to longitude, remind them of the fact that the world is divided into different time zones.

For more information, go online to the *Atlas* at **www.sfsocialstudies.com.**

Latitude and Longitude in the West

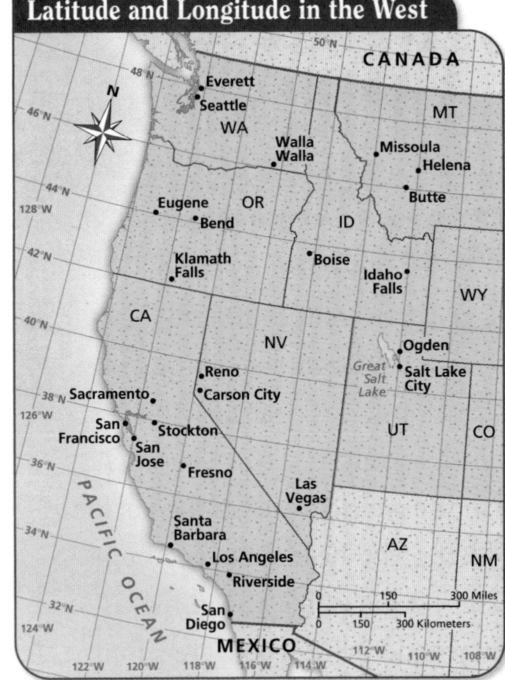

Lines of **longitude** (LON ji tood) extend north and south. They are also called meridians (muh RID ee uhns). Lines of longitude are used to determine how far east or west of the prime meridian a place is located.

The prime meridian is the starting point for measuring longitude. It is labeled 0°, or zero degrees, longitude. Longitude is measured in degrees east and west of the prime meridian.

Find the prime meridian on the globe on the right (page 408). Notice that the lines of longitude east of the prime meridian are marked with an *E*. The lines west of the prime meridian are marked with a *W*. The 180th meridian is just labeled 180° without an *E* or *W*. This is because 180°E and 180°W are the same meridian. 3

Why? The lines of latitude and longitude together form a grid. You can see this grid on the map to the left. You can use this grid to locate places on Earth. 4

How? To find what city is located near 44°N, 116°W on the map at the left, first find the latitude line labeled 44°N. Then run your finger along that line until it crosses 116°W. What city is located nearest this point?

1. What cities are located near 48°N, 122°W?
2. What city is located nearest to 34°N, 120°W?
3. What is the closest **longitude** and **latitude** for Butte, Montana?

1 **Lines of latitude also can be called "parallels." How does this meaning of *parallel* relate to the mathematical meaning of *parallel*?** In both cases, a parallel is a line that is always the same distance apart from another line. **Compare and Contrast**

2 **What is the special name of the line at 0° latitude? What lies at 90° latitude?** The equator; the Poles **Main Idea and Details**

3 **The equator divides Earth into the Northern and Southern Hemispheres. What hemispheres are roughly divided at the prime meridian and at 180° longitude?** The Eastern and Western Hemispheres **Apply Information**

4 **Why is it important for all countries in the world to use the same system of latitude and longitude?** Possible answers: To avoid confusion when referring to locations; to help in planning air and sea routes **Draw Conclusions**

3 Close and Assess

Think and Apply

1. Everett and Seattle, Washington
2. Santa Barbara, California
3. 46°N, 112°W

SOCIAL STUDIES STRAND
Geography

The following map resources are available:

- Big Book Atlas
- Student Atlas
- Outline Maps
- Desk Maps
- Map Resources CD-ROM

Workbook, p. 94

Understand Latitude and Longitude

Also on Teacher Resources CD-ROM.

Business and Pleasure

Objectives

- Compare and contrast the cities of Los Angeles and Salt Lake City.
- Name some of the industries found in Los Angeles, Seattle, and Salt Lake City.
- Explain how climate can affect tourism in selected western cities.
- Identify products that the United States exports to and imports from the Pacific Rim countries.

Vocabulary

computer software, p. 412;
international trade, p. 414

Resources

- Workbook, p. 95
- Transparency 14
- Every Student Learns Guide, pp. 170–173
- Quick Study, pp. 86–87

Quick Teaching Plan

If time is short, have students record key information in a table.

- Have students create a table with columns labeled *Los Angeles, Seattle,* and *Salt Lake City,* and rows labeled *Climate, Business,* and *Other Information.*
- Then have students read the lesson and complete the table.

1 Introduce and Motivate

Preview To activate prior knowledge, ask students what place they think of when someone mentions moviemaking. Tell them they will learn more about Los Angeles and other western cities as they read Lesson 3.

As a class, discuss how students might react if they saw a movie being filmed. Compare that with how someone from Los Angeles might react.

LESSON 3

PREVIEW

Focus on the Main Idea
Cities in the West have many different kinds of businesses and attractions.

PLACES
Los Angeles, California
Seattle, Washington
Salt Lake City, Utah

VOCABULARY
computer software
international trade

Business and Pleasure

You Are There You are enjoying another beautiful, sunny day of vacation in southern California. Yesterday you went hiking in the Santa Monica Mountains near Los Angeles. Today, you just want to relax on the beach and splash in the gentle waves of the Pacific Ocean. Suddenly, you hear shouts coming from the water. It looks like a swimmer is in trouble. You wonder why people are simply standing around and watching. Then you see a person behind a big camera. A woman shouts into the megaphone, "Cut!" The swimmer laughs. It's then that you realize they are making a movie!

Compare and Contrast As you read, compare and contrast the businesses that can be found in each of the cities mentioned.

Practice and Extend

READING SKILL Compare/Contrast

In the Lesson Review, students complete a graphic organizer like the one below. You may want to provide students with a copy of Transparency 14 to complete as they read the lesson.

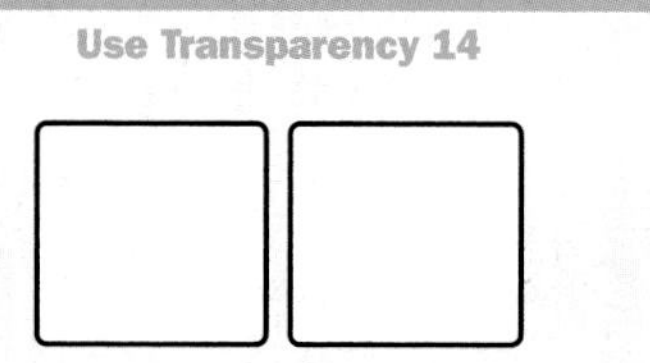

VOCABULARY Individual Word Study

Originally, the word *computer* was used to describe a person who was using a mathematical process to find an answer. In the late 1800s, the term was first used to describe a device that could compute. At first, computers were entirely mechanical—there was nothing except hardware. When electric, digital computers came along, programs, not gears, did the computing. These programs were called *software,* to contrast them with hardware.

Fun in the Sun

Many movies are made in **Los Angeles, California**—and for a good reason. Because California has a sunny, pleasant climate, the area around Los Angeles is an excellent location for filming movies and television shows. Over time, the ❶ entertainment industry has grown in Los Angeles.

The pleasant climate around Los Angeles has drawn many other businesses to the area. People from across the United States and around the world come to Los Angeles to live and work. The rapid growth of Los Angeles has made it the second largest city in the United States. ❷

People also travel to Los Angeles to visit its many attractions. Tourism is an important industry. Whether they are relaxing on the beach or riding on a roller coaster, people enjoy visiting Los Angeles.

▶ There are many amusement parks in and around Los Angeles.

REVIEW What are some reasons people come to Los Angeles? Main Idea and Details

▶ The famous Hollywood sign has become a symbol of the movie industry in Los Angeles.

411

2 Teach and Discuss

PAGE 411

Fun in the Sun

Quick Summary A pleasant climate makes Los Angeles an excellent location for filmmaking, business, and tourism.

SOCIAL STUDIES STRAND History

Hollywood, a district of Los Angeles, was founded in 1887 by Horace Wilcox, who hoped it would grow into a devout religious community. However, by 1915, Hollywood had become the capital of U.S. filmmaking.

❶ **Why did the entertainment industry develop in Hollywood?** The climate of Los Angeles was ideal for filming movies and television shows. Apply Information

Test Talk

Use Information from the Text

❷ **What facts and details from the text support the statement, "Los Angeles is a popular place for people to live and work"?** Have students make notes from the lesson to answer the question. Students should reread the question and check their notes. Students should ask themselves, "Do I have enough information to answer the question?" The rapid growth of Los Angeles has made it the second largest city in the United States. Main Idea and Details

✓ **REVIEW ANSWER** Possible answers: To enjoy the pleasant climate; to live and work in the entertainment industry or other businesses; to see and experience its many attractions Main Idea and Details

SOCIAL STUDIES STRAND History

Filmmaking in Hollywood

- Thomas Edison's company produced the first commercial motion-picture machine—called a *kinetoscope*—for display at the World's Columbian Exposition of 1893.
- Motion pictures in the early years of American filmmaking were made in a number of places, including New York City, New Jersey, Chicago, and Florida.
- Soon motion-picture producers were drawn to southern California. There they found a variety of scenic landscapes and a climate suitable for year-round filming.

Two Western Cities

Quick Summary Seattle and Salt Lake City are very different places, but both are examples of cities with varied and strong economies in the West.

3 What are some of the high-tech industries that are located in or around Seattle? Computer software companies and manufacturers of ships and jet airplanes **Main Idea and Details**

SOCIAL STUDIES STRAND
Geography

The Great Salt Lake is located in an arid climate and is one of the saltiest inland lakes in the world. On its shores are sand, salt land, and marshland. Although the environment is harsh, parts of the lake are mined for salt and other minerals, used for recreation, and serve as important wildlife preserves.

4 What are some of the natural resources found near Salt Lake City? Salt, copper, lead, silver
Main Idea and Details

✓ **REVIEW ANSWER** Alike: both cities are located in the West, industry is important to both economies, and tourists enjoy visiting both cities; Different: Seattle's economy depends on the industries of computer software manufacturing and ship and jet manufacturing. Salt Lake City's economy relies on mining.
Compare and Contrast

Two Western Cities

The cities of the West are as varied as the region's landscape. About a thousand miles north of Los Angeles lies the city of **Seattle, Washington.**

Seattle's economy depends on a number of different industries. Many companies that make **computer software**—programs that help computers run certain functions—have their headquarters in or near Seattle. Ships and jet airplanes are also built
3 in the area.

Tourists to Seattle enjoy the city's historic districts and parks. Sightseers can ride the Monorail—an elevated train—through the city to the Space Needle. This tall tower has a wide view of the Seattle area and nearby mountains.

Salt Lake City, Utah, is hundreds of miles south and east of Seattle. Salt Lake City lies on the shore of the Great Salt Lake, from which the city takes its name. Like Seattle, Salt Lake City's economy depends on varied industries.

Salt is an important resource in the Salt Lake City area. The Great Salt Lake is a saltwater lake. About 2.5 million tons of salt are drawn each year from the area surrounding the lake.

Mining is also important to Salt Lake City. One of the world's largest open-pit copper mines is located near the city. Valuable minerals such as lead and
4 silver are mined as well.

Tourists come to Salt Lake City to enjoy its rich history. Nearby mountains also attract people who enjoy skiing and other winter sports.

Seattle and Salt Lake City are very different places. Still, they are both examples of the strong, busy cities of the West.

REVIEW Name ways that Seattle and Salt Lake City are alike and different.
Compare and Contrast

▶ **Bingham Canyon Mine, one of the world's largest open-pit copper mines, is located in the mountains west of Salt Lake City.**

Practice and Extend

MEETING INDIVIDUAL NEEDS
Leveled Practice

Demonstrate the Usefulness of Software Have students evaluate the usefulness of computer software and the importance of the software industry.

Easy Have students show examples of tasks that can be completed using word-processing, spreadsheet, or other basic software. **Reteach**

On-Level Have students explain orally how each type of software demonstrated above allows people to complete work faster, more easily, and/or more accurately. **Extend**

Challenge Have students research and write a paragraph explaining how the software industry impacts the economy, technology, or culture of the United States. **Enrich**

For a Lesson Summary, use Quick Study, p. 86.

FACT FILE

The bar graph shows the increase in population in the metropolitan areas of Los Angeles, California; Seattle, Washington; and Salt Lake City, Utah from 1990 to 2000. The pie chart shows the populations of these three Western cities in relation to each other.

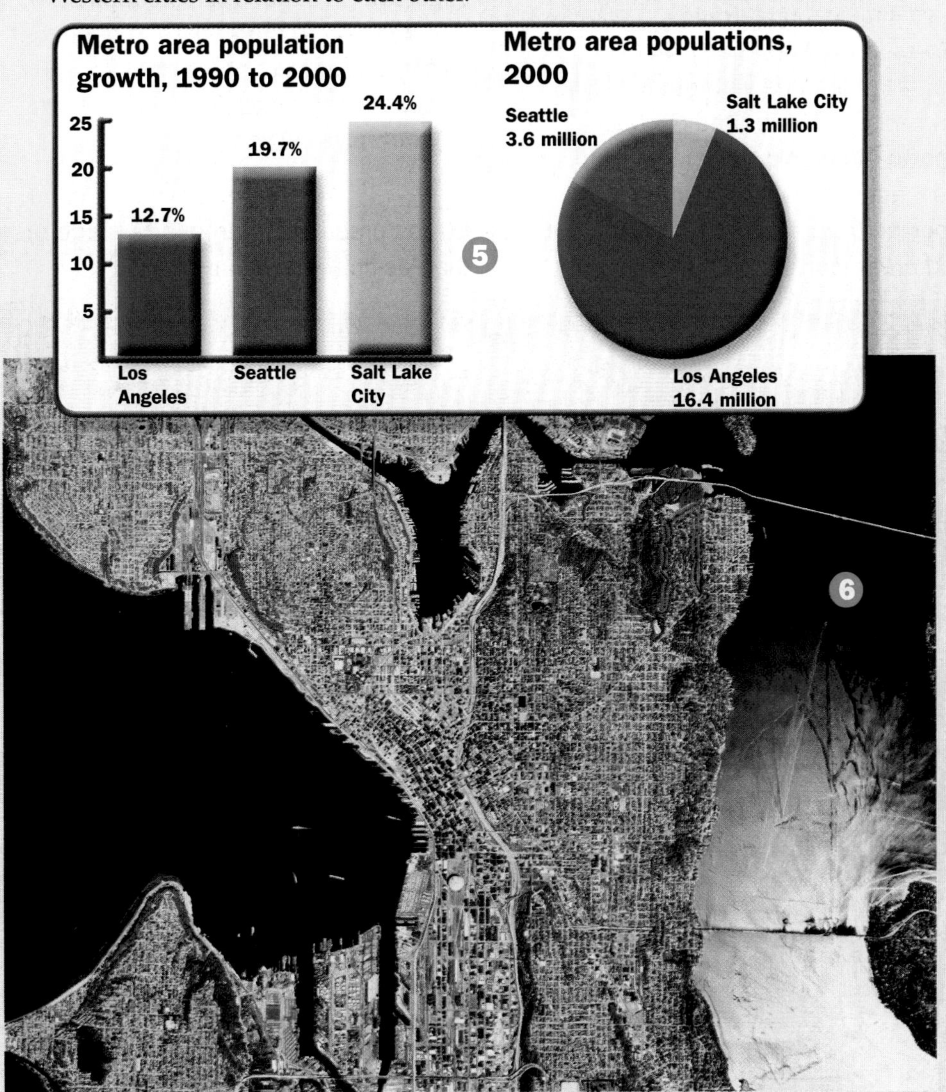

▶ This satellite image of Seattle, Washington, shows a densely populated city.

413

FACT FILE

5 Which city had the fastest rate of growth between 1990 and 2000? Which city had the highest population in 2000? Salt Lake City; Los Angeles **Interpret Graphs**

6 In the picture, how can you tell that an area is densely populated? The houses and other buildings are located very close together. **Analyze Pictures**

CURRICULUM CONNECTION Math

Create a Local Fact File

- Have students research the 1990 and 2000 populations of their community and two other communities in their state.
- Have students determine the percentage of change for each location. (Subtract the smaller number from the larger number and divide the result by the 1990 figure. If the 1990 figure is larger than the 2000 figure, express the rate as a negative percentage.)
- Tell students to record their data in a Fact File like the one above.

SOCIAL STUDIES Background

About Los Angeles

- Los Angeles was founded as a mission in 1771 and became a cow town in the mid-1800s. It prospered during the Gold Rush, when miners hungrily consumed local beef.
- After railroads linked the city to the East, settlers were encouraged to move to the "New Eden." As a result, the city's population more than quadrupled in just ten years!

PAGE 414

Trade and the Pacific Rim

Quick Summary The states of the West engage in a great deal of international trade with the countries of the Pacific Rim.

7 What kinds of goods does the United States export to many Pacific Rim countries? Movies made in Los Angeles, computer software made in Seattle, agricultural products from Hawaii Main Idea and Details

SOCIAL STUDIES STRAND
Economics

Shipping companies carry goods from one place to another on ships, trains, airplanes, or trucks.

8 Why might a shipping company become involved in both importing and exporting? Possible answer: It could fill a container with domestic goods, deliver them to a distant location, refill the container with foreign goods, and transport them back home.
Make Inferences

Ongoing Assessment

If... students have difficulty seeing the similarities in the importing and exporting processes,

then... have them list the basic steps involved in each type of transaction. Then ask them which steps (and costs) they could reduce if they combined the two processes.

REVIEW ANSWER The United States exports goods such as movies, computer software, and agricultural products to Pacific Rim countries. The United States also imports electronics, cars, and other goods from other Pacific Rim countries. Summarize

DIAGRAM SKILL Answer automobiles, electronics, and machinery

Trade and the Pacific Rim

Pacific Rim countries are nations that border the Pacific Ocean. The United States trades many resources, goods, and services with these countries. Trade between countries is called **international trade.**

Ports in the West carry on international trade with other Pacific Rim nations. The United States imports electronic equipment and cars from Japan. Meat and minerals are imported from Australia. Clothing and food are imported from China.

The United States also exports products to Pacific Rim countries. Movies made in Los Angeles and computer software made in Seattle are important U.S. exports. Hawaii exports agricultural products such as sugarcane, coffee, and pineapples. 7 8

In addition to the exchange of goods between these countries, ideas, languages, and traditions pass along this international trade route.

REVIEW Summarize how the United States practices international trade on the Pacific Rim. Summarize

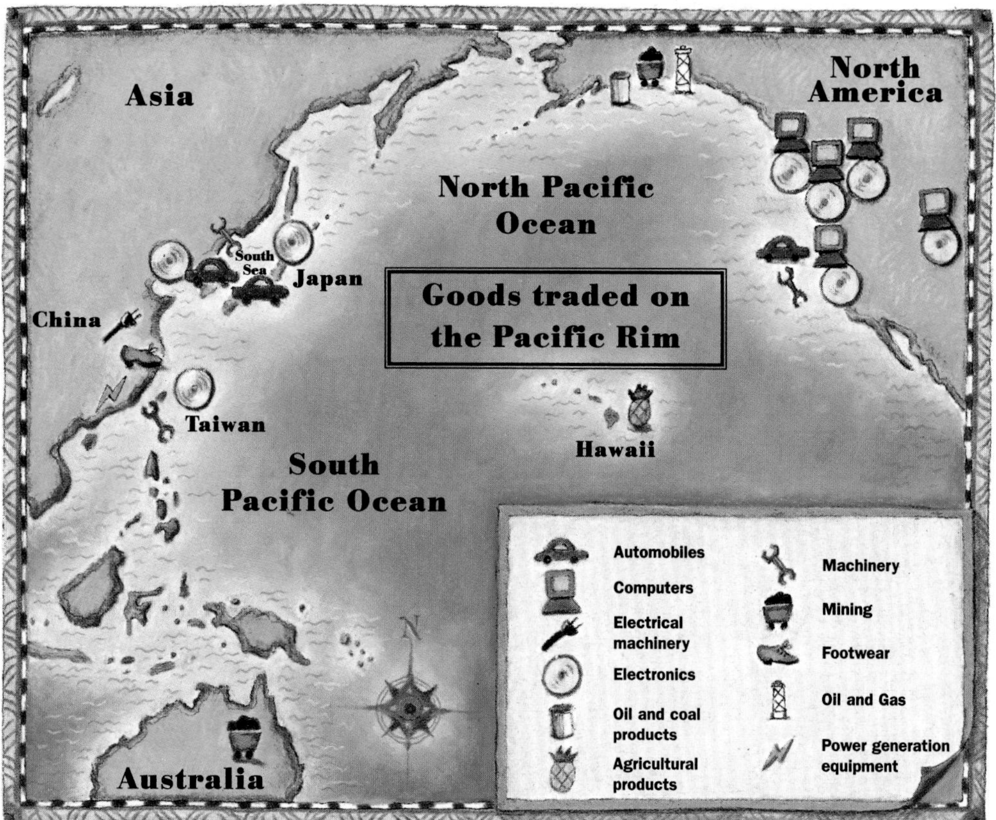

DIAGRAM SKILL *According to the map, what goods and services are manufactured both in Asia and North America?* automobiles, electronics, machinery

Practice and Extend

EXTEND LANGUAGE
ESL Support

Examine Root Words Explain to students that the root *port* means "to carry." Relate the concept to the words *import* and *export.*

Beginning Have students use a dictionary to find definitions for the words *import* and *export.*

Intermediate Have students research and define at least two more words that use the root *port* (e.g. *portable, transportation, report*).

Advanced Have students work in pairs to research a product that is imported by the United States, and one that is exported by the U.S. Encourage students to report their findings to the class.

For additional ESL support, use Every Student Learns Guide, pp. 170–173.

Westward Bound

You have read many reasons why the West is a great place to live in or visit. You can enjoy viewing the region's natural beauty and wildlife. You can climb up mountains or ski down them in many Western states. You can live and work in a place with many natural resources. The West has something for everyone. 9

REVIEW Why is the West an interesting region to live in or visit? Main Idea and Details

Summarize the Lesson

- **The climate and industries in Los Angeles have helped it to grow in population.**
- **Seattle and Salt Lake City are examples of strong Western cities.**
- **The United States and the countries of the Pacific Rim trade many resources, goods, and services.**

▶ **Whale watching is an attraction on the Pacific coast.**

LESSON 3 REVIEW

Check Facts and Main Ideas

1. Compare and Contrast On a separate sheet of paper, compare Los Angeles and Salt Lake City. Describe similarities.

Similarities	Differences
Near water Many tourists Large cities in the West Near mountains	• Los Angeles is on the Pacific Ocean. • Salt Lake City is inland. • Los Angeles is famous for movies. • Salt Lake City is known for mining.

2. Name some of the different industries found in Los Angeles, Seattle, and Salt Lake City.
3. What is the effect of climate on the tourism industries in Los Angeles and Salt Lake City?
4. What goods does the United States import from and export to Pacific Rim countries? Use the term **international trade** in your answer.
5. **Critical Thinking:** ***Point of View*** Of the cities described in this lesson, which one would you most like to visit? Why?

Link to Writing

Pen Pal Postcards Write a postcard to a person living in one of the cities from the lesson. Compare and contrast your community with theirs. Describe similarities and differences.

SOCIAL STUDIES Background

About Western Cities

- Los Angeles sprawls over 464 square miles between the San Gabriel Mountains and the ocean.
- Seattle was named for Chief Seattle, an important leader of the Suquamish and Duwamish peoples of the West.
- Salt Lake City was founded in 1847 by a group of Mormons (the Church of Jesus Christ of Latter-day Saints) seeking religious freedom.

Workbook, p. 95

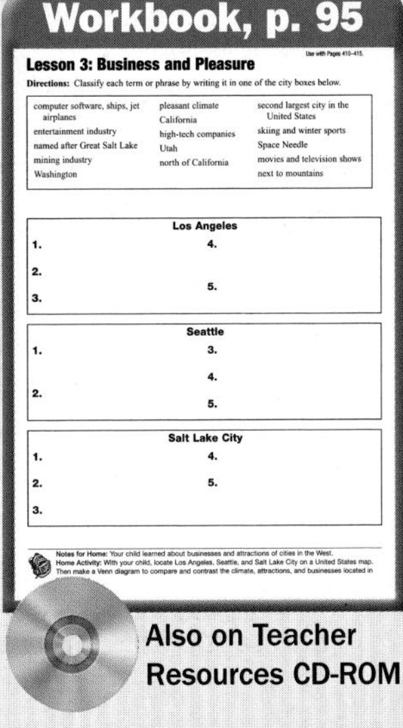

Also on Teacher Resources CD-ROM.

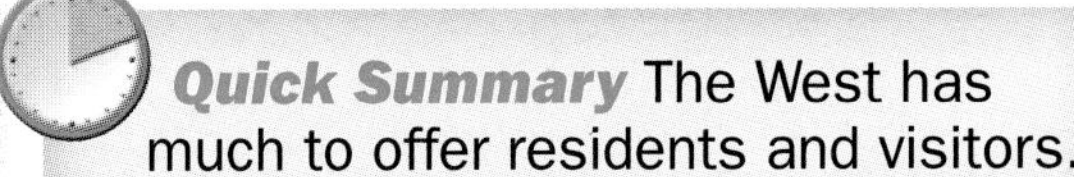

Westward Bound

Quick Summary The West has much to offer residents and visitors.

9 **What are some of the natural attractions of the West? the cultural attractions?** Possible answers: Natural: ocean, coast, wildlife, mountains; Cultural: cities, amusement parks, entertainment industry Summarize

✓ **REVIEW ANSWER** Possible answers: People can view the natural scenery, climb mountains, ski, or watch movies being made. Main Idea and Details

3 Close and Assess

Summarize the Lesson

Have students take turns reading the three main points. Then have students write a broad generalization that summarizes all three points. (e.g., There are many reasons for the growth of the West.)

✓ **LESSON 3 REVIEW**

1. **Compare and Contrast** For possible answers, see the reduced pupil page.
2. Possible answers: Los Angeles: entertainment and tourism; Seattle: computer software manufacturing; Salt Lake City: tourism and mining
3. The sunny, warm climate of Los Angeles makes outdoor attractions popular there; winter sports are popular among tourists in and around Salt Lake City.
4. International trade includes imports such as electronic equipment, cars, meat, minerals, and clothing; and exports such as movies, computer software, and agricultural products.
5. **Critical Thinking: *Point of View*** Students should draw on material from the lesson to formulate their answers.

Link to Writing

Encourage students to include information about climate, natural attractions, and businesses.

Building a City

Objective

- Identify individuals such as Thomas Bradley who exemplify good citizenship.

1 Introduce and Motivate

Preview To activate prior knowledge, ask volunteers to describe a time when they felt something was not fair. Discuss how ordinary citizens might work to correct each situation.

2 Teach and Discuss

1 **What problem did Mayor Bradley observe in Los Angeles? How did he solve this problem?** He saw that some people had difficulty traveling around the city; He had the Metro Rail system built to provide mass transit. Summarize

SOCIAL STUDIES STRAND
Citizenship

2 **How did Bradley show his belief in fairness?** Possible answers: He worked to find a way to help all people get around Los Angeles. Draw Conclusions

CITIZEN HEROES

Building a City

▶ Mayor Thomas Bradley

Thomas Bradley "was a builder... encouraging a thriving downtown and improving mass transit. Just as important, he built bridges across the lines that divide us, uniting people of many races and backgrounds in the most diverse city in America."

—President William Jefferson Clinton

Thomas Bradley was mayor of Los Angeles for twenty years. He thought his city was a great place to live, and he wanted everyone to have a fair chance to enjoy it. One problem Bradley saw was his city's transportation system. Bradley knew that most people used cars for transportation. People without cars often had a hard time getting around.

Bradley felt it was not fair that some people had difficulty enjoying his city. He knew that sometimes people could not take good jobs because they had no way to get to work. He knew that some people paid more for food and other needs because they could not get to inexpensive supermarkets and

Practice and Extend

CURRICULUM CONNECTION
Science

Investigate Engineering

The development of highways and public transportation systems requires the skills of transportation and civil engineers.

- Have students report how each type of engineer above contributes to the creation or implementation of transportation systems.
- Encourage students to interview local engineers about their jobs and report their findings to the class.

SOCIAL STUDIES
Background

About Transportation in California

- California has more motor vehicles and more miles of freeway than any other state.
- A driver can get on a freeway in San Diego and drive almost 500 miles north through Los Angeles and the Central Valley without ever seeing a stop sign or traffic signal.
- Los Angeles lacks a traditional city center, which made the construction of a public transportation system especially difficult.

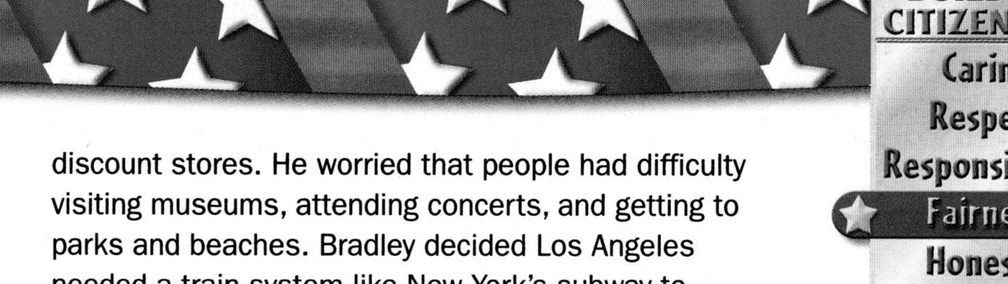

BUILDING CITIZENSHIP
Caring
Respect
Responsibility
Fairness
Honesty
Courage

discount stores. He worried that people had difficulty visiting museums, attending concerts, and getting to parks and beaches. Bradley decided Los Angeles needed a train system like New York's subway to help make transportation fairer.

Over many years Bradley worked to have the Metro Rail system built. Now many people ride these trains to jobs, stores, museums, parks, and other places. The Metro Rail system 1 and other projects Bradley began have helped make Los Angeles a fairer place to live. 2 3

Thomas Bradley believed that all people should follow their dreams. He said,

> *"The only thing that can stop you is you. Dream big dreams, work hard, study hard, and listen to your teachers. Above all get along with each other. You can be* 4 *anything your heart wants to be."*

Los Angeles Metro Rail System

Fairness in Action

Other people in United States history have taken action when they saw people being treated unfairly. Research a person who has worked for fairness toward immigrants, workers, or people of a different race or religion. You may choose an important figure in history or someone from your own community.

417

3 **How do you think Bradley's Metro Rail system may have helped some people achieve their dreams?** Possible answer: It may have given some people access to better jobs or learning opportunities that led to the achievement of specific goals. Make Inferences

Primary Source

4 **In the quote, Bradley implies that it is not enough to dream. What does he say people should do to achieve their dreams?** Work hard, study hard, listen to teachers, and get along with each other. Analyze Primary Sources

3 Close and Assess

Fairness in Action

- Encourage students to share the results of their research.
- Ask students to describe the problem their subject tackled and what he or she did to combat it.

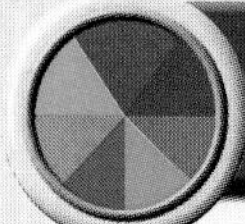

CURRICULUM CONNECTION
Writing

Write a Story About Unfairness

- Have students write a story in which the main character notices and remedies an unfair situation.
- Encourage students to write about characters and situations that are familiar to them, such as a school, community, or family situation.
- Tell students that the plot of the story should center on how the problem is solved.
- Ask volunteers to share their stories with the class.

WEB SITE
Technology

Students can find out more about Thomas Bradley by clicking on *Meet the People* at **www.sfsocialstudies.com.**

Resources

- Assessment Book, pp. 69–72
- Workbook, p. 96: Vocabulary Review

Chapter Summary

For possible answers, see the reduced pupil page.

Vocabulary

1. Images of animals and people are carved into a totem pole to tell a story.
2. The potlatch is a Tlingit tradition that celebrates important events in a family's life.
3. During the mid-1800s many prospectors came to California in search of riches.
4. The California Gold Rush gave rise to a number of boom towns.
5. When people left the boom towns in search of other opportunities, the boom towns became ghost towns.
6. Seattle is home to many businesses that make computer software.
7. The United States participates in international trade with many Pacific Rim countries.

People and Places

1. Juneau, Alaska
2. Junípero Serra
3. Sutter's Mill
4. Levi Strauss
5. Salt Lake City

CHAPTER 13 REVIEW

1750 — 1800 — 1850

1769 Father Serra established the first California mission.

1841 Wagon trains traveled West.

1848 The United States won the territory of California from Mexico. Gold was discovered in California.

Chapter Summary

Compare and Contrast

On a separate sheet of paper, fill in the diagram to list similarities and differences in the ways in which Alaska and Hawaii became states.

Similarities	Differences
Both had to wait much longer than other U.S. territories before they became states.	The United States bought Alaska prior to making it a state, but made Hawaii a territory.

▶ Sunset in Barrow, Alaska

Vocabulary

Use each word in a sentence that explains the meaning of the word.

1. **totem pole** (p. 395)
2. **potlatch** (p. 396)
3. **prospector** (p. 402)
4. **boom town** (p. 403)
5. **ghost town** (p. 403)
6. **computer software** (p. 412)
7. **international trade** (p. 414)

People and Places

Write these sentences on a separate sheet of paper. Fill in the blank with the name of a person or place from this chapter.

1. The Tlingit's governing council meets in _________. (p. 397)
2. A priest, _________, built the first mission in California. (p. 401)
3. In 1848 John Marshall discovered gold in California at _________. (p. 402)
4. _________ sold sturdy pants during the Gold Rush in California. (p. 403)
5. _________ is a city in Utah that was named for a nearby body of water. (p. 412)

418

Practice and Extend

Assessment Options

✓ Chapter 13 Assessment

- Chapter 13 Content Test: Use Assessment Book, pp. 69–70.
- Chapter 13 Skills Test: Use Assessment Book, pp. 71–72.

Standardized Test Prep

- Chapter 13 Tests contain standardized test format.

✓ Chapter 13 Performance Assessment

- Have students work in small groups to review the information in this chapter.
- Tell students to take turns reading the title of each lesson subsection and then summarizing the section's important details.
- Observe students as they work. If they seem to be missing key ideas, ask targeted questions.

1867 The United States purchased Alaska from Russia.

1883 "Buffalo Bill" Cody started his Wild West show.

1900 The United States claimed Hawaii as a territory.

1959 Alaska and Hawaii were granted statehood.

Facts and Main Ideas

1. What is the purpose of a totem pole?
2. How did some missions in California grow and change?
3. **Time Line** How many years passed between the year the United States purchased Alaska and the year the United States claimed Hawaii?
4. **Main Idea** Describe the Tlingit way of life.
5. **Main Idea** How did the discovery of gold change the West?
6. **Main Idea** What are some products that are traded among the Pacific Rim countries?
7. **Critical Thinking:** ***Make Inferences*** Why is the West Coast a convenient place for international trade?

Write About History

1. **Write a journal entry** describing how you might feel if you learned that gold had been discovered in your state. Would you believe it? Would you want to become a prospector?
2. **Write a newspaper report** about a local potlatch. Tell why the potlatch was held, who attended, and what kinds of gifts were given.
3. **Write a travel brochure** about a city in the West. Choose one western city to research and write about. Include information about things to see and do in and around the city.

Apply Skills

Understand Latitude and Longitude

1. What is the approximate latitude and longitude of Denver?
2. What is the approximate latitude and longitude of Pikes Peak?
3. What national monument is between 40°N, 109°W and 41°N, 109°W?
4. Name the Colorado cities that are located at about 105°W.

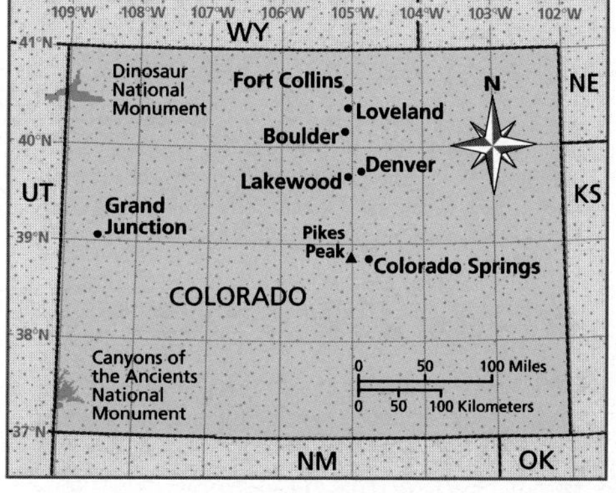

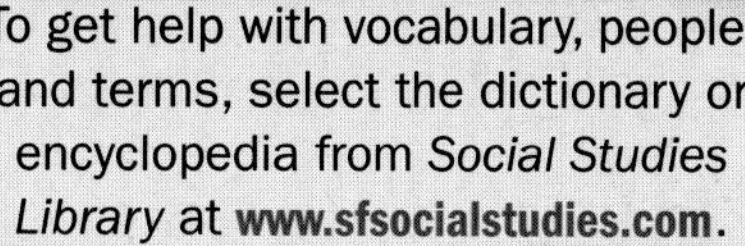

To get help with vocabulary, people, and terms, select the dictionary or encyclopedia from *Social Studies Library* at **www.sfsocialstudies.com**.

Facts and Main Ideas

1. A totem pole shows the history of the family who owns it through the use of important symbols.
2. As more people moved to the missions, these settlements grew into cities such as San Francisco and Los Angeles.
3. 33 years
4. The Tlingit use the natural resources around them, make and trade various goods and crafts, and continue many of their traditions even today.
5. Towns sprang up in the West wherever gold was found, and their populations soared. Some boom towns later grew into cities.
6. Possible answers: Movies, computer software, cars, food products, clothes
7. Because the West Coast is on the Pacific Ocean, trade with Pacific Rim countries is convenient.

Write About History

1. Students should include personal thoughts and opinions in their journal entries.
2. Newspaper reports should include detailed information based on the lesson.
3. Travel brochures should include interesting facts about the chosen city. Students can use the Internet to find out more information about their cities.

Apply Skills

1. 40°N, 105°W
2. 39°N, 105°W
3. Dinosaur National Monument
4. Fort Collins, Loveland, Boulder, Denver, Lakewood, Colorado Springs

Hands-on Unit Project

Unit 6 Performance Assessment

- See p. 424 for information about using the Unit Project as a means of performance assessment.
- A scoring guide is provided on p. 424.

WEB SITE Technology

For more information, students can select the dictionary or encyclopedia from *Social Studies Library* at **www.sfsocialstudies.com.**

Workbook, p. 96

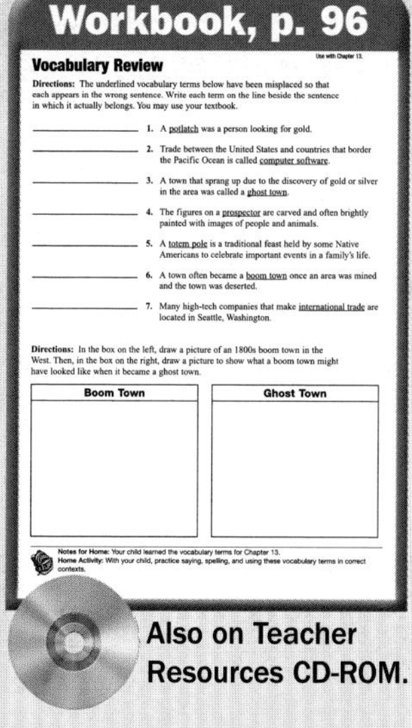

Use with Chapter 13.

Vocabulary Review

Directions: The underlined vocabulary terms below have been misplaced so that each appears in the wrong sentence. Write each term on the line beside the sentence in which it actually belongs. You may use your textbook.

_______ 1. A potlatch was a person looking for gold.

_______ 2. Trade between the United States and countries that border the Pacific Ocean is called computer software.

_______ 3. A town that sprang up due to the discovery of gold or silver in the area was called a ghost town.

_______ 4. The figures on a prospector are carved and often brightly painted with images of people and animals.

_______ 5. A totem pole is a traditional feast held by some Native Americans to celebrate important events in a family's life.

_______ 6. A town often became a boom town once an area was mined and the town was deserted.

_______ 7. Many high-tech companies that make international trade are located in Seattle, Washington.

Directions: In the box on the left, draw a picture of an 1800s boom town in the West. Then, in the box on the right, draw a picture to show what a boom town might have looked like when it became a ghost town.

Boom Town	Ghost Town

Notes for Home: Your child learned the vocabulary terms for Chapter 13.
Home Activity: With your child, practice saying, spelling, and using these vocabulary terms in correct contexts.

Also on Teacher Resources CD-ROM.

Sweet Betsy from Pike

Objectives

- Identify geographic locations in songs.
- Identify historical events in songs.
- Explain how examples of music reflect the times in which they were written.

Resource

- Transparency 64

1 Introduce and Motivate

Preview To activate prior knowledge, ask students if they know any songs that tell stories. Explain that "Sweet Betsy from Pike" tells the story of two people moving west in the 1800s.

2 Teach and Discuss

1 How would you describe Betsy and Ike's journey from Missouri to California? Possible answer: It was a long, hard journey over rough terrain. **Express Ideas**

2 What obstacles did Betsy and Ike face on their journey to California? Possible answers: It was a long trip, the rooster ran off, oxen died, the desert was hot, they had to cross rivers and mountains, and they fought hunger and rattlers. **Main Idea and Details**

UNIT 6 End with a Song

Sweet Betsy

Sweet Betsy was a fictional woman who left Pike County, Missouri and headed for the California gold mines. This song celebrates all the hearty people who traveled westward to California after gold was found there in 1848.

Folk Song from the United States
Adapted and arranged by Lillian Wiedman
A
C G7 C
1. Oh, don't you re - mem - ber sweet Bet - sy from Pike?
2. One ev' - ning quite ear - ly they camped on the Platte,
C D7 G
She crossed the wide prai - ries with her hus - band, Ike,
'Twas near by the road on a green shad - y flat.
C F C
With two yoke of ox - en, an old yel - low dog,
Poor Bet - sy, quite tired, ___ lay down for re - pose,
C G7 C
A ___ tall Shang - hai roost - er and one spot - ted hog.
And ___ Ike sat and gazed at his Pike Coun - ty rose.

420

Practice and Extend

SOCIAL STUDIES
Background

"Sweet Betsy from Pike"

- "Sweet Betsy from Pike" describes the long and difficult journey many gold seekers and other settlers made to California during the 1800s.
- The route described in the song is the Overland Trail, established in part in 1862 by the new Overland Mail Route.
- In the mid-1860s, hundreds of thousands of settlers traveled to the West on the Overland, Oregon, California, Mormon, and Santa Fe Trails.

AUDIO CD
Technology

Play the CD *Songs and Music* to listen to "Sweet Betsy from Pike."

from Pike

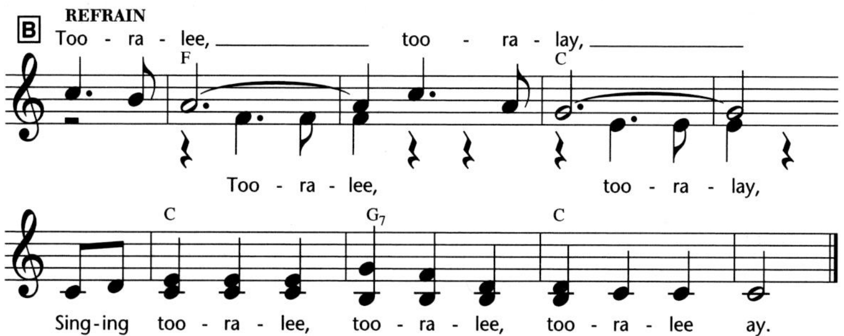

REFRAIN
B
Too - ra - lee, too - ra - lay,
F C
Too - ra - lee, too - ra - lay,
C G7 C
Sing-ing too - ra - lee, too - ra - lee, too - ra - lee ay.

3. They soon reached the desert where Betsy gave out.
And down on the sand she lay rolling about.
While Ike, in great tears, looked on in surprise:
Said, "Betsy, get up, you'll get sand in your eyes." *Refrain*

4. The rooster ran off and the oxen all died:
The last piece of bacon that morning was fried.
Poor Ike got discouraged and Betsy got mad:
The dog wagged his tail and looked awfully sad. *Refrain*

5. The alkali desert was burning and hot,
And Ike, he decided to leave on the spot:
"My dear old Pike County, I'll go back to you."
Said Betsy, "You'll go by yourself if you do." *Refrain* ③

6. They swam the wide rivers, they crossed the tall peaks,
They camped out on prairies for weeks and for weeks,
Fought hunger and rattlers and big storms of dust,
① ② Determined to reach California or bust. *Refrain* ④

PIKE

421

③ **How do you think Betsy's and Ike's points of view about the journey differed?** Possible answer: Betsy was able to bounce back from all the hardships of the trip and was determined to reach California no matter what. Ike was less determined and wanted to give up. **Point of View**

④ **Do you think Betsy and Ike eventually reached California? Why or why not?** Possible answer: Yes; they already had proven that they could overcome obstacles, and they were determined to reach California. **Predict**

3 Close and Assess

- Have students discuss ways to perform this song. Students who play musical instruments may be interested in playing the song for the class.
- Ask students what conclusions they can draw about the trip west for many settlers during the 1800s. (Possible answers: Many settlers dreamed of moving to California to find wealth and better lives; the long journey west could be physically and emotionally draining.)

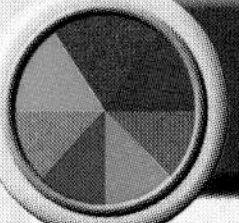

CURRICULUM CONNECTION
Art

Trace a Route on a Map

- Tell students that the song "Sweet Betsy from Pike" describes settlers' journey along the Overland Trail to the West.
- Have them work in groups of two or three to research the route of the Overland Trail.
- Then, have them trace the route on an outline map of the United States.
- Using their research and the words of the song, have students add to their maps the geographic landforms and other features Betsy and Ike would have encountered on their journey.
- Have students present their maps to the class.

Resource

- Assessment Book, pp. 73–76

Main Ideas and Vocabulary

1. c, **2.** d, **3.** b, **4.** c

People and Places

Possible answers:

1. Yellowstone National Park is located in Wyoming, Idaho, and Montana. It is the world's oldest national park.
2. Death Valley, California, is a desert area that is a part of the Great Basin.
3. Many fruits and vegetables are grown in Willamette Valley, Oregon.
4. Juan Rodríguez Cabrillo probably was the first European to see California.
5. In 1769, Father Junípero Serra built the first mission in California.
6. In 1848, gold was discovered at Sutter's Mill, owned by John Sutter.
7. Levi Strauss invented blue jeans and built a successful business.

Test Talk

Write Your Answer to Score High
Use People and Places, Question 1, to model the Test Talk strategy.

Make sure the answer is correct. Students should make sure their written answer has only correct details.

Make sure the answer is complete.

Make sure the answer is focused. Students should make sure their written answer has only details that answer the question.

UNIT 6 Review

Main Ideas and Vocabulary

Read the passage below and use it to answer the questions that follow.

Many people think of the West as a region of mountains. The Rocky Mountains, which are the largest system of mountain ranges in North America, are located in the West. So are the Sierra Nevada and the Cascade Range. Mount McKinley, the highest point in North America, is located in the western state of Alaska.

Yellowstone, the nation's oldest national park, is located in the mountains of Wyoming, Idaho, and Montana. It is famous for its scenery, wildlife, and hot springs. Some hot springs, such as the famous Old Faithful, are geysers. An eruption from Old Faithful sends boiling water more than 100 feet into the air.

The West is much more than mountains, however. The Great Basin is a desert that is often quite hot. Death Valley, California is more than 200 feet below sea level. It is the lowest elevation in North America. Parts of the West produce lots of fruit and vegetables. California's Central Valley and Oregon's Willamette Valley are famous for their farm products. Tropical Hawaii produces crops such as sugarcane and pineapples.

The history and culture of the West is as varied as the region's landscape. In 1848 gold was discovered at Sutter's Mill in California. This triggered the Gold Rush. Soon prospectors from around the world came to California to search for gold. Merchants followed, hoping to make money by selling goods to the miners. Cities throughout the West grew as gold, silver, and other valuable ores were discovered.

Today the West is home to many different cultures. Some, such as the Tlingit, have lived in southern Alaska for hundreds of years. One Tlingit tradition is the carving and displaying of totem poles. The carvings on a totem pole include symbols of a family's history. Another Tlingit tradition is the potlatch, a feast where gifts are given. Potlatches can last many days.

1. According to the passage, what is the highest place in North America?
   A Death Valley
   B Yellowstone
   C Mount McKinley
   D The Great Basin

2. In the passage, the word *geysers* means
   A lakes made by humans
   B very old trees
   C wildlife of the West
   D hot springs that erupt

3. In the passage, the word *prospectors* means
   A people opening stores
   B people searching for valuable ore
   C people going on vacation
   D people climbing mountains

4. What item below is not a part of Tlingit culture?
   A a totem pole
   B a potlatch
   C a pineapple
   D gift-giving

422

Practice and Extend

Assessment Options

✓Unit 6 Assessment

- Use Unit 6 Content Test: Use Assessment Book, pp. 73–74.
- Use Unit 6 Skills Test: Use Assessment Book, pp. 75–76.

Standardized Test Prep

- Unit 6 Tests contain standardized test format.

✓Unit 6 Performance Assessment

- See page 424 for information about using the Unit Project as a means of performance assessment.
- A scoring guide for the Unit 6 Project is provided in the teacher's notes on p. 424.

Test Talk

- Test Talk Practice Book

WEB SITE Technology

For more information, you can select the dictionary or encyclopedia from *Social Studies Library* at **www.sfsocialstudies.com.**

Is your answer complete, correct, and focused?

People and Places

Write a sentence or two explaining why each of the following people or terms is important.

1. **Yellowstone National Park** (p. 370)
2. **Death Valley, California** (p. 380)
3. **Willamette Valley, Oregon** (p. 385)
4. **Juan Rodríguez Cabrillo** (p. 401)
5. **Junípero Serra** (p. 401)
6. **John Sutter** (p. 402)
7. **Levi Strauss** (p. 403)

Apply Skills

Write Notes and Outlines

Choose one topic covered in Unit 6, such as Yellowstone National Park, the Tlingit culture, or the Gold Rush, and do research on it. As you do your research, take notes. Then use your notes to write an outline about the topic. Illustrate the outline, if you wish.

Upper Geyser Basin
- Old Faithful
- Castle Geyser
- Morning Glory Pool

Things to See in Yellowstone National Park
- I. Upper Geyser Basin
  - A. Old Faithful
  - B. Castle Geyser
  - C. Morning Glory Pool
- II. Mammoth Hot Springs
  - A. Minerva Terrace
  - B. Canary Spring
  - C. Elk

Write and Share

Write and Share a Story With a group of classmates, write a story about a person who comes to California seeking his or her fortune during the Gold Rush. Choose one person from the group to read the whole story, or split the story into sections and let each group member read.

Read on Your Own

Look for books like these in the library.

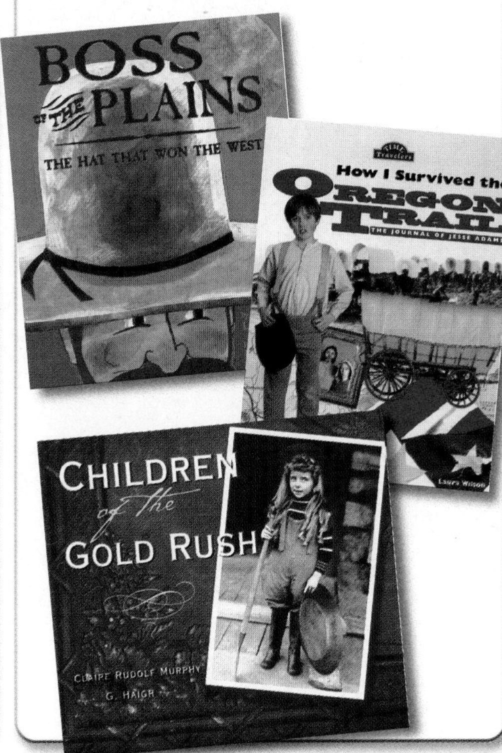

423

Apply Skills

Students' notes and outlines should follow the style set forth in the Research and Writing Skills feature on pp. 376–377.

Write and Share

- Encourage students to brainstorm before they begin writing. Reviewing the facts in the textbook may help them generate ideas.
- Remind students to practice reading beforehand. Tell them to work on reading with feeling and making eye contact.
- Use the following scoring guide.

✓Assessment Scoring Guide

Write and Share a Story	
6	Story is accurate with clear beginning, middle, and end. Reader speaks clearly, with emotion and eye contact.
5	Story is accurate with clear beginning, middle, and end. Reader speaks clearly with some eye contact.
4	Story lacks coherence or is not entirely accurate; reader does not speak clearly or make eye contact.
3	Story lacks coherence and is not entirely accurate; reader mumbles or reads with no emotion.
2	Story is uneven and mostly inaccurate; reader seems under-rehearsed.
1	Story is uneven and lacks coherence and attention to detail; reader seems under-rehearsed.

If you prefer a 4-point rubric, adjust accordingly.

Read on Your Own

Have students prepare oral reports, using the following books.

Boss of the Plains: The Hat That Won the West, by Laurie Carlson (DK Publishing, ISBN 0-7894-2657-9, 2000) **Easy** ***ALA Notable Book***

How I Survived the Oregon Trail: The Journal of Jesse Adams, by Laura Wilson (Beech Tree Books, ISBN 0-688-17276-8, 1999) **On-Level**

Children of the Gold Rush, by Claire Rudolf Murphy, Jane G. Haigh (Alaska Northwest Books, ISBN 0-88240-548-9, 2001) **Challenge**

Revisit the Unit Question

✓Portfolio Assessment

- Have students look at the lists they compiled throughout Unit 6 of how the resources and people of the West make the region unique.
- Have them share their lists with a partner and discuss any items that differ between the two lists.
- Allow students to add to or edit their lists to accurately reflect their knowledge of the West.
- Tell students to write a summary expressing how the resources and people of the West make the region unique.
- Have students add these lists and summaries to their Social Studies Portfolio.

Unit Project

Great State

Objective

- Describe a current event in your state and make a prediction about the future.

Resource

- Workbook, p. 97

Materials

paper, pencils, crayons, markers, sample travel guides, books, and magazines

Follow This Procedure

- Tell students they will present a testimonial about a current event in the state and predict its effects. Explain that a testimonial usually offers proof of positive characteristics.
- Brainstorm current events with students, including those related to government, cities, technology, education, and so on.
- Divide students into groups. Ask students to write a paragraph about a current event and illustrate it.
- Have students write a prediction about the effects of their current event. Make a booklet of predictions and pictures.
- Invite each group to present its booklets and testimonials to the class.
- Use the following scoring guide.

✓ Assessment Scoring Guide

Great State	
6	Provides detailed, informative descriptions; accurate content; clear illustrations; and precise word choices
5	Provides informative descriptions, accurate content and illustrations, and good word choices
4	Provides some informative descriptions, mostly accurate content and illustrations, and good word choices
3	Provides few informative descriptions, mostly accurate content and illustrations, and appropriate word choices
2	Provides few descriptions, some unclear illustrations, and vague word choices
1	Provides no descriptions, few clear illustrations, and incorrect word choices

If you prefer a 4-point rubric, adjust accordingly.

Unit 6 Project

Great State

Create a booklet that shows what's great about your state today—and what will be great in the future.

1 **Form** a group. Choose a current event in your state.

2 **Write** a paragraph about the event. Predict what will happen in the future and write several sentences.

3 **Draw** or find pictures that illustrate the event today and what might occur in the future.

4 **Put** your group's paragraphs and pictures together into a booklet. Share it with the class.

Internet Activity

Learn more about the West. Go to **www.sfsocialstudies.com/activities** and select your grade and unit.

Practice and Extend

Hands-on Unit Project

✓ Performance Assessment

- The Unit Project can also be used as a performance assessment activity.
- Use the scoring guide to assess each group's work.

WEB SITE

Technology

Students can launch the Internet Activity by clicking on *Grade 4, Unit 6* at **www.sfsocialstudies.com/activities.**

Workbook, p. 97

Unit 6 Project Great State

Directions: In a group, prepare a booklet that shows what's great about your state today—and what will be great in the future.

1. Our current event is ______.
2. This is a description of the current event:
3. This is our prediction of what will happen in the future:
4. This is a description of the pictures we will include in our booklet:

1st picture: ______

2nd picture: ______

3rd picture: ______

4th picture: ______

Checklist for Students

____ We chose a current event about our state.
____ We wrote a paragraph about the current event.
____ We wrote predictions about the future.
____ We illustrated the current event.
____ We shared our booklet with the class.

Notes for Home: Your child learned about current events in your state.
Home Activity: With your child, discuss some events that occurred in the past in your state. Share details about the event, and discuss how the event has affected your state today.

Also on Teacher Resources CD-ROM.

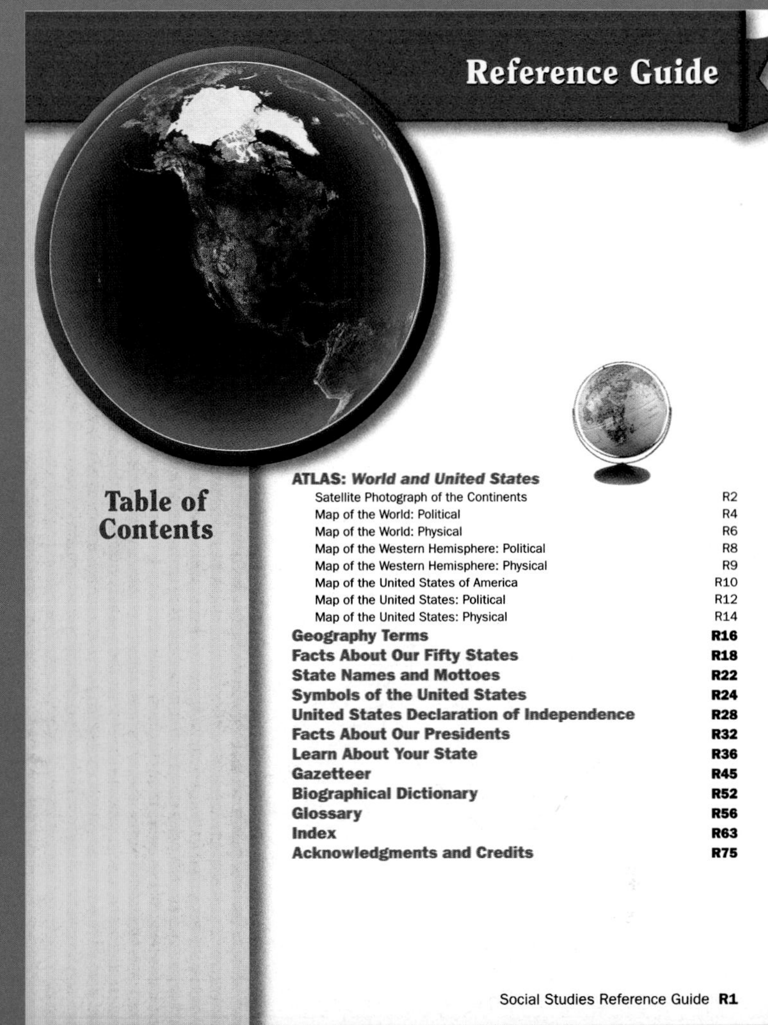

Reference Guide

Table of Contents

ATLAS: *World and United States*

- Satellite Photograph of the Continents R2
- Map of the World: Political R4
- Map of the World: Physical R6
- Map of the Western Hemisphere: Political R8
- Map of the Western Hemisphere: Physical R9
- Map of the United States of America R10
- Map of the United States: Political R12
- Map of the United States: Physical R14

Geography Terms R16
Facts About Our Fifty States R18
State Names and Mottoes R22
Symbols of the United States R24
United States Declaration of Independence R28
Facts About Our Presidents R32
Learn About Your State R36
Gazetteer R45
Biographical Dictionary R52
Glossary R56
Index R63
Acknowledgments and Credits R75

Social Studies Reference Guide **R1**

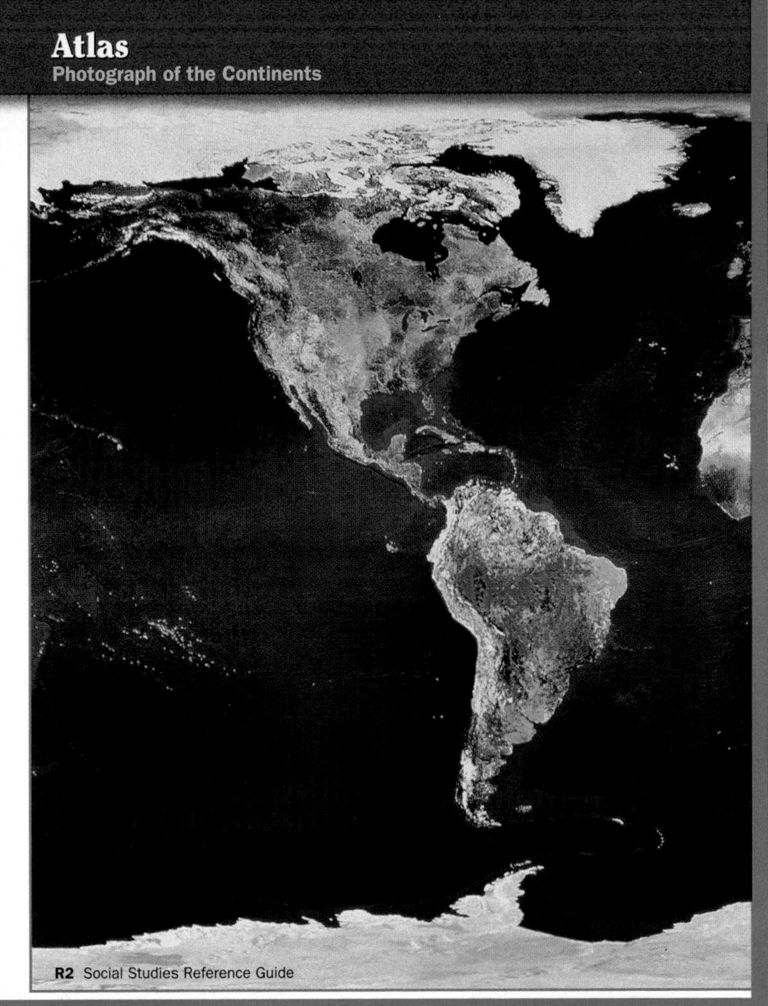

Atlas

Photograph of the Continents

R2 Social Studies Reference Guide

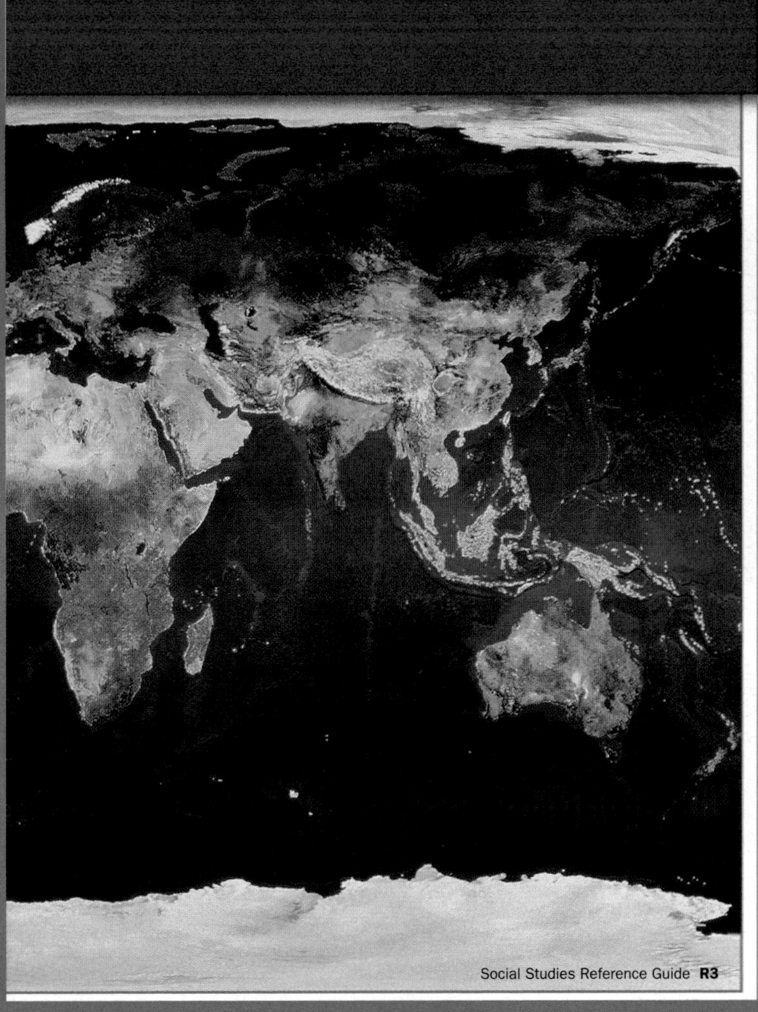

Social Studies Reference Guide **R3**

Atlas
Map of the World: Political

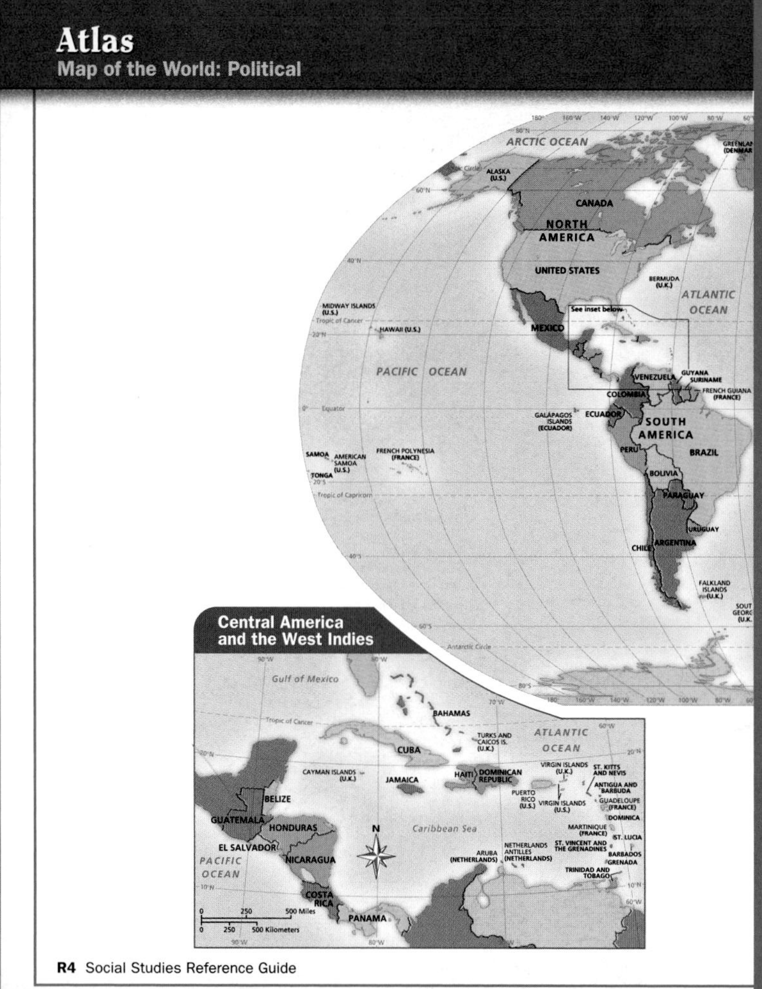

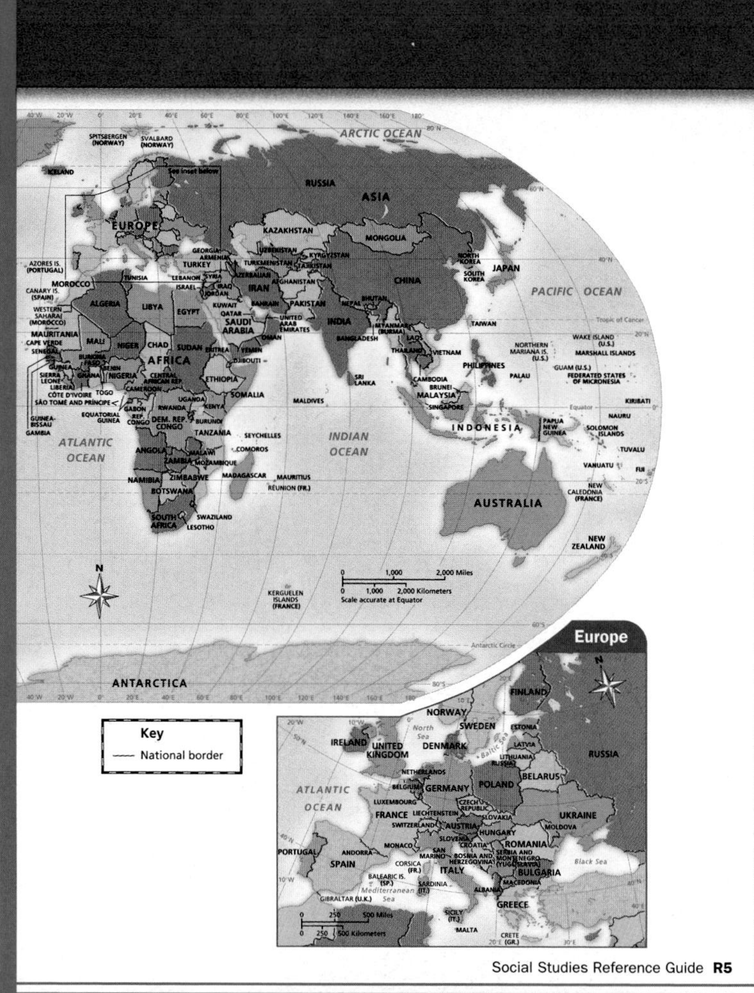

Atlas
Map of the World: Physical

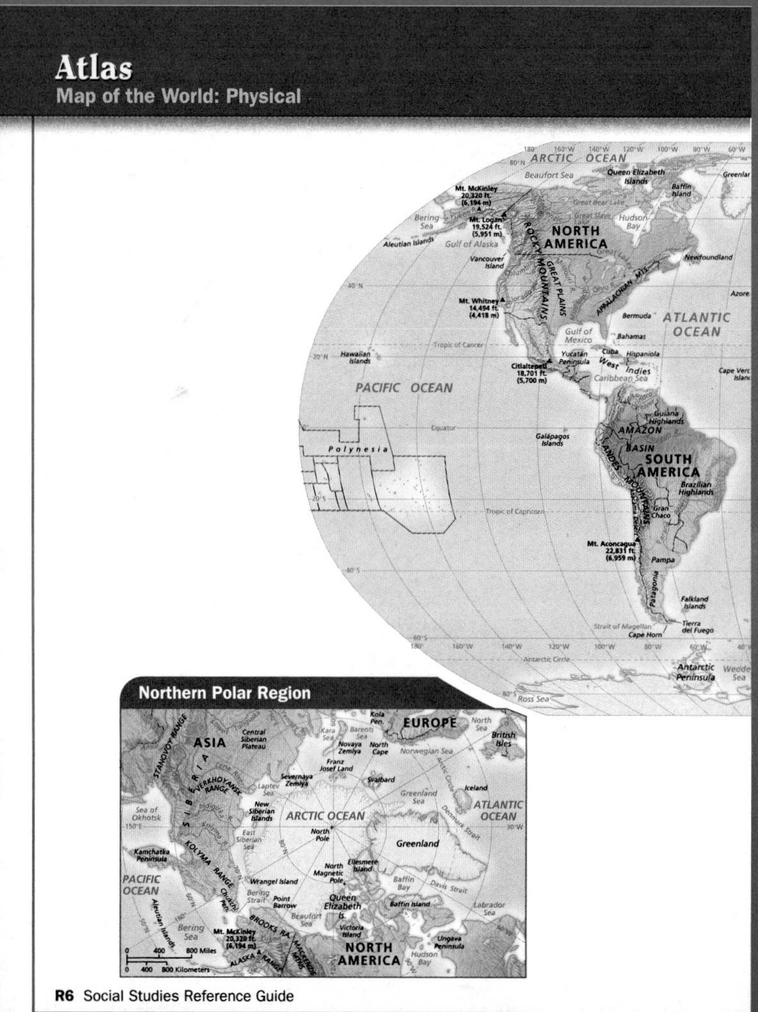

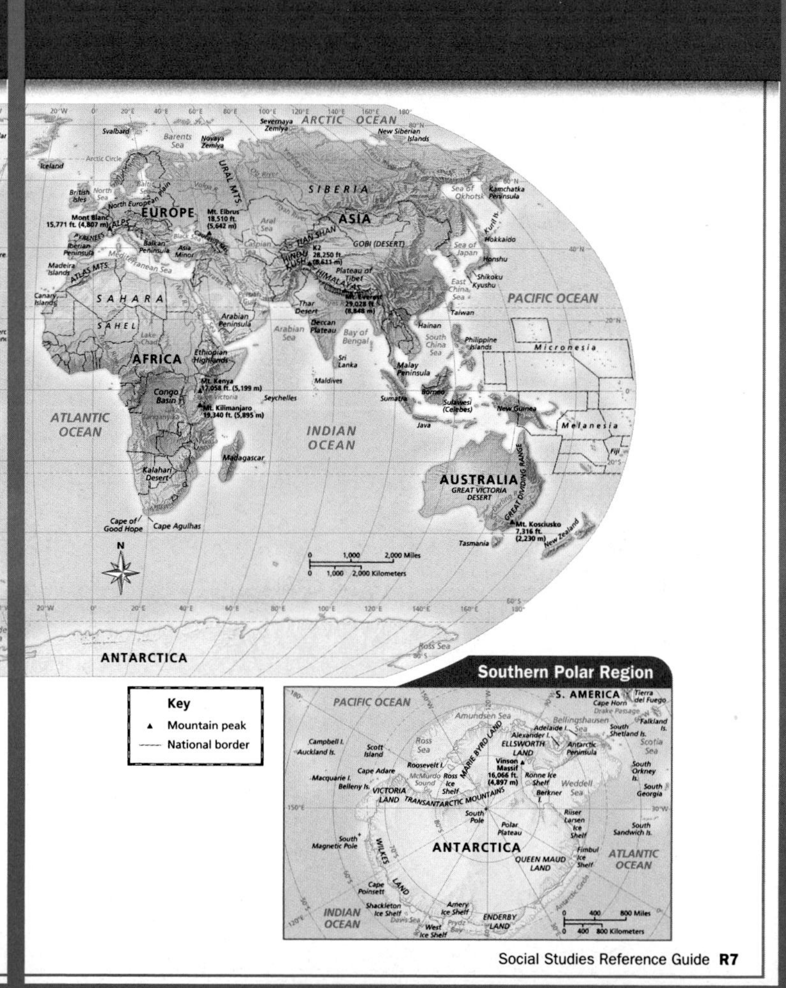

Atlas

Map of the Western Hemisphere: Political

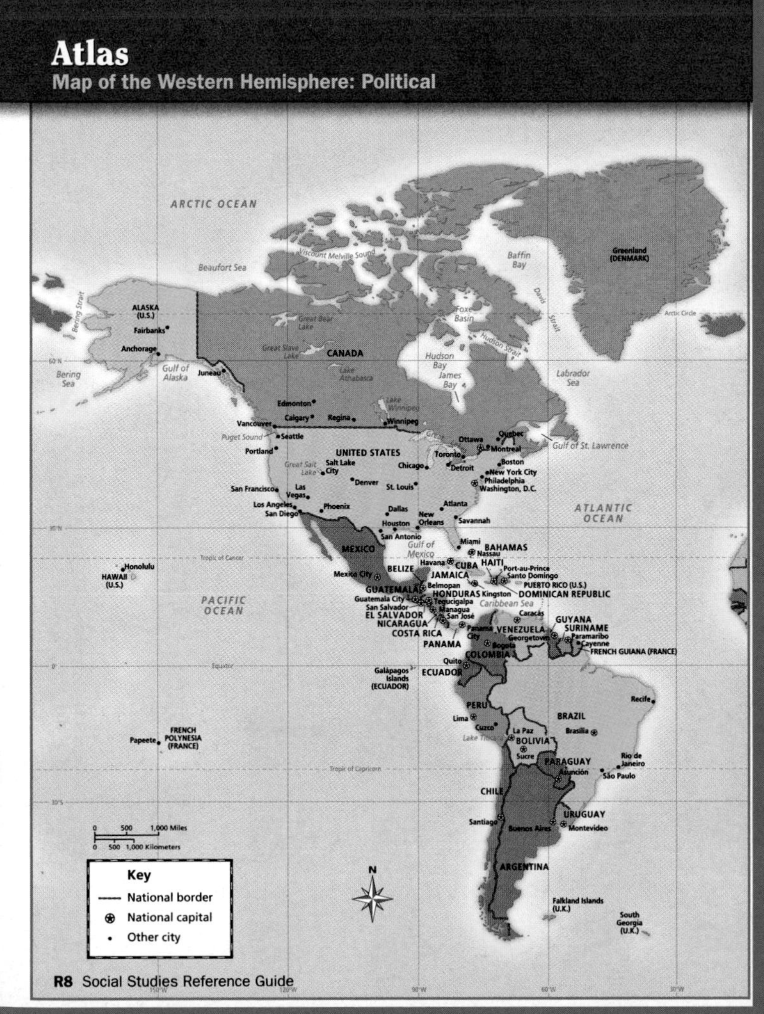

Map of the Western Hemisphere: Physical

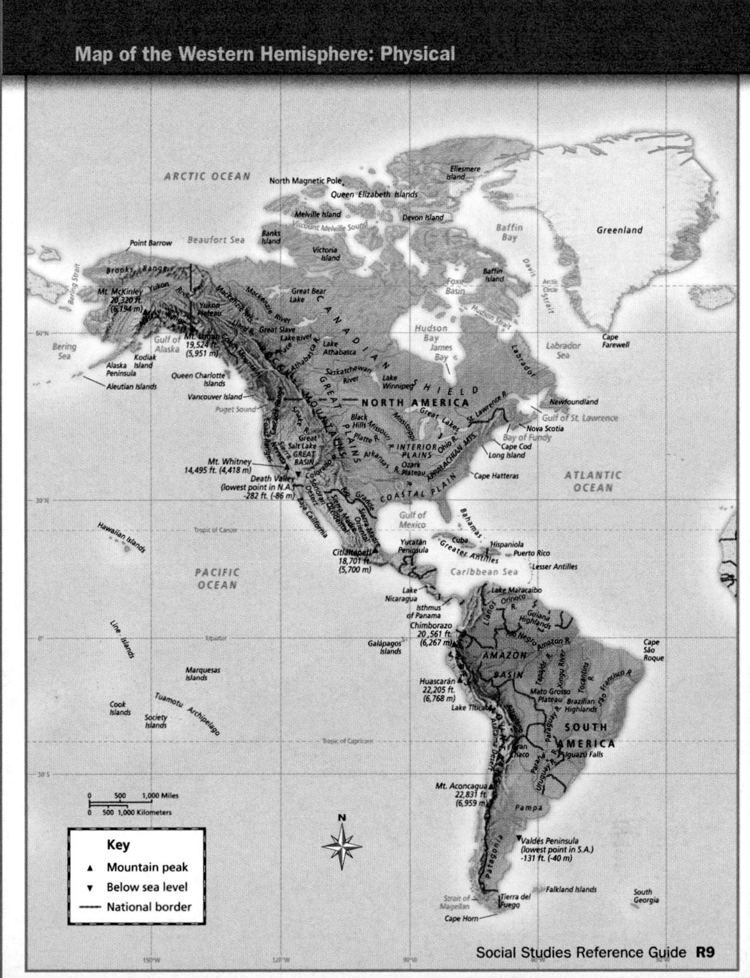

Atlas

Map of the United States of America

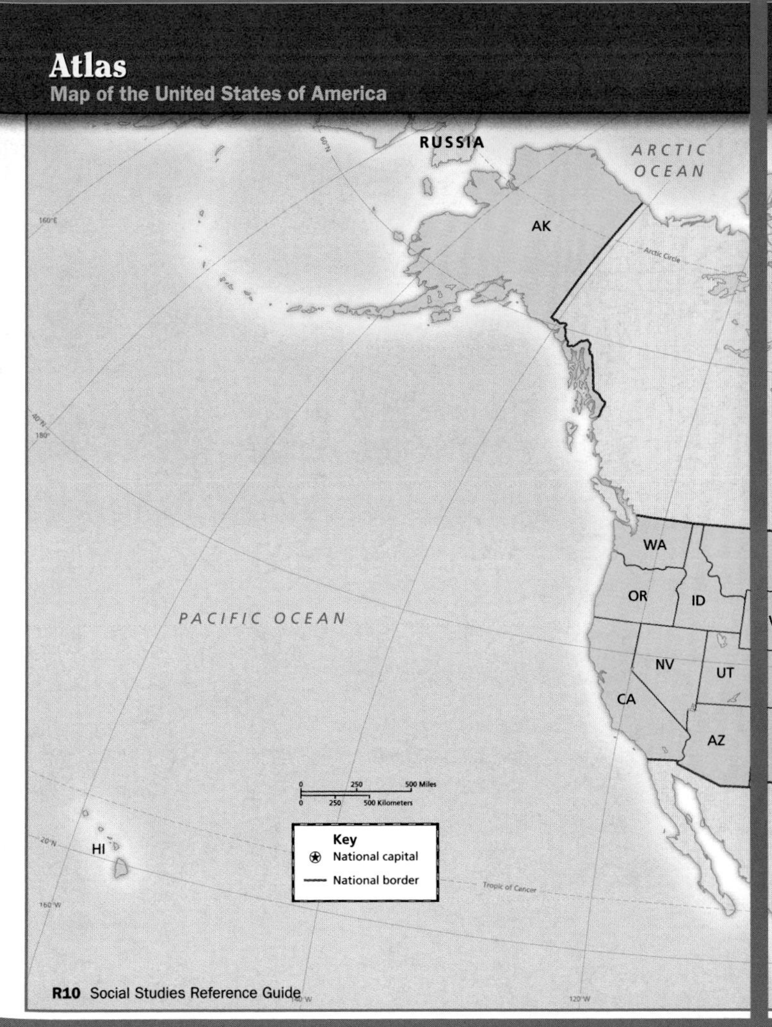

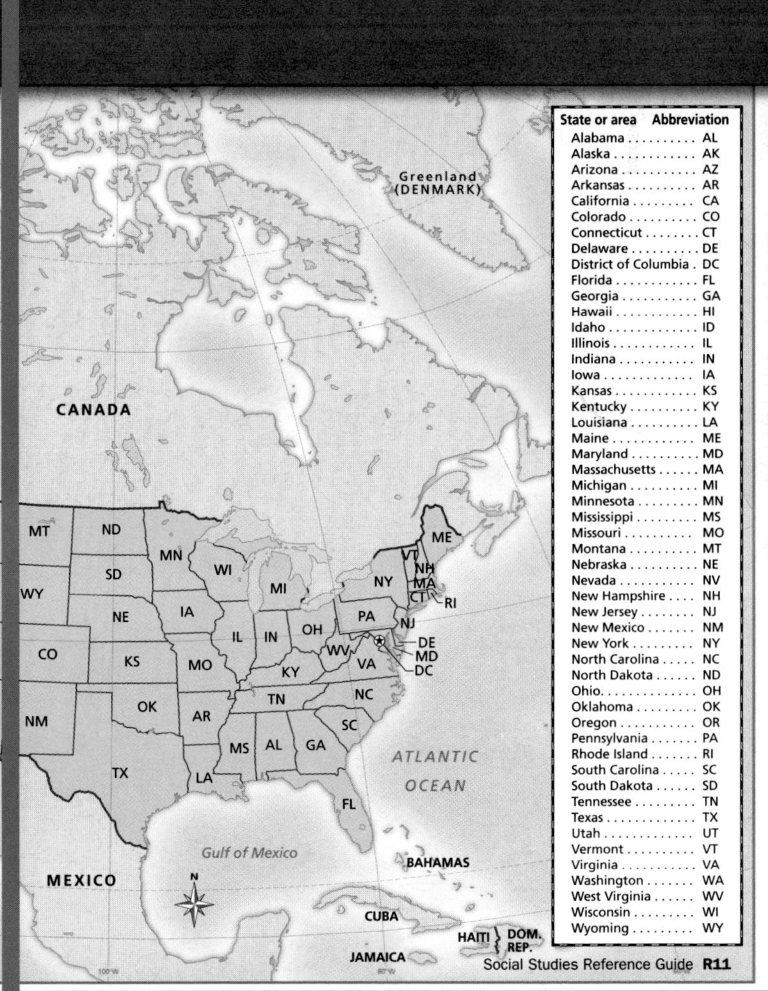

State or area	Abbreviation
Alabama	AL
Alaska	AK
Arizona	AZ
Arkansas	AR
California	CA
Colorado	CO
Connecticut	CT
Delaware	DE
District of Columbia	DC
Florida	FL
Georgia	GA
Hawaii	HI
Idaho	ID
Illinois	IL
Indiana	IN
Iowa	IA
Kansas	KS
Kentucky	KY
Louisiana	LA
Maine	ME
Maryland	MD
Massachusetts	MA
Michigan	MI
Minnesota	MN
Mississippi	MS
Missouri	MO
Montana	MT
Nebraska	NE
Nevada	NV
New Hampshire	NH
New Jersey	NJ
New Mexico	NM
New York	NY
North Carolina	NC
North Dakota	ND
Ohio	OH
Oklahoma	OK
Oregon	OR
Pennsylvania	PA
Rhode Island	RI
South Carolina	SC
South Dakota	SD
Tennessee	TN
Texas	TX
Utah	UT
Vermont	VT
Virginia	VA
Washington	WA
West Virginia	WV
Wisconsin	WI
Wyoming	WY

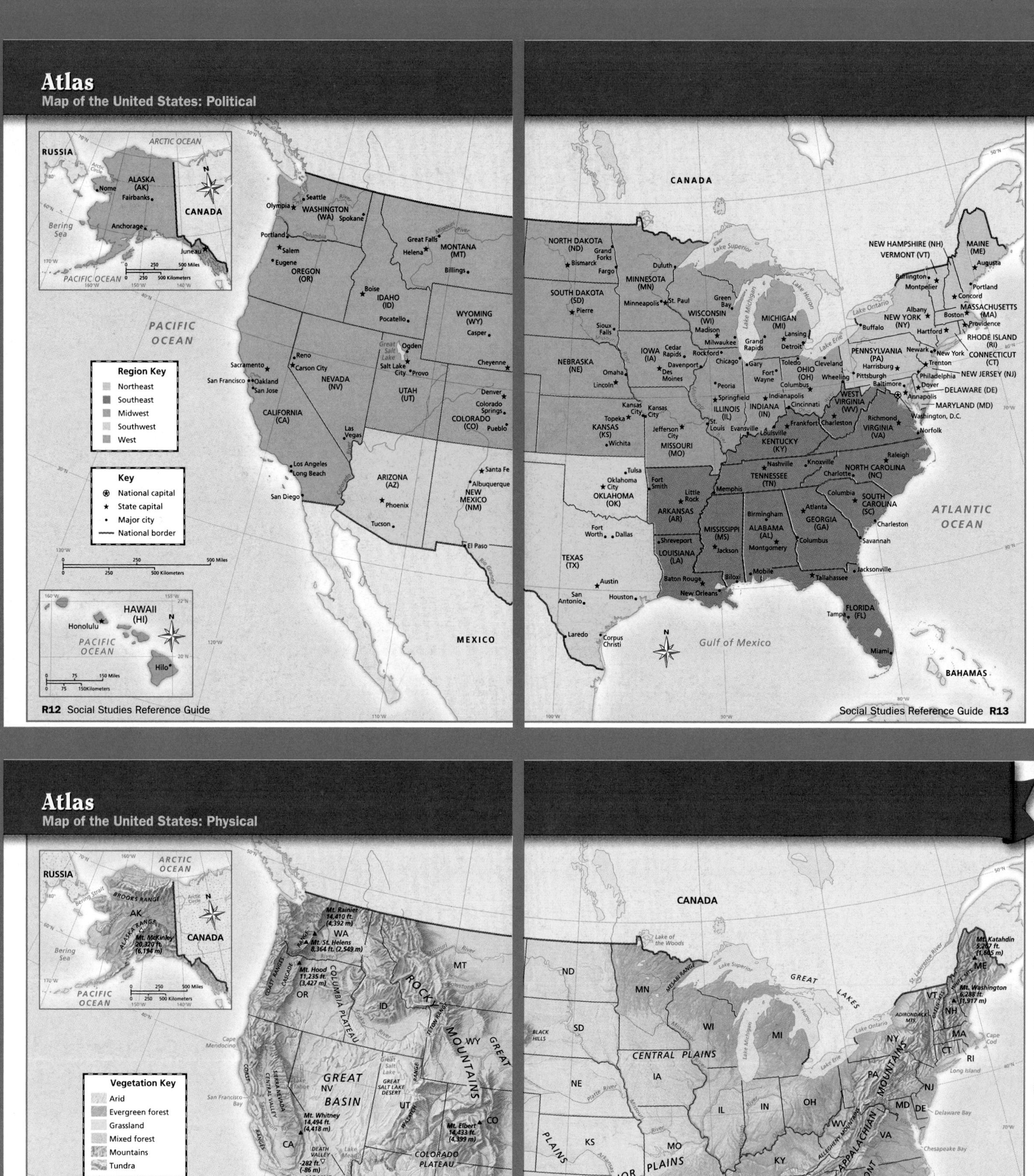

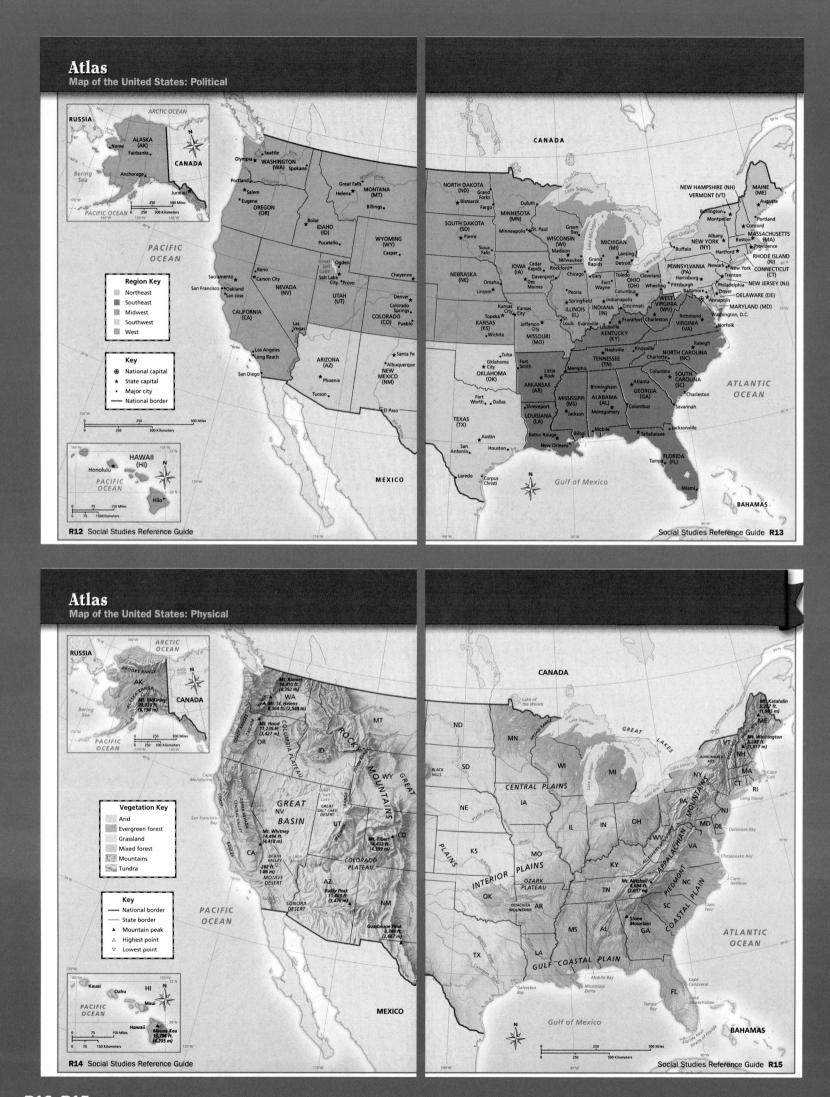

Atlas
Map of the United States: Political
Region Key
Northeast
Southeast
Midwest
Southwest
West
Key
National capital
State capital
Major city
National border
ARCTIC OCEAN
RUSSIA
ALASKA (AK)
CANADA
PACIFIC OCEAN
ATLANTIC OCEAN
Gulf of Mexico
MEXICO
BAHAMAS
HAWAII (HI)
R12 Social Studies Reference Guide
Social Studies Reference Guide R13
Atlas
Map of the United States: Physical
Vegetation Key
Arid
Evergreen forest
Grassland
Mixed forest
Mountains
Tundra
Key
National border
State border
Mountain peak
Highest point
Lowest point
ROCKY MOUNTAINS
GREAT BASIN
COLUMBIA PLATEAU
COLORADO PLATEAU
CENTRAL PLAINS
INTERIOR PLAINS
GREAT LAKES
APPALACHIAN MOUNTAINS
PIEDMONT
COASTAL PLAIN
GULF COASTAL PLAIN
OZARK PLATEAU
Mt. McKinley 20,320 ft. (6,194 m)
Mt. Rainier 14,410 ft. (4,392 m)
Mt. St. Helens 8,364 ft. (2,549 m)
Mt. Hood 11,235 ft. (3,427 m)
Mt. Whitney 14,494 ft. (4,418 m)
Death Valley -282 ft. (-86 m)
Mt. Elbert 14,433 ft. (4,399 m)
Baldy Peak 11,403 ft. (3,476 m)
Guadalupe Peak 8,749 ft. (2,667 m)
Mt. Mitchell 6,684 ft. (2,037 m)
Stone Mountain
Mt. Washington 6,288 ft. (1,917 m)
Mt. Katahdin 5,267 ft. (1,605 m)
Mauna Kea 13,796 ft. (4,205 m)
R14 Social Studies Reference Guide
Social Studies Reference Guide R15

Geography Terms

basin bowl-shaped area of land surrounded by higher land

bay narrower part of an ocean or lake that cuts into land

canal narrow waterway dug across land mainly for ship travel

canyon steep, narrow valley with high sides

cliff steep wall of rock or earth, sometimes called a bluff

coast land at the edge of a large body of water such as an ocean

coastal plain area of flat land along an ocean or sea

delta triangle-shaped area of land at the mouth of a river

desert very dry land

fall line area along which rivers form waterfalls or rapids as the rivers drop to lower land

forest large area of land where many trees grow

glacier giant sheet of ice that moves very slowly across land

gulf body of water, larger than most bays, with land around part of it

harbor sheltered body of water where ships safely tie up to land

hill rounded land higher than the land around it

island land with water all around it

lake large body of water with land all or nearly all around it

mesa flat-topped hill with steep sides

mountain a very tall hill; highest land on Earth

mountain range long row of mountains

mouth place where a river empties into another body of water

ocean any of the four largest bodies of water on Earth

Sea Level
Peninsula
Ocean
Gulf
Prairie
Volcano
Valley
Coast
Waterfall
Plateau
Canyon
Cliff or Bluff
Mesa
Fall Line
Coastal Plain
Lake
Port
Sea
Island
Harbor

peak pointed top of a mountain

peninsula land with water on three sides

plain very large area of flat land

plateau high, wide area of flat land, with steep sides

port place, usually in a harbor, where ships safely load and unload goods and people

prairie large area of flat land, with few or no trees, similar to a plain

river large stream of water leading to a lake, other river, or ocean

riverbank land at a river's edge

sea large body of water somewhat smaller than an ocean

sea level an ocean's surface, compared to which land can be measured either above or below

slope side of a mountain or hill

source place where a river begins

swamp very shallow water covering low land filled with trees and other plants

tributary stream or river that runs into a larger river

valley low land between mountains or hills

volcano mountain with an opening at the top, formed by violent bursts of steam and hot rock

waterfall steep falling of water from a higher to a lower place

Peak
Mountain
Glacier
Mountain Range
Slope
Source
Basin
Hill
River
Tributary
Plain
Swamp
Forest
Riverbank
Desert
Mouth
Bay
Canal
Delta

Facts About Our Fifty States

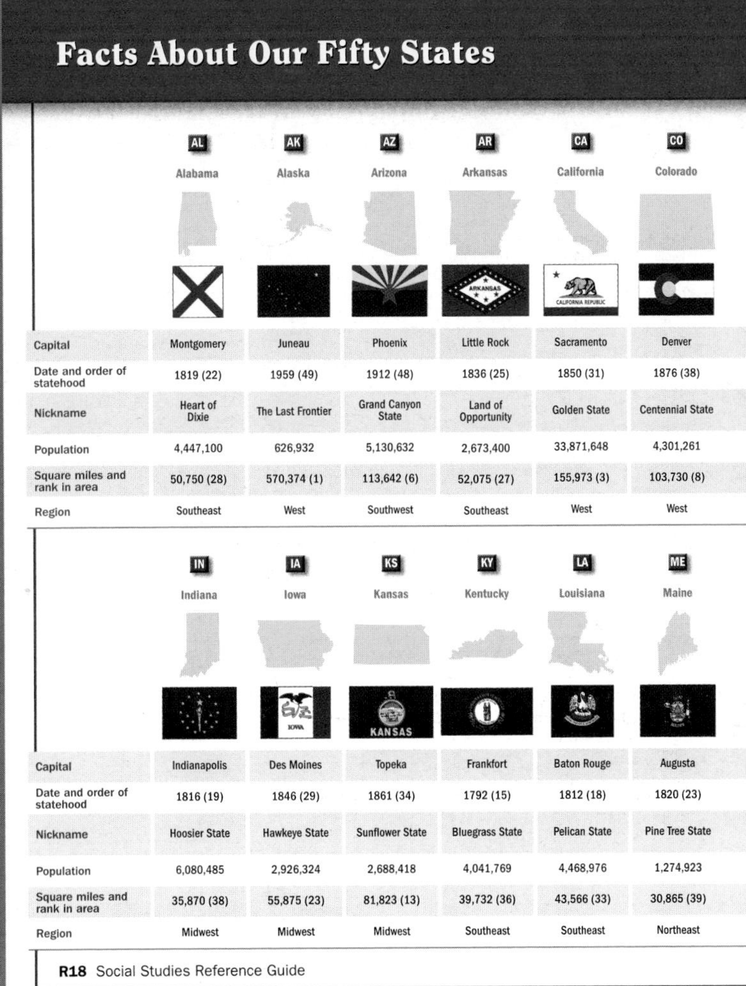

	AL Alabama	AK Alaska	AZ Arizona	AR Arkansas	CA California	CO Colorado
Capital	Montgomery	Juneau	Phoenix	Little Rock	Sacramento	Denver
Date and order of statehood	1819 (22)	1959 (49)	1912 (48)	1836 (25)	1850 (31)	1876 (38)
Nickname	Heart of Dixie	The Last Frontier	Grand Canyon State	Land of Opportunity	Golden State	Centennial State
Population	4,447,100	626,932	5,130,632	2,673,400	33,871,648	4,301,261
Square miles and rank in area	50,750 (28)	570,374 (1)	113,642 (6)	52,075 (27)	155,973 (3)	103,730 (8)
Region	Southeast	West	Southwest	Southeast	West	West

	IN Indiana	IA Iowa	KS Kansas	KY Kentucky	LA Louisiana	ME Maine
Capital	Indianapolis	Des Moines	Topeka	Frankfort	Baton Rouge	Augusta
Date and order of statehood	1816 (19)	1846 (29)	1861 (34)	1792 (15)	1812 (18)	1820 (23)
Nickname	Hoosier State	Hawkeye State	Sunflower State	Bluegrass State	Pelican State	Pine Tree State
Population	6,080,485	2,926,324	2,688,418	4,041,769	4,468,976	1,274,923
Square miles and rank in area	35,870 (38)	55,875 (23)	81,823 (13)	39,732 (36)	43,566 (33)	30,865 (39)
Region	Midwest	Midwest	Midwest	Southeast	Southeast	Northeast

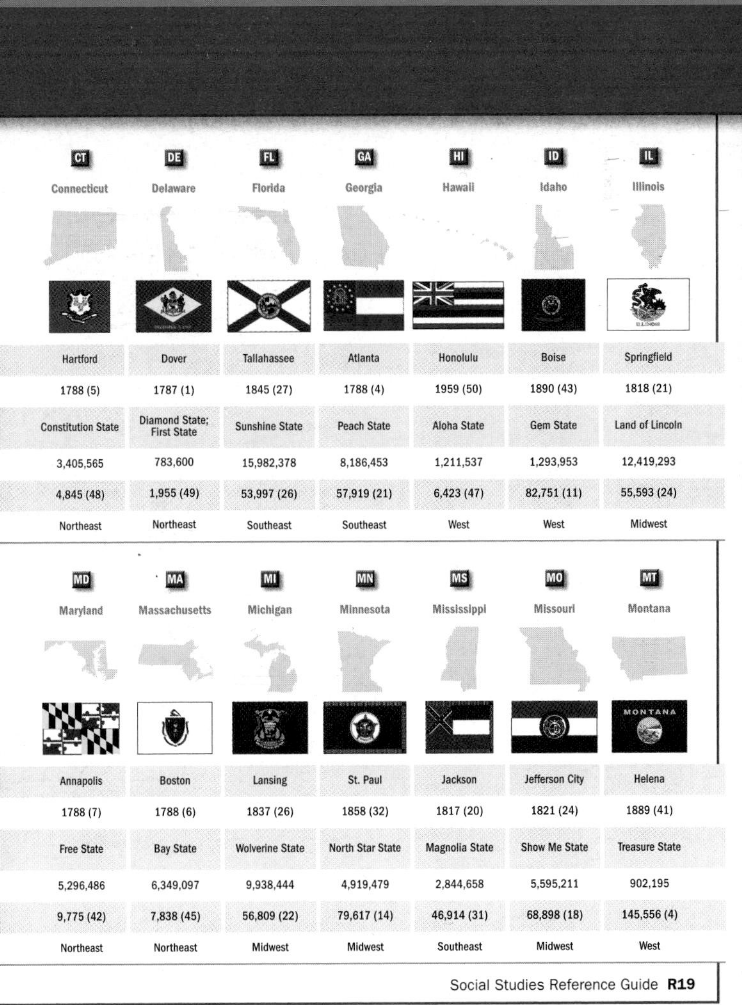

	CT Connecticut	DE Delaware	FL Florida	GA Georgia	HI Hawaii	ID Idaho	IL Illinois
Capital	Hartford	Dover	Tallahassee	Atlanta	Honolulu	Boise	Springfield
Date and order of statehood	1788 (5)	1787 (1)	1845 (27)	1788 (4)	1959 (50)	1890 (43)	1818 (21)
Nickname	Constitution State	Diamond State; First State	Sunshine State	Peach State	Aloha State	Gem State	Land of Lincoln
Population	3,405,565	783,600	15,982,378	8,186,453	1,211,537	1,293,953	12,419,293
Square miles and rank in area	4,845 (48)	1,955 (49)	53,997 (26)	57,919 (21)	6,423 (47)	82,751 (11)	55,593 (24)
Region	Northeast	Northeast	Southeast	Southeast	West	West	Midwest

	MD Maryland	MA Massachusetts	MI Michigan	MN Minnesota	MS Mississippi	MO Missouri	MT Montana
Capital	Annapolis	Boston	Lansing	St. Paul	Jackson	Jefferson City	Helena
Date and order of statehood	1788 (7)	1788 (6)	1837 (26)	1858 (32)	1817 (20)	1821 (24)	1889 (41)
Nickname	Free State	Bay State	Wolverine State	North Star State	Magnolia State	Show Me State	Treasure State
Population	5,296,486	6,349,097	9,938,444	4,919,479	2,844,658	5,595,211	902,195
Square miles and rank in area	9,775 (42)	7,838 (45)	56,809 (22)	79,617 (14)	46,914 (31)	68,898 (18)	145,556 (4)
Region	Northeast	Northeast	Midwest	Midwest	Southeast	Midwest	West

Facts About Our Fifty States

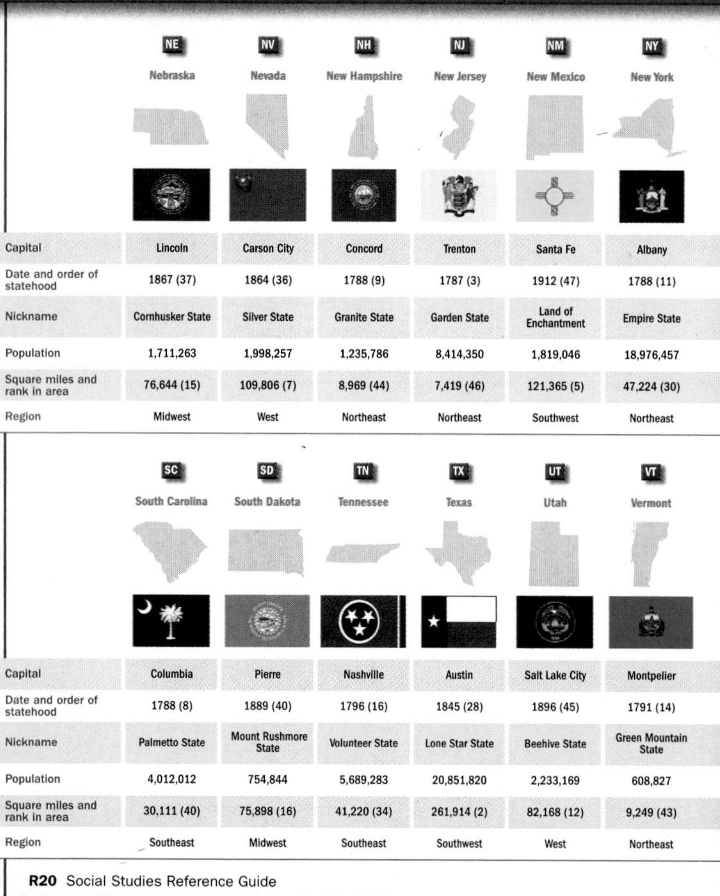

	NE Nebraska	NV Nevada	NH New Hampshire	NJ New Jersey	NM New Mexico	NY New York
Capital	Lincoln	Carson City	Concord	Trenton	Santa Fe	Albany
Date and order of statehood	1867 (37)	1864 (36)	1788 (9)	1787 (3)	1912 (47)	1788 (11)
Nickname	Cornhusker State	Silver State	Granite State	Garden State	Land of Enchantment	Empire State
Population	1,711,263	1,998,257	1,235,786	8,414,350	1,819,046	18,976,457
Square miles and rank in area	76,644 (15)	109,806 (7)	8,969 (44)	7,419 (46)	121,365 (5)	47,224 (30)
Region	Midwest	West	Northeast	Northeast	Southwest	Northeast

	SC South Carolina	SD South Dakota	TN Tennessee	TX Texas	UT Utah	VT Vermont
Capital	Columbia	Pierre	Nashville	Austin	Salt Lake City	Montpelier
Date and order of statehood	1788 (8)	1889 (40)	1796 (16)	1845 (28)	1896 (45)	1791 (14)
Nickname	Palmetto State	Mount Rushmore State	Volunteer State	Lone Star State	Beehive State	Green Mountain State
Population	4,012,012	754,844	5,689,283	20,851,820	2,233,169	608,827
Square miles and rank in area	30,111 (40)	75,898 (16)	41,220 (34)	261,914 (2)	82,168 (12)	9,249 (43)
Region	Southeast	Midwest	Southeast	Southwest	West	Northeast

	NC North Carolina	ND North Dakota	OH Ohio	OK Oklahoma	OR Oregon	PA Pennsylvania	RI Rhode Island
Capital	Raleigh	Bismarck	Columbus	Oklahoma City	Salem	Harrisburg	Providence
Date and order of statehood	1789 (12)	1889 (39)	1803 (17)	1907 (46)	1859 (33)	1787 (2)	1790 (13)
Nickname	Tar Heel State	Sioux State	Buckeye State	Sooner State	Beaver State	Keystone State	Ocean State
Population	8,049,313	642,200	11,353,140	3,450,654	3,421,399	12,281,054	1,048,319
Square miles and rank in area	48,718 (29)	68,994 (17)	40,953 (35)	68,679 (19)	96,003 (10)	44,820 (32)	1,045 (50)
Region	Southeast	Midwest	Midwest	Southwest	West	Northeast	Northeast

	VA Virginia	WA Washington	WV West Virginia	WI Wisconsin	WY Wyoming
Capital	Richmond	Olympia	Charleston	Madison	Cheyenne
Date and order of statehood	1788 (10)	1889 (42)	1863 (35)	1848 (30)	1890 (44)
Nickname	Old Dominion	Evergreen State	Mountain State	Badger State	Equality State
Population	7,078,515	5,894,121	1,808,344	5,363,675	493,782
Square miles and rank in area	39,598 (37)	66,582 (20)	24,087 (41)	54,314 (25)	97,105 (9)
Region	Southeast	West	Southeast	Midwest	West

State Names and Mottoes

Northeast

Connecticut .... From an Algonquian word meaning "beside the long river." **Motto** He who transplanted still sustains

Delaware .... Named in honor of a colonial governor of Virginia, Lord De La Warr. **Motto** Liberty and Independence

Maine .... May be a reference to the fact that the state's land is part of the mainland. **Motto** I direct

Maryland .... Named in honor of Henrietta Maria, queen of Charles I of England. **Motto** Strong deeds, gentle words

Massachusetts .... From a Massachusett word meaning "at or about the great hill." **Motto** By the sword we seek peace, but peace only under liberty

New Hampshire .... Named for Hampshire, a county in England. **Motto** Live free or die

New Jersey .... Named for island named Jersey off the coast of England. **Motto** Liberty and Prosperity

New York .... Named in honor of England's Duke of York. **Motto** Excelsior; Ever upward

Pennsylvania .... In honor of Admiral William Penn, father of the state's founder, William Penn. It means "Penn's woods." **Motto** Virtue, Liberty, and Independence

Rhode Island .... Named for the Greek Island of Rhodes. **Motto** Hope

Vermont .... From French *verts monts*, meaning "green mountains." **Motto** Freedom and Unity

Southeast

Alabama .... Named for the Alabama, Native Americans who lived in the area. **Motto** We Dare Defend Our Rights

Arkansas .... From a Lakota word meaning "downstream place." **Motto** The people rule

Florida .... From the Spanish phrase "feast of flowers," meaning Easter. **Motto** In God We Trust

Georgia .... Named in honor of King George II of England. **Motto** Wisdom, justice, and moderation

Kentucky .... From an Iroquois word meaning "land of tomorrow." **Motto** United we stand, divided we fall

Louisiana .... Named in honor of King Louis XIV of France. **Motto** Union, justice, and confidence

Mississippi .... From a Native American word meaning "father of waters." **Motto** By valor and arms

North Carolina .... Named in honor of England's King Charles I. **Motto** To be rather than to seem

South Carolina .... Named in honor of England's King Charles I. **Mottoes** While I breathe I hope

Tennessee .... From the Cherokee word *Tanasi*, meaning "villages." **Motto** Agriculture and Commerce

Virginia .... From a nickname for England's Queen Elizabeth I. **Motto** Thus Always to Tyrants

West Virginia .... From a nickname for England's Queen Elizabeth I. **Motto** Mountaineers are always free

Midwest

Illinois .... From an Algonquian word meaning "superior men." **Motto** State Sovereignty, National Union

Indiana .... Means "land of the Indians." **Motto** The Crossroads of America

Iowa .... From a Native American word meaning "beautiful land." **Motto** Our liberties we prize and our rights we will maintain

Kansas .... From a Lakota word meaning "people of the south wind." **Motto** To the stars through difficulties

Michigan .... From an Ojibwa word meaning "great water" or "great lake." **Motto** If you seek a pleasant peninsula, look about you.

Minnesota .... From a Dakota word meaning "sky-tinted water." **Motto** The star of the north

Missouri .... Named after the Missouri, Native Americans who lived in the region and whose name means "town of the large canoes." **Motto** The welfare of the people shall be the supreme law

Nebraska .... From an Oto word that means "flat water," referring to the Platte River. **Motto** Equality before the law

North Dakota .... Dakota is a Native America word meaning "friend." **Motto** Liberty and union, now and forever, one and inseparable

Ohio .... From the Iroquois word meaning "good river." **Motto** With God, all things are possible

South Dakota .... Dakota is a Native American word meaning "friend." **Motto** Under God, the people rule

Wisconsin .... From an Ojibwa word, *Ouisconsin*, believed to mean "grassy place." **Motto** Forward

Southwest

Arizona .... From a Pima word meaning "little spring." **Motto** God enriches

New Mexico .... Named by the Spanish for lands north of Mexico. **Motto** It grows as it goes

Oklahoma .... From Native American words meaning "red man." **Motto** Work conquers all things

Texas .... From a Caddo word meaning "friends." **Motto** Friendship

West

Alaska .... From an Aleut word meaning "great land." **Motto** North to the Future

California .... Named for a mythical island in a Spanish story. **Motto** Eureka

Colorado .... From the Spanish word for "red," to describe the Colorado River. **Motto** Nothing without Providence

Hawaii .... May be named for Hawaiki, the traditional Polynesian homeland. **Motto** The life of the land is perpetuated in righteousness

Idaho .... An invented name the meaning of which is unknown. **Motto** It is forever

Montana .... From the Spanish word for "mountainous." **Motto** Gold and Silver

Nevada .... From a Spanish word meaning "snow-capped." **Motto** All for our country

Oregon .... May have come from a river shown as "Ouaricon-sint" on a 1715 French map. **Motto** She flies with her own wings

Utah .... Named after the Ute, Native Americans who lived in the region and whose name means "people of the mountains." **Motto** Industry

Washington .... Named in honor of George Washington. **Motto** Bye and Bye

Wyoming .... From a Native American word meaning "large prairie place." **Motto** Equal Rights

Symbols of the United States

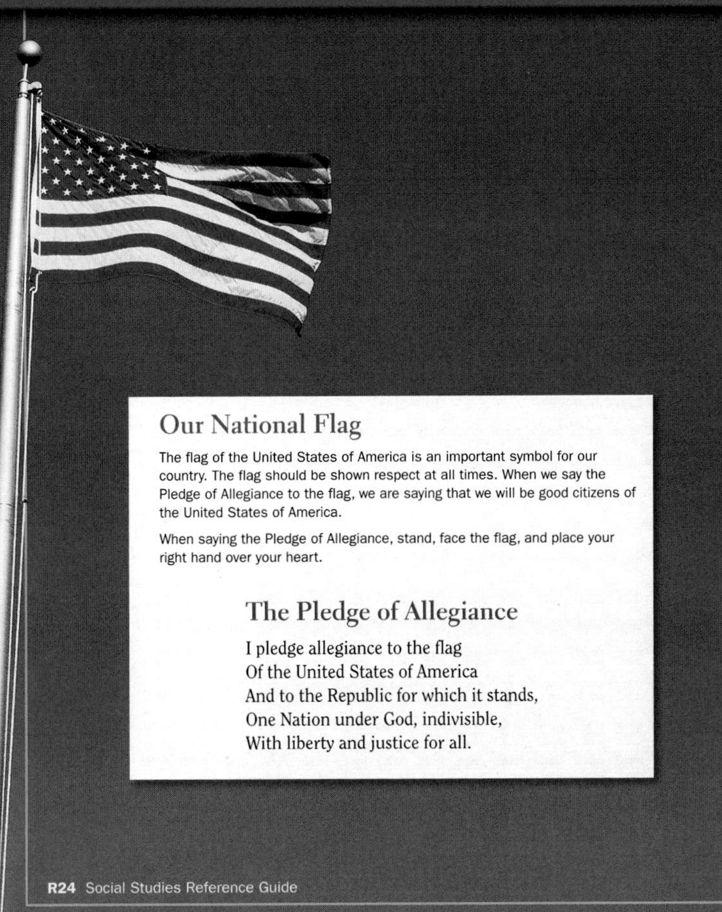

Our National Flag

The flag of the United States of America is an important symbol for our country. The flag should be shown respect at all times. When we say the Pledge of Allegiance to the flag, we are saying that we will be good citizens of the United States of America.

When saying the Pledge of Allegiance, stand, face the flag, and place your right hand over your heart.

The Pledge of Allegiance

I pledge allegiance to the flag
Of the United States of America
And to the Republic for which it stands,
One Nation under God, indivisible,
With liberty and justice for all.

Displaying the Flag

Display the flag only from sunrise to sunset, except when bad weather might damage the flag.

No other flag or pennant should be placed above the U.S. flag. If another flag is displayed on the same level, it should be to the right of the flag of the United States of America.

When the flag passes in a parade, stand and put your hand over your heart.

When singing the National Anthem, everyone should rise and stand at attention. A man should remove his hat with his right hand and place the palm of his right hand over his heart.

Flag Holidays

The flag of the United States should be flown every day, but especially on these holidays:

New Year's Day . . . . January 1
Inauguration Day . . . . January 20
Lincoln's Birthday . . . . . . February 12
Washington's Birthday . . third Monday in February
Easter Sunday . . . . varies
Mother's Day . . . . second Sunday in May
Armed Forces Day . . . . . . third Saturday in May
Memorial Day . . . . last Monday in May (half-staff until noon)
Flag Day . . . . June 14
Independence Day . . . . . . July 4
Labor Day . . . . first Monday in September
Constitution Day . . . . September 17
Columbus Day . . . . second Monday in October
Navy Day . . . . October 27
Veteran's Day . . . . November 11
Thanksgiving Day . . . . . . fourth Thursday in November
Christmas Day . . . . December 25

By Executive Order, the flag flies 24 hours a day at the following locations:

The Betsy Ross House, Philadelphia, Pennsylvania

The White House, Washington, D.C.

The United States Capitol, Washington, D.C.

Iwo Jima Memorial to U.S. Marines, Arlington, Virginia

Battleground in Lexington, MA (site of the first shots in the Revolutionary War)

Winter Encampment Cabins, Valley Forge, Pennsylvania

Fort McHenry, Baltimore, Maryland (A flag flying over Fort McHenry after a battle during the War of 1812 provided the inspiration for "The Star-Spangled Banner.")

The Star-Spangled Banner Flag House, Baltimore, Maryland (This is the site where the famous flag over Fort McHenry was sewn.)

Jenny Wade House, Gettysburg, Pennsylvania (Jenny Wade was the only civilian killed at the battle of Gettysburg.)

USS *Arizona* Memorial, Pearl Harbor, Hawaii

Our National Anthem

Francis Scott Key wrote the words of "The Star-Spangled Banner" during the War of 1812. After a heavy battle, he was proud to see that the American flag was still flying over a fort that had been heavily damaged during the night. This song became the official national anthem in 1931.

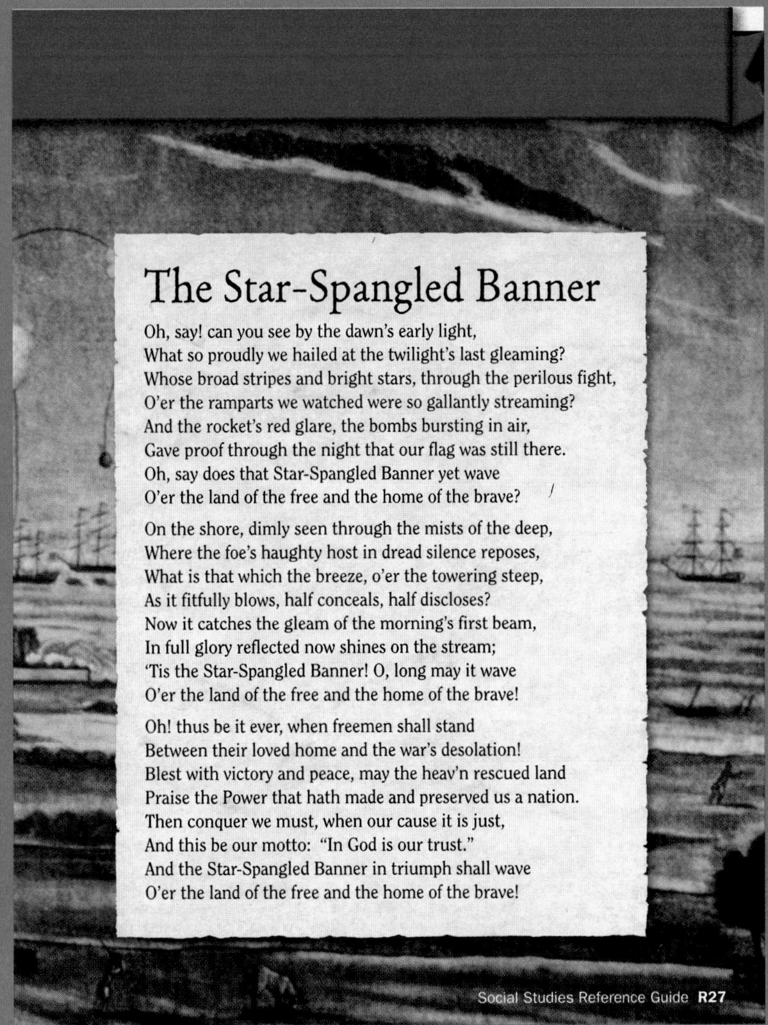

The Star-Spangled Banner

Oh, say! can you see by the dawn's early light,
What so proudly we hailed at the twilight's last gleaming?
Whose broad stripes and bright stars, through the perilous fight,
O'er the ramparts we watched were so gallantly streaming?
And the rocket's red glare, the bombs bursting in air,
Gave proof through the night that our flag was still there.
Oh, say does that Star-Spangled Banner yet wave
O'er the land of the free and the home of the brave?

On the shore, dimly seen through the mists of the deep,
Where the foe's haughty host in dread silence reposes,
What is that which the breeze, o'er the towering steep,
As it fitfully blows, half conceals, half discloses?
Now it catches the gleam of the morning's first beam,
In full glory reflected now shines on the stream;
'Tis the Star-Spangled Banner! O, long may it wave
O'er the land of the free and the home of the brave!

Oh! thus be it ever, when freemen shall stand
Between their loved home and the war's desolation!
Blest with victory and peace, may the heav'n rescued land
Praise the Power that hath made and preserved us a nation.
Then conquer we must, when our cause it is just,
And this be our motto: "In God is our trust."
And the Star-Spangled Banner in triumph shall wave
O'er the land of the free and the home of the brave!

In Congress, July 4, 1776

When, in the course of human events, it becomes necessary for one people to dissolve the political bands which have connected them with another, and to assume, among the powers of the earth, the separate and equal station to which the laws of nature and nature's God entitle them, a decent respect to the opinions of mankind requires that they should declare the causes which impel them to the separation.

We hold these truths to be self-evident; that all men are created equal, that they are endowed by their Creator with certain unalienable rights, that among these are life, liberty, and the pursuit of happiness.

That to secure these rights, governments are instituted among men, deriving their just powers from the consent of the governed; that whenever any form of government becomes destructive of these ends, it is the right of the people to alter or to abolish it, and to institute new government, laying its foundation on such principles, and organizing its powers in such form, as to them shall seem most likely to effect their safety and happiness.

Prudence, indeed, will dictate that governments long established should not be changed for light and transient causes; and accordingly all experience hath shown that mankind are more disposed to suffer, while evils are sufferable, than to right themselves by abolishing the forms to which they are accustomed. But when a long train of abuses and usurpations, pursuing invariably the same object, evinces a design to reduce them under absolute despotism, it is their right, it is their duty, to throw off such government, and to provide new guards for their future security.

Such has been the patient sufferance of these colonies; and such is now the necessity which constrains them to alter their former systems of government. The history of the present king of Great Britain is a history of repeated injuries and usurpations, all having in direct object the establishment of an absolute tyranny over these states. To prove this, let facts be submitted to a candid world.

Sometimes in history it becomes necessary for a group of people to break political ties with the country that rules it. When this happens, it is proper to explain the reasons for the need to separate.

We believe that all men are created equal and given by their Creator certain rights that cannot be taken away. People have the right to live, be free, and seek happiness.

Governments are established to protect these rights. The government gets its power from the support of the people it governs. If any form of government tries to take away the basic rights, it is the right of the people to change or end the government and to establish a new government that seems most likely to result in their safety and happiness.

Wise judgment will require that long-existing governments should not be changed for unimportant or temporary reasons. History has shown that people are more willing to suffer under a bad government than to get rid of the government they are used to. But when there are so many abuses and misuses of power by the government, it is the right and duty of the people to throw off such government and form a new government to protect their basic rights.

The colonies have suffered patiently, and now it is necessary for them to change the government. The king of Great Britain has repeatedly abused his power over these states. To prove this, the following facts are given.

He has refused his assent to laws the most wholesome and necessary for the public good. He has forbidden his governors to pass laws of immediate and pressing importance, unless suspended in their operation till his assent should be obtained; and when so suspended, he has utterly neglected to attend to them.

He has refused to pass other laws for the accommodation of large districts of people, unless those people would relinquish the right of representation in the legislature, a right inestimable to them, and formidable to tyrants only.

He has called together legislative bodies at places unusual, uncomfortable, and distant from the depository of their public records, for the sole purpose of fatiguing them into compliance with his measures.

He has dissolved representative houses repeatedly, for opposing, with manly firmness, his invasions on the rights of the people.

He has refused, for a long time after such dissolutions, to cause others to be elected; whereby the legislative powers, incapable of annihilation, have returned to the people at large for their exercise; the state remaining, in the meantime, exposed to all the dangers of invasion from without and convulsions within.

He has endeavored to prevent the population of these states; for that purpose obstructing the laws for the naturalization of foreigners, refusing to pass others to encourage their migrations hither, and raising the conditions of new appropriations of lands.

He has obstructed the administration of justice, by refusing his assent to laws for establishing judiciary powers.

He has made judges dependent on his will alone for the tenure of their offices, and the amount and payment of their salaries.

He has erected a multitude of new offices, and sent hither swarms of officers to harass our people and eat out their substance.

He has kept among us, in times of peace, standing armies, without the consent of our legislatures.

He has affected to render the military independent of, and superior to, the civil power.

He has combined with others to subject us to a jurisdiction foreign to our constitution and unacknowledged by our laws, giving his assent to their acts of pretended legislation:

The king has not given his approval to needed laws. He has not allowed his governors to pass laws needed immediately. The king has made the governors delay laws until they can get his permission and then he has ignored the laws.

He has refused to pass other laws to help large districts of people, unless those people would give up the right of representation in the legislature, a right priceless to them and threatening only to tyrants.

He has called together legislative bodies at unusual and uncomfortable places, distant from where they store their public records, and only for the purpose of tiring them into obeying his measures.

He has repeatedly done away with legislative groups that firmly opposed him for taking away the rights of the people.

After he has dissolved these representative meetings, he has refused to allow new elections. Because of this lack of legislative power, the people are exposed to the dangers of invasion from without and violence within.

He has tried to prevent people from immigrating to these states by blocking the process for foreigners to become citizens, refusing to pass laws to encourage people to travel to America, and making it harder to move to and own new lands.

He has interfered with the administration of justice by refusing to approve laws for establishing courts.

He has made judges do what he wants by controlling how long they serve and how much they are paid.

He has created many new government offices and sent many officials to torment our people and live off of our hard work.

In times of peace, he has kept soldiers among us, without the consent of our legislatures.

He has tried to make the military separate from, and superior to, the civil government.

He and others have made us live under laws that are different from our laws. He has given his approval to these unfair laws that parliament has adopted:

For quartering large bodies of armed troops among us;

For protecting them, by a mock trial, from punishment for any murders which they should commit on the inhabitants of these states;

For cutting off our trade with all parts of the world;

For imposing taxes on us without our consent;

For depriving us, in many cases, of the benefits of trial by jury;

For transporting us beyond seas, to be tried for pretended offenses;

For abolishing the free system of English laws in a neighboring province, establishing therein an arbitrary government, and enlarging its boundaries, so as to render it at once an example and fit instrument for introducing the same absolute rule into these colonies;

For taking away our charters, abolishing our most valuable laws, and altering fundamentally the forms of our governments;

For suspending our own legislatures, and declaring themselves invested with power to legislate for us in all cases whatsoever.

He has abdicated government here, by declaring us out of his protection and waging war against us.

He has plundered our seas, ravaged our coasts, burned our towns, and destroyed the lives of our people.

He is at this time transporting large armies of foreign mercenaries to complete the works of death, desolation, and tyranny already begun with circumstances of cruelty and perfidy scarcely paralleled in the most barbarous ages, and totally unworthy the head of a civilized nation.

He has constrained our fellow citizens, taken captive on the high seas, to bear arms against their country, to become the executioners of their friends and brethren, or to fall themselves by their hands.

He has excited domestic insurrection among us, and has endeavored to bring on the inhabitants of our frontiers, the merciless Indian savages, whose known rule of warfare is an undistinguished destruction of all ages, sexes, and conditions.

In every stage of these oppressions we have petitioned for redress in the most humble terms; our repeated petitions have been answered only by repeated injury. A prince, whose character is thus marked by every act which may define a tyrant, is unfit to be the ruler of a free people.

For forcing us to feed and house many British soldiers;

For using pretend trials to protect British soldiers from punishment for murdering people in America;

For cutting off our trade with the world;

For taxing us without our consent;

For taking away, in many cases, the benefits of trial by jury;

For taking us to Great Britain to be tried for made-up offenses;

For doing away with the free system of English laws in a neighboring province and establishing a harsh government there, enlarging its boundaries as a way to introduce the same absolute rule into these colonies;

For taking away our governing documents, doing away with our most valuable laws, and changing our governments completely;

For setting aside our own legislatures and declaring that Great Britain has power to make laws for us in all cases whatsoever.

He has deserted government here, by not protecting us and by waging war against us.

He has robbed our ships on the seas, destroyed our coasts, burned our towns, and destroyed the lives of our people.

He is at this time sending large armies of foreign hired soldiers to complete the works of death, destruction, and injustice. These deeds are among the cruelest ever seen in history and are totally unworthy of the head of a civilized nation.

He has forced our fellow citizens, who were captured on the high seas, to fight against America, to kill their friends and family, or to be killed themselves.

He has stirred up civil disorder among us and has tried to cause the merciless killing of the people living on the frontiers by the American Indians, whose rule of warfare includes the deliberate killing of people regardless of age, sex, or conditions.

In every stage of these mistreatments we have asked for a solution in the most humble terms; our repeated requests have been answered only by more mistreatment. A leader who is so unfair and acts like a dictator is unfit to be the ruler of a free people.

Nor have we been wanting in attentions to our British brethren. We have warned them, from time to time, of attempts by their legislature to extend an unwarrantable jurisdiction over us. We have reminded them of the circumstances of our emigration and settlement here. We have appealed to their native justice and magnanimity; and we have conjured them, by the ties of our common kindred, to disavow these usurpations, which would inevitably interrupt our connections and correspondence. They, too, have been deaf to the voice of justice and consanguinity. We must, therefore, acquiesce in the necessity which denounces our separation, and hold them, as we hold the rest of mankind, enemies in war; in peace, friends.

We, therefore, the representatives of the United States of America, in General Congress assembled, appealing to the Supreme Judge of the world for the rectitude of our intentions, do, in the name and by the authority of the good people of these colonies, solemnly publish and declare that these United Colonies are, and of right ought to be, free and independent states; that they are absolved from all allegiance to the British crown, and that all political connection between them and the state of Great Britain is, and ought to be, totally dissolved; and that, as free and independent states, they have full power to levy war, conclude peace, contract alliances, establish commerce, and do all other acts and things which independent states may of right do. And, for the support of this declaration, with a firm reliance on the protection of Divine Providence, we mutually pledge to each other our lives, our fortunes, and our sacred honor.

Button Gwinnett (GA)	Thomas Nelson, Jr. (VA)	Richard Stockton (NJ)
Lyman Hall (GA)	Francis Lightfoot Lee (VA)	John Witherspoon (NJ)
George Walton (GA)	Carter Braxton (VA)	Francis Hopkinson (NJ)
William Hooper (NC)	Robert Morris (PA)	John Hart (NJ)
Joseph Hewes (NC)	Benjamin Rush (PA)	Abraham Clark (NJ)
John Penn (NC)	Benjamin Franklin (PA)	Josiah Bartlett (NH)
Edward Rutledge (SC)	John Morton (PA)	William Whipple (NH)
Thomas Heyward, Jr. (SC)	George Clymer (PA)	Samuel Adams (MA)
Thomas Lynch, Jr. (SC)	James Smith (PA)	John Adams (MA)
Arthur Middleton (SC)	George Taylor (PA)	Robert Treat Paine (MA)
John Hancock (MA)	James Wilson (PA)	Elbridge Gerry (MA)
Samuel Chase (MD)	George Ross (PA)	Stephen Hopkins (RI)
William Paca (MD)	Caesar Rodney (DE)	William Ellery (RI)
Thomas Stone (MD)	George Read (DE)	Roger Sherman (CT)
Charles Carroll (MD)	Thomas McKean (DE)	Samuel Huntington (CT)
George Wythe (VA)	William Floyd (NY)	William Williams (CT)
Richard Henry Lee (VA)	Philip Livingston (NY)	Oliver Wolcott (CT)
Thomas Jefferson (VA)	Francis Lewis (NY)	Matthew Thornton (NH)
Benjamin Harrison (VA)	Lewis Morris (NY)	

We have also asked for help from the British people. We have warned them, from time to time, of attempts by their government to extend illegal power over us. We have reminded them why we came to America. We have appealed to their sense of justice and generosity; and we have begged them, because of all we have in common, to give up these abuses of power. They, like the king, have not listened to the voice of justice and brotherhood. We must, therefore, declare our separation. In war the British are our enemies. In peace, they are our friends.

We therefore, as the representatives of the people of the United States of America, in this General Congress assembled, appealing to God for the honesty of our purpose, do solemnly publish and declare that these United Colonies are, and rightly should be, free and independent states. The people of the United States are no longer subjects of the British crown. All political connections between the colonies and Great Britain are totally ended. These free and independent states have full power to declare war, make peace, make treaties with other countries, establish trade, and do all other acts and things which independent states have the right to do. To support this declaration, with a firm trust on the protection of God, we pledge to each other our lives, our fortunes, and our sacred honor.

"Among the natural rights of the Colonists are these: First, a right to life; Secondly, to liberty; Thirdly, to property; together with the right to support and defend them in the best manner they can."

Samuel Adams, The Report of the Committee of Correspondence to the Boston Town Meeting.

"All, too, will bear in mind this sacred principle, that though the will of the majority is in all cases to prevail, that will to be rightful must be reasonable; that the minority possess their equal rights, which equal law must protect, and to violate would be oppression."

Thomas Jefferson, First Inaugural Address.

Facts About Our Presidents

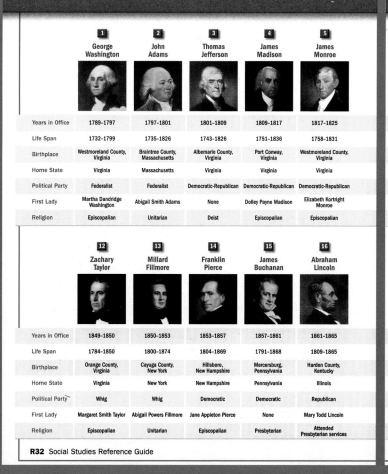

	1 George Washington	2 John Adams	3 Thomas Jefferson	4 James Madison	5 James Monroe
Years in Office	1789–1797	1797–1801	1801–1809	1809–1817	1817–1825
Life Span	1732–1799	1735–1826	1743–1826	1751–1836	1758–1831
Birthplace	Westmoreland County, Virginia	Braintree County, Massachusetts	Albemarle County, Virginia	Port Conway, Virginia	Westmoreland County, Virginia
Home State	Virginia	Massachusetts	Virginia	Virginia	Virginia
Political Party	Federalist	Federalist	Democratic-Republican	Democratic-Republican	Democratic-Republican
First Lady	Martha Dandridge Washington	Abigail Smith Adams	None	Dolley Payne Madison	Elizabeth Kortright Monroe
Religion	Episcopalian	Unitarian	Deist	Episcopalian	Episcopalian

	12 Zachary Taylor	13 Millard Fillmore	14 Franklin Pierce	15 James Buchanan	16 Abraham Lincoln
Years in Office	1849–1850	1850–1853	1853–1857	1857–1861	1861–1865
Life Span	1784–1850	1800–1874	1804–1869	1791–1868	1809–1865
Birthplace	Orange County, Virginia	Cayuga County, New York	Hillsboro, New Hampshire	Mercersburg, Pennsylvania	Harden County, Kentucky
Home State	Virginia	New York	New Hampshire	Pennsylvania	Illinois
Political Party	Whig	Whig	Democratic	Democratic	Republican
First Lady	Margaret Smith Taylor	Abigail Powers Fillmore	Jane Appleton Pierce	None	Mary Todd Lincoln
Religion	Episcopalian	Unitarian	Episcopalian	Presbyterian	Attended Presbyterian services

	6 John Quincy Adams	7 Andrew Jackson	8 Martin Van Buren	9 William H. Harrison	10 John Tyler	11 James K. Polk
Years in Office	1825–1829	1829–1837	1837–1841	1841	1841–1845	1845–1849
Life Span	1767–1848	1767–1845	1782–1862	1773–1841	1790–1862	1795–1849
Birthplace	Braintree, Massachusetts	Waxhaw, South Carolina	Kinderhook, New York	Charles City County, Virginia	Charles City County, Virginia	Mecklenburg County, North Carolina
Home State	Massachusetts	Tennessee	New York	Ohio	Virginia	Tennessee
Political Party	Democratic-Republican	Democratic	Democratic	Whig	Whig	Democratic
First Lady	Louisa Johnson Adams	None	None	Anna Symmes Harrison	Letitia Christian Tyler; Julia Gardiner Tyler	Sarah Childress Polk
Religion	Unitarian	Presbyterian	Dutch Reformed	Episcopalian	Episcopalian	Presbyterian

	17 Andrew Johnson	18 Ulysses S. Grant	19 Rutherford B. Hayes	20 James A. Garfield	21 Chester A. Arthur	22 24 Grover Cleveland
Years in Office	1865–1869	1869–1877	1877–1881	1881	1881–1885	1885–1889; 1893–1897
Life Span	1808–1875	1822–1885	1822–1893	1831–1881	1829–1886	1837–1908
Birthplace	Raleigh, North Carolina	Point Pleasant, Ohio	Delaware, Ohio	Orange, Ohio	Fairfield, Vermont	Caldwell, New Jersey
Home State	Tennessee	Illinois	Ohio	Ohio	New York	New York
Political Party	Democratic	Republican	Republican	Republican	Republican	Democratic
First Lady	Eliza McCardle Johnson	Julia Dent Grant	Lucy Webb Hayes	Lucretia Rudolph Garfield	None	Frances Folsom Cleveland
Religion	No specific affiliation	Methodist	Methodist	Disciples of Christ	Episcopalian	Presbyterian

Facts About Our Presidents

	23 Benjamin Harrison	25 William McKinley	26 Theodore Roosevelt	27 William H. Taft	28 Woodrow Wilson
Years in Office	1889–1893	1897–1901	1901–1909	1909–1913	1913–1921
Life Span	1833–1901	1843–1901	1858–1919	1859–1930	1856–1924
Birthplace	North Bend, Ohio	Niles, Ohio	New York, New York	Cincinnati, Ohio	Staunton, Virginia
Home State	Indiana	Ohio	New York	Ohio	New Jersey
Political Party	Republican	Republican	Republican	Republican	Democratic
First Lady	Caroline Scott Harrison	Ida Saxton McKinley	Edith Carow Roosevelt	Helen Herron Taft	Ellen Axson Wilson; Edith Galt Wilson
Religion	Presbyterian	Methodist	Dutch Reformed	Unitarian	Presbyterian

	35 John F. Kennedy	36 Lyndon B. Johnson	37 Richard M. Nixon	38 Gerald R. Ford	39 James E. Carter
Years in Office	1961–1963	1963–1969	1969–1974	1974–1977	1977–1981
Life Span	1917–1963	1908–1973	1913–1994	1913 -	1924–
Birthplace	Brookline, Massachusetts	Stonewall, Texas	Yorba Linda, California	Omaha, Nebraska	Plains, Georgia
Home State	Massachusetts	Texas	California	Michigan	Georgia
Political Party	Democratic	Democratic	Republican	Republican	Democratic
First Lady	Jacqueline Bouvier Kennedy	Claudia "Lady Bird" Taylor Johnson	Thelma "Pat" Ryan Nixon	Elizabeth (Betty) Warren Ford	Rosalynn Smith Carter
Religion	Roman Catholic	Disciples of Christ	Quaker	Episcopalian	Southern Baptist

	29 Warren G. Harding	30 Calvin Coolidge	31 Herbert Hoover	32 Franklin D. Roosevelt	33 Harry S. Truman	34 Dwight D. Eisenhower
Years in Office	1921–1923	1923–1929	1929–1933	1933–1945	1945–1953	1953–1961
Life Span	1865–1923	1872–1933	1874–1964	1882–1945	1884–1972	1890–1969
Birthplace	Morrow County, Ohio	Plymouth, Vermont	West Branch, Iowa	Hyde Park, New York	Lamar, Missouri	Denison, Texas
Home State	Ohio	Massachusetts	California	New York	Missouri	Kansas
Political Party	Republican	Republican	Republican	Democratic	Democratic	Republican
First Lady	Florence DeWolfe Harding	Grace Goodhue Coolidge	Lou Henry Hoover	Anna Eleanor Roosevelt	Bess Wallace Truman	Marie "Mamie" Doud Eisenhower
Religion	Baptist	Congregational	Quaker	Episcopalian	Baptist	Presbyterian

	40 Ronald Reagan	41 George H. W. Bush	42 William J. Clinton	43 George W. Bush
Years in Office	1981–1989	1989–1993	1993–2001	2001–
Life Span	1911–	1924–	1946–	1946–
Birthplace	Tampico, Illinois	Milton, Massachusetts	Hope, Arkansas	New Haven, Connecticut
Home State	California	Texas	Arkansas	Texas
Political Party	Republican	Republican	Democratic	Republican
First Lady	Anne "Nancy" Davis Reagan	Barbara Pierce Bush	Hillary Rodham Clinton	Laura Welch Bush
Religion	Disciples of Christ	Episcopalian	Baptist	Methodist

Learn About Your State

You read about different regions of the United States. You read about many general things about your region. You may have found out some things about your state when you were reading about your region. Your state has its own special landforms, climate, history, economics, and culture.

Use reference materials in your classroom or library to write a guidebook about your state. What makes your state special? The skills you learned in this book will help you organize material about your state. Here are some things to include.

Your State's Geography

Find out some facts about your state's geography. In what region is your state? What is the state capital? What are the populations of some of the large cities? What states are neighbors of your state?

Make a chart with some facts about your state. Here is a chart that some students in Pennsylvania made. What special facts about your state would you add?

Facts About Pennsylvania

Region: Northeast

Large Cities: Philadelphia, Pittsburgh, Erie, Scranton, Harrisburg

State Capitol: Harrisburg

Nickname: The Keystone State

Neighbor States: New York, New Jersey, Delaware, Maryland, West Virginia, Ohio

Pennsylvania state capitol building in Harrisburg

Your State's Landforms

Use reference materials to find out about rivers and landforms in your state. Include the information in your guidebook. Do mountain ranges go through your state? Is your state on the coast of an ocean? Does your state have a desert area?

Make a physical map of your state. Use reference materials to find out about landforms and their elevations. Mark the highest point and the lowest point in your state. Include some rivers and cities. Here is a map that some students in North Carolina made.

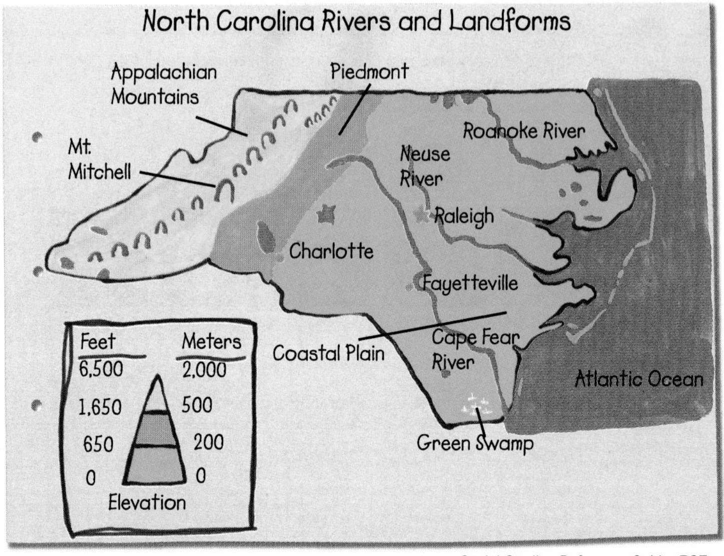

Your State's Climate

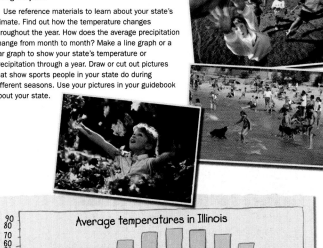

What are some outdoor sports that people in your state can do in the winter? How can you describe the climate of your state? Does your state have very cold winters and hot summers, or is your state warm for much of the year? How much rain and snow falls in your state during the year?

Use reference materials to learn about your state's climate. Find out how the temperature changes throughout the year. How does the average precipitation change from month to month? Make a line graph or a bar graph to show your state's temperature or precipitation through a year. Draw or cut out pictures that show sports people in your state do during different seasons. Use your pictures in your guidebook about your state.

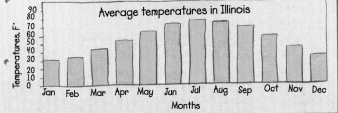

Plants and Animals in Your State

Do saguaros grow near your home? If you live in the Southwest, you might see saguaros growing. But if you live in the Northeast, you would see different plants. You know that certain plants and animals are more likely to live in some regions than in others. Alligators might be swimming in wetlands of the Southeast, but it is not likely that you would see them in the rivers of the West.

What animals and plants might you see in your state? Add the plants and animals that live in your state to your guidebook. Include your official state animal, tree, and flower. Are any animals and plants in your state endangered species?

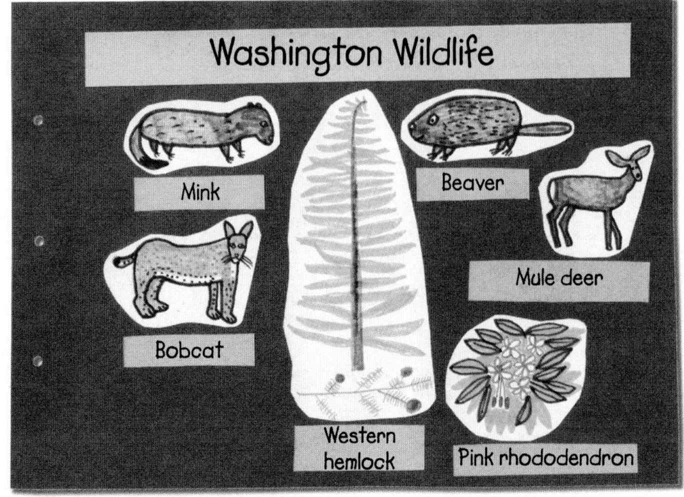

Your State's Resources

Some states have lots of rich farmland, others have oil or mineral resources, and still other states have thick forests. Your state might have all of these! Natural resources can be found on Earth's surface or can be mined from deep inside Earth.

Some natural resources are used within the state to make materials and products. Natural resources are also shipped to other states and countries where they can be used.

Make a list of natural resources found in your state. Choose one resource from the list. Make a diagram that shows where in your state the resource is found, and then show some ways that the resource is used. If the resource is shipped to other places, show the shipping method most often used.

Natural Resources of Minnesota
- Fertile soil for farming
- Trees
- Water in lakes and rivers
- > Iron ore

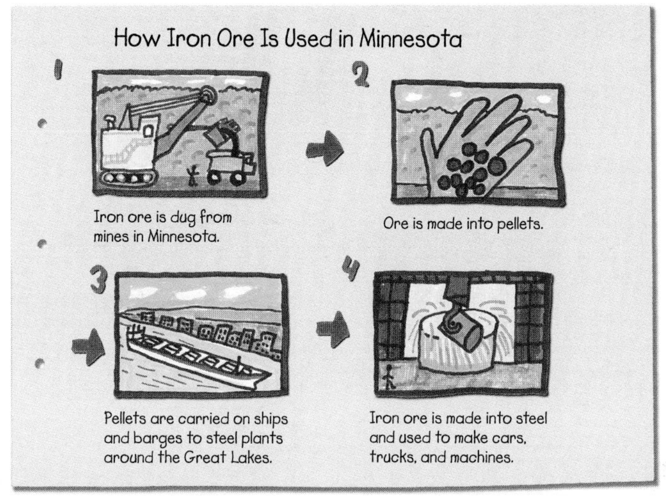

How Iron Ore Is Used in Minnesota
1
Iron ore is dug from mines in Minnesota.
2
Ore is made into pellets.
3
Pellets are carried on ships and barges to steel plants around the Great Lakes.
4
Iron ore is made into steel and used to make cars, trucks, and machines.

Your State's Economy

The natural resources of an area can help its businesses grow. A state's climate can also affect its businesses.

Find out about the main kinds of businesses in your state. How do the businesses use the natural resources of the area? Does the climate affect your state's businesses?

Do research to find out about businesses in your state. Include a section in your state guidebook that shows how one type of business depends on the resources or climate of your state. Here's a picture that some students in New Mexico made.

▶ In October, people come to the International Balloon Fiesta in Albuquerque.

▶ Tourism is a business in New Mexico

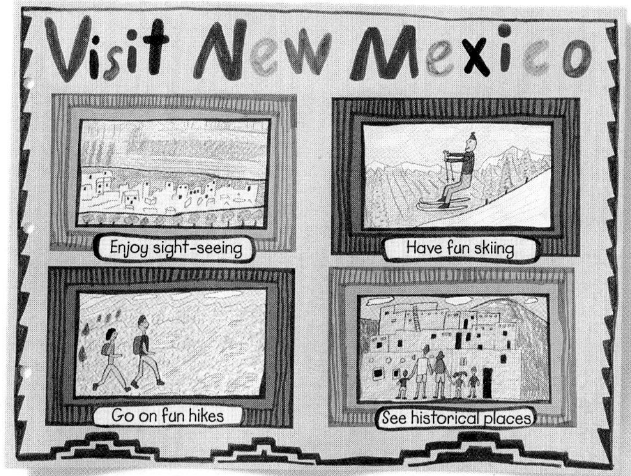

Visit New Mexico
Enjoy sight-seeing
Have fun skiing
Go on fun hikes

Your State's History

People and events make up the history of a place. Many groups of people have come to live in each state. Native Americans, explorers, and settlers have lived throughout the country. Events have brought changes to every area.

Use reference materials to learn about the history of your state. Find out about the earliest groups of people who lived in your state. Research the explorers who visited your state. Then, find out about other people who settled in your state. What events brought major changes to your state?

Make a time line for your state. Include at least five dates in your time line. Here is a time line that some students in Alaska made.

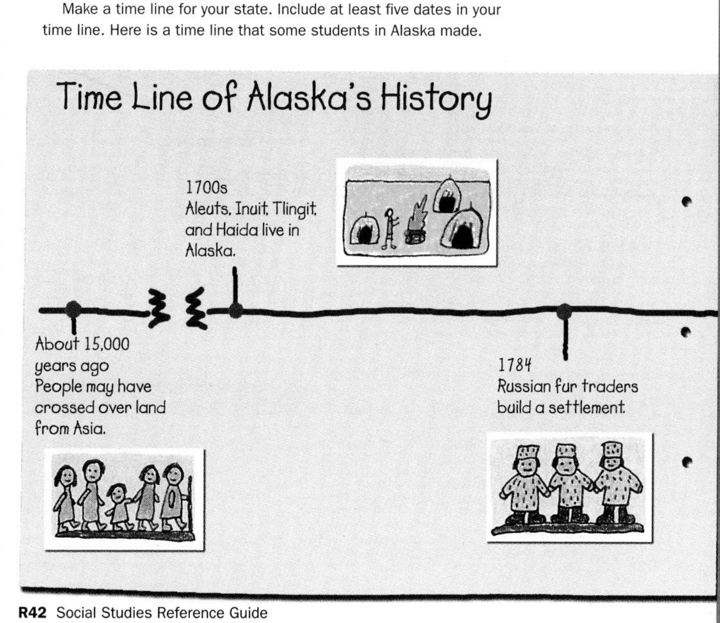

Time Line of Alaska's History
About 15,000 years ago
People may have crossed over land from Asia.
1700s
Aleuts, Inuit, Tlingit, and Haida live in Alaska.
1784
Russian fur traders build a settlement.

▶ These people in Barrow, Alaska are watching the sun setting over the Arctic Ocean.

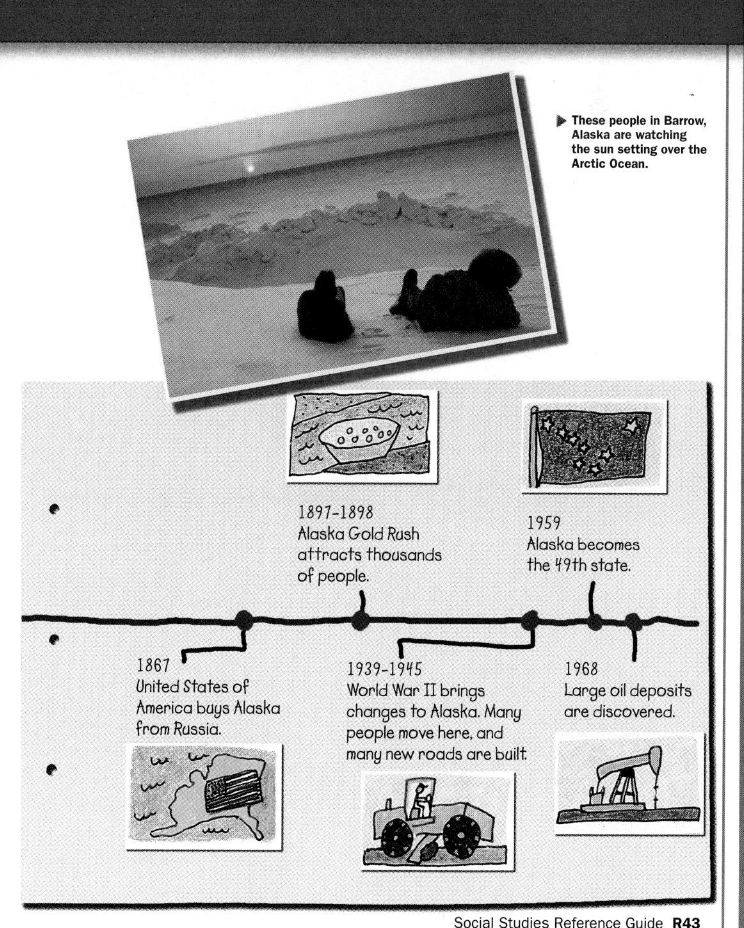

1867
United States of America buys Alaska from Russia.
1897–1898
Alaska Gold Rush attracts thousands of people.
1939–1945
World War II brings changes to Alaska. Many people move here, and many new roads are built.
1959
Alaska becomes the 49th state.
1968
Large oil deposits are discovered.

People from Your State

You can learn a lot about your state's history by reading about famous people who have lived in your state. Some famous people from your state have also made a difference in the whole country.

Do research to find out about famous people from your state. Choose one person you admire and make a picture card about him or her. On your card, list the dates and place in which the person lived. Then list some reasons why the person became well-known. Your class might display all the cards as a set of State Heroes. Students in Massachusetts made cards like these.

State Heroes of Massachusetts

Crispus Attucks
1723–1770
- Crispus Attucks was an African American who lived in Boston.
- He led a group of colonists against British soldiers.
- He was the first American to die in the Revolutionary War.

Susan B. Anthony
1820–1906
- Susan B. Anthony was born in Adams.
- She fought for women getting the right to vote.
- She worked for equal rights for women.

Alexander Graham Bell
1847–1922
- Alexander Graham Bell lived in Boston.
- He had a school for teachers of the deaf.
- He invented the telephone.

John F. Kennedy
1917–1963
- John F. Kennedy was born in Brookline.
- He was the 35th President of the United States of America.
- He said, "Ask what you can do for your country."

Gazetteer

This Gazetteer is a geographic dictionary that will help you locate and pronounce the names of places in this book. Latitude and longitude are given for many cities. The page numbers tell you where each place appears on a map (m) or in the text (t).

A

Acadia National Park (ə kā′ de ə nash′ə nəl pärk) Area in eastern Maine famous for its cliffs and rocky coastline. (t. 108)

Alabama (al′ ə bam′ ə) One of the states in the Southeast region of the United States. (m. 160)

Alaska (ə las′ kə) A West region state that lies northwest of Canada. (m. 362; t. 378, 405)

Albuquerque (al′ bə kėr′ kē) City in New Mexico where new technological products are developed; 35°N, 106°W. (m. 314, t. 316)

American River (ə mer′ ə kən riv′ ər) River in Colorado where gold was discovered in 1848. (t. 402, m. 403)

Appalachia (ap′ ə lā′ chə) Mountainous area in the eastern United States, covering parts of eleven states. (t. 169)

Appalachian Mountain Range (ap′ ə lā′ chən moun′tən rānj) Oldest range of mountains in the United States, extending from eastern Canada to Alabama. (m. 98, t. 106)

Arizona (ar′ə zo′ nə) One of the states in the Southwest region of the United States. (m. 294)

Arkansas (är′ kən sȯ) One of the states in the Southeast region of the United States. (m. 160)

Atlanta (at lan′ tə) Capital of Georgia and a major business and transportation center; 33°N, 84°W. (m. 210, t. 211)

Atlantic City (at lan′ tik sit′ ē) Vacation and resort city along the Atlantic coast in New Jersey; 39°N, 74°W. (t. 109)

B

Badlands National Park (bad′ landz′ nash′ ə nəl pärk) Area of South Dakota where wind and water have carved the soft rock into jagged ridges and sharp spires. (m. 242, t. 244)

Beaumont (bō′ mont) City in southeastern Texas where major oil fields are located; 30°N, 94°W. (m. 314, t. 315)

Bering Strait (bir′ ing strāt) Narrow body of water in the north Pacific Ocean that separates North America from Asia. (t. 39)

Big Springs (big springz) Town located in Nebraska around which much wheat and sunflowers are grown; 41°N, 102°W. (m. 247, t. 247)

Bosque Redondo (bos′ kā rē don′ dō) Area in New Mexico where the Long Walk by the Navajo ended in 1864. (m. 326, t. 326)

Boston (bȯ′ stən) Capital and largest city in Massachusetts and a center for culture, transportation, and commerce; 42°N, 71°W. (m. 142, t. 143)

Pronunciation Key

a	in hat	ō	in open	sh	in she
ā	in age	ȯ	in all	th	in thin
â	in care	ô	in order	ᴛʜ	in then
ä	in far	oi	in oil	zh	in measure
e	in let	ou	in out	ə	= a in about
ē	in equal	u	in cup	ə	= e in taken
ėr	in term	ů	in put	ə	= i in pencil
i	in it	ü	in rule	ə	= o in lemon
ī	in ice	ch	in child	ə	= u in circus
o	in hot	ng	in long		

Gazetteer

C

Cahokia (kə hō′ kē ə) French trading post on the eastern side of the Mississippi River near St. Louis; 38°N, 90°W. (m. 276, t. 277)

California (kal′ə fôr′ nyə) One of the states in the West region of the United States. (m. 362)

Capitol (kap′ə təl) Building in Washington, D.C., where Congress meets. (t. 50)

Cascade Range (ka skād′ rānj) Pacific coast mountain range formed by volcanoes, where rainfall is heavy. (m. 372, t. 382)

Catskill Mountains (kats′ kil moun′ tənz) Smaller part of the Appalachian Mountain Range, located in eastern New York State. (m. 98, t. 107)

Central Plains (sen′ trəl plānz) Grassy region in the eastern part of the Midwest, drained by the Great Lakes and the Mississippi River basin. (m. 247, t. 247)

Central Valley (sen′ trəl val′ ē) A major fruit-growing area in California. (m. 384, t. 385)

Charleston (chärlz′ tən) Seaport in South Central South Carolina in whose harbor the Civil War began; 32°N, 80°W. (m. 202, t. 203)

Charlestown (chärlz′ toun) Native American reservation in Rhode Island where the Narragansett live today; 41°N, 71°W. (m. 126, t. 128)

Chesapeake Bay (ches′ə pēk′ bā) Bay in the Atlantic Ocean between the states of Maryland and Virginia. (m. 116, t. 117)

Colorado (kol′ə rad′ ō) One of the states in the West region of the United States. (m. 362)

Connecticut (kə net′ə kət) One of the states in the Northeast region of the United States. (m. 98)

Continental Divide (kon′ tə nen′ tl də vīd′) Ridge in the Rocky Mountains that divides streams flowing toward the Pacific Ocean from those flowing toward the Atlantic Ocean. (t. 369)

D

Dahlonega (dä′ lon ē′ gə) Town in mountainous area of northern Georgia near where gold was discovered in 1828; 34°N, 84°W. (m. 210, t. 211)

Death Valley (deth val′ ē) Dry valley in southern California that has the lowest elevation in North America. (m. 372, t. 382)

Delaware (del′ə wâr) One of the states in the Northeast region of the United States. (m. 98)

Delaware Bay (del′ə wâr bā) Inlet of the Atlantic Ocean between the states of Delaware and New Jersey. (m. 98, t. 119)

Duluth (də lüth′) City in Minnesota on Lake Superior near where the Ojibwa settled; 46°N, 92°W. (m. 256, t. 257)

Dust Bowl (dust bōl) Area in the Great Plains where a long drought occurred in the 1930s, causing many farmers to suffer. (t. 272)

E

Ellis Island (el′ is ī′ lənd) Small island in New York City harbor that served as the main point of arrival for many immigrants from 1892–1943; 41°N, 74°W. (m. 130, t. 132)

Everglades National Park (ev′ər glādz′ nash′ə nəl pärk) Large area of wetlands in southern Florida. (m. 178, t. 179)

F

Florida (flôr′ə də) One of the states in the Southeast region of the United States. (m. 160)

Florida Keys (flôr′ə də kēz) Chain of small islands located off the southern coast of Florida between the Atlantic Ocean and the Gulf of Mexico. (m. 167, t. 173)

Fort Canby (fôrt kan′ bē) Place known today as Fort Defiance in New Mexico, where many Navajo surrendered in 1864; 35°N, 109°W. (m. 326, t. 326)

G

Georgia (jôr′ jə) One of the states in the Southeast region of the United States. (m. 160)

Grand Canyon National Park (grand kan′ yən nash′ə nəl pärk) Deep gorge in northern Arizona formed by the Colorado River. (m. 300, t. 304)

Great Basin (grāt bā′ sn) Large desert region that covers most of the state of Nevada. (m. 378, t. 380)

Great Lakes (grāt lāks) Largest set of freshwater lakes in the world, located between the United States and Canada. (m. 233, t. 233)

Great Plains (grāt plānz) Grassy area in the western part of the Midwest region, in the rain shadow of the Rocky Mountains. (m. 247, t. 247)

Green Mountains (grēn moun′ tənz) Smaller part of the Appalachian Mountain Range that runs north and south through Vermont into Massachusetts and Connecticut. (m. 98, t. 106)

H

Hawaii (hə wī′ ē) State in the eastern part of the Pacific Ocean, made up of a group of islands. (m. 362)

Hoopeston (hüp′ stən) Town located in Illinois around which large crops of corn and soybeans are grown; 40°N, 87°W. (m. 246, t. 247)

Houston (hyü′ stən) Major city in southeastern Texas where the Johnson Space Center and the Texas Medical Center are located; 29°N, 95°W. (m. 314, t. 317)

I

Idaho (ī′ də hō) One of the states in the West region of the United States. (m. 362)

Illinois (il′ə noi′) One of the states in the Midwest region of the United States. (m. 226)

Illinois Waterway (il′ə noi′ wȯ′tər wā′) Several rivers and canals that connect Lake Michigan with the Mississippi River. (m. 234, t. 234)

Indiana (in′ dē a′nə) One of the states in the Midwest region of the United States. (m. 226)

Inner Coastal Plain (in′ər kō′ stl plān) Land area in the Southeast region lying between the Outer Coastal Plain and the Piedmont area. (m. 167, t. 167)

Iowa (ī′ə wə) One of the states in the Midwest region of the United States. (m. 226)

J

Jamestown (jāmz′ toun) Village that was the first permanent English settlement in North America, on the James River in Virginia; 37°N, 76°W. (m. 194, t. 196)

Juneau (jü′ nō) Capital of the state of Alaska, where the Tlingit governing council meets; 58°N, 134°W. (m. 394, t. 397)

Pronunciation Key

a	in hat	ō	in open	sh	in she
ā	in age	ȯ	in all	th	in thin
â	in care	ô	in order	ᴛʜ	in then
ä	in far	oi	in oil	zh	in measure
e	in let	ou	in out	ə	= a in about
ē	in equal	u	in cup	ə	= e in taken
ėr	in term	ů	in put	ə	= i in pencil
i	in it	ü	in rule	ə	= o in lemon
ī	in ice	ch	in child	ə	= u in circus
o	in hot	ng	in long		

Gazetteer

K

Kansas (kan′ zəs) One of the states in the Midwest region of the United States. (t. 21, m. 226)

Kentucky (kən tuk′ ē) One of the states in the Southeast region of the United States. (m. 160)

Key West (kē west) Island and seaport in the Florida Keys, which lie off the coast of southern Florida; 24°N, 81°W. (m. 172, t. 173)

King Ranch (king ranch) A large ranch in Texas that is also used for the scientific study of cattle. (m. 338, t. 343)

L

Lake Seneca (lāk sen′ə kə) Largest of the Finger Lakes in upstate New York, noted for its large vineyards. (t. 113)

Lexington (lek′ sing tən) Town in Massachusetts near Boston where the first shots of the American Revolution were fired; 42°N, 71°W. (m. 130, t. 131)

Los Alamos (lòs al′ ə mōs) Town in northern New Mexico where nuclear energy is studied; 36°N, 106°W. (m. 314, t. 316)

Los Angeles (lòs an′ jə ləs) City in southern California that is the second largest city in the United States; 34°N, 118°W. (m. 410, t. 411)

Louisiana (lü ē′ zē an′ə) One of the states in the Southeast region of the United States. (m. 160)

Louisiana Territory (lü ē′ zē an′ə ter′ə tôr′ ē) Area purchased by the United States in 1803 that included much of the land west of the Mississippi River to the Rocky Mountains. (m. 41, t. 41)

M

Mackinaw (mak′ə nò) City in the far northern part of the Lower Peninsula of the state of Michigan where the French colonial fort of Michilimackinac was located; 45°N, 84°W. (m. 264, t. 265)

Maine (mān) One of the states in the Northeast region of the United States. (m. 98)

Maryland (mer′ə lənd) One of the states in the Northeast region of the United States. (m. 98)

Massachusetts (mas′ə chü′ sits) One of the states in the Northeast region of the United States. (m. 98)

Massachusetts Bay (mas′ə chü′ sits bā) Bay near the city of Boston; a center for fishing and boating. (m. 98, t. 119)

Michigan (mish′ə gən) One of the states in the Midwest region of the United States. (m. 226)

Midwest Region (mid′ west′ rē′ jən) Region of the United States that has flat grassy plains and large areas of forests. (m. 4, 10; t. 12)

Milwaukee (mil wò′ kē) City in Wisconsin near where the Ojibwa settled; 43°N, 88°W. (m. 256, t. 257)

Minnesota (min′ə so′ tə) One of the states in the Midwest region of the United States. (m. 226)

Mississippi (mis′ə sip′ ē) One of the states in the Southeast region of the United States. (m. 160)

Mississippi River (mis′ə sip′ ē riv′ ər) Major river in the United States that flows through the Midwest south from Minnesota to the Gulf of Mexico. (m. 38, 234; t. 41, 234)

Missouri (mə zùr′ ē) One of the states in the Midwest region of the United States. (m. 226)

Mitchell (mich′ əl) Town in South Dakota where the Corn Palace is located; 43°N, 98°W. (m. 246, t. 247)

Montana (mon tan′ ə) One of the states in the West region of the United States. (m. 362)

Monticello (mon′ tə chel′ ō) Home of Thomas Jefferson, located near Charlottesville, Virginia. (t. 197)

Mount McKinley (mount mə kin′ lē) Highest peak in North America, located in Alaska. (m. 372, t. 379)

Mount Pleasant (mount plez′ nt) Town in Michigan where some members of the Saginaw Nation of Native Americans live; 43°N, 84°W. (m. 256, t. 257)

Mount Waialeale (mount wī ə lā ä′ lē) Mountain in Hawaii that receives the heaviest annual rainfall in the United States. (t. 382)

Myrtle Beach (mėr′ tl bēch) Atlantic coast resort city in South Carolina; 33°N, 79°W. (m. 166, t. 167)

N

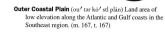

Nebraska (nə bras′ kə) One of the states in the Midwest region of the United States. (m. 226)

Nevada (nə vad′ ə) One of the states in the West region of the United States. (m. 362)

New Hampshire (nü hamp′ shər) One of the states in the Northeast region of the United States. (m. 98)

New Jersey (nü jėr′ zē) One of the states in the Northeast region of the United States. (m. 98)

New Mexico (nü mek′ sə ko) One of the states in the Southwest region of the United States. (m. 294)

New York (nü yôrk) One of the states in the Northeast region of the United States. (m. 98)

New York City (nü yôrk sit′ ē) Largest city in the United States, located in southeast New York; served as the first capital of the United States; 41°N, 74°W. (t. 131, 143; m. 142)

Niagara Falls (nī ag′ rə fòlz) Great waterfall on the Niagara River on the boundary between the United States and Canada; a city in the western part of New York State; 43°N, 79° W. (m. 104, 105; t. 105)

North Carolina (nôrth kar′ə lī′ nə) One of the states in the Southeast region of the United States. (m. 160)

North Dakota (nôrth də kō′ tə) One of the states in the Midwest region of the United States. (m. 226)

Northeast Region (nôrth′ ēst′ rē′ jən) Region in the United States that contains the country's oldest mountains, the Appalachian Mountain Range. (m. 4, t. 12)

O

Ohio (ō hī′ ō) One of the states in the Midwest region of the United States. (m. 226)

Oklahoma (ō′ klə hō′ mə) One of the states in the Southwest region of the United States. (m. 294)

Oregon (ôr′ə gən) One of the states in the West region of the United States. (m. 362)

Outer Coastal Plain (ou′ tər kō′ stl plān) Land area of low elevation along the Atlantic and Gulf coasts in the Southeast region. (m. 167, t. 167)

P

Pennsylvania (pen′ səl vā′ nyə) One of the states in the Northeast region of the United States. (m. 98)

Philadelphia (fil′ə del′ fē ə) City in southeastern Pennsylvania where the Declaration of Independence was signed and which served as the second capital of the United States from 1790 to 1800; 40°N, 75°W. (m. 130; t. 131, 137, 143)

Phoenix (fē′ niks) Capital of the state of Arizona, irrigated from the California State Water Project; 33°N, 112°W. (m. 346, t. 347)

Piedmont (pēd′ mont) Upland area in the Southeast region, located between the coastal plains and the Appalachian Mountains. (m. 167, t. 168)

Pittsburgh (pits′ berg′) City in southwestern Pennsylvania where three major rivers meet and which became a leading iron- and steel-making center; 40°N, 80°W. (m. 142, t. 143)

Plymouth (plim′ əth) Town located in eastern Massachusetts that was one of the first English settlements in North America; 42°N, 70°W. (m. 130, t. 131)

Pronunciation Key

a	in hat	ō	in open	sh	in she
ā	in age	ò	in all	th	in thin
â	in care	ô	in order	ᴛʜ	in then
ä	in far	oi	in oil	zh	in measure
e	in let	ou	in out	ə	= a in about
ē	in equal	u	in cup	ə	= e in taken
ėr	in term	ů	in put	ə	= i in pencil
i	in it	ü	in rule	ə	= o in lemon
ī	in ice	ch	in child	ə	= u in circus
o	in hot	ng	in long		

Gazetteer

Q

Qualla Boundary (kwä′ la boun′ dər ē) An Eastern Cherokee reservation in western North Carolina. (m. 188, t. 191)

R

Rhode Island (rōd ī′ lənd) One of the states in the Northeast region of the United States. (m. 98)

Roanoke Island (rō′ə nōk ī′ lənd) Island in present-day North Carolina along the Outer Banks where the English tried but failed to establish a colony in 1587, which was called the "Lost Colony." (t. 196)

Rocky Mountains (rok′ ē moun′ tənz) Chief group of mountain ranges in the western part of the United States, extending from Alaska to New Mexico. (m. 368, t. 369)

S

Saguaro National Park (sə gwär′ ō nash′ə nəl pärk) Park outside Tucson, Arizona, where the saguaro cactus grows. (m. 308, t. 310)

Salt Lake City (sòlt lāk sit′ ē) Capital and largest urban center in the state of Utah; 40°N, 112°W. (m. 410, t. 412)

San Antonio (san an tō′ nē ō) City in southern Texas where the San Jose Mission was built and where the first air-conditioned office building was located; 28°N, 97°W. (m. 332; t. 334, 341)

San Francisco (san frən sis′ kō) Major port city in California whose bay connects with the Pacific Ocean; 37°N, 122°W. (m. 400, t. 402)

Santa Fe (san′ tə fā) Capital of the state of New Mexico, founded by the Spanish in about 1609; 35°N, 106°W. (m. 332, t. 336)

Sault Sainte Marie (sü′ sānt mə rē′) City in Michigan that began as a French fort and later became a trading post; 46°N, 84°W. (m. 264, t. 265)

Seattle (sē at′ l) Largest city and major Pacific Ocean port in the state of Washington; 47°N, 122°W. (m. 410, t. 412)

Seneca Falls (sen′ə kə fòlz) Village in west-central New York State where the National Women's Hall of Fame is located; 43°N, 76°W. (m. 136, t. 138)

Sonoran Desert (sə nôr′ ən dez′ərt) Dry area in Arizona where saguaro cactuses grow. (m. 309, t. 310)

South Carolina (south kar′ə lī′ nə) One of the states in the Southeast region of the United States. (m. 160)

South Carver (south kär′ vər) Town in Massachusetts that is home to the annual Massachusetts Cranberry Harvest Festival; 41°N, 70°W. (m. 112, t. 113)

South Dakota (south də kō′ tə) One of the states in the Midwest region of the United States. (m. 226)

Southeast Region (south′ ēst′ rē′ jən) Region in the United States where the Appalachian Mountains gradually flatten into the Atlantic Coastal Plain. (m. 4, t. 12)

Southwest Region (south′ west′ rē′ jən) Region in the United States that is very dry, with many deserts, canyons, and plateaus. (m. 4, t. 13)

St. Albans (sānt òl′ bənz) Town in Vermont that hosts the Vermont Maple Festival each year; 44°N, 73°W. (m. 112, t. 114)

St. Augustine (sānt ò′ gə stēn′) City on the coast of eastern Florida, founded by the Spanish in 1565; 30°N, 81°W. (m. 195, t. 196)

St. Lawrence Seaway (sānt lôr′ əns sē′ wā′) Waterway that links the Great Lakes with the Atlantic Ocean. (m. 234, t. 234)

St. Louis (sānt lü′ is) City in Missouri on the Mississippi River where a French trading center was located in the 1600s and 1700s and which became the Midwest transportation hub in the early 1800s; 38°N, 90°W. (m. 72, 276; t. 73, 277)

Sutter's Mill (sut′ tərz mil) Location in California where gold was discovered in 1848. (t. 400, 402, m. 403)

T

Tennessee (ten′ ə sē′) One of the states in the Southeast region of the United States. (m. 160)

Texas (tek′ səs) One of the states in the Southwest region of the United States. (m. 294)

Tlingit Cultural Region (klin′ git kul′ chər əl rē′ jən) Area along the southeastern coast of Alaska and the northern part of British Columbia in Canada where the Tlingit people live. (m. 394, t. 395)

Tucson (tü′ son) City in the state of Arizona where new technological products are developed and which is watered by irrigation from the California State Water Project; 32°N, 111°W. (m. 346, t. 347)

U

Utah (yü′ tò) One of the states in the West region of the United States. (m. 362)

V

Vermont (vər mont′) One of the states in the Northeast region of the United States. (m. 98)

Virginia (vər jin′ yə) One of the states in the Southeast region of the United States. (m. 160)

W

Wapello County (wə pel′ ō koun′ tē) A part of Iowa where the first Midwest land rush took place in 1843. (m. 268, t. 269)

Washington (wäsh′ ing tən) One of the states in the West region of the United States. (m. 362)

Washington, D.C. (wäsh′ ing tən) The capital city of the United States, located in the District of Columbia; 39°N, 77°W. (t. 14, 48; m. 46)

West Region (west rē′ jən) Region in the United States that has extremes both in temperatures and landforms. (m. 4, t. 13)

West Virginia (west vər jin′ yə) One of the states in the Southeast region of the United States. (m. 160)

White Mountains (wīt moun′ tənz) Small part of the Appalachian Mountain Range that extends from the western part of Maine through New Hampshire. (m. 98, t. 106)

Willamette Valley (wil a′ met val′ ē) Area in Oregon where a variety of fruits and vegetables are grown. (m. 384, t. 385)

Window Rock (win′ dō rok) Capital of the Navajo Nation in Arizona; 35°N, 109°W. (m. 324, t. 327)

Wisconsin (wi skon′ sən) One of the states in the Midwest region of the United States. (m. 226)

Wyoming (wī ō′ ming) One of the states in the West region of the United States. (m. 362)

Y

Yellowstone National Park (yel′ ō stōn′ nash′ə nəl pärk) Oldest national park in the world, located mostly in northwestern Wyoming, famous for its scenery, hot springs, and geysers. (m. 368, t. 370)

Pronunciation Key

a	in hat	ō	in open	sh	in she
ā	in age	ò	in all	th	in thin
â	in care	ô	in order	ᴛʜ	in then
ä	in far	oi	in oil	zh	in measure
e	in let	ou	in out	ə	= a in about
ē	in equal	u	in cup	ə	= e in taken
ėr	in term	ů	in put	ə	= i in pencil
i	in it	ü	in rule	ə	= o in lemon
ī	in ice	ch	in child	ə	= u in circus
o	in hot	ng	in long		

Biographical Dictionary

This Biographical Dictionary tells you about the people in this book and how to pronounce their names. The page numbers tell you where the person first appears in the text.

Adams, John (ad′ əmz) 1735–1826 Signer from Massachusetts of the Declaration of Independence and second President of the United States. (p. 131)

Albright, Madeleine (ȯl′ brīt) 1937– Immigrant from eastern Europe who became the first female United States Secretary of State. (p. 132)

Anthony, Susan B. (an′ thə nē) 1820–1906 Leader in the women's rights movement who helped to organize the Seneca Falls Convention. (p. 138)

Armour, Philip (är′ mər) 1832–1901 Businessman who started a meat-packing industry in Chicago. (p. 339)

Bell, Alexander Graham (bel) 1847–1922 Scottish immigrant who invented the telephone. (p. 132)

Bradley, Thomas (brad′ lē) 1917–1998 First African American mayor of Los Angeles. (pp. 416–417)

Cabrillo, Juan Rodríguez (kä brē′ yō) died in 1543 Spanish explorer who first saw the coast of present-day California. (pp. 400–401)

Calamity Jane (kə lam′ ə tē jān) 1852–1903 Nickname for Martha Canary, a famous cowgirl, who also performed shooting displays. (p. 340)

Canonicus (ka non′ ə kəs) c. 1565–1647 Native American ruler of the Narragansett who sold land to Roger Williams for the colony of Rhode Island. (p. 128)

Cárdenas, García López de (kär dā′ näs) (dates unknown) Spanish explorer who traveled near the Grand Canyon and the Colorado River in 1540. (p. 302)

Carnegie, Andrew (kär nā′gē) 1835–1919 Business leader who developed the steel industry in Pennsylvania. (pp. 132, 147)

Carrier, Willis (kar′ ē ər) 1876–1950 Engineer responsible for reducing air moisture at his printing plant in Brooklyn, New York, in 1902, which led the way for the development of modern air conditioning. (pp. 348, 349)

Carson, Kit (kär′ sən) 1809–1868 Soldier who helped stop conflicts in 1863 between the Navajos and white settlers in New Mexico. (p. 326)

Chisholm, Jesse (chiz′ əm) c. 1806–1868 American trader who marked a trail from San Antonio, Texas, to Abilene, Kansas. (p. 341)

Clark, William (klärk) 1770–1838 Explorer who helped lead an expedition to find a water route to the Pacific Ocean through the Louisiana Territory in 1804–1805. (pp. 42, 278)

Cobb, Geraldyn (Jerri) (kob) 1931– First woman who trained as an astronaut, but who received the Nobel Peace Prize for piloting airplanes to take medicines, clothing, food, and doctors to people in the Amazon rain forest. (pp. 318–319)

Columbus, Christopher (kə lum′ bəs) c. 1451–1506 Spanish explorer who landed on North America in 1492. (pp. 38–39)

Coronado, Francisco Vásquez de (kôr′ə nä′ dō) 1510–1554 Spaniard who led an expedition through parts of the Southwest looking for the Seven Cities of Gold in the early 1540s. (p. 302)

Deere, John (dir) 1804–1886 Inventor of the steel plow in 1838, which made farming grasslands much easier in the Midwest. (pp. 271, 273)

De Soto, Hernando (di sō′ tō) c. 1500–1542 Spanish explorer who sailed around Florida in 1539 and then traveled along the southeast coast as far as the Mississippi River. (p. 195)

Dodge, Henry Chee (doj) 1857–1947 First chairman of the Navajo Tribal Council. (pp. 327, 329)

Douglass, Frederick (dug′ ləs) c. 1817–1895 Former slave who became an Abolitionist newspaper editor and who spoke in favor of women's right to vote. (p. 137)

Du Sable, Jean Baptiste Pointe (dü sa′ bəl) c. 1745–1818 Free man of African ancestry, born in Haiti, who became known as the "Father of Chicago" when he set up a successful trading post in the area in 1784. (pp. 266, 267)

Einstein, Albert (in′ stin) 1879–1955 German immigrant who became one of the world's most important scientists. (p. 132)

Franklin, Benjamin (frang′ klən) 1706–1790 Signer of the Declaration of Independence who was from Pennsylvania; later was a member of the Constitutional Convention. (p. 131)

Garrison, William Lloyd (gar′ə sən) 1805–1879 Abolitionist who began publishing a newspaper called *The Liberator* in 1833. (p. 137)

Grimké, Angelina (grim′ kē) 1805–1879 Southern-born woman who wanted to end slavery and who wrote letters and pamphlets attacking its evils. (pp. 200–201)

Grimké, Sarah (grim′ kē) 1792–1873 Abolitionist sister of Angelina who also wrote about the evils of slavery. (pp. 200–201)

Hendrickson, Sue (hen′ drik sən) 1949– Archaeologist who discovered dinosaur bone fossils in South Dakota. (pp. 242, 243)

Higgins, Pattillo (hig′ ənz) 1863–1955 Scientist who discovered natural gas escaping from a stream near Spindletop Hill in Beaumont, Texas, in 1901, which soon led to the discovery of oil. (p. 315)

Inouye, Daniel (en′ ō wā) 1924– U.S. representative from Hawaii who was the first Japanese American to be elected to Congress. (p. 53)

Pronunciation Key

a in hat	ō in open	sh in she
ā in age	ȯ in all	th in thin
â in care	ô in order	ᴛʜ in then
ä in far	oi in oil	zh in measure
e in let	ou in out	ə = a in about
ē in equal	u in cup	ə = e in taken
ėr in term	u̇ in put	ə = i in pencil
i in it	ü in rule	ə = o in lemon
ī in ice	ch in child	ə = u in circus
o in hot	ng in long	

Biographical Dictionary

Jackson, Andrew (jak′ sən) 1767–1845 Seventh President of the United States, who was born in present-day South Carolina and was very popular with the common people. (p. 197)

Jefferson, Thomas (jef′ər sən) 1743–1826 Virginian who wrote the Declaration of Independence, served as the third President of the United States, and purchased the Louisiana Territory from France in 1803. (pp. 42, 197)

Jolliet, Louis (jō′ lē et) 1645–1700 French explorer who traveled down Lake Michigan and the Illinois and Mississippi Rivers in 1673. (p. 265)

King, Martin Luther, Jr. (king) 1929–1968 African American leader who believed in the use of non-violent civil disobedience to gain civil rights in the 1950s and 1960s. (p. 206)

Kino, Eusebio (kē′ nō) 1645–1711 Spanish priest who founded three missions in present-day Arizona in 1687 where he taught Native Americans. (p. 334)

La Guardia, Fiorello (lə gwär′ dē ə) 1882–1947 United States congressman and later mayor of New York City. (p. 45)

La Salle, Robert (le sal) 1643–1687 French explorer who sailed down the Ohio and Mississippi Rivers in 1682, reaching the Gulf of Mexico. (p. 195)

Lewelling, Seth (lü wel′ ling) 1820–1896 Fruit grower from Oregon who helped to develop the Bing cherry. (p. 389)

Lewis, Meriwether (lü′ is) 1774–1809 Explorer who helped lead an expedition to find a water route to the Pacific Ocean through the Louisiana Territory in 1804–1805. (pp. 42, 278)

Lincoln, Abraham (ling′ kən) 1809–1865 Sixteenth President of the United States, from 1861 to 1865, during the Civil War. (p. 203)

Lucas, Anthony (lü′ kəs) 1855–1921 A mining engineer hired to drill for oil at Spindletop Hill in Texas in 1901. (p. 315)

Madison, James (mad′ə sən) 1751–1836 Important delegate at the Constitutional Convention who later served as the fourth President of the United States. (p. 197)

Marquette, Jacques (mär ket′) 1637–1675 French explorer who traveled down Lake Michigan and the Illinois and Mississippi Rivers in 1673. (p. 265)

Marshall, James (mär′ shəl) 1810–1885 Worker who discovered gold in California in 1848 while building a sawmill for John Sutter. (p. 402)

Mott, Lucretia (mot) 1793–1880 Women's rights leader who worked with Elizabeth Cady Stanton and Susan B. Anthony. (p. 138)

Oakley, Annie (ō′klē) 1860–1926 Famous cowgirl who took part in rodeos and Wild West shows. (p. 340)

Parks, Rosa (pärks) 1913– African American woman who protested bus segregation in Montgomery, Alabama, in 1955, leading to a bus boycott. (p. 207)

Podlasek, Joseph (pō la′ sek) Native American who is the executive director of the American Indian Center in Chicago. (pp. 260–261)

Ponce de León, Juan (pons də lē′ ən) c. 1460–1521 Spanish explorer who traveled through Florida in 1513 looking for the "fountain of youth." (p. 195)

Powell, John Wesley (pou′əl) 1834–1902 Explorer of the Grand Canyon and the Colorado Plateau in 1869 who wrote reports about his findings. (pp. 302, 305)

Roosevelt, Theodore (rō′ zə velt) 1858–1919 United States President who signed a law making the Grand Canyon a national monument. (p. 303)

Sequoyah (si kwoi′ə) c. 1763–1843 Cherokee who developed a written alphabet for his people in 1821. (pp. 190, 193)

Serra, Junípero (ser′ rä) 1713–1784 Spanish priest who set up missions in California beginning in 1769. (p. 401)

Stanton, Elizabeth Cady (stan′ tən) 1815–1902 Women's rights leader who helped write the "Declaration of Sentiments" at the Seneca Falls Convention. (pp. 138, 139)

Strauss, Levi (strous) 1829–1902 Inventor of sturdy blue jeans in the 1850s for miners in California. (pp. 403, 407)

Sutter, John (sut′ tər) 1803–1880 Owner of sawmill in California where gold was discovered in 1848. (p. 402)

Truth, Sojourner (trüth) 1797–1883 African American woman who addressed Abolitionist meetings and told about her early life as a slave. (p. 137)

Twain, Mark (twān) 1835–1910 Literary name of Samuel Clemens, who wrote books about life along the Mississippi River. (p. 283)

Washington, George (wäsh′ ing tən) 1732–1799 Virginian who led American troops in the Revolutionary War and who served as the first President of the United States, making him the "Father of the Country." (p. 190)

Williams, Roger (wil′ yəmz) c. 1603–1683 English colonist who bought land from the Narragansetts in 1636 for a colony which became Rhode Island. (p. 128)

Pronunciation Key

a in hat	ō in open	sh in she
ā in age	ȯ in all	th in thin
â in care	ô in order	ᴛʜ in then
ä in far	oi in oil	zh in measure
e in let	ou in out	ə = a in about
ē in equal	u in cup	ə = e in taken
ėr in term	u̇ in put	ə = i in pencil
i in it	ü in rule	ə = o in lemon
ī in ice	ch in child	ə = u in circus
o in hot	ng in long	

Glossary

This Glossary will help you understand the meanings and pronounce the vocabulary words in this book. The page numbers tell you where the word first appears.

A

abolitionist (ab′ ə lish′ ə nist) a reformer who believed that slavery should be erased from the law (p. 137)

adobe (ə dō′ bē) a kind of mud brick (p. 302)

agriculture (ag′ rə kul′ chər) the raising of crops or animals (pp. 28, 180)

amendment (ə mend′ mənt) a change to the Constitution of the United States (p. 52)

aqueduct (ak wə dukt) a pipe used to bring water from a distance (p. 347)

arid (ar′ id) dry, but not desert-like (p. 309)

B

backwoodsman (bak′ wu̇dz′ mən) a person who lives in forests or wild areas far away from towns (p. 198)

badlands (bad′ landz′) a region of dry hills and sharp cliffs (p. 243)

barge (bärj) a flat-bottomed boat that carries goods through lakes and rivers (p. 236)

barrier island (bar′ ē ər ī′ lənd) a narrow island between the ocean and the mainland (p. 167)

barter (bär′ tər) trading one kind of good or service for another (p. 73)

bay (bā) part of a sea or lake that cuts into a coastline (p. 117)

bayou (bī′ ü) marshy river (p. 163)

Bill of Rights (bil əv rīts) the first ten amendments to the United States Constitution; they state the basic rights of United States citizens (p. 52)

bog (bog) an area of soft, wet, spongy ground (p. 113)

boom town (büm′ toun′) fast-growing town, usually located near where gold or silver have recently been discovered (p. 403)

boundary (boun′ dər ē) a line or natural feature that separates one area or state from another (p. 14)

boycott (boi′ kot) refusing to buy something as a form of protest (p. 207)

C

canal (kə nal′) a waterway that has been dug across land for ships to travel through (p. 234)

canyon (kan′ yən) a deep valley with steep rocky walls (p. 13)

capital resource (kap′ ə təl rē′ sôrs) something people make in order to produce other products (p. 28)

Capitol (kap′ ə təl) the building where the Congress of the United States meets (p. 50)

citizen (sit′ ə zən) an official member of a country (p. 47)

civil rights (siv′ əl rīts) the rights of a citizen, including the right to vote and protection under the law (p. 205)

Civil War (siv′ əl wôr) the United States Civil War, fought between Northern and Southern states from 1861 to 1865 (p. 203)

climate (klī′ mit) the weather patterns in one place over a long period of time (p. 19)

colony (kol′ ə nē) a settlement of people who come from one country to live in another land (p. 131)

commerce (kom′ ərs) the buying and selling of goods, especially in large amounts between different places (p. 141)

communication (kə myü′ nə kā′ shən) the way that people send and receive information (p. 84)

computer software (kəm pyü′ tər sôft′ wâr′) programs that help computers perform certain functions (p. 412)

confederacy (kən fed′ ər ə sē) a union of groups, countries, or states that agree to work together for a common goal (p. 129)

Confederacy (kən fed′ ər ə sē) the name of the Southern states in the United States Civil War (p. 203)

consensus (kən sen′ səs) a method of decision-making in which all come to agreement (p. 189)

conserve (kən sərv′) to use resources carefully (p. 29)

Constitution (kon stə tü′ shən) the written plan for governing the United States of America (p. 48)

consumer (kən sü′ mər) a person who buys goods and services (p. 74)

convention (kən ven′ shən) a meeting held for a certain purpose (p. 138)

cooperation (kō op′ ə rā′ shən) to work together to get things done (p. 127)

crab pot (krab pot) a large wire cage with several sections that crabs swim into but from which they cannot escape (p. 117)

crop rotation (krop rō tā′ shən) the planting of different crops in different years (p. 248)

culture (kul′ chər) a way of life followed by a group of people (p. 43)

D

demand (di mand′) the amount of an item that consumers are willing to buy at different prices (p. 77)

democracy (di mok′ rə sē) a system of government in which every citizen has a right to take part (p. 47)

desert (dez′ ərt) an area that receives less than ten inches of rain in one year (pp. 13, 309)

diverse (də vėrs′) varied (p. 145)

drought (drout) a long period with little or no rain (p. 272)

Dust Bowl (dust bōl) an area of the Midwest and Southwest that was struck by years of drought in the 1930s (p. 272)

E

economy (i kon′ ə mē) the way in which the resources of a country, state, region, or community are managed (p. 76)

elevation (el′ ə vā′ shən) how high a place is above sea level (pp. 21, 167)

endangered species (en dān′ jərd spē′ shēz) a kind of animal or plant that is in danger of becoming extinct (p. 179)

equator (i kwā′ tər) the imaginary line that circles the center of Earth from east to west (p. 21)

erosion (i rō′ zhən) the process by which wind and water wear away rock (p. 244)

executive branch (eg zek′ yə tiv branch) the part of government that enforces the laws (p. 51)

export (ek′ spôrt) an item sent from one country to be sold in another (p. 143)

extinct (ek stingkt′) no longer existing (p. 179)

Pronunciation Key

a in hat	ō in open	sh in she
ā in age	ȯ in all	th in thin
â in care	ô in order	ᴛʜ in then
ä in far	oi in oil	zh in measure
e in let	ou in out	ə = a in about
ē in equal	u in cup	ə = e in taken
ėr in term	u̇ in put	ə = i in pencil
i in it	ü in rule	ə = o in lemon
ī in ice	ch in child	ə = u in circus
o in hot	ng in long	

Glossary

F

fall line (fȯl līn) a line of waterfalls that marks the boundary between the Piedmont and the coastal plains (p. 168)

federal (fed′ ər əl) a system of government in which the national and state governments share power (p. 48)

fossil fuel (fos′ əl fyü′ əl) a fuel formed in the earth from the remains of plants and animals (p. 183)

free enterprise system (frē en′ tər prīz sis′ təm) a system in which businesses have the right to produce any good or provide any service that they want (p. 76)

frigid (frij′ id) very cold (p. 379)

fur trade (fėr trād) the trading of goods for animal skins (p. 258)

G

geyser (gī′ zər) a hot spring that erupts and sends hot water from the Earth into the air (p. 370)

ghost town (gōst toun) a town where all of the people have moved away (p. 403)

glacier (glā′ shər) huge sheets of ice that cover land (p. 105)

globalization (glō′ bə liz ā′ shən) the process by which a business makes something or provides a service in different places around the world (p. 82)

gold rush (gōld rush) a sudden movement of people to an area where gold has been found (p. 211)

gorge (gôrj) a deep, narrow valley (p. 105)

government (guv′ ərn mənt) the laws that are followed and the people that run a country (p. 47)

greenhouse (grēn′ hous′) an enclosed structure that allows light to enter and keeps in heat and moisture (p. 385)

gusher (gush′ ər) an oil well that produces a large amount of oil (p. 315)

H

harvest (här′vist) cut for use, as a crop (p. 27)

hogan (hō′ gän′) a one-room Navajo home with a door facing east (p. 325)

homestead (hōm′ sted′) land given to settlers by the United States government if they lived and raised crops on it (p. 342)

hub (hub) a center of activity (p. 280)

human resource (hyü′ mən rē′ sôrs) a person that makes products or provides services (p. 31)

humidity (hyü mid′ ə tē) the amount of moisture in the air (pp. 20, 348)

hurricane (hėr′ ə kān) a violent storm with high winds and heavy rain that forms over an ocean (p. 174)

hurricane season (hėr′ ə kān sē′ zn) the time of the year when hurricanes mainly occur (p. 174)

hydroelectricity (hī′ drō i lek′ tris′ ə tē) electricity produced by flowing water (p. 105)

hydropower (hī′ drō pou′ ər) power produced by capturing the energy of flowing water (p. 105)

I

immigrant (im′ ə grənt) a person who comes to live in a new land (p. 43)

import (im′ pôrt) an item brought from abroad to be offered for sale (p. 143)

industry (in′ də strē) a business that makes a product or provides a service (p. 28)

inlet (in′ let) a narrow opening in a coastline (p. 117)

interdependent (in′ tər di pen′ dənt) when regions rely on one another for goods, services, or resources (p. 81)

international trade (in′ tər nash′ ə nəl trād) trade between different countries (p. 414)

Interstate highway system (in′ tər stāt′ hī′ wā′ sis′ təm) a system of interconnected highways in the United States (p. 282)

irrigation (ir′ ə gā′ shən) the process of bringing water to crops (p. 248)

J

judicial branch (jü dish′ əl branch) the part of government, made up of courts and judges, that interprets laws (p. 51)

jury (ju̇r′ ē) a panel of ordinary citizens who make decisions in a court of law (p. 58)

K

key (kē) a low island (p. 173)

L

landform (land′ fôrm′) a natural feature of the earth's surface (p. 11)

latitude (lat′ ə tüd) measurement of how far north or south of the equator a place is located (p. 408)

lava (lä′ və) molten rock (magma) that rises and flows on the surface of the earth (p. 372)

legislative branch (lej′ ə slā′ tiv branch) the part of government that makes laws (p. 50)

lighthouse (līt′ hous′) a tall tower with a very strong light used to guide ships (p. 108)

livestock (līv′ stok′) animals raised on farms and ranches for human use (p. 386)

lock (lok) a gated part of a canal or river used to raise and lower water levels (p. 234)

longitude (lon′ jə tüd) measurement of how far east or west of the prime meridian a place is located (p. 409)

The Long Walk (ᴛʜə lȯng wok) a forced journey of hundreds of miles by the Navajo in the 1800s (pp. 326–327)

M

magma (mag′ mə) molten rock beneath the surface of the earth (p. 370)

manufacturing (man′ yə fak′ chər ing) making things to use or sell (p. 28)

meridian (mə rid′ ē ən) line of longitude (p. 409)

mineral (min′ ər əl) metals and other resources dug from the ground (p. 115)

mission (mish′ ən) a settlement set up by a religious group to teach religion and help area people (p. 265)

missionary (mish′ ə ner′ ē) a person sent by a religious organization to spread its beliefs (p. 334)

mound (mound) a pile of earth or stone constructed by early Native Americans for a variety of purposes (p. 277)

mountain (moun′ tən) a very high landform, often with steep sides (p. 12)

Pronunciation Key

a in hat	ō in open	sh in she
ā in age	ȯ in all	th in thin
â in care	ô in order	ᴛʜ in then
ä in far	oi in oil	zh in measure
e in let	ou in out	ə = a in about
ē in equal	u in cup	ə = e in taken
ėr in term	u̇ in put	ə = i in pencil
i in it	ü in rule	ə = o in lemon
ī in ice	ch in child	ə = u in circus
o in hot	ng in long	

Glossary

N

natural resource (nach′ ər əl rē′ sôrs) something in the environment that can be used (p. 27)

need (nēd) something that a person must have in order to live (p. 73)

nonrenewable resource (non′ ri nü′ ə bəl rē′ sôrs) a resource that cannot be replaced (p. 29)

Northern Hemisphere (nôr′ ᴛʜərn hem′ ə sfir) the half of Earth north of the equator (p. 408)

O

opportunity cost (op′ ər tü′ nə tē kost) what is given up when one thing is chosen over another (p. 78)

P

passport (pas′ pôrt) a paper or booklet that gives a person permission to travel to other countries (p. 57)

peninsula (pə nin′ sə lə) a piece of land almost surrounded by water (p. 108)

pioneer (pī′ ə nēr′) a person who settles in a part of a country and prepares it for others (p. 198)

plain (plān) an area of flat land that often is covered with grass or trees (p. 12)

plantation (plan tā′ shən) a large farm that produces crops to sell (p. 198)

plateau (pla tō′) a large, flat, raised area of land (p. 13)

polar climate (pō′ lər klī′ mit) areas around the North and South Poles with the coldest temperatures (p. 22)

potlatch (pot′ lach′) a feast held by Native Americans of the Northwest to celebrate important events (p. 396)

powwow (pou′ wou′) a Native American festival (p. 128)

prairie (prâr′ ē) an area where grass grows well, but trees are rare (p. 245)

precipitation (pri sip′ ə tā′ shən) the amount of moisture that falls as rain or snow (p. 19)

primary source (prī′ mer′ ē sôrs) an eyewitness account or observation of an event (p. 330)

prime meridian (prīm mə rid′ ē ən) the starting point for measuring longitude (p. 409)

process (pros′ es) to change something so that people can use it (p. 27)

producer (prə dü′ sər) a person who makes goods or products to sell (p. 74)

product (prod′ əkt) something that people make or grow (p. 28)

profit (prof′ it) the money left over after costs are paid (p. 76)

prospector (pros′ pek tər) someone who searches for valuable minerals (p. 402)

public transportation system (pub′ lik tran′ spər tā′ shən sis′ təm) the trains and buses that carry people through a city (p. 212)

pueblo (pweb′ lō) a Spanish word that means "village" and which refers to some Native American groups in the Southwest (p. 302)

pulp (pulp) a combination of wood chips, water, and chemicals used to make paper (p. 182)

Q

quarry (kwôr′ ē) a place where stone is dug, cut, or blasted out of the ground (p. 115)

R

rain shadow (rān shad′ ō) the side of a mountain chain that receives less precipitation than the other side (p. 382)

raw material (ró mə tir′ ē əl) something that is changed so that people can use it (p. 27)

Reconstruction (rē′ kən struk′ shən) the period of time after the United States Civil War when the South was rebuilt (p. 205)

recycle (rē sī′ kəl) to use something more than once (p. 29)

refinery (ri fī′ nər ē) a factory that separates crude oil into different groups of chemicals (p. 315)

reforest (rē fôr′ ist) to plant new trees to replace ones that have been cut down (p. 388)

region (rē′ jən) a large area in which places share similar characteristics (p. 11)

renewable resource (ri nü′ ə bəl rē′ sôrs) a natural resource that can be replaced (p. 29)

represent (rep′ ri zent′) the act of leaders making decisions for those who elected them (p. 47)

republic (ri pub′ lik) a type of government in which people elect leaders to represent them (p. 47)

reservation (rez′ ər vā′ shən) an area of land set aside by the United States for Native Americans (p. 128)

revolution (rev′ ə lü′ shən) a fight to overthrow a government (p. 131)

rural (rúr′ əl) in small towns or farms (p. 71)

S

sachem (sā′ chəm) a ruler over a portion of Narragansett territory (p. 127)

sap (sap) a liquid carrying water and food that circulates through a plant (p. 114)

savanna (sə van′ ə) a grassy plain with few trees (p. 310)

sea level (sē lev′ əl) the same height as the surface of the ocean (p. 170)

search engine (sėrch en′ jən) a special Web site that locates other Web sites (p. 262)

secede (si sēd′) to pull out of or separate from (p. 203)

secondary source (sek′ ən der′ ē sôrs) secondhand account of history (p. 330)

segregate (seg′ rə gāt′) to separate people according to their race (p. 205)

service (sėr′ vis) job that someone does for others (p. 31)

slave (slāv) a person who is owned as property by another person and is forced to work (pp. 137, 198)

sod (sod) the grass, roots, and dirt that form the ground's top layer (p. 270)

Southern Hemisphere (suᴛʜ′ ərn hem′ ə sfir) the half of Earth south of the equator (p. 408)

steamboat (stēm′ bōt′) a boat powered by a steam engine (p. 280)

subarctic climate (sub ärk′ tik klī′ mit) an area with short, warm summers and ground covered in snow for most of the rest of the year (p. 22)

supply (sə plī′) the amount of an item someone has to sell (p. 77)

Supreme Court (sə prēm′ côrt) the highest court of the United States (p. 51)

Pronunciation Key

a in hat	ō in open	sh in she
ā in age	ò in all	th in thin
â in care	ô in order	ᴛʜ in then
ä in far	oi in oil	zh in measure
e in let	ou in out	ə = a in about
ē in equal	u in cup	ə = e in taken
ėr in term	ù in put	ə = i in pencil
i in it	ü in rule	ə = o in lemon
ī in ice	ch in child	ə = u in circus
o in hot	ng in long	

Glossary

T

tallow (tal′ ō) animal fat used for making candles and soap (p. 339)

tax (taks′) money the government collects to pay for its services (p. 58)

technology (tek nol′ ə jē) the development and use of scientific knowledge to solve practical problems (p. 70)

temperate climate (tem′ pər it klī′ mit) moderate area between the tropical and subarctic climates (p. 23)

temperature (tem′ pər ə chər) a measurement telling how hot or cold something is (p. 19)

timberline (tim′ bər lin′) the elevation on a mountain above which trees cannot grow (p. 369)

totem pole (tō′ təm pōl) a tall post carved with images of people and animals to represent family history (p. 395)

trading post (trā′ ding pōst) a kind of store in which goods are traded (p. 266)

Trail of Tears (trāl əv tirz) the forced journey of the Cherokees to land set aside for them by the United States in what is now Oklahoma (p. 191)

transcontinental railroad (tran′ skon tə nen′ tl rāl′ rōd′) a rail line that crosses an entire country (p. 281)

transportation (tran′ spər tā′ shən) the moving of goods, people, or animals from one place to another (p. 81)

tropical climate (trop′ ə kəl klī′ mit) an area that is usually very warm all year (p. 22)

tundra (tun′ drə) a cold, flat area where trees cannot grow (p. 379)

U

Union (yü′ nyən) the name for the Northern states during the American Civil War (p. 203)

urban (ėr′ bən) in the city (p. 71)

V

vaquero (vä ker′ ō) Spanish word for "cowboy" (p. 336)

viceroy (vīs′ roi) an early governor of Mexico (p. 333)

vineyard (vin′ yərd) a place where grapevines are planted (p. 113)

volcano (vol kā′ nō) a type of mountain with an opening through which ash, gas, and lava are forced (p. 372)

W

want (wänt) something that a person would like to have but can live without (p. 73)

watermen (wò′ tər mən) men or women who gather different kinds of seafood and fish in different seasons (p. 117)

waterway (wò′ tər wā′) a system of rivers, lakes, and canals, through which ships travel (p. 234)

weather (weᴛʜ′ ər) the condition of the air at a certain time and place (p. 19)

wetland (wet′ land′) land that is covered with water at times (p. 167)

White House (wīt hous) the place where the President of the United States lives and works (p. 51)

wigwam (wig′ wäm) a Narragansett hut made of wooden poles covered in bark (p. 127)

Index

This Index lists the pages on which topics appear in this book. Page numbers after an *m* refer to a map. Page numbers after a *p* refer to a photograph. Page numbers after a *c* refer to a chart or graph.

Abilene, Kansas, 341, *m*54
abolitionism, 137, 200, 201
Acadia National Park, 108
Adams, John, 131
Adirondack Mountains, 107, *m*H13, *m*98
adobe, 302, 325, 333
African Americans, 136, 137, 205–207, 208
agriculture
- in Arizona, 347
- Cherokees and, 189, 190
- in the Midwest, 247–249
- resources and, 28
- in the Southeast, 180, *m*181
- in the West, 384–387, *m*387, *p*384–386

air conditioning, 348, 349, *p*348
airplane, 135, *p*317
Alabama, R18
Alamo, 198, 335, *p*335
Alaska
- climate of, 22, 378, 379
- crops in, 385
- facts about, R18
- fishing industry in, 386
- government of, 50
- inset maps of, 24, *m*24, 25
- map of, *m*362
- mountains in, 13, 372, *m*372
- Native Americans of, 395, 397
- Russian claim to, 401, *m*401
- statehood of, 405, *c*405

Albright, Madeleine, 132
Albuquerque, New Mexico, 316, *m*309, *m*326
Aleutian Range, 372, *m*372
alligator, 179, *p*178
alphabet, 188, 190, 193, *p*188
Amazon rain forest, 318, 319, *p*319
amendment, 52
"America," 90–91
American Civil War. *See* Civil War
American Falls, 104
American Indians. *See* Native Americans
American Revolution, 131, 197
American River, 402, *m*403
Among the Sierra Nevada Mountains, California, *p*362
Anasazi, 295, 302, 306
Anthony, Susan B., 138, *p*138
Appalachia, 169, 183
Appalachian Mountain Range, 12, 106, 169, 179, *m*160, *m*167, *m*247
Appalachian Trail, 106, *p*106
apple, 384, 385, *m*387, *p*384, *p*385
aqueduct, 347
arid, 309
Arizona, 309, 310, 316, 328, 334, 346, 347, R18, *m*309, *m*347, *p*295
Arkansas, 180, R18, *m*160
Armour, Philip, 339
Asia, 16, 39, 40, *m*408
astronaut, 317, 318
astronomy, 316
Atlanta, Georgia, 210–212, *m*187, *p*211
Atlantic Coastal Plain, 12, *m*11
Atlantic Ocean, 108, 369, 400, *m*H13, *m*H15, *m*11, *m*40, *m*133
automobile, 135, 282, 414

backwoodsman, 198
badlands, 242–245, *m*226
Badlands National Park, 244, *m*231, *p*244
baobab tree, 312, *p*313
barge, 236, 237, *p*236
bar graph, 240, 241
barrier islands, 167, *m*167
Barrow, Alaska, 379
barter, 73, *p*73
bay, 117–119
bayou, 163
Beaumont, Texas, 314, 315, *m*299, *m*309
beef, 339, 386
Bell, Alexander Graham, 132, 135
Bering Strait, 39
Big Springs, Nebraska, 246, 247, *m*247
Bill of Rights, 52
Bimini, 194, 195
Bing, Ah, 389
Bing cherry, 389
Bingham Canyon Mine, *p*412

Index

Bird of Paradise, *p*383
bison, 245, 269, 370, *p*245, *p*370–371
Black Hills, 243, *m*226
blacksmith, 275
blanket, 395, *p*325, *p*396
Blue Ridge Mountains, 169, *m*160, *m*167
Bodie, California, 404, *p*404
Bodie Island, *p*174, *p*175
bog, 113, *p*113
boomtown, 403, 404
Boone, Daniel, 198
Bosque Redondo, New Mexico, 326, 327, *m*326
Boston, Massachusetts, 142, 143
boundaries, 14
boycott, 207
Bradley, Thomas, 416, 417, *p*416
Britain. *See* England, Great Britain
British Columbia, 395, *m*394
broccoli, *m*387
buckaroo, 354
buffalo, 245, 271, 370, *p*245, *p*370
"Buffalo Bill's Wild West" show, 404, *p*404

Cabrillo, Juan Rodríguez, 400, 401, *p*400
cactus, 310
Cahokia, Illinois, 277
Cahokia Mounds State Park, 277, *p*277
Calamity Jane (Martha Canary), 340, *p*340
California, 13, 50, 69, 380, 385, 401–404, 407, 411, R18, *m*362, *m*403, *c*405
***California* clipper ship,** 402, *m*402
California State Water Project, 347
Callasaja Falls, *p*168
Canada, 104, 105, 128, *m*11, *m*19, *m*25, *m*103, *m*105
canal, 234, R16
Canonicus, 128
canyon, 13, *p*13, R16
Cape Cod, 108, *m*98
Cape Hatteras, 174, *m*174
Capitol, 50, *m*35
car. *See* automombile
Cárdenas, García López de, 302
cardinal direction, H16, H17
Carnegie, Andrew, 132, 145, 147 *p*147
Carrier, Willis Haviland, 348, 349, *p*348, *p*349
Carson City, Nevada, 403, *m*403
Carson, Kit, 326, *p*326
Cartier, Jacques, 41
Cascade Mountains, 365, 382, 383, *m*372, *p*365
Castillo de San Marcos, 196, *p*196
Catskill Mountains, 106, 107, *m*H13, *m*98
cattle, 249, 336–343, 385, 404, *m*387, *p*339
cause and effect, 228, 229
cave system, 12
Centennial Olympic Park, 210
Central Plains, 247, 248, *m*247
Central Valley, California, 385, *m*367, *m*372
Charleston, South Carolina, 203, 212, 214, 215, *m*187, *p*161, *p*214
Charlestown, Rhode Island, 128, *m*125, *m*126
Cherokee, 188–193
Cherokee language, 192, 193
Cherokee *Phoenix*, 190, 193
cherries, 389, *m*387
Chesapeake Bay, 116–119, *m*35, *m*98, *m*103, *m*167
Chesapeake Bay Foundation, 118
Chicago, Illinois, 266, 267, 280, 281, 350, *m*H14, *m*19
Chicago River, 232, 234, 235, *m*234, *m*265
Chilkat blanket, 395
Chisholm, Jesse, 341
Chisholm Trail, 341, *m*341
***Cinco de Mayo*,** 336, *p*336
cities, 71, 142–146, 211–213
citizen, 47, 133
citizenship (Citizen Heroes)
caring, H2, 318–319
courage, H2, 200–201
fairness, H2, 416–417
honesty, H2, 60–61
respect, H2, 260–261
responsibility, H2, 148–149
citrus fruit, 180
civil rights, 205, 206
Civil Rights Act of 1964, 206
Civil War, 137, 187, 202–205, 281, *p*204
clan, 325
Clark, William, 42, 278, 279, *p*278
Clemens, Samuel Langhorne, 283, *p*283
cliff dwelling, *p*306
cliff, R16
climate, 7, 18–23, 309, 378–383, *m*19, *m*20, *m*22, *m*309

Clinton, William Jefferson, 416
cloud, 382, 383
coal, 70, 183, *p*183
coast, R16
coastal plain, 179, 180, R16, *m*11, *m*167, *m*247
coastline, 108, 109, 117, 167, 175
Cobb, Geraldyn (Jerrie), 318, 319, *p*318
Cody, William "Buffalo Bill," 404, *p*404
colony, 128, 131, 196, 401
Colorado, 382, 403, R46, *m*362, *m*419, *c*405
Colorado Plateau, 13, *m*11
Colorado River, 301, 302, 305, 347, *m*11, *m*372, *m*381, *p*301
Columbus, Christopher, 38–40, *m*40
commerce, 142, 143
communication, 84
compare and contrast, 364
compass rose, H16, H17
computer, 82, 83, 316, 412, 414, *p*82
computer software, 412
conclusion, 296, 297
confederacy, 129
Confederacy, the, 203
Confederate States of America, 203
Congress, 50–52, *p*52
Connecticut, R19, *m*98
consensus, 189
conserve, 29
Constitutional Convention, 197
Constitution of the United States of America, 48–52, 137, 138, 144, 204
consumer, 74, 84
Continental Divide, 369, *m*372
convention, 138
cooperation, 127
copper mine, 412, *p*412
corn, 246, 248, *p*246
Corn Belt, 248
Corn Palace, 246, 247, *p*246
Coronado, Francisco Vásquez de, 40, 302, 333, *m*40
corral, 337
cotton, 28, 199
cotton gin, 135
covered wagon, *p*270
cowboy, 336, 340, 341, 344, 354, 355, 404, *p*340, *p*344, *p*345
***Cowboy Country*,** 354, 355
cowgirl, 340, 344, *p*344
cow town, 404
crab pot, 116, 117, *p*117
crabs, 116, 117, 386, *p*116
cranberry, 113, *m*114, *p*113
Crockett, David "Davy," 198, *p*198
crop rotation, 248
cross-section diagram, 110, 111
crude oil, 315
culture, 39, 43

Dahlonega, Georgia, 211, *m*210
Dahlonega Courthouse, 211
dam, 347, *m*347
Dead Sea, 16, *m*16
Death Valley, California, 13, 380, 382, *m*16
Declaration of Independence, 131, 144, 197, R28–R31
Deere, John, 273, 275, *p*275, R53
degree, H14, H15, *p*H15
Delaware, R19, *m*98
Delaware Bay, 119, *m*98
delta, 163, R16, *m*167
demand, 77
democracy, 47, 48, 52, 53
denim, 407
Denver, Colorado, 403, *m*20, *m*89
desert, 13, 309, 310, 346, 347, 380, R16, *p*13, *p*310, *p*380
"Desert Is Theirs, The," 310
de Soto, Hernando, 40, 195, *m*40, *m*195, R53
details, 162, 296
***Diez y seis de Septiembre*,** 336
dinosaur, 242, 244, *p*242, *p*243
Dismal Swamp, 167, *m*167, *m*170
District of Columbia, 14
diverse, 145
Dodge, Henry Chee, 327, 329, *p*329, R53
dogsled race, 378, 379, *p*378
Douglass, Frederick, 136, 137, *p*136, R53
Dr. Martin Luther King, Jr. National Historic Site, 210
drought, 274
Duluth, Minnesota, 257, *m*255
Du Sable, Jean Baptiste Point, 266, 267, *p*267, R53
Dust Bowl, 274

Eastern Cherokee, 191
economy, 76, 81, 82, 145
Edison, Thomas Alva, 135
Einstein, Albert, 133, R53

Index

election, 50, 51
electricity, 70, 105, 110, 111, 135, 183
electric light bulb, 135
elevation, 21, 167
elevation map, 170, 171, *m*170, *m*372
elk, 369, 370, *p*369
Ellis Island, New York, 132, *m*125
Empire State Building, 142
endangered species, 179
England, 131
entrepreneur, 273
***E pluribus unum*,** 44
equator, 21, 22, 408, H1, *m*21, *m*408, *p*H1
Erie Canal, 143, 280
Erie, Lake, 113, 143, 233, 235, *m*226, *m*234
erosion, 244, 301
Europe, 40, 127, 128, 132, 190, 195, 196, 269, 401, *m*40, *m*133, *m*195
Everglades National Park, 179, *m*165, *m*167
executive branch, 51
exploration, 39–41, 68, 302, 332–337, 400, 401, *m*40, *m*333
export, 141, 414
extinct, 179

fact, 208, 209
fall line, 169, R16, *m*167
farm equipment, 274, 275, *p*275
farmhouse, 272, *p*272
federal government, 48
Finger Lakes Region, 113
fishing, 116–118, 386, 395
Florida, 14, 22, 40, 42, 43, 173, 179, 180, 195, 196, 212, R19, *m*160, *m*173, *p*41
Florida Keys, 173, *m*160, *m*167
flour, 248
flowers, 386
folklore, 198
forest, R16
forest products, *m*387
fort, 266
Fort Canby, Arizona, 326, *m*326
Fort Ross, 401
Fort Sumter, 202, 203, *p*203
forty-niners, 403
fossil, 242–244, *p*242, *p*243
fossil fuel, 183
fountain of youth, 194, 195
Four Corners, *p*15
France, 41, 265, 266, 278, *m*40
Franciscan missions, 401
Franklin, Benjamin, 131
Freedmen's Bureau, 205
freedoms, political. *See* specific freedoms
Freedom Trail, 142
free enterprise system, 76, 77, *c*76
freight train, 237, *p*237
French Quarter, *p*161
freshwater, 233
frigid, 379
Frost, Robert, 107
fruit, 180, 385
fuel, 29
fur trade, 258, 264–267, 278, 401, 405

Garrison, William Lloyd, 137, R53
Gateway Arch, 276, *p*227, *p*276
generalizations, make, 306, 307
generator, 111, *p*110
geography terms, R16, *p*R16
Georgia, 173, 180, 211, R19, *m*160
Georgia State Capitol, 211
Germany, 132, *m*130
geyser, 370
ghost town, 403, 404
gila monster, *p*346
glacier, 105, 167, 233, R16
globalization, 82, 83, *m*83
globe, H12, H13, *p*H12, *p*H13
gold, 333
Golden Gate Bridge, *p*363
gold rush, 69, 211, 393, 402–404, 405, 407, *m*402, *p*69
gorge, 105
government
Cherokee and, 191
free trade and, 76
Narragansett and, 127
Navajo and, 327
United States and, 47–52
Grand Canyon National Park, 13, 297, 299–307, *m*299, *p*293, *p*301, *p*303, *p*304
Grand Teton National Park, H6–H7, *m*H6, *p*H6–H7
Granite State, 115
grape, 112, 113, *m*114, *p*112 *m*387
graphs, 240, 241
grazing, 341, 342
Great Basin, 380, 381, *m*367, *m*381
Great Britain, 132, 401, *m*133

Great Council, 129
Great Lakes, 13, 232–235, 238, 257, 280, *m*234, *p*233
Great Plains, 243, 247, 248, 258, *m*247
Great Salt Lake, 381, 412, *m*372
Great Shellfish Bay, 117
Great Smoky Mountains, 169, *m*167
greenhouse, 385
greenhouse products, 386
Green Mountains, 106, *m*H13, *m*98
Green River, 305
grid, 409
Grimké, Angelina and Sarah, 200, 201, *p*200, *p*201
growing season, 180, 347
gusher, 314, 315, *p*314

Haida, 397, 398, *p*399
haiku, 385
harvest, 27, 113, 117, 385
Havasupai, 302
Hawaii
climate of, 18, 22, 380, 382, *m*381
crops of, 385, *p*363
facts about, R19
fishing industry in, 386
Inouye and, 53
inset maps of, 24, *m*24, *m*25, *p*362
mountains in, 373, *m*372
Pacific Rim trade and, 414
statehood of, 405, 406, *c*405
Hendrickson, Sue, 242, 243, *p*242
Higgins, Pattillo, 315
highway, 282
hogs, 249
hogan, 325, 326, 328, *p*325
Hoh Rain Forest, *p*380
Hollywood, *p*411
homestead, 342
Hoopeston, Illinois, 247, *m*231
Hoover Dam, *p*363
Horseshoe Falls, 104, *m*105
hot spot, 370
hot spring, 370, *p*370
Houston, Texas, 317, *m*309
hub, 280
Hudson River, 280
humidity, 348, 349
hunting, 189
Huron, Lake, 233, *m*226, *m*234, *m*265
hurricane, 174
hurricane season, 174
hydroelectricity, 105, 110, 111, *p*110
hydropower, 105, 110, 111, *m*105, *p*110

ice age, 233
Idaho, 379, 385, 386, R19, *m*362, *c*405
Iditarod, 378, 379, *p*378
Illinois, R19, *m*226
Illinois River, 234, *m*234, *m*265
Illinois Waterway, 234, *m*234
immigrant, 45, 132, 133
import, 141, 414
Inca empire, 398
independence, 131
Independence Hall, 144
Indiana, R18, *m*226
Indians. *See* Native Americans
Indian Territory, 295, 341
Industrial Revolution, 70, 71
industry, 28, 70, 71, 143
inlet, 117
Inner Coastal Plain, 167
Inouye, Daniel, 53
inset map, 24, 25, *m*24
interdependent, 81, 82
international trade, 414, *m*414
Internet, 262, 263
interstate highway system, 282
invention, 132, 135
Iowa, R18, *m*226
Ireland, 132, *m*132
Iroquois Confederacy, 129
irrigation, 248, 347, *p*347
"I've Been Working on the Railroad," 286–287

Jackson, Andrew, 197
Jamestown, Virginia, 196, *m*195
Japanese American, 53
Jefferson, Thomas, 41, 197, 278
"Jim Crow" laws, 225
Jolliet, Louis, 41, 265, *m*40
***Josefina Saves the Day*,** 74
judicial branch, 51
justice, 51

Index

Kansas, 21, R18, *m*226
Kentucky, R18, *m*160
key, 173, H16
Key West, Florida, 173, *m*165
keyword, 262, 263
Kilauea, Mount, 373
King, Dr. Martin Luther, Jr., 206
King Ranch, Texas, 343, *m*323, *p*343
Kino, Father Eusebio, 334

La Guardia, Fiorello, 45
lake, R16
Lake Placid, New York, 107
landform, 7, 11–15, *p*12, 13
landmarks, 142
land rush, *p*271
La Salle, Robert, 195, *m*40, *m*195
lasso, 337
latitude, 408, 409, H14, H15, *p*H15, *m*409
lava, 372
law, 47, 50–52
legends, 198
legislative branch, 50
lei, *p*406
lettuce, *m*387
Levi Strauss & Company, 407
Lewelling, Seth, 389, *p*389
Lewis and Clark Expedition, 41, 278, 279, *m*279
Lewis, Meriwether, 42, 278, 279, *p*278
Lexington, Massachusetts, 131, *m*130
liberator, 137
Liberty Bell, 144
lighthouse, 108, 174, 175, *p*108, *p*174, *p*175
Lincoln, Abraham, 203, *p*203
line graph, 240, 241
livestock, 28, 385, 386, *p*386
local government, 48
locator, H16
lock, 234, 235, *p*235
longitude, 408, 409, H14, H15, *p*H15, *m*409
Long Walk, the, 326, 327, 329, *m*326
Los Alamos, New Mexico, 316
Los Angeles, California, 411, 416, 417, *m*393, *m*410, *c*413
lost colony, 196
Louis XIV, 195
Louisiana, 12, 41, 173, 195, R18, *m*160
Louisiana Territory, 41, 197, *m*41
Lucas, Anthony, 315
Lyndon B. Johnson Space Center, 295, 317, *p*294

Mackinaw, Michigan, 265
Madison, James, 197
Magazine Mountain, *m*170, *p*171
magma, 370, 372
magnolia, *p*161
Maid of the Mist, 101
mail delivery, 81
Maine, 108, R18, *m*98
main idea, 162
Mammoth Cave system, 12
manatee, 179, *p*161
Mandan Village, 279, *m*279
manufacturing, 28
maple syrup, 114, *m*114
maps
climate, *m*19, *m*20, *m*22
elevation, 170, 171, *m*170, *m*171, *m*372
inset maps, 24, 25, *m*24, *m*25, *m*35
Northeast, *m*H13
physical, *m*11, *m*R6–R7, R9, H17, *p*H17
political, R4–R5, R8, H16, *p*H16
road, *m*86, *m*89
satellite, R2–R3
Southeast, *m*H15
time-zone, 54, 55, *m*54, *m*55, *m*63, *p*55
United States, R10–R15
Western Hemisphere, R8–R9
world, *m*R4–R7
Marconi, Guglielmo, 135
Marquette, Jacques, 41, 265, *m*40
marsh, 310, 311, *p*311
Marshall, James, 402
MARTA, 212, *p*212
Maryland, 117, R19, *m*98
mask, 398, *p*189, *p*398, *p*399
Massachusetts, 108, 113, 118, 128, 131, R19, *m*98
Massachusetts Bay, 119, *m*H13, *m*98
McKinley, Mount (Denali), 13, 379, *p*379
meat packing, 339
Menotti, Gian Carlo, 214
meridian, 409
mesa, R16
metal ore, 403
Metro Rail system, 417, *m*417
Mexican Independence Day, 336

Mexican War, 41
Mexico, 41, 333–336, 340, 401, *m*11, *m*40
Mexico, Gulf of, 163, *m*19, *m*40
Michigan, 43, 249, 265, R19, *m*226, *m*265, *c*241
Michigan, Lake, 43, 232–235, 267, *m*226, *m*234, *m*265, *p*233
Michilimackinac, Michigan, 265, *m*265
Middle Atlantic states, 117, *m*98
Midwest Region
Badlands in, 242–245
boundaries of, 14
farming in, 246–249, 273–275
fur trade in, 264–266, *m*265
Great Lakes in, 233–235
immigration to, 132
landforms in, 11–13
map of, *m*226, *m*250
Native Americans in, 245, 256–259, 264–266, 271, 277
pioneers of, 270, 271
population of, *c*240, 241
rainfall patterns in, 229, 247, *m*247
resources of, 28
shipping and, 236, 237, 273, 280, 282
transportation in, 277–282
Milam Building, 348
Milwaukee, Wisconsin, 257, *m*20
mineral, 114, 115
mining, 114, 115, 183, 297, 303, 327, 402, 403, 412, 414, *p*115
Minnesota, 257, 258, R19, *m*226, *m*255
mission, 265, 334–336, 401, *p*334, *p*335
missionary, 334, 339
Mission Dolores, 334
Mission San José, 334
Mississippi, 12, R19, *m*160
Mississippi River, 12, 41, 163, 195, 234, 235, 283, *m*11, *m*38, *m*265, *p*163, *p*280
Missouri, R19, *m*226, *c*241
Missouri River, 278, *m*11, *m*279
Mitchell, Mount, 169
Mitchell, South Dakota, 246, 247
money, 74, 75, *p*75
Monks Mound, 277, *p*277
Montana, 386, R19, *m*362, *c*405
Monticello, 197, *p*197
Mott, Lucretia, 138
mound, 277
mountain, 11–13, R16. *See also* specific mountains
mountain range, R16
Mount Everest, 16, *m*16
Mount Katahdin, H13, *m*H13
Mount Kilauea, 373
Mount McKinley, 17, 379, *m*16, *m*372
Mount Mitchell, 169, *m*170, *m*185
Mount Pleasant, Michigan, 257
Mount Rushmore, *p*227
Mount St. Helens, 365
Mount Washington, H13, *m*H13
mouth, R16
movie industry, 411
Muir, John, 361
museum, 351
Myrtle Beach, South Carolina, 167, 212, *m*165

Nantucket Island, Massachusetts, 118
Narragansett Bay, 127, *m*126
Narragansett Indians, 126–128, *p*128
NASA, 317, 318
National Association for the Advancement of Colored People (NAACP), 207
national government, 48
national park, 108, 297, 370
Native Americans
Columbus and, 39
in the Midwest, 245, 256–259, 264–266, 271, 277, *p*257, *p*258
in the Northeast, 126–129, *p*128, *p*129
in the Southwest, 302, 324–329, 334–336, 340, 342, 347, *m*326, *p*295, *p*326, *p*327, *p*328
in the West, 394–399, 401
natural resources, 27–29, 76, 183, 315, 395, *p*29
Navajo, 325–328, *p*325, *p*326, *p*327 *p*328
Navajo Code Talker, 329, 330, *p*331
Navajo language, 328
Navajo Tribal Council, 327, 329
Nebraska, R20, *m*226
need, 73
Nevada, 386, 403, R20, *m*362, *m*403, *c*405
New England, 108, *m*98
New England landscape, *p*97
New Hampshire, 106, R20, *m*98
New Jersey, 108, 109, R20, *m*98
New Mexico, 294, 309, 316, 326–328, 333, 334, 336, R20, *m*274, *m*295, *m*309
newspaper, 330
New York City, New York, 45, 105, 131, 142–144, *m*142, *p*142
New York State, 43, 105, 107, R20, *m*98
"Niagara," 152

Index

Niagara Falls, 101, 104, 105, 152, *m*103, *m*105, *p*101, *p*152, *p*153
Niagara River, 105, *m*105
Nineteenth Amendment, 138
Nobel Peace Prize, 319
nonrenewable resource, 29, 183, 315
nonviolence, 206
North America, 39, 68, *m*40, *m*195, *m*401, *m*408
North Carolina, 173, 191, 196, R21, *m*160, *m*173, *m*174
North Dakota, R21, *m*226
Northeast Region
abolitionists in, 137
boundaries of, 14
cities in, 140–144, *m*142
colonies in, 131
immigration to, 132
landforms of, 12, 106–109
Native Americans in, 126–129
Niagara Falls in, 104, 105, *p*105
resources of, 28, 112–115
Northern Hemisphere, 408, H13, *p*H13
North Pole, 408, *m*408
notes, 376, 377
nuts, 180, *m*387
Nyiri Desert, 312, *m*312

Oakley, Annie, 340
ocean, 21, R16. *See also* specific oceans
Ocracoke Island, *p*174
Ohio, R21, *m*226
oil, 70, 314, 315, 327, 405, *m*414, *c*315
Ojibwa, 256–258, 264, 266, *p*257, *p*259
Oklahoma, 191, 295, 309, 317, 341, R21, *m*294, *m*309
Old Faithful, 370
Olympia National Park, *p*380
Olympic Mountains, 372, *m*372
Olympic Peninsula, 382
Ontario, Lake, 233, *m*234
On the Banks of Plum Creek, 271
opinion, 208, 209
opportunity cost, 78
Oregon, 13, 385, 401, R21, *m*362, *c*405
Oregon Territory, 42
Ottawa Indians, 259
otter, *p*363
Outer Coastal Plain, 167
outline, 376, 377
overfishing, 118

Pacific Ocean, 369, 383, 400, *m*H12, *m*11
Pacific Rim, 414, *m*414
paper, 388
parallel, 408
Parks, Rosa, 207, *p*207
peanut, 180, *p*161
Pearl Harbor, 406
peninsula, 108
Pennsylvania, 108, R21, *m*98
Philadelphia, Pennsylvania, 131, 137, 141, 142, *m*130, *m*136, *m*142
Phoenix, Arizona, 347, *m*346, *m*347
phonograph, 135
Piedmont, 168, 169, 179, m167, *p*168
Pikes Peak, 368, 369, *m*372
Pima Air and Space Museum, 316, *p*316
pineapple, *m*387
pioneer, 198, 271, 272
Pittsburgh, Pennsylvania, 141, 143, 145, *m*125, *m*142, *p*143
plain, 12, 28, 229
plantation, 198, 199, *p*199
plant nursery, 389
plants, 310, 311, 386, 389, *p*310, *p*311
plateau, 13
Platte River, *m*279
plow, 273–274, *p*273
plumb, *m*387
Plymouth, Massachusetts, 131, *m*130
Pocono Mountains, 107, *m*H13, *m*98
polar climate, 22
pollution, 118, 143, 145
Ponce de León, Juan, 40, 195, *m*40, *m*195, *p*194
Pony Express, 80
population, *c*240, *c*241, *c*413
port cities, 141, 143, 163, 237
Port of South Louisiana, 163
potato, 385, *m*387
Potawatomi Indians, 259
potlatch, 396, *p*396
Powell, John Wesley, 297, 302, 305, 306, *p*305
Powhatan Indians, 196
powwow, 128
prairie, 245, 272
prairie dog, 279

precipitation. *See* rainfall, snowfall
president, 51, 197
press, freedom of the, 52
primary source, H16, 3, 53, 61, 97, 159, 206, 207, 225, 239, 244, 261, 293, 305, 310, 329, 330, 331, 351, 353, 357, 361, 385, 416, 417, R24, R27, R28–R31
prime meridian, 409
process, 27
producers, 75
products, 28
profit, 76
Prospect Creek, Alaska, 379
prospector, 402, 403
public transportation system, 212, 416, 417, *p*212
pueblo, 302, 335
Pueblo peoples, 302, 325
Puerto Rico, 195, *m*40
pulp, 182

Qualla Boundary, North Carolina, 191, 192, *m*187, *m*188
quarry, 115, *m*114, *p*115
Quivira, 333

radio, 135
radio telescope, 316, *p*316
railroad, 54, 70, 212, 281, 286, 339, 341, 342, 403, 404, *m*281
rainfall, 229, 247, 309, 347, 365, 382, 383, *m*247, *m*309
Rainier Paradise Ranger Station, 382
rain shadow, 382, 383, *c*382
ranch, 338–343, *p*342
raw materials, 27, 70
Reconstruction, 205
recycle, 29
Red River, 12, *m*11
redwood tree, *p*363
refinery, 315
reforestation, 182, 388
region, 7, 11–15, 28, 81, *m*11
religion, freedom of, 52
renewable resource, 29, 182, 388, *p*29
represent, 47
Representatives, House of, 50
republic, 47
research, 262, 263
reservation, 128, 258, 327, 328
reservoir, 347
revolution, 131
Rhode Island, 127, 128, R21
rice, 180
river, 11
riverboat, 283
road maps, *m*86, *m*89
roadrunner, *p*295
Roanoke Island, 196
rock squirrel, *p*300
Rocky Mountains, 243, 363, 365, 369, *m*367, *m*372, *p*363, *p*365
Roosevelt, Theodore, 297, 303
Route 66, 350–351, *m*351
rural, 71
Russia, 401, 405, *m*54, *m*372

sachem, 127
saguaro, 310, 312, *p*312
Saguaro National Park, 310, *m*299
salmon, *m*387
salt, 412
Salt Lake City, Utah, 412, *m*20, *c*413
San Antonio, Texas, 334, 335, 341, 348, *m*20, *m*309, *m*332
Sandburg, Carl, 152
San Diego, California, 401, *m*H12, *m*19, *m*409
San Francisco, California, 401–403, *m*20, *m*402
Santa Barbara, California, 401
Santa Fe, New Mexico, 336, *m*309, *m*323, *m*332, *p*337
Santa Monica, California, 350
sap, 114
Sault Sainte Marie, Michigan, 265, 266, *m*255, *m*265
savanna, 310
Scandinavia, 132, *m*132
seafood, 116, 117
Sealaska Corporation, 397
sea level, 16, 170
search engine, 262, 263
sea shanty, 218
Seattle, Washington, 412, *m*20, *p*413, *c*413
secede, 203
secondary source, 330, 331
segregate, 205, 206
Senate, 50, 51
Seneca Falls, New York, 138, *m*125, *m*136

Index

Seneca, Lake, 113
sequence of events, 100, 101
Sequoyah, 190, 193, *p*193
Serra, Junipero, 401
shanty, 218
Shark Bay, 120–121, *m*121
sheep, 325, 385
shellfish, 116–118, 386
"Shenandoah," 218, 219
Shenandoah River, 218
shipping, 236, 237, 273, 277, 280, 282
Sierra Nevada, 229, 372, *m*372, *p*361, *p*373
Silver Lake, Colorado, 382
Sioux Indians, 258
slavery, 136, 137, 187, 198–201
Slavery as It Is: Testimony of a Thousand Witnesses, 201
snowfall, 382, 383
sod, 272, *p*272
software, 412
soil, 29, 168
songs
"America," 90–91
"Shenandoah," 218–219
"I've Been Working on the Railroad," 286–287
"Sweet Betsy from Pike," 420–421
Sonora Desert, 310, 312, 347, *m*309
Sonora, Mexico, 334
South Carolina, 173, 212, R20, *m*160
South Carver, Massachusetts, 113, *m*112
South Dakota, 242–247, R20, *m*226
Southeast Region
agriculture in, 180, *m*181
boundaries of, 14
Cherokee culture in, 188–193
cities of, 210–215
civil rights movement and, 206, 207
Civil War in, 187, 202–205, 208, 209, *p*204
climate and weather of, 173–175
early history of, 194–201
landforms of, 12, 167–171, *m*167, *m*170
map of, *m*160
resources of, 28, 178–183
Southern Hemisphere, 408, H13, *p*H13
South Pole, 408, *m*408
Southwest Region
boundaries of, 14
climate of, 308, 309, *m*309
desert in, 309, 346, 347
Grand Canyon in, 297, 299–307, *m*299, *p*293, *p*301, *p*303, *p*304
landforms of, 11, 13
map of, *m*294, *m*309
Native Americans in, 302, 324–329, 334–336, *m*326, *p*295, *p*327, *p*328
oil and, 314, 315, *p*314, *c*315
plants of, 310, 311, *p*310, *p*311
ranching in, 338–343, *m*341, *m*343, *p*339, *p*342, *p*343
resources of, 28
Spain and, 302, 332–337
technology in, 316, 317
soybeans, 180, 248
space flight, 317
Space Needle, 412
space shuttle, *p*160
Spain
explorers from, 40, 190, 195, 196, 401, *m*40, *m*401, *m*195
Southwest and, 302, 332–337, *m*333
territory purchased from, 41
Spanish language, 337
speech, freedom of, 52
Spindletop Hill, 314, 315
Spoleto Festival of Two Worlds, 214, 215, *m*215, *p*215
SR-71 Blackbird, *p*317
St. Albans, Vermont, 114, *m*103
St. Augustine, Florida, 196, *m*187, *m*195
St. Helens, Mount, 365
St. Lawrence Seaway, 234, 235, *m*234
St. Louis, Missouri, 73, 237, 276–280, *m*255, *m*279
Stanton, Elizabeth Cady, 138, 139, *p*139
state government, 48
Statue of Liberty, 142, 144, *p*99
steamboat, 280, *p*280
steamship, 135
steel, 70, 143, 145
"Stopping by Woods on a Snowy Evening," 107
Stowe, Harriet Beecher, 201
Strauss, Levi, 403, 407, *p*407
subarctic climate, 22, 23
"Sue," 242, *p*243
sugar beet, *m*387
sugar house, 114
sugar maple tree, 114
summary, 6
summer, 21, 22
superhighway, 282
Superior, Lake, 233, *m*226, *m*234
supply, 77
supporting details, 162
Supreme Court, 51, 115, *p*51
Sutter, John, 402
Sutter's Mill, 402, *m*393, *m*403
swamp, 179
"Sweet Betsy from Pike," 420–421
syllabary, 193

talking stick, 256, *p*256
tallow, 339
technology, 70, 316, 317
telephone, 132, 135
telescope, 316, *p*316
temperature, 13, 309, 349, 379, 380, *m*173, *m*309, *m*381
temperature climate, 23
Tennessee, 198, R20, *m*160
Texas, 41, 294, 309, 314, 315, 317, 339–341, 343, R20, *m*294, *m*309
Thailand, 250–251, *m*250
Thirteenth Amendment, 137, 204
"This Land Is Your Land," 3
Thoreau, Henry David, 97
timber, 388
timberline, 369
time line, 134, 135
time zone, 7, 54, 55, *m*54, *m*55
Tlingit, 394–399
Tlingit Cultural Region, 395, *m*393
tomato, *m*387
totem pole, 395, *p*395
trade
barter as, 73, *p*73
Cahokia and, 277
Cherokee culture and, 190
communication and, 84
European explorers and, 40, 127
free enterprise system and, 76, 77
Jefferson and, 278
Northeastern cities and, 141
Ojibwa and, 258, 264, 266
Pacific Rim and, 414
St. Louis and, 280
Tlingit and, 395
trading post, 266, 267
Trail of Tears, 191, *p*191
train, 237, *p*237
transcontinental railroad, 281, *m*281
transportation, 81–84, 141, 212, 236, 237, 277–283
tree, 29, 182, 369, 388, *p*363
Triangle Region, 213
tropical climate, 22, 23, 380
Troy Female Seminary, 139
trucks, 236, 237
Truth, Sojourner, 137
Tucson, Arizona, 346, 347, *m*323, *m*347
tugboat, *p*236
tuna, *m*387
tundra, 379
turbine, 111, *p*110
Twain, Mark, 283, *p*283
Tyrannosaurus rex, 242–243, *p*242, *p*243
Uncle Tom's Cabin, 201
Union, 203
United States
boundaries in, 14, 15
Cherokees and, 190
Civil War in, 202–205, 281, *p*204
climates of, 22, 23, *m*22
communication in, 84
culture and, 43
exploration of, 39–41, 401, *m*40
government of, 47–52, *c*50
immigration to, 132, 133
independence of, 131
industry in, 70, 71
inset maps of, 24, *m*4, *m*24, *m*25
international trade and, 414
landforms in, 12, 13
money in, 74, 75, *p*75
natural resources of, 27, 28
regions of, 11–15, *m*4, *m*11
slavery in, 136, 137
time zone maps of, *m*54, *m*55
trade in, 73, 75, 76
transportation in, 81–84, 281, *m*281
women's rights in, 138, 139
urban, 71
Utah, 328, 381, 386, 412, R20, *m*362, *c*405

Index

Valdez, Alaska, 405
vaquero, 336, 340
vegetable, 385
Vermont, 43, 106, 108, 114, 115, R20, *m*98
Vermont Maple Festival, 114
vertical time line, 134, 135
Very Large Array, 316, *p*316
vice president, 51
viceroy, 333, 335
vineyard, 113
Virginia, 173, 196, R21, *m*160
volcano, 365, 372–373, 374–375, 377
vote, right to, 138, 205

Waialeale, Mount, 382
Walden, 97
want, 73
Wapello County, Iowa, 270, 271, *m*255, *m*270
War Between the States, 203
Washington, 382, 385, 386, 401, R21, *m*362, *c*405
Washington, D.C., 14, 48, 51, 131, *m*35, *m*98
Washington, George, 131, 190, 197
water, 29
waterfall, 168, *p*168
watermen, 116, 117, *p*117
waterway, 234, *m*234
weather, 18–23, 173, 174, *m*173
Web site, 262
Weld, Theodore Dwight, 201
Welland Ship Canal, 235, *m*105, *m*234
Western Australia, 120, *m*121
Western Cherokee, 191
West Region, 11, 13, 14, 28, 69
cities of, 411–413, 416, 417
climate of, 378–383
exploration and growth of, 400–406, *m*401
map of, *m*362, *m*372, *m*381
mountains in, 365, 368, 369, 372–373, 377, *m*372, *p*369, *p*373, *p*379
Native Americans of, 394–399
Pacific Rim trade and, 414
resources in, 384–389
Yellowstone National Park in, 370–371
West Virginia, R21, *m*160
wetlands, 167, 179, 310–311, *p*311
whale watching, *p*415
whaling, 118, *p*118
wheat, 27, 248, *m*387
White House, 51, *m*35
White, John, 196
White Mountains, 106, *m*H13, *m*98
wigwam, 127, *p*127
Wilderness Road, 198
wildfire, 371
wildlife, 370
Wild West, 340, 404
Willamette Valley, Oregon, 385
Williams, Roger, 128
Window Rock, Arizona, 327, *m*323, *m*324
winter, 21, 379, 380
Wisconsin, 249, R21, *m*226
women's rights movement, 138, 139, 140, 141
wood, 388
World Trade Center, 148
World War II, 53, 329, 330, 405, 406
World Wide Web, 262
Wright, Orville and Wilbur, 135
Wyoming, 370, R21, *m*362, *c*405

Yakima, Washington, 382
Yearling, The, 179
Yellowstone National Park, 370, 371, *m*368, *p*370, *p*371

zebra mussels, 238, *p*238

Credits

TEXT: Dorling Kindersley (DK) is an international publishing company specializing in the creation of high-quality reference content for books, CD-ROMs, online and video. The hallmark of DK content is its unique combination of educational value and strong visual style. This combination allows DK to deliver appealing, accessible and engaging educational content that delights children, parents and teachers around the world. Scott Foresman is delighted to have been able to use selected extracts of DK content within this Social Studies program.

140–141 from *First Ladies* by Amy Pastan in association with the Smithsonian Institution. Copyright © 2001 by Dorling Kindersley Limited and the Smithsonian Institution.

176–177 from Eyewitness: Hurricane & Tornado by Jack Challoner. Copyright © 2000 by Dorling Kindersley Limited.

374–375 from Eyewitness: Volcano & Earthquake by Susanna Van Rose. Copyright © 1992 by Dorling Kindersley Limited.

From *The Yearling* by Marjorie Kinnan Rawlings. Text copyright © 1938 Marjorie Kinnan Rawlings; copyright renewed © 1966 Norton Baskin. Reprinted with the permission of Atheneum Books for Young Readers, an imprint of Simon & Schuster Children's Publishing Division and Brandt & Hochman Literary Agents, Inc. p.179

"Ripening Cherries" by Florence Vilén. Reprinted by permission of the author. p.385

"Sweet Betsy from Pike" adapted and arranged by Lillian Wiedman. Reprinted by permission of Pearson Education, Inc. p.420

Text excerpt from *Cowboy Country* by Ann Herbert Scott. Text copyright © 1993 by Ann Herbert Scott. Reprinted by permission of Clarion Books/Houghton Mifflin Company. All rights reserved. p.354

Illustration from *Cowboy Country* by Ann Herbert Scott, pictures by Ted Lewin. Illustrations copyright © 1993 by Ted Lewin. Reprinted by permission of Clarion Books/Houghton Mifflin Company. All rights reserved. p.354

"Stopping by Woods on a Snowy Evening" by Robert Frost from *The Poetry of Robert Frost*, Edward Connery Lathem. Copyright © 1969 by Henry Holt and Co., copyright © 1951 by Robert Frost. Reprinted by permission of Henry Holt and Company, LLC. p.107

From *The Desert Is Theirs* by Byrd Baylor. Copyright © 1975 by Byrd Baylor. Reprinted by permission of Atheneum Books for Young Readers, an imprint of Simon & Schuster Children's Publishing. p.310

From *On the Banks of Plum Creek* by Laura Ingalls Wilder. Text copyright © 1937 by Laura Ingalls Wilder. Copyright renewed © 1965 Roger L. MacBridge. Used by permission of HarperCollins Publishers. p.273

Reprinted from *Josefina Saves the Day* by Valerie Tripp with permission from Pleasant Company. p.74

"Niagara" from *The People, Yes* by Carl Sandburg, copyright © 1936 by Harcourt Brace & Company and renewed 1964 by Carl Sandburg. Reprinted by permission. p.152

From "This Land Is Your Land" words and music by Woody Guthrie. TRO Copyright © 1956 (Renewed) 1958 (Renewed) 1970 (Renewed) Ludlow Music, Inc., New York, New York. Used by permission. p.iii, 3

MAPS: MapQuest.com, Inc.

ILLUSTRATIONS:
16, 17, 21, 382, R16, R17 Leland Klanderman; 36 Paul Bachem; 48, 50 Paul Perreault; 67 Neal Armstrong; 83 Joe LeMonnier; 110 Robert Lawson; 119, 402 Mike Reagan; 174, 181, 387, 389 Susan J. Carlson; 200, 201 Robert Gunn; 208 Julian Mulock; 235 Robert Van Nutt; 239, 303 Albert Lorenz; 279 Guy Porfirio; 286, 350 Darryl Ligasan; 354, 355 © Ted Lewin 389 Richard Waldrep; 414, 417 Peter Siu; 414 Elizabeth Wolf; 420 John Sandford

PHOTOGRAPHS:
Every effort has been made to secure permission and provide appropriate credit for photographic material. The publisher deeply regrets any omission and pledges to correct errors called to their attention in subsequent editions.

Unless otherwise acknowledged, all photographs are the property of Scott Foresman, a division of Pearson Education.

Cover: © Panoramic Images, Chicago, (BR) © F. Schussler/PhotoLink/PhotoDisc
Endsheets: Front - Left page: (BCL), (TL), (TR) Hemera Technologies, (BC) © Richard Price/Getty Images, (BL) © Reza Estakhrian/Getty Images, (BR) © Adam Woolfitt/Corbis, (CR) PhotoDisc, Front - Right page: © Panoramic Images, Chicago, (BC) © Amanda Clement/PhotoDisc, (TR) © Kunio Owaki/Corbis Stock Market, (CR) © C. Borland/PhotoLink/PhotoDisc (BR) Hemera Technologies, (BL) Superstock, (RC) © F. Schussler/PhotoLink/PhotoDisc, Back - Left page: (BL) © Joseph Sohm/Visions of America/Corbis, (TR) © Joseph Sohm/Chromosohm/Photo Researchers, Inc., (CR) Hemera Technologies, Back - Right page: (BL) Hemera Technologies, (CR) © Laurie Rubin/Getty Images, PhotoDisc
Front Matter:
E1 (TL) © Corbis, (C) © Heidi Zeiger Photography, (BCL) © Brian Post/Mount Washington Observatory, (CR, Bkgd) © Hemera Technologies, (B) © David R. Frazier Photolibrary, (BL) © Ed Pritchard/Getty Images; E2 (BCL) © Geoffrey Clements/Corbis, © eStock Photo, (TCL) © Corbis, (BCL) © MAPS.com/Corbis; E3 (BCL) © M. Gibson/Robertstock.com, (BCL) © Corbis, (BCL) © Steve Dunwell/Folio Inc., (Bkgd) © Mark E. Gibson Stock Photography, (BCL) © Bob Rowan, Progressive

Credits

Image/Corbis; E4 (BCL) © Flip Chalfant/Getty Images, © Ed Young/Corbis; E4-5 (C) © David W. Hamilton; E5 (BCL) © Terres du Sud/Sygma/Corbis, © Comstock Inc., © Getty Images; E6 (Inset) Corbis, (BCL) © Hulton-Deutsch Collection/Corbis; E6-7 (BCL) © A & L Sinibaldi/Getty Images; E7 (BCL) © G. Brad Lewis/Photo Researchers, Inc., © Galen Rowell/Corbis; E8-9 (Bkgd) © David Metsky; E9 (CC) © C.W. Biedel, M.D./Photri – Microstock, (BCL) © Christopher J. Morris/Corbis, © Brian Post/Mount Washington Observatory, © Cosmo Condina/Getty Images; E10 © B.S.P. I./Corbis; E10-11 (TCL, TR, TCR, CL) © Heidi Zeiger Photography, (Bkgd) © Getty Images; E11 (TCL) © Getty Images, (R) © Robert Holmes/Corbis, (BR) © Volker Mohrke/Corbis; E12-13 (CR) © Richard Cummins/Corbis; E13 (Inset) © Courtesy Women's Museum; E14 (BL) © Dave G. Houser/Houserstock, Inc., (CL) © James A. Sugar/Getty Images; E14-15 (BC, C, L) © David R. Frazier Photolibrary, (BL) © James Randklev/Getty Images, (BR) © David Hughes/Alamy.com; E15 (CR) © David W. Hamilton/Getty Images, (CR) © A. Witte/ C. Mahaney/Getty Images, (CR) © David Olsen/Getty Images, (BC) © Getty Images; E16 (TC) © Gary Randall/Getty Images. (CL) © Ed Pritchard/Getty Images; iv SuperStock v Art Resource, NY vi Jacquelyn Modesitt Schindehette vii (Detail) Estate of Grant Wood/Licensed by VAGA, New York, NY/Joslyn Museum, Omaha, NE/SuperStock viii Christie's Images/Corbis ix Geoffrey Clements/Corbis x (C) Julie Habel/Corbis, (T) Earth Imaging/Stone xii, xiii © Panoramic Images, Chicago H4 Colonial Williamsburg Foundation H5 Colonial Williamsburg Foundation H6 (Bkgd) Index Stock Imagery, (R) © Raymond Gehman/Corbis, (L) © David Muench/Corbis H7 (R) Greg Martin/SuperStock, (L) © Dewitt Jones/Corbis H8 Earth Imaging/Getty Images H17 © David Young-Wolff/Getty Images

Unit 1:

5 (TL) © Panoramic Images, Chicago, (BL) Laurence Parent, (BR) © Panoramic Images, Chicago, (CL) © Kathleen Brown/Corbis, (TR) © Walter Bibikow/Getty Images 8 (B) SuperStock, (C) © Julie Habel/ Corbis, (T) © Mark Wagner/Getty Images 10 Tom Burnside/Photo Researchers, Inc. 12 (B) © Bob Krist/Getty Images, (T) © Ron Thomas/Getty Images, (Bkgd) © Chris Sanders/Getty Images 13 (R) Jack Hoehn/Index Stock Imagery, (L) Larry Lefever/Grant Heilman Photography 14 (B) © Joseph Sohm/Corbis, (T) L © Kevin R. Morris/ Corbis 15 © Dave G. Houser/Corbis 18 NOAA /Weatherstock 22 Carl Purcell/Words and Pictures 23 (L) © Doug Wilson/Corbis, (R) PhotoDisc 26 Texas Department of Transportation 27 (TC) PhotoDisc, (BR) Eascott/ Momatuk/Animals Animals/Earth Scenes, (TR) Artville, (BL) Steve Satushek 28 (T) PhotoDisc, (B) © Comstock Inc. 29 (B) Mark E. Gibson/Visuals Unlimited, (T) Grelad & Buff Corsi/Visuals Unlimited 30 Jim Emery/Folio Inc. 31 Mark E. Gibson/Visuals Unlimited 33 (BCC) Leonard Lee Rue/Bruce Coleman Collection, (TL) © David W. Hamilton/Getty Images, (TCL) © Aldo Torelli/Getty Images, (BCL) René Burri/© Magnum Photos, (BL) © A. & L. Sinibaldi/Getty Images, (TCCL) © Dorling Kindersley, (TCCR) © Gary Irving/Getty Images, (TC) PhotoDisc, (TR) © Gene Ahrens, (BR) © Dorling Kindersley, (TCR) Dennis Stock/© Magnum Photos, (BCR) © Richard Hamilton Smith/Corbis 34 Patrick J. Endres/Visuals Unlimited 36 (B) © Andy Sacks/Getty Images, (C) Robert Clay/Visuals Unlimited 38 Museum of the History of Science, Oxford 39 Breck P. Kent/Animals Animals/Earth Scenes 41 Corbis 42 (T) Courtesy National Archives of the United States (from THE NATIONAL ARCHIVES OF THE UNITED STATES by Herman J. Viola, ©1984 Harry N. Abrams, Inc. New York), (B) SuperStock 43 SuperStock 44 Sandy Vanderlaan/Visuals Unlimited 45 Bettmann/Corbis 47 Mike Pattisall/Photri, Inc. 49 (B) Don Farrall/PhotoDisc, (C) Phil Martin/PhotoEdit, (T) SuperStock 51 Supreme Court Historical Society/Richard W. Strauss/Smithsonian Institution 52 Vivian Ronay 53 (Bkgd) © David Muench/Corbis, (L) Corbis, (BR) Courtesy, Senator Daniel Inouye 57 Photri, Inc. 58 (B) Jeff Cadge 59 © Andy Sacks/Getty Images 60, 61 Ruben R. Ramirez/El Paso Times 62 PhotoDisc 64 (C) Hulton Archive, (B) © Lawrence Manning/Corbis, (T) © Mike McQueen/Getty Images 66 N. Carter/North Wind Picture Archives 67 Museum of Mankind/© Dorling Kindersley 68 Culver Pictures Inc. 69 (B) The Granger Collection, New York, (T) © Mike McQueen/Getty Images 70 Detroit Industry, North Wall (Detail), 1932-1933, Diego M. Rivera, Gift of Edsel B. Ford, photograph ©2001/Detroit Institute of Arts 72 Gallo Images/Corbis 73 Hulton/Archive/Getty Images 75 British Museum/© Dorling Kindersley 77 (T) Jeff Greenberg/Visuals Unlimited, (B) Reuters/ Corbis 78 (L) © Kelly-Mooney Photography/Corbis, (R) A. Ramey/PhotoEdit 79 © Tessa Codrington /Getty Images 80 St. Joseph Museum, St. Joseph, Missouri 81 (T) Bettman/Corbis, (B) © Bruce Hands/Getty Images 82 (R) © Jim Sugar/Corbis, (L) Robert Holmgren/Peter Arnold, Inc. 83 (R) Robert Holmgren/Peter Arnold, Inc., (L) © Lester Lefkowitz/ Getty Images, (C) L. O'Shaughnessy/H. Armstrong Roberts 85 Siede Preis/PhotoDisc 88 PhotoDisc 90, 91 (Bkgd) © Panoramic Images, Chicago

Unit 2:

95, 96, 97 Art Resource, NY 98 (B) © Walter Bibikow/Getty Images 99 (TCL) © Bob Rowan/Corbis, (BCL) Randa Bishop, (CC) Donovan Reese/PhotoDisc, (R) © V.C.L/Getty Images 101 SuperStock 102 (T) © Cosmo Condina/Getty Images, (B) © Lynda Richardson/Corbis, (C) ©Jonathan Blair/Corbis 104 © Paul A. Souders/Corbis 106 © Raymond Gehman/Corbis 107 (T) AFP/Corbis, (B) © Susan Rosenthal/Corbis 108 © Buddy Mays/Corbis 109 Preston J. Garrison/Visuals Unlimited 112 © Kunio Owaki/Corbis Stock Market 113 Marilyn "Angel" Wynn/Nativestock 114 Ted Levin/Animals Animals/ Earth Scenes 115 © Joseph Sohm; ChromoSohm Inc/Corbis 116 © Lynda Richardson/Corbis 117

Credits

Sonda Dawes/Image Works 118 (B) SuperStock, (T) Courtesy Nantucket Historical Association 119 © Josh Reynolds/Image Works 120 (T) H. Armstrong Roberts, (Bkgd) Viesti Collection, Inc. 121 (T) James Watt/ Animals Animals/Earth Scenes, (C) Eric Kamp/ Index Stock Imagery, (B) © Paul A. Souders/ Corbis 122 © Lowell Georgia/Corbis 124 (TC) SuperStock, (BC) Hulton-Deutsch Collection Limited/Corbis, (B) SuperStock, (T) North Wind Pictures/North Wind Picture Archives 126 AP/Wide World Photos 127 (B) North Wind Pictures/North Wind Picture Archives, (T) Marilyn "Angel" Wynn/Nativestock 128 AP/Wide World 129 Marilyn "Angel" Wynn/ Nativestock 130 SuperStock 131 SuperStock 132 Bettmann-Corbis 135 (T), (CC), (CBC), (BC), (B) Stock Montage Inc., (TC) The Granger Collection, New York 136 The Granger Collection, New York 137 Bettmann/Corbis 138 Library of Congress/Corbis 139 (Bkgd) AP/Wide World, (R) Bettmann Archive/Bettmann-Corbis, (L) Corbis, (Bkgd) Hulton-Deutsch Collection/Corbis, (Bkgd) Library of Congress/Corbis, (Bkgd) Hulton/Archive/ Getty Images 140, 141 140 National Museum of American History, Behring Center/Smithsonian Institution 141 (TL, TR) National Museum of American History, Behring Center/Smithsonian Institution, (B) Library of Congress 143 Hulton/Archive/Getty Images 145 SuperStock 146 © Richard T. Nowitz/Corbis 147 (R) SuperStock, (L) © Patrick Ward/Corbis, (Bkgd) © Steven Rothfeld/Getty Images 148, 149 Ethan Moses 150 Marilyn "Angel" Wynn/Nativestock 152, 153 Brooklyn Museum of Art, New York, USA/Bridgeman Art Library International Ltd.

Unit 3:

157, 158, 159 Jacquelyn Modesitt Schindehette 160 © Panoramic Images, Chicago 161 (TL) © Ken Reid/Getty Images, (CL) Laszlo Selly/FoodPix, (BL) Cousteau Society/Getty Images, (CR) Benn Mitchell, (TR) PhotoDisc 163 George Gerster/Photo Researchers, Inc. 164 (T) © Michael T. Sedham/ Corbis, (C) SuperStock, (B) © Kevin Fleming/Corbis 166 © Randy Faris/Corbis 168 (T) ©James Carmichael/Getty Images, (B) © David Muench/Corbis 171 Laurence Parent 172 (R) © Nicole Duplaix/ Corbis, (L) © Forest Johnson/Corbis 175 Michael Brindle/ BrindlePix 176 (T) © David Toase/Travel Ink, (BL) © Dr. A. C. Waltham/Robert Harding 176 (BR) © Gary Williams/Getty Images 177 (R) © Volvox/Index Stock Imagery 178 SuperStock 179 Rick Baetsen/ Visuals Unlimited 180 SuperStock 182 (T) PhotoDisc, (B) © Ric Ergenbright/Corbis 183 (T) Breck P. Kent/Animals Animals/Earth Scenes 184 Colorstock/ Getty Images 185 Warren Faidley/ Weatherstock 186 (TC) © Karen Huntt Mason/Corbis, (B) SuperStock, (T) Marilyn "Angel" Wynn/Nativestock, (BC) Fort Sumpter/Visuals Unlimited 188 North Wind Picture Archives 189 (C), (B) Marilyn "Angel" Wynn/ Nativestock, (T) Richard A. Cooke/Corbis 190 The Granger Collection, New York 191 The Granger Collection, New York 192 Marilyn "Angel" Wynn/ Nativestock 193 (L) © Galen Rowell/Corbis, (R) Newberry Library, Chicago/SuperStock, (Bkgd) Marilyn "Angel" Wynn/Nativestock 194 SuperStock 195 North Wind Picture Archives 196 © Karen Huntt Mason/Corbis 197 (T) Monticello/Thomas Jefferson Foundation, Inc., (B) North Wind Picture Archives 198 (L) Burstein Collection/Corbis 199 (TL) © Franz-Marc Frei/Corbis 201 AP/Wide World 202 Fort St. Joseph Museum 203 (B) North Wind Picture Archives, (T) Stock Montage Inc. 204 Photri, Inc. 205 The Granger Collection, New York 206 © Flip Schulke/Corbis 207 (B) Carlos Osorio/AP/Wide World, (Bkgd) Bettmann/ Corbis, (T) Rus Baxley Photography 210 © Joseph Sohm; ChromoSohm/ Corbis 211 Hulton/Archive/ Getty Images 212 David Sailors Photography 213 © Eric Horan 214 (BL) © Annie Griffiths Belt/Corbis, (BR) William Struhs, (TL) Margot Granitsas/Image Works 215 (TR) Wade Spees/AP/ Wide World, (C) Margot Granitsas/Image Works 216 (TR) Marilyn "Angel" Wynn/Nativestock 218, 219 (Bkgd) © Richard A. Cooke/Corbis

Unit 4:

223, 224, 225 (C) (Detail) Estate of Grant Wood/Licensed by VAGA, New York, NY/Joslyn Museum, Omaha, NE/SuperStock 226 © Panoramic Images, Chicago 227 (TL) © James L. Amos/Corbis, (TR) Larry Lefever/Grant Heilman Photography, (BL) © Vladimir Pcholkin /Getty Images, (BR) SuperStock, (CL) Joel Sartore/Grant Heilman Photography 229 Detail) Estate of Grant Wood/Licensed by VAGA, New York, NY/Joslyn Museum, Omaha, NE/SuperStock 230 B) © Patti McConville/Getty Images, (TC) © Dave G. Hauser/Corbis, (T) John Sohlden/Visuals Unlimited, (C) Tim Brown/Index Stock Imagery 232 Wendella Sightseeing Boats 233 B) © Macduff Everton/Corbis, (T) WorldSat International/ Science Source/Photo Researchers, Inc. 236 © Bruce Forster/Getty Images 237 Skip Nall/PhotoDisc 238 (T) Peter Yates/TimePix, (B) Dave Haas/The Image Finders 242 Emile Wamsteker/AP/Wide World 243 Reuters/NewMedia, Inc./Corbis 244 Tim Brown/Index Stock Imagery 245 SuperStock 246 (R) © Tom Bean/Corbis, (L) Artville 248 TL) © Wayne Eastep/Getty Images, (TR) © Charles O'Rear/Corbis, (BL) Zefa Visual Media - Germany/Index Stock Imagery, (BC) Inga Spence/Index Stock Imagery, (BR) Nigel Cattlin/H.S. Int./Photo Researchers, Inc., (TC) © Willard Clay/Getty Images 249 (T) © Macduff Everton/Corbis, (B) Judd Pilossof/FoodPix 250 (B) Getty Images, (CR) © Jim Richardson/ Corbis 251 (T) © Yann Layma/Getty Images, (BR) SuperStock 252 N. Carter/North Wind Picture Archives 254 TC) © Layne Kennedy/Corbis, (B) PhotoDisc, (T) Minnesota Historical Society, (BC) Fred Hultstrand History in Pictures Collection, NDSU-NDIRS, Fargo 256 Marilyn "Angel" Wynn/Nativestock 257 Minnesota Historical Society 258 © Peter Turnley/Corbis 259 © Phil Schermeister/Corbis 264 © Lowell Georgia/Corbis 266 © Layne Kennedy/Corbis 267 © Dallas and John Heaton/Corbis 268-269 © Colonial Williamsburg Foundation 270 Fred Hultstrand History in Pictures Collection, NDSU-NDIRS, Fargo 271 Michael Maslan

Credits

Historic Photographs/Corbis 272 Corbis 273 B) "Detail image" of John Deere Carries New Plow to Test Site by Walter Haskell Hinton, oil on canvas, 11x16 inches/Courtesy of the John Deere Art Collection, (T) Wallace Kirkland/TimePix, (Bkgd) PhotoDisc 274, 275 (B) Smithsonian Institution 276 (BL) PhotoDisc 277 Cahokia Mounds State Historic Site 278 R) North Wind Pictures/North Wind Picture Archives, (L), (C) Independence National Historical Park 280 Currier & Ives/The Granger Collection, New York 283 R) The Granger Collection, New York, (CL) Lowell Observatory/AURA/NOAO/NSF 284 Marilyn "Angel" Wynn/Nativestock

Unit 5:

291, 292, 293 Christie's Images/Corbis 294 (B) Laurence Parent 295 CL) Hal Gage/Index Stock Imagery, (CR) Corbis, (TR) Jess Alford/ PhotoDisc, (BC) © Steve Bly/Getty Images, (TL) © Dewitt Jones/Corbis 297 © Eddie Hironaka/Getty Images 298 T) © John Beatty/Getty Images, (C) © Art Wolfe/Getty Images, (B) © David Muench/Corbis 301 © John Beatty/Getty Images 302 © Buddy Mays/ Corbis 303 SuperStock 304 © Marc Romanelli/Getty Images 305 Bkgd) © Marc Romanelli/Getty Images, (L), (R) © John K. Hillers/Corbis 306 (B) R. Kord/H. Armstrong Roberts 308 T) © Frank Lane Picture Agency/Corbis, (B) © Art Wolfe/Getty Images 310 T) © Granitsas/Getty Images, (B) © Charles C. Place/Getty Images 311 R) © David Muench/Corbis, (L) Jack Ryan/Photo Researchers, Inc. 312 L) © Dallas and John Heaton/Corbis, (R) © David Muench/ Corbis 313 (B) © Papilio/Corbis, (T) © Gallo Images/ Corbis 314 Hulton/Archive/Getty Images 316 B) © Roger Ressmeyer/Corbis, (TR) Courtesy of the Pima Air & Space Museum 317 James P. Rowan Stock Photography 318 AP/Wide World Photos 319 B) Rhoda Sidney/PhotoEdit, (T) Courtesy Jerrie Cobb Foundation, Inc. 320 T) © John Beatty/Getty Images, (B) © John K. Hillers/Corbis 322 BC) King Ranch, Inc., Kingsville, Texas, (B) Bob Rowan; Progressive Image/Corbis, (T) Rachel Epstein/Image Works, (TC) Danny Lehman/Corbis 324 Tom Bean 325 B) North Wind Picture Archives, (TR) American Museum of Natural History/© Dorling Kindersley 326 B) Arthur Olivas, Detail, #38194/Museum of New Mexico, (T) Bettmann/Corbis 328 SuperStock 329 Bkgd) Corbis, (R) Arthur Olivas, Detail, #15950/Ben Wittick/Courtesy of Museum of New Mexico, (L) Edmond Van Hoorick/PhotoDisc 331 Marine Corps/Department of Defense 332 Wallace Collection, London, UK/Bridgeman Art Library International Ltd. 335 © Sandy Felsenthal/ Corbis 336 Kolvoord/Image Works 337 © Danny Lehman/Corbis 338 Mark Culbertson/Index Stock Imagery 339 Inga Spence/Visuals Unlimited 340 (T) Corbis-Bettmann, (B) Corbis 342 Archives and Manuscripts Division of the Oklahoma Historical Society 343 King Ranch, Inc., Kingsville, Texas 344, 345 Smithsonian Institution 346 (BR) © Brian Kenney 347 © Thomas Wiewandt/Getty Images 348 Carrier Corporation 349 B) Bettmann Archive/Corbis, (T) Corbis, (Bkgd) Eddie Stangler/Index Stock Imagery 350, 351 Alan Rose 352 SuperStock 356 © Gary Randall/Getty Images 357 Arthur Olivas Detail, #15950/Ben Wittick/Courtesy of Museum of New Mexico

Unit 6:

359, 360, 361 Geoffrey Clements/Corbis 362 (B) © Kathleen Brown/Corbis 363 TL) © Stuart Westmorland/Getty Images, (TC) PhotoDisc, (BL) Eyewire, Inc., (C) © Robert Cameron/Getty Images, (TR) V.C.L./Getty Images 365 L) © Craig Aurness/Corbis, (R) L. Carstens/H. Armstrong Roberts 366 B) Carmen Northen/Index Stock Imagery, (T) Raymond K. Gehman/NGS Image Collection, (C) Neil Gilchrist/© Panoramic Images, Chicago 368 © Joseph Sohm/Corbis, (B) Richard Day/© Panoramic Images, Chicago 369 Tom J. Ulrich/Visuals Unlimited 370 (B) © Panoramic Images, Chicago 371 C) Chuck Nacke/Woodfin Camp & Associates, (T) Ken M. Johns/Photo Researchers, Inc. 373 © George D. Lepp/Corbis 374 TR) © Photri/Robert Harding, (TL), (BR) © Gary Rosenquist, 1980, (BL) © Dorling Kindersley, (CL) University of California/GSF 375 TL) Robert Harding, (TR), (C) © Lawrence Burr/Getty Images, (B) © Gary Rosenquist, 1980 378 Alaska Stock 379 © Harvey Lloyd/Getty Images 380 A&E Morris/Visuals Unlimited 381 Richard Olsenius/NGS Image Collection 383 Jeff Greenberg/Image Works 384 Burke/Triolo Productions/FoodPix 385 © Phil Degginger/Getty Images 386 T) Vanessa Vick/Photo Researchers, Inc., (B) Peter Adams/Index Stock Imagery 388 Gary C. Will/Visuals Unlimited 389 (C) Grant Symon, (Bkgd) Ross Frid/Visuals Unlimited 390 © Craig Aurness/Corbis 392 T) AK/Haines/Photri, Inc., (C) Hulton/Archive/Getty Images, (B) Mark Richards/PhotoEdit 394 Porterfield/Chickerine/Photo Researchers, Inc. 395 Jeff Greenberg/Image Works 396 B) Marilyn "Angel" Wynn/ Nativestock, (T) Lawrence Migdale/Photo Researchers, Inc. 398 BL) Adam Woolfit/Woodfin Camp & Associates, (TR) Robert Frerck/Woodfin Camp & Associates 399 Canadian Museum of Civilization 400 Chuck Place Photography 403 Hulton/Archive/Getty Images 404 T) Corbis-Bettmann, (B) Geoff Clifford/Woodfin Camp & Associates 405 One Mile Up, Inc. 406 (CL) PhotoDisc 407 L) Nancy Richmond/Image Works, (Bkgd) Corbis, (R) SuperStock 410 © James Cotier/Getty Images 411 (B) © Kurt Krieger/Corbis, (T) © Robert Landau/Corbis 412 © Scott T. Smith/Corbis 413 Stocktrek/PhotoDisc 415 © Paul Chesley/Getty Images 416 B) © Shelley Gazin/Corbis, (T) Lester Sloan/Woodfin Camp & Associates 418 © Galen Rowell/Corbis

End Matter:

R1 Earth Imaging/Getty Images R2 Earth Imaging/ Getty Images R18, R19 One Mile Up, Inc. R20, R21 One Mile Up, Inc. R24 One Mile Up, Inc. R26, R27 (Bkgd) Bettmann/Corbis R38 BR) © Sandy Felsenthal/Corbis, (TR) SuperStock, (TR) © Peter Cade/Getty Images, (L) © Julie Habel/Corbis R43 © Galen Rowell/Corbis

08160, 08161, 08162, 08163, 08164

Facing Fear: Helping Students Cope with Tragic Events

Together, we can save a life

As much as we would like to protect our children, we cannot shield them from personal or community tragedies. We can, however, help them to be prepared for unforeseen dangerous events and to learn about facing and moving beyond their fears and related concerns.

Common Responses to Trauma and Disaster

Young people experience many common reactions after a trauma. These include reexperiencing the event (for example, flashbacks), avoidance and numbing of feelings, increased agitation, and changes in functioning. These reactions may be manifested in clingy behaviors, mood changes, increased anxieties, increased startle responses (for example, more jumpy with noises), physical complaints, and regressive behavior. Increased aggressive behaviors may also be seen. When the trauma or disaster is human-made, such as a terrorist event, young people may react with hurtful talk, behaviors, or play. All of these reactions are normal responses and will, in general, dissipate with time. However, should these persist or increase over time, a referral to a mental health professional might be considered. Similarly, should these reactions result in a danger to self or others, immediate action is warranted.

Issues of Safety, Security, and Trust

In the aftermath of terrorism or other tragic events, students can feel overwhelmed with concerns of safety, security, and trust. Worries about their own safety as well as the safety of those important in their lives are likely heightened. Although they have developed a sense of empathy and are concerned about others, their immediate needs for personal reassurance will take priority. They will need repeated reassurances about their safety and the safety of those around them. They may have concerns about the event reoccurring; this concern may be exacerbated by repeated exposure to media images. At times students may feel as if they are reexperiencing the event. They may have triggers for memories, such as noises, sights, or smells. These "flashbacks" may also occur without an obvious reminder. Reexperiencing can be very frightening for students this age. They may try (without success) to NOT think about the event. Their inability to block the thoughts may produce increased levels of stress. Although students will continue to process recent events, a return to a classroom routine is one of the best ways to reinforce a sense of security and safety.

Expressing Thoughts and Feelings

Young people seven to twelve years old have the ability to understand the permanence of loss from trauma. They may become preoccupied with details of it and want to talk about it continually. The questions and the details discussed are often disturbing to adults (for example, talk of gore and dismemberment). Such discussions are not meant to be uncaring or insensitive but rather are the way that many students attempt to make sense of a tragedy. Since their thinking is generally more mature than that of students under seven, their understanding of the disaster is more complete. They understand the irreversibility of death but may continue to ask questions about death and dying as they try to understand the repercussions of the event.

Students this age will attempt to create the "story" of the terrorist action or tragic event. Unfortunately, their attempts will contain misinformation as well as misperceptions. Unless addressed directly, the misunderstanding may be perpetuated and lead to increased levels of stress. Students are trying to make the story "fit" into their concept of the world around them. Questions related to the trauma may be equally repetitive. Teachers may answer students' questions only to have the same questions repeated within a few minutes. Having the same answer will increase the students' sense of security and help them process the trauma.

One result of a human-made tragedy may be intense feelings of anger and a sense of revenge. With an inaccurate understanding of events, these feelings may develop into hateful/hurtful talk or play. It may be directed toward classmates or groups of people. This behavior should be immediately addressed. Open discussions with these young students may improve their understanding of the event as well as reduce inappropriate direction of anger toward others.

Identifying Factors to Predict Students at Greatest Risk

Feelings accompanying the event may overwhelm elementary-aged students. In addition to the anger, they may also have feelings of guilt and intense sadness; nervousness is also seen. As they attempt to process these feelings, a change in school performance may be seen. Some students will have a drop in school performance as attention to and concentration on their work are diminished. They may not be able to grasp new concepts as easily as before the event, and grades may show a decline. Students may become more active in their behaviors as well as more impulsive and reckless. These behaviors often appear similar to attention deficit hyperactivity disorder and/or learning disabilities. Although either may be present, the impact of the event as a reason for the behavior changes should be considered. Students may develop problems in sleep and appetite after a traumatic event or disaster. These changes may contribute to a decrease in school performance.

It is important to note that some students may try to handle feelings of guilt and worry by an intense attention to schoolwork. These students may be worried about disappointing teachers and parents. Through their intense focus on school, they may be attempting to avoid activities and thoughts that are disturbing.

Students' anxiety and fear may be seen in an increased number of physical complaints. These may include headaches, stomachaches, feelings of nausea, or vague aches and pains. Expression of these emotions may also be seen in mood changes.

(continued on the following page)

De la escuela al hogar

Unidad 1 **Boletín**

Estas son las ideas principales que estamos estudiando:

- ★ Los Estados Unidos se dividen en cinco regiones, además del Distrito de Columbia.
- ★ Hay muchos factores que influyen en el clima, que varía de una región a otra.
- ★ Cada región tiene recursos especiales.
- ★ Los Estados Unidos son una nación diversa que cuenta con personas de muy distintas procedencias y culturas.
- ★ El gobierno de los Estados Unidos da a los ciudadanos el poder de elegir a representantes que redactan y hacen cumplir las leyes.
- ★ Los ciudadanos tienen derechos y responsabilidades.
- ★ La riqueza de recursos de los Estados Unidos ha atraído a muchas personas al continente y a regiones específicas durante nuestra historia.
- ★ Las personas comercian con los bienes y servicios que necesitan y quieren.
- ★ Las regiones de los Estados Unidos y las naciones del mundo dependen unas de otras.

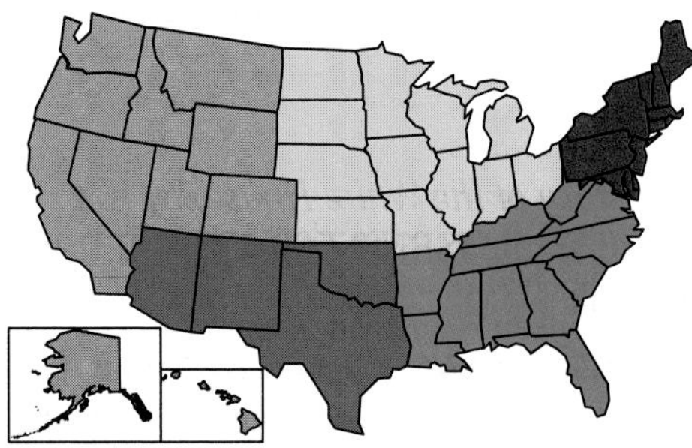

Datos curiosos

El monte McKinley, en Alaska, con una altura de 20,320 pies, es el lugar más alto de los Estados Unidos. Badwater, en el valle de la Muerte, California, con una altura de 282 pies por debajo del nivel del mar, es el punto más bajo.

Actividades en familia

Para conversar

Hable con su niño o niña acerca de las regiones de los Estados Unidos y los accidentes geográficos de cada una. Comenten cómo es el clima de su región. Hablen acerca de formas en que los accidentes geográficos y el clima pueden afectar la comunicación y el transporte en los Estados Unidos.

Para aprender juntos

Ayude a su niño o niña a aprender cosas sobre la comunicación y el transporte en los Estados Unidos.

- ✔ En una hoja de papel, hagan una tabla de dos columnas.
- ✔ Escriba *Comunicación y transporte en el pasado* en la parte de arriba de la primera columna y *Comunicación y transporte en el presente* en la parte de arriba de la segunda columna.
- ✔ Trabaje con su niño o niña para escribir en las columnas medios de comunicación y transporte del pasado y del presente en los Estados Unidos.

Para leer juntos

Dana, Yo soy de los Estados Unidos, por Carole Nicholas (La Galera, ISBN 84-246-9404-X, 1997)

¿Quién es de aquí?, por Magy Burns Knight y Anne Sibley O'Brien (ilustradora) (Tilbury House, ISBN 0-88448-159-X, 1993) Best Multicultural Book, Publisher's Weekly

Guía para los niños que quieren salvar el planeta, por Patricia Hume (Diana, ISBN 968-13-2118-9, 1991)

Para encontrar más actividades, visite **www.estudiosocialessf.com**

¡Gracias por apoyar la educación de sus hijos en Estudios sociales!

School to Home

Unit 2 **Newsletter**

Here are the main ideas that we are learning:

★ The Northeast region is one of incredible scenery and magnificent natural formations.

★ The Northeast produces products for the world to enjoy.

★ Chesapeake Bay and other bays in the Northeast provide seafood for millions.

★ The Narragansett lived in the Northeast region before European settlers came to North America.

★ The Northeast saw the beginnings of the American Revolution, the writing of our nation's Constitution, and the start of many new lives as immigrants arrived in the United States.

★ The Northeast was the birthplace of the abolitionist movement and the women's rights movement.

★ Northeastern cities and their industries have grown and changed.

Fast Facts

Eight of the ten smallest states in area are in the Northeast region. Rhode Island, with an area of about 1,500 square miles, is the smallest state. If all states were its size, the United States would have over 2,400 states!

Family Activities

Talk Together

Talk with your child about the states that make up the Northeast region. Help your child name some of the cities in the Northeast region such as Boston, New York, Philadelphia, and Baltimore. Ask your child to tell what they know about each.

Learn Together

Help your child learn more about people and places of the Northeast.

✔ Say each of the following names to your child and ask your child to tell you one fact about each place or person:

– Niagara Falls
– Roger Williams
– Chesapeake Bay
– Benjamin Franklin
– Ellis Island
– Elizabeth Cady Stanton
– Seneca Falls, New York
– Pittsburgh

Read Together

If Your Name Was Changed at Ellis Island, by Ellen Levine (Scholastic Trade, ISBN 0-590-43829-8, 1994)

Sojourner Truth: Ain't I a Woman? by Patricia C. and Fredrick McKissack (Scholastic Trade, ISBN 0-590-44691-6, 1994) ALA Notable Book, Coretta Scott King Honor Book

Waterman's Boy, by Susan Sharpe (Simon & Schuster, ISBN 0-027-82351-2, 1990)

Go online to find more activities at **www.sfsocialstudies.com**

Thank you for supporting your child's Social Studies education!

De la escuela al hogar

Unidad 2

Boletín

Estas son las ideas principales que estamos estudiando:

★ La región del Noreste cuenta con paisajes increíbles y formaciones naturales magníficas.

★ Del Noreste provienen muchos productos de los que disfruta todo el mundo.

★ La bahía de Chesapeake y otras bahías en el Noreste proveen pescado y marisco para millones de personas.

★ Los indígenas narragansets vivían en la región del Noreste antes de que llegaran los colonos europeos a América del Norte.

★ El Noreste fue testigo de los principios de la Guerra de Independencia, la redacción de la Constitución de nuestra nación y el comienzo de muchas nuevas vidas a medida que los inmigrantes llegaban a los Estados Unidos.

★ El Noreste fue el lugar de nacimiento del movimiento abolicionista y del movimiento a favor de los derechos de la mujer.

★ Las ciudades del Noreste y sus industrias han crecido y han cambiado.

Datos curiosos

Ocho de los diez estados de menor superficie están en la región del Noreste. Rhode Island, con un área de unas 1,500 millas cuadradas, es el estado más pequeño. Si todos los estados tuvieran este tamaño, ¡los Estados Unidos tendrían más de 2,400 estados!

Actividades en familia

Para conversar

Hable con su niño o niña sobre los estados que componen la región del Noreste. Ayúdele a nombrar algunas de las ciudades de la región tales como Boston, Nueva York, Filadelfia y Baltimore. Pida a su niño o niña que le cuente lo que sabe de cada una.

Para aprender juntos

Ayude a su niño o niña a aprender más cosas sobre las personas y los lugares del Noreste.

✔ Diga cada uno de los nombres siguientes a su niño o niña y pídale que le dé un dato sobre cada persona o lugar:

- cataratas del Niágara
- Roger Williams
- bahía de Chesapeake
- Benjamin Franklin
- isla Ellis
- Elizabeth Cady Stanton
- Seneca Falls, Nueva York
- Pittsburgh

Para leer juntos

Botes y barcos, por Jason Cooper (Rourke, ISBN 0-86592-474-0, 1991)

El pollo de los domingos, por Patricia Polacco (Lectorum, ISBN 0-8037-1662-1, 1983)

Nightjohn: El esclavo que me enseñó a leer, por Gary Paulsen (Bronce, ISBN 84-8453-003-5, 2000)

Para encontrar más actividades, visite **www.estudiosocialessf.com**

¡Gracias por apoyar la educación de sus hijos en Estudios sociales!

School to Home

Unit 3 **Newsletter**

Here are the main ideas that we are learning:

- ★ The main areas of the Southeast region include the coastal plains, the Piedmont, and Appalachia.
- ★ The mild climates of the coastal areas of the Southeast bring many tourists, but the area has some natural hazards.
- ★ The Southeast is rich in different resources. These resources are used in different industries throughout the region.
- ★ The Cherokee have contributed greatly to the history of the Southeast.
- ★ Exploration, settlements, agriculture, and slavery all shaped the early growth of the Southeast region.
- ★ The Civil War had a major impact on the history of the Southeast.
- ★ Cities in the Southeast are growing and changing.

Fast Facts

Eight Presidents of the United States—George Washington, Thomas Jefferson, James Madison, James Monroe, William Henry Harrison, John Tyler, Zachary Taylor, and Woodrow Wilson—were born in the state of Virginia.

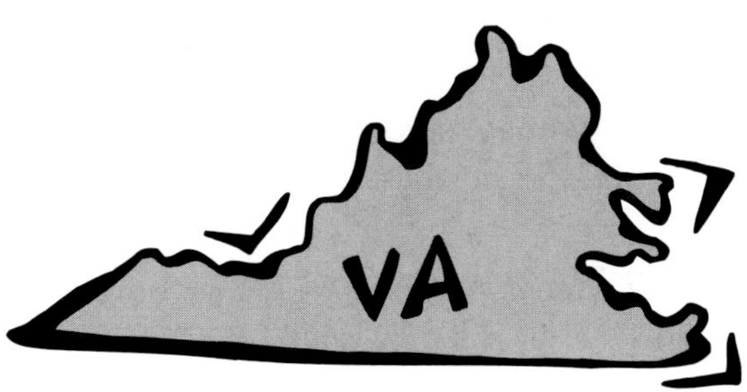

Family Activities

Talk Together

Encourage your child to tell you about the history of the Southeast region. Ask your child to identify changes that have occurred in the Southeast region over time.

Learn Together

Help your child appreciate the importance of the Thirteenth Amendment and the Civil Rights Act of 1964.

- ✔ Make a two-column chart.
- ✔ In Column 1, write the heading *Law;* and in Column 2, write the heading *What the Law Did.*
- ✔ Write *Thirteenth Amendment* as the first entry in Column 1. Have your child identify what this amendment did for African Americans. Ask your child to write his or her response in Column 2.
- ✔ Then write *Civil Rights Act of 1964* as the next entry in Column 1. Ask your child to write in Column 2 what this law did.

Read Together

Monticello, by Leonard Everett Fisher (Holiday House, ISBN 0-823-41406-X, 1998)

Freedom's Children: Young Civil Rights Activists Tell Their Own Stories, by Ellen Levine (Puffin, ISBN 0-698-11870-7, 2000) Jane Addams Book Award

Go online to find more activities at **www.sfsocialstudies.com**

Thank you for supporting your child's Social Studies education!

De la escuela al hogar

Unidad 3

Boletín

Estas son las ideas principales que estamos estudiando:

★ Entre las áreas principales de la región del Sureste se incluyen las Llanuras Costeras, el Piedmont y los Apalaches.

★ El clima suave de las zonas costeras del Sureste atrae a muchos turistas, pero esta región contiene algunos peligros naturales.

★ El Sureste es rico en diferentes recursos. Éstos se usan en diversas industrias de toda la región.

★ Los cheroquíes han contribuido mucho a la historia del Sureste.

★ La exploración, los asentamientos, la agricultura y la esclavitud conformaron las primeras etapas de crecimiento de la región de Sureste.

★ La Guerra Civil tuvo un gran impacto en la historia del Sureste.

★ Las ciudades del Sureste están creciendo y cambiando.

Datos curiosos

Ocho presidentes de los Estados Unidos —George Washington, Thomas Jefferson, James Madison, James Monroe, William Henry Harrison, John Tyler, Zachary Taylor y Woodrow Wilson— nacieron en el estado de Virginia.

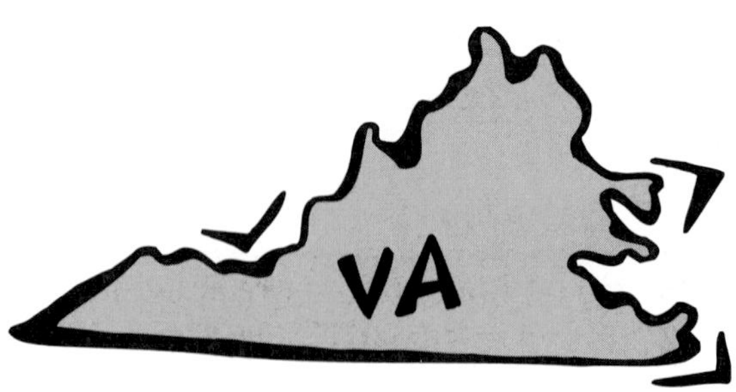

Actividades en familia

Para conversar

Anime a su niño o niña a que le cuente cosas sobre la historia de la región del Sureste. Pídale que identifique los cambios que se han producido con el tiempo en la región del Sureste.

Para aprender juntos

Ayude a su niño o niña a apreciar la importancia de la Decimotercera Enmienda y la Ley de los Derechos Civiles de 1964.

✔ Prepare una tabla de dos columnas.

✔ En la Columna 1, escriba el título *Ley;* y en la Columna 2, escriba el título *Lo que hizo la ley.*

✔ Escriba *Decimotercera Enmienda* como primer dato de la Columna 1. Pida a su niño o niña que identifique lo que significó esta enmienda para los afroamericanos. Pídale que escriba su respuesta en la Columna 2.

✔ Después, escriba *Ley de los Derechos Civiles de 1964* en la Columna 1. Pídale que escriba en la Columna 2 lo que significó esta ley.

Para leer juntos

PREMIO *Los huevos parlantes,* por Jerry Pinkney (Ilusteador), Robert D. San Souci (Penguin Putnam, 0-8037-1991-4, 1996)

La peineta colorado, por Fernando Picó y María Ordoñez (Ekaré Ediciones, ISBN 980-257-174-1, 1999)

Lloro por la tierra, por Mildred Taylor (Norma S.A., ISBN 958-04-4388-2, 1999)

Para encontrar más actividades, visite **www.estudiosocialessf.com**

¡Gracias por apoyar la educación de sus hijos en Estudios sociales!

School to Home

Unit 4 **Newsletter**

Here are the main ideas that we are learning:

★ The Great Lakes link the Midwest region to the Gulf of Mexico and to the Atlantic Ocean.

★ Erosion has shaped the South Dakota Badlands.

★ The Midwest is one of the world's leading farming regions.

★ The Ojibwa have maintained important cultural traditions and have contributed to the culture of the Midwest.

★ European settlement in the Great Lakes region and the Mississippi valley began with the fur trade. Many of the region's cities and towns began as fur trading centers.

★ Many settlers came to the Midwest in the 1800s to farm the land.

★ The Midwest has been a trade and transportation hub, from long ago to the present.

Fast Facts

On October 8, 1871, huge fires swept through Chicago and northeastern Wisconsin. On that day, about 300 people lost their lives in the Great Chicago Fire and around 1,200 people died in the Peshtigo forest fire in Wisconsin.

Family Activities

Talk Together

Discuss with your child the importance of Midwest farms to the United States. Help your child name some of the foods and products in your home that may have come from farms of the Midwest region.

Learn Together

Help your child learn about important features of the Midwest.

✔ Write each set of words on a separate sheet of paper.
- *corn, crop rotation, soybeans*
- *St. Lawrence River and Seaway, Great Lakes, Atlantic Ocean*
- *erosion, Badlands, dinosaur fossils*
- *fur trade, John Baptiste Du Sable, Chicago*

✔ Ask your child to choose a sheet of paper and explain how the words on the sheet are related.

✔ For example, for *corn, crop rotation,* and *soybeans,* your child might say, "Some farmers *rotate* their *crops* from year to year by growing *corn* one year and *soybeans* the next."

Read Together

Little Town on the Prairie, by Laura Ingalls Wilder (HarperCollins, ISBN 0-06-52242-9, 2003) Newbery Honor Book

Heartland, by Diane Siebert (HarperCollins Juvenile Children's Books, ISBN 0-064-43287-4, 1999) Notable Children's Trade Book in Social Studies

Caddie Woodlawn, by Carol Ryrie Brink (Simon & Schuster, ISBN 0-689-86225-3, 2003) Newbery Honor Book

Go online to find more activities at **www.sfsocialstudies.com**

Thank you for supporting your child's Social Studies education!

De la escuela al hogar

Unidad 4

Boletín

Estas son las ideas principales que estamos estudiando:

- ★ Los Grandes Lagos unen la región del Medio Oeste con el golfo de México y el océano Atlántico.
- ★ La erosión ha dado forma a los Badlands de Dakota del Sur.
- ★ El Medio Oeste es una de las regiones agrícolas más importantes del mundo.
- ★ Los ojibwas han mantenido tradiciones culturales importantes y han contribuido a la cultura del Medio Oeste.
- ★ El asentamiento europeo en la región de los Grandes Lagos y en el valle del Mississippi empezó con el comercio de pieles. Muchas de las ciudades y poblaciones de la región tuvieron sus orígenes como centros de comercio de pieles.
- ★ Muchos colonos llegaron al Medio Oeste en el siglo XIX para cultivar la tierra.
- ★ El Medio Oeste ha sido un centro comercial y de transporte desde tiempos muy antiguos hasta el presente.

Datos curiosos

El 8 de octubre de 1871, se produjeron grandes incendios que arrasaron Chicago y el noreste de Wisconsin. Ese día, unas 300 personas perdieron la vida en el Gran Incendio de Chicago y unas 1,200 murieron en el incendio forestal de Peshtigo, en Wisconsin.

Actividades en familia

Para conversar

Hable con su niño o niña sobre la importancia de la agricultura del Medio Oeste para los Estados Unidos. Ayúdele a nombrar algunos de los alimentos y productos en su casa que hayan podido venir desde granjas de esa région.

Para aprender juntos

Ayude a su niño o niña a aprender las características importantes del Medio Oeste.

- ✔ Escriba cada conjunto de palabras en una hoja de papel separada:
  - *maíz, rotación de cultivos, habas de soya*
  - *río San Lorenzo, Grandes Lagos, océano Atlántico*
  - *erosión, Badlands, fósiles de dinosaurio*
  - *comercio de pieles, John Baptiste Du Sable, Chicago*
- ✔ Pida a su niño o niña que escoja una hoja de papel y explique la forma en que están relacionadas las palabras de la hoja.
- ✔ Por ejemplo, para *maíz, rotación de cultivos y habas de soya,* su niño o niña podría decir: "Algunos agricultores *rotan* sus *cultivos* de un año a otro plantando *maíz* un año y *habas de soya* el siguiente".

Para leer juntos

PREMIO *Ani y la anciana*, por Miska Miles y Peter Parnall (ilustrador) (Lectorum, ISBN 9-6816374-8-8, 1992) Newbery Honor Book

PREMIO *Sarah, sencilla y alta,* por Patricia MacLachlan (Noguer, ISBN 84-279-3421-1, 1996) Newbery Award, IBBY Honor List

Para encontrar más actividades, visite **www.estudiosocialessf.com**

¡Gracias por apoyar la educación de sus hijos en Estudios sociales!

School to Home

Unit 5 **Newsletter**

Here are the main ideas that we are learning:

★ The Grand Canyon dazzles visitors with its size and beauty.

★ The Southwest climate can vary greatly. It is dry in some places and moist in others.

★ The Southwest is a region of discovery and research.

★ The Navajo have lived in the Southwest for centuries.

★ Explorers and missionaries brought a Spanish presence to the Southwest.

★ The cattle industry boomed in the Southwest in the 1800s. The cowboys who herded cattle became part of our nation's lore.

★ High temperatures and a shortage of water can make living in the desert a challenge.

Fast Facts

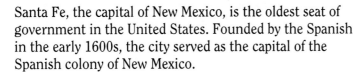

Santa Fe, the capital of New Mexico, is the oldest seat of government in the United States. Founded by the Spanish in the early 1600s, the city served as the capital of the Spanish colony of New Mexico.

Family Activities

Talk Together

Talk with your child about the role oil and cattle played in the development of the Southwest. Discuss what industries, including high technology industries, are important to the Southwest region today.

Learn Together

Help your child learn about important features, people, places, and events of the Southwest region.

✔ Make a tic-tac-toe grid and write one of the following in each square: *Grand Canyon, cactus, Spindletop, Los Alamos, Navajo, missionary, cowboy, viceroy,* and *Chisholm Trail.*

✔ With your child, play a game of tic-tac-toe. Take turns choosing a square, reading the word or term in the square, and describing how it relates to the Southwest region.

✔ In the squares, draw an *X* or *O* for correct answers. Use the textbook to check answers.

✔ Repeat the activity, using other features, people, places, and events of the Southwest region.

Read Together

Old Blue, by Sibyl Hancock (Penguin Putnam, ISBN 0-399-61141-X, 1980) ALA Notable Book

The Diary of John Wesley Powell (In My Own Words), by John Wesley Powell (Benchmark Books, ISBN 0-761-41013-9, 2000)

Out of the Dust, by Karen Hesse (Scholastic Paperbacks, ISBN 0-590-37125-8, 1999) Newbery Medal

Go online to find more activities at **www.sfsocialstudies.com**

Thank you for supporting your child's Social Studies education!

De la escuela al hogar

Unidad 5

Boletín

Estas son las ideas principales que estamos estudiando:

★ El Gran Cañón deslumbra a los visitantes por su tamaño y belleza.

★ El clima del Suroeste puede variar considerablemente. En algunos lugares es seco y en otros es húmedo.

★ El Suroeste es una región de descubrimientos e investigaciones.

★ Los navajos han vivido en el Suroeste durante siglos.

★ Los exploradores y misioneros fueron responsables de la presencia española en el Suroeste.

★ La industria ganadera tuvo un gran auge en el Suroeste en el siglo XIX. Los vaqueros dedicados al arreo de ganado se convirtieron en parte de nuestra tradición nacional.

★ Las temperaturas altas y la escasez de agua pueden hacer que la vida en el desierto sea un desafío.

Datos curiosos

Santa Fe, la capital de Nuevo México, es la sede de gobierno más antigua de los Estados Unidos. Fundada por los españoles a principios del siglo XVII, la ciudad sirvió como capital de la colonia española de Nuevo México.

Actividades en familia

Para conversar

Hable con su niño o niña sobre la función que desempeñaron el petróleo y el ganado en el desarrollo del Suroeste. Hablen sobre qué industrias, incluidas las de alta tecnología, son importantes hoy en día en la región.

Para aprender juntos

Ayude a su niño o niña a aprender las características, personas, lugares y acontecimientos importantes de la región del Suroeste.

✔ Haga una cuadrícula de tres en raya y escriba uno de los términos siguientes en cada recuadro: *Gran Cañón, cactus, Spindletop, Los Álamos, navajo, misionero, vaquero, virrey y Camino Chisholm.*

✔ Juegue con su niño o niña a tres en raya con una variación. Túrnense para escoger un recuadro, lean la palabra o el término del recuadro y describan cómo está relacionado con la región del Suroeste.

✔ En los recuadros, tracen una *X* o un *O* para las respuestas correctas. Use el libro de texto para comprobar las respuestas.

✔ Repitan la actividad, cuando otras características, personas, lugares y acontecimientos de la región del Suroeste.

Para leer juntos

El gigante del desierto, por Barbara Bash (Scholastic, ISBN 0-590-47429-4, 1993)

Charro, por George Ancona (Harcourt, ISBN 0-15-202026-8, 1999)

Para encontrar más actividades, visite **www.estudiosocialessf.com**

¡Gracias por apoyar la educación de sus hijos en Estudios sociales!

School to Home

Unit 6 **Newsletter**

Here are the main ideas that we are learning:

★ Many parts of the West are mountainous.

★ The climate in different areas of the West varies greatly.

★ The West is rich in natural resources.

★ The Tlingit live in the northern part of the West.

★ Explorers from Spain and settlers seeking gold helped shape the West.

★ Cities in the West have many different kinds of businesses and attractions.

Fast Facts

Established in 1872, Yellowstone National Park is the world's oldest national park. It boasts spectacular hot springs and geysers, including Old Faithful, a geyser that erupts on average about every 90 minutes.

Energy companies in California and Oregon are building windfarms to generate electricity.

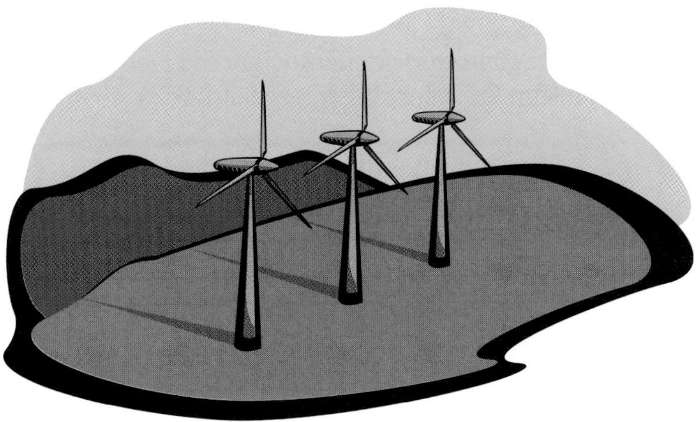

Family Activities

Talk Together

Talk with your child about the geography of the West, focusing on mountain ranges. Help your child name some mountains and the states in which they are found.

Learn Together

Help your child understand what different states in the West have to offer.

✔ Choose a well-known tune, such as "Old MacDonald Had a Farm" or "Row, Row, Row Your Boat."

✔ Together with your child, write new lyrics, focusing on one of the states in the West.

✔ Your child may enjoy sharing your new lyrics with his or her class.

Read Together

Mountain Town, by Bonnie Geisert (Houghton Mifflin Co., ISBN 0-395-95390-1, 2000) Parents' Choice Gold Award

How I Survived the Oregon Trail: The Journal of Jesse Adams, by Laura Wilson (Morrow/Avon, ISBN 0-688-17276-8, 1999)

The Eagle's Shadow, by Nora Martin (Scholastic Trade, ISBN 0-590-36087-6, 1997)

Go online to find more activities at **www.sfsocialstudies.com**

Thank you for supporting your child's Social Studies education!

De la escuela al hogar

Unidad 6 **Boletín**

Estas son las ideas principales que estamos estudiando:

- ★ Muchas partes del Oeste son montañosas.
- ★ El clima de distintas áreas del Oeste varía considerablemente.
- ★ El Oeste es rico en recursos naturales.
- ★ Los tlingits viven en la parte norte del Oeste.
- ★ Los exploradores de España y los colonos en busca de oro ayudaron a conformar el Oeste.
- ★ Las ciudades del Oeste tienen muchas clases de comercios y atracciones.

Datos curiosos

Establecido en 1872, el Parque Nacional Yellowstone es el parque nacional más antiguo del mundo. Tiene unos manantiales calientes y géiseres espectaculares, incluido Old Faithful, un géiser que entra en erupción aproximadamente cada 76 minutos.

Las empresas proveedoras de energía de California y Oregón están construyendo "granjas de viento" para generar electricidad.

Actividades en familia

Para conversar

Hable con su niño o niña sobre la geografía del Oeste, concentrándose en las cordilleras. Ayude a su niño o niña a nombrar algunas montañas y los estados en que se encuentran.

Para aprender juntos

Ayude a su niño a entender lo que ofrecen los distintos estados del Oeste.

- ✔ Escoja una melodía bien conocida, como "Old MacDonald Had a Farm" o "Row, Row, Row Your Boat".
- ✔ Escriban juntos una letra nueva concentrándose en uno de los estados del Oeste.
- ✔ Su niño o niña quizá quiera compartir su nueva letra con la clase.

Para leer juntos

César Chávez: Una biografía ilustrada con fotografías, por Lucile Davis (Bridgestone Books, ISBN 1-56065-808-8, 1999)

Por la gran cuchara de cuerno!, por Sid Fleischman (Lectorum Publ, Inc, ISBN 1-880507-08-0, 1994)

Para encontrar más actividades, visite **www.estudiosocialessf.com**

¡Gracias por apoyar la educación de sus hijos en Estudios sociales!

08160, 08161, 08162, 08163, 08164

Calendar Pages

Each month of the year provides new opportunities for students to learn about history, geography, government, good citizenship, economics, culture, and technology through holidays, "firsts," and important birthdays and anniversaries. The 12-month format is ideal for year-round schools and summer schools but also provides a wealth of information for students who attend a standard 9-month school.

The following pages offer an entire year of calendar activities, including:

- A list of facts about the month: birthdays, holidays, and other red-letter days
- Detailed instructions for constructing a bulletin board for each month
- At least one additional activity per month
- A selection of books for students to read about a monthly subject
- A Web link for *This Day in History,* part of the Scott Foresman Social Studies Web site

An extra page is given for you to note state or community celebrations.

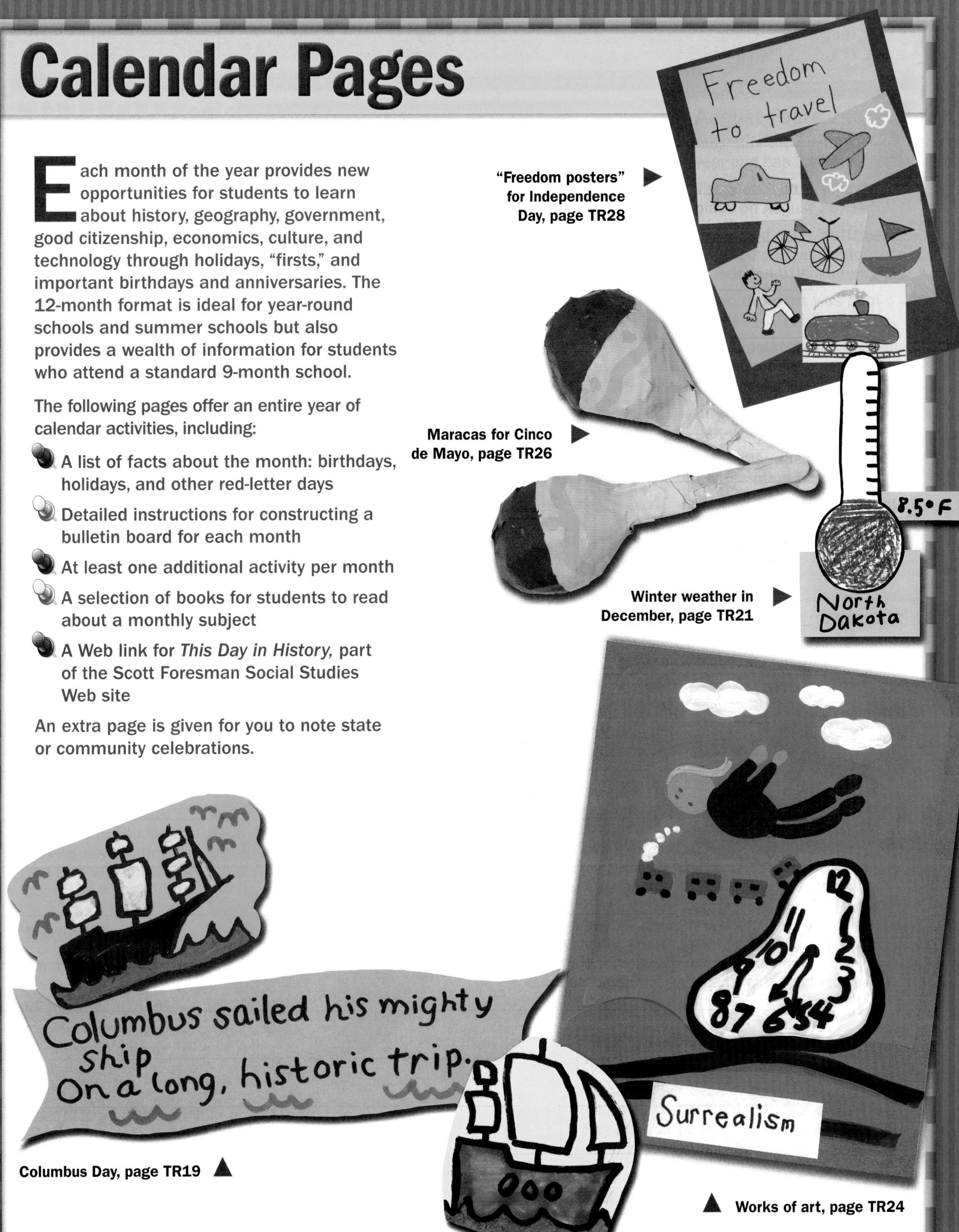

"Freedom posters" for Independence Day, page TR28

Maracas for Cinco de Mayo, page TR26

Winter weather in December, page TR21

Columbus Day, page TR19

Works of art, page TR24

September

Up, Up and Away!

September Facts

- September is the ninth month of the year and has 30 days. Autumn begins in September.
- **Labor Day** is celebrated on the first Monday in September.
- **National Hispanic Heritage Month** begins in September.
- **National Grandparents' Day** is the first Sunday in September.
- On September 19, 1863, President Lincoln delivered the **Gettysburg Address.**
- The **Moon Festival** in China is celebrated in September.
- The **first solo balloon flight across the Atlantic** began on September 14, 1984.
- **Rosh Hashanah,** the Jewish New Year, is usually observed in September.

Activities

First Solo Balloon Fight Across Atlantic—September 14, 1984

Ask students to research the history of hot air balloons and find out more about the first solo flight across the Atlantic in 1984. Have students look up information about hot air balloon designs. What materials are used to make them? What makes them go up, and how can they be brought back down safely? Students can try designing their own hot air balloons. Ask each student to draw a picture of his or her design. Then ask students where they would like to travel in their balloons. Have students pick a spot somewhere in the United States or the world, then measure the miles on a map "as the crow flies" to that destination. Ask them to write the location along with number of miles on the basket below the balloon. Display the balloons on a bulletin board titled, "UP, UP, and AWAY!"

Moon Festival in China

For more information on the **Moon Festival** in China look for books such as these:

Moon Festival, by Ching Yeung Russell (Boyds Mills Press, ISBN 1-59078-079-5, 2003)

Moonbeams, Dumplings and Dragon Boats: A Treasury of Chinese Holiday Tales, Activities and Recipes by Nina Simonds (Harcourt, ISBN 0-15-201983-9, 2002)

National Hispanic Heritage Month

Ask students what Spanish words they know. Write the words on the board, along with their English translations. Now have students make a list of English words they would like to translate into Spanish. Have students look for a Spanish-English dictionary from the library to find translations. Then ask students to make illustrations to match the translations for a class dictionary.

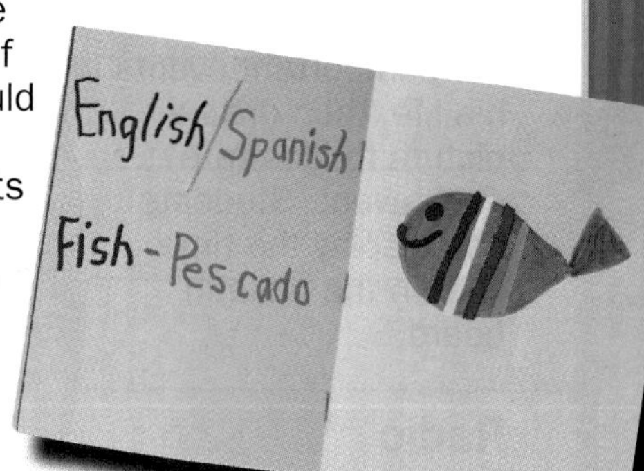

This Day in History

For additional September events, go to *This Day in History* at **www.sfsocialstudies.com**. Select a birthday or historic event for any day in September and base an activity on it.

Alternatively, have students go to this Web site and choose an event in September on which to do a project or report.

October

Never Before Seen National Memorials

October Facts

- October is the tenth month of the year and has 31 days.
- **Columbus Day** is celebrated on the second Monday in October.
- The comic strip **"Peanuts"** debuted on October 2, 1950.
- October is **National Stamp Collecting Month.**
- The **first World Series game** was played on October 1, 1903.
- **Mount Rushmore** was completed on October 31, 1941.
- **General Cornwallis surrendered to General George Washington** at Yorktown, Virginia, on October 19, 1781.

Activities

Mount Rushmore

Find out what the students know about Mount Rushmore. Ask them to research this national memorial and find out who designed it, how long it took to complete, and who is depicted on this giant monument. Have students compare its size to other statues and buildings in the United States and the world. You might want to help the class make a graph to compare sizes. Now ask students to design their own national memorials or statues and draw pictures of their monuments. Under each picture, students can include information such as what it is made of, how long it took to make, and who or what it commemorates. Display the new memorials on a bulletin board titled "Never Before Seen National Memorials."

Stamp Collecting

For more information on **stamp collecting,** look for books such as these:

The Postal Service Guide to U.S. Stamps, by The United States Postal Service (HarperResource, ISBN 0-06-095856-1, 2002)

Stamps, by Jennifer Abeyta (Children's Press, ISBN 0-516-23534-6, 2000)

Columbus Day Journals

After studying about Columbus and his travels across the Atlantic Ocean in 1492, have each student write a story about Columbus and a day on his trip. Ask students to write about what they think Columbus would see, hear, touch, taste, and smell that day on the ship more than 500 years ago. Bind all entries into a classroom book.

This Day in History

For additional October events, go to *This Day in History* at **www.sfsocialstudies.com**. Select a birthday or historic event for any day in October and base an activity on it.

Alternatively, have students go to this Web site and choose an event in October on which to do a project or report.

November

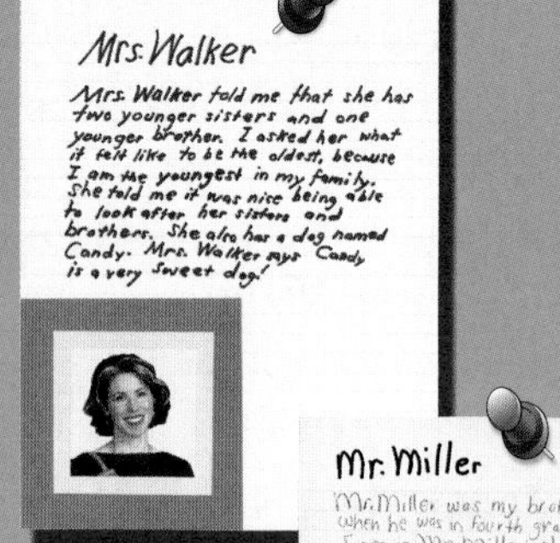

November Facts

- November is the eleventh month of the year and has 30 days.
- **Election Day** is the first Tuesday in November. Every four years there is a Presidential Election.
- November 11 is **Veterans Day.**
- **Thanksgiving** is the fourth Thursday in November.
- **American Education Week** is the third week in November.
- November is **International Drum Month.**
- **Sandwich Day** is November 3.

Activities

American Education Week

To celebrate American Education Week, have students honor the teachers in your school. Let your students become reporters. Have them take pictures of all the teachers in the school. Then have them set up interviews to find out more about the teachers. Ask students to make up a list of interview questions about background, family, and formal education. Have students ask teachers about the importance of education in their own lives. After the interviews, have students write essays about the teachers they spoke to. Display the pictures and stories on a school-wide bulletin board for everyone to enjoy.

Thanksgiving

For more information on **Thanksgiving,** look for books such as these.

Nickommoh!: A Thanksgiving Celebration, by Jackie French Koller (Atheneum Books for Young Readers, ISBN 0-689-81094-6, 1999)

Thanksgiving on Thursday, by Mary Pope Osborne (Random House, 0-375-90615-0, 2002)

Election Day

Help students research the candidates in your area. Ask students to find out to which party the candidates belong and for which office they are running. Gather political information on each candidate, and have students read over the materials. Discuss each candidate's views and make a chart

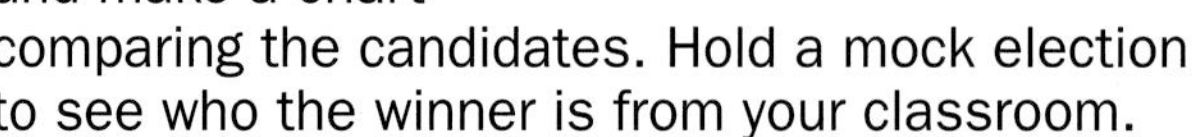

comparing the candidates. Hold a mock election to see who the winner is from your classroom.

This Day in History

For additional November events, go to *This Day in History* at **www.sfsocialstudies.com**. Select a birthday or historic event for any day in November and base an activity on it.

Alternatively, have students go to this Web site and choose an event in November on which to do a project or report.

December

The Boston Tea Party

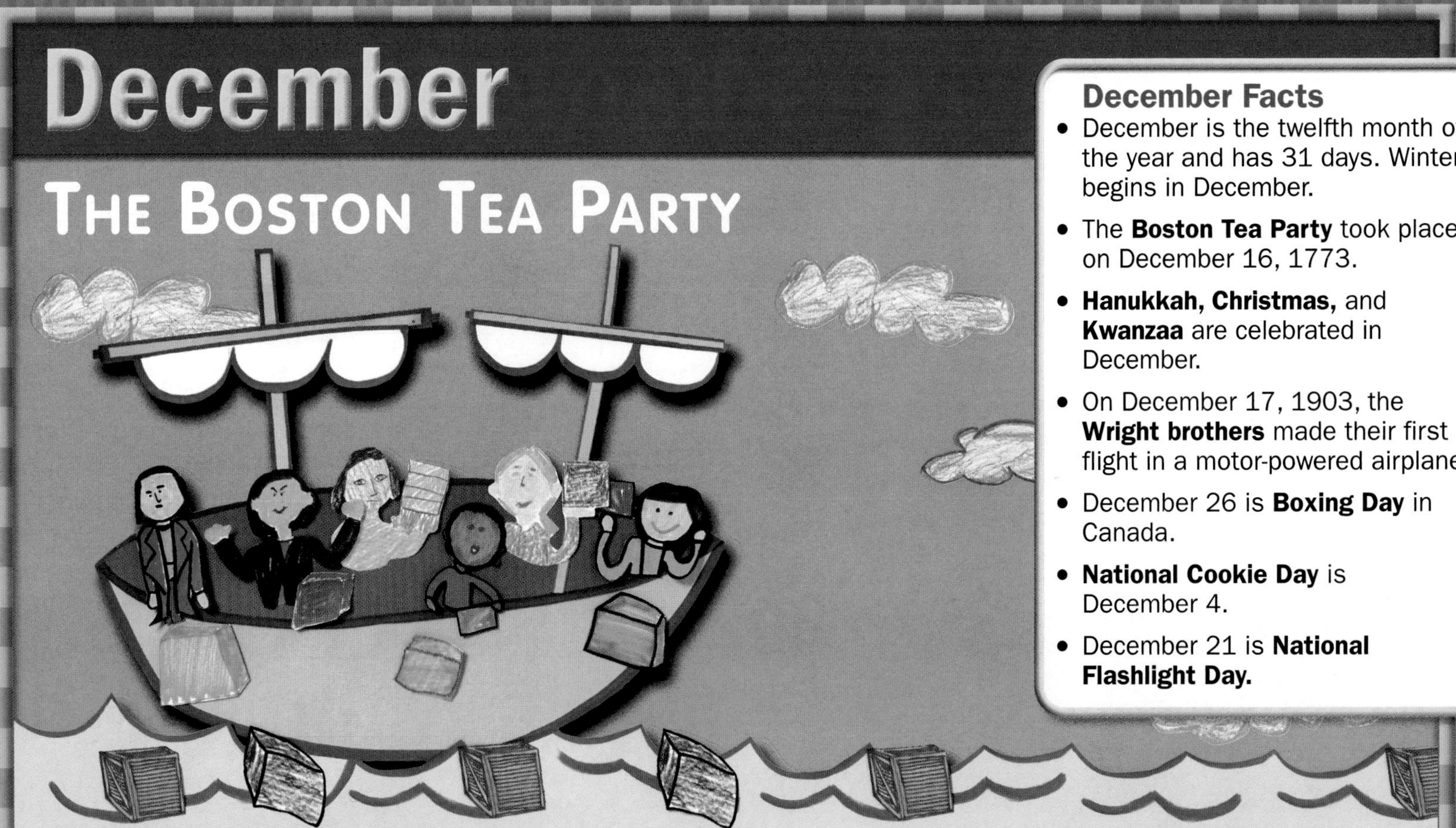

December Facts

- December is the twelfth month of the year and has 31 days. Winter begins in December.
- The **Boston Tea Party** took place on December 16, 1773.
- **Hanukkah, Christmas,** and **Kwanzaa** are celebrated in December.
- On December 17, 1903, the **Wright brothers** made their first flight in a motor-powered airplane.
- December 26 is **Boxing Day** in Canada.
- **National Cookie Day** is December 4.
- December 21 is **National Flashlight Day.**

Activities

The Boston Tea Party

Find out what students know about the Boston Tea Party. Have students research the names of the three ships docked in the Boston Harbor on the night of December 16, 1773. Ask them to find out how much tea was on each ship, and why the patriots dumped the tea into the harbor. Ask students how they think the colonists felt that night. Then have students draw one of the patriots who took part in the Boston Tea Party. Ask each student to draw two or three crates of tea. Make a large boat out of brown butcher paper and put it on the bulletin board. Cut out some blue paper "water" to put under the ship. Have students add the drawings of the patriots and the crates of tea to the bulletin board. Title it "The Boston Tea Party."

Boxing Day in Canada

For more information on **Canada,** look for books such as these:

Canada: The Culture, by Bobbie Kalman (Crabtree, ISBN 0-7787-9360-5, 2002)

Welcome to Canada, by Meredith Costain (Chelsea House Publishers, ISBN 0-7910-6873-0, 2002)

National Flashlight Day

In honor of National Flashlight Day, ask students to bring flashlights to school. Working in small groups, have students brainstorm all the uses for a flashlight. Ask groups to share their ideas. Now challenge each group to come up with a game or activity that requires the use of flashlights. Each group must explain their activity or give the rules of their game. Allow the class to try each game or activity out. Students can vote on their favorite activity by a show of flashlights.

This Day in History

For additional December events, go to *This Day in History* at **www.sfsocialstudies.com**. Select a birthday or historic event for any day in December and base an activity on it.

Alternatively, have students go to this Web site and choose an event in December on which to do a project or report.

January

January Facts

- January is the first month of the year and has 31 days.
- January 1 is the birthday of **Paul Revere** (1735) and **Betsy Ross** (1752).
- **Martin Luther King, Jr. Day** is celebrated on the third Monday in January.
- January is **National Hobby Month** and **National Soup Month.**
- **National Puzzle Day** is January 29.
- January 14 is **National Dress Up Your Pet Day.**
- **Jackie Robinson** was born on January 31, 1919.
- January 20 is the presidential **Inauguration Day** every four years.

Activities

National Puzzle Day

In honor of National Puzzle Day, make a bulletin board that will "put together" special events and holidays in January. Have students make large uppercase letters to spell out JANUARY. Then help students cut the letters apart to resemble a jigsaw puzzle. Give each student or group of students a piece of the puzzle. Assign a different holiday or event from the month of January to each group. Have students research their special day, cut out pictures or make drawings to represent that event, and use them to decorate the puzzle piece. Students can put the puzzle together to complete the bulletin board.

Jackie Robinson

For more information on **Jackie Robinson,** look for books such as these:

Jackie Robinson, by Lucia Raatma (World Almanac Library, ISBN 0-8368-5072-6, 2002)

Jackie Robinson, by Tony De Marco (Child's World, ISBN 1-56766-918-2, 2001)

Inauguration Day

Ask students what they know about Inauguration Day. Ask if anyone has ever seen a U.S. President sworn into office. Research presidential inauguration speeches with the class. Have volunteers read excerpts from some of them aloud to the class. Then ask students to write their own inauguration speeches. What important message would they like to share with American citizens? Students can give their speeches on January 20.

This Day in History

For additional January events, go to *This Day in History* at **www.sfsocialstudies.com**. Select a birthday or historic event for any day in January and base an activity on it.

Alternatively, have students go to this Web site and choose an event in January on which to do a project or report.

February

Plenty of Predictions

February Facts

- February is the second month of the year and has 28 days. It is the shortest month of the year.
- Every four years February has 29 days. This is called a **Leap Year.**
- **Valentine's Day** and **Presidents' Day** are celebrated in February.
- February is **Black History Month.**
- February is **National Dental Health Month.**
- **Groundhog Day** is February 2.
- **Weatherperson's Day** is February 5.
- **John Glenn** became the first U.S. astronaut to orbit Earth on February 20, 1962.

Activities

Weatherperson's Day

Display a February weather map of the United States, and ask students what they already know about the different symbols pictured there. Discuss the weather patterns in the different regions of the country and the different seasons of the year. Ask students to watch the weather over a week's period of time. How did the weather change? Why did it change? How important is it to know the weekly forecast? Then ask each student to create his or her own country. Have each student draw a February weather map of the new country, complete with cold fronts, warm fronts, and symbols for snow, rain, or sun. Have each student be the top weatherperson for the new country and predict the weather for the coming week. Display the weather maps and weather forecasts on a bulletin board titled "Plenty of Predictions."

Dental Health Month

For more information on **Dental Health Month,** look for books such as these:

The Dentist and You, by Diane Swanson, (Firefly Books, ISBN 1-55037-729-9, 2002)

Staying Healthy: Dental Care, by Alice B. McGinty (Franklin Watts, ISBN 0-531-11661-1, 1998)

Groundhog Day

Ask students to explain the legend of Groundhog Day. Why do the students think the groundhog was chosen to make this seasonal weather prediction? Have students research information about the groundhog as well as other hibernating animals. Then ask students to choose an animal and make up a new weather legend.

This Day in History

For additional February events, go to *This Day in History* at **www.sfsocialstudies.com**. Select a birthday or historic event for any day in February and base an activity on it.

Alternatively, have students go to this Web site and choose an event in February on which to do a project or report.

March

Read All About It!

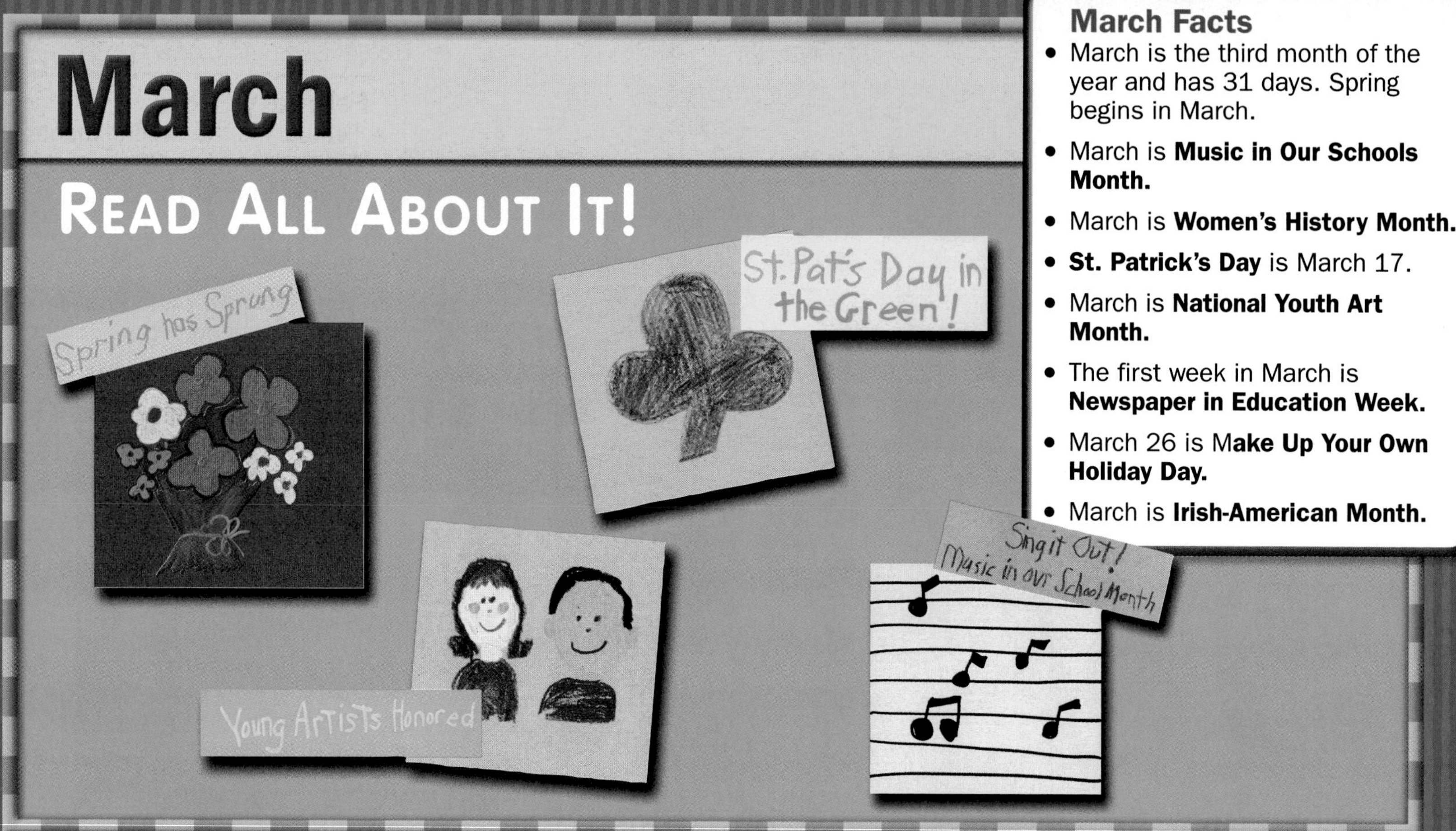

March Facts

- March is the third month of the year and has 31 days. Spring begins in March.
- March is **Music in Our Schools Month.**
- March is **Women's History Month.**
- **St. Patrick's Day** is March 17.
- March is **National Youth Art Month.**
- The first week in March is **Newspaper in Education Week.**
- March 26 is M**ake Up Your Own Holiday Day.**
- March is **Irish-American Month.**

Activities

Newspaper in Education Week

Have students read and discuss local and national newspaper headlines. Without reading the articles, can students guess what the stories will be about? Talk about how a headline is written. Is it a complete sentence? Point out that the most important information or idea from the article must be covered in just a few words. Now challenge groups of students to write their own headlines about school activities or March events. Ask them to write the headlines in big, bold letters and display them on a bulletin board titled "Read All About It."

Irish-American Month

For more information on **Irish Americans,** look for books such as these:

Irish Americans, by Margaret Hall (Heinemann Library, ISBN 1-40340-734-7, 2003)

Irish Americans, by Sarah De Capua (Child's World, ISBN 1-56766-155-6, 2003)

Music in Our Schools Month

Have students research the instruments in an orchestra. Ask each student to find out more about one kind of instrument, then draw a picture or find one to illustrate. Put the instruments into categories, such as string, wind, or percussion. Now challenge students to create new instruments to go into each category. How would the instrument look? How would it be played? From what materials would it be made? Students can draw pictures of these new creations or even create the instruments to share with the class.

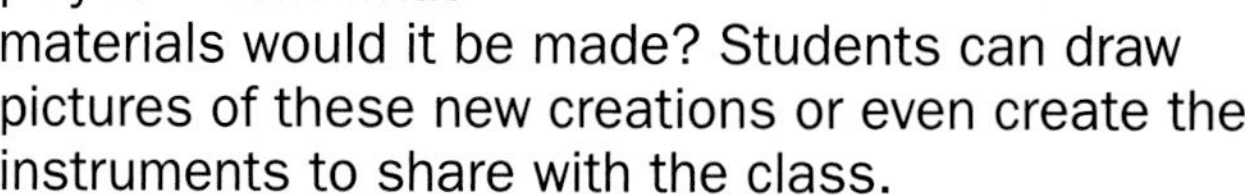

This Day in History

For additional March events, go to *This Day in History* at **www.sfsocialstudies.com.** Select a birthday or historic event for any day in March and base an activity on it.

Alternatively, have students go to this Web site and choose an event in March on which to do a project or report.

April

The Libraries Of The Future

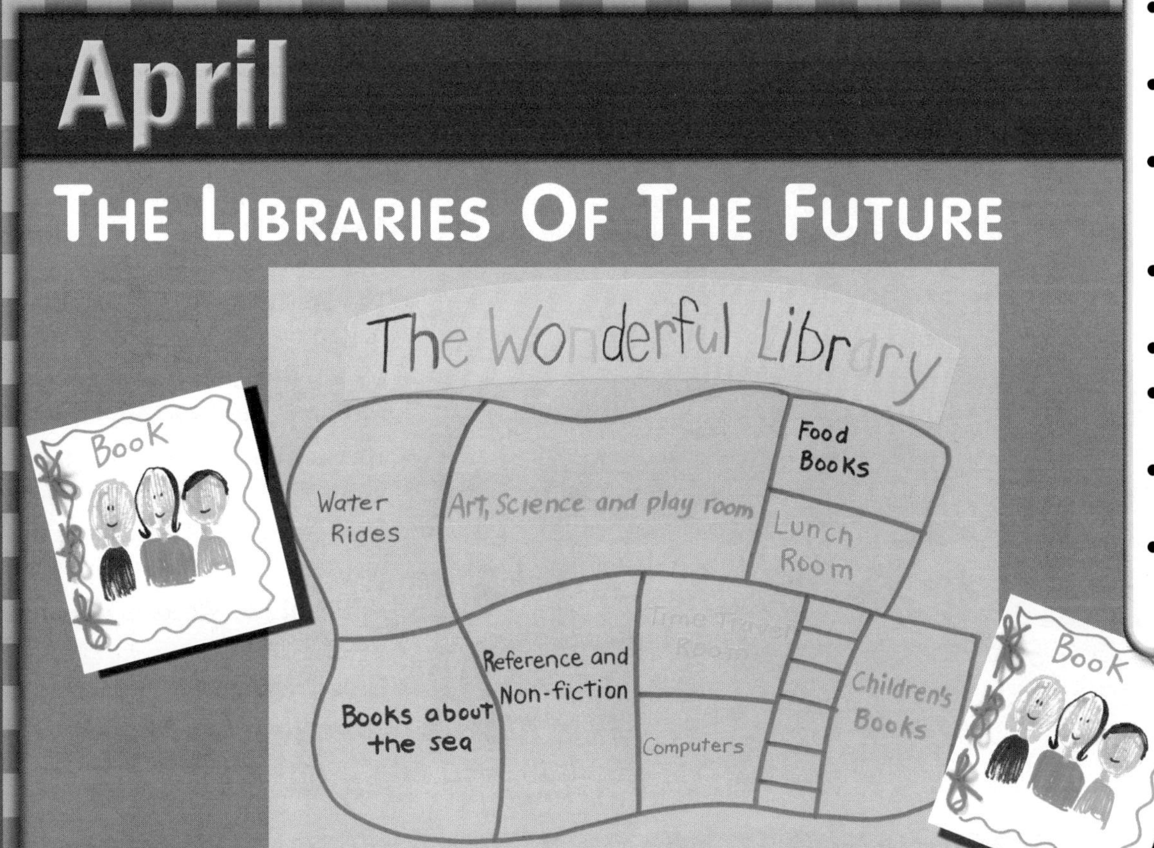

April Facts

- April is the fourth month of the year and has 30 days.
- **Thomas Jefferson** was born on April 13, 1743.
- The United States **Civil War** started (1861) and ended (1865) in April.
- April is **Math Education Month** and **National Poetry Month.**
- **Earth Day** is April 22.
- The **midnight ride of Paul Revere** started on April 18, 1776.
- **National Library Week** is the second week in April.
- On April 14, 1828, the **first American Dictionary** was published by Noah Webster.

Activities

National Library Week

Have students research the history of public libraries. Students can look at layouts of some of the country's famous libraries. Discuss why each one is organized the way it is. Where are the children's books? The magazines? The resource materials? The computers? Now ask students what they would like to see in the libraries of the future. Ask students to create their own libraries by drawing floor plans. Have each student create a name for the library, then display the libraries on a bulletin board titled "The Libraries of the Future." Ask each student to explain why he included what he did in his plans.

Paul Revere's Ride

For more information on **Paul Revere's ride,** look for books such as these.

The Midnight Ride of Paul Revere, by Henry Wadsworth Longfellow (National Geographic Society, ISBN 0-7922-6558-0, 2002)

Paul Revere: American Patriot, by JoAnn A. Grote (Chelsea House Publishers, ISBN 0-7910-5355-5, 2000)

Civil War

Ask students what they know about the Civil War. Talk about the mid-1800s and what was going on in the South and the North. Display pictures of Civil War soldiers and families from that time period. Ask students to select a photo and have them write a story about one of the people in that picture. Put the stories together in a "Civil War Journal."

This Day in History

For additional April events, go to *This Day in History* at **www.sfsocialstudies.com**. Select a birthday or historic event for any day in April and base an activity on it.

Alternatively, have students go to this Web site and choose an event in April on which to do a project or report.

May

Kentucky Derby Winners

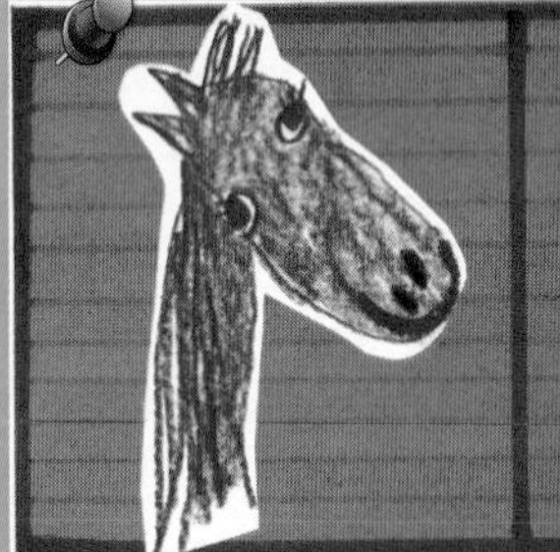

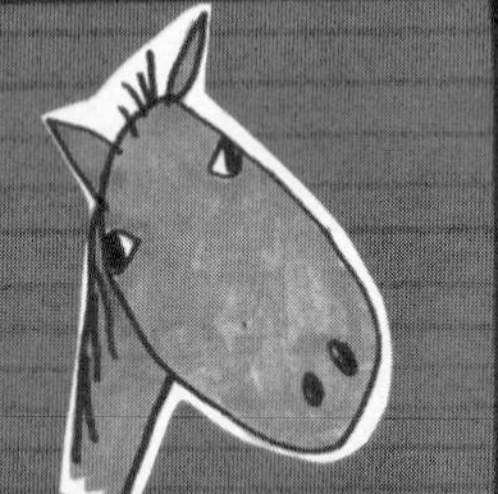

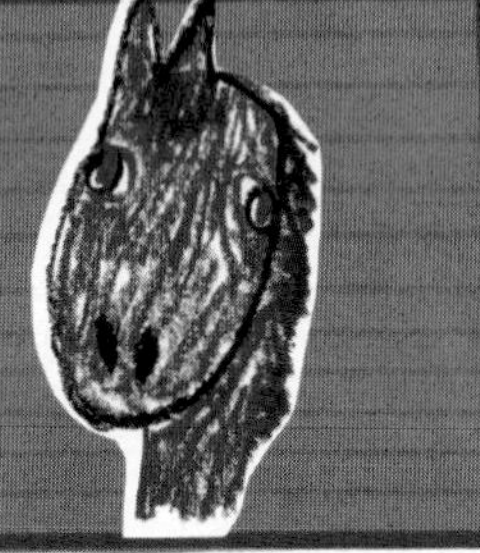

Funny Cide

In 2003, Funny Cide Won the Kentucky Derby. The jockey's name was J. Santos and the winning time was 2:01.19

Secretariat

In, 1973, Secretariat Won the Kentucky Derby. The jockey's name was R. Turcotte and the winning time was 1:59 2/5

Flying Ebony

In 1925, Flying Ebony won the Kentucky Derby. The Jockey's name was E. Sande, and the winning time was 2:07 3/5

Aristides

In 1875, Aristides won the Kentucky Derby. The jockey's name was O. Lewis, and the winning time was 2:37 3/4

May Facts

- May is the fifth month of the year and has 31 days.
- **Memorial Day** is the last Monday in May.
- The **Lewis and Clark Expedition** began on May 14, 1804.
- May is **National Book Month** and **National Transportation Month.**
- The **Kentucky Derby** takes place on the first Saturday in May.
- The Mexican holiday **Cinco de Mayo** is celebrated on May 5.
- **National Pet Week** is the first week in May.
- **Limerick Day** is May 12.

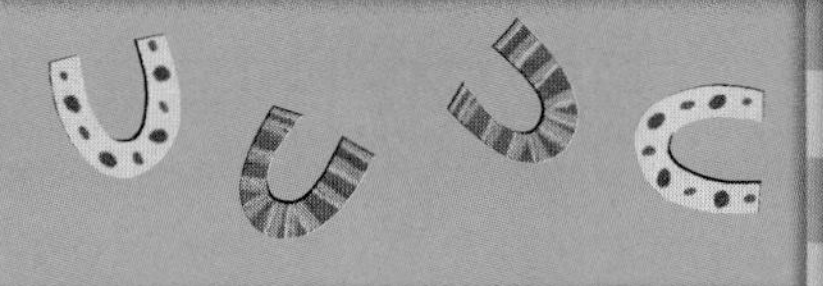

Activities

The Kentucky Derby

Research the history of the Kentucky Derby. Make a list of the winning horses from each year the race has been run. Have students work in small groups to select a horse to research. Ask students to write down the history of the horse. Have them include the horse's jockey at the Kentucky Derby, its owner, its trainer, and its number and race colors. Have students write down their information and draw a picture of their horse's head to be used for a bulletin board titled "Kentucky Derby Winners."

Limerick Day

For more information on **limericks,** look for books such as these:

The Kingfisher Book of Funny Poems, selected by Roger McGough (Kingfisher, ISBN 0-7534-5480-7, 2002)

Knock at a Star: A Child's Introduction to Poetry, compiled by X.J. Kennedy and Dorothy Kennedy (Little, Brown and Company, ISBN 0-316-48800-3, 1999)

Cinco de Mayo

Cinco de Mayo is a celebration of Mexican customs, culture, food and music. It honors a group of Mexican militia who stopped the French army from advancing to Mexico City in 1862. Have students research this holiday and choose an activity, game, custom, or recipe to share with the class. Plan a Cinco de Mayo fiesta and invite another class to join the fun!

This Day in History

For additional May events, go to *This Day in History* at **www.sfsocialstudies.com**. Select a birthday or historic event for any day in May and base an activity on it.

Alternatively, have students go to this Web site and choose an event in May on which to do a project or report.

June

New Signs Of Safety

Watch your step

Slow Down

cat Crossing

Keep off

June Facts

- June is the sixth month of the year and has 30 days. Summer begins in June.
- **Flag Day** is June 14.
- The third Sunday in June is **Father's Day.**
- On June 20, 1782, the **Great Seal of the United States** was adopted by Congress.
- June is **National Dairy Month** and **National Safety Month.**
- **World Juggling Day** is June 14.
- June 1 is **Doughnut Day.**
- June 18 is **International Picnic Day.**

Activities

National Safety Month

In honor of National Safety Month, have students research different types of safety signs that are used in stores, in businesses, in schools, and on roads. With the class, discuss the size, shape, and color of these signs. Discuss the words and lettering used on each sign. Now ask students to design their own safety signs, keeping in mind what they have learned about the real signs. Display the signs on the bulletin board titled "New Signs of Safety."

The Great Seal of the United States

For more information on the **Great Seal of the United States,** look for books such as these.

The American Eagle: The Symbol of America, by Jon Wilson (Child's World, ISBN 1-56766-545-4, 1999)

The Bald Eagle, by Debbie L. Yanuck (Capstone Press, ISBN 0-7368-1629-1, 2003)

International Picnic Day

Plan a picnic for the entire class! Have students work in small groups to plan the menu, the destination, the supply list, and the total cost of such an event. Ask students to use grocery store ads from the newspaper to get an idea of the cost of food and other items. If possible, gather the goods and get going on a picnic adventure!

This Day in History

For additional June events, go to *This Day in History* at **www.sfsocialstudies.com**. Select a birthday or historic event for any day in June and base an activity on it.

Alternatively, have students go to this Web site and choose an event in June on which to do a project or report.

July

Fun and Games Are Everywhere

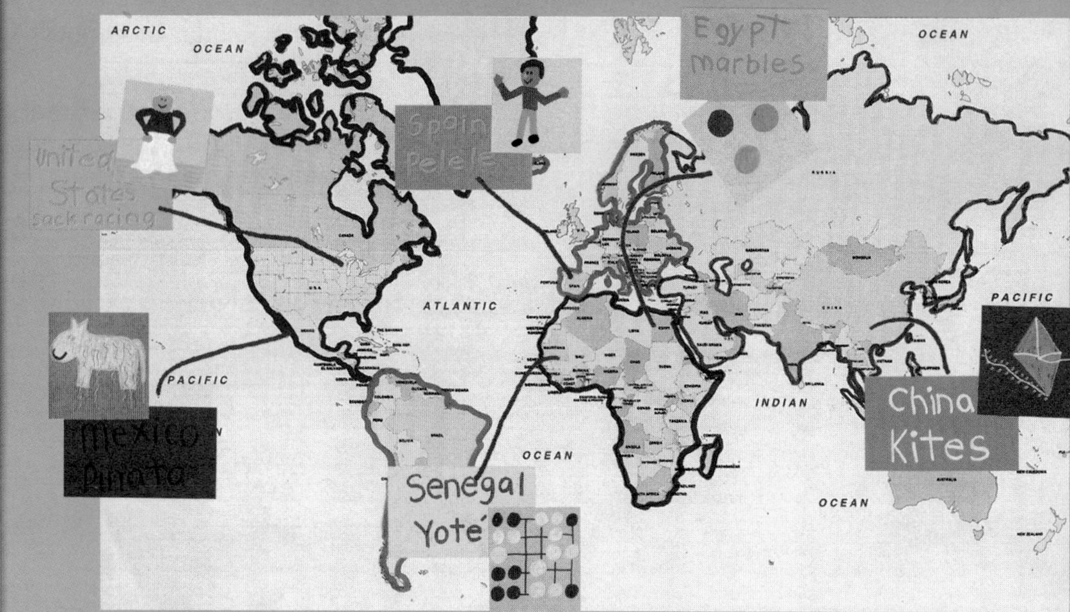

July Facts

- July is the seventh month of the year and has 31 days.
- **Independence Day** is July 4.
- The **first moon landing** was on July 20, 1969.
- July is **National Hot Dog Month.**
- July is **Recreation and Parks Month.**
- July is **National Ice Cream Month.**
- The **Liberty Bell** cracked on July 8, 1835.
- **P. T. Barnum,** circus owner, was born on July 5, 1810.

Activities

Recreation and Parks Month

Help students research games that are played in different parts of the world for a special classroom Recreation Day. Have students choose a country and find out what group games and sports are played there. Ask students to mark the country on a world map. Then have them find or draw a picture of people playing a traditional game from that country. The map and pictures can be displayed on a bulletin board titled "Fun and Games Are Everywhere." Rules for each game can be posted beside each picture.

P.T. Barnum

For more information on **P.T. Barnum,** look for books such as these:

P.T. Barnum, by David K. Wright (Raintree Steck-Vaughn, ISBN 0-8172-4456-5, 1997)

P.T. Barnum: Genius of the Three-Ring Circus, by Karen Clemens Warrick (Enslow, ISBN 0-7660-1447-9, 2001)

Liberty Bell

Ask students what they know about the Liberty Bell. Then have them do further research to find out when it was made and what materials were used. Ask students why the Liberty Bell was rung on July 8, 1835. Had it been rung before then? Why was the crack not repaired? Ask students how they would fix the Liberty Bell if they could.

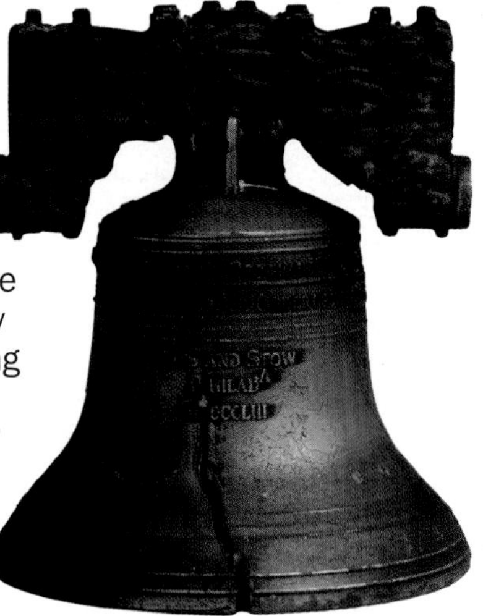

This Day in History

For additional July events, go to *This Day in History* at **www.sfsocialstudies.com.** Select a birthday or historic event for any day in July and base an activity on it.

Alternatively, have students go to this Web site and choose an event in July on which to do a project or report.

08160, 08161, 08162, 08163, 08164

Writing Rubrics

Narrative Writing TR30

Persuasive Writing TR32

Expressive/Descriptive Writing TR34

Expository Writing TR36

Rubric for Narrative Writing

	6	5	4
Content Quality and Idea Development	• well-focused on topic and purposeful • ideas thoroughly developed • reflects insight into writing situation • conveys sense of completeness	• focused on topic • ideas developed • reflects firm grasp of writing situation • conveys sense of completeness	• fairly focused on topic • moderately developed ideas • may include extraneous or loosely related material • conveys some sense of completeness
Voice	• clear and fitting for topic • expressive and engaging • well-suited for audience and purpose	• clear and fitting for topic • engaging • suited for audience and purpose	• fairly clear and seems to fit topic • fairly engaging style • suited for audience and purpose
Organization	• logical progression of ideas • sequence very clear	• logical progression of ideas • sequence clear	• organizational pattern apparent • some lapses may occur in organization • sequence fairly clear
Word Precision	• demonstrates mature command of language • precise and interesting word choice • wide variety of word choice	• demonstrates command of language • interesting word choice • variety of word choice	• adequate word choice • some variety of word choice
Sentence Fluency	• uses complete sentences • varied sentence structures and lengths	• uses complete sentences • varied sentence structures	• uses complete sentences • varied sentence structure attempted • some simple sentence structures
Mechanics	• correct spelling, punctuation, and capitalization • proper grammar and usage • errors do not prevent understanding	• few errors in spelling, punctuation, and capitalization • proper grammar and usage • errors do not prevent understanding	• mostly correct spelling, punctuation, and capitalization • few errors in grammar and usage • errors do not prevent understanding
If using a four-point rubric	**4**	**4**	**3**

3	2	1	Cannot be scored
• generally focused on topic • ideas may be vague • erratic development of ideas • some loosely related material • conveys some sense of completeness	• somewhat related to topic • insufficient development of ideas • includes extraneous or loosely related material • may lack sense of completeness	• minimally focused on topic • little, if any, development of ideas • lacks sense of completeness	• no focus on topic • no development of ideas • incomplete
• generally clear and seems to fit topic • engaging at times • generally suited for audience and purpose	• rarely comes through • basic attempt to engage reader • ill-suited for audience and purpose	• weak • basic attempt to engage reader • not suited for audience or purpose	• no attempt to engage reader • unaware of audience or purpose
• organizational pattern attempted • sequence generally clear	• little evidence of organizational pattern • sequence may be unclear	• no organizational pattern evident • sequence unclear	• no attempt at organization present • no sequence • cannot follow
• adequate word choice • limited, predictable, or occasionally vague word choice • some variety of word choice	• word choice limited, inappropriate, or vague • little variety of word choice	• limited or inappropriate word choice may obscure meaning • words/phrases repetitive and show minimal variety	• incorrect word choice • word choice shows no variety
• uses complete sentences • varied sentence structure attempted • generally simple sentence structures	• occasional sentence fragment or run-on sentence • limited to simple sentence structure	• excessive use of sentence fragments or run-on sentences • limited to simple sentence structure • sentences difficult to understand	• no complete sentences • sentence structure basic/below grade level
• generally correct spelling, punctuation, and capitalization • some errors in grammar and usage • errors do not prevent understanding	• some errors in spelling, punctuation, and capitalization • errors in grammar and usage • errors may prevent understanding	• errors in spelling, punctuation, and capitalization • frequent errors in grammar and usage • errors prevent understanding	• critical errors in spelling, punctuation, and capitalization/below grade level • critical errors in grammar and usage/below grade level • errors prevent understanding
3	**2**	**1**	

Rubric for Persuasive Writing

	6	5	4
Content Quality and Idea Development	• well-focused on topic • clear position stated • many facts and opinions to support position • convincing argument • conveys sense of completeness	• focused on topic • clear position stated • ample support • presents convincing argument • conveys sense of completeness	• fairly focused on topic • position apparent • adequate support, though perhaps uneven • may include extraneous or loosely related material • presents reasonable argument • conveys some sense of completeness
Voice	• clear and fitting for topic • confident, engaging, and credible • well-suited for audience and purpose	• clear and fitting for topic • engaging and credible • suited for audience and purpose	• fairly clear and seems to fit topic • fairly engaging • suited for audience and purpose
Organization	• logical organization with reasons presented in clear order • clearly contains beginning, middle, and end • easy to follow argument	• logical organization with reasons presented in order • contains beginning, middle, and end • easy to follow argument	• organizational pattern apparent • some lapses may occur in organization • vaguely contains beginning, middle, and end • fairly easy to follow argument
Word Precision	• demonstrates mature command of language • precise, persuasive, and interesting word choice • wide variety of word choice	• demonstrates command of language • interesting word choice • variety of word choice	• adequate word choice • some variety of word choice
Sentence Fluency	• uses complete sentences • varied sentence structures and lengths	• uses complete sentences • varied sentence structures	• uses complete sentences • varied sentence structure attempted • some simple sentence structures
Mechanics	• correct spelling, punctuation, and capitalization • proper grammar and usage • errors do not prevent understanding	• few errors in spelling, punctuation, and capitalization • proper grammar and usage • errors do not prevent understanding	• mostly correct spelling, punctuation, and capitalization • few errors in grammar and usage • errors do not prevent understanding
If using a four-point rubric	**4**	**4**	**3**

3	2	1	Cannot be scored
• generally focused on topic • position may be present • some support included, but erratic development • includes loosely related material • presents mediocre argument • conveys some sense of completeness	• somewhat related to topic • position may be unclear • inadequate support • includes extraneous or unrelated material • may lack sense of completeness	• minimally focused on topic • position unclear • little, if any, development of support • lacks sense of completeness	• no focus on topic • no position • no development of support • incomplete
• generally clear and seems to fit topic • engaging at times • generally suited for audience and purpose	• rarely comes through • basic attempt to engage reader • ill-suited for audience and purpose	• weak • basic attempt to engage reader • not suited for audience or purpose	• no attempt to engage reader • unaware of audience or purpose
• organizational pattern attempted • attempts to contain beginning, middle, and end • generally easy to follow argument	• little evidence of organizational pattern • somewhat difficult to follow argument	• no organizational pattern evident • difficult to follow argument	• no attempt at organization present • cannot follow argument
• adequate word choice • limited, predictable, or occasionally vague word choice • some variety of word choice	• word choice limited, inappropriate, or vague • little variety of word choice	• limited or inappropriate word choice may obscure meaning • words/phrases repetitive and show minimal variety	• incorrect word choice • word choice shows no variety
• uses complete sentences • varied sentence structure attempted • generally simple sentence structures	• occasional sentence fragment or run-on sentence • limited to simple sentence structure	• excessive use of sentence fragments or run-on sentences • limited to simple sentence structure • sentences difficult to understand	• no complete sentences • sentence structure basic/below grade level
• generally correct spelling, punctuation, and capitalization • some errors in grammar and usage • errors do not prevent understanding	• some errors in spelling, punctuation, and capitalization • errors in grammar and usage • errors may prevent understanding	• errors in spelling, punctuation, and capitalization • frequent errors in grammar and usage • errors prevent understanding	• critical errors in spelling, punctuation, and capitalization/below grade level • critical errors in grammar and usage/below grade level • errors prevent understanding
3	**2**	**1**	

Rubric for Expressive/Descriptive Writing

	6	5	4
Content Quality and Idea Development	• well-focused on topic • ideas supported with interesting and vivid details • "paints a picture" for reader • conveys sense of completeness	• focused on topic • ideas supported with details • sustains interest of reader • conveys sense of completeness	• fairly focused on topic • ideas supported with adequate detail, but development may be uneven • may include extraneous or loosely related material • conveys some sense of completeness
Voice	• clear and fitting for topic • thoughtful, expressive, and engaging • well-suited for audience and purpose	• clear and fitting for topic • expressive and engaging • suited for audience and purpose	• fairly clear and seems to fit topic • fairly engaging with some expression • suited for audience and purpose
Organization	• logical progression of ideas • easy to follow	• logical progression of ideas • easy to follow	• organizational pattern apparent • some lapses may occur in organization • fairly easy to follow
Word Precision	• demonstrates mature command of language • precise, vivid, and interesting word choice • wide variety of word choice	• demonstrates command of language • interesting word choice • variety of word choice	• adequate word choice • some variety of word choice
Sentence Fluency	• uses complete sentences • varied sentence structures and lengths	• uses complete sentences • varied sentence structures	• uses complete sentences • varied sentence structure attempted • some simple sentence structures
Mechanics	• correct spelling, punctuation, and capitalization • proper grammar and usage • errors do not prevent understanding	• few errors in spelling, punctuation, and capitalization • proper grammar and usage • errors do not prevent understanding	• mostly correct spelling, punctuation, and capitalization • few errors in grammar and usage • errors do not prevent understanding
If using a four-point rubric	**4**	**4**	**3**

3	2	1	Cannot be scored
• generally focused on topic • ideas may be vague • some details included, but erratic development • some loosely related material • conveys some sense of completeness	• somewhat related to topic • inadequate details • includes extraneous or unrelated material • may lack sense of completeness	• minimally focused on topic • little, if any, development of ideas • lacks sense of completeness	• no focus on topic • no development of ideas • incomplete
• generally clear and seems to fit topic • engaging at times • generally suited for audience and purpose	• rarely comes through • basic attempt to engage reader • ill-suited for audience and purpose	• weak • basic attempt to engage reader • not suited for audience or purpose	• no attempt to engage reader • unaware of audience or purpose
• organizational pattern attempted • generally easy to follow	• little evidence of organizational pattern • somewhat difficult to follow	• no organizational pattern evident • difficult to follow	• no attempt at organization present • cannot follow
• adequate word choice • limited, predictable, or occasionally vague word choice • some variety of word choice	• word choice limited, inappropriate, or vague • little variety of word choice	• limited or inappropriate word choice may obscure meaning • words/phrases repetitive and show minimal variety	• incorrect word choice • word choice shows no variety
• uses complete sentences • varied sentence structure attempted • generally simple sentence structures	• occasional sentence fragment or run-on sentence • limited to simple sentence structure	• excessive use of sentence fragments or run-on sentences • limited to simple sentence structure • sentences difficult to understand	• no complete sentences • sentence structure basic/below grade level
• generally correct spelling, punctuation, and capitalization • some errors in grammar and usage • errors do not prevent understanding	• some errors in spelling, punctuation, and capitalization • errors in grammar and usage • errors may prevent understanding	• errors in spelling, punctuation, and capitalization • frequent errors in grammar and usage • errors prevent understanding	• critical errors in spelling, punctuation, and capitalization/below grade level • critical errors in grammar and usage/below grade level • errors prevent understanding
3	2	1	

Rubric for Expository Writing

	6	5	4
Content Quality and Idea Development	• well-focused on topic • ideas supported with interesting details • conveys sense of completeness	• focused on topic • ideas supported with details • conveys sense of completeness	• fairly focused on topic • ideas supported with adequate detail, but development may be uneven • may include extraneous or loosely related material • conveys some sense of completeness
Voice	• clear and fitting for topic • engaging • well-suited for audience and purpose	• clear and fitting for topic • engaging • suited for audience and purpose	• fairly clear and seems to fit topic • fairly engaging • suited for audience and purpose
Organization	• logical progression of ideas • excellent transitions • easy to follow	• logical progression of ideas • good transitions • easy to follow	• organizational pattern apparent • some lapses may occur in organization • some transitions • fairly easy to follow
Word Precision	• demonstrates mature command of language • precise, interesting word choice • wide variety of word choice	• demonstrates command of language • precision in word choice • variety of word choice	• adequate word choice • some variety of word choice
Sentence Fluency	• strong topic sentence • uses complete sentences • varied sentence structures and lengths	• good topic sentence • uses complete sentences • varied sentence structures	• adequate topic sentence • uses complete sentences • varied sentence structure attempted • some simple sentence structures
Mechanics	• correct spelling, punctuation, and capitalization • proper grammar and usage • errors do not prevent understanding	• few errors in spelling, punctuation, and capitalization • proper grammar and usage • errors do not prevent understanding	• mostly correct spelling, punctuation, and capitalization • few errors in grammar and usage • errors do not prevent understanding
If using a four-point rubric	**4**	**4**	**3**

3	2	1	Cannot be scored
• generally focused on topic • some loosely related material • some details included, but erratic development	• somewhat related to topic • inadequate details • includes extraneous or unrelated material • may lack sense of completeness	• minimally focused on topic • little, if any, development of ideas • lacks sense of completeness	• no focus on topic • no development of ideas • incomplete
• generally clear and seems to fit topic • engaging at times • generally suited for audience and purpose	• rarely comes through • basic attempt to engage reader • ill-suited for audience and purpose	• weak • basic attempt to engage reader • not suited for audience or purpose	• no attempt to engage reader • unaware of audience or purpose
• organizational pattern attempted • few transitions • generally easy to follow	• little evidence of organizational pattern • no transitions • somewhat difficult to follow	• no organizational pattern evident • difficult to follow	• no attempt at organization present • cannot follow
• adequate word choice • limited, predictable, or occasionally vague word choice • some variety of word choice	• word choice limited, inappropriate, or vague • little variety of word choice	• limited or inappropriate word choice may obscure meaning • words/phrases repetitive and show minimal variety	• incorrect word choice • word choice shows no variety
• adequate topic sentence • uses complete sentences • varied sentence structure attempted • generally simple sentence structures	• weak topic sentence • occasional sentence fragment or run-on sentence • limited to simple sentence structure	• topic sentence not evident • excessive use of sentence fragments or run-on sentences • limited to simple sentence structure • sentences difficult to understand	• no topic sentence • no complete sentences • sentence structure basic/below grade level
• generally correct spelling, punctuation, and capitalization • some errors in grammar and usage • errors do not prevent understanding	• some errors in spelling, punctuation, and capitalization • errors in grammar and usage • errors may prevent understanding	• errors in spelling, punctuation, and capitalization • frequent errors in grammar and usage • errors prevent understanding	• critical errors in spelling, punctuation, and capitalization/below grade level • critical errors in grammar and usage/below grade level • errors prevent understanding
3	**2**	**1**	

Unit 1 Bibliography

Death Valley National Park, by David Petersen (Children's Press, ISBN 0-516-26095-2, 1997) **Easy**

Ellis Island: New Hope in a New Land, by William J. Jacobs (Atheneum, ISBN 0-684-19171-7, 1990) **Easy**

How We Crossed the West: The Adventures of Lewis & Clark, by Rosalyn Schanzer (National Geographic Society, ISBN 0-7922-3738-2, 1997) **Easy**

Indians of the Northeast, by Colin G. Callaway (Facts on File, ISBN 0-8160-2389-1, 1991) **Easy**

Recycle! A Handbook for Kids, by Gail Gibbons (Little Brown & Co., ISBN 0-316-30943-5, 1996) **Easy**

The Story of Money, by Betsy Maestro (William Morrow, ISBN 0-688-13304-5, 1995) **Easy**

The Story of the White House, by Kate Waters (Scholastic Trade, ISBN 0-590-43334-2, 1992) **Easy**

America's Top 10 Natural Wonders, by Edward Ricciuti (Blackbirch Marketing, ISBN 1-56711-192-0, 1997) **On-Level**

Bold Journey: West with Lewis and Clark, by Charles Bohner (Houghton Mifflin Co., ISBN 0-395-54978-7, 1989) **On-Level**

The Dead Sea: The Saltiest Sea, by Aileen Weintraub (PowerKids Press, ISBN 0-8239-5637-7, 2000) **On-Level**

Girl of the Shining Mountains: Sacagawea's Story, by Connie Roop and Peter Roop (Hyperion Press, ISBN 0-7868-0492-0, 1999) **On-Level**

Quilted Landscape: Conversations with Young Immigrants, by Yale Strom (Simon & Schuster, ISBN 0-689-80074-6, 1996) **On-Level**

Shh! We're Writing the Constitution, by Jean Fritz (PaperStar, ISBN 0-698-11624-0, 1997) **On-Level** ***ALA Notable Book***

How the Weather Works, by Michael Allaby (Reader's Digest Assn., ISBN 0-7621-0234-9, 1999) **Challenge**

Legends of Landforms: Native American Lore and the Geology of the Land, by Carole Garbuny Vogel (Millbrook Press, ISBN 0-7613-0272-7, 1999) **Challenge**

Meet the Wild Southwest: Land of Hoodoos and Gila Monsters, by Susan J. Tweit (Graphic Arts Center Publishing Co., ISBN 0-88240-468-7, 1995) **Challenge**

Native American Rock Art: Messages from the Past, by Yvette La Pierre (Lickle Publishing, ISBN 1-56566-064-1, 1994) **Challenge**

To the Top of Everest, by Laurie Skreslet and Elizabeth MacLeod (contributor) (Kids Can Press, ISBN 1-55074-721-5, 2001) **Challenge**

Westward Expansion: Primary Sources, by Tom Pendergast and Sara Pendergast (U*X*L, ISBN 0-7876-4864-7, 2001) **Challenge**

Where Do You Think You're Going, Christopher Columbus? by Jean Fritz (PaperStar, ISBN 0-698-11580-5, 1997) **Challenge** ***ALA Notable Book***

Globalization and the Challenges of the New Century: A Reader, Patrick O'Meara, Howard D. Mehlinger, and Matthew Krain, eds. (Indiana University Press, ISBN 0-253-21355-X, 2000) **Teacher reference**

It Happened in the White House: Extraordinary Tales from America's Most Famous Home, by Kathleen Karr (Hyperion Press, ISBN 0-7868-1560-4, 2000) **Teacher reference**

Undaunted Courage: Meriwether Lewis, Thomas Jefferson, and the Opening of the American West, by Stephen E. Ambrose (Touchstone Books, ISBN 0-684-82697-6, 1997) **Teacher reference**

***Discovery Channel School* Video**

The Frontier Discover how two cultures clashed to create a new balance. (Item #716704E, 26 minutes)

 Look for this symbol throughout the Teacher's Edition to find **Award-Winning Selections**.

The Ballot Box Battle, by Emily Arnold McCully (Dragonfly, ISBN 0-679-89312-1, 1998) **Easy**

Cranberries: Fruit of the Bogs, by Diane L. Burns (Lerner Publishing, ISBN 0-87614-964-6, 1994) **Easy**

Dancing on the Sand: A Story of an Atlantic Blue Crab, by Kathleen M. Hollenbeck (Soundprints Corp Audio, ISBN 1-56899-730-2, 1999) **Easy**

If Your Name Was Changed at Ellis Island, by Ellen Levine (Scholastic Trade, ISBN 0-590-43829-8, 1994) **Easy**

Square Dancing, by Mark Thomas (Children's Press, ISBN 0-516-23070-0, 2001) **Easy**

The Tower to the Sun, by Colin Thompson (Knopf, ISBN 0-679-98334-1, 1997) **Easy**

Way to Go, Alex! by Robin Pulver (Albert Whitman & Company, ISBN 0-807-51583-3, 1999) **Easy**

Awesome Chesapeake: A Kid's Guide to the Bay, by David Owen Bell (Tidewater Publishing, ISBN 0-87033-457-3, 1994) **On-Level**

Eagle Song, by Joseph Bruchac (Puffin, ISBN 0-14-130169-4, 1999) **On-Level**

Famine, by Christopher F. Lampton (Millbrook Press, ISBN 1-56294-317-0, 1994) **On-Level**

Rhode Island, by Kathleen Thompson (Raintree/Steck-Vaughn, ISBN 0-8114-7466-6, 1996) **On-Level**

The Road to Seneca Falls, by Gwenyth Swain (Lerner Publishing, ISBN 1-57505-025-0, 1996) **On-Level**

Sojourner Truth: Ain't I a Woman? by Patricia C. McKissack and Fredrick McKissack (Scholastic Trade, ISBN 0-590-44691-6, 1994) **On-Level** ***ALA Notable Book, Coretta Scott King Honor Book***

Sugaring Time, by Kathryn Lasky (Aladdin, ISBN 0-689-71081-X, 1986) **On-Level**

The Maple Syrup Book, by Marilyn Linton (Kids Can Press, ISBN 0-919964-52-4, 1993) **Challenge**

Roger Williams, by Mark Ammerman (Barbour Publishing, ISBN 1-55748-761-8, 1996) **Challenge**

Waterman's Boy, by Susan Sharpe (Simon & Schuster, ISBN 0-02-782351-2, 1990) **Challenge**

Where Did All the Water Go? by Carolyn Stearns (Tidewater Publishers, ISBN 0-87033-506-5, 1998) **Challenge**

Women Win the Vote, by JoAnn A. Grote (Barbour & Company, ISBN 1-57748-452-5, 1998) **Challenge**

Women's Rights and Nothing Less, by Lisa Frederiksen Bohannon (Morgan Reynolds, ISBN 1-883846-66-8, 2001) **Challenge**

You Want Women to Vote, Lizzie Stanton? by Jean Fritz (PaperStar, ISBN 0-698-11764-6, 1999) **Challenge**

The Great Irish Potato Famine, by James S. Donnelly, (Sutton Publishing, ISBN 0-7509-2928-6, 2003) **Teacher reference**

The Industrial Revolution, by James A. Corrick (Lucent Books, ISBN 1-56006-318-1, 1998) **Teacher reference**

Watching Nature: A Mid-Atlantic Natural History, by Mark S. Garland (Smithsonian Institution Press, ISBN 1-56098-742-1, 2000) **Teacher reference**

***Discovery Channel School* Video**

Understanding: Cities Explore "The Big Apple" and four other great cities around the world, examining how they function, their history, and their evolution. (Item #717611, 52 minutes)

 Look for this symbol throughout the Teacher's Edition to find **Award-Winning Selections**.

I Am Rosa Parks, by Rosa Parks (Puffin, ISBN 0-14-130710-2, 1999) **Easy**

Manatee Blues, by Laurie Halse Anderson (Pleasant Company Publications, ISBN 1-58485-049-3, 2000) **Easy**

Mathew Brady: Civil War Photographer, by Elizabeth Van Steenwyk (Franklin Watts, ISBN 0-531-20264-X, 1997) **Easy**

Mist Over the Mountains: Appalachia and Its People, by Raymond Bial (Houghton Mifflin, ISBN 0-395-73569-6, 1997) **Easy**

Thomas Jefferson, by Lucia Raatma (Compass Point Books, ISBN 0-7565-0070-2, 2001) **Easy**

Thomas Jefferson: A Picture Book Biography, by James Cross Giblin (Scholastic Trade, ISBN 0-590-44838-2, 1994) **Easy**

Together in Pincone Patch, by Thomas F. Yezerski (Farrar, Straus & Giroux, ISBN 0-374-37647-6, 1998) **Easy**

The Trail of Tears, by Joseph Bruchac (Random House, ISBN 0-679-89052-1, 1999) **Easy**

Young Rosa Parks: A Civil Rights Heroine, by Anne Benjamin (Troll Associates, ISBN 0-8167-3775-4, 2003) **Easy**

Boy of the Deeps, by Ian Wallace (Dorling Kindersley Publishing, ISBN 0-7894-2569-6, 1999) **On-Level**

The Boys' War: Confederate and Union Soldiers Talk About the Civil War, by Jim Murphy (Clarion Books, ISBN 0-395-66412-8, 1993) **On-Level** ***Golden Kite Award***

The Day Martin Luther King, Jr., Was Shot: A Photo History of the Civil Rights Movement, by Jim Haskins (Scholastic Inc., ISBN 0-590-43661-9, 1992) **On-Level**

Georgia, by Nancy Robinson Masters (Children's Press, ISBN 0-516-20685-0), 1999) **On-Level**

Let It Shine: Stories of Black Women Freedom Fighters, by Andrea Davis Pinkney (Gulliver Books, ISBN 0-15-201005-X, 2000) **On-Level** ***Coretta Scott King Honor Book***

Monticello, by Leonard Everett Fisher (Holiday House, ISBN 0-8234-1406-X, 1996) **On-Level**

Rosa Parks: From the Back of the Bus to the Front of a Movement, by Camilla Wilson (Scholastic Paperbacks, ISBN 0-439-16330-7, 2001) **On-Level**

Strange But True Civil War Stories, by Nancy Clayton (Lowell House Juvenile Books, ISBN 0-7373-0110-4, 1999) **On-Level**

Tom Jefferson: Third President of the United States, by Helen Albee Monsell (Aladdin Paperbacks, ISBN 0-689-71347-9, 1989) **On-Level**

Dancing Drum: A Cherokee Legend, by Terri Cohlene (Troll Associates, ISBN 0-8167-2362-1, 2003) **Challenge**

Freedom's Children: Young Civil Rights Activists Tell Their Own Stories, by Ellen Levine (Puffin, ISBN 0-698-11870-7, 2000) **Challenge** ***Jane Addams Book Award***

George Washington, by Wendie C. Old (Enslow Publishers, ISBN 0-89490-832-4, 1997) **Challenge**

Growing Up in a Holler in the Mountains: An Appalachian Childhood, by Karen Gravelle (Franklin Watts, ISBN 0-531-11452-X, 1997) **Challenge**

Growing Up in Coal Country, by Susan Campbell Bartoletti (Houghton Mifflin, ISBN 0-395-77847-6, 1996) **Challenge** ***ALA Notable Book, Jane Addams Book Award***

Jammin' on the Avenue: Going to New Orleans, by Whitney Stewart (Four Corners Publishing, ISBN 1-893577-06-6, 2001) **Challenge**

Now Is Your Time! The African-American Struggle for Freedom, by Walter Dean Myers (HarperCollins Juvenile Books, ISBN 0-06-446120-3, 1992) **Challenge** ***ALA Notable Book, Coretta Scott King Award***

Roll of Thunder, Hear My Cry, by Mildred D. Taylor (Puffin, ISBN 0-14-038451-0, 1997) **Challenge** ***Newbery Medal Winner***

Rosa Parks: My Story, by Rosa Parks (Puffin, ISBN 0-14-130120-1, 1999) **Challenge**

The Education of Little Tree, by Forrest Carter, (University of New Mexico Press, ISBN 0-8263-2809-1, 2001) **Teacher reference** ***American Bestsellers Book of the Year***

Why We Can't Wait, by Martin Luther King, Jr. (Signet Classic, ISBN 0-451-52753-4, 2000) **Teacher reference**

***Discovery Channel School* Video**

Native Americans This video shows how Native American groups were affected by the arrival of European settlers. (Item #745299, 52 minutes)

 Look for this symbol throughout the Teacher's Edition to find **Award-Winning Selections**.

 ***I Have Heard of a Land,*** by Joyce Carol Thomas (HarperTrophy, ISBN 0-06-443617-9, 2000) **Easy** ***ALA Notable Book, Coretta Scott King Honor Book***

If You're Not from the Prairie..., by David Bouchard (Aladdin Paperbacks, ISBN 0-689-82035-6, 1998) **Easy**

 ***Little Town on the Prairie,*** by Laura Ingalls Wilder (HarperTrophy, ISBN 0-06-440007-7, 1953) **Easy** ***Newbery Honor Book***

The Messenger of Spring: A Chippewa/ Ojibwa Legend, by C. J. Taylor (Tundra Books, ISBN 0-88776-413-4, 1997) **Easy**

Pioneer Girl: The Story of Laura Ingalls Wilder, by William Anderson (HarperTrophy, ISBN 0-06-446234-X, 2000) **Easy**

 ***The Story of Jumping Mouse,*** by John Steptoe (William Morrow, ISBN 0-688-08740-X, 1989) **Easy** ***Caldecott Honor Book***

The Big Rivers: The Missouri, the Mississippi, and the Ohio, by Bruce Hiscock (Atheneum, ISBN 0-689-80871-2, 1997) **On-Level**

Children of the Dust Bowl: The True Story of the School at Weedpatch Camp, by Jerry Stanley (Crown Publishing, ISBN 0-517-88094-6, 1993) **On-Level**

Grandpa's John Deere Tractors, by Roy Harrington (American Society of Agricultural Engineers, ISBN 0-929355-81-4, 1996) **On-Level**

 ***Heartland,*** by Diane Siebert (HarperCollins Children's Books, ISBN 0-06-443287-4, 1999) **On-Level** ***Notable Children's Trade Book in Social Studies***

Laura's Album: A Remembrance Scrapbook of Laura Ingalls Wilder, by William Anderson (HarperCollins Juvenile Books, ISBN 0-06-027842-0, 1998) **On-Level**

One Nation, Many Tribes: How Kids Live in Milwaukee's Indian Community, by Kathleen Krull (Viking Penguin, ISBN 0-14-036522-2, 1999) **On-Level**

The Adventures of Tom Sawyer, by Mark Twain (Viking Children's Books, ISBN 0-670-86985-6, 1996) **Challenge**

 ***Caddie Woodlawn,*** by Carol Ryrie Brink (Aladdin Paperbacks, ISBN 0-689-81521-2, 1997) **Challenge** ***Newbery Honor Book***

Laura Ingalls Wilder: A Biography, by William Anderson (HarperCollins, ISBN 0-06-446103-3, 1995) **Challenge**

Lewis and Clark for Kids: Their Journey of Discovery with 21 Activities, by Janis Herbert (Chicago Review Press, ISBN 1-55652-374-2, 2003) **Challenge**

My Face to the Wind: The Diary of Sarah Jane Price, a Prairie Teacher, Broken Bow, Nebraska, 1881, by Jim Murphy (Scholastic Trade, ISBN 0-590-43810-7, 2001) **Challenge**

 ***Sarah, Plain and Tall,*** by Patricia MacLachlan (HarperCollins, ISBN 0-06-440205-3, 1987) **Challenge** ***ALA Notable Book, Newbery Medal Winner***

Cahokia: City of the Sun, by Claudia G. Mink (Cahokia Mounds Museum Society, ISBN 1-881563-00-6, 1995) **Teacher reference**

Meeting the Neighbors: Sketches of Life on the Northern Prairie, by W. Scott Olsen (North Star Press of St. Cloud, ISBN 0-878-39080-4, 1993) **Teacher reference**

 Look for this symbol throughout the Teacher's Edition to find **Award-Winning Selections.**

Cowboys & the Trappings of the Old West, by William Manns, Elizabeth Clair Flood (Zon International Publishing Co., ISBN 0-939549-13-1, 1997) **Easy**

Cowboys: Roundup on an American Ranch, by Joan Anderson (Scholastic Trade, ISBN 0-590-48424-9, 1996) **Easy**

Exploring the Earth with John Wesley Powell, by Michael Elsohn Ross (Carolrhoda Books, ISBN 1-57505-254-7, 2000) **Easy**

Here is the African Savanna, by Madeleine Dunphy (Hyperion Press, ISBN 0-7868-0162-X, 1999) **Easy**

The Legend of the African Bao-Bab Tree, by Bobbie Dooley Hunter (Africa World Press, ISBN 0-86543-422-0, 1994) **Easy**

The Navajos: A First Americans Book, by Virginia Driving Hawk Sneve (Holiday House, ISBN 0-8234-1168-0, 1993) **Easy**

Old Blue, by Sibyl Hancock (Penguin Putnam, ISBN 0-399-61141-X, 1980) **Easy** ***ALA Notable Book***

The Unbreakable Code, by Sara Hoagland Hunter (Northland Publishing, ISBN 0-87358-638-7, 1996) **Easy**

Anasazi, by Leonard Everett Fisher (Atheneum, ISBN 0-689-80737-6, 1997) **On-Level**

Calamity Jane, by Calamity Jane (Applewoods Books, ISBN 1-55709-369-5, 1997) **On-Level**

The Colorado River, by Carol B. Rawlins (Franklin Watts, ISBN 0-531-16421-7, 2000) **On-Level**

The Diary of John Wesley Powell, by John Wesley Powell (Benchmark Books, ISBN 0-7614-1013-9, 2000) **On-Level**

In the Days of the Vaqueros: America's First True Cowboys, by Russell Freedman (Clarion Books, ISBN 0-395-96788-0, 2001) **On-Level**

A Right Fine Life: Kit Carson on the Santa Fe Trail, by Andrew Glass (Holiday House, ISBN 0-8234-1326-8, 1997) **On-Level**

Tree of Life: The World of the African Baobab, by Barbara Bash (Sierra Club Books, ISBN 1-57805-086-3, 2002) **On-Level**

Valleys and Canyons, by Larry Dane Brimner (Children's Press, ISBN 0-516-27193-8, 2001) **On-Level**

Annie Oakley: Young Markswoman, by Ellen Wilson (Aladdin Paperbacks, ISBN 0-689-71346-0, 1989) **Challenge**

Desert Giant: The World of the Saguaro Cactus, by Barbara Bash (Econo-Clad Books, ISBN 0-8335-4225-7, 1999) **Challenge**

The Deserts of the Southwest, by Maria Mudd Ruth (Marshall Cavendish Corp., ISBN 0-7614-0899-1, 1999) **Challenge**

Get Along, Little Dogies: The Chisholm Trail Diary of Hallie Lou Wells: South Texas, 1878, by Lisa Waller Rogers (Texas Tech University Press, ISBN 0-89672-446-8, 2001) **Challenge**

In Search of the Grand Canyon: Down the Colorado with John Wesley Powell, by Mary Ann Fraser (Henry Holt & Company, ISBN 0-8050-5543-6, 1997) **Challenge**

John Wesley Powell: Explorer of Grand Canyon, by Roger A. Bruns (Enslow Publishers, ISBN 0-89490-783-2, 1997) **Challenge**

Out of the Dust, by Karen Hesse (Scholastic Paperbacks, ISBN 0-590-37125-8, 1999) **Challenge** ***Newbery Medal Winner***

Richard King: Texas Cattle Rancher, by Carl R. Green, William R. Sanford (Enslow Publishers, ISBN 0-89490-673-9, 1997) **Challenge**

Business Builders in Oil, by Nathan Aaseng (Oliver Press, ISBN 1-881508-56-0, 2000) **Teacher reference**

Cowboys in the Old West, by Gail B. Stewart (Lucent Books, ISBN 1-56006-077-8, 1995) **Teacher reference**

***Discovery Channel School* Video**

The Battle of the Alamo This video uses recent footage of the fort along with historic artwork from American hero Davy Crockett to re-create the Battle of the Alamo. (Item #715870, 52 minutes)

Look for this symbol throughout the Teacher's Edition to find **Award-Winning Selections**.

Unit 6 Bibliography

AWARD ***Boss of the Plains: The Hat That Won the West,*** by Laurie Carlson (Dorling Kindersley Publishing, ISBN 0-7894-2657-9, 2000) **Easy** ***ALA Notable Book***

Cut and Make Mexican Masks, by A. G. Smith and Josie Hazen (Dover Publications, ISBN 0-486-28794-7, 1995) **Easy**

Earthdance: How Volcanoes, Earthquakes, Tidal Waves and Geysers Shake Our Restless Planet, by Cynthia Pratt Nicolson (Kids Can Press, ISBN 1-55074-155-1, 1994) **Easy**

Giant Sequoia Trees, by Ginger Wadsworth (Lerner Publications Company, ISBN 0-8225-3001-5, 1995) **Easy**

AWARD ***Mountain Town,*** by Bonnie Geisert (Houghton Mifflin Co., ISBN 0-395-95390-1, 2000) **Easy** ***Parents' Choice Gold Award***

Nine for California, by Sonia Levitin (Orchard Books, ISBN 0-531-07176-6, 2000) **Easy**

The Wave of the Sea-Wolf, by David Wisniewski (Houghton Mifflin Co., ISBN 0-395-96892-5, 1999) **Easy**

Buried Treasures of the Rocky Mountain West: Legends of Lost Mines, Train Robbery Gold, Caves of Forgotten Riches, and Indians' Buried Silver, by W. C. Jameson (August House Publications, ISBN 0-87483-272-1, 1993) **On-Level**

Geysers: When Earth Roars, by Roy A. Gallant (Franklin Watts, ISBN 0-531-15838-1, 1998) **On-Level**

Glaciers, by John Ewart Gordon (Voyageur Press, ISBN 0-89658-559-X, 2001) **On-Level**

How I Survived the Oregon Trail: The Journal of Jesse Adams, by Laura Wilson (Beech Tree Books, ISBN 0-688-17276-8, 1999) **On-Level**

Northwest Coast Indian Punch-Out Masks, by A. G. Smith and Josie Hazen (Dover Publications, ISBN 0-486-29055-7, 1996) **On-Level**

Seeds of Hope: The Gold Rush Diary of Susanna Fairchild, California Territory, 1849, by Kristiana Gregory (Scholastic Trade, ISBN 0-590-51157-2, 2001) **On-Level**

World Book Looks at the American West, Brian Williams; Brenda Williams (World Book, Inc., ISBN 0-7166-1805-2, 1997) **On-Level**

Children of the Gold Rush, by Claire Rudolf Murphy and Jane G. Haigh (Alaska Northwest Books, ISBN 0-88240-548-9, 2001) **Challenge**

Cloud: Wild Stallion of the Rockies, by Ginger Kathrens (BowTie Press, ISBN 1-889540-70-6, 2001) **Challenge**

The Eagle's Shadow, by Nora Martin (Scholastic Trade, ISBN 0-590-36087-6, 1997) **Challenge**

The Hoover Dam, by Elizabeth Mann (Mikaya Press, ISBN 1-931414-02-5, 2003) **Challenge**

In the Heart of the Rockies, by G. A. Henty (Lost Classics Book Company, ISBN 1-890623-08-3, 1998) **Challenge**

Lost in Death Valley: The True Story of Four Families in California's Gold Rush, by Connie Goldsmith (Twenty First Century Books, ISBN 0-7613-1915-8, 2001) **Challenge**

Masks Tell Stories, by Carol Gelber (Millbrook Press, ISBN 1-56294-224-7, 1993) **Challenge**

The Tlingit: An Introduction to Their Culture & History, by Wallace M. Olson (Heritage Research, ISBN 0-965-90090-8, 1997) **Teacher reference**

The World Rushed In: The California Gold Rush Experience, by J. S. Holliday (Touchstone Books, ISBN 0-671-25538-X, 1983) **Teacher reference**

The Yellowstone Story: A History of Our First National Park, by Aubrey L. Haines (University Press of Colorado, ISBN 0-87081-390-0, 1996) **Teacher reference**

Discovery Channel School **Video**

How the West Was Lost Explore Native Americans' struggle to maintain their lands, lives, and cultures as settlers began moving west. (Item #716233, 52 minutes)

Look for this symbol throughout the Teacher's Edition to find **Award-Winning Selections**.

08160, 08161, 08162, 08163, 08164

Main Idea and Details

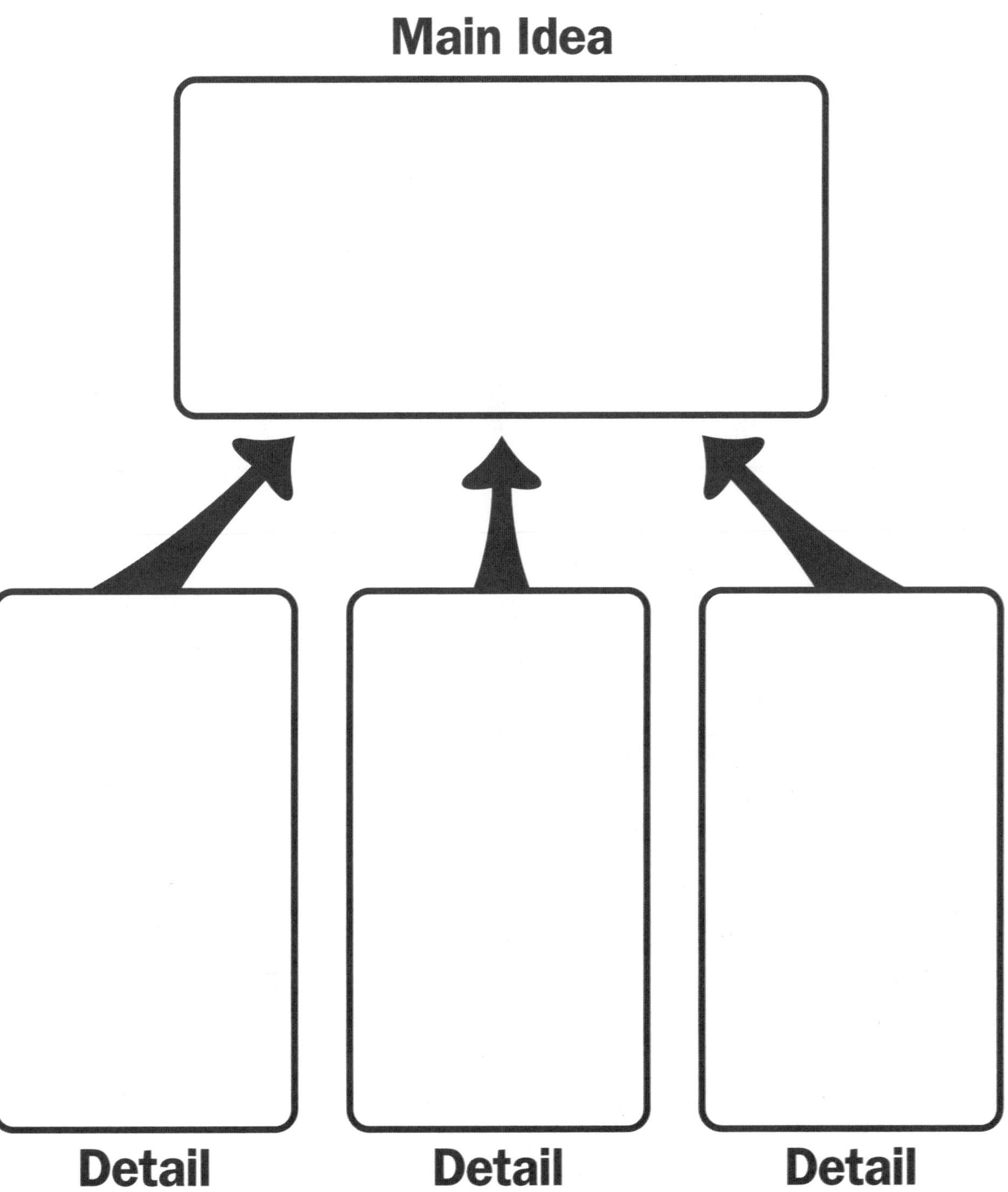

Sequence

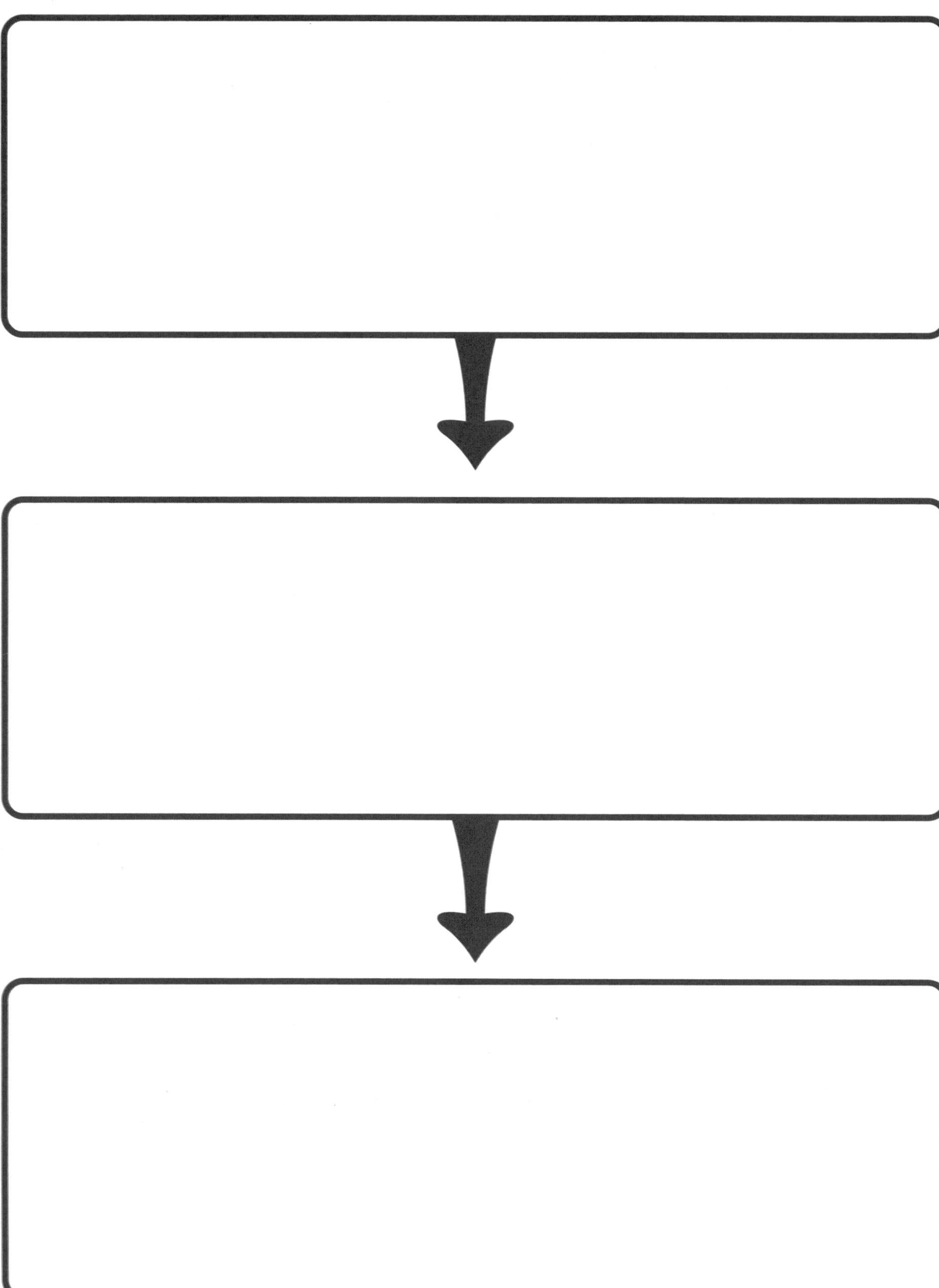

Cause and Effect

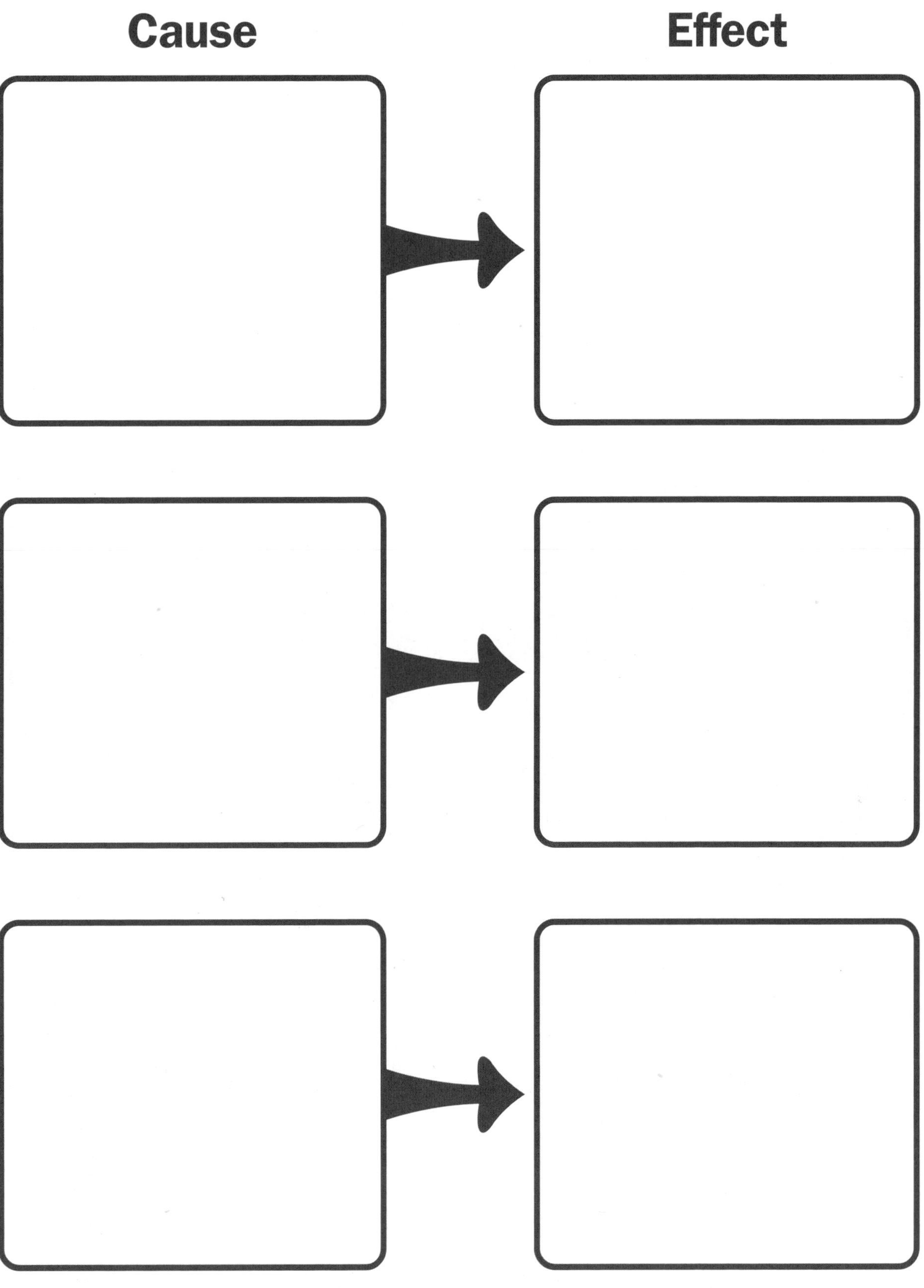

Compare and Contrast

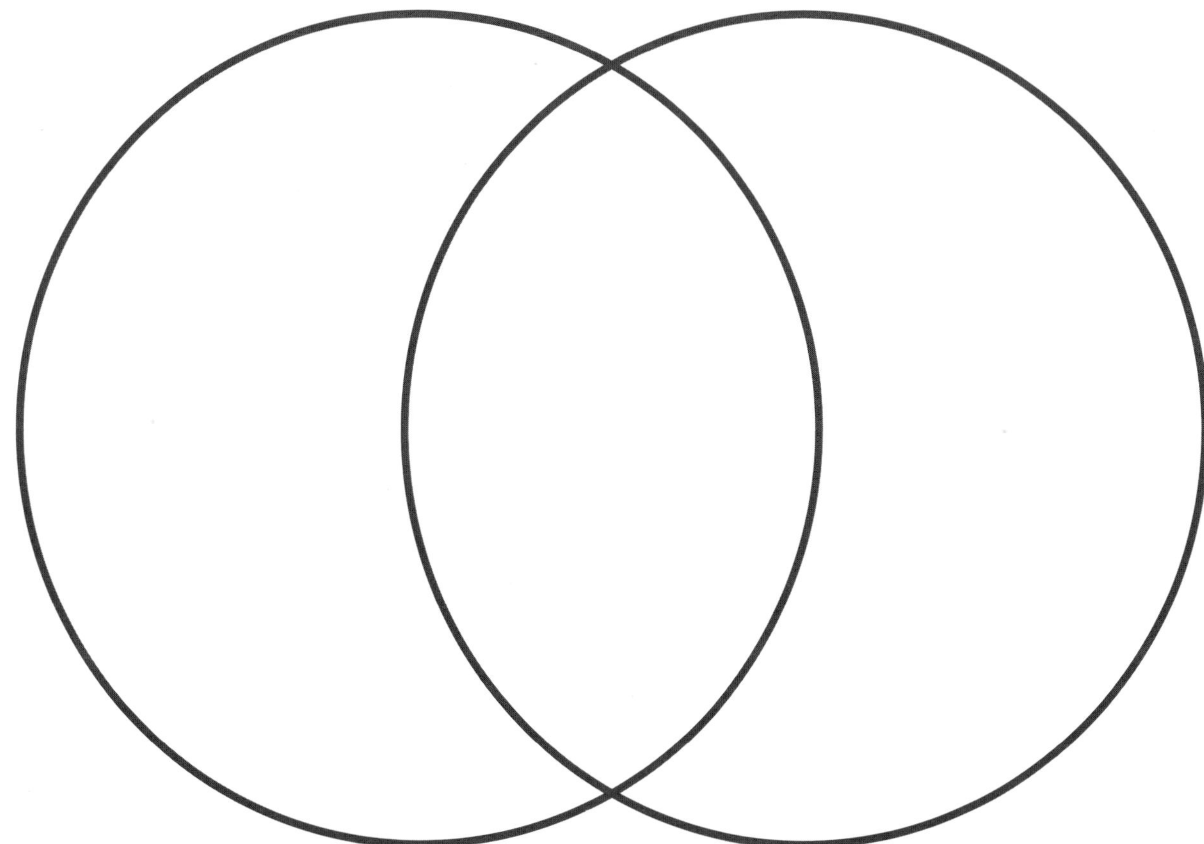

Compare and Contrast

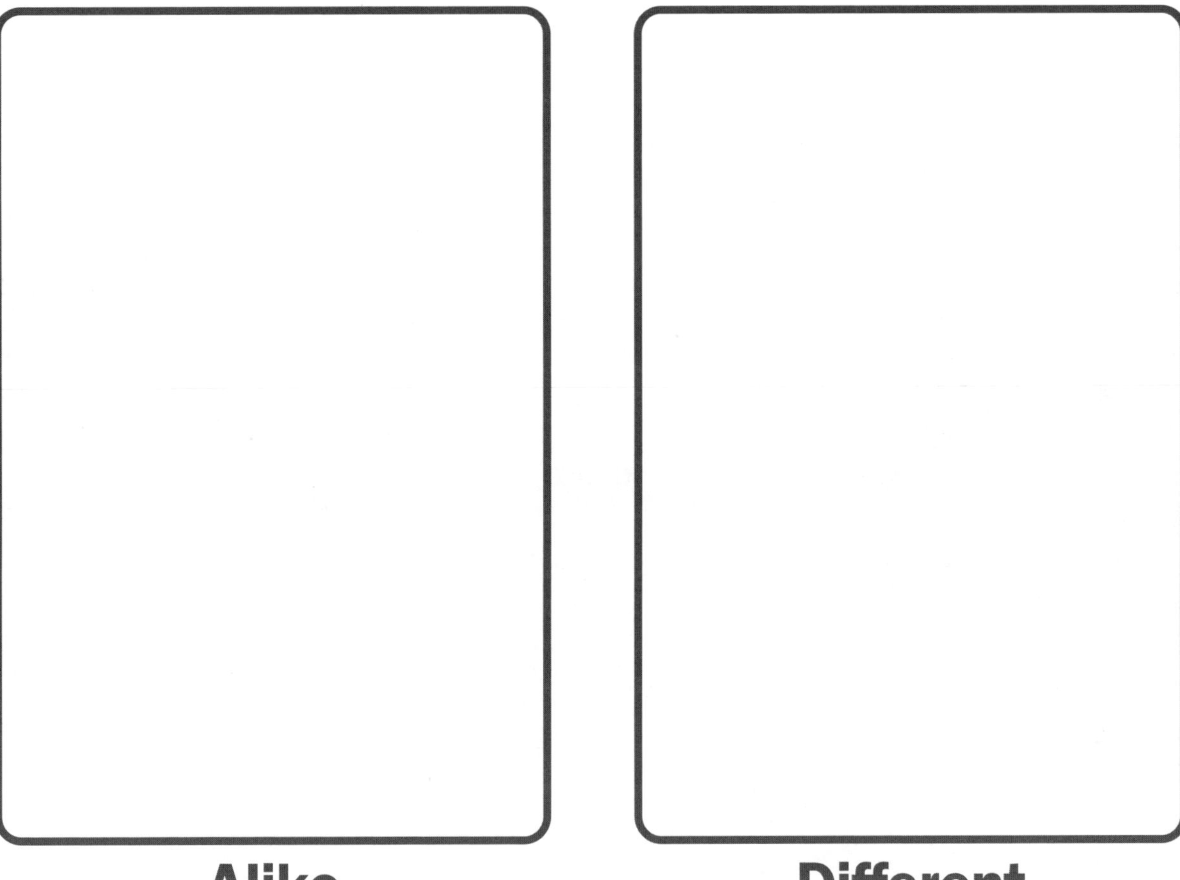

Summarize

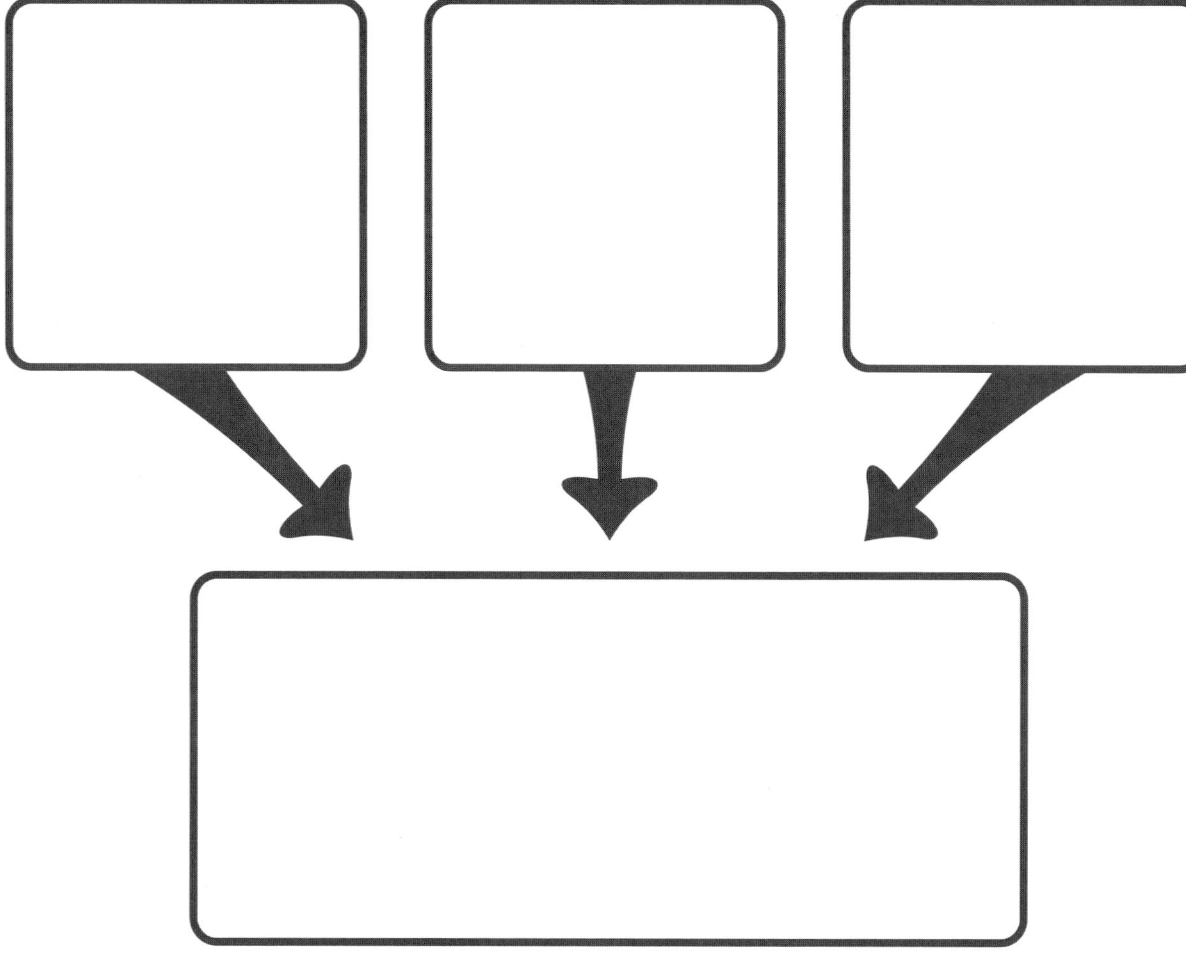

Draw Conclusions

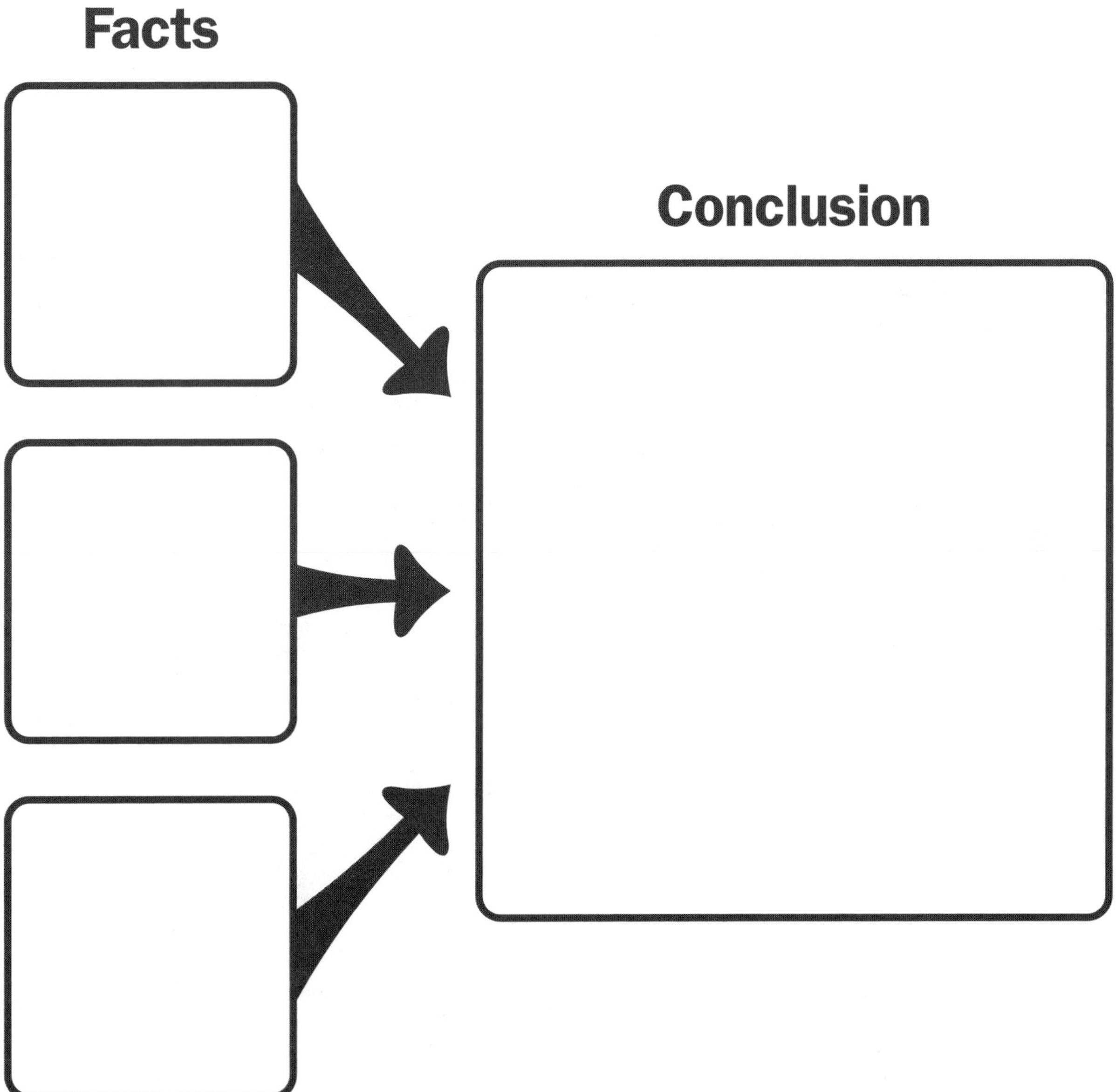

Make Generalizations

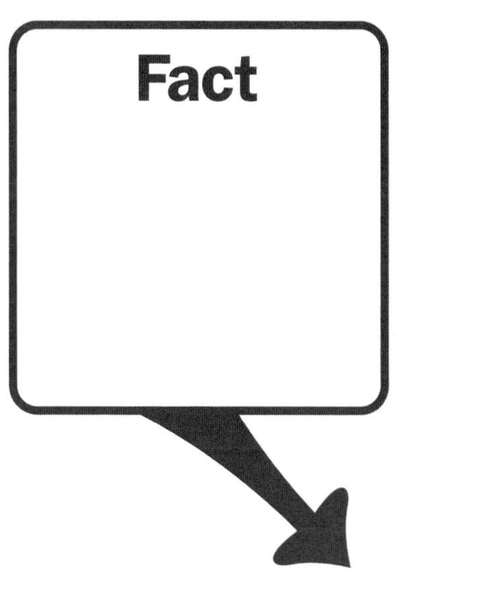

Generalization

K-W-L Chart

Topic ____________________

What We Know	What We Want to Know	What We Learned

K-W-L Interactive Reading Strategy was developed and is reprinted by permission of Donna Ogle, National-Louis University, Evanston, Illinois.

Event Summary

Name of event ______________________________

WHO? **Who was part of this event?**

WHAT? **What happened?**

WHEN? **When did this happen?**

WHERE? **Where did this happen?**

WHY? **Why did this happen?**

Lesson Summary

Chapter______ Lesson______ Title________________________________

Section Title	Notes
Summary	

Section Title	Notes
Summary	

Section Title	Notes
Summary	

Section Title	Notes
Summary	

Categorize

Topic	Category 1	Category 2	Category 3	Category 4

Social Studies Daily Journal

Today I learned...

Some new words I learned...

One way this relates to me...

I would like to learn more about...

Current Event Organizer

Article Title ____________________

Article Source ____________________ Article Date ____________

(magazine/newspaper title)

TOPIC?
What is the article about?

WHAT?
What is the issue or event?

WHY?
Why is the event taking place? Why is it important?

WHERE?
Where is the event taking place?

WHEN?
When did the event take place? Is it still going on?

WHO?
Who are the people involved?

My reaction to this issue/event:

Solve a Problem

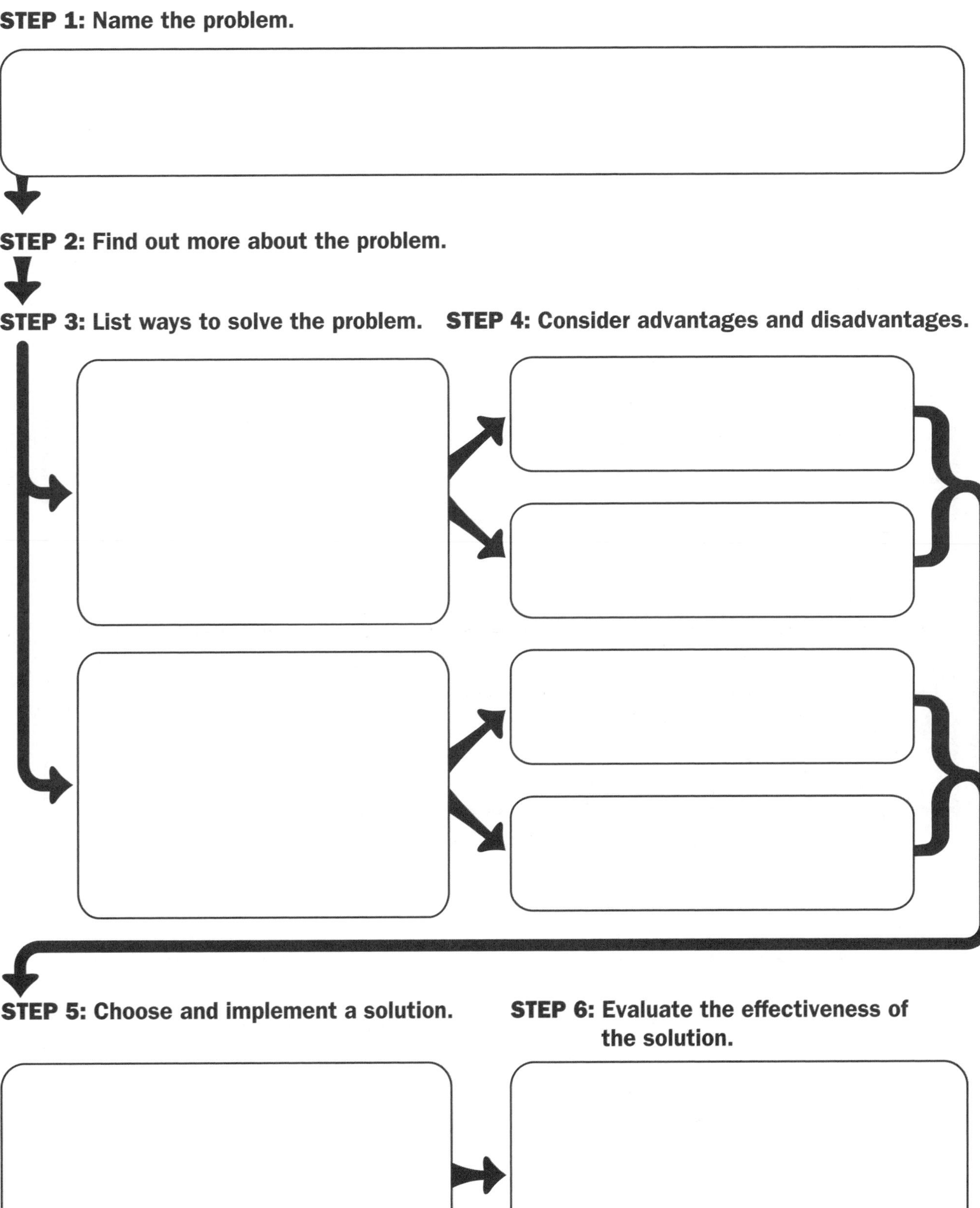

STEP 1: Name the problem.
STEP 2: Find out more about the problem.
STEP 3: List ways to solve the problem.
STEP 4: Consider advantages and disadvantages.
STEP 5: Choose and implement a solution.
STEP 6: Evaluate the effectiveness of the solution.

Vocabulary Organizer

Word	Definition
One thing I learned about this word...	

Word	Definition
One thing I learned about this word...	

Word	Definition
One thing I learned about this word...	

Word	Definition
One thing I learned about this word...	

Writing Organizer

Topic of Writing Piece	Audience	Purpose

Main Idea	Supporting Details

Transition Sentence

Main Idea	Supporting Details

Transition Sentence

Main Idea	Supporting Details

Artifact Analysis

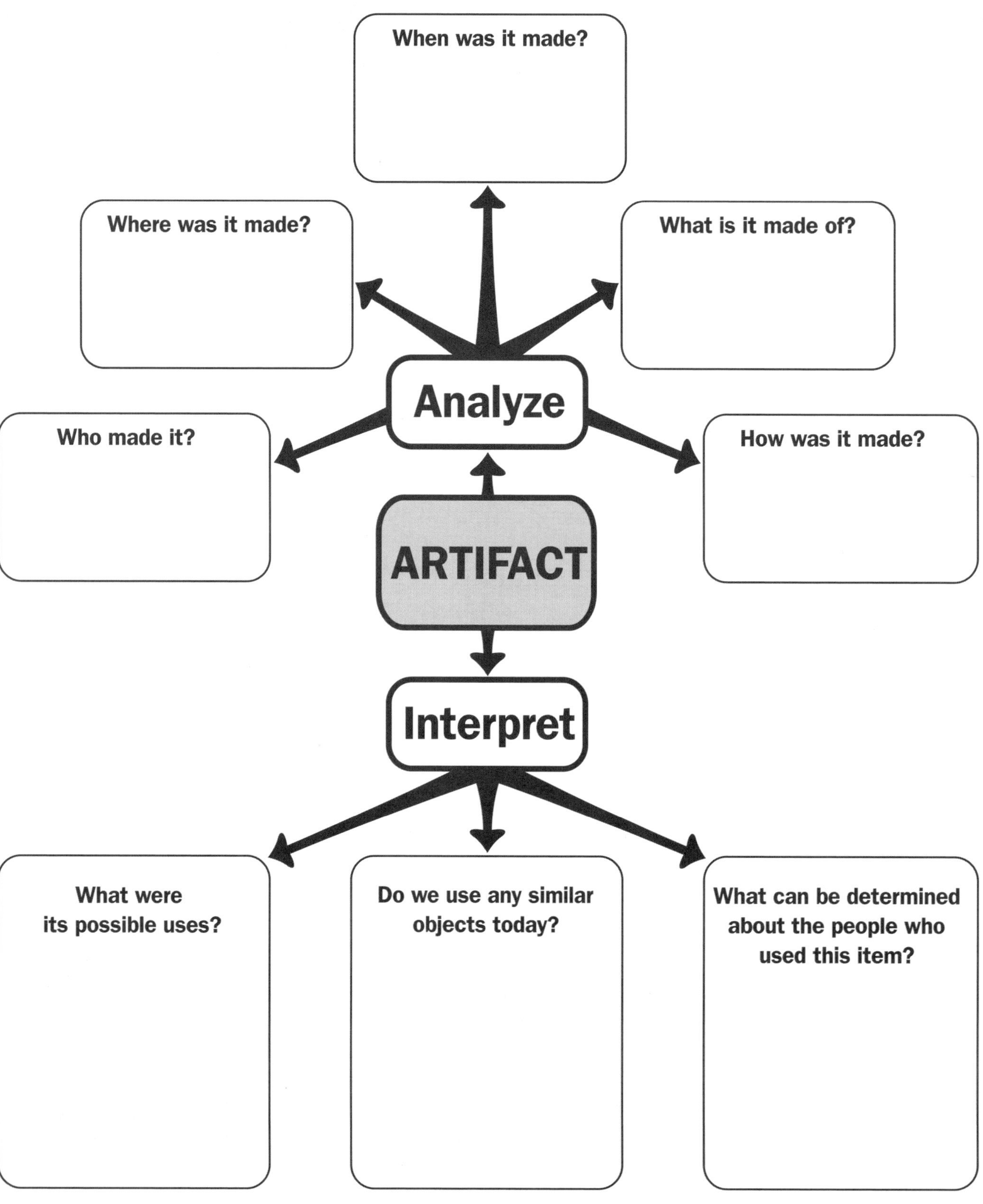
When was it made?
Where was it made?
What is it made of?
Analyze
Who made it?
How was it made?
ARTIFACT
Interpret
What were its possible uses?
Do we use any similar objects today?
What can be determined about the people who used this item?

Document Analysis

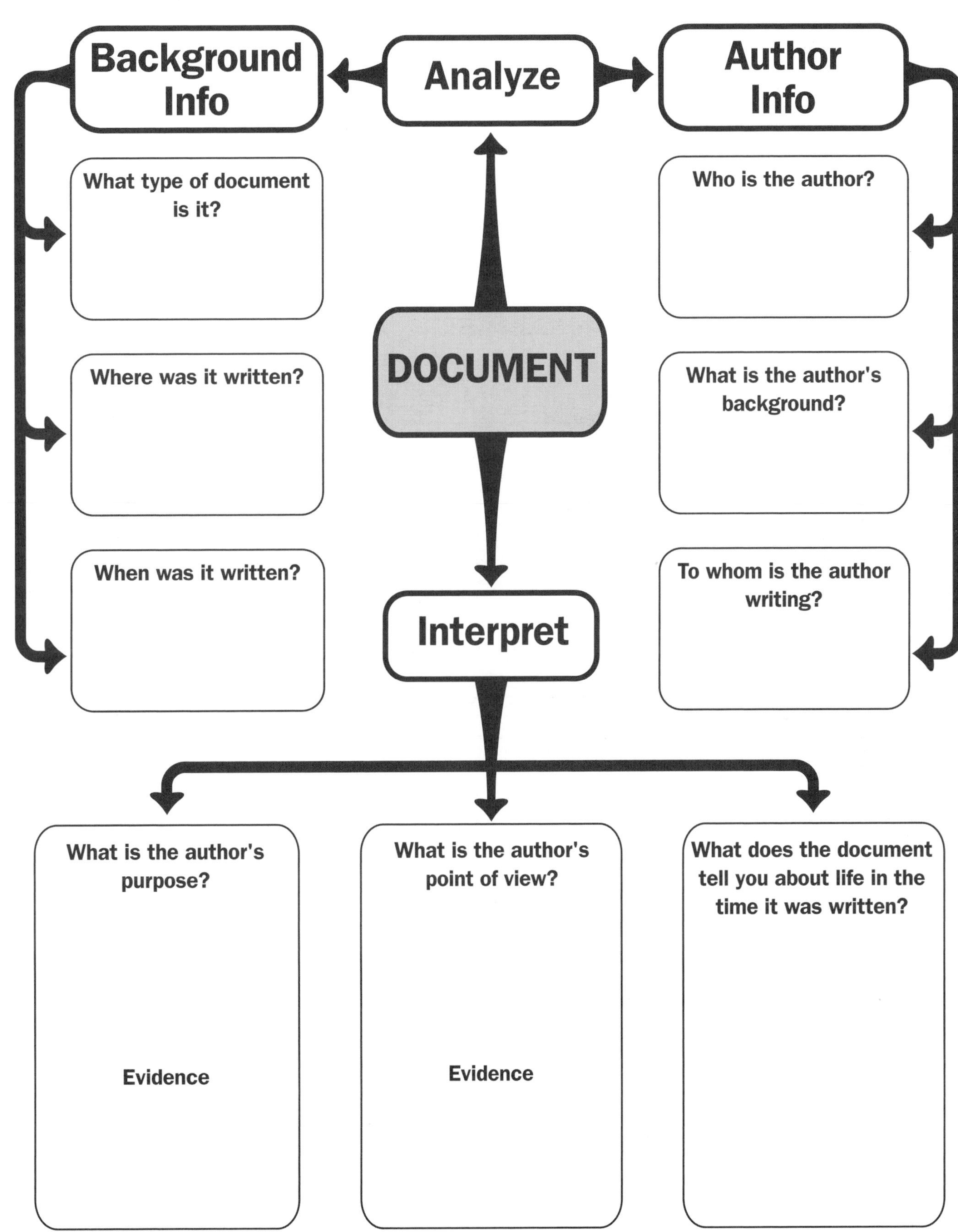
Background Info
Analyze
Author Info
What type of document is it?
Where was it written?
When was it written?
DOCUMENT
Who is the author?
What is the author's background?
To whom is the author writing?
Interpret
What is the author's purpose?
Evidence
What is the author's point of view?
Evidence
What does the document tell you about life in the time it was written?

Graph Paper

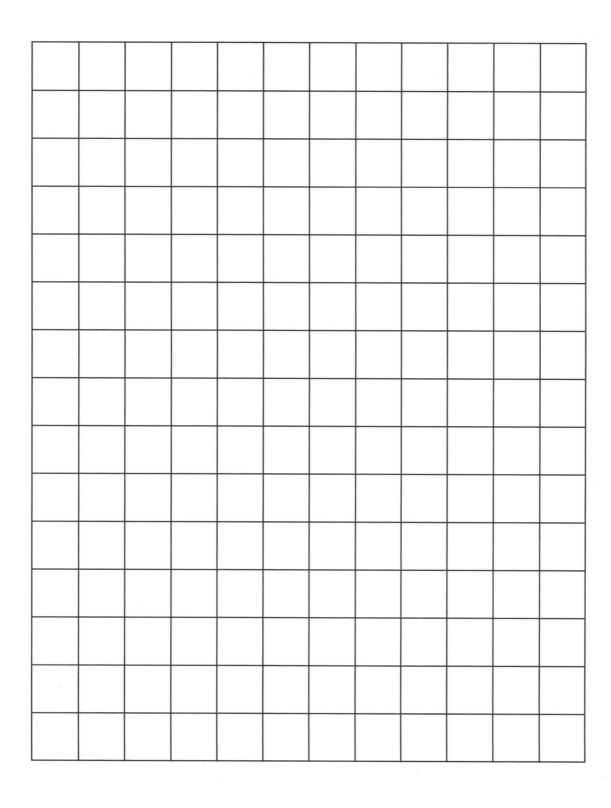

Time Line

Grid

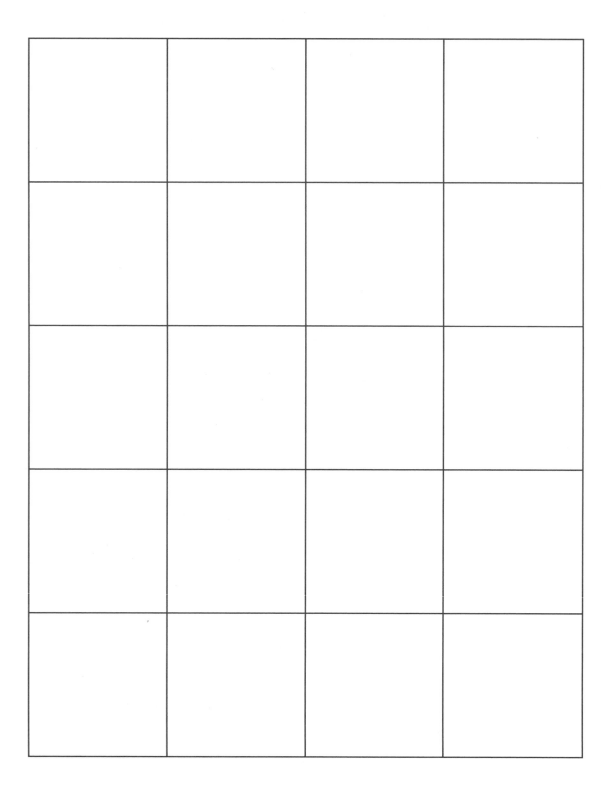

Name ____________________________ Date __________

The World

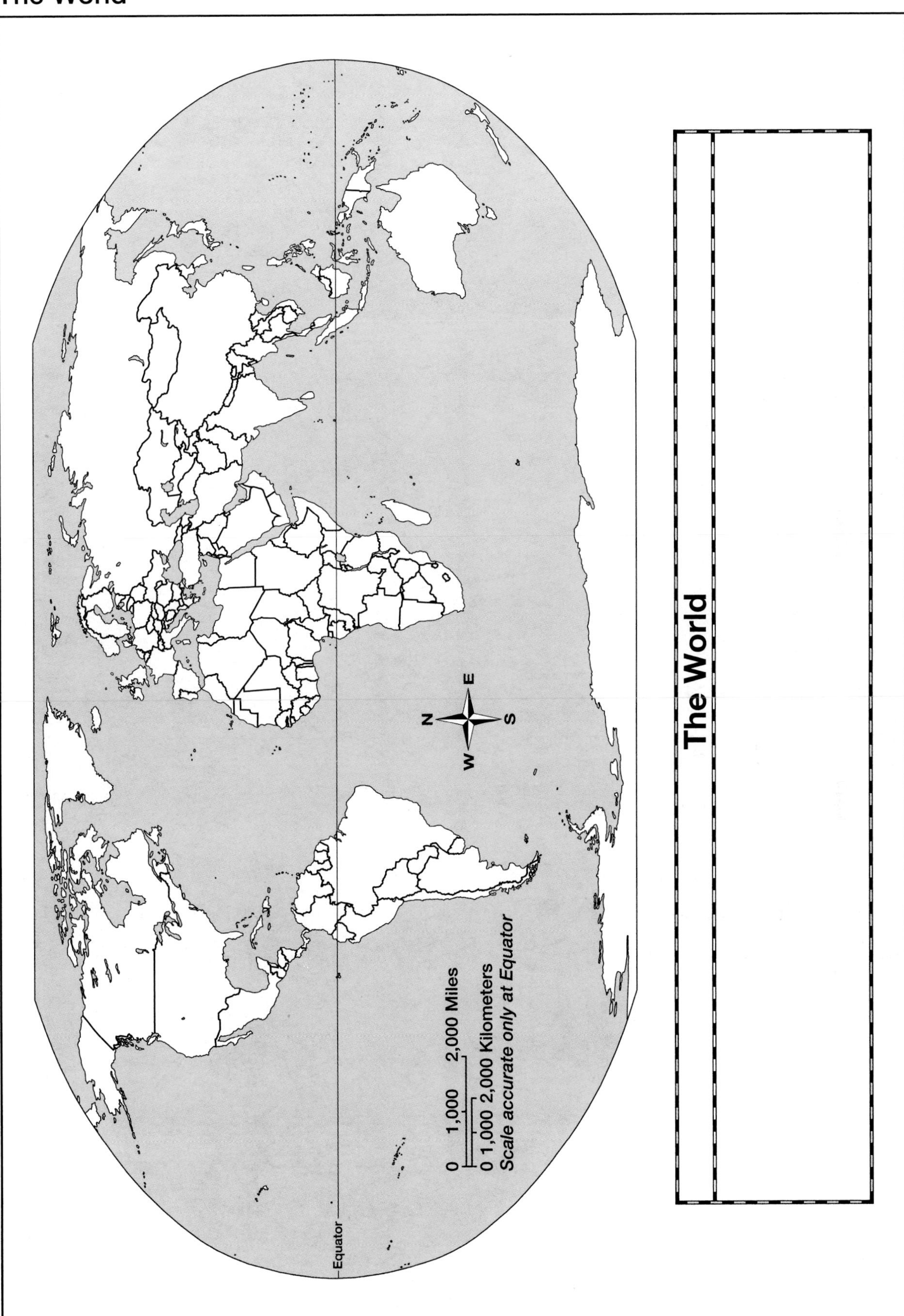

Name ______________________________ Date __________

North America

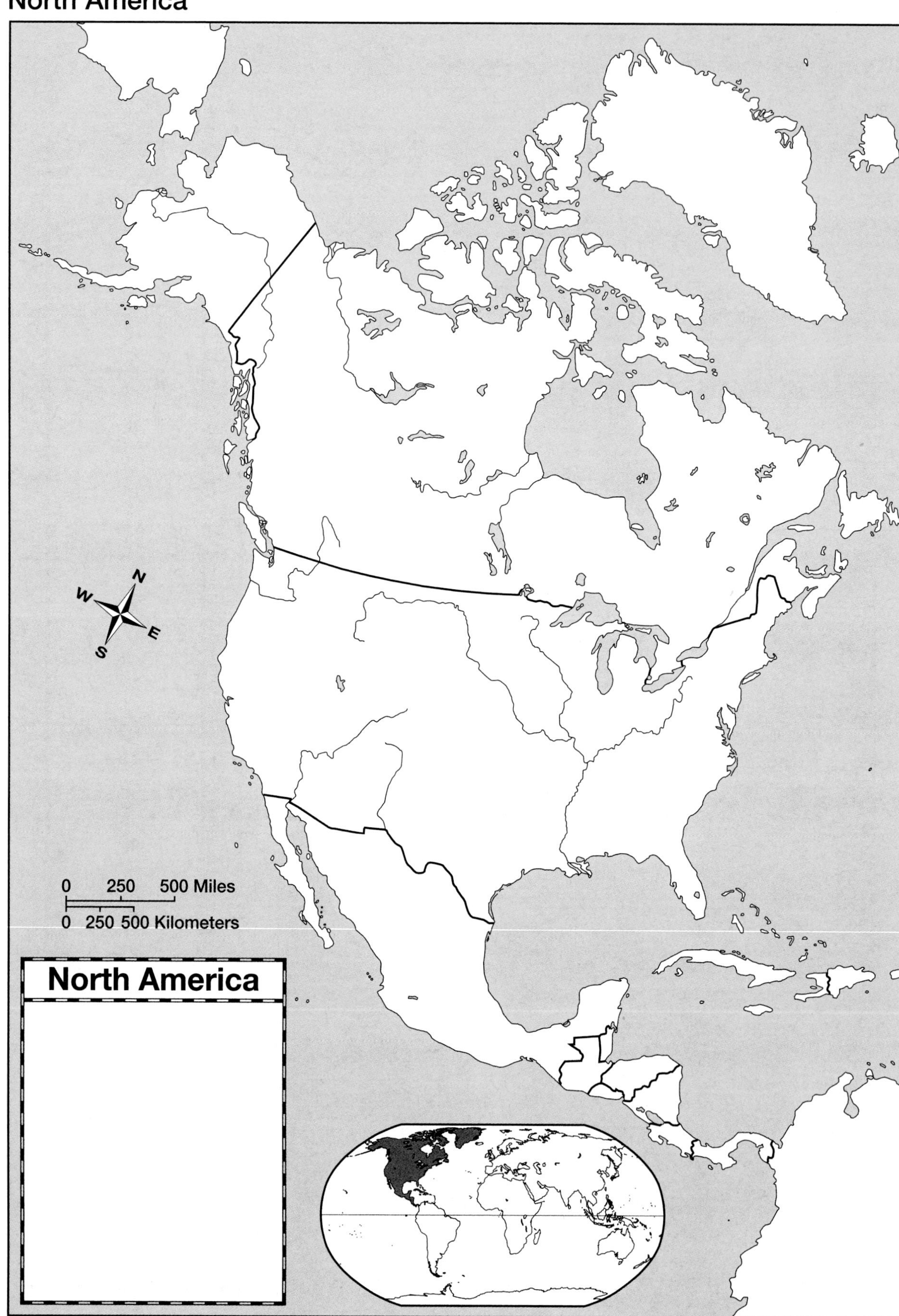

Name ______________________ Date __________

The United States

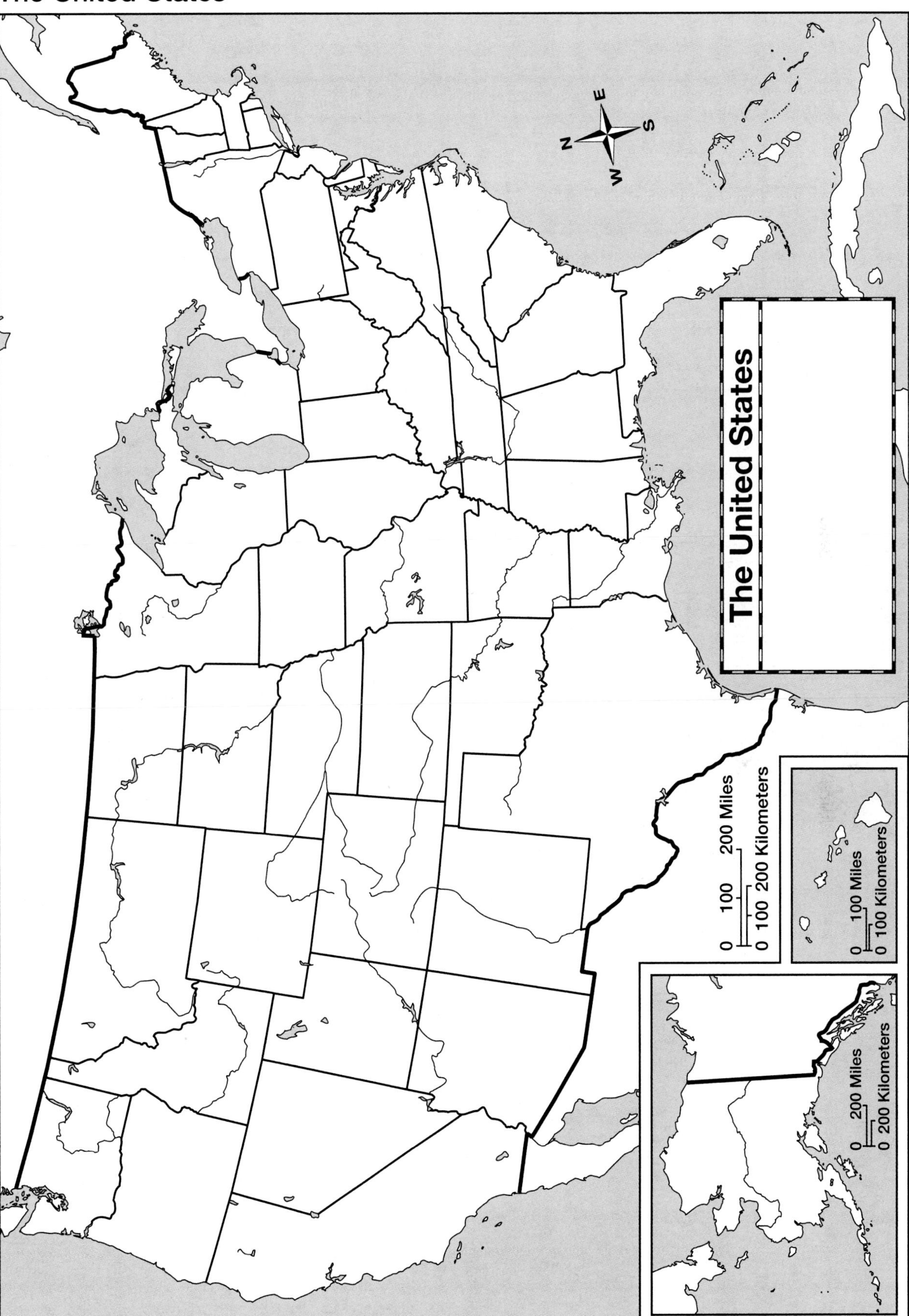

Calendar

____

Sunday	Monday	Tuesday	Wednesday	Thursday	Friday	Saturday

08160, 08161, 08162, 08163, 08164

Index

Activate Prior Knowledge (*see* ESL Support)
Analyze Information (*see* Reading Skills)
Analyze Pictures (*see* Reading Skills)
Analyze Primary Sources (*see* Reading Skills, Primary Sources)
Anthropology (*see* Culture)
Apply Information (*see* Reading Skills)

Art
- **Artistic Learning** (*see* Meeting Individual Needs, Learning Styles)
- **Curriculum Connection,** H5, H9, H13, 1f, 3, 13, 52, 77, 95f, 140, 147, 148, 157f, 170, 192, 201, 223f, 225, 268, 291f, 293, 307, 337, 359f, 383, 395, 421
- **Link to Art,** 15, 52, 129, 274, 328, 397

Auditory Learning (*see* Meeting Individual Needs, Learning Styles)

Assessment
- **Chapter Reviews,** 34–35, 62–63, 88–89, 122–123, 150–151, 184–185, 216–217, 252–253, 284–285, 320–321, 352–353, 390–391, 418–419
- **ExamView® Test Bank CD-ROM,** 1c, 8b, 8e, 36b, 36e, 64b, 64e, 95c, 102b, 102e, 124b, 124e, 157c, 164b, 164e, 186b, 186e, 223c, 230b, 230e, 254b, 254e, 291c, 298b, 298e, 322b, 322e, 359c, 366b, 366e, 392b, 392e
- **Formal,** 1e, 95e, 157e, 223e, 291e, 359e
- **Informal,** 1e, 95e, 157e, 223e, 291e, 359e
- **Lesson Reviews,** 15, 23, 31, 44, 52, 59, 71, 79, 85, 109, 115, 119, 129, 133, 138, 146, 169, 175, 183, 192, 199, 206, 213, 237, 245, 249, 259, 266, 274, 282, 304, 311, 317, 328, 337, 343, 348, 373, 383, 388, 397, 406, 415
- **Ongoing,** 1e, 14, 21, 30, 39, 48, 70, 77, 95e, 106, 115, 117, 127, 131, 138, 157e, 167, 174, 180, 189, 203, 212, 223e, 233, 243, 249, 257, 265, 272, 280, 291e, 301, 309, 319, 327, 335, 341, 348, 359e, 371, 382, 388, 395, 404, 414
- **Performance,** 1e, 1, 34, 35, 62, 63, 88, 89, 92, 94, 95e, 95, 122, 123, 150, 151, 154, 156, 157e, 157, 184, 185, 216, 217, 220, 222, 223e, 223, 252, 253, 284, 285, 288, 290, 291e, 291, 320, 321, 352, 356, 358, 359e, 359, 390, 391, 418, 419, 422, 424
- **Portfolio,** 1e, 1, 2, 93, 95e, 95, 96, 155, 157e, 157, 158, 221, 223e, 223, 224, 289, 291e, 291, 292, 357, 359e, 359, 360, 423
- **Scoring Guides (Rubrics),** 93, 94, 155, 156, 221, 222, 289, 290, 357, 358, 423, 424
- **Support,** 8e–8f, 36e–36f, 64e–64f, 102e–102f, 124e–124f, 164e–164f, 186e–186f, 230e–230f, 254e–254f, 298e–298f, 322e–322f, 366e–366f, 392e–392f
- **Unit Reviews,** 92–93, 154–155, 220–221, 288–289, 356–357, 422–423

Atlas
- **Big Book Atlas,** H11, 1c, 8b, 24, 36b, 64b, 95c, 102b, 124b, 157c, 164b, 186b, 223c, 230b, 254b, 291c, 298b, 322b, 359c, 366b, 392b, 409
- **Social Studies Reference Guide,** R2–R15
- **Student Atlas,** H11, 1c, 8b, 24, 36b, 64b, 95c, 102b, 124b, 157c, 164b, 186b, 223c, 230b, 254b, 291c, 298b, 322b, 359c, 366b, 392b, 409

AudioText (*see* Technology)
Auditory Learning (*see* Meeting Individual Needs, Learning Styles)
Authors, 1g, 95g, 157g, 223g, 291g, 359g

Background
- **Abolitionists,** 201
- **Alaska,** 406
- **"America,"** 90
- **"America, the Beautiful,"** 224
- **Atlases,** 32
- **Badlands,** 243
- **Baobab,** 313
- **Blue Jeans,** 407
- **Branding Cattle,** 354
- **Cahokia Mounds,** 277
- **California Gold Rush,** 69
- **Cherokee,** 190
- **Cherries,** 389
- **Cities of Gold,** 333
- **Climate Data,** 22
- **Confederacy,** 203
- **Continental Drift Theory,** H12
- **Corn Palace,** 247
- **Cranberries,** 113
- **Deere, John,** 275
- **Ellis Island Ownership,** 14
- **Essential Elements of Geography,** H10
- ***Evangeline*,** 158
- **Exploration of the West Coast,** 401
- **Flag Etiquette,** 3
- **Geography of Rice-Growing,** 251
- **Grand Canyon,** 292, 303
- **Guthrie, Woody,** 2
- **Hawaii,** 406
- **Highest and Lowest Points,** 16
- **History of MapMaking,** H17
- **Homestead Act,** 270
- **Hurricanes,** 177
- **Internet,** 262
- **"I've Been Working on the Railroad,"** 286
- **Latitude and Longitude,** 408
- **Lewis and Clark Expedition,** 278
- **Logging Companies,** 182
- **Los Angeles,** 413
- **Moran's *The Grand Canyon of the Yellowstone*,** 361
- **Mount St. Helens,** 374
- **Muir, John,** 360
- **Narragansett People,** 127
- **National Register of Historic Places,** 351
- **Native Americans Today,** 39
- **Natural Resources,** 27
- **Navajo Code Talkers,** 330
- **Navajo Reservation,** 328
- **Primary Documents,** H4
- **Ranchers and Cowhands,** 344
- **Rights of Citizens vs. Non-citizens,** 59
- **Sandburg, Carl,** 152
- **September 11, 2001,** 149
- **Shark Bay,** 120
- **"Shenandoah,"** 218
- **"Sweet Betsy from Pike,"** 420
- **Thoreau's Walden,** 96
- **Time Zones,** 54
- **Trade and Culture,** 268
- **Transportation in California,** 416
- **Union,** 203
- **U.S. Route 40,** H22
- **Volcanoes,** 376
- **Western Cities,** 415
- **Zebra Mussels,** 238

Bibliography
- **Grade-Level,** TR39–TR44
- **Unit-Level,** 1h, 95h, 157h, 223h, 291h, 359h

Biography
- **Carnegie, Andrew,** 147
- **Carrier, Willis Haviland,** 349
- **Deere, John,** 275
- **Dodge, Henry Chee,** 329
- **Du Sable, Jean Baptiste Point,** 267
- **Inouye, Daniel,** 53
- **LaGuardia, Fiorello,** 45
- **Lewelling, Seth,** 389
- **Parks, Rosa,** 207

Index

Powell, John Wesley, 305
Sequoyah, 193
Stanton, Elizabeth Cady, 139
Strauss, Levi, 407
Twain, Mark, 283

Build Background, 1h, 95h, 157h, 223h, 291h, 359h (see ESL Support, Build Background)
Building Citizenship Skills (see Citizenship)

Calendar Activities, TR15–TR28
Categorize (see Reading Skills)
Cause and Effect (see Reading Skills)
Chapter Reviews, 34–35, 62–63, 88–89, 122–123, 150–151, 184–185, 216–217, 252–253, 284–285, 320–321, 352–353, 390–391, 418–419
Character (see Citizenship)

Chart and Graph Skills
Compare Line and Bar Graphs, 240–241
Read a Cross-Section Diagram, 110–111
Use a Vertical Time Line, 134–135

Citizen Heroes
Caring, 318–319
Courage, 200–201
Fairness, 416–417
Honesty, 60–61
Respect, 260–261
Responsibility, 148–149

Citizenship
Building Citizenship Skills, H2–H3
Decision Making, H3
Problem Solving, H3
Social Studies Strand, H2, 45, 61, 128, 141, 148, 200, 207, 260, 274, 275, 318, 354, 416

Colonial Williamsburg, H4–H5, 268–269
Compare and Contrast (see Reading Skills)
Critical Thinking (see Lesson Review Critical Thinking Questions and Issues and Viewpoints)
Cross-Curricular Links (see Art; Drama; Literature; Mathematics; Music; Reading; Science; Writing)
Culture
Social Studies Strand, 43, 82, 205, 215, 257, 269, 302, 336, 342, 345, 398

Curriculum Connections (see Art; Drama; Literature; Mathematics; Music; Reading; Science; Writing)

DK (Dorling Kindersley), 1c, 32–33, 95c, 140–141, 157c, 176–177, 223c, 291c, 344–345, 359c, 374–375
Decision Making, H3, H20, 14, 28, 49, 51, 76, 78, 111, 118, 174, 180, 200, 265, 339, 341, 380, 402 (see *also* Problem Solving; Reading Skills; Thinking Skills)
Discovery Channel School
Unit Projects, 94, 156, 222, 290, 358, 424
Videos, 1h, 95h, 157h, 223h, 291h, 359h
Drama
Curriculum Connection, 1f, 28, 47, 61, 84, 95f, 107, 133, 148, 157f, 176, 199, 223f, 291f, 329, 359f, 369, 404

Draw Conclusions (see Reading Skills)

ESL Support
Access Content, H14, 6, 11, 29, 50, 70, 105, 117, 131, 157g, 168, 173, 179, 244, 279, 291g, 309, 317, 327, 370, 403
Activate Prior Knowledge, 1g, 21, 42, 100, 162, 228, 249, 267, 296, 341, 364, 396
Build Background, H18, 257, 287
Extend Language, 57, 75, 81, 95g, 105, 114, 128, 137, 143, 189, 198, 205, 211, 223g, 234, 265, 271, 302, 306, 318, 335, 336, 348, 359g, 379, 385, 414
Professional Development (Dr. Jim Cummins), 1g, 95g, 157g, 223g, 291g, 359g
Economics
Social Studies Strand, 27, 73, 182, 250, 315, 387, 403, 414

English Language Learners (see ESL Support)
Enrich Activities (see Meeting Individual Needs, Leveled Practice—Easy, On-Level, Challenge Activities)
Evaluate (see Reading Skills)
ExamView® Test Bank CD-ROM, 1c, 8b, 8e, 36b, 36e, 64b, 64e, 95c, 102b, 102e, 124b, 124e, 157c, 164b, 164e,i 186b, 186e, 223c, 230b, 230e, 254b, 254e, 291c, 298b, 298e, 322b, 322e, 359c, 366b, 366e, 392b, 392e
Explore the United States, E1–E24
Express Ideas (see Reading Skills)
Extend Activities (see ESL Support, Extend Language; Meeting Individual Needs, Leveled Practice—Easy, On-Level, Challenge Activities)
Extend Language (see ESL Support)

Facing Fear: Helping Students Cope with Tragic Events, TR1–TR2
Fact and Opinion (see Reading Skills)
Fact File, 30, 42, 49, 75, 106, 248, 303, 315, 413
Family Activities, TR3–TR14
Fast Facts, H2, 196, 236, 250, 331

Generalize (see Reading Skills)
Geography
Link to Geography, 138, 373
Social Studies Strand, H11, 9, 15, 24, 37, 40, 65, 69, 103, 125, 165, 170, 173, 187, 196, 211, 231, 255, 283, 299, 323, 367, 393, 409, 412
Themes of Geography, H10–H11
Government
Social Studies Strand, 43, 51, 189, 282
Graphic Organizers
Graphic Organizers, E17–E24, 10, 18, 26, 38, 46, 56, 66, 72, 80, 104, 112, 116, 126, 130, 136, 142, 166, 172, 178, 188, 194, 202, 210, 232, 242, 246, 256, 264, 270, 276, 300, 308, 314, 324, 332, 338, 346, 368, 378, 384, 394, 400, 410
Teacher Resources Tab Section, TR45–TR70

Hands-on Unit Project (Discovery Channel School), 1, 35, 63, 89, 94, 95, 123, 151, 156, 157, 185, 217, 222, 223, 253, 285, 290, 291, 321, 353, 358, 359, 391, 419, 422, 424
Helping Students Cope with Tragic Events, TR1–TR2

Here and There, 16–17, 120–121, 214–215, 250–251, 312–313, 398–399

History
Social Studies Strand, H8, 51, 70, 127, 143, 168, 179, 190, 204, 205, 268, 319, 326, 331, 335, 411

Holidays (*see* Social Studies Plus!)
Hypothesize (*see* Reading Skills)

Individual Learning (*see* Meeting Individual Needs, Learning Styles)
Internet (*see* Technology)
Interpret Charts (*see* Chart and Graph Skills; Reading Skills)
Interpret Graphs (*see* Chart and Graph Skills; Reading Skills)
Interpret Maps (*see* Map and Globe Skills; Reading Skills)
Interpret Time Lines (*see* Reading Skills)
Interpret Visuals (*see* Reading Skills)

Issues and Viewpoints
Critical Thinking, 23, 28, 41, 258, 282, 315, 319, 326, 371
Invasion of the Zebra Mussels, 238–239
Save "America's Main Street"? 350–351

Kinesthetic Learning (*see* Meeting Individual Needs, Learning Styles)

Learning Styles (*see* Meeting Individual Needs, Learning Styles)
Lesson Review Critical Thinking Questions, 15, 23, 31, 44, 52, 59, 71, 79, 85, 109, 115, 119, 129, 133, 138, 146, 169, 175, 183, 192, 199, 206, 213, 237, 245, 249, 259, 266, 274, 282, 304, 311, 317, 328, 337, 343, 348, 373, 383, 388, 397, 406, 415
Leveled Practice—Easy, On-Level, Challenge Activities (*see* Meeting Individual Needs, Leveled Practice—Easy, On-Level, Challenge Activities)
Linguistic Learning (*see* Meeting Individual Needs, Learning Styles)

Literature
Bibliography, Unit Level, 1h, 95h, 157h, 223h, 291h, 359h, TR39–TR44
Curriculum Connection, H3, 1f, 4, 17, 41, 95f, 98, 115, 139, 157f, 160, 183, 197, 206, 207, 223f, 226, 273, 291f, 294, 305, 312, 345, 359f, 362, 373, 399
End with a Poem
"Niagara," 152–153
End with Literature
Cowboy Country, 354–355
Literature and Social Studies, 74, 107, 179, 271, 310, 385,
Trade Books, 1h, 95h, 157h, 223h, 291h, 359h
Logical Learning (*see* Meeting Individual Needs, Learning Styles)

Main Idea and Details (*see* Reading Skills)
Make Decisions (*see* Decision Making; Problem Solving; Reading Skills, Decision Making; Thinking Skills)
Make Inferences (*see* Reading Skills)

Map and Globe Skills
Elevation Maps, 170–171
Grid, H20
Inset Maps, 24–25
Latitude and Longitude, H15, H21, 408–409
Map Features, H16–H17
Road Map and Scale, H19, H22, 86–87
Time-Zone Map, 54–55

Map and Globe Skills Review, H10–H22
Map Resources CD-ROM, 1c, 8b, 24, 36b, 64b, 95c, 102b, 124b, 157c, 164b, 186b, 223c, 230b, 254b, 291c, 298b, 322b, 359c, 366b, 392b, 409
MapQuest, SF4

Maps
Atlas, 1c, 8b, 24, 36b, 64b, 95c, 102b, 124b, 157c, 164b, 186b, 223c, 230b, 254b, 291c, 298b, 322b, 359c, 366b, 392b, 409
Map Adventure, 83, 144, 174, 279, 341, 402

Mathematics
Curriculum Connection, H16, H19, H22, 1f, 25, 53, 74, 83, 95f, 135, 157f, 171, 196, 223f, 248, 283, 291f, 309, 339, 359f, 382, 405, 413
Link to Mathematics, 259

Meeting Individual Needs, Learning Styles
Artistic, 30
Auditory, 30, 214, 261, 350, 387
Individual, 281
Kinesthetic, 68, 78, 119, 175, 261, 310, 387
Linguistic, 141, 398
Logical, 30, 78, 175, 281, 350, 387
Musical, 68, 119, 214, 245
Social, 43, 261
Verbal, 141, 214, 245, 310, 398
Visual, 43, 68, 78, 119, 141, 175, 214, 245, 281, 310, 350, 398

Meeting Individual Needs, Leveled Practice
Easy, On-Level, Challenge Activities, H21, 12, 19, 31, 40, 48, 58, 67, 73, 82, 86, 108, 110, 113, 118, 129, 132, 134, 138, 145, 167, 174, 181, 191, 195, 204, 208, 212, 233, 240, 243, 247, 259, 263, 266, 272, 280, 301, 311, 316, 325, 334, 343, 347, 372, 377, 381, 386, 397, 402, 412

Music
Curriculum Connection, H3, 1f, 13, 44, 91, 95f, 105, 153, 157f, 180, 213, 219, 223f, 258, 274, 291f, 304, 340, 359f, 382, 395
End with a Song
"America," 90–91
"I've Been Working on the Railroad," 286–287
"Shenandoah," 218–219
"Sweet Betsy from Pike," 420–421
Link to Music, 183, 406
Musical Learning (*see* Meeting Individual Needs, Learning Styles)
***Songs and Music* CD,** 1c, 95c, 157c, 223c, 291c, 359c

Objectives
Lesson Objectives, 10, 16, 18, 24, 26, 32, 38, 45, 46, 53, 54, 56, 60, 66, 72, 80, 86, 104, 110, 112, 116, 120, 126, 130, 134, 136, 139, 140, 142, 147, 148, 166, 170, 172, 176, 178, 188, 193, 194, 200, 202, 207, 208, 210, 214, 232, 238, 240, 242, 246, 250, 256, 260, 262, 264, 267, 270, 275, 276, 283, 300, 305, 306, 308, 312, 314, 318, 324, 329, 330, 332, 338, 344, 346, 349, 350, 368, 374, 376, 378, 384, 389, 394, 398, 400, 407, 408, 410, 416

Unit Objectives, 1d, 95d, 157d, 223d, 291d, 359d

Pacing, 1b, 8a, 36a, 64a, 95b, 102a, 124a, 157b, 164a, 186a, 223b, 230a, 254a, 291b, 298a, 322a, 359b, 366a, 392a
Patriotism, H2–H3, 140–141, 224

Planning Guides
Chapter Planning Guides, 8a–8f, 36a–36f, 64a–64f, 102a–102f, 124a–124f, 164a–164f, 186a–186f, 230a–230f, 254a–254f, 298a–298f, 322a–322f, 366a–366f, 392a–392f
Unit Planning Guides, 1b–1h, 95b–95h, 157b–157h, 223b–223h, 291b–291h, 359b–359h
Poems, 1h, 95h, 157h, 223h, 291h, 359h
Point of View (see Reading Skills)
Predict (see Reading Skills)

Primary Sources
Begin with a Primary Source, 2–3, 96–97, 158–159, 224–225, 292–293, 360–361
Primary Source, H6, 2–3, 53, 57, 60–61, 75, 96–97, 118, 135, 140–141, 148–149, 158–159, 206–207, 224–225, 239, 244, 261, 278, 292–293, 305, 329, 330–331, 333, 344–345, 351, 353, 357, 360–361, 398–399, 404, 416–417, R28–R31

Problem Solving, H3, 29, 260, 281, 304, 349 (*see also* Citizenship; Decision Making)
Professional Development, 1g, 95g, 157g, 223g, 291g, 359g
Projects, (see Hands-on Unit Project [Discovery Channel School])
Providing More Depth, 1c, 8b, 36b, 64b, 95c, 102b, 124b, 157c, 164b, 186b, 223c, 230b, 254b, 291c, 298b, 322b, 359c, 366b, 392b

Quick Teaching Plan, 10, 18, 26, 38, 46, 56, 66, 72, 80, 104, 112, 116, 126, 130, 136, 142, 166, 172, 178, 188, 194, 202, 210, 232, 242, 246, 256, 264, 270, 276, 300, 308, 314, 324, 332, 338, 346, 368, 378, 384, 394, 400, 410

Read Aloud, 1h, 95h, 157h, 223h, 291h, 359h
Reading
Curriculum Connection, 1f, 95f, 153, 157f, 223f, 291f, 359f
Link to Reading, 59, 79, 119, 146, 199, 388

Reading Skills
Analyze Information, H19, 12, 25, 28, 30, 48, 50, 67, 71, 74, 82, 99, 106, 152, 196, 207, 219, 236, 273, 302, 303, 307, 342, 350, 363, 377, 405
Analyze Pictures, 5, 27, 39, 47, 68, 69, 99, 111, 153, 159, 161, 204, 279, 293, 295, 301, 315, 334, 345, 399, 413
Analyze Primary Sources, 53, 91, 149, 158, 244, 261, 292, 351, 417
Apply Information, H2, 14, 20, 21, 25, 49, 50, 58, 70, 73, 76, 84, 106, 111, 114, 117, 131, 137, 141, 145, 175, 176, 180, 190, 197, 204, 209, 211, 235, 236, 237, 247, 274, 275, 280, 283, 315, 329, 334, 348, 354, 370, 385, 395, 396, 409, 411
Categorize, 11, 14, 73, 214, 336, 372, 377
Cause and Effect, 28, 39, 40, 43, 69, 77, 81, 115, 117, 132, 137, 141, 142, 143, 146, 179, 190, 196, 198, 199, 212, 232, 233, 235, 237, 238, 242, 243, 245, 246, 248, 249, 256, 258, 259, 264, 266, 267, 270, 271, 273, 274, 276, 277, 280, 281, 282, 315, 324, 326, 327, 328, 333, 337, 342, 346, 348, 382, 385, 395, 401, 404
Compare and Contrast, H6, H10, H11, H12, 13, 23, 31, 33, 51, 71, 74, 76, 107, 115, 117, 132, 136, 138, 139, 143, 147, 159, 167, 183, 189, 191, 193, 195, 197, 199, 212, 215, 233, 234, 250, 257, 259, 272, 280, 309, 327, 335, 336, 339, 344, 368, 369, 371, 373, 374, 378, 379, 380, 381, 383, 385, 386, 396, 401, 406, 409, 410, 412, 415
Draw Conclusions, H11, H13, 3, 5, 16, 19, 21, 28, 29, 30, 33, 40, 43, 45, 51, 52, 57, 60, 61, 70, 73, 74, 75, 76, 77, 79, 91, 107, 113, 119, 121, 127, 129, 133, 137, 140, 141, 146, 149, 152, 161, 168, 169, 173, 177, 181, 183, 191, 192, 206, 211, 212, 214, 218, 227, 234, 236, 241, 245, 249, 257, 266, 267, 272, 274, 281, 286, 287, 300, 301, 302, 303, 304, 305, 308, 311, 314, 315, 316, 317, 318, 325, 327, 328, 332, 334, 335, 337, 338, 343, 344, 345, 347, 354, 355, 361, 371, 375, 380, 388, 389, 398, 400, 401, 402, 403, 404, 405, 406, 407, 409, 416
Evaluate, H7, 59, 61, 74, 106, 140, 141, 149, 180, 200, 207, 215, 237, 239, 249, 258, 317, 319, 328, 333, 337, 347, 350, 385
Express Ideas, 19, 47, 53, 107, 144, 148, 261, 272, 327, 335, 385, 420
Fact and Opinion, 85, 213, 351, 389
Generalize, 5, 42, 114, 119, 260, 307, 309, 311, 313, 316, 382, 406
Hypothesize, 3, 16, 74, 75, 118, 145, 148, 153, 233, 277, 278, 310, 325, 331, 333, 340, 399
Interpret Charts, 248, 313, 413
Interpret Graphs, 241, 313
Interpret Maps, H12, H13, H14, H16, H22, 5, 11, 17, 19, 20, 22, 32, 40, 41, 55, 83, 87, 105, 120, 127, 133, 167, 171, 173, 181, 195, 227, 265, 281, 309, 347, 372, 381, 387, 401, 403
Interpret Time Lines, 135
Interpret Visuals, 413
Main Idea and Details, H2, H6, H7, H16, H17, H18, 11, 12, 13, 14, 19, 21, 26, 27, 28, 29, 30, 31, 33, 38, 39, 40, 41, 43, 44, 45, 47, 48, 57, 58, 67, 68, 73, 76, 79, 81, 82, 105, 108, 113, 114, 118, 120, 121, 127, 128, 129, 131, 132, 137, 138, 139, 143, 144, 145, 146, 147, 161, 166, 167, 168, 169, 172, 173, 174, 175, 176, 177, 178, 179, 180, 182, 183, 188, 189, 190, 191, 192, 193, 194, 195, 196, 197, 198, 199, 200, 202, 203, 204, 205, 206, 209, 210, 211, 213, 214, 227, 233, 234, 236, 238, 239, 241, 243, 244, 247, 248, 249, 250, 257, 259, 263, 265, 271, 272, 273, 278, 281, 295, 301, 307, 309, 310, 311, 317, 318, 325, 327, 328, 333, 336, 339, 340, 341, 343, 347, 349, 355, 363, 369, 370, 371, 372, 375, 379, 380, 381, 383, 388, 395, 397, 398, 402, 404, 409, 411, 412, 414, 415, 420
Make Decisions, H3, 14, 28, 44, 49, 51, 76, 78, 111, 118, 174, 180, 200, 245, 265, 339, 341, 380, 402
Make Inferences, H6, 15, 17, 21, 22, 29, 31, 33, 43, 55, 58, 60, 77, 78, 82, 99, 108, 111, 115, 121, 127, 128, 133, 138, 152, 175, 189, 196, 201, 219, 251, 258, 265, 266, 271, 277, 279, 283, 287, 295, 301, 305, 312, 329, 331, 345, 354, 355, 373, 386, 396, 397, 398, 404, 405, 414, 417

Point of View, 60, 90, 138, 139, 199, 259, 282, 303, 326, 337, 348, 383, 415, 421
Predict, 3, 51, 105, 179, 244, 304, 333, 421
Sequence, 20, 27, 42, 84, 104, 105, 107, 109, 112, 113, 115, 116, 118, 119, 126, 129, 130, 131, 133, 143, 145, 171, 193, 209, 235, 263, 266, 374, 405
Solve Problems, H3, 29, 109, 182, 260, 281, 304, 343, 349
Summarize, 6, 10, 11, 13, 15, 16, 18, 19, 20, 22, 23, 25, 30, 40, 42, 44, 46, 47, 48, 49, 52, 56, 57, 59, 66, 69, 71, 72, 74, 79, 80, 85, 132, 148, 167, 203, 204, 205, 206, 257, 260, 282, 325, 342, 363, 377, 383, 384, 386, 388, 394, 396, 397, 401, 405, 406, 414, 415, 416

Research and Writing Skills
Identify Primary and Secondary Sources, 330–331
Take Notes and Write Outlines, 376–377
Use a Search Engine on the Internet, 262–263

Reteach Activities (*see* Meeting Individual Needs, Leveled Practice)
Rubrics (*see* Assessment, Scoring Guides [Rubrics], Writing Rubrics)

Science
Curriculum Connection, H15, 1f, 20, 49, 55, 71, 83, 84, 95f, 109, 121, 128, 157f, 159, 176, 182, 215, 223f, 248, 251, 257, 278, 291f, 339, 359f, 369, 375, 416
Link to Science, 23, 85, 115, 169, 175, 237, 245, 304, 317, 348, 383

Science and Technology
Social Studies Strand, 16, 21, 55, 144, 145, 278, 313, 315, 342, 398

Sequence (*see* Reading Skills)
Skills (*see* Chart and Graph Skills; Lesson Review Critical Thinking Questions; Map and Globe Skills; Reading Skills; Research and Writing Skills)
Social Learning (*see* Meeting Individual Needs, Learning Styles)
Social Studies Strand (*see* Citizenship; Culture; Economics; Geography; Government; History; Science and Technology)
Sociology (*see* Culture)
Solve Problems (*see* Reading Skills)
Songs (*see* Music)
Songs and Music (*see* Music; Technology)
Standardized Test Prep, 7, 34, 62, 88, 92, 101, 122, 150, 154, 163, 184, 216, 220, 229, 252, 284, 288, 297, 320, 352, 356, 365, 390, 418, 422
Summarize (*see* Reading Skills)

Technology
Additional Internet Links, 1c, 8b, 36b, 64b, 95c, 102b, 124b, 157c, 164b, 186b, 223c, 230b, 254b, 291c, 298b, 322b, 359c, 366b, 392b
Audio CD, 90, 218, 286, 420
AudioText, 1c, 8b, 36b, 64b, 95c, 102b, 124b, 157c, 164b, 186b, 223c, 230b, 254b, 291c, 298b, 322b, 359c, 366b, 392b
ExamView® Test Bank CD-ROM, 1c, 8b, 8e, 36b, 36e, 64b, 64e, 95c, 102b, 102e, 124b, 124e, 157c, 164b, 164e, 186b, 186e, 223c, 230b, 230e, 254b, 254e, 291c, 298b, 298e, 322b, 322e, 359c, 366b, 366e, 392b, 392e
Key Internet Search Terms, 1c, 8b, 36b, 64b, 95c, 102b, 124b, 157c, 164b, 186b, 223c, 230b, 254b, 291c, 298b, 322b, 359c, 366b, 392b
Songs and Music, 1c, 95c, 157c, 223c, 291c, 359c
Teacher Resources CD-ROM, 1c, 7, 8b, 8c, 8e, 8, 15, 23, 25, 31, 35, 36b, 36c, 36e, 36, 44, 52, 55, 59, 63, 64b, 64c, 64e, 64, 71, 79, 85, 87, 89, 94, 95c, 101, 102b, 102c, 102e, 102, 109, 111, 115, 119, 123, 124b, 124c, 124e, 124, 129, 133, 135, 138, 141, 146, 151, 156, 157c, 163, 164b, 164c, 164e, 164, 169, 171, 175, 183, 185, 186b, 186c, 186e, 186, 192, 199, 206, 209, 213, 217, 222, 223c, 229, 230b, 230c, 230e, 230, 237, 241, 245, 249, 253, 254b, 254c, 254e, 254, 259, 263, 266, 269, 274, 282, 285, 290, 291c, 297, 298b, 298c, 298e, 298, 304, 307, 311, 317, 321, 322b, 322c, 322e, 322, 328, 331, 337, 343, 345, 348, 353, 358, 359c, 365, 366b, 366c, 366e, 366, 373, 377, 383, 388, 391, 392b, 392c, 392e, 392, 397, 406, 409, 415, 419, 424
Video Field Trips, 1c, 95c, 157c, 223c, 291c, 359c
Web Site (www.sfsocialstudies.com), H17, 1c, 5, 8b, 9, 17, 33, 35, 36b, 37, 45, 53, 63, 64b, 65, 66, 87, 89, 92, 94, 95c, 97, 99, 102b, 103, 121, 123, 124b, 125, 130, 139, 142, 147, 151, 154, 156, 157c, 161, 164b, 165, 185, 186b, 187, 193, 207, 215, 217, 220, 222, 223c, 227, 230b, 231, 239, 253, 254b, 255, 267, 275, 283, 285, 288, 290, 291c, 295, 298b, 299, 305, 312, 319, 321, 322b, 323, 329, 330, 346, 349, 351, 353, 356, 358, 359c, 361, 363, 366b, 367, 389, 391, 392b, 393, 399, 404, 407, 417, 419, 422, 424

Test Prep (*see* Standardized Test Prep)

Test Talk
Choose the Right Answer, 1e, 95e, 157e, 220, 223e, 291e, 359e
Locate Key Words in the Question, 1e, 49, 92, 95e, 107, 157e, 157, 179, 223e, 280, 291e, 316, 359e, 370
Locate Key Words in the Text, 1e, 12, 74, 95e, 117, 154, 157e, 204, 223e, 239, 291e, 302, 359e, 386
Use Information from Graphics, 1e, 68, 95e, 111, 157e, 171, 223e, 235, 291e, 309, 356, 359e, 372, 403
Use Information from the Text, 1e, 50, 95e, 114, 157e, 191, 223e, 288, 291e, 340, 359e, 382, 411
Write Your Answer to Score High, 1e, 23, 95e, 133, 157e, 169, 223e, 259, 291e, 345, 359e, 422

Then and Now, 118, 197, 277, 335, 404

Thinking Skills
Identify Fact and Opinion, 208–209
Make Generalizations, 306–307

Unit Project, (*see* Discovery Channel School)
Unit Reviews, 92–93, 154–155, 220–221, 288–289, 356–357, 422–423

Verbal Learning (*see* Meeting Individual Needs, Learning Styles)
Visual Learning (*see* Meeting Individual Needs, Learning Styles)

Index

Vocabulary

Lesson Vocabulary, 10, 18, 24, 26, 38, 46, 56, 66, 72, 80, 104, 112, 116, 126, 130, 136, 142, 166, 170, 172, 178, 188, 194, 200, 202, 207, 210, 232, 242, 246, 256, 262, 264, 270, 275, 276, 300, 308, 314, 324, 330, 332, 338, 346, 368, 376, 378, 384, 394, 400, 408, 410

Preview, 8, 36, 64, 102, 124, 164, 186, 230, 254, 298, 322, 366, 392

Word Exercise, 7, 10, 18, 26, 38, 46, 56, 66, 72, 80, 101, 104, 112, 116, 126, 130, 136, 142, 163, 166, 172, 178, 188, 194, 202, 210, 229, 232, 242, 246, 256, 264, 270, 276, 297, 300, 308, 314, 324, 332, 338, 346, 365, 368, 378, 384, 394, 400, 410

Workbook

Workbook Support, 7, 8c–8d, 8, 15, 23, 25, 31, 35, 36c–36d, 36, 44, 52, 55, 59, 63, 64c–64d, 64, 71, 79, 85, 87, 89, 94, 101, 102c–102d, 102, 109, 111, 115, 119, 123, 124c–124d, 124, 129, 133, 135, 138, 141, 146, 151, 156, 163, 164c–164d, 164, 169, 171, 175, 183, 185, 186c–186d, 186, 192, 199, 206, 209, 213, 217, 222, 229, 230c–230d, 230, 237, 241, 245, 249, 253, 254c–254d, 254, 259, 263, 266, 269, 274, 282, 285, 290, 297, 298c–298d, 298, 304, 307, 311, 317, 321, 322c–322d, 322, 328, 331, 337, 343, 345, 348, 353, 358, 366c–366d, 365, 366, 373, 377, 383, 388, 391, 392c–392d, 392, 397, 406, 409, 415, 419, 424

Writing

Curriculum Connection, H2, H18, 1f, 20, 45, 47, 60, 74, 79, 85, 91, 95f, 106, 140, 144, 146, 157f, 169, 193, 197, 209, 223f, 235, 273, 291f, 293, 340, 355, 359f, 388, 417

Link to Writing, 31, 44, 71, 109, 133, 192, 206, 213, 249, 266, 282, 311, 337, 343, 415

Writing Rubrics, TR29–TR37

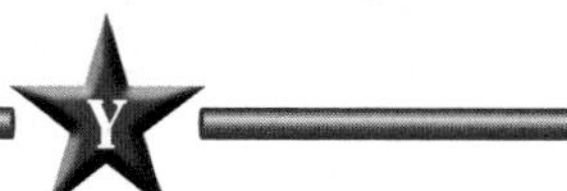

You Are There, 10, 18, 26, 38, 46, 56, 66, 72, 80, 104, 112, 116, 126, 130, 136, 142, 166, 172, 178, 188, 194, 202, 210, 232, 242, 246, 256, 264, 270, 276, 300, 308, 314, 324, 332, 338, 346, 368, 378, 384, 394, 400, 410

Credits

Maps:

Mapquest.com, Inc.

Illustrations:

223H Eric Reese

Photographs:

Every effort has been made to secure permission and provide appropriate credit for photographic material. The publisher deeply regrets any omission and pledges to correct errors called to its attention in subsequent editions.

Unless otherwise acknowledged, all photographs are the property of Scott Foresman, a division of Pearson Education.

Photo locators denoted as follows: Top (T), Center (C), Bottom (B), Left (L), Right (R), Background (Bkgd)

Cover: ©Panoramic Images, Chicago, ©F. Schussler/PhotoLink/Getty Images; **Front Matter:** SF1 ©Panoramic Images, Chicago; SF4 Smithsonian Institution; SF6 Lexington Historical Society; SF12 Getty Images; **Unit 1:** 1C Photri, Inc.; 1D ©Dorling Kindersley; 1H (TL) Carl Purcell/Words and Pictures, (TR) ©Doug Wilson/Corbis; 8A ©Comstock Inc.; 8B NOAA/Weatherstock; 36A ©Bettman/Corbis; 36B Museum of the History of Science, Oxford; 64A Getty Images; 64B ©Gallo Images/Corbis; **Unit 2:** 95A Art Resource, NY; 95B The Granger Collection; 95C SuperStock; 95D ©Bob Rowan/Corbis; 95H ©Paul A. Souders/Corbis; 102A ©Lynda Richardson/Corbis; 102B SuperStock; 124A ©Bettmann Archive/Corbis; 124B AP/Wide World; **Unit 3:** 157A Jacquelyn Modesitt Schindehette; 157B The Granger Collection; 157C Breck P. Kent/Animals Animals/Earth Scenes; 157D ©Randy Faris/Corbis; 157H Warren Faidley/Weatherstock; 164A SuperStock; 164B ©James Carmichael/Getty Images; 186A Fort St. Joseph Museum; 186B North Wind Picture Archives; **Unit 4:** 223A SuperStock; 223B ©Hulton Archive/Getty Images; 223C ©Wallace Kirkland/Getty Images; 223D Artville; 230A ©Reuters/NewMedia, Inc./Corbis; 230B ©Peter Yates/Getty Images; 254B Minnesota Historical Society; **Unit 5:** 291A ©Christie's Images/Corbis; 291B American Museum of Natural History/©Dorling Kindersley; 291C ©Eddie Hironaka/Getty Images; 291D ©Dallas and John Heaton/Corbis; 291H ©Hulton Archive/Getty Images; 298A ©John K. Hillers/Corbis; 298B Hal Gage/Index Stock Imagery; 322A Kolvoord/Image Works; 322B Ben Wittick/Courtesy of Museum of New Mexico; **Unit 6:** 359A ©Geoffrey Clements/Corbis; 359B Marilyn "Angel" Wynn/Nativestock; 359C Jeff Greenberg/Image Works; 359D ©V.C.L./Getty Images; 359H Jeff Greenberg/Image Works; 366A Burke/Triolo Productions/FoodPix; 366B ©George D. Lepp/Corbis; 392A ©James Cotier/Getty Images; 392B AK/Haines/Photri, Inc.; End Matter; TR11 Hallogram Publishing; TR13 Hallogram Publishing; TR19 Getty Images; TR21 Bill Fitzpatrick/The White House; TR24 Library of Congress; TR25 ©Comstock Inc.; TR59 St. Joseph Museum; TR60 ©Bettmann/Corbis; TR61 Marilyn "Angel" Wynn/Nativestock; TR62 SuperStock; TR63 ©Tim Flach/Getty Images; TR64 ©Paul Souders/Getty Images; **End Matter:** TR17 (L) Burstein Collection/Corbis, (R) Corbis; TR22 Bill Fitzpatrick/The White House; TR25 Library of Congress; TR26 Comstock, Inc.; TR27 Hemera Technologies; TR28 Comstock, Inc.

Notes

Notes

Notes